TRACING YOUR IRISH ANCESTORS:
THE COMPLETE GUIDE

Fourth Edition

The Author

John Grenham writes the 'Irish Roots' column in *The Irish Times* and runs the *Irish Times* Irish Ancestors website. He is a fellow of The Irish Genealogical Research Society and The Genealogical Society of Ireland.

John came to professional genealogy in 1981, as one of the panel of researchers in the Office of the Chief Herald of Ireland. As in-house researcher for that Office in 1990–91, he was instrumental in setting up the Consultation Service, the forerunner of the current Genealogical Advisory Services in the National Library and National Archives and was a founder member of The Association of Professional Genealogists in Ireland in 1986.

Among his publications are *Clans and Families of Ireland* (1995), *Generations* (1996), 'The Genealogical Office and its Records' in *The Genealogical Office* (1999), *Grenham's Irish Recordfinder* (CD-ROM, 1995–2006), *Grenham's Irish Surnames* (CD-ROM, 2003) and numerous articles and columns in the UK magazine *Your Family Tree*. His website is <*www.johngrenham.com*>.

TRACING YOUR IRISH ANCESTORS: THE COMPLETE GUIDE

Fourth Edition

JOHN GRENHAM ~

Genealogical Publishing Co., Inc.

Published in Ireland by Gill & Macmillan
Hume Avenue, Park West, Dublin 12, Ireland

First edition 1992
Second edition 1999
Third edition 2006

Fourth edition published in the USA and Canada, 2012,
by arrangement with Gill & Macmillan
by Genealogical Publishing Company
3600 Clipper Mill Rd., Suite 260
Baltimore, Maryland 21211-1953

Printed in the UK by MPG Books Ltd, Cornwall

Library of Congress Catalogue Card Number 2011943970
ISBN: 978-0-8063-1897-4

Yet again, for Doireann and Eoin

CONTENTS

ACKNOWLEDGMENTS

Without the encouragement and enthusiasm of Mr Donal Begley, this work would never have been started. I also owe a great deal over the years and over the editions to the other members and former members of staff at the Genealogical Office, in particular to the present Chief Herald, Colette O'Flaherty, to Bernard Devaney and to the late Willie Buckley, and to the former Chief Herald, Mr Fergus Gillespie. My colleagues in the Association of Professional Genealogists in Ireland have once again tolerated me spilling the professional beans and contributed very welcome advice and suggestions. I am also grateful to the staff of the National Library, the General Register Office, the Public Record Office of Northern Ireland, the National Archives and the Department of Arts, Heritage and the Gaeltacht for all their help over the years. Jonathan Hession's unswerving dedication to friendship, rest, recreation and photographs continues. Again, my deepest thanks to my family, especially Eoin, whose grace and good humour never flagged.

ABBREVIATIONS

AA	Armagh Ancestry
AH	*Analecta Hibernica*
BBHC	Brú Boru Heritage Centre
BFA	British Film Area
BL	British Library
BM	British Museum
C of I	Church of Ireland
CAI	Cork Archives Institute
CCAP	Cork City Ancestral Project
CCL	Clare County Library
CGP	Carlow Genealogy Project
CHGC	Cavan Heritage and Genealogy Centre
Clare HGC	Clare Heritage and Genealogical Centre
DA	Donegal Ancestry
DCL	Donegal County Library
DCLA	Dublin City Library and Archive
DGC	Derry Genealogy Centre
DHG	Dublin Heritage Group
DLGSJ	*Dún Laoghaire Genealogical Society Journal*
DLHS	Dún Laoghaire Heritage Society
DSHGC	Dún na Sí Heritage and Genealogical Centre
EGFHS	East Galway Family History Society Ltd
GAS	Genealogy Advisory Service
GFHSW	Galway Family History Society West Ltd
GO	Genealogical Office
GPC	Genealogical Publishing Company, Inc.
GRO	General Register Office
IA	*Irish Ancestor*
IFH	*Irish Family History: Journal of the Irish Family History Society*
IFHF	Irish Family History Foundation
IG	*Irish Genealogist*
IGRS	Irish Genealogical Research Society
IMA	Irish Midlands Ancestry
IMC	Irish Manuscripts Commission
IR	*Irish Roots*

IS	*Irish Sword: Journal of the Military History Society of Ireland*
IW	Irish World
JCHAS	*Journal of the Cork Historical and Archaeological Society*
JCLAHS	*Journal of the County Louth Archaeological and Historical Society*
JGAHS	*Journal of the Galway Archaeological and Historical Society*
JKAHS	*Journal of the Kerry Archaeological and Historical Society*
JKAS	*Journal of the Kildare Archaeological Society*
JNMAS	*Journal of the North Munster Archaeological Society*
JPRS	*Journal of the Parish Register Society*
JRSAI	*Journal of the Royal Society of Antiquaries of Ireland*
JWHS	*Journal of the Wexford Historical Society*
JWSEIAS	*Journal of the Waterford and South-East of Ireland Archaeological Society*
KCL	Kildare County Library
KG	Kildare Genealogy
KGC	Killarney Genealogical Centre
LC	Local Custody
LCL	Leitrim County Library
LDS	Latter-Day Saints
LEC	Landed Estates Court
Leitrim GC	Leitrim Genealogy Centre
LG	Limerick Genealogy
LGC	Longford Genealogy Centre
LHL	Linen Hall Library (Belfast)
LOC	Library of Congress
Louth CL	Louth County Library
MG	Monaghan Genealogy
MHC	Mallow Heritage Centre
MHGC	Meath Heritage and Genealogy Centre
MNFHRC	Mayo North Family History Research Centre
MSFHC	Mayo South Family Heritage Centre
NA (Kew)	National Archives (England and Wales)
NAI	National Archives of Ireland
NIFHS	North of Ireland Family History Society
NLA	National Library of Australia
NLC	National Library of Canada
NLI	National Library of Ireland
NLNZ	National Library of New Zealand

NLS	National Library of Scotland
NLSA	National Library of South Africa
NTGC	North Tipperary Genealogy Centre
O'K.	*O'Kief, Coshe Mang etc.* (ed. Albert Casey)
Ph.	Phillimore & Co. publication
Pos.	Positive (National Library of Ireland microfilm)
Pres.	Presbyterian
Pres. NS	Presbyterian Non-Subscribing
PRIA	*Proceedings of the Royal Irish Academy*
PRO	Public Record Office (London)
PRONI	Public Record Office of Northern Ireland
PRS	Parish Register Society publication
RC	Roman Catholic
RCBL	Representative Church Body Library
RDKPRI	*Report of the Deputy Keeper of Public Records of Ireland*
RHGC	Roscommon Heritage and Genealogy Centre
RHK	Rothe House, Kilkenny
RIA	Royal Irish Academy
SA	*Seanchas Ardmhacha*
SHC	Swords Heritage Centre
SHGS	Sligo Heritage and Genealogy Society
SMFRC	South Mayo Family Research Centre
TCD	Trinity College, Dublin
TFHR	Tipperary Family History Research
UHF	Ulster Historical Foundation
UHGGN	*Ulster Historical and Genealogical Guild Newsletter*
UJA	*Ulster Journal of Archaeology*
WCHC	West Cork Heritage Centre
WCL	Westmeath County Library
WFHC	Wicklow Family History Centre
WHGC	Waterford Heritage and Genealogy Centre
WHGS	Wexford Heritage and Genealogy Service
WXCL	Wexford County Library

LIST OF ILLUSTRATIONS

PREFACE TO THE FOURTH EDITION

Tracing Your Irish Ancestors was first published in 1992, at a time when genealogy in Ireland was barely respectable. The change has been extraordinary. Family history now figures on the agendas of Government departments in a way that was scarcely imaginable then. All Irish record-holding institutions—local and national archives, libraries and private institutions—have now recognised that genealogists are one of their largest constituencies, and they are providing dedicated research rooms, personalised consultations, expanded finding aids and, above all, digitised records. Computerising records not only improves speed and removes drudgery but can qualitatively alter the kinds of information that become available and can increase by orders of magnitude the number of people who can access it. Such websites as the National Archives census site, *<www.census.nationalarchives.ie>*, the Library Council's Griffith's Valuation site, *<www.askaboutireland.ie>*, the church records sites, *<www.rootsireland.ie>* and *<www.irishgenealogy.ie>*, and the newspapers archives at *<www.irishnewsarchive.com>* and *<www.irishtimes.com/archive>* are slowly but surely changing the everyday relationship that people in Ireland, and people of Irish heritage outside the island, have with their family's past, and by extension with their country's past. This can only be a good thing.

This edition reflects the profound change in the connection between Irish research and the internet that has taken place since 2005. Then, any online copies of records were piecemeal and amateur—very welcome, but afterthoughts to the main business of hands-on research in Irish repositories. Now the internet is at the heart of any Irish family history research project, and the entire edition has been rewritten to incorporate that change. Where online transcripts exist, these are listed alongside the descriptions of the original records, and research strategies are supplied for any major dedicated websites.

The reference section has also been greatly enlarged, and an index has been added. As before, any material removed for reasons of space will be found at the Irish Ancestors website, *<www.irishtimes.com/ancestor>*.

INTRODUCTION

The aim of this book is to provide a comprehensive guide for anyone wanting to trace his or her Irish ancestors. As the individual circumstances of each family are unique, the relevant areas of research vary widely from case to case. While some areas will be important for almost all researchers, others are more specialised and are therefore extremely important only in particular cases. This book is structured to reflect that division: the first five chapters examine the basic sources and the internet; the following seven chapters detail sources with a narrower application; and the final three chapters consist of a number of reference guides to facilitate quick access to a range of research materials, including county-by-county source lists and Roman Catholic records.

How you use the book depends very much on your individual circumstances. For someone with no experience of genealogical research in Ireland it would be best to start from this Introduction and work through the early chapters, leaving the rest until the basic materials have been exhausted. Someone who has already covered parish registers, land records, census returns and the state records of births, marriages and deaths may wish to start from Chapter 5. Others may simply want to use the reference guides as a basis for planning and directing their research. However, as anyone who regularly uses Irish records will know, one of the pleasures of research is the constant discovery of new sources of information, and new aspects of familiar sources. The information in this book is the result of many years of such discoveries in the course of full-time research, and it is quite possible that even a hard-bitten veteran will find something new in the account of the basic records given in the early chapters.

WHERE TO START
The first question asked by anyone embarking on ancestral research is 'What do I need to know before I start?' Unfortunately, there are as many answers as there are families. Although the painstaking examination of original documents has its own pleasures, in genealogy it is usually better to arrive than to travel hopefully. So, while it is theoretically possible to start from your own birth and work back through records of births, marriages and deaths, parish records and census records, in practical terms the more you can glean from older family members or from family documents the better: there is no point in combing through decades of parish records to uncover your great-grandmother's maiden name if you could find the answer simply by asking Aunt Agatha. Nor does the information you initially acquire this way need to be absolutely precise. At this point in your research, quantity is more important than quality. Later on, something that

seemed relatively insignificant—the name of a local parish priest, the story of a contested will, someone's unusual occupation, even a postmark—may well prove to be the vital clue that enables you to trace the family further back. In any case, whether or not such information eventually turns out to be useful, it will certainly be of interest and will help to flesh out the picture of earlier generations. For most people the spur to starting research is curiosity about their own family, and the kind of anecdotal information provided by the family itself rarely emerges from the official documents.

To use the record resources fully and successfully, three strands of information are vital: dates, names and places. Dates of emigration, births, marriages and deaths; names of parents, siblings, cousins, aunts, in-laws; addresses, townland names, parishes, towns, counties . . . Needless to say, not all of this is essential, and again absolute accuracy is not vital to start out with. A general location and siblings' names can be used to uncover parents' names and addresses, and their parents' names. A single precise name and date can be enough to unlock all the other records. Even a name alone, if it is sufficiently unusual, can sometimes be enough. In general, though, the most useful single piece of information is the precise locality of origin of the family. The county of origin would normally be the minimum information necessary, though in the case of a common surname (of which there are only too many) even this may not be enough. For the descendants of Irish emigrants the locality is often one of the most difficult things to discover. There are a variety of ways of doing this, however, both in the records of the destination country and in Irish records online. The best time to do it is certainly before coming to Ireland. A guide to staring research online will be found below, and the most useful Australian, American and British sources for uncovering the locality of origin of Irish emigrants are detailed at the end of this Introduction.

The only absolute rule in family history research is that you should start from what you know, and use that to find out more. Every family's circumstances are unique, and where your research leads you will depend very much on the point from which you start. So, for example, knowing where a family lived at about the turn of the century will allow you to uncover a census return with the ages of the individuals, leading to birth or baptismal records giving parents' names and residence, leading on in turn to early land records, which may permit the identification of generations before the start of parish records. At each stage of such research the next step should always be determined by what you have just found out: each discovery is a stepping-stone to the next. As a result, it is simply not possible to lay down a route that will serve every reader. It is possible, however, to say that there is no point in taking, say, a seventeenth-century pedigree and trying to extend it forwards to connect with your family. Although there may very well be a connection, the only way to prove it is by expanding your own family information and then working backwards.

WHAT YOU CAN EXPECT TO FIND

What you will uncover about your family history depends on the quality of the surviving records for the area of origin and, again, on the point from which you start. In the majority of cases, that is, for the descendants of Catholic tenant-farmers, the limit is generally the starting date of the local Catholic parish records, which varies widely from place to place. However, it would be unusual for records of such a family to go back much earlier than the 1780s, and for most people the early 1800s is the more likely limit. In Gaelic culture genealogy was of crucial importance, but the collapse of that culture in the seventeenth century, and its subsequent impoverishment and oppression in the eighteenth century, have left a gulf that is almost unbridgeable. That said, exceptions immediately spring to mind. One Australian family, starting with only the name of their great-grandfather, his occupation and the date of his departure from Ireland, uncovered enough information through parish registers and state records of births, marriages and deaths to link him incontestably to the Garveys of Mayo, for whom an established pedigree is registered in the Genealogical Office stretching back to the twelfth century. An American family, knowing only a general location in Ireland and a marriage that took place before emigration, discovered that marriage in the pedigree of the McDermotts of Coolavin, which is factually verified as far back as the eleventh century. Discoveries like this are rare, however, and are much likelier for those of Anglo-Irish extraction than for those of Gaelic or Scots Presbyterian extraction.

Whatever the outcome, genealogical research offers pleasures and insights that are unique. The desire that drives it is simple and undeniable: it is the curiosity of the child asking, 'Where did I come from?' All history starts from here, and genealogy is the most basic form of history—tracing the continual cycle of family growth and demise, unravelling the individual strands of relationship and experience that are woven together in the great patterns of historical change. Reconstructing the details of our own family history is a way of understanding, immediately and personally, the connection of the present with the past—a way of understanding ourselves.

STARTING RESEARCH ONLINE

The internet is now the first stop for most people beginning family history research, and transcripts of the four major record sources of universal relevance for Irish research are now online. Or rather part-transcripts are partly online. As we shall see, the devil is in the detail.

For someone who had an ancestor living in Ireland in the first decades of the twentieth century, the National Archives of Ireland census website, <*www.census.nationalarchives.ie*>, is the obvious starting point. It is completely free, leaving plenty of scope for trial and error; every item on every return from 1901 and 1911 is searchable; and it includes images of all the returns, which are printed and follow a thoroughly consistent format. The sheer ease of use of the site means that even someone whose ancestors left Ireland long before 1901 can glean extremely useful information. Perhaps your great-great-grandfather emigrated in 1850, but if you can pick out his nephews and nieces in 1901 you're well on the way to identifying living relatives in Ireland. For more, see Chapter 2: Census Records, 'Using the 1901 and 1911 censuses online'.

The next step in most cases will be to General Register Office records; the state registered all births, marriages and deaths from 1864. The Mormon website <*www.familysearch.org*> has a complete transcript of the central indexes to these registrations up to 1922 for the entire island of Ireland, and to 1958 for the Republic. The site also has part-transcripts of the actual birth registrations up to 1881. Another website, the pay-per-record <*www.rootsireland.ie*>, has full transcripts of civil registrations up to 1900, but only for a minority of areas. Otherwise it is necessary to use the index entry obtained online to purchase a print-out of the registration entry from the GRO itself. See Chapter 1: General Register Office Records for more detail.

Once research goes back past the start of civil registration only two classes of record are invariably useful: the property tax records of Griffith's Valuation and church baptismal, marriage and burial registers. Griffith's is freely searchable at <*www.askaboutireland.ie*> and can provide valuable information about a family's location and economic circumstances, as well as a key to the (offline) records used in drawing it up and in keeping it up to date. See Chapter 4: Property and Valuation Records.

Church records, probably the most valuable source for genealogical research, are transcribed online in two main places, <*www.irishgenealogy.ie*> and <*www. rootsireland.ie*>. The former is free, the latter paying. Only some of the transcripts on <*www.irishgenealogy.ie*> are accompanied by record images, which means that a certain amount of interaction with offline microfilm and original records becomes necessary in most cases. For Catholic records the National Library of Ireland (<*www.nli.ie*>) is aiming to make images created from its microfilm copies of pre-1880 parish registers available online in the near future. Some caution is needed in using online transcripts of church records: the originals can be in poor condition or fragmented, and the transcriptions can be poor. See Chapter 3: Church Records for more detail.

The internet has been a wonderful boon to Irish genealogy, bringing distant records closer and making opaque records transparent. But it has its dangers. The sheer ease it brings to research can be all too seductive, masking gaps in the originals and flaws in the transcripts. Anyone tracing their ancestors online has to keep in mind that everything, absolutely everything, they are searching is merely a copy of the original, with an inevitable layer of error. This means that knowing precisely what records you are looking at becomes more, not less, important. Saying 'I found it on the internet' is the equivalent of saying 'I don't know where I found it'. And if you don't know where you found information, you don't know what it means.

US SOURCES FOR IDENTIFYING IRISH PLACE OF ORIGIN

Naturalisation records: These may contain the date of birth, place of birth, occupation and place of residence of the immigrant as well as the name of the ship on which they arrived. They are unlikely to give a precise place of origin in Ireland. The records are still for the most part in the courts where the naturalisation proceedings took place. Some records are now in Federal Record Centres. Indexes for the states of Maine, Massachusetts, New Hampshire and Rhode Island before 1906 are available at the National Archives, Washington. A good guide to which records are online is at <*www.germanroots.com*>.

Cemetery and burial records: There are two kinds of potentially valuable records: gravestone inscriptions and sextons' records. These vary enormously in usefulness but may sometimes specify the exact place of origin. Good guides are at <*www.deathindexes.com*> and <*www.cyndislist.com*>.

Immigration records and passenger lists: These are now mostly in the National Archives in Washington. The Customs Passenger Lists, dating from 1820, give only the country of origin. The Immigration Passenger Lists, from 1883, include details of the last place of residence. See also Chapter 8 for details of other sources. A good online guide is at <*www.genealogybranches.com*>.

Military records: Depending on place or branch of service, these may specify the place, or at least the county, of origin. First World War draft cards asked for date and location of birth and are online at <*www.ancestry.com*>. A good guide to online US military records is <*www.militaryindexes.com*>.

Church records: These may in some cases, particularly for the marriages of recently arrived immigrants, include details of the Irish place of origin of the persons recorded. Most Catholic records are still in the parishes. The records of other denominations may be held locally or deposited with a variety of institutions, including public libraries, universities and diocesan archives. Good guides are at <*www.genealogybranches.com*> and <*www.cyndislist.com*>.

Biographies in county histories: Many counties in the United States have printed county histories, which can often contain biographical information about families living there. The catalogue of the Library of Congress, <*catalog.loc. gov*>, can be good, as can the LDS Family History Library, <*www.familysearch. org/#form=catalog*>.

Vital records: Death records in particular may be of value, since they generally supply parents' names.

CANADIAN SOURCES FOR IDENTIFYING IRISH PLACE OF ORIGIN

National and Provincial Archives: The vast bulk of information of genealogical interest can be found in the National and Provincial Archives of Canada, which are familiar with the needs of genealogical research and very helpful. The National Archives (395 Wellington Street, Ottawa ON K1A 0N3; tel. 613-995-5138) publish a useful twenty-page booklet, *Tracing Your Ancestors in Canada,* which is available by post. Some of the information held in the

Provincial Archives, in particular the census records, is also to be found in Ottawa; but in general the Provincial Archives have a broader range of information relating to their particular areas. Some of the Provincial Archives now have excellent websites with very good immigration information. New Brunswick is an excellent example.

Civil records: In general the original registers of births, marriages and deaths, which have widely varying starting dates, are to be found in the offices of the Provincial Registrars-General, although microfilm copies of some may also be found in the Provincial Archives.

Census records: Countrywide censuses are available for 1851, 1861, 1871, 1881 and 1891. There are, however, many local returns available for earlier years, which record a wide variety of information. The largest collection is in the Ottawa National Archives.

Other sources: Cemetery and burial records, gravestone inscriptions, passenger lists, church registers and land records may all be of value. The best comprehensive guide is in Angus Baxter's *In Search of Your Canadian Roots* (3rd ed., 2000), which gives details of a wide range of records to be found in the National and Provincial Archives.

AUSTRALIAN SOURCES FOR IDENTIFYING IRISH PLACE OF ORIGIN

Convict transportation records: A database index of Dublin Castle records of those transported from Ireland to Australia was presented to Australia as part of the Bicentennial celebrations of 1988. It often includes details of the conviction and place of residence. Further information on the records it covers will be found in Chapter 8. It is widely available in the Australian State Archives, in the National Archives and on the internet (<*www.nationalarchives.ie*>). Many other classes of record, originating both in Australia and in England, also exist and can be found in most Australian repositories.

Assisted immigration records: A detailed record was kept of those who availed of assisted passages to Australia. See the New South Wales State Archives' *Guide to Shipping and Free Passenger Lists*. See also 'Australia' in Chapter 8.

Civil records: Australian state death records provide a wealth of family detail, in most cases including precise places of origin. Marriage records also supply places of birth and parents' names. A good guide is at the Society of Australian Genealogists website, <*www.sag.org.au*>.

BRITISH SOURCES FOR IDENTIFYING IRISH PLACE OF ORIGIN

England and Wales

Civil registration of births, marriages and deaths: Registration began in 1837 and records the same details as those given in Irish records (see Chapter 1). Unfortunately, the marriage records very rarely give exact Irish addresses for parents. It is sometimes worthwhile extending research into the broader Irish community in a given area. Our perennial clannishness, and the mechanics of chain migration, meant that people from a particular area of Ireland tended to gravitate towards each other.

Census records: Seven sets of census returns are available between 1841 and 1901. Those from 1871 to 1901 are online at various locations, and most allow a search on place of birth. Again it is rare to find a precise place of birth in Ireland recorded, though the county is sometimes given. Investigation of the local Irish immigrant populace can yield circumstantial evidence. Almost all nineteenth and early twentieth-century censuses of England and Wales are online at <www.ancestry.co.uk>, <www.findmypast.co.uk> and <www.thegenealogist. co.uk>.

Church records: Marriage records for recent immigrants may give the place of origin in Ireland.

Scotland

Civil registration of births, marriages and deaths: Registration began in 1855 and recorded substantially more detail than in Ireland or England. In particular, birth records show a place and date of marriage, and death records supply parents' names.

Census records: Census returns are similar to those for England and Wales. A computerised index to the 1891 census is available.

Civil and census records are available at the General Register Office (New Register House), Princes Street, Edinburgh EH1 3YT. The Scottish Record Office is next door and holds a vast array of relevant archive material. Cecil Sinclair's *Tracing Your Scottish Ancestors: a guide to ancestry research in the Scottish Record Office* (Edinburgh: 1990; rev. ed., 1997) is the standard guide. Almost all relevant records are now searchable online at <www.scotlandspeople.gov.uk>.

THE CHURCH OF JESUS CHRIST OF LATTER-DAY SAINTS

Because of the central importance of the family in its teachings, the Church of Jesus Christ of Latter-Day Saints, also known as the Mormons, places great emphasis on family history. For many decades the Family History Library in Salt Lake City has been collecting copies of records of genealogical value as aids to its members' research. The collection is now extraordinary: its Irish section includes all of the GRO indexes and a good quantity of the registers, a large proportion of church records, the records of the Genealogical Office and the Registry of Deeds, and much more. More detail is given in the individual chapters.

To work on these records it is not necessary to visit the library in person. Every Mormon temple has a family history section open to non-church members that can request copies of any of the microfilms from Salt Lake City—in effect providing a worldwide system of access to copies of the original records. To those for whom a research visit to Ireland is impractical, the LDS Family History Centres are almost as good. Many LDS records are searchable online at <www.familysearch.org>.

Chapter 1 ∿

GENERAL REGISTER OFFICE RECORDS

HISTORY

Registration of non-Roman Catholic marriages began in Ireland in 1845, but the full registration system only came into operation in 1864, when all births, marriages and deaths began to be registered. These dates are relatively late, at least when compared with the starting years of the civil registration systems in other parts of what was then the United Kingdom of Great Britain and Ireland. Full registration was introduced in 1837 in England and Wales and in 1855 in Scotland.

To appreciate the nature of the records it created it is necessary to have some idea of how registration began. It was an offshoot of the Victorian public health system in Ireland, in turn based on the Poor Law, an attempt to provide some measure of publicly funded relief for the most destitute. Between 1838 and 1852, 163 workhouses were built throughout Ireland, each at the centre of an area known as a Poor Law Union. The workhouses were commonly situated in a large market town, and the Poor Law Union comprised the town and its catchment area, with the result that in many cases the Unions ignored many existing parish and county boundaries. This had consequences for research, as we will see below.

In the 1850s a large-scale public health system was created, based on the areas covered by the Poor Law Unions. Each Union was divided into Dispensary Districts, with an average of six to seven Districts per Union. A Medical Officer, normally a doctor, was given responsibility for public health in each District. With the introduction of the registration of all births, deaths and marriages in 1864, these Dispensary Districts did double duty as Registrar's Districts, with a Registrar responsible for collecting the registrations within this District. In most cases, the Medical Officer for the Dispensary District now also acted as the Registrar for the same area. The superior of the Registrar was the Superintendent Registrar, responsible for all the Registrars within the old Poor Law Union.

The day-to-day system worked as follows: when a local Registrar had filled a registration volume it was forwarded to the Superintendent Registrar, who made a copy of this register and forwarded the copy to the GRO in Dublin; these copies were then used to create centralised all-Ireland indexes; and these indexes and their corresponding copy registers then formed the basis for research in the records, by both GRO staff and the public.

Because of its origins, responsibility for registration in the Republic rested with the Department of Health until 2004. The Civil Registration Act (2004) then transferred responsibility for the GRO to the Department of Social Protection, with local Registrars in each Health Service Executive Area still part of the Department of Health. Although the current registration system is completely digitised, the historical local registers are still held by the Superintendent Registrars. The GRO public research facility, at 8–11 Lombard Street East, Dublin 2, has the master indexes to all 32 counties up to 1921 and to the 26 counties of the Republic after 1921, as well as digital copies of the centrally copied historical registers. The administrative headquarters of the GRO is now at Convent Road, Roscommon.

ACCESS IN THE REPUBLIC
To recap: under the original system the local Registrars passed completed copies of their registers to their Superintendent Registrar, who made copies and sent these to the central GRO in Dublin, where master indexes were created from them. This index-to-register system is still the basis of all research in these records.

1. Official access: In the Republic the only legal access to the historical records is to the centralised indexes and copy registers via the research room of the GRO in the Irish Life Centre in Lower Abbey Street, Dublin. Researchers pay €2 to search five years of a single-event index or €20 for a full day's access to all indexes of either births, marriages or deaths. These indexes record surname, forename, registration district, volume and page number. Death indexes also record the reported age at death. From 1903, birth indexes record the mother's maiden name. To see the complete details in an original register transcript entry, a researcher fills out a request form with the details extracted from the index volume, pays €4 and waits for a member of the counter staff to find the entry in the digitised system, print it out and bring it back to the counter. There is a limit of five print-outs per researcher per day, though members of staff will post on any requests above that number. Limited research is carried out by the staff in response to postal queries.
2. <www.certificates.ie>: This Health Service Executive website operates an online certificates-only service covering births from 1864, marriages from 1920 and deaths from 1924. The system is designed to produce certificates for current use, but it could in theory be used in conjunction with the LDS system (see below) to obtain a full transcript of information in historical birth registrations. Orders are fulfilled from Joyce House, 8–11 Lombard Street East, Dublin 2.
3. LDS: The Church of Jesus Christ of Latter-Day Saints, the Mormons, have microfilm copies of all the indexes to 1958, of the birth registers 1864–81, 1900–1913 and 1933–50, of marriage registers 1845–70 and of death registers 1864–70. They also have microfilm copies of the birth registers 1930–58. These

microfilms have long been available for research via the Family History Centres attached to most Mormon temples (see below). Over the past few years they have begun to make transcripts from the microfilms available on their website, <*www.familysearch.org*>. For more details see 'GRO research online' below.

4. Heritage centres: As part of the Irish Genealogical Project it was planned that a network of local heritage centres would transcribe the historical registers still held locally by the Superintendent Registrars. Five centres have completed transcriptions of these registers for their county, generally up to 1920, and six more have very extensive but still incomplete transcripts. These are searchable on a pay-per-view basis at <*www.rootsireland.ie*>. No further transcription by the centres will take place.

ACCESS IN NORTHERN IRELAND

In Northern Ireland the only official access to the historical records is via the public search room of GRONI in Chichester Street, Belfast. Unlike in the Republic, public access to digitised versions of the records is well advanced. Transcription of the original register entries is taking place, creating a much more flexible research system independent of the old index-to-register search model.

Since the summer of 2010 the results of this transcription project have been available in the public search room. There is partial public access to the transcript database, combined with manual print-outs from digital images of the registers. A single daily fee covers access to the database and a specified number of print-outs. Above this number, users pay on a *pro rata* basis. GRONI plans to eventually migrate all historical indexes and records (births over 100 years, marriages over 75 years and deaths over 50 years) to its website. Access will require payment, but precise details of payment mechanisms have yet to be decided. It is anticipated that the entire project will take three years, with a completion date of 2014, but interim access will be provided in the public search room.

THE MORMONS

In the late 1950s and early 60s the LDS Library carried out a huge microfilming programme on GRO records, and it now has several thousand films of both the centralised indexes and the corresponding registers. Almost every Mormon temple includes a Family History Centre, which can order copies of any of the LDS microfilms. Unfortunately, the collection is not complete: in particular, the birth registers for the last two decades of the nineteenth century, and marriage and death registers after 1870, are missing—a lack that is now unlikely to be made good. Details of the full LDS holdings are given below.

LDS copies of GRO records

BIRTHS

Area	Indexes	Film	Online	Registers	Film
All Ireland	1864–1921	0101041–01001079	Yes	1864–1st qtr 1881	0101080–0257861
					1419540–1419541
				1900–1913	0257861–0258168
				1930–55	0258169–0258441
Republic of Ireland	1922–58	0101229–0101240, 0231962–0231969	No	1922–59	0231970–0259147
Northern Ireland	1922–59	0231962–0231969	No		

MARRIAGES

Area	Indexes	Film	Online	Registers	Film
All Ireland	1845–1921	0101241–0101264	Yes	1845–70	0101265–0101572
Republic of Ireland	1922–58	0101575–0101581, 0257850–0257852	Yes		
Northern Ireland	1922–59	0232169–0232173	No	1922–59	0232174–0232471

DEATHS

Area	Indexes	Film	Online	Registers	Film
All Ireland	1864–1921	0101582–0101608	Yes	1864–70	0101609–0101727
Republic of Ireland	1922–58	0101735–0101744, 0257853–0257856	Yes		
Northern Ireland	1922–59	0232472–0232478	No	1922–59	0232479–0259139

The LDS website, <*www.familysearch.org*>, includes a complete transcript copy of the indexes to 1958 as well as partial transcripts of the earliest registers (births 1864–81, marriages 1864–70 and deaths 1864–70). See 'GRO research online' below.

INFORMATION RECORDED

One of the peculiarities of the system of registration is that, although the local Registrars were responsible for the registers, the legal obligation to register births and deaths actually rested with the public and was enforced with hefty fines. Marriage registration, on the other hand, was generally the responsibility of the officiating clergyman. The classes of people required to carry out registration in each of the three categories are given below, along with a detailed account of the information they were required to supply. It should be remembered that not all of this information is relevant to genealogical research.

Births

Persons required to register births were:

- the parent or parents, or in the case of death or inability of the parent or parents
- the occupier of the house or tenement in which the child was born, or
- the nurse, or
- any person present at the birth of the child.

The information they were required to supply was:

- the date and place of birth;
- the name (if any);
- the sex;
- the name, surname and dwelling-place of the father;
- the name, surname, maiden surname and dwelling-place of the mother;
- the rank, profession or occupation of the father.

The informant and the Registrar were both required to sign each entry, which was also to include the date of registration, the residence of the informant and his or her 'qualification' (for example 'present at birth'). Notice of the birth was to be given to the Registrar within twenty-one days, and full details within three months. It was not obligatory to register a first name for the child. The very small proportion for which no first name was supplied appear in the indexes as, for example, 'Kelly (male)' or 'Murphy (female)'.

Deaths

Persons required to register deaths were:

- some person present at death, or
- some person in attendance during the last illness of the deceased, or
- the occupier of the house or tenement where the death took place, or
- someone else residing in the house or tenement where the death took place, or
- any person present at, or having knowledge of the circumstances of, the death.

The information they were required to supply was:

- the date and place of death;
- the name and surname of the deceased;
- the sex of the deceased;
- the condition of the deceased as to marriage;
- the age of the deceased at last birthday;
- the rank, profession or occupation of the deceased;
- the certified cause of death and the duration of the final illness.

Again, the informant and the Registrar were both required to sign each entry, which was also to include the date of registration, the residence of the informant and his or her 'qualification' (for example 'present at death'). Notice of the death was to be given to the Registrar within seven days, and full details within fourteen days.

Marriages

From 1864 any person whose marriage was to be celebrated by a Roman Catholic clergyman was required to have the clergyman fill out a certificate containing the information detailed below and to forward it within three days of the marriage to the Registrar. In practice, as had already been the case for non-Catholic marriages since 1845, the clergyman simply kept a civil register separate from the church register, filled it in after the ceremony and forwarded it to the local Registrar when it was full. The information to be supplied was:

- the date when married;
- the names and surnames of each of the parties marrying;
- their age;
- their condition (i.e. bachelor, spinster, widow, widower);
- their rank, profession or occupation;
- their residences at the time of marriage;
- the name and surname of the fathers of each of the parties;
- the rank, profession or occupation of the fathers of each of the parties.

The certificate was to state where the ceremony had been performed and be signed by the clergyman, the parties marrying and two witnesses.

GENEALOGICAL RELEVANCE

From a genealogical point of view, only the following information is of genuine interest:

Births: the name, the date of birth, the place of birth; the name, surname and dwelling-place of the father; the name, surname and dwelling-place of the mother; and, occasionally, the name, residence and qualification of the informant.

Marriages: the parish in which the marriage took place; the names, ages, residences and occupations of the persons marrying; the names and occupations of their fathers.

Deaths: the place of death; the age of death and, occasionally, the name, residence and qualification of the informant.

Of the three categories the most useful is certainly the marriage entry, both because it provides fathers' names, thus giving a direct link to the preceding generation, and because it is the easiest to identify from the indexes, as we will see below. Birth entries are much more difficult to identify correctly from the indexes without precise information about date and place, and even with such information the high concentration of people of the same surname within particular localities can make it difficult to be sure that a particular birth registration is the relevant one. Unlike in many other countries, death records in Ireland are not very useful for genealogical purposes, because there was no obligation to record family information, and the 'age at death' is often very imprecise. That said, these records can sometimes be of value. The person 'present at death' was often a family member, and the relationship is sometimes specified in the register entry. Even the age recorded may be useful, since it at least gives an idea of how old the person was thought to be by family or neighbours.

A general word of warning about civil registration is necessary: some proportion of all three categories simply went unregistered, particularly in the two decades up to 1884. It is impossible to be sure how much is not there, since the thoroughness of local registration depended very much on local conditions and on the individuals responsible; but experience in cross-checking from other sources, such as parish and census records, suggests that as much as 10–15 per cent of marriages and births simply do not appear in the registers.

RESEARCH IN THE INDEXES

When carrying out research in all three areas, a large dose of scepticism is necessary with regard to the dates of births, marriages and deaths reported by family members before 1900. This is especially true for births: the ages given in census returns, for example, are almost always inaccurate, and round figures—50, 60, 70 etc.—must be treated with particular caution. The actual date of birth is almost always well before the one reported, sometimes by as much as fifteen years. Why this should be is a matter for speculation, but probably neither vanity nor mendacity is to blame. It seems more likely that until quite recently very few people actually knew their precise date of birth. And as most people don't feel their age, after middle age at least, a guess will usually produce an underestimate. Whatever the explanation, charitable or otherwise, it is always wiser to search a range of the indexes before the reported date, rather than after it.

From 1864 to 1877 the indexes consist of a single yearly volume in each category—births, marriages and deaths—covering the entire country and recording all names in a straightforward alphabetical arrangement. The same

INDEX to BIRTHS REGISTERED in IRELAND in 1866.

District.	Vol.	Page
....	7	411
....	13	328
....	20	266
....	6	991
elin. Lisburn .	1	659
....	17	715
....	11	893
th............	7	572
....	5	140
....	11	222
....	20	104
....	11	782
....	7	937
....	7	732
....	3	447
rick	20	432
....	19	500
....	14	82
....	14	476
....	10	128
....	6	178
orth........	7	549
....	15	394
....	20	154
....	10	735
....	2	728
....	11	112
....	6	613
....	14	376
....	1	173
....	3	701
hdown	17	889
....	5	232
....	1	264
. Parsonstown	18	599
trick........	11	531
....	11	834
....	2	463
....	17	386
....	7	653
lin, South ...	17	622
....	10	665
oth........	7	672
....	16	281
....	12	892
....	2	750
....	15	244
....	20	179
....	14	905
....	9	950
....	19	655
....	9	370
....	3	571
h............	11	82
uth........	7	813
....	1	757
, North	2	690
gh........	11	82
....	8	503
....	17	38
, North.....	2	630
orth.......	12	547
....	1	838
....	16	788
....	11	43
....	9	871
....	5	175
....	11	26

Name and Registration District.	Vol.	Page
PELL, John Joseph. Dublin, North	12	584
PELLETT, Anna Maria. Dublin, South	12	656
PELLICAN, John. Listowel	10	500
PELLY, Catherine. Ballinasloe	19	37
—— Catherine Evangiline. Dublin, South	2	745
—— John Joseph. Dublin, South	2	737
—— Mary. Portumna	14	946
PEMBERTON, Marian Sydney. Dublin, North	17	527
—— (female). Dublin, South	7	811
PEMBROKE, Ellen. Tralee	20	627
—— Ellen. Tralee	15	596
—— Margaret. Kilkenny	8	603
—— Mary. Dingle	15	207
—— Mary Eliza. Kilkenny	3	609
—— Patrick. Listowel	10	501
PENDER, Anne. Enniscorthy	14	725
—— Bernard. Carrick-on-Shannon	18	65
—— Bridget. Enniscorthy	4	814
—— Bridget. Enniscorthy	9	753
—— Daniel. Gorey	7	876
—— Daniel. Gorey	7	877
—— Elizabeth. Nenagh	3	651
—— Elizabeth. Carlow	13	447
—— Ellen. Ballymoney	6	194
—— Ellen. Rathdown	12	920
—— Ellen. Enniscorthy	19	764
—— James. Waterford	9	951
—— John. Carlow	8	507
—— John. Enniscorthy	14	722
—— John. Mullingar	13	317
—— Joseph. Athy	13	406
—— Laurance. Carlow	13	436
—— Mary. Wexford	14	911
—— Mary Anne. Carlow	3	505
—— Mary Catherine. Carlow	18	427
—— Mathew. Wexford	14	910
—— Michael. Carlow	3	494
—— Peter. Rathdrum	2	1061
—— Thomas. Ballinasloe	19	31
—— William. Waterford	19	925
—— (female). Limerick	10	454
PENDERGAST, Anne. Roscommon	18	353
—— Bridget. Tulla	19	606
—— Catherine. Swineford	4	579
—— Ellen. Castlereagh	19	161
—— Margaret. Castlereagh	19	162
—— Margaret. Killarney	5	400
—— Mary. Bawnboy	3	51
—— Mary. Castlebar	19	133
—— Myles. Wexford	19	955
—— Pat. Ballinrobe	4	51
—— Patrick. Rathdown	17	891
—— Patrick. Monaghan	8	330
PENDERGAST, Anne. New Ross	4	969
—— Ellen. Killarney	15	315
—— Michael. Killarney	15	316
PENDERS, Mary. Nenagh	13	584
PENDLETON, Essie. Lurgan	16	673
PENGELLY, Michael James. Cork	20	193
PENNAPATHER, (male). Rathkeale	10	621
PENNAMEN, Mary Jane Fraser. Belfast	11	277
PENNEFATHER, John Thomas. Dublin, North	2	608
—— Richard Dymock. Cashel	3	531
PENNELL, (male). Cork	15	101
PENNINGTON, Charles. Banbridge	16	229
PENNY, John. Ballymena	11	113
—— (male). Wexford	14	922
PENNYCOOK, Janet. Athy	8	459

Name and Reg...
PERCY, Robert Henry ...
—— William. Antrim...
PERDUE, John. Callar...
—— Mary Anne. Ti...
PERIL, Patrick. Gort...
PERKINS, Cornelius. ...
—— Joseph John. D...
—— Patrick. Naas ...
—— Robert Henry. ...
—— Thomas. Ought...
—— (female). Ballin...
PERKINSON, Barkly. A...
PERKISSON, Briget. T...
PERRILL, Patrick. Cli...
PERRIN Ellen. Dublin...
—— Henrietta. Rath...
—— William Alexand...
—— (female). Cavan...
PERROT, Catherine. D...
—— Sarah. Clonakilt...
PERROTT, Margaret. ...
—— Robert. Cork ..
—— William Cooke ...
—— William Thomas...
PERRY, Agnes. Belfas...
—— Agnes. Lisburn...
—— Angelina Margare...
—— Ann. Downpatri...
—— Ann Jane. Bally...
—— Anthony. Ennis...
—— Catherine. Balti...
—— Eliza. Ballymah...
—— Eliza. Naas ....
—— Eliza. Belfast ..
—— Elizabeth. Bally...
—— Elizabeth. Larn...
—— Ellen. Ballymen...
—— Etheld Letitia. ...
—— Hannah. Larne...
—— Helena Jane. L...
—— Henry. Newry ...
—— James. Dundalk...
—— James. Dublin...
—— James. Baltingl...
—— Jane. Banbridg...
—— Jane Eleanor. ...
—— John. Lisburn ...
—— John. Naas ...
—— Joseph. Ballym...
—— Letitia Anne. ...
—— Martin. Newtow...
—— Mary. Ballymal...
—— Mary Anne. Ba...
—— Rebecca. Bally...
—— Robinson Gale...
—— Sarah. Downpa...
—— Sarah. Newtow...
—— Sarah. Ballyme...
—— Susanna. Down...
—— Thomas. Trim...
—— Thomas. Belfas...
—— Thomas Shanklin...
—— William. Tippe...
—— William Gardine...
—— William Richard...
—— William Robinso...
—— (male). Clonme...
—— (male). Armag...

General Register Office births index.

(Courtesy of the National Library of Ireland)

arrangement also applies to the non-Roman Catholic marriages registered from April 1845. From 1878 the yearly volume is divided into four quarters, each one covering three months and being indexed separately. This means that a search for a name in, for example, the 1877 births index means looking in one place in the index, while it is necessary to check four different places in the 1878 index, one in each of the four quarters. Between 1903 and 1928 a supplementary series of unofficial indexes exists for births only, once again covering the entire year and also supplying the mother's maiden name. These indexes were not microfilmed by the LDS and thus do not form part of the online FamilySearch index transcripts (see 'GRO research online' below). Starting in 1928, the official birth indexes do supply mothers' maiden names, and these are online. In all three categories each index entry provides surname, first name, registration district, volume and page number. The death indexes also give the reported age at death. The 'volume and page number' simply make up the reference for the original register entry, necessary in order to identify it and, in the GRO research room, to obtain a print-out of the full information given in that entry. The remaining three items—surname, first name and registration district—are dealt with in detail below.

Surname: The order followed in the indexes is strictly alphabetical, but it is always necessary to keep possible variants of the surname in mind. In the late nineteenth century, when a large majority of the population were illiterate, the precise spelling of their surname was a matter of indifference to most people, so members of the same family may be registered as, for example, Kilfoyle, Gilfoyle or Guilfoile. The question of variants is particularly important for names beginning with 'O' or 'Mac'. Until the Irish revival in the last decades of the nineteenth century these were often treated as entirely optional and, in the case of the 'O's particularly, more often omitted than included. Before starting a search in the indexes, therefore, it is essential to have as clear an idea as possible of the variants to be checked. Otherwise it may be necessary to cover the same period as many as three or four times.

First name: The range of first names in use in the nineteenth century was severely limited among the vast majority of the population. Apart from some localised names—'Cornelius' in south Munster, 'Crohan' in the Caherdaniel area of the Iveragh Peninsula, 'Sabina' in the east Galway and north Roscommon area—the anglicisation of the earlier Irish names was restrictive and unimaginative. In all parts of the country, John, Patrick, Michael, Mary and Bridget occur with almost unbelievable frequency. Combined with the intensely localised nature of surnames, which reflect the earlier tribal areas of the country, this can present intense difficulties when using the indexes. For example, a single quarter of 1881, from January to March, might contain twenty or more John (O')Reilly (or Riley) registrations, all in the same registration district of Co. Cavan. A further obstacle is the fact that it is very rare for more than one first name to be registered. Therefore someone known to the family as John James (O')Reilly will almost certainly appear in the index simply as 'John'. It is of course possible to examine all the original register entries, but unless some other piece of information, such as the parents' names or the townland address, can be used to cross-check, it will almost certainly not be possible to identify which, if any, of the original register entries is the relevant one. This uncertainty is further compounded by the persistent imprecision regarding ages and dates of birth, which means that over the seven or eight-year period during which the relevant birth could have taken place there might be fifty or sixty births of the same name in the one county.

Registration district: As a result of the original arrangements for administering the system, the registration districts used were, and still are, largely identical to the old Poor Law Unions. As these were based on natural catchment areas, normally consisting of a large market town and its rural hinterland, rather than on the already existing administrative divisions of townland, parish and county, registration districts for births, marriages and deaths cut right across these earlier boundaries—a fact that can be very significant for research. For example, Waterford registration district, centred in the town of Waterford, also takes in a large part of rural south Co. Kilkenny. The only comprehensive guide listing the towns and townlands contained in each registration district is to be found in a series of pamphlets produced in the nineteenth century by the Registrar-General's Office for the use of each of the local registrars. This is now republished in George B. Handran (ed.), *Townlands in Poor Law Unions: a reprint of poor law union pamphlets of the general registrar's office with an introduction, and six appendices relating to Irish genealogical research* (Salem, Mass.: Higginson Book, 1997; NLI Ir 9291 h 5, 616 p.). This work is particularly useful when a problem arises in identifying a variant version of a townland name given in the original register entry for a birth, marriage or death. By scanning the lists of townlands in the relevant district in which the entry is recorded, it is almost always possible to identify the standard version of the name and, from this, to go on to census, parish and land records.

To go in the other direction, that is, to find out which registration district a particular town or townland is in, the standard source is the *Alphabetical Index to the Towns, Townlands and Parishes of Ireland*. Three editions of this were published, based on the census returns for 1851, 1871 and 1901. In the first two the registration district is recorded as the Poor Law Union; in the 1901 index it does not appear in the body of the work but may be found as an appendix. Copies of these can be found on open access in NLI, NAI, the GRO itself or in any library. The 1851 index is by far the most widely available and can be found online at <*www.seanruad.com*> and <*www.irishtimes.com/ancestor/placenames*>. If the original townland or address of the family being researched is known, and the search narrowed to a single registration district, at least some of the problems in picking out the relevant entry, in the births indexes particularly, can be significantly reduced.

GRO RESEARCH ONLINE

A project to transcribe all GRO indexes and to image the corresponding registers began in the Republic in 1995. It was suspended in 2004, on the move of the GRO to Roscommon. The aim of the project was to retain the index-to-register search system but improve its efficiency beyond recognition by creating a database of the index entries linked to digital images of the corresponding register pages. By the time the project was suspended, digital images had been created for all the central copy registers, along with fully validated index transcripts for births from 1864, marriages from 1920 and deaths from 1924. These transcripts and images form part of the live registration system. Unvalidated transcripts were created for the remaining indexes. These transcripts, linked to the corresponding images, are accessible to staff in the GRO in Roscommon and in the GRO research room. No public access is available to either part of the system. Under the legislation currently in force in the Republic the only legal public research access is via the printed volumes in the GRO research room. Change is devoutly to be wished.

Legal or not, several ways to access GRO records online exist. First and most important are the transcripts of the LDS microfilms of GRO indexes up to 1922 for the 32 counties, and to 1958 for the Republic, at <*www.familysearch.org*>. To search these it is necessary to drill down from the FamilySearch home page, using 'browse by location', to Europe, then Ireland, then 'Ireland, Civil Registration Indexes, 1845–1958'. The 'advanced search' option then allows the search to be restricted to the birth, marriage or death indexes, and by period and registration district.

It is vital to keep in mind that these are only the indexes: even though the search options allow a user to specify spouses' or parents' names, none of these appear in the indexes until 1928, when the mother's maiden name is given in the birth indexes. So entering these names will result in a negative search. In most cases the full register information is only available from the registers at the GRO. To obtain it you must use the index information on year, quarter, volume and page to purchase a print-out of the register entry, either in person or by correspondence, costing €4 in both cases. It is possible to use the online marriage index transcripts in the same way as the hard-copy indexes to zero in on the relevant marriage by cross-referencing the two names. (See 'Research techniques' below.) The death indexes supply a reported age at death, and FamilySearch automatically subtracts this age from the year of registration to come up with a year of birth. This is then returned for any search of births, meaning that it is impossible to confine a search strictly to the birth indexes.

FamilySearch also has partial transcripts of the LDS microfilm copies of the birth registers to 1881 and some of the marriage and death registers 1864–70. These online records seem to be the result of several separate transcription projects. In some cases the same record appears to have been transcribed three times. Unfortunately, none of the transcriptions include all the information recorded in the originals—townland addresses are missing from all.

Heritage centre transcripts at <*www.rootsireland.ie*> are the other major source of online registration records. These are based on the original local

Registrar's records, rather than on the central copies used by the GRO for its indexes. Five counties—Clare, Donegal, Mayo, Roscommon and Tipperary—have complete transcripts to 1900 for all records in their area, while Galway, Kilkenny, Limerick and Sligo have almost complete coverage. Two things need to be kept in mind: the originals used for these transcripts have fewer errors than the central GRO copies, because they are closer to the original event; and the advanced (and free) index search on <*www.rootsireland.ie*> allows more precise targeting of individual records than FamilySearch. It is of course possible to use the index search on FamilySearch and then check full transcripts on <*www.rootsireland.ie*>.

Part-transcripts of individual areas' records have also been put online. Where these are substantial they are noted under the individual county in Chapter 13.

RESEARCH TECHNIQUES

Births: As highlighted above, it is important to approach the birth indexes with as much information as possible from other sources. If the birth took place between 1864 and 1880 it may be possible to identify it from the FamilySearch birth register transcripts. If the area is known, but not the date, it may be useful to search the online 1901 and 1911 census returns to obtain at least an approximate age and, hence, date of birth. If the names of siblings and the order of their birth are known, but the area and date are not, it may be necessary to search a wide range of years in the indexes, noting all the names of the births that occur in the family, and then try to work out which births of the relevant names occur in the right order in the same registration district. If the name is unusual enough, of course, none of this may be necessary. In Ireland, however, few of us are lucky enough to have an ancestor called Horace Freke-Blood or Euphemia Thackaberry.

Marriages: As long as care is taken over the question of surname variants, and the names of both parties are known, research in the marriage indexes is straightforward. If two people married each other then obviously the registration district, volume and page-number references for them in the indexes must be the same. Therefore it is only necessary to cross-check the two names in the indexes, working back from the approximate date of birth of the eldest child, if this is known, until two entries are found in which all three references correspond. This process is slightly more cumbersome with the FamilySearch online transcripts but still perfectly possible. Marriage records are especially important in the early years of civil registration, as they record the names of the fathers of people born c.1820 to c.1840, as well as their approximate ages, thus providing evidence that can be used to establish earlier generations in parish records. For non-Roman Catholic families the value of these records is even greater, as the records of non-Roman Catholic marriages start in 1845.

Deaths: As in the case of births, it is essential to uncover as much information as possible from other sources before starting a search of the death indexes. Therefore if a date of birth is known from parish or other records, the 'age at death' given in the index, together with the registration district, provides at least a rough guide as to whether or not the death recorded is the relevant one. If the location of a family farm is known, the approximate date of death can often be worked out from the changes in occupier recorded in the Valuation Books of the Land Valuation Office (see Chapter 4). Similarly, if the family had property the Will Calendars of the National Archives after 1858 (see Chapter 6) can be the easiest way to pinpoint the precise date of death. With such information it is then usually a simple matter to pick out the relevant entry from the indexes. Information from a marriage entry may also sometimes be useful: together with the names of the fathers of the parties marrying, the register entry sometimes also specifies that one or both of the fathers are deceased. There is no rule about this, however. The fact that a father is recorded as, say, 'John Murphy, labourer' does not necessarily mean that he was alive at the time of the marriage. If an individual is recorded as 'deceased' this does at least provide an end point for any search for his death entry. As already pointed out, however, death records give no information on preceding generations and only occasionally name a surviving family member.

LIVING RELATIVES

It is very difficult to use the records of the GRO to trace descendants, rather than forebears, of a particular family. From 1903, as already noted, the birth indexes do record the mother's maiden name, as well as the name and surname of the child, so it can be straightforward to trace all the births of a particular family from that date forward. Uncovering the subsequent marriages of those children without knowing the names of their spouses is a much tougher proposition, however. To take one example, the likely range of years of marriage for a Michael O'Brien born in 1905 would be 1925–40; there are certainly hundreds of marriages recorded in the indexes under that name. One could, of course, purchase copies of all the original register entries in the hope that one entry might show the relevant address and father's name and then investigate births of that marriage; but in most cases the work involved makes the task impractical. There are, however, other ways of tracking descendants through land, census, voters' and, sometimes, parish records (Chapters 2, 3 and 4).

LATE REGISTRATIONS, ARMY RECORDS ETC.

Late registrations: A significant proportion of all births, marriages and deaths were simply not registered, as mentioned above. When the individuals concerned, or their relatives, later needed a certificate for official purposes, it became necessary to register the event. The index references for these late registrations are included in the volume for the year in which the event took place. Therefore, for example, the index reference for someone born in 1880 but whose birth was not registered until 1900 is to be found in the index for 1880. In the case of births and deaths these references are indexed separately from the main body of the index, at the back of the volume. For marriages, late registrations are written in by hand at the relevant point in the main body of the index. Although the chances of finding a missing registration among these are quite slim, it is still necessary to include them in any thorough search of the indexes.

Maritime records: From 1864 to the present the GRO has kept a separate Marine Register of births and deaths of Irish subjects that took place at sea. There are 12,382 records between 1864 and 1922. From 1886 only, a printed index to this register is bound into the back of the births and deaths index for each year. For earlier registers the indexes are in GRO headquarters in Roscommon and have to be requested from there. No separate register was kept for marriages at sea. The LDS copy is on film 101765.

Army records: The Births, Deaths and Marriages (Army) Act (1879) required these events to be registered with the Office of the Registrar-General in Dublin, where they affected Irish subjects serving in the British army abroad. There are 15,436 registrations recorded between 1883 and 1922. Separate indexes, bound into the backs of the main yearly indexes, start from 1888 and continue until 1930 for births and until 1931 for marriages and deaths. The deaths index for 1902 also contains an index to 'Deaths of Irish Subjects pertaining to the South African War (1898–1902)'. There is also a separate register of deaths of 'Irish NCOs and men who died in the Great War', with 28,044 entries.

The Foreign Register: From 1864 the GRO was required to keep a separate register of births, marriages and deaths of Irish subjects abroad, where such births were notified to the relevant British consul. There is no index to this register, which contains only 208 entries. It is held in GRO headquarters in Roscommon.

The Schulze Register: The GRO also holds the 'General Index to Baptisms and Marriages purported to have been celebrated by the Rev. J.F.G. Schulze, 1806–1837'. Schulze was one of a group of eleven Dublin clergymen, known with Dublin bluntness as 'couple-beggars' or 'tack 'ems', who specialised in clandestine marriages between 1799 and 1844. The records of the other ten were destroyed in the Public Record Office in 1922, but a court challenge in the 1870s resulted in Schulze's marriages being declared legally sound, and two volumes of his records were acquired by the GRO. They record 55 baptisms and c.14,000 marriages. Most of the marriages, celebrated at the German Lutheran Church in Poolbeg Street, Dublin, are for the years 1825–37 and record only the names of the contracting parties. The original is held in GRO headquarters in Roscommon. The LDS copy is on film 101771.

USING CIVIL RECORDS WITH OTHER SOURCES

Some of the areas in which information from other sources may be used to simplify research in civil records have already been outlined. What follows is an expanded guide to the ways in which civil records can supplement, or be supplemented by, those other sources.

Births: Ages recorded in 1901 and 1911 census returns (see Chapter 2) can be used to narrow the range of years to be searched. If the birth registration is uncovered first, it records the precise residence of the parents, which can then lead to the relevant census returns, providing fuller information on other members of the family.

Marriages: The 1911 census records the number of years a couple have been married, the number of children born and the number of those children still living. This information is obviously very useful in narrowing the range of years to be searched for a particular marriage. In the case of names common in a particular area, the fathers' names supplied in the marriage record are often the only firm evidence with which to identify the relevant baptismal record in the parish registers. Once a marriage has been located in civil records, thus showing the relevant parish, it is always worthwhile to check the church record of the same marriage. As church marriage registers were standardised, from the 1860s on, they became more informative, in many cases supplying the names, addresses and occupations of both the mother and father of the parties marrying. In the case of most Dublin Roman Catholic parishes this information is recorded from about 1856.

Deaths: The records of the Valuation Office (Chapter 4) or the testamentary records of the National Archives (Chapter 6) can be used to pinpoint the year of death, thus making a successful search more likely. The place of death given, if it is not the home of the deceased person, may be the home of a relative. This can be investigated firstly through land records (Chapter 4) and then through parish and census records, and may provide further information on other branches of the family.

Chapter 2 ∿

CENSUS RECORDS

OFFICIAL CENSUSES IN IRELAND

Full government censuses of the whole island were taken in 1821, 1831, 1841, 1851, 1861, 1871, 1881, 1891, 1901 and 1911. The first four—1821, 1831, 1841 and 1851—were largely destroyed in the fire at the Public Record Office in 1922; surviving fragments are detailed below. Those for 1861, 1871, 1881 and 1891 were completely destroyed prior to 1922, by order of the government. This means that the earliest surviving comprehensive returns are for 1901 and 1911. Because of this, the normal rule that census returns should not be available to the public for a hundred years was suspended in the Republic in the 1960s, and microfilm copies of both 1901 and 1911 can be consulted in NAI and online at its census website, <*www.census.nationalarchives.ie*>. Microfilm copies are also available via the LDS Family History Library in Salt Lake City.

1901 AND 1911
Information given

Although these returns are very late and therefore of limited value for some purposes, the information they contain can still be extremely useful. The 1901 returns record the following:

- name;
- relationship to the head of the household;
- religion;
- literacy;
- occupation;
- age;
- marital status;
- county of birth;
- ability to speak English or Irish.

The returns also record details of the houses, giving the number of rooms, outhouses and windows and the type of roof. Family members of those not present when the census was taken are not given. The same information was again collected in 1911, with one important addition: married women were required to state the number of years they had been married, the number of children born alive and the number of children still living. Unfortunately, widows were not required to give this information, although a good number obliged in any case. Only the initials, not the full names, of policemen, soldiers and inmates of mental hospitals are recorded.

USES

(i) *Age:* The most obviously useful information given in 1901 and 1911 is age; unfortunately, this is also the information that needs to be treated with the most caution. Precious few of the ages given in the two sets of returns actually match precisely. Indeed in the decade between the two censuses, most people appear to have aged significantly more than ten years. The introduction of the Old Age Pension in 1908 may have been influential. Of the two censuses, 1901 seems to be the less accurate, with widespread underestimation of age. Nonetheless, if used with caution the returns do provide a rough guide to age, which can help to narrow the range of years to be searched in earlier civil records of births, marriages and deaths, or in parish records.

(ii) *Location:* When the names of all or most of the family are known, together with the general area (but not the precise locality), it is possible to search all the returns for that area to identify the relevant family, and thus pinpoint them. This can be particularly useful when the surname is very common: the likelihood of two families of Murphys in the same area repeating all the children's names is slight. For migrants to cities such as Dublin, Belfast and Limerick, the 'where born' column can be the only clue that allows a link with earlier records.

(iii) *Cross-checking:* In some instances, again when a name is common, it is impossible to be sure from information uncovered in civil or parish records that a particular family is the relevant one. In such cases, when details of the subsequent history of the family are known—dates of death or emigration, or siblings' names, for instance—a check of the 1901 or 1911 census for the family can provide useful circumstantial evidence. More often than not, any certainties produced will be negative, but the elimination of false trails is a vital part of any research. An illustration will show why: Peter Barry, born Co. Cork c.1880, parents unknown, emigrated to the United States in 1897. A search of civil birth records shows four Peter Barrys recorded in the county between 1876 and 1882, with no way of distinguishing which, if any, of them is the relevant one. A search of the 1901 census returns for the addresses given in the four birth entries shows two of the four still living there. These can now be safely eliminated and research concentrated on the other two families.

(iv) *Marriages:* The requirement in the 1911 census for married women to supply the number of years of marriage is obviously a very useful aid when subsequently searching civil records for a marriage entry. Even in 1901 the age of the eldest child recorded can give a rough guide to the latest date at which a marriage is likely to have taken place.

(v) *Living relatives:* Children recorded in 1901 and 1911 are the grandparents of people still living. The ages—generally much more accurate than those given for older members of the family—can be useful in trying to uncover later marriages in civil records. When used together with Valuation Office records (see Chapter 4) or the voters' lists at NAI or DCLA, they can provide an accurate picture of the passing of property from one generation to another. Fortunately, the Irish attitude to land means that it is quite unusual for rural property to pass out of a family altogether.

(vi) *Extended family:* The ease of access created by having both censuses freely searchable online makes it well worthwhile to trawl for other, related households. As well as expanding the family history, this increases the chances of picking up collateral information: because members of each household were required to describe their connection to the head of the household, the names of grandmothers, cousins or in-laws can often provide excellent clues for use in other records.

USING THE 1901 AND 1911 CENSUSES ONLINE
The format used

Both 1901 and 1911 censuses are online at *<www.census.nationalarchives.ie>*. A complete database transcript of all Form As (the household returns) is searchable, with search results linked to images of the original return, to the enumerator's abstract for the townland or street (Form N), to the House and Building Return (Form B1), which gives details of the nature of the dwelling and the names of landholders for each household, and to the Out-Offices and Farm-Steadings Return (Form B2) for farms.

The images were created from the LDS microfilm copies of the originals. This means that the sequence of images online follows the sequence on the microfilm, which in turn follows the arrangement of the originals: the returns for each townland or street are grouped together and preceded by Form N, Form B1 and, if one exists, Form B2. There is no facility on the site to browse through the returns sequentially, as they appear on the microfilm, but it is possible to do this simply by adding or subtracting 1 from the file number (starting 'nai') in your browser's address bar. This can be useful if you suspect that a household return has been omitted from the transcription. At the time of writing, a significant number of returns, particularly related to single-street villages, remain untranscribed, but it is possible to track down the images.

One further consequence of the use of the microfilm copies is worth keeping in mind: the microfilm of 1901 omitted the reverse of the majority of returns. This is where specific place-identifying information was recorded—street numbers, townlands, parishes—and its omission is regrettable. However, almost all the information can be reconstructed from the enumerator's abstract (Form N).

Unlike most if not all the overseas census material now searchable online, the Irish 1901 and 1911 returns are the originals filled out by the householders themselves and have a vivid immediacy that can be very poignant.

National Archives of Ireland census search form, with all options displayed
(<*census.nationalarchives.ie/search/#searchmore*>). (*Courtesy of the National Archives of Ireland*)

The search form

The search function on the site is very powerful and very flexible. A few points need to be kept in mind:

- Every single item recorded on Form A is searchable. This means that virtually any information already known can be leveraged to identify a relevant return. For example, there were 736 John Byrnes in Dublin in 1911. But if you know that your John Byrne was married and had two children in 1911, the number of potential candidates is immediately reduced to just 14. Sometimes thinking laterally is useful. An unusual sibling's name, a specific occupation, a cousin who joined the Plymouth Brethren—virtually anything recorded by the census can be used as the key to finding the right household.

- The search form has an ambivalent relationship with wild cards and spaces. Entering 'Abbey Street' (without the quotation marks) in the Townland/Street field and selecting Dublin as the county will return all townlands or streets in Dublin city and county that contain either 'Abbey' or 'Street', which is not terribly useful. Entering 'Sackville Street' (with the quotation marks) will return all townlands or streets that contain those exact letters, so returning 'Sackville Street Upper' and 'Sackville Street Lr' but not 'Sackville St'. The '*' wild card can be used in any text field to represent any sequence of letters, so 'Mor*' will return Moran, Morin, Moriarty . . . But it is not possible to use the wild card at the beginning of a word, so it is impossible to search for all surnames ending in 'orum', for example.

- There is no surname variant function on the site and, as with the Townland/Street search, by default all entries that include the sequence of

CENSUS OF IRELAND, 1901.

(Two Examples of the mode of filling up this Table are given on the other side.)

FORM A.

No. on Form B. 5

RETURN of the MEMBERS of this FAMILY and their VISITORS, BOARDERS, SERVANTS, &c. who slept or abode in this House on the night of SUNDAY, the 31st of MARCH, 1901.

No.	NAME and SURNAME	RELATION to Head of Family	RELIGIOUS PROFESSION	EDUCATION	AGE	SEX	RANK, PROFESSION, OR OCCUPATION	MARRIAGE	WHERE BORN	IRISH LANGUAGE	If Deaf and Dumb; Dumb only; Blind; Imbecile or Idiot; or Lunatic.
1	Bernard McEnert	Head of Family	Roman Catholic	Read & Write	50	M	Farmer	Married	Co Cavan	Irish & English	—
2	Mary McEnert	Wife	do Catholic	Read & Write	48	F	Farmers Wife	Married	Co Cavan	Irish & English	—
3	Marie McEnert	Daughter	do Catholic	Read & Write	23	F	Farmers Daughter	not married	Co Cavan	English	—
4	Ellen McEnert	Daughter	do Catholic	Read & Write	19	F	Farmers Daughter	not married	Co Cavan	English	—
5	John McEnert	Nephew	do Catholic	Read & Write	6	M	Scholar	not married	Co Cavan	English	—
6											
7											
8											
9											
10											
11											
12											
13											
14											
15											

I hereby certify, as required by the Act 63 Vic, cap. 6, s 6 (1), that the foregoing Return is correct, according to the best of my knowledge and belief.

Michael Lillen (Signature of Enumerator)

I believe the foregoing to be a true Return.

Bernard McEnert (Signature of Head of Family).

Form A, 1901 census (<census.nationalarchives.ie/reels/nai000436430/>). (*Courtesy of the National Archives of Ireland*)

Form A, 1911 census (<census.nationalarchives.ie/reels/naioo1737740/>). (*Courtesy of the National Archives of Ireland*)

letters entered as a distinct word are returned. Searching for 'Mahon' returns all 'Mahons' and 'Mc Mahons' (with a space) but no 'McMahons' (without a space). The site does give ample warning of the slipperiness of both surnames and placenames.

The 'browse' function and DEDs

The site also allows users to browse by geographical area. The hierarchy used is County—District Electoral Division—Townland/Street.

District Electoral Divisions originated as subdivisions of a Poor Law Union, grouping together a number of townlands to create a constituency for the election of members to a Poor Law Board of Guardians. As the Poor Law was funded by property taxes, the aim in creating the DEDs was to have areas that produced roughly similar tax takes. This meant that their boundaries ignored natural community borders, such as counties or parishes. It also means that it can be difficult to work out the geographical relationship between DEDs. The only readily accessible map of DEDs dates from the 1930s and can be found on the website of the Irish Placenames Commission, <*www.loganim.ie*>, under 'Information resources'/'The Placenames Branch'.

In urban areas the problems posed by DEDs are even more acute. A boundary could run down the middle of a street or bisect it in other ways, with a slightly different spelling in the other DED. The only way to reconstruct all the returns for a particular street is to use great care and many wild-card searches in the Townland/Street field.

The most straightforward, though cumbersome, way to cover a large area is to take all the townlands in a particular civil parish and check their DEDs in the 1901 *Townlands Index*. The 1841 *Townlands Index,* also known as *Addenda to the 1841 Census,* available on request from the NAI reading room staff or in the National Library (Ir 310 c 1), organises townlands alphabetically within civil parishes.

NINETEENTH-CENTURY CENSUS FRAGMENTS

1821

This census, organised by townland, civil parish, barony and county, took place on 28 May 1821 and aimed to cover the entire population. It recorded the following information:

- name;
- age;
- occupation;
- relationship to the head of the household;
- acreage of land-holding;
- number of storeys of house.

Almost all the original returns were destroyed in 1922, with only a few volumes surviving for parts of Cos. Cavan, Fermanagh, Galway, Meath and Offaly (King's

Col. 1. No. of House.	Col. 2. No. of Stories	Column 3. NAMES OF INHABITANTS.	Col. 4. AGE.	Column 5. OCCUPATION.	Col. 6. No. of Acres.
		No. 38 Townland of *Tulrahen* in the Parish of *Castlerahan* Ba			
		N. B.—In Counties where Plowlands or other denominations or sub-denominations are in use, the word " Townland" is to be			
		Eliza Fitzsimmons Daughter	15	Spinner	
8	1	Garrett Fitzsimmons	60	Farmer	12
		Cath. Fitzsimmons his Wife	57	Spinner	
		Patrick Fitzsimmons his Son	32	Labourer	
		Thos Fitzsimmons Do	27	Labourer	
		John Fitzsimmons Do	23	Labourer	
		Mary Smyth	20	House Servt	
9	1	John Gilroy	39	Farmer	16
		Margt Gilroy his Wife	33	Spinner	
		Patrick Gilroy his Son	10		
		Owen Gilroy his Son	1		
		Mary Gilroy Daughter	15	Spinner	
		Margt Gilroy Do	13	Same	
		Bridget Gilroy Do	7		
		Anne Gilroy Do	5		
10	1	Peter Lynch	64	Farmer	15
		Eliza Lynch his Wife	61	Spinner	
		Hugh Lynch his Son	32	Labourer	
		Lawce Lynch his Son	16	Labourer	
		Anne Lynch Daughter	25	Spinner	
		Mary Lynch Daughter	23	Spinner	
		John Lynch his Nephew	1		
11	1	John Flood	33	Farmer	4½
		Anne Flood his Wife	30	Spinner	
		John Flood his Son	8		
		Mary Flood Daughter	10		
		Cath. Flood Do	6		
		Anne Flood Do	3		
12	1	John Smyth	55	Mason	
		Peter Smyth his Son	25	Labourer	
		James Smyth his Son	22	Labourer	
		Patk Smyth Do	15	Labourer	

1821 census return (NAI: CEN 1821/3; MFGS 34/001). (*Courtesy of the National Archives of Ireland*)

County). These are now in NAI, and full details of call numbers and areas covered will be found in Chapter 13 under the relevant county. The overall reliability of the population figures produced by the 1821 census has been questioned, but there is no doubt as to the genealogical value of the returns. Once again, however, the ages given need to be treated with scepticism. NAI is currently engaged in a collaboration with the Family History Library of the LDS church to digitise all surviving records and make them available free online.

1831

Again organised by townland, civil parish, barony and county, this census recorded the following:

- name;
- age;
- occupation;
- relationship to the head of the household;
- acreage of land-holding;
- religion.

Very little of this survives, with most of the remaining official fragments relating to Co. Derry. This was the first census to record religion and was therefore of interest in ongoing local sectarian arguments, and quite a few local copies were made to provide ammunition. Details of locations and call numbers of any such copies are in Chapter 13 under the relevant county. NAI is currently engaged in a collaboration with the Family History Library of the LDS church to digitise these records and make them available free online.

1841

Unlike in the two earlier censuses, the householders themselves filled out these returns, rather than government enumerators. The information supplied was:

- name;
- age;
- occupation;
- relationship to the head of the household;
- date of marriage;
- literacy;
- absent family members;
- family members who died since 1831.

Only one set of original returns survived 1922, that for the parish of Killeshandra in Co. Cavan. There are, however, a number of transcripts of the original returns. The 1841 census was the earliest to be of use when state Old Age Pensions were introduced in the early twentieth century, and copies of the household returns from 1841 and 1851 were sometimes used as proof of age. The forms detailing the results of searches in the original returns to establish age have survived and are found in NAI for areas in the Republic, and in PRONI for areas now in its jurisdiction. Copies of the Northern Ireland returns are also available at the LDS Library. County-by-county indexes to the areas covered, giving the names of the individuals concerned, are found on open shelves in the NAI reading room.

There are a number of other miscellaneous copies, some also related to the Old Age Pension, and mostly relating to northern counties. They are detailed (though not indexed) in the pre-1901 census catalogue of NAI on open shelves in the reading room. There are also a number of researchers' transcripts and abstracts compiled from the original returns before their destruction and donated to public institutions after 1922 in an attempt to replace some of the lost records. As the researchers were usually interested in particular families, rather than in whole areas, these are generally of limited value. The most significant collections are the Walsh-Kelly Notebooks, which also abstract parts of the 1821, 1831 and 1851 returns and relate particularly to south Kilkenny, and the Thrift Abstracts in NAI. Details of dates, areas covered and locations for the Walsh-Kelly Notebooks will be found under Co. Kilkenny in Chapter 13. The Thrift Abstracts are listed in detail in the NAI pre-1901 census catalogue under 'miscellaneous copies'. Counties for which significant numbers exist are given under the relevant county in Chapter 13.

1851
This recorded the following:

- name;
- age;
- occupation;
- relationship to the head of the household;
- date of marriage;
- literacy;
- absent family members;
- family members who died since 1841;
- religion.

Most of the surviving returns relate to parishes in Co. Antrim, and details will be found in Chapter 13. An online transcript, of doubtful accuracy, is also available. The comments above on transcripts and abstracts of the 1841 census also apply to 1851.

1861, 1871, 1881, 1891
The official destruction of the returns for these years was commendably thorough: virtually nothing survives. The only transcripts are contained in the Catholic registers of Enniscorthy (1861) and Drumcondra and Loughbraclen, Co. Meath (1871). Details appear in Chapter 13.

CENSUS SUBSTITUTES

Almost any document that records more than a single name can be called a census substitute, at least for genealogical purposes. What follows is a listing, chronological where possible, of the principal such substitutes. It is intended as a gloss on some of the sources given county-by-county under 'Census returns and substitutes' in Chapter 13, and as a supplement covering sources that do not fit the county-by-county format. Any material given in the source lists of Chapter 13 that is self-explanatory is not dealt with here.

SIXTEENTH AND SEVENTEENTH CENTURIES

1521–1603: *Fiants*
The Irish fiants of the Tudor sovereigns during the reigns of Henry VIII, Edward VI, Philip & Mary, and Elizabeth I (4 vols., Dublin: Edmund Burke, 1994; NLI Ir 94105 i 1). These documents, unique to Ireland, were created to facilitate the issuing of royal grants and were originally published as a series of appendices to the *Reports of the Deputy Keeper of Public Records in Ireland* in the late nineteenth century. For many of those Irish chieftains who submitted to English authority under the policy of surrender and regrant, they give long lists of extended family and followers.

1612–13: *'Undertakers'*
The Historical Manuscripts Commission Report, 4 (Hastings Mss.), gives lists of English and Scottish large landlords granted land in the northern counties of Cavan, Donegal and Fermanagh.

1630: *Muster Rolls*
These are lists of large landlords in Ulster and the names of the able-bodied men they could assemble to fight if the need arose. They are arranged by county, and by district within the county. The Armagh County Museum copy is available in NLI (Pos. 206). Published lists are noted under the relevant county in Chapter 13, along with later lists from 1642/3 in PRONI.

1641: *Books of Survey and Distribution*
After the wars of the mid-seventeenth century the English government needed solid information on land ownership throughout Ireland to carry out its policy of land redistribution. The Books of Survey and Distribution record ownership before the Cromwellian confiscations (c.1641) and after (c.1666–8). The books for Cos. Clare, Galway, Mayo and Roscommon have been published by the Irish Manuscripts Commission. See *<www.irishmanuscripts.ie>*. For other counties, manuscript copies are available at NLI. Details will be found under the relevant counties in Chapter 13.

1641: *Depositions*
These are eye-witness testimonies given mainly by Protestants, but also by some Catholics, from all social backgrounds, concerning their experiences of the 1641

Rebellion in Ireland. They provide vivid accounts of the events of that year and also list large numbers of people accused of participation in the rebellion or claiming to have suffered loss. Along with the victories of King William at the Boyne in 1690 and Aughrim in 1691, and the Battle of the Somme in 1916, the events they record have long been fundamental to the identity and culture of Unionist Protestants in Ireland, especially in Ulster. They are now all online at <*1641.tcd.ie*>.

1654–6: *Civil Survey*
This was a record of land ownership in 1640, compiled between 1655 and 1667 and fuller than the Books of Survey and Distribution. It contains a great deal of topographical and descriptive information as well as details of wills and deeds relating to land title. It has survived for twelve counties only: Cork, Derry, Donegal, Dublin, Kildare, Kilkenny, Limerick, Meath, Tipperary, Tyrone, Waterford and Wexford. These have all been published by the Irish Manuscripts Commission. Details will be found under the relevant counties in Chapter 13.

1659: *Pender's 'Census'*
This was compiled by Sir William Petty, also responsible for the Civil Survey, and records the names of titled individuals ('tituladoes'), the number of English and Irish people living in each townland and the principal Irish names in each barony. It is not a census in any modern sense of the word. Five counties are not covered: Cavan, Galway, Mayo, Tyrone and Wicklow. The work was edited by Seamus Pender and published in 1939 (NLI I 6551 Dublin).

1662–6: *Subsidy Rolls*
These list the nobility, clergy and laity who paid a grant in aid to the King. They supply name and parish and, sometimes, amount paid and occupation. They relate principally to counties in Ulster.

1664–6: *Hearth Money Rolls*
The Hearth Tax was levied on the basis of the number of hearths in each house; these rolls list the householders' names as well as this number. They seem to be quite comprehensive. Details of surviving lists will be found under the relevant counties in Chapter 13. For the copies of the Hearth Money Rolls listed in PRONI under T.307, an index is available on the public search room shelves.

Various dates: Cess tax accounts
'Cess' (from an abbreviation of 'assessment') was a very elastic term, which could be applied to taxes levied for a variety of reasons. In Ireland it was very often related to taxes used to support a military garrison. The accounts generally consist of lists of householders' names, along with amounts due.

EIGHTEENTH AND NINETEENTH CENTURIES

1703–1838: Converts

The Convert Rolls, ed. Eileen O'Byrne, IMC, 1981; NLI Ir 2741 c 25, 308 p.

A list of those converting from Catholicism to the Church of Ireland. The bulk of the entries date from 1760 to 1790.

1740: Protestant householders

For parts of Cos. Antrim, Armagh, Derry, Donegal and Tyrone. Arranged by barony and parish, it gives names only. Parts are at the Public Record Office of Northern Ireland, the Genealogical Office, the National Library and the Representative Church Body Library. Included in the Name Search at *<www.proni.gov.uk>*. Details will be found under the relevant counties in Chapter 13.

1749: Elphin Diocesan Census

Arranged by townland and parish, and listing householders, their religion, the numbers, sex and religion of their children, and the numbers, sex and religion of their servants. Elphin diocese includes parts of Cos. Galway, Roscommon and Sligo. Details of the parishes covered, along with indexes or online transcripts, will be found under the relevant counties in Chapter 13.

1766: Census

In March and April 1766, on the instructions of the government, Church of Ireland rectors were asked to compile complete returns of all householders in their parishes, showing their religion and giving an account of any Catholic clergy active in their area. The result was extraordinarily inconsistent, with some rectors producing only numerical totals of population and some drawing up partial lists. The most conscientious detailed all householders and their addresses individually. All the original returns were lost in 1922, but extensive transcripts survive for some areas and are deposited with various institutions. The only full listing of all surviving transcripts and abstracts is in the NAI reading room, on the open shelves. However, this does not differentiate between those returns that supply names and those that merely give numerical totals. The details given under the relevant counties in Chapter 13 refer only to those parishes for which names are given.

1775: Dissenters' petitions

A series of petitions to the Irish Parliament protesting against an Act of 1774 excluding dissenters from voting at vestry meetings of the Church of Ireland. The originals were destroyed in 1922, but a series of transcripts had been made by Arthur Tenison Groves, which is now in PRONI and is searchable via their online Name Search.

1790–1880: Official Papers, petitions

The Official Papers form part of the incoming correspondence records of the Office of the Chief Secretary to the Lord Lieutenant of Ireland, usually known simply as the Chief Secretary's Office, the main organ of central administration in Ireland for the period. Two main series exist in NAI, 1790–1831 and 1832–80, the former calendared and classified by year and subject, the latter covered by card indexes. As well as records of the administration of justice (see Chapter 12, 'Convicts'), they also include a long series of petitions to the Lord Lieutenant from around the country, generally described as 'memorials', which very often include long lists of names or signatures. The mother of all memorials is the William Smith O'Brien petition from 1848/9, a plea for clemency for the main instigator of an abortive rising in 1848, the so-called 'battle of Widow McCormack's cabbage patch'. It includes almost 90,000 names from all over Ireland as well as from Irish people in England. Ruth Lawler's transcription has been published on CD-ROM by Eneclann (ENEC002) and is searchable online at <www.findmypast.ie>.

Many smaller petitions also exist, ranging from pleas for relief from distress among weavers to an appeal for a road from Kanturk to Cork city. The largest numbers relate to changes made in the arrangements for local court sittings (Quarter Sessions) in 1837–8. Bids to host the courts poured in from all over the country—the economic spin-offs must have been considerable. At least forty of these smaller petitions have been identified and are listed under the relevant county in Chapter 13, with estimates of the number of names they contain. No doubt there are many more.

1795–1862: *Charlton Trust Fund marriage certificates*
As an encouragement to Protestant population growth, the Charlton Trust Fund offered a small marriage gratuity to Protestant day labourers. To qualify, a marriage certificate—recording occupations and fathers' names and signed by the local Church of Ireland clergyman—had to be submitted, and these are now in NAI. They are particularly useful for the years before the start of registration of non-Catholic marriages in 1845. The areas covered by the fund were mainly in Cos. Meath and Longford, but a few certificates exist for parts of Cos. Cavan, Offaly (King's), Louth and Westmeath, as well as Dublin city. They are indexed in NAI Accessions Vol. 37.

1796: *Spinning-Wheel Premium Entitlement Lists*
As part of a government scheme to encourage the linen trade, free spinning-wheels or looms were granted to individuals planting a prescribed area of land with flax. The lists of those entitled to the awards, covering almost sixty thousand individuals, were published in 1796. They record only the name of the individual and the civil parish in which the recipient lived. As might be expected, the majority, more than 64 per cent, were in Ulster, but some names appear from every county except Dublin and Wicklow. In the county-by-county source lists, only those counties with significant numbers include a reference. A microfiche index to the lists is available in NAI and PRONI, and online at <www.failteromhat.com>.

No.   *No in Receipt.*

CHARLETON'S CHARITABLE FUND.

County of LONGFORD, To Wit.

WE, the Undersigned, Minister and Church Wardens of the Parish of *Ardagh* in the County of Longford, DO CERTIFY, that *James Burtey* of *Slenagh* in the Parish of *Killcomic* in said County, was duly married to *Elizabeth* otherwise *Burtey* on the *twenty fifth* day of *January* in 13 *thirteen* in our presence, and that the said Marriage was solemnized with the consent of the parents of the said *several parties* who were also present and expressed their approbation thereof; AND WE DO FURTHER CERTIFY, that *William* the father of the said *James Burtey* was at the time of said Marriage, and for *59* years previous thereto, a resident day labourer of the said County of Longford, and that the father of the said was also at the time of the said marriage, and for *many* years previous thereto, a resident day labourer of the said County of Longford, and that we know the said *James* to have been aged more than fifteen years and less than thirty years at the time of the said marriage, and that we know the said *Elizabeth Young* to have been aged more than fifteen years and less than forty years at the time of the said marriage.

Given under our hands this *Eleventh* day of *April*   1832

Rich Thos Hearn   } Minister of the Parish of *Ardagh for the time then being* in the County of Longford.

John Morris   } Church Wardens of the said Parish.

There is only one church warden at present within

Charleton Marriage Fund (NAI: Charleton Funds: Longford A-K). (*Courtesy of the National Archives of Ireland*)

1798: *Persons Who Suffered Losses in the 1798 Rebellion*

This comprises a list of claims for compensation from the government for property destroyed by the rebels during the insurrection of 1798 and is particularly useful for the property-owning classes of Cos. Wexford, Carlow, Dublin, Kildare and Wicklow. Where significant numbers are recorded, these are supplied in the county source lists in Chapter 13. (NLI I 94107.)

1803: *Agricultural censuses of Cos. Antrim and Down*

As part of the preparations for a possible French invasion in the aftermath of the abortive rebellion of 1803, plans were drawn up for the evacuation of coastal areas. A survey of livestock, crops, wagons and horses was ordered, but it appears to have been carried out only in Cos. Antrim and Down. In most cases, occupiers' names are also recorded. Eleven parishes in Antrim are covered (see Chapter 13) in NAI Official Papers (OP 153/103/1–16), with a copy in PRONI. For Down the survey survived as part of the papers of the 1st Marquess of Londonderry and is available in PRONI. Fifty Down parishes are covered, with returns for thirty, including at least some occupiers' names. Ian Maxwell's *Researching Down Ancestors* (UHF, 2004) provides a parish-by-parish description.

1822–54: *Loan Fund records*

In the mid-nineteenth century, when the practice was at its peak, hundreds of local loan funds took deposits and made loans to the poorest classes in Ireland. One estimate puts the number of loans at 500,000 a year in the early 1840s, covering nearly a fifth of the households in the country. The system originated in 1822, when a severe but localised famine drew a great deal of attention in England and a committee based in London 'for the relief of the distressed Irish' collected more than £300,000. More than £55,000 of this remained after the famine abated, and the committee decided to establish a Reproductive Loan Fund to make small loans to the 'industrious poor' of the ten most needy counties. The fund was reproductive in the sense that the loan would, in theory at least, finance an asset from which an income could be derived to pay the instalments. Legislation was passed in 1823, and again in 1836 and 1838, to encourage such funds and to create a regulatory body, the Loan Fund Board. By 1843 some three hundred local funds were registered with it, over and above the fifty to a hundred funds created by the Reproductive Institution, which were exempt and administered from London. In 1843, at the prompting of the commercial banks, more legislation was passed, sharply reducing the interest rates the funds could charge. The effect was an immediate rise in the number of funds closing and a sharp drop in the number of loans. The Great Famine took hold in 1845, magnifying further the destructive effects of the change. A large number of funds failed and closed.

Records of the Loan Funds: Virtually no detailed records survive from the institutions administered by the Loan Fund Board—the only exceptions currently known are the Tanderagee Estate Fund, preserved in PRONI as part of the more general Tanderagee estate records (D1248/LF/3) and the Shirley Estate Loan Book in Carrickmacross Library, Co. Monaghan. However, the records produced by the original Reproductive Institution itself have survived almost entire. After lending ceased at the end of 1848, all the records were eventually returned to its headquarters in London and are now in NA (Kew), series T/91. As well as the notes of security for the loans, there are loan ledgers, repayment books and defaulters' books for the local associations and the county committees. The minimum information supplied is the name and address, but much additional detail is often given in the local association records, including notes on health, occupation, family circumstances and emigration. The local records generally run from the late 1830s to the mid-1840s and are available for the following associations:

Clare: County Account Book and Minutes.
Cork: Baltimore, Castletown, Castle Townsend, Cloyne, Creagh, Kilmoe and Crookhaven, Schull.
Galway: Ahascragh, Ballygar, Castle Hackett, Clifden, Kilconickny, Outerard, Galway town.
Limerick: A single association covered the entire county.
Mayo: Ballina or Carramore, Ballindine, Ballinrobe, Castlebar, Claremorris, Kilmore, Swineford.
Roscommon: Aughnasurn, Ballinlough, Ballymoe, Clonfinlough, Elphin, Mosshill, Rockville, Tybohan.
Sligo: Templehouse.
Tipperary: Tipperary town.

A large obstacle to using these records is that they are extremely extensive, unindexed and, to researchers outside London, inaccessible. However, a subsidiary website of the NA, <*movinghere.org.uk*>, scanned and indexed part of the records in 2003 to make them more widely available. The records chosen for scanning were the Returns to the Clerk of the Peace of each county, created as part of the process of winding up the funds. For each local fund, these generally consist of two parts:

1. An overall account, usually dated 1846–8, showing the names and addresses of the borrower and of their two sureties or guarantors, along with amounts outstanding.
2. A more detailed townland-by-townland listing, organised by constabulary sub-district and carried out by the local RIC in 1853–4, recording details of deaths, economic circumstances and emigration.

No Return to the Clerk of the Peace appears to survive for Co. Clare, and the return for Co. Sligo was not scanned. For Cos. Cork, Galway, Limerick, Mayo, Roscommon and Tipperary almost 40,000 names are indexed. The indexing is imperfect, the organisation of the records is confusing and a broadband connection is essential, but for the areas they cover the records are superb, providing in many cases a before-and-after survey of the effect of the Famine on a particular locality.

To take one example, Philip Ebzery of the townland of Doonscardeen in the parish of Robertstown in Limerick is recorded in the overall account (T/91/180/0060) as having borrowed four pounds from the Limerick Fund on

23 Nov 1846, with the entire amount still outstanding as of 1848. His sureties were John Ebzery and Michael Ryan, both also of Doonscardeen. In the 1853 constabulary account (T/91/180/0448) he is recorded as having lived in Doonscardeen in 1846: 'a farmer, was poor, died about 4 years ago, family all emigrated'. And the two sureties are also there: John Ebzery 'was a farmer, went to Australia about four years since with his mother and sisters'; and Michael Ryan was 'a poor labourer, supporting his mother and sisters, emigrated to America with his family in 1847'.

1823–38: Tithe Applotment Books
See Chapter 4.

1831–1921: National School records
In 1831 a countrywide system of primary education was established under the control of the Board of Commissioners for National Education. The most useful records produced under this system are the school registers themselves, which record the age of the pupil, their religion, their father's address and occupation, and general observations. In the Republic very little effort has been made to centralise these records: most remain in the custody of local schools or churches. NAI has c.145 registers, mostly dating from the 1870s and 80s. PRONI has a collection of more than 1,500 registers for schools in the six counties of Northern Ireland. The administrative records of the Board of Commissioners itself are now held by NAI in Dublin. These include teachers' salary books, which can be very useful if an ancestor was a teacher. See also Chapter 12: Occupational Records.

1838–: Workhouse records
The 130 Poor Law Unions established in 1838, rising to 163 by 1852, had responsibility for administering what little public relief there was and dealt with huge numbers during the Great Famine. Unfortunately, most of the records of interest to family historians, in particular the workhouse admissions registers, do not appear to have survived, and what does exist is scattered and somewhat piecemeal. No comprehensive guide exists. The closest is *Records of the Irish Famine: a guide to local archives, 1840–1855* by Deirdre Lindsay and David Fitzpatrick (Dublin: Irish Famine Network, 1993). See also *The Workhouses of Ireland* by John O'Connor (Dublin: Anvil Books, 1995). The best single collection is held by PRONI, covering the 27 Poor Law Unions that were established in the counties of Northern Ireland. Any surviving admission and discharge registers are listed under the relevant county in Chapter 13. An excellent guide to the history of workhouses throughout the British Isles is at <*www.workhouses.org.uk*>.

1847–64: Griffith's Valuation
See Chapter 4.

1876: *Landowners*

Landowners in Ireland: Return of owners of land of one acre and upwards . . . (London: HMSO, 1876; reissued Baltimore, Md.: GMC, 1988). This records 32,614 owners of land in Ireland in 1876, identifying them by province and county; the entries give the address of the owner, along with the extent and valuation of the property. Only a minority of the population actually owned the land they occupied, but the work is invaluable for those who did. It is online at *<www.failte romhat.com>*.

VARIOUS DATES
Freeholders

Freehold property is held either by fee simple (where one has absolute freedom to dispose of it) or by fee tail (where the disposition is restricted to a particular line of heirs or by a life tenure). From the early eighteenth century, freeholders' lists were drawn up regularly, usually in connection with the right to vote, which went with freehold of property over a certain value. It follows that such lists are of genealogical interest only for a minority of the population. Details of surviving lists will be found under the relevant counties in Chapter 13.

Voters' lists and poll books

Voters' lists cover a slightly larger proportion of the population than freeholders' lists, because freehold property was not the only determinant of the franchise. In particular, freemen of the various corporation towns and cities had a right to vote in some elections at least. As membership of a trade guild carried with it admission as a freeman, and as this right was hereditary, a wider range of social classes is covered. Details of surviving lists will be found under the relevant counties in Chapter 13. Poll books are the records of votes actually cast in elections.

Electoral records

No complete collection of the electoral lists used in the elections of this century exists. This is unfortunate, since they can be of great value in tracing living relatives, listing as they do all eligible voters by townland and household. The largest collection of surviving electoral registers is to be found in NAI, but even here the coverage of various areas is quite skimpy. The best collection for the twentieth century is in DCLA, which has made part of them searchable online at *<www.dublinheritage.ie>*.

Valuations

Local valuations and revaluations of property were carried out with increasing frequency from the end of the eighteenth century, usually for electoral reasons. The best of these record all householders. Again, details are given under the relevant counties in Chapter 13.

Chapter 3

CHURCH RECORDS

THE PARISH SYSTEM

After the coming of the Reformation to Ireland in the sixteenth century the parish structures of the Roman Catholic Church and the Anglican Church of Ireland diverged. The Church of Ireland retained the medieval parochial divisions and became the state church, in effect an arm of the government. Its parish framework then came to be used for administrative purposes by the secular authorities. Therefore civil parishes—the geographical basis of early censuses, tax records and land surveys—are almost identical to Church of Ireland parishes. The Roman Catholic Church, on the other hand, weakened by the confiscation of its assets and the restrictions on its clergy, had to create larger and less convenient parishes. In some ways, this weakness produced more flexibility, allowing parishes to be centred on new, growing population centres and, in the nineteenth century, permitting the creation of new parishes to accommodate this growth in population.

The differences in the parish structures of the two churches are reflected in their records. Even allowing for the fact that members of the Church of Ireland were almost always a small minority of the total population, the records of each parish are proportionately less extensive than Roman Catholic records, and cover a smaller area, and so are relatively easy to search in detail. Catholic records, by contrast, cover the majority of the population and a much larger geographical area and as a result can be very time-consuming to search in detail by hand. The creation of new Catholic parishes in the nineteenth century can also mean that the registers relevant to a particular area may be split between two parishes.

Both Roman Catholic and Church of Ireland parishes are organised on the diocesan basis first laid out in the Synod of Kells in the Middle Ages, and the dioceses remain almost identical, although the Catholic system has amalgamated some of the smaller medieval dioceses.

ROMAN CATHOLIC RECORDS

Dates

For dates before the start of civil registration for all in 1864, virtually the only direct sources of family information for the great majority of the population are the local parish records. The intense hostility shown by the state to the Roman Catholic Church from the sixteenth to the nineteenth centuries made efficient record-keeping an understandably low priority, and very few registers survive from before the latter half of the eighteenth century. The earliest Roman Catholic parish records in the country appear to be the fragments for the towns of Waterford and Galway, dating from the 1680s, and for Wexford, dating from 1671. Generally speaking, early records tend to come from the more prosperous and anglicised areas, in particular from the towns and cities of the eastern half of the island. In the poorest and most densely populated rural parishes of the west and north, which saw most emigration, the parish registers very often do not start until the middle or later part of the nineteenth century. However, the majority of Catholic registers begin in the first decades of the nineteenth century, and even in poor areas, if a local tradition of Gaelic scholarship survived, records were often kept from an earlier date.

The list given in Chapter 14 reflects the state of knowledge of the dates of Roman Catholic registers at the time of writing (mid-2011). No listing can ever be definitive, however. The number of parishes covered by the local heritage centres will continue to grow, the National Library microfilming programme will carry on to completion, online transcripts will continue to appear, and almost certainly there are still some unrecorded registers awaiting discovery in sacristies around the country.

Nature of the records

Roman Catholic registers consist mostly of baptismal and marriage records. The keeping of burial records was much less thorough than in the Church of Ireland, with fewer than half the parishes in the country having a register of burials before 1900; and even where they do exist, these records are generally intermittent and patchy. For some reason almost all Roman Catholic burial registers are for the northern half of the island. Baptisms and marriages are recorded in either Latin or English—never in Irish. Generally, parishes in the more prosperous areas, where English was more common, tended to use English, while in Irish-speaking parishes Latin was used. There is no absolute consistency, however. The Latin presents very few problems, as only first names were Latinised, not surnames or placenames, and the English equivalents are almost always self-evident. The only difficulties or ambiguities are *Carolus* (Charles), *Demetrius* (Jeremiah, Jerome, Darby, Dermot), *Gulielmus* (William), *Eugenius* (Owen or Eugene), *Jacobus* (James), *Ioannes* or *Joannes* (John) and *Honoria* (Hannah, Nora).

Apart from names, the only other Latin in need of explanation is that used in recording marriage dispensations. These were necessary when those marrying were related—*consanguinati*—and the relationship was given in terms of degrees, with siblings first degree, first cousins second degree, and second cousins third degree. Thus a couple recorded as *consanguinati in tertio grado* are second cousins—information that can be of value in disentangling earlier generations. A less frequent Latin comment, *affinitatus*, records an earlier relationship, but only by marriage, between the two parties, which could create an impediment to the marriage.

Baptisms

Roman Catholic baptismal registers almost invariably contain the following information:

- date;
- child's name;
- father's name;
- mother's maiden name;
- names of sponsors (godparents).

In addition, most registers also record the residence of the parents. A typical Latin entry in its full form would read:

> *Baptisavi Johannem, filium legitimum Michaeli Sheehan et Mariae Sullivan de Lisquill.*
> *Sponsoribus, Danielus Quirk, Johanna Donoghue.*
> Much more often the entry is abbreviated to:
> *Bapt. Johannem, f.l. Michaeli Sheehan et Mariae Sullivan, Lisquill,*
> *Sp: Daniel Quirk, Johanna Donoghue.*

Translated, this is simply 'I baptised John, legitimate son of Michael Sheehan and Mary Sullivan of Lisquill, with godparents Daniel Quirk and Johanna Donoghue'. In many cases even the abbreviations are omitted, and the entries simply consist of dates, names and places.

Marriages

The information given in marriage records is more variable but always includes at least the following:

- date;
- names of persons marrying;
- names of witnesses.

Other information that may be supplied includes:

- residences (of all four people);
- ages;
- occupations;
- fathers' names.

In some rare cases the relationship of the witnesses to the people marrying is also specified. Some Dublin city registers from the middle of the nineteenth century

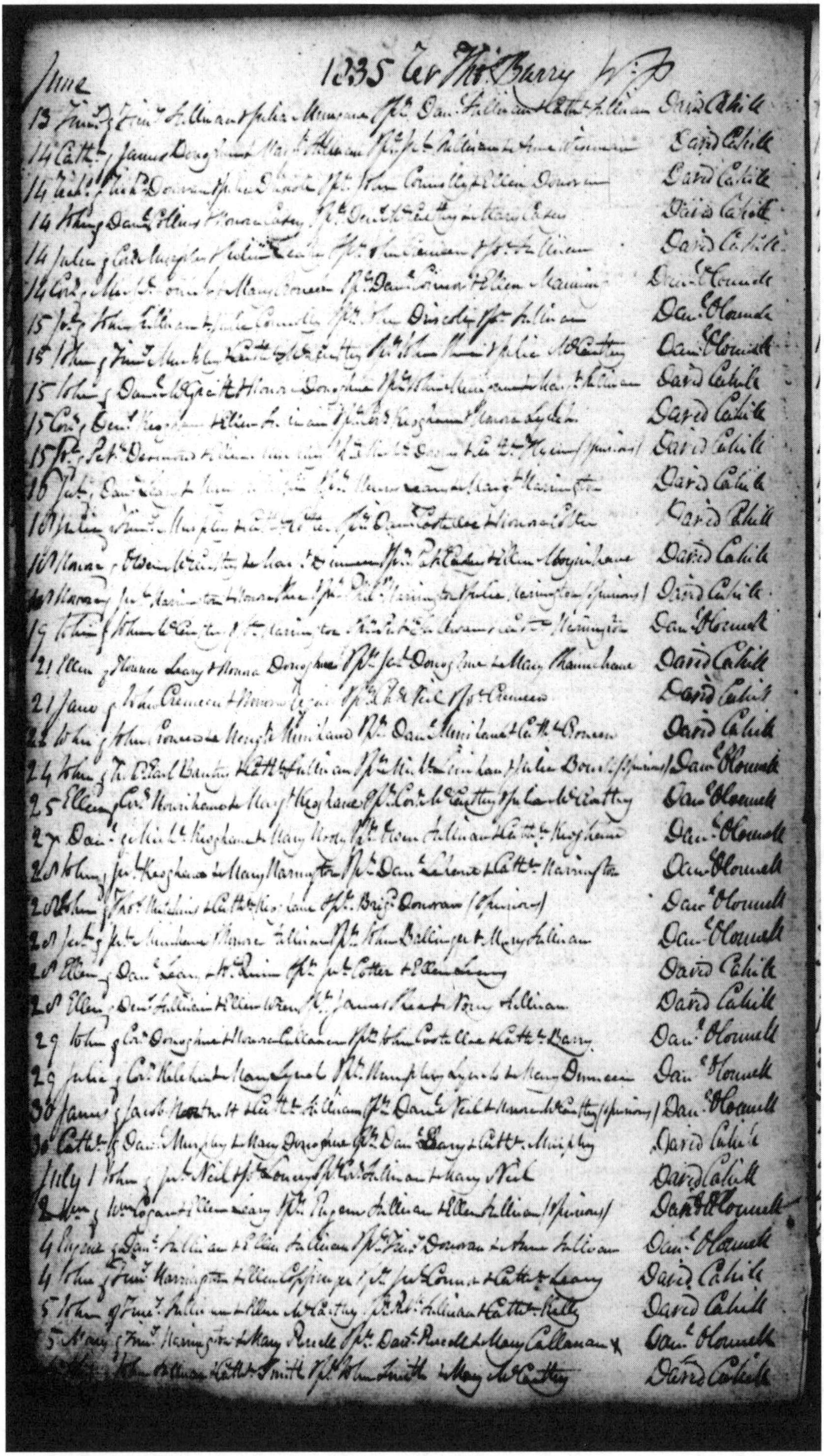

Bantry Roman Catholic baptisms, June (facing page) to August 1835. (*Courtesy of* <*www.irishgenealogy.ie*>)

record the full names and addresses of the parents of both bride and groom—a wonderful innovation. The typical Latin marriage entry would read:

In matrimonium coniunxi sunt Danielum McCarthy et Brigidam Kelliher, de Ballyboher.
Testimonii: Cornelius Buckley, Margarita Hennessy.

Abbreviated, this entry reads:

Mat. con. Danielum McCarthy et Brigidam Kelliher, Ballyboher.
Test. Cornelius Buckley, Margarita Hennessy.

Meaning simply: 'Daniel McCarthy and Brigid Kelliher of Ballyboher are joined in matrimony; witnesses, Cornelius Buckley, Margaret Hennessy.'

Locations

In the 1950s and early 60s the National Library of Ireland carried out a project of microfilming the surviving Roman Catholic parish registers of the entire island up to 1880. Microfilming of the few parishes missed by this project took place again in the late 1990s and early 2000s, and the cut-off year for these registers was set at 1900. Among very few parishes still not covered are Rathlin Island (Co. Antrim), Killorglin (Co. Kerry), Kilmeena (Co. Mayo), Rathcore and Rathmolyon (Co. Meath) and the Dublin city and county parishes of Clontarf, Naul and Santry. Almost all of these appear to have registers earlier than 1880 in local custody. In addition, the parishes of St John's (Sligo town), Cappawhite (Co. Tipperary) and the city of Waterford have registers held locally that are fuller than those microfilmed by the library. All these microfilms are available for public research in NLI. The library has begun (2011) a project to create digital images from all the parish register microfilms it holds, comprising some 390,000 individual frames, and make them freely available through its website. See 'What's online?' below.

A separate microfilming project was carried out by the Public Record Office of Northern Ireland for areas under its jurisdiction to supplement copies of the NLI microfilms it had acquired. For its own microfilms, PRONI used a later cut-off date. See Chapter 14 for details.

The Church of Jesus Christ of Latter-Day Saints, the Mormons, also has an extensive collection of Roman Catholic parish register microfilms, made up partly of copies of some of the NLI films and partly of material microfilmed by the church itself. Of the 1,153 parishes in the country, the LDS Library has records of 398. (See Chapter 14 for details.) Any volunteer transcripts and extracts appearing on the internet are usually from these LDS microfilms.

Apart from research in the original records, or in microfilm copies, one other access route exists to the information recorded in parish registers: the network of local heritage centres that has come into being throughout the country since about 1980. Using state-funded community employment schemes, or retraining programmes for the unemployed, these centres undertook the transcription (initially to card index, then to database) of the Catholic Church records in their districts. The project eventually spread to other genealogical records, but the Catholic registers were the starting point, and they are the area in which the centres made most progress. Since 2007 the centres have been making their records searchable online via the Irish Family History Foundation pay-per-view website, <*www.rootsireland.ie*>. There are now records for 27 of the 32 counties on this site, though not all records for all 27 counties are there. A separate site funded by the Department of Arts, Heritage and the Gaeltacht, <*www.irishgenealogy.ie*>, is aiming to cover areas not included in <*www.rootsireland.ie*>. See 'What's online?' below for more detail.

Research in Roman Catholic records

As the records are so extensive, as there are so many parishes and as many Irish surnames are extremely common, the first step in any research must be to try to identify the relevant parish. In the ideal case, where a precise town or townland is known, this is relatively simple. Any of the *Townland Indexes,* from 1851, 1871 or 1901, will show the relevant civil parish. The 1851 *Townland Index* is searchable online at <*www.seanruad.com*> and <*www.irishtimes.com/ancestor/placenames*>. There are then a number of ways to uncover the corresponding Roman Catholic parish. The Irish Ancestors site, <*www.irishtimes.com/ancestor*>, provides click-though maps and identifies surviving church records for the three major denominations. Lewis's *Topographical Dictionary of Ireland* (1837), available on open access at most libraries, gives an account, in alphabetical order, of all the civil parishes of Ireland and specifies the corresponding Roman Catholic parish. Brian Mitchell's *Guide to Irish Parish Records* (Baltimore, Md.: GPC, 1987) contains a county-by-county alphabetical reference guide to the civil parishes of Ireland and the Roman Catholic parishes of which they are part.

For the city of Dublin the procedure is slightly different. Where the address is known, the relevant civil parish can be found in the street-by-street listings of the Dublin directories, Pettigrew and Oulton's *Dublin Almanac and General Register of Ireland* (yearly from 1834 to 1849) and Thom's *Irish Almanac and Official Directory* (yearly from 1844). More details of these will be found in Chapter 11. The corresponding Roman Catholic parishes can then be found in Mitchell's *Guide* or in James Ryan's *Tracing Your Dublin Ancestors* (Flyleaf Press, 1988).

Unfortunately, in most cases a precise address is not known. How this is to be overcome depends, obviously, on what other information exists. Where a birth, marriage or death took place in the family in Ireland after the start of civil registration in 1864, state records are the first place to look, particularly if the birth took place between 1864 and 1880, and should therefore be part-transcribed at <*www.familysearch.org*>. Where a mother's maiden name is known, the free index-search on <*www.rootsireland.ie*> might uncover at least a county. When the occupation is known, records relating to this may supply the vital link (see Chapter 12). For emigrants, the clue to the relevant area might be provided by passenger and immigration lists, naturalisation papers, burial or death records, or even the postmarks on old family letters. In general, unless the surname is quite rare, the minimum information needed to start research on parish records with any prospect of success is the county of origin. An online service at <*www. irishtimes.com/ancestor*> allows the identification of counties and parishes where households of a particular surname are found in the mid-nineteenth-century Griffith's Valuation. The full online version of Griffith's at <*www.askabout ireland.ie*> can also be invaluable.

Because of the creation of new Roman Catholic parishes in the nineteenth century, the apparent starting dates of many Roman Catholic registers are sometimes deceptive. Quite often, earlier records for the same area can be found in the registers of what is now an adjoining parish. To take an example, the Roman Catholic parish of Abbeyleix in Co. Laois (Queen's County) has records listed in the NLI catalogue, and on <*www.rootsireland.ie*>, as starting in 1824. In fact the parish was only created in that year, and before then its records will be found in Ballinakill, which has records from 1794. Where surviving records appear too late to be of interest, therefore, it is always advisable to check the surrounding parishes for earlier registers. The maps of Roman Catholic parishes accompanying Chapter 14 are intended to simplify this task. These maps are not intended to be geographically precise: their aim is merely to show the positions of Roman Catholic parishes relative to each other. There are online versions at <*www.irishtimes.com/ancestor*>. As the only published source of information on nineteenth-century Roman Catholic parishes is Lewis's *Topographical Dictionary of Ireland,* which was published in 1837, and as the power and public presence of the church expanded greatly after Catholic Emancipation in 1829, some caution is needed in identifying which sets of records are relevant to a particular area.

At first sight, parish registers, particularly on microfilm, can appear quite daunting. The mass of spidery, abbreviated Latin, complete with blots and alterations, and cross-hatched with the scratches of a well-worn microfilm, can strike terror into the heart of even the most seasoned researcher. Some registers are a pleasure to use, with decade after decade of carefully laid-out copperplate handwriting; many more, unfortunately, appear to have been intended by local clergymen as their revenge on posterity. The thing to remember is that it is neither possible nor desirable to read every word on every page. The aim is to extract efficiently any relevant information, and the way to do this is by scanning the pages rather than reading them. In general, each parish takes a particular format and sticks to it. The important point is to identify this format and where within it the relevant information is given. For most purposes the family surname is the crucial item, so that in the baptismal example given above the best procedure would be to scan fathers' surnames, stopping to read fully, or note, only those recording the relevant surname. For other formats, such as

John Maguire of Patrick and Mary Reilly
Sp. Thos McKiernan, Rose Smith,

in which the family surname is given with the child's name, rather than with the father's, it is the child's surname that must be scanned. Even with very efficient scanning, however, there are registers that can be deciphered only line by line, that change format every page or two, or that are simply so huge that nothing but hours of eye strain can extract any information. The most notorious are the registers for St Catherine's (Dublin), Cork city, Clonmel (Co. Tipperary) and Clifden (Co. Galway).

In searching parish records, as for census returns and state records of births, marriages and deaths, a large measure of scepticism must be applied to all reported ages. In general, a five-year span around the reported date is the minimum that can be expected to yield results, and ten years is even better, with emphasis on the years before the reported date. A very open mind should also be kept on surname variants: widespread illiteracy made consistency and exactness of spelling extremely rare. It is essential to keep a written note of the precise period and parishes searched, especially where online transcripts are concerned; if you don't it is horribly inevitable that you will have to search the same records again. Duplication such as this is an endemic hazard of genealogy, as the nature of the research is such that the relevance of particular pieces of evidence often emerges only with hindsight; this is especially true of research in parish records. One example: a search in parish records for Ellen, daughter of John O'Brien, born c.1840. The search starts in 1842 and moves back through the baptismal registers. There are many baptisms recording different John (O')Briens as father, but no Ellen recorded until 1834. If it is then necessary to check the names of her siblings, much of what has already been researched will have to be covered again, unless all the baptisms recording John O'Brien as father have already been noted, even though there is a possibility (in most cases a probability) that none of them will ultimately turn out to have been relevant. This can be very costly on a pay-per-view site, and difficult even on the most user-friendly web-search interface.

Apart from the obvious family information they record, Roman Catholic parish registers may also include a wide variety of incidental information: details of famine relief, parish building accounts, marriage dispensations, local censuses, even personal letters. Anything of immediate genealogical interest is noted under the relevant county in Chapter 13.

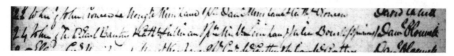

The baptism of the son of the Earl of Bantry on 24 June 1835. (*Courtesy of* <*www.irishgenealogy.ie*>)

CHURCH OF IRELAND RECORDS

Dates
Records of the Established Church, the Church of Ireland, generally start much earlier than those of the Roman Catholic Church. From as early as 1634, local parishes were required to keep records of christenings and burials in registers supplied by the church authorities. As a result, a significant number, especially of urban parishes, have registers dating from the middle of the seventeenth century. The majority, however, start in the years between 1770 and 1820. The only countrywide listing of all Church of Ireland parish records that gives full details of dates is the NAI catalogue, a copy of which is also to be found at NLI. In addition, the Irish Family History Society has published *A Table of Church of Ireland Parochial Records* (ed. Noel Reid, 1994; 2nd ed., 2002); and the *Guide to Church Records: Public Record Office of Northern Ireland* (online, PRONI, 2010) gives details of PRONI's holdings. The largest collection of original registers is in the RCBL. An up-to-date listing can be found at their website, <*www.ireland. anglcian.org*>.

The nature of the records
Burials: Unlike their Roman Catholic counterparts, the majority of Church of Ireland clergymen recorded burials as well as baptisms and marriages. These burial registers are often also of interest for families of other denominations; the sectarian divide appears to have narrowed a little after death. The information given for burials rarely consists of more than the name, age and townland, making definite family connections difficult to establish. However, as early burials generally record the deaths of those born well before the start of the register, they can be the only evidence on which to base a picture of preceding generations, and are particularly valuable because of this.

Baptisms: Church of Ireland baptismal records almost always supply only

- the child's name;
- the father's name;
- the mother's first name;
- the name of the officiating clergyman.

Quite often, the address is also given, but this is by no means as frequent as in the case of Roman Catholic registers. The omission of the mother's maiden name can be a serious obstacle to further research. From about 1820 the father's occupation is supplied in many cases.

Marriages: As the Church of Ireland was the Established Church, the only legally valid marriages, in theory at least, were those performed under its aegis. In practice, of course, *de facto* recognition was given to marriages of other

1857

Richard son of Richard Adderley & Ellen his wife. Born February 28th. Baptised April 19 1857.

Andrew, son of Robert & Jeannette Rutherford Born 13th May. Baptised 6th June 1857 —

Thomas Eld son of Thomas Heffernan of Newtown Esq & Rose his wife, Born February 18th 1851 on Received into Church November 22 1857 ...

Sponsors { Thomas Eld
{ Thomas Heffernan & Fanny Eld.

Mary Eld daughter of Thomas Heffernan of Newtown Esq. & Rose his wife Born Nov 10th 1854 Baptised November 22 1857 —

Sponsors { Mary Bernard
{ Rose Heffernan & Thomas Heffernan

George Thomas son of Edward Thomas of Cooltown Parish of Drumdowney & Marianne his wife, Born Nov 29th Baptised Dec 20th 1857.

1858 John, son of Michael Farmer & Anne his wife Baptised March 21st 1858.

William John, son of Denis Lynch of Ballinaphy and Ellen his wife Born April 8th Baptised April 24th ...

Ballymodan Church of Ireland baptismal register (NAI MFCI reel 30). (*Courtesy of the National Archives of Ireland*)

denominations. Nonetheless, the legal standing of the Church of Ireland meant that many marriages, of members of other Protestant churches in particular, are recorded in Church of Ireland registers. The information given is not extensive, consisting usually of the names of the parties marrying and the name of the officiating clergyman. Even addresses are not usual, unless one of the people is from another parish. More comprehensive material is included in records of marriage banns, where these exist. (Although it was obligatory for notification of the intention to marry to be given in church on three consecutive Sundays, written records of these are relatively rare.) After 1845, when non-Roman Catholic marriages were registered by the state, the marriage registers record all the information contained in state records, including occupations, addresses and fathers' names.

Marriage Licence Bonds: As an alternative to marriage banns, members of the Church of Ireland could take out a Marriage Licence Bond. The parties lodged a sum of money with the diocese to indemnify the Church against there being an obstacle to the marriage; in effect, the system allowed the better-off to purchase privacy by insuring the Church against future liability. The original bonds were all destroyed in 1922, but the original indexes are available at NAI and on LDS microfilm. Some transcriptions are appearing online (see Chapter 13). The Dublin diocesan index was published as part of the Index to Dublin Will and Grant Books, RDKPRI, 26, 1895 (1270–1800), and RDKPRI, 30, 1899 (1800–1858), online at <www.findmypast.ie>. The Genealogical Office holds abstracts of Prerogative Marriage Licence Bonds from 1630 to 1858 (GO 605–607), as well as marriages recorded in Prerogative Wills (GO 255–6). For an explanation of the Prerogative Court see Chapter 6: Wills.

Other: As well as straightforward information on baptisms, marriages and burials, Church of Ireland parish records very often include vestry books. These contain the minutes of the vestry meetings of the local parish, which can supply detailed information on the part played by individuals in the life of the parish. It should be kept in mind that as the Church of Ireland was in effect an arm of government, matters concerning non-Anglicans, such as poor relief, are also treated in these books. They are not generally included with the parish registers in NAI, but PRONI and the RCBL in Dublin have extensive collections.

Locations

After the Church of Ireland ceased to be the Established Church in 1870, its marriage records before 1845 and baptismal and burial records before 1871 were declared to be the property of the state: public records. Unless the local clergyman was in a position to demonstrate that he could house these records safely, he was required to deposit them in the Public Record Office. By 1922 the original registers of nearly a thousand parishes, more than half the total for the country, were stored at the PRO, and these were all destroyed in the fire there on 28 June that year.

Fortunately, 637 registers had been kept locally in secure storage, and local rectors had in many cases made a transcript before surrendering the originals. In addition, local historians and genealogists using the PRO before 1922 amassed collections of extracts from the registers. All these factors mitigated, to some extent, the loss of such a valuable collection. However, it has also meant that surviving registers, transcripts and extracts are now held in a variety of locations. The Appendix to the *28th Report of the Deputy Keeper of Public Records in Ireland* lists the Church of Ireland parish records for the entire island, giving full details of the years covered and specifying those that were in the PRO at the time of its destruction. No information on locations is included. A more comprehensive account is supplied by the NAI catalogue of Church of Ireland records, available in the NAI reading room and at the National Library in *A Table of Church of Ireland Parochial Records* (ed. Noel Reid, IFHS, 1994; 2nd ed., 2002) and in the Representative Church Body Library's *Handlist of Church of Ireland Registers*, online at <*www.ireland.anglican.org/library*>. As well as the dates of the registers, the NAI catalogue also gives some details of locations, but only when the archives hold the originals, a microfilm copy, a transcript or abstracts on open access, when the RCBL in Dublin holds original registers for dates that make them public records, or when they are still held in the parish. The catalogue does not indicate when microfilm copies are held by the RCBL, PRONI or NLI, simply specifying 'local custody'. This is accurate in that the originals are indeed held locally, but it is unhelpful to researchers.

The RCBL is the Church of Ireland's own repository for its archives and manuscripts, and it holds the original records of more than a thousand parishes, not all of them of genealogical interest. Except where the originals are too fragile, these records are open for public research. Their own *Handlist* is the only comprehensive published guide.

In general, for the northern counties of Antrim, Armagh, Cavan, Derry, Donegal, Down, Fermanagh, Leitrim, Louth, Monaghan and Tyrone, surviving registers have been microfilmed by PRONI and are available to the public in Belfast. The *Guide to Church Records: Public Record Office of Northern Ireland* (PRONI, 2010; also online) gives details. For those counties that are in what is now the Republic—Cavan, Donegal, Leitrim, Louth and Monaghan—copies of the PRONI microfilms are available to the public at the RCBL. The vast majority of all surviving historical records for the rest of the Republic are now in the RCBL, with some transcripts and images online. See 'What's online?' below. If the surviving records really are only available locally, the current *Church of Ireland Directory* will supply the relevant name and address.

PRESBYTERIAN RECORDS

Dates

In general, Presbyterian registers start much later than those of the Church of Ireland, and early records of Presbyterian baptisms, marriages and deaths are often to be found in the registers of the local Church of Ireland parish. There are exceptions, however. In areas that had a strong Presbyterian population from an early date, particularly in the north-east, some registers date from the late seventeenth and early eighteenth centuries. The only published listing remains that included in Margaret Falley's *Irish and Scotch-Irish Ancestral Research* (reprinted GPC, 1988). This, however, gives a very incomplete and out-of-date picture of the extent and location of the records. For the six counties of Northern Ireland, and many of the adjoining counties, the PRONI *Guide to Church Records* provides a good guide to the dates and locations of surviving registers.

The nature of the records

Presbyterian registers record the same information as that given in the registers of the Church of Ireland (see above). It should be remembered that after 1845 all non-Roman Catholic marriages, including those of Presbyterians, were registered by the state. From that year, therefore, Presbyterian marriage registers contain all the invaluable information given in state records.

Locations

Presbyterian registers are in three main locations: in local custody, in PRONI and at the Presbyterian Historical Society in Belfast. PRONI also has microfilm copies of almost all registers in Northern Ireland that have remained in local custody and also lists those records held by the Presbyterian Historical Society. For the rest of Ireland almost all the records are in local custody. It can be very difficult to locate these, as many congregations in the South have moved, amalgamated or simply disappeared over the last sixty years. The very congregational basis of Presbyterianism further complicates matters, as it means that Presbyterian records do not cover a definite geographical area: the same town often had two or more Presbyterian churches drawing worshippers from the same community and keeping distinct records. In the early nineteenth century especially, controversy within the Church fractured the records, with seceding and non-seceding congregations in the same area often in violent opposition to each other. Apart from the PRONI listing, the only guide is *History of Congregations* (Belfast: PHS, 1982; NLI Ir 274108 p 11), which gives a brief historical outline of the history of each congregation. An online version at <*www.presbyterianhistoryireland.com*> is more up to date. Lewis's *Topographical Dictionary of Ireland* (1837) records the existence of Presbyterian congregations within each civil parish, and Pettigrew and Oulton's *Dublin Almanac and General Register of Ireland* (1835) includes a list of all Presbyterian ministers in the country, along with the names and locations of their congregations. Brian Mitchell's *A New Genealogical Atlas of Ireland* (Baltimore, Md.: GPC, 2nd ed., 2002; NLI RR 9292 m 36) maps the locations of historical Presbyterian congregations in the nine counties of Ulster. A brief bibliography of histories of Presbyterianism is given under 'Clergymen' in Chapter 12. For Dublin especially, Steven Smyrl's *Dictionary of Dublin Dissent: Dublin's Protestant Dissenting Meeting Houses, 1660–1920* (Dublin: A. & A. Farmer, 2009) is an excellent guide to the congregations and their records.

METHODIST RECORDS

Despite the hostility of many of the clergy of the Church of Ireland, the Methodist movement remained unequivocally a part of the Established Church from the date of its beginnings in 1747, when John Wesley first came to Ireland, until 1816, when the movement split. Between 1747 and 1816, therefore, records of Methodist baptisms, marriages and burials will be found in the registers of the Church of Ireland. The split in 1816 took place over the question of the authority of Methodist ministers to administer sacraments, and it resulted in the 'Primitive Methodists' remaining within the Church of Ireland and the 'Wesleyan Methodists' authorising their ministers to perform baptisms and communions. (In theory at least, up to 1844 only marriages carried out by a minister of the Church of Ireland were legally valid.) The split continued until 1878, when the Primitive Methodists united with the Wesleyan Methodists, outside the Church of Ireland. What this means is that the earliest surviving registers that are specifically Methodist date from 1815–16 and relate only to the Wesleyan Methodists. The information recorded in these is identical to that given in the Church of Ireland registers.

There are a number of problems in locating Methodist records that are specific to that Church. Firstly, the origins of Methodism, as a movement rather than as a church, gave its members a great deal of latitude in their attitude to Church membership, so that records of the baptisms, marriages and burials of Methodists may also be found in Quaker and Presbyterian registers, as well as in the registers of the Church of Ireland. In addition, the ministers of the Church were preachers on a circuit, rather than administrators of a particular area, and they moved frequently from one circuit to another. Quite often the records moved with them. Tracking the minister is often the only way of locating the relevant records. *An Alphabetical Arrangement of all the Wesleyan Methodist Preachers and Missionaries (Ministers, Missionaries and Preachers on Trial), etc.* (Bradford: T. Inkersley), originally by William Hill and republished twenty-one times between 1819 and 1927, tracks all ministers in Britain and Ireland. At the time of writing (mid-2011), three editions—1827, 1858 and 1862—are online at Google Books.

For the nine historical counties of Ulster, the PRONI *Guide to Church Records* has a county-by-county, parish-by-parish listing of the surviving registers and their dates and locations. No such listing exists for the rest of the country. Again, Pettigrew and Oulton's *Dublin Almanac and General Register of Ireland* (1835 and subsequent years) provides a list of Methodist preachers and their stations, which will give an indication of the relevant localities. The next step is then to identify the closest surviving Methodist centre and to enquire of them about surviving records. Many of the local county heritage centres also hold database copies of surviving Methodist records and have made them searchable at <*www. rootsireland.ie*> (see Chapter 15).

QUAKER RECORDS

From the time of their first arrival in Ireland in the seventeenth century, the Society of Friends, the Quakers, kept rational and systematic records of the births, marriages and deaths of all their members, and in most cases these continue without a break up to the present. Parish registers as such were not kept. Each of the local weekly meetings reported any births, marriages and deaths to a larger Monthly Meeting, which then entered them in a register. Monthly Meetings were held in the following areas: Antrim, Ballyhagan, Carlow, Cootehill, Cork, Dublin, Edenderry, Grange, Lisburn, Limerick, Lurgan, Moate, Mountmellick, Richhill, Tipperary, Waterford, Wexford and Wicklow. For all but Antrim and Cootehill, registers have survived from an early date and are detailed below.

The entries for births, marriages and deaths do not themselves contain information other than the names and addresses of the immediate parties involved, but the centralisation of the records, and the self-contained nature of the Quaker community, make it a relatively simple matter to establish family connections; many of the local records are given in the form of family lists, in any case.

There are two main repositories for records: the libraries of the Society of Friends in Dublin and Lisburn. The LDS Library in Salt Lake City has microfilm copies of the records of the Dublin Society of Friends' Library. PRONI has microfilm copies of records from Ulster. As well as the records outlined below, these records also include considerable collections of letters, wills and family papers, together with detailed accounts of the discrimination suffered by the Quakers in their early years.

Births, marriages and burials

Ballyhagan Marriages, Library of the Society of Friends, Lisburn. Also NLI Pos. 4127 and PRONI.

Bandon, 1672–1713, in Albert Casey (ed.), O'K., Vol. 11.

Carlow births, marriages and deaths up to 1859, Library of the Society of Friends, Dublin. Also NLI Pos. 1021.

Cork, births, marriages and deaths up to 1859, Library of the Society of Friends, Dublin. (NLI Pos. 1021.) See also *Cork (seventeenth to nineteenth centuries),* NLI Pos. 5530.

Dublin, births, marriages and deaths up to 1859, Library of the Society of Friends, Dublin. Also NLI Pos. 1021 (births and marriages) and 1022 (burials).

Edenderry, births, marriages and deaths up to 1859, Library of the Society of Friends, Dublin. Also NLI Pos. 1022; 1612–1814 (in the form of family lists), NLI Pos. 5531.

Grange, births, marriages and deaths up to 1859, Library of the Society of Friends, Dublin. Also NLI Pos. 1022.

Lisburn, births, marriages and deaths up to 1859, Library of the Society of Friends, Dublin. Also NLI Pos. 1022, PRONI.

Limerick, births, marriages and deaths up to 1859, Library of the Society of Friends, Dublin. Also NLI Pos. 1022.

Lurgan, births, marriages and deaths up to 1859, Library of the Society of Friends, Dublin. (NLI Pos. 1022.) See also *Lurgan Marriage Certificates,* Library of the Society of Friends, Lisburn. (NLI Pos. 4126.) Also PRONI.

Moate, births, marriages and deaths up to 1859, Library of the Society of Friends, Dublin. Also NLI Pos. 1022.

Mountmellick, births, marriages and deaths up to 1859, Library of the Society of Friends, Dublin. Also NLI Pos. 1023 and Pos. 5530.

Mountrath, Library of the Society of Friends, Dublin. Also NLI Pos. 5530.

Richhill, births, marriages and deaths up to 1859, Library of the Society of Friends, Dublin. Also NLI Pos. 1023.

Tipperary, births, marriages and deaths up to 1859, Library of the Society of Friends, Dublin. Also NLI Pos. 1024.

Waterford, births, marriages and deaths up to 1859, Library of the Society of Friends, Dublin. Also NLI Pos. 1024.

Wexford, births, marriages and deaths up to 1859, Library of the Society of Friends, Dublin. Also NLI Pos. 1024.

Wicklow, births, marriages and deaths up to 1859, Library of the Society of Friends, Dublin. Also NLI Pos. 1024.

Youghal, births, marriages and deaths up to 1859, Library of the Society of Friends, Dublin. Also NLI Pos. 1024.

Births, Marriages and Deaths throughout Ireland, 1859–1949, Library of the Society of Friends, Dublin. Also NLI Pos. 1024.

Also

Leinster Province, births, marriages and deaths, seventeenth century, Library of the Society of Friends, Dublin. (NLI Pos. 5530.)

Munster Province, births, marriages and deaths, 1650–1839, Library of the Society of Friends, Dublin. (NLI Pos. 5531.)

Ulster Province Meeting Books, 1673–1691, Library of the Society of Friends, Lisburn. (Also PRONI and NLI Pos. 3747.)

Ulster Province Meetings Minute Books to 1782, Library of the Society of Friends, Lisburn. (Also PRONI and NLI Pos. 4124 and 4125.)

Other records
(1) Published

Butler, David M., *Quaker Meeting Houses of Ireland,* Dublin: Historical Committee of Friends in Ireland, 2004. 256 p.

Eustace, P.B., and Goodbody, O., *Quaker Records, Dublin, Abstracts of Wills* (2 vols., 1704–1785), IMC, 1954–8. NLI Ir 289 e 6, 136 p.

Goodbody, Olive, *Guide to Irish Quaker Records, 1654–1860, with contribution on Northern Ireland records by B.G. Hutton,* IMC, 1967. NLI Ir 2896 g 4, 237 p.

Grubb, Isabel, *Quakers in Ireland,* London: Swarthmore Press, 1927. NLI Ir 2896 g 3, 128 p.

Harrison, Richard S., *Cork City Quakers, 1655–1939: a brief history,* the author, 1991. NLI Ir 289 h 3.

Harrison, Richard S., *A Biographical Dictionary of Irish Quakers,* Dublin: Four Courts Press, 2nd ed. 2008. NLI, 123 p.

Impey, E.J.A., *A Roberts Family, quondam Quakers of Queen's Co.*, privately printed, 1939. NLI Ir 9292 r 3.

Leadbetter, *Biographical Notices of the Society of Friends.* NLI J 2896.

Lunham, T.A., *Early Quakers in Cork: and Cork topographical notes*, Cork: Guy, 1904. NLI Large Pamphlets LP 2.

Myers, A.C., *Immigration of Irish Quakers into Pennsylvania*, Baltimore, Md.: GPC, 1969 (repr. of 1902 ed.). NLI Ir 2896 m 2 and 4.

(2) *Manuscript*

Quaker Pedigrees. Library of the Society of Friends, Dublin. Also NLI Pos. 5382–5.

Quaker Wills and Inventories. Library of the Society of Friends, Lisburn. Also NLI Pos. 4127.

Manuscript records of the Quaker Library (see guide above): Quaker House, Stocking Lane, Rathfarnham, Dublin 16. Tel. +353 (0) 1 4950021 ext. 222. Open Thurs., 11 a.m. to 1 p.m.

JEWISH RECORDS

There have been Jews in Ireland since the Middle Ages, but a sizeable community developed only in the second half of the nineteenth century, and it began to shrink again from about the 1950s. One man, Stuart Rosenblatt, has devoted decades to collecting all the surviving records of this community and has collated them on the website <*www.irishjewishroots.com*>. He has also published twenty-six volumes of extracts from his databases.

WHAT'S ONLINE?

Three websites hold significant quantities of material transcribed from Irish church records.

1. <*www.roostireland.ie*> This is the website of the Irish Family History Foundation, the umbrella body for local genealogy centres around the country. It is pay-per-view, but an advanced index search is free once a user has registered and logged in. Employed judiciously, this index search alone can be very helpful. By far the most useful aspect of the site is the ability to search (almost) all their records at once to identify a place of origin in Ireland. It now contains about 80 per cent of pre-1900 Roman Catholic records, perhaps 50 per cent of Church of Ireland records and about 10–15 per cent of other congregations' records. For particular centres, such as Limerick, Sligo and Mayo, these proportions are 100 per cent. No further transcription is likely to be undertaken.

   A number of points should be kept in mind when using the site. The system of red and green colour-coding used to indicate which centres have uploaded records is misleadingly simple. Even if a centre has few or no records for an area, when that area forms part of the designated catchment of the centre it will appear green, as having records. For example, Irish World Heritage Centre has responsibility for Cos. Fermanagh and Tyrone, and has made its records searchable on <*www.roostireland.ie*>. So Fermanagh is coloured green on the site's map of Ireland. But there are no church record transcripts for Co. Fermanagh on the site, only civil record transcripts. Similar omissions occur for almost every centre. The list of sources supplied by each centre and the separate drop-down list titled 'Parish/District' on the search form itself do not match in some cases. For example, the Catholic parish of Athlone (St Peter's) in Co. Roscommon has been transcribed by the Roscommon Heritage and Genealogy Society and is listed by the centre as among the sources online, but nothing from this parish ever appears among search results. Similar examples are widespread. The implication is clear: be sceptical, and satisfy yourself that everything the site claims to have searchable is in fact present.

The search interface in use is clear and relatively straightforward. The only serious flaw is the lack of forename variants and wild-card functions: searching for 'Mathew' will return results different from those returned for 'Matthew'. The surname variants system is, if anything, too comprehensive. It is available to browse at <*www.rootsireland.ie/ifhf/surnames.php*>.

The site reflects the intensely disparate and jealously local nature of the groups that make up the Irish Family History Foundation and is designed to allow these groups to maintain their distinct identities and receive payment purely for the use made of their records. In other words, the site reflects the demands of the component centres rather than the needs of researchers. In addition, the lack of record images means that an examination of the NLI microfilms remains essential. This much having been said, the site is a remarkable achievement and is now an indispensable part of any Irish family history project.

2.   <*www.irishgenealogy.ie*> This site is run by the Department of Arts, Heritage and the Gaeltacht and aims to cover areas not included by <*www.roostireland.ie*>. At present (2011) it has the record transcripts of two former IFHF centres—Dublin city and Co. Kerry—its own transcripts of the Roman Catholic records of Cork city, west Cork and Dublin city, and the Church of Ireland records of Dublin city and Cos. Carlow and Kerry. The major differences with <*www.rootsireland.ie*> are that the site is completely free and that the fresh transcripts are accompanied by images of the records, generally from NLI microfilm in the case of the Catholic records and new, high-quality colour scans in the case of the Church of Ireland records.

The basic search interface is non-standard, a misguided attempt to be as unintimidating as possible, which has ended up causing much initial confusion. However, with trial and error it is possible to retrieve almost everything a search could aim for. Wild cards (*) are allowed in all the text fields, and a decent (and improving) surname and forename variants system is in use. Above all, the fact that the majority of record transcripts are accompanied by images of the originals means that the most sceptical researcher can check (and correct) what the database tells them.

3. <*www.familysearch.org*> The main Mormon website has a significant number of transcripts from its copies of NLI microfilms. It can be extraordinarily difficult to discern precisely what the site holds, but it has at least two major collections. The first is the twelve or so parishes from the diocese of Elphin that were transcribed and originally made available on the LDS CD-ROM *British Isles Vital Records Index* (2nd ed.). These transcripts are listed in Chapter 14. The site also appears to have copies of the transcripts made by Albert Casey for his monumental *O'Kief, Coshe Mang* series, consisting of parish registers for areas close to the Sliabh Luachra area on the Cork-Kerry border. Where there is an O'Kief transcript, this is also noted in Chapter 14. Despite the fact that the LDS Family History Library holds close to 40 per cent of historical Roman Catholic records on microfilm, there appears to be no concerted effort to transcribe these.

4. Other sites: Volunteers, especially in North America, have made transcripts of parish registers from LDS microfilms for areas they are researching and have put them on various websites. Where there are significant numbers, these sites are noted in Chapter 13 under the relevant county.

The largest commercial genealogy site, <*www.ancestry.com*>, added transcripts of the records of forty-seven Catholic parishes in September 2011. These are based on a small selection of the NLI microfilms and cover forty-seven parishes, almost all in the diocese of Meath, representing perhaps 5 per cent of the NLI total.

At the time of writing, NLI has begun the process of creating digital images from all its parish register microfilms, with the aim of making them freely available on its website. In itself this would revolutionise Irish research: a visit to the NLI microfilm room could take place from anywhere on the planet with a broadband connection. Inevitably, once the images are available, transcription will follow—most likely volunteer transcription.

Chapter 4 ～

PROPERTY AND VALUATION RECORDS

IRISH PLACENAMES

The smallest official geographical division used in Ireland is the townland. Loosely related to the customary rural and agricultural divisions used in post-medieval Ireland—the 'ballybetagh' in the north-west, the 'cappel' lands and 'ploughlands' in the south-east, the *ceathrú* (quarter) in the west—townlands began to undergo standardisation from the seventeenth century. They retain a loose relationship with agricultural value and can therefore vary enormously in size, from a single acre or less to several thousand acres. There are more than 64,000 townlands in Ireland. The final standardisation was carried out by the Ordnance Survey in the 1830s, and the versions they chose (or imposed) are still in use today. Standardisation resulted in the loss of a large number of traditional names, later referred to as 'sub-denominational'. A guide to sources useful in identifying Irish placenames will be found in the introduction to Chapter 13.

Anything from five to thirty townlands may be grouped together to form a civil parish. These are a legacy of the Middle Ages, pre-dating the formation of counties and generally co-extensive with the parishes of the Established Church, the Church of Ireland. They are not to be confused with Catholic parishes, which are usually much larger. In turn, civil parishes are collected together in baronies. Originally related to the tribal divisions, the *tuatha*, of Celtic Ireland, these were multiplied and subdivided over the centuries up to their standardisation in the 1500s, so that the present names represent a mixture of Irish, Anglo-Norman and English influences. A number of baronies, from five in Co. Leitrim to twenty-two in Co. Cork, then go to make up the modern county. Baronies and civil parishes are no longer in use as administrative units.

These geographical units are the basis of the only two nineteenth-century property surveys to cover the entire country. Because of the destruction of early-century census returns, the Tithe Applotment Books of c.1823–38 and Griffith's Valuation, dating from 1847 to 1864, have acquired a somewhat unnatural importance.

41   PARISH OF *Castlerahan*

TOWNLANDS AND LAND-LORDS.	OCCUPIERS.	1st Quality			2nd			3rd			4th			
		A.	R.	P.	A.	R.	P.	A.	R.	P.	A.	R.	P.	A
Aghlion	forwarded	52	1	20	73	2	25	10	0	05	4	0	00	
"	Peter Lynch &c.	4	2	~	5	~	~	2	2	~	~	~	~	
"	T.B.&I. Lynch	10	~	~	17	~	~	5	~	~	~	~	~	
"	I.&P. Krogan	3	~	~	24	1	~	4	~	~	~	~	~	
"	I. Kilroy & Brady	4	~	~	12	~	~	3	~	~	7	2	~	
"	Garret Fitzsimon	3	~	~	7	~	~	1	1	15	~	~	~	
"	Jn. Fitzsimons	4	~	~	7	~	~	~	2	15	~	~	~	
"	John Brady	~	~	1	~	~	~	~	~	~	~	~	~	
"	Luke Maginis	1	0	30	4	~	~	~	~	~	1	~	~	
"	Nich. Glannon	1	~	~	1	~	~	~	~	~	~	~	~	
		83	1	10	150	3	25	24	1	35	12	2	~	

Tithe Applotment Book, Aghalion, Co. Cavan (NAI 4/32, MFA 53/7, Film 5B). (*Courtesy of the National Archives of Ireland*)

TITHE APPLOTMENT BOOKS

The Composition Act (1823) specified that tithes due to the Established Church, the Church of Ireland, which had hitherto been payable in kind, should now be paid in money. As a result, it was necessary to carry out a valuation of the entire country, civil parish by civil parish, to determine how much would be payable by each landholder. This was done over the ensuing fifteen years, up to the suspension of tithe payments in 1838. Not surprisingly, those who were not members of the Church of Ireland fiercely resented tithes, all the more so because the tax was not payable on all land; the exemptions produced spectacular inequalities. In parts of Munster, for instance, tithes were payable on potato patches but not on grassland, with the result that the poorest had to pay most. The exemptions also mean that the Tithe Books are not comprehensive. Apart from the fact that they omit entirely anyone not in occupation of land, certain categories of land, varying from area to area, are simply passed over in silence. They are not a full list of householders. Nonetheless, they do constitute the only countrywide survey for the period and are valuable precisely because the heaviest burden of tithes fell on the poorest, for whom few other records survive.

From a genealogical point of view, the information recorded in the Tithe Books is quite basic, consisting typically of townland name, landholder's name, area of land and tithes payable. In addition, many books also record the landlord's name and an assessment of the economic productivity of the land. The tax was based on the average price of wheat and oats over the seven years up to 1823, and it was levied at a different rate according to the quality of the land.

Microfilm copies of the Tithe Books for all of Ireland are available in NAI, NLI and via the LDS Family History Library. Those for the nine counties of Ulster are available in PRONI. At the time of writing (2011), NAI is engaged with the LDS Family History Library in a project to make transcriptions and digital images of the complete set of Tithe Books searchable online, probably at <www.familysearch.org>.

The usefulness of the Tithe Books can vary enormously, depending on the nature of the research. As only a name is given, with no indication of family relationships, any conclusions drawn are inevitably somewhat speculative. However, for parishes where registers do not begin until after 1850 they are often the only surviving written records. They can provide valuable circumstantial evidence, especially where a holding passed from father to son in the period between the Tithe Survey and Griffith's Valuation. The surnames in the Tithe Books have been roughly indexed in NLI 'Index of Surnames', described more fully below. A full index is available at <www.ancestry.com>.

An organised campaign of resistance to the payment of tithes, the so-called Tithe War, culminated in 1831 in large-scale refusals to pay the tax. To apply for compensation for the resultant loss of income, local Church of Ireland clergymen were required to produce lists of those liable for tithes who had not paid, the 'tithe defaulters'. The lists can provide a fuller picture of tithe-payers than the original Tithe Book and can be useful for cross-checking against it, especially if it dates from before 1831. Of these lists 127 survive, in the NAI Chief Secretary's Office, Official Papers series. They relate principally to Cos. Kilkenny and Tipperary, with some coverage also of Cos. Carlow, Cork, Kerry, Laois, Limerick, Louth, Meath, Offaly, Waterford and Wexford. A full list was published in the *Irish Genealogist*, Vol. 8, No. 1, 1990. County-by-county microfiche indexes have been produced by Data Tree Publishing (<www.alphalink.com.au/~datatree>). These are available at NLI. An online version is available at <www.findmypast.ie>.

Valuation of Tenements.

ACTS 15 & 16 VIC., CAP. 63, & 17 VIC., CAP. 8.

COUNTY OF CAVAN.

BARONY OF CASTLERAHAN.

UNION OF OLDCASTLE.

PARISH OF CASTLERAHAN.

No. and Letters of Reference to Map.		Names.		Description of Tenement.	Area.	Rateable Annual Valuation.		Total Annual Valuation of Rateable Property.
		Townlands and Occupiers.	Immediate Lessors.			Land.	Buildings.	
		AGHALION. (Ord. S. 39.)			A. R. P.	£ s. d.	£ s. d.	£ s. d.
1	a	John Lynch,	C. T. Nesbit,	House, offices, and land,	14 2 28	6 5 0	0 10 0	6 15 0
–	b	C. T. Nesbit,	In fee,	Land,	0 3 30	0 5 0	—	0 5 0
2	{ a	Bryan McDonald, }	C. T. Nesbit,	{ Herd's house & land, }	19 3 22	{ 4 0 0	1 5 0	5 5 0
	{ –	John Fitzsimon, }		{ Land,		4 0 0	—	4 0 0
3		John Fitzsimon,	Same.	House, offices, and land,	5 1 34	2 0 0	1 0 0	3 0 0
4		John Fitzsimon,	Same,	Land,	4 1 34	2 0 0	—	2 0 0
–	a	Rose Fitzsimon,	Same,	House.	—	—	0 10 0	0 10 0
5	a	John Fitzsimon, jun.,	Same,	House, offices, and land,	8 1 35	4 0 0	1 0 0	5 0 0
–	b	John Fitzsimon,	Same,	Land,	0 2 15	0 5 0	—	0 5 0
6	c {	John Flood,	Same.	{ Land (gardens),	0 1 24	0 5 0	—	0 5 0
	– {			House, offices, and land,	17 2 8	8 0 0	1 15 0	9 15 0
7	{	Michael Cogan,	Same.	{ House, offices, and land,	31 0 12	10 0 0	1 5 0	} 14 0 0
8	{			Land.	7 2 16	2 15 0	—	
9	a	Peter Lynch,	Same.	{ House, offices, and land,	5 0 22	1 18 0	0 10 0	} 2 15 0
				Bog,	7 0 17	0 7 0	—	
–	b }	Joseph Brady,	Same,	{ Ho., off., & sm. garden,	—	—	0 10 0	0 10 0
10	{			Land,	1 1 33	0 10 0	—	0 10 0
11		Catherine Fitzsimon,	Same,	House and land,	2 0 4	0 10 0	0 5 0	5 0 0
12		Matthew Cogan,	Same.	House, office, and land,	13 0 9	4 10 0	0 10 0	5 0 0
13	{			Land,	11 0 24	4 0 0	—	
14	{	Patrick Cogan,	Same.	{ House, offices, and land,	23 3 18	12 0 0	1 5 0	} 22 5 0
15	{			Land,	8 2 21	4 0 0	—	
16	{			Land.	1 2 2	1 0 0	—	
–	a	John Lynch,	Same,	Land,	0 1 24	0 4 0	—	0 4 0
17	a	Terence & Patk. Cogan,	Same,	House, offices, and land,	38 0 30	15 0 0	1 0 0	16 0 0
–	b	Vacant,	Terence & Patk. Cogan,	House,	—	—	0 5 0	0 5 0
–	c	Vacant,	Same,	House,	—	—	0 10 0	0 10 0
18		Michael Brady,	C. T. Nesbit,	House, office, and land,	8 2 20	4 0 0	0 15 0	4 15 0
19	a	James Bennett,	Same,	House, offices, and land,	34 2 18	17 10 0	1 5 0	18 15 0
–	b	Margaret Gilroy,	James Bennett,	House,	—	—	0 10 0	0 10 0
–	c	Anne Tinmon,	Same,	House,	—	—	0 5 0	0 5 0
–	d	Peter Lynch,	C. T. Nesbit,	Land,	0 0 20	0 1 0	—	0 1 0
–	e	Joseph Brady,	Same.	Land,	0 0 20	0 1 0	—	0 1 0
20		Anthony Brady,	Same.	House, offices, and land,	12 0 14	5 15 0	1 0 0	6 15 0
21		John Lynch,	Same.	House, offices, and land,	12 1 18	6 5 0	1 0 0	7 5 0
22		Edward Fitzsimons,	Same.	House, office, and land,	6 2 16	3 0 0	0 10 0	3 10 0
23	a	Michael Brady,	Same.	Herd's house and land,	14 3 13	7 10 0	0 10 0	8 0 0
–	b	Terence & Patk. Cogan,	Same.	Land,	0 1 24	0 5 0	—	0 5 0
24		Peter Brady,	Same,	Land,	7 0 31	3 0 0	—	3 0 0
25		John Brady,	Same.	Herd's house and land,	34 3 2	16 0 0	0 5 0	16 5 0
26		Patrick Brady,	Same.	House, offices, and land,	18 1 17	8 15 0	1 15 0	10 10 0
27		C. T. Nesbit,	In fee.	Land,	14 0 13	0 15 0	—	0 15 0

B

Griffith's Valuation, Aghalion, Co. Cavan. (*Courtesy of the Genealogical Office*)

GRIFFITH'S VALUATION

From the 1820s to the 1840s a complex process of reform attempted to standardise the basis of local taxation in Ireland. The first steps were to map and fix administrative boundaries through the Ordnance Survey and the associated Boundary Commission. The next step was to assess the productive capacity of all property in the country in a thoroughly uniform way. Richard Griffith, a geologist based in Dublin, became Boundary Commissioner in 1825 and Commissioner of Valuation in 1827. The results of his great survey, the Primary

Valuation of Ireland, were published between 1847 and 1864. The valuation is arranged by county, barony, Poor Law Union, civil parish and townland, and it lists every landholder and every householder in Ireland. Apart from townland address and householder's name, the particulars given are:

- name of the person from whom the property was leased ('immediate lessor');
- description of the property;
- acreage;
- valuation.

The only directly useful family information supplied is in areas where a surname was particularly common. The surveyors often adopted the traditional Irish practice of using the father's first name to distinguish between individuals of the same name, so that 'John Reilly (James)' is the son of James, while 'John Reilly (Michael)' is the son of Michael. For similar reasons, occupations are also sometimes used to tell 'John Ryan (weaver)' from 'John Ryan (farmer)'. Copies of Griffith's Valuation are widely available in major libraries and record offices, both on microfiche and in their original published form. A free online version is at <www.askaboutireland.ie>. The dates of first publication will be found under the individual counties in Chapter 13.

The valuation was never intended as a census substitute, and if the 1851 census had survived it would have little genealogical significance. As things stand, however, it gives the only detailed guide to where in Ireland people lived in the middle of the nineteenth century and to what property they occupied. In addition, a huge quantity of material was produced both before publication and in subsequent revisions, making it possible in many cases to identify occupiers before the publication date and to trace living descendants of those originally listed by Griffith. (See 'Valuation Office records' below.)

USING GRIFFITH'S ONLINE

In the early 2000s, Eneclann, the National Library of Ireland and the Origins Network put together the most complete set of Griffith's Valuation ever assembled, digitally imaged it and an accompanying set of valuation maps, made a database transcription of the published volumes and had the result searchable online for a fee at <www.origins.net> and free in NLI. In 2009 the Library Council of Ireland acquired a licence from this consortium for the digital images and the transcripts and made them searchable free at <www.askaboutireland.ie>, linked to a set of Ordnance Survey maps the council acquired separately. The full original set—images, transcripts and maps—has since also been licensed by the Origins Network consortium to another paying website, <www.findmypast.ie>. Consequently, the same database transcript of Griffith's is searchable on two paying sites and one free site.

The major differences between <www.askaboutireland.ie> and the paying sites lie in the search interface and the maps. Searching on the free site permits only a very weak surname variant option, no wild cards and no variant option at all for its placenames search. It is not possible to combine a personal name and townland name search. The placenames used in Griffith's are the versions earlier standardised by the Ordnance Survey and used in the 1851 census, so the 1851 *Townlands Index*, freely searchable using wild cards at *<www.irishtimes.com/ ancestor/placenames>* and *<www.seanruad.com>*, can remedy the lack of flexibility in the placenames search.

The difference in the links to the Ordnance Survey maps accompanying Griffith's is more complex and needs a little explanation. The leftmost column in the printed valuation is headed 'No and Letters of Reference to map'. Each holding within a townland or street is numbered sequentially in order of valuation, not of geographical contiguity. In general, on the accompanying map each townland is surrounded by a thick line, with the numbered subdivisions outlined inside lighter lines. Within these numbered subdivisions in the printed valuation, letters are sometimes included. Capital letters after the subdivision number (e.g. '2A, B, C') indicate separate parcels of property in the townland held by the same individual. So if a John Kelly leased two separate fields in the townland of Ballymore, these will be listed within the townland under his name following each other as 2A, B. Lower-case letters after the holding number (e.g. '2a, b, c') indicate a house situated within a parcel of property. Where a number of houses are situated on a parcel held in common by a number of listed occupiers, large braces enclose them {like this}. This was common in rural areas in early and mid-nineteenth-century Ireland, especially in the west, with anything up to twenty families farming an area in common.

In theory, all three online versions of Griffith's allow a user to go from the printed valuation to the corresponding os map and thus identify precisely a particular holding. In practice, this is sometimes difficult. The map set used by the Origins Network and *<www.findmypast.ie>* is more or less contemporaneous with Griiffith's Valuation and so corresponds more closely to it, but the maps are often badly worn, and the images are in black and white and are presented very awkwardly. The *<www.askaboutireland.ie>* maps are very clean, are in full colour and have been stitched together and overlaid on a contemporary Google map, making them much easier to manipulate and to match to modern roads and villages. But the map set is not contemporary with the printed valuation: it appears to be at least thirty years older, with the result that many of the subdivision boundaries no longer match those recorded in Griffith's.

OTHER INDEXES TO GRIFFITH'S AND TITHE BOOKS
In the early 1960s the National Library of Ireland undertook a project to part-index the surnames occurring in Griffith's Valuation and the Tithe Books, which produced the county-by-county series known as the Index of Surnames or Householders' Index. This records the occurrence of households of a particular surname in each of the civil parishes of a county, giving the exact number of households in the case of Griffith's, and provides a summary of the total number

17.

Surname			Barony
Fitzgerald	G2		Loughtee L.
Fitzgerald	G	T	Loughtee U.
Fitzgerald		T	Tullygarvey
Fitzgerald	G2	T	Clankee
Fitzgerald	G2		Clanmahon
Fitzmaurice	G		Tullyhunco
Fitzpatrick	G25	T	Tullyhaw
Fitzpatrick	G114	T	Loughtee L.
Fitzpatrick	G24	T	Tullyhunco
Fitzpatrick	G73	T	Loughtee U.
Fitzpatrick	G30	T	Tullygarvey
Fitzpatrick	G9	T	Clankee
Fitzpatrick	G33	T	Clanmahon
Fitzpatrick	G10	T	Castlerahan
Fitzsimmons		T	Tullyhunco
Fitzsimmons	G	T	Loughtee U.
Fitzsimmons	G	T	Clanmahon
Fitzsimon	G	T	Tullyhunco
Fitzsimon	G2	T	Loughtee U.
Fitzsimon	G7	T	Tullygarvey
Fitzsimon	G	T	Clankee
Fitzsimon	G		Clanmahon
Fitizsimon	G5	T	Castlerahan
Fitzsimon	G39	T	Castlerahan
Fitzsimons	G	T	Tullyhaw
Fitzsimons	G6	T	Loughtee L.
Fitzsimons	G12	T	Loughtee U.
Fitzsimons	G8	T	Tullygarvey
Fitzsimons	G7	T	Clankee
Fitzsimons	G14	T	Clanmahon
Fitzsimons	G6	T	Castlerahan
Flack		T	Tullyhunco
Flack	G2	T	Tullygarvey
Flack	G3	T	Clankee
Flaherty		T	Loughtee L.
Flanagan	G14	T	Tullyhaw
Flanagan	G3	T	Loughtee L.
Flanagan	G		Tullyhunco
Flanagan	G10	T	Loughtee U.
Flanagan	G	T	Tullygarvey
Flanagan	G4	T	Clankee
Flanagan	G3	T	Clanmahon
Flanagan	G14	T	Castlerahan
Flanigan	G2	T	Tullyhaw
Flanigan	G		Loughtee L.
Flanigan		T	Loughtee U.
Flannagan	G		Loughtee L.
Flannery	G		Loughtee U.
Fleming	G		Tullyhaw
Fleming	G	T	Loughtee L.
Fleming	G3	T	Tullyhunco
Fleming	G8	T	Loughtee U.
Fleming	G	T	Tullygarvey
Fleming	G	T	Clankee
Fleming	G9	T	Clanmahon
Fleming	G7	T	Castlerahan
Fletcher	G		Loughtee U.
Fleuker	G	T	Clankee
Flewker	G2	T	Clankee
Flinn		T	Clankee
Flinn	G	T	Clanmahon
Flood	G	T	Tullyhaw
Flood	G8	T	Loughtee L.
Flood	G3	T	Tullyhunco

Surname			Barony
Flood	G21	T	Loughtee U.
Flood	G18	T	Tullygarvey
Flood	G4	T	Clankee
Flood	G14	T	Clanmahon
Flood	G29	T	Castlerahan
Floody	G3	T	Tullygarvey
Floyd	G2	T	Loughtee U.
Flynn	G13	T	Tullyhaw
Flynn	G6	T	Loughtee L.
Flynn	G		Tullyhunco
Flynn	G3	T	Loughtee U.
Flynn		T	Tullygarvey
Flynn	G		Clankee
Flynn	G9	T	Clanmahon
Flynn	G20	T	Castlerahan
Foghlan	G		Tullyhaw
Polbus		T	Tullyhunco
Foley	G2		Tullygarvey
Follett	G		Loughtee U.
Fonor		T	Castlerahan
Forbes	G	T	Tullyhunco
Forbes	G	T	Clankee
Ford	G		Tullyhaw
Ford	G		Loughtee U.
Ford	G2	T	Tullygarvey
Ford	G		Clankee
Forde	G	T	Tullyhaw
Foreman	G6	T	Clankee
Forest		T	Loughtee U.
Forster		T	Loughtee U.
Forster	G10	T	Clanmahon
Forster	G3	T	Castlerahan
Forsyth	G3	T	Clanmahon
Forsythe		T	Tullygarvey
Fosqua	G	T	Tullyhaw
Foster	G6	T	Loughtee U.
Foster	G5		Tullygarvey
Foster	G9	T	Clanmahon
Foster	G3	T	Castlerahan
Fotton		T	Tullygarvey
Fottrell	G		Clankee
Fox	G2	T	Tullyhaw
Fox	G2	T	Tullyhunco
Fox		T	Loughtee U.
Fox	G4	T	Tullygarvey
Fox	G15	T	Clankee
Fox	G2	T	Clanmahon
Fox	G36	T	Castlerahan
Foy	G3	T	Loughtee L.
Foy	G2	T	Loughtee U.
Foy	G26	T	Tullygarvey
Foy	G5	T	Clankee
Foy	G	T	Clanmahon
Foy		T	Castlerahan
Foy		T	Tullygarvey
Foyragh	G	T	Clankee
Frances		G	Clankee
Francey	G3		Clankee
Francis		T	Loughtee L.
Fraser	G3	T	Tullyhaw
Frazer	G		Tullyhaw
Frazer	G		Loughtee U.
Prazor		T	Tullyhunco
Freeland	G	T	Castlerahan
Freeman	G2	T	Tullygarvey

'Index of Surnames', Co. Cavan. (*Courtesy of the Genealogical Office*)

in each barony of the county. As it is not a true index, providing only an indication of the presence or absence of a surname in the Tithe Books, together with the number of householders bearing the surname in Griffith's, its usefulness is limited. In any case, Griffith's is now well indexed elsewhere. For names that are relatively uncommon it can still have a role to play, but it is of little help for a county in which a particular surname is plentiful. The county volumes include outline maps of the civil parishes covered and a guide to the corresponding Catholic parishes. Full sets of the Index of Surnames can be found at NAI, NLI, PRONI and the LDS Library. Irish Ancestors, at <*www.irishtimes.com/ancestor*>, reproduces online the functionality of the Index of Surnames, giving counts of householders by county (free) and parish (paying).

For the Tithe Books, the Index of Surnames remains the only free countywide guide until the NAI-LDS digitisation project comes to fruition. The website <*www.ancestry.com*> has recently made a transcript of the NAI-LDS microfilms available to subscribers. However, it does not include record images. A CD-ROM index to the Tithe Books of the six counties of Northern Ireland, *International Land Records: Tithe Applotment Books, 1823–38,* was published by FamilyTreeMaker in 1999 and is now available to subscribers at <*www.genealogy.com*>, and various volunteer transcripts from the LDS microfilms are also online (see Chapter 13).

VALUATION OFFICE RECORDS

Pre-publication records
The gestation of Griffith's Valuation was a complex one. Three separate valuation methods were used prior to publication, each producing its own distinct set of records. Firstly, the initial Townland Valuation Act (1826) allowed for a complete assessment of every parcel of land and tenement (building) in Ireland, to enable an equitable replacement for the unevenly applied local cess taxes. However, after Griffith began surveying in Londonderry in 1831 it quickly became apparent that this was far too ambitious for the resources available. A lower threshold of £3 was adopted for buildings to be assessed, excluding the large majority of householders but still covering a significant number of dwellings and commercial premises, especially in towns. The valuation continued on this basis for the next seven years, covering eight of the northern counties. By 1838, however, it was clear that even with a £3 threshold the surveying would last for a very long time indeed. In that year the threshold was raised to £5, covering only the most substantial buildings.

The year 1838 was also that of the introduction of the Irish Poor Law, a system of relief for the most destitute, and its funding, based on property assessments carried out for the local Board of Guardians of each of the 138 Poor Law Unions, soon became a source of contention, with widespread accusations of bias in the valuations. It became obvious fairly quickly that it made no sense to have two separate systems of local taxation, based on differing valuations of the same property. In 1844, with so-called townland valuations complete for 27 of the 32 counties, Griffith was told to change the basis of assessment by dropping the

£5 threshold and covering all property in the remaining counties, all in Munster. The aim was to see if a uniform basis could be created for unifying Poor Law rates and cess. The experiment was an almost unqualified success, and the Tenement Valuation Act (1852) authorised Griffith to extend the system throughout Ireland—a procedure he had in fact already begun. The results were published between 1847 and 1864, generally with the southern counties earlier and the northern counties later.

In the course of this long-drawn-out administrative saga, large quantities of manuscript records were produced. Firstly, the pre-1838 valuation of the northern counties, based on the £3 building threshold, created local valuers' 'house books' and 'field books', the former including the names of occupiers, the latter concerned purely with soil quality. The originals are in NAI and PRONI, with microfilm copies in the LDS Family History Library. They are particularly useful for urban or semi-urban areas in northern counties before 1838.

After the change in the basis of assessment in 1844, the main categories of valuers' notebooks continued to be known as house books and field books, but the distinction became more than a little blurred, with information on occupiers appearing in both. To add to the merriment, other classes of notebook were also created:

- tenure books, showing landlord and lease information;
- rent books, showing rents paid, as an aid to valuation;
- quarto books, covering towns;
- perambulation books, recording valuers' visits; and
- mill books.

There are far fewer of these than of the house books and field books. Copies of all of them are available at NAI and the LDS Library, though not in PRONI, with some still in the Valuation Office itself.

A number of points need to be kept in mind. Firstly, pre-publication manuscript valuation records do not survive for all parishes. The only way to find out if something is there is to check the NAI, LDS, PRONI or Valuation Office catalogues. Secondly, the categories into which the records are sorted were somewhat hazy to begin with and have only become hazier over the years. Check under all the categories and investigate anything that survives for an area you're interested in. And you should remember that Griffith's, far from being the record of a settled population, is in fact a snapshot of the aftermath of a catastrophe, the Great Famine of 1845 to c.1850. In many areas enormous changes took place between the original and the published valuations.

Post-publication records

The 1852 act envisaged annual revisions to the valuations to record any changes in occupier, size of holding, lessor or value. In practice, revisions were relatively rare until well into the 1860s. From about that time until the 1970s, a system of handwritten amendments, coded by colour for each year, was employed, with a new manuscript book created when the number of alterations threatened legibility. These are the Cancelled Land Books, still available at the Valuation Office itself, now in the Irish Life Centre, Lower Abbey Street, Dublin. The LDS Family History Library has microfilm copies, unfortunately in black and white.

The Cancelled Land Books can be very useful in pinpointing a possible date of death or emigration, or in identifying a living relative. A large majority of those who were in occupation of a holding by the 1890s, when the Land Acts began to subsidise the purchase by tenant-farmers of their land, have descendants or relatives still living in the same area. The Cancelled Land Books for Northern Ireland are now in PRONI. Full revaluations of areas in Northern Ireland took place in 1935, 1956/7 and 1975, with revisions for the intervening years and up to 1993. These are open to the public at PRONI.

ESTATE RECORDS

Throughout most of the eighteenth and nineteenth centuries the vast majority of the Irish population lived as small tenant-farmers on large estates owned for the most part by English or Anglo-Irish landlords. The administration of these estates inevitably produced large quantities of records: maps, tenants' lists, rentals, account books, lease books etc. Over the course of the twentieth century, as the estates have been broken up and sold off, many collections of these records have found their way into public repositories, and they constitute a largely unexplored source of genealogical information.

There are, however, good reasons for their being unexplored. Firstly, it was quite rare for a large landowner to have individual rental or lease agreements with the huge number of small tenants on his land: instead he would let a significant area to a middleman, who would then sublet to others, who might in turn rent out parts to the smallest tenants. It is very rare for estate records to document the smallest landholders, as most of these had little or no right of tenure in any case.

A related problem is the question of access. The estate records in the two major Dublin repositories, NAI and NLI, are not catalogued in detail. The only comprehensive guide is given in Richard Hayes's *Manuscript Sources for the History of Irish Civilisation* and its supplements, copies of which can be found in NLI and NAI and online at *<sources.nli.ie>*. This catalogues the records by landlord's name and by county, with entries such as 'NL Ms. 3185. Rent Roll of Lord Cremorne's estate in Co. Armagh, 1797.' Hayes gives no more detail of the areas of the county covered, and it can be difficult to ascertain from the Tithe Books or Griffith's just who the landlord was; Griffith's supplies only the name of the immediate lessor. The holdings of PRONI are catalogued more comprehensively but still do not relate the papers to the exact areas covered. Again, it is necessary to know the landlord's name. In addition, it should be noted that some of the collections in NLI have still not been catalogued at all.

There are a number of ways to overcome, or partially overcome, this obstacle. With common sense it is often possible to identify the landlord by examining

Griffith's for the surrounding areas: the largest lessor is the likeliest candidate. If the immediate lessor in Griffith's is not the landlord but a middleman it can be useful to try to find this middleman's own holding or residence and see who he was leasing from. Two publications may also be of value. U.H. Hussey de Burgh's *The Landowners of Ireland* provides a guide to the major landowners, the size of their holdings and where in the country they were situated. *Landowners in Ireland: Return of owners of land of one acre and upwards . . .* (London: 1876; online at *<www.failteromhat.com/lo1876.htm>*) is comprehensive to a fault and is organised more awkwardly, alphabetically within county.

The largest collection of estate records, the Landed Estate Court records, also known as the Encumbered Estate Courts, is in NAI, not catalogued in Hayes. The court was set up to facilitate the sale of estates whose owners could not invest enough to make them productive, and between 1849 and 1857 it oversaw the sale of more than three thousand Irish estates. Its records contain many rentals and maps drawn up for the sales, but they are so close in time to Griffith's as to make them of limited use except in very particular circumstances. NAI has an index to the townlands covered by the records. Since 2011 the records have been searchable at the subscription site *<www.findmypast.ie>*.

Despite all the problems, research in estate records can be very rewarding, especially for the period before the major nineteenth-century surveys. To take one example, the rent rolls of the estate of Charles O'Hara in Cos. Sligo and Leitrim, which date from c.1775, record a large number of leases to smaller tenants and supply the lives named in the leases, often specifying family relationships. It must be emphasised, however, that information of this quality is rare: the majority of the rentals and tenants' lists surviving only give details of major tenants.

A more detailed guide to the dates, areas covered and class of tenants recorded in the estate papers of NLI and NAI has been produced by NLI in collaboration with the Irish Genealogical Society of Minnesota. To date, Cos. Armagh, Carlow, Cavan, Clare, Cork, Donegal, Fermanagh, Kerry, Kildare, Leitrim, Limerick, Longford, Galway, Mayo, Monaghan, Roscommon, Sligo, Tyrone, Waterford, Westmeath and Wicklow have been covered, and a brief outline of the results will be found in Chapter 13 under these counties. In addition, the continuing expansion of the PRONI online catalogue has allowed the identification of parishes in the six counties of Northern Ireland covered by estate records held in PRONI. Again, an outline of the results is in Chapter 13 under these counties.

Chapter 5 ∽

| THE INTERNET

RESEARCH ONLINE

At its most basic, genealogy is information pure and simple and, as such, is ideally suited for digitisation and online research. For a long time Ireland lagged behind other countries in making record transcripts available online. That has changed radically over the last few years, and the success of the sites that have made records available has focused official attention on genealogy. Over the coming years the process of simplifying and expanding online access will undoubtedly continue.

Internet research, wonderful as it is, brings with it difficulties of its own, and a few points need emphasising:

1. There are no records on the internet. There are extracts, abstracts, partial transcripts—at best a more-or-less complete copy with an accompanying image. But there are no actual records. For anyone doing research online, this is a very basic point but one that can be difficult to grasp. The original records are all offline. The seductive ease of access that the internet allows can mask great gulfs in apparently continuous runs of records, transcription errors that compound record-keeping errors, and large flaws in search technology. Online research depends absolutely on the very first principle of all research: know absolutely, precisely, exactly what records you've searched, their dates, page numbers, locations, shelf references, lacunae, original purposes . . . If you don't, and you find nothing, you will certainly end up searching the same records all over again at some point in the future. If you do find something and don't know the details of the record source, it becomes impossible to interpret.

   The rule is simple: if you don't know what you've searched, you don't know what you've found.

2. If you can't find something, blame yourself first. By far the most common reason for failed research online is a flaw in the information entered in the search form. The most common is the simplest: entering a surname in a forename field, or vice versa. If you don't find what you were expecting, first check the information you've used to search.

3. Search is cheap, so squander it. The second most common cause of failed research is the use of search terms that are too precise. You may know that

your ancestor was John Thomas Bourke, son of Patrick and Mary, and that the family was very fussy about the middle name and the spelling of the surname. But was the record-keeper that fussy? Or the transcriber? Why not start off with all B*urk* entries, then all B*urk* entries, with a Pat* as father, and start whittling down from there? The wider your trawl, the likelier it is to turn something up eventually. If you're paying per record, this needs a little more care, of course.

SOURCES ONLINE

Major sources

General Register Office records
The Republic GRO website is at <*www.groireland.ie*>, and the Northern Ireland office is at <*www.groni.gov.uk*>. Neither has any online search facility at present, although GRONI plans to have paying online access before 2014. The nineteenth-century records for the rest of the island will also certainly be online at some point. For the moment, the two main sites are the LDS's <*www.familysearch. org*> and that of the heritage centres at <*www.rootsireland.ie*>.

<*www.familysearch.org*> The LDS site includes complete transcripts of the central all-Ireland GRO indexes to 1922 and the Republic indexes to 1958, and partial transcripts of the central birth registers from 1864 to the first quarter of 1881 and the central marriage registers from 1864 to 1870. Some of the central death registers, but not all, between 1864 and 1870 have been partially transcribed.

<*www.rootsireland.ie*> Many Irish Family History Foundation heritage centres made full transcripts of the civil registers still held locally in their areas, and these are now searchable on this pay-per-record site. For the Republic, there appear to be complete transcripts from all registration districts in Cos. Clare, Donegal, Mayo, Roscommon and Tipperary, while Galway, Kilkenny, Limerick and Sligo have near-complete transcripts. For Northern Ireland the situation is less clear. Some, at least, of the local civil marriage and birth registers are online from Cos. Antrim, Down and Tyrone, as are all the birth and marriage registers to 1921 for Co. Derry and all the marriage records for Co. Armagh to 1921. Some Armagh birth registers have also been transcribed.

<*www.certificates.ie*> This is the service of the HSE geared to producing birth, marriage and death certificates for use in interactions with state agencies in the Republic.

<*www.waterfordcountylibrary.ie*> Waterford County Library has made local death registrations available and freely searchable from 1864 to 1901.

<*freepages.genealogy.rootsweb.ancestry.com/~mturner*> Partial transcripts for Co. Cork are available on Margaret Grogan's site.

There are quite a few sites that invite users to submit records they have transcribed themselves. The best organised are at *<www.cmcrp.net>*. The problems are self-evident: accuracy is always doubtful, and in most cases it is not clear what proportion of the records is included. Irish Ancestors at the website of the *Irish Times, <www.irishtimes.com/ancestor>*, provides county-by-county links to transcripts.

Census records

The National Archives of Ireland transcriptions of the 1901 and 1911 censuses have transformed Irish research. The ease of access and flexible search interface mean that even those whose ancestors left Ireland fifty years before 1901 can often glean useful information. For the fragments of earlier censuses, NAI is engaged in a collaboration with the LDS Family History Library to make transcripts and record images available. Only the most extensive transcripts currently available are listed below. For county-by-county listings see *<www. census-online.com>, <www.censusfinder.com>* and *<www.irishtimes.com/ ancestor>*, as well as *<www.cyndislist.com/ireland.htm>*.

<www.census.nationalarchives.ie> This is the site of the National Archives 1901 and 1911 censuses. For detailed advice on research techniques see Chapter 2: Census Records, 'Using the 1901 and 1911 censuses online'.

<www.leitrim-roscommon.com> Before the launch of the NAI site this was the best place to find Irish census transcripts. It remains very useful as a second opinion if the NAI site has errors or omissions. As well as having an almost complete database of the 1901 returns for Cos. Leitrim and Roscommon, the site contains large numbers of transcripts from Cos. Mayo, Sligo, Westmeath and Wexford. Unlike many other sites, there is a systematic account of which records are complete and which are still to be added. The quality of the transcripts is consistently good.

<www.clarelibrary.ie> Clare County Library has a full transcript of the 1901 census for the county. Again, useful as a second opinion.

<freepages.genealogy.rootsweb.ancestry.com/~mturner> Margaret Grogan's site has a large number of transcripts for Cork, for both 1901 and 1911, submitted by volunteers.

<freepages.genealogy.rootsweb.com/~donegal/census.htm> This page has volunteer transcripts for 1901 and 1911 for parts of Co. Donegal.

Parish records

The two largest church record sites are *<www.rootsireland.ie>* and *<www. irishgenealogy.ie>*. The former is paying, the latter free. There are also free piecemeal transcripts, largely a result of the availability of LDS microfilms to volunteer transcribers. County-by-county listings are at *<www.irishtimes. com/ancestor/browse/links/counties.htm>*, and a general listing is at *<www.cyndislist.com/ireland.htm>*. See also Chapter 14: Roman Catholic Parish Registers.

<www.rootsireland.ie> This is the umbrella site of the Irish Family History Foundation. It should be remembered that not all heritage centres are members of the IFHF, that not all members of the IFHF have put their records on the site, and that many centres with transcripts on the site have other copies of other records still only held in the centre itself. For more detail see Chapter 3: Church Records, 'What's online?' and Chapter 14: Roman Catholic Parish Records.

<www.irishgenealogy.ie> This state-run site aims to complete the imaging and transcription of areas not covered by the IFHF, and it currently has Roman Catholic and Church of Ireland records for the city of Dublin and for Cos. Carlow, Cork and Kerry. For more detail see Chapter 3: Church Records, 'What's online?' and Chapter 14: Roman Catholic Parish Records.

<www.nli.ie> The National Library of Ireland website has no records online at the time of writing (mid-2011) but has begun the process of creating digital images from its parish register microfilms with a view to making them available online. Its site will report on the project's progress.

<www.familysearch.org> The LDS website includes the records of twelve Roman Catholic parishes in Co. Kerry and north-west Cork, which were published by Albert Casey in *O'Kief, Coshe Mang etc.* (16 vols., 1964–72). As transcripts of transcripts, they need to be approached with caution. A number of other parishes, mainly in Cos. Galway, Roscommon and Sligo, are also included. Most were originally published in the second edition of the LDS CD-ROM *British Isles Vital Records Index* (2002).

<www.rootsweb.com/~irllog/churchrecs.htm> This site gives the records of five Longford Roman Catholic parishes.

<www.ancestry.co.uk> This site has transcriptions of the NLI microfilms of the records of forty-seven Roman Catholic parishes, almost all in Meath diocese. See Chapter 14.

Property records

Because of the lack of nineteenth-century census material, the two property surveys, Griffith's Valuation (1847–64) and the Tithe Applotment Books (1823–38), have acquired unusual importance. Griffith's is the most widely available source online. Watch the NAI website for news on the transcription of the Tithe Books.

<www.askaboutireland.ie> The Library Council of Ireland site has a comprehensive database transcript of Griffith's linked to digital images and maps. The same database, with a different search interface and a different set of maps, is on two paying sites, *<www.irishorigins.com>* and *<www.findmypast.ie>*.

<www.irishtimes.com/ancestor> This site has a count of the number of Griffith's householders of a particular surname by county (free) and parish (paying).

<www.leitrim-roscommon.com> On this site there are Griffith's transcripts for 22 parishes in Co. Roscommon, 24 in Co. Limerick and 10 in Co. Galway—always useful as a cross-check with the *<www.askaboutireland.ie>* transcripts.

<www.landedestates.ie> The site of the Moore Institute at the National University of Ireland, Galway, brings together precise location data, photographs, published material and information on the scope and location of surviving records for estates in Connacht and Munster.

<sources.nli.ie> This is the NLI's online version of the Hayes Catalogue, with details of Irish estate collections in Irish and overseas repositories.

<www.ancestry.com> This site has a transcript of the Tithe Books made from the LDS microfilms but without record images.

Other sources

Migration records

The vast majority of records relate to North America and Australia.

<www.immigrantships.net> The major site for ships' lists, copied by volunteers.

<www.ellisisland.org> The Ellis Island site has New York arrivals records from 1892 to 1924.

<www.castlegarden.org> Records of 11 million immigrants arriving in New York between 1820 and 1892.

<www.ancestry.com> A good collection of ships' lists and immigration records.

<aad.archives.gov/aad/subject-list.jsp> The US National Archives has a database of Irish Famine immigrants to New York, 1846–51.

<www.genealogybranches.com/irishpassengerlists> The Irish Passenger Lists Research Guide gives a good overview of the available records.

<www.irishtimes.com/ancestor/browse/links/passship-a.htm> A selection of links to ships' lists.

<www.nationalarchives.ie/search01.html> The NAI site has an extensive but incomplete database of transportation records from Ireland to Australia up to 1868.

<www.pcug.org.au/~ppmay/convicts.htm> This site has details of convict arrivals in Australia, 1791–1820, a period for which the National Archives transportation registers have not survived.

Gravestone inscriptions and cemetery records

<www.interment.net/ireland> This provides web space in which volunteers can submit transcriptions and compilations. The site is well organised, and many of the transcripts are extensive, though most appear to be incomplete.

<www.webone.com.au/~sgrieves/cemeteries__ireland.htm> This page has a good, reliable selection, mostly from Co. Tipperary.

<www.historyfromheadstones.com> The Ulster Historical Foundation and Irish World have made their collection of headstone transcripts for the six counties of Northern Ireland searchable online, for a fee.

<www.dublinheritage.ie/graveyards> Dublin City Library and Archive has put its Directory of Graveyards in the Dublin Area online, with guides to surviving cemetery records and gravestone transcripts.

<www.glasnevintrust.ie> Glasnevin Trust in Dublin has made its burial records dating from 1828 searchable online. These very often include names and addresses of next of kin and can be invaluable for those who lived in or near Dublin.

<www.findmypast.ie> This site has copies of the Cantwell gravestone transcriptions, completely covering Cos. Wexford and Wicklow, as well as areas near the Atlantic seaboard in Cos. Galway and Mayo.

Military and police records

<www.ancestry.com> This site has the Royal Irish Constabulary List, an index to the LDS microfilms of the original service registers and also the 'burnt documents', British army service records of the First World War.

<www.cwgc.org> The Commonwealth War Graves Commission is probably the best online military database.

<www.greatwar.ie> The Royal Dublin Fusiliers Association has excellent information on the Irish in the First World War.

<www.findmypast.co.uk> Royal Hospital, Chelsea, Pension Records, 1760–1915, and index to regimental registers of births, 1761–1924.

<www.nationalarchives.gov.uk/documentsonline> Medal Rolls Index Cards of the First World War, 1914–20.

<www.findmypast.ie> This site has transcripts of almost all surviving prison registers for areas now in the Republic, as well as *Ireland's Memorial Records* (Dublin: 1923), an eight-volume commemorative publication listing the Irish men and women killed during the First World War.

Loan Fund records

<www.movinghere.org.uk>, a subsidiary site of the National Archives (Kew), has scanned and indexed a large proportion of the Reproductive Loan Fund records, c.1838–52. The indexing is peculiar and the layout of the site confusing, but it is worth persevering. See Chapter 3 and the county source lists for Cork, Galway, Limerick, Mayo and Tipperary.

Newspapers

<www.ucs.louisiana.edu/bnl> The *News Letter* (Belfast): biographical material.

<www.irishnewsarchive.com> A subscription full-text search of a number of newspapers now part of the Independent Group. Most are twentieth century, but the *Freeman's Journal* runs from 1763 to 1924, with some gaps. Free to users of the National Library of Australia.

<www.irishtimes.com/archive> The *Irish Times* began publication in 1859. Its full archive is searchable with a daily subscription.

<www.britishnewspaperarchives.co.uk> The British Library's subscription newspapers site includes full-text searches of the *Freeman's Journal*, 1820 to 1900, the *News Letter* (Belfast), 1828–1900, and *The Cork Examiner* (1841–6).

Wills

<www.proni.gov.uk> The PRONI website has Calendars of Wills and Administrations from 1858 to 1943 for areas now in Northern Ireland, along with District Registry Will Books, 1858–1900, and pre-1858 diocesan indexes.

<www.findmypast.ie> This site has a digital copy of the NAI testamentary card index, along with various printed pre-1858 indexes.

Directories

<www.failteromhat.com> has Pigot's (1824), Pettigrew and Oulton's (Dublin: 1842), Slater's (1846) and Taylor and Skinner's *Road Maps of Ireland* (1778).

<books.google.com> has Thom's *Dublin Directory* of 1850 and 1852.

<www.irishfamilyresearch.co.uk> has a number of local nineteenth-century trade directories (paying).

<www.proni.gov.uk> has an excellent collection of Belfast and Ulster directories.

<www.corkpastandpresent.ie> has a superb collection of Cork city and county directories.

<www.findmypast.ie> has a large collection of local directories

STARTING POINTS

Research guides

Good basic guides can be found at the National Archives of Ireland site, *<www.nationalarchives.ie/genealogy>*, and the National Library of Ireland site, *<www.nli.ie>*. A more detailed treatment can be found at *<www.irishtimes.com/ancestor>*. The 'Browse' section gives detailed accounts of all the record sources used in Irish research.

Other brief guides include:

- Sean Murphy's Beginner's Guide, *<homepage.eircom.net/~seanjmurphy/dir/guide.htm>*
- The Fianna Homepage, *<www.rootsweb.com/~fianna>*, which presumes that research is being done via the Family History Centres of the Church of Jesus Christ of Latter-Day Saints.

Listings sites

There are numerous listings sites that provide links to Irish genealogy sites. Since many of these sites themselves consist largely of listings, a frustrating amount of travelling in circles is inevitable. The sites listed below are the largest and most stable. For a more detailed treatment of the structure of the first two in particular see Peter Christian's *The Genealogist's Internet* (National Archives, 4th ed., 2009), by far the most comprehensive publication on genealogy and the internet. Of their nature, all these sites suffer from a certain amount of link-rot.

- The mother of all genealogy site lists is Cyndi Howell's <*www.cyndislist.com*>, which categorises and cross-references online genealogical resources. The Irish section is at <*www.cyndislist.com/ireland.htm*>. With more than 300,000 links, the sheer scale of the enterprise is very impressive.
- A more discriminating guide can be found at Genuki, <*www.genuki.org.uk/ contents/IRLcontents.shtml*>, where a good attempt is made to give a comprehensive overview of the relevant records, with links listed where there are matching online resources.
- The WorldGenWeb project is a volunteer-run survey of sources relating to particular localities. The county-by-county listings for the twenty-six counties of the Republic can be found at <*www.irelandgenweb.com*> and those for the six counties of Northern Ireland at <*www.rootsweb.ancestry. com/~nirwgw*>. The quality of the listings depends very much on the enthusiasm and discrimination of the individuals responsible. Some counties are superb.
- The Irish Ancestors listings, <*www.irishtimes.com/ancestor/browse/links*>, attempt to present a county-by-county listing of what online source materials are available, as well as passenger lists and family sites.

Other sites with valuable listings include:

- <*www.genealogylinks.net/uk/ireland*> A good listing, despite the irritating identification of Ireland as a region of the United Kingdom.
- <*www.tiara.ie/links.php*> Another well-maintained and comprehensive site is that of the Irish Ancestral Research Association

DISCUSSION GROUPS

Usenet
Discussion or news groups were one of the first uses of the internet and can still be extremely interesting. Most browsers now provide a news reader, but the simplest means of access is through <*groups.google.com*>. The Irish group is soc.genealogy.ireland, which was set up in August 1997 (messages before that date will be in soc.genealogy.uk+ireland). A less widely used news group, also available as above, is soc.genealogy.surnames.ireland.

GEOGRAPHY
A specific townland address of origin is the key to most Irish sources. *The General Alphabetical Index to the Townlands and Towns, Parishes and Baronies of Ireland* (reprinted GPC, 1981), first published in 1861 and based on the 1851 census, is the standard source. It is freely searchable on two sites:

<*www.seanruad.com*>, which has a straightforward interface and includes information on acreage and barony
<*www.irishtimes.com/ancestor/placenames*>, which allows wild-card searches and complete listings for individual parishes. The free historical maps section of

the Ordnance Survey of Ireland site at <*maps.osi.ie*> is a superb resource, allowing the layering of modern and historical maps and including a good placenames search function. The site of the Irish Placenames Commission, <*www.logainm.ie*>, is mainly concerned with researching the Irish originals of anglicised placenames but has a search feature that covers many geographical features, such as rivers and mountains, omitted from other sources.

SURNAME SITES

Many of those who have done a good deal of research will publish it on a website, partly through straightforward altruism, partly through enlightened self-interest: the more people publish, the greater the chance that someone from a related branch of the family will see the information and be able to add to it. The information provided ranges from superb to abysmal. There are now millions of personal family history sites, and tracking down any relevant ones can be difficult.

<*www.cyndislist.com*> has an enormous list, indexed alphabetically.
<*freepages.rootsweb.ancestry.com*> is the largest provider of free genealogy pages.
<*www.genealogy.com*> also gives users free web pages and allows searches.
<*www.irishtimes.com/ancestor/surnames*> provides links to surname sites.
<*www.google.com*> A straightforward search on a site such as Google or Yahoo—
   'Murphy Family History'—can often be surprisingly rewarding.

ARCHIVES AND LIBRARIES

Web addresses will be found in Chapter 15.

ONLINE FAMILY TREES

Many sites allow users to begin creating a family tree online. In some cases this is part of a subscription package to an online records site, such as <*www.ancestry.com*>; in others it is part of a broader social-networking service (<*www.geni.com*>), while still others provide a purely commercial service (<*www.tribalpages.com*>). These trees can be extremely useful ways of sharing information with extended family and of flushing out corrections. For all of them, two main questions need to be asked:

1. Does the site allow me to export my information in an easily portable format, specifically GEDCOM? Don't be held prisoner.
2. What is the site's privacy policy? It's important to be able to control the level of access to the information you put up.

COMMERCIAL SITES

<*www.irishorigins.com*> includes Griffith's Valuation (see above), as well as many of the sources published on CD-ROM by Eneclann. These include the William Smith O'Brien Petition (see Chapter 2: Census Substitutes), the index to the Dublin city census of 1851 and the NAI Wills Index.

<www.findmypast.ie> duplicates much of the content of <www.irishorigins.com> but is adding many so-called 'second-line' sources that can be extremely useful, such as prison records, Landed Estate Court rentals and court records.

<www.ancestry.com> The biggest commercial genealogy site has the RIC index (see above), US passenger and immigration lists, British military and census records, a transcript of the Tithe Applotment Books, a copy of the LDS transcripts of GRO records and the records of forty-seven Catholic parishes, mainly in Meath diocese.

<www.ancestryireland.com> The Ulster Historical Foundation has a wide range of sources relating to Ulster, including indexes to its database transcripts of Down and Antrim church records, as well as some with wider relevance, such as the Irish Will Calendars, 1858–1900.

<www.irishtimes.com/ancestor> provides personalised guidance on relevant sources. Most of the site is free to view, including civil and Roman Catholic parish maps.

<www.rootsireland.ie> The Irish Family History Foundation is the umbrella organisation for local heritage centres, and its site holds copies of most, but not all, of their record transcriptions.

COMMISSIONING RESEARCH

- The NLI, NAI and NA (Kew) websites include lists of researchers willing to carry out commissioned research, purely as a convenience.
- <www.apgi.ie> is the home site of the Association of Professional Genealogists in Ireland.

LOST WEBSITES

A perennial problem with online information is that websites, especially small personal sites with family or record details, are very perishable. The Internet Archive Project at <web.archive.org> is a brave attempt to store the web. Its Wayback Machine holds copies of virtually all sites that have appeared and disappeared since 1998 and is readily searchable.

Chapter 6 ∾

WILLS

PART 1: BACKGROUND

Wills have always been an extremely important source of genealogical information about the property-owning classes, in Ireland as elsewhere. They provide a clear picture of a family at a particular point in time and can often supply enough details of a much larger network of relationships—cousins, nephews, in-laws and others—to produce quite a substantial family tree. Apart from their genealogical significance, wills can also vividly evoke the way of life of those whose final wishes they record.

Information supplied

The minimum information to be found in a will is:

1. the name, address and occupation of the testator;
2. the names of the beneficiaries;
3. the name(s) of the executor(s);
4. the names of the witnesses;
5. the date on which the will was made;
6. the date of probate of the will.

Specific properties are usually, though not always, mentioned. The two dates, that of the will itself and of its probate, give a period during which the testator died. Up to the nineteenth century most wills were made close to the date of death, and witnesses were normally related to the person making the will. As well as the minimum information, of course, many wills also contain much more, including at times addresses and occupations of beneficiaries, witnesses and executors, and details of family relationships—quarrels as well as affection.

Testamentary Authority before 1857

Before 1857 the Church of Ireland, as the Established Church, had charge of all testamentary affairs. Consistorial Courts in each diocese were responsible for granting probate, that is, for legally authenticating a will and conferring on the executors the power to administer the estate. The courts also had the power to issue letters of administration to the next of kin or the main creditor on the estates of those who died intestate. Each court was responsible for wills and administrations in its own diocese. However, when the estate included property worth more than £5 in another diocese, responsibility for the will or administration passed to the Prerogative Court, under the authority of the Archbishop of Armagh.

Consistorial wills and administrations

The wills and administration records of the Consistorial Courts were held locally in each diocese up to the abolition of the testamentary authority of the Church of Ireland in 1857. After that date the Public Record Office began the slow process of collecting the original records and transcribing them into Will and Grant Books. The Office then indexed the wills and administration bonds (the sureties the administrators had to produce as a guarantee that the estate would be properly administered). None of the Consistorial Courts had records of all the wills or administrations they had dealt with. Very little earlier than the seventeenth century emerged, and the majority of the courts appear to have had serious gaps before the middle of the eighteenth century.

All the original wills and administrations in the Public Record Office were destroyed in 1922, along with almost all the Will and Grant Books into which they had been transcribed. The only exceptions are the Will Books for Down (1850–58) and Connor (1853–8), and the Grant Books for Cashel (1840–45), Derry and Raphoe (1818–21) and Ossory (1848–58).

The indexes to wills and administration bonds were not destroyed, although a number were badly damaged. These are available in the reading room of NAI. The wills indexes are alphabetical and normally give the testator's address and the year of probate as well as occasionally specifying his occupation. The administration bonds indexes are not fully alphabetical, being arranged year by year under the initial letter of the surname of the deceased person. They give the year of the bond, the full name and usually the address of the deceased, and sometimes their occupation. Many of the wills indexes have been published, and details of these will be found at the end of this chapter.

Prerogative wills and administrations

To recap: an estate was dealt with by the Prerogative Court, rather than a Consistorial Court, if it covered property worth more than £5 in a second diocese. In general, then, prerogative wills and administrations tend to cover the wealthier classes, merchants with dealings in more than one area, and those who lived close to diocesan borders. Up to 1816 the Prerogative Court was not housed in a single place, with hearings generally held in the residence of the presiding judge. From 1816 the King's Inns building in Henrietta Street, Dublin, provided a permanent home. For this reason the records of the court before 1816 cannot be taken as complete. After 1857 all these records were transferred to the Public Record Office, where the original wills and grants of administration were transcribed into Prerogative Will and Grant Books and indexed. The indexes survived 1922, but all the original wills and grants, and almost all the Will and Grant Books, were destroyed. Details of those books that survived will be found at the end of this chapter.

The loss of the original prerogative wills is mitigated to a large extent by the project carried out in the early decades of the nineteenth century by Sir William Betham, Ulster King of Arms. As well as preparing the first index of testators, up to 1810, he also made abstracts of the family information contained in almost all the wills before 1800. The original notebooks in which he recorded the information are now in the National Archives, and the Genealogical Office has his sketch pedigrees based on these abstracts and including later additions and amendments. PRONI has a copy of the Genealogical Office series made by a successor of Betham's, Sir John Burke (T/559), but without the additions and amendments. Betham also made a large number of abstracts from prerogative grants up to 1802. The original notebooks for these are also in NAI. The Genealogical Office transcript copy (GO 257–60) is fully alphabetical, unlike the notebooks.

The first index to prerogative wills, up to 1810, was published in 1897 by Sir Arthur Vicars, Burke's successor as Ulster King of Arms, as *Index to the Prerogative Wills of Ireland (1536–1810)*, and can be used as a guide to Betham's abstracts and sketch pedigrees, with the proviso that wills from the decade 1800–1810 are not covered by Betham. The book is widely available online, including at <*www.archive.org*>. The manuscript index for the period 1811–57 is in the NAI reading room. As with the consistorial administration bonds indexes, the prerogative grants indexes are not fully alphabetical but are simply arranged year by year under the initial letter of the surname of the deceased person.

Testamentary authority after 1857

The Probate Act (1857) did away with the testamentary authority of the Church of Ireland. Instead of the Consistorial Courts and the Prerogative Court, power to grant probate and issue letters of administration was vested in a Principal Registry in Dublin and eleven District Registries. Rules similar to those governing the geographical jurisdiction of the ecclesiastical courts applied, with the Principal Registry taking the place of the Prerogative Court, as well as covering Dublin and a large area around it. Transcripts of the wills proved and administrations granted were made in the District Registries, and the originals were forwarded to the Principal Registry. Almost all the records of the Principal Registry were destroyed in 1922. The few surviving Will and Grant Books are detailed below. The Will Book transcripts made by the District Registries survived, however. The records of those districts covering areas now in the Republic—Ballina, Cavan, Cork, Kilkenny, Limerick, Mullingar, Tuam and Waterford—are in NAI. For districts now in Northern Ireland—Armagh, Belfast and Londonderry—the Will Books are in PRONI and are searchable through the PRONI website.

Fortunately, from 1858 a new system of indexing and organising wills and administrations had been devised. A printed, alphabetically ordered *Calendar of*

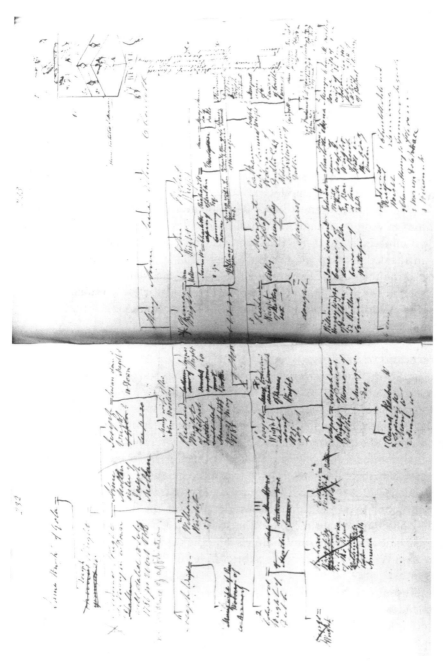

Betham's 'Sketch Pedigrees from Will Abstracts'. (*Courtesy of the Genealogical Office*)

Wills and Administrations was produced for every year, and copies of all of these have survived. For each will or administration, these record:

1. the name, address and occupation of the deceased person;
2. the place and date of death;
3. the value of the estate;
4. the name and address of the person or persons to whom probate or administration was granted.

In many cases the relationship of the executor is also specified. This means that, despite the loss of so much original post-1857 testamentary material, some information at least is available on all wills or administrations from this period. Very often, much that is of genealogical value can be gleaned from the calendars, including such information as exact dates of death, places of residence and indications of economic status. A consolidated index covers the period 1858–77, making it unnecessary to search each yearly calendar. The calendars are on open access in the NAI reading room, with a copy also in PRONI. Calendar entries relating to the three district registries of Armagh, Belfast and Londonderry are searchable at <*www.proni.gov.uk*>. The Ulster Historical Foundation has transcribed the calendar information for all of Ireland to 1900. It is on the UHF subscription website, <*www.ancestryireland.com*>.

Abstracts and transcripts

As well as the original consistorial and prerogative wills and grants, together with the transcripts made of them in the Will and Grant Books, a wide range of other sources exists, particularly for material before 1857. The most important of these is the collection of NAI itself, gathered after 1922 in an attempt to replace some at least of what had been lost. As well as original wills from private legal records and individual families, this ever-expanding collection also includes pre-1922 researchers' abstracts and transcripts. It is covered by a card index in the reading room, which also gives details of those wills and grants in the surviving pre-1857 Will and Grant Books. Separate card indexes cover the Thrift, Jennings and Crosslé Collections of abstracts and the records of Charitable Donations and Bequests. PRONI has made similar efforts, and the copies it holds are indexed in the Pre-1858 Wills Index, part of the Subject Index in the public search room.

Inland Revenue records

The Inland Revenue in London kept a series of annual Indexes to Irish Will Registers and Indexes to Irish Administration Registers from 1828 to 1879, which are now in NAI. These give the name and address of both the deceased and the executor or administrator. As well as the Indexes, the Archives also hold a set of the actual Inland Revenue Irish Will Registers and Irish Administration Registers for the years 1828–39, complete apart from the Wills Register covering January to June 1834. The Will Registers are not exact transcripts of the original wills, but

270   WILLS AND ADMINISTRATIONS. 1871.

HORGAN Daniel.

[191]   Effects under £200.

20 March.   Letters of Administration of the personal estate of Daniel Horgan late of Great George's-street **Cork** Builder deceased who died 21 February 1870 at same place were granted at **Cork** to Michael Joseph Horgan of the South Mall in said City Solicitor the Nephew of said deceased for the benefit of Catherine Horgan Widow John Horgan the Reverend David Horgan Ellen Gillman Mary Daly and Margaret Horgan only next of kin of said deceased.

HORNE Christopher.

[67]   Effects under £100.

7 March.   Letters of Administration of the personal estate of Christopher Horne late of Ballinasloe County **Galway** Gentleman a Widower deceased who died 21 March 1867 at same place were granted at the **Principal Registry** to Patrick Horne of Ballinasloe aforesaid M.D. the only Brother of said deceased.

HORNER Isabella.

[17]   Effects under £100.

29 April.   Letters of Administration of the personal estate of Isabella Horner late of Rahaghy County **Tyrone** Widow deceased who died 13 April 1871 at same place were granted at **Armagh** to James Horner of Rahaghy (Aughnacloy) aforesaid **Farmer** the Son and one of the next of kin of said deceased.

HORNIDGE John Isaiah.

[79]   Effects under £450.

8 June.   Letters of Administration (with the Will annexed) of the personal estate of John Isaiah Hornidge late of the South Dublin Union Workhouse **Dublin** Master of said Workhouse a Widower deceased who died 22 April 1871 at same place were granted at the **Principal Registry** to James Seymour Longstaff of Stephen's-green Dublin Merchant and William Thomas Orpin of George's-terrace George's-avenue Blackrock County Dublin Accountant the Guardians during minority only of the Daughter and only next of kin of deceased.

HOUSTON Eliza.

[337]   Effects under £200.

22 September.   Letters of Administration of the personal estate of Eliza Houston late of Gortin County Done...

Calendar of Wills and Administrations, 1871. (*Courtesy of the National Archives of Ireland*)

they supply a good deal of detailed information, including the precise date of death, the principal beneficiaries and legacies, and a brief inventory of the estate. The Administration Registers are less informative but still include details of the date of death, the administrator and the estate.

Estate Duty Office records
Between 1812 and 1857 copies of all wills liable for estate duty proved in English Prerogative and Diocesan Courts of testators with an Irish address, almost 3,000 in all, were sent to the Estate Duty Office in London. They remained there until some point after 1922, when 1,370 of them, dating from 1821 to 1857, were transferred to PRONI. They are indexed in PRONI's Pre-1858 Wills Index. They concern testators from the entire island of Ireland.

Land Commission records
Under the provisions of the Land Purchase Acts, which subsidised the purchase of smallholdings by the tenants who occupied them, it was necessary for those wishing to sell to produce evidence of their ownership to the Irish Land Commission. As a result, more than ten thousand wills were deposited with the commission, the majority from the nineteenth century but many earlier. The National Library and PRONI hold a card index to the testators. The original documents remain unavailable to the public and are housed in the Land Commission (Records Branch, Unit 11, Clonminam Industrial Estate, Port Laoise; tel. +353 57 8634988).

The Registry of Deeds
The registration of wills was normally carried out because of a legal problem anticipated by the executor or executors in the provisions, almost certainly the exclusion of parties who would feel they had some rights over the estate. Because of this, wills at the Registry of Deeds cannot be taken as providing a complete picture of the family. Abstracts of all wills registered from 1708 (the date of foundation of the Registry) to 1832 were published in three volumes by the Irish Manuscripts Commission between 1954 and 1986. These are available on open shelves at the National Library and NAI. Although the abstracts record and index all the persons named—testators, beneficiaries and witnesses—they do not show the original provisions of the wills. These can be found in the original memorials in the Registry.

The Genealogical Office
Most of the will abstracts held by the Genealogical Office are covered by the Office's own index, GO Ms. 429, which was published in *Analecta Hibernica*, No. 17, 1949 (NLI Ir 941 a 10). The manuscript index has since been added to but is still not entirely comprehensive, excluding all the Betham material and many of the collections relating to individual families. A guide to the major collections is included in the reference guide at the end of this chapter.

English records

If a testator held property in both Ireland and England or Wales, a grant of probate was made both in England and in Ireland. Almost all wills proved before the Prerogative Court of Canterbury are available online at *<www. documentsonline.pro.gov.uk>*. Many of the indexes of the Society of Genealogists to other English and Welsh wills are available for a fee at Origins, *<www. originsnetwork.com>*.

Other sources

There are many other collections of will abstracts and transcripts in such public repositories as the National Library, the Representative Church Body Library, the Royal Irish Academy, PRONI and Trinity College Library. There are no separate indexes to these testamentary collections. Where a significant group of abstracts or transcripts exists, this is noted in the reference guide that follows.

PART 2: A REFERENCE GUIDE

What follows is an attempt to provide a series of checklists and guides to the various testamentary sources. Because of the changes in testamentary jurisdiction in 1858, it is divided into two sections, dealing with records before and after that date. Section 1: Pre-1858 includes (1) a general checklist of surviving indexes; (2) a list of surviving Will and Grant Books; (3) a list of major collections of abstracts and transcripts, divided into (*a*) general collections, (*b*) those relating to particular surnames and (*c*) those relating to particular diocesan jurisdictions; and (4) a detailed list of surviving consistorial wills and administrations indexes, both published and in the National Archives. Section 2: Post-1858 covers (1) the yearly calendars and (2) original wills and transcripts.

Section 1: Pre-1858

1. General indexes

1. Card indexes, NAI search room, published on CD-ROM by Eneclann, *Irish Records Index, Vol. 1: Index of Irish Wills, 1484–1858*, Dublin: 1999. Online at *<www.findmypast.ie>*.
2. Pre-1858 Wills Index, PRONI reading room and part of the 'Name Search' at *<www.proni.gov.uk>*.
3. Indexes to consistorial wills and administrations, diocese by diocese. See below for details.
4. Indexes to Prerogative Wills.
   (*a*) Sir Arthur Vicars, *Index to the Prerogative Wills of Ireland, 1536–1810* (1897).
   (*b*) Ms. index, 1811–58, NAI, PRONI.
5. Index to Prerogative Grants, NAI, PRONI.
6. Index to Wills in the records of the Land Commission, card index, NLI.

PUBLIC RECORD OFFICE OF IRELAND.

Class—Testamentary. *Diocese - Cork & Ross* Sub-Class.—Wills.
District Registry - Cork.

Testator's Name.		Year of Probate.	Bay.	Tray.	Number.	
O'Coghlane	Donell Reigh Crookhaven	1620	1A	36	1	
O'Comon	Connor Twrmore	1675				
O'Conohan	Teige Cork	1664				
O'Connor	Joshua Cork	1796				
"	Patrick	1851				
O'Crouly	Teige Behegallane	1683				
O'Crowly	Revd Jas. Patrick Ballinriskig	1829				
"	Timothy P.P. Killmocomoy	1789				
O'Daniel	Theophilus Cork	1736				
O'Dea als Walsh	Beale	1649				
O'Donnell	James Ballyeurrig	1781				
"	Mary Cork	1845				
O'Donoghue	Elizabeth Cork	1809				

Diocesan Wills Index, Cork and Ross. (*Courtesy of the National Archives of Ireland*)

2. Surviving Will and Grant Books

1. Prerogative Will Books: 1664–84, 1706–1708 (A–W), 1726–8 (A–W), 1728–9 (A–W), 1777 (A–L), 1813 (K–Z), 1834 (A–E), NAI. Included in card index, online at <*www.findmypast.ie*>.
2. Prerogative Administrations: Grants, 1684–8, 1748–51, 1839; Day Books, 1784–8, NAI.
3. Consistorial Will Books: Connor (1853–8); Down (1850–58), NAI.
4. Consistorial Grant Books: Cashel (1840–45); Derry and Raphoe (1812–21); Ossory (1848–58), NAI.

3. Abstracts and transcripts

(i) General collections

1. Betham abstracts from Prerogative Wills, to c.1800. NAI (notebooks); GO and PRONI (sketch pedigrees). See Vicars above.
2. Betham abstracts from Prerogative Administrations, to c.1800. NAI (notebooks); GO (alphabetical listing), online at <*www.findmypast.ie*>.
3. Indexes to Irish Will Registers, 1828–79 (Inland Revenue). NAI. See Testamentary Catalogue, online at <*www.findmypast.ie*>.
4. Irish Will Registers, 1828–39 (Inland Revenue). NAI. See Testamentary Catalogue, online at <*www.findmypast.ie*>.
5. Indexes to Irish Administration Registers, 1828–79 (Inland Revenue). NAI. See Testamentary Catalogue, online at <*www.findmypast.ie*>.
6. Irish Administration Registers, 1828–39 (Inland Revenue). NAI. See Testamentary Catalogue, online at <*www.findmypast.ie*>.
7. Index to Will Abstracts at the Genealogical Office. *Analecta Hibernica*, 17. GO Ms. 429.
8. P.B. Phair and E. Ellis (eds.), *Abstracts of Wills at the Registry of Deeds (1708–1832)*, IMC, 1954–88.
9. Abstracts of wills of Irish testators registered at the Prerogative Court of Canterbury, 1639–98. NLI Ms. 1397.
10. Abstracts of miscellaneous eighteenth-century wills made by the Protestant clergy and their families. RCBL. (For the years 1828–39 see also NLI Ms. 2599.)
11. Leslie Collection. 981 wills. NLI Ms. 1774. See also NLI Pos. 799.
12. Ainsley Will Abstracts. GO 535 and 631.
13. Wilson Collection. NLI Pos. 1990.
14. Welply Collection. 1,500 wills, 100 administrations. RCBL. Indexed in *IG*, 1985/6.
15. Richey Collection, NLI Mss. 8315–16.
16. Upton Collection, RIA. Also NLI Pos. 1997. Principally families in Co. Westmeath, with some from Cos. Cavan and Longford.
17. MacSwiney Papers, RIA. Mainly Cos. Cork and Kerry.
18. Westropp Manuscripts, RIA. Mainly Cos. Clare and Limerick.

(ii) By surname

Burke: GO Ms. 707.

Butler: Wallace Clare, *The Testamentary Records of the Butler Family*, 1932. NLI Ir 9292 b 11.

Dawson: Almost all eighteenth-century Dawson wills. NLI Ms. 5644/5.

Domville: NLI Mss. 9384–6.

Drought: Crosslé Abstracts, NAI. Also GO 417/18.

Gordon: GO Ms. 702. Abstracts of most Irish Gordon wills.

Greene: See NAI card index.

Griffith: NLI Ms. 8392.

Hamilton, Co. Down: PRONI T.702A.

Hill: GO Ms. 691–2.

Kelly: GO Ms. 415.

Manley: NLI D.7075–86. The Manley family of Dublin and Offaly.

Mathews: Prerogative wills and administrations. PRONI T.681.

O'Loghlen, Co. Clare: NLI Pos. 2543.

Skerrett: *IA*, Vol. 5, No. 2, 1975.

Young: NLI Pos. 1276.

(iii) By diocese

A word of warning is necessary: the identification of a collection of abstracts or transcripts under a particular diocese does not necessarily mean that all the wills it covers belong to that diocese. In the case of the larger collections especially, it is just not possible to be absolutely precise about the areas covered.

Armagh

'Four Wills of old English merchants of Drogheda, 1654–1717', JCLAHS, Vol. 20, 2, 1982.

'Alphabetical list of the prerogative wills of residents of Co. Louth up to 1810'. NLI. Ms. 7314.

'Index to wills of Dundalk residents'. JCLAHS, Vol. 10, No. 2, 1942, pp. 113–15.

Cashel and Emly

White, J.D., 'Extracts from original wills, formerly in the consistorial office, Cashel, later moved to Waterford Probate Court', *Kilkenny and South of Ireland Archaeology Society Journal*, Ser. 2, Vol. 2, Pt 2, 1859; Vol. 4, 1862.

Clogher

Swanzy Collection, NAI T. 1746 (1C-53-16). Copies also at the Genealogical Office (GO 420, indexed in 429) and RCBL. Abstracts from Clogher and Kilmore Will Books, Marriage Licence Bonds, Administrations and militia lists. Principal names include Beatty, Nixon, Armstrong, Young, Veitch, Jackson, Mee, Noble and Fiddes.

Clonfert
GO 707: Numerous abstracts, mainly relating to wills mentioning Burke families.

Cloyne
Welply Abstracts (4 vols.), RCBL. Indexed in *IG*, 1985/6.
'Index to Will Abstracts at the Genealogical Office', *AH*, 17; GO Ms. 429.

Connor
Connor Will Book, 1818–20, 1853–8. NAI.
Stewart-Kennedy Notebooks, will abstracts, many from Down and Connor. Principal families include Stewart, Clarke, Cunningham, Kennedy and Wade. Trinity College Library and PRONI. See also NLI Pos. 4066.

Cork and Ross
Welply Abstracts (4 vols.), RCBL. Indexed in *IG*, 1985/6.
Caulfield transcripts, mainly sixteenth century, RCBL. See also *JCHAS*, 1903/4.
Notes from wills of Cork diocese, 1660–1700. NA M. 2760.

Derry
Amy Young, *300 Years in Inishowen* (NLI Ir 9292 y 1). Contains forty-six Co. Donegal wills.

Down
Down Will Book, 1850–58. NAI and PRONI.
Stewart-Kennedy Notebooks, will abstracts, many from Down and Connor. Principal families include Stewart, Clarke, Cunningham, Kennedy and Wade. Trinity College Library and PRONI.

Dublin and Glendalough
Lane-Poole Papers, NLI Ms. 5359 (abstracts).
Abstracts of wills proved in Dublin diocesan court, 1560–1710, A–E only. GO Ms. 290.

Elphin
Wills and Deeds from Co. Sligo, 1605–1632. NLI Ms. 2164.

Kildare
Betham Collection, NAI. Abstracts of almost all Kildare wills up to 1827. Also NLI Pos. 1784–5.

Killaloe and Kilfenora
O'Loghlen wills from Co. Clare. NLI Pos. 2543.
Wills and administrations from Cos. Clare and Limerick. Westropp manuscript volume, 3A 39. RIA.

Kilmore

Swanzy Collection, NAI T. 1746 (1C-53-16). Copies also at the Genealogical Office (GO 420, indexed in 429) and RCBL. Abstracts from Clogher and Kilmore Will Books, Marriage Licence Bonds, Administrations and militia lists. Principal names include Beatty, Nixon, Armstrong, Young, Veitch, Jackson, Mee, Noble and Fiddes.

Leighlin

Carrigan Collection. NLI Pos. 903. (952 wills, mainly Ossory and Leighlin.) Indexed in *IG*, 1970.
Abstracts from Ossory and Leighlin Admins. *IG*, 1972.

Limerick

R. Hayes, 'Some old Limerick wills', *JNMAS*, Vol. 1, pp. 163–8; Vol. 2, pp. 71–5.
Wills and administrations from Cos. Clare and Limerick. Westropp manuscript volume, 3A 39. RIA.

Meath

Alphabetical list of the prerogative wills of residents of Co. Louth up to 1810. NLI Ms. 7314.
G. Rice, 'Extracts from Meath priests' wills, 1658–1782', *Ríocht na Midhe*, Vol. 4, No. 1, 1967, pp. 68–71.

Ossory

Carrigan Collection. NLI Pos. 903. (952 wills, mainly Ossory and Leighlin.) Indexed in *IG*, 1970.
Abstracts from Ossory and Leighlin Admins., *IG*, 1972.
T.U. Sadleir, Abstracts from Ossory Admins., 1738–1884. NAI.
Calendar of Administrations, Ossory. NA T. 7425.
GO 683–6. Walsh-Kelly Notebooks. Will abstracts, mainly from Ossory.

Raphoe

Amy Young, *300 Years in Inishowen* (NLI Ir 9292 y 1). Contains forty-six Donegal wills.

Tuam

GO 707. Numerous abstracts, mainly relating to wills mentioning Burke families, 1784–1820.

Waterford and Lismore

Wills relating to Waterford. *Decies* 16, 17, 19, 20, 22, 23.
Jennings Collection. NAI and *Decies* (above).
166 Waterford wills and administrations. NLI D. 9248–9413.

4. *Consistorial wills and administration bonds indexes, published and in the National Archives*

Diocese	Wills	Admin. bonds
Ardagh	1695–1858 (also IA, 1970)	1697–1850
Ardfert and Aghadoe	1690–1858 (Ph., 1690-1800; o'k., Vol. 5, 1690–1858)	1782–1858 (o'k., Vol. 5, 1782–1858)
Armagh	1666–1837 (A–L) 1677–1858 (M–Y) Drogheda District, 1691–1846	
Cashel and Emly	1618–1858 (Ph., 1618–1800)	1644–1858
Clogher	1661–1858	1660–1858
Clonfert	1663–1857 (IA, 1970)	1771–1857 (IA, 1970)
Cloyne	1621–1858 (Ph., 1621–1800 o'k., Vol. 8 (1547–1858)	1630–1857 (o'k., Vol. 6)
Connor	1680–1846 (A–L) 1636–1857 (M–Y)	1636–1858
Cork and Ross	1548–1858 (Ph. and o'k., Vol. 8, 1548–1800; JCHAS, 1895–8, 1548–1833)	1612–1858 (o'k., Vol. 5)
Derry	1612–1858 (Ph.)	1698–1857
Down	1646–1858	1635–1858
Dromore	1678–1858 with Newry and Mourne, 1727–1858 (Ph.)	1742–1858 with Newry and Mourne, 1811–45 (IA, 1969: Newry and Mourne)
Dublin and Glendalough	1536–1858 (RDKPRI, Nos. 26 and 30)	1636–1858 (RDKPRI, Nos. 26 and 30)
Elphin	1650–1858 (fragments)	1726–1857
Ferns	1601–1858 (fragments) 1603–1838 (F–V) 1615–1842 (unproved, W only) (Ph., 1601–1800)	1765–1833
Kildare	1661–1858 (Ph., 1661–1800; JKAS, 1905: 1661–1858)	1770–1848 (JKAS, 1907: 1770–1858)
Killala and Achonry	1756–1831 (fragments)	1779–1858 (IA, 1975)
Killaloe and Kilfenora	1653–1858 (fragments) (Ph., 1653–1800)	1779–1858 (IA, 1975)
Kilmore	1682–1858 (damaged)	1728–1858
Leighlin	1642–1858 (Ph., 1642–1800)	1694–1845 (IA, 1972)
Limerick	1615–1858 (Ph., 1615–1800)	1789–1858
Meath	1572–1858 (fragments, partial transcript, 1635–1838), NAI	1663–1857

Diocese	Wills	Admin. bonds
Ossory	1536–1858 (fragments) (Ph., 1536–1800)	1660–1857
Raphoe	1684–1858 (damaged) (Ph.)	1684–1858
Tuam	1648–1858 (damaged)	1692–1857
Waterford and Lismore	1648–1858 (damaged) (Ph., 1648–1800)	1661–1857

Section 2: Post-1858
1. Yearly calendars of wills and administrations, 1858 to date
These provide name, address and occupation of the deceased; place and exact date of death; names and addresses of grantees of probate or administration, and relationship; exact date of probate; value of the estate.

On open access in the search room of the National Archives and PRONI. The consolidated index, 1858–77, is only in NAI.

2. Original wills or transcripts
  (a) Card index, NAI search room.
  (b) Surviving Will and Grant Books in NAI, as follows:
    (i) Principal Registry Wills: 1874, G–M
         Principal Registry Wills: 1878, A–Z
         Principal Registry Wills: 1891, G–M
         Principal Registry Wills: 1896, A–F
         Principal Registry Wills, Dublin District: 1869, G–M
         Principal Registry Wills, Dublin District: 1891, M–P
         Principal Registry Wills, Dublin District: 1901, A–F
    (ii) Principal Registry Grants: 1878, 1883, 1891, 1893
    (iii) District Registry Will Books:
         Ballina, 1865 to date
         Cavan, 1858–1909
         Cork, 1858–1932
         Kilkenny, 1858–1911
         Limerick, 1858–99
         Mullingar, 1858–1901
         Tuam, 1858–1929
         Waterford, 1858–1902
  (c) District Registry Will Books in PRONI and online at <www.proni.gov.uk>:
         Armagh, 1858–1900 (MIC 15C)
         Belfast, 1858–1900 (MIC 15C)
         Londonderry, 1858–1900 (MIC 15C)

Chapter 7 ∽

| THE GENEALOGICAL OFFICE

The Genealogical Office is the successor to the office of Ulster King of Arms, also known simply as the Office of Arms, which was created in 1552 when King Edward VI designated Bartholomew Butler the chief heraldic authority in Ireland, with the title of Ulster King of Arms. The reasons for the choice of 'Ulster' rather than 'Ireland' are somewhat unclear; it seems likely that the older title of Ireland King of Arms was already in use among the heralds at the College of Arms in London. Whatever the reason, Ulster King of Arms acquired full jurisdiction over coats of arms in Ireland and retained it for almost four hundred years, until 1943, when the office was taken over by the Irish Government and renamed the Genealogical Office and the post of Ulster King of Arms was replaced by that of Chief Herald of Ireland, with substantially the same powers as his predecessor. The Genealogical Office is now a department of the NLI.

At the outset the authority of Ulster King of Arms was limited to those areas of the country under English authority; heraldry, as a feudal practice, was in any case quite alien to Gaelic culture. Up to the end of the seventeenth century the functions of the office remained purely heraldic: ascertaining and recording what arms were in use and by what right families used them. From the late seventeenth century Ulster began to acquire other duties, as an officer of the Crown intimately linked to the government. These duties were largely ceremonial: deciding and arranging precedence on state occasions, introducing new peers to the Irish House of Lords and recording peerage successions. In essence, these two areas—the heraldic and the ceremonial—remained the principal functions of the office over the succeeding three centuries, with Ulster becoming registrar of the chivalric Order of St Patrick, instituted in 1783, and continuing to have responsibility for the ceremonial aspects of state occasions at the court of the Lord Lieutenant.

The functioning of the office depended to an inordinate degree on the personal qualities of Ulster, and an unfortunate number of the holders of the position, in the eighteenth century especially, appear to have regarded it as a sinecure, paying little attention to the keeping of records and treating the manuscript collection as their personal property. It was only with the arrival of Sir William Betham in the early nineteenth century that the business of the office was put on a sound footing and serious attention paid to the collection and care of manuscripts. As a consequence, although a number of the official records are much earlier, the vast majority of the office's holdings do not pre-date the nineteenth century.

In the course of carrying out its heraldic functions the office inevitably acquired a large amount of material of genealogical interest, as the right to bear arms is strictly hereditary. Nonetheless, the new title given to the office in 1943, Genealogical Office, was somewhat inaccurate. Its principal function continues to be heraldic: the granting and confirmation of official achievements to individuals and corporate bodies. Up to the 1980s the office also carried out commissioned research into family history. This service has been discontinued.

An excellent account of the history of the office is Susan Hood's *Royal roots—republican inheritance: the survival of the Office of Arms* (Dublin: Woodfield Press, 2002, 285 p.)

GENEALOGICAL OFFICE RECORDS

Manuscripts
The manuscripts of the Genealogical Office are numbered in a single series from 1 to 822. They are, however, of a very mixed nature, a reflection of the office's changing functions over the centuries, and they are best dealt with in categories based on those functions. The following account divides them into (1) official records, (2) administrative records and reference works and (3) research material.

(1) *Official records*
A manuscript-by-manuscript listing of the holdings of the office can be found in the 'Browse' section of Irish Ancestors at <*www.irishtimes.com/ancestor*>.

A number of sets of manuscripts are direct products of the official functions of the office and may be termed official records. On the heraldic side, the principal records are the Visitations (GO 47–9), the Funeral Entries (GO 64–79), the official grants and confirmations of arms (GO 103–111g) and the Registered Pedigrees (GO 156–82). In addition to these, four other manuscript groups reflect duties that Ulster's office acquired over the centuries. These are the Lords' Entries (GO 183–8), Royal Warrants for Changes of Name (GO 26 and 149–54A), Baronets' Records (GO 112–14) and Gaelic Chieftains (GO 610 and 627).

The visitations were an attempt to carry out in Ireland heraldic visitations along the lines of those the College of Arms had been using in England for almost a century to control the bearing of arms. The results were meagre, confined to areas close to Dublin and almost certainly incomplete even for those areas. The following places were covered: Dublin and parts of Co. Louth, 1568–70; Drogheda and Ardee, 1570; Swords, 1572; Cork, 1574; Limerick, 1574; the city of Dublin, 1607; the county of Dublin, 1610; and Wexford, 1610. They are indexed in GO 117.

The Funeral Entries, covering the period 1588–1691, make up some of the deficiencies of the Visitations. Their aim was to record the name, wife and issue of deceased nobility and gentry, along with their arms. In addition, many of the entries include very beautiful illustrations of the arms and armorial devices used at the funeral, as well as notes on the ordering of the funeral processions and ceremonies. An index to the entries is found in GO 386.

One of the later effects of the lack of visitations was to make it difficult for Ulster to verify from his own records that a particular family had a right to its arms. This gave rise to the practice, peculiar to Ireland, of issuing 'confirmations' of arms, which were taken as official registrations and were dependent on an applicant being able to show that the arms in question had been in use in their family for three generations or a hundred years. The records of these confirmations, and of actual grants of arms, are found in GO 103–111g, dating from 1698 and still current. Earlier grants and confirmations are scattered through the manuscript collection; a complete index to all arms officially recorded in the office is to be found in GO 422–3. Hayes's *Manuscript Sources for the History of Irish Civilisation* reproduces this and includes a summary of any genealogical information; this is now online at <*sources.nli.ie*>.

As the right to bear arms is hereditary, the authentication of arms required the collection of a large amount of genealogical material. This is undoubtedly the origin of the Registered Pedigrees, GO 156–82, but the series very quickly acquired a life of its own, and the majority of entries are now purely genealogical. It is particularly important for the collection of eighteenth-century pedigrees of Irish émigrés to France, produced in response to their need to prove membership of the nobility: admission to such a position carried very substantial privileges, and the proofs required included the signature of Ulster. The series continues up to the present and is indexed in GO 469, as well as in Hayes's *Manuscript Sources.*

Partly as a result of difficulties concerning the status of lords who had supported King James II, from 1698 one of the duties of Ulster became the keeping of an official list of Irish peers, Ulster's Roll. In theory, all those entitled to sit in the Irish House of Lords, whether by creation of a new peerage or by succession, were obliged to inform Ulster before they could be officially introduced to the house; in practice, the vast bulk of the information collected relates to successions, with the heirs supplying the date of death and place of burial, arms, marriages and issue. The series covers the period from 1698 to 1939 and is indexed in GO 470.

To regulate the assumption of arms and titles, after 1784 it became necessary to obtain a warrant from the King for a change of name and arms. From 1795 the Irish House of Lords made it obligatory to register such a warrant in Ulster's office. The result is the manuscript series known officially as 'royal warrants for changes of name and licences for changes of name'. Most of the nineteenth-century changes came about as a result of wills, with an inheritance made conditional on a change of name. Hayes's *Manuscript Sources* indexes the series.

A similar need to regulate the improper assumption of titles produced the Baronets' Records, GO 112–14. A royal warrant of 1789 for 'correcting and preventing abuses in the order of baronets' made registration of their arms and pedigrees with Ulster obligatory. The volumes are indexed in GO 470.

The records of 'Gaelic Chieftains' in GO 610 and 627 are the consequence of a revival instituted in the 1940s by Edward MacLysaght, the first Chief Herald of Ireland. He attempted to trace the senior lineal descendants in the male line of the last recorded 'Chief of the Name', who was then officially recognised as the contemporary holder of the title. The practice met with mixed success, as the collapse of Gaelic culture in the seventeenth century left an enormous gulf to be bridged, and the chieftainships were not in any case originally passed on by primogeniture but by election within the extended kin-group, the *deirbhfhine*. Nonetheless, more than twenty chiefs were recognised, and the records of the research that went into establishing their right to the title are extremely interesting. Following a controversy over the recognition of MacCarthy Mór in the 1990s, the practice was discontinued.

(2) *Administrative records and reference works*

Many of the documents now part of the general manuscript series simply derive from the paperwork necessary for running an office. These include cash books, receipts, Ulster's diaries, letter books, day books and records of fees due for the various functions carried out by Ulster. Of these the most interesting from a genealogical point of view are the letter books (GO 361–78), copies of all letters sent out from the office between 1789 and 1853; and the Betham letters (GO 580–604), a collection of the letters received by Sir William Betham between c.1810 and 1830 and purchased by the Genealogical Office in 1943. The former are indexed volume by volume; the latter are of more potential value. The only index, however, comes in the original catalogue of the sale of the letters, dated 1936, a copy of which is to be found at the office, though not numbered among the manuscripts. The catalogue lists the letters alphabetically by addressor, and a supplementary surnames index provides a guide to the families dealt with. Another eight volumes of the series, unindexed, are to be found in NAI (M.744–51).

As well as documents produced in the day-to-day running of the office, a large number of manuscripts relate to the ceremonial functions performed by Ulster. These include official orders relating to changes of insignia, papers dealing with precedence and protocol, records of official functions at the Viceregal court, and the records of the Order of St Patrick. There is little of genealogical interest in these.

In the course of their heraldic and genealogical work Ulster and his officers accumulated a large series of manuscripts for use as reference works. These include manuscript armories, ordinaries of arms, treatises on heraldry and precedence, a series of English Visitations, and blazons of arms of English and Scottish peers. The bulk of the material is heraldic, but there is a good deal of incidental genealogical information, particularly in the seventeenth-century ordinaries of arms.

(3) *Research material*

The most useful manuscripts in the Genealogical Office collection are those acquired and created to provide sources for genealogical research. The policy was begun in the early nineteenth century by Sir William Betham and was continued by his successors, and it has produced a wide range of material, much of it based on records that were destroyed in the Public Record Office in 1922. It may be divided into three broad categories: (i) Betham's own compilations, (ii) the collections of later genealogists and (iii) other records. The sheer diversity of these documents makes a complete account impractical here; what follows is a broad outline.

The greatest work produced by Betham is the collection of abstracts of family information from prerogative wills. These are divided into a number of series. GO 223–6 ('Old Series', Vols. 1–4) covers wills before 1700, and GO 227–54 ('New Series', Vols. 1–31) covers wills from 1700 to c.1800. The series is roughly alphabetical, with each volume containing its own index. Sir Arthur Vicars's *Index to the Prerogative Wills of Ireland, 1536–1810* (online at <www.archive.org>) provides a guide to wills covered. Many of the sketch pedigrees include later amendments and additions from other sources. GO Mss. 255–6 index all the marriage alliances recorded in the wills. Another series, GO 203–214 ('Will Pedigrees', Vols. 1–12), represents an unfinished attempt to rearrange all these sketch pedigrees into strictly alphabetical order. Betham also produced a large number of sketch pedigrees based on other sources, collected as 'Ancient Anglo-Irish Families', Vols. 1–6 (GO 215–19), 'Milesian Families', Vols. 1–3 (GO 220–22), and the '1st series', Vols. 1–16 (GO 261–76), and '2nd series', Vols. 1–7 (GO 292–8). These are all indexed in GO 470.

As well as the sketch pedigrees and the letters (covered above under 'Administrative records and reference works') there are two other sources in the collection that owe their origin to Betham. The first of these, genealogical and historical excerpts from the plea rolls and patent rolls from King Henry III to King Edward VI (GO 189–93), constitute the most important source of information on Anglo-Norman genealogy in Ireland. Betham's transcript of Roger O'Ferrall's 'Linea Antiqua', a collation of earlier genealogies compiled in 1709, is the office's most extensive work on Gaelic, as opposed to Anglo-Irish, genealogy. This copy (in three volumes, GO 145–7, with an index to the complete work in GO 147) also contains Betham's interpolations and additions, unfortunately not giving sources. It records the arms of many of the Gaelic families covered, without giving any authority for them, and is the source of most of the arms illustrated in MacLysaght's *Irish Families*.

Pedigrees and research notes produced by later amateur and professional genealogists make up a large part of the office's manuscript collection. Among those who have contributed to these are Sir Edmund Bewley, Denis O'Callaghan Fisher, Arthur Tenison Groves, Alfred Molony, T.U. Sadleir and the Rev. H.B. Swanzy. For the most part their records concern either particular groups of families or particular geographical areas. Some of these have their own indexes, some are covered by GO 470 and 117, and others have will abstracts only indexed in GO 429.

As well as these, some of the results of Ulster's own research in the late nineteenth and early twentieth centuries are classed as manuscripts, GO 800–822. These constitute no more than a fraction of the total research information produced by the Genealogical Office. They are indexed in Hayes's *Manuscript Sources.*

A final class of records consists of extremely diverse documents, having only their potential genealogical usefulness in common. It includes such items as freeholders' lists from different counties, extracts from parish registers, transcripts of the Dublin city roll of freemen, transcripts of returns from the 1766 census, transcripts of city directories from various periods and militia lists. The most useful of these are referred to in the county source lists in Chapter 13.

Archives

As well as the manuscripts series, now closed, the Genealogical Office has extremely extensive archive records of the commissioned research it carried out up to the 1980s. For the closing decades of the nineteenth century and the early decades of the twentieth century these records are still largely concerned with the Anglo-Irish. Manuscripts 800–822 cover perhaps 5 per cent of this material.

After the creation of the Genealogical Office in 1943 the focus of the commissioned research shifted, with most work now carried out on behalf of the descendants of emigrants to Australia and North America. There are more than twenty thousand research files giving details of the results of this research.

RESEARCH IN GENEALOGICAL OFFICE MANUSCRIPTS

The biggest obstacle to research in GO manuscripts is the lack of a single, comprehensive index, though this has been mitigated to some extent by the recent work of Virginia Wade McAnlis (see below). Many attempts have been made over the centuries of the office's existence to produce a complete index; the result has been a proliferation of partial indexes, each covering some of the collection, none covering it all. These are dealt with below. In addition, the policy used in the creation of manuscripts appears to have become somewhat inconsistent from the 1940s. Before then only the earliest and most heterogeneous manuscripts had been numbered in a single series, with each of the other groups simply having its own volume numbers, 'Lords' Entries, Vol. 2' or 'Registered Pedigrees, Vol. 12', for example. The laudable attempt to produce a consistent numbering system, beginning at GO 1 and moving through the collection, seems to have given rise to the piecemeal addition of material that was more properly the preserve of NLI. The subsequent transfers to the library and renumbering of remaining material produced a virtual collapse of the system in the upper numbers: no manuscripts exist for many of the numbers between 600 and 800. The numerical list of manuscripts at <*www.irishtimes.com/ancestor/browse/records/genealogical*> reflects the present situation, with titles no longer in the office given in brackets.

In recent years Virginia Wade McAnlis has taken on the task of creating a consolidated index for Genealogical Office manuscripts, working from the microfilm copies available through the Family History Centres of the Church of

Jesus Christ of Latter-Day Saints, the Mormons. This work, in four volumes, is available at the NLI (Ir 9291 c 11/1) and online at *<www.nli.ie/en/heraldry-catalogues-and-databases.aspx>*. The McAnlis index brings together the references from the indexes numbered as GO Mss. 117, 148, 255–60, 386, 422–3 and 470. Details of these are found below. In addition to the page references included in these indexes, McAnlis also includes microfilm references for the Latter-Day Saints collection.

Indexes

GO 59   A detailed calendar of manuscripts 1–58, particularly useful as many of these consist of very early heterogeneous material bound together for preservation.

GO 115   Indexes the following: Arms, A–C; Grants and Confirmations, A and B; Visitations; British Families; Funeral Entries; and Registered Pedigrees, Vols. 1–10. Only the Visitations (GO 47–9) and British Families (GO 44–6) are not indexed more fully elsewhere.

GO 116   An unfinished index.

GO 117   Duplicates much of the material indexed in GO 422, GO 470 and Hayes's *Manuscript Sources*. Only the following are not covered elsewhere: Antrim Families (GO 213); Fisher Mss. (GO 280–85); Irish Arms at the College of Heralds (GO 37); Irish Coats of Arms (Fota) (GO 526); Heraldic Sketches (GO 125); Betham Letter Books (GO 362–78); Ecclesiastical Visitations (GO 198–9); and Reynell Mss. (GO 445).

GO 148   Index to 'Linea Antiqua'. The version at the end of GO 147, 'Linea Antiqua', Vol. 3, is more complete.

GO 255–6 Index to Alliances in Prerogative Wills (Betham).

GO 386   Index to the Funeral Entries.

GO 422–3 Index to arms registered at the Genealogical Office.

GO 429   Eustace Index to Will Abstracts at the Genealogical Office. The published version in *Analecta Hibernica*, Vol. 17, is less extensive than the manuscript copy.

GO 469   Index to Registered Pedigrees. This appears to be less complete than the version included in Hayes's *Manuscript Sources*. Attached to it is a typescript copy of the index to the Genealogical Office collection of pedigree rolls.

GO 470   Index to Unregistered Pedigrees. This is the most useful index in the office, covering the Lords' Entries, the Betham pedigrees and many of the genealogists' pedigree collections. It is divided into three separate parts and gives the descriptive titles in use before the adoption of the single GO numbering system. The flyleaf lists the manuscripts covered.

GO 476   Numerical listing of GO manuscripts dating from the 1950s and now inaccurate for the higher numbers.

See also Hayes's *Manuscript Sources* (*<sources.nli.ie>*). This indexes the Registered Pedigrees, GO 800–822, and Fisher Mss. (GO 280–85).

Access

Access to the Genealogical Office collection is through the manuscript reading room of the National Library at 2 Kildare Street, Dublin, the same building that houses the office itself. For the most valuable manuscripts, in general those in the lower numbers, only microfilm copies are accessible, in the National Library microfilm reading room. A complete listing of microfilm copies can be found at <*www.nli.ie/en/heraldry-catalogues-and-databases.aspx*>.

Chapter 8 ～

EMIGRATION AND THE
IRISH ABROAD

For anyone descended from an Irish emigrant it is natural to look to emigration records for information on family or place of origin. Unfortunately, no centralised records of emigration exist. For emigration to North America in particular, where any ships' passenger lists have survived they were deposited at the port of arrival rather than at the port of departure; the authorities were more concerned with recording those entering a country than those leaving one. The most comprehensive records for the United States, therefore, are the Customs Passenger Lists, dating from 1820, and the Immigration Passenger Lists, dating from 1883, both in the US National Archives in Washington. The earlier lists are not very informative, giving only the country of origin of the emigrant. They have been collected by the US National Archives for the most important immigrant ports: Boston, New York, Baltimore and Philadelphia, as well as Mobile, New Bedford and New Orleans. Microfilm copies of the lists for New York and Boston are available at the National Library of Ireland. No index to these is available, making them very difficult to use if a relatively precise date of arrival is not known. A good guide is at <*www. genealogybranches.com/irishpassengerlists*>.

As well as these, however, there are many less comprehensive lists, published and unpublished, which record intending and actual emigrants and ships' passengers to North America. A number of attempts have been made to systematise access to these. The most important are the *Passenger and Immigration Lists Index* (multi-volume, ed. P. William Filby and Mary K. Meyer, Detroit: Gale, ongoing; NL: RR 387 p 7), a consolidated index to a wide variety of lists relating to North American immigration from all over the world, and *The Famine Immigrants* (7 vols., indexed, Baltimore, Md.: GPC, 1988; NLI Ir 942 g 12), which records more than half a million Irish arrivals in New York between 1846 and 1851. Even these, however, cover only a small fraction of the material of potential value.

For Australia and New Zealand the situation is somewhat better. Because of the distance, very few emigrants could afford the journey themselves, and most, whether assisted free settlers or transported convicts, are therefore quite well documented. Transportation from Ireland, or for crimes committed in Ireland, lasted from 1791 to 1853, ending some fifteen years earlier than transportation from England. The only mass transportation later than 1853 was of sixty-three Fenians, who were sent to Western Australia in 1868 aboard the last convict ship from England to Australia. The records of the Chief Secretary's Office, which had responsibility for the penal system, are the major Irish source of information on transportees. Not all the relevant records have survived, particularly for the period before 1836, but what does exist can provide a wealth of information. The records were formerly housed in the State Paper Office in Dublin Castle, which is now part of NAI. The principal classes of relevant records are as follows:

1. *Prisoners' Petitions and Cases, 1788–1836:* These consist of petitions to the Lord Lieutenant for commutation or remission of sentence and record the crime, trial, sentence, place of origin and family circumstances.
2. *State Prisoners' Petitions:* These specifically concern those arrested for participation in the 1798 Rebellion and record the same information as the main series of petitions.
3. *Convict Reference Files, from 1836:* These continue the earlier petitions series and may include a wide range of additional material.
4. *Transportation Registers, from 1836:* These record all the names of those sentenced to death or transportation, giving the name, age, date of trial, county of trial, crime and sentence. Other details, including the name of the transport ship or the place of detention, are sometimes also given.
5. *Male Convict Register, 1842–7:* In addition to the information supplied by the Transportation Registers, this volume also gives physical descriptions.
6. *Register of Convicts on Convict Ships, 1851–3.* This gives the names, dates and counties of trial of those transported to Van Diemen's Land (Tasmania) and Western Australia for the period covered.
7. *Free Settlers' Papers, 1828–52:* After serving a minimum of four years, male convicts had the right to request free passage for their wife and family. The papers contain lists of those making such a request, along with transportation details and the name and address of the wife. A number of petitions from husbands and wives, together with prisoners' letters, are also included.

To celebrate the Australian Bicentenary of 1988 all these records were microfilmed, and a computerised database of the surnames they contain was created. Copies of the microfilms and the database were presented to the Australian government and can now be found in many state archives. NAI also retains copies, and the database in particular can save a great deal of time and effort. It supplies enough details from the originals to identify the relevant record. It is available online at <*www.nationalarchives.ie*>. Early convict arrivals records, making up some of the gaps in the NAI material, are online at Irish Convicts to Australia, 1791–1815, <*www.pcug.org.au/~ppmay/convicts.htm*>.

For obvious reasons, the records relating to free settlers are more scattered and less easily researched. The most useful source for early settlers, also invaluable for convicts, is the 1828 census of New South Wales, published by the Library of Australian History in 1980. Although the precise place of origin is not recorded, the details include age, occupation, marital status and household. An online transcript is at <*www.ancestry.com.au*>. For later settlers the University of Wollongong in New South Wales has produced on microfiche a complete index and transcript of all information concerning immigrants of Irish origin recorded on ships' passenger lists between 1848 and 1870. The later lists in particular are extremely useful, often recording the precise place of origin as well as parents' names. Australian state archives have free online databases of convict and free settler arrivals at the Public Record Office of Victoria (<*www.prov.vic.gov.au*>) and the State Records Authority of New South Wales (<*www.records. nsw.gov.au*>).

Other than these, the principal records likely to be of relevance are in the Colonial Office Papers of the Public Record Office at Kew (class reference CO 201). This class contains a wide variety of records, including petitions for assisted passages, emigrants' lists, records of emigrants on board ship, petitions from settlers for financial assistance, and much else. A number of these have been published in David T. Hawkings's *Bound for Australia* (Chichester, Sussex: Phillimore & Co., 1987). The Society of Australian Genealogists (<*www.sag.org. au*>) provides excellent guidance.

Almost everyone now living in Ireland has links with what came to be known as the 'Irish diaspora'. Because of the disastrous loss of Irish records in 1922, records of these relatives, however distant, can often be used not only to fill in the extended family but also to retrieve information on parentage and place of origin. To take one example: Massachusetts marriage records from the early decades of the twentieth century require the names and addresses of the parents of both parties; for some parts of Ireland where parish registers may not start until the 1880s, this can be the only concrete evidence of these names.

The remainder of this chapter is an attempt to present a systematic guide to published material covering the Irish abroad. Any passenger lists given separately in earlier editions are now included under the general area of arrival. Lists relating to emigrants from specific localities in Ireland are shown in the county source lists in Chapter 13.

AFRICA

South Africa

Akenson, D.H., *Occasional papers on the Irish in South Africa*, Grahamstown: Institute of Social and Economic Research, Rhodes University, 1991. NLI Ir 942 a 15, 101 p.

Blake, J.Y.F., *A West Pointer with the Boers*, Boston. Irish in the Anglo-Boer War.

Davitt, Michael, *The Boer Fight for Freedom,* New York: Funk & Wagnalls, 1902. Irish in the Anglo-Boer War.

Dickason, G.D., *Irish settlers to the Cape: history of the Clanwilliam 1820 settlers from Cork Harbour*, Cape Town: A. A. Balkema, 1973. NLI Ir 968 d 7, 113 p.

Irish Republican Association of South Africa, *The Irish in South Africa, 1920–1921*, Cape Town: Die Nasionale Pers Beperk, 1921. NLI Ir 968 i 2, 183 p.

Liggett, Neville D., *The Longbottom family: Dublin to South Africa, c.1781 to 1994*, Beacon Bay: N.D. Liggett, 1995. LC, 39 p.

McCracken, D.P., *The Irish Pro-Boers, 1877–1902*, Perskor, Johannesburg.

—— 'The Irish Transvaal Brigades', *IS*, 1974 (winter).

—— 'Odd man out: the South African experience' in Andy Bielenberg (ed.), *The Irish Diaspora*, Harlow, Middx, and New York: Longman, 2000. NLI, 368 p.

McCracken, D.P., (ed.), 'The Irish in Southern Africa, 1795–1910,' *Southern African-Irish Studies*, Vol. 2, 1991.

—— 'Irish Settlement and Identity in South Africa before 1910,' *Southern African-Irish Studies*, Vol. 1, 1991.

McCracken, J.L., *New Light at the Cape of Good Hope: William Porter, the Father of Cape Liberalism*, Belfast: UHF, 1993. NLI Ir 92 p 201, 160 p.

Murphy, David, *The Irish Brigades, 1685–2006*, Dublin: Four Courts Press, 2007. 304 p. For South African Irish regiments, 1885–2006.

Naidoo, Indren, 'The Irish diaspora and its impact on the Eastern and Western Cape in the colonial era,' 1994. NLSA (microform), MF.1163, 6 microfiches. Originally presented as MA thesis, University of Durban-Westville, 1994.

Vincent, John, 'A new Era for the Irish in South Africa', *IR*, No. 4, 13 (1994). NLI.

AUSTRALASIA

Australia

Adam-Smith, Patsy, *Heart of exile: Ireland, 1848, and the seven patriots banished, their adventures, loneliness, and loves in three continents as they search for refuge*, Melbourne, Vic: Nelson, 1986. NLI Ir 94108 a 5, 369 p.

Akenson, D.H., 'Reading the texts of rural immigrants: Letters from the Irish in Australia, New Zealand and America', *Canadian papers in Rural History*, Vol. 7, 1990, Gananoque, Ont.: Langdale Press, c.1978–c.1996. NLC.

Amos, Keith, *The Fenians in Australia, 1865–1880*, Kensington, NSW: New South Wales University Press, 1988. NLI Ir 994 a 18, 330 p.

Australian Journal of Irish Studies, Perth, W. Aus.: Centre for Irish Studies, Murdoch University, 2001–. NLI 1H 94.

Brownrigg, Jeff (ed.), *Echoes of Irish Australia: rebellion to republic: a collection of essays*, Galong, NSW: St Clement's Retreat and Conference Centre, 2007. NLI, 269 p. Co-editors, Cheryl Mongan and Richard Reid.

Bull, Philip, *Ireland and Australia, 1798–1998: studies in culture, identity and migration*, Sydney: Crossing Press, 2000. NLA, 367 p. Co-editors, Francis Devlin-Glass and Helen Doyle.

Cam, A.M., *Irish freemasonry in Australasia*, South Plympton, S. Aus.: the author, 2006. NLI, 523 p.

Campbell, Malcolm, 'A comparative study of Irish rural settlement in nineteenth-century Minnesota and New South Wales', in Bielenberg, *The Irish Diaspora*. See McCracken under 'Africa'.

—— *Ireland's New Worlds: immigrants, politics, and society in the United States and Australia, 1815–1922*, Madison, Wis.: University of Wisconsin Press, 2008. NLI, 249 p.

Cleary, P.J.S., *Australia's Debt to Ireland's Nation-builders*, Sydney: Angus & Robertson, 1933. NLI Ir 994 c 6, 280 p.

Clinton, Brian Hankard, *Clinton our name, from Erin we came*, Wamberal, NSW: the author, 1995. LC, 201 p. Patrick and Charles Clinton, who came from Ireland to Australia in 1877.

Coffey, Hubert W., *Irish Families in Australia and New Zealand, 1788–1979*, Melbourne: the author, 1979–94. NLI Ir 942 c 14. Four-volume biographical dictionary. Co-author, Marjorie Jean Morgan.

Conlon, Bernard, *The travels of Bernard Conlon: Sessiamagaroll to San Francisco, New York, New Zealand and New South Wales, recorded as a memoir by his son Proinsias Ó Conluain*, Dungannon: O'Neill Country Historical Society, 2004. NLI, 36 p.

Costello, Con, *Botany Bay*, Cork: Mercier Press, c.1987. NLI Ir 942 c 27, 172 p.

Curry, C.H., *The Irish at Eureka*, Sydney: 1954. NLI Ir 993 c 7.

Davis, Richard, *Ireland and Tasmania, 1848: sesquicentenary papers*, Sydney: Crossing Press, 1998. NLI Ir 990 d 23, 152 p. Richard Davis and Stefan Petrow, editors.

—— *Irish traces on Tasmanian history, 1803–2004*, Sandy Bay, Tas.: Sassafras Books, 2005. NLI, 208 p.

Donohoe, H., *The convicts and exiles transported from Ireland, 1791–1820*, Sydney: the author, 1992. NLI Ir 942 p 17(3).

Donohoe, James Hugh, *The bibliography of the convict transports*, Sydney: the author, 1988. NLI 016 p 5(3).

Evans, A. G., *Fanatic heart: a life of John Boyle O'Reilly, 1844–1890*, Boston, Mass.: Northeastern University Press, 1999. NLI Ir 92 o 529, 280 p.

Fitzpatrick, David, *Home or Away?: Immigrants in Colonial Australia*, Canberra: Australian National University, 1992. NLA, 130 p.

—— *Oceans of Consolation*, Cork: Cork University Press, 1994. NLI Ir 942 f 12. Personal accounts of Irish emigration to Australia.

Forth, G.J., *A biographical register and annotated bibliography of Anglo-Irish colonists in Australia*, Warrnambool, Vic.: Deakin University, 1992. NLI Ir 942 b 23, 85 p.

Geary, Laurence, *Ireland, Australia and New Zealand: history, politics and culture*, Dublin: Irish Academic Press, 2008. NLI, 270 p.

Gleeson, Damian John, *Carlon's town: a history of the Carolan/Carlon sept and related Irish pioneer families in New South Wales*, Sydney: the author, 1998. NLI Ir 9292 g 38, 100 p.

Graham, John, *Far from Owenreagh: memories of John Graham (1899–1893)*, Draperstown, Co. Derry: Moyola Books, 1990. NLI Ir 92 p 172(2), 36 p.

Greiner, Alyson Lee, 'British and Irish immigration to rural nineteenth-century Australia: sources and destinations,' 1996. NLA (microform), 318 p. PhD thesis, University of Texas, Austin, 1996.

Grimes, Seamus, *The Irish-Australian Connection*, Galway: Irish Academic Press, 1989. NLI Ir 999 g 20, 159 p. Irish-Australian Bicentenary Conference. Co-editor, Gearóid Ó Tuathaigh.

Hall, Barbara, *Death or liberty: the convicts of the Britannia: Ireland to Botany Bay, 1797*, Coogee, NSW: the author, 2006. NLI, 258 p.

—— *A desperate set of villains: the convicts of the Marquis Cornwallis, Ireland to Botany Bay, 1796*, the author, 2000. NLI, 287 p.

—— *The Irish vanguard: the convicts of the Queen, Ireland to Botany Bay, 1791*, Sydney: the author, 2009. NLI, 238 p.

—— *A nimble fingered tribe: the convicts of the Sugar Cane, Ireland to Botany Bay, 1793*, the author, 2002. NLI 3A 1267.

—— *Of infamous character: the convicts of the Boddingtons, Ireland to Botany Bay, 1793*, Sydney: the author, 2004. NLI, 242 p.

Hawkings, David T., *Bound for Australia*, Chichester, Sussex: Phillimore & Co., 1987.

Hogan, J., *The Irish in Australia*, Melbourne: G. Robertson, 1888. NLI Ir 9940.

Hughes, Robert, *The Fatal Shore*, London: Collins Harvill, 1988. NLI 993 h 11.

The Irish link: the Irish family history magazine, South Melbourne, Vic.: Irish Link, 1984–. NLI Ir 9292 i 2.

Kiernan, T.J., *The Irish exiles in Australia*, Dublin: Clonmore & Reynolds, 1954. NLI Ir 994 k 1, 196 p. Irish exiles of 1848.

Kildea, Jeff, *Anzacs and Ireland*, Cork: Cork University Press, 2007. NLI, 295 p.

Langmead, Donald, *Accidental architect*, Sydney: Crossing Press, 1994. NLI 92 K n 13, 280 p. On George Strickland Kingston (1807–1880).

Larkin, David A., *'Here lyeth O'Flaherty': some notable Irish buried in Brisbane*, Brisbane: O'Lorcan, David Austin, 1991. NLA, 63 p.

—— *Irish research compendium: guide and directory of sources available in Australia*, Burpengary, Qld.: the author, c.1999. NLA, 236 p.

—— *Memorials to the Irish in Queensland*, Brisbane: Genealogical Society of Queensland, 1988. NLA, 143 p.

—— *Pushing up shamrocks: index to biographies*, Burpengary, Qld.:, Larkin Clan Association, 1998. NLA, 158 p. Irish in Queensland.

Maher, Brian, *Planting the Celtic cross: foundations of the Catholic Archdiocese of Canberra and Goulburn*, Canberra: the author, 1997. NLA, 379 p.

McClaughlin, Trevor, *Barefoot and Pregnant: Irish Famine Orphans in Australia*, Melbourne: GSV, 1991. NLI Ir 942 b 20, 256 p.

—— *From shamrock to wattle: digging up your Irish ancestors*, Melbourne: Genealogical Society of Victoria, 2nd ed., 1990. NLA, 158 p.

—— *Irish women in colonial Australia*, St Leonards, NSW: Allen & Unwin, 1998. NLI Ir 990 i 47, 229 p.

McConville, Chris, *Croppies, Celts and Catholics: the Irish in Australia*, Caulfield East, Vic.: Edward Arnold, 1987. NLA, 167 p.

McDonagh, Oliver, and Mandle, W.F., *Australia and Ireland, 1788–1988*, Dublin: 1988. NLI Ir 942 a 9.

—— *Ireland and Irish-Australians*, Sydney: 1982. NLI Ir 942 i 12.

McIntyre, Perry, *Fair Game: Australia's first immigrant women*, Spit Junction, NSW: Anchor Books Australia, 2010, 256 p. 'In 1832, the British government sent 400 young single women to Sydney and Hobart to balance the male-dominated societies . . . the "Red Rover" from Cork and the "Princess Royal" from London.'

—— *Free passage: the reunion of Irish convicts and their families in Australia, 1788–1852*, Dublin: Irish Academic Press, 2010. NLI, 344 p.

Mitchell, Brian, *Australia: the early years: from reports in the Derry Journal*, Derry: Genealogy Centre, 1988. NLA, 68 p.

Murphy, David, *The Irish Brigades, 1685–2006*. See 'South Africa'.

Neary, Bernard, *Irish Lives: the Irish in Western Australia*, Dublin: Lenhar Publications, 1989. NLI Ir 92001 p 8(1).

O'Brien, John (ed.), *The Irish Emigrant Experience in Australia*, Dublin: Poolbeg Press, 1991. NLI Ir 942 i 25, 279 p. Co-editor, Pauric Travers.

O'Farrell, Patrick, *The Catholic Church in Australia: a short history, 1788–1967*, London: Chapman, 1969. NLI 282099 o 2, 294 p.

—— *The Irish in Australia* (rev. ed.), Cork: Cork University Press, 2001. NLI Ir 942 o 29/1A 3224.

—— *Letters from Irish Australia*, Sydney: New South Wales University Press, and Belfast: UHF, 1984. NLI Ir 942 o 31. Co-editor, Brian Trainer.

—— *Through Irish eyes: Australian and New Zealand images of the Irish, 1788–1948*, Richmond, Vic.: Aurora Books, 1994. NLI Ir 942 o 43, 131 p.

—— *Vanished kingdoms: Irish in Australia and New Zealand: a personal excursion*, Kensington, NSW: New South Wales University Press, 1990. NLI Ir 942 o 34, 310 p.

O'Hearn, D., *Erin Go Bragh: Advance Australia Fair*, Melbourne: Celtic Club, 1990, 86 p. History of the Celtic Club, Melbourne.

O'Leary, J., *A Catholic miscellany: containing items of interest to Queenslanders, Irishmen and Irish Australians*, Brisbane, Qld.: Father O'Leary, 1914. NLA, 207 p.

Ó Lúing, Seán, *Fremantle mission*, Tralee: Anvil Books, 1965. NLI Ir 993 o 11, 183 p.

O'Mahoney, C., *Poverty to promise: the Monteagle emigrants, 1838–58*, Sydney: Crossing Press, 1994. NLI Ir 993 o 40. Co-author, Valerie Thompson.

O'Sullivan, Margaret Mary Kathleen, *A cause of trouble?: Irish nuns and English clerics*, Sydney: Crossing Press, 1995. NLI Ir 994 o 51. Irish Sisters of Charity.

Patrick, Ross, *Exiles undaunted: the Irish rebels, Kevin and Eva O'Doherty*, St Lucia, Qld.: University of Queensland Press, 1989. NLA, 293 p. Irish exiles of 1848.

Patterson, Brad (ed.), *Ireland and the Irish Antipodes: one world or worlds apart?: papers delivered at the 16th Australasian Irish Studies Conference . . .* Spit Junction, NSW: Anchor Books Australia, 2010. NLI, 306 p.

Pawsey, Margaret M., *The Popish plot: culture clashes in Victoria, 1860–1863*, Manly, NSW: Catholic Theological Faculty, St Patrick's College, 1983. NLA, 211 p.

Press, Kate, *West Limerick families abroad*, Melbourne: the author, 2001. NLA, 217 p. Co-author, Valerie Thompson.

Reece, Bob, *Exiles from Erin: Convict life in Ireland and Australia*, Basingstoke, Hants: Macmillan, 1991. NLI Ir 994 r 16, 336 p.

—— *Irish convict lives*, Sydney: Crossing Press, 1993. NLI Ir 942 i 35, 266 p.

—— *Irish convicts: the origins of convicts transported to Australia*, Dublin: Dept of History, University College, 1989. NLI Ir 942 r 9, 191 p.

—— *The origins of Irish convict transportation to New South Wales: mixture of breeds*, Basingstoke, Hants: Macmillan, 2000. NLI Ir 942 r 22, 392 p.

Reid, Richard, *The Irish Australians*, Belfast: UHF, and Sydney: Society of Australian Genealogists, 1984. NLI 3B 842, 56 p. Co-editor, Keith Johnson.

—— '*A decent set of girls . . .': the Irish Famine Orphans of the Thomas Arbuthnot, 1849–1850*, Yass, NSW: Yass Heritage Project, 1996. NLI Ir 942 r 17, 130 p.

—— *Farewell, my children: Irish emigration to Australia, 1848–1870*, Spit Junction, NSW: Anchor Books Australia, 2011. NLA.

—— *Not just Ned: a true history of the Irish in Australia*, Canberra: National Museum of Australia Press, 2011. NLA.

Richards, Eric (ed.), *Poor Australian immigrants in the nineteenth century*: Canberra: Australian National University, 1991. NLI.

—— *Visible immigrants: neglected sources for the history of Australian immigration*, Canberra: Australian National University, 1989. NLI. Co-authors, Richard Reid and David Fitzpatrick.

Robinson, Portia, *The hatch and brood of time: a study of the first generation of native-born white Australians, 1788–1828*, Melbourne and New York: Oxford University Press, 1985. NLI Ir 993 r 5.

Robson, L.L., *The convict settlers of Australia*, Melbourne: Melbourne University Press, 1965. NLI 325 r 2, 257 p.

Ronayne, Jarlath, *The Irish in Australia: rogues and reformers: First Fleet to federation*, Camberwell, Vic.: Viking Penguin, c.2003. NLA, 252 p. Previously published as *First Fleet to federation: Irish supremacy in Colonial Australia*, Dublin: Trinity College Dublin Press, 2002.

Sheedy, Kieran, *The Tellicherry Five: the transportation of Michael Dwyer and the Wicklow rebels*, Dublin: Woodfield Press, 1997. NLI Ir 92 d 268, 182 p.

Simons, P. Frazer, *Tenants no more: Voices from an Irish Townland, 1811–1901, and the Great Migration to Australia and America*, Richmond, Vic.: Prowling Tiger Press, 1996. NLI Ir 994 s 32, 288 p. Clay family from Gurteen, Co. Offaly (King's County), and Methodist emigrants to the United States and Australia.

Trainor, Brian (ed.), *Researching Irish Australians: directory of research*, Belfast: UHF, 1998. NLA, 87 p.

The Ulster Link, Magazine of the Northern Irish in Australia and New Zealand. NLI Ir 994 u 1.

Whitaker, Anne-Marie, 'Armagh convicts in Australia, 1800–1806', SA, 16, No. 1, 1994, pp. 100–102.

—— *Unfinished revolution: United Irishmen in New South Wales, 1800–1810*, Darlinghurst, NSW: Crossing Press, 1994. NLI Ir 993 w 15, 275 p.

New Zealand

Akenson, D.H., *Half the world from home: perspectives on the Irish in New Zealand, 1860–1950*, Wellington: Victoria University Press, 1990. NLI Ir 942 a 14, 250 p.

—— 'The Irish in New Zealand', *Familia: Ulster Genealogical Review*, 2, 5, 1989.

—— 'Reading the texts of rural immigrants: Letters from the Irish in Australia, New Zealand and America', *Canadian papers in Rural History*, 7, 1990, Gananoque, Ont.: Langdale Press, c.1978 to c.1996. NLC.

—— *Small differences: Irish Catholics and Irish Protestants, 1815–1922: an international perspective*, Dublin: Gill & Macmillan, 1991. NLI Ir 94108 a 7, 236 p.

Bellam, Michael, 'The Irish in New Zealand', *Familia: Ulster Genealogical Review*, 2, 1, 1985.

Benfell, Janet, *Shamrock and tussock: the Irish Atkinsons as remembered by their descendants*, Ashburton: Benfell, 2007. NLNZ, 63 p.

Boyd, Murray A., *From Donegal to Blackguard's Corner*, Kaikoura: 1992. NLI 2C 9, 448 p.

Cam, A.M., *Irish freemasonry in Australasia*. See 'Australia'.

Coffey, Hubert W., *Irish Families in Australia and New Zealand, 1788–1979*, Melbourne: the author, 1979–94. NLI Ir 942 c 14. Four-volume biographical dictionary. Co-author, Marjorie Jean Morgan.

Davis, Richard, *Irish issues in New Zealand politics, 1868–1922*, Dunedin: University of Otago Press, 1974. NLI Ir 942 d 15, 248 p.

—— *The Whistling Irish bushrangers: Tasmania and South Australia, 1848–63*, Sandy Bay, Tas.: Sassafras Books, c.2002. NLI 3A 150, 40 p.

Downey, David, *What's the weather like?: the story of a New Zealand pioneer family*, Auckland: Downey, 2004. NLNZ, 68 p.

Eccleston, Norman, *Irish Kiwi*, Levin: Levin Chronicle for Palmerston North Newspapers, 1977. NLNZ, 112 p.

'Family Migration to New Zealand: the Bassett Family of Ballygawley, Downpatrick, Co. Down', *Familia: Ulster Genealogical Review*, Vol. 2, No. 5, 1989.

Fraser, Lyndon, *A distant shore: Irish migration and New Zealand settlement*, Dunedin: University of Otago Press, 2000. NLNZ, 196 p.

—— *Castles of gold: a history of New Zealand's West Coast Irish*, Dunedin: Otago University Press, 2007. NLA, 203 p.

—— *To Tara via Holyhead: Irish Catholic immigrants in nineteenth-century Christchurch*, Auckland: Auckland University Press, 1997. NLI Ir 990 f 16, 208 p.

Gardner, Iris, *The family of Steele: the history of the Steele family in New Zealand*, Christchurch: Private Lane Publishing, 2003. NLNZ, 85 p.

Geary, Laurence, *Ireland, Australia and New Zealand: history, politics and culture*. See 'Australia'.

Golden, John, *Some old Waikato days*, Dunedin: NZ Tablet Printing and Publishing Co., 1922. NLNZ, 57 p.

Gray, Arthur J., *An Ulster plantation: the story of the Katikati settlement*, Wellington: A.H. & A.W. Reed, 1950. NLI Ir 970.g17, 154 p.

Graydon, E., *People of Irish descent: biographical notes on New Zealanders of Irish descent*, Tauranga: E.M. Graydon, 1992. NLNZ.

Hansen, Karen, *New Zealand Irish voices: stories from Irish migrants and their descendants*, Wellington: Hansen, 2008. NLA, 246 p.

Horn, Gerard, '*Fine representatives of the old band of genuine pioneers': Irish migration to Wellington, 1840–1853*, Wellington: Wellington Historical and Early Settlers' Association, 2008. NLNZ, 19 p.

The Irish link: the Irish family history magazine, South Melbourne, Vic.: Irish Link, 1984–. NLI Ir 9292 i 2.

King, Michael, *God's farthest outpost: a history of Catholics in New [sic] New Zealand*, Auckland: Penguin, 1997. NLNZ, 208 p.

McCann, Patrick D., *In quest of roots: the Dooney family of County Kildare in Ireland and Hawke's Bay District in New Zealand*, Dublin: [De La Salle Provincialate], 1977. NLI GO 475, 62 p.

McCarthy, Angela, '"The desired haven"?: impressions of New Zealand in letters to and from Ireland, 1840–1925', in Bielenberg, *The Irish Diaspora*. See McCracken under 'Africa'.

—— *Irish Migrants in New Zealand, 1840–1937: The Desired Haven*, Woodbridge: Boydell Press, 2005.

—— *Scottishness and Irishness in New Zealand since 1840*, Manchester: Manchester University Press, c.2011. NLA, 235 p.

McGill, David, *The lion and the wolfhound: the Irish rebellion on the New Zealand goldfields*, Wellington: Grantham House, 1990. NLI Ir 994 m 49, 178 p.

McGuire, Hugh, *A brief family account of Laurence and Anne, 1865–1990, first compiled by Elizabeth Coombes and Leonie Flower*, Auckland: 1999. NLI Ir 9292 m 85, 95 p. Rev. ed., Hugh McGuire.

McIlrath, James, *The McIlrath letters: sent from Killinchy, New Zealand to Killinchy, County Down, 1860–1915*, Belfast: Killyleagh Branch of the NIFHS, 2009. NLI, 143 p.

Moriarty, Brian, *A Moriarty story: a record of Irish folk who emigrated from Coom, County Kerry, Ireland, to New Zealand in the late 1870's*, Nelson: Moriarty Family Trust, 2003. NLNZ, 288 p.

O'Farrell, Patrick, *Through Irish eyes: Australian and New Zealand images of the Irish, 1788–1948*, Richmond, Vic.: Aurora Books, 1994. NLI Ir 942 o 43, 131 p.

—— *Vanished kingdoms: Irish in Australia and New Zealand: a personal excursion*, Kensington, NSW: New South Wales University Press, 1990. NLI Ir 942 o 34, 310 p.

Patterson, Brad, *The Irish in New Zealand: historical contexts and perspectives*, Wellington: Stout Research Centre, University of Wellington, 2002. NLNZ, 212 p.

—— *Ulster-New Zealand migration and cultural transfers.* Dublin: Four Courts Press, 2006. NLI, 286 p.

Patterson, Brad (ed.), *Ireland and the Irish Antipodes: one world or worlds apart?* See 'Australia'.

Phillips, Jock, *Settlers: New Zealand immigrants from England, Ireland and Scotland, 1800–1945*, Auckland: Auckland University Press, 2008. NLNZ, 221 p.

Reiher, Gwen, *Irish Interest Group, NZSG* [New Zealand Society of Genealogists] *newsletter supplement,* Irish Interest Group, 1998–2002. NLNZ.

—— *Suggestions for research in Ireland,* Auckland: Irish Interest Group, New Zealand Society of Genealogists, 1999. NLNZ, 28 p.

Rogers, Anna, *A lucky landing: the story of the Irish in New Zealand,* Auckland and London: Random House, 1996. NLI Ir 300 r 22, 246 p.

Rombouts, Michael, *A register of Irish settlers to Otago-Southland,* Dunedin: M.J. Rombouts, 2002. NLNZ, 518 p.

——*More Irish settlers to Otago-Southland,* Dunedin: Rombouts, 2004. NLNZ, 252 p.

Sharp, C.A., *The Dillon letters: the letters of the Hon. Constantine Dillon, 1842–1853,* Wellington: A.H. & A.W. Reed, 1954. NLI 2A 1205, 174 p.

Shaw, M. Noeline, *The history of the McKay family of Wyndham,* Waikanae: Heritage Press, 1986. NLI GO 110, 295 p.

Stewart, George Vesey, *Notes on the origin and prospects of the Stewart special settlement, Kati-Kati, New Zealand, and on New Zealand as a field for emigration,* Omagh: N. Carson, 1877. NLNZ, 128 p.

Went, A.E.J., 'William Spotswood Green', *Scientific proceedings of the Royal Dublin Society,* Ser. B, Vol. 2, No. 3, 1967, pp. 17–35, Dublin: Royal Dublin Society. NLI Ir 506 r 12.

Wily, Henry E.R.L., *Robert Maunsell: a New Zealand pioneer, his life and times,* Dunedin: A.H. & A.W. Reed, 1938. NLI Ir 92 m 191, 189 p. Co-author, Herbert Maunsell.

See also:

- 'List of New Zealand's Irish immigrants', online: <*www.geocities.ws/ nziconnection/immlist.htm*>.
- 'The Irish in New Zealand', online: <*www.teara.govt.nz*>.

EUROPE

General

O'Connor, Thomas, *The Irish in Europe, 1580–1815,* Dublin and Portland, Oreg.: Four Courts Press, 2001. NLI, 219 p.

Austria

Murphy, David, *The Irish Brigades, 1685–2006,* Dublin: Four Courts Press, 2007, 304 p. Irish soldiers in Austrian service, 1689–1918.

Walsh, V. Hussey, 'The Austrian branches of the family of Walsh,' *The Genealogist,* new series, 18 (1901), pp. 79–88.

France

General

'A Maguire family in France', *Clogher Record*, 5 (1a), pp. 222–6.

'An O'Brien family in France', *IG*, 8, No. 2, 1994, pp. 207–9.

Barnwell, Stephen B., 'Some Irish nuns in 18th century France', *IG*, 8, No. 2, 1994, p. 213.

Boyle, Patrick, *The Irish College in Paris from 1578 to 1901, with a brief account of the other Irish Colleges in France: viz., Bordeaux, Toulouse, Nantes, Poitiers, Douai, and Sille*, London: Art and Book Co., and New York: Benziger Bros., 1901. NLI Ir 28207 b 1, 236 p.

Forgues, E., *Histoire d'un sept irlandais: Les Macnamara*, Paris: Bureaux de la Revue Britannique, 1901. NLI Ir 9292 m 22, 54 p.

Griffin, G.T., *The Wild Geese: pen portraits of famous Irish exiles*, London: Jarrolds, 1938. NLI Ir 920041 g 5, 288 p.

Hayes, Richard, *Biographical Dictionary of Irishmen in France*, Dublin: M.H. Gill, 1949. NLI Ir 9440 h 16, 332 p.

—— *Ireland and Irishmen in the French Revolution*, Dublin: Phoenix Publishing Company, 1932. NLI Ir 94404 h 1, 314 p.

—— *Irish Swordsmen of France*, Dublin: M.H. Gill & Son, 1934. NLI Ir 94404 h 3, 307 p. Dillon, O'Moran, Lally, Kilmaine, Warren.

—— *Old Irish Links with France: some echoes of exiled Ireland*, Dublin. NLI Ir 944 h 11, 230 p.

Hennessy, Maurice, *The Wild Geese: the Irish soldier in exile*, London: Sidgwick & Jackson, 1973. NLI Ir 942 h 10, 227 p.

Holohan, Renagh, *The Irish Chateaux: in search of descendants of the Wild Geese*, Dublin: Lilliput Press, 1989. NLI Ir 942 h 21, 187 p. Co-author, Jeremy Williams.

Jones, Paul, *The Irish Brigade*, Washington: R.B. Luce, 1969. NLI Ir 942 j 3.

Lee, G.A., *Irish Chevaliers in the Service of France*. NLI Ir 340 l 3.

Murphy, David, *The Irish Brigades, 1685–2006*, Dublin: Four Courts Press, 2007, 304 p. The exiled Stuart army in France and Irish regiments in French service, 1685–1871.

McDonnel, Hector, *The Wild Geese of the Antrim McDonnells*, Blackrock, Co. Dublin: Irish Academic Press, 1996. NLI Ir 942 m 46.

McLaughlin, Mark G., *The Wild Geese: the Irish Brigades of France and Spain*, London: Osprey, 1980. NLI Ir 358 m 20, 40 p. Colour plates by Chris Warner.

O'Callaghan, J.C., *History of the Irish Brigades*, New York: P. O'Shea, 1874. NLI Ir 944 o 13, 649 p.

O'Connell, M.J., *The Last Colonel of the Irish Brigade: Count O'Connell, 1745–1833*, London: Trubner & Co., 1892 (2 vols.). NLI Ir 92027.

O'Connor, Thomas H., *An Irish theologian in Enlightenment France: Luke Joseph Hooke, 1714–96*, Blackrock, Co. Dublin: Four Courts Press, 1995. NLI Ir 92 h 171, 218 p.

Ó hAnnracháin, Eoghan, 'Irish veterans in the Invalides: the Tipperary contingent', *Tipperary Historical Journal (Irisleabhar Staire Thiobraid Árann)*, 1998–.

O'Reilly, Andrew, *Reminiscences of an emigrant Milesian: the Irish abroad and at home, in the camp, at the court: with souvenirs of 'the Brigade'*, London: R. Bentley, 1853. NLI Ir 94107 o 6, 358 p. Also New York: D. Appleton & Co., 1856.

Swords, Liam, *The Irish-French connection, 1578–1978*, Paris: Irish College, 1978. NLI Ir 942 i 6, 177 p.

Terry, James, *Pedigrees and Papers*. NLI Ir 9292 t 7. Part of the collection of pedigrees taken to France by Terry in the early eighteenth century.

Walsh, V. Hussey, 'The French branches of the family of Walsh', *The Genealogist*, new series, 17 (1900–1901), pp. 36–43, 90–99, 153–8.

Bordeaux

Clark de Dromentin, Patrick, *Les oies sauvages: mémoires d'une famille irlandaise réfugiée en France (Nantes, Martinique, Bordeaux, 1691–1914)*, Bordeaux: Presses Universitaires de Bordeaux, 1995. NLI Ir 942 c 37.

Hayes, Richard, *Les Irlandais en Aquitaine*, Bordeaux: Héritiers E.-F. Miailhe, 1971. NLI 3B 811, 61 p. Co-authors, Christopher Preston and Col. J. Weygand.

Walsh, T.J., *The Irish Continental College movement: the colleges at Bordeaux, Toulouse, and Lille*, Dublin: Golden Eagle Books, 1973. NLI Ir 271 w 8, 202 p.

Brittany

Dagier, Patricia, *Les réfugiés Irlandais au 17ème siècle en Finistère*, Quimper: Genealogie Cornouaille, 1999. NLI Ir 944 d 21, 357 p.

Brive

La colonie Irlandaise de Brive (Corrèze), 1662 et 1762–1792: d'après le fonds Pataki aux AD Lot (30J), Noisy-le-Grand, Paris: 1994. NLI 1B 793, 15 p.

Grenoble

Barnwell, Stephen B., 'Some Irish in Grenoble, France, 1694–1771', *IG*, 8, No. 2, 1994, pp. 210–12.

Lille

Walsh, T.J., *The Irish Continental College movement: the colleges at Bordeaux, Toulouse, and Lille*, Dublin: Golden Eagle Books, 1973. NLI Ir 271 w 8, 202 p.

Nantes

Clark de Dromentin. See 'Bordeaux'.

Mathorez, J., *Les irlandais nobles ou notables à Nantes aux XVIIe et XVIIIe siècles*. NLI Ir 941 p 20.

Toulouse

Walsh, T.J., *The Irish Continental College movement: the colleges at Bordeaux, Toulouse, and Lille*, Dublin: Golden Eagle Books, 1973. NLI Ir 271 w 8, 202 p.

Great Britain

General

Clancy, Mary, *The emigrant experience: papers presented at the Second Annual Mary Murray Weekend Seminar, Galway, 30 Mar.–1 Apr. 1990*, Galway: Galway Labour History Group, 1991. NLI Ir 942.i.26, 142 p.

Connolly, Tracey, 'Emigration from Ireland to Britain during the Second World War', in Bielenberg, *The Irish Diaspora*. See McCracken under 'Africa'.

Davis, Graham, *The Irish in Britain, 1815–1914*, Dublin: Gill & Macmillan, 1991.

—— 'The Irish in Britain, 1815–1939', in Bielenberg, *The Irish Diaspora*. See McCracken under 'Africa'.

MacRaild, Donald M., *Irish migrants in modern Britain, 1750–1922*, Basingstoke, Hants: Macmillan Press, 1999, 230 p. NLI Ir 942 m 62.

McRonald, Malcolm, *The Irish boats: Vol. 1, Liverpool to Dublin*, Stroud, Glos.: Tempus, 2005. NLI, 255 p.

—— *The Irish boats: Vol. 2, Liverpool to Cork and Waterford*, Stroud, Glos.: Tempus, 2006. NLI, 256 p.

——*The Irish boats: Vol. 3, Liverpool to Belfast*, Stroud, Glos.: Tempus, 2007, 256 p. NLI

Vaughan, W.E. (ed.), *A New History of Ireland, Vol. 5: Ireland under the Union*, Oxford.

Durham

Duffy, G., 'County Monaghan immigrants in the Consett area of County Durham, England, 1842–1855', *Clogher Record*, Vol. 16, No. 1, 1997, pp. 37–45.

Liverpool

Brady, L.W., *T.P. O'Connor and the Liverpool Irish*, London: Royal Historical Society, 1983. NLI Ir 92 o 340, 304 p.

Gallman, J. Matthew, *Receiving Erin's children: Philadelphia, Liverpool, and the Irish famine migration, 1845–1855*, Chapel Hill: University of North Carolina Press, c.2000. NLI A 3A 2106, 306 p.

Kelly, Michael, *Liverpool: the Irish connection: the story of some notable Irish people who helped create the great city of Liverpool*, Southport: the author, 2003. NLI 148 p.

McRonald, Malcolm. See 'Great Britain: General'.

Neal, Frank, *Sectarian violence: the Liverpool experience, 1819–1914: an aspect of Anglo-Irish history*, Manchester: Manchester University Press, 1988. NLI Ir 942 n 7, 272 p.

Scotland

Aspinwall, Bernard, 'A long journey: the Irish in Scotland', in Patrick O'Sullivan (ed.), *Religion and identity*, London: Leicester University Press, 1996. HP2.201.01540, p. 146–82 (Irish world wide series: History, heritage, identity, Vol. 5).

Devine, T.M., *Irish immigrants and Scottish society in the nineteenth and twentieth centuries: proceedings of the Scottish Historical Studies Seminar, University of Strathclyde, 1989–90*, Edinburgh: John Donald, c.1991. NLI Ir 942 i 34, 141 p.

Dickson, David, *Ireland and Scotland: Nation, Region, Identity*, Dublin: Centre for Irish-Scottish Studies, 2001. NLI 113 pp. Co-editors Seán Duffy, Cathal Ó hÁinle and Ian Campbell Ross.

Gallagher, Tom, *Glasgow: the uneasy peace: religious tension in modern Scotland, 1819–1914*, Manchester: Manchester University Press, c.1987. NLI G 305 g 2, 383 p.

McCready, Richard B., 'Revising the Irish in Scotland: the Irish in nineteenth- and early twentieth-century Scotland', in Bielenberg, *The Irish Diaspora*. See McCracken under 'Africa'.

McFarland, E.W., *Ireland and Scotland in the age of revolution: planting the green bough*, Edinburgh: Edinburgh University Press, c.1994. NLI Ir 94107 m 24, 272 p.

—— *Protestants first: Orangeism in nineteenth century Scotland*, Edinburgh: Edinburgh University Press, c.1990. NLI 941508 m 15, 255 p.

Mitchell, Martin J., *The Irish in the west of Scotland, 1797–1848: trade unions, strikes and political movements*, Edinburgh: John Donald, 1998. NLI Ir 942 m 57, 286 p.

Sloan, William, 'Employment opportunities and migrant group assimilation: Highlanders and Irish in Glasgow, 1840–1860', in A.J.G Cummings (ed.), *Industry, business and society in Scotland since 1700*, Edinburgh: c.1994, pp. 197–217. Co-editor, T.M. Devine.

Tyneside

Barrington, Mary A., *The Irish independence movement on Tyneside, 1919–1921*, Dún Laoghaire: Dún Laoghaire Genealogical Society, 1999. NLI, 40 p.

York

Clancy, Mary, *The emigrant experience: papers presented at the Second Annual Mary Murray Weekend Seminar, Galway, 30 Mar.–1 Apr. 1990*, Galway: Galway Labour History Group, 1991. NLI Ir 942.i.26, 142 p.

Portugal

Notas e documentos genealogicos a'cerca de familia O'Neill, Lisbon: Imprensa Minerva, 1893. NLI GO 480, 22 p. The O'Neills in Portugal.

Spain

General

Fannin, Samuel, 'Carew, Langton and Power: an Irish trading company in 18th century Spain', *IG*, 11, 1, 2002, pp. 53–9.

Henry, Gráinne, *The Irish Military Community in Spanish Flanders, 1586–1621*, Dublin: Irish Academic Press, 1992. NLI Ir 942 h 23.

McDonnel, Hector, *The Wild Geese of the Antrim McDonnells*, Blackrock, Co. Dublin: Irish Academic Press, 1996. NLI Ir 942 m 46.

McLaughlin, Mark G., *The Wild Geese: the Irish Brigades of France and Spain*, London: Osprey, 1980. NLI Ir 358 m 20, 40 p. Colour plates by Chris Warner.

MacSwiney de Mashanaglass, Patrice, Marquis, *Notes on the early services of 'Irlanda el famoso': with reference to a recent paper on the Irish regiments in the service of Spain*, Dublin: 1930. NLI Ir 94107 m 4, 12 p.

Murphy, David, *The Irish Brigades, 1685–2006*, Dublin: Four Courts Press, 2007, 304 p. Irish regiments in Spanish service, 1709–1939.

O'Ryan, W.D., 'The family of O'Mulryan in Spain', *IG*, 3, 1961, pp. 195–7.

—— 'O'Ryan of Mallorca', *IG*, 3, 1962, pp. 266–9.

Santiago, Mark, *The Red Captain: the life of Hugo O'Conor, commandant inspector of the interior provinces of New Spain*, Tucson, Ariz.: Arizona Historical Society, 1994. NLI, 127 p.

Schüller, Karin, *Die Beziehungen zwischen Spanien und Irland im 16. und 17. Jahrhundert: Diplomatie, Handel und die Soziale Integration Katholischer Exulanten*, Münster: Aschendorff, 1999. NLI Ir 946 s 43, 280 p.

Stradling, R.A., *The Spanish Monarchy and Irish Mercenaries: the Wild Geese in Spain, 1618–68*, Dublin: Irish Academic Press, 1994. NLI Ir 94106 s 13.

Terry, Kevin 'The Ryan and Terry families in Spain', *IG*, 10, 2, 1999, pp. 245–9.

—— 'Some Spanish Terrys of Irish origin', *IG*, 10, 1, 2000, pp. 372–3.

Walsh, Micheline, *An Exile of Ireland: Hugh O'Neill*, Dublin: Four Courts Press, 1996. NLI Ir 92 o 491, 154 p.

—— *Spanish knights of Irish origin: documents from Continental archives*, Dublin: IMC, 1960. NLI Ir 946 w 3.

Bilbao

Bilbao Acedos, Amaia, *The Irish Community in the Basque Country, c.1700–1800*, Dublin: Geography Publications, 2003. NLI 114 p.

INDIA

Foley, Tadhg (ed.), *Ireland and India: colonies, culture and empire*, Dublin: Irish Academic Press, 2007, 306 p. Co-editor, Maureen O'Connor.

Hewson, Eileen, *A handbook for Irish war graves in India, Burma and beyond: 1914–45*, Wem, Sussex: Kabristan Archives, 2005. NLI, 92 p.

—— *The Forgotten Irish: Memorials of the Raj*, Wem, Sussex: Kabristan Archives, 2004. NLI, 320 p. 'A detailed account of the Irish and their memorials in India, Ireland and the Far East during the 18th and 19th centuries.'

Holmes, Michael, 'The Irish and India: imperialism, nationalism and internationalism', in Bielenberg, *The Irish Diaspora*. See McCracken under 'Africa'.

Silvestri, Michael, *Ireland and India: nationalism, empire and memory*, Basingstoke, Hants: Palgrave Macmillan, 2009. NLI, 298 p.

NORTH AMERICA

General

Adams, William Forbes, *Ireland and Irish Immigration to the New World: From 1815 to the Famine*, Baltimore, Md.: GPC, 1980. NLI, Ir 3252 a 6.

Akenson, D.H., *Being had: historians, evidence, and the Irish in North America*, Port Credit, Ont.: P.D. Meany, 1985. NLI Ir 973 a 10, 243 p.

—— 'Irish migration to North America, 1800–1920', in Bielenberg, *The Irish Diaspora*. See McCracken under 'Africa'.

Blake, J.W. (ed.), *The Ulster-American Connection*, Coleraine: New University of Ulster. NLI Ir 942 u 3.

Bolton, C.K, *Scotch Irish pioneers in Ulster and America*, Baltimore, Md.: GPC, 1986. NLI Ir 973 b 14, 398 p.

Bradley, A.K., *History of the Irish in America*, Chartwell, 1986. NLI Ir 942 b 19.

Concannon, John Joseph, and Cull, Frank, *Irish-American Who's Who*, New York: Irish-American's Who's Who, 1984. NLI Ir 942 i 13, 981 p.

Dickson, R.J., *Ulster Emigration to Colonial America, 1718–75*, Belfast: UHF, 1988. NLI Ir 9411 d 22, 320 p.

Dobson, David, *Irish emigrants in North America*, Baltimore, Md.: reprinted for Clearfield Co. by GPC, 1997–2000. LC. Originally published in five volumes, St Andrews, Fife: 1994–9.

—— 'Scottish Emigration to Colonial America: An Overview', *Familia: Ulster Genealogical Review*, No. 18, 2002.

—— *Ships from Ireland to early America, 1623–1850*, Baltimore, Md.: GPC, c.1999. LC, 153 p.

Doyle, David Noel, and Dudley Edwards, Owen (eds.), *America and Ireland, 1776–1976*, Westport, Conn.: Greenwood Press, 1980. NLI Ir 973 a 5. The proceedings of the United States Bicentennial Conference of Cumann Merriman, Ennis, August 1976.

Drudy, P.J., *The Irish in America: emigration, assimilation, and impact*, Cambridge and New York: Cambridge University Press, 1985. NLI Ir 942 i 9, 359 p.

Glasgow, M., *Scotch-Irish in Northern Ireland and the American Colonies*, New York: 1936. NLI Ir 973 g 16.

Glazier, Michael, *The encyclopedia of the Irish in America*, Notre Dame, Ind.: University of Notre Dame Press, 1999. NLI RR 970 e 11, 988 p.

Green, E.R.R., *Essays in Scotch-Irish History*, Belfast: UHF, 1992. NLI Ir 942 p 14(2), 110 p.

Griffin, William D., *The Irish in America, 1550–1972: a chronology and fact book*, Dobbs Ferry, NY: Oceana Publications, 1973. NLI Ir 942 g 5, 154 p.

Harris, Ruth-Ann, *The Search for Missing Friends: Vols. 1–4, 1831–1860*, Boston, Mass.: New England Historic Genealogical Society, 1989–93. NLI Ir 942 s 22. Irish immigrant advertisements placed in the *Pilot* (Boston). Co-editors, D.M. Jacobs and B.E. O'Keeffe. Online at <*infowanted.bc.edu*>.

Hotten, J.C., *Original Lists of Persons of Quality emigrating to America, 1600–1700*, London: 1874. NLI. 'Emigrants; religious exiles; political rebels; serving men sold for a term of years; apprentices; children stolen; maidens pressed; and others who went from Great Britain to the American plantations, 1600–1700; with their ages, the localities where they formerly lived in the mother country, the names of the ships in which they embarked, and other interesting particulars, from mss. preserved in the state paper department of Her Majesty's public record office.' Reprint, GPC, 1968 and 2003.

King, Joseph A., *The uncounted Irish in Canada and the United States*, Toronto: P.D. Meany, c.1990. NLI GR 192. Co-author, Margaret E. Fitzgerald.

Knowles, Charles, *The Petition to Governor Shute in 1718: Scotch-Irish Pioneers in Ulster and America*. NLI.

Laxton, Edward, *The famine ships: the Irish exodus to America, 1846–51*, London: Bloomsbury, 1997. NLI Ir 94108 L 22, 250 p.

Linehan, John C., *Irish Schoolmasters in the American Colonies, 1640–1775*, Washington: American-Irish Historical Society, 1898. NLI Ir 942 r 9, 31 p. (With a continuation of the subject during and after the War of the Revolution.)

Lockhart, Audrey, *Some aspects of emigration from Ireland to the North American colonies between 1660 and 1775*, New York: Arno Press, 1976. NLI Ir 973 l 5, 243 p.

Maguire, John, *The Irish in America*, London: Longmans, Green & Co., 1868. NLI Ir 973 m 3, 653 p.

Marshall, W.F., *Ulster Sails West*, Baltimore, Md.: GPC, 1996. NLI Ir 973 m 59.

McDonnell, Frances, *Emigrants from Ireland to America, 1735–1743*, Baltimore, Md.: GPC, 1992. NLI Ir 94107 e 10, 134 p. A transcription of the report of the Irish House of Commons into enforced emigration to America.

McGee, Thomas D'Arcy, *A history of the Irish settlers in North America: from the earliest period to the census of 1850*, New York: 1852. NLI Ir 970 m 1. Reprint, Baltimore, Md.: GPC, 2003.

Metress, Seamus P., *The Irish-American experience: a guide to the literature*, Washington: University Press of America, c.1981. NLI Ir 942 m 21, 220 p.

—— *The Irish in North America: a regional bibliography*, Toronto: P.D. Meany Publishers, c.1999. NLI GR 2602, 227 p. Co-author, Donna M. Hardy-Johnston.

Miller, K.A., *Exiles and Emigrants*, Oxford: 1985. NLI Ir 942 m 26.

—— *Ireland and Irish America: culture, class, and transatlantic migration*, Dublin: Field Day, 2008. NLI, 411 p.

—— *Irish immigrants in the land of Canaan: letters and memoirs from colonial and revolutionary America, 1675–1815*, Oxford and New York: Oxford University Press, 2003, 788 p.

—— *Out of Ireland: the story of Irish emigration to America*, Washington: Elliott & Clark Publishing, c.1994. LC, 132 p. Co-author, Paul Wagner.

—— '"Scotch-Irish", "Black Irish" and "Real Irish": emigrants and identities in the old South', in Bielenberg, *The Irish Diaspora*. See McCracken under 'Africa'.

—— '"Scotch-Irish" myths and "Irish" identities in eighteenth- and nineteenth-century America', in Fanning, *New perspectives . . .* See USA, 'General'.

Mitchell, Brian, *Irish Emigration Lists, 1833–39*, Baltimore, Md.: GPC, 1989. Cos. Antrim and Derry.

Mulrooney, Margaret M., *Fleeing the Famine: North America and Irish refugees, 1845–1851*, Westport, Conn.: Praeger, 2003. NLC, 154 p.

O'Brien, M.J., *Irish Settlers in America: A consolidation of articles from the Journal of the American-Irish Society*, Baltimore, Md.: GPC, 1979. NLI Ir 942 O 23.

Quinn, David B., *Ireland and America their early associations, 1500–1640*, Liverpool: Liverpool University Press, 1991. NLI Ir 942 p 14(1), 57 p.

Schrier, Arnold, *Ireland and the American emigration, 1850–1900*, Chester Springs, Pa.: Dufour, 1997. NLI Ir 94108 s 31, 210 p.

Shannon, W.V., *The American Irish*, New York: Macmillan, 1963. NLI Ir 973 s 3, 458 p.

Shaw, James, *The Scotch-Irish in History*, Springfield: 1899. NLI Ir 942 s 13.

'Sources for the identification of emigrants from Ireland to North America in the 19th century', *Ulster Historical and Genealogical Guild Newsletter*, 1979, Vol. 1, Nos. 2 and 3, Belfast: UHF. NLI, Ir 9292 u 3.

Weaver, Jack W., *Migrants from Great Britain and Ireland: a guide to archival and manuscript sources in North America compiled*, Westport, Conn.: Greenwood Press, 1986. NLI Ir 016 w 2, 129 p. Co-editor, DeeGee Lester.

Wokeck, Marianne S., *Trade in strangers: the beginnings of mass migration to North America*, University Park, Pa.: Pennsylvania State University Press, 1999. NLI Ir 324 w 6, 319 p.

Passenger lists

Adams, Raymond D., *An Alphabetical Index to Ulster Emigrants to Philadelphia, 1803–1850*, Baltimore, Md.: GPC, 1992. Family Archive CD 7257. From PRONI records.

Begley, D.F., *Handbook on Irish Genealogy*, Dublin: Heraldic Artists, 1984 (6th ed.), pp. 101–110, p. 115 (1803/4).

Coldham, Peter Wilson, *The Complete Book of Emigrants in Bondage, 1614–1775*, Baltimore, Md.: GPC, 1988 (and supplements). NLI Ir 973 c 47, 600 p.

Glazier, Ira A. (ed.), *The Famine immigrants: lists of Irish immigrants arriving at the port of New York, 1846–1851*, Baltimore, Md.: GPC, 7 vols. NLI Ir 942 g 12. Associate editor, Michael Tepper.

Hackett, J. Dominick, and Early, Charles M., *Passenger Lists from Ireland*, Baltimore, Md.: GPC, 1998 (1811, 1815–16, from *Journal of the American Irish Historical Society*, Vols. 28 and 29).

Lancour, Harold, *A bibliography of ship passenger lists, 1538–1825: being a guide to published lists of early immigrants to North America*, New York: New York Public Library, 1963, 3rd ed., rev. Richard J. Wolfe. NLI G 387 L 14, 137 p.

Form 500 B
Department of Commerce and Labor
IMMIGRATION SERVICE

SALOON, CABIN, AND STEERAGE ALIENS MUST BE COMPLETELY MANIFESTED.

LIST OR MANIFEST OF ALIEN PASSENGERS FOR THE UNITED

Required by the regulations of the Secretary of Commerce and Labor of the United States, under Act of Congress approved February 20, 1907, to be delivered

S. S. _Caronia_ sailing from _Queenstown_, _Sept October 6th, 1912._

No. on List.	NAME IN FULL.		Age.		Sex.	Married or Single.	Calling or Occupation.	Able to—		Nationality. (Country of which citizen or subject.)	Race or People.	*Last Permanent Residence.		The name and complete address of nearest relative or friend in country whence alien came.	Final Destination. *(Intended future permanent residence.)	
	Family Name.	Given Name.	Yrs.	Mos.				Read.	Write.			Country.	City or Town.		State.	City or Town.
X	Winter	Bridget	18		F	S	dom.	yes	yes	British	Irish	Ireland	Tullamore	Father John Winter, Tullamore, Co. Galway	U.S.	Buffalo
2	Manning	Catherine	22				"	"	"	"	"	"	"	Father C. Manning, Clonan	"	"
3	"	Nellie	21				"	"	"	"	"	"	"	Clonan Gardy	"	"
4	Sullivan	Johanna	20				"	"	"	Ireland	Dingle	Mother, Mary Sullivan, Ballyeagh, Dingle, Co. Kerry	"	"
5	Hannifin	Mary	20		F	S	S.s. maid	"	"	"	"	St. Louis	Father John B. Hannifin	St. L. St Louis

Filby, P. William, and Meyer, Mary K. (eds.), *Passenger and immigration lists bibliography, 1538–1900: being a guide to published lists of arrivals in the United States and Canada* (3 vols.), Gale, Detroit: 1981. NLI RR, 387 p. Revision of Lancour, below.

McDonnell, Frances, *Emigrants from Ireland to America, 1735–1743*, Baltimore. Md.: GPC, 1992. Family Archive CD 7257. Records the names of almost two thousand convict transportees.

Maher, James P., *Returning Home: Transatlantic Migration from North America to Britain and Ireland, 1858–1870*, Dublin: Eneclann (ENEC010), 2005. British and Irish incoming passenger lists.

Mitchell, Brian, *Irish Emigration Lists, 1833–1839*, Baltimore, Md.: GPC, 1989. Family Archive CD 7257. From Co. Antrim and Co. Derry OS letters.

—— *Irish Passenger Lists, 1803–1806*, Baltimore, Md.: GPC, 1995. Family Archive CD 7257. Departure lists: Dublin, Belfast, Newry and Londonderry.

—— *Irish Passenger Lists, 1847–1871*, Baltimore, Md.: GPC, 1989. Family Archive CD 7257. Londonderry, Cooke & McCorkell Shipping.

Schlegel, Donald M., *Passengers from Ireland: lists of passengers arriving at American ports between 1811 and 1817*, Baltimore, Md.: GPC, 1980. Family Archive CD 7257 (transcribed from the Shamrock or Hibernian chronicle).

Tepper, Michael, *New England Passengers to America*, Baltimore, Md.: GPC, 1986. NLI 387 p 6, 554 p.

Tepper, Michael, *Passenger arrivals at the Port of Philadelphia, 1800–1819: the Philadelphia baggage lists*, Baltimore, Md.: GPC, 1986. NLI Ir 970 p 12, 913 p.

United States, Department of State, *Passengers Arriving in the U.S., 1821–1823*, Baltimore, Md.: Magna Carta Book Co., 1969. NLI G 3251 u 1, 427 p.

See also:
- The Immigrant Ships Transcribers' Guild: <*www.immigrantships.net*>
- The Irish Passenger Lists Research Guide: <*www.genealogybranches.com/irishpassengerlists*>
- Ellis Island: <*www.ellisisland.org*>
  Also 'Migration records' in Chapter 5: The Internet

Canada

General

Cowan, Helen I., *British emigration to British North America, 1773–1837*, Toronto: University of Toronto Library, 1928. NLC, 275 p.

Davin, N.F., *The Irishman in Canada*, Shannon. NLI Ir 971 d 1.

Elliott, B.S., *Irish Migrants in the Canadas: A New Approach*, Montréal and Kingston, Ont.: McGill-Queen's University Press, 2002. NLI Ir 942 e 7, 408 p. Irish Protestants from North Tipperary especially.

Fromers, V., 'Irish Emigrants to Canada in Sussex Archives, 1839–47,' *IA*, pp. 31–42.

Houston, Cecil J., *Irish Emigration and Canadian Settlement: Patterns, Links and Letters,* Toronto: University of Toronto Press, and Belfast: UHF, 1990. NLI Ir 942 h 20, 370 p. Co-author, William J. Smyth.

Leeson, F., *Irish Emigrants to Canada, 1839–47.* From the Wyndham estates in Cos. Clare (especially), Limerick and Tipperary.

MacKay, Donald, *Flight from famine: the coming of the Irish to Canada,* Toronto and London: McClelland & Stewart, 1992. NLI Ir 942 m 45, 368 p.

Mannion, John J., *Irish settlements in eastern Canada: a study of cultural transfer and adaptation,* Toronto: University of Toronto Press, c.1974. NLI Ir 971 m 11, 219 p.

O'Driscoll, R., and Reynolds, L. (eds.), *The Untold Story: the Irish in Canada* (2 vols.), Toronto: Celtic Arts of Canada, 1988. NLI Ir 971 o 67.

Typed transcripts of Canadian newspaper notices querying the whereabouts of emigrants, 1984, PRONI, D/3000/82. Mainly the *New Brunswick Courier* (1830–46) and the *Toronto Irish-Canadian* (1859).

Wilson, David A., *The Orange Order in Canada,* Dublin: Four Courts Press, 2007. NLI, 213 p.

New Brunswick

Cook, Jane L., 'Scots and Irish in the lower St John River Valley, 1815–1851', in *Coalescence of styles: the ethnic heritage of St John River Valley regional furniture, 1763–1851,* pp. 112–50, Montréal: McGill-Queen's Studies in Ethnic History, 2000. NLS.

Cushing, J.E., *Irish Immigration to St John, New Brunswick, 1847,* St John, NB: New Brunswick Museum, 1979. NLI Ir 942 c 16.

Daley, Caroline, *Middle Island: before and after the tragedy,* Miramichi, NB: Middle Island Irish Historical Park, 2002. NLI. Co-author Anna Springer.

Dallison, Robert L., *Turning back the Fenians: New Brunswick's last colonial campaign,* Fredericton, NB: Goose Lane Editions, 2006. NLI, 132 p.

Jack, D.R., *Centennial Prize Essay on the History of the City and County of St. John,* St John, NB: J. & A. McMillan, 1883.

Johnson, Daniel F., *Irish emigration to New England through the port of Saint John, New Brunswick, Canada, 1841 to 1849,* Baltimore, Md.: Clearfield, 1997. NLI Ir 274 j 4, 284 p.

King, Joseph A., *Ireland to North America: emigrants from West Cork,* Lafayette, Calif.: K&K Publications, and Toronto: P.D. Meany, 1994. NLI Ir 942 k 7, 124 p. Schull to Miramichi River Region, NB.

—— Joseph A., *The uncounted . . .* See North America, 'General'.

McDevitt, Mary Kilfoil, *We Hardly Knew Ye: St. Mary's Cemetery: An Enduring Presence,* St John, NB: Irish Canadian Cultural Association, 1990. NLI Ir 942 p 16(4), 140 p.

McGahan, Elizabeth, 'The Port in the City: Saint John, NB (1867–1911), and the Process of Integration,' PhD thesis, University of New Brunswick.

Murphy, David, *The Irish Brigades, 1685–2006,* Dublin: Four Courts Press, 2007, 304 p. Irish regiments in North and South America.

Murphy, Peter, *Poor, ignorant children: Irish famine orphans in Saint John, New Brunswick*, Halifax, NS: D'Arcy McGee Chair of Irish Studies, Saint Mary's University, 1999. NLI Ir 942 m 63, 83 p.

—— *Together in Exile*, 1991. Carlingford emigrants to St John, New Brunswick.

Power, Thomas P., *The Irish in Atlantic Canada, 1780–1900*, Fredericton, NB: New Ireland Press, 1979. NLI Ir 942 p 15, 210 p.

Punch, T.M., *Erin's Sons: Irish arrivals in Atlantic Canada, 1761–1853*, Baltimore, Md.: GPC, 2007.

—— *Erin's Sons: Irish arrivals in Atlantic Canada, 1761–1853, Vol. 2*, Baltimore, Md.: GPC, 2009, 190 p.

Rees, J., *Surplus people: the Fitzwilliam clearances, 1847–1856*, Cork: Collins Press, 2000. NLI, 156 p.

Rees, Ronald, *Some other place—than here: St Andrews and the Irish emigrant*, Fredericton, NB: New Ireland Press, c.2000. NLI 3B 919, 81 p.

Rogers, Ralph W., Jr, *The Rogers family of Northampton Parish, New Brunswick, and some descendants*, Homosassa, Fla.: R.W. Rogers, 1989. LC, 65 p.

See, Scott W., *Riots in New Brunswick: Orange nativism and social violence in the 1840s*, Toronto: University of Toronto Press, 1993. NLI Ir 942 s 28, 266 p.

Toner, P.M., *An index to Irish immigrants in the New Brunswick census of 1851*, Fredericton, NB: Provincial Archives of New Brunswick, c.1991. NLI Ir 942 t 2, 378 p.

——*New Ireland Remembered: historical essays on the Irish in New Brunswick*, 1988.

—— *The green fields of Canada: Irish immigration and New Brunswick settlement, 1815–1850*, Fredericton, NB: Provincial Archives of New Brunswick, c.1991. NLI.

Newfoundland

Clancy, Mary, *The emigrant experience*. See Great Britain, 'General'.

'County Wexford priests in Newfoundland', *JWHS*, No. 10, 1984/5, pp. 55–68.

Greene, John Carrick, *Of fish and family: family trees and family histories of Tilting, set against the background of historical developments in the Newfoundland fisheries, 1700–1940*, St John's, Nfld: Triumphant Explorations, 2002. NLC, 731 p.

McCarthy, Michael, *The Irish in Newfoundland, 1600–1900: their trials, tribulations and triumphs*, St John's, Nfld: Creative, 1999. NLI GR 515, 216 p.

Mannion, John J., 'Kilkennymen in Newfoundland', *Old Kilkenny Review*, 1987, 358 p.

Punch, T.M.: See 'New Brunswick'.

Nova Scotia

Blois, Ralph S., *The Joshua Smith family of Ireland and Hants County, NS*, Woodburn, Oreg.: R.S. Blois, 1994. LC, 224 p.

MacKenzie, A.A., *The Irish in Cape Breton*, Antigonish, NS: Formac Pub. Co., 1988. NLI Ir 942 m 20, 129 p.

Punch, T.M., *Irish Halifax: the immigrant generation, 1815–1859*, Halifax, NS: International Education Centre, St Mary's University, 1981. NLI Ir 942 p 11, 86 p.

—— *Some Sons of Erin in Nova Scotia*, Halifax, NS: Petheric Press, 1980. NLI Ir 971 p 10, 127 p.

Punch, T.M.: See also 'New Brunswick'.

Smith, Col. Leonard H., Jr, *Nova Scotia Immigrants to 1867*, Baltimore, Md.: GPC, 1992. NLI GAS, 542 p.

—— *Nova Scotia Immigrants to 1867, Vol. 2, from non-Nova Scotia Periodicals and from Published Diaries and Journals*, Baltimore, Md.: GPC, 1994. NLI GAS, 291 p. Co-author, Norma H. Smith.

Stewart, H.L., *The Irish in Nova Scotia: annals of the Charitable Irish Society of Halifax (1736–1836)*, Kentville, NS: Kentville Pub. Co. 1949. NLI Ir 971 s 2, 199 p.

Ontario

Akenson, D.H., *The Irish in Ontario: a study in rural history*, Kingston, Ont.: McGill, 1985. NLI Ir 971 a 8, 404 p.

Elliott, B.S. *The McCabe list: early Irish in the Ottawa Valley*, Toronto: Ontario Genealogical Society, 2002. NLI, 82 p.

Heald, Carolyn A., *The Irish Palatines in Ontario: Religion, Ethnicity and Rural Migration*, Garanoque, Ont.: Langdale Press.

McCuaig, Carol Bennett, *Leinster to Lanark*, Renfrew, Ont.: Juniper Books, 2010. NLC, 284 p. Post-1798 migrants from Cos. Carlow, Kilkenny, Wexford and Wicklow to Lanark County, Ottawa.

—— *The Kerry chain: the Limerick link*, Renfrew, Ont.: Juniper Books, c.2003. NLI, 178 p.

McGowan, Mark, *Death or Canada: The Irish Famine Migration to Toronto, 1847*, Toronto: Novalis, 2009. NLA.

Trew, Johanne Devlin, *Place, culture and community: the Irish heritage of the Ottawa Valley*, Newcastle: Cambridge Scholars, 2009. NLI, 336 p.

Prince Edward Island

O'Grady, Brendan, *Exiles and Islanders: The Irish Settlers of Prince Edward Island*, Montréal: McGill-Queen's Studies in Ethnic History, 2004. NLI, 313 p.

Punch, T.M.: See 'New Brunswick'.

Québec

Dagneau, G.-H., *Révélations sur les trois frères O'Leary de Québec*, Société Historique de Québec, 1998. NLC, 117 p.

Grace, Robert J., *The Irish in Quebec: an introduction to the historiography*, Québec: Institut Québécois de Recherche sur la Culture, 1993. NLC, 265 p. Followed by *An annotated bibliography on the Irish in Quebec* (Fernand Harvey).

Guerin, T., *The Gael in New France*, Montréal: 1946. NLI Ir 971 g 4, 134 p.

O'Farrell, John, *Irish Families in Ancient Quebec Records*, Montréal: 1908.

O'Gallagher, Marianna, *St Patrick's and St Brigid's, Québec*, Québec: Carraig Books, 1981. NLI Ir 942 o 29, 124 p.

———— *The shamrock trail: tracing the Irish in Quebec City*, Sainte-Foy, Que.: Livres Carraig Books, 1998. NLC, 35 p.

Redmond, P.M., *Irish Life in Rural Quebec*, Duquesne, 1983. NLI Ir 942 r 6.

Rees, J., *Surplus people*. See 'New Brunswick'.

Sheehy, Réjeanne, *L'alliance Irlandaise Sheehy au Québec*, Chicoutimi, Que.: Éditions Entreprises, c.2000. LC, 118 p.

Thibault, Michel, *Catalog of Catholic immigrants from the British Isles before 1825*, Montréal: Société de Recherche Historique Archiv-Histo, 1988, NAI GAS. Co-author, Norman Robert. Extracted from Québec Roman Catholic marriages, 1731–1825.

Timbers, Wayne, 'Britannique et Irlandaise: l'identité ethnique et démographique des Irlandais protestants et la formation d'une communauté à Montréal, 1834–1860,' MA thesis, McGill University, c.2001. NLC, 107 leaves.

Trew, Johanne Devlin: see 'Ontario'.

Trigger, Rosalyn, 'The role of the parish in fostering Irish-Catholic identity in nineteenth-century Montreal,' MA thesis, McGill University, c.1997. NLC.

Saskatchewan

Coughlin, Jack, *The Irish colony of Saskatchewan*, Scarborough, Ont.: Lochleven Publishers, c.1995. NLC, 108 p.

Mexico

Davis, Graham, *Land!: Irish pioneers in Mexican and revolutionary Texas*, College Station, Tex.: A&M University Press, 2002. NLI 3A 2048, 304 p.

Hogan, Michael, *Los soldados Irlandeses de México*, Guadalajara: Fondo Editorial Universitario, 1999. NLI GR 175, 268 p.

Murphy, David, *The Irish Brigades, 1685–2006*, Dublin: Four Courts Press, 2007. 304 p. Irish regiments in North and South America.

Santiago, Mark, *The Red Captain: the life of Hugo O'Conor, commandant inspector of the interior provinces of New Spain*, Tucson, Ariz.: Arizona Historical Society, 1994. NLI, 127 p.

USA

General

Akenson, D.H., *The United States and Ireland*, Cambridge, Mass.: Harvard University Press, 1973. NLI Ir 941 a 15.

Beller, Susan Provost, *Never were men so brave: the Irish Brigade during the Civil War*, New York: Margaret K. McElderry Books, 1998. NLI Ir 9737 b 25, 98 p.

Blessing, Patrick J., *The Irish in America: a guide to the literature and the manuscript collections*, Washington: Catholic University of America Press, 1992. NLI Ir 016 b 9, 347 p.

Bradley, A.K., *History of the Irish in America*, Chartwell, 1986. NLI Ir 942 b 19.

Bric, Maurice J., 'Patterns of Irish emigration to America, 1783–1800', *Éire-Ireland: A Journal of Irish Studies*, 36, pp. 1–2, 2001.

Byron, Reginald, *Irish America*, Oxford and New York: Oxford University Press, 1999. NLI Ir 973 b 30, 317 p.

Cobb, Irvin, *The lost tribes of the Irish in the South*, New York: 1917. LC, 5 p.

D'Arcy, William, *The Fenian movement in the United States, 1858–1886*, Washington: Catholic University of America Press, 1947. NLI Ir 94108 d 15, 453 p.

Dezell, Maureen, *Irish America: coming into clover: the evolution of a people and a culture*, New York: Doubleday, 2000. LC, 259 p.

Diner, Hasia R., *Erin's daughters in America: Irish immigrant women in the nineteenth century*, Baltimore, Md.: Johns Hopkins University Press, c.1983. NLI Ir 942 d 14, 192 p.

Doerries, Reinhard R., *Iren und Deutsche in der Neuen Welt: Akkulturationsprozesse in der Amerikanischen Gesellschaft im Späten Neunzehnten Jahrhundert*, Stuttgart: F. Steiner, 1986. NLI 3A 117, 363 p.

Donohoe, H., *The Irish Catholic Benevolent Union.* NLI Ir 973 d 6.

Doyle, D., *Ireland, Irishmen, and Revolutionary America*, Dublin: Mercier Press, 1981. NLI Ir 942 d 12, 257 p.

Drudy, P.J., *The Irish in America: emigration, assimilation, and impact*, Cambridge and New York: Cambridge University Press, 1985. NLI Ir 942 i 9, 359 p.

Duff, John B., *The Irish in the United States*, Belmont, Calif.: Wadsworth Pub. Co., 1971. LC.

Dunne, Robert, *Antebellum Irish immigration and emerging ideologies of 'America': a Protestant backlash*, Lewiston, NY: Edwin Mellen Press, c.2002. LC, 148 p.

Durney, James, *The Mob: The history of Irish gangsters in America*, Naas, Co. Kildare: Leinster Leader. NLI Ir 330 D 32, 208 p.

'Early Irish emigrants to America, 1803, 1806,' *Recorder*, 1926, New York: American Irish Historical Society, 1901. NLI Ir 973 r 1.

Fanning, Charles (ed.), *New perspectives on the Irish diaspora*, Carbondale, Ill.: Southern Illinois University Press, c.2000. NLI, 329 p.

Fallows, Marjorie R., *Irish Americans: identity and assimilations*, Englewood Cliffs, NJ: Prentice-Hall, 1979. NLI Ir 942 f 2, 158 p.

Femminella, Francis X., *Italians and Irish in America: proceedings of the Sixteenth Annual Conference of the American Italian Historical Association*, New York: American Italian Historical Association, 1985. NLI Ir 973 f 7, 308 p.

Ferrie, Joseph P., *Yankeys now: immigrants in the antebellum United States, 1840–1860*, New York: Oxford University Press, 1999. NLI, 233 p.

Foy, R.H., *Dear Uncle: immigrant letters to Antrim from the USA: the Kerr letters . . .* Antrim: Antrim and District Historical Society, 1991. NLI Ir 842 f 9, 117 p.

Funchion, M.F., *Irish American voluntary organizations*, Westport, Conn.: Greenwood Press, 1983, NAI, Ir 942 i 10, 323 p.

Gleeson, Ed, *Erin go gray!: an Irish rebel trilogy*, Carmel, Ind.: Guild Press of Indiana, 1997. NLI GR 1476, 148 p.

Golway, Terry, *The Irish in America*, New York: Hyperion, c.1997. LC, 272 p.

Goodwin, Donn, *Look Back upon Erin*, Milwaukee: Woodland Books, c.1980. LC, 171 p.

Greeley, Andrew M., *The Irish Americans: the rise to money and power*, New York: Harper & Row, c.1981. NLI Ir 942 g 11, 215 p.

Gribben, Arthur, *The Great Famine and the Irish diaspora in America*, Amherst, Mass.: University of Massachusetts Press, 1999. NLI Ir 970 g 30, 268 p.

Griffin, William D., *A Portrait of the Irish in America*, Dublin: Academy Press, 1981. NLI 2B 785, 260 p.

Hartigan, J., *The Irish in the American Revolution*, Washington: 1908. NLI Ir 973 h 8.

Hayden, Tom, *Irish on the inside: in search of the soul of Irish America*, London and New York: Verso, 2001. NLI, 312 p.

History of the Friendly Sons of St. Patrick and of the Hibernian Society for the Relief of Emigrants from Ireland: March 17, 1771–March 17, 1892. NLI Ir 973 c 1.

The Irish-American Genealogist, Torrance, Calif.: Irish Genealogy and Research Committee of the Augustan Society, 1973–. NLI Ir 9291 i 3.

Johnson, James E., *The Irish in America*, Minneapolis: Lerner Publications, 1978. NLI Ir 973.j4, 80 p.

Journal of the American-Irish Historical Society. NLI Ir 973 a 1.

Kennedy, John F., *A Nation of Immigrants*, London: Hamish Hamilton.

Kenny, Kevin, *The American Irish: a history*, Harlow, Middx: Longman, 2000. NLI Ir 973 k 16, 328 p.

—— *New directions in Irish-American history*, Madison, Wis.: University of Wisconsin Press, c.2003. LC, 334 p.

Knobel, Dale T., *Paddy and the Republic: ethnicity and nationality in antebellum America*, Middletown, Conn.: Wesleyan University Press, 1986. NLI Ir 942 k 5, 251 p.

Linehan, John C., *The Irish Scots and the 'Scotch-Irish'*, Bowie, Md.: Heritage Books, 1997. LC, 138 p.

Lynch, Mary C., *O'Sullivan Burke, Fenian*, Carrigadrohid, Co. Cork: Ebony Jane Press, 1999. NLI, 247 p. Co-author, Seamus O'Donoghue.

McCaffrey, Lawrence J., *The Irish Catholic diaspora in America*, Washington: Catholic University of America Press, 1997. NLI Ir 973 m 55, 253 p.

—— *The Irish diaspora in America*, Bloomington, Ind.: Indiana University Press, c.1976. NLI Ir 973 m 13.

—— *Textures of Irish America*, Syracuse, NY: Syracuse University Press, 1992. NLI Ir 970 m 40, 236 p.

McGrath, Thomas F., *A history of the Ancient Order of Hibernians.* NLI 1B 3243, 180 p.

McKenna, Erin, *A student's guide to Irish American genealogy*, Phoenix, Ariz.: Oryx Press, 1996. NLI Ir 9291 m 25, 168 p.

MacMaster, Richard K., *Scotch-Irish merchants in Colonial America*, Belfast: UHF, 2009. NLI.

Meagher, T.J., *From Paddy to Studs: Irish-American communities in the turn of the century era, 1880 to 1920*, Westport, Conn.: Greenwood Press, 1986. NLI Ir 942 f 8, 202 p.

Mullin, James V., *The Irish Americans*, Evanston, Ill.: Nextext, c.2001. LC, 224 p. 'A historical reader'.

Murphy, David. See 'Mexico'.

O'Brien, M.J., *A Hidden Phase of American History*, Baltimore, Md.: 1973. NLI Ir 9733 o 25. Irishmen in the American Revolution.

O'Brien, Sean Michael, *Irish Americans in the Confederate Army*, Jefferson, NC: McFarland & Co., 2007. NLI, 256 p.

O'Carroll, Ide, *Models for Movers*, Dublin: Attic Press. Women emigrants.

O'Dea, John, *History of the Ancient Order of Hibernians and Ladies' Auxiliary*, Notre Dame, Ind.: University of Notre Dame Press, 1994. 3 vols. NLI Ir 942 o 6.

O'Donovan, Jeremiah, *Irish immigration in the United States: immigrant interviews*, New York: Arno Press, 1969. NLI Ir 942.033, 382 p.

O'Grady, Joseph P., *How the Irish became Americans*, New York: Twayne Publishers, 1973. NLI Ir 973 o 15, 190 p.

O'Hanlon, John, *Irish-American history of the United States*, Bristol: Thoemmes Press, 2003. NLI 2 v, 798 p.

Padden, Michael, *May the road rise to meet you: everything you need to know about Irish American history*, New York: Plume, c.1999. NLI Ir 942 p 21, 332 p. Co-author, Robert Sullivan.

Potter, G., *To the Golden Door: the story of the Irish in Ireland and America*, Boston, Mass.: Little, Brown, 1960. NLI Ir 973 p 4, 631 p.

Reynolds, F., *Ireland's Important and Heroic Part . . .* Chicago: Daleiden. NLI Ir 973 r 3, 322 p. Irish in the American Revolution.

Ridge, John T., *Erin's Sons in America*, New York: 1986. NLI Ir 973 r 7. The Ancient Order of Hibernians.

Roberts, E.F., *Ireland in America*, New York and London: G.P. Putnam's Sons, 1931. NLI Ir 973 r 2, 218 p.

Rose, Walter R., *A bibliography of the Irish in the United States*, Afton, NY: Tristram Shanty Publications, 1969. LC, 18 leaves.

Samito, Christian G., *Becoming American under fire: Irish Americans, African Americans, and the politics of citizenship during the Civil War era*, Ithaca, NY: Cornell University Press, 2006. NLI, 127 p.

Sawyer, Kem Knapp, *Irish Americans*, Carlisle, Mass.: Discovery Enterprises, 1998. NLI Ir 973 i 48, 64 p. Sources.

Seagrave, Pia Seija, *The history of the Irish Brigade: a collection of historical essays*, Fredericksburg, Va.: Sergeant Kirkland's Museum and Historical Society, 1997. NLI GR 261, 225 p.

Simons, P. Frazer, *Tenants no more*. See 'Australia'.

Spalding, J.L., *The religious mission of the Irish people and Catholic colonization*, New York: Christian Press Association, c.1900. NLI Ir 942.s18, 339 p.

Tucker, Phillip Thomas, *The history of the Irish Brigade: a collection of historical essays*, Fredericksburg, Va.: Sergeant Kirkland's Museum and Historical Society, c.1995. LC, 223 p.

Vernon, T. Foy, *American outsider: stories from the Irish Traveller diaspora*, Newcastle: Cambridge Scholars Pub., 2007. NLI, 144 p.

Wakin, Edward, *Enter the Irish-American*, New York: Crowell, c.1976. NLI Ir 973 w 9, 189 p.

Walsh, James P., *Ethnic militancy: an Irish Catholic prototype*, San Francisco: R and E Research Associates, 1972. NLI GR 308, 145 p.

—— *The Irish: America's political class*, New York: Arno Press, 1976. NLI Ir 973 w 8, 350 p.

Wells, Ronald A., *Ulster migration to America: letters from three Irish families*, New York: P. Lang, c.1991. LC, 170 p. 'Irish studies, Vol. 2'.

Werkin, E., *Enter the Irish-American*, New York: Crowell, 1976. NLI Ir 973 w 9, 189 p.

Williams, Richard, *Hierarchical structures and social value: the creation of Black and Irish identities in the United States*, Cambridge and New York: Cambridge University Press, 1990. LC, 190 p.

Wilson, David A., *United Irishmen, United States: immigrant radicals in the early republic*, Dublin: Four Courts Press, 1998. NLI Ir 973 w 21, 223 p.

Wittke, C, *The Irish in America*, Baton Rouge: Louisiana State University Press, 1956. NLI Ir 973 w 2, 319 p.

Regional

The South

Gleeson, David T., *The Irish in the South, 1815–1877*, Chapel Hill, NC: University of North Carolina Press, 2001. NLI A 2A 1609, 278 p.

McCullough, Eileen, *More than blarney: the Irish influence in Appalachia*, Old Fort, NC: Wolfhound Press, c.1997. LC, 165 p.

The West

Emmons, David A. *Beyond the American pale: the Irish in the West, 1845–1910*, Norman, Okla.: University of Oklahoma Press, 2010. NLI, 472 p.

Maume, Patrick, *19th-century Irish and Irish-Americans on the Western frontier*, Fort Lauderdale, Fla.: Department of Liberal Arts, Nova Southeastern University, c.2000. LC, 18 p. Co-author, Marguerite Quintelli-Neary.

Quigly, Hugh, *The Irish Race in California and on the Pacific Coast*, San Francisco: A. Roman & Co., 1878. NLI Ir 973 q 1, 548 p.

O'Laughlin, M., *Irish settlers on the American frontier*, Kansas City, Mo.: Irish Genealogical Foundation, 1984. LC.

Sarbaugh, Timothy J., *The Irish in the West*, Manhattan, Kans.: Sunflower University Press, c.1993. LC, 116 p. Co-editor, James P. Walsh.

New England

Cahill, Robert Ellis, *The old Irish of New England*, Peabody, Mass.: Chandler-Smith, c.1985. NLI GR 3019, 48 p.

Johnson, Daniel F., *Irish emigration . . . See 'New Brunswick'.*

New England Irish Guide, 1987, Boston, Mass.: Quinlin Campbell Publishers, 1987. NLI Ir 973 n 6, 171 p.

O'Brien, M.J., *Pioneer Irish in New England*, Baltimore, Md.: GPC, 1998. NLI Ir 974 o 66, 325 p.

O'Connor, Thomas H., *The Irish in New England*, Boston, Mass.: New England Historic Genealogical Society, 1985. NLI Ir 9292 p 25(5). Sources on Irish-American genealogy and the Kennedys of Massachusetts.

Scotch-Irish Heritage Festival, Rock Hill, SC: Winthrop College, 1981. NLI Ir 942 s 15.

The Midwest

Benson, James K., *Irish and German families and the economic development of Midwestern cities, 1860–1895*, New York: Garland, 1990. LC, 418 p.

Herr, Cheryl Temple, *Critical regionalism and cultural studies: from Ireland to the American Midwest*, Gainesville, Fla.: University Press of Florida, c.1996. LC, 233 p.

Wyman, Mark, *Immigrants in the Valley: Irish, Germans, and Americans in the upper Mississippi country, 1830–1860*, Chicago: Nelson-Hall, c.1984. LC, 258 p.

Arkansas

Rees, J., *A farewell to famine*, Arklow: Arklow Enterprise Centre, 1994. NLI Ir 94138 r 6, 174 p.

California

Burchell, R.A., *San Francisco Irish, 1848–1880*, Manchester: Manchester University Press, 1979. NLI Ir 973 b 12, 227 p.

Calhoon, F. D., *49er Irish: one Irish family in the California mines*, Hicksville, NY: Exposition Press, c.1977. LC, 194 p. McGuire family.

Campbell, Malcolm, *Ireland's New Worlds: immigrants, politics, and society in the United States and Australia, 1815–1922*, Madison, Wis.: University of Wisconsin Press, 2008. NLI, 249 p.

Conlon, Bernard. See under 'Australia'.

Dillon, Richard H., *Iron men: California's industrial pioneers, Peter, James, and Michael Donahue*, Point Richmond, Calif.: Candela Press, c.1984. LC, 334 p. San Francisco.

Dowling, Patrick J., *California, the Irish dream*, San Francisco: Golden Gate Publishers, 1988. NLI GR 2938, 429 p.

—— *Irish Californians: historic, benevolent, romantic*, San Francisco: Scottwall Associates, 1998. NLI Ir 973 d 25, 515 p.

Emmons. See 'Regional: The West'.

Fox, John, *Macnamara's Irish colony and the United States taking of California in 1846*, Jefferson, NC: McFarland, c.2000. NLI Ir 973 f 19, 230 p.

O'Brien Hickey, Anne, *Ballroom of romance: the KRB revisited: a collection of memoirs*, San Francisco: California Pub. Co., c.2000. LC, 306 p. An account of the social life of Irish-Americans in San Francisco centred around the 'Knights of the Red Branch' Hall.

Prendergast, T.F, *Forgotten Pioneers: Irish Leaders in Early California*, San Francisco: Trade Pressroom, 1942. NLI Ir 942 p 13, 278 p.

Sarbaugh, Timothy J., *Post Civil War fever and adjustment: Fenianism in the Californian context, 1858–1872*, Boston, Mass.: Northeastern University, c.1992. LC, 30 leaves.

Shaw, Eva, *The sun never sets: the influence of the British on early Southern California: contributions of the English, Irish, Scottish, Welsh, and Canadians*, Irvine, Calif.: Dickens Press, 2001. LC, 177 p.

Walsh, James P., *The San Francisco Irish, 1850–1976*, San Francisco: Irish Literary and Historical Society, 1978. LC, 150 p.

Connecticut

Hogan, Neil, *The cry of the famishing: Ireland, Connecticut and the potato famine*, East Haven, Conn.: Connecticut Irish-American Historical Society, 1998. NLI GR 1736, 201 p.

——*The wearin' o' the green: St. Patrick's Day in New Haven, Connecticut, 1842–1992*, Connecticut Irish-American Historical Society, 1992. NLI GR 1758, 234 p.

Stone, Frank Andrews, *The Irish: in their homeland, in America, in Connecticut: a curriculum guide*, Storrs, Conn.: School of Education, University of Connecticut, c.1975. LC, 113 p.

—— *Scots and Scotch Irish in Connecticut: a history*, Storrs, Conn.: University of Connecticut, 1978. NLI Ir 929 p 5, 69 p.

Toole, Arthur T., 'Roll of the 2nd Connecticut Volunteer Heavy Infantry, 1862–1865', *IG*, 9, 4, 1997, pp. 530–65.

Delaware

Mulrooney, Margaret M., *Black powder, white lace: the Du Pont Irish and cultural identity in nineteenth-century America*, Hanover, NH: University Press of New England, c.2002. LC, 296 p. Brandywine Creek Valley (Pennsylvania and Delaware).

Purcell, R.J. 'Irish settlers in early Delaware', *Pennsylvania History*, 1947 (April). NLI Ir 973 p 2.

Wokeck, Marianne S., 'Family and servants: Critical links in the 18th century immigration chain to the Delaware Valley', *Familia: Ulster Genealogical Review*, No. 18, 2002.

Georgia

Callahan, Dave, *The Callihans of Fannin County, Georgia, 1843 to 2003*, Leesburg, Va.: the author, 2003. LC, 632 p.

Constitution of the Hibernian Society of the City of Savannah, 1812, Philadelphia: F. McManus Jr & Co., 1887. NLI LO p 341, 61 p.

Fogarty, William L., *The days we've celebrated: St. Patrick's Day in Savannah*, Savannah, Ga.: Printcraft Press, c.1980. NLI GR 1746, 206 p.

Jones, Patricia K., *Across the ocean of promise: the Irish in Georgia* (2 vols.), Oakwood, Ga.: P.K. Jones, 2005. NLI.

Illinois

Barry, P.T., *The first Irish in Illinois: reminiscent of old Kaskaskia days*, Chicago: Chicago Newspaper Union, 1902. LC, 16 p.

Columb, Frank, *Chicago May: queen of the blackmailers*, Cambridge: Evod Academic Publishing Co., 1999. NLI Ir 92 c 400, 195 p.

Curtin, Paul J., *West Limerick Roots: the Laurence Curtin family of Knockbrack, Co. Limerick*, Austin, Tex.: P.J. Curtin, 1995. NLI Ir 9292 c 47, 424 p. Christian County, Illinois.

Fanning, Charles, *Mr Dooley and the Chicago Irish*, New York: 1976. NLI Ir 973 d 10.

—— *Nineteenth century Chicago Irish: a social and political portrait*, Chicago: Center for Urban Policy, Loyola University of Chicago, 1980. LC, 46 p. Co-authors, Ellen Skerrett and John Corrigan.

Funchion, M.F., *Chicago's Irish Nationalists, 1881–1890*, New York: Arno Press, 1976. NLI Ir 973 f 1, 160 p.

—— *The Irish in Chicago*, Chicago: 1987. NLI Ir 970 i 15.

Hilton, Dolores, *Cemetery inscriptions, records, early history, and biographies of St. Patrick's Irish Grove, Rock Run Township, Stephenson County, Illinois*, Pecatonica, Ill.: D. Hilton, c.1981. LC, 83 p.

Koos, Greg, *Irish immigrants in McLean County, Illinois*, Bloomington, Ill.: McLean County Historical Society, c.2000. LC, 81 p.

McCaffrey, Lawrence J., *The Irish in Chicago*, Urbana, Ill.: University of Illinois Press, c.1987. NLI Ir 970 i 15, 171 p.

McMahon, Eileen M., *What parish are you from?: a Chicago Irish community and race relations*, Lexington, Ky.: University Press of Kentucky, 1995. NLI Ir 300 m 37, 226 p.

Metress, Seamus P., *The Irish in the Great Lakes region: a bibliographic survey*, Toledo, Ohio: 1990. NLI GRP 47, 52 p. Co-author, Kathleen R. Annable.

O'Neill, Francis, *Chief O'Neill's sketchy recollections of an eventful life in Chicago*, Dingle: Brandon, 2008. NLI, 302 p.

Skerrett, Ellen, *At the crossroads: Old Saint Patrick's and the Chicago Irish*, Chicago: Wild Onion Books, c.1997. LC, 171 p.

Skerrett, Ellen, 'The Irish of Chicago's Hull-House neighborhood', in Fanning (ed.), *New perspectives. See USA, 'General'.*

Walsh, James B., 'J.R. Walsh of Chicago' in *The Irish: America's political class*, New York: Arno Press, 1976. NLI Ir 973 w 8, 350 p.

Wyman. See 'The Midwest'.

Indiana

Burr, David, *The Irish War*, Fort Wayne, Ind.: 1953. LC, 8 p.

Driscoll, Allen W., *Driscolls and more Driscolls: from County Cork (Ireland) to Township York (Noble County, IN)*, Wawaka, Ind.: the author, c.1998. LC, 436 p.

Iowa

Costello, Timon, *Shining emeralds*, Fond du Lac, Wis.: T. Costello, c.1994. LC, 302 p. McGalloway family.

Mullaley, Robert C., *History of the Mullaleys: a twelve hundred year journey from County Galway to Iowa*, Los Altos, Calif.: R.C. Mullaley, c.1993. LC, 214 p.

Naughton, Michael L., *A genealogical history of the Naughton family: from Ireland to Iowa and beyond*, Aurora, Colo.: M.L. Naughton, 1989. NLI GO 593, 108 leaves.

Sinclair Tierney, Evelyn, *But of course they were Irish*, Moravia, Iowa: E. Sinclair Tierney, c.1984. LC, F629.M446 T54, 491 p. Melrose, Iowa.

Wallace, Gene, *Emeralds of the heartland: a story of Irish Catholic immigrants of the nineteenth century, based on the family history stories of John M. Sheehan*, Santa Paula, Calif.: Wallace Pub., c.1994. LC, 275 p. Iowa: Adair County.

Ward, Leo R., *Holding up the hills: the biography of a neighborhood*, New York: Sheed & Ward, 1941. LC, 202 p.

Wyman. See 'The Midwest'.

Kansas

Gillespie, LaRoux K., *The Iretons of Kansas and Oklahoma*, Kansas City, Mo.: Family History and Genealogy Center, c.1985. NLI GO 37, 296 p.

Kentucky

Crews, Clyde F., *Mike Barry and the Kentucky Irish American: an anthology*, Lexington, Ky.: University Press of Kentucky, c.1995. LC, 167 p.

Fitzpatrick, Edward, 'Early Irish settlers in Kentucky', *Journal of the American-Irish Historical Society*, 2, 1899, pp. 139–44. NLI Ir 973 a 1.

Kelly, Mary Ann, *My old Kentucky home, good-night*, Hicksville, NY: Exposition Press, c.1979. LC, 310 p. Ludlow (Kentucky).

Kendall, Margaret M.G., *Irish in the 1850 Mason County, Ky. federal census*, Maysville, Ky.: the author, 1980. LC, 30 leaves.

Linehan, John C., 'Irish pioneers and builders of Kentucky', *Journal of the American-Irish Historical Society*, 3, 1900, pp. 78–88. NLI Ir 973 a 1.

Louisiana

Finn, John, *New Orleans Irish: famine exiles*, Luling, La.: Holy Family Church, 1997. LC, 683 p.

Niehaus, E.F., *The Irish in New Orleans, 1800–1860*, Baton Rouge: Louisiana State University Press, 1965. NLI Ir 973 n 3, 194 p.

Walsh, Terence G., *James Joseph Walsh: a chronicle of his life and that of Mary Ann McConochie*, Dallas, Tex.: T.G. Walsh, 1988. NLI B 2B 535, 89 p. Orleans Parish (Louisiana).

Maine

Connolly, Michael C., *They change their sky: the Irish in Maine*, Orono, Maine: University of Maine Press, 2004. NLI, 414 p.

Mundy, James H., *Hard times, hard men: Maine and the Irish, 1830–1860*, Scarborough, Maine: Harp Publications, 1990. NLI Ir 942 m 12, 209 p.

Thibadeau, W.J., *The Irishman: a factor in the development of Houlton: A history of the Parish of St Mary's*, Augusta, Maine: O'Ceallaigh Publications, 1992. NLI Ir 970 t 1, 109 p.

Maryland

A salute to the Maryland Irish: a Bicentennial publication of the Ladies' Auxiliary to the Ancient Order of Hibernians, Baltimore, Md.: Uptown Press, 1976. LC, 63 p.

Athy, Lawrence F., Jr, *Captain George Athy (of Galway and Maryland) and his descendants: a guide to the first six generations of the Athy, Athey, Atha, Athon family in America*, Houston, Tex.: L.F. Athy, 1987. LC, 140 p.

Hoffman, Ronald, *Princes of Ireland, planters of Maryland: a Carroll saga, 1500–1782*, Chapel Hill, Va.: University of North Carolina Press, 2000. NLI Ir 9292 c 59, 429 p.

Moore-Colyer, Richard, 'The Moores of Londonderry and Baltimore: a study in Scotch-Irish eighteenth-century emigration', *Familia: Ulster Genealogical Review*, 19, 2003, pp. 11–40.

O'Brien, M.J., 'The Irish in Montgomery and Washington Counties, Maryland in 1778', *Journal of the American-Irish Historical Society*, 24, 1925, pp. 157–61. NLI Ir 973 a 1.

—— 'Irish pioneers in Maryland', *Journal of the American-Irish Historical Society*, 14, 1915, pp. 207–19. NLI Ir 973 a 1.

Riley, Robert Shean, *The colonial Riley families of the Tidewater frontier*, Utica, Ky.: McDowell Publications, c.1999. NLI G 9292 r 23, 2 vols. 'A history of several Riley families of Maryland and Virginia.'

Williams, H.A., *History of the Hibernian Society of Baltimore, 1803–1951*, Baltimore, Md.: 1951. NLI Ir 942 w 1.

Massachusetts

Beatty, Jack, *The Rascal King: the life and times of James Michael Curley, 1874–1958*, Reading, Mass.: Addison-Wesley, c.1992. NLI GR 1632.

Blanchette, Joseph P., *The view from Shanty Pond: an Irish immigrant's look at life in a New England mill town, 1875–1938*, Charlotte, Vt.: Shanty Pond Press, 1999. NLI 2A 929, 222 p. Lawrence (Massachusetts).

Charitable Irish Society of Boston, *The Constitution and by-laws of the Charitable Irish Society of Boston: Instituted 1737, adopted March 17th 1876, with a list of officers and members . . .* Boston, Mass.: James F. Cotter, 1876. NLI GR 757, 127 p.

Coelho, Anthony, *A row of nationalities: life in a working class community: the Irish, English, and French Canadians of Fall River, Massachusetts, 1850–1890*, c.1981. NLI Fiche 327(4), 300 leaves.

Cullen, J.B., *Story of the Irish in Boston*, Boston, Mass.: H.A. Plimpton, 1893. NLI Ir 973 c 8, 630 p.

Curley, James Michael, *I'd do it again: a record of all my uproarious years*, Englewood, NJ: Prentice-Hall, 1957. NLI Ir 92 c 129, 372 p.

Daly, Marie E., *Gravestone inscriptions from Mount Auburn Catholic Cemetery, Watertown, Massachusetts*, Waltham, Mass.: M.E. Daly, 1983. LC, 92 leaves.

Dauwer, Leo P., *Boston's St. Patrick's Day Irish: being an account of life among the piety, political, noteworthy and ordinary*, Plymouth, Mass.: American Heritage Home, c.1980. NLI Ir 399041.d.10, 143 p.

Donovan, G.F., *The pre-revolutionary Irish in Massachusetts, 1620–1775*, Menasha, Wis.: George Banta Pub. Co., 1931. NLI Ir 9744 d 2, 158 p.

Edmonds, John Henry, 'Dorman Mahoone alis Mathews': an early Boston Irishman. NLI GRP 70, 29 p.

Evans, A. G., *Fanatic heart: a life of John Boyle O'Reilly, 1844–1890*, Boston, Mass.: Northeastern University Press, 1999. NLI Ir 92 o 529, 280 p.

Fanning, Patricia J., 'Epidemics, influenza, and the Irish: Norwood, Massachusetts, in 1918', in Fanning, *New perspectives . . .* See USA, 'General'.

Gardner, H. C., *Glimpses of our lake region in 1863*, New York: Nelson & Phillips, and Cincinnati: Hitchcock & Walden, 1874. LC, microfilm 24936 PS, 420 p. Plymouth County.

Gearan, Marie M., *The Early Irish Settlers in the Town of Gardner, Massachusetts*, Gardner, Mass.: Marie M. Gearan, 1932. NLI Ir 9744 g 1, 73 p.

Handlin, Oscar, *Boston's immigrants, 1790–1880: a study in acculturation*, Cambridge, Mass.: Belknap Press of Harvard University Press, 1991. NLI Ir 300 h 11, 382 p.

Hartford, William F., *Working people of Holyoke: class and ethnicity in a Massachusetts mill town, 1850–1960*, New Brunswick, NJ: Rutgers University Press, c.1990. NLI Ir 331 h 17, 294 p.

Kimball, Charles N., *Descendants of John Riley, Jeremiah Coakley, Felix Sharkey: natives of Ireland who came to Charlestown, Massachusetts in the 1840s*, Kansas City, Mo.: C.N. Kimball, 1986. LC, 216 p. Edited by Joan F. Curran.

Kohl, Lawrence Frederick (ed.), *Irish green and Union blue: the Civil War letters of Peter Welsh, color sergeant 28th Regiment Massachusetts Volunteers*, New York: Fordham University, 1986. NLI Ir 9237 w 6, 170 p. With Margaret Casse Richard.

MacDonald, Michael Patrick, *All Souls: a family story from Southie*, Boston: Beacon Press, 1999. NLI Ir 921 m, 266 p.

McKean, David Duncan, *The cross and the shamrock*, Lowell, Mass.: Archives of St Patrick Parish, c.1997. LC, 32 p. Lowell (Massachusetts).

Macnamara, Daniel George, *The history of the Ninth Regiment, Massachusetts Volunteer Infantry, June, 1861–June, 1864*, New York: Fordham University Press, 2000. LC, 557 p. With an introduction by Christian G. Samito.

Meagher, T.J., *Inventing Irish America: generation, class, and ethnic identity in a New England city, 1880–1928*, Notre Dame, Ind.: University of Notre Dame Press, c.2001. NLI 2A 969, 523 p. Worcester (Massachusetts).

Mitchell, Brian C., *The Paddy camps: the Irish of Lowell, 1821–61*, Urbana, Ill.: University of Illinois Press, c.1988. NLI GR 1003, 247 p.

Moreton, Cole, *Hungry for home: leaving the Blaskets: a journey from the edge of Ireland*, London: Viking, 2000. NLI Ir 94146 m 13, 287 p. Springfield (Massachusetts) in particular.

O'Connor, Thomas H., *The Boston Irish: a political history*, Boston, Mass.: Northeastern University Press, 1995. NLI Ir 942 o 38, 363 p.

—— *South Boston, my home town: the history of an ethnic neighborhood*, Boston, Mass.: Quinlan Press, c.1988. NLI GR 196, 259 p.

Panas, Leo, *The Irish came to Lowell: journalists' observations of 19th century Irish in Lowell, Massachusetts*, Lowell, Mass.: L. Panas, 1985. LC, 58 p.

Pierce, R. Andrew, *The stones speak: Irish place names from inscriptions in Boston's Mount Calvary Cemetery*, Boston, Mass.: New England Historic Genealogical Society, c.2000. NLI Ir 9291 p 19, 246 p.

Powers, Vincent Edward, *Invisible immigrants: the pre-Famine Irish community in Worcester, Massachusetts, from 1826 to 1860*, New York: Garland Pub., 1989. LC, 549 p.

Riley, George R., *Reilly to Riley, Galway to Quincy: Book of Rileys*, Boston, Mass.: Recollections Bound, c.1986. NLI GR 659, 342 leaves.

Ryan, D.P., *Beyond the Ballot Box: Boston Irish, 1845–1917*, London: 1983. NLI Ir 973 r 4, 173 p.

Ryan, Michael, *The Irish in Boston*, Boston, Mass.: Boston 200, c.1975. NLI Ir 800 p 33, 31 p.

Samito, Christian G., *Commanding Boston's Irish Ninth: the Civil War letters of Colonel Patrick R. Guiney, Ninth Massachusetts Volunteer Infantry*, New York: Fordham University Press, 1998. NLI GR 382, 280 p.

Walsh, Louis S., *The early Irish Catholic schools of Lowell*, Boston, Mass.: Press of T.A. Whalen & Co., 1901. LC, 20 p.

Wood, S.G., *Ulster Scots and Blandford Scouts*, West Medway, Mass.: Wood, 1928. NLI Ir 973 w 1, 438 p.

Michigan

Doby, J., *The last full measure of devotion*, Raleigh, NC: Pentland Press, c.1996. NLI GR 2967, 216 p. 15th Michigan Infantry Regiment, 1862–5.

Duncan, Mary Lou Straith, *Passage to America, 1851–1869: the records of Richard Elliott, passenger agent, Detroit, Michigan*, Detroit: Detroit Society for Genealogical Research, 1999. LC, 194 p.

McGee, John Whalen, *The passing of the Gael: our Irish ancestors, their history and exodus*, Grand Rapids, Mich.: Wolverine Printing Co., c.1975. LC, 332 p. Kent County.

Marman, Ed, *Modern journeys: the Irish in Detroit*, Detroit: United Irish Societies, 2001. NLI A 2A 973, 237 p.

Metress, Seamus P., *Irish in Michigan*, East Lansing, Mich.: Michigan State University Press, 2006. NLI, 92 p.

—— See also 'Illinois'.

Vinyard, Jo Ellen, *The Irish on the urban frontier: Nineteenth century Detroit, 1850–1880*, New York: Arno Press, 1976. NLI Ir 973 v 1, 446 p.

Minnesota

Campbell, Malcolm, 'A comparative study of Irish rural settlement in nineteenth-century Minnesota and New South Wales', in Bielenberg, *The Irish Diaspora*. See McCracken under 'Africa'.

Condon Johnston, Patricia, *Minnesota's Irish*, Afton, Minn.: Johnston Pub., c.1984. NLI GR 1959, 92 p.

Connelly, Bridget, *Forgetting Ireland*, St Paul, Minn.: Borealis Books, c.2003. LC, 263 p. Graceville.

Donahue, Deborah Bozell, *The light of the future: the O'Donoghue story*, Ormond Beach, Fla.: Donahue Pub., c.2000. LC, 184 p.

Metress. See 'Illinois'.

Regan, Ann, *Irish in Minnesota*, St Paul, Minn.: Minnesota Historical Society Press, c.2002. NLI B 3B 853, 89 p.

Rogers, Ralph W., Jr, *The Rogers family of Northampton Parish, New Brunswick, and some descendants*, Homosassa, Fl.: R.W. Rogers, 1989. LC, 65 p.

Shannon, James P., *Catholic colonization on the western frontier*, New York: Arno Press, 1976. NLI G 2820973 s 1, 302 p.

Smith, Alice E., *The Sweetman Irish colony*. LC.

Wingerd, Mary Lethert, *Claiming the city: politics, faith, and the power of place in St. Paul*, Ithaca, NY: Cornell University Press, 2001. LC, 326 p. Twentieth century.

Wyman. See 'The Midwest'.

Missouri

Cochran, Alice Lida, *The saga of an Irish immigrant family: the descendants of John Mullanphy*, New York: Arno Press, 1976. NLI Ir 973 c 12, 270 p. St Louis.

Faherty, William B., *The St. Louis Irish: an unmatched Celtic community*, St Louis: Missouri Historical Society Press, c.2001. NLI A 3A 467, 270 p.

O'Leary, Cornelius F., 'The Irish in the early days of St Louis', *Journal of the American-Irish Historical Society*, 9, 1910, pp. 206–13. NLI Ir 973 a 1.

O'Neill, Pat, *From the bottom up: the story of the Irish in Kansas City*, Kansas City, Mo.: Seat o' the Pants Pub., c.2000. LC, 244 p.

'Passenger list of *Ticonderoga*, 1850' (New Wexford, Missouri), *The Past: The Organ of the Uí Ceinnsealaigh Historical Society*, 12 (1978), pp. 49–52. NLI Ir 941382 p 1.

Montana

Connelly Sullivan, Mary, *A Montana saga: 'our yesterdays'*, Great Falls, Mont.: H.S. Pannell, c.1984. LC, F730.S84 1984, 112 p. 'With Helena Sullivan Pannell's story.'

Emmons, David A., *The Butte Irish: an American Mining Town, 1875–1925*, Chicago: University of Illinois Press, 1998. NLI Ir 942 e 8, 443 p.

—— See also 'The West'.

Nebraska

DeVries, Ellen M., *Irish and Scotch-Irish who made a declaration of intention to naturalize from Cass, Douglas, Lancaster, Nemaha, Otoe, Richardson, Sarpy, and York counties in Nebraska, 1855–1940+*, Lincoln, Neb.: Nebraskans of Irish and Scotch-Irish Ancestry, c.1997. LC, 152 p. Co-author, Raymond D. De Vries.

New Hampshire

Brennan, James F., *The Irish settlers of southern New Hampshire*, [Peterborough?]: 1910. LC 11 p.

O'Brien, M.J., Irish pioneers in New Hampshire, *Historical papers: reprinted from the Journal of the American Irish Historical Society*, 1926. NLI GR 2240, Vol. 25.

New Jersey

Quinn, Dermot, *The Irish in New Jersey: four centuries of American Life*, New Brunswick, NJ: Rutgers University Press, c.2004. 226 p.

Shaw, Douglas V., *The making of an immigrant city: ethnic and cultural conflict in Jersey City, New Jersey, 1850–1877*, New York: Arno Press, 1976. NLI G 32373 S 8, 273 p.

New York

Bannan, Theresa, *Pioneer Irish of Onondaga (about 1776–1847)*, New York and London: G.P. Putnam's Sons, 1911. NLI Ir 971 b 2, 333 p.

Bayor, Ronald H., *Neighbors in conflict: the Irish, Germans, Jews, and Italians of New York City, 1929–1941*, Baltimore, Md.: Johns Hopkins University Press, c.1978. NLI, 232 p.

—— *The New York Irish*, London and Baltimore, Md.: Johns Hopkins University Press, 1996. NLI Ir 937 n 2, 743 p. Co-editor, Timothy J. Meagher.

Beadles, John Asa, *The Syracuse Irish, 1812–1928: immigration, Catholicism, socio-economic status, politics, and Irish nationalism*, Syracuse, NY: Beadles, 1974. NLI Pos. 8719, 501 leaves.

Bennett., Brian A., *The beau ideal of a soldier and a gentleman: the life of Col. Patrick Henry O'Rorke from Ireland to Gettysburg*, Wheatland, NY: Triphammer Pub., c.1996. LC, 196 p. Rochester, New York.

Bigelow, Bruce, *Ethnic separation in a pedestrian city: a social geography of Syracuse, New York, in 1860*, Syracuse, NY: Department of Geography, Syracuse University, 1987. LC.

Bilby, Joseph G., *Remember Fontenoy!: the 69th New York and the Irish Brigade in the Civil War*, Hightstown, NJ: Longstreet House, 1997. NLI GR 1478, 270 p. Irish soldiers in the Army of the Potomac.

Blake Stevenson, Lenore, *From Cavan to the Catskills: an informal history of the Conerty, Finigan and Smith families of upstate New York*, Baltimore, Md.: Gateway Press, 1989. NLI GR 2767, 230 p.

Buckley, John Patrick, *The New York Irish: their view of American foreign policy, 1914–1921*, New York: Arno Press, 1976. NLI G 327973 b 9, 395 p.·

DeBartolo Carmack, Sharon, *My wild Irish rose: the life of Rose (Norris) (O'Connor) Fitzhugh and her mother, Delia (Gordon) Norris*, Boston, Mass.: Newbury Street Press, 2001. LC, 84 p. 'A study in the lives of Irish immigrant women in America with a summary of matrilineal generations.'

Dolan, Jay P., *The immigrant church: New York's Irish and German Catholics, 1815–1865*, Baltimore, Md.: Johns Hopkins University Press, 1975. NLI G 2820973 d 1, 221 p.

Dunkak, Harry M., *Freedom, culture, labor: the Irish of early Westchester County, New York*, New Rochelle, NY: Iona College Press, 1994. NLI GR 1737, 145 p.

Dowling Almeida, Linda, *Irish immigrants in New York City, 1945–1995*, Bloomington, NY: Indiana University Press, c.2001. NLI GR 2832, 211 p.

Emigrant Savings Bank Records (New York), New York: New York Public Library. NLI Pos. 9179–87, 1850–77. Indexed. Nine microfilm reels. See Rich, below.

English, T. J., *The Westies: inside the Hell's Kitchen Irish mob*, New York: Putnam, 1990. NLI GR 1927, 384 p.

Gibson, Florence Elizabeth, *The attitudes of the New York Irish toward state and national affairs, 1848–1892*, New York: Columbia University Press, 1951. LC, 480 p.

Glasco, Laurence Admiral, *Ethnicity and social structure: Irish, Germans, and native-born of Buffalo, NY, 1850–*, New York: Arno Press, 1980. LC, 366 p.

Gordon, Michael A., *The Orange riots: Irish political violence in New York City, 1870 and 1871*, London and Ithaca, NY: Cornell University Press, 1993. NLI Ir 942 g 21, 263 p.

Henderson, Thomas M., *Tammany Hall and the new immigrants: the progressive years*, New York: Arno Press, 1976. NLI Ir 973 h 12, 314 p.

Lizzi, Dominick C., *Governor Martin H. Glynn: forgotten hero*, Valatie, NY: Valatie Press, c.1994. LC, 122 p.

McDonald, Brian, *My father's gun: one family, three badges, one hundred years in the NYPD*, New York: Dutton, 1999. LC, 309 p.

Mann, A.P., 'The Irish in New York in the early 1860s', *Irish Historical Studies*, 7, 1950, pp. 87–108.

New York Irish History: Journal of the New York Irish History Roundtable, New York: 1986–. NLI Ir 973 n 13.

New York Irish History Roundtable: Newsletter (spring 1998–). NLI Ir 970 n 14.

O'Brien, M.J., *In Old New York: Irish Dead in Trinity and St Paul's Churchyards*, New York: 1928. NLI Ir 973 o 8.

Raghallaigh, Eibhilín, *St. Paul's Roman Catholic Church, Court Street, Brooklyn, New York: baptism register, July 22, 1839–July 12, 1857: marriage register, August 7, 1839–August 18, 1857*, Salt Lake City: Redmond Press, 1996. LC, 282 p.

—— *St. Paul's Roman Catholic Church, Brooklyn, New York: the Irish parish: baptism and marriage registers, 6 September 1857–30 December 1900*, Floral Park, NY: Delia Publications, LLC, 2001. LC, 440 leaves.

Rich, Kevin J., *Irish immigrants of the Emigrant Industrial Savings Bank: Volume I, 1850–1853*, New York: Broadway-Manhattan Co., 2001?. NLI B 3B 1134, 285 p.

Ridge, John T., *The Flatbush Irish*, New York: Division 35 Ancient Order of Hibernians, c.1983. NLI 3B 900, 44 p.

—— *Sligo in New York: the Irish from County Sligo, 1849–1991*, New York: County Sligo Social and Benevolent Association, c.1991. NLI Ir 947 r 21, 157 p.

—— *The St. Patrick's Day Parade in New York*, New York: Patrick's Day Parade Committee, 1988. NLI Ir 973 r 12, 204 p.

Rowley, William E., 'The Irish aristocracy of Albany, 1798–1878', *New York History*, 52, 1971, pp. 275–304.

Ruddock, George, *Linen threads and broom twines: an Irish and American album and directory of the people of the Dunbarton Mill, Greenwich, New York, 1879–1952*, Bowie, Md.: Heritage Books, 1997 (2 vols.). NLI Ir 9292 r 27.

Shea, Ann M., *The Irish experience in New York City: a select bibliography*, New York: New York Irish History Roundtable, c.1995. NLI, 130 p. Co-author, Marion R. Casey.

Silinonte, Joseph M., *Tombstones of the Irish born: cemetery of the Holy Cross, Flatbush, Brooklyn*, Bowie, Md.: Heritage Books, 1994. NLI Ir 9292 s 29, 112 p.

Smith, Dennis, *A song for Mary: an Irish-American memory*, New York: Warner Books, 1999. NLI GR 2466, 369 p.

Toole, Arthur T., 'Roll of the 10th NY Volunteer Infantry, 1861–1865', *IG*, 9, 2, 1995, pp. 238–81.

Trimble, Richard M., *Brothers 'til death: the Civil War letters of William, Thomas, and Maggie Jones, 1861–1865: Irish soldiers in the 48th New York Volunteer Regiment*, Macon, Ga.: Mercer University Press, 2000. LC, 173 p.

Waters, Maureen, *Crossing Highbridge: a memoir of Irish America*, Syracuse, NY: Syracuse University Press, 2001. NLI 2A 192, 149 p.

North Carolina

'Irish builders in North Carolina', *Journal of the American-Irish Historical Society*, 10, 1911, pp. 258–61. NLI Ir 973 a 1.

Lynch Deans, Frances, *The Lynches, from Ireland to eastern North Carolina: in the counties of Craven, Johnston, Bobbs, Wayne*, Goldsboro: F.L. Deans, c.1989. LC, 577 p.

McGinn, Brian, 'The Irish on Roanoake Island', *IR*, 3 (1993), p. 21. NLI.

O'Brien, M.J., 'North Carolina: Some early MacCarthys, McGuires . . . *Journal of the American-Irish Historical Society*, 12, 1913, pp. 161–7. NLI Ir 973 a 1.

Ohio

Callahan, Nelson J., *Irish-Americans and their Communities of Cleveland*, Cleveland, Ohio: Cleveland State University, 1978. NLI Ir 942 c 23, 254 p.

Wolf, Donna M., *Irish immigrants in nineteenth century Ohio: naturalizations: selected years*, Apollo, Pa: Closson Press, 1999. LC, 166 p.

—— *Irish immigrants in nineteenth century Ohio: a database*, Apollo, Pa: Closson Press, c.1998. LC, 216 p.

—— *The Irish in central Ohio: baptisms and marriages, 1852–1861, St. Patrick Roman Catholic Church, Columbus, Ohio*, Columbus, Ohio: D.M. Wolf, 1991?. LC, 71 p.

Oklahoma

Blessing, Patrick J., *The British and Irish in Oklahoma*, Norman, Okla.: University of Oklahoma Press, c.1980. NLI GR 1748, 57 p.

Gillespie. See 'Kansas'.

Oregon

Emmons. See 'The West'.

'The Irish of Morrow County, Oregon', *Historical Quarterly* (June 1968).

Ó Longaigh, David, *We Irish in Oregon: a historical account of the Irish in Oregon from the pioneer times to the present day*, Portland, Oreg.: All-Ireland Cultural Society of Oregon, 1998. NLI Ir 942 w 22, 103 p.

Pennsylvania

Adams, E., and O'Keeffe, B.B., *Catholic Trails West: The Founding Catholic Families of Pennsylvania*, Baltimore, Md.: GPC, 1988, Vol. 1: St Joseph's Church, Philadelphia.

Armor, William C., *Scotch-Irish Bibliography of Pennsylvania*, Nashville, Tenn.: Barbee & Smith, 1896.

Brauer, Carl M., *The man who built Washington: a life of John McShain*, Wilmington, Del.: Hagley Museum and Library, c.1996. NLI Ir 92 m 582, 298 p.

Burstein, Alan Nathan, *Residential distribution and mobility of Irish and German immigrants in Philadelphia, 1850–1880*, 1975. NLI Pos. 7838, microfilm, 355 leaves.

Campbell, John H., *History of the Friendly Sons of St. Patrick and of the Hibernian Society for the Relief of Emigrants from Ireland, March 17, 1771–March 17, 1892*, Philadelphia: Hibernian Society, 1892. NLI Ir 973 c 1, 570 p.

Chambers, George, *A tribute to the principles, virtues, habits and public usefulness of the Irish and Scotch early settlers of Pennsylvania, by a descendant*, Chambersburg, Pa.: printed by M. Kieffer & Co., 1856. LC, 171 p.

Clark, Dennis, *Erin's heirs: Irish bonds of community*, Lexington, Ky.: University Press of Kentucky, c.1991. LC, 238 p. Irish-American families in Philadelphia.

—— *A history of the Society of the Friendly Sons of St. Patrick for the Relief of Emigrants from Ireland in Philadelphia, 1951–1981*, Philadelphia: the society, c.1982. NLI Ir 973 c 22.

—— *The Irish in Pennsylvania: a people share a commonwealth*, University Park, Pa.: Pennsylvania Historical Association, 1991. NLI GR 3017, 56 p.

—— *The Irish in Philadelphia: ten generations of urban experience*, Philadelphia: Temple University Press, 1973. NLI Ir973 c 11, 246 p.

—— *The Irish relations: trials of an immigrant tradition*, Rutherford, Pa.: Fairleigh Dickinson University Press, 1982. NLI Ir 973 c 26, 255 p. Irish-Americans in Philadelphia.

Coleman, J. Walter, *The Molly Maguire riots: industrial conflict in the Pennsylvania coal region*, Richmond, Va.: Garrett & Massie, 1936. NLI Ir 3318.c.49, 189 p.

Cummings, H.M., *Scots Breed*, Pittsburgh, Pa.: 1964. NLI Ir 942 c 17. Scotch-Irish in Pennsylvania.

Dougherty, Daniel J., *History of the Society of the Friendly Sons of St. Patrick for the Relief of Emigrants from Ireland of Philadelphia, March 17, 1771–March 17, 1892*, Philadelphia: the society, 1952. NLI Ir 973 c 24, 448 p.

Dunaway, W., *Scotch-Irish of Colonial Pennsylvania*, Baltimore, Md.: GPC, 1985. NLI Ir 974 d 16.

Gallman, J. Matthew, *Receiving Erin's children: Philadelphia, Liverpool, and the Irish famine migration, 1845–1855*, Chapel Hill, NC: University of North Carolina Press, c.2000. NLI A 3A 2106, 306 p.

Gudelunas, William A., Jr, *Before the Molly Maguires: the emergence of the ethno-religious factor in the politics of the lower anthracite region, 1844–1872*, New York: Arno Press, 1976. NLI Ir 973 g 7, 165 p. Co-author, William G. Shade. Schuylkill County.

Hackett, Dominic J., 'Philadelphia Irish', *Journal of the American-Irish Historical Society*, 30, 1932, pp. 103–17. NLI Ir 973 a 1.

Hood, Samuel, *A brief account of the Society of the Friendly Sons of St. Patrick*, Philadelphia: by order of the Hibernian Society, 1844. LC, 112 p.

Kenny, Kevin, *Making sense of the Molly Maguires*, New York and Oxford: Oxford University Press, 1998. NLI Ir 300 k 16, 336 p.

Laughlin, Ledlie Irwin, *Joseph Ledlie and William Moody, early Pittsburgh residents: their background and some of their descendants*, Pittsburgh, Pa.: University of Pittsburgh Press, 1961. NLI GO 147, 208 p.

Light, Dale B., *Class, ethnicity, and the urban ecology in a nineteenth century city: Philadelphia's Irish, 1840–1890*, 1979. NLI Fiche 199(3), microfiche, 246 leaves.

List of members of the Hibernian Society for the Relief of Emigrants from Ireland, together with the list of members of the Friendly Sons of St. Patrick, 1771–1884, Philadelphia: published by authority of the society, 1884. NLI GR 2945, 42 p.

Lynott, William J., *The Lynotts of Ireland and Scranton: the story of Peter Lynott and his descendants*, Scranton, Pa.: William J. Lynott, 1996. NLI Ir 9292 L 23, 43 p.

McMaster, Richard K, 'James Fullton: A Philadelphia merchant and his customers', *Familia: Ulster Genealogical Review*, No. 17, 2001, pp. 23–4.

Mahony, M.E., *Fág an bealach: the Irish contribution to America and in particular to Western Pennsylvania*, Pittsburgh, Pa.: United Irish Societies Bicentennial Committee of Western Pennsylvania, 1977. NLI Ir 973 m 16, 132 p. Allegheny and Washington counties.

Mulholland, St Clair A., *The story of the 116th Regiment Pennsylvania Volunteers in the War of the Rebellion*, New York: Fordham University Press, 1996. NLI G 9737 m 11, 480 p. Edited, with an introduction, by Lawrence Frederick Kohl.

Mulrooney. See 'Delaware'.

O'Brien, M.J. 'Irish pioneers in Berks County, Pennsylvania', *Journal of the American-Irish Historical Society*, 27, 1928, pp. 39–45. NLI Ir 973 a 1.

Searight, James A., *A record of the Searight family*, Uniontown, Pa.: 1893. NLI LO 5287, 'Londonderry . . . to Lancaster County, Pennsylvania, about 1740,' 228 p.

Silcox, Harry C., *Philadelphia politics from the bottom up: the life of Irishman William McMullen, 1824–1901*, London and Cranbury, NJ: Associated University Presses, c.1989. NLI GR 2249, 175 p.

Rhode Island

'A seed drops on a distant land: The emigration of Patrick McMahon', *IG*, 9, No. 2 (1995), pp. 188–94.

Conley, Patrick T., *The Irish in Rhode Island: a historical appreciation*, Providence, RI: Rhode Island Heritage Commission, Rhode Island Publications Society, 1986. NLI GRP 87, 46 p.

McCarron, E.T., 'Altered states: Tyrone migration to Providence, Rhode Island, during the nineteenth century', *Clogher Record*, Vol. 16, No. 1 (1997), pp. 145–61.

McMahon, Timothy E., *The McMahon chronicles: the story of an Irish-American family in Rhode Island, 1870–1995*, Pawtucket, RI: Taurus House Publications, 1995. LC, 88 p.

Molloy, Scott, *Irish titan, Irish toilers: Joseph Banigan and nineteenth-century New England labor*, Durham, NH: University of New Hampshire Press, 2008. NLI, 309 p.

Murray, Thomas Hamilton, *The Irish vanguard of Rhode Island*, Boston, Mass.: 1904. LC, 27 p.

South Carolina

Gleeson, David T., The Irish in the Atlantic world, Columbia, SC: University of South Carolina Press, c.2010, 341 p. The Irish community at Saint Croix in the Danish West Indies.

Jones, Patricia K., *Across the ocean of promise: the Irish of Charleston, South Carolina*, Oakwood, Ga.: P.K. Jones, 2006, 642 p. Data compiled from federal census records, 1850 to 1900.

Peckham Motes, Margaret, *Irish Found in South Carolina: 1850 Census*, Baltimore, Md.: GPC, 2003. LC, 209 p.

O'Brien, M.J., 'The Irish in Charleston, South Carolina', *Historical papers: reprinted from the Journal of the American Irish Historical Society*, 1926. NLI GR 2240, Vol. 25.

—— 'Lymerick Plantation, Berkeley County, SC', *Historical papers: reprinted from the Journal of the American Irish Historical Society*, 1926. NLI GR 2240, Vol. 25.

O'Connor, M.P., *The life and letters of M.P. O'Connor*, New York: Dempsey & Carroll, 1893. LC, 561 p.

Stephenson, Jean, *Scotch-Irish Migration to South Carolina*, Strasburg, Va.: the author, 1971. Includes methodology on connecting families in South Carolina and Ireland using newspapers, records and other sources.

South Dakota

Kemp, David, *The Irish in Dakota*, Sioux Falls, S. Dak.: Mariah Press, 1995. NLI GR 2555, 158 p.

McDonald, Bill, *The Nunda Irish: a story of Irish immigrants: the joys and sorrows of their life in America and Dakota*, Stillwater, Minn.: Farmstead Publishing, 1990. NLI Ir 942 m 41, 237 p.

Mulrooney, Margaret M., *Fleeing the famine: North America and Irish refugees, 1845–1851*, Westport, Conn.: Praeger, 2003. NLC, 154 p.

Tennessee

Gleeson, Ed, *Rebel sons of Erin: a Civil War unit history of the Tenth Tennessee Infantry Regiment (Irish), Confederate States Volunteers*, Indianapolis, Ind.: Guild Press of Indiana, c.1993. LC, 429 p.

—— 'Tennessee Irishmen in Confederate service', in D. O'Hearn (ed.), *Erin Go Bragh: Advance Australia Fair*, Melbourne: Celtic Club, 1990, 86 p. History of the Celtic Club, Melbourne.

Taylor, Carol Sue, *The arrow and the shillelagh*, Knoxville, Tenn.: Tennessee Valley Pub., c.1996. LC, 74 p. Edward Henry and Jeanette McCarthy.

Texas

Bluntzer Hébert, Rachel, *The forgotten colony: San Patricio de Hibernia: the history, the people, and the legends of the Irish colony of McMullen-McGloin*, Burnet, Tex.: Eakin Press, c.1981. NLI GR 1383, 459 p.

Davis. See under 'Mexico'.

Flannery, J.B., *The Irish Texans*, San Antonio, Tex.: University of Texas, Institute of Texan Cultures at San Antonio, 1980. NLI Ir 973 f 4, 173 p.

Linehan, John C., 'The Irish pioneers of Texas', *Journal of the American-Irish Historical Society*, 2, 1899, pp. 120–38. NLI Ir 973 a 1.

Oberste, W.H., *Knights of Columbus in Texas, 1902–1952*, Austin, Tex.: Von Boeckmann-Jones Co., 1952. LC, 298 p.

—— *Texas Irish empresarios and their colonies: Power and Hewetson, McMullen and McGloin, Refugio—San Patricio*, Austin, Tex.: Von Boeckmann-Jones Co., 1953. NLI Ir 973 o 10, 310 p.

Rice, Bernardine, 'The Irish in Texas', *Journal of the American-Irish Historical Society*, 30, 1932, pp. 60–70. NLI Ir 973 a 1.

Roche, Richard, *The Texas connection: the story of the Wexford colony in Refugio*, Wexford: Wexford Heritage Committee, 1989. NLI Ir 942 r 10, 59 p.

Santiago, Mark, *The Red Captain: the life of Hugo O'Conor, commandant inspector of the interior provinces of New Spain*, Tucson, Ariz.: Arizona Historical Society, 1994. NLI A 2A 217, 127 p.

Vermont

Dunn, Mary Lee, *Ballykilcline rising: from famine Ireland to immigrant America*, Amherst, Mass.: University of Massachusetts Press, 2008. NLI, 218 p.

Murphy, Ronald Chase, *Irish famine immigrants in the state of Vermont: gravestone inscriptions*, Baltimore, Md.?: Clearfield, c.2000. LC, 723 p. Co-author, Janice Church Murphy.

Virginia

Chalkey, Lyman, *The Scotch-Irish Settlement in Virginia (Vols. 1–3)*, Baltimore, Md.: GPC, 1989 (reprint). Exhaustive compendium.

'Grantees of land in Virginia', *Journal of the American-Irish Historical Society*, 13. NLI Ir 973 a 1.

'Irish settlers on the Opequan', *Journal of the American-Irish Historical Society*, 6, 1906, pp. 71–4. NLI Ir 973 a 1.

Jamieson, Jean, *Jamieson and O'Callaghan ancestors*, 1978. LC, 124 p.

Lawless, Joseph T., 'Some Irish settlers in Virginia', *Journal of the American-Irish Historical Society*, 2, 1899, pp. 161–6. NLI Ir 973 a 1.

Linehan, John C., 'Early Irish settlements in Virginia', *Journal of the American-Irish Historical Society*, 4, 1904, pp. 30–42. NLI Ir 973 a 1.

McGinn, Brian, 'Virginia's lost Irish colonists', *IR*, No. 4 (1994), pp. 21–4. NLI.

O'Brien, M.J., 'Pioneer Irish families in Virginia, the Meades and Sullivans', *Historical papers: reprinted from the Journal of the American Irish Historical Society*, 1926. NLI GR 2240, Vol. 25.

O'Grady, Kelly J., *Clear the Confederate way!: the Irish in the army of Northern Virginia*, Mason City, Iowa: Savas, c.2000. NLI 1A 3081, 348 p.

Riley, Robert Shean, *The colonial Riley families of the Tidewater frontier*, Utica, Ky.: McDowell Publications, c.1999 (2 vols.). NLI G 9292 r 23. 'A history of several Riley families of Maryland and Virginia.'

West Virginia

Cook, Samuel R., *Monacans and miners: Native American and coal mining communities in Appalachia*, Lincoln, W.Va.: University of Nebraska Press, c.2000. LC, 329 p. Wyoming county.

Maloney, Charles R., *Devoted to Sunday: the meaning of the name Maloney: a West Virginia genealogy*, Charleston, W.Va: C.R. Maloney, 1988. LC, 127 leaves.

Wisconsin

Beaudot, William J.K., *An Irishman in the Iron Brigade: the Civil War memoirs of James P. Sullivan, Sergt., Company K, 6th Wisconsin Volunteers*, New York: Fordham University Press, 1993. NLI GR 1694, 189 p. Co-editor, Lance J. Herdegen.

Doran Barlow, Carol, *Chronicles of the Smith-Crowleys of Ireland and Iowa County, Wisconsin*, Roseville, Calif.: Roseville Printing Co., 1999. LC.

—— *Descendants of the Walsh-Dorans of Ireland and Rock County, Wisconsin*, Roseville, Calif.: Roseville Printing Co., c.2000. LC, 315 p.

Conzen, Kathleen Neils, *Immigrant Milwaukee, 1836–1860: accommodation and community in a frontier city*, Cambridge, Mass.: Harvard University Press, 1976. NLI G 977 c 18, 300 p.

Costello, Timon, *Shining emeralds*. See under 'Iowa'.

—— *Transplanted Shamrocks: the story of Daniel and Ann Claugher Costello coming to Byron, Wisconsin, from County Sligo, Ireland, in 1859*, Appleton, Wis.: St Patrick Press, c.1989. LC, 265 p.

Gorman, Elizabeth Joyce, *Edmund and Elizabeth (Patterson) Greany and their descendants from Ireland, 1848, to Wisconsin, 1856*, Janesville, Wis.: J. Gorman, 1989. LC, 1989, 128 p.

Holmes, David G., *Irish in Wisconsin*, Madison, Wis.: Wisconsin Historical Society Press, 2004. LC, 86 p.

Irish Genealogical Quarterly, Irish Genealogical Society of Wisconsin. NLI.

Kennedy, Genieve C., *The descendants of Charles Flynn and Margaret Faherty, County Longford, Ireland, and Crawford County, Wisconsin, 1850–1998*, Chula Vista, Calif.: G.C. Kennedy, 1998. LC, 239 p.

Kinney, Thomas P., *Irish settlers of Fitchburg, Wisconsin, 1840–1860*, Fitchburg, Wis.: Fitchburg Historical Society, 1993. NLI Ir 942 k 10, 111 p.

McDonald, M. Justille, *History of the Irish in Wisconsin in the nineteenth century*, Washington: Catholic University of America Press, 1954. NLI Ir 973 m 9, 324 p.

Metress. See under 'Illinois'.

Michaels, Bernard L., *A bit of the old sod: the account of the Byron-Lima settlement*, B.L. Michaels, c.1999. LC, 163 p.

Murphy Thibaudeau, May, *I shall not die, I shall live on in you*, South Milwaukee, Wis.: Ramur Pub., c.1990. LC, 167 p. Calvy and Green families.

Reardon Childs, Blanche, *A Reardon family history*, Evanston, Wis.: the author, 1991. NLI Ir 9292 r 16. Co. Tipperary to St Croix, Wisconsin.

Sheahan, Thomas J., *All those folks from Saint Patrick's: the Irish community of rural Maple Grove, Wisconsin*, Reedsville, Wis.: Friends of St Patrick's, c.2001. LC, 125 p.

U'Ren, William, *The Albany Vindicator Index: Green Co., WI, 1911–1925*, Rock Co. Genealogical Society, 2000. LC.

Ward Ryan, Carol, *Descendants of two Irish families: Ryan and Moore, from Ireland to Wisconsin, 1780's–1979*, Green Bay, Wis.: C.W. Ryan, 1979. LC, 162 p.

Wyoming

Emmons. See under 'The West'.

Ward, Harry Arundel, *Register: the story of Casper's Irish colony*, Bantry Publications, 2002. NLI A 2A 2777. Online at <*www.casperirish.com*>.

West Indies

General

Coldham, Peter Wilson, *The Complete Book of Emigrants in Bondage, 1614–1775*, GPC, 1988 (and supplements). NLI Ir 973 c 47, 600 p.

Gwynn, A., 'Documents relating to the Irish in the West Indies, with accounts of Irish Settlements, 1612–1752', *AH*, Vol. 4, pp. 140–286.

Kirby, Peadar, *Ireland and Latin America*, Dublin: Trócaire and Gill & Macmillan, 1992. NLI.

MacInery, M.H., *Irish slaves in the West Indies*, Dublin: Sealy, Bryers & Walker, 1909. NLI Ir 3269 m 1, 52 p.

Oliver, Vere Langford, *Caribbeana: Miscellaneous Papers Relating to the History, Topography, Genealogy and Antiquities of the British West Indies*, London: 1900–1919 (6 vols.). NLI 9729 O 1.

—— *The monumental inscriptions in the churches and churchyards of the island of Barbados, British West Indies*, London: 1915. BL; reprinted Glendale, Calif.: Sidewinder Press, 1988.

Antigua

Oliver, Vere Langford, *The History of the island of Antigua . . . from the first settlement in 1635 to the present time*, London: Mitchell & Hughes, 1894–9. BL, 3 vols.

Barbados

Lane, Geraldine, *Tracing Ancestors in Barbados: a practical guide*, Baltimore, Md.: GPC, 2007.

O'Callaghan, Sean, *To Hell or Barbados: The Ethnic Cleansing of Ireland*, Dingle: Brandon, 2000. NLI 240 p.

Williams, Joseph J., *Whence the 'black Irish' of Jamaica?* New York: L. MacVeagh, Dial Press, 1932. NLI Ir 94106 w 3, 97 p.

Jamaica

Williams. See under 'Barbados'.

Martinique

Clark de Dromentin. See under 'France: Bordeaux'.

Montserrat

Akenson, D.H., *If the Irish ran the world: Montserrat, 1630–1730*, Liverpool: Liverpool University Press, 1997. NLI Ir 94106 a 5, 372 p.

Clancy, Mary, *The Emigrant Experience*. See under 'Great Britain: General'.

McGinn, Brian, 'How Irish is Montserrat?' *IR*, Nos. 1 and 2 (1994), pp. 15–17 and 21–3. NLI.

St Croix

Gleeson, David T., *The Irish in the Atlantic world*, Columbia, SC: University of South Carolina Press, c.2010. 341 p. The Irish community at St Croix in the Danish West Indies.

South America

General

Cayol, Rafael, *El Barón de Ballenary*, Buenos Aires: 1989. Ambrose O'Higgins.

de Courcy Ireland, John, 'Irish soldiers and seamen in Latin America', *is*, Vol. 1, No. 4 (1952–3), pp. 296–303.

Kirby, Peadar, *Ireland and Latin America*, Dublin: Trócaire and Gill & Macmillan, 1992. NLI.

Lambert, Eric, 'Irish soldiers in South America, 1818–1830', *is*, Vol. 16, No. 62 (summer 1984), pp. 22–35.

—— *Voluntarios Británicos e Irlandeses en la Gesta Bolivariana*, Caracas: Dirección de Artes Gráficas del Ministerio de la Defensa, 1993, 3 vols. NLI Ir 942 L 14.

MacErlean, John, 'Irish Jesuits in foreign missions from 1574 to 1773', *Irish Jesuit directory and year book*, 1930, pp. 127–38. NLI Ir 2715 i 1.

McGinn, Brian, 'The South American Irish', *IR*, Nos. 25–8 (1998). NLI.

MacLoughlin, Guillermo, 'The Irish in South America', in M.D. Evans (ed.), *Aspects of Irish Genealogy: proceedings of the . . . Irish Genealogical Congress*, pp. 170–77, Dublin: Irish Genealogical Congress Committee, 1993. NLI Ir 9291 a 3. Co-editor, Eileen Ó Dúill.

MacMurrough Mulhall, Marion, 'Erin in South America', *Irish Rosary*, Vol. 12, No. 11 (November 1908), pp. 810–19. NLI Ir 05 i 21.

Marshall, Oliver, *European Immigration and Ethnicity in Latin America: A Bibliography*, London: Institute of Latin American Studies, 1991.

Mulhall, Michael G., *The English in South America*, Buenos Aires: Standard Office, 1878. LC, F2239.B8 M9 1977, reprinted New York: Arno Press, 1977.

Murphy, David, *The Irish Brigades, 1685–2006*, Dublin: Four Courts Press, 2007. 304 p. Irish regiments in North and South America.

Read, Jan, *The New Conquistadors*, London: Evans Brothers, 1980. Foreign officers in South America.

Ready, William B., 'The Irish and South America', *Éire-Ireland: A Journal of Irish Studies*, Vol. 1, No. 1 (1966), pp. 50–63.

Vicuna Mackenna, Benjamin, *Vida del General D. Juan Mackenna*, Santiago: Imprenta del Ferrocarrill, 1856.

Vila, Manuel Pérez, *Vida de Daniel Florencio O'Leary: Primer Edecán del Libertador*, Caracas: Imprenta Nacional, 1957. LC, F2235.5.O5 P4, 619 p.

Williams, W.J., 'Bolivar and his Irish Legionaires', *Studies: An Irish Quarterly Review*, Vol. 18, 1929, pp. 619–32. NLI Ir 05 s 7.

Argentina

Belgrano, Mario, *Repatriación de los restos del general Juan O'Brien, Guerrero de la Independencia Sud Americana*, Buenos Aires: Guillermo Kraft, 1938.

Brabazon, John, *Andanzas de un Irlandés en el Campo Porteño (1845–1864)*, Buenos Aires: Ediciones Culturales Argentinas, Secretaría de Estado de Cultura, 1981. NLI GO 441, 207 p.

Brown, Guillermo, *Memorias del Almirante Brown*, Buenos Aires: Academia Nacional de la Historia, 1957.

Bulfin, William, *Rambles in Eirinn*, London: Sphere, 1981. NLI Ir 9141 b 128, 2 vols. (reprint).

Coghlan, Eduardo, *El Aporte de los Irlandeses a la formación de la nación Argentina*, Buenos Aires: Librería Alberto Casares, 1982.

—— *Los Irlandeses en Argentina*, Buenos Aires: 1987. NLI LO 5273, 963 p.

de Courcy Ireland, John, *The admiral from Mayo: a life of Almirante William Brown of Foxford . . .* Dublin: E. Burke, c.1995. NLI Ir 92 b 472, 159 p.

—— 'Admiral William Brown', *IS*, Vol. 6, No. 23 (1962), pp. 119–21.

Fleming de Cornejo, Margarita, *Detrás de los retratos*, Salta: M. Fleming de Cornejo, 2000. LC, 259 p. Fleming family.

Gaynor, John, *The History of St. Patrick's College in Mercedes*, Buenos Aires: Southern Cross, 1958.

Graham-Yooll, Andrew, *The Forgotten Colony: A History of the English-Speaking Communities in Argentina*, London: Hutchinson, 1981. NLI G 982 g 3, 317 p.

Gwynn, A., 'The first Irish priests in the New World', *Studies: An Irish Quarterly Review*, Vol. 21, No. 82, June 1932, pp. 213–28. NLI Ir 05 s 7.

Harrington, Isabel H., *Un criollo irlandés*, Buenos Aires: 1976. LC, GV1010.32.H37 H37, 99 p. Life of Alfredo Harrington, Argentine polo-player.

Hayes, Seán S., 'Hurling in Argentina', *A Century of Service*, pp. 80–82, Dublin: Cumann Lúthchleas Gael, 1984. NLI Ir 396 g 18.

Julianello, Maria Theresa, 'The Story of Camilla O'Gorman', *IR*, No. 3 (1996), pp. 18–19. NLI.

Kelly, Helen, *Irish 'Ingleses': The Irish Immigrant Experience in Argentina, 1840–1920*, Dublin: Irish Academic Press, 2009. NLI, 250 p.

King, Seamus J., 'Hurling in Argentina,' in *The Clash of the Ash in Foreign Fields: Hurling Abroad*, Cashel: King, 1998. NLI.

Korol, Juan Carlos, *Cómo fue la inmigración irlandesa en la Argentina*, Buenos Aires: Plus Ultra, 1981. NLI Ir 942 k 4, 213 p.

Landaburu, Roberto E., *Irlandeses: Eduardo Casey, vida y obra*, Venado Tuerto: Fondo Editorial Mutual Venado Tuerto, 1995. LC, HC172.5.C37 L36 1995, 220 p. Founder of the city of Venado Tuerto.

'The Lynch family of Argentina', *IR*, No. 2 (1993), pp. 11–14. NLI.

MacLoughlin, Guillermo, 'Argentina: The forgotten people', *IR*, 4 (1993), pp. 6–7. NLI.

—— 'Casey and the one-eyed deer', *IR*, No. 3 (1994), p. 20. NLI.

—— 'The Hibernian-Argentinian', *IG*, 9, No. 4 (1997), pp. 423–7.

McKenna, Patrick, 'Irish emigration to Argentina: a different model', in Bielenberg, *The Irish Diaspora*. See McCracken under 'Africa'.

MacMurrough Mulhall, Marion, *Between the Amazon and the Andes; or, Ten years of a lady's travels in the pampas, Gran Chaco, Paraguay and Matto Grosso*, London: E. Stanford, 1881. LC, F2217.M95, 340 p.

Murray, John, 'The Irish and others in Argentina', *Studies: An Irish Quarterly Review*, No. 38, 1949, pp. 377–88. NLI Ir 05 s 7.

Murray, Thomas, *The story of the Irish in Argentina*, New York: P.J. Kenedy & Sons, 1919. NLI Ir 982 m 8, 512 p.

Nally, Pat, 'Los Irlandeses en la Argentina', *Familia: Ulster Genealogical Review*, Vol. 2, No. 8, 1992, pp. 69–77.

O'Sullivan, Patrick, 'Irish migration to Argentina', in *Patterns of migration*, Leicester: Leicester University Press, 1992. NLI Ir 324 o 8 Vol. 1, 231 p.

Platt, D.C.M., 'British agricultural colonization in Latin America', *Inter-American Economic Affairs*, 18, No. 3 (winter 1964), pp. 3–38.

Pyne, Peter, *The invasions of Buenos Aires, 1806–1807: the Irish dimension*, Liverpool: University of Liverpool, Institute of Latin American Studies, 1996. NLI Ir 982 p 20, 102 p.

—— 'A soldier under two flags: Lieutenant-Colonel James Florence Burke: Officer, adventurer and spy', *Études irlandaises* (spring 1996), Villeneuve-d'Ascq: CERIUL. NLI Ir 05 e 7.

Rodriguez, Horácio, *King*, Buenos Aires: Instituto Browniano, 1995. Argentine naval hero Juan (John) King from Westport, Co. Mayo.

Saez-Germain, Alejandro, 'Siempre al frente: Los Lynch: casi mil años de historia', *Noticias Magazine* (20 March 1994), pp. 44–51. Buenos Aires.

Share, Bernard, 'Tan gaucho como los gauchos: The Irish in Argentina', *Cara*, Vol. 16, No. 5 (Sep.–Oct. 1983), pp. 42–66.

The Southern Cross, Buenos Aires: 1875–.

Ussher, Santiago M., 'Irish immigrants in Argentina', *Irish Ecclesiastical Record*, 5th Ser., Vol. 70, pp. 385–92. NLI Ir 282 i 4.

—— *Las Hermanas de la Miseracordia (1856–1956)*, Buenos Aires: 1956.

—— *Los capellanes irlandeses en la collectividad hiberno-argentina durante el siglo XIX*, Buenos Aires: 1954.

—— *Padre Fahy, biografía de Antonio Domingo Fahy, OP, misionero irlandés en la Argentina, 1805–1871*, Buenos Aires: 1952. NLI Ir 92 f 84, 219 p.

Walsh, Micheline, 'Unpublished Admiral Brown documents in Madrid', *IS*, Vol. 3, No. 10, 1957, pp. 17–19.

White, Arden C., 'Irish immigration to Argentina: An historical focus', *The Irish at Home and Abroad*, Vol. 4, No. 3 (3rd qtr), 1997, pp. 133–4, Salt Lake City: 1993–2001. NLI Ir 9292 i 6.

—— 'Researching the Irish in Argentina', *The Irish at Home and Abroad*, Vol. 5, No. 1 (1st qtr), 1998, pp. 26–30, Salt Lake City: 1993–2001. NLI Ir 9292 i 6.

Bolivia

Burdett O'Connor, Francis, *Un Irlandés con Bolívar*, Caracas: El Cid Editor, 1977.

'Francis Burdett O'Connor', *IS*, Vol. 13, No. 51 (winter 1977), pp. 128–33.

Brazil

ABEI Newsletter (Brazilian Association for Irish Studies), University of São Paulo.

Basto, Fernando Lázaro de Barros, *Ex-combatentes irlandeses em Taperoá*, Rio de Janeiro: Editorial Vozes, 1971. NLI Ir 360 p 13, 52 p.

de Araujo Neto, Miguel Alexandre, 'An Anglo-Irish newspaper in nineteenth century Brazil: The Anglo-Brazilian Times, 1865–84', *ABEI Newsletter (Brazilian Association for Irish Studies)*, No. 8, 1994, pp. 11–13, University of São Paulo.

Gwynn, A., 'An Irish settlement on the Amazon', *PRIA*, Vol. 41, Section C, No. 1, 1932, pp. 1–54. NLI Ir 7941 O 3 (27).

—— *Father Thomas Field, SJ*, Dublin: Irish Messenger Publications, 1924.

Lauth, Aloisius Carlos, *A Colônia Príncipe Dom Pedro: um caso de politica imigratória no Brasil Império*, Brusque: Museo Arquidiocesano Dom Joaquim, 1987.

Lorimer, Joyce, *English and Irish settlement on the River Amazon, 1550–1646*, London: Hakluyt Society, 1989. NLI G 325 L 6, 499 p.

McCann, William, *Two Thousand Miles' Ride through the Argentine Provinces*, London: 1853. 2 vols. Reprinted New York: AMS Press, 1971.

McGinn, Brian, 'The Irish in Brazil', *IR*, No. 22, 1997, pp. 25–6. NLI.

Mulhall. See under 'Argentina'.

Ó Maidín, Pádraig, 'An Irish mutiny in Brazil and a betrayal', *Cork Examiner*, 21 May 1981.

von Allendorfer, Frederic, 'An Irish regiment in Brazil, 1826–8', *IS*, Vol. 3, No. 10, 1957, pp. 18–31.

Chile

Clissold, Stephen, *Bernardo O'Higgins and the Independence of Chile*, London: Hart-Davis, 1968. NLI G 983 0 4, 254 p.

Figueroa, Pedro Pablo, *Historia del popular escritor Don Benjamin Vicuna Mackenna, su vida, su carácter i sus obras*, Santiago de Chile: Imprenta Barcelona, 1903.

—— *Vida del General Don Juan O'Brien, Héroe de la Independencia Sud Americana, Irlandés de nacimiento, chileno de adopción*, Santiago de Chile: Imprenta Mejia, de A. Poblete Garin, 1904.

Vicuna Mackenna, Benjamin, *Vida de O'Higgins: La corona del héroe*, Santiago de Chile: Universidad de Chile, 1936. Bernardo O'Higgins.

Yáñez, Raúl Tellez, *El General Juan MacKenna*, Santiago de Chile: Editorial Francisco de Aguirre, 1976.

Colombia

Puyana, Edmundo Harker, *Bucaramanga y los Puyana: mi pueblo y mi gente*, Bucaramanga: Editorial Camara de Comercio de Bucaramanga, 1984. LC, F2291.B77 H36 1984, 160 p. How Francis O'Farrell founded the Puyana family.

Ecuador

de Courcy Ireland, John, 'Thomas Charles Wright: soldier of Bolivar, founder of the Ecuadorian Navy', *IS*, Vol. 6, No. 25 (winter 1964), pp. 271–5.

Lambert, Eric, 'Arthur Sandes of Kerry', *IS*, Vol. 12, No. 47 (winter 1975), pp. 139–46.

Paraguay

Brodsky, Alyn, *Madame Lynch and friend: the true account of an Irish adventuress and the dictator of Paraguay who destroyed that American nation*, London: Cassell, 1976. NLI Ir 92 L 7.3, 312 p.

Caraman, Philip, *The Lost Paradise: an account of the Jesuits in Paraguay, 1607–1768*, London: Sidgwick & Jackson, 1975.

'The First Irish priests in the New World', *Studies: An Irish Quarterly Review*, Vol. 11, No. 82 (June 1932), pp. 213–28. NLI Ir 05 s 7.

Gwynn, A., *Father Thomas Field, SJ*, Dublin: Irish Messenger Publications, 1924.

Mulhall. See under 'Argentina'.

Peru

McGinn, Brian, 'Saint Patrick's Day in Peru', *IR*, No. 1 (1995), pp. 26–7. NLI.

Venezuela

'General O'Leary and South America', *IS*, Vol. 11, No. 43 (winter 1973), pp. 57–74.

Lambert, Eric, *Carabobo*, Caracas: Fundación John Boulton, 1974. NLI G 987 l 2. Vital battle for Venezuela's independence in 1821; includes Irish participants.

McGinn, Brian, 'Venezuela's Irish legacy', *Irish America Magazine*, November 1991, pp. 34–7.

Vila, Manuel Pérez, *Vida de Daniel Florencio O'Leary: Primer Edecán del Libertador*, Caracas: Imprenta Nacional, 1957. LC, 619 p.

Chapter 9 ∾

THE REGISTRY OF DEEDS

THE SCOPE OF THE RECORDS

Because research in the Registry of Deeds can be laborious and time-consuming, it is a good idea to be aware of the limitations of its records before starting work there. The Registry was set up by the Irish Parliament in 1708 to help regularise the massive transfer of land ownership from the Roman Catholic, Anglo-Norman and Gaelic populations to the Protestant Anglo-Irish that had taken place over the preceding century. The registration of deeds was not obligatory: the function of the Registry was simply to provide evidence of legal title in the event of a dispute. These two facts—the voluntary nature of registration and the general aim of copperfastening the Cromwellian and Williamite confiscations—determine the nature of the records held by the Registry. The overwhelming majority deal with property-owning members of the Church of Ireland, and a disproportionate number of these relate to transactions that carried some risk of legal dispute. In other words, the deeds registered are generally of interest only for a minority of the population and constitute only a small fraction of the total number of property transactions carried out in the country.

The implications of these facts are worth spelling out in detail. Over the most useful period of the Registry's records, the non-Roman Catholic population of Ireland comprised, at most, a fifth of the total. A high proportion of these were dissenting Presbyterians, largely concentrated in the north and suffering restrictions on their property rights similar to, though not as severe as, those imposed on Catholics; very few deeds made by dissenting Protestants are registered. Of the remaining non-Roman Catholics the majority were small farmers, tradesmen or artisans, usually in a position of economic dependence on those with whom they might have property transactions and therefore in no position to dispute the terms of a deed. As a result, the records of the Registry cover only a small number of the non-Roman Catholic minority. There are exceptions, of course, for example large landlords who made and registered great numbers of leases with their smaller tenants; marriage settlements between families of relatively modest means; the business transactions of the small Catholic merchant class; or the registration of the holdings of the few surviving Catholic landowners after the relaxation of the Penal Laws in the 1780s. These are definitely exceptions, however, and for the vast bulk of the population—the Catholic tenant-farmers—the possibility of a deed having been registered can almost certainly be discounted, as they owned virtually nothing and had only tenuous legal rights to the property they occupied.

A further limit to the scope of the records is the scant use made of the Registry before the middle of the eighteenth century. It was only from about that time that registration became even relatively widespread, and its major genealogical usefulness is for the century or so from then until the 1850s, when it is generally superseded by other sources.

With these caveats in mind, it should now be said that for those who made and registered deeds, the records of the Registry can often provide superb information. The inclination to register deeds appears to have run in families: a single document can name two or three generations and can also lead back to a chain of related records that give a picture of the family's evolving fortunes and the network of its collateral relationships.

REGISTRATION

Registration worked in the following way. After a deed had been signed and witnessed, one of the parties to it had a copy made, known as a 'memorial', signed it and had it in turn witnessed by two people, at least one of whom had to have also witnessed the original. The memorial was then sworn before a justice of the peace as a faithful copy of the original and sent to the Registry. Here it was transcribed into a large manuscript volume and indexed. The original memorial was retained and stored, and these are all still preserved in the vaults of the Registry. For research purposes, however, the large manuscript volumes containing the transcripts of the memorials are used. The registration of a deed normally took place fairly soon after its execution, within a month or two in most cases, although delays of up to two years are quite common. If the gap between the execution and the registration of a deed is much longer, this may be significant: it indicates an impending need for one of the parties to the deed, or their heirs, to be able to show legal proof of its execution. The most common reason for such a necessity would have been the death of one of the parties.

THE INDEXES

The indexing system used by the Registry is complicated and incomplete. There are two sets of indexes: one by grantor's name (i.e. the name of the party disposing of the asset), the other by the name of the townland or street in which the property was situated. The Grantors Index is fully alphabetical and is divided into a number of sets covering different initial letters and periods. Between 1708 and 1833 the Grantors Index records the name of the grantor, the surname of the first grantee, and the volume, page and memorial number. No indication is given of the location of the property concerned—an omission that can make a search for references to a family with a common surname very tedious indeed. After 1833 the index is more comprehensive, listing the county in which the property was situated. In general, the index is remarkably accurate, but there are some mistakes, particularly in the volume and page references. In such instances the memorial number can be used to trace the transcript; several transcribers worked simultaneously on different volumes, and the volume numbers were sometimes transposed. If, for example, Volume 380 is not the correct reference, Volumes 378–82 may contain the transcript. Within each volume the transcripts are numerically consecutive.

The Lands Index is subdivided by county and is roughly alphabetical within each county, with townland names grouped together under their initial letter. This means that a search for deeds relating to, say, Ballyboy, Co. Roscommon, involves a search through all the references to Co. Roscommon townlands that start with the letter 'B'. The information given in the index is brief, recording only the surnames of two of the parties and the volume, page and deed numbers. As with the Grantors Index, the index is divided into a number of sets covering different periods. After 1828 it further subdivides the townlands by barony, making research a good deal more efficient. Alongside the county volumes there are separate indexes for corporation towns and cities. The subdivisions within these are somewhat eccentric, particularly in the case of Dublin, making it necessary to search even more widely than in the rural indexes. It should be pointed out that the Registry does not make it possible for the history of all the transactions in which a property was involved to be traced, because inevitably some of the deeds recording the transactions have not been registered.

In general, of the Registry's two sets of indexes the Grantors Index is the most genealogically useful, because it is strictly alphabetical and lists transactions by person rather than by property. The greatest omission in the Registry is of an index to the grantees: given the distribution of wealth in the country, the social range covered would be enhanced greatly by the production of such an index. Microfilm copies of both the Lands Index and the Grantors Index, amounting to more than four hundred reels, are available at NLI, PRONI and the LDS Family History Library. Volume 1 of Margaret Falley's *Irish and Scotch-Irish Ancestral Research*, available on open shelves in the NLI reading room, gives a complete breakdown of the locations and microfilm numbers of the NLI indexes up to 1850 (pp. 71–90). The only online access is by means of the Registry of Deeds Index Project at <*freepages.genealogy.rootsweb.ancestry.com/~registryofdeeds*>, a valiant attempt to index all the names in the eighteenth-century memorials using the LDS microfilms.

THE NATURE OF THE RECORDS

The archaic and legalistic terminology used in deeds can make it extremely difficult to work out what precisely the parties to a deed intended it to do. This is particularly true in cases where earlier agreements are referred to but not recited in full. However, from a genealogical point of view the precise nature of the transaction recorded is not always vital, and with a little practice it becomes relatively easy to pare the document down to the essentials of dates, placenames and personal names. It should be kept in mind that all personal names—buyers, sellers, trustees, mortgagees, witnesses—may be important and should be noted. There are, however, numerous cases in which the nature of the deed is of interest, and some advance knowledge will speed up the process of interpretation. So what follows here is an attempt to clarify some of the less familiar terms and to describe the most common or useful documents likely to be encountered.

The most important part of most deeds is the opening, and it follows an almost invariable pattern. After the phrase 'A memorial of', which indicates that the transcript is of a copy rather than the original, the following are stated: (1) the nature of the deed, (2) the date on which the original was made and (3) the names of the parties to the deed. It must be remembered that a number of people could constitute a single party for the purposes of a legal transaction. A typical opening would then be:

> A memorial of an indented deed of agreement dated October 13th 1793 between John O'Hara of Oak Park, Co. Meath, farmer, and George O'Hara of Balltown, Co. Meath, farmer, his eldest son of the first part, William Coakley of Navan, Co. Meath, merchant, of the second part, and Christopher French of Navan, gentleman, of the third part, in which . . .

Very often it is necessary to read no more than this to know that a deed is not relevant. If, for example, the research is on the O'Haras of Sligo, it is evident at a glance that the above document has no direct relevance. But, as happens so often in genealogy, the significance of information in a deed may only become clear retrospectively, in the light of something uncovered later. When carrying out a search for a particular family it is therefore a good idea to note briefly the important points in all deeds examined—names, addresses and occupations— whether or not they seem immediately relevant. That way, if it subsequently emerges that, for example, the O'Haras of Sligo and Meath are in fact related, the relevant deeds can be readily identified again.

Categorising the kinds of deeds that appear in the Registry can be difficult, as many of them are not what they appear to be. The most common misleading description in the opening of the memorial is the 'deed of lease and release', which may in fact be a conveyance or sale, a mortgage, a marriage settlement or a rent charge. 'Lease and release' was a legal device whereby the obligation to record a conveyance publicly could be avoided; it was not obligatory to record a transaction to a tenant or lessee already in occupation, and it was not obligatory to record a lease for one year only. Accordingly, a lease for one year was first granted and then the true transaction—conveyance, mortgage, marriage settle- ment or other—was carried out. It remained popular as a method of conveyance until 1845, when the Statute of Uses, which made it possible, was repealed.

Despite the difficulties created by such disguises as the lease and release, the underlying transactions fall into a number of broad classes:

1. Leases

By far the most common of the records in the Registry, leases could run for any term between 1 and 999 years, could depend on the lives of a number of persons named in the document or could be a mixture of the two, lasting three lives or sixty years, whichever was longer. Only leases for more than three years could be registered. The most genealogically useful information in such leases is the lives they mention. The choice of lives generally rested with the lessee or grantee, and in most cases those chosen were related. Often the names and ages of the grantee's children appear—an extremely valuable piece of information for families in the eighteenth century. Leases for 900 years, or for lives renewable in perpetuity, were much more common in Ireland than elsewhere and amounted to a permanent transfer of the property, although the grantor remained the nominal owner. As might be imagined, such leases provided a rich basis for legal disputes.

2. Marriage settlements

Any form of pre-nuptial property agreement between the families of the prospective bride and groom was known as a 'marriage settlement', or as 'marriage articles'. A variety of transactions can therefore be classed in this way. What they have in common is their aim to provide security, to women in particular: as married women could hold no property in their own right, it was common practice for the dowry to be granted to trustees rather than directly to the future husband, which allowed the women some degree of independence. It was also common for the family of the prospective husband, or the husband himself, to be granted an annuity out of the income of his land to the future wife and children should he predecease them. The information given in settlements varies, but in general it should at least include the names, addresses and occupations of the bride, groom and bride's father. In addition, other relatives— brothers, uncles etc.—may also put in an appearance. For obvious reasons, marriage settlements are among the most useful of the records held in the Registry. The period during which they were most commonly registered appears to have been the three decades from 1790 to 1820. When searching the Grantors Indexes for them it should be remembered that they are not always indicated as such and that the formal grantor may be a member of either family, making it necessary to search under both surnames.

3. Mortgages

In the eighteenth and nineteenth centuries, mortgages were very commonly used as a form of investment on the one hand and as a way of raising short-term cash on the other. Generally they do not provide a great deal of family information, but as they were an endless source of legal disputes they form a disproportionate number of the deeds registered. It was quite common for mortgages to be passed on to third or fourth parties, each hoping to make money, so the resulting deeds can be very complicated.

4. Bills of discovery

Under the Penal Laws, Catholics were not allowed to possess more than a very limited amount of land, and a Protestant who discovered a Catholic in possession of more than the permitted amount could file a bill of discovery to claim it. In practice, most bills appear to have been filed by Protestant friends of Catholic landowners to pre-empt hostile discovery and as a means of allowing them to remain in effectual possession. Registered bills are not common, but they are extremely interesting, both genealogically and historically.

5. Wills

Only those wills likely to be contested legally were registered, in other words those that omitted someone—almost certainly a family member who might have a legitimate claim. Abstracts of the personal and geographical information in all the wills registered between 1708 and 1832 have been published in P.B. Phair and E. Ellis (eds.), *Abstracts of Wills at the Registry of Deeds* (3 vols., Dublin: IMC, 1954–88), online at <*www.irishmanuscripts.ie*>. The full provisions of the wills are to be found only in the original memorials.

6. Rent charges

These were annual charges of a fixed sum payable out of the revenue generated by nominated lands. They were used to provide for family members in straitened circumstances or to pay off debts or mortgages in instalments. Once made, they could be transferred to others and were valuable assets in their own right. Depending on the terms, they can provide useful insights into family relationships and family fortunes.

Other, miscellaneous classes of deed also appear in the Registry of Deeds. As outlined above, the only common feature is that they record a property transaction of some description; any family information they may contain is a matter of luck.

Chapter 10 ～

NEWSPAPERS

Newspapers are one of the most enjoyable but also one of the most difficult of genealogical sources. Faced with so much of the everyday particularity of the past, it is impossible to confine oneself to biographical data; again and again research is sidetracked by curiosity. In addition to this, the endemic imprecision of family information means that it is almost always necessary to search a wide range of dates. A sustained search for genealogical information in original copies of newspapers is extremely time-consuming. If the efficient use of research time is a priority, newspapers are certainly not the place to start.

This proviso notwithstanding, the destruction of so many Irish records in 1922 gives a disproportionate importance to Irish newspapers, and when they do throw up information it can be extremely rewarding. Events are reported virtually as they happen, within a few weeks at most, and the reports have an authority and accuracy that is hard to match, even making allowances for journalistic errors. In addition, as more and more Irish newspapers become available in online archives, the balance between research time and results has shifted dramatically; the ability to quickly trawl entire decades of publications has made them much more genealogically useful.

INFORMATION GIVEN
There are two principal formats in which useful information appears in early newspapers: biographical notices and, in the earliest publications, advertisements. Up to the 1850s the former consist largely of marriage announcements and obituaries; birth announcements tend to be sparse, to relate only to the wealthiest classes and often to give no more than the father's name, taking the form 'on the 12th, the lady of George Gratton Esq., of a son'. After the middle of the nineteenth century the number of birth notices rises sharply, but they remain relatively uninformative.

Marriage announcements contain a much broader range of information, from the bare minimum of the names of the two parties to comprehensive accounts of the addresses, occupations and fathers' names. In the majority of cases the name of the bride's father and his address are supplied, in a form such as 'married on Tuesday last, Michael Thomson Esq. to Miss Neville, eldest daughter of James Neville of Bandon Esq.' For many eighteenth-century marriages a newspaper announcement may be the only surviving record, particularly where the relevant Church of Ireland register has not survived.

Obituaries are by far the most numerous newspaper announcements, and they cover a much broader social spectrum than either births or marriages. Again, the kind of information given can vary widely, from the barest 'died at Tullamore, Mr. Michael Cusack' to the most elaborate, giving occupation, exact age and family relationships: 'died at the house of her uncle Mr. Patrick Swan in George's St. in the 35th year of her age, Mrs. Burgess, relict of Henry Burgess Esq., late of Limerick.' This amount of information is rare, however: most announcements confine themselves to name, address, occupation and place of death. Because of the paucity of Catholic burial records, newspaper obituaries are the most comprehensive surviving records of the deaths of the majority of the Catholic middle classes. From about the 1840s the number of both obituaries and marriage announcements rose sharply; unfortunately, these events are by then usually more easily traceable in parish or civil records. In the twentieth century the newspaper death notice became an obligatory part of Irish life, often recording age, extended family and place of death. The online availability of complete runs of all three national dailies—the *Irish Times*, *Irish Press* and *Irish Independent*—has made these death notices a very significant element in any search for living relatives in Ireland.

Advertisements, especially in the early newspapers, were more often paid announcements than true advertisements in the modern sense, and an extraordinary variety of information can be gleaned from them. The most useful types are as follows:

(i)   *Elopements:* A husband would announce that his wife had absconded and disclaim all responsibility for any debts she might contract. Usually his address and her maiden name are given.

(ii) *Business announcements:* The most useful are those that record the place and nature of the business, a change of address or ownership for the business, or the succession of a son to a business after his father's death.

(iii) *Bankruptcies:* These generally request creditors to gather at a specified time and place, and they can be useful in narrowing the focus of a search for relevant transactions in the Registry of Deeds.

As well as their advertisements and biographical notices, of course, newspapers naturally reported the news of the day, concentrating on the details of court cases with particular relish. For an ancestor who was a convict these hold great interest, because much of the evidence was reported verbatim and may provide vital clues for further research. The full-text searches available in the online archives provide ways to retrieve these reports relatively easily. These searches also expand the range of individuals for whom newspaper research may be relevant. Many reports of court cases during the Land War of the 1870s and 80s supply long lists of tenants involved in opposing evictions, for instance.

PERSONS COVERED

Apart from reports of trials, the genealogical information to be gleaned from early newspapers relates to fairly well-defined social groups. Firstly, the doings of the nobility were of general interest, and their births, marriages and deaths are extensively covered. Next to be covered are the merchant and professional classes of the towns in which the newspapers were published. These would include barristers and solicitors, doctors, masters of schools, military officers and clergy, together with the more prosperous business people. It should be remembered that, from about the 1770s, this would include the growing Catholic merchant class. Next are the farming gentry from the surrounding areas. After them come the less well-off traders, traceable largely through advertisements. Finally, the provincial papers also cover the inhabitants of neighbouring towns in these same classes, albeit sparsely at times. No information is to be found concerning anyone at or below middling farmer level—the great bulk of the population, in other words. This remains true even from the third and fourth decades of the nineteenth century, when the number of announcements rose markedly and the social classes covered broadened somewhat.

As literacy grew, and as newspaper circulation expanded from the late nineteenth century into the early twentieth, this broadening of the social classes continued. Then, as now, publishing long lists of individuals—amateur football teams, successful candidates in the Intermediate Certificate examination, complete memberships of dramatic societies—was a way of ensuring that everyone on the list would buy the paper. With online full-text search it is possible to retrieve individuals from these lists quickly and painlessly.

DATES AND AREAS

The earliest Irish newspapers were published in Dublin at the end of the seventeenth century. However, it was not until the middle of the eighteenth century that they became widespread and began to carry information of genealogical value. The period of their prime usefulness is from about this time to about the middle of the nineteenth century, when other sources become more accessible and thorough. Obviously, not all areas of the country were equally well served, particularly at the beginning of this period. Publications tended to be concentrated in particular regions, as follows:

(i) *Dublin:* The most important eighteenth-century publications were the *Dublin Evening Post,* begun in 1719, *Faulkner's Dublin Journal* (1725), the *Freeman's Journal* (1763) and the *Dublin Hibernian Journal* (1771). As well as carrying plentiful marriage and obituary notices relating to Dublin and surrounding areas from about the middle of the century, these papers also reproduced notices that had first appeared in provincial papers—something that should be kept in mind in cases where the original local newspapers have not survived. From the early nineteenth century there was a great proliferation of publications; unfortunately, the custom of publishing family notices fell into disuse in the first decades of the century and did not resume until well into the 1820s. A full-text search of the *Freeman's Journal* is available at *<www.irishnewsarchive.com>*.

(ii) *Cork:* After Dublin, Cork was the area of the country best served by newspapers, with many publications following the lead of the *Corke Journal*, which began in 1753. As well as publishing notices relating specifically to Cork city and county, these papers also carried much of interest for other Munster counties, notably Co. Kerry. Like the Dublin papers, they republished notices relating to Munster that had originally appeared in other publications. An index exists to newspaper biographical notices relating to Cos. Cork and Kerry between 1756 and 1827, details of which will be found below. Some extracts from early editions of the *Corke Journal* are online at *<www.corkgen.org>*.

(iii) *Limerick and Clare:* There was a great deal of overlap between the earliest Clare newspapers— the *Clare Journal* from 1787 and the *Ennis Chronicle* from 1788—and those of Limerick, where the first publications were the *Munster Journal* (1749) and the *Limerick Chronicle*. Both groups of papers also had extensive coverage of Co. Tipperary, and in the case of the Limerick publications this coverage also extended to Cos. Kerry and Galway. The Molony series of manuscripts in the Genealogical Office (see Chapter 7) includes extensive abstracts from the Clare papers. Details of a more accessible and far-ranging set of abstracts will be found below. Obituaries and funeral notices from the *Limerick Chronicle* are transcribed in the 'Local studies' section of the Limerick City Library website, *<www.limerickcity.ie/Library>*.

(iv) *Carlow and Kilkenny:* This area was covered by a single publication, *Finn's Leinster Journal,* which began in 1768. Although the advertisements are useful, early biographical notices are sparse. The earliest have been published in the *Irish Genealogist* (1987/8). A full-text search is available at *<www.irishnewsarchive.com>*.

(v) *Waterford:* The earliest newspapers here were the *Waterford Chronicle* (1770), the *Waterford Herald* (1791) and the *Waterford Mirror* (1804). Few of the earliest issues appear to have survived. For surviving issues before 1800 the *Irish Genealogist* has published the biographical notices (1974 and 1976–80, inclusive). Notices to 1821 are included with the abstracts for Cos. Clare and Limerick.

(vi) *Belfast and Ulster:* The most important newspaper in this area is the *News Letter* (Belfast), which began publication in 1737. It had a wider geographical range than any of the Dublin papers, covering virtually all of east Ulster. Biographical material to 1800 is indexed at *<www.ucs.louisiana.edu/bnl>*. A full-text search 1828–190 is at *<www.britishnewspaperarchive.co.uk>*. Editions after 1900 are searchable at *<www.newsletter.co.uk>*. Outside Belfast, the most significant publications were the *Londonderry Journal,* from 1772, which also covered a good area of Cos. Donegal and Tyrone, and the *Newry Journal* and *Strabane Journal,* of which very few, if any, early issues survive.

LOCATIONS

Offline

The best repository for Irish newspapers is the British Library. After 1826 it was obliged to hold a copy of all Irish publications, and from that date its collection is virtually complete. It also has an extensive, though patchy, collection before that date. In Ireland the largest collection is held by the National Library of Ireland, though this is by no means comprehensive. Many unique copies are held in local libraries and other repositories. The *Report* of the NEWSPLAN Project in Ireland (NLI, 2nd ed., 1998) lists all known hard-copy and microfilm holdings of Irish newspapers. It is available as a database on the NLI website, <*www.nli.ie*>.

Online

Two major online Irish newspaper archives exist, <*www.irishnewsarchive.com*> and <*www.irishtimes.com/archive*>. The former has full-text searches of the stable of newspapers now part of the Independent Group, including many provincial titles of the nineteenth and early twentieth century. Its earliest titles are the *Freeman's Journal* from 1763 and *Finn's Leinster Journal* from 1768. The bulk of its collection comprises twentieth-century newspapers, including complete runs of the *Irish Independent* from 1905 and the *Irish Press* from 1931, and it can be very useful in tracking living relatives, by means of death notices in particular. The *Irish Times* archive includes an almost complete run of the paper from its foundation in 1859. For Irish newspapers in the British Library, see <*www.british newspaperarchive.co.uk*>.

INDEXES

A number of indexes exist to the biographical material to be found in newspapers, and they can greatly lighten the burden of research. The following list orders them by date.

1730–40	*Pue's Occurrences* and the *Dublin Gazette*. Marriages and deaths. NLI Ms. 3197.
1737–1800	*News Letter* (Belfast). Biographical material. Online: <*www.ucs.louisiana.edu/bnl*>.
1756–1827	Rosemary ffolliott's 'Index to Biographical Notices Collected from Newspapers, Principally Relating to Cork and Kerry, 1756–1827' transcribes all the notices from eleven Cork newspapers, together with relevant notices from a further eight Dublin and Leinster publications. Her 'Index to Biographical Notices in the Newspapers of Limerick, Ennis, Clonmel and Waterford, 1758–1821' covers eleven provincial and five Dublin newspapers. Between the two works almost all the surviving eighteenth-century notices for the southern half of the country are extracted. Copies are available in local libraries, DCLA, NLI and the library of the Society of Australian Genealogists.

1771–1818	*Hibernian Chronicle* (1771–1802) and *Cork Mercantile Chronicle* (1803–1818). Biographical notices. IGRS, London.
1772–84	Donald M. Schlegel, *Irish Genealogical Abstracts from the Londonderry Journal, 1772–1784* (Baltimore, Md.: 1990; reprinted 2001).
1772–1812	Henry Farrar, *Biographical Notices in Walker's Hibernian Magazine, 1772–1812* (Dublin: 1889). Online: <*www.celticcousins.net*>, among other places.
1792–1964	*Northern Star* (1792–7), *Northern Herald* (1833–6), *Downpatrick Recorder* (1836–86), *Co. Down Spectator* (1904–1964), *Mourne Observer* (1949–80), *Newtownards Chronicle* (1871–3). Southern Education and Library Board (Northern Ireland).
1828–64	Vol. 6 of Albert Casey's *O'Kief, Coshe Mang etc.* reprints the biographical notices from the *Kerry Evening Post* from 1828 to 1864 and includes them in the general index at the back of the volume.
1829–69	Births, marriages and deaths from the *Ballymoney Northern Herald and Ulster General Advertiser* (1860–63), the *Coleraine Chronicle* (1844–69) and the *Londonderry Sentinel* (1829–69). NIFHS CD-ROMS.
1841–6	*The Cork Examiner*, <*www.britishnewspaperarchive.co.uk*>.

Chapter 11 ✍

┃ DIRECTORIES

For those areas and classes they cover, Irish directories are an excellent source, often supplying information not readily available elsewhere. Their most obvious and practical use is that of finding out where precisely in the larger towns a family lived; but for members of the gentry and for the professional, merchant and trading classes they can show much more, providing indirect evidence of reversals of fortune or growing prosperity, of death or emigration. In many cases, directory entries are the only precise indication of occupation. The only classes totally excluded from all directories are, once again, the most disadvantaged: small tenant-farmers, landless labourers and servants. Virtually all classes other than these are at least partly included, in some of the nineteenth-century directories in particular. One point to be kept in mind when using any directory is that every entry is at least six months out of date by the time of publication.

The account that follows divides directories into Dublin directories, countrywide directories and provincial directories, supplying in each case the dates, locations and information included, followed, in the first two categories, by a chronological checklist.

DUBLIN DIRECTORIES
The Gentleman's and Citizen's Almanack, produced by John Watson, began publication in Dublin in 1736 and continued until 1844. However, the first true trade directories in Ireland were those published by Peter Wilson for the city of Dublin, beginning in 1751 and continuing until 1837, with a break from 1754 to 1759. From the outset these were considered as supplements to *Watson's Almanack* and were regularly bound with it. In 1787 the two publications were put together with the *English Court Registry,* and, until it ceased publication in 1837, the whole was known as the *Treble Almanack.*

Initially the information supplied in *Wilson's Directory* consisted purely of alphabetical lists of merchants and traders, supplying name, address and occupation. In the early years these were quite scanty, but they grew steadily over the decades, from less than a thousand names in the 1752 edition to almost five thousand in 1816. The last decades of the eighteenth century also saw the inclusion of separate lists of those who might now be termed the 'establishment':

officers of the city guilds and of Trinity College, state officials, those involved in the administration of medicine and the law, Church of Ireland clergy etc. The range of people covered expanded markedly, if a little eccentrically, in the early nineteenth century. The most permanent addition was a new section, added in 1815, that covered the nobility and gentry. A number of other listings of potential use to readers were also added, though some appear only intermittently. Persons covered by these lists include pawnbrokers, bankers, apothecaries, police, dentists, physicians, militia officers and ships' captains.

The most significant difference between the *Treble Almanack* and Pettigrew and Oulton's *Dublin Almanac and General Register of Ireland,* which began annual publication in 1834, is the inclusion in the latter of a street-by-street listing, initially only of the inhabitants of Dublin proper but enlarged annually to encompass the suburbs. From 1835 this listing was supplemented by an alphabetical list of the individuals recorded. In theory at least, the combination of the two listings should now make it possible to track the movements of individuals around the city—an important feature, as changes of address were very frequent in the nineteenth century, when the common practice was to rent rather than purchase. Unfortunately, in practice the alphabetical list is much less comprehensive than the street list.

Pettigrew and Oulton also extended even further the range of persons covered. The officers of virtually every Dublin institution, club and society are recorded, as are clergy of all denominations. Another significant difference from the earlier *Treble Almanack* that should be kept in mind is the extension of the coverage outside the Dublin area. Under the rubric 'Official Authorities of Counties and Towns', Pettigrew and Oulton recorded the names of many of the rural gentry and of more prosperous inhabitants of the large towns, in their guise as local administrators. This is particularly useful for areas that were not served by a local directory or for which none has survived. Similarly, the officials of many of the better-known institutions and societies in the larger country towns are also recorded, together with the more important provincial clergy.

An important competitor to Pettigrew and Oulton was the *Post Office Annual Directory and Calendar,* published by John S. Folds between c.1832 and c.1858. Although it does not include a street directory, almost three hundred pages give alphabetical listings of the nobility, gentry, merchants and traders of Dublin—a very comprehensive record of the pre-Famine city. There are also separate directories for the professions, including attorneys, barristers, benchers of the King's Inns, medical practitioners, surgeons and apothecaries. The *Annual Directory* was eventually put out of business by Thom's.

Alexander Thom's *Irish Almanac and Official Directory,* which began in 1844 and has continued publication up to the present, is by far the best-known Irish directory. As the name implies, it continued Pettigrew and Oulton's extension of coverage outside Dublin. To take one year as an example, the 1870 edition includes, as well as the alphabetical and street listings for Dublin, alphabetical lists of the following for the entire country: army officers; attorneys, solicitors and

1 N.—Bessborough-avenue.
Off North-strand-road.

1 Boyd, Mrs.	8*l.*
2 Flanagan, Mr. Thomas	
3 Preest, Mr. Patrick,	9*l.*
4 M'Carthy, Mr. Patk. J. G.P.O.	7*l.*
5 Hutchin, Mrs.	7*l.*
6 Purcell, Mr. Thomas,	10*l.*
7 Conroy, Mr. John,	10*l.*
8 Hatchell, Geo. master mariner,	8*l.*
9 Harbron, Mr. Wm. J.	9*l.*
10 Bell, Mr. Peter,	9*l*
11 Keane, Alphons., photographer, and 94 North-strand,	9*l.*
12 Byrne, Mr. Joseph,	8*l.*
13 Goulding, Daniel, carpenter,	7*l.*
14 O'Kelly, Mr. Alexander,	7*l.*
15 Curtis, Mrs.	8*l*
16 O'Callaghan, Mrs.	8*l.*
Link Line	
19 Frazer, Mr. James,	7*l.*
20 Reynolds, Mr. Thomas,	6*l.*
21 Robinson, Mr. Charles,	6*l.*
22 Armstrong, Mr. Andrew,	6*l.*
Link Line.	
24 Wren, Mr. James,	6*l.*
25 Carroll, Mr. Patrick,	7*l.*
26 Byrne, Mr. Patrick,	7*l.*
27 M'Cauley, Mr. Peter,	7*l.*
28 Gregan, Mr. Hugh,	
Drumcondra Link Line Railway	
32 Tomlinson, Mr. William,	12*l.*
33 Halliday, Mr. Thomas,	9*l.*
34 Grimes, James, engineer,	9*l.*
35 Wilcocks, Mr. Joseph,	9*l.*
36 Dillon, Mr. Andrew,	9*l.*
37 Lacy, Mr. James,	9*l.*
38 Scott, Mr. William,	9*l.*
39 Lambert, Mr. Thomas	7*l.*
40 Mooney, Mr. Mathew,	7*l.*
41 Hayden, Mr. John,	7*l.*
42 Smith, Mrs.	7*l.*
43 Hendry, Mr. William,	7*l.*
44 Sweny, Mr. Herbert Sidney,	7*l.*
45 Tuites, Mr. R.	7*l.*
46 Griffith, John,	7*l.*
47 Homan, Mr. Thomas,	4*l.* 10*s.*
48 Kennedy, Mrs.	4*l.* 10*s.*
49 Murphy, Mrs.,	6*l.*
50 Holmes, Mr. William,	6*l.*
51 Langan, Mr. John	

Bethesda-place.
Upper Dorset-street.
Three small cottages

3 S.—Bishop-street.

22½ Dunne, J. fishmonger,	7*l.*
23 Tenements,	16*l.*
24 Hayden, Mrs. board & lodging,	16*l.*
here Redmond's-hill & Peter's-row inters.	
25 Kelly, James, grocer, wine and spirit dealer, & 13 Peter's-row,	58*l.*
26, 27, 27A, 28 to 39 Jacob, W. R. & Co. (limited)	
40, 41 & 42 Tonge and Taggart, *South City* foundry and iron works,	37*l.*, 17*l.*
43 to 45 Tenements,	14*l.* to 17*l.*
46 Jacob, W. R. and Co. (limited) stores,	17*l.*
..........*here Bishop-court intersects........*	
47 to 49 Tenements,	20*l.* 9*l.*
50 Jacob, W. R. and Co. stores,	30*l.*
51 Tenements,	26*l.*
52 & 53 Tenements,	21*l.*, 24*l.*
54 & 55 Tenements,	17*l.*, 16*l.*
56 Leigh, P. provision merchant,	21*l.*

Black-street.
Infirmary-road.
Twenty small houses — Artizan's Dwellings company.

3 N.—Blackhall-parade.
From Blackhall-street to King-street, Nth.
P. St. Paul.—Arran-quay W.

1 Bourke, Mr. James,	9*l.*
2 Duffy, Mrs. lodgings,	9*l.*
3 Murphy, Mrs. M.	13*l.*
4 & 5 Condron, J. horseshoer and farrier,	8*l.*
6 & 7 Chew T. C. & Co. wool merchants, with 55 and 56 Queen-street, and 27 Island-street	
8 Dardis, Mr. M.	17*l.*
9 Clarke, Joseph, watch maker,	14*l.*
10 Tenements,	14*l.*
11 Duignan, Mrs.	14*l.*

3 N.—Blackhall-place.
From Ellis's-quay to Stoneybatter.
P. St. Paul.—Arran-quay W.

KING'S, OR BLUE COAT HOSPITAL—
George R. Armstrong, esq. agent and registrar; Rev. T. P. Richards, M.A. chaplain & head master

1 and 2 Menton, Denis, dairy, and 17 King-street, north,	59*l.*
3 and 4 Losty, Mr. M. J.	30*l.* 34*l.*
5 Young, Mr. William	
6 and 7 Paul and Vincent, farming implement manufs. millwrights, and iron founders, chemical ma-	

30 McKeever, Mr. J.	
34 Dixon, Mrs.	
35 King, Mrs. M.	
36 Kirk, Mr. B.	
37 Muldoon, Mr. T.	
38 Behan, Mr. P.	
39 Donovan, Mr. Henry,	
40 *Dublin Prison Gate Mission* Laun. workroom, and dormitories—J. C. Wilkinson, secretary.	

3 N.—Blackhall-street.
From Queen-street to Blackhall-pl
P. St. Paul.—Arran-quay W.

1 Gorman, Mrs.	
2 Hopkins, Mr. Robert,	
........*here Blackhall-parade inters.*	
3 Gordon, Samuel, wholesale manufacturer,	
4 *The National Hotel*—John We proprietor,	
5 Baird, Mrs.	
6 Clancy, Mrs. Mary,	
,, Doyle, Mr. T. M.	
,, Montgomery, Mr. James	
7 Dillon, Mr. John,	
8 Lemass, Mr. Joseph,	
9 Nurses' Training Institu Miss Tierney Superintende	
10 Mooney, Mrs.	
11 and 12 Ruins,	
13 Keogh, Mrs. J.	
14 Vacant,	
15 Tenements,	
........*here Blackhall-place inters*	
16 to 18 Fitzgerald, P. corn an stores,	16*l.*
19 & 20 Hickey & Co. stores off	
21 & 22 *Cairn's Memorial Home*,	
23 Correll, Mr. J.	
24 Doran, Mr. C. J.	
25 Leahy, Mr. W. J.	
26 Doheney, Mr. Joseph	
27 Eivers & Rispin, cattle sales	
,, Curtis, T. H. forage contrac	
28 Ralph, Mrs.,	
29 Hickey, Paul, & Co. cattle s corn, hay, and wool facto	
30 Scott, Mr. John F.	
31 Byrne, Mr. P. J.	
32 Cobbe, Mrs.	

3 S.—Blackpitt
From New-row, South, to Gra
P. St. Nicholas Without, east si
Luke, west.—M. rchauts'
.......LETTER BOX.

Thom's Dublin Directory, 1901. (*Courtesy of the Genealogical Office*)

barristers; bankers; Catholic, Church of Ireland and Presbyterian clergy; coastguard officers; doctors; members of Parliament; magistrates; members of the Irish Privy Council; naval and marine officers; officers of counties and towns; and peers. Although Thom's is generally regarded as a Dublin directory, its usefulness goes well beyond Dublin.

Dublin was also included in the countrywide publications of Pigot and Slater, issued at intervals during the nineteenth century. The only significant difference is the arrangement of the individuals listed under their trades, making it possible to identify all those engaged in the same occupation—important at a time when many occupations were handed down from one generation to the next. These directories are dealt with more fully below.

Checklist

1751–1837: Wilson's Directory. From 1787 it was issued as part of the *Treble Almanack.*

c.1832–c.58: Folds's *Post Office Annual Directory and Calendar.*

1834–49: Pettigrew and Oulton's *Dublin Almanac and General Register of Ireland.*

1844–: Thom's *Irish Almanac and Official Directory.*

See also Pigot's and Slater's countrywide directories from 1820.

NLI and NAI have extensive collections, but Dublin City Library and Archive hold the most comprehensive set. Access in DCLA is still to the published volumes, making research much easier than on microfilm or CD. Archive CD Books Ireland (<*www.archivecdbooks.ie*>) began the process of republishing early directories on CD-ROM in early 2005 and have now republished five editions of the *Treble Almanack* between 1783 and 1822, two editions of Pettigrew and Oulton from 1835 and 1842, Folds's *Post Office Annual Directory and Calendar* for 1843 and 1858, and four editions of Thom's between 1868 and 1910. All of these are also available through <*www.findmypast.ie*>. Pettigrew and Oulton (1842) is also available at <*www.failteromhat.com*>. The *Treble Almanack* from 1832 is now on <*books. google.com*>, along with Thom's from 1850 and 1852.

COUNTRYWIDE DIRECTORIES

Until the productions of Pigot and Co. in the early nineteenth century, very little exists that covers the entire country. Although not true directories in the sense of the Dublin publications, four works may be used in a similar way, at least as far as the country gentry are concerned. The earliest of these is Taylor and Skinner's *Road Maps of Ireland* (1778), which prints maps of the principal routes from Dublin to the country towns, including the major country houses and the surnames of their occupants, with an alphabetical index to these surnames. The aim of William Wilson's *Post-Chaise Companion* (1786) is similar, providing a discursive description of what might be seen on various journeys through the countryside. These descriptions include the names of the country houses and, again, their owners' surnames. There is no index. The next publications were the two editions, those of 1812 and 1814, of Ambrose Leet's *Directory*. This contains an alphabetical listing of placenames—with towns, villages, country houses and townlands in an arbitrary mix—showing the county, the nearest post town and, in the case of the houses, the full name of the occupant. These names are themselves indexed at the back of the volume.

The earliest countrywide directory covering more than the gentry was Pigot's *Commercial Directory of Ireland* (1820). This goes through the towns alphabetically, supplying the names of nobility and gentry living in or near the town and arranging the traders of each town according to their trade. Pigot published a subsequent edition in 1824, and his successor, Slater, issued expanded versions in 1846, 1856, 1870, 1881 and 1894. These followed the same basic format, dividing the country according to its four provinces and then dealing with towns and villages alphabetically within each province. With each edition the scope of the directory was steadily enlarged, including ever more towns and villages. Chapter 4: Guide to Irish Directories of *Irish Genealogy: A Record Finder* (ed. Donal Begley; Dublin: Heraldic Artists, 1981) includes a detailed county-by-county listing of the towns and villages covered by each edition. Another guide to the towns covered is available at <*www.irishtimes.com/ancestor*>. The most important differences between the various editions are as follows:

1824: Includes a countrywide alphabetical index to all the clergy, gentry and nobility listed in the entries for individual towns, omitted in subsequent issues.

1846: Includes the names of schoolteachers for the towns treated—a practice continued in later editions.

1881: Supplies the names of the principal farmers near each of the towns treated, giving the relevant parish. This feature was continued in the 1894 edition.

From 1824, separate alphabetical listings are given for the clergy, gentry and nobility of Dublin and for most of the larger urban centres.

Checklist

1778: Taylor and Skinner's *Road Maps of Ireland* (reprinted 1969: Irish University Press). NLI Ir 9141 t 1. Republished by Archive CD Books Ireland, CD ROM #IET0027, 2005. <*www.failteromhat.com*>.

1786: William Wilson's *The Post-Chaise Companion*. NLI J 9141 w 13. <*books.google.com*>.

1812: Ambrose Leet, *A List of... noted places*. NLI Ir 9141 l 10; LDS film 990023, item 2.

1814: Ambrose Leet, *A Directory to the Market Towns, Villages, Gentlemen's Seats and other noted places in Ireland*. NLI Ir 9141 l 10. <*www.findmypast.ie*>.

1820: J. Pigot, *Commercial Directory of Ireland*. NLI Ir 9141 c 25.

1824: J. Pigot, *City of Dublin and Hibernian Provincial Directory*. NLI Ir 9141 p 75. Republished by Archive CD Books Ireland, CD ROM #IET0005, 2005. <*www.failteromhat.com*>.

1846: Slater's *National Commercial Directory of Ireland*. NLI Ir 9141 s 30. <*www.findmypast.ie*>.

1856: Slater's *Royal National Commercial Directory of Ireland.*
1870: Slater's *Royal National Commercial Directory of Ireland.* <*www.findmypast.ie*>.
1881: Slater's *Royal National Commercial Directory of Ireland.* <*www.findmypast.ie*>.
1894: Slater's *Royal National Commercial Directory of Ireland.* <*www.findmypast.ie*>.
See also Dublin directories from 1834.

Eneclann's collection of CD-ROM versions is online at <*www.findmypast.ie*> and includes Pigot's (1824) and Slater's (1846, 1870, 1881 and 1894). Pigot's (1824) and Slater's (1846) are also at <*www.failteromhat.com*>, along with Taylor and Skinner's *Road Maps of Ireland* (1778).

PROVINCIAL DIRECTORIES

John Ferrar's *Directory of Limerick* (1769), online at <*www.celticcousins.net*>, was the first directory to deal specifically with a provincial town, and the practice spread throughout Munster in the remaining decades of the eighteenth century, with Cork particularly well covered. In the nineteenth century, local directories were produced in abundance, especially in areas with a strong commercial identity, such as Belfast, the north-east and, again, Munster. The quality and coverage of these varies widely, from the street-by-street listings in Martin's 1839 *Belfast Directory* to the barest of commercial lists. The best online collections are for the city and county of Cork at Cork City Library's site, <*www.corkpastandpresent.ie*>, and for Belfast and Ulster generally at PRONI, <*www.proni.gov.uk*>. A guide to the principal local directories is included in the county source lists in Chapter 13. These lists cannot, however, be regarded as complete: many small, local publications, especially from the first half of the nineteenth century, are now quite rare, with only one or two surviving copies. Locating these can be extremely difficult. Some guides are:

Carty, James, *Bibliography of Irish history, 1870–1911*, Dublin: NLI, 1940. NLI RR, 319 p.
Evans, Edward, *Historical and Bibliographical Account of Almanacks, Directories etc., in Ireland from the Sixteenth Century*, Dublin: 1897. NLI Ir 9410016 e 3. 149 p. Reprinted Blackrock, Co. Dublin: Carraig Books, 1976.
Keen, M.E., *A Bibliography of Trade Directories of the British Isles in the Victoria and Albert Museum*, London: Victoria and Albert Museum, 1979. NLI G 01742 v 1. 121 p.

In addition, Archive CD Books are uncovering forgotten local directories in the copyright library of Trinity College, Dublin, and republishing them. Their website, <*www.archivecdbooks.ie*>, gives details.

Chapter 12 ∽

| OCCUPATIONAL RECORDS

PART 1: ARMY, LAWYERS, MEDICS, CLERGY, TEACHERS

British army

Which records are relevant depends on whether your ancestor was a soldier or an officer and on the period in which they served. Almost all the records are in the English National Archives.

Soldiers

From the late eighteenth century a very large proportion of the rank and file of the British army consisted of Irishmen: one estimate for the middle of the nineteenth century is 40 per cent. You should remember that these men served throughout the army and not exclusively in the Irish regiments.

Soldiers' documents (discharges)

wo 97 contains records of discharges from the army between 1760 and 1913 and can often provide details of place of birth, age and appearance, and, after 1882, next of kin. The records up to 1882 only cover soldiers discharged to pension; after that year all discharges are recorded. Before 1873 the records are organised by regiment, but a name index exists for the period 1760–1854. For dates between 1854 and 1873 you must know the regiment to use the records. From 1873 to 1882 they are organised under the collective headings 'Artillery', 'Cavalry', 'Corps' and 'Infantry', and then within these alphabetically. From 1883 they are alphabetical. Many of the early discharge papers are summarised in the National Archives online catalogue, <*www.catalogue.nationalarchives.gov.uk*>. It can be worth while simply to enter the name of the individual, or the county militia, in the National Archives search page and see what emerges.

Only a minority of soldiers were actually discharged to pension; if your soldier does not appear in the soldiers' documents you many find him in one of the sources below.

Pension records

If a soldier was discharged to pension or as medically unfit in Ireland between 1760 and 1822, detailed information will be found in the registers of the Royal

Hospital, Kilmainham, wo 119, which contain the Certificates of Service. These records are searchable by name in the National Archives online catalogue. Go to <*www.nationalarchives.gov.uk/catalogue/search.asp*> and confine the search under 'department or series code' to wo 119.

In-pensioners' records (for those actually resident in the institution) go from 1704 to 1922 and are in wo 118. Irish out-pensioners (those receiving a pension but not resident) were administered from the Royal Hospital, Chelsea, after 1822 (wo 116 and 117). The pension records (1760–1915) of the Royal Hospital, Chelsea, are on <*www.findmypast.co.uk*>. Regimental Registers of Admissions to Pension also exist, indexed from 1806 to 1836; otherwise, each regimental volume includes an index. The NAI also has microfilm copies of the Kilmainham records.

You should remember that it was quite common for Irishmen to be discharged outside Ireland, in which case pension papers would be in the Chelsea records, even between 1760 and 1822, and that, again, only a minority of those who served are covered.

Pay lists and musters
Each regiment made a quarterly return of all personnel from the early eighteenth century to 1878. From the 1860s these also included details of wives and children living in married quarters. These are obviously much more comprehensive than the pensions and discharge records and can supply fascinating detail about individuals. The date of enlistment can be used for searching the relevant muster, which should give birthplace, age and former occupation. The records are in wo 10–13. However, it is necessary to know the regiment before using these records, which can be a serious obstacle.

Other records

Casualties and deserters
Soldiers who died on active service are recorded in the regimental returns of casualties from 1795 to 1875 in wo 25 and are indexed. Additional material, such as wills, lists of effects and details of next of kin, may also be found. The same series also includes details of absentees and registers of deserters for the first half of the nineteenth century. There is also an incomplete card index at the National Archives (Kew) to army deserters (1689–1830).

Description books
Also in wo 25 are the regimental description books—the earliest from 1756, the latest from 1900—which give physical details as well as service history. They are not comprehensive and do not cover the entire period.

Regimental registers of births, 1761–1924
The index to regimental registers of births, 1761–1924, gives the regiment and place of birth of children born to the wives of serving soldiers, if they were

attached to the regiment. The indexes are online at <*www.findmypast.co.uk*>. Full certificates can then be ordered online at <*www.gro.gov.uk*>.

Finding the regiment

For most of the pre-1873 records, knowing the regiment is vital. It can be quite difficult.

1. *Uniforms:* Wikipedia has an excellent list of British army cavalry and infantry regiments for 1881. Also useful is D.J. Barnes, 'Identification and Dating: Military Uniforms', in *Family History in Focus,* edited by D.J. Steel and L. Taylor (Guildford, Surrey: 1984), and the National Army Museum (<*www.national-army-museum.ac.uk*>).
2. The regimental registers of births (see above) can help if you have some idea of the names of children or the areas a soldier served in.
3. Wills of soldiers dying overseas were proved at the Prerogative Court of Canterbury (PROB 11). These are searchable online at <*www.nationalarchives. gov.uk/documentsonline*>. The registers of next of kin in WO 25 may also be useful.
4. If you have an idea where a soldier was stationed, and approximately when, J.M. Kitzmiller's *In Search of the Forlorn Hope: A Comprehensive Guide to Locating British Regiments and Their Records* (Salt Lake City: 1988) will help you to identify which regiments were stationed where.
5. David Murphy's *The Irish Brigades, 1685–2006: A Gazetteer of Irish Military Service, Past and Present* (Dublin: Four Courts Press, 2007) is a comprehensive account of Irish regiments in foreign armies

Later records

The Irish Soldiers' and Sailors' Fund
This fund was set up to provide cottages for Irishmen who had served in the armed forces during the First World War, and it helped build more than four thousand cottages up to the 1930s. (In Northern Ireland, cottages were built up to 1952.) The records are organised by place; there is no name index. The tenancy files for 1920–77 are in AP 7.

Anglo-Boer War
The Family Record Centre has separate indexes to the deaths of army personnel in the Anglo-Boer War, from 1899 to 1902. The GRO in Dublin also has an index to 'Deaths of Irish Subjects pertaining to the South African War (1898–1902)' in the deaths index for 1902. Certified copies of the original entries include regiment and rank.

First World War
Of the 6½ million service records of servicemen in the First World War originally held at the War Office Record Store, more than 4 million were destroyed in the

Second World War. Those that survived were charred or suffered water damage and are consequently unavailable for research. A microfilming project to make these records (generally known as the 'burnt documents') publicly accessible was completed in the summer of 2002, and the films are now available at the National Archives, through the LDS Family History Centres and online at <*www.ancestry. co.uk*>, which also has pension records, 1914–1920. More than 2 million individuals are covered, with a variety of records. Among the most common are attestation papers, which give information about name, address, date of birth and next of kin. The National Archives (Kew), <*www.nationalarchives.gov.uk/documentsonline*>, has the Medal Rolls Index Cards (1914–20) of the First World War.

Ireland's Memorial Records (Dublin: 1923) is an eight-volume commemorative publication listing the Irish men and women killed during the war and those of other nationalities who died while serving with Irish regiments. It is not, however, a complete list of all Irishmen killed while serving. It also supplies the place of origin. Online at <*www.findmypast.ie*>. (Eneclann CD ENEC011, 2004.)

The Commonwealth War Graves Commission

The commission maintains graves in more than 150 countries, covering more than 925,000 individuals—those members of the forces of the Commonwealth killed in the First and Second World Wars. Its website, <*www.cwgc.org*>, includes extensive details on those buried.

Officers

Lists

The official *Army List* was published at least annually from 1740, and it records all officers. *Hart's Army List* was published from 1839 to 1915 and supplies more information about individuals' army careers. Both publications are available at the Public Record Office. Annotated copies, sometimes including supplementary details, are in WO 65 (1754–1879) and WO 66 (1879–1900). A large collection of army lists is online at <*www.thegenealogist.co.uk*>.

Commissions

Records concerning the purchase and sale of the commissions of Irish officers from 1768 to 1871 can be found in HO 123. Correspondence relating to commissions generally between 1793 and 1871 is in WO 31. The records are arranged chronologically, can be extremely informative and are relatively simple to use, as the date of commission is supplied by the *Army List*.

Service records

These records, in WO 25, are not comprehensive, consisting of a series of surveys carried out every fifteen to twenty years between 1809 and 1872. The early returns concentrate on military service, with some biographical detail supplied in the later ones. The records are covered by an alphabetical card index on open access, which also takes in WO 75, an episodic series of regimental service returns between 1755 and 1954.

A Chelsea pensioner's enlistment record, 1869. (*British Army Service Records, reproduced courtesy of <www.findmypast.co.uk> and the National Archives, Kew.* © *Crown Copyright*)

Pensions
Up to 1871, if an officer did not sell his commission on retirement he went on half-pay (a retainer that meant he was theoretically available for service). Records of these payments, as well as widows' and dependants' pensions, can provide detailed biographical information. The half-pay ledgers of payment from 1737 to 1921 are in PMG 4, arranged by regiment up to 1841 and thereafter alphabetically. WO 25 also contains much detail on pensions and dependants.

Other
Many officers' original baptismal certificates are included in War Office records, for 1777–1868 in WO 32/8903 to WO 32/8920 (code 21A) and for 1755–1908 in WO 42. Both are indexed.

Attorneys and barristers
Up to 1867, in order to be admitted to the King's Inns Society it was necessary to become either a barrister or attorney (solicitor). Roman Catholics were excluded until 1794. To gain admission to the society as either an apprentice (to become a solicitor) or a student (to become a barrister), a good deal of family information had to be submitted. The earlier papers relating to admission are incomplete, but what survives has been published in *King's Inns admission papers, 1607–1867*, edited by Edward Keane, P. Beryl Phair and Thomas U. Sadleir (Dublin: Stationery Office, for the IMC, 1982). A companion volume, omitting solicitors, is Kenneth Ferguson's *King's Inns barristers, 1868–2004* (Dublin: King's Inns, 2005).

In following the later careers of lawyers, directories (in particular Dublin directories) are the major source.

Clergymen

Roman Catholic
As Roman Catholic priests did not marry, their usefulness for genealogical research is limited, but their relative prominence means that they left records that can lead to other members of their families. Obituaries are relatively common from the latter half of the nineteenth century, and the information in their seminary records can lead to a precise place of origin.

Until the 1790s all Irish Catholic clergy were educated on the Continent, because of the legal restrictions of the Penal Laws. When these were lifted, two seminaries were founded in short order, St Patrick's in Carlow and St Patrick's in Maynooth. Some of the records of both have been published.

Carlow College, 1793–1993: the ordained students and the teaching staff of St. Patrick's College, Carlow (J. McEvoy; Carlow: St Patrick's College, 1993).
Maynooth students and ordinations index, 1795–1895 (Birr, Co. Offaly: P.J. Hamell, 1992).

The *Irish Catholic Directory* was published annually from 1836 and lists priests by diocese and parish. Volumes 1 and 2 are available from Eneclann at <*www.eneclann.ie*>.

Church of Ireland

Biographical details of Church of Ireland clergy can be found in the Leslie Biographical Index, a far-reaching compendium originated by the Rev. James Leslie held at the Representative Church Body Library in Dublin. Additional information is also available in Leslie's Succession Lists, chronological accounts arranged by diocese and parish. The succession lists for sixteen dioceses have been published. The RCBL has these and the remaining dioceses in typescript.

Church of Ireland directories were also published, intermittently but frequently in the first half of the nineteenth century and annually from 1862. The 1862 and 1865 editions are now (2011) available on <*books.google.com*>.

Methodist

The essential work for Methodist clergy is *An Alphabetical Arrangement of All the Wesleyan Methodist Preachers and Missionaries (Ministers, Missionaries and Preachers on Trial), etc.* (Bradford: T. Inkersley), originally by William Hill but republished twenty-one times between 1819 and 1927. It covers all clergy in Britain and Ireland, giving locations and year of service. The 1827 and 1862 editions are now (2011) available on <*books.google.com*>.

C.H. Crookshank's *History of Methodism in Ireland, 1740–1860* (3 vols., Belfast: 1885–8) records brief biographical details of preachers. It is continued in H. Lee Cole's *History of Methodism in Ireland, 1860–1960* (Belfast: 1961).

Presbyterian

Two works cover almost all ministers. The Rev. James McConnell's *Fasti of the Irish Presbyterian Church, 1613–1840* (Belfast: 1938) covers the early years of the Synod of Ulster, and John M. Barkly's *Fasti of the General Assembly of the Presbyterian Church in Ireland, 1840–1910* (3 vols., Presbyterian Historical Society, 1986–7) takes things up to 1910. The Presbyterian Historical Society of Ireland maintains a very useful database covering six hundred historical and contemporary congregations at <*www.presbyterianhistoryireland.com*>. Other useful sources include:

Ferguson, Rev. S., *Brief Biographical Notices of some Irish Covenanting Ministers who laboured during the latter half of the eighteenth century*, Londonderry: J. Montgomery, 1897. NLI Ir 285 f 1.
History of Congregations. NLI Ir 285 h 8.
Irwin, C.H., *A History of Presbyterians in Dublin and the South and West of Ireland*, Dublin: Mecredy & Kyle, 1890. NLI Ir 285 i 1.
Latimer, W.T., *History of the Irish Presbyterians*, Belfast: J. Cleeland, 1902. NLI Ir 285 l 1.
McComb's Presbyterian Almanack, Belfast: W. McComb, 1841–1886? NLI Ir 285 m 1.

McConnell, J., *Fasti of the Irish Presbyterian Church*, Belfast: 1938. NLI Ir 285 m 14.

Marshall, W.F., *Ulster Sails West*, Baltimore, Md.: GPC, 1996. NLI Ir 973 m 59.

New Plan for Education in Ireland, 1838 (Part 1, pp. 200–205). Names of Presbyterian clergymen and their congregations in Cos. Antrim, Armagh, Down, Donegal, Fermanagh, Tyrone, Cork, Dublin, King's (Offaly), Louth, Westmeath and Mayo, 1837. NLI.

Reid, James Seiton, *History of the Presbyterian Church*, London: 1853. NLI Ir 285 r 1. Online: <*books.google.com*>.

Smith's *Belfast Almanack*, 1820. See Chapter 13, 'Antrim'.

Stewart, Rev. D., *The Seceders in Ireland, With Annals of Their Congregations*, Belfast: Presbyterian Historical Society, 1950. NLI Ir 285 s 5.

Witherow, Thomas, *Historical and Literary Memorials of Presbyterianism in Ireland, 1731–1800*, London: W. Mullan, 1880. NLI Ir 285 w 1.

Doctors

Because medical practice was only partly regulated before the middle of the nineteenth century, early records of medical education are patchy. The major Irish institutions were the Dublin Guild of Barber-Surgeons (from 1576), the Royal College of Physicians of Ireland (from 1667), the Royal College of Surgeons in Ireland (from 1784) and Apothecaries' Hall (from 1747). In addition, the University of Dublin (Trinity College) had a School of Physic (Medicine) from 1711. Many Irish medical men also trained in Britain or on the Continent.

The records of the Dublin Guild of Barber-Surgeons are in Trinity College, Dublin (Ms. 1447), and the Royal College of Physicians of Ireland has registers from the seventeenth century. However, both sources are difficult to access and use. In most cases, Dublin directories and freemen's lists are just as informative and easier to use. The records of Apothecaries' Hall from 1747 to 1833 are on microfilm in the National Library (Pos. 929). *Alumni Dublinenses* (eds. George D. Burtchaell and Thomas U. Sadleir; Dublin: 1935) contains detailed records of Trinity College students up to 1860.

For tracing the careers of medical practitioners, the major sources are Dublin directories, which list physicians and surgeons from 1761 and apothecaries from 1751; local, generally later, directories (see Chapter 11); and Irish Medical Directories, published intermittently between 1843 and the end of the nineteenth century.

Another, less conventional source is the 'Biographical file on Irish medics', compiled by T.P.C. Kirkpatrick, which is a compendium of biographical material on Irish medics up to 1954 held in the Royal College of Physicians. The college and the National Library both hold a copy of the index.

A bibliography of published works will be found in the checklist in Part 2.

Policemen

From the late eighteenth century a police force operated in Dublin city, with a part-time, *ad hoc* constabulary in the rest of the country. In 1814 the armed Peace

Preservation Force was created, followed in 1822 by the full-time County Constabulary. These two were amalgamated in 1836 to form the Irish Constabulary, renamed the Royal Irish Constabulary (better known as the RIC) in 1867. The separate Dublin force remained in existence and was known as the Dublin Metropolitan Police (DMP). With the creation of the Irish Free State in 1922, the RIC was disbanded. Responsibility for policing passed to the Garda Síochána in the 26 Counties and to the newly formed Royal Ulster Constabulary in the six counties of Northern Ireland.

Excellent personnel records were kept from 1816. The General Register from that date to 1922 is now in the National Archives, Kew (HO 184), with microfilm copies in NAI, the LDS Family History Library and PRONI. For each recruit it includes a brief service record, a date of marriage and wife's native county, and the name of the individual who recommended him. This can be important in helping to identify an exact place of origin, as the recommendations usually came from local clergymen or magistrates who knew the recruit personally. Thom's *Directories* (see Chapter 11) can pinpoint their address. HO 184 also includes a separate Officers' Register.

The partly alphabetical index to the registers included in HO 184 has now been superseded by Jim Herlihy's *The Royal Irish Constabulary: a complete alphabetical list of officers and men, 1816–1922* (Dublin: Four Courts Press, 1999), which supplies the service number needed to use the registers quickly and easily.

A further source, available only at the National Archives, Kew, is PMG 48, 'Pensions and allowances to officers, men and staff of the Royal Irish Constabulary and to their widows and children'. This dates from the 1870s and usually gives the address of the recipient.

An online discussion forum is at <*www.irishconstabulary.com*>.

Part of the RIC service register, showing enlistments for 1828. (*Courtesy of the National Archives of Ireland*)

The DMP register is now held by NAI and is available on microfilm. It does not give marriage details, but it supplies a parish of origin. See Jim Herlihy's *The Dublin Metropolitan Police: A short history and genealogical guide* (Dublin: Four Courts Press, 2001). Herlihy's website is *<www.esatclear.ie/~ric>*.

Teachers

Irish education was relatively informal until quite recently. Until the last quarter of the nineteenth century a large majority of Irish teachers had received no training.

The Society for Promoting the Education of the Poor of Ireland, better known as the Kildare Place Society, was the first attempt to provide systematic non-denominational primary education. Founded in 1811, it trained several thousand teachers and supported schools throughout the country. Its personnel records from 1814 to 1854 are now held by the Church of Ireland College of Education, Upper Rathmines Road, Dublin 6. Its website is at *<www.cice.ie>*.

Appendix 22 of the *Irish Education Enquiry, 1826, 2nd Report* (4 vols.) lists all parochial schools in Ireland in 1824, including names of teachers and other details. It is indexed in *Schoolmasters and schoolmistresses in Ireland, 1826–1827* (1982) by Dorothy Rines Dingfelder (NLI Ir 372 d 38).

The Irish Education Enquiry was set up because of the objections of the Roman Catholic hierarchy to the non-denominational nature of the Kildare Place schools. Its outcome was the establishment of the Board of National Education in 1831, which ended state support for the Kildare Place schools and placed control of elementary education in the hands of the local clergy in the form of national schools—a system that still exists.

The principal source for teachers in the national schools is the series of Teachers' Salary Books from 1834 to 1855 held by the National Archives. These are not particularly informative from a genealogical point of view, but they sometimes include comments that can be of interest. They are organised by school, so it is necessary to know where your teacher was working. (See also the bibliography of published sources in Part 2.)

PART 2: CHECKLIST OF SOURCES

Apothecaries

Admissions to the guilds of Dublin, 1792–1837; Reports from Committees; Parliamentary Papers, 1837, Vol. 11 (ii).

Ancient Dublin Freemen. Online: *<www.dublinheritage.ie>*.

Apothecaries, apprentices, journeymen and prosecutions, 1791–1829. GO Ms. 648.

List of Licensed Apothecaries of Ireland, 1872. NLI Ir 61501 i 1.

McWalter, James Charles, *A history of the Worshipful Company of Apothecaries of the City of Dublin*, Dublin: E. Ponsonby, 1916. NLI Ir 615 m 1. 166 p.

NLI Report on Private Collections No. 208.

Records of Apothecaries' Hall, Dublin: 1747–1833. NLI Pos. 929.

Architects

Irish Architectural Archive: *Dictionary of Irish Architects, 1720 to 1940*. Online: <*www.dia.ie*>.

Loeber, Rolf, *A biographical dictionary of architects in Ireland, 1600–1720*, London: J. Murray, 1981. NLI Ir 9291 L 2. 127 p.

Artists

Breeze, George, *Society of Artists in Ireland: index of exhibits, 1765–80*, Dublin: National Gallery of Ireland, 1985. NLI Ir 708 b 11. 57 p.

Crookshank, Ann, and Glin, Knight of, *The painters of Ireland, c.1660–1920*, London: Barrie & Jenkins, 1978. NLI Ir 750 c 2.

Murray, Peter, *Cork artists in the 19th century*, Cork: 1991. Catalogue of Crawford Gallery exhibition. NLI Ir 708 c 7.

Stewart, Ann M., *Royal Hibernian Academy of Arts: index of exhibitors and their works, 1826–1979*. Dublin: Manton, 1986 (3 vols.). NLI Ir 921 r 2.

Strickland, Walter G., *A dictionary of Irish artists*, Shannon: Irish University Press, 1969 (2 vols.). Reprint of the 1913 edition. NLI RR 750941.

Williams, John, *Artists of Ireland*, 1796. NLI Ir 9275 w 3.

Aristocracy and gentry

Bence-Jones, Mark, *Burke's Guide to Country Houses, Vol. 1: Ireland*, London: Burke's, 1978. A clear guide to families who owned particular houses.

Burke's Commoners of Great Britain and Ireland, 1837 (3 vols.).

Burke's Extinct Peerages . . . 1831. Five subsequent editions.

Burke's Landed Gentry of Great Britain and Ireland (4 vols.). Subsequent editions 1858, 1863, 1871, 1879, 1886, 1894, 1898 and 1937. (Irish supplement.)

Burke's Landed Gentry of Ireland. Subsequent editions 1904, 1912 and 1958.

Burke's Peerage and Baronetage of the United Kingdom . . . 1826. 106 subsequent editions.

Debrett's Peerage, Baronetage, Knightage and Companionage, 1852. Many subsequent editions.

Leet, Ambrose, *A Directory to the Market Towns, Villages, Gentlemen's Seats and other Noted Places in Ireland*, 1812 and 1814. Shows country houses and their owners. NLI Ir 9141 l 10.

The Post-Chaise Companion through Ireland (1783). Descriptions of journeys along the main coach roads, including the names of country houses and their owners' surnames. NLI. <*books.google.com*>.

Taylor and Skinner's *Road Maps of Ireland*, 1778; reprinted 1969: Irish University Press. Shows homes of gentlemen along the major routes through the country; the surnames are alphabetically indexed. NLI Ir 9414 t 1. Online: <*www.failteromhat.com*>.

A Visitation of Seats and Arms of the Noblemen and Gentlemen of Great Britain and Ireland (1852–3). See Hugh Montgomery-Massinberd, *Burke's Family Index* (London: Burke's, 1976) for a composite index.

Walford, E., *The County Families of the United Kingdom*, London: Chatto & Windus, 1877. Subsequent editions annually. 1919 edition at *<www.archive. org>*, 1913 edition at *<books.google.com>*.

Bakers

Admissions to the guilds of Dublin, 1792–1837: Reports from Committees, Parliamentary Papers, 1837, Vol. 11 (ii).
Ancient Dublin Freemen. Online: *<www.dublinheritage.ie>*.
Freemen's Rolls of the city of Dublin, 1468–85 and 1575–1774, in (i) GO 490–93 (Thrift Abstracts), (ii) DCLA (Original Registers) and (iii) NLI Mss. 76–9.

Barbers and surgeons

Admissions to the guilds of Dublin, 1792–1837: Reports from Committees, Parliamentary Papers, 1837, Vol. 11 (ii).
Freemen's Rolls of the city of Dublin, 1468–85 and 1575–1774, in
 (i) GO 490–93 (Thrift Abstracts), (ii) DCLA (Original Registers) and (iii) Ancient Dublin Freemen. Online: *<www.dublinheritage.ie>*.

Board of Ordnance employees

'Mainly concerned with the upkeep of fortifications and harbours, with some of the principal locations being Buncrana, Enniskillen, Ballincollig, Cóbh, Spike Island,' *IG*, 1985.

Booksellers and printers

Dix, E.R. McClintock, *Dictionary of Printers and Booksellers, 1668–1775*. NLI 6551 b 1 and 6551 b 4. See also under 'Dix' in NLI Author Catalogue for various provincial centres.
Irish Booksellers and English Authors, Dublin: R.C. Cole, 1954.
Kirkpatrick, T.P.C., *Notes on Dublin Printers in the Seventeenth Century*, Dublin: University Press, 1929. NLI Ir 65510941 k 1.
Pollard, A.W., *A short title catalogue of books printed in England, Scotland and Ireland . . . 1475–1640*, Bibliographical Society, 1986–91 (3 vols.). Joint editor, G.R. Redgrave. Vol. 3 includes an index of printers and publishers.

Brewers

Old Kilkenny Review, 1988, p. 583.

Bricklayers

See 'Barbers and surgeons'.
'Dublin city tradesmen employed by Board of Works', *Dún Laoghaire Genealogical Society Journal*, Vol. 4 (2), 1995.
Records of the Bricklayers' and Stonemasons' Guild, from 1830. NA Acc. 1097.

Carpenters

See 'Barbers and surgeons'.

Clark, Mary, 'The Dublin Guild of Carpenters, 1656', *IG*, 8, No. 3 (1992), pp. 333–5.

'Dublin city tradesmen employed by Board of Works', *Dún Laoghaire Genealogical Society Journal,* Vol. 4 (2), 1995.

Clockmakers

Fennell, Geraldine, *A List of Irish Watch- and Clockmakers*, Dublin: Stationery Office, 1963. NLI Ir 681 f 10. 42 p.

National Museum Ms., 'List of Watch and Clockmakers in Ireland, 1687–1844'. NLI Pos. 204.

Coachbuilders

Cooke, Jim, *Ireland's premier coachbuilder, John Hutton & Sons, Summerhill, Dublin, 1779–1925*, Dublin: 1993. NLI Ir 670 p 33(2).

Coastguard

See 'Navy'.

<www.coastguardsofyesteryear.org>.

Cooks and vintners

See 'Barbers and surgeons'.

Convicts

Eighteenth and early nineteenth centuries Prisoners' petitions. NAI.

1796   Return of prisoners who were discharged out of the Four Courts Marshalsea by virtue of the Acts of Insolvency from the 9th day of February 1796 to the 10th day of January, 1798. 160 names. NAI OP 52/16.

1798–   Original Prison Registers for more than forty individual prisons, in many cases giving details of prisoners' families; unindexed, in chronological order. Most date from the 1840s, but some start much earlier, for example Kilmainham (1798), Cork City Gaol (1822), Limerick Gaol (1830), Sligo Gaol (1836) and Trim Gaol (1837). NAI. Online at <www.findmypast.ie>.

1800   List of boys sent to New Geneva Prison, Feb. 13, 1800. 19 names. NAI OP 87/3.

1806   List of debtors confined in the Marshalsea of Clonmel. Calendar of Prisoners found guilty and executed—together with those tried and found guilty and now confined in the Gaol of Clonmel, 30 Dec. 1806. 51 names. NAI OP 245/1.

1808   List of persons in Limerick Gaol admitted to bail: charged by L. Burke [*sic*], 10 Dec. 1808. NAI OP 267/19.

1809   Calendars of prisoners in Waterford Gaol detained for trial at the next assizes, 29 Jan. 1809. 21 names. NAI OP 267/2.

1810   Calendars of Prisoners not tried and confined in the Gaols of Limerick city and county, Waterford and Clonmel. 148 names. NAI OP 308/15b, c, d, e.

1810   Prisoners for trial, Co. Kilkenny, Dec. 4 1810. Six names. NAI OP 308/15a.

1810   Lists of Prisoners: Croom, Kilross, Rathkeale and Kilfinnane Bridewells, Co. Limerick. Dec. 17 1810. NAI OP 308/16a and b.

1811   Calendar of prisoners in Limerick Gaol, Jan. 1811. NAI OP 347/1.

1812   Quarterly reports of the Governors of the House of Industry on Dublin Penitentiaries, James' St, Smithfield and Kilmainham, 5 July 1812. Listing all prisoners, with detailed notes; includes prisoners convicted outside Dublin. NAI OP 373/15.

1814–23   *Parliamentary Papers, Vol. 22 (1824): Convictions, 1814–23, Limerick City Assizes and Quarter sessions.* All persons committed for trial under the Insurrection Act (1823–4) in Cos. Clare, Cork, Kerry, Kildare, Kilkenny, King's, Limerick and Tipperary. NLI.

1815   Return of boys committed to Smithfield Penitentiary. Jan 1815 to Jan 1821. NAI OP 538/1.

1815   Return of Convicts (with name, age, crime etc.) sentenced to death or transportation at spring and summer assizes, 1815: Cos. Antrim, Armagh, Cavan, Donegal, Down, Drogheda, Fermanagh, Leitrim, Longford, Louth, Meath, Monaghan, Tyrone and Tipperary, July and Aug. 1815. Part only. 102 names. NAI OP 439/15.

1816   List of Prisoners in Roscommon Gaol who solicit that their sentences may be speedily put in execution. Nov. 8 1816. NAI OP 462/20.

1817   Calendars of prisoners confined in various gaols, Dec. 31 1817. NAI OP 488/50.

1817   Convictions at Downpatrick Assizes, Mar. 31 1817. NAI OP 488/36.

1818   Lists of Convicts under sentence of Death or Transportation in the Gaol of Newgate. Mar. 5 1818. NAI OP 515/2.

1818   Lists of Convicts under sentence of Death or Transportation in the several Gaols of Ireland (names, ages, crimes etc.), Feb. 1818. NAI OP 515/1.

1821   A calendar of prisoners in the custody of Henry Green Barry, Esq., High Sheriff of Co. Cork, at summer assizes, 1821, with details of crimes, sentences etc. CAI.

1832   Register of persons convicted at the Assizes and Petty Sessions in Co. Kerry, 1832–99. NLI Ms. 906.

1842–3   Prosecutions at Spring Assizes, 1842–43. *Parliamentary Papers, 1843, Vol. 50*, pp. (619) 34ff.

See also NAI Registered Papers Indexes and Calendar.

Doctors

See Part 1 of this chapter.

Cameron, Charles A., *History of the Royal College of Surgeons in Ireland, and of the Irish schools of medicine, including numerous biographical sketches, also a medical bibliography*, Dublin: Fannin, 1916. NLI Ir 6107 c 1.

Doolin, W., *Dublin's surgeon-anatomists and other essays: a centenary tribute*, Dublin: Department of History of Medicine, RCSI, 1987. NLI Ir 610 d 8.

Fleetwood, John F., *The history of medicine in Ireland*, Dublin: Skellig Press, 1983. NLI Ir 610 f 3, 373 p.

Lyons, J.B., *Brief lives of Irish doctors*, Dublin: Blackwater Press, c.1978. NLI Ir 921 L 1, 182 p.

—— *A pride of professors: the professors of medicine at the Royal College of Surgeons in Ireland, 1813–1985*, Dublin: A. & A. Farmar, 1999. NLI Ir 610 L 3.

—— *The quality of Mercer's: the story of Mercer's Hospital, 1734–1991*, Dún Laoghaire, Co. Dublin: Glendale Press, 1991. NLI Ir 362 L 2. 215 p.

—— *St Michael's Hospital, Dún Laoghaire, 1876–1976*, Dalkey, Co. Dublin: 1976. NLI Ir 610 L 1, 47 p.

O'Sullivan, Denis J., *The Cork School of Medicine: a history*, Cork: UCC Medical Alumni Association, 2007. NLI.

Sheppard, Julia, *Guide to the Contemporary Medical Archives Centre in the Wellcome Institute for the History of Medicine*, the institute, 1971. BL YK.1991.a.10735.

Wallis, P.J., and Wallis, R.V., *Eighteenth century medics: subscriptions, licences, apprenticeships*, Newcastle-upon-Tyne: Project for Historical Bio-bibliography, 1985. With the assistance of T.D. Whittet. NLI Ir 610 w.

Widdess, J.D.H, *The Charitable Infirmary, Jervis Street, Dublin, 1718–1968*, Dublin: Hely Thom, 1968. NLI 1B 2988. 68 p.

—— *A history of the Royal College of Physicians of Ireland, 1654–1963*, Edinburgh: E. & S. Livingstone, 1963. NLI Ir 6107 w 2.

—— *The Richmond, Whitworth and Hardwicke Hospitals: St Laurence's, Dublin, 1772–1972*, 1972. NLI Ir 362 w 2.

—— *The Royal College of Surgeons in Ireland and its medical school, 1784–1984*, Dublin: RCSI, 1984. NLI Ir 61709 w 2.

Dublin trade guilds

Ancient Freemen of Dublin, 1461–91 and 1564–1774. Online: <*www.dublinheritage.ie*>.

Engineers

Cox, Ronald C., *Engineering Ireland*, Cork: Collins Press, 2005. NLI. 371 p.

Loeber, Rolf, 'Biographical dictionary of engineers in Ireland, 1600–1730', *IS*, Vol. 13, No. 52 (1978–9), pp. 230–55. NLI Ir 355 i 6.

O'Donoghue, Brendan, *The Irish County Surveyors, 1834–1944: a biographical dictionary*, Dublin: Four Courts Press, 2007. NLI, 332 p.

Goldsmiths

Admissions to the Freedom of Dublin. Online: <*www.dublinheritage.ie*>.

Assay Office, Registrations of gold- and silversmiths (1637–). Also NLI Pos. 6851 (1637–1702); Pos. 6785 (1704–1855, with some gaps); Pos. 6782: freemen (1637–1779); Pos. 6784, 6788, 6851: apprentices.

Fitzgerald, Alison, 'The business of being a goldsmith in eighteenth-century Dublin', in Gillian O'Brien and Finola O'Kane-Crimmins (eds.), *Georgian Dublin*, Dublin: 2008, pp. 127–35.

—— 'The production of silver in late-Georgian Dublin', *Irish Architectural and Decorative Studies: The Journal of the Irish Georgian Society*, 4 (2001), pp. 8–48. With Conor O'Brien.

GO 665; LDS British Film 100213, item 9. Dublin: Goldsmiths, 1675–1810.

Jackson, Charles James, *English Goldsmiths and Their Marks*, New York: Dover Publications, 1964. Contains extensive information on Irish goldsmiths and silversmiths. NLI RR 73931 j 1.

JCHAS, Ser. 2, Vol. 8, 1902.

'Notes and pamphlets relating to goldsmiths and silversmiths in Cork, Dublin and Galway'. NAI M.465.

Linen-workers and weavers

1796 Linen Board premiums for growing flax. NLI Ir 633411 i 7. Online: Hayes.

Admissions to the Freedom of Dublin. Online: <*www.dublinheritage.ie*>.

'Workers and Manufacturers in Linen', in *The Stephenson Reports, 1755–84*. NLI Ir 6551.

Masons

See 'Barbers and surgeons'.

'Dublin city tradesmen employed by Board of Works', *Dún Laoghaire Genealogical Society Journal*, Vol. 4 (2), 1995.

Members of Parliament

Johnston-Liik, Edith Mary, *History of the Irish Parliament, 1692–1800: commons, constituencies and statutes*, Belfast: UHF, 2002. NLI RR 94107 j 7.

NLI Mss. 184 and 2098. Details of Irish members of Parliament.

Walker, B.M, *Parliamentary Election Results in Ireland, 1801–1922*, Dublin: RIA, 1978. NLI Ir 324 w 4, 438 p.

—— *Parliamentary Election Results in Ireland, 1918–1992*, Dublin: RIA, 1992. NLI Ir 324 p 7, 358 p.

See also local history source lists under the relevant county in Chapter 13.

Merchants

See 'Barbers and surgeons' and also 'Local directories' under the county source lists in Chapter 13.

Militia

The English National Archives has more than eight hundred muster books and pay lists of Irish county militia and volunteer regiments (WO 13/2574 to WO 13/3370) dating from the end of the eighteenth century to the late nineteenth century—a seriously under-explored source. Musters may also show enrolment and discharge information. Separate from these are the militia attestation papers, 1806–1915 (WO 96). These record the service details of large numbers of Irishmen, mainly from the second half of the nineteenth century, and are online at <*www.findmypast.co.uk*>. GO Ms. 608 has 1761 militia lists for Cos. Cork, Derry, Donegal, Down, Dublin, Kerry, Limerick, Louth, Monaghan, Roscommon, Tyrone and Wicklow.

Millers

See 'Barbers and surgeons'.
Hogg, William E., *The Millers and Mills of Ireland . . . of about 1859*, Dublin: 1997. NLI Ir 620 h 2.

Navy

The Navy List, 1814, 1819, 1827–79, 1885 et seq., NLI 35905 Top floor. Seniority and disposition lists of all commissioned officers, masters, pursers, surgeons, chaplains, yard officers, coast guards, revenue cruisers and packets. See also <*www.books.google.com*>.
O'Byrne, W.R, *A Naval Biographical Dictionary,* London: J. Murray, 1849 (3 vols.). NLI 9235 o 1/3B 2676–8.
Rodger, N.A.M., *Naval Records for Genealogists,* London: HMSO, 1984. Records of the National Archives, Kew.
Royal Marines Registers of Service (1842–1925). Online database: <*www.national archives.gov.uk/documentsonline*>.
Royal Naval Seamen (1853–1923). Online database: <*www.nationalarchives.gov. uk/documentsonline*>.

Paper-makers

Muir, Alison, 'The Eighteenth-century Paper-makers of the north of Ireland', *Familia: Ulster Genealogical Review,* 7, No. 2 (2005), pp. 37–73.

Plumbers

See 'Barbers and surgeons'.
'Dublin city tradesmen employed by Board of Works', *Dún Laoghaire Genealogical Society Journal,* Vol. 4 (2), 1995.

Post Office employees

Correspondence and reports to 1835. Sub-section in pre-1831 Calendars of Official Papers, NAI.
'Dublin city tradesmen employed by Board of Works', *Dún Laoghaire Genealogical Society Journal,* Vol. 4 (2), 1995.

Records of the Post Office, reports, minutes and pensions, 1686–1920 (all Ireland), 1920 to date (NI). British Postal Museum and Archive. Online: <*postalheritage.org.uk*>.

Prison warders
General Prisons Board applications for employment. NAI. From 1847.

Publicans
Excise Licences in premises valued under £10, 1832–1838: Reports from Committees, Parliamentary Papers, 1837–38, Vol. 13 (ii), pp. 558–601 and 602–607.

Railway workers
1870s–1950s: Irish Transport Genealogical Archives, Irish Railway Record Society, Heuston Station, Dublin. <*www.irrs.ie*> and irishrailwayrecords@gmail.com.

Lecky, Joseph, *Records of the Irish Transport Genealogical Museum,* Irish Railway Record Society. NLI Ir 385 L 8.

McCamley, Bill, *Dublin tram workers, 1872–1945,* Dublin: Labour History Workshop, 2008. NLI. 275 p.

Revenue officers
Employees of the Irish Revenue Service in 1709: <*www.from-ireland.net/history/Revenue-Officers%2C-1709*>.

Seamen
Agreements and Crew Lists series, NAI.

Agreements and Crew Lists series, National Archives, Kew.

Cox, N.G., 'The records of the Registrar General of Shipping and Seamen', *Maritime History,* Vol. 2, 1972.

Deceased Seamen, 1887–1949. Names (and other information) for seamen whose deaths were reported to the GRO. NLI 31242 d.

Irish-born merchant seamen in the British merchant marine, 1918–21. 23,000 names. Online: <*www.irishmariners.ie*>.

Murphy, Frank, 'Pursuit of seafaring ancestors', *Decies,* 16. NLI Ir 9414 d 5.

RNLI volunteers. Online: <*www.rnli.org.uk*>.

Silversmiths
See 'Goldsmiths'.

Smiths
See 'Barbers and surgeons'.

'Dublin city tradesmen employed by Board of Works', *Dún Laoghaire Genealogical Society Journal,* Vol. 4 (2), 1995.

Stonemasons
See 'Bricklayers'.

Teachers
Akenson, D.H., *The Irish Education Experiment*, London: Routledge & Kegan Paul, 1970. NLI Ir 372 a 4.

Brennan, M., *Schools of Kildare and Leighlin, 1775–1835*, Dublin: M.H. Gill & Son, 1935. NLI Ir 37094135 b 4, 616 p.

Corcoran, T.S., *Some lists of Catholic lay teachers and their illegal schools in the later Penal times*, Dublin: M.H. Gill & Son, 1932. NLI Ir 370941 c 12.

de Brún, Pádraig, *Scriptural Instruction in the Vernacular: the Irish Society and its teachers, 1818–1827*, Dublin: Dublin Institute for Advanced Studies, 2009. NLI, 680 p.

ffolliott, R. 'Some schoolmasters in the diocese of Killaloe, 1808', *JNMAS*, Vol. 11, 1968.

Handwritten list of national school teachers, 1905. NAI PCO/R/1 3/760/3.

'The Irish Society's Bible teachers, 1818–1827', *Éigse: A Journal of Irish Studies*, Vol. 18, Nos. 1 and 2. NLI Ir 8916205 e 4.

Linehan, John C., 'Irish school-masters in the American colonies', *Catholic Bulletin*, Vol. 29, pp. 784–8. NLI Ir 942 l 9.

'Some early schools of Kilkenny', *Old Kilkenny Review*, 3, 1960.

'Teachers of Cashel and Emly, 1750–60', *Catholic Bulletin*, Vol. 29, pp. 784–8.

Vintners
See 'Barbers and surgeons'.

Watchmakers
See 'Clockmakers'.

Weavers
See 'Linen-workers and weavers'.

Chapter 13 ∿

| COUNTY SOURCE LISTS

T he source lists included here are intended primarily as working research tools, with references as specific as possible, and very little explanation of the records given. An outline of the mechanics of the categories used is therefore necessary here.

CENSUS RETURNS AND SUBSTITUTES
Where no indication of the nature of the record is given, a description should be found in Chapter 2: Census Records. Griffith's Valuation and the Tithe Books are dealt with in Chapter 4: Property and Valuation Records. Locations are given in the text for all records mentioned, with, if possible, exact reference numbers. National Library call numbers for published works should be found in the 'Local histories etc.' or 'Local journals' sections. More recent additions are flagged 'NLI'. The precise call number is easily retrievable from the NLI online catalogue. The absence of an LDS reference does not mean that the work is not in the Library.

THE INTERNET
References are generally given only to the home page of the relevant site, unless the records are especially well hidden. To preserve clarity, cross-references from the main record categories mainly use the title of the website, rather than the full online address (URL). The URL will be found in the 'Online' section. Only websites referred to directly in the census, parish or other county listings are given here. Other, more general sites are dealt with in Chapter 5.

LOCAL HISTORIES ETC.
The bibliographies given are by no means exhaustive, and the works cited vary enormously in their usefulness. I have tried, where possible, to give a sample location and reference number for each work. The lists also include some unpublished material, where this is relevant.

LOCAL JOURNALS
The journals noted are those originating in or covering part of the particular county. Where possible, National Library of Ireland call numbers are given. The

absence of the number means that the journal started publication relatively recently and, at the time of writing, had not yet been assigned a number.

GRAVESTONE INSCRIPTIONS

Many of the largest collections of indexed transcripts of gravestone inscriptions are now held by local heritage centres. For counties where this is the case, the name of the relevant centre is supplied. Further details will be found in Chapter 15, 'Research services'. This section does not cover the transcripts published in the *Journal of the Association for the Preservation of the Memorials of the Dead,* as the records are not treated in a geographically consistent way. Nonetheless, over the forty-seven years of its existence, between 1888 and 1934, the *Journal* published a huge volume of inscriptions, many of which have since been destroyed. A composite index to surnames and places for the first twenty years of publication was published in 1910; the remaining volumes have their own indexes. Again, National Library call numbers for the local history journals or local histories will be found in the sections dealing specifically with the journals and histories. The online listings for gravestone transcripts are not comprehensive. The largest sites for volunteer-submitted transcripts are *<www.findagrave.com>* and *<www.interment. net>*. Many of the transcripts on these are only partial. The most durable site is *<www.interment.net>*, and where it holds significant numbers for a county this is indicated.

ESTATE RECORDS

A summary is given of relevant, catalogued records in the National Archives, National Library and county archives for Cos. Armagh, Carlow, Cavan, Clare, Cork, Donegal, Fermanagh, Galway, Kerry, Kildare, Leitrim, Limerick, Longford, Mayo, Monaghan, Roscommon, Sligo, Tyrone, Waterford and Westmeath. The estate record holdings of the Public Record Office of Northern Ireland are also included, covering mainly the six counties now part of Northern Ireland—Cos. Antrim, Armagh, Derry/Londonderry, Down, Fermanagh and Tyrone—but also parts of Cos. Cavan, Donegal, Longford, Leitrim, Monaghan and Sligo. The identification of these records, and the parishes they relate to, was made possible by the depth of coverage provided by PRONI's own online eCatalogue, and the chance it supplied to correlate placenames with Griffith's in *<www. askaboutireland.ie>*.

It should be kept in mind that these lists omit other repositories. A great deal of material covering all areas of Ireland survives in county libraries, in private collections and in the English national and local archives. A more detailed account of the nature of these records is given at the end of Chapter 4: Property and Valuation Records.

PLACENAMES

References given in earlier editions to works dealing with placenames on a county basis are now incorporated in the local history section. Material of more general use in identifying Irish placenames for the entire island is as follows:

Townlands Indexes: Produced on the basis of the returns of the 1851, 1871 and 1901 censuses, these list all the townlands in the country in strict alphabetical order. The 1851 Index uses the forms of placenames standardised by the Ordnance Survey. The full 1851 *Townlands Index* is now available online at *<www.irish times.com/ancestor>* and *<www.leitrim-roscommon.com>*. The 1901 *Townlands Index* has been transcribed to database by Perry McIntyre and Terry Eakin in Australia and is available from *<www.irelandhome.com.au>*.

Addenda to the 1841 Census: Also known as the 1841 *Townlands Index,* this is also based on the census returns but organises townlands on a different basis. They are grouped alphabetically within civil parishes, which are then grouped alphabetically within baronies, which are grouped by county. The organisation is very useful in tracking down variant townland spellings, once it is known that a particlar townland is to be found in a particular area; but if the later *Townlands Indexes* do not record it, the general area can be searched in the 1841 *Addenda* for names which are close enough to be possible variants. NLI Ir 310 c 1.

Townlands in Poor Law Unions: Produced by the Office of the Registrar-General for use by local registration officers, this series of pamphlets lists townlands in each Registration District, or Poor Law Union (see Chapter 1, 'Using civil 2records with other sources'). It is useful in attempting to identify placenames given in civil records. NLI Ir 9141 b 35. It has been reprinted as *Townlands in Poor Law Unions* (ed. Handran, Salem, Mass.: Higginson, 1997).

Topographical Dictionary of Ireland by Samuel Lewis, 1837: This goes through civil parishes in alphabetical order, giving a brief history, an economic and social description, and the names and residences of the 'principal inhabitants'. It also records the corresponding Catholic parish, and the locations of Methodist and Presbyterian congregations. The entire text is downloadable free from the Ordnance Survey of Ireland Historic Archive *<shop.osi.ie>*. The accompanying Atlas is useful in determining the precise relative positions of the parishes.

Ordnance Survey of Ireland: There are three main OSI sources of value in tracking down the many unapproved or 'sub-denominational' placenames that escaped standardisation in the 1830s:

1. Manuscript indexes to placenames on the original OSI 6-inch (six inches to a mile) maps include many sub-townland names which are not found elsewhere. Microfilm copies in NLI are

> Pos. 4621: Cos. Cork, Clare, Kerry
> Pos. 4622: Cos. Tipperary, Galway, Leitrim, Mayo
> Pos. 4623: Cos. Sligo, Antrim, Armagh, Cavan, Donegal, Roscommon, Waterford, Limerick
> Pos. 4624: Cos. Kildare, Carlow, Down, Dublin, Fermanagh, Kilkenny, Offaly, Longford, Louth, Meath, Monaghan

Pos. 4625: Cos. Laois, Tyrone, Westmeath, Wexford, Wicklow and Derry/Londonderry.

2. Ordnance Survey Name Books, complied by John O'Donovan in the course of the Survey, record local naming practices and traditions. Microfilm copies are at NLI, with microfilms for Ulster at Queen's University, Belfast.

3. OSI's Historic Archive at <*maps.osi.ie*> has a free fully searchable version of the current map of Ireland, which can be overlaid on superbly clear copies of the original 1840s 6-inch maps and the much more detailed 25-inch maps from the 1890s and early 1900s. These can be invaluable not only in identifying a placename but in judging the geographical and topographical relationships between areas where different families may have lived. The Ordnance Survey of Northern Ireland (<*maps.osni.gov.uk*>) has an equally detailed, though less addictive, service for the six counties.

Placenames Commission: The Irish Placenames Commission was established in 1946 to research the Irish-language origins of placenames and to provide authoritative Irish forms of those names for official and public use. Its website, <*www.logainm.ie*>, gives access to almost all the research carried out over the last seventy years. It is most useful for the origins of names—for local history rather than genealogy, in other words—but its database includes thousands of placenames—rivers, mountains, local nicknames—that are not covered in any of the official nineteenth-century publications.

Other works of general interest include Yann Goblet's *Index to Townlands in the Civil Survey, 1654–6* (IMC, 1954), *Locations of Churches in the Irish Provinces* (Church of Jesus Christ of Latter-Day Saints, 1978), NLI Ir 7265 i 8, and *The Parliamentary Gazetteer of Ireland* (1846), NLI Ir 9141 p 30.

ANTRIM

Census returns and substitutes

1614/15	'Carrickfergus merchants and ships' captains', *Carrickfergus and District Historical Society Journal*, Vol. 2, 1986.
1630	Muster Roll of Ulster. Armagh County Library; PRONI D.1759/3C/3, T. 808/15164; NLI Pos. 206. Part online: McAfee.
1641	Testimonies of 330 witnesses to the 1641 Rebellion. Online: 1641.
1642	Muster Roll. PRONI T.3726/2; also LDS SLC film 897012. Marquis of Argyll's Regiment, Ballycastle, Ballintoy and Dunluce.
1642	Muster Roll, Belfast and Dunmurry. PRONI T. 563.
1659	Pender's 'Census'.
1661	Books of Survey and Distribution. PRONI T.370/A and MIC 532.
1666	Hearth Money Roll. NLI Pos. 207; also PRONI T/307.
1666	Subsidy Roll. PRONI T/808/14889.

1669	Hearth Money Roll. NLI Ms. 9584; PRONI T.307 Online: McAfee.
1720	Down and Antrim landed gentry. RIA 24 k 19.
1734	'Religious census of part of the barony of Cary', *The Glynns*, 1993, 1994. Householder's names.
1740	Protestant householders in the parishes of Ahoghill, Armoy, Ballintoy, Ballymoney, Ballywillin, Billy, Drummaul, Duneane, Dunluce, Finvoy, Kilraghts, Kirkinriola, Loughguile, Ramoan, Rasharkin, Rathlin Island. PRONI T808/15258. Online: PRONI name search. GO 539.
1746	Freeholders: voters and registrations, 1746–1840. Online: Freeholders.
1766	Ahoghill, Ballintoy, Ballymoney, Ballynure. Online: PRONI name search.
1768	Pipewater rent, Lisburn. From Wallace estate papers. PRONI D.195.
1775	Dissenters' petitions from Antrim, Ballyclare, Ballymena, Ballynure, Belfast, Carnmoney, Carrickfergus, Donegore, Kilbride and Nilteen, Drumbeg, Lisburn, Larne, Raloo, Carncastle, Kilwaughter, Glenarm and Ballyeaston. Online: PRONI name search.
1779	Map of Glenarm, including tenants' names, *The Glynns*, No. 9, 1981.
1796	Spinning-Wheel Premium List. 1,125 names for Co. Antrim. Online: Hayes.
1798	Persons who suffered losses in the 1798 Rebellion. Propertied classes only. c.140 names. NLI I 94107. Online: FindMyPast.
1799–1800	Militia Pay Lists and Muster Rolls. PRONI T.1115/1A and B.
1803	Ballintoy inhabitants. C of I registers. PRONI T.679/68–9, MIC.1/111 p.
1803	Agricultural survey recording householders, occupations and agricultural possessions. Covers Armoy, Ballymoney, Ballyrashane, Billy, Culfeightrin, Derrykeighan, Dunluce, Kilraghts, Loughguile, Ramoan, Rathlin Island. NAI OP 153/103/1–16; also PRONI. Online: UHF; part online: McAfee.
1804–1810	Ballymoney inhabitants listed by street, *North Antrim Roots*, Vol. 2 (3), 1989.
1813	Census of Ballyeaston Presbyterian Congregation in Ballycor, Donagore, Glenwhirry, Grange of Doagh, Kilbride and Rashee, Co. Antrim. LDS Fiche 6026299, LDS film 100173.
1820	Lisburn householders. PRONI T679/107–112.
1821	Various fragments. NAI Thrift Abstracts.
1823	Parishioners' list, C of I parish of Layd, Co. Antrim. PRONI T.679/359–63.
1823–38	Tithe Books.
1833–9	*Emigrants from Antrim. Irish Emigration Lists, 1833–9*, Baltimore, Md.: GPC, 1989. Online: Olive tree.
1834	Carrickfergus freeholders, leaseholders and householders. From Court of Quarter Sessions. LDS film 990408.

1837	House Book for Belfast. House-by-house valuation, giving house-holders' names. Date not completely certain. NAI OL 70001 VO Quarto book.
1837	Valuation of towns returning MPs (occupants and property values), Lisburn. Parliamentary Papers, 1837, Reports from Committees.
1837–8	Memorials from inhabitants for quarter sessions. (1837: Lisburn, c.70 names, Ballycastle, c.100 names, Glenarm, c.65 names; 1838: Ballynure, Ballylinny, Ballycorr, Rashee (commonly called Ballyeaston) and the Grange of Doagh, c.350 names.) Many with occupations. NAI OP 1837/10.
1839–1948	Some material, including admissions registers and relief registers, survives for all the unions of Co. Antrim. PRONI BG Series; LDS holds microfilm copies of Ballymena (259181–5), Belfast (259177), Ballymoney (259174–5), Ballycastle (259173) and Lurgan (259166–72).
1851	Partial: Ahoghill—Craigs townland only; Aghagallon—M to T only; Ballymoney—Garryduff only; Killead—A to C only; Rasharkin—K to T only. PRONI MIC. 5A/11–26; also NAI. Online: 1851.
1856	Census of united parishes of Glenavy, Camlin and Tullyrusk, Co. Antrim, taken in 1856–7, revised 1858–9 and 1873; with Glenavy C of I registers. PRONI MIC.1/43–4, 44A, 74, C.R.1/53, T.679/1, 74.
1856–7	Voters. NLI ILB 324.
1861–2	Griffith's Valuation. Online: Askaboutireland.
1870	Parishioners list, Carnmoney, Co. Antrim; with C of I parish registers. PRONI T.679/325–9, 332, D.852/8, 48, 85, 91, 105, 122, 125.
1901	Government Census. Online: NAI.
1911	Government Census. Online: NAI.
1912	The Ulster Covenant. Almost half a million original signatures and addresses of those who signed. Online: Covenant.

Online

1851	<www.searchforancestors.com>	1851 census extracts
Askaboutireland	<www.askaboutireland.ie>	Griffith's Valuation
Ballymoney	<www.ballymoneyancestry.com>	Wide range of Ballymoney sources
Bann Valley	<www.torrens.org.uk/Genealogy/BannValley>	Records from the Antrim-Derry border
Covenant	<www.proni.gov.uk/ulstercovenant>	
FindMyPast	<www.findmypast.ie>	Subscription site
Freeholders	<www.proni.gov.uk/freeholders>	
Hayes, John	<www.failteromhat.com>	
Headstones	<www.historyfromheadstones.com>	Comprehensive collection of inscriptions

History	<www.antrimhistory.net>	Glens of Antrim Historical Society
McAfee	<www.billmacafee.com>	Large range of North Antrim sources
NAI	<www.census.nationalarchives.ie>	1901 and 1911 censuses, complete
News Letter (Belfast)	<www.ucs.louisiana.edu/bnl>	Index, 1737–1800
Olive tree	<www.rootsweb.ancestry.com/~ote>	
PRONI	<www.proni.gov.uk>	
Rathlin	<www.rathlin-island.info>	Extraordinary collection of Rathlin sources
UHF	<www.ancestryireland.co.uk>	Parish records online
Ulsterancestry	<www.ulsterancestry.com>	Many transcribed early sources

Publications

Local histories etc.

Castlereagh: some local sources, Ballynahinch: South Eastern Education and Library Service, 1980. NLI Ir 914115 p 15, 27 p.

Listing Mid-Antrim Presbyterians in 1864, Ballymena: Mid-Antrim Historical Group, 1996. NLI, 96 p.

Old Randalstown and District, Randalstown: Randalstown Historical Society, 2007, 93 p.

'Presbyterians in Glenarm', *The Glynns*, Vol. 9, 1981.

Allen, Andrew W., *Old Ballyclug*, Ballymena: Ballymena Borough Council, 1994. NLI Ir 9295 p, 17 p.

—— *Skerry burying ground*, Ballymena: Ballymena Borough Council. NLI 4B 1704, 4 p.

Akenson, D.H., *Between two revolutions: Islandmagee, County Antrim, 1798–1920*, Port Credit, Ont.: P. D. Meany, 1979. NLI Ir 94111 a 3, 221 p.

—— *Local poets and social history: James Orr, bard of Ballycarry*, Belfast: PRONI, 1977. NLI Ir 82189 o 107, 130 p.

Barr, W.N., *The oldest register of Derryaghy, Co. Antrim, 1696–1772*. NLI Ir 9293 b 3.

Benn, George, *A History of the Town of Belfast*, London: 1877–80 (reprinted, archivecdbooks, #IE0102).

Boyd, H.A., *A History of the Church of Ireland in Ramoan Parish*, Belfast: R. Carswell, 1930. NLI Ir 2741 b 9, 232 p.

Carmody, V. Rev. W.P., *Lisburn Cathedral and Its Past Rectors*, Belfast: R. Carswell & Son, 1926. NLI Ir 27411 c 2, 190 p.

Cassidy, William, *Gravestone inscriptions in Lambeg churchyard*. PRONI.

Clarke, Harry Jessop St John, *Thirty centuries in south-east Antrim: The parish of Coole or Carnmoney*, Belfast: Quota Press, 1938. NLI Ir 274111 c 3, 319 p.

Cox, John H.R., *Cromwellian Settlement of the parish of Kilbride*, 1959.

Day, Angelique, and McWilliams, Patrick (eds.), *Ordnance Survey Memoirs of Ireland Series*, Belfast: Institute of Irish Studies, and RIA, 1990–97.

—*Vol. 2: Co. Antrim I* (1990): Ballymartin, Ballyrobert, Ballywalter, Carnmoney, Mallusk. NLI Ir 914111 o 11.

—*Vol. 8: Co. Antrim II* (1991): Blaris (Lisburn), Derryaghy, Drumbeg, Lambeg. NLI Ir 9141 o 80.

—*Vol. 10: Co. Antrim III* (1991): Carncastle and Killyglen, Island Magee, Kilwaughter, Larne.

—*Vol. 13: Co. Antrim IV* (1992): Ardclinis, Dunaghy, Dundermot, Layd, Inispollan, Loughguile, Newton Crommelin, Racavan, Skerry, Tickmacrevan. NLI Ir 914111 o 11.

—*Vol. 16: Co. Antrim V* (1992): Ballymoney, Ballyrashane, Ballywillin, Billy, Derrykeighan, Drumtullagh, Dunluce, Kilraughts. NLI Ir 914111 o 11.

—*Vol. 19: Co. Antrim VI* (1993): Ballyscullion, Connor, Cranfield, Drummaul, Duneane, Shilvodan. NLI Ir 9141 o 84.

—*Vol. 21: Co. Antrim VII* (1993): Aghagallon, Aghalee, Ballinderry, Camlin, Glenavy, Lough Neagh, Magheragall, Magheramesk, Tullyrusk. NLI Ir 9141 o 83.

—*Vol. 23: Co. Antrim VIII* (1993): Ahoghill, Ballyclug, Finvoy, Killagan, Kirkinriola, Rasharkin. NLI Ir 9141 o 80.

—*Vol. 24: Co. Antrim IX* (1994): Armoy, Ballintoy, Culfeightrin, Ramoan, Rathlin Island. NLI Ir 9141 o 80.

—*Vol. 26: Co. Antrim X* (1994): Glynn, Inver, Kilroot, Templecorran. NLI Ir 94111 o 7.

—*Vol. 29: Co. Antrim XI* (1995): Antrim, Doagh, Donegore, Kilbride. NLI Ir 9141 o 80.

—*Vol. 32: Co. Antrim XII* (1995): Ballycor, Ballylinny, Ballynure, Glenwhirry, Raloo, Rashee. NLI Ir 9141 o 80.

—*Vol. 35: Co. Antrim IIII* (1996): Carmavy, Killead, Muckamore, Nilteen, Templepatrick, Umgall. NLI Ir 9141 o 80.

—*Vol. 37: Co. Antrim XIV* (1996): Carrickfergus. NLI Ir 9141 o 80.

Dunlop, Bill, *Ahoghill, Part 1: Buick's Ahoghill: a filial account (1910) of seceders*, Ballymena: Mid-Antrim Historical Group, 1987. NLI Ir 94111 a (1), 113 p.

—— *Ahoghill, Part 2: Ahoghill folk: photographs of people of the Fourtowns and round about*, Ballymena: Mid-Antrim Historical Group, 1989. NLI Ir 94111 a (2), 96 p.

—— *Ahoghill, Part 3: Around Ahoghill: further photographs and other . . .* Ballymena: Mid-Antrim Historical Group, 1990. NLI Ir 94111 p 5 (8), 96 p.

—— *McIlmoyle of Dervock: pastor of two*, Ballymena: Mid-Antrim Historical Group, 1991. NLI Ir 92 m 505, 180 p.

—— Round 'Kells and Conyer' [Part 1], Ballyclare: Kells and Connor Luncheon Club, 1989. NLI Ir 94111 d 8, 101 p.

—— Mid-Antrim, Part 2: further articles on Ballymena and district, Ballymena: Mid-Antrim Historical Group, 1991. NLI Ir 94111 d 9, 208 p.

Fulton, Eileen, A history of the Parish of St. Joseph's, Hannahstown, Co. Antrim, 1826–1993, Detailing the Names of the Graves . . . Ulster Journals, 1993.

Gaston, Stephen, Inscriptions in first and second Killymurris Presbyterian burying-grounds, Ballymena: Ballymena Borough Council, 1996. NLI Ir 285 p, 45 p.

Gillespie, Raymond, Irish Historic Towns Atlas, 12: Belfast, Part 1, 1840, Dublin: RIA, 2002. NLI.

—— Early Belfast: the origins and growth of an Ulster town to 1750, Belfast: UHF, 2007, 182 p.

IGRS, Tombstone inscriptions, Vol. 1, Dublin: IGRS Tombstone Committee, 2001. NLI, 850 p.

Jackson, Bill, The Bells of Trummery and beyond: 350 years of an Irish Quaker family, York: Sessions, 2005, 241 p.

Joy, Henry, Historical Collections relative to the town of Belfast, Belfast: 1817.

Kingston, Simon, Ulster and the Isles in the fifteenth century: the lordship of the Clann Domhnaill of Antrim, Dublin and Portland, Oreg.: Four Courts Press, 2004, 256 p.

Lee, Rev. W.H.A., St Colmanell, Aghoghill: A History of its Parish, Belfast: Newton Publishing Co., 1939. LHL BPB1939.11.

Liggett, Michael, A district called Ardoyne: a brief history of a Belfast Community, Belfast: Glenravel Publications, 1994. NLI Ir 9411 P 41(3).

McConnell, Charles, The witches of Islandmagee, Antrim: Carmac, 2000. NLI Ir 9411 m 45, 78 p.

M'Meekin, D., Memories of '59, or the revival movement as manifested itself at Ahoghill, Grange, Longstone, New Ferry, Ballymena, Broughshane, Cullybackey, Teeshan, and Whiteside's Corner, Hull: M. Harland, 1908. LHL U.28/MACM.

McNeill, Hugh, The annals of the Parish of Derrykeighan from AD 453 to AD 1890, compiled by Hugh McNeill, Ballymena: Mid-Antrim Historical Group, 1993. NLI, 81p.

McRonald, Malcolm, The Irish boats, Vol. 3: Liverpool to Belfast, Stroud, Glos.: Tempus, 2007, 256 p.

McSkimin, Samuel, The History and Antiquities of the Town of Carrickfergus, 1318–1839, Belfast: 1909.

Marshall, Rev. H.C., The Parish of Lambeg, Lisburn: Victor McMurray, 1933. NLI Ir 27411 m 2, 127 p.

Marshall, J.D.C, Discovering Mosside: the history of an Ulster Scots village, Ballymoney: Clenagh House, 2008, 171 p.

Millin, S.S, Sidelights on Belfast History, 1932.

Mullin, Julia, A history of Dunluce Presbyterian church, 1995. NLI Ir 285 m 37.

NIFHS, These Hallowed Grounds: Lisburn, Kilrush and St. Patrick's Cemeteries, Belfast: NIFHS, 2001. LHL I/929.5041619.

—— *Carved in stone: a record of memorials in the ancient graveyard around the Church* . . . Belfast: NIFHS, 1994. NLI.

—— *Mallusk Memorials,* Belfast: NIFHS, 1997. NLI Ir 9295 m 4, 108 p.

Observer (Ballymena), *Old Ballymena: a history of Ballymena during the 1798 Rebellion,* 1857.

Owen, D.J, *History of Belfast,* Belfast: W. & G. Baird, 1921. NLI Ir 94111 o 1, 459 p.

Rankin, Kathleen, *The linen houses of the Lagan Valley: the story of their families,* Belfast: UHF, 2002. NLI, 221 p.

Robinson, Rev. Aston, *The presbytery of Ballymena, 1745–1945,* Ballymena: Mid-Antrim Historical group, 1949. NLI.

Robinson, Philip, *Irish Historic Towns Atlas, 2: Carrickfergus,* Dublin: RIA, 1986. NLI ILB 941 i 3 (2).

Rosenblatt, Stuart, *Belfast: Irish Jewish Memorial Inscriptions, Carnmoney (1912–2003) and City Centre (1873–1995) Cemeteries,* Dublin: the author, 2005. NLI.

Royle, Stephen A., *Irish Historic Towns Atlas, 17: Belfast, Part II, 1840 to 1900,* Dublin: RIA, 2007.

Rutherford, George, *Gravestone Inscriptions, County Antrim, Vol. 1,* Belfast: UHF, 1977. NLI Ir 9295 c 1.

—— *Gravestone Inscriptions, County Antrim, Vol. 4: Old Families of Larne and District from Gravestone Inscriptions, Wills and Biographical Notes,* Belfast: UHF, 2004. NLI, 224 p.

—— *Gravestone Inscriptions, County Antrim, Vol. 2,* Belfast: UHF, 1980. NLI Ir 94111 c 4.

Sharpe, Robert, *'By the light of the hurricane lamp': growing up in Glenariffe in the thirties,* the author, 2004. NLI, 119 p.

Shaw, William, *Cullybackey: the Story of an Ulster Village,* Edinburgh: Macdonald, 1913. NLI Ir 91411 s 1, 201 p.

Smyth, Alastair, *The story of Antrim,* Antrim: Antrim Borough Council, 1984. NLI Ir 94111 s 9, 116 p.

St John Clarke, H.J., *Thirty centuries in south-east Antrim: the Parish of Coole or Carnmoney,* Belfast: 1938. NLI Ir 27411 c 3.

Walker, B.M., *Sentry Hill: an Ulster farm and family,* Dundonald: Blackstaff Press, 1981. NLI Ir 9292 w 19, 167 p.

Watson, Charles, *The Story of the United Parishes of Glenavy, Camlin and Tullyrusk* . . . Belfast: McCaw, Stevenson & Orr, 1892, reprinted 1982. NLI Ir 94111 w 1, 63 p.

Watson, Sandy, *Old Antrim coast,* Catrine, Ayrshire: Stenlake Publishing, 2004, 48 p.

Young, Robert M., *Historical Notices of Old Belfast and Its Vicinity,* 1896.

—— *The Town Book of the Corporation of Belfast, 1613–1816,* 1892. Includes freemen, 1635–1796. LDS SLC film 0990294.

Local journals
Carrickfergus and District Historical Society Journal. NLI Ir 9411 c 5.
Down and Connor Historical Society Magazine. NLI Ir 94115 d 1.
East Belfast Historical Society Journal. LHL.
The Glynns: Journal of the Glens of Antrim Historical Society. LHL.
Historical Belfast Magazine. LHL.
Irish Family Links. NLI Ir 9292 f 19.
Lisburn Historical Society Journal. LHL.
North Belfast Historical Society Magazine. NLI Ir 94111 n 1.
North Irish Roots: Journal of the North of Ireland Family History Society. NLI Ir
     92905 n 4.
Ulster Journal of Archaeology. NLI Ir 794105 u 1.

Directories
Thirty Belfast and Ulster directories are online at PRONI.

1807/8	Joseph Smith, *Belfast Directories*, reprinted as J.R.R. Adams (ed.), *Merchants in Plenty*, Belfast: UHF, 1992. NLI Ir 914111.s.27.
1811	Holden's *Annual London and country directory of the United Kingdoms and Wales, in three volumes, for . . . 1811.* Facsimile reprint, Norwich: M. Winton, 1996. NLI G 942 h 23; LDS film 258722 item 2.
1820	*Belfast Almanack.* NLI JP 5331.
1820	J. Pigot, *Commercial Directory of Ireland.* PRONI; NLI Ir 9141 p 107; LDS film 962702 item 1. Online: Hayes.
1831–2	Donaldson's *Belfast Directory.* LDS film 258724 item 2.
1835	*Matier's Belfast Directory.* PRONI; NLI Ir 9141111 m 5; LDS film 258724; Archive CD Books Ireland.
1839	Martin, *Belfast Directory.* PRONI; NLI Ir 9141111 m 4.
1841	Martin, *Belfast Directory,* reprinted Ballymena: Mid-Antrim Historical Group, 1992. PRONI; NLI Ir 914111 m 24; LDS film 258724/5.
1843–52	Henderson's *Belfast and Province of Ulster Directory.* PRONI; NLI Dix Belfast (1852); LDS film 908816 item 1.
1846	Slater's *National Commercial Directory of Ireland.* Online: Hayes.
1854–	*Belfast and Province of Ulster Directory.* Also 1856, 1858, 1861, 1863, 1865, 1868, 1870, 1877, 1880, 1884, 1887, 1890, 1894, 1900. PRONI; LDS (various years).
1856	Slater's *Royal National Commercial Directory of Ireland.* NLI; LDS film 1472360 item 1.
1860	Hugh Adair, *Belfast Directory.* NLI Dix Belfast 1860; LDS film 990275 item 4.
1865	R. Wynne, *Business Directory of Belfast.* NLI Ir 91411 b 2.
1870	Slater's *Directory of Ireland.* NLI.
1881	Slater's *Royal National Commercial Directory of Ireland.* NLI.
1887	*Derry Almanac and Directory* (Portrush only).

1888   George Henry Bassett, *The Book of Antrim*. Reprinted Belfast: Friar's Bush Press, 1989. NLI Ir 94116 b 29.

1894   Slater's *Royal Commercial Directory of Ireland*. NLI.

Gravestone inscriptions

The Ulster Historical Foundation has transcripts for 151 graveyards in Co. Antrim and Belfast. Irish World has transcripts of 32 graveyards. These are searchable online for a fee at <*www.historyfromheadstones.com*>. Published or freely available transcripts are given below. Full publication details are in the publications list above.

Ahoghill: Cullybackey Old Methodist. *Ballymena Borough gravestone series*, Vol. 3, 1994. NLI.

Ardclinis: Carrivemurphy, RC, *The Glynns*, Vol. 4.

Belfast:

    Christ Church interior, C of I, Clarke, R.S.J., *Gravestone Inscriptions*, Belfast, Vol. 1.

    City centre: Rosenblatt, *Irish Jewish Memorial Inscriptions*.

    Clifton St, Clarke, R.S.J., *Gravestone Inscriptions, Belfast, Vol. 4 (Old Belfast Families and the New Burying Ground)*, UHF, 1991. NLI Ir 9295 o 1.

    Milltown, RC, Clarke, R.S.J., *Gravestone Inscriptions, Belfast*, Vol. 2, UHF, 1986.

    Friar's Bush, RC, Clarke, R.S.J., *Gravestone Inscriptions, Belfast*, Vol. 2, UHF, 1986.

    Hannahstown: St Joseph's, Hannahstown, RC, in Fulton, *A history of the Parish of St. Joseph's, Hannahstown*, 1993.

    St George's interior, C of I, Clarke, R.S.J., *Gravestone Inscriptions, Belfast*, Vol. 1, UHF, 1982.

    Shankill, Clarke, R.S.J., *Gravestone Inscriptions, Belfast*, Vol. 1.

Blaris: Lisburn, Carmody, *Lisburn*.

St Patrick's: *These Hallowed Grounds*.

Ballyclug: Ballymarlagh (Ballyclug), Allen, *Old Ballyclug*.

Camlin, Ballydonagh, NIFHS, *These Hallowed Grounds*.

Carnmoney: Carnmoney, NIFHS, *Carved in stone*.

Connor: St Saviour's, Kells. Ballymena Borough gravestone series, Vol. 4, 1995. NLI.

Culfeightrin: Cross, *IA*, Vol. 2, No. 2.

Culfeightrin: Bonamargy, IGRS, *Tombstones, 1*.

Drumbeg: C of I, Clarke, *Down*, Vol. 3.

Grange of Killyglen: Dromain, Rutherford, *Antrim*, Vol. 4.

Glynn: Glynn, Rutherford, *Antrim*, Vol. 2.

Islandmagee: Ballyprior More, Rutherford, *Antrim*, Vol. 1.

Islandmagee: Ballykeel, Rutherford, *Antrim*, Vol. 1.

Kilroot: Rutherford, *Antrim*, Vol. 2.

Kilwaughter (New and Old): Rutherford, *Antrim*, Vol. 4.

Lambeg: Lambeg North, C of I, Cassidy, William, *Inscriptions on Tombstones in Lambeg Graveyard.*

Larne, St Macnissi's, Chaine, Rutherford, *Antrim*, Vol. 4.

Layd: Kilmore, *The Glynns*, Vol. 4.

Layd: Layd, *Survey of Layde Graveyard*, Glens of Antrim Historical Society, 1991. NLI Ir 9295 s 2.

Magheragall: Magheragall, C of I, *Family Links*, Vol. 1, Nos. 2 and 3, 1981.

Muckamore (Grange of): Muckamore, *Carved in stone: a record of memorials in the ancient graveyard around the Church* . . . NIFHS, 1994.

Newton Cromlin, Skerry East, Allen, *Old Ballyclug.*

Raloo: Ballyvallagh, Rutherford, *Antrim*, Vol. 2.

Rasharkin, Dromore/Killymurris?, Gaston, *Inscriptions.*

Templecorran: Forthill (Ballycarry?), C of I, Rutherford, *Antrim*, Vol. 2.

Templepatrick: Grange of Molusk, *Mallusk Memorials*, NIFHS, 1997.

Estate records

Adair. Rentals, 1795–1805, 1808–1900. PRONI T. 1333/1–3, D.929, Kirkinriola. May cover areas in other parishes.

Agnew. Rentals, 1647–1880. PRONI Calendar to D.282, Kilwaughter, Larne.

Agnew. Maps of townlands with names of tenants, 1788. PRONI T2309/1. Online: McAfee. Kilraghts.

Allen. Rentals, 1832–9. PRONI T. 734/9–57. Derrykeighan, Lisconnon and Dervock.

Antrim, Earls of. Rentals, 1603–1900. PRONI D.2977, Ahoghill, Antrim, Ardclinis, Armoy, Ballintoy, Ballymartin, Ballyrashane, Ballywillin, Billy, Carncastle, Culfeightrin, Derrykeighan, Dunaghy, Duneane, Dunluce, Finvoy, Grange of Drumtullagh, Grange of Killyglen, Island Magee, Killagan, Kilraghts, Kilwaughter, Larne, Layd, Loughguile, Newton Cromlin, Ramoan, Rasharkin, Rathlin, Skerry, Tickmacrevan. May cover areas in other parishes. Also a rent roll. All tenants, 1779–81, NAI M524, similar area.

Darcus. Register of deed and memorials of leases: 1830. PRONI T.528/29, Island Magee, Larne.

Dungannon, Lord. Rental, 1839. PRONI, Raloo. May cover areas in other parishes.

Edmonstone. Rent roll, 1777. PRONI T.561/2, Red Hall, Carrickfergus. May cover areas in other parishes.

Farrell. Rental, 1824. PRONI D.282/60, Ballywillin, Carncastle, Glynn. May cover areas in other parishes.

Foster/Massereene. Rentals, 1830. PRONI D. 1739, Aghnamullen, Antrim, Connor, Killead, Muckamore (Grange of). May cover areas in other parishes.

Gage. Estate papers and accounts, 1789–1900. PRONI D.463/1, D.1375, Rathlin.

Hertford. Rental, 1719–23, 1728–30. PRONI D.427/1–27, Aghagallon, Aghalee, Ballinderry, Blaris, Derryaghy, Glenavy, Lambeg, rental of the Manor of Killyleagh, London, Lisburn, Lambeg, Derryaghy, Magheragall, Magheramesk, Aghalee, Aghagallon, Ballinderry and Gleanvy.

Hutchinson. Maps of townlands with names of tenants, 1805. PRONI D408/1. Online: McAfee. Ballymoney.

Ker. Rentals, 1740–1930. PRONI D.892/I/l–2, 7, Templecorran. May cover areas in other parishes.

Kirk. Rental account: 1827–8; rent roll, 1842–3. PRONI D.1255/5/1–6, D.2121/1–8, Carrickfergus.

Lecky. Rentals, 1829–1933. PRONI D.1946/1–4, Billy. Four rentals of property in Aird, Ballymoy, Bushmills, Castlemagee, Carnkirk, Clogher and Kilcoobin.

Macartney. Rent rolls, 1768–89, 1801; 1816; 1828. PRONI D.426/3,5; D.572/21, Loughguile. Rent roll of Loughgall [i.e. Loughguile] estate.

McGildowny. Rentals and maps, 1800–1900. PRONI D.1011, Ramoan.

Massereene and Ferrard, Viscount. Rent roll, 1700–1715. PRONI D.562/57–8, 210, 216, 834, 991, Aghalee, Connor, Grange of Shilvodan, Killead, Muckamore (Grange of).

Montgomery. Maps of townlands with names of tenants: 1788. PRONI T1638,21/1. Online: McAfee. Kilraghts.

Montgomery. Rent roll, 1800–1815. PRONI T.1638/30–31, Dunluce, Layd, Loughguile, Ramoan; rent roll for the estate in the baronies of Dunluce, Kilconway. Townlands of Benvarden, Bantown, Kilmoyle, Ballyness, Ballyleckan, Ballytaggart, Tonygoogan, Ballylough, Legawherry, Toberbilly etc. Online: McAfee.

Moore. Rentals, 1704–1936. PRONI D.2171/8–132, Finvoy. Estate papers, including leases, assignments, rents, conveyance.

Mussenden. Rent rolls and returns, 1750. PRONI D.354/292, Carnmoney, c.1750. Rent rolls for Whitehouse, Jordanstown, Carnmoney, Ballycraigy, Ballyhenry etc.

O'Neill of Shane's Castle. Rentals, 1812–31. PRONI T.1024/2–4, D.1374/1, D.1470/1–6, Antrim, Killead, Drummaul.

Pakenham. Rent ledger: 1822–8. PRONI D.2827/1, Killead.

Saunders. Rent roll, 1771–8. PRONI D.1759/3B/7, Carrickfergus, rent roll for Newtownards, Comber, Belfast and Carrickfergus.

Skeffington. Rentals, 1813–43. PRONI D.1835/42/2–3, Ballymoney.

Stewart-Moore. Rentals and accounts, 1829–1900. PRONI D.915, Derrykeighan.

Wallace, Sir Richard. Rent roll, 1728–30. PRONI D.427/1–3, Blaris.

ARMAGH

Census returns and substitutes

1625–7	Leet Court Rolls. Jurors and litigants in Armagh Manor, Arboe, Ardtrea, Donaghmore (Co. Tyrone), Termonfeckin (Co. Louth). SA, Vol. 11, No. 9, 1957, pp. 295–322.
1630	Muster Roll of Ulster. PRONI T. 808/15164; NLI Pos. 206.
1631	Muster Roll of Armagh. SA, Vol. 5, No. 2, 1970.
1634	Subsidy roll, Portadown area. NAI M. 2471, 2475, Shankill and Seagoe; PRONI T/808/14950.

1641	Testimonies of 135 witnesses to the 1641 Rebellion. Online: 1641.
1654–6	*Civil Survey.* NLI Ir 31041 c 4.
1659	Pender's 'Census', reprinted GPC, 1997; IMC, 2002. LDS film 924648.
1660	Poll Tax Returns, Co. Armagh. PRONI MIC15A/75, T808/14950.
1661	Books of Survey and Distribution. PRONI T370/A and D.1854/1/8.
1664	Hearth Money Roll. *Archivium Hibernicum*, 1936. NLI Ms. 9586; PRONI T.604.
1670/71	Armagh diocese, gentry, clergy and parishioners supporting the Franciscans. SA, Vol. 15, No. 1, 1992, pp. 186–216.
1689	Protestants attainted by James II. PRONI T808/14985. List of names only.
1737	Tithe-payers, Drumcree. NLI I 920041 p 1.
1738	Freeholders. NLI Pos. 206; also Armagh County Library.
1740	Protestant householders: Creggan, Derrynoose, Loughgall, Mullaghbrack, Shankill, Tynan. NAI; also GO 539; PRONI T808/15258 (part online: PRONI name search); LDS film 258517; Portadown, LDS film 1279357 item 8, and SA, Vol. 18, 2, 2001.
1753	Poll Book. NAI M. 4878; also GO 443; PRONI T808/14936; LDS film 1279237. Online: Freeholders.
1766	(1) Creggan Parish. NAI Parl. Ret. 657; also GO 537; PRONI T808/14936 (Online: PRONI name search); LDS film 100173; JCLAHS, 8 (2); transcripts for parts of Armagh, Ballymore, Creggan, Drumcree, Kilmore, Loughgall, Tartaraghan. PRONI T/808/15265–7, T/3709, Lurgan; NAI M2476; RCBL Ms. 23.
1770	Armagh town householders. NLI Ms. 7370; also PRONI T808/14977; LDS film 258621.
1775	Dissenters' petitions. Armagh Parish, Benburb town and neighbourhood, Clare Congregation. Online: PRONI name search.
1793–1908	Armagh Militia Records. NLI Pos. 1014; also Armagh County Library.
1796	Spinning-Wheel Premium List. 3,100 names for Co. Armagh. Online: Hayes.
1796	Catholics emigrating from Ulster to Co. Mayo. SA, 1958, pp. 17–50. See also 'Petition of Armagh migrants in the Westport area', *Cathair na Mart*, Vol. 2, No. 1 (Appendix).
1799–1800	Militia Pay Lists and Muster Rolls. PRONI T.1115/2A–2C.
1803–1831	Armagh Freeholders and Poll Books. PRONI ARM 5/2/1–17, D 1928; also NLI Ir 94116 a 1, Ir 352 p 2 (baronies of Tiranny, Lower Fews and Upper Fews, 1821–31). Online: Freeholders.
1821	Kilmore Parish, PRONI T. 450. Portadown, PRONI T/281/7; also LDS films 258511/258621. Forkhill, in Walsh, *Kick Any Stone.* Parts of Drumcree and Mullaghbrack online: Armagh Ancestry.
1821	Various fragments. NAI Thrift Abstracts.
1823–38	Tithe Books. NAI.

1828–57	Seven volumes of cash books from the Caledon estate, containing entries of payments made to emigrating tenants. PRONI D.266/337.
1831	Memorial of the inhabitants of part of Cos. Down and Armagh praying for relief, 21 April 1831. More than 1,300 names, 'more particularly in the neighbourhood of Shane Hill'—Knocknashane, Shankill Parish? NAI OP 974/122.
1834–7	Valuation of Armagh town (heads of households). *Parliamentary Papers, 1837, Reports from Committees*, Vol. 2 (1), Appendix G.
1836	Memorial from inhabitants of Moyntaghe and Seagoe Parishes, 'on behalf of Mr. Handcock.' More than 1,000 names. NAI OP 1836/20.
1837	Marksmen (i.e. illiterate voters), Armagh borough. *Parliamentary Papers, 1837, Reports from Committees*, Vol. 2 (1), Appendix A.
1838	Memorial from inhabitants of Portadown for quarter sessions. c.90 signatures. NAI OP 1837/10.
1839	Valuation of Co. Armagh. NLI Pos. 99; also Armagh County Library.
1840	Ratepayers for the Union of Armagh. PRONI D/1670/13/6.
1840–55	Emigrants from Derrynoose to the United States and Scotland; with parish registers. PRONI MIC.1/158.
1842–1904	Workhouse records: Armagh Union, indoor and outdoor relief registers. PRONI BG/2; LDS film 259166–72, Castleblayney Union, MG.
1843	Armagh voters. NAI 1842/85.
1851	Various fragments. NAI Thrift Abstracts.
1851–73	Persons entitled to vote. Armagh County Museum D7; also LDS film 1279325.
1864	Tynan Parish, c.1864. *The History of Charlemont Fort and Borough*, 1921.
1864	Griffith's Valuation. Online: Askaboutireland.
1868	Census of the C of I parish of Shankill, Cos. Armagh and Down. With the local clergyman.
1871	Creggan Upper. *Archivium Hibernicum*, Vol. 3.
1901	Census. Online: NAI.
1911	Census. Online: NAI.
1912	The Ulster Covenant. Almost half a million original signatures and addresses of those who signed. Online: Covenant.

Online

1641	<www.1641.tcd.ie>	
Armagh Ancestry	<www.rootsireland.ie>	
Askaboutireland	<www.askaboutireland.ie>	Griffith's Valuation
Bagenals Castle	<www.bagenalscastle.com>	Newry and Mourne
Covenant	<www.proni.gov.uk/ulstercovenant>	PRONI transcription of the Covenant
Hayes, John	<www.failteromhat.com>	Large compendium of transcribed records

Headstones	<www.historyfromheadstones.com>	Comprehensive collection of inscriptions
Freeholders	<www.proni.gov.uk/freeholders>	74 freeholders' and voters' lists for Co. Armagh, 1712–1832
Lurgan	<www.lurganancestry.net>	Wide range of Lurgan sources
NAI	<www.census.nationalarchives.ie>	1901 and 1911 censuses, complete
PRONI	<www.proni.gov.uk>	
South Armagh	<www.sagp.org>	South Armagh Genealogy Project

Publications

Local histories etc.

Armagh Road Presbyterian Church, Portadown (1868–1968). NLI Ir 2741 p 25.

Armagh Royal School: Prizes and prizemen, 1854. NLI P 439.

Balleer School: Copy-book of letters, 1827–29. NLI Ir 300 p 106.

'Life and Times of Fr. Edmund Murphy, Killeavy, 1680,' *JCLAHS,* 7 (3), 1931, pp. 336–81. Lists Catholic residents.

Mullaghbrack from the tithepayers' list of 1834. NLI I 920041 p 1.

Provisional list of pre-1900 School Registers in the Public Record Office of Northern Ireland. *UHGGN,* 9, 1986, pp. 60–71.

Atkinson, Edward D., *Dromore: an Ulster diocese,* Dundalk: W. Tempest, 1925. NLI Ir 274116 a 1, 317 p.

Blaney, Roger, Blaney of Lurgan, Co. Armagh, *IG,* 3, 1, 1971, pp. 32–9.

Canavan, T., *Frontier town: an illustrated history of Newry,* Belfast: Blackstaff Press, 1989.

Coffey, Hubert W., *A history of Milltown Parish, the Birches, North-West Armagh,* Portadown: 1950? Jackson family (Stonewall Jackson). NLI Ir 283 p 5, 86 p.

Coyle, Michael F., *Genealogy of the Smyths of Carrickaduff in the Parish of Derrynoose, Carnagh, Keady, Co. Armagh,* Dunleer, Co. Louth: the author, 1980. NLI GO 613, 22 leaves.

Day, Angelique, *Ordnance Survey Memoirs of Ireland, Vol. 1: Parishes of County Armagh, 1835–8,* Belfast: Institute of Irish Studies, 1990. Co-editor, Patrick McWilliams. All of Co. Armagh, except the town. NLI Ir Ir 914116 o 10, 144 p.

Donaldson, John, *A Historical and Statistical Account of the Barony of Upper Fews.*

Ferrar, Major M.L., *Register of the Royal School, Armagh,* Belfast: 1933. NLI Ir 37941 f 5, 235 p.

Galogly, John, *The History of St Patrick's Parish, Armagh,* 1880.

Gwynn, A., *The medieval province of Armagh,* Dundalk: 1946. NLI Ir 27411 g 1.

Hogg, Rev. M.B., *Keady Parish: A Short History of its Church and People,* 1928.

Hughes, A.J., *Armagh: history and society*, Dublin: Geography Publications, 2001. NLI, 1,080 p.

Lockington, John W., *A history of the Mall Presbyterian Church, Armagh, 1837–1987*, Belfast: Ulster Services, 1987. NLI, 56 p.

McCorry, F.X., *Lurgan: an Irish Provincial Town*, Inglewood Press, 1993.

McCullough, Catherine, *Irish Historic Towns Atlas, 18: Armagh*, Dublin: RIA, 2007.

McGleenon, C.F., '17th and 18th century patterns of settlement in the Catholic parishes of Ballymore and Mullaghbrack,' *SA*, 15, No. 2, 1993, pp. 51–83.

Madden, Kyla, *Forkhill Protestants and Forkhill Catholics, 1787–1858*, Liverpool: Liverpool University Press, and Montréal: McGill-Queen's, 2005, 240 p.

Mallon, Seamus, *Historical sketches of the parish of Tynan and Middletown*, Tynan: County Armagh Parish Council, 1995. NLI Ir 274111 L 11, 301 p.

Marshall, J.J., *History of the parish of Tynan in the County of Armagh: with notices of the O'Neill, Hovenden, Stronge and other families connected with the district*, Dungannon: 1932. NLI Ir 94116 m 1, 83 p.

—— *The History of Charlemont Fort and Borough . . .* Dungannon: 1921.

Maxwell, Ian, *Researching Armagh ancestors: a practical guide for the family and local historian*, Belfast: UHF, 2000. NLI, 180 p.

—— *Armagh History and Guide*, Dublin: Nonsuch Press, 2009, 160 p.

Moore, Rev. H.H., *Three hundred years of Congregational life: the story of the First Presbyterian Church, Markethill, Co. Armagh, established AD 1609*, Armagh: R.P. M'Watters, 1909. NLI LO 5327, 65 p.

Murray, Rev. Lawrence P., *History of the Parish of Creggan in the Seventeenth and Eighteenth Centuries*, Dundalk: 1940.

Nelson, Simon, *History of the Parish of Creggan in Cos. Armagh and Louth from 1611 to 1840*, Belfast: PRONI, 1974. 'Copied from the original mss. . . . with a new introduction . . . by Rev. Tomás Ó Fiaich.' NLI Ir 941 p 43, 37 p.

Patterson, T., *Armagh Manor Court Rolls, 1625–7, and incidental notes on 17th century sources for Irish surnames in Co. Armagh*, 1957, *SA*, pp. 295–322.

Richardson, James N., *The Quakri at Lurgan, by two of themselves*, 1899. Richardson family and the Society of Friends, Lurgan. NLI Ir 82189 Irish r 7, 160 p.

Stewart, James, *Historical Memoirs of the City of Armagh*, Dublin: 1900, ed. Ambrose Coleman.

Swayne, John, *The register of John Swayne, Archbishop of Armagh and Primate of Ireland*.

Walsh, Una, and Murphy, Kevin, *Kick Any Stone: Townlands, People and Stories from Forkhill Parish*, Forkhill: Mullaghbawn Community Association, 2003. (Includes 1821 Forkhill census.) NLI.

Local journals
Craigavon Historical Society Review. LHL.
Irish Family Links. NLI Ir 9292 f 19.
Mullaghbawn Historical and Folk-Lore Society. NLI Ir 800 p 50.

North Irish Roots: Journal of the North of Ireland Family History Society. NLI Ir
　92905 n 4.

Seagoe Magazine. NLI I r 94116 s 4.

Seanchas Ardmhacha: Journal of the Armagh Diocesan Historical Society. NLI Ir
　27411 s 4.

Seanchas Dhroim Mór: Journal of the Dromore Diocesan Historical Society. NLI Ir
　94115 s 3.

Ulster Journal of Archaeology. NLI Ir 794105 u 1.

Directories

A large selection of Ulster directories are online at PRONI.

1819	Thomas Bradshaw's *General Directory of Newry, Armagh, and the Towns of Dungannon, Portadown, Tandragee, Lurgan, Waringstown, Banbridge, Warrenpoint, Rosstrevor, Kilkeel, Rathfriland, 1820.* PRONI; NLI Ir 91411 b 18; LDS film 258723. Online: Armagh History (Armagh town).
1820	J. Pigot, *Commercial Directory of Ireland.* PRONI; NLI Ir 9141 p 107; LDS film 962702 item 1.
1824	J. Pigot & Co., *City of Dublin and Hibernian Provincial Directory.* NLI; LDS film 451787 Online: Armagh History, Hayes.
1839	Martin, *Belfast Directory.* PRONI; NLI Ir 9141111 m 4.
1843–52	Henderson's *Belfast and Province of Ulster Directory.* PRONI; NLI Dix Belfast (1852); LDS film 908816 item 1.
1846	Slater's *National Commercial Directory of Ireland.* PRONI; NLI LO; LDS film 1696703 item 3. Online: Hayes.
1854–	*Belfast and Province of Ulster Directory.* Also 1856, 1858, 1861, 1863, 1865, 1868, 1870, 1877, 1880, 1884, 1887, 1890, 1894, 1900. PRONI; LDS (various years).
1856	Slater, *Royal National Commercial Directory of Ireland.* NLI; LDS film 1472360 item 1.
1865	R. Wynne, *Business Directory of Belfast.* NLI Ir 91411 b 2.
1870	Slater, *Directory of Ireland.* NLI.
1881	Slater, *Royal National Commercial Directory of Ireland.* NLI. Online: FindMyPast.
1883	S. Farrell, *County Armagh Directory and Almanac.*
1888	George Henry Bassett, *The Book of Armagh,* reprinted Belfast: Friar's Bush Press, 1989. NLI Ir 94116 b 3.
1894	Slater, *Royal Commercial Directory of Ireland.* NLI.

Gravestone inscriptions

The Ulster Historical Foundation has transcripts for 135 graveyards in Co.
Armagh. Heritage World has transcripts of 54 graveyards. These are searchable

online for a fee at <*www.historyfromheadstones.com*>. Published or publicly available transcripts are given below.

Armagh: Sandy Hill, sa, Vol. 11, 2, 1985.
Creggan: Creggan Bane Glebe, C of I, sa, Vol. 4, 1976.
Kilclooney: lds film 1279354.
Mullaghbrack: lds film 1279384.

Estate records

[No landlord given]. Tenants list, 1714. nli Ms. 3922. All tenants. Covering areas in the civil parishes of Armagh, Clonfeacle, Derrynoose, Drumcree, Killyman, Kilmore, Tynan.

Alexander, Earls of Caledon. Rentals, 1766–1916. proni D.2433. Covering areas in the civil parishes of Eglish, Tynan. May cover areas in other parishes.

Anglesea. Tenants list, 1856. Most tenants. Covering Newry-Crobane, Derryleckagh, Desert, Sheeptown in the civil parish of Newry. *jclahs*, 12 (2), 1950, pp. 151–3.

Armagh Diocesan Registry. Rentals, 1628–1878. proni D/848. Covering areas in the civil parishes of Armagh, Ballymore, Drumcree, Eglish, Kilmore, Lisnadill, Loughgall, Mullaghbrack, Shankill, Tynan. May cover further parishes.

Bacon (Richardson). Rentals, 1822–30. proni D.1606/6C/1–6. Covering areas in the civil parish of Kilmore.

Blacker. Rentals, 1827–77. proni D.959. Covering areas in the civil parish of Seagoe. Three rentals.

Brownlow. Lease books and rentals, 1710–1891. proni D.1928. Covering areas in the civil parishes of Drumcree, Magheralin, Montiaghs, Seagoe, Shankill, Tartaraghan.

Caledon. Rentals, 1766–1916. proni D.2433. Covering areas in the civil parish of Eglish. Rentals, including violated rentals for 1766, 1774, 1800–1810.

Charlemont. 800 expired leases: 1782–1904. proni D.1644/1–30. Covering areas in the civil parishes of Eglish, Grange, Kilclooney, Lisnadill, Mullaghbrack, Tartaraghan.

Charlemont. Rental, 1752–65. proni T.1175/2. Clonfeacle, Loughgall, mainly in the Charlemont, Blackwatertown and Loughgall areas.

Charlemont. Freeholders list, 1820. nli Ms. 3784. Rentals, 1798–1802. nli Ms. 2702. Major tenants only. Covering areas in the civil parishes of Eglish, Forkill, Grange, Keady, Kilclooney, Killevy, Lisnadill, Loughgall, Loughgilly, Mullaghbrack, Tartaraghan.

Charlemont. Partial rentals, 1798–1802. Major tenants only. nli Ms. 2702. Covering areas in the civil parishes of Clonfeacle, Donaghmore, Eglish, Forkill, Grange, Keady, Kilclooney, Killevy, Lisnadill, Loughgall, Loughgilly, Mullaghbrack, Tartaraghan.

Commissioners of Education. Rentals, 1846–54. nli Ms. 16924. All tenants. Covering areas in the civil parish of Loughgilly.

Cope. Rentals, 1629–1920. PRONI D.1345. Covering areas in the civil parish of Loughgall.

Dawson. Rent rolls, 1787 (NLI Ms. 3183, 3283), 1797 (NLI Ms. 3185), 1812 (NLI Ms. 3188), 1838–9 (NLI Ms. 3189), 1846 (NLI Ms. 1648), 1852–3 (NLI Ms. 5674). All tenants. Covering areas in the civil parish of Clonfeacle.

Dawson. Rentals, 1817–1900. PRONI D.526. Covering areas in the civil parish of Clonfeacle.

De Salis. Tenants list, 1733–87. PRONI D.763/1–6. Covering areas in the civil parishes of Ballymore, Kilmore, Mullaghbrack.

Gosford. Rentals and account books, 1787–1959. c.40,000 documents. PRONI D.1606. Covering areas in the civil parishes of Kilclooney, Kilmore, Mullaghbrack.

Gosford, Earls of. Rentals, 1787–1824. PRONI D/1606. Covering areas in the civil parishes of Kilclooney, Kilmore, Lisnadill, Loughgilly, Mullaghbrack, Tynan. May cover further parishes.

Hall. Rentals, 1814–1914. PRONI D.2090/2–7. Covering areas in the civil parishes of Ballymore and Killevy.

Irwin. Rentals, 1750–1870. PRONI D.2523/1-M. Covering areas in the civil parish of Keady.

Johnston. Rentals, 1791–1802, 1853 (with observations). NAI M. 3508. All tenants. Covering areas in the civil parish of Eglish.

Kilmorey, Viscounts. Rental, 1816. PRONI D/2638. Covering areas in the civil parishes of Kilkeel, Magheralin, Newry. May cover further parishes.

McGeough-Bond. Rentals, 1790–1930. PRONI D.288. Covering areas in the civil parish of Grange.

Manchester, Duke of. Rentals, 1715–1932. PRONI D.2862. Covering areas in the civil parishes of Drumcree, Seagoe.

Maxwell. Rentals, 1823–1960. PRONI D.3727. Covering areas in the civil parish of Tynan. Armstrong Papers, c.5,000 documents and volumes. May cover areas in other parishes.

Maxwell, Robert. Rental, 1770–71. PRONI T.1307/1. Covering areas in the civil parish of Tynan.

Moore. Rentals, 1848. NAI M.2977. All tenants. Covering areas in the civil parish of Seagoe.

Obins. Rent roll, 1753 (major tenants only), 1770 (all tenants). NLI Ms. 4736. Covering areas in the civil parish of Drumcree.

Obre. Rentals, 1800–1870. PRONI D.1719/1–6. Covering areas in the civil parish of Tartaraghan.

Verner. Rentals, 1788–1890. PRONI D.236/51–455. Covering areas in the civil parish of Clonfeacle.

Verner/Wingfield. Rental. PRONI D/2538, 1830. Covering areas in the civil parishes of Killyman, Kilmore, Lisnadill and Tartaraghan. May cover further parishes.

Wallace, Sir Richard. Rent roll, 1728–30. PRONI D.427/1–3. Covering areas in the civil parishes of Drumcree, Magheralin, Montiaghs, Mullaghbrack, Seagoe, Shankill, and Tartaraghan.

CARLOW

Census returns and substitutes

1641	Book of Survey and Distribution. NLI Ms. 971.
1641	Testimonies of 212 Carlow and Kilkenny witnesses to the 1641 Rebellion. Online: 1641.
1659	Pender's 'Census', reprinted GPC, 1997; IMC, 2002. LDS film 924648.
1669	Carlow Parish housholders. *JKAS*, 10, 1918–21, pp. 255–7.
1767	Co. Carlow Freeholders. *IG*, 1980.
1797	Chief Catholic inhabitants, parishes of Graiguenamanagh and Knocktopher. *IA*, 1978.
1798	Persons who suffered losses in the 1798 Rebellion. Propertied classes only. c.300 names. NLI I 94107. Online: FindMyPast.
1817	Emigrants from Cos. Carlow and Wexford to Canada. *Wexford: History and Society*. Online: Emigrants.
1823–38	Tithe Books. NAI, LDS.
1832–7	Voters registered in Carlow borough. *Parliamentary Papers, 1837: Reports from Committees*, Vol. 2 (2), 193–6.
1835	List of electors, with addresses. NLI Ms. 16899.
1837	Marksmen (illiterate voters) in parliamentary boroughs: Carlow. *Parliamentary Papers, 1837: Reports from Committees*, Vol. 2 (1), Appendix A.
1843	Co. Carlow voters. NAI 1843/55.
1852–3	Griffith's Valuation. Online: Askaboutireland.
1901	Census. Online: NAI.
1911	Census. Online: NAI.

Online

1641	*<www.1641.tcd.ie>*
Askaboutireland	*<www.askaboutireland.ie>*
Emigrants	*<www.bytown.net/wexlist.htm>*
Hayes, John	*<www.failteromhat.com>*
IGP Carlow	*<www.rootsweb.com/~irlcar2>*
NAI	*<www.census.nationalarchives.ie>*

Publications

Local histories etc.
Carlow Parliamentary Roll, 1872. NLI Ir 94138 m 1.
Kavanagh papers (Borris, Co. Carlow), *AH*, 25, 15–30.
Vigors papers (Burgage, Co. Carlow), *AH*, 20, 302–310.
Bennett McCuaig, Carol, *Leinster to Lanark,* Renfrew, Ont.: Juniper Books, 2010. Post-1798 emigrants from Cos. Carlow, Kilkenny, Wexford and Wicklow to Lanark County, Ottawa. NLI, 284 p.

Blackall, Sir Henry, 'The Blackneys of Ballyellin, Co. Carlow', *IG*, 3, 1957–8, pp. 44–5, 116.

Brennan, M., *Schools of Kildare and Leighlin, 1775–1835*, Dublin: M.H. Gill & Son, 1935. NLI Ir 37094135 b 4, 616 p.

Brophy, M., *Carlow past and present: a brochure containing short historical notes and miscellaneous gleanings of the town and county of Carlow*, Carlow: 1888. NLI Ir 94138 b 1, 138 p.

Coleman, James, 'Bibliography of the counties Carlow, Kilkenny and Wexford', *Waterford and South-East of Ireland Archaeological Society Journal*, 2, 1907. NLI 794105 w 1.

Coyle, James, *The Antiquities of Leighlin*, Dublin: Browne & Nolan, n.d. NLI Ir 94138 c 1.

Doyle, Owen, *Tinnahinch: a village within a town: the story of a changing village*, Graiguenamanagh Historical Society, 2003. NLI, 176 p.

Farrell, Noel, *Exploring Family Origins in Carlow Town*, Longford: Noel Farrell, [2004?], 48 p.

Gallwey, Hubert, 'Tobin of Caherlesk and Tobinstown', *IG*, 5, 1979, pp. 760–62.

Hood, Susan, 'Marriage in Ireland before the famine: case study of Rathvilly parish', *Journal of the West Wicklow Historical Society*, 3, 1989, pp. 33–40.

Hore, H.F., *The Social State of the Southern and Eastern Counties of Ireland in the Sixteenth Century, being the presentments of the gentlemen, commonalty, and citizens of Carlow, Cork, Kilkenny, Tipperary, Waterford, and Wexford, made in the reigns of Henry VIII. and Elizabeth. Printed from the originals in the Public Record Office, London. Edited by the late Herbert J. [i.e. F.] Hore . . . and the Rev. James Graves*. Dublin: 1870. NLI Ir 794105 r 2.

IGRS, Tombstone Inscriptions, Vol. 1, Dublin: IGRS Tombstone Committee, 2001. NLI, 850 p.

Joyce, John, *Graiguenamanagh: a town and its people: an historical and social account of Graiguenamanagh and Tinnahinch*, Graiguenamanagh: Graigue Publications, 1993. NLI Ir 94139 j 2, 198 p.

—— *Graiguenamanagh and the South Carlow-Kilkenny area in 1798*, Graignamanagh Historical Society, 1998. NLI 1A 337, [20 p.].

King, Thomas, *Carlow: the manor and town, 1674–1721* (Maynooth Studies in Irish Local History, No. 12), Dublin: Irish Academic Press, 1997. NLI Ir 94138 k 5, 72 p.

McGrath, Thomas F., *Carlow History and Society*, Dublin: Geography Publications, 2008. NLI, 1,070 p.

Mac Suibhne, Peadar, *Ballon and Rathoe*, Carlow: Nationalist and Leinster Times, 1980. NLI, 117 p.

—— *Clonegal Parish*, Carlow: 1975. NLI Ir 2741 m 14, 190 p.

Morris, Andrew, *Dunleckney Headstone Inscriptions*, Morris, 1987. NLI GS, 66 p.

Muintir na Tíre, *Co. Carlow Tombstone Inscriptions*, St Mullins: St Mullins Muintir na Tíre, 1985. NLI Ir 9295 c 3.

Murphy, Phillip E., *The O'Leary footprint: an anthology of the publications of the O'Leary family on Graignamanagh, Tinnahinch, Ullard and St. Mullins, 1895–1926*, Graignamanagh: O'Leary Archive, 2004. NLI, 420 p.

O'Donovan, John, *Ordnance Survey Letters: Carlow* [1838], Dublin: 1927. NLI Ir 9141 O 2.

O'Toole, Edward, *The Parish of Ballon, Co. Carlow*, Dublin: Thom, 1933. NLI Ir 94138 o 3.

Quane, Michael, *D'Israeli School, Rathvilly*, Dublin: Royal Society of Antiquaries, 1948. NLI, 23 p.

Ryan, John, *The history and antiquities of the County Carlow*, Dublin: R.M. Times, 1833. NLI Ir 94138 r 1, 388 p.

Veale, T., *Richard Lucas, 1788: directory extract for south east of Ireland*, Dublin: Veale, 1995. NLI Ir 9414 v.

—— *Index of Surnames in 'The New Commercial Directory for the cities of Waterford and Kilkenny and the towns of Clonmel, Carrick-on-Suir, New Ross and Carlow'*, Dublin: Veale, 1996. NLI Ir 9414 p.

White, W.D., *Heirs to a heritage: a story of the people and places of the Clonegal area of Clonegal Parish*, Clonegal: 1992. NLI Ir 941 p 132 (2), 72 p.

Local journals
Carloviana. NLI Ir 94138 c 2.
Carlow Past and Present. NLI Ir 94138 c 3.
The Carlovian. NLI Ir 379 c 29.

Directories

1788	Richard Lucas, *General Directory of the Kingdom of Ireland*. Reprinted in Veale, *Lucas*, *IG*, 1965, 1966, 1967, 1968. Online: Rootsweb Carlow. NLI Pos. 3729.
1820	J. Pigot, *Commercial Directory of Ireland*. PRONI; NLI Ir 9141 p 107; LDS film 962702 item 1.
1824	J. Pigot & Co., *City of Dublin and Hibernian Provincial Directory*. NLI; LDS film 451787. Online: Hayes.
1839	T. Shearman, *New Commercial Directory for the cities of Waterford and Kilkenny, Towns of Clonmel, Carrick-on-Suir, New Ross and Carlow*. Indexed in Veale.
1840	*New Trienniel Commercial Directory for 1840, 1841, 1842* (Carlow town).
1846	Slater's *National Commercial Directory of Ireland*. PRONI; NLI LO; LDS film 1696703 item 3. Online: Hayes.
1856	Slater, *Royal National Commercial Directory of Ireland*. NLI; LDS film 1472360 item 1.
1870	Slater, *Directory of Ireland*. NLI.
1881	Slater, *Royal National Commercial Directory of Ireland*. NLI. Online: FindMyPast.
1894	Slater, *Royal Commercial Directory of Ireland*. NLI.

Gravestone inscriptions

Parts (at least) of ten Co. Carlow graveyards are transcribed at <*www. interment.net*>.

Aghade: in Ryan, *History and Antiquities*. Online: Rootsweb Carlow.
Ballyellin: Ballyellin and Tomdarragh, Muintir na Tíre, *Inscriptions*, Vol. 4.
Clonygoose: Borris, Muintir na Tíre, *Inscriptions*, Vol. 2.
Clonygoose: Ballycoppigan, New, Muintir na Tíre, *Inscriptions*, Vol. 2.
Clonygoose: Muintir na Tíre, *Inscriptions*, Vol. 2.
Dunleckny: Morris, *Dunleckney*.
Killerrig: IGRS, Vol. 1.
Kiltennell: Rathanna, RC, Muintir na Tíre, *Inscriptions*, Vol. 3.
Kiltennell: Killedmond, C of I, Muintir na Tíre, *Inscriptions*, Vol. 3.
Kiltennell: Ballinvalley and Kiltennell, Muintir na Tíre, *Inscriptions*, Vol. 2.
Rathvilly: Kellymount (Mountkelly), Muintir na Tíre, *Inscriptions*, Vol. 4.
St Mullins: C of I, Muintir na Tíre, *Inscriptions*, Vol. 1.
St Mullins: Ballymurphy, RC, Muintir na Tíre, *Inscriptions*, Vol. 3.
Tullowmagimma: Linkardstown, IGRS, Vol. 1.
Wells: Muintir na Tíre, *Inscriptions*, Vol. 4.

Estate records

[No landlord given]. Survey, 1170–1623. NLI Pos. 1707 [Lambeth Palace Library Ms. 635 (extracts)]. Coverage unclear. Covering areas in the civil parishes of Agha, Ballyellin, Clonygoose, Cloydagh, Dunleckny, Fennagh, Killinane, Kiltennell, Lorum, Myshall, Nurney, Oldleighlin, Sliguff, Tullowcreen, Ullard and Wells.

Bindon, Lady Henrietta. Rental and accounts, 1705–1709. NLI Ms. 3071. Principally major tenants. Covering areas in the civil parishes of Aghade, Ballinacarrig, Carlow, Clonmelsh and Killerrig.

Cuffe, Sir Wheeler. Map and survey, 1807. NLI Ms. 2148. All tenants. Covering areas in the civil parish of Moyacomb.

Dawson. Rental and map, 1852. NLI Ms. 8391. Coverage unclear. Covering areas in the civil parish of Killerrig.

Farnham. Rentals, 1818–30. NLI Mss. 3133, 3502. All tenants. Covering areas in the civil parish of Barragh.

Fishbourne, William. Rental, 1830. NLI Ms. 10,078 (5). Most tenants. Covering areas in the civil parish of Carlow.

Hamilton, James Hans. Rentals and accounts, 1822–33. NLI Mss. 6000, 5885. All tenants. Covering areas in the civil parish of Carlow.

Kavanagh. Tithe book, 1829. NLI Pos. 7156. Principally major tenants. Covering areas in the civil parish of St Mullins.

Kavanagh, Thomas. Map, 1738–58. NLI Pos. 576; rent ledger: 1755–1810. NLI Pos. 7155. Map and rent ledger: 1736–68. NLI Pos. 4645. Major tenants only. Covering areas in the civil parishes of Ballyellin, Clonygoose, Kiltennell, St Mullins and Ullard.

O'Brien. Rentals, 1690. NLI Pos. 4769. Principally major tenants. Covering areas in all civil parishes.

Ormond, Duke of. Survey, 1690. NLI Ms. 10, 469. Major tenants only. Covering areas in the civil parishes of Ardristan, Ballon, Ballyellin, Barragh, Fennagh, Gilbertstown, Kellistown, Myshall, Templepeter, Tullowmagimma. Rent rolls, 1690–91, 1689–1704, 1703–1728, 1706. NLI Mss. 2562, 2561, 23,790, 23,789. Major tenants only. Covering areas in the civil parishes of Agha, Aghade, Ardristan, Ballinacarrig, Ballon, Barragh, Carlow, Clonmore, Clonygoose, Cloydagh, Fennagh, Gilbertstown, Kellistown, Killerrig, Kiltennell, Kineagh, Rahill, Rathvilly, Sliguff, St Mullins, Tullowcreen, Tullowphelim and Urglin.

Paul, Sir R.J. Map, 1843. NLI Ms. 21.F.136. Most tenants. Covering areas in the civil parish of Tullowphelim.

Vigors. Account book, 1826. NLI Pos. 7629. Most tenants. Covering areas in the civil parish of Oldleighlin.

CAVAN

Census returns and substitutes

1612–13	*Survey of Undertakers Planted in Co. Cavan: Historical Manuscripts Commission Report, No. 4* (Hastings Mss.), 1947, pp. 159–82.
1630	Muster Roll of Ulster. Armagh County Library; PRONI D.1759/3C/1, T. 808/15164. NLI Pos. 206.
1641	Testimonies of 263 witnesses to the 1641 Rebellion. Online: 1641.
1660–1834	Belturbet Corporation records: Annual lists of court cases, commons grazing payments, charitable payments. Some gaps. NAI MFP 4.1.
1664	Hearth Money Roll, parishes of Killeshandara, Kildallan, Killenagh, Templeport, Tomregan. PRONI T808/15142.
1703–1704	Tenants in Kildallan and Killeshandara. *IA*, 8 (2), pp. 86–7.
1719–27	Account Book of Tithes of the parishes of Mostrim, Granard, Columkille, Drumlumman and Ballymacormick, Templemichael. NAI M1502.
1761	Poll Book. PRONI T1522. Online: Freeholders.
1766	Protestants in parishes of Kinawley, Lavey, Lurgan, Munterconnaught. NAI M 2476(e); also RCBL; GO Ms. 536/7; LDS film 258517, 100173. Online: PRONI name search.
1796	Spinning-Wheel Premium List. 2,400 names for Co. Cavan.
1802	Protestants in Enniskeen Parish. *IA*, Vol. 8 (2), 1973, pp. 86–7.
1813–21	Freeholders. NLI Ir 94119 c 2.
1814	Youthful Protestants in the parishes of Drung and Larah. *IA*, 1978.
1821	Parishes of Annagelliff, Ballymachugh, Castlerahan, Castleterra, Crosserlough, Denn, Drumlumman, Drung, Kilbride, Kilmore, Kinawley, Larah, Lavey, Lurgan, Mullagh, Munterconnaught. LDS films 597154–8; CHGC; NAI; LDS films 597154–8. Part online: Cmcrp (Cavan).

1823–38	Tithe Books.
1833	Arms registered with the Clerk of the Peace, April. More than 1,500 names. NLI ILB 04 p 12.
1838	Householders, Mullinanalaghta RC parish. Contributors to new church. *Teathbha*, 1 (3), 1978, pp. 244–51.
1841	Part of Killashandra parish only. Also some certified copies of census returns for use in claims for old-age pensions. NAI.
1843	Voters' list. NAI 1843/71.
1845–1913	Enniskillen Union Workhouse records. PRONI BG/14; also LDS films 25914–53.
1851	List of inhabitants of Castlerahan barony, c.1851. With Killinkere Parish registers. NLI Pos. 5349.
1851	Some certified copies of census returns for use in claims for old-age pensions. NAI.
1856–7	Griffith's Valuation. Online: Askaboutireland.
1901	Census. Online: NAI.
1911	Census. Online: NAI.
1912	The Ulster Covenant. Almost half a million original signatures and addresses of those who signed. Online: Covenant.

Online

1641	<www.1641.tcd.ie>
Askaboutireland	<www.askaboutireland.ie>
Beagan, Al	<www.rootsweb.ancestry.com/~irlcav/cavan2.htm>
Clogher	<www.clogherhistory.ie>
Cmcrp (Cavan)	<www.cmcrp.net/OtherCty/Cavan1821-1.htm>
Covenant	<www.proni.gov.uk/ulstercovenant>
Freeholders	<www.proni.gov.uk/freeholders>
Genweb Cavan	<www.rootsweb.ancestry.com/~irlcav2/cavan.html>
Hayes, John	<www.failteromhat.com>
Killeshandra	<www.iol.ie/~galwill/welcome.htm>
NAI	<www.census.nationalarchives.ie>
PRONI name search	<www.proni.gov.uk>
Townland Maps	<freepages.genealogy.rootsweb.com/~colin/Ireland/CAV/Maps>

Publications

Local histories etc.

A list of the freeholders, registered in the county of Cavan since 1st Jan. 1813 with those of £50 and £20 previously registered, Cavan: 1821. NLI Ir 94119 c 2.

'As time goes by—' compiled by Kingspan and Kingscourt Community Council, Vol. 1, Kingscourt: the council, 1994. NLI Ir 94119 a 1, 100 p.

Nugent papers (Mount Nugent, Co. Cavan), AH, 20, 126–215.

'The Volunteer Companies of Ulster, 1778–93, III: Cavan', *IS*, 7, 1906, pp. 308–310.

Cavan County Library, *Guide to Local Studies Dept.*, Cavan: 1982. 14 sheets. NLI Ir 0179 p 6.

Clarke, Desmond, *List of subscribers to Kilmore Academy, Co. Cavan, 1839*, Dublin: the compiler, 1999. NLI Ir 260 L 6.

Cullen, Sara, *Castlerahan*, Cavan: 1981. NLI Ir 94119 g 3, 58 p.

Cunningham, T.P., *The Ecclesiastical History of Larah Parish*, Larah, Co. Cavan: Rev. Michael Canon O'Reilly, 1984. NLI Ir 27412 c 2, 84 p.

Day, Angelique, *Ordnance Survey Memoirs of Ireland, Vol. 40: Counties of South Ulster, 1834–8: Cavan, Leitrim, Louth, Monaghan and Sligo*, Belfast: Institute of Irish Studies, 1997. Co-editor, Patrick McWilliams. Co. Cavan: Drumgoon, Drumloman, Drung, Enniskeen, Killdrumsherdan, Laragh. NLI Ir 9141 o 80, 216 p.

Elliott, David R., *Enniskillen Poor Law Union outdoor relief register (1847–99)*, covering parts of counties Fermanagh, Cavan, and Tyrone, Parkhill, Ont.: Kinfolk Finders, 2009. NLI, 88 p.

Farrell, Noel, *Exploring Family origins in Cavan*, Longford: the author, 1993. NLI Ir 941 p 118(1), 47 p.

Flood, Cathal, *Greaghrahan National School, 1871–2001: a history*, Greaghrahan: Greaghrahan National School Committee, 2001. NLI 2A 2123, 157 p.

Gallogly, Dan, *The diocese of Kilmore, 1800–1950*, Cavan: Bréifne Historical Society, 1999. 466 p. NLI.

Gammons, James, *Virginia then and now: a look at Virginia and Virginians*, Virginia, Co. Cavan: Old Virginia, 2004. 80 p. NLI.

Gillespie, Raymond, *Cavan: Essays on the History of an Irish County*, Dublin: Irish Academic Press, 1995. NLI Ir 94119 c 4, 240 p.

Hall, Juanita Arundell, *The John Hall family from Cootehill, Cavan County, Ireland*, Baltimore, Md.: Gateway Press, 1990. NLI Ir 9292 h 21, 482 p.

Keogh, Marie, *Crosserlough, Co. Cavan, 1821 census*, Dún Laoghaire: Genealogical Society of Ireland, 2000. NLI Ir 9291 g 7, 298 p.

Kernan, John Devereux, *The Utica Kernans, descendants of Bryan Kernan, gent. . . . of the townland of Ned in the parish of Killeshandra, barony of Tullyhunco, county of Cavan*, Hamden, Conn.: Kernan Enterprises, 1969. NLI Ir 9292 k 7, 101 p.

—— *Supplement to 'The Utica Kernans: descendants of Bryan Kernan'*, J.D. Kernan, 1993. NLI GO 36, 107 p.

McCullam, R., *Sketches of the Highlands of Cavan, and of Shirley Castle, in Farney, taken during the Irish famine, by a Looker-On*, Belfast: J. Reed, 1856. NLI Dix Belfast 1856, 316 p.

McGuinn, James, *Staghall: a history*, Belturbet: Staghall Church Committee, 1995. NLI Ir 94119 s 4, 451 p.

MacKiernan, Francis J., *The college boys: students of the Kilmore Academy and St Patrick's College, Cavan, 1839–2000*, Cavan: Bréifne Historical Society, 2008. NLI, 362 p.

MacNamee, James J., *History of the Diocese of Ardagh*, Dublin: Browne & Nolan, 1954. NLI Ir 274131 m 5, 858 p.

Masterson, Josephine, *A transcription and index of the 1841 census for Killeshandra Parish, County Cavan, Ireland,* Indianapolis: Masterson. Also FamilyTreeMaker CD ROM 7275. 1990. NLI.

Monahan, Rev. J., *Records Relating to the Diocese of Ardagh and Clonmacnoise*, Dublin: M.H. Gill & Son, 1886. NLI Ir 27413 m 3, 400 p.

Mullagh Historical Committee, *Portrait of a Parish: Mullagh, Co. Cavan*, Mullagh: Mullagh Historical Committee, 1988. NLI 1, 396 p.

O'Brien, Hugh B., *St. Michael's, Cootehill: a brief history of the Church, its buildings, its people*, Cootehill: St Michael's Church, 1993. NLI Ir 282 o 16, 124 p.

O'Connell, Philip, *The Diocese of Kilmore: its History and Antiquities*, Dublin: Browne & Nolan, 1937. NLI Ir 274119 o 3, 579 p.

—— *The schools and scholars of Breiffne*, Dublin: Browne & Nolan, 1942. NLI Ir 370941 o 3, 669 p.

Scott, Brendan, *Culture and society in early modern Breifne/Cavan*, Dublin: Four Courts Press, 2004. 241 p. NLI.

—— *Cavan, 1609–53: plantation, war and religion*, Dublin: Four Courts Press, 2007. NLI, 63 p.

Smyth, T.S., *A civic history of the town of Cavan*, Cavan: 1934. NLI Ir 94119 s 1.

Stewart, Herbert, *Billis school revisited: a history of Billis school, 1826–2002*, 2002. NLI 4A 1775, 66 p.

Sullivan, Tom, *Drumkilly: from Ardkill Mountain to Kilderry Hill*, Drumkilly History Committee, 2001. NLI Ir 94119 d 4, 503 p.

Swanzy, Rev. H.B., Some account of the family of French of Belturbet, *UJA*, 2nd Ser., 8, 1902, pp. 155–60.

Local journals
Ardagh and Clonmacnoise Historical Society Journal. NLI Ir 794105.
Bréifne: Journal of Cumann Seanchais Bhréifne. NLI Ir 94119 b 2.
The Drumlin: a Journal of Cavan, Leitrim and Monaghan. NLI Ir 05 d 345.
Heart of Breifny. NLI Ir 94119 h 1.

Directories

1820	J. Pigot, *Commercial Directory of Ireland*. PRONI; NLI Ir 9141 p 107; LDS film 962702 item 1.
1824	J. Pigot & Co., *City of Dublin and Hibernian Provincial Directory*. NLI; LDS film 451787. Online: Hayes.
1846	Slater's *National Commercial Directory of Ireland*. PRONI; NLI LO; LDS film 1696703 item 3. Online: Hayes.
1852	*Belfast and Province of Ulster Directory*. Also 1856, 1858, 1861, 1863, 1865, 1868, 1870, 1877, 1880, 1884, 1887, 1890, 1894, 1900. Online: PRONI; LDS (various years); NLI Dix Belfast 1852.

1856	Slater, *Royal National Commercial Directory of Ireland*. NLI; LDS film 1472360 item 1.
1870	Slater, *Directory of Ireland*. NLI.
1881	Slater, *Royal National Commercial Directory of Ireland*. NLI. Online: FindMyPast.
1894	Slater, *Royal Commercial Directory of Ireland*. NLI.

Gravestone inscriptions

Parts (at least) of ten Co. Cavan graveyards are transcribed at <*www. interment.net*>. Eileen Hewson (<*www.kabristan.org.uk*>) has transcribed and published five volumes of transcripts for Co. Cavan. They are available at NLI. It is not clear if the transcripts are complete for each graveyard. Other published or freely available transcripts are given below.

Annagh: Clonosey, CHGC.
—— Killoughter, CHGC.
Ballintemple: Ballintemple, C of I, CHGC.
—— Pottahee (Brusky?), RC, CHGC.
Castlerahan: Castlerahan, C of I, *Bréifne*, 1925/6. Also CHGC.
Castleterra: RC, CHGC.
Crosserlough: Kill, *Bréifne*, 1976. Also CHGC.
—— Crosserlough, RC, CHGC.
Denn: Denn Glebe, C of I, *Bréifne*, 1924.
Drumgoon: Drumgoon, CHGC.
Drumlane: Drumlane, *Bréifne*, 1979.
Drung: Magherintemple, *Bréifne*, 1963.
—— Drung, CHGC.
Kilbride: Gallonreagh (Kilbride?), CHGC.
Killeshandra (Old): Online: Killeshandra.
Killinagh: Termon (Killinagh Old?), C of I, CHGC.
Killinkere: Gallon, CHGC.
Kilmore: Trinity Island (St Mogue's?), CHGC.
Larah: CHGC.
Lavey: C of I, GO; also CHGC.
Lurgan: *Bréifne*, 1961. Also CHGC.
Mullagh: Mullagh (Raffoney?), C of I, CHGC.
Munterconnaught: Knockatemple, RC, *Bréifne*, 1927/8. Also CHGC.
Scrabby: Cloone, C of I, SA, Vol. 10, No. 1, 1980–81.
Templeport: Port, *Bréifne*, 1971.
Urney: Cavan, Church Lane, *Bréifne*, 1986.

Estate records

Annesley. Maps, with tenants' names, 1805–1817. NLI Ms. 2730. Coverage unclear. Covering areas in the civil parishes of Annagh, Denn, Drumlumman, Drung, Kilmore, Larah, Lavey, Templeport, Urney.

Commissioners of Education. Rentals, 1818–45. NLI Ms. 16920(5), 1837–42. NLI Ms. 16926. All tenants. Covering areas in the civil parish of Annagelliff.

Craigies, Robert. Tenants list, 1703–1704, *IA*, 1978. Coverage unclear. Covering areas in the civil parishes of Kildallan and Killashandra.

Crofton. Rent rolls, 1792. NLI Ms. 4530, 1796–1831. NLI Ms. 8150. Major tenants only. Covering areas in the civil parish of Kinawley.

Farnham, Earl of. Rent rolls etc.: 1718–90. NLI Ms. 11491. Major tenants only. Rentals, 1820. NLI Ms. 350; 1841–8: NLI Ms. 5012–13; 1842–3: NLI Ms. 18624. All tenants. Covering areas in the civil parishes of Ballintemple, Ballymachugh, Castlerahan, Crosserlough, Denn, Drumlane, Drumlumman, Kilbride, Kildallan, Killashandra, Killinkere, Kilmore, Lurgan and Urney.

Fingall, Earl of. Rent rolls, 1750. NLI Ms. 8024. Major tenants only. Covering areas in the civil parishes of Loughan or Castlekeeran Lurgan, Mullagh, Munterconnaught.

Garvagh, Lord. Rentals, 1829–48, NAI M5535. All tenants. Covering areas in the civil parishes of Drumgoon, Knockbride and Larah.

Gosford, Earls of. Rentals, 1787–1824. PRONI D/1606. Covering areas in the civil parishes of Ballintemple; Killashandra; Scrabby. May cover further parishes.

Greville, William. Rentals, surveys etc., 1810–48, NAI M6178 (1–89). All tenants. Covering areas in the civil parishes of Drumgoon and Knockbride.

Groome, Edward. Rentals, with observations, 1822, NAI M5559. All tenants. Covering areas in the civil parishes of Bailieborough, Knockbride and Moybolgue.

Hamilton. Rentals, with observations: 1851, NAI M5571 (1–39). All tenants. Covering areas in the civil parishes of Kildallan, Killashandra and Kilmore.

Hodson. Rentals, 1811–24. NLI Ms. 16397–8. All tenants. Covering areas in the civil parishes of Bailieborough and Knockbride.

Mayne, Robert. Map, 1780. NAI M1853. All tenants. Map of Begleive and Killcross in Knockbride Parish.

O'Reilly, James. Rentals, 1815–16, NAI M.6962. All tenants. Covering areas in the civil parishes of Annagelliff, Castlerahan, Crosserlough, Denn and Kilbride.

Pratt. Rentals. 1837–63. NLI Ms. 3021, 1837–55. NLI Ms. 3284. All tenants. Covering areas in the civil parish of Enniskeen.

Saunderson. Rent roll, 1779. NLI Ms.13340. Major tenants only. Covering areas in the civil parishes of Annagelliff, Killinkere and Lavey.

Tennison. Rentals, 1846–54. NLI Ms. 1400–1409. All tenants. Covering areas in the civil parish of Annagelliff.

CLARE

Census returns and substitutes

1641	*Book of Survey and Distribution*, Dublin: IMC, 1947. Also NLI Ms. 963. Transcribed online: Clare County Library.
1659	Pender's 'Census'. Reprinted GPC, 1997; IMC, 2002. LDS film 924648.
1745	Voters. TCD Ms. 2059.
1778	Militia volunteers in Ennis. *JNMAS*, 6 (4), 1952, pp. 143–51.
1821	Part of Ennis. NAI. See pre-1901 census catalogue.
1823–38	Tithe Books. Transcribed online: Clare County Library.
1829	Freeholders. NLI P.5556.
1837	Marksmen (illiterate voters) in parliamentary boroughs: Ennis. *Parliamentary Papers, 1837: Reports from Committees*, Vol. 2 (i), Appendix A.
1843	Clare voters. NAI 1843/68.
1848–9	Smith O'Brien Petition, Eneclann CD ENEC002. Almost 4,000 names for Ennis/Tulla. See '1790–1800: Official Papers, petitions' in Chapter 2.
1849	Evictions in Kilrush Union. Online: Clare County Library.
1850	Deaths in Kilrush and Ennistymon workhouses, hospitals, infirmaries, 25/3/1850–25/3/1851. *Accounts and Papers (Parliamentary Papers), 1851*, Vol. 49, pp. (484) 1–47.
1855	Griffith's Valuation. Online: Askaboutireland; Clare County Library.
1866	Kilfenora. NLI Pos. 2440.
1901	Census. Online: NAI, Clare County Library.
1911	Census. Online: NAI.

Online

Askaboutireland	*<www.askaboutireland.ie>*
Aughty	*<www.aughty.org>*
Celtic Cousins	*<www.celticcousins.net>*
Clare County Library	*<www.clarelibrary.ie>*
Clare Roots Society	*<www.clareroots.org>*
Connors	*<www.connorsgenealogy.com>*
Hayes, John	*<www.failteromhat.com>*
NAI	*<www.census.nationalarchives.ie>*

Publications

Local histories etc.

A Guide to Ennistymon Union, 1839–50, Ennistymon: North Clare Historical Society, 1992. NLI Ir 360 g, 47 p.

'Businessmen of Ennis early in the Napoleonic wars', *IA*, 16 (1), 1984, pp. 6–8.

Páirtín, 1885–1985: Parteen centenary book, Parteen: the Club, 1985. NLI Ir 396 p 56(1), 176 p.

Visions of Famine in West Clare: 'vultures in the wild bogs': pictures of yesterday, words of today, Westwords, n.d. NLI 1A 501, 40 p.

[Unknown], *The Pope's own Irish parish*, Dublin: n.d. A history of Liscannor. 102 p.

Ainsworth, J.F., *The Inchiquin Manuscripts*, Dublin: IMC, 1960. NLI Ir 091 a 1, 749 p.

Bourke, Freddie, *Kiltenanlea Parish Church and its community, Clonlara, Co. Clare, 1782–1992*, Clonlara: Clonlara Development Association, 1992. NLI Ir 941 p 116(4), 36 p.

Brew, Frank, *The parish of Kilkeedy: a local history compiled*, Tubber: Frank Brew, 1998. NLI Ir 94143 b 10, 310 p.

Clancy, John, Rev. Canon, 'Gleanings in 17th century Kilrush', *North Munster Antiquarian Society Journal*, 1942–3.

—— *Short History of the Parish of Killanena or Upper Feakle*, Ennis: Clare Champion, 1954. NLI Ir 941 p 27, 27 p.

Coffey, Thomas, *The Parish of Inchicronan (Crusheen)*, Mountshannon: Ballinakella Press, 1993. NLI Ir 94143 c 10.

Coleman, James, Limerick and Clare Bibliography, *Limerick Field Club Journal*, No. 32, 1907.

Comber, Maureen, *Poverty before the famine: County Clare, 1835: first report from His Majesty's Commissioners into the Condition of the Poorer Classes in Ireland*, Ennis: CLASP Press, 1995. Edited and indexed by Maureen Comber. NLI Ir 94143 p 2, 170 p.

Cooralclare-Cree Historical Society, *Cooraclare and Cree: Parish of Kilmacduane: History and Folklore*, 2002. 460p.

Cotter, Maura, *Parish of Kilmihil: Historical, cultural and sporting achievements*, n.d. Co-authors, Marian Moran and Annette Collins. NLI Ir 94143 c 6, 264 p.

Craig, Edward Thomas, *An Irish commune: the experiment at Ralahine, County Clare, 1831–3*, Dublin: Irish Academic Press, c.1983. NLI Ir 630941 c 38, 208 p.

Dwyer, Philip, *A handbook to Lisdoonvarna and its vicinity: giving a detailed account of its curative waters, and tours to the principal places of interest in the County Clare*, Dublin: Hodges, Foster, 1876. NLI Ir 914143 l 4, 86 p.

—— *The Diocese of Killaloe, from the Reformation to the Close of the Eighteenth Century*, Dublin: Hodges, Foster & Figgis, 1878. NLI Ir 94143 d 11, 602 p. Reprinted Newmarket-on-Fergus: O'Brien Book Publications, 1997.

Flanagan, John, *Kilfenora: a history*, Lahinch: John Flanagan, 1991. NLI Ir 94143.f.7, 141 p.

Frost, James, *The history and topography of Co. Clare from the earliest times to the beginning of the eighteenth century*, Dublin: 1893. Reprinted Newmarket-on-Fergus: O'Brien Book Publications, 1997. NLI Ir 94143 f 3.

Glynn, Rose, *The Story of Aughinish*, Ballyvaughan: Glynn, 2002. Clare County Library.

Gwynn, A., *A history of the diocese of Killaloe*, Dublin: M.H. Gill & Son, 1962. NLI Ir 27414.g.3, 566 p.

Hacker, Bryan and Jenny, *The Gormans, master mariners of Kilrush*, Kenmore Hills, Qld: the authors, 2006. NLI. 195 p.

Hayes-McCoy, G.A., *Index to 'The Compossicion Booke of Connoght, 1585'*, Dublin: IMC, 1945. NLI Ir 9412 c 1, 179 p.

Herbert, Robert, *Worthies of Thomond: a compendium of short lives of the most famous men and women of Limerick and Clare*, Limerick: published by the author, 1946. NLI, 3 parts.

Holohan, Pat, *Cill Mhuire na nGall: a history of Kilmurry, 1891–1991, written by the people of Kilmurry*, Kilmurry: Kilmurry Centenary Committee, 1991. NLI Ir 94143.k.7, 172 p.

IGRS, *Tombstone inscriptions, Vol. 1*, Dublin: IGRS Tombstone Committee, 2001. NLI, 850 p.

Jones, Anne, *The scattering: images of emigrants from an Irish county*, Dublin: A. & A. Farmar, 2000. Text by Ray Conway. NLI 4B 2178, 256 p.

Kelly, John S., *The Bodyke evictions*, Scariff: Fossabeg Press, 1987. NLI Ir 94143 k 6, 184 p.

Kierse, Sean, *The famine years in the parish of Killaloe, 1945 [sic]–1851*, Clare: Boru Books, 1984. NLI Ir 94143 k 5, 86 p.

—— *Land and people of Killaloe Parish*, Killaloe: Boru Books, 2008. NLI. 383 p.

—— *Priests and religious of Killaloe Parish, Co. Clare*, Killaloe: Boru Books, 2000. NLI. 54 p.

—— *Historic Killaloe: a guide to its antiquities*, Killaloe: Boru Books, 1983. NLI Ir 941 p 77, 46 p.

Lane, Michael, *Church of St. Sena, Clonlara: parish of Doonass and Truagh*, Clonara: M. Lane, 1984. NLI Ir 270 p 15, 36 p.

Lee, David, *Ralahine land war and the co-operative*, Limerick: Bottom Dog, in association with Co-op Books, 1981. NLI Ir 333 p 52, 56 p.

Lloyd, A.R., *Lloyd's tour of Clare, 1780 (from Henn's exact reprint of 1893)*, Whitegate: Ballinakella, c.1986. NLI Ir 914143 L 15, 60 p.

Lynch, Mathew, and Nugent, Patrick, *Clare: History and Society*, Dublin: Geography Publications, 2008. NLI, 789 p.

McAuliffe, E.J., *Notes on the parishes of Kilmurry McMahon and Killofin, Co. Clare and tombstone inscriptions from Kilrush*, Dublin: McAuliffe, 1989. NLI Ir 941 p 137(4), 31 p.

McCarthy, Daniel, *Ireland's banner county: Clare from the fall of Parnell to the Great War, 1890–1918*, Ennis: Saipan Press, 2002. NLI 3A 1777, 213 p.

McGuane, James T., *Kilrush from olden times*, Indreabhán, Co. Galway: Clódóirí Lurgan, 1984. NLI Ir 94143 m 11, 114 p.

Mac Mathúna, Seosamh, *Kilfarboy: a history of a west Clare parish*, Milltown Malbay: S. Mac Mathúna, 1976?

Madden, Gerard, *Holy Island: jewel of the Lough: A history*, Tuamgraney: East Clare Heritage Centre, 1990. NLI Ir 941 p 102(1), 39 p.

—— *For God or King: the history of Mountshannon, Co. Clare, 1742–1992*,

Tuamgraney: East Clare Heritage, 1993. NLI Ir 94143 f 8, 204 p.

—— A history of Tuamgraney and Scariff since earliest times, Tuamgraney: East Clare Heritage, 2000. NLI Ir 94143 m 19, 208 p.

Markham, Paul, Kilmurry Mcmahon and Killofin remembered: an accurate and detailed account—past and present—of a rural parish in the barony of Clonderlaw, Co. Clare, Ireland, s.n. NLI Ir 94143 m 18, 236 p.

Mayer, John, Families of Kilmaley Parish: A Two-Hundred Year Review, Kilmaley: John Mayer, 2011. Clare County Library, 603 p.

Murphy, Ignatius, Father Michael Meehan and the Ark of Kilbaha, Ennis: Rev. Michael Greene, 1980. NLI Ir 920041 p 7, 16 p.

—— The Diocese of Killaloe, 1800–50, Dublin: Four Courts Press, 1992. NLI Ir 27414 m 7, 488 p.

—— Before the Famine struck: life in West Clare, 1834–45, Blackrock, Co. Dublin: Irish Academic Press, 1996. NLI Ir 94143 m 16, 105 p.

—— A People Starved: Life and Death in West Clare, 1845–51, Dublin: Irish Academic Press, 1995. NLI Ir 94143 m 15, 113 p.

—— The Diocese of Killaloe, 1850–1904, Dublin: Four Courts Press, 1995. NLI Ir 27414 m 9, 527 p.

—— The diocese of Killaloe in the eighteenth century, Dublin: Four Courts Press, 1991. NLI Ir 27414 m 8, 373 p.

Murphy, Paul, Cuchulain's Leap: a history of the parishes of Carrigaholt and Cross, Carrigaholt: Carrigaholt and Cross Heritage Group, 1992. NLI Ir 94143 m 12, 288 p.

O'Brien, Grania Rachel, These my friends and forebears: the O'Briens at Dromoland Castle, Whitegate: Ballinakella Press, 1991. NLI Ir 9292 O 54, 259 p.

O'Cillin, Sean P., Travellers in Co. Clare, 1459–1843, Galway: S.P. O'Cillin and P.F. Brannick, 1977. NLI Ir 914143 o 16, 55 p.

Ó Conchúir, M.F., O Conor Corcomroe: a bilingual history, M.F. Ó Conchúir, 1996. NLI Ir 9292 o 68, 293 p.

Ó Dálaigh, Brian, Corporation book of Ennis, 1660–1810, Dublin: Irish Academic Press, 1990. NLI Ir 94143 c 8, 455 p.

—— Ennis in the 18th century: portrait of an urban community (Maynooth Studies in Local History, No. 3), Dublin: Irish Academic Press, 1995. NLI Ir 94143 o 9, 62 p.

Ó Dálaigh, Brian, and Holton, Clare, Irish villages: studies in local history, Dublin: Four Courts Press, 2003. Sixmilebridge. NLI. 326 p.

O'Donovan, John, The antiquities of County Clare … collected during the progress of the Ordnance Survey in 1839, and letters and extracts relative to ancient territories in Thomond [1841], Ennis: CLASP Press, 1997. John O'Donovan and Eugene Curry; edited and indexed by Maureen Comber. NLI Ir 94143 o 10, 323 p.

O'Gorman, Michael, A pride of paper tigers: a history of the Great Hunger in the Scariff Workhouse Union from 1839 to 1853, Tuamgraney: East Clare Heritage, 1994. NLI Ir 94143 o 8, 82 p.

O'Mahoney, Dr C., 'Emigration from Kilrush Workhouse, 1848–59', *The Other Clare*, 1983.

Ó Murchadha, Ciarán, *County Clare studies: essays in memory of Gerald O'Connell, Seán Ó Murchadha, Thomas Coffey and Pat Flynn*, Ennis: Clare Archaeological and Historical Society, 2000. NLI 3B 466, 271 p.

Ó Riain, Dónal, *The history and folklore of Parteen and Meelick*, Parteen: Ó Riain, 1991. NLI 360 p.

Power, Joseph, *A history of Clare Castle and its environs*, Ennis: Power, 2004. NLI 4B 1621, 646 p.

Scanlan, Senan, *Inhabitants of Scattery Island, Shannon Estuary, County Clare*, the author, 2007. NLI. 197 p.

Shiely, James F., Jr, *The Shealys (Shielys) of Kilrush, County Clare, Ireland, and Minnesota, USA*, Prescott, Wis.: J.F. Shiely, Jr, 1998. NLI Ir 94143 s 14.

Simington, Robert C., *The transplantation to Connacht, 1654–58*, Shannon: Irish University Press, for IMC, 1970. NLI Ir 94106 s 9, 306 p.

Spellisy, Seán, *The merchants of Ennis*, Blarney: On Stream Publications, for Ennis Chamber of Commerce, 1996. NLI Ir 380 s 10, 200 p.

—— *A history of County Clare*, Dublin: Gill & Macmillan, 2003. NLI, 156 p.

Starkie, Virginia, *Indexed abtracts from Co. Clare civil records, 1864–80*, Vienna, Va.: the author, 1990. LDS Family History Library, film 1696528.

Swinfen, Averin, *Forgotten stones: ancient church sites of the Burren and environs*, Dublin: Lilliput Press, 1992. NLI Ir 726 s 19, 151 p.

Weir, H., *Historical, genealogical, architectural notes on some houses of Clare*, Whitegate, Co. Clare: Ballinakella Press, 1999. NLI Ir 728 w 12, 285 p.

Westropp, Westropp Manuscripts, RIA. Will abstracts mainly for Cos. Clare and Limerick.

White, Rev. P., *History of Clare and the Dalcassian Clans of Tipperary, Limerick and Galway*, Dublin: 1893. Reprinted Newmarket-on-Fergus: O'Brien Book Publications, 1997. NLI Ir 94143 w 4, 398 p.

Local journals
Dál gCais. NLI Ir 94143 d 5.
Journal of the North Munster Archaeological Society. NLI Ir 794105 n 1.
The Other Clare (Journal of the Shannon Archaeological and Historical Society). NLI Ir 9141 p 71.
Shannonside Annual (1956–60). Ir 94146 s 2.
Sliabh Aughty: East Clare Heritage Journal. Ir 94133.s.

Directories
1788   Richard Lucas, *General Directory of the Kingdom of Ireland.* NLI Pos. 3729. Reprinted in Veale, *Lucas, IG*, 1965, 1966, 1967, 1968. Online: Clare County Library.

1820	J. Pigot, *Commercial Directory of Ireland,* PRONI; NLI Ir 9141 p 107; LDS film 962702 item 1. ·
1824	J. Pigot & Co., *City of Dublin and Hibernian Provincial Directory.* NLI; LDS film 451787. Online: Hayes.
1842	Hogan's *Directory of Kilkee.* NLI Ir 61312 k 1. Online: Clare County Library.
1846	Slater's *National Commercial Directory of Ireland.* PRONI; NLI LO; LDS film 1696703 item 3. Online: Hayes.
1856	Slater, *Royal National Commercial Directory of Ireland.* NLI; LDS film 1472360 item 1.
1863	Hogan's *Directory of Kilkee.* Online: Clare County Library.
1866	George Henry Bassett, *Directory of the City and County of Limerick, and of the Principal Towns in the Cos. of Tipperary and Clare.* NLI Ir 914144 b 5.
1866–80	Bassett's *Directory of Limerick City and County and Principal Towns of Clare, Tipperary and Kerry.* 1875 and 1880 Clare towns online: Clare County Library.
1867	Henry and Coughlan's *General Directory of Cork and Munster,* Archive CD Books.
1870	Slater, *Directory of Ireland.* NLI. Online: Clare County Library.
1881	Slater, *Royal National Commercial Directory of Ireland.* NLI. Clare towns online: Clare County Library.
1886	Francis Guy, *Postal Directory of Munster.* NLI Ir 91414 g 8; LDS film 1559399 item 8.
1893	Francis Guy, *Directory of Munster.* NLI Ir 91414 g 8. Clare towns online: Clare County Library.
1894	Slater, *Royal Commercial Directory of Ireland.* NLI.

Gravestone inscriptions

The Clare Genealogy Centre has transcripts for eighty graveyards in the county. Contact details will be found in Chapter 15. Clare County Library has online transcripts of almost a hundred graveyards. It also has Co. Clare entries from the *Journal of the Association for the Preservation of the Memorials of the Dead, Ireland, 1888–1916.* Parts (at least) of twenty-three Co. Clare graveyards are transcribed at *<www.interment.net>.* Published transcripts are given below.

Feakle: Online: Clare County Library.
Kilrush: Kilrush, Grace St, C of I, IGRS, Vol. 1, also McAuliffe, *Notes.*

Estate records

Arthur, Thomas. Map, 1823. Major tenants only. NLI Ms. 21 f 75 (3). Covering areas in the civil parishes of Kilballyowen and Moyarta.
Brown, John. Rental, 1828–32. NLI Ms. 8990. Principally major tenants. Covering areas in the civil parishes of Killaloe, Killilagh, Kiltenanlea and Templemaley.

Buckingham, Duke of. Estate sale and map, 1848. NLI Ms. 14.A.20. All tenants. Covering areas in the civil parishes of Drumcreehy, Killinaboy and Rathborney.

Burton, Edward William. Rental, 1828. NLI Ms. 8683. All tenants. Covering areas in the civil parishes of Feakle, Kilballyowen, Kilfenora, Killinaboy, Kilmurry and Kiltoraght.

Butler. Rentals, undated (late nineteenth century). NAI M. 3703 (179) and (180). All tenants. Covering areas in the civil parishes of Clondagad, Doon, Inchicronan and Mungret.

Inchiquin. Rentals, 1840–60. NLI Ms. 14355ff. All tenants. Full; approximate dates. Covering areas in the civil parish of Kilnasoolagh.

O'Brien, Sir Donat. Rent rolls, 1688–1717. NLI Mss. 14353–410. Principally major tenants. Covering areas in the civil parishes of Clonloghan, Doora, Drumline, Kilfintinan, Kilnasoolagh, Kilseily, Quin, Templemaley, Tomfinlough and Tulla.

O'Brien, Sir Lucius. Map, 1768–81. NLI Maps 21 f 138. Major tenants only. Covering areas in the civil parishes of Clareabbey, Killinaboy, Kilnasoolagh and Tomfinlough.

O'Callaghan-Westropp. Rentals, barony of Tulla Upper. NLI Ms. 867.

Roxton. Rentals, Inchiquin barony, 1834. NA Ms. 5764.

Stacpoole Kenny. Rental, 1824–6. NLI Ms. 18910. Most tenants. Clonloghan, 1851–3, NLI Ms. 18913. Covering areas in the civil parish of Killaspuglonane.

Studdert. (1830s?) Tenants, 'List of persons who are in want of immediate employment in the different townlands in the parish of Kilballyowen'; tenants' names; number in each family; number able to work; observations. NLI Ms. 20640.

Vandeleur: Note on the Leconfield estate papers at the National Archives, Accession No. 1074. (Vandeleur leases, Kilrush, 1816–1929, Lord Leconfield rentals, 1846–1917, including comments on age, health, poverty etc.) *North Munster Antiquarian Journal*, Vol. 23, 1981.

Westby, Nicholas. Survey, 1842 NLI Ms. map 21 f 85. Major tenants only. Ennis town.

Westropp. Map, 1844–95. NLI Ms. maps 21 f 126. Most tenants. Covering areas in the civil parishes of Clareabbey, Doora, Kilmacduane, Kilmihil, Kilnoe and Quin.

CORK

Census returns and substitutes

1500–1650   The Pipe Roll of Cloyne. *JCHAS*, 1918.

1641   Testimonies of 2,033 witnesses to the 1641 Rebellion. Online: 1641.

1641   Book of Survey and Distribution. Proprietors in 1641, grantees in 1666–8. NLI Ms. 966–7.

1641   Survey of Houses in Cork city, listing tenants and possessors. NAI Quit Rent Office Papers.

1654	*Civil Survey*, Vol. 6.
1659	Pender's 'Census'. Reprinted GPC, 1997; IMC, 2002. LDS film 924648.
1662–7	Subsidy rolls. Extracts for Condons and Clangibbons baronies. NAI M.4968, M.2636.
1700–1752	Freemen of Cork city. NAI M. 4693.
1753	Householders in St Nicholas' Parish, Cork city. Also later years. NAI MFCI 23, 24, 25; M 6047.
1761	Militia list of Co. Cork. NAI.
1766	Aghabulloge, Aghada, Ardagh, Ballintemple, Ballyhay, Ballynoe, Carrigdownane, Carrigrohanebeg, Castlelyons, Castletownroche, Churchtown, Clenor, Clondrohid, Clondulane, Clonfert, Clonmeen, Clonmult, Clonpriest, Cloyne, Coole, Farahy, Garrycloyne, Glanworth, Grenagh, Ightermurragh, Imphrick, Inishcarra, Kildorrery, Kilmahon, Kilnamartry, Kilshannig, Kilworth, Knockmourne, Lisgoold, Litter, Macroney, Macroom, Magourney, Mallow, Marshalstown, Matehy, Middleton, Mogeely, Mourneabbey, Roskeen, Shandrum, St Nathlash, Templemolaga, Whitechurch, and Youghal, M5036a; Rathbarry and Ringrone, NAI; Parl. Ret., 773, 774; Dunbulloge, *JCHAS*, Vol. 51; Kilmichael, Vol. 26. Part online: Prendergast, Swanton. Youghal online: PRONI name search.
1783	Freemen and freeholders, Cork city. NLI P 2054.
1792	Kinsale Loyalty Petition. *Freeman's Journal*, 5 January 1793. Online: Hall #2.
1793	Householders in the parish of St Anne's, Shandon. Also includes householders of additional houses built up to 1853. *JCHAS*, Vol. 47, pp. 87–111.
1796	Spinning-Wheel Premium List. 1,170 names for Co. Cork.
1814	Jurors, Co. Cork. NAI M2637, Grove-White Abstracts.
1817	Freemen, Cork city. NLI P 722.
1821	Eighteen townlands in Inchigeelagh. Online: Grogan.
1823–38	Tithe Books. Part online: Prendergast.
1830	House-owners, St Mary's, Shandon. *JCHAS*, Vol. 49.
1830–37	Registered householders, Cork city (alphabetical). *Parliamentary Papers, 1837: Reports from Committees*, 1837/8, Vol. 13 (2), pp. 554–7.
1831	Memorial of inhabitants of Kanturk for Kanturk–Mallow–Cork road, 12 July 1831 (128 names). NAI OP 974/132.
1832–7	Voters, Cork city. *Parliamentary Papers, 1837: Reports from Committees*, 1837/8. Vol. 13 (1), pp. 320–21.
1834	Protestant families, Magourney Parish; with C of I Registers. NAI M 5118.
1834	Protestant parishioners, Bandon town (Ballymodan only). NLI Ms. 675.
1834–7	Valuation of Bandonbridge, Kinsale and Youghal towns (£5 householders). *Parliamentary Papers, 1837: Reports from Committees*, Vol. 2 (1), Appendix G.

1834–52   Kingwilliamstown Crown estate censuses, 1834, 1849–52. NLI Pos. 1873; also LDS film 101767.

1836   Memorials for quarter sessions at Kanturk (c.120 signatures), Middleton (c.40 names), Mitchelstown (c.100 signatures, with addresses) and Mallow (c.85 signatures). NAI OP 1836/130.

1837   Marksmen (i.e. illiterate voters), Bandonbridge, Kinsale and Youghal boroughs. *Parliamentary Papers, 1837: Reports from Committees, 1837,* Vol. 2 (1), Appendix A.

1837   Lists of waste and poor Cork city parishes. *Parliamentary Papers, 1837: Reports from Committees,* 1837–8, Vol. 13 (1), pp. 324–34.

1838–52   Reproductive Loan Fund records. Parishes of Ballinadee, Brigown, Castlehaven, Cloyne, Durrus, Inch, Kilcaskan, Kilcatherine, Kilfaughnabeg, Killaconenagh, Kilmacabea, Kilmeen (East Carbery), Kilmocomoge, Kilmoe, Kinsale, Marshalstown, Ringcurran, Ross, Skull and Tullagh. 5,000+ names, with accounts of deaths and emigration. NA (Kew) T 91. Partly online: Moving Here.

1841–51   Extensive extracts for Kilcrumper, Leitrim and Kilworth Parishes. NAI M4685. Also abstracts used in application for old-age pensions. See Masterson ('Local history', below).

1842   Cork voters. NAI. West OP 1842/26, East OP 1842/23.

1842   Census of the Catholic parish of Middleton. Online: IGP-WEB.

1843–50   Records of Easter and Christmas dues, Catholic parish of Ballyclogh; includes names of parishioners, with children. NLI Pos. 5717.

1848   Memorial from inhabitants of Cork city for additional quarter sessions. c.80 names. NAI OP 1836/130.

1848–1925   Youghal Workhouse records, including indoor relief registers, 1848–51. CAI BG/163.

1851   Extracts for Kilcrumper, Kilworth, Leitrim and Macroney. Online: Swanton.

1851–3   Griffith's Valuation. Online: Askaboutireland; Clare County Library.

1901   Census. Online: NAI.

1911   Census. Online: NAI.

Online

1641	<www.1641.tcd.ie>	
Askaboutireland	<www.askaboutireland.ie>	Griffith's Valuation
Aubane	<www.aubanehistoricalsociety.org>	
Castlemagner	<www.iol.ie/~edmo>	Castlemagner Historical Society
Cork City Library	<www.corkpastandpresent.ie>	
Grogan, Margaret	<http://freepages.genealogy.rootsweb.ancestry.com/~mturner/smith/index.htm>	Volunteer-transcribed Cork records
Hall, Brendan	<homepage.tinet.ie/~jbhall>	

Hayes, John	*<www.failteromhat.com>*	Compendium of Irish records, esp. Clonakilty
Limerick Archives	*<www.limerickcity.ie>*	
Moving Here	*<www.movinghere.org.uk/search>*	
NAI	*<www.census.nationalarchives.ie>*	1901 and 1911 censuses, complete
Prendergast, Jean	*<www.corkgen.org/publicgenealogy/cork/potpourri>*	
PRONI name search	*<www.proni.gov.uk>*	
Swanton, Ginni	*<www.ginnisw.com/corkmain.html>*	Assorted records for most areas of Co. Cork
Turner, Paul	*<www.paulturner.ca>*	Ballymoney, Kinneigh, Bandon
Waterford Archives	*<www.waterfordcoco.ie>*	

Publications

Local histories etc.

Cill na Martra, Múscraí, Co. Chorcaí, Kilnamartyra: Coiste Forbartha Chill na Martra, 1995. NLI Ir 94145 c 28, 151 p.

A vision fulfilled, 1846–1996: a Skibbereen school, Skibbereen: St Fachtna's De La Salle Past Pupils' Union, 1996. NLI Ir 373 v 1, 92 p.

Ahern, Madge, *Inniscarra looks back through the avenues of time*, Cork: St Coleman's, 1995. NLI Ir 94145 a 1, 97 p.

Allen, D.H., *Áth Trasna: a history of Newmarket, County Cork*, Cork: Cork Historical Guides Committee, 1973. NLI 3A 2157, 104 p.

Aubane Historical Society, *A Millstreet medley*, Millstreet: Aubane Historical Society, 2001. NLI 1B 388, 47 p.

—— *Aubane: notes on a townland*, Aubane: Aubane Historical Society, 1996. This is the text of a talk in Aubane School on 26 August 1996. NLI 1B 1100, 51 p.

—— *Aubane school and its roll books, 1913–74*, Aubane: Aubane Historical Society, 1998. NLI 2B 667, 50 p.

—— *250 years of the butter road*, Millstreet: Aubane Historical Society, 1997. NLI 1B 482, 50 p.

Ballynoe Cemetery Committee, *Ballynoe Cemetery: a guide and brief history*, Ballynoe: 1993. NLI Ir 9295 p 3(1).

Ballynoe National School, *Ballynoe national schools, 1850–1990*, Ballynoe: Ballynoe National School, 1990. NLI Ir 372.b.66, 160 p.

Ballyvongane Committee, *Ballyvongane N.S., 1845–1995: Béal Átha na Marbh, Aghinagh: a rural community*, Ballyvongane: 150th Anniversary Committee, 1995. NLI Ir94145 b 18, 239 p.

Barry, E., *Barrymore: the records of the Barrys of Co. Cork*, Cork: Guy, 1902, 214 p. NLI Ir 9292 b 19.

Barry, J.M., *Old Glory at Queenstown: American maritime activity in the*

Queenstown era, 1800–1922, Cork: Sidney Publishing, 1999. NLI Ir 94145 b 21, 206 p.

—— *Queenstown for orders: contributions to the maritime history of Queenstown Harbour, the Cove of Cork*, Cork: Sidney Publishing, 1999. NLI 3B 1733, 185 p.

—— *The Victoria Hospital, Cork: a history*, Cork: 1992. NLI Ir 362 b 8, 310 p.

Bennett, G., *The history of Bandon and the principal towns of the West Riding of Cork*, Cork: Francis Guy, 1869. NLI Ir 94145 b 1, 572 p. Online: Turner.

Bolster, Evelyn, *A history of the Diocese of Cork: from the Reformation to the Penal Era*, Cork: Tower Books, 1982. NLI, 355 p.

—— *A history of the diocese of Cork: from the earliest times to the Reformation*, Shannon: Irish University Press, 1972. NLI Ir 27414 b 6, 548 p.

Bowen, Elizabeth, *Bowen's Court*, London: 1944. NLI Ir 9292 b 18.

Brady, W. Maziere, *Clerical and Parochial Records of Cork, Cloyne and Ross*, Dublin: printed for the author, 1864. NLI Ir 27414 b 4, 3 vols.

Broderick, Mary, *A History of Cóbh*, Cóbh: Mary Broderick, 1989. NLI Ir 94145 p 7(3), 169 p.

Browne, Fergal, *Tracton: where the abbey lies low*, Tracton: Knochnamanagh Old School, 2007. Co-editors, Eileen McGough and Lesley Roberts. NLI, 380 p.

Brunicardi, Niall, *Fermoy to 1890: a local history*, Fermoy: Éigse na Mainistreach, 1975. NLI Ir 94145 p 2, 210 p.

Cadogan, Tim, *Tracing your Cork Ancestors*, Dublin: Flyleaf Press, 1998. Co-editor, Tony McCarthy. NLI, Genealogy Service, 123 p.

—— *A biographical dictionary of Cork*, Dublin: Four Courts Press, 2006. Co-editor, Jeremiah Falvey. NLI, 361 p.

Casey, Albert, *O'Kief, Cosh Mang, Slieve Lougher, and Upper Blackwater in Ireland*, Privately printed, 1962–74. Massive multi-volume compendium of information on the Sliabh Luachra and Blackwater Valley area on the Cork-Kerry border. NLI Ir 94145 c 12. Index online at Cork City Library.

Caulfield, R., *Council Book of the Corporation of Kinsale*, Guildford, Surrey: 1879. NLI Ir 94145 c 3, 447 p.

—— *Council Book of the Corporation of Youghal (1610–59, 1666–87 and 1690–1800)*, Guildford, Surrey: 1878. NLI Ir 94145 c 4, 637 p.

—— (ed.), *Annals of the Cathedral of St. Coleman, Cloyne*, Cork: Purcell, 1882. NLI Ir 7266 c 2, 59 p.

—— (ed.), *The pipe roll of Cloyne*, Cork: Guy, 1918. (From the original, formerly preserved in the registry of the ancient cathedral church of Cloyne, now in the Public Record Office, Dublin.) Latin transcribed by Dr Caulfield; English version by Rev. Canon O'Riordan PP; annotated by James Coleman. NLI Ir 94145 c 1.

Cole, Rev. J.H., *Church and Parish Records of the United Dioceses of Cork, Cloyne and Ross*, Cork: Guy & Co., 1903. Supplements the clerical and parochial records of Cork, Cloyne and Ross by W.M. Brady. NLI Ir 274145 c 1, 347 p.

Connolly, Sean, *The Bandon River from source to sea*, 1993. NLI Ir 94145 p 6(5), 100 p.

Coombes, James, *A history of Timoleague and Barryroe*, Timoleague: Muintir na Tíre (Friary Preservation Committee), 1969. NLI Ir 941 p 134(3), 89 p.

Cork Archives Institute, *The Poor Law records of County Cork*, Cork: Archives Institute, 1995. A list of the records of County Cork Poor Law Unions transferred from St Finbar's Hospital, Cork, to the Cork Archives Institute. NLI Ir 94145 c 30, 80 p.

Courtney, Sean, *Memories of Kilcorney and Rathcoole*, Mallow: Kilcorney-Rathcoole Historical Society, 1998. NLI Ir 94145 c 37, 152 p.

Cox, Richard, *Description of the County and City of Cork, between the years 1680 and 1690*, Dublin: 1903. Edited, with notes, by T.A. Lunham. NLI Ir 94145 c 6, 23 p.

Cronin, Maura, *Country, class or craft?: the politicisation of the skilled artisan in nineteenth-century Cork*, Cork: Cork University Press, 1994. NLI Ir 94145 c 27, 294 p.

Cusack, Mary F., *A History of the City and County of Cork*, Dublin: McGlashan & Gill, 1875. NLI Ir 94145 c 8, 586 p.

d'Alton, Ian, *Protestant society and politics in Cork, 1812–44*, Cork: Cork University Press, 1980. NLI Ir 94145 d 4, 264 p.

Daly, Eugene, *Heir Island / Inis Uí Drisceoil: its history and people*, Leap: Heron's Way Press, 2004. NLI, 324 p.

—— *Leap and Glandore: fact and folklore*, Leap: Heron's Way Press, 2005. NLI, 264 p.

Darling, John, *St Multose Church, Kinsale*, Cork: 1895.

Dennehy, Ven. Archdeacon, *History of Queenstown*, Cork: 1923.

Denny, H.L.L, *The family of Limrick, of Schull, Co. Cork*, 1907. NLI GO 413, 8 p.

Dickson, David, *Old world colony: Cork and South Munster, 1630–1830*, Cork: Cork University Press, 2005. NLI, 726 p.

Donnelly, James S., Jr, *The land and the people of nineteenth-century Cork: the rural economy and the land question*, London and Boston: Routledge & Kegan Paul, 1975. NLI Ir 333 d 14, 440 p.

Duhallow Heritage Project, *Newmarket Court (1725–1994)*, Newmarket: Duhallow Heritage Project, 1994. NLI Ir 720 n 10, 88 p.

Ellis, Éilís, *Emigrants from Ireland, 1847–52*, Baltimore, Md.: GPC, 1977. NLI Ir 325 e 5.

Falvey, Jeremiah, *The chronicles of Midleton, 1700–1900*, Cloyne: Sira Publications, 1998. NLI Ir 94145 f 4, 356 p.

Farrell, Noel, *Youghal family roots: exploring family origins in Youghal*, Longford: Noel Farrell, 2001. NLI 1B 3029, 48 p.

—— *Kinsale family roots: exploring family origins in Kinsale*, Longford: Noel Farrell, 2001. NLI 3B 563, 48 p.

FÁS Community Training, *Buttevant, Co. Cork: a short history*, Buttevant: Buttevant Community Council, 1991. NLI Ir 941 p 134(2), 48.

Fisher, William A., *Appeal for improvements at 'The church of the poor near Crookhaven'*, 1851. Includes list of subscribers. NLI JP 4271.

Fitzgerald, Séamus, *Mackerel and the making of Baltimore, County Cork, 1879–1913* (Maynooth Studies in Irish Local History, No. 22), Dublin and Portland, Oreg.: Irish Academic Press, 1999. NLI Ir 94145 f 5, 64 p.

Foley, Con, *A history of Douglas*, Douglas: Con Foley, 1991. NLI Ir 94145 f 2, 185 p.

Gaughan, Rev. J.A., *Doneraile*, Dublin: Kamac Publications, 1970. NLI Ir 94145 g 1, 171 p.

Gibson, C.B., *The history of the county and city of Cork*, London: 1861. NLI J 94145.

Grove-White, Col. James, *History of Kilbryne, Doneraile, Cork*, Cork.

—— *Historical and Topographical Notes etc. on Buttevant, Castletownroche, Doneraile, Mallow, and places in their vicinity*, Cork: Guy & Co., 1905–1916. NLI Ir 94145 w 1.

Hajba, Anna-Maria, *Historical, genealogical, architectural notes on some houses of Cork, Vol. 1: North Cork*, Whitegate, Co. Clare: Ballinakella Press, 2002. NLI 2B 1080, 414 p.

Harrington, Gerard (Gerdie), *Beara: history and stories from the peninsula*, Cork: Beara Historical Society, 2005. NLI, 305 p.

Harrison, Richard S., *Béara and Bantry Bay: history of Rossmacowen*, Bantry: Rossmacowen Historical Society, 1990. NLI Ir 94145.h.5, 236 p.

—— *Cork City Quakers, 1655–1939: a brief history*, the author, 1991. NLI Ir 289.h.3, 91 p.

—— *Bantry in olden days*, Bantry: the author, 1992. NLI Ir 94145 p 7(4), 62 p.

—— *Four hundred years of Drimoleague*, Drimoleague: Sruth Fán, 1999. NLI Ir 94145 h 10, 96 p.

Hawke, Siobhán, *A social and economic history of Bere Island, 1900–20*, Castletownbere: The Shell, 2004. NLI 4A 2152, 81 p.

Hayman, S., *The handbook for Youghal*, Youghal: J.W. Lindsay, 1852. 'Containing an account of St Mary's Collegiate Church (including memorials of the Boyles), the College, Sir Walter Raleigh's house, the Franciscan and Dominican Friaries, the Templar's house at Rhincrew, and the Monastery of St John's; with the historical annals of the town.' NLI Dix Youghal 1852, 96 p.

Hayman, Samuel, *The Handbook for Youghal*, Youghal: John Lindsay, 1858. NLI Dix Youghal 1858, 76 p.

Healy, Dan, *Cork national school registers*, Cork: Cork Genealogical Society, 2000. NLI 1B 3144, 62 p.

Henchion, Richard, *East to Mahon: the story of Blackrock, Ballintemple, Ballinlough, Ballinure and Mahon and how they were shaped . . .* Cork: Dahadore Publications, 2005. NLI, 214 p.

—— *Donoughmore and All Around: A Record of the Families Commemorated in the Old and New Cemeteries of Donoughmore Cross and Stuake, Co. Cork*, Donoughmore: Donoughmore Historical Society, 2010. NLI, 316 p.

—— *The Graveyard Inscriptions of St. John the Baptist Cemetery, Midleton. Co. Cork*, Cloyne: Cloyne Literary and Historical Society, 2009. NLI, 194 p.

—— *The gravestone inscriptions of the Cathedral cemetery of Cloyne, Co. Cork*, Cloyne: Cloyne Literary and Historical Society, 1999. 194 p.

Hickey, Nora M., *St. Peter's, Ballymodan, Bandon, Co. Cork: Gravestone Inscriptions*, Bandon: Droichead na Bandan Community Co-operative Society, 1986. NLI Ir 9295 p 3(3), 45 p.

—— *Kilbrogan, Roman Catholic, Bandon, Co. Cork: Gravestone Inscriptions*, Bandon: Droichead na Bandan Community Co-operative Society, 1985. NLI Ir 9295 p 3(4), 44 p.

Holland, Rev. W., *History of West Cork and the Diocese of Ross*, Skibbereen: Southern Star, 1949. NLI Ir 94145 h 3, 427 p.

Hore, H.F., *The Social State of the Southern and Eastern Counties of Ireland in the Sixteenth Century*, Dublin: 1870. NLI Ir 794105 r 2. (See Carlow.)

Hurley, Frank, *St. Joseph's Convent of Mercy, Kinsale: a celebration of 150 years, 1844–1944*, Kinsale: St Joseph's Convent of Mercy, 1994. NLI Ir 270 s 20, 156 p.

Hurley, Mícheál, *Home from the sea: the story of Courtmacsherry lifeboat, 1825–1995*, Courtmacsharry: Mícheál Hurley, 1995. NLI Ir 363 h 10, 133 p.

Hyde, Fr John, SJ, *Ballycotton long 'go by*, Ballycotton: Margaret Hyde, 1990. NLI Ir 941 p 110(3), 63 p.

IGRS, *Tombstone inscriptions, Vol. 1*, Dublin: IGRS Tombstone Committee, 2001. NLI, 850 p.

Jefferies, Henry A., *Cork: historical perspectives*, Dublin and Portland, Oreg.: Four Courts Press, 2004. NLI, 261 p.

Jephson, M.D., *An Anglo-Irish Miscellany: some records of the Jephsons of Mallow*, Dublin: Allen Figgis, 1964. NLI Ir 9292 j 2, 434 p.

Jordan, Kieran, *Kilworth and Moore Park British Army camps from 1896 to 1922*, Fermoy: Strawhall Press, 2004. Kilworth Ranges Historical Project. NLI 5A 741, 126 p.

Keane, Leonard M., Jr, *Ancestors and descendants of John Keane and Elizabeth Leader of Keale, Milistreet, County Cork, Ireland, and related female lines*, Wakefield, Mass.: L.M. Keane, c.1984. LC CS71.K225 1984.

Kelleher, B.J., *Kelleher family, of Knockraheen, Carriganimma, Macroom, Co. Cork, Ireland and Australia and USA*, Chadstone, Vic.: Kelleher, 1970. NLI GO 443, 42 leaves.

Kelleher, George D., *The gunpowder mill at Ballincollig: an extract from Gunpowder to guided missiles . . .* Inniscarra, Co. Cork: John F. Kelleher, 1993. NLI Ir 3380 p 42(5), 89 p.

Killavullen Community Council, *The History of Killavullen*, Killavullen: Killavullen Community Council, 1986. NLI 2A 3213, 16 p.

King, Joseph A., *Ireland to North America: emigrants from West Cork*, Lafayette, Calif.: K&K Publications, 1994. Also Toronto: P.D. Meany. Schull to Miramichi River Region, NB. NLI Ir 942 k 7, 124 p.

Kingston, W.J., *The story of West Carbery*, Waterford: Friendly Press, 1985. NLI Ir 94145 k 2, 133 p.

Lane, Fintan, *In search of Thomas Sheahan: radical politics in Cork, 1824–36* (Maynooth Studies in Irish Local History, No. 37), Dublin and Portland, Oreg.: Irish Academic Press, 2001. NLI 2A 497, 69 p.

Lankford, Máirín, *The cloth-capped men: the story of a West Cork slate quarry, 1841–1962*, Cork: Celum Publishing, 2005. Slate quarry at Curraghalicky, Drinagh, Cork. NLI, 101 p.

Lannin, Joseph, *The Wilcox family of Ardravinna, Goleen, Co. Cork*, Dublin: Joseph Lannin, 1995. NLI Ir 9292 w, 54 p.

—— *The Lannin family of Gubbeen, Schull, Co. Cork*, Dublin: the author, 1994. NLI Ir 941 p 140(5), 181 p.

Leland, Mary, *That endless adventure: a history of the Cork Harbour Commissioners*, Cork: Port of Cork Co., 2001. NLI 2A 675, 272 p.

Lindsay, John W., *An account of the present state of Youghal Church*, Youghal: John W. Lindsay, 1850. NLI Ir 94145 d 1, 52 p.

Lomasney, Michael, *Ballynoe Cemetery: a guide and brief history*, Ballynoe, Co. Cork: Ballynoe Cemetery Committee, 1993. Edited by John Gough Nichols. NLI Ir 9295 p 3(1).

Mac Carthaigh, David, *The Gurranabraher story: a history of the place and its people*, Cork: 1997. NLI 3A 3243, 69 p.

MacCarthy, John George, *The history of Cork*, Cork: Miros Press, 1974. Reprint of 3rd ed., Cork: F. Guy, 1870. NLI Ir 94145 m 5, 47 p.

McCarthy, M., *Kinsale inscriptions (Church of Ireland)*, Kinsale: the author.

McRonald, Malcolm, *The Irish boats, vol. 2: Liverpool to Cork and Waterford*, Stroud, Glos.: Tempus, 2006. NLI, 256 p.

Mac Suibhne, Máire, *Famine in Muskerry: an Drochshaol: an outline of conditions in the sixteen parishes of Macroom Poor Law Union, Co. Cork, during the Great Famine, 1845–'51*, Macroom: Cúilín Gréine Press, 1997. NLI Ir 94145 m 10, 160 p.

MacSwiney, Unpublished manuscripts, RIA. Historical notes and will abstracts, mainly from Cos. Cork and Kerry, RIA.

Masterson, Josephine, *County Cork, Ireland: a collection of 1841/1851 census records*, Indianapolis, Ind.: Masterson. Also FamilyTreeMaker CD ROM 7275. 1993. NLI Ir 94145 m 11.

Mercer, J. Douglas, *Record of the North Cork Regiment of Militia, with sketches extracted from history of the times in which its services were required, from 1793 to 1880*, Dublin: 1886, 128 p. NLI Ir 355942 m 4.

Mooney, Canice, *The friars of Broad Lane: the story of a Franciscan friary in Cork, 1229–1977*, Cork: Tower Books, 1977. Revised and extended by Bartholomew Egan. NLI Ir 27414 m 4, 101 p.

Murphy, Donal, *Tuath na Dromann: a history of Cill na Martra*, Dublin: Original Writing, 2008. NLI, 173 p.

Murphy, Ina, *Speaking of Lyre, 1844–1994*, Lyre: Lyre Community Association, 1994. NLI Ir 372 m 136, 175 p.

Murphy, John A., *The College: a history of Queen's/University College, Cork, 1845–1995*, Cork: Cork University Press, 1996. NLI Ir 37841 m 24, 469 p.

Murphy, Pat, *The magic of west Cork*, Dublin: Mercier Press, 1978. Crookhaven, social life and customs. BL X.708/21438, 94p.

Myers, Declan, *My own place: Ballyphelane*, Ballyphelane: the author, 1995. NLI Ir 94145 m 9, 202p.

O'Brien, Brigid, *From Ilen to Roaring Water Bay: reminiscences from the Parish of Aughadown*, Aughadown Guild of the ICA, 2000. Editors Brigid O'Brien and Mary Whooley. NLI 2A 2753, 160 p.

O'Brien, Niall, *Blackwater and Bride: navigation and trade, 7,000 BC to 2007*, Ballyduff Upper: Niall O'Brien Publishing, 2008. NLI, 562 p.

O'Brien, Susan, *A history of Bessborough House and the Pike family*, Cork. With Karan Mullan. 52 p.

Ó Coindealbháin, Seán, *The story of Iveleary: the history, antiquities and legends of Uibh-Laoghaire*, Dundalk: Dundalgan Press, 1921. NLI 4A 922, 54 p.

O'Connell, Mary, *Tullylease: Pride of Place: Our History and Heritage*, Tullylease: Tullylease Community Council. NLI, 40 p.

O'Connor, W.R., *The New Cork Guide . . . names and dwelling of . . . physicians, lawyers, merchants, bankers, teachers, shopkeepers, architects, mechanics, publicans, &c.* (satire in verse), Cork: 1803. NLI Dix Cork [1803?] [P 4.], 10 p.

O'Donoghue, Brendan, *In search of fame and fortune: the Leahy family of engineers, 1780–1888*, Dublin: Geography Publications, 2006. NLI, 338 p.

O'Donoghue, Bruno, *Parish histories and place names of West Cork*, Tralee: Kerryman, 1986. Cork County Library 941.95, 345 p.

O'Donovan, Derry, *Ballinspittle and De Courcy country: historical landscapes*, Bray, Co. Wicklow: Wordwell, 2003. NLI 3B 1751, 276 p.

O'Dwyer, Riobárd, *Who Were my Ancestors?: Family Trees of Eyeries Parish*, Astoria, Ill.: K.K. Stevens Publishing Co., 1976. NLI.

—— *Who Were my Ancestors? Family Trees of Allihies Parish*, Astoria, Ill.: K.K. Stevens Publishing Co., 1988. NLI Ir 9292 o 60, 307 p.

—— *Who Were my Ancestors? Family Trees of Castletownbere and Bere Island Parishes*, Astoria, Ill.: K.K. Stevens Publishing Co., 1989. NLI Ir 9292 o 61 and 62, 292 p.

O'Flanagan, Patrick, *Irish Historic Towns Atlas, 3: Bandon*, Dublin: RIA, 1988. NLI ILB 941 p 13 (1).

O'Flanagan and Buttimer, *Cork History and Society*, Dublin: Geography Publication, 1994. NLI Ir 94145 c 25, 1,000 p.

O'Keeffe, Alison, *St John the Baptist National School, Midleton: a history*, Midleton: St John the Baptist National School, 2008. NLI.

O Mahony, Colman, *In the shadows: life in Cork, 1750–1930*, Ballincollig: Tower Books, 1997. NLI Ir94145 o 19, 396 p.

—— *Cork's Poor Law palace: workhouse life, 1838–90*, Cork: Rosmathún Press, 2005. NLI, 338 p.

O'Mahony, Frank, *Kilcrohane: the holy ground, Book 1: O'Mahony: the diary of Frank. —Book 2: Frank O'Mahony*, Dromkeal: Frank O'Mahony, 1990. NLI Ir 9292 o 57, 148 p.

O'Mahony, Jeremiah, *West Cork and its story*, Tralee: Kerryman, 1961. NLI 1A 3496, 288 p.

—— *West Cork parish histories and place-names*, Tralee: Kerryman, 1959. NLI Ir 94145 o 12, Ir 94145 o 12.

O'Mahony, Michelle, *The famine in Cork city: Famine life at Cork Union Workhouse*, Cork: Mercier Press, 2005. NLI.

Ó Murchadha, D., 'Diary of Gen. Richard O'Donovan, 1819–23', *JCHAS*, 1986. (Lands in West Cork.)

—— *Family Names of Co. Cork*, Dublin: Glendale Press, 1985. NLI Ir 9291 o 11.

O'Rahilly, Ronan, *A history of the Cork Medical School, 1849–1949*, Cork: Cork University Press, 1949. NLI Ir 6109 o 1, 69 p.

Ó Ríordáin, John J., *Where Araglen so gently flows*, Tralee: Kerryman, 1989. NLI Ir 94145 o 16, 304 p.

O'Sullivan, Florence, *The History of Kinsale*, Dublin: 1916.

O'Sullivan, John L., *By Carraigdonn and Owenabue*, Ballinhassig: Ballyheeda Press, 1990. NLI Ir 94145.0.15, 442 p.

—— *The Cork City Gaol*, Ballinhassig, Co. Cork: Ballyheada Press, 1996. NLI Ir 366 o, 169 p.

O'Sullivan, Ted, *Bere Island: a short history*, Cork: Inisgragy Books, 1992. NLI Ir 94145 p 8(1), 128 p.

Pettit, S.F., *This city of Cork, 1700–1900*, Cork: Studio Publications, 1977. NLI Ir 94145 p 1, 304 p.

Power, Bill, *From the Danes to Dairygold: a history of Mitchelstown*, Mitchelstown: Mount Cashell Books, 1996. NLI Ir 94145 p 10, 150 p.

—— *White knights, dark earls: the rise and fall of an Anglo-Irish dynasty*, Cork: Collins Press, 2000. King family, Earls of Kingston. NLI 2A 439, 303 p.

—— *Mitchelstown through seven centuries: being a concise history of Mitchelstown, County Cork*, Fermoy: Éigse Books, c.1987. NLI Ir 94145 p 4, 138 p.

—— *Another side of Mitchelstown: a street and townland by townland history of people, events and places associated with one of Ireland's best planned historic towns*, Mitchelstown: PsyOps Books, 2008. NLI, 269 p.

Power, Very Rev. P., *Waterford and Lismore: A Compendious History of the Dioceses*, Dublin: Cork University Press, 1937. NLI Ir 274141 p 1, 402 p.

Pratt, John, *Pratt Family Records: an account of the Pratts of Youghal and Castlemartyr and their Descendants*, Millom, Cumb.: P.C. Dickinson & Sons, 1931. NLI Ir 9292 p 15, 82 p.

—— *The Family of Pratt of Gawsworth, Carrigrohane, Co. Cork*, Millom, Cumb.: 1925. NLI Ir 9292 p 3.

Prentice, Sydney, *Bear and forbear: a genealogical study of the Prentice, Barnard and related families in Great Britain, Ireland and Australia*, Taringa, Qld.: S.A & M. Prentice, 1984. Bandon. NLI Ir 9292 p 32, 285 p.

Quane, Michael, *Midleton School, Co. Cork*, Dublin: Royal Society of Antiquaries, 1952. NLI 1B 2041, 27 p.

Quinlan, P., *Old Mitchelstown and the Kingston family*, Kilworth: the author, 1980. NLI Ir 941 p 66, 21 p.

Reedy, Rev. Donal A., *The diocese of Kerry (formerly Ardfert)*, Killarney: Catholic

Truth Society, 1937. NLI A 3A 2620, 46 p.

Robinson, A.C., *St. Fin Barre's Cathedral, Cork: historical and descriptive*, Cork: Guy & Co., 1897. Cork City Library, 87 p.

Roche, Christy, *The Ford of the apples: a history of Ballyhooly*, Fermoy: Éigse, 1988. NLI Ir 91414 r 5.

Ryan, Eileen, *Mohera National School: a history, 1847–1996*, 1996. NLI Ir94145 r 3, 157 p.

Rynne, Colin, *At the sign of the cow: the Cork Butter Market, 1770–1924*, Cork: Collins Press, 1998. NLI 4B 1336, 118 p.

St James's, Durrus, *St. James', Durrus: a parish history: published for the bi-centenary of the Church, 1992*, Cloghroe, Co. Cork: Forum Publications, 1992. NLI 1A 1224, 80 p.

St Leger, Alicia, *Silver, sails and silk: Huguenots in Cork, 1685–1850*, Cork: Cork Civic Trust, 1991. NLI Ir 283 s 2, 71 p.

Smith, Charles, *The ancient and present state of the county and city of Cork*, Dublin: 1750. Reprinted Cork: Guy & Co., 1893–94. NLI Ir 94145 s 1.

Sullivan, T.D., *Bantry, Berehaven and the O'Sullivan sept* and *The O'Dalys Muintiravara: the story of a bardic family, by D.D.*, Cork: Tower Books of Cork, 1978. *The O'Dalys Muintiravara*, by Dominick Daly, was originally published 1821. NLI Ir 94145 s 4, 119 p.

Swanzy, Rev. H.B., *The family of Nixon of Nixon Hall, Co. Fermanagh, and Nixon Lodge, Co. Cavan: with a short account of the families of Erskine of Cavan and Allin of Youghal, by a descendant*, Dublin: Thom, 1899. NLI GO 513, 45 p.

Tangney, Denis, *St. Anna's Church, Millstreet: a history*, Millstreet: Millstreet Museum Society, 1995. NLI 1A 1222, 56 p.

Thompson, Francis, *Families of the Catholic Parish of Carrigaline-Crosshaven, 1826–80*, 1986. LDS film 1441035.

Troy, Bartholemew, *Ballycotton wrecks and rescues, 1800–55*. NLI 3A 1457, 43 p.

—— *The cemetery, Church of Our Lady of the Most Holy Rosary, Midleton, Co. Cork: gravestone inscriptions*, Midleton: Troy, 1994. NLI Ir 9295 t 1 224 p.

Tucker, Sean, *The origin and development of the parish of Millstreet, Aubane*, Millstreet: Aubane Historical Society, 2008. NLI, 51 p. Online: Aubane.

Tuckey, Francis, *The County and City of Cork Remembered*, Cork: O. Savage & Son, 1837. NLI Dix Cork 1837, 352 p.

Twomey, Francis, *Beara: the unexplored peninsula*, Dublin: Woodpark Publications, 2007. NLI, 120 p.

Veale, T., *Richard Lucas, 1788: directory extract for south east of Ireland*, Dublin: Veale, 1995. NLI Ir 9414 v.

W., T.J., *The parish of Blackrock: a retrospect*, Cork: St Michael's Parish, 1962. NLI 1A 347, 27 p.

Wain, H., *Eochoill: the history of Youghal*, Cork: Cork Historical Guides Committee, 1965. NLI Ir 94145 w 8, 72 p.

Walshe, Denis, *Bishops, priests and religious of Cloyne Parish, County Cork*, Cloyne: 1994. NLI 1A 1223.

West, Trevor, *Midleton College, 1696–1996: a tercentenary history*, Midleton: Midleton College, 1996. NLI Ir 379 w 4, 57 p.

—— *Malting the barley: John H. Bennett, the man and his firm: 200 years of malting barley in Ballinacurra*, Ballinacurra: Charleston House, 2006. NLI, 171 p.

West, W., *Directory and picture of Cork*, 1810. NLI J 914145.

Williams, R. Allan, *The Berehaven Copper Mines, Allihies, Co. Cork*, Sheffield: Northern Mine Research Society, 1991. Puxley family. NLI Ir 621 w 5, 228 p.

Windele, J., *Cork: historical and descriptive notices . . . to the middle of the 19th century*, Cork: 1910. NLI Ir 94145 w 3.

Local journals

Bandon Historical Journal. NLI Ir 794105 c 1.

Bantry Historical and Archaeological Society Journal. NLI Ir 94145 b 27.

Canovee: An Historical Society Magazine. 1986–. NLI Ir 914145 c 35.

Donoughmore Remembers: Journal of Times Past. Vol. 1 (2004). NLI 1 F 233.

Harbour Lights: Journal of the Great Island Historical Society. 1988–. NLI Ir 94145 h 6.

Journal of the Ballincollig Community School Local History Society. NLI Ir 94145 b 15.

Journal of the Cork Genealogical Society. NLI. <www.corkgenealogicalsociety.com>.

Journal of the Cork Historical and Archaeological Society. NLI Ir 794105 c 1. <www.ucc.ie/chas>.

Kinsale Historical Journal. Annual from 1986. NLI Ir 95145 k 5.

Mallow Field Club Journal. NLI r 94145 m 6. <www.rootsweb.ancestry.com/~irlmahs>.

Mizen Journal. 1995–. NLI Ir 794105 m 1.

Ogham Magazine: Ballindangan and District Review. One issue. NLI Ir 94145 o 22.

Old Blarney: Journal of the Blarney and District Historical Society. 1989–. NLI 1H 359.

Seanchas Chairbre. NLI Ir 94145 s 6.

Seanchas Dúthalla: Duhallow Magazine. NLI Ir 94145 s 3.

Directories

1787   Richard Lucas, *Cork Directory.* NLI. *Journal of the Cork Hist. and Arch. Soc.*, 1967. Online: Cork City Library ('Places').

1788   Richard Lucas, *General Directory of the Kingdom of Ireland.* NLI Pos. 3729. Reprinted in Veale, *Lucas, 1G*, 1965, 1966, 1967, 1968.

1797   John Nixon, *Cork Almanack.* NLI Pos. 3985.

1809   Holden's *Annual London and country directory of the United Kingdoms and Wales, in three volumes, for . . . 1811.* Facsimile reprint, Norwich: M. Winton, 1996. NLI G 942 h 23; LDS film 258722 item 2.

1810   William West, *Directory of Cork.* NLI Pos. 3985. Online: Cork City Library ('Places').

1812   John Connor, *Cork Directory.* Also 1817, 1826, 1828. NLI Pos. 3985.

1820   J. Pigot, *Commercial Directory of Ireland.* PRONI. NLI Ir 9141 p 107; LDS film 962702 item 1.

1824   J. Pigot & Co., *City of Dublin and Hibernian Provincial Directory.* NLI; LDS film 451787.

1844–5   Aldwell's *County and City of Cork P.O. General Directory.* Online: Cork City Library ('Places').

1846   Slater's *National Commercial Directory of Ireland.* PRONI. NLI LO; LDS film 1696703 item 3. Online: Hayes.

1856   Slater, *Royal National Commercial Directory of Ireland.* NLI. LDS film 1472360 item 1.

1863   Laing's *Cork Mercantile Directory.* Online: Cork City Library ('Places').

1867   Henry and Coughlan's *General Directory of Cork and Munster.* Online: FindMyPast.

1870   Slater, *Directory of Ireland.* NLI.

1871   Fulton's *City of Cork Directory, incorporating the Commercial Directory of Queenstown.* Online: Cork City Library ('Places').

1875   Francis Guy, *City and County Cork Almanack and Directory.* NLI Ir 91414 g 9. Online: Cork City Library ('Places').

1881   Slater, *Royal National Commercial Directory of Ireland.* NLI. Online: FindMyPast.

1884   Guy's *City and County Cork Almanac and Directory.* Online: Cork City Library ('Places').

1886   Francis Guy, *Postal Directory of Munster.* NLI Ir 91414 g 8; LDS film 1559399 item 8.

1889   Francis Guy, *City and County Cork Almanack and Directory.* Annually from this year. 1891, 1907, 1913, 1921, 1945. Online: Cork City Library ('Places').

1894   Slater, *Royal Commercial Directory of Ireland.* NLI.

Gravestone inscriptions

Abbeystrowry: C of I, IGRS, Vol. 1.
—— Skibbereen, St Patrick's RC church interior, IGRS, Vol. 1.
Aghadown: Glebe, C of I, IGRS, Vol. 1.
Aghinagh: Caum, *JCHAS*, No. 216, 1967. Also O'K., Vol. 8.
—— Ballaghboy, Cork County Library.
Ballyclogh: Village of Ballyclogh, Main St, O'K., Vol. 8.
Ballycurrany: Ballycurrany West, *JCHAS*, No. 237, 1978.
—— Ballydesmond, O'K., Vol. 6.
—— Ballyhoolahan East, O'K., Vol. 6.
Ballymartle: Mill-land, C of I, *JCHAS*, 235, 1989.
Ballymodan: Clogheenavodig (Kilbeg?), WCHC.
Ballymodan: Knockanreagh, RC?, WCHC.
Ballymodan: Knockaveale, Hickey, *St Peter's.*
—— Ballynamona, O'K., Vol. 11.
Ballynoe: *Ballynoe Cemetery.*
Ballyvourney: Glebe, C of I, O'K., Vol. 6.

Brinny: C of I, wchc.

Buttevant: Templemary, o'k., Vol. 11.

Caheragh: Caheragh, rc, igrs, Vol. 1.

—— Cappyaughna, rc, igrs, Vol. 1.

Carrigrohane: Ballincollig British Military Graveyard: <*www.interment.net*>.

Carrigrohanebeg: *jchas*, No. 218, 1968.

—— Castle-land (Buttevant?), C of I, o'k., Vol. 11.

Castlemagner: o'k., Vol. 6.

Churchtown: Village of Churchtown, George's St, o'k., Vol. 11.

Clondrohid: o'k., Vol. 6.

—— Clonfert, o'k., Vol. 6.

Clonfert: Newmarket, Main St, C of I, o'k., Vol. 6.

Clonmeen: Clonmeen North, C of I, o'k., Vol. 7.

Clonmult: Ballyeightragh, *jchas*, No. 223/4/5, 1976/7.

—— Cloonaghlin West (Killaconenagh?), Cork County Library.

Cloyne: Church St, C of I, Henchion *Cloyne*.

Cullen: Cullen, o'k., Vol. 6.

Dangandonovan: Kilcounty, *jchas*, No. 229, 1974.

Desertmore: Kilcrea, *jchas*, No. 219, 1969.

Doneraile: Oldcourt (Donraile), o'k., Vol. 11.

Donaghmore (Muskerry): Coolicka, Henchion, *Donoughmore*.

—— Lackabane, Henchion, *Donoughmore*.

Drishane: Millstreet, o'k., Vol. 6.

—— Dromtariff, o'k., Vol. 6.

Dromtarriff: Garraveasoge or Dromagh, o'k., Vol. 8.

Dunderrow: Horsehill More North, *jchas*, No. 224, 1971.

Fermoy: Carrignagroghera, *is*, Nos. 51/3, 1977/9 (military only).

—— Inchigeelagh interior, o'k., Vol. 6.

—— Inchigeelagh New, o'k., Vol. 6.

Inchigeelagh: Glebe, C of I, o'k., Vol. 6.

Kilbrin: Castlecor Demesne (Kilbrin?), o'k., Vol. 8.

Kilbrogan: Kilbrogan, rc, C of I, Hickey, *Kilbrogan*.

Kilcaskan: Adrigole, C of I, igrs, Vol. 1. Also Cork County Library.

Kilcatherine: Gortgarriff igrs, Vol. 1.

Kilcoe: igrs, Vol. 1.

Kilcorney: o'k., Vol. 7.

—— Kilcrea Friary, *jchas*, No. 226, 1972.

Kilgrogan: o'k., Vol. 11.

Killaconenagh: Clanlaurence, Cork County Library.

Ballynakilla, Castletown Berehaven, igrs, Vol. 1.

Curradonohoe, Bere Island, igrs, Vol. 1.

Cloonaghlin West (Killaconenagh?), igrs, Vol. 1.

Killeagh: Town of Killeagh, Main St, C of I, *jchas*, No. 226, 1972.

Kilmeen: Glebe (Boherbue?), C of I, o'k., Vol. 6.

Kilmocomoge: Bantry (St Finbarr's), IGRS, Vol. 1.

Kilmonoge: Coolnagaug (Kilmonoge?), JCHAS, 251, 1987.

Kilnaglory: Kilnaglory, JCHAS, No. 220, 1969.

Kilnamanagh: Cloan (Kilnamanagh?), Cork County Library, IGRS, Vol. 1.

Kilnamartry: Glebe, O'K., Vol. 6.

Kinsale: Kinsale, Church St, C of I, McCarthy, *Kinsale inscriptions.*

—— Kishkeam, O'K., Vol. 6.

Liscarroll: Village of Liscarroll, Main St, O'K., Vol. 11.

Lisgoold: Lisgoold East, C of I, JCHAS, No. 237, 1978.

Macloneigh: O'K., Vol. 8.

Macroom: Castle St, C of I, O'K., Vol. 8.

Magourney: Coachford, O'K., Vol. 11.

—— Mallow, Main St, C of I, O'K.

Mallow: Mallow, Main St, RC, O'K., Vol. 8.

Middleton: Middleton, RC, Troy, *The cemetery.*

—— Middleton Church Lane, C of I. Henchion *Midleton.*

Mourneabbey: Kilquane (Mourneabbey?), O'K., Vol. 11.

—— Nohaval Lower, O'K., Vol. 8.

Nohavaldaly: Knocknagree, O'K., Vol. 6.

Rathgoggan: Charleville, Main St, C of I, O'K., Vol. 11.

—— Rossmackowen, Cork County Library.

Shandrum: Dromina, O'K., Vol. 11.

St Finbar's: Curraghconway, C of I, *St Finbarr's Cathedral,* 1897.

St Peter's: Duncan St, JCHAS, 252, 1988.

Timoleague: Castle Lower, C of I, GO.

Tisaxon: Tisaxon Beg, JCHAS, No. 222, 1970.

Titeskin: JCHAS, No. 221, 1970.

Tullylease: Tulllylease, O'K., Vol. 8.

Youghal: Nelson Place, Hayman, *The Handbook for Youghal.*

Estate records

[**Barrymore barony**]. 'Tenant Farmers on the Barrymore Estate', JCHAS, Vol. 51, pp. 31–40.

[**No landlord given**]. Rental, c.1835–7. Major tenants only. Covering townlands in the civil parishes of Castlelyons, Gortroe, Knockmourne and Rathcormack. NLI Ms. 13018.

[**No landlord given**]. Rentals, 1821, covering all tenants. Townlands in the civil parish of Kilmocomoge. NLI Ms. 3273.

Arden, Lord. Rentals, 1824–30. All tenants. Covering townlands in the civil parishes of Bregoge, Buttevant, Castlemagner, Clonfert, Dromtarriff and Dungourney. NLI Ms. 8652.

Bantry, Earl of. Rentals, 1829. All tenants. Covering townlands in the civil parishes of Kilcaskan, Kilcatherine and Killaconenagh. NLI Ms. 3273.

Bennett. Rental, 1770, mainly Cork city and surrounding areas. NLI Pos. 288.

Benn-Walsh, Sir John. J.S. Donnelly, 'The journals of Sir John Benn-Walsh relating to the management of his Irish estates (1823–64)', *JCHAS*, Vol. 81, 1975.

Bishop of Cork. Rentals, 1807–31. Major tenants only. Townlands in the civil parishes of Aghadown, Ardfield, Fanlobbus, Kilbrogan, Kilmocomoge, Kilsillagh, Ross, St Finbarr's and Skull. NA M6087.

Boyle/Cavendish. The Lismore Papers. Rentals, valuations, lease books and account books for the estates of the Earls of Cork and the Dukes of Devonshire, 1570–1870. NLI Mss. 6136–898. Generally covering only major tenants. A detailed listing is given in NLI Special List 15. Covering townlands in the civil parishes of Ahern, Ardagh, Ballymodan, Ballynoe, Brinny, Clonmult, Clonpriest, Ightermurragh, Kilbrogan, Killeagh, Killowen, Kinneigh, Knockmourne, Lismore, Mogeely, Murragh, St Finbarr's and Youghal. See also 'Lismore Castle Estate Emigration Database'. Online: Waterford Archives.

Courtenay, Viscount. Rental, 1762. Townlands in the parish of Moviddy. LCA IE LA P6. Online: Limerick Archives.

Cox, Richard. Rentals, 1839. Major tenants only. Townlands in the civil parishes of Aghinagh, Clondrohid, Desertserges, Fanlobbus, Kilcaskan, KIlmeen, Kilmichael, Kilnamartery and Macloneigh. NA Gordon Presentation 214.

Doneraile, Lord. Rent roll, 1777, 'of the right honble Lord Donneralle's Estate at Ballyhooly'. NLI Ms. 10933.

Earbery estates. Rentals, 1788–1815. NLI Ms. 7403. Principally major tenants. NLI Ms. 5257: Full tenants list, 1800. Townlands in the civil parishes of Aghabulloge, Clondrohid, Donoghmore and Kilmurry.

Edgeworth, Richard. Rental, accounts, valuations: 1760–68. All tenants. Covering townlands in the civil parish of Clontead. NAI M.1503.

Eyre, Robert Hodges. Rentals of the Bere Island estate, 1833 and 1835. NLI Mss. 3273, 3274. All tenants. Civil parish of Killaconenagh.

Graham, James. Rentals, c.1763. NAI M2329. Major tenants only. Covering townlands in the civil parish of Killathy.

Lombard, Rev. Edmund. Rentals, 1795. NLI Ms. 2985. Major tenants only. Covering townlands in the civil parishes of Kilmacdonagh and Kilshannig.

Neville, Richard. Rentals of lands in Cos. Cork, Kildare and Waterford. NLI Ms. 3733. Principally major tenants. Covering townlands in the civil parishes of Aglishdrinagh and Cooliney.

Newenham. Rentals, c.1825. NLI Ms. 4123. All tenants. Covering townlands in the civil parishes of Kilcrumper, Kilworth, Leitrim and Macroney.

Perceval, Lord Egmont. Rentals, 1688–1750. Major tenants only. NLI Pos. 1355 (1688); NLI Pos. 4674 (1701–12, 1713–14); NLI Pos. 4675 (1714–19); NLI Pos. 4676 (1720–24, 1725–7); NLI Pos. 4677 (1728–33); NLI Pos. 4678 (1734–8); NLI Pos. 4679 (1739–41, 1742–6); NLI Pos. 4680 (1747–50). Covering townlands in the civil parishes of Aglishdrinagh, Ballyclogh, Bregoge, Brigown, Britway, Buttevant, Castlemagner, Churchtown, Clonfert, Cullin, Dromtarriff,

Hackmys, Imphrick, Kilbrin, Kilbrogan, Kilbroney, Kilcaskan, Kilgrogan, Kilmichael, Kilroe, Liscarroll, Rathbarry.

Putland, George. NLI Mss 1814–27. Eleven rentals of land in Cos. Cork, Carlow, Kilkenny, Tipperary and Wicklow. Principally major tenants. Covering townlands in the civil parishes of Garrycloyne, Matehy and Templeusque.

Ronayne, Thomas. Rentals, 1755–77. NLI Ms. 1721. Major tenants only. Covering townlands in the civil parishes of Carrigaline, Clonmel, Killanully, Kilquane, Middleton and Templerobin.

Sarsfield. Rentals, 1817–23. NLI Ms. 3638. Major tenants only. Covering townlands in the civil parishes of Kilmoney, Kinsale, St Finbar's and Templerobin.

Shuldam. Estate map, 1801–1803, with some tenants' names given. Covering townlands in the civil parishes of Dreenagh, Fanlobbus, Iveleary and Kilmichael. NLI Ms. 3025.

Standish Barry. Maps (1846) and tenants list (1840?). Covering townlands in the civil parishes of Ballycurrany and Lisgoold. Cork County Library.

DERRY/LONDONDERRY

Census returns and substitutes

1618	Survey of Derry city and county. TCD Ms. 864 (F.I.9).
1620–22	Muster Roll. PRONI T510/2.
1630	Muster Roll of Ulster. Armagh County Library and PRONI D.1759/3C/2. NLI Pos. 206.
1654–6	*Civil Survey*, Vol. 3. NLI I 6551.
1659	Pender's 'Census'. Reprinted GPC, 1997; IMC, 2002. LDS film 924648.
1660	Poll Tax Returns. PRONI MIC/15A/82.
1661	Books of Survey and Distribution. PRONI D.1854/1/23 and T370/C.
1663	Hearth Money Roll. PRONI T307; also NLI Ms. 9584 (indexed in Ms. 9585). Online: McAfee.
1670–71	Armagh diocese gentry, clergy and parishioners supporting the Franciscans. SA, 15, No. 1, 1992, pp. 186–216.
1740	Protestant householders, Aghadowey, Aghanloo, Artrea, Ballinderry, Ballyaghran, Ballynascreen, Ballyrashane, Ballyscullion, Ballywillin, Balteagh, Banagher, Bovevagh, Clondermot, Coleraine, Cumber Lower, Cumber Upper, Derryloran, Desertlyn, Desertmartin, Desertoghill, Drumachose, Dunboe, Dungiven, Errigal, Faughanvale, Kilcronaghan, Killelagh, Killowen, Kilrea, Lissan, Macosquin, Maghera, Magherafelt, Tamlaght, Tamlaght Finlagan, Tamlaght O'Crilly, Templemore and Termoneeny. PRONI T808/15258. Online: PRONI Name Search; also GO 539; LDS films 100182, 1279327. Magherafelt NAI M2809. Online: McAfee.
1752–1930	Tenants lists, Ballylifford (Ballinderry Parish), Ballyheifer, Ballymilligan (Ballymoghan?) and Aghaskin (Magherafelt Parish)

only. 1752, 1795, 1812, 1825, 1845, 1859, 1900, 1930. *South Derry Historical Society Journal*, 2, 1991/2.

1766	Artrea, Desertlyn, Magherafelt, NAI Parl. Ret. 650, 659, 674; Boveagh, Comber, Drumachose, Inch, NAI 2476; Protestants in Ballynascreen, Banagher, Donaghedy, Dungiven, Leck, NAI M2476; Desertmartin (all), RCBL M23; also PRONI T808/15264–7. Online: PRONI name search.
1775	Arboe Parish census. With C of I registers. PRONI T.679/111, 115–19, D.1278.
1775	Dissenters' petitions, Londonderry City, Coleraine, Killowen. Online: PRONI name search.
1796	Census of Garvagh First Presbyterian congregation, also 1840, 1850. PRONI MIC.1P/257.
1796	Spinning-Wheel Premium List. 4,900 names for Co. Derry/Londonerry. Online: Hayes.
1797–1804	Yeomanry muster rolls. PRONI T1021/3; also LDS film 993910.
1803	Faughanvale local census, with C of I registers. PRONI MIC1/7B; also Genealogy Centre (database) and UHGGN, 1 (10), 1984, pp. 324–32.
1808–1813	Freeholders. NAI M.6199.
1808	Memorial from the mayor and inhabitants of Coleraine to the Privy Council on the scarcity of provisions, 5 May 1808. 51 names. NAI OP 268/7.
1813	Freeholders (A–L). PRONI T2123. Online: Freeholders.
1823–38	Tithe Books.
1829	Census of Protestants, Chapel of the Woods Parish. PRONI T308.
1830	Census of Drumachose Parish; with C of I Registers. PRONI T.679/3, 394, 396–7, 416–17.
1831	Aghadowey, Aghanloo, Agivey, Arboe, Artrea, Ballinderry, Balteagh, Banagher, Ballyaughran, Ballymoney, Ballynascreen, Ballyrashane, Ballyscullion, Ballywillin, Boveagh, Clondermot, Coleraine, Cumber, Desertlyn, Derryloran, Desertmartin, Desertoghill, Drumachose, Dunboe, Dungiven, Errigal, Faughanvale, Kilcrea, Kilcunaghan, Killeagh, Killowen, Lissane, Maghera, Magherafelt, Macosquin, Tamlaght, Tamlaght Finlagan, Tamlaght O'Crilly, Tamlaghtard, Templemore, Termoneny and Killdollagh (Glendermot). NAI; PRONI MIC5A/6–9; TGC (database). Online index: McAfee.
1831–2	Derry, *First Valuation*. LDS fiche 6342808; also NAI.
1832	Voters, (1) Londonderry city, PRONI T1048/1–4. Online: Freeholders, (2) Coleraine. NAI Outrage papers 1832/2188.
1833–4	Emigrants to the US. Martin, *Historical gleanings*.
1833–9	Emigrants list. Mitchell, *Emigration Lists*. Originals in PRONI MIC.6. Online: Olive tree.
1837	Marksmen (illiterate voters) in parliamentary boroughs, Londonderry and Coleraine. *Parliamentary Papers, 1837: Reports from Committees*, Vol. 2 (i), Appendix A.

1837	Aldermen, Burgesses and Freemen of Coleraine. *Parliamentary Papers, 1837: Reports from Committees*, Vol. 2 (2), Appendix B.
1837	Memorial of c.50 individuals (mainly from Buncrana and Derry) to have quarter sessions at Buncrana. NAI OP 1851/79.
1840	Freeholders. PRONI D834/1.
1842–99	Magherafelt Workhouse records. PRONI; also LDS film 259179–80.
1850	Census of Magilligan Presbyterian congregation, c.1850. PRONI MIC 1P/215.
1858–9	Griffith's Valuation. Online: Askaboutireland.
1864–1927	Limavady Workhouse records. PRONI; also LDS film 259176.
1868	Voters' list. PRONI D1935/6; NLI JP 733.
1888	Ballinascrpeen local census; with C of I registers. PRONI T.679/45, 206–208, 227.
1901	Census. Online: NAI.
1911	Census. Online: NAI.
1912	The Ulster Covenant. Almost half a million original signatures and addresses of those who signed. Online: Covenant.

Online

Aghadowey	<www.rootsweb.ancestry.com/~nirldy/aghadowey/ag_index.htm>
Askaboutireland	<www.askaboutireland.ie>
Bann Valley	<www.torrens.org.uk/Genealogy/BannValley>
Covenant	<www.proni.gov.uk/ulstercovenant>
Freeholders	<www.proni.gov.uk/freeholders>
Grieves	<members.iinet.net.au/~sgrieves>
Hayes, John	<www.failteromhat.com>
Headstones	<www.historyfromheadstones.com>
Lavey	<www.lmi.utvinternet.com>
McAfee	<www.billmacafee.com>
Olive tree	<www.rootsweb.ancestry.com/~ote>
NAI	<www.census.nationalarchives.ie>
PRONI name search	<www.proni.gov.uk>
Ulsterancestry	<www.ulsterancestry.com>

Publications

Local histories etc.

A Register of Trees for Co. Londonderry, 1768–1911, Belfast: PRONI, 1984. 80 p. Including names of tenant planters.

Bernard, Nicholas (ed.), *The Whole Proceedings of the Siege of Drogheda [and] Londonderry*, Dublin: 1736.

Boyle, E.M.F-G., *Records of the town of Limavady, 1609–1808*, Londonderry: 1912. NLI Ir 94112 b 2.

—— *Genealogical Memoranda relating to the family of Boyle of Limavady*, Londonderry: Sentinel, 1903. NLI Ir 9292 b 8.

Campbell, Barry L., *The Campbell's [sic] . . . from Tamlaght O'Crilly (Ireland) to Tallygaroopna (Victoria, Australia)*, Turramurra, NSW: B.L. Campbell, c.1999. LC CS2009.C35 1999. 'A history of the Campbell, Weston, Caldwell, Killough, McInnes, Sandilands, Wilson, Winnett, Pollock, Pavey and Thompson families.'

Canning, Bernard J., *By Columb's footsteps trod: the long tower's holy dead, 1784–1984*, Ballyshannon: Donegal Democrat, 198–. NLI Ir 27411 c 8.

Carson, W.R.H., *A bibliography of printed material relating to the county and county borough of Londonderry*, 1969. NLI Ir 914112 c 8.

Cooke, Sholto, *The maiden city and the western ocean: a history of the shipping trade between Londonderry and North America in the nineteenth century*, Dublin: Morris, 1960. NLI Ir 387 c 13, 223 p.

Daly, Edward, *The clergy of the diocese of Derry: an index*, Dublin: Four Courts Press, 2009. NLI, 244 p.

Day, Angelique, and McWilliams, Patrick (eds.), Ordnance Survey Memoirs of Ireland series, Belfast: Institute of Irish Studies and RIA, 1990–1997.

—*Vol. 6: Co. Londonderry I* (1990): Arboe, Artrea, Ballinderry, Ballyscullion, Magherafelt, Termoneeny. NLI Ir 914111 o 15.

—*Vol. 9: Co. Londonderry II* (1991): Balteagh, Drumachose (Newtownlimavady). NLI Ir 9141 o 15.

—*Vol. 11: Co. Londonderry III* (1991): Aghanloo, Dunboe, Magilligan (Tamlaghtard).

—*Vol. 15: Co. Londonderry IV* (1992): Dungiven. NLI Ir 914111 o 15.

—*Vol. 18. Co. Londonderry V* (1992): Maghera and Tamlaght O'Crilly. NLI Ir 914111 o 15.

—*Vol. 22: Co. Londonderry VI* (1993): Aghadowey, Agivey, Ballyrashane, Kildollagh, Macosquin. NLI Ir 9141 o 85.

—*Vol. 25: Co. Londonderry VII* (1993): Bovevagh, Tamlaght Finlagan. NLI Ir 9141 o 80.

—*Vol. 27: Co. Londonderry VIII* (1993): Desertoghill, Errigal, Killelagh, Kilrea. NLI Ir 9141 o 86.

—*Vol. 28: Co. Londonderry IX* (1994): Cumber (Upper and Lower). NLI Ir 9141 o 80.

—*Vol. 30: Co. Londonderry X* (1994): Banagher. NLI Ir 94111 o 6.

—*Vol. 31: Co. Londonderry XI* (1995): Londonderry, Ballynascreen, Desertlyn, Desertmartin, Kilcronaghan, Lissan. NLI Ir 9141 o 80.

—*Vol. 33: Co. Londonderry XII* (1995): Ballyaghran, Ballywillin, Coleraine, Killowen. NLI Ir 9141 o 80.

—*Vol. 34: Co. Londonderry XIII* (1996): Clondermot and the Waterside. NLI Ir 9141 o 80.

—*Vol. 36: Co. Londonderry XIV* (1996): Faughanvale. NLI Ir 9141 o 80.

Deery, Leo, *The schools of Ballinascreen (1823–1990)*, Ballinascreen: Ballinascreen Historical Society, 2007. NLI, 122 p.

Derry Youth and Community Workshop, *First Valuation of the City of Derry, parish of Templemore, 1832*, Derry: Derry Youth and Community Workshop, 1984. LDS fiche 6342808; also NAI.

Durnin, Patrick, *The workhouse and the famine in Derry*, Derry: Guildhall Press, 2001. NLI, 186 p.

—— *Tillies: Tillie and Henderson Shirt Factory*, Derry: Guildhall Press, 2005. NLI, 144 p.

Ewart, L.M., *Handbook to the dioceses of Down, Connor and Dromore*, Belfast: 1886. NLI Ir 27411 e 1. 123 p.

Ferguson, Rev. S., *Some items of Historic Interest about Waterside, Londonderry, 1902, with tables of householders in Glendermot Parish*, 1663, 1740.

Gavin, Robert, *Atlantic gateway: the port and city of Londonderry since 1700*, Dublin and Portland, Oreg.: Four Courts Press, 2009. Co-authors, William Kelly and Dolores O'Reilly. NLI, 382 p.

Graham, John, *Far from Owenreagh: memories of John Graham (1899–3)*, Draperstown: Moyola Books, 1990. NLI Ir 92 p 172(2), 36 p.

Graham, Rev. John, *Derriana: a History of the Siege of Derry and the Defence of Enniskillen in 1688 and 1689, with Biographical Notes*, Londonderry: the author, 1823. NLI J94112, 64 p.

Henry, Samuel, *The Story of St Patrick's Church, Coleraine*, Coleraine: Coleraine Chronicle, 1941. NLI Ir 7265 h 3, 108 p.

Hughes, Samuel, *City on the Foyle*, Londonderry: 1984.

Innes, R., *Natural History of Magiligan Parish in 1725*.

Kernohan, J.W, *The County of Londonderry in Three Centuries*, Belfast: 1921.

—— *The parishes of Kilrea and Tamlaght O'Crilly: a sketch of their history, with an account of Boveedy congregation*, Coleraine: Chronicle Office, 1912. Reprinted 1993. NLI Ir 94112 k 3, 80 p.

King, R.G.S, *A particular of the houses and families in Londonderry, 15/5/1628*, Londonderry: Sentinel Office, 1936. NLI Ir 94112 l 1; also LDS films 1363860 and 990087.

Macafee, William, *Researching Derry and Londonderry Ancestors: A practical guide for family and local historians* (CD, MacAfee, 2010).

McMahon, Kevin, *Guide to Creggan Church and Graveyard*, Creggan: Creggan Historical Society, 1988. NLI Ir 9295 p 3(2) 48 p.

MacRory, Patrick, *Days that are gone*, Limavady: North-West Books, 1983. NLI Ir 92 m 346, 167 p. Also Pottinger family.

Maitland, W.H., *History of Magherafelt*, 1916. Reprinted Moyarta Books, 1988, 1991. Online: <www.readanybook.com>

Martin, Samuel, *Historical gleanings from Co. Derry, and some from Co. Fermanagh*, Dublin: 1955. NLI Ir 94112 m 2.

Mitchell, Brian, *Derry: A City Invincible*, Eglinton: 1990.

—— *Irish Emigration Lists, 1833–39*, Baltimore, Md.: GPC, 1988.

—— *Derry: Sources for Family History*, Derry: Genealogy Centre, 1992.

Moody, T.W., *The Londonderry plantation, 1609–41*, Belfast: 1939; GPC, 1989. NLI Ir 94112 m 2.

Mullin, Julia, *The Presbytery of Limavady*, Limavady: 1989.

Mullin, T.H., *Ulster's Historic City, Derry, Londonderry,* Coleraine: 1986.

—— *Families of Ballyrashane: a district in Northern Ireland,* Belfast: News Letter Printing Co., 1969. 386 p. NLI Ir 9292 m 33.

—— *Aghadowey,* Coleraine: Mullin, 1971. NLI Ir 94112 m 8, 255 p.

Mullin, T.H. and J., *The Ulster clans: O'Mullan, O'Kane and O'Mellan,* Limavady: North-West Books, 1984. NLI Ir 9292 m 54, 249 p.

Murphy, Desmond, *Derry, Donegal, and modern Ulster, 1790–1921,* Londonderry: Aileach Press, 1981. NLI Ir 94112 m 11, 294 p.

O'Brien, Gerard, *Derry and Londonderry: history and society,* Dublin: Geography Publications, 1999. NLI Ir 94112 d 13, 741 p.

O'Donovan, John, *Ordnance Survey letters: Londonderry* [1834], Draperstown: Ballinascreen Historical Society, 1992. NLI Ir 94112 o 3, 140 p.

Phillips, Sir Thomas, *Londonderry and the London Companies,* Belfast: PRONI, 1928.

Reeves, William, *Ecclesiastical Antiquities of Down, Connor and Dromore,* 1847.

Simpson, Robert, *The Annals of Derry,* Londonderry: 1847.

Thomas, Avril, *Irish Historic Towns Atlas, 15: Derry/Londonderry,* Dublin: RIA, 2005. NLI.

Witherow, Thomas, *A True Relation of the Twenty Week Siege . . .* London: 1649.

—— *Derry and Enniskillen, in the year 1689,* 1873, 1885, Belfast: W. Mullen & Son, 1895. NLI Ir 94112 w 8, 419 p.

Local journals
Benbradagh (Dungiven parish magazine).
Derriana: The Journal of the Derry Diocesan Historical Society.
Irish Family Links. NLI Ir 9292 f 19.
North Irish Roots: Journal of the North of Ireland Family History Society. NLI Ir 92905 n 4.
Seanchas Ardmhacha. NLI Ir 27411 s 4.
South Derry Historical Society Journal. NLI Ir 914112 s 21.

Directories
Thirty Belfast and Ulster directories are online at PRONI.

1820	J. Pigot, *Commercial Directory of Ireland.* PRONI; NLI Ir 9141 p 107; LDS film 962702 item 1.
1824	J. Pigot & Co., *City of Dublin and Hibernian Provincial Directory.* NLI; LDS film 451787. Online: Hayes.
1835	William T. Matier, *Belfast Directory.*
1839	Mathew Martin, *Belfast Directory.* Also 1841, 1842.

1846   Slater's *National Commercial Directory of Ireland*. PRONI; NLI LO; LDS film 1696703 item 3. Online: Hayes.

1852   James A. Henderson, *Belfast and Province of Ulster Directory*. Issued also in 1854, 1856, 1858, 1861, 1863, 1865, 1868, 1870, 1877, 1880, 1884, 1887, 1890, 1894 and 1900. Online: PRONI; LDS (various years).

1856   Slater, *Royal National Commercial Directory of Ireland*. NLI; LDS film 1472360 item 1.

1865   R. Wynne, *Business Directory of Belfast*. NLI Ir 91411 b 2.

1870   Slater, *Directory of Ireland*. NLI.

1881   Slater, *Royal National Commercial Directory of Ireland*. NLI. Online: FindMyPast.

1887   *Derry Almanac and Directory*. NLI Ir 914112 d 1.

1888   George Henry Bassett, *The Book of Antrim*. Reprinted Belfast: Friar's Bush Press, 1989. NLI Ir 94116 b 29 (Portglenone only).

1894   Slater, *Royal Commercial Directory of Ireland*. NLI.

Gravestone inscriptions

The Ulster Historical Foundation has transcripts for 76 graveyards in Co. Derry. Heritage World has transcripts of 42 graveyards. These are searchable online for a fee at <www.historyfromheadstones.com>. Published or publicly available transcripts are given below.

Aghanloo: Rathfad (Aghanloo Old?), *Irish Family Links*, 1985, 2 (3).
—— Derramore, Pres., *Irish Family Links*, 2 (4), 1985.
—— Drumbane, C of I, *Irish Family Links*, 1985, 2 (3).
Artrea: Ballyeglish Old, *South Derry Historical Society Journal*, 1981/2.
Ballinderry: Ballinderry, Methodist, *South Derry Historical Society Journal*, 1982/3.
Ballynascreen: Draperstown, RC, 'St. Patrick's', <www.interment.net>.
Balteagh: Lislane, Pres., *Irish Family Links*, 2 (4), 1985.
Carrick: Largy, Pres., *Irish Family Links*, 2 (5), 1985.
Clondermot: Glendermot Old, online: Grieves.
Coleraine: Coleraine, Church St, C of I, Samuel Henry, *The Story of St Patrick's Church, Coleraine*, 1941.
Drumachose: Limavady, First Pres., *Irish Family Links*, 2 (5), 1985.
—— Rathbrady More, Pres., *Irish Family Links*, 2 (5), 1985.
—— Limavady, Myroe, Pres., *Irish Family Links*, 2 (5), 1985.
—— Limavady, RC, *Irish Family Links*, 2 (5), 1985.
—— Drummond (Drumachose Old?), *Irish Family Links*, 2 (4), 1985.
Magherafelt: Magherafelt, Castledawson St, C of I, *South Derry Historical Society Journal*, 1980/81.
Magilligan: Tamlaght, RC, *Irish Family Links*, 2 (5), 1985.
—— Magilligan, Pres., *Irish Family Links*, 2 (5), 1985.
Tamlaght Finlagan: Ballykelly town, *Irish Family Links*.
—— Oghill, RC, *Irish Family Links*, 2 (5), 1985.

—— Ballykelly town, Pres., *Irish Family Links*.
Templemore: Creggan, McMahon, *Guide to Creggan*.
Templemore: Derry, Glendermot, C of I, NAI.

Estate records

[No landlord given]. Tenants lists, Magherafelt and Ballinderry parishes (Aghaskin, Ballyheifer, Ballylifford, Ballymilligan), 1752–1930. *South Derry Historical Society Journal*, 1 (2).

Bruce. Rentals, 1838–76, PRONI D.1514/2/1. Covering areas in the civil parishes of Dunboe, Macosquin, Magilligan and Templemore.

Clothworkers' Estate. Administration book, 1840–60, PRONI D2738/8/2/11. Covering areas in the civil parish of Dunboe.

Conolly. Rentals and accounts, 1718–1802, PRONI T.2825/C/11, T.2825/C/15–16. Covering areas in the civil parish of Drumachose.

Desertmartin. Rentals. *Derriana*, 1981–2.

Drapers' Company. Rents, leases, petitions, 1610–18, PRONI T635/1–1. Rentals, 1640–1793, PRONI D3632/K/1–6. Covering areas in the civil parishes of Arboe, Artrea, Ballynascreen, Derryloran, Desertmartin, Kilcronaghan and Lissan.

Garvagh, Lord. Rentals, 1815–1930, PRONI D1550/20–24, 34–8. Covering areas in the civil parishes of Aghadowey, Desertmartin, Desertoghill and Errigal.

Goldsmiths' Company. Rental, 1722, PRONI D3482/1. Covering areas in the civil parishes Clondermot and Cumber Lower.

Grocers' Company. Rentals of the Limavady estate, 1729–1800, PRONI D.2094/26–79. Covering areas in the civil parish of Drumachose.

Grocers' Company. Rentals, 1824–46, PRONI MIC9B/2. Covering areas in the civil parishes of Clondermot, Cumber Lower and Faughanvale.

Irish Society. Rent roll ('estates in and near Londonderry and Coleraine'), 1756–94. PRONI D573/1 and 2 or MIC15D3. Covering areas in the civil parishes of Ballyaghran, Ballywillin, Clondermot, Coleraine, Kildollagh and Templemore.

Lenox-Conyngham. Rentals for the Springhill estate, 1786–1914, PRONI D.1449/1–7. Covering areas in the civil parishes of Arboe, Artrea and Tamlaght.

Londonderry, Marquis of. PRONI D/654. Rentals, 1750–1940. Covering townlands in the civil parishes of Faughanvale and Magherafelt. May cover further parishes.

McCausland, Marcus. Rent rolls, 1830–60, PRONI D1550/42. Covering areas in the civil parishes of Balteagh, Desertoghill, Drumachose and Tamlaght Finlagan.

Merchant Taylors' Company. Rental, 1729, PRONI T.656, boxes 126–9. Aghadowey, Errigal and Macosquin.

Phillips. Rentals and accounts ('including a list of tenants who had left their farms for New England in 1718'), 1718–29, PRONI T2825/C/11/1–9. Accounts, 1684–94, PRONI T2825/C/5/1. Rentals, 1781–4, PRONI T2825/C/15/1–33. Rent roll (includes Limavady town), 1800, PRONI D2094/79. Valuation, 1782, PRONI D2094/61. Rent roll, 1802, PRONI T2825/C/16/1. Covering areas in the civil parishes of Bovevagh, Drumachose and Tamlaght Finlagan.

Salters' Company. Rentals, 1752–90, PRONI D4108/15G/1, 16O, 16R, 16Y, 16Z/8, 17B. Covering areas in the civil parishes of Artrea, Desertlyn, Desertmartin and Magherafelt (1752 rental in Maitland, Magherafelt).

Skinners' Company. Rent roll and more, 1794–1865, PRONI D573/2–6, 10, 11. Covering areas in the civil parishes of Banagher, Cumber Lower, Cumber Upper, Dungiven and Learmount.

Staples: Rent roll, 1812, PRONI D476/114. Covering areas in the civil parish of Lissan.

Stewart, Alexander. Rent roll, 1768, PRONI D654/R4/1. Covering areas in the civil parish of Kilrea. May cover areas in other parishes.

Vintners' Company. Rental, 1718, PRONI D2094/21. Rent roll, 1729, PRONI D2094/29–30. All tenants; rentals, 1775–6, PRONI D2094/50–51. Rentals, 1788–93, PRONI D2094/76–8. Rentals, 1795–1801 and 1818, PRONI T2825/C/19/1–13. Rentals, 1817–42, PRONI T3110/1/180–93. See also MIC273. Rent ledger, 1838–82, PRONI D1062/1/2. Lease renewal book, 1839–1941, PRONI D1062/1/13. Covering areas in the civil parishes of Ballyscullion, Desertmartin, Killelagh, Kilrea, Maghera, Magherafelt and Tamlaght O'Crilly. Part online: McAfee.

DONEGAL

Census returns and substitutes

1612–13	'Survey of Undertakers Planted in Co. Donegal', *Historical Manuscripts Commission Report*, No. 4 (Hastings Mss.), 1947, pp. 159–82.
1630	Muster Roll of Ulster. Armagh County Library and PRONI D.1759/3C/1, T. 808/15164. NLI Pos. 206. Part (?) online: McAfee.
1641	Book of Survey and Distribution. NLI Ms. 968.
1654	*Civil Survey*, Vol. 3. Dublin. NLI I 6551.
1659	Pender's 'Census'. Reprinted GPC, 1997; IMC, 2002. LDS film 924648.
1665	Hearth Money Roll. PRONI T.307/D; also GO 538. NLI Ms. 9583. Part online: Ulster Ancestry, Buckley.
1669	Subsidy Roll, covering baronies of Kilmacrenan, Raphoe, Tirhugh and Taughboyne. PRONI T 307; also LDS film 258502.
1740	Protestant householders: parishes of Clonca, Clonmany, Culdaff, Desertegny, Donagh, Fahan, Moville and Templemore. GO 539. LDS film 100182. Online: PRONI name search.
1761–75	Freeholders. PRONI T.808/14999; also GO 442. NLI P.975; LDS film 100181. Online: Freeholders.
1766	Diocesan census, Donoghmore Parish. NA m 207/8. Protestants in Leck and Raphoe. NA M2476. Inch and Leck online: PRONI name search.
1770	Freeholders entitled to vote. NLI Mss. 787–8.
1782	Persons in Culdaff. Young, *300 Years in Inishowen*.

1796	Spinning-Wheel Premium List. 7,525 names for Co. Donegal. Online: Hayes.
1796	Clondevaddock local census; with C of I registers. PRONI MIC.1/164.
1799	Protestant householders, Templecrone Parish. IA, 1984.
1802–1803	Protestants in part of Culdaff Parish. Young, *300 Years in Inishowen*.
1823–38	Tithe books.
1836–44	Memorials from the inhabitants of the towns of Ballyshannon, Pettigo and Bundoran (1836, c.70 names), Buncrana and Derry (1837, c.50 names) and Leterkenny (1844, c.130 names). NAI OP 1851/79.
1843	Voters. NAI OP1843/56.
1857	Griffith's Valuation. Online: Askaboutireland.
1860–67	Emigrants to North America from Inver; with C of I registers. PRONI MIC.1/158.
1862–83	Strabane Union Workhouse records. PRONI BG/27; also LDS film 259164–5.
1901	Census. Online: NAI.
1911	Census. Online: NAI.
1912	The Ulster Covenant. Almost half a million original signatures and addresses of those who signed. Online: Covenant.

Online

Askaboutireland	*<www.askaboutireland.ie>*
Buckley	*<freepages.genealogy.rootsweb.ancestry.com/~donegal>*
Covenant	*<www.proni.gov.uk/ulstercovenant>*
Donegal	*<www.donegalhistory.com>*
Freeholders	*<www.proni.gov.uk/freeholders>*
Hayes	*<www.failteromhat.com>*
Kilcar	*<www.personal.psu.edu/faculty/j/w/jwd6/kilcar.htm>*
NAI	*<www.census.nationalarchives.ie>*
Palmer	*<www.benpalmer.co.uk/movillerecords.htm>*
PRONI name search	*<www.proni.gov.uk>*
Ulsterancestry	*<www.ulsterancestry.com>*

Publications

Local histories etc.

Historical notes of Raphoe, Vol. 3: Finn Valley, Lifford and Twin towns, Stranorlar: Knights of Columbanus, 1991. NLI Ir 94113 b 8.

A golden jubilee story and index to contents of fifty annuals, Donegal: County Donegal Historical Society, 1995. NLI Ir 94113 d 14, 76 p.

Aalen, F.H., *Gola: the life and last days of an island community*, Cork: Mercier Press, 1969. NLI Ir 914113 a 2, 127 p.

Allingham, Hugh, *Ballyshannon: its history and antiquities (with some account of the surrounding neighbourhood)*, Londonderry: 1879. Reprinted Ballyshannon: 1937. NLI Ir 94113 p 2(3), 112 p.

Beattie, Seán, *The book of Inistrahull*, Carndonagh: Lighthouse, 1992. 24 p.NLI Ir 941 p 115(4).

Begley, Anthony, *Ballyshannon and surrounding areas: history, heritage and folklore*, Ballyshannon: Carrickboy Publishing, 2009. NLI, 500 p.

Bonner, Brian, *Where Aileach guards a millennium of Gaelic civilisation*, Pallaskenry: Salesian Press Trust, 1986? NLI Ir 94113 b 7, 150 p.

Briody, Liam, *Glenties and Iniskeel*, Ballyshannon: Donegal Democrat, 1986. 320 p. NLI

Campbell, Patrick, *Memories of Dungloe*, the author, 1993. NLI Ir 92 c 360, 149 p.

—— *Death in Templecrone: an account of the Famine years in northwest Donegal, 1845–50*, P.H. Campbell, 1995. NLI Ir 94113 c 7, 193 p.

Carville, Geraldine, *Assaroe: abbey of the morning star*, Abbey Mill Wheel Trust, 1989. NLI Ir 27411 c 9, 63 p.

Caulfield, Debbie, *Hands across the Foyle: reflections of our culture, landscape and history: Moville, Greencastle and the Roe Valley*, Limavady: Ageing Well Roe Valley, 2004. NLI 128 p.

Conaghan, Charles, *History and antiquities of Killybegs*, Ballyshannon: Donegal Democrat, 1975.

Conaghan, Pat, *The Zulu Fishermen: Forgotten Pioneers of Donegal's First Fishing Industry*, Aghayeevoge, Co. Donegal: Bygones Enterprise, 2003. NLI 3A 3994, 340 p.

—— *Bygones: New Horizons on the History of Killybegs*, Killybegs: the author, 1989. NLI Ir 94113 c 6, 399 p.

—— *The Great Famine in South-West Donegal, 1845–50*, Aghayeevoge, Co. Donegal: Bygones Enterprise, 1997. NLI, 280 p.

Conn, Nancy H., *From Drumholm, Donegal to Cartwright, Upper Canada: the Dinsmore-Freeborn-Strong families*, Toronto: Stewart Publishing, 1998. Donegal County Library, 322p.

Daly, Edward, *The clergy of the diocese of Derry: an index*, Dublin: Four Courts Press, 2009. NLI, 244 p.

Day, Angelique, and McWilliams, Patrick (eds.), *Ordnance Survey Memoirs of Ireland, Vol. 39: Parishes of County Donegal II, 1835–6: Mid, West and South Donegal*, Belfast: Institute of Irish Studies, 1997. NLI Ir 9141 o 80, 216 p. Clonleigh, Convoy, Conwal, Donaghmore, Donegal, Drumhome, Glencolmbcille, Inishkeel, Kilbarron, Killea and Taughboyne, Killymard, Kilteevoge, Leck, Raphoe, Raymoghy, Taughboyne, Templecarn, Tullaghobegley, Urney.

—— *Ordnance Survey Memoirs of Ireland, Vol. 38: Parishes of County Donegal I, 1833–5, North-East Donegal*, Belfast: Institute of Irish Studies, 1997. NLI Ir 9141 o 80, 168 p. Clondavaddog, Clonmany, Culdaff, Desertegney, Donagh, Killygarvan, Kilmacrenan, Mevagh, Mintiaghs (Bar of Inch), Moville, Muff, Tullyaughnish, Lough Swilly (with Burt and Inch).

Devine, Donn, *Devine family genealogy, Conwal Parish, County Donegal*, Philadelphia, Pa., and Wilmington, Del.: the author, 1985. NLI, 22 p.

Devitt, James W., *Boyds of Loughros Point: The Rosses, America, Australia, and New Zealand*, J.W. Devitt, 1994. LC CS71.B79 1994.

Doherty, William J., *The abbey of Fahan in Inishowen, Co. Donegal*, Dublin: P. Traynor, 1881.

—— *Inis-Owen and Tirconnel: being some account of the antiquities . . . of Donegal*, Dublin: 1895. NLI Ir 94113 d 1.

Duffy, Godfrey F., *A guide to tracing your Donegal ancestors*, Dublin: Flyleaf Press, 1996. NLI Ir 941 D 9, 94 p.

Duffy, Margaret, *Inishfree: a tribute to a Donegal Island and its people*, Burtonport, Co. Donegal: M.M. Duffy, 2004. NLI, 302 p.

Durnin, Patrick, *The workhouse and the famine in Derry*, Derry: Guildhall Press, 2001. NLI, 186 p.

Egan, Bernard, *Drumhome*, Ballyshannon: Donegal Democrat, 1986. NLI, 93 p.

Farrell, Noel, *Exploring family origins in Ballyshannon*, Longford: Noel Farrell, 1998. NLI, 48 p.

—— *Exploring Family origins in Ballybofey/Stranorlar and Killygordon*, Longford: the author, 1994. NLI, 48 p.

—— *Exploring Family origins in Letterkenny*, Longford: the author, 1997. NLI, 47 p.

—— *Exploring family origins in Mountcharles, Inver and Donegal town*, Longford: Noel Farrell, 1997. NLI, 48 p.

Fitzgerald, Barbara, *Our McMenamin story: starting in Carrickalangan, Co. Donegal, Ireland and stretching to other areas of the world*, Dandenong North, Vic.: the authors, 1999. Co-author, Noel Fitzgerald. Donegal County Library, 404 p.

Fleming, Sam, *Letterkenny: past and present*, Ballyshannon: Donegal Democrat, 197–. NLI Ir 94113 f 1, 88 p.

Fox, Robin, *The Tory islanders, a people of the celtic fringe*, Notre Dame and London: University of Notre Dame Press, 1995. NLI Ir 914111 f 10, 210 p.

Friel, Deirdra, *St. Mary's Church, the Lagg, 1829–1961*, Milford: Deirdra Friel, 1996. NLI, 31 p.

Gallagher, Barney, *Arranmore Links: the families of Arranmore*, Dublin: Aiden Gallagher, 1986. NLI Ir 94109 g 18.

Harkin, M., *Inishowen: its history, traditions, and antiquities . . . by Maghtochair*, Carndonagh: M. Harkin, 1935. NLI Ir 94113 h 1, 227 p.

Harkin, William, *Scenery and Antiquities of North West Donegal*, Londonderry: 1893. NLI Ir 914113 h 1, 120 p.

Harvey, G.H., *The Harvey families of Inishowen, Co. Donegal, and Maen, Cornwall*, Folkestone: F. Weatherhead, 1927. NLI Ir 9292 h 3, 178 p.

Hill, Rev. George, *Facts from Gweedore*, Dublin: 1854. NLI P 1191 (10), 64 p.

Hunter, Jim, *The waves of Tory / Tonnta Thoraí: the story of an Atlantic community / scéal pobail Atlantaigh*, Gerrards Cross, Bucks: Colin Smythe, 2006. NLI, 136 p.

IGRS, *Tombstone inscriptions, Vol. 1*, Dublin: IGRS Tombstone Committee, 2001. NLI, 850 p.

Jensen, Marjorie Molloy, *The family of Big Jimmy McLaughlin of Dreenagh, Malin Head, Donegal, Ireland*, Golden, Colo.: M.M. Jansen, 1999. LC CS71.M1617 1999.

Keaveney, J.J., *Róise Rua, an island memoir*, Cork: Mercier Press, 2009. Arranmore Island. NLI, 286 p.

Killybegs Community Response Scheme, *St Catherine's Church and graveyard project, Killybegs*, Killybegs: Killybegs Community Response Scheme, 2008. NLI, 104 p.

Knights of St Columbanus C.K. 56., *Ballybofey and Stranorlar historical notes*, Stranorlar: 1987. NLI Ir 94113 b 8.

Lawrenson, Leslie Robert, *The parish of Conwall, Aughawawshin, and Leck*, Letterkenny: the parish, 1944. NLI Ir 2741 p 41, 36 p.

Lecky, Alexander G., *The Laggan and its Presbyterianism*, Belfast: Davidson and M'Cormack, 1905. NLI Ir 285 L 7, 211 p.

Leiball, Abigail Cone, *The Coane family of Ballyshannon, Donegal*, Stamford, Conn.: the author, 2002. NLI 3B 120.

Lucas, Leslie W., *Mevagh Down the Years*, Portlaw: Volturna, 1972. NLI Ir 94113 l 1, 214 p.

—— *More about Mevagh*, Belfast: Appletree Press, 1982. NLI Ir 941 p 22, 93 p.

McCarron, Edward, *Life in Donegal, 1850–1900*, Dublin: Mercier Press, c.1981. NLI Ir 92 m 321, 140 p.

McClintock, May, *The heart of the Laggan: the history of Raymoghy and Ray National School*, Letterkenny: An Taisce, 1990. NLI Ir 372.m.109, 93 p.

—— *After the battering ram: the trail of the dispossessed from Derryveagh, 1861*, Letterkenny: An Taisce, 1991. NLI Ir 941 p 102(3), 20 p.

McCreadie, John, *Glenwar and Oughterlin*, Carndonagh: Foyle Press, 198–.

MacDonagh, J.C.T., 'Bibliography of Co. Donegal', *Donegal Historical Society Journal*, 1947–50, pp. 217–30.

McGarrigle, Joe, *Donegal Past and present*, Donegal: McGarrigle family, 1995. NLI r 94113 m 11, 195 p.

McGinley, Niall, *Donegal, Ireland and the First World War*, Leitir Ceanainn: An Crann, 2005. NLI, 431 p.

McLaughlin, Gerry, *Cloughaneely: myth and fact*, Johnswood Press, 2002. NLI, 304 p.

Mac Laughlin, Jim, *Donegal: the making of a northern county*, Dublin: Four Courts Press, 2007. NLI, 382 p.

McLaughlin, John A., 'Carrowmenagh: history of a Donegal village and townland', *JAML*, 2001. NLI, 118 p.

Maguire, Edward, *Letterkenny past and present*, Letterkkenny: McKinney and O'Callaghan, 192–.

—— *Ballyshannon past and present*, Bundoran: Stepless, 193–.

Maguire, V. Rev. Canon, *The History of the Diocese of Raphoe*, Dublin: Browne & Nolan, 1920. NLI Ir 274113 m 1, 2 vols.

Manning, Aidan, *Glencolumbkille, 3000 BC–1985 AD*, Ballyshannon: Donegal Democrat, 1985.

Meehan, Helen, *Inver Parish in History*, Mountcharles: the author, 2005. 731 p.

Montgomery, H.H., *A history of Moville and its neighbourhood by Rt. Rev. Bishop Henry Montgomery*, Crawford Norris and C. Doherty, 1992. NLI r 94113 p 2(2), 52 p.

Mullin, T.H., *The kirk and lands of Convoy since the Scottish settlement*, Belfast: News Letter, 1960.

Murphy, Desmond, *Derry, Donegal, and modern Ulster, 1790–1921*, Londonderry: Aileach Press, 1981. NLI Ir 94112 m 11, 294 p.

Nolan, W., *Donegal History and Society*, Dublin: Geography Publications, 1995. Co-editors, Liam Ronayne and Mairead Dunlevy. NLI Ir 94113 d 12, 920 p.

O'Carroll, Declan, *Rockhill House, Letterkenny, Co. Donegal: a history*, Ballyshannon: Donegal Democrat, 1984.

Ó Ceallaigh, Seosamh, *Aspects of our rich inheritance*, Dúlra, 2000. NLI Ir 94113 c 8, 240 p.

O'Donnell, Ben, *History of the parish of Templecrone*, Donegal: 1999. Donegal County Library 941.693 (photocopy).

—— *The Story of The Rosses*, Lifford: Caoran Publ., 1999. Much detail on local families. Donegal County Library, 441 p.

O'Donnell, Vincent, *Ardaghey Church and people*, Ardaghey: St Naul's Church, 1995. NLI Ir 94113 a 5, 146 p.

O'Donovan, John, *Ordnance Survey letters, Donegal: letters containing information relative to the antiquities of the County of Donegal collected during the progress of the Ordnance Survey in 1835*, Dublin: Four Masters Press, 2000. Edited with an introduction by Michael Herity; preface by Brian Friel. NLI LO 8194, 148 p.

Ó Gallachair, P., *Where Erne and Drowes meet the sea: Fragments from a Patrician parish*, Ballyshannon: Donegal Democrat, 1961, 118 p.

—— *The history of landlordism in Donegal*, Ballyshannon: Donegal Democrat, 1962. NLI Ir 94113 o 5, 192 p.

Ó Searcaigh, Cathal, *Tulach Beaglaoich inné agus inniú (Tullaghobegley past and present)*, Fál Carrach: Glór na nGael, 1993. NLI Ir 27411 o, 68 p.

Parke, W.K., *The parish of Inishmacsaint*, Fermanagh, 1982. NLI Ir 27411 p 6, 73 p.

Patterson, W.J., *Rossnowlagh remembered*, Ballyshannon: Donegal Democrat, 1992. NLI Ir 94113 p.

Patton, Billy, *Lifford, seat of power*, Lifford: Lifford Tidy Towns Committee, 2008. NLI, 106 p.

Ronayne, Liam, *The Battle of Scariffhollis, 1650*, Letterkenny: Eagráin Dhún na nGall, 2001. NLI 3B 561, 72 p.

Rural Schools Reunion Committee, *Schools of yesteryear, memories of the rural schools of Donegal town*, Donegal: 2006. NLI, 220 p.

Smeaton, Brian, *The parish of Kilmacrennan now and then with a history of the Parish Church of Saint Finian and Saint Mark 1846–1996*, 1995. NLI Ir 9411 p, 40 p.

Strong, Dale G., *The descendants of John Strong (1770–1837) and Martha Watson (1772–1851) of Drumhome Parish, Co. Donegal, Ireland*, Cassatt, sc: Mr and Mrs D.G. Strong, 1983. LC CS71.S923 1983a, 98 leaves.

Swan, H.P., *The Book of Inishowen*, Buncrana: 1938. NLI Ir 94113 s 1, 192 p.

Trimble, H., *Killymard ancient and modern*, Killymard: 2001. NLI, 240 p.

Trimble, T.H., *The legacy that is Laughey Community and Church*, Letterkenny: printed by Browne Printers, 2000. NLI, 160 p.

Ward, Brid, *St. John's Point, County Donegal: In Former Days and Now*, Inver: Brid Ward, 2010. Killaghtee. Donegal County Library, 410 p.

Young, Amy, *300 Years in Inishowen*, Belfast: M'Caw, Stevenson & Orr, 1929. NLI Ir 9292 y 1, 357 p.

Local journals
Donegal Annual.
Journal of the Donegal Historical Society. NLI Ir 94113 d 3.
Ulster Journal of Archaeology. NLI Ir 794105 u 1.

Directories

1824	J. Pigot & Co., *City of Dublin and Hibernian Provincial Directory*. NLI; LDS film 451787. Online: Hayes.
1839	*Directory of the Towns of Sligo, Enniskillen, Ballyshannon, Donegal [. . .]*
1846	Slater's *National Commercial Directory of Ireland*. PRONI; NLI LO; LDS film 1696703 item 3. Online: Hayes.
1852	James A. Henderson, *Belfast and Province of Ulster Directory*. Issued also in 1854, 1856, 1858, 1861, 1863, 1865, 1868, 1870, 1877, 1880, 1884, 1887, 1890, 1894, 1900. Online: PRONI; LDS (various years).
1856	Slater, *Royal National Commercial Directory of Ireland*. NLI; LDS film 1472360 item 1.
1870	Slater, *Directory of Ireland*. NLI.
1881	Slater, *Royal National Commercial Directory of Ireland*. NLI. Online: FindMyPast.
1887	*Derry Almanac and Directory*. NLI Ir 914112 d 1.
1894	Slater, *Royal Commercial Directory of Ireland*. NLI.

Gravestone inscriptions

Eileen Hewson (<*www.kabristan.org.uk*>) has transcribed and published almost seven thousand inscriptions in seven volumes for Co. Donegal. Most are available at NLI. It is not clear if the transcripts are complete for each graveyard.

Aghanunshin: Kiltoy, DA.
—— Killydonnell, DA.
Aughnish: Tullyaughnish, DA.
Fahan Lower: Buncrana town, C of I, HW.

Gartan: Churchtown (Gartan?), DA.

Inishmacsaint: Assaroe Abbey; online: Ulsterancestry.

Ballyshannon town (Assaroe?), RC, DA.

Ballyshannon, St Anne's C of I: <*www.interment.net*>.

—— Finner, Ó Gallachair, *Where Erne*.

—— Finner, <*www.interment.net*>.

Inver: Cranny Lower (Old Inver?), C of I, DA.

—— Cranny Lower (Old Inver?), C of I, IGRS, Vol. 1.

Kilbarron: Ballyshannon, Church Lane, C of I, *Donegal Annual*, Vol. 12, No. 2.

Killaghtee: Beaugreen Glebe (Old Killaghtee?), DA.

Killybegs Upper: St Catherine's, DA.

Kilmacrenan: Kilmacrenan town, DA.

Kilteevoge: <*www.interment.net*> (part).

Letterkenny: Gartan <*www.interment.net*>.

Leck: Leck, DA.

Muff: Muff, Scared Heart, RC, HW.

Taughboyne: St Johnstown town, Pres., HW.

Tullaghobegly: Magheragallan, DA.

—— Ballintemple (Tullaghobegly?), Ó Searcaigh, *Tulach Beaglaoich*, Vol. 8.

Estate records

[No landlord given]. Visiting book, with observations, 1842–3. NLI Ms. 7938. Coverage unclear. Covering areas in the civil parish of Inishkeel.

Abercorn, Dukes of. Rent account books, 1794–1911. PRONI D623/C/4. Covering areas in the civil parishes of Raphoe, Raymoghy and Taughboyne.

Abercorn, Earls of. Tenants list, 1799, in Lecky, *The Laggan*. Covering townlands in the civil parishes of Clonleigh, Taughboyne and Urney.

Alexander, Earls of Caledon. Rentals, 1839–40. PRONI D.2433. Covering areas in the civil parishes of Moville Lower and Moville Upper.

Connolly. Rent rolls, 1724–1831, intermittent. NLI Ms. 17302; NAI M. 6917 (1–17). Major tenants only. Covering areas in the civil parishes of Drumhome, Glencolumbkille, Inishkeel, Inishmacsaint, Kilbarron, Kilcar, Killybegs Upper and Killymard.

Connolly. Rent rolls, 1724–1831, NLI Ms. 17302. Major tenants only. Rent rolls, 1772–93, NAI M. 6917 (1–17). Major tenants only. Rent rolls, 1848, NAI M. 6917 (18). Major tenants only. Covering areas in the civil parishes of Drumhome, Glencolumbkille, Inishkeel, Inishmacsaint, Kilbarron, Kilcar, Killybegs Upper and Killymard.

Ferguson, Andrew. Maps, with names, 1790, NLI Ms. 5023. Major tenants only. Rentals, 1838–42, NLI Ms. 8410 (2). All tenants. Tenants list, 1840, NLI Ms. 8410 (3). All tenants. Covering areas in the civil parish of Donagh.

Forward, William. Valuation and survey, 1727, NLI Ms. 4247. Major tenants only. Maps, with tenants, 1727, NLI Ms.2614. All tenants. Covering areas in the civil parishes of Allsaints and Burt.

Hamilton, John. Estate Rental, 1818–49. DA. Covering areas in the civil parishes of Inishkeel, Bellanamore and Fintown.

Hart. Rentals, 1757–67. NLI Ms. 7885. All tenants. Covering areas in the civil parishes of Clonca and Muff.

Leslie. Rentals, 1819–37. NLI Ms. 5811–12. All tenants. Covering areas in the civil parish of Templecarn.

Leslie. Valuation, with names and observations, 1833, NLI Ms. 5813. All tenants. Rental, 1846, NLI Ms. 5813. All tenants. Covering areas in the civil parish of Templecarn.

Londonderry estate. Rentals, 1750–1800, PRONI D.654. Covering areas in the civil parishes of Allsaints, Clonleigh.

Maxwell. Valuation, with names, 1807, NLI Ms. 5357. All tenants. Covering areas in the civil parishes of Clonleigh and Fahan Upper.

Murray Stewart, Horatio Granville. Rental, 1749–1880, DA. Covering areas in the civil parishes of Kilcar, Killaghtee, Killybegs Lower and Killybegs Upper. May cover further parishes in south Donegal.

Stewart. Rentals, 1813–53. NAI BR DON 21/1/1–3. All tenants. Covering areas in the civil parishes of Clondahorky, Clonmany, Raymunterdoney and Tullyfern.

Stuart-Murray. Rentals, 1842–50, NLI Ms. 5465–70. All tenants. Rentals, 1849, NLI Ms. 3084. All tenants. Rentals, 1851–9, NLI Ms. 5472–6, 5892–6. Covering areas in the civil parishes of Inishkeel Kilcar, Killaghtee, Killea, Killybegs Lower and Killymard.

Styles, Sir Charles. Valuation and survey, 1773. NLI Ms. 402. Major tenants only. Covering areas in the civil parish of Kilteevoge.

Wicklow, Lord. Rent roll, with leaseholders, 1780. NLI Ms. 9582. Major tenants only. Covering areas in the civil parishes of Allsaints, Burt, Raymoghy and Taughboyne.

DOWN

Census returns and substitutes

1641	Testimonies of 144 witnesses to the 1641 Rebellion. Online: 1641.
1642	Muster Roll, Donaghadee. PRONI T.3726/1.
1642–3	Muster Roll. PRONI T.563/1.
1659	Pender's 'Census'. Reprinted GPC, 1997; IMC, 2002. LDS film 924648.
1660	Poll Tax Returns, Co. Down. PRONI MIC/15A/76, LDS film 993164.
1661	Books of Survey and Distribution. PRONI T.370/A and D.1854/1/18.
1663	Subsidy Roll. NAI M. 2745; also NLI Pos. 206; PRONI T.307; LDS film 1279356.
1669	Newry and Mourne Poll Tax Returns. PRONI T1046.
1708	Householders in Downpatrick town. R.E. Parkinson, *The City of Downe.*
1720	Down and Antrim landed gentry. RIA 24 k 19.
1722–1970	Records of Southwell Charity School, Downpatrick. PRONI D/2664.

1740 Protestant householders (Kilbroney and Seapatrick). PRONI T.808/15258. Online: PRONI name search.

1746–89 'Deputy Court Cheque Book'—freeholders A–G only. PRONI D.654/A3/1B. Online: Freeholders.

1766 Kilbroney, Seapatrick, Inch: Online: PRONI name search. Shankill. NLI Ms. 4173; Lurgan NAI M2476; RCBL Ms. 23.

1775 Dissenters' petitions. Presbyterians in Ballee, Comber, Donacloney, Dundonald, Dromore, Dromara, Drumballyroney, Drumgooland, Killyleagh, Newry, Rathfriland, Seapatrick and Tullylish. PRONI T/808/14977; NLI Ms. 4173.

1777–95 Freeholders Registers. PRONI DOW 5/3/1 and 2 (1777, 1780, 1795), Lecale barony only, c.1790. PRONI T.393/1. Online: Freeholders.

1789 'Deputy Court Cheque Book' (votes cast). PRONI D.654/A3/1B. Online: Freeholders.

1796 Spinning-Wheel Premium List. 2,975 names for Co. Down. Online: Hayes.

1798 Persons who suffered losses in the 1798 Rebellion. Propertied classes only. c.180 names. NLI I 94107.

1799–1800 Militia Pay Lists and Muster Rolls. PRONI T.1115/4A C.

1803 Agricultural survey, recording householders, occupations and agricultural possessions. Covers parts at least of thirty parishes. See Maxwell, *Down Ancestors,* for details. More than 11,000 names. PRONI D/654/A2/1–37A-C.

1813–21 Freeholders. PRONI T.761/19; LDS film 258701. Online: Freeholders.

1815–46 Downpatrick electors. NLI Ms. 7235.

1820 Lisburn householders. PRONI T679/107–112.

1821 Some extracts. NAI Thrift Abstracts.

1823–38 Tithe Books.

1824 Freeholders. PRONI T.761/20. Online: Freeholders.

1831 Memorial of the inhabitants of part of Cos. Down and Armagh praying for relief, 21 April 1831. More than 1,300 names, 'more particularly in the neighbourhood of Shane Hill'—Knocknashane, Shankill Parish? NAI OP 974/122.

1837 Valuation of Newry town (heads of households). *Parliamentary Papers, 1837: Reports from Committees,* Vol. 2 (1), Appendix G.

1837 Marksmen (illiterate voters) in parliamentary boroughs: Newry and Downpatrick. *Parliamentary Papers, 1837: Reports from Committees,* Vol. 2 (i), Appendix A.

1837 Memorial from inhabitants of Lisburn. NAI OP 1837/10.

1839–1948 Some material, including admissions registers and relief registers, survives for all the unions of Co. Down. PRONI; LDS holds microfilm copies of Lurgan (259166–72) and Downpatrick (993164 part, 259159–61).

1841–61 Religious censuses: Aghaderg. RCBL Ms. 65.

1842	Voters. OP 1842/113.
1851	Some extracts. NAI Thrift Abstracts.
1851	Presbyterians only, Loughinisland. *Family Links*, Vol. 1, Nos. 5 and 7, 1982/3.
1851	Inhabitants of Scarva. Also Church of Ireland parishioners, 1858, 1860, 1861. RCBL Ms. 65.
1852	Poll Book (votes cast). Incomplete. PRONI D.671/02/5–6, D.671/02/7–8; LDS film 993158.
1861	Loughinisland. Presbyterians only. *Family Links*, Vol. 1, Nos. 5 and 7, 1982/3.
1863–4	Griffith's Valuation. Online: Askaboutireland.
1868	Census of the Church of Ireland parish of Shankill, Cos. Armagh and Down. Local clergyman.
1873	Census of the congregation of the Church of Ireland parish of Knockbreda, Co. Down. Also 1875; with Church of Ireland registers.
1884	A list of inhabitants of the Manor of Ardkeen. Savage estate. PRONI D.2223/15/10.
1901	Census. Online: NAI.
1911	Census. Online: NAI.
1912	The Ulster Covenant. Almost half a million original signatures and addresses of those who signed. Online: Covenant.

Online

Askaboutireland	<www.askaboutireland.ie>	
Bagenals Castle	<www.bagenalscastle.com>	Newry and Mourne
Covenant	<www.proni.gov.uk/ulstercovenant>	
Freeholders	<www.proni.gov.uk/freeholders>	34 Freeholders and voters' lists for Co. Down, 1746–1831
Hayes	<www.failteromhat.com>	
Headstones	<www.historyfromheadstones.com>	Comprehensive collection of inscriptions
Lecale	<www.lecalehistory.co.uk>	Lecale and Downe Historical Society
NAI	<www.census.nationalarchives.ie>	
PRONI name search	<www.proni.gov.uk>	

Publications

Local histories etc.

Clandeboye: a reading guide, Ballynahinch: South Eastern Education and Library Service, 1981. Blackwood family bibliography. NLI Ir 914115 p 15.

Donaghadee: a local history list, Ballynahinch: South Eastern Education and Library Service, 1981. NLI Ir 9411 s 12, 38 p.

Killyleagh and Crossegar: a local history list, Ballynahinch: South Eastern Education and Library Service, 1981. NLI Ir 914115 p 15, 18 p.

Atkinson, Edward D., *An Ulster Parish: Being a History of Donaghcloney*, Dublin: Hodges, Figgis, 1898. Jenny and Warren families. NLI Ir 94115 a 1, Waringstown, Co. Down.

—— *Dromore: an Ulster diocese*, Dundalk: W. Tempest, 1925. NLI Ir 274116 a 1, 317 p.

Barden, Sean, *Elm Park, 1626–1954: country house to preparatory school*, Belfast: UHF, 2004. NLI, 139 p.

Barry, J., *Hillsborough: a parish in the Ulster Plantation*, Belfast: W. Mullan, 1982. Ed. Wm. Mullin. NLI Ir 94115 b 3, 129 p.

Bowsie, George A., *Carryduff, 2000: a chronological record of events in the life and development of Carryduff, past and present, and memoirs of the district from bygone days*, 2000. Co-author, Graham Murphy. NLI Ir 94115 b 8, 90 p.

Buchanan, Rev. James, *An historical sketch of the Reformed Presbyterian Church of Rathfriland*, Newry: Newry Telegraph, 1908. NLI LO P 560, 23 p.

Buchanan, R.H., *Irish Historic Towns Atlas, 8: Downpatrick*, Dublin: RIA, 1997. NLI.

Cairns, Ann, *The Church and Community of St. John the Evangelist, Gilford: Sesquicentennial, 1850–2000*, Befast: Inglewood Press, 2002. Cardinal Tomás Ó Fiaich Library.

Canavan, T., *Frontier town: an illustrated history of Newry*, Belfast: Blackstaff Press, 1989.

Carr, P., *The most unpretending of places: a history of Dundonald*, Belfast: White Row Press, 1987. NLI Ir 94115 c 13, 252 p.

—— *Portavo, an Irish townland and its peoples, Part 1: earliest times to 1844*, Belfast: White Row Press, 2003. NLI, 339 p.

Clarke, R.S.J., *Gravestone Inscriptions, Co. Down, Vols. 1–20*, Belfast: UHF, 1971–89. NLI Ir 9292 c 43. See 'Gravestone inscriptions' below.

Cohen, Marilyn, *Linen, family and community in Tullylish, County Down, 1690–1914*, Dublin: Four Courts Press, 1997. NLI 94115 c 11, 287 p.

Cowan, J. Davison, *An Ancient Parish, Past and Present; being the Parish of Donaghmore, County Down*, London: D. Nutt, 1914. NLI Ir 94115 c 1, 402 p.

Crossle, Francis, *Local Jottings of Newry, Collected and Transcribed, Vols. 1–34*, Newry: 1890–1910.

Crowther, J.A. Claire, *The Cloughley family of Loughans, Co. Down, Ireland*, Claire Crowther, 1985. NLI GO 573.

Day, Angelique, and McWilliams, Patrick (eds.), *Ordnance Survey Memoirs of Ireland Series*, Belfast: Institute of Irish Studies and RIA, 1990–1997.
   —*Vol. 3: Co. Down I* (1990): Clonallan, Clonduff, Donaghmore, Drumballyroney, Drumgath, Drumgooland, Kilbroney, Kilcoo, Kilkeel, Kilmegan, Newry, Warrenpoint. NLI Ir 914111 o 12.
   —*Vol. 7: Co. Down II* (1991): Ardkeen, Ardquin, Ballyhalbert (Saint Andrew's), Ballyphilip, Ballytrustan, Ballywalter, Bangor, Castleboy, Comber, Donaghadee, Drumbeg, Drumbo, Dundonald, Grey Abbey, Holywood,

Inishargy, Kilinchy, Kilmood, Knockbreda, Newtownards, Saintfield, Slanes, Tullynakill, Witter. NLI Ir 9141 o 80.

—*Vol. 12: Co. Down III* (1993): Aghaderg, Annaclone, Annahilt, Blaris, Donaghcloney, Dromara, Dromore, Garvaghy, Hillsborough, Magheralin, Magherally, Moira, Seapatrick, Shankill, Tullylish. NLI Ir 914115 o 12.

—*Vol. 17: Co. Down IV* (1992): Ardglass, Ballee, Ballyculter, Ballykinler, Bright, Down, Dunsfort, Inch, Kilclief, Killyleagh, Kilmore, Loughinisland, Magheradrool, Rathmullan, Saul. NLI Ir 914111 o 12.

Ewart, L.M., *Handbook to the dioceses of Down, Connor and Dromore.*

Fisher Schmidt, Joanne C., *Tombstones of Ireland: Counties Down and Roscommon*, Bowie, Md.: Heritage Books, c.2000. LC CS448.D68, S36 2000, 110 p.

Haddock, Josiah, *A Parish Miscellany: Donaghcloney*, Lurgan: Mail Press, 1948. 41 p.

Hill, Rev. George, *Montgomery Manuscripts, 1603–1706*, Belfast: 1869.

Irwin, David, *Tide and Times in the 'Port: a narrative history of the Co. Down village of Groomsport*, Groomsport: Groomsport Presbyterian Church, 1993.

James, W.V., *Strangford: The Forgotten Past of Strangford Village*, Belfast: Northern Whig, 1994.

Keenan, Padraic, 'Clonallon Parish: its annals and antiquities', *JCLAHS*, Vol. 10. NLI.

—— *Historical Sketch of the Parish of Clonduff*, Newry: 1941.

Kelly, Charles, *The Kelly's of County Down: a record of . . . the Kelly's of County Down, with particular reference to Newtownards and surrounding parishes*, Ayr: C. Kelly, 1999? NLI GO 112, 132 p.

Knox, Alexander, *History of the County Down*, Dublin: 1875. NLI Ir 94115 k 2, 724 p. Reprinted Davidson Books, 1982.

Lamont, J.A., *Presbyterianism in Holywood: Bangor Road Congregation*, Bangor: 1967. NLI, 50 p.

Linn, Capt. Richard, *A history of Banbridge*, Belfast: 1935. Ed. W.S. Kerr. Including Tullylish.

Little, Canon G.L., *Historical Highlights: Parish of Aghaderg, Diocese of Dromore, Co. Down*, Banbridge: 1989. None specified.

Lockington, John W., *Robert Blair of Bangor*, Belfast: Presbyterian Historical Society of Ireland. Biographical portrait of Robert Blair (1593–1666), Presbyterian minister in Ulster and Scotland.

Lowrie, T.K., *The Hamilton Mss.: settlement of Clandeboye, Great Ardes, and Dufferin . . . by Sir James Hamilton, Knight (Viscount Claneboye) . . . reigns of James I and Charles I (with his family)*, Belfast: Archer & Sons, 1867. NLI Ir 94115 h 1, 166 p.

McCavery, T., *A covenant community: a history of Newtownards Reformed Presbyterian Church*, Newtownards: 1997. NLI Ir 285 m 40, 186 p.

—— *Newtown: a history of Newtownards*, Belfast: White Row Press, 1994. NLI Ir 94115 m 6, 221 p.

McCullogh, S., *Ballynahinch, Centre of Down*, Ballynahinch: Chamber of Commerce, 1968.

McIlrath, James, *The McIlrath letters: sent from Killinchy, New Zealand to Killinchy, County Down, 1860–1915*, Belfast: Killyleagh Branch, NIFHS, 2009. NLNZ, 143 p.

Monroe, Horace, *Foulis Castle and the Monroes of Lower Iveagh*, London: Mitchell, Hughes & Clarke, 1929. NLI Ir 9292 m 10, 83 p.

Nangle, F.R. and J.F.T., *A short account of the Nangle family of Downpatrick*, F. Nangle, 1986. NLI Ir 9292 n 8, 46 p.

O'Donovan, John, *Letters containing information relative to the [history and] antiquities of the County of Down (1834)*, Dublin: Browne & Nolan, 1909. NLI Ir 94115 o 1, 92 p.

O'Laverty, Rev. James, *An Historical Account of the Dioceses of Down and Connor*, Dublin: 1878–89, 4 vols.

Parkinson, Edward, *The City of Down from its earliest days*, Bangor: Donard Publishing Co., 1977. Reprint of 1928 edition. NLI Ir 94115 p 1, 162 p.

Patton, W.D., *A short history of First Dromore Presbyterian Church, 1660–1981*, Banbridge: Review Press, 1982. NLI, 55 p.

Pilson, A., *Downpatrick and its Parish Church*, 1852. Including lists of clergy and churchwardens. NLI P 1938.

Pooler, L.A., *Down and its Parishes*, 1907.

Proudfoot, Lindsey, *County Down: history and society*, Dublin: Geography Publications, 1997. NLI Ir 94115 d 2, 698.

Rankin, Kathleen, *The linen houses of the Lagan Valley: the story of their families*, Belfast: UHF, 2002. NLI, 221 p.

Redpath, Beverly J., *The Monk family from Bally William, Co. Down, Ireland: across the world, a family history*, Avoca, Vic.: B. and A. Redpath, 1989. LC CS71.M73715 1989.

Reeves, William, *Ecclesiastical Antiquities of Down, Connor and Dromore*, 1847.

Reilly, E.J.S., *A genealogical history of the family of Montgomery, comprising the lines of Eglinton and Braidstane in Scotland, and Mount-Alexander and Grey-Abbey in Ireland*, 1942. NLI Ir 9292 m 24, 84 p.

Reside, S.W., *St Mary's Church, Newry: its History*, 1933.

Roden, Clodagh Rose Jocelyn, Countess of, *Kilcoo Parish Church, Bryansford*, 1971. NLI, 31 p.

Rudnitzky, Honor, *Killinchy Parish Church: [written] to celebrate the 150th anniversary of the consecration of the present church*, Killinchy: 1980. NLI, 19.

Smith, Charles, *The Ancient and Present State of the County of Down*, Dublin: 1744. Co-author, Walter Harris. NLI I 94115 h 2. Reprinted Ballynahinch: Davidson Books, 1977.

Smith, K., *Bangor Reading List*. NLI, 'Journal of the Bangor Historical Society'.

Wilson, A.M., *Saint Patrick's town: a history of Downpatrick and the Barony of Lecal*, Belfast: Isabella Press, 1995. NLI Ir 94115 w 5, 243 p.

Local journals
12 Miles of Mourne: Journal of the Mourne Local Studies Group. NLI Ir 94115 T 1.
Craigavon Historical Society Review. LHL.
Down and Connor Historical Society's Journal. LHL.
Irish Family Links. NLI Ir 9292 f 19.
Journal of the Bangor Historical Society. NLI Ir 94115 b 4.
Lecale Miscellany.
Lisburn Historical Society Journal. LHL.
North Irish Roots: Journal of the North of Ireland Family History Society. NLI Ir
    92905 n 4.
Old Newry Journal.
Saintfield Heritage. LHL.
Seanchas Dhroim Mór: Journal of the Dromore Diocesan Historical Society. NLI Ir
    94115 s 3.
Ulster Journal of Archaeology. NLI Ir 794105 u 1.

Directories
Thirty Belfast and Ulster directories are online at PRONI.

1807/1808	Joseph Smith, *Belfast Directories.* Reprinted as J.R.R. Adams (ed.), *Merchants in Plenty*, Belfast: UHF, 1992. NLI Ir 914111.S.27.
1811	Holden's *Annual London and country directory of the United Kingdoms and Wales, in three volumes, for . . . 1811.* Facsimile reprint, Norwich: M. Winton, 1996. NLI G 942 h 23; LDS film 258722 item 2.
1819	Thomas Bradshaw's *General directory of Newry, Armagh, and the towns of Dungannon, Portadown, Tandragee, Lurgan, Waringstown, Banbridge, Warrenpoint, Rosstrevor, Kilkeel, Rathfriland, 1820.* PRONI; NLI Ir 91411 b 18; LDS film 258723.
1820	Joseph Smyth, *Directory of Belfast and its Vicinity.*
1820	J. Pigot, *Commercial Directory of Ireland.* PRONI; NLI Ir 9141 p 107; LDS film 962702 item 1.
1824	J. Pigot & Co., *City of Dublin and Hibernian Provincial Directory.* NLI; LDS film 451787. Online: Hayes.
1835	Matier's *Belfast Directory.* PRONI; NLI Ir 9141111 m 5; LDS film 258724.
1839	Martin, *Belfast Directory*, PRONI; NLI Ir 9141111 m 4. Also 1841, 1842.
1843–52	Henderson's *Belfast and Province of Ulster Directory.* PRONI; NLI Dix Belfast (1852); LDS film 908816 item 1.
1846	Slater's *National Commercial Directory of Ireland.* PRONI; NLI LO; LDS film 1696703 item 3. Online: Hayes.
1854	James A. Henderson, *Belfast and Province of Ulster Directory.* Issued also in 1854, 1856, 1858, 1861, 1863, 1865, 1868, 1870, 1877, 1880, 1884, 1887, 1890, 1894 and 1900.
1856	Slater, *Royal National Commercial Directory of Ireland.* NLI; LDS film 1472360 item 1.

1865	R. Wynne, *Business Directory of Belfast*. NLI Ir 91411 b 2.
1870	Slater, *Directory of Ireland*. NLI.
1881	Slater, *Royal National Commercial Directory of Ireland*. NLI. Online: FindMyPast.
1883	Farrell, *County Armagh Directory and Almanac* (Newry).
1888	George Henry Bassett, *The Book of Antrim*. Lisburn and Dromara. Reprinted Belfast: Friar's Bush Press, 1989. NLI Ir 94116 b 29.
1888	George Henry Bassett, *The Book of Armagh* (Donaghcloney, Moira, Waringstown).
1894	Slater, *Royal Commercial Directory of Ireland*. NLI.

Gravestone inscriptions

The Ulster Historical Foundation has transcripts for 128 graveyards in Co. Down. Heritage World has transcripts of 56 graveyards. These are searchable online for a fee at <*www.historyfromheadstones.com*>. Published or freely available transcripts are given below, ordered by civil parish.

Gravestone Inscriptions, Co. Down, Vols. 1–20, R.S.J. Clarke, 1966–81. NLI Ir 9295 c 1.

Annaclone: Ballydown, Pres. Vol. 20.
Annahilt: Cargacreevy, Pres. Vol. 18.
Cargygary (Loughaghery), Pres. Vol. 18.
—— Glebe (Annahilt), C of I. Vol. 18.
Ardglass: Ardglass town, C of I. Vol. 8.
Ardkeen: Ardkeen. Vol. 13.
—— Kirkistown, C of I. Vol. 13.
—— Ballycran Beg, RC (one inscription). Vol. 13.
—— Lisbane, RC. Vol. 13.
Ardquin: Ardquin, C of I. Vol. 13.
Ballee: Church Ballee, C of I. Vol. 8.
—— Church Ballee, Pres. NS/Unitarian. Vol. 8.
Ballyculter: Ballyculter Upper, C of I. Vol. 8.
—— Strangford Lower, C of I. Vol. 8.
Ballykinler: Ballykinler Upper, RC. Vol. 16.
—— Ballykinler Upper, RC. Vol. 9.
Ballyphilip: Portaferry town (Ballyphilip). Vol. 13.
—— Ballygalget, RC. Vol. 13.
Ballytrustan: Ballytrustan, RC. Vol. 13.
Ballywalter: Whitechurch. Vol. 15.
Bangor: Castle Park, Bangor (one inscription). Vol. 17.
—— Conlig town, Pres. Vol. 17.
—— Groomsport, Pres. Vol. 17.
—— Groomsport, C of I. Vol. 17.
—— Ballyleidy (Clandeboye House), family graveyard. Vol. 17.

—— Bangor Church, C of I interior. Vol. 17.

—— Bangor Abbey. Vol. 17.

—— Ballygilbert Church, Pres. (one inscription). Vol. 17.

—— Copeland Island. Vol. 16.

—— Bangor, Pres. (First). Vol. 17.

Blaris: Maze, Pres. Vol. 18.

—— Blaris. Vol. 5.

—— Eglantine, C of I. Vol. 18.

—— Eglantine, C of I. Vol. 18.

Bright: Bright, C of I and mixed. Vol. 8.

Castleboy: Cloghy/Clough, Pres. Vol. 14.

Comber: Comber, the Square, C of I. Vol. 5.

—— Gransha, Pres. Vol. 1.

—— Moneyreagh, Pres. NS (Unitarian). Vol. 1.

Donaghadee: Templepatrick. Vol. 14.

—— Ballymacruise (Millisle), Pres. Vol. 16.

—— Ballycopeland, Pres. Vol. 16.

—— Donaghadee, Church Lane, C of I, Vol. 16.

—— Ballyrawer, C of I. Vol. 14.

Donaghcloney: Donaghcloney. Vol. 19.

—— Waringstown town, C of I. Vol. 19.

Down: Downpatrick, Church Lane, C of I. Vol. 7.

—— Downpatrick, Fountain St, Pres. Vol. 7.

—— Downpatrick, Stream St, RC. Vol. 7.

—— Downpatrick, Stream St, Unitarian (Pres. NS). Vol. 7.

—— Downpatrick, English St, C of I. Vol. 7.

Dromara: Finnis, RC. Vol. 19.

—— Drumgavlin, Magherahamlet. Vol. 9.

—— Dromara, C of I. Vol. 19.

—— Drumgavlin, Magherahamlet Pres. Vol. 9.

Dromore: Dromore, Church St, C of I. Vol. 19.

—— Drumlough. Vol. 19.

Drumbeg: Drennan, Pres. (Baileysmill). Vol. 2.

—— Drumbeg, C of I. Vol. 3.

Drumbo: Ballycarn, Pres. Vol. 1.

Knockbreckan, Pres. (reformed). Vol. 1.

—— Edenderry House, Dunlop family. Vol. 3.

—— Carrickmaddyroe, Pres. Vol. 2.

—— Drumbo, Pres. Vol. 4.

—— Carryduff, Pres. Vol. 1.

—— Ballelessan, C of I. Vol. 1.

—— Legacurry, Pres. Vol. 2.

—— Ballelessan, C of I. Vol. 18.

—— Carryduff, Pres. Vol. 18.

Dundonald: Dundonald town, C of I. Vol. 2.
Dunsfort: Dunsfort, C of I. Vol. 8.
—— Dunsfort, St Mary's, RC. Vol. 8.
Garvaghy: Fedany (Garvaghy?), C of I. Vol. 19.
—— Kilkinamurry, Pres. Vol. 19.
—— Ballooly. Vol. 19.
Greyabbey: Rosemount, Grey Abbey grounds and graveyard. Vol. 12.
Hillsborough: Hillsborough, Main St, C of I. Vol. 18.
—— Ballykeel Edenagonnell (Annahilt), Pres. Vol. 18.
—— Corcreeny, Moravian. Vol. 18.
—— Corcreeny, C of I. Vol. 19.
—— Hillsborough, Park St, Quaker. Vol. 18.
—— Reillys Trench, RC. Vol. 18.
—— Corcreeny, C of I. Vol. 18.
Holywood: Holywood, Old Church Lane, Priory? Vol. 4.
Inch: Inch, C of I. Vol. 7.
Inishargy: Balliggan, C of I. Vol. 14.
—— Kircubbin, Pres. Vol. 12.
—— Inishargy, Old. Vol. 14.
Kilclief: Kilclief, C of I. Vol. 8.
—— Kilclief, St Malachy's, RC. Vol. 8.
Kilkeel: Kilkeel, Bridge St, Vol. 10.
—— Mourne Abbey, one inscription only. Vol. 10.
—— Glasdrumman, RC, Vol. 10.
—— Moneydorragh More, C of I (Kilhorne). Vol. 10.
—— Kilkeel, Newry St, C of I. Vol. 10.
Kilkeel, Greencastle St, Pres. (Mourne). Vol. 10.
—— Ballymartin, RC. Vol. 10.
—— Ballymageogh, RC. Vol. 10.
—— Kilkeel, Newcastle St, Moravian. Vol. 10.
Killaney: Carrickmaddyroe, Pres. (Boardmills). Vol. 2.
—— Killaney, C of I. Vol. 2.
Killinchy: Ballygowan (Killinchy?), Pres. Vol. 5.
—— Killinakin, two inscriptions only. Vol. 6.
—— Ballymacashen, Pres. (reformed). Vol. 6.
—— Ravara, Unitarian. Vol. 5.
—— Killinchy, C of I. Vol. 5.
—— Balloo, Pres. Vol. 6.
—— Drumreagh (Kilcarn?), RC. Vol. 5.
Killyleagh: Killyleagh, Church Hill St, C of I. Vol. 6.
—— Killyleagh, The Plantation, Pres. Vol. 7.
—— Toy and Kirkland, Killaresy graveyard. Vol. 6.
—— Killyleagh Old. Vol. 6.
—— Tullymacnous, one inscription. Vol. 6.

Kilmegan: Moneylane (Kilmegan?), C of I. Vol. 9.
—— Aghalasnafin, RC. Vol. 9.
Kilmood: Kilmood and Ballybunden, C of I. Vol. 5.
—— Ballyministragh, Pres. Vol. 5.
Kilmore: Barmaghery, one inscription only. Vol. 1.
—— Carnacully (Kilmore?), C of I. Vol. 3.
—— Drumaghlis, Pres. (Kilmore). Vol. 3.
—— Rademan, Pres. NS (Unitarian). Vol. 3.
Lambeg: Lisnatrunk, Pres. (Hillhall). Vol. 1.
Loughinisland: Tievenadarragh, Mixed. Vol. 9.
—— Seaforde town, C of I. Vol. 9.
—— Clough town, Pres. Vol. 9.
—— Clough town, Unitarian. Vol. 9.
—— Drumaroad, RC. Vol. 9.
Magheradrool: Ballynahinch, C of I. Vol. 9.
—— Ballynahinch, Windmill St, Pres. Vol. 9.
—— Ballynahinch, Dromore St, Pres. Vol. 9.
Magheralin: Ballymakeonan (Magheralin?). Vol. 19.
Magherally: Magherally, C of I. Vol. 20.
—— Magherally, Pres. Vol. 20.
Moira: Moira (Clare). Vol. 18.
—— Moira, Pres. NS. Vol. 18.
—— Lurganville, RC. Vol. 18.
—— Moira, Pres. Vol. 18.
Newtownards: Ballyblack, Pres. Vol. 12.
—— Milecross, RC (Killysuggan). Vol. 5.
—— Movilla. Vol. 11.
—— Newtownards Chuch interior, C of I. Vol. 11.
—— Newtownards Priory. Vol. 11.
Rathmullan: Rathmulland Upper, C of I. Vol. 9.
—— Rossglass, RC. Vol. 8.
—— Killough, Palatine Square, C of I. Vol. 8.
Saintfield: Saintfield town, Pres. Vol. 3.
—— Saintfield town, C of I. Vol. 3.
—— Saintfield, Cow Market, Pres. Vol. 3.
Saul: Saul, C of I. Vol. 7.
—— Ballysugagh (Saul?), RC. Vol. 8.
Seapatrick: Banbridge, Scarva St, Vol. 20.
—— Kilpike (Seapatrick?). Vol. 20.
Slanes: Slanes. Vol. 14.
St Andrews alias Ballyhalbert: Ballyesborough, C of I. Vol. 15.
—— Ballyhemlin, Pres. NS and Unitarian. Vol. 14.
—— Ballyhalbert. Vol. 15.
—— Glastry, Pres. Vol. 15.

Tullylish: Tullylish, C of I. Vol. 20.
——— Moyallon, Quaker. Vol. 20.
——— Laurencetown. Vol. 20.
——— Clare. Vol. 19.
Tullynakill: Tullynakill, C of I. Vol. 1.

Estate records

Anglesea. Tenants on the Anglesea estate, 1856, *JCLAHS*, 12 (2), 1950, pp. 151–3, covering areas in the civil parish of Newry.

Annesley, Earls. Rentals, 1650–1950. PRONI D/1503. Covering townlands in the civil parishes of Clonduff, Drumballyroney, Drumgooland, Kilcoo and Kilmegan. May cover further parishes.

Bangor, Lord. Rent account book, 1801–1809. PRONI T.1128/70. Covering areas in the civil parish of Ballyculter.

Bateson. Arrears of rent, 1820–27; Rentals of c.25 townlands, 1830–41, 1820–41. PRONI MIC.77. Covering areas in the civil parish of Moira.

Blackwood Price. 1840–1920. PRONI D.2223/20/1–4. Covering areas in the civil parishes of Comber, Dunsfort and Saintfield.

Burgess. Rentals for Gilford, 1800. PRONI D.1594. Covering areas in the civil parish of Tullylish.

Chichester Fortescue. Rental, 1817. NAI, M3610. Covering areas in the civil parishes of Donaghcloney, Magherally, Seapatrick and Donaghadee.

Clanbrassil. Rent roll with early eighteenth-century annotations. Much detail on tenants, 1670. PRONI T.2253. Covering areas in the civil parishes of Ballyhalbert, alias St Andrews, Ballywalter, Bangor, Donaghadee, Holywood and Inishargy.

Clanwilliam. Rentals, 1829–1939. PRONI D.3044/A/1–7. Covering areas in the civil parish of Dromore.

Cleland. Rentals, 1854–1912. PRONI D.2223/4/1–9. Covering areas in the civil parishes of Ballyhalbert, alias St Andrews, Castleboy, Donaghadee, Drumgooland, Dunsfort, Greyabbey and Kilmore.

Crommelin. Rentals, 1609–1860. PRONI D.2223/9/1–26. Covering areas in the civil parishes of Comber and Donaghadee.

De Clifford. Rental, 1789–92. PRONI D.3696/C/6. Covering areas in the civil parishes of Ballee, Down, Inch and Saul.

Downshire. Rentals, 1650–1880. PRONI D.671. Covering areas in the civil parishes of Ballykinler, Clonduff, Hillsborough and Kilmegan.

Dungannon. Rentals, 1818–1900. PRONI D.1954/1–7. Covering areas in the civil parish of Drumbo. May cover areas in other parishes.

Fitzgerald. Leases (information on holdings, leases and tenants), 1814. PRONI T.3670. Covering areas in the civil parish of Ballyculter.

Ford. Rentals, 1714–1876. PRONI D.566. Covering areas in the civil parishes of Dromara, Kilmore, Loughinisland and Magheradrool.

Hall. Rentals, 1814–1914. PRONI D.2090/2–7. Covering areas in the civil parishes of Ballymore, Killevy and Warrenspoint.

Ker. Rentals, 1731–1944. PRONI D.2223/2/1–29. Covering areas in the civil parishes of Bangor, Holywood, Kilclief and Saintfield.

Kilmorey. Rental, 1816 PRONI D/2638. Covering townlands in the civil parishes of Kilkeel and Magheralin and Newry. May cover further parishes.

Londonderry, Marquis of. Rentals, 1750–1800. PRONI D.654. Covering areas in the civil parishes of Ballee, Ballywalter, Comber, Greyabbey, Killinchy, Kilmood and Newtownards.

Martin. Rents, 1817–53. PRONI D.2722/7. Covering areas in the civil parish of Magherally.

Nugent. Rentals, 1641–1952. PRONI D552/B/3/1/1–184. Covering areas in the civil parishes of Ardquin, Ballyphilip, Ballytrustan and Witter.

Perceval-Maxwell. Rentals, 1803–1922. PRONI D.1556. Covering areas in the civil parishes of Ballee, Bangor and Inch.

Price. Rental, 1788–1802. PRONI T.2101/3–4. Covering areas in the civil parish of Saintfield.

Saunders. Rent roll for Newtownards, Comber, Belfast and Carrickfergus, 1771–8. PRONI D.1759/3B/7.

Wallace. Rent roll for Ravara, Lisowen and Downpatrick, 1824–5. PRONI D.2223/11/3. Covering areas in the civil parishes of Down, Killinchy and Saintfield.

Whyte. Rentals and rent accounts, Loughbrickland, 1738–1910. PRONI D.1167. Covering areas in the civil parish of Aghaderg.

DUBLIN

Census returns and substitutes

1461–1774	Admissions to the freedom of Dublin. Online: Dublin Heritage.
1568	Herald's Visitation of Dublin. GO 46; also NLI Pos. 957.
1607–1610	Herald's Visitation of Dublin city and county. GO 48; NLI Pos. 957.
1621	St John's Parish cess lists. Also for years 1640 and 1687. JPRS, Appendix to Vol. 1, 1906. LDS film 82407.
1634	Book of Survey and Distribution. NLI Ms. 964.
1641	Testimonies of 474 witnesses to the 1641 Rebellion. Online: 1641.
1652	Inhabitants of the baronies of Newcastle and Uppercross. NAI M.2467.
1654–6	*Civil Survey*, Vol. 7.
1659	Pender's 'Census'. Reprinted GPC, 1997; IMC, 2002. LDS film 924648.
1663–8	Subsidy roll for Co. Dublin. NAI NA M.2468.
1664	Persons with six hearths or upwards, Dublin city. RDKPRI, No. 57, p. 560.
1667–1810	Assessments for the parish of St Bride's. TCD M. 2063.
1680	Pipe water accounts. IG, 1987; also 1703–1704, IG, 1994.
1680–86	Index only to an applotment book for Dublin city. NAI M. 4979.
1684	List of those eligible for jury service. IG, 8, No. 1, 1990, pp. 49–57.
1711–1835	Annual cess applotment books of St Michan's Parish. RCBL.

1730–40	Index to marriages and deaths in *Pue's Occurrences* and the *Dublin Gazette*. NLI Ms. 3197.
1756	'Inhabitants of St Michael's Parish', *Irish Builder*, Vol. 33, pp. 170–71.
1761	Dublin city voting freemen and freeholders. NLI I 6511 Dubl.
1766	Crumlin. RCBL; also in GO 537; Castleknock, RCBL Ms. 37; Taney, NAI M2478; LDS film 258517. Castleknock, Clonsilla and Taney online: PRONI name search.
1767	Freeholders. NAI M. 4910–12.
1778–82	Catholic Merchants, Traders and Manufacturers of Dublin. *Reportorium Novum*, 2(2), 1960, p. 298, 323.
1791–1831	Register of children at Baggot St School (Incorporated Society for Promoting Protestant Schools). NLI Pos. 2884.
1791–1957	Register of Admissions to Pleasant's Female Orphan Asylum, including places of birth and families. NLI Ms. 1555. See also Mss. 1556 and 1558.
1793–1810	Census of Protestants in Castleknock. GO 495; LDS film 100225.
1798	Persons who suffered losses in the 1798 Rebellion. Propertied classes only. c.100 names. NLI I 94107. Online: Hayes.
1798–1831	Register of children at Santry School (Incorporated Society for Promoting Protestant Schools). NLI Pos. 2884.
1805–1839	Register of children at Kevin St School (Incorporated Society for Promoting Protestant Schools). NLI Pos. 2884.
1806	Voters' lists, by occupation. NLI Ir 94133 d 13.
1807	Board of Works tradesmen's names and occupations, Dublin city, *DLGSJ*, 4 (2), 1995.
1820	Freemen voters. NLI P 734.
1821	Some extracts. NAI Thrift Abstracts.
1823–38	Tithe Books.
1826	Labourers' accounts, May–June 1826. c.300 names. NAI OP 727 1–199. Relief tickets, June–Sept. 1826. NAI OP 726. Almost all weavers from the Liberties. See Magee, *Weavers* (1993).
1828–2006	Glasnevin Cemetery burial records, many including details of addresses and next of kin. Online: Glasnevin.
1830	Freeholders. NLI Ms. 11,847.
1831	Householders in St Bride's Parish. NLI P. 1994.
1834–5	Returns of those liable for paying tax. Inquiry into the impeachment of Alderman Richard Smith (formerly in State Paper Office). NAI.
1835	Alphabetical list of voters, with addresses and occupations. NLI Ir 94133 d 12.
1835–7	Dublin county freeholders and leaseholders. NLI Ms. 9363.
1837	Memorial from Balbriggan for General Sessions (c.300 names). NAI OP 1837/413 c.
1840–1938	Admissions and discharge registers for Dublin city workhouses (North BG/78 and South BG/79). NAI.

1841	Some extracts. NAI Thrift Abstracts.
1843	Voters. NAI 1843/52.
1844–50	Householders, St Peter's Parish. RCBL P45/15/1, 2.
1847–51	Griffith's Valuation. Online: Askaboutireland.
1848–9	Smith O'Brien Petition. Eneclann CD ENEC002. More than 40,000 names for Dublin. Online: FindMyPast.
1851	Index only to heads of households, by street and parish. NAI Cen 1851/18/1; Eneclann CD ENEC003. Online: Origins, FindMyPast.
1864	City of Dublin Voters' List, by district and street. NLI Ir 94133 d 16.
1865–6	Voters. NLI Ir 94133 d 15.
1878	Voters, South Dock Ward only. NLI ILB 324 d.
1901	Census. Online: NAI.
1911	Census. Online: NAI.

Online

1641	<www.1641.tcd.ie>	
Askaboutireland	<www.askaboutireland.ie>	
Chapters	<www.chaptersofdublin.com>	Many Dublin histories
Dublin Heritage	<www.dublinheritage.ie>	Voters, graveyeards, freemen and more
Hayes, John	<www.failteromhat.com>	
FindMyPast	<www.findmypast.ie>	
Glasnevin	<www.glasnevintrust.ie>	
Loughman, Trish	<www.dublin1850.com>	
NAI	<www.census.nationalarchives.ie>	
Origins	<www.originsnetwork.com>	
Uphill, Christine	<freepages.genealogy.rootsweb.com/~chrisu>	Howth

Publications

Local histories etc.

Here Lyeth . . . a record and description of the graveyards of Grange Abbey, Coolock, Raheny and Kilbarrack and a summary of the history of their parishes, Dublin: Grange Abbey Restoration Committee, 1987. DCLA, 89 p.

St Peter's Parochial Male and Female Boarding Schools, Sunday, Daily and Infant Schools: Reports, 1850–60. NLI P. 439.

Aalen, F.H., *Dublin city and county: From prehistory to present,* Dublin: Geography Publications, 1992. Co-editor, Kevin Whelan. NLI Ir 94133 d 48, 450 p.

Adams, B.N, *History and Description of Santry and Cloghran Parishes,* London: Mitchell & Hughes, 1883. NLI Ir 94133 a 1, 144 p.

Appleyard, D.S, *Green Fields Gone Forever,* Coolock: Coolock Select Vestry, 1985. Coolock and Artane area. NLI Ir 94133 a 5, 214 p.

—— *In and out of school: over two centuries of Coolock and Raheny School,* Governors of Raheny and Coolock Schools, 1989. NLI 120 p.

Ball, F.E., *A history of the County of Dublin, Vol. 1–6,* Dublin: 1902–1920. NLI Ir 94133 b 1. Online: Chapters.

1. Monkstown, Kill of the Grange, Dalkey, Killiney, Tully, Stillorgan, Kilmacud.
2. Donnybrook, Booterstown, St Bartholemew, St Mark, Taney, St Peter, Rathfarnham.
3. Tallaght, Cruagh, Whitechurch, Kilgobbin, Kiltiernan, Rathmichael, Old Connaught, Saggart, Rathcoole, Newcastle.
4. Clonsilla, Leixlip, Lucan, Aderrig, Kilmactalway, Kilbride, Kilmahuddrick, Esker, Palmerstown, Ballyfermot, Clondalkin, Drimnagh, Crumlin, St Catherine, St Nicholas Without, St James, St Jude, Chapelizod.
5. Howth.
6. Castleknock, Mulhuddert, Cloghran, Ward, St Margaret's, Finglas, Glasnevin, Grangegorman, St George, Clonturk.

—— *The Parish of Taney,* Dublin: 1895. NLI Ir 94133 b 2, 256 p.

Blacker, Rev. Beaver H., *Sketches of the Parishes of Booterstown and Donnybrook,* Dublin: 1860–74. NLI Ir 94133 b 6, 488 p.

Byrne, Joseph, *War and peace: the survival of the Talbots of Malahide, 1641–71,* Dublin: Irish Academic Press, 1997. NLI Ir 94133 b 17, 76 p.

Byrne, Roy H., *From generation to generation: Clondalkin, village, parish and neighbourhood,* Clondalkin: the authors, 1990.

Cantwell, Brian, *Memorials of the Dead, North-East Wicklow* (1) (typescript), 1974. NLI Ir 9295 c 2, Master Index, Vol. 10.

—— *Memorials of the Dead: South Dublin,* Dublin: Genealogical Office, 1990.

Carroll, Frieda, *Booterstown, Co. Dublin, Ireland school registers, 1861–72 and 1891–1939,* Dún Laoghaire: Dún Laoghaire Genealogical Society, 1998. NLI Ir 9291 g 7.

Clare, Liam, *Enclosing the commons: Dalkey, the Sugar Loaves and Bray, 1820–70,* Dublin: Four Courts Press, 2004. NLI 4A 3362, 64 p.

Clarke, H.B., *Irish Historic Towns Atlas, 11: Dublin, Part 1 to 1610,* Dublin: RIA, 2002. NLI.

Clarke, Mary, *Sources for Genealogical Research in Dublin Corporation Archives.* IG, 1987. NLI.

Collins, James, *Life in old Dublin: historical associations of Cook Street: three centuries of Dublin printing: reminiscences of a great tribune,* Dublin: J. Duffy, 1913. NLI Ir 94133 c 6. Online: Chapters.

Collins, Sinéad, *Balrothery Poor Law Union, County Dublin, 1839–51,* Dublin: Four Courts Press, 2005. NLI, 64 p.

Connell, Carmel, *Glasnevin Cemetery, Dublin, 1832–1900,* Dublin: Four Courts Press, 2004. NLI 4A 3360, 72 p.

Coote, Michael H., *A short history of Taney Parish,* Dublin: Select Vestry of Taney Parish, 1969. Research by R.C.H. [i.e. R.H.C.] Townshend, compiled and edited by Michael H. Coote. NLI Ir 2741 p 41, 84 p.

Costello, Peter, *Dublin Churches*, Dublin: Gill & Macmillan, 1989. NLI Ir 720 c 23, 238 p.

Craig, Maurice, *Dublin, 1660–1800*, London: Penguin, 1992. NLI Ir 91433 c 25, 367 p.

Crawford, John, *Among the graves: inscriptions in St. Audoen's Church, Cornmarket, Dublin*, Dublin: Select Vestry of St Patrick's Cathedral Group of Parishes, 1990. DCLA.

—— *St Catherine's Parish Dublin, 1840–1900: portrait of a Church of Ireland community*, Blackrock, Co. Dublin: Irish Academic Press, 1996. NLI Ir 27413 c 11, 57 p.

—— *Within the walls: the story of St. Audoen's Church, Cornmarket, Dublin*, Dublin: Select Vestry of St Patrick's Cathedral Group of Parishes, 1986. NLI.

Cronin, Elizabeth, *Fr Michael Dungan's Blanchardstown, 1836–68*, Dublin: Four Courts Press, 2002. NLI, 64 p.

Cullen, L.N, *Princes and Pirates: the Dublin Chamber of Commerce, 1783–1983*. NLI Ir 94133 c 17.

D'Alton, John, *The history of the County of Dublin*, Dublin: Hodges & Smith, 1838. NLI Ir 94133 d 1, 943 p. Online: Chapters.

Donnelly, Nicholas, *Series of short histories of Dublin parishes*, Dublin: Catholic Truth Society of Ireland, 1905. NLI Ir 27413 d 1.

Doolin, W., *Dublin's surgeon-anatomists and other essays: a centenary tribute*, Dublin: Dept. of History of Medicine, RCSI, 1987. NLI Ir 610 d 8, 232 p.

Dublin Public Libraries, *Dublin in Books: A reading list from the stock of Dublin Public Libraries*, Dublin: 1982. NLI Ir 941 p 127(1), 22 p.

Egan, Michael E., *Memorials of the Dead: Dublin City and County*, Vols. 1–10 (typescript), 1992–2004. NLI; NAI.

Fingal Heritage Group, '*In Fond Remembrance*': Headstone Inscriptions, No. 2: St. Columba's Graveyard, Dublin: 1990. NLI Ir 9295 p 1(2), 24 p.

Finlayson, Rev. John, *Inscriptions on the monuments, mural tablets etc. at present existing in Christ Church Cathedral*, Dublin: Hodges, Foster & Figgis, 1878. NLI Ir 9295 f 1, 110 p.

Fitzpatrick, William J., *History of the Dublin Catholic cemeteries*, Dublin: Catholic Cemeteries Committee, 1900. NLI Ir 71941 f 1, 235 p. Online: Chapters.

Flanagan, John, *Malahide Past and Present*, Malahide: the author, 1986. NLI Ir 94133 f 8, 176 p.

Gilbert, Sir John T., *A History of the City of Dublin*, Dublin: 1885–9. NLI Ir 94133 g 3, 3 vols. Online: Chapters.

Gilbert Library, *Dublin and Irish Collections*, Dublin. NLI Ir 02 p 50.

Goodbody, Rob, *Sir Charles Domvile and the management of his Shankill estate, Co. Dublin, 1857–68*, Dublin: Four Courts Press, 2003. NLI, 64 p.

Guilfoyle, Eithne, *Harold (Boys') School, Glasthule, County Dublin: Registers, 1904–48*, Dún Laoghaire: Dún Laoghaire Genealogical Society, 1998. NLI Ir 9291 g 7, 145 p.

Harris, Walter, *The History and Antiquities of the city of Dublin*, Dublin: 1776. Online: Chapters.

Harrison, W., *Dublin Houses, or Memorable Dublin Houses*, Dublin: 1890. NLI Ir 94133 h 5.

Joyce, Weston St John, *The neighbourhood of Dublin, its topography, antiquities and historical associations*, Dublin: M.H. Gill & Son, 1939. NLI Ir 914133 j 4.

Keane, Rory, et al. (eds.), *Ardgillan Castle and the Taylor Family*, Balbriggan, Co. Dublin: Ardgillan Castle, 1995. NLI Ir 94133 a 8, 65 p.

Kelly, James, *The Liberty and Ormond Boys: factional riots in eighteenth-century Dublin*, Dublin: Four Courts Press, 2005. NLI, 64 p.

Kingston, Rev. John, *The Parish of Fairview*, Dundalk: Dundalgan Press, 1953. 'Including the present parishes of Corpus Christi, Glasnevin, Larkhill, Marino, and Donnycarney.' NLI Ir 94133 k 2, 121 p.

Lacey, Jim, *A candle in the window: a history of the barony of Castleknock*, Cork: Mercier Press, 2007. NLI, 224 p.

Leeper, A., *Historical handbook to the monuments, inscriptions, &c., of the collegiate, national and cathedral church of St. Patrick, Dublin*, Dublin: Hodges, Foster & Figgis, 1878. NLI Ir 7266 L 11, 74 p.

Le Fanu, T.P., *The Huguenot Churches of Dublin and their Ministries*, 1905. NLI P. 2274.

Lennon, Colm, *Irish Historic Towns Atlas, 19: Dublin, Part II, 1610 to 1756*, Dublin: RAI, 2008. NLI. Online: <*www.logainm.ie*>.

—— *The lords of Dublin in the age of Reformation*, Dublin: Irish Academic Press, 1989. NLI Ir 94133 L 12, 357 p.

McCamley, Bill, *Dublin tram workers, 1872–1945*, Dublin: Labour History Workshop, 2008. NLI, 275 p.

McCready, C.T., *Dublin street names, dated and explained*, Dublin: Hodges, Figgis, 1892. NLI Ir 92941 m 1, 160 p. Online: Chapters.

McDonnell, Annette, *Petitioners against closure of Kill o' the Grange Cemetery, County Dublin, 1864*, Dún Laoghaire: Dún Laoghaire Genealogical Society, 1998. NLI Ir 9291 g 7, 134 p.

Mac Giolla Phádraig, Brian, *History of Terenure*, Dublin: Veritas, 1954.

MacSorley, Catherine M., *The Story of Our Parish: St Peter's Dublin*, Dublin: 1917. NLI P 1173(10).

Magee, Seán, *Weavers of Prosporous, County Kildare, Balbriggan, County Dublin and Tullamore, County Offaly in memorials of 1826*, Dún Laoghaire: Dún Laoghaire Genealogical Society, 1998. NLI Ir 9291 g 7.

—— *Dublin street index, 1798, extracted from Whitelaw's census*, Dún Laoghaire: Dún Laoghaire Genealogical Society, 1998. NLI Ir 9291 g 7, 47 p.

—— *Weavers and related trades in Dublin, 1826*, Dún Laoghaire: Dún Laoghaire Genealogical Society, 1993. Includes 'Labourers on Account' (1,522 names) and 'List of Food Recipients on Account'. NLI Ir 9292.

Manning, Conleth, *Dublin and beyond the Pale: studies in honour of Patrick Healy*,

Bray, Co. Wicklow: Wordwell, in association with Rathmichael Historical Society, 1998. NLI Ir 7941 d 6, 290 p.

Maxwell, Constantia, *Dublin under the Georges, 1714–1830*, London: 1956. NLI Ir 94133 h 5.

Milne, Kenneth, *The Dublin Liberties, 1600–1850*, Dublin: Four Courts Press, 2009. NLI, 55 p.

Monks, W., *Lusk: a Short History*, Lusk: Old Fingal Society, 1978. NLI Ir 9141 p 85, 8 p.

Mulhall, Mary, *A History of Lucan*, Lucan: 1991.

Murphy, Sean, *Memorial Inscriptions from St. Catherine's Church and Graveyard*, Dublin: Divellina, 1987. NLI.

—— *Bully's Acre and Royal Hospital, Kilmainham, graveyards: history and inscriptions*, Dublin: Divellina, 1989. NLI Ir 9295 p 2(2), 48 p.

Ó Broin, Seán, *The book of Finglas*, Dublin: Kincora Press, c.1980. NLI Ir 94133 o 6, 96 p.

O'Connor, Barry, *Memorial inscriptions of Dún Laoghaire-Rathdown, Co. Dublin, Ireland, Vol. 1*, Dún Laoghaire: Genealogical Society of Ireland, 2000. Co-complier, Brian Smith. NLI Ir 9295 m 7.

Ó Dálaigh, Brian, Clare, Liam, and Holton, Karina, *Irish villages: studies in local history*, Dublin: Four Courts Press, 2003. Kilmainham. NLI, 326 p.

O'Doherty, Tony, *A History of Glasnevin: Its Village, Lands and People*, Dublin: Original Writing, 2011. 284 p.

O'Donovan, John, *Ordnance Survey Letters, Dublin (1837)*, Dublin: Fourmasters Press, 2001. NLI LO 8195, 94 p.

O'Driscoll, J., *Cnucha: a history of Castleknock and district*. NLI Ir 94133 o 9.

Ó Maitiú, Séamas, *The humours of Donnybrook: Dublin's famous fair and its suppression*, Blackrock, Co. Dublin: Irish Academic Press, 1995. NLI Ir 94133 o 19, 56 p.

O'Sullivan, Peter, *Newcastle Lyons, A Parish of the Pale*, Dublin: Geography Publications, 1986. NLI Ir 941233 o 13, 139 p.

Parkinson, Danny, *Huguenot Cemetery, 1693*, Dublin: Dublin Family History Society, 1988. NLI Ir 941 p 105 (4), 49 p.

Poyntz, S.G., *St. Ann's: the church in the heart of the city*, Dublin: Representative Church Body Library, 1976. NLI Ir 200 p 10, 105 p.

Refaussé, Raymond, *Directory of historic Dublin guilds*, Dublin: Dublin Public Libraries, 1993. NLI Ir 94133 d 40, 65 p.

Robinson Tweed, Carol, *Taney: portrait of a parish: a social and historical profile of the parish of Taney in Dublin*, Dundrum: Taney Parish, 1994. NLI Ir 27413 t 3, 136 p.

Rosenblatt, Stuart, *Irish Jewish Museum, Dublin, 1992: 12,300 listings*, Dublin: the author, 2004. NLI, 341 p. See also <*www.irishjewishroots.com*>.

St Maelruan's Teamwork Project, *St Maelruan's and Tallaght, Dublin*, Tallaght: St Maelruan's Teamwork Project. NLI Ir 94133 p 15(1), 80 p.

Shepherd, W.E., *Behind the Scenes: the story of Whitechurch district*, Dublin: Whitechurch Publications, 1983. 80 p. NLI Ir 94133 s 8.

Smith, Charles V., *Dalkey society and economy in a small medieval Irish town*, Blackrock, Co. Dublin: Irish Academic Press, 1996. NLI Ir 94133 s 15, 63 p.

Smyrl, Steven C., *Dictionary of Dublin dissent: Dublin's Protestant dissenting meeting houses, 1660–1920*, Dublin: A. & A. Farmar, 2009. NLI, 358 p.

TCD, *Alphabetical list of the constituency of the University of Dublin*, Dublin: 1865. NLI Ir 37841 t 2. —1832. NLI JP 1375; also LO.

Twomey, Brendan, *Smithfield and the parish of St Paul, Dublin, 1698–1750*, Dublin: Four Courts Press, 2005. NLI, 64 p.

Tyrrell, J.H., *Genealogical History of the Tyrrells of Castleknock in Co. Dublin, Fertullagh in Co. Westmeath and now of Grange Castle, Co. Meath*, 1904. NLI Ir 9292 t 6, 202 p.

Walsh, John Edward, *Sketches of Ireland sixty years ago*, Dublin: McGlashan, 1849. NLI J 94107, 180 p. Online: Chapters.

Warburton, John, *History of the City of Dublin*, London: 1818. Co-authors, James Whitlow, Robert Walsh. NLI Ir 94133 w 2, 2 vols.

Local journals
Dublin Historical Record (Journal of the Old Dublin Society). NLI Ir 94133 d 23.
Genealogical Society of Ireland Journal. NLI Ir 9292 d 20.
Reportorium Novum: Dublin Diocesan Historical Record. NLI Ir 27413 r 3.

Directories

1738 Dublin Corporation Public Libraries, *A directory of Dublin for the year 1738: compiled from the most authentic sources*, Dublin: 2000. NLI Ir 94133 d 63.

1751 Peter Wilson, *An Alphabetical List of Names and Places of Abode of the Merchants and Traders of the City of Dublin* (annual to 1837). NLI LO 85.

1820 J. Pigot, *Commercial Directory of Ireland*. PRONI; NLI Ir 9141 p 107; LDS film 962702 item 1.

1824 J. Pigot & Co., *City of Dublin and Hibernian Provincial Directory*. NLI; LDS film 451787. Online: Hayes.

1834 Pettigrew and Oulton, *Dublin Almanack and General Register of Ireland*. NLI 1824. Online: Hayes.

1844 Alexander Thom, *Irish Almanack and Official Directory*. NLI; LDS (various years). Online (1850 and 1852): Google Books.

1846 Slater's *National Commercial Directory of Ireland*. PRONI; NLI LO; LDS film 1696703 item 3. Online: Hayes.

1850 Henry Shaw, *New City Pictorial Directory of Dublin City*. NLI Ir 914133 n 1. Online: Loughman.

1856 Slater, *Royal National Commercial Directory of Ireland*. NLI; LDS film 1472360 item 1.

1870 Slater, *Directory of Ireland*. NLI.

1881   Slater, *Royal National Commercial Directory of Ireland*. NLI. Online: FindMyPast.

1894   Slater, *Royal Commercial Directory of Ireland*. NLI.

Gravestone inscriptions

Parts (at least) of thirty Dublin graveyards are transcribed at <*www.interment. net*>. An online map of all Dublin city and county graveyards, with details of transcripts of inscriptions and burial records, is at <*www.dublinheritage.ie*>.

MDDCC: *Memorials of the Dead: Dublin City and County, Vols. 1–10*, Dublin: 1988–2004. Compiled and edited by Dr Michael T.S. Egan. NAI open shelves and NLI.

MDSD: *Memorials of the Dead: South Dublin*, Dublin: 1990. Complied and edited by Brian Cantwell. NAI open shelves and NLI.

Aderrig, MDSD, MDDCC, Vol. 9.

Baldongan: MDDCC, Vol. 9.

Baldoyle: Grange, MDDCC, Vol. 4.

Ballyboghil: MDDCC, Vol. 6.

Ballymadun: MDDCC, Vol. 5.

Balrothery: Balbriggan, George's St, C of I, MDDCC, Vol. 6.

—— Balrothery town, C of I, MDDCC, Vol. 6.

—— Bremore, MDDCC, Vol. 6.

—— Balrothery Union, MDDCC, Vol. 6.

Balscaddan: Tobertown (Balscaddan Old), MDDCC, Vol. 6.

—— Balscaddan New, MDDCC, Vol. 6.

Booterstown: church interior, RC, MDSD.

Castleknock: Abbotstown, MDDCC, Vol. 3; slso GO 622, p. 82.

Chapelizod: C of I, IG, Vol. 5, No. 4, 1977.

Cloghran: C of I. B.N. Adams, *History and Description of Santry and Cloghran Parishes*, Dublin: 1883.

—— Cloghran-Hidart, MDDCC, Vol. 4.

—— Cloghran, MDDCC, Vol. 4.

Clondalkin: Mount St Joseph, MDDCC, Vol. 2.

Clonmethan: Glebe (Clonmethan), C of I, MDDCC, Vol. 5.

Clonsilla: MDDCC, Vol. 8.

Coolock: St John the Evangelist Churchyard, MDDCC, Vol. 10.

Cruagh: MDDCC, Vol. 4.

Crumlin: C of I, IG, Vol. 7, No. 2, 1988.

—— Mount Argus interior, RC, MDSD.

Dalkey: Dalkey, MDSD, also IG, Vol. 5, No. 2, 1975.

Donabate: Kilcrea, MDSD, MDDCC, Vol. 8.

—— Donabate: MDDCC, Vol. 8.

Donnybrook: Irishtown (St Mathew's), C of I, MDDCC, Vol. 2.

—— Merrion, MDDCC, Vol. 2.

—— St Bartholomew's interior, C of I, MDSD.

—— Church of the Sacred Heart interior, RC, MDSD.

—— Sandymount: Star of the Sea, RC interior, MDSD.

Drimnagh: Bluebell, MDDCC, Vol. 3.

Garristown: Garristown, C of I, MDDCC, Vol. 5.

Grallagh: Grallagh, MDDCC, Vol. 5.

Hollywood: Hollywood Great, MDDCC, Vol. 5.

—— Damastown, MDDCC, Vol. 5.

Holmpatrick: Skerries, South Strand St: MDDCC, Vol. 7.

Kilbride: Kilbride, IG, Vol. 6, No. 3, 1982.

—— Kilbride, MDDCC, Vol. 2.

Kilgobbin: Kilgobbin, MDDCC, Vol. 2.

—— Kilgobbin New, MDDCC, Vol. 3.

Kill: Kill of the Grange, IG, Vol. 4, No. 5, 1972.

—— Deansgrange. *Memorial Inscriptions of Deangrange Cemetery, Blackrock, Co. Dublin*, Dún Laoghaire Genealogical Society, 1993. NLI Ir 9295 d.

Killeek: Killeek, MDDCC, Vol. 5.

Killiney: Killiney, IG, Vol. 4, No. 6, 1973.

—— Killiney, MDSD.

—— Ballybrack, RC interior, MDSD.

Killossery: MDDCC, Vol. 5.

Kilmactalway: MDDCC, Vol. 2, IG, Vol. 6, No. 3, 1982.

—— Loughtown Lower, MDDCC, Vol. 2.

Kilmahuddrick: Kilmahuddrick, MDDCC, Vol. 2.

Kilsallaghan: Castlefarm (Kilsallaghan), C of I, MDDCC, Vol. 4.

—— Corrstown (Chapelmidway), MDDCC, Vol. 5.

Kiltiernan: Kiltiernan, MDDCC, Vol. 2, also MDSD, and O'Connor, *Memorial Inscriptions.*

—— Glencullen, RC, MDSD.

Lucan: Lucan and Pettycannon (St Mary's), RC, MDDCC, Vol. 2. Also IG, Vol. 5, No. 6, 1976.

Lusk: Whitestown: MDDCC, Vol. 8.

—— Lusk town (RC): MDDCC, Vol. 8.

—— Lusk town (C of I): MDDCC, Vol. 8.

—— St Macculllin's (RC): MDDCC, Vol. 10.

Monkstown: York Road interior, Pres., MDSD.

—— St Paul's Glenageary, C of I interior, MDSD.

—— Northumberland Avenue interior, Methodist, MDSD.

—— Mariner's Church interior, C of I, MDSD.

—— Christ Church Kingstown interior, C of I, MDSD.

—— Monkstown, IG, Vol. 4, Nos. 3, 4, 1970/71.

—— Monkstown interior, C of I, MDSD.

Mulhuddart: Buzzardstown (Mulhuddart), MDDCC, Vol. 4; also GO Ms. 622 p. 96.

Naul: C of I, MDDCC, Vol. 5.

Newcastle: Colmanstown, MDDCC, Vol. 3.

—— Glebe, C of I, MDDCC, Vol. 2.

—— Esker, Old, MDDCC, Vol. 2.

—— Newcastle, RC, MDDCC, Vol. 2.

Oldconnaught: St James' interior, C of I, MDSD.

—— Little Bray, RC, *Memorials of the Dead, North-East Wicklow* (1).

—— Oldconnaught, MDSD, and O'Connor *Memorial Inscriptions.*

Palmerstown: Palmerstown (Oldtown), IG, Vol. 5, No. 8, 1978.

—— Palmerstown (Oldtown), MDDCC, Vol. 4.

Portmarnock: Burrow: MDDCC, Vol. 10.

—— Portmarnock (C of I): MDDCC, Vol. 7.

Raheny: Raheny town: *Here Lyeth.*

Rathcoole: Rathcoole, C of I, MDDCC, Vol. 2.

—— Rathcoole, C of I, IG, Vol. 6, No. 4, 1983.

Rathfarnham: Rathfarnham, IG, 1987.

—— Rathfarnham interior, RC, MDSD.

Rathmichael: Rathmichael interior, C of I, MDSD.

—— Rathmichael: O'Connor *Memorial Inscriptions.*

Saggart: Newtown Upper, MDDCC, Vol. 3.

—— Saggart New, MDDCC, Vol. 3.

Santry: Adams [. . .] *Santry and Cloghran.*

St Peter's: Adelaide Road, Pres., MDSD.

—— Rathmines interior, RC, MDSD.

Stillorgan: Stillorgan South, C of I, MDSD.

Swords: Swords Glebe. C of I. Fingal Heritage, '*In Fond Remembrance*'.

Swords: Swords, St Colmcille's RC. Fingal Heritage, '*Rest in Peace*'.

Tallaght: Templeogue, MDDCC, Vol. 2.

—— Tallaght, C of I, IG, Vol. 4, No. 1, 1968.

Taney: Dundrum, Churchtown Road. Ball, *Taney.*

—— Dundrum interior, RC, MDSD.

Tully: Laughanstown, O'Connor, *Memorial Inscriptions.*

—— Laughanstown, MDSD.

Ward: Ward Lower, MDDCC, Vol. 4.

Westpalstown: Westpalstown, MDDCC, Vol. 5.

Whitechurch: Whitechurch New, MDDCC, Vol. 4.

—— Whitechurch, MDDCC, Vol. 3; also IG, 1990.

Dublin City

St Andrew's: St Andrew's St, C of I, MDSD.

—— St Andrew's (coffin plates), IG, Vol. 5, No. 1, 1974.

St Anne's: Dawson St, C of I, MDSD.

St Audoën's: St Audoën's Church: Crawford, *Among the graves.*

St Bride's: Peter St, French Protestant, MDSD.

—— Bride St, C of I. DCLA (unpublished).

St Catherine's: Thomas St, C of I. Murphy, *Memorial Inscriptions.*

St James's: Military Road. Murphy, *Bully's Acre.*

—— Goldenbridge North, MDDCC, Vol. 1.

—— Royal Hospital, Murphy *Bully's Acre.*

—— James's St, C of I, NAI open shelves.

St John's: SS. Michael and John, RC (coffin plates), *IG*, Vol. 5, No. 3, 1976.

St Michael's: Merchants' Quay interior, RC, MDSD.

St Nicholas' Without: St Nicholas' interior, RC, MDSD.

—— St Patrick's Cathedral, Leeper, *Historical Handbook.*

St Paul's: St Paul's, C of I, *JRSAI*, Vol. 104, 1974.

St Peter's: Harrington St interior, RC, MDSD.

—— Kevin St Lower, C of I, MDSD.

—— Merrion Row, French Protestant, MDDCC, Vol. 2, and Parkinson, *Huguenot Cemetery, 1693.*

FERMANAGH

Census returns and substitutes

1612–13	*Survey of Undertakers Planted in Co. Fermanagh: Historical Manuscripts Commission Report, No. 4* (Hastings Mss.), 1947, pp. 159–82.
1630	Muster Roll of Ulster. Armagh County Library and PRONI D.1759/3C/1, T/934; NLI Pos. 206.
1630–1800	Church of Ireland Marriage Licence Bonds, Diocese of Clogher. Online: Ulsterancestry.
1631	Muster Roll. Trimble, *History of Enniskillen.* Online: Ulsterancestry.
1641	Testimonies of 152 witnesses to the 1641 Rebellion. Online: 1641.
1659	Pender's 'Census'. Reprinted GPC, 1997; IMC, 2002. LDS film 924648.
1660	Poll Tax Returns. PRONI MIC/15A/80.
1661	Books of Survey and Distribution. PRONI T.370/B and D.1854/1/20.
1662	Subsidy roll, Enniskillen town. NLI Ms. 9583; also PRONI T.808/15068.
1665–6	Hearth Money Roll. NLI Ms. 9583; PRONI T.808/15066. Lurg barony, *Clogher Record,* 1957.
1747	Poll Book (votes cast). PRONI T.808/15063. Online: Freeholders.
1766	Derryvullen, Devenish, Kinawley, Rossory. Online: PRONI name search. Boho also NAI m. 2476d.
1770	Freeholders. NLI Ms. 787–8; also GO 443.
1785	Male Protestants aged over seventeen—Magheracloone, Errigal Trough and Trory. LDS film 258517.
1788	Poll Book (votes cast). PRONI T.808/15075, T.543, T.1385; LDS films 100181, 1279356. Online: Freeholders.
1794–9	Militia Pay Lists and Muster Rolls. PRONI T.1115/5A-C.
1796	Spinning-Wheel Premium List. 2,500 names for Co. Fermanagh. Online: Hayes.

1796–1802	Freeholders. PRONI D.1096/90. Online: Freeholders.
1797	Yeomanry Muster Rolls. PRONI T.1021/3.
1821	Parishes of Derryvullan and Aghalurcher (part only). NAI; PRONI. Online: Fermanagh Genweb.
1823–38	Tithe Books.
1832	Enniskillen registered voters. *Parliamentary Papers, 1837, Reports from Committees*, Vol. 13 (2), pp. 554–7.
1836	Memorials from the inhabitants of the towns of Ballyshannon, Pettigo and Bundoran (c.70 names). NAI OP 1851/79 1836.
1837	Freeholders. *Parliamentary Papers, 1837: Reports from Committees*, Vol. 11 (1), pp. (39) 7–21.
1841	Certified copies of census returns for use in claims for old-age pensions. NAI; PRONI; LDS film 258357.
1842	Voters. NAI OP 1842/114.
1845	Workhouse records, Irvinestown (1845–1918) and Enniskillen (1845–1913). PRONI; also LDS films 259187–90 and 25914–53, respectively.
1846	Voters. NAI OP 1846/145.
1851	Townland of Clonee only. NAI CEN 1851/13/1.
1851–2	Galloon parish. PRONI D.2098.
1861	Boho parish. Protestants only, c.1861. NAI T.3723.
1862	Griffith's Valuation. Online: Askaboutireland.
1874	Census of Devenish C of I parish. Local custody.
1901	Census. Online: NAI.
1911	Census. Online: NAI.
1912	The Ulster Covenant. Almost half a million original signatures and addresses of those who signed. c.15,000 names for Co. Fermanagh. Online: Covenant.

Online

1641	<www.1641.tcd.ie>	
Askaboutireland	<www.askaboutireland.ie>	
Covenant	<www.proni.gov.uk/ulstercovenant>	
Fermanagh Genweb	<www.rootsweb.com/~nirfer>	
Freeholders	<www.proni.gov.uk/freeholders>	Five freeholders' and voters' lists, 1747–1802
Gold	<www.fermanagh-gold.com>	
Hayes	<www.failteromhat.com>	
Headstones	<www.historyfromheadstones.com>	Comprehensive collection of inscriptions
NAI	<www.census.nationalarchives.ie>	
Ulsterancestry	<www.ulsterancestry.com>	Assorted records

Publications

Local histories etc.

Belmore, Earl of, *Parliamentary Memoirs of Fermanagh and Tyrone, 1613–1885*, Dublin: Alex. Thom & Co., 1887. NLI Ir 94118 b 1, 368 p.

Bradshaw, W.H., *Enniskillen Long Ago: an Historic Sketch of the Parish . . .* Dublin: G. Herbert, 1878. NLI Ir 274118 b 1, 159 p.

Busteed, Mervyn, *Castle Caldwell, County Fermanagh: life on a west Ulster estate, 1750–1800*, Dublin: Four Courts Press, 2006. NLI, 68 p.

Cunningham, J.B., *John O'Donovan's letters from County Fermanagh (1834)*, Belleek: St Davog's Press, 1993. NLI Ir 94118 o 2.

Day, Angelique, and McWilliams, Patrick (eds.), *Ordnance Survey Memoirs of Ireland Series*, Belfast: Institute of Irish Studies and RIA, 1990–97.

—*Vol. 4: Co. Fermanagh I* (1990): Aghalurcher, Aghavea, Clones, Derrybrusk, Drummully, Enniskillen, Galloon, Kinawley, Tomregan. NLI Ir 914111 o 13.

—*Vol. 14: Co. Fermanagh II* (1992): Belleek, Boho, Cleenish, Derryvullan, Devenish, Drumkeeran, Inishmacsaint, Killesher, Magheracross, Magheraculmoney, Rossorry, Templecarn, Trory. NLI Ir 9141 o 13.

Duffy, Joseph, *A Clogher Record Album: a diocesan history*, Enniskillen: Cumann Seanchais Chlochair, 1975. NLI Ir 94114 c 3, 340 p.

Duffy, Patrick, *Landscapes of South Ulster: a parish atlas of the diocese of Clogher*, Belfast: Institute of Irish Studies, 1993. NLI ILB 270 d 1, 131 p.

Dundas, W.H., *Enniskillen parish and town*, Dundalk: 1913. NLI Ir 94118 d 2, 197 p.

Elliott, David R., *Cemetery Transcription series*, Parkhill, Ont.: Kinfolk Finders, 2007–2011. NLI.

—— *Enniskillen Poor Law Union outdoor relief register (1847–99), covering parts of Counties Fermanagh, Cavan, and Tyrone*, Parkhill, Ont.: Kinfolk Finders, 2009. NLI, 88 p.

Elliott, E.G., *The parish of Devenish and Boho*, Enniskillen: Elliott, 1990. NLI Ir 27411 e 2, 198 p.

Gallogly, Dan, *The diocese of Kilmore, 1800–1950*, Cavan: Bréifne Historical Society, 1999. NLI, 466 p.

Glassie, Henry, *Passing the time in Ballymeno: culture and history of an Ulster community*, Bloomington and Indianapolis, Ind.: Indiana University Press, 1995. NLI, 852 p.

Graham, Rev. John, *Derriana: a History of the Siege of Derry and the Defence of Enniskillen in 1688 and 1689, with Biographical Notes*, Londonderry: the author, 1823. NLI J94112, 64 p.

King, Sir Charles (ed.), *Henry's 'Upper Lough Erne in 1739'*, Dublin: 1892. NLI Ir 914118 h 6, 95 p.

Livingstone, Peadar, *The Fermanagh story: a documented history of the County Fermanagh from the earliest times to the present day*, Enniskillen: Clogher Historical Society, 1969. NLI Ir 94118 L 1, 570 p.

McCusker, Breege, *Lowtherstown Workhouse,* Irvinestown: Necarne Press, 1997. NLI, 37 p.

MacDonald, Brian, *Time of Desolation: Clones Poor Law Union, 1845–50,* Monaghan: Clogher Historical Society, 2002. Monaghan County Library 941.67.

McKenna, J.E., *Devenish, its history, antiquities and traditions,* Dublin: Gill, 1897. NLI Ir 914118 m 2, 134 p.

Maguire, Dermot, *Drumlone at the crossroads: a country area in Co. Fermanagh: history and heritage,* 2006. NLI, 264 p.

Maguire, Thomas, *Fermanagh: its Native Chiefs and Clans,* Omagh: S.D. Montgomery, 1954. NLI Ir 914118 m 9.

Martin, Samuel, *Historical gleanings from Co. Derry, and some from Co. Fermanagh,* Dublin: 1955. NLI Ir 94112 m 2.

Moran, T. Whitley, *The Whitleys of Enniskillen,* Hoylake: T.W. Moran, 1962. NLI GO 343, 39 leaves.

O'Connell, Philip, *The Diocese of Kilmore: its History and Antiquities,* Dublin: Browne & Nolan, 1937. NLI Ir 274119 o 3, 579 p.

Parke, W.K., *The parish of Inishmacsaint,* Fermanagh: Select Vestry, 1982. NLI Ir 27411 p 6, 73 p.

Roslea Community Historical Society, *Roslea remembers,* Fermanagh: 2001? NLI, 152 p.

Steele, W.B., *The parish of Devenish,* Enniskillen: Fermanagh Times Office, 1937. NLI Ir 914118 s 12, 172 p.

Swanzy, Rev. H.B., *The later history of the Family of Rosborough of Mullinagoan, Co. Fermanagh,* 1898. Mullynagowan, Galloon Parish. LHL 929.2/ROSB.

Trimble, W.C., *The history of Enniskillen, with reference to some manors in Co. Fermanagh, and other local subjects,* Enniskillen: W. Trimble, 1919–21. McGuire family. NLI Ir 94118 t 1, 3 vols.

Witherow, Thomas, *Derry and Enniskillen, in the year 1689, 1873, 1885,* Belfast: W. Mullen & Son, 1895. NLI Ir 94112 w 8, 419 p.

Local journals
Clogher Record. NLI Ir 94114 c 2.
North Irish Roots: Journal of the North of Ireland Family History Society. NLI Ir 92905 n 4.
Irish Family Links. NLI Ir 9292 f 19.
Ulster Journal of Archaeology. NLI Ir 794105 u 1.

Directories
Thirty Belfast and Ulster directories are online at PRONI.

1824   J. Pigot & Co., *City of Dublin and Hibernian Provincial Directory.* NLI; LDS film 451787. Online: Hayes.
1839   *Directory of the Towns of Sligo, Enniskillen, Ballyshannon, Donegal . . .*

1846   Slater's *National Commercial Directory of Ireland*. PRONI; NLI LO; LDS film 1696703 item 3. Online: Hayes.

1848   Macloskie, *Directory of Fermanagh*. Online: FindMyPast.

1852   James A. Henderson, *Belfast and Province of Ulster Directory*. Issued also in 1854, 1856, 1858, 1861, 1863, 1865, 1868, 1870, 1877, 1880, 1884, 1887, 1890, 1894 and 1900. PRONI; LDS (various years).

1856   Slater, *Royal National Commercial Directory of Ireland*. NLI; LDS film 1472360 item 1.

1870   Slater, *Directory of Ireland*. NLI.

1881   Slater, *Royal National Commercial Directory of Ireland*. NLI. Online: FindMyPast.

1887   *Derry Almanac and Directory* (Enniskillen). NLI Ir 914112 d 1.

1894   Slater, *Royal Commercial Directory of Ireland*. NLI.

Gravestone inscriptions

Heritage World has transcripts for forty-six graveyards in Co. Fermanagh. These are searchable online for a fee at <*www.historyfromheadstones.com*>. Eileen Hewson (<*www.kabristan.org.uk*>) has transcribed and published eight volumes of transcripts for Co. Fermanagh. They are available at NLI. It is not clear if the transcripts are complete for each graveyard. Other published or freely available transcripts are given below.

Aghavea: Aghavea, C of I, *Clogher Record*, Vol. 4, Nos. 1, 2, 1960/61.
Boho: Carrickbeg, Elliott, *Cemetery transcription series*.
Cleenish: Templenaffrin, *Clogher Record*, Vol. 2, No. 1, 1957.
Mullaghdun, RC, Elliott, *Cemetery transcription series*.
Clones: Rosslea. St Tierney's, RC, *Clogher Record*, 1982–4.
Derryvullan: Monea, C of I, Steele, *The parish of Devenish*.
Devenish: St Molaise's and Devenish Abbey, J.E. MacKenna, *Devenish, its history*.
Garrison, C of I, Elliott, *Cemetery transcription series*.
Drummully: *Clogher Record*, Vol. 1, No. 2, 1954.
Enniskillen: St Macartin's, C of I, Dundas, W.H., *Enniskillen*.
Galloon: Galloon, *Clogher Record*, Vol. 10, No. 2, 1980.
Galloon: Donagh, *Clogher Record*, Vol. 1, No. 3, 1955.
Inishmacsaint: Benmore, RC, Elliott, *Cemetery transcription series*.
Old Derrygonnelly, Elliott, *Cemetery transcription series*.
Slawin, Elliott, *Cemetery transcription series*.
Magheracross: Bellanamallard town, C of I, Elliott, *Cemetery transcription series*.
Bellanamallard, Methodist, Elliott, *Cemetery transcription series*.
Magheracross, Elliott, *Cemetery transcription series*.
Rossorry: Mullanacaw C of I, Elliott, *Cemetery transcription series*.
Rossorry, Elliott, *Cemetery transcription series*.
Trory: C of I. Elliott, *Cemetery transcription series*.

Estate records

Archdale. Rental, 1753. Online: Ulsterancestry. Devinish parish.

Balfour family. Tenants list, 1735. NLI Mss. 10259, 10305. Major tenants only. Rentals, 1735–89. NLI Ms. 10259. Major tenants only. Rentals, 1818–22. NLI Ms. 10260. All tenants. Covering areas in the civil parishes of Aghalurcher and Kinawley.

Belmore, Earls of. Rentals, 1759–1946. PRONI D.3007. Covering areas in the civil parishes of Derrybrusk, Derryvullan, Enniskillen, Templemichael and Termonmaguirk.

Belmore, Earls of. Tenants on the Belmore estates, 1843–4. PRONI D.3007/D/1–15. Covering areas in the civil parishes of Derrybrusk, Derryvullan and Enniskillen.

Brooke. Rentals, 1795–1885. PRONI D3004/B. Covering areas in the civil parishes of Aghalurcher, Aghavea, Cleenish, Clones, Derrybrusk, Devenish, Enniskillen, Inishmacsaint, Killesher, Kinawley, Magheraculmoney and Rossorry.

Broomfield, J.C. Rentals, 1810–20, NAI M.3563. All tenants. Covering areas in the civil parish of Belleek.

Commissioners of Education. Rentals, 1832–51. NLI Ms. 17956. All tenants. Covering areas in the civil parishes of Cleenish and Killesher.

Enniskillen, Earls of. Rentals, 1810–76. PRONI D.1702. Covering areas in the civil parishes of Aghalurcher, Aghavea, Cleenish, Derryvullan, Drumkeeran, Drummully, Enniskillen, Inishmacsaint, Killesher, Kinawley, Rossorry and Trory.

Erne, Earls of. Rentals, 1824–1931. PRONI D.1939/4, 7. Covering areas in the civil parishes of Aghalurcher, Boho, Cleenish, Clones, Devenish, Enniskillen, Galloon, Inishmacsaint and Kinawley. Much earlier rentals for the Balfour estate portion, around Lisnaskea (Aghalurcher) D.1939/17.

Hassard family. Rentals, 1810–20, NAI M3136. Major tenants only. Covering areas in the civil parish of Enniskillen.

Hume. Rental, 1793. PRONI D.580. Covering areas in the civil parishes of Devenish, Inishmacsaint, Killesher, Rssorry and Trory.

Hume, Nicholas (Ely estate). Online: Fermanagh Genweb.

Irwin. Rentals and more, 1802–1930. PRONI D.1096/59/1–9. Covering areas in the civil parish of Trory.

Madden. Manor Waterhouse estate, near Rosslea. Rentals and accounts, 1775–1929. PRONI D.3465. Covering areas in the civil parish of Clones.

Montgomery. Rent rolls and more, 1650–1900. PRONI D627. Covering areas in the civil parish of Enniskillen.

Montgomery. Rental, 1792–4. PRONI D.464/74. Covering areas in the civil parish of Enniskillen.

Tennent. Rent rolls, 1799–1831. PRONI D2922. Covering areas in the civil parish of Enniskillen.

GALWAY

Census returns and substitutes

1640	Irish Papist Proprietors, Galway town. Hardiman, *History of . . .*
1641–1703	Book of Survey and Distribution. NLI Ms. 969.
1657	English Protestant proprietors, Galway town. Hardiman, *History of . . .*
1724	Galway town Hearth Money Roll. *JGAHS*, Vol. 35, 1976, pp. 105–128.
1727	A Galway election list. *JGAHS*, 1976.
1749	Ahascra, Athleague, Ballynakill, Drimatemple, Dunamon, Kilbegnet, Killian, Killosolan. NAI MFS 6; LDS film 101781. See Manning, *Elphin Index*. Online: FindMyPast. Ballynakill, Dunamon, Kilbegnet. Online: Creggs.
1791	Survey of Loughrea town (occupiers). *JGAHS*, Vol. 24, No. 3.
1794	Catholic Freemen of Galway town. *JGAHS*, Vol. 9, No. 1.
1798	Convicted rebels from Galway *JGAHS*, Vol. 23, No. 1.
1798	Persons who suffered losses in the 1798 Rebellion. Propertied classes only. c.100 names. NLI I 94107.
1806–1810	Catholic householders, Killalaghten; in the Catholic parish registers of Cappataggle. NLI. Pos. 2431.
1810–19	Names in account books of C. St George, Oranmore town, *IG*, Vol. 7 (1) 1986, pp. 101–112.
1821	Parishes of Aran, Athenry, Kilcomeen, Kiltallagh, Killimore, Kilconickny, Kilreekill. NAI CEN 1821/18–25; LDS film 597734. Also Loughrea (fragments) GO Ms. 622, pp. 53ff.
1823–38	Tithe Books.
1827	Protestants in Aughrim parish. NA M 5359.
1830	Memorials: 1. Killyan barony (Athleague, Kilroran, Killyan and Tisrara), 1830, c.130 names, NAI OP 974/148. 2. Galway town, 1830, c.100 signatures. NAI OP 974/145. 3. Fishermen of Claddagh, 1831, 59 names. NAI OP 974/101. 4. Urrismore [Errismore], 1831, 85 names. NAI OP 974/121.
1834	List of parishioners, Kinvara and Killina. NLI Pos. 2442; also GFHSW. Online: Celtic Cousins.
1837	Valuation of towns returning members of Parliament (occupants and property values): Galway. *Parliamentary Papers, 1837: Reports from Committees,* Vol. 2 (i), Appendix G.
1838–52	Reproductive Loan Fund records. Records of loan associations at Ahascragh, Ballygar, Castlehacket, Clifden, Corrandulla, Furbo, Loughrea, Galway town, Mountshannon (now in Co. Clare) and Mountbellew, covering more than 50 parishes and 8,000 individuals. NA (Kew). T 91. Partly online: Moving Here.
1839–46	List of subscribers to the RC Chapel at Dunmore, with name, townland and donation, 1839–46. NLI Pos. 4211.

1841   Fragments, for Loughrea town. NAI M 150(2); also GO 622, pp. 53ff.
1848–52 Ahascragh assisted passages. AH, Vol. 22, 1960. Also Ellis, *Emigrants.*
1850–59 Emigrants to Australia and the United States from the parish of Kilchreest, with some from the parishes of Killogilleen, Killinane, Killora, Kilthomas and Isertkelly. GO Ms. 622.
1851   Fragments, for Loughrea town. NAI M 150.
1855   Griffith's Valuation. Online: Askaboutireland.
1901   Census. Online: NAI.
1911   Census. Online: NAI.

Online

Askaboutireland	*<www.askaboutireland.ie>*	
Aughty	*<www.aughty.org>*	Slieve Aughty uplands in Cos. Clare and Galway
Celtic Cousins	*<www.celticcousins.net/ireland>*	Assorted records, Beagh and Gort areas
Creggs	*<www.strandnet.com/creggs>*	North-east Galway
Egan	*<homepages.rootsweb.ancestry. com/~egan>*	
Galway Library	*<places.galwaylibrary.ie/history>*	
Hayes, John	*<www.failteromhat.com>*	
Lally, Joseph	*<www.lalley.com>*	
Leitrim-Roscommon	*<www.leitrim-roscommon.com>*	
Moving Here	*<www.movinghere.org.uk/search>*	
NAI	*<www.census.nationalarchives.ie>*	

Publications

Local histories etc.
Dillon Papers (Clonbrock, Co. Galway), AH, 20, 17–55.
Dunsandle papers, AH, 15, 392, 405.
'The ethnography of the Aran Islands', PRIA, 3rd Ser., Vol. 2, 1891–3, pp. 827–9.
'The ethnography of the Carna and Mweenish in the Parish of Moyruss', PRIA, 3rd Ser., Vol. 6, 1900–1902, pp. 503–534.
Barna-Furbo ICA, *Barna and Furbo: A Local history*, Barna: Barna-Furbo Irish Countrywomen's Association, 1982.
Beirne, Francis, *A history of the parish of Tisrara*, Tisrara: Tisrara Heritage Society, 1997. NLI Ir 94125 h 5, 219 p.
Berry, J.F, *The Story of St Nicholas' Church, Galway*, 1912. NLI Ir 7265 b 5.
Blackmore, Liz (ed.), *The parish of Lackagh Turloughmore*, Lackagh: Lackagh Museum Committee, 2001. Includes 1901 census. NLI, 292 p.
Breatnach, Caoilte, *Memories in Time: Folklore of Beithe, 1800–2000*, Tubber, Co. Galway: Beagh Integrated Rural Development Association, 2003. NLI, 224 p.

Breathnach, Pádraic, *Maigh Cuilinn: a táisc agus a tuairisc,* Indreabhán: Cló Chonamara, 1986. NLI Ir 94124 m 6, 298 p.

Candon, Geraldine, *Headford, County Galway, 1775–1901,* Dublin: Four Courts Press, 2003. NLI, 64 p.

Cantwell, Ian, *Memorials of the Dead, Counties Galway and Mayo (Western Seaboard),* Eneclann CD ENEC004, Dublin: Eneclann, 2002. Online: FindMyPast.

Carroll, Michael H., *Of beauty rarest: a history of Clydagh National School, Headford, Co. Galway,* Headford: Michael H. Carroll, 2000. NLI, 206 p.

—— *Valley of the Milk: a history of the Carroll Family of Luggawannia, Headford, Co. Galway,* Headford: M.H. Carroll, 2000. NLI Ir 9292 c 65, 221 p.

Claffey, John A., *Glimpses of Tuam since the famine,* Tuam: Old Tuam Society, 1997 NLI [Ir] 94124 g 10, 254 p.

—— *History of Moylough-Mountbellew, Part 1: from the earliest times to 1601,* Tuam: Claffey, 1983. NLI Ir 94124 c 13, 168 p.

—— *Irish Historic Towns Atlas, 20: Tuam,* Dublin: RIA, 2009. NLI. Online: <*www.logainm.ie*>.

Claregalway Historical and Cultural Society, *Claregalway parish history, 750 years / Stair pharóiste Bhaile Chláir na Gaillimhe,* Claregalway: Claregalway Historical and Cultural Society, 1999. NLI Ir 94124 c 14, 277 p.

Clarke, Joe, *Christopher Dillon Bellew and his Galway estates, 1763–1826,* Dublin: Four Courts Press, 2003. NLI, 64 p.

Connemara Orphans' Nursery, *The story of the Connemara Orphans' Nursery from its commencement to the year 1876,* Glasgow: Campbell & Tudhope, 1877. Records of the Connemara Orphans' Nursery. NLI Ir 361.s, 213 p.

Conwell, John Joe, *A Galway landlord and the Famine: Ulick John de Burgh,* Dublin: Four Courts Press, 2003. NLI, 64 p.

—— *Lickmolassy by the Shannon: a history of Gortanumera and surrounding parishes,* Galway: Conwell, 1998. NLI, 343 p.

Cronin, Denis, *A Galway gentleman in the age of improvement: Robert French of Monivea, 1716–76,* Blackrock, Co. Dublin: Irish Academic Press, 1995. NLI Ir 94124 c 12.

Cunningham, John, *'A Town tormented by the sea': Galway, 1790–1914,* Dublin: Geography Publications, 2004. NLI, 408 p.

D'Alton, E., *History of the Archdiocese of Tuam,* Dublin: Phoenix, 1928. NLI Ir 27412 d 1, 2 vols.

Donnelly, Fr James, *Family history of the Donnellys and the Crushells of Belmont, Co. Galway,* Kathmandu: the author, 1990. Including references to Maloney (Lissananny), Dowd (Kilconly), Devaney (Kilconly) and Donnelly (Ballyglass, Co. Mayo), NLI Ir 921 d.

Dwyer, Philip, *The Diocese of Killaloe, from the Reformation to the Close of the Eighteenth Century,* Dublin: Hodges, Foster & Figgis, 1878. NLI Ir 94143 d 11, 602 p. Reprinted Newmarket-on-Fergus: O'Brien Book Publications, 1997.

Egan, Patrick K., *The parish of Ballinasloe: its history from the earliest times to the present day,* Galway: Kenny's Bookshops, 1994. NLI Ir 94124 e 2, 355 p.

Ellis, Éilís, *Emigrants from Ireland, 1847–52*, Baltimore, Md.: GPC, 1977. NLI Ir 325 e 5.

Faherty, Padhraic, *Barna: A History*, Barna: Faherty, 2000.

Fahey, Jerome, *The History and Antiquities of the Diocese of Kilmacduagh*. Reprinted Galway: Kildare Genealogy, 1986. NLI r 274124 f 2, 480 p.

Fahy, Mary de Lourdes, *Kiltartan: many leaves, one root: a history of the parish of Kiltartan*, Gort: Kiltartan Gregory Cultural Society, 2004. NLI, 349 p.

Farrell, Noel, *County Galway, Tuam family roots: exploring family origins in Tuam*, Longford: Noel Farrell, 2004. NLI, 48 p.

—— *Exploring family origins in Ballinasloe town*, Longford: Noel Farrell, 1998. NLI 1B 2235, 48 p.

FÁS Galway Family History Project, *Forthill graveyard*, Galway: Galway Family History Society West, 1992. NLI Ir 941 p 118 (4).

Finnegan, Eileen, *A History of the parish of Templetogher and the town of Williamstown, from earliest times to 1990*, Williamstown: Finnegan, 1990. NLI Ir 94124 p 5(3), 56 p.

Flynn, John S., *Ballymacward: the story of an east Galway parish*, Mullingar: John S. Flynn, 1991. NLI Ir 94124.f.3, 238 p.

Forde, Joseph, *The District of Loughrea, Vol. 1: History, 1791–1918*, Loughrea: Loughrea History Project, 2003. Co-editors, Christina Cassidy, Paul Manzor and David Ryan. NLI.

—— *The District of Loughrea, Vol. 2: Folklore, 1860–1960*, Loughrea: Loughrea History Project, 2003. NLI, 326 p.

Furey, Brenda, *Oranmore Maree: a history of a cultural and social heritage*, Galway: the author, 1991. NLI Ir 94124 f 4, 116 p.

Glynn, Sean M., *Williamstown, County Galway: Historical Sketch and Records*, Galway: Galway Printing Co., 1966. Galway County Library.

Goaley, Rev. M., *History of Annaghdown*, Westport: Berry's Printing Works, 197–. NLI Ir 274 p 31.

Gorman, Thomas, *Clanricarde Country and the land campaign*, Woodford: Woodford Heritage Group, 1987. NLI Ir 94124 c 4.

Hardiman, James, *History of the town and county of Galway . . . to 1820*. Reprinted Galway: Kenny's Bookshops and Art Galleries, 1975. NLI Ir 94124 h 1, 320 p. Archive CD Books Ireland.

Harvey, Karen J., *The Bellews of Mount Bellew: a Catholic gentry family in eighteenth-century Ireland*, Dublin: Four Courts Press, 1998. NLI Ir 94107 h 12, 218 p.

Hayes-McCoy, G.A., *Index to 'The Compossicion Booke of Connoght, 1585'*, Dublin: IMC, 1945. NLI Ir 9412 c 1, 179 p.

Higgins, Jim, *St. Mary's Cathedral (Church of Ireland), Tuam: an architectural, archaeological and historical guide*, Tuam: Friends of St Mary's Cathedral, c.1995. Co-author, Aisling Parsons. NLI Ir 27412 s 1, 182 p.

—— *The White Canons, Abbeytown, Cill-Na-Manach, 1260–1990: a history of the monastery of the White Canons, and other historical places in the District of Maigh Seola*, Galway: Crow's Rock Press, 1990. NLI Ir 7941 w 34, 143 p.

IGRS, *Tombstone inscriptions, Vol. 1*, Dublin: IGRS Tombstone Committee, 2001. NLI, 850 p.

Irish Countrywomen's Association, *Portrait of a Parish: Ballynakill, Connemara*, Renvyle: Irish Countrywomen's Association, 1985. NLI, 142 p.

Jordan, Kieran, *Kiltullagh/Killimordaly as the centuries passed: a history from 1500 to 1900*, Kiltullagh: Kiltullagh-Killimordaly Historical Society, 2000. NLI A 5A 46, 378 p.

Kavanagh, Michael V., *A Bibliography of the Co. Galway*, Galway: Galway County Libraries, 1965. NLI Ir 801 K 6, 187 p.

Kenney, James C., *Pedigree of the Kenney family of Kilclogher, Co. Galway*, Dublin: 1968. Killaclogher, Monivea.

Knox, H.T., *Notes on the Early History of the Dioceses of Tuam, Killala and Achonry*, Dublin: Hodges Figgis, 1904. NLI Ir 27412 k 1, 410 p.

—— Portumna and the Burkes, *JGAHS*, 6, 1909, pp. 107–109.

Lackagh Parish History Committee, *The parish of Lackagh Turloughmore*, Turloughmore: Lackagh Parish History Committee, 1990. Includes the 1901 census. NLI Ir 94124 f 2, 292 p.

Lynch, Ronan, *The Kirwans of Castlehacket, Co. Galway: history, folklore and mythology in an Irish horseracing family*, Dublin: Four Courts Press, 2006. NLI, 200 p.

Mac Lochlainn, Tadhg, *A Historical summary on the Parish of Ahascra, Caltra and Castleblakeney*, Ballinasloe: Mac Lochlainn, 1979. NLI Ir 9141 p 79, 92 p.

—— *Ballinasloe inniu agus inné: a story of a community over the past 200 years*, Galway: Galway Printing Co., 1971? NLI Ir 94124 m 1, 223 p.

—— *The Parish of Aughrim and Kilconnell*, London: Mac Lochlainn, 1980. NLI Ir 94124 m 4, 79 p.

—— *The Parish of Laurencetown and Kiltormer*, Ballinasloe: Mac Lochlainn, 1981. NLI Ir 94124 m 5, 73 p.

—— *A short history of the Parish of Killure, Fohenagh and Kilgerrill*, Galway: MacLochlainn, 1975. NLI Ir 9141 p 74, 54 p.

McNamara, Marie, *Beagh: a history and heritage*, Beagh: Beagh Integrated Rural Development Association, 1995? Co-author, Maura Madden. NLI Ir 94124 b 4, 276 p.

Madden, Gerard, *For God or King: the history of Mountshannon, Co. Clare, 1742–1992*, Tuamgraney, Co. Clare: East Clare Heritage, 1993. NLI Ir 94143 f 8, 204 p.

Maguire, Samuel J., *Galway Reader*. Online: Galway Library.

Manning, Peter, *Elphin Diocesan census, 1749: surname index*, Rainham, Kent: Manning, 1987. NLI Ir 27412 m 20.

Mulvey, Con, *The memorial inscriptions and related history of Kiltullagh, Killimordaly and Esker graveyards*, Kiltullagh: Kiltullagh Community Council, 1998. NLI Ir 9295 m 5/1, 146 p.

Naughton, M., *The History of St Francis' Parish, Galway*, Galway: Corrib Printers, 1984. NLI Ir 27412 n 1, 60 p.

Ní Dhomhnaill, Cáit, *An Cheathrú Rua*, Baile Átha Cliath: An tOireachtas, 1984. NLI, 33 p.

Ó Concheanainn, Peadar, *Innismeadhoin: seanchas agus sgéalta*, Baile Átha Cliath: Oifig Díolta Foillseacháin Rialtais, 1931. NLI Ir 89162 Oc 25, 76 p.

O'Connor, Gabriel, *A place of genius and gentility: insights into our past: Kilkerrin, Co. Galway: historical essays on a north Galway parish*, Kilkerrin: Oidhreacht Chill Choirín, 2006. NLI, 192 p.

Ó Dálaigh, Brian, *Irish villages: studies in local history*, Dublin: Four Courts Press, 2003. Williamstown. NLI. 326 p.

O'Donnell, Paul, *A Mullagh Miscellany, Vol. 1*, Galway Rural Development, 2002. Galway County Library, 49 p.

O'Donovan, John, *Ordnance Survey letters . . . the County of Galway . . . 1838 and 1839*, Dublin: Fourmasters Press, 2009. NLI, 215 p.

—— *The Tribes and customs of Hy-Many, commonly called O'Kelly's country*, Dublin: for the Irish Archaeological Society, 1843. NLI Ir 9412 o 1/1.

O'Flaherty, Roderic, *A chorographical description of West or H-Iar Connaught: written AD 1684*, Dublin: for the Irish Archaeological Society, 1846. Reprinted Galway: Kenny's Bookshops and Art Galleries, 1978. NLI Ir 94124 o 2.

O'Gorman, Michael, *A pride of paper tigers: a history of the Great Hunger in the Scariff Workhouse Union from 1839 to 1853*, Tuamgraney, Co. Clare: East Clare Heritage, 1994. NLI Ir 94143 o 8, 82 p.

O'Gorman, Tony, *History of Fohenagh*, Galway: Fohenagh Community Council, 2000? NLI, 167 p.

Ó Laoi, Pádraic, *History of Castlegar Parish*, Galway: Ó Laoi, 1998? NLI Ir 94124 o 14, 216 p.

O'Neill, T.P., *The Tribes and other Galway families: Galway quincentennial, 1484–1984*, Galway: Connaught Tribune, 1984. NLI Ir 927 p 5, 32 p.

O'Regan, Carol, *Moylough: a people's heritage*, Moylough: Moylough Community Council, 1993. Co-editor, John Jones. NLI Ir 94124 p 5(4), 138 p.

O'Regan, Finbarr, *The Lamberts of Athenry: a book on the Lambert families of Castle Lambert and Castle Ellen, Co. Galway*, Athenry: Finbarr O'Regan, for the Lambert Project Society, 1999. NLI Ir 9292 L 24, 254 p.

O'Sullivan, M.D., *Old Galway: the history of a Norman colony in Ireland*, Cambridge: W. Heffer & Sons, 1942. NLI Ir 94124 o4, 488 p.

Qualter, Aggie, *Athenry history from 1780: folklore, recollections*, Galway: Qualter, 1989. NLI Ir 94124 p 3(2), 66 p.

Regan, Carol, *Moylough: a people's heritage*, Moylough: Moylough Community Council, 1993. NLI Ir 94124 p 5(4), 138 p.

Regan, D., *Abbeyknockmoy: a time to remember*, Abbeyknockmoy: Abbeyknockmoy Community Council, 1996. NLI Ir 94124 a 4.

Robinson, Tim, *Connemara after the Famine: journal of a survey of the Martin Estate by Thomas Colville Scott, 1853*, Dublin: Lilliput Press, 1995. NLI Ir 94124 s 10, 102 p.

Rynne, Etienne, *Athenry: a medieval Irish town*, Athenry: Athenry Historical Society, 1992. NLI Ir 941 p 132(1).

Shiel, Michael, *A Forgotten Campaign and aspects of the heritage of south-east Galway*, Galway: East Galway Centenary Committee. Co-author, Desmond Roche. Land wars and evictions, c.1886. NLI Ir 94124 f.

Simington, Robert C., *The transplantation to Connacht, 1654–58*, Shannon: Irish University Press, for IMC, 1970. NLI Ir 94106 s 9, 306 p.

Smythe, Colin, *A guide to Coole Park, Co. Galway, home of Lady Gregory*, Gerrards Cross, Bucks: Colin Smythe, 1995. With a foreword by Anne Gregory. 3rd ed. (rev.). NLI Ir 94124 s 9.

Tourelle, John F., *Forde, Forde, Forde: from Annagh West, Co. Galway, Ireland to Southland, New Zealand*, Alexandra: J.F. Tourelle, 1998. NLNZ P q929.2 FOR TOU 1998, 180 p.

Villiers-Tuthill, Kathleen, *History of Clifden, 1810–60*, Dublin: the author, c.1981. Dorsey family. NLI Ir 94124 V 1, 88 p.

—— *Patient endurance: the great famine in Connemara*, Dublin: Connemara Girl Publications, 1997. NLI Ir 94123 v 1, 189 p.

—— *Beyond the Twelve Bens: a history of Clifden and district, 1860–1923*, Dublin: the author, 1990. NLI Ir 94124.v.3, 252 p.

White, Rev. P., *History of Clare and the Dalcassian Clans of Tipperary, Limerick and Galway*, Dublin: 1893. Reprinted Newmarket-on-Fergus: O'Brien Book Publications, 1997. NLI Ir 94143 w 4, 398 p.

Wilde, Sir William R., *Lough Corrib, its shores and islands: with notices of Lough Mask*, Dublin: McGlashan & Gill, 1867. NLI J 7941, 306 p.

Local journals
Galway Roots: Journal of the Galway Family History Society West. NLI.
Journal of the Galway Archaeological and Historical Society. NLI Ir 794105 g 1.

Directories

1820	J. Pigot, *Commercial Directory of Ireland.* PRONI; NLI Ir 9141 p 107; LDS film 962702 item 1.
1824	J. Pigot & Co., *City of Dublin and Hibernian Provincial Directory.* NLI; LDS film 451787. Online: Hayes.
1846	Slater's *National Commercial Directory of Ireland.* PRONI; NLI LO; LDS film 1696703 item 3. Online: Hayes.
1856	Slater, *Royal National Commercial Directory of Ireland.* NLI; LDS film 1472360 item 1.
1870	Slater, *Directory of Ireland.* NLI.
1881	Slater, *Royal National Commercial Directory of Ireland.* NLI. Online: FindMyPast.
1894	Slater, *Royal Commercial Directory of Ireland.* NLI.

Gravestone inscriptions

Galway Family History Society West Ltd has transcripts for sixty-one graveyards, mainly in the west of the county. Contact details will be found in Chapter 15. Parts (at least) of eleven Co. Galway graveyards are transcribed at <*www.interment.net*>. Published transcripts are given below.

Ballynakill (Ballynahinch), Ballynakill. Cantwell, *Memorials.*
Drumacoo: Drumacoo: IGRS, Vol. 1.
Kilcummin, Canrawer West (Carraroe?). Cantwell, *Memorials.*
Oughterard, Main St, C of I. Cantwell, *Memorials.*
Killannin, Cloghmore. Cantwell, *Memorials.*
Killimordaly, Killimor, RC. Mulvey, *Memorial inscriptions.*
Kilmacduagh: Lisnagyreeny: IA. NLI Ir 9205 i 3, Vol. 7, No. 1, 1975.
Kiltullagh, Kiltullagh North (Esker?). Mulvey, *Memorial inscriptions.*
Kiltullagh. Mulvey, *Memorial inscriptions.*
Moycullen, Moycullen. Cantwell, *Memorials.*
Spiddle town. Cantwell, *Memorials.*
Moyrus, Ardbear. Cantwell, *Memorials.*
Roundstone town, C of I. Cantwell, *Memorials.*
Omey, Clifden, Chapel Lane, RC. Cantwell, *Memorials.*
Clifden, Church St, C of I. Cantwell, *Memorials.*
Rahoon, Rahoon (Barna, RC?). Cantwell, *Memorials.*
St Nicholas: Galway, Forthill Road: RC: *Forthill graveyard.*
St Nicholas' Church: C of I. Higgins, *Monuments of St. Nicholas.*
Tuam, Tuam. Church Lane (St Mary's?). Higgins, *St Mary's Cathedral.*

Estate records

[**No landlord given**]. NLI 21 g 76 (14) and 21 g 76 (26). Maps of the townlands of Cloonfane and Carogher in Dunmore parish, with tenants' names. Mid-nineteenth century.

[**No landlord given**]. NLI Ms. 4633. Survey of occupiers, townlands of Ballinasoora, Streamsfort, Fortlands and Woodlands, parish of Killimordaly. 1851.

[**No landlord given**]. NLI Mss. 2277–80. Rentals, 1854–5, townlands of Ballyargadaun, Leitrim More, Kylebrack and Knockash in the civil parishes of Leitrim and Kilteskil.

Bellew. Estate wages book, 1679–75. NLI Ms. 9200.

Blake Knox, Francis. Rental, 1845–66. NLI Ms. 3077. Covering townlands in the civil parishes of Annaghdown, Kilmacduagh and Kilmoylan.

Browne, Col. John. NLI Pos. 940. Account of the sales of the estates of Col. John Browne in Cos. Galway and Mayo, compiled in 1778, giving names of major tenants and purchasers, 1698–1704, and those occupying the estates in 1778. Covering townlands in the civil parishes of Ballynakill, Cong, Kilcummin, Killannin, Omey and Ross.

Clanmorris, Lord. Estate rental, 1833. NLI Ms. 3279. All tenants. Covering townlands in the civil parish of Claregalway.

Dillon, Barons Clonbrock. NLI Ms. 19501; tenants ledger, 1801–1806, indexed. NLI Mss. 19585–608 (24 vols.); rentals and accounts, 1827–40. All tenants. NLI Mss. 22008, 22009; maps of the Co. Galway estates, with full valuation of all tenants' holdings. NLI Mss. 19609–616; rentals and accounts, 1840–44. All tenants. Covering townlands in the civil parishes of Ahascragh, Aughrim, Fohanagh, Kilcoona, Killaan, Killallaghtan, Killosolan and Kilteskil.

French family. NLI Ms. 4920; rent ledger, Monivea estate, 1767–77. Major tenants only. NLI Ms. 4929; estate accounts and wages book, 1811/12. All tenants, with index. NLI Ms. 4930; accounts and wages book, 1830–33. Covering townlands in the civil parishes of Abbeyknockmoy, Athenry, Cargin, Claregalway, Monivea, Moylough and Oranmore.

Hodson, Lieut Edward. NLI Ms. 2356. Rent rolls and tenants' accounts, 1797–1824, indexes. Covering townlands in the civil parish of Kiltormer.

St George, Richard St George Mansergh. NLI Pos. 5483. (*a*) Rental of Headford town (all tenants) and (*b*) estate rentals (major tenants only), both 1775. Covering townlands in the civil parishes of Cargin, Donaghpatrick, Kilcoona, Kilkilvery and Killursa.

Shee, George. NA M3105–120. Yearly rentals of the estate in and around Dunmore, 1837–59. All tenants. Covering townlands in the civil parishes of Addergoole, Boyounagh, Clonbern and Dunmore.

Trench. NLI Ms. 2577. Estate rental, 1840–50. Covering townlands in the civil parishes of Ballymacaward, Kilbeacanty, Killaan and Killimordaly.

Wolfe, Theobold. NLI Ms. 3876. Estate maps, with names of major tenants, 1760, indexed. Covering townlands in the civil parishes of Kilmallinoge and Tiranascragh.

KERRY

Census returns and substitutes

1586	Survey of the estates of the Earl of Desmond, recording leaseholders. NAI M.5037.
1641	Book of Survey and Distribution. NLI Ms. 970.
1654	*Civil Survey*, Vol. 4: Dysert, Killury, Rathroe. NLI I 6551 Dublin.
1659	Pender's 'Census'. Reprinted GPC, 1997; IMC, 2002. LDS film 924648. Online: Genweb, Kerry.
1799	Petition of 300 prominent Catholics of Co. Kerry. *Dublin Evening Post*, 9 June 1799.
1809	List of pupils at Tarbert School. NLI Ms. 17935.
1821	Some extracts for Tralee and Annagh. NAI Thrift Abstracts.
1821	Parish of Kilcummin. RIA, McSwiney papers, parcel f, No. 3. LDS film 596419.
1823–38	Tithe Books. NAI.

1834–5	Householders, parishes of Dunquin, Dunurlin, Ferriter, Killemlagh, Kilmalkedar, Kilquane, Marhin and Prior. *JKAHS*, 1974–5. Part online: Ballyferriter.
1835	Tralee Voters. *JKAHS*, No. 19, 1986.
1847–51	Assisted passages, Castlemaine estate, Kiltallagh parish. *AH*, Vol. 22, 1960.
1852	Griffith's Valuation. Indexed online: Hayes.
1901	Census. Online: NAI.
1911	Census. Online: NAI.

Online

Askaboutireland	*<www.askaboutireland.ie>*
Ballyferriter	*<www.rootsweb.ancestry.com/~irlker/mansfieldballyferriter.html>*
Cork City Library	*<www.corkpastandpresent.ie>*
Genweb, Kerry	*<www.rootsweb.ancestry.com/~irlker>*
Hayes, John	*<www.failteromhat.com>*
NAI	*<www.census.nationalarchives.ie>*

Publications

Local histories etc.

Allman, J., *Causeway, location, lore and legend*, Naas: Leinster Leader, 1983. NLI Ir 94146 a 2, 117 p.

Barrington, T.J., *Discovering Kerry*, Dublin: 1976. NLI Ir 94146 b 5, 363 p.

Bary, V.A., *Houses of Co. Kerry*, Clare: Ballinakella Press, 1994. NLI Ir 720 b 32, 247 p.

Brady, W. Maziere, *The McGellycuddy Papers*, London: 1867. NLI Ir 9292 m 3, 209 p.

Brosnan, D.P., *The Brosnans of Glounlea, Co. Kerry*, Tucson, Ariz.: D.P. Brosnan, 1990. LC CS71.B87417 1990.

Browne, Bernard, *In the shadow of Sliabh Mish: Blennerville, Tonevane, Annagh, Curraheen, Derryquay, Derrymore*, Derryquay: Derryquay ICA, 2001. NLI, 176 p.

Casey, Albert, *O'Kief, Cosh Mang, Slieve Lougher, and Upper Blackwater in Ireland*, Privately printed, 1962–74. Massive multi-volume compendium of information on the Sliabh Luachra and Blackwater Valley area on the Cork-Kerry border. NLI Ir 94145 c 12. Index online at Cork City Library.

Costello, Michael, *The famine in Kerry*, Tralee: Kerry Archaeological and Historical Society, 1997. NLI Ir 94146 f 6, 108 p.

Cusack, Mary F., *History of the kingdom of Kerry*, Boston, Mass.: Donohoe, 1871. NLI Ir 94146 c 1, 453 p.

Denny, H.A., *A Handbook of Co. Kerry Family History etc.*, 1923. NLI Ir 9291 d 1.

Dickson, David, *Old World colony: Cork and south Munster, 1630–1830*, Cork: Cork University Press, 2005. NLI, 726 p.

Donovan, T.M., *A Popular History of East Kerry*, Dublin: Talbot Press, 1931. NLI Ir 94146 d 2, 230 p.

Farrell, Noel, *Killarney family roots book: exploring family origins in Killarney*, Longford: Noel Farrell, 2000. NLI, 48 p.

Finuge Heritage Society, *A span across time: Finuge, a folk history*, Finuge Heritage Society.

Gaughan, Rev. J.A., *Listowel and its vicinity*, Cork: Mercier Press, 1973 NLI Ir 94146 g1, 611 p.

Guerin, Michael, *Listowel Workhouse Union*, Listowel: Michael Guerin, 1996. NLI Ir 94146 g 27, 86 leaves.

Harrington, Gerard (Gerdie), *Beara: history and stories from the peninsula*, Cork: Beara Historical Society, 2005. NLI, 305 p.

Herlihy, John, *Footsteps, fiddles, flagstones, and fun: Kilcummin's living tradition*, Kilcummin: Craobh Chill Chuimín, Comhaltas Ceoltóirí Éireann, 2004. NLI, 219 p.

Hickson, Mary, *Selections from Old Kerry Records, Historical and Genealogical*, London: Watson & Hazell, 1872–4. NLI Ir 94146 h 1, 337 p.

IGRS, *Tombstone inscriptions, Vol. 1*, Dublin: IGRS Tombstone Committee, 2001. NLI, 850 p.

Keane, L., *Knocknagoshel: then and now*, Kerry County Library, 1985.

Kelly, Liam, *Blennerville: gateway to Tralee's past*, Tralee: Community Response Programme, 1989. Co-authors, Geraldine Lucid and Maria O'Sullivan. NLI Ir 94146 k 8, 463 p.

Kilcummin Rural Development Group, *Kilcummin: Glimpses of the Past*, Kilcummin: Kilcummin Rural Development Group, 1998.

King, Jeremiah, *County Kerry, Past and Present*, Dublin: Hodges, Figgis & Co., 1931. NLI Ir 94146 k 3, 338 p.

—— *King's history of Kerry, or, History of the parishes in the county, Part IV*, Tralee: 191–. NLI Dix Tralee 284–353 p.

Lansdowne, Marquis of, *Glanerought and the Petty-Fitzmaurices*, London and New York: Oxford University Press, 1937. NLI Ir 94146 L 1, 226 p.

Larner, Jim, *Killarney, history and heritage*, Cork: Collins Press, 2005. NLI, 320 p.

Lucey, Donnacha Seán, *The Irish National League in the Dingle Poor Law Union, 1885–91*, Dublin: Four Courts Press, 2003. NLI, 64 p.

Lynch, Patrick J., *Tarbert, an unfinished biography*, 2008. NLI, 512 p.

Lyne, G.J., *The Lansdowne Estate in Kerry under the agency of William Steuart Trench, 1849–72*, Dublin: Geography Publications, 2001. NLI Ir 94146 L 3, 764 p.

MacLysaght, Edward, *The Kenmare Manuscripts*, Dublin: IMC, 1947.

MacMahon, Bryan, *The story of Ballyheigue*, Baile Uí Thaidhg: Oidhreacht, 1994. NLI Ir 94146 m 9, 264 p.

McMoran, R., *Tralee: a short history and guide to Tralee and environs*, 1980.

MacSwiney, Unpublished manuscripts, RIA. Historical notes and will abstracts, mainly from Cos. Cork and Kerry.

Mitchell, Frank, *Man and Environment in Valencia Island*, Dublin: RIA, 1989. NLI Ir 914146 p 19(4), 130 p.

Moreton, Cole, *Hungry for home: leaving the Blaskets; a journey from the edge of Ireland*, London: Viking, 2000. Emigration to Springfield, Mass., especially. NLI Ir 94146 m 13, 287 p.

O'Carroll, Gerald, *Mr Justice Robert Day (1746–1841): the Diaries (1801–29) and the Addresses (Charges) to Grand Juries (1793–1810)*, Tralee: Polymath Press, 2004. Kerry County Library, 317 p.

Ó Concubhair, Pádraig, *A remote outpost: the story of the Methodist Society in Tarbert, County Kerry, 1820–1960*, the author, 2005. NLI, 96 p.

O'Connor, Michael, *A Guide to Tracing your Kerry Ancestors*, Dublin: Flyleaf Press, 1994. NLI Ir 9291 o 6, 96 p.

O'Connor, T., *Ardfert in times past*, Ardfert: Foilseacháin Bhréanainn, 1990. History of Ardfert parish. NLI Ir 94146 oo 11.

O'Donovan, John, Ordnance Survey Letters: Kerry, 1841; Bray, 1927. Typewritten. 15NLI, Ir 9141 O 8, 222 f.

Ó Loingsigh, Pádraig, *Bórdóinín: a history of the parish of Caherdaniel*, Kerry: Oidhreacht na Stéige, 1999. NLI Ir 94146 o 14, 331 p.

O'Shea, Kieran, *Castleisland: church and people*, Castleisland: the author, 1981. NLI Ir 94146 o 6, 88 p.

—— *Knocknagoshel Parish*, 1991. NLI Ir 270 p 21(1), 47 p.

Palmer, A.H., *Genealogical and historical account of the Palmer family of Kenmare, Co. Kerry*, 1872.

Pochin Mould, Daphne D.C., *Valentia: portrait of an island*, Dublin: Blackwater Press, 1978. NLI Ir 914146 m 7, 143 p.

Prendergast, James, *The Prendergast letters: correspondence from famine-era Ireland, 1840–50*, Amherst, Mass.: University of Massachusetts Press, 2006. Milltown, Co. Kerry. NLI 202 p.

Quane, Michael, *Castleisland Charter School*, Kerry Archaeological and Historical Society, 1968. NLI, 15 p.

Reedy, Rev. Donal A., *The diocese of Kerry (formerly Ardfert)*, Killarney: Catholic Truth Society, 1937. NLI, 46 p.

Siepmann, Dennis, *I am of Ireland: a family social history of the descendants of Dennis Scanlon and Mary Mullen of Lisselton Cross, County Kerry, Ireland, 1798–2002*, Knoxville, Tenn.: Tennessee Valley Pub., c.2002. LC CS71.S285 2002, 647 p.

Smith, Charles, *The Ancient and Present State of the County of Kerry: being a natural, civil, ecclesiastical, historical and topographical description thereof*, Dublin: 1756. Reprinted Dublin: Mercier Press, 1979. NLI Ir 94145 s 5.

Stoakley, T.E., *Sneem: The Knot in the Ring*, Sneem: Sneem Tourism Association, 1986. NLI Ir 94146 s 7, 140 p.

Twomey, Francis, *Beara: the unexplored peninsula*, Dublin: Woodpark Publications, 2007. NLI, 120 p.

Windele, J., Unpublished manuscripts. NLI Pos. 5479. Information on Cork and Kerry families, including Coppinger, Cotter, Crosbie, O'Donovan, O'Keeffe, McCarthy, Sarsfield and others. See also Casey, O'K., Vol. 7.

Local journals
Journal of the Kerry Archaeological and Historical Society. NLI Ir 794105 k 1.
Kenmare Literary and Historical Society Journal.

Directories

1824   J. Pigot & Co., *City of Dublin and Hibernian Provincial Directory.* NLI;
        LDS film 451787. Online: Hayes.

1846   Slater's *National Commercial Directory of Ireland.* PRONI; NLI LO; LDS
        film 1696703 item 3. Online: Hayes.

1856   Slater, *Royal National Commercial Directory of Ireland.* NLI; LDS film
        1472360 item 1.

1867   Henry and Coughlan's *General Directory of Cork and Munster.* Archive
        CD Books Ireland

1870   Slater, *Directory of Ireland.* NLI.

1881   Slater, *Royal National Commercial Directory of Ireland.* NLI. Online:
        FindMyPast.

1886   Francis Guy, *Postal Directory of Munster.* NLI Ir 91414 g 8; LDS film
        1559399 item 8.

1893   Francis Guy, *Directory of Munster.* NLI Ir 91414 g 8.

1894   Slater, *Royal Commercial Directory of Ireland.* NLI.

Gravestone inscriptions

The situation with transcripts compiled by the Kerry Genealogical Society and
Finuge Heritage Society is unclear. They may be available through Killarney
Library, Rock Road, Killarney. Kerry local authority burial registers, 1898–2008,
are online at <*www.kerrylaburials.ie*>.

Aghadoe: Parkavonear (Fossa?), O'K., Vol. 6.
Aghadoe: Knoppoge (Aghadoe?), C of I, O'K., Vol. 6.
Aghavallen: Rusheen, C of I, Kerry Genealogical Society.
Aglish: C of I, O'K., Vol. 6.
Ardfert: Ardfert town, C of I, O'K., Vol. 8.
Ballincuslane: Cordal East, O'K., Vol. 6.
Ballincuslane: Kilmurry, O'K., Vol. 6.
Ballymacelligott: C of I, O'K., Vol. 8.
—— Ballymacelligot, O'K., Vol. 11.
Ballynahaglish: Spa, O'K., Vol. 11.
Brosna: O'K., Vol. 6.
Caher: Cahersiveen (Killevanoge), IGRS Collection, GO.
Caher: Caherciveen Marian Place, IGRS Collection, GO. Also Finuge Heritage
    Society.
Castleisland: Church Lane, C of I, O'K., Vol. 6.
—— Kilbannivane, O'K., Vol. 6.
—— Meenbannivane (Dysert?), O'K., Vol. 6.

Clogherbrien: Clogherbrien, *o'k.*, Vol. 8.
Currans: Ardcrone, *o'k.*, Vol. 6.
Dingle: Raheenyhooig, IGRS, Vol. 1.
Duagh: Islandboy (Duagh?), *o'k.*, Vol. 11.
Dysert: Kilsarkan East, *o'k.*, Vol. 6.
Finuge: Finuge Heritage Society. Also Kerry Genealogical Society.
Kilcummin: Glebe, *o'k.*, Vol. 6.
—— Gneevegullia, *o'k.*, Vol. 6.
Kilcummin: Kilquane, *o'k.*, Vol. 6.
Killarney: Muckross, *o'k.*, Vol. 6.
—— Killarney (new), *o'k.*, Vol. 6.
Killeentierna: C of I, *o'k.*, Vol. 6.
Killehenny: (Ballybunion?), *o'k.*, Vol. 11.
Killorglin: *o'k.*, Vol. 11.
—— Dromavally (Killorglin?), *o'k.*, Vol. 8.
Kilnanare: Kilnanare, *o'k.*, Vol. 6.
Listowel: Listowel, *o'k.*, Vol. 11.
Molahiffe: Castlefarm (Molahiff?), *o'k.*, Vol. 6.
Murher: Murher, Kerry Genealogical Society.
Nohaval: Ballyregan, *o'k.*, Vol. 8.
—— Nohaval, *o'k.*, Vol. 11.
O'Brennan: *o'k.*, Vol. 11.
—— Crag, *o'k.*, Vol. 8.
Tralee: Tralee, Nelson St, C of I, *o'k.*, Vol. 8.
—— Tralee, Brewery Road, *o'k.*, Vol. 8.
—— Tralee, Castle St Lower, C of I, *o'k.*, Vol. 8.

Estate records

[**No landlord given—Locke?**]. Rental of the Feale river fishery, early nineteenth century. NAI M3296. Major tenants only. Covering townlands in the civil parishes of Ballyconry, Duagh, Dysert (Listowel), Finuge, Killeentierna, Killehenny, Listowel and Rattoo.

Asgill. Account book, 1709. NAI M 1854. Major tenants only. Covering townlands in the civil parishes of Currans, Kilbonane, Kilcredane, Killarney, Killeentierna, Kiltomy and Tuosist.

Browne, Earls of Kenmare. Assorted rentals, maps and estate accounts for areas around Kenmare and in the barony of Dunkerron, from 1620 to 1864, in Edward MacLysaght, *The Kenmare Manuscripts*, Dublin: 1942. See also *O'Kief, Coshe Mang etc.*, Vols. 6, 7, 9.

Crosbie, John, Viscount. Rent ledger, 1805–1812. NLI Ms. 5033. Most tenants. Indexed, with detailed abstracts of lives in leases. Covering townlands in the civil parishes of Currans, Kilbonane, Kilcredane, Killarney, Killeentierna, Kiltomy and Tuosist.

Fitzmaurice, F.T. Seven sets of rentals, 1742–86, with comments on lives in leases. NLI Pos. 176–7 (Paris, Archives Nationales). Major tenants only. Covering townlands in the civil parishes of Aghavallen, Ardfert, Ballyconry, Ballynahaglish, Duagh, Dysert (Listowel), Fenit, Finuge, Galey, Kilcaragh, Kilcolman, Kilconly, Kilcredane, Kilfeighny, Killahan, Killeentierna, Killehenny, Killury, Kilmoyly, Kilnanare, Kilshenane, Kiltomy, Knockanure, Lisselton, Listowel, O'Dorney and Rattoo.

Gun Mahoney. Map, 1832. NLI Ms. 26812 (6). All tenants. Covering townlands in the civil parishes of Aghavallen, Ardfert, Galey and Kilcrohane.

Herbert. Rent rolls, 1760 and 1761. NAI M 1864. Covering townlands in the civil parishes of Aghadoe, Aglish, Ballincuslane, Brosna, Castleisland, Cloghane, Dingle, Dysert (Trughanacmy), Garfinny, Kilcredane, Kilcrohane, Kilcummin, Killaha, Killarney, Killeentierna, Killorglin, Kilnanare, Knockane, Valencia and Ventry.

Herbert, Richard Townsend. Account book, 1709. NAI M 1854. Major tenants only. Covering townlands in the civil parishes of Currans, Kilbonane, Kilflyn and Killeentierna. Rent and account book, 1741–52. NAI M 1854. Covering townlands in the civil parishes of Aghadoe, Aglish, Ballymacelligott, Ballynacourty, Brosna, Caher, Duagh, Dysert (Listowel), Galey, Garfinny, Kilbonane, Kilcredane, Kilcrohane, Kilcummin, Kilgarrylander, Killaha, Killarney, Killeentierna, Killorglin, Kilnanare, Kilquane, Kiltomy, Knockane, Minard, Molahiffe, Nohavaldaly and O'Brennan.

Kerry, Earl of. Rent roll, 1761–4. NAI M 3302. Major tenants only. Covering townlands in the civil parishes of Aghavallen, Ardfert, Ballymacelligott, Ballynahaglish, Dingle, Duagh, Dysert (Listowel), Fenit, Finuge, Galey, Kilcaragh, Kilcummin, Kilfeighny, Killahan, Killehenny, Kilmoyly, Kilshenane, Kiltomy, Lisselton, Listowel, O'Dorney and Rattoo.

Lefroy, Thomas. Abstract of leases, 1781. NLI Ms. 10933 (Part 5). Major tenants only. Covering townlands in the civil parishes of Ballymacelligott, Kilmoyly and Kiltallagh.

Listowel, Earl of. Tithes, 1838. NAI M2356. Most tenants. Covering the civil parishes of Ardfert, Galey, Kilcaragh, Killahan, Kilshenane, Kiltomy and O'Dorney.

Locke. Summary of leases, 1801, with many comments on lives in leases. NAI M3284. Major tenants only. Covering townlands in the civil parishes of Ardfert, Ballincuslane, Duagh, Dysert (Listowel), Fenit, Kilcaragh, Kilfeighny, Killehenny, Kilshenane, Kiltomy, Lisselton and Rattoo.

MacGillicuddy. NLI Ms. 3014, MacGillicuddy papers. Rentals, 1707 (p. 186), 1777 (p. 176) n.d (early eighteenth century?) (p. 172). Major tenants only. Covering townlands in the civil parishes of Kilbonane, Kilcummin, Killarney, Killorglin, Knockane and Tuosist.

Monsell. Rental, 1842. NLI Ms. 7868. All tenants. Covering townlands in the civil parishes of Ballycahane, Kilkeedy, Killeely, Kiltallagh, Mungret and Rathronan.

Naper, James Lenox. Rental, mainly Co. Meath, 1733–1814. NLI Ms. 3031. Major tenants only. Covering townlands in the civil parish of Knockane.

Orpen. 'Land Tenure in Tuosist and Kenmare', *JKAHS*, 1976, 1978, 1979. Rentals. All tenants. Covering townlands in the civil parishes of Kenmare and Tuosist.

Rice, Stephen Edward. Summary of rents of Coolkeragh, Co. Kerry, parish of Galey, 1806–1823. NLI Ms. 605 F. All tenants.

Sandes, Thomas. Rental of the estate, 1792–1828. Covering parts of the parishes of Aghavallin, Kilnaughtin and Murher. NLI Ms. 1792.

Talbot-Crosbie, William. Rental, 1845–9. NLI Ms. Ms. 5035. All tenants, with some comments on tenancies. Covering townlands in the civil parishes of Ardfert, Duagh, Kilbonane, Kilgobban, Killahan, Kilmoyly, Kiltomy, O'Dorney and Rattoo.

KILDARE

Census returns and substitutes

1641	Testimonies of 331 witnesses to the 1641 Rebellion. Online: 1641.
1641	Book of Survey and Distribution. Also NLI Ms. 971. JKAS, Vol. 10, 1922–8.
1654	*Civil Survey*, Vol. 8.
1659	Pender's 'Census'. Reprinted GPC, 1997; IMC, 2002. LDS film 924648.
1766	Catholic householders in Kilrush and Comerford. Collections relating to Kildare and Leighlin. Ballycommon, parish of Clonaghlis, JKAS, 7 (4), 1913, pp. 274–6, Ballymore Eustace and Tipperkevin. Online: PRONI name search.
1798	Persons who suffered losses in the 1798 Rebellion. Propertied classes only. c.320 names. NLI I 94107.
1804	Yeomanry Order Book for the tpwnland of Millicent, giving names and addresses of officers and men. JKAS, 13 (4), 1953, pp. 211–19.
1807	Tithe estimate, Kildare parish. NAI MFCI 70.
1823–38	Tithe Books.
1831	Kilcullen. Protestant returns only. NAI; also GO Ms. 622, pp. 53ff; NAI M 150(2).
1837	Memorial from inhabitants of Ballymore Eustace. c.100 names. NAI OP 1837/397.
1837	Voters. NLI Ms. 1398.
1840	Castledermot and Moone. NLI Pos. 3511.
1843	Voters. NAI OP 1843/53.
1851	Griffith's Valuation. Online: Askaboutireland.
1901	Census. Online: NAI.
1911	Census. Online: NAI.

Online

Askaboutireland	*<www.askaboutireland.ie>*
Ehistory	*<www.kildare.ie/library/ehistory>*
Hayes, John	*<www.failteromhat.com>*
PRONI name search	*<www.proni.gov.uk>*
NAI	*<www.census.nationalarchives.ie>*

Publications

Local histories etc.

Andrews, J.H., *Irish Historic Towns Atlas, 1: Kildare*, Dublin: RIA, 1989. NLI ILB 941 i 3(1).

Archbold, W.D., *The Archbolds of Roseville: an anthology of the Archbold family of Eadestown, County Kildare, Ireland, in the colony of New South Wales*, Birrong, NSW: Bill Archbold Ministries, 1997. Rathmore parish. NLI, 177 p.

Athy Union, *Athy Union list of destitute persons relieved out of the workhouse in the Stradbally District, Athy Union*, Naas: Athy Union, 1845. NLI, Poster.

Brennan, M., *Schools of Kildare and Leighlin, 1775–1835*, Dublin: M.H. Gill & Son, 1935. NLI Ir 37094135 b 4, 616 p.

Bunbury, Turtle, *The Landed Gentry and Aristocracy of Co. Kildare*, Wexford: Irish Family Names, 2004. Aylmer, Barton, de Burgh, Clements, Conolly, Guinness, Henry, Fennell, FitzGerald, Latten, La Touche, Mansfield, Maunsell, Medlicott, More O'Ferrall, Moore, de Robeck and Wolfe.

Carey, Michael, Journal of Michael Carey, Athy, Co. Kildare. Letters, leases, social commentary, 1840–59. NLI Ms. 25299.

Carville, Geraldine, *Monasterevin, Valley of Roses*, Monasterevin: 1989.

Colgan, John, *Leixlip, County Kildare, Vol. 1*, Leixlip: Tyrconnell Press, 2005. NLI, 268 p.

Comerford, Rev. M., *Collections relating to Kildare and Leighlin*, Dublin: J. Duffy, 1883–6. NLI Ir 27413 c 4, 3 vols.

Connolly, Mary, *From Connell to Droichead Nua*, Naas: Leinster Leader, 2003.

Corrigan, Mario, *All that Delirium of the brave: Kildare in 1798*, Naas: Kildare County Council, 1998. NLI Ir 94135 c 12, 143 p.

—— *Cill Dara Historical Society, essays from the Kildare Nationalist, 6 March–30 December, 2009, and An Tóstal souvenir booklet, 1953*, Kildare: Cill Dara Historical Society, 2009. Kildare town. NLI, 176 p.

Costello, Con, *A most delightful station: the British Army on the Curragh of Kildare, Ireland, 1855–1922*, Cork: Collins Press, 1996. NLI Ir 355 c 18, 431 p.

—— *Kildare: Saints, Soldiers and Horses*, Naas: Leinster Leader, 1991. NLI Ir 94135.c.8184 p, 184 p.

—— *Looking Back: Aspects of History, Co. Kildare*, Naas: Leinster Leader, 1988. NLI Ir 94135 c 7, 113 p.

Coyle, James, *The Antiquities of Leighlin*, Dublin: Browne & Nolan, n.d. NLI Ir 94138 c 1.

Cullen, Seamus, *Unity in division: a history of Christianity in Kilcock and Newton Parish, 400–2000*, Kilcock: Kilcock Publication Millennium Committee, 1999. NLI, 197 p.

Doohan, Tony, *A History of Celbridge*, Dublin: n.d. NLI Ir 94135 d 2, 88 p.

Duggan, John, *250 years at Highfield, Co. Kildare: a short history of the Duggan family, researched, compiled and edited by John Duggan*. Highfield Publications. NLI, 64 p.

Dunlop, Robert, *Waters under the bridge: the saga of the La Touches of Harristown, John Ruskin and his Irish Rose*, Brannockstown: 1988. NLI Ir 9292 p 29(3), 64 p.

Durney, James, *Far from the short grass: Kildare men in the two World Wars*, Durney, 1999. NLI Ir 94135 d 4, 259 p.

Flynn, Michael, *Outline histories . . . Kelly of Youngstown, Kilmead, Athy, Co. Kildare, Murphy of Togher, Roundwood, Co. Wicklow, Masterson family of Ardellis, Athy, Co. Kildare (with descendants)*. Mullingar: Michael P. Flynn, 1997. NLI Ir 9292 f.

Gibson, Comdt W.H., *St. Peter's Church, Two-Mile-House, 1790–1990*, Naas: St Peter's Church Bi-centenary Committee, 1990. NLI Ir 27413 s 6, 176 p.

Hickey, Stan, *Nás na Ríogh: From Poorhouse road to the Fairy Flax: an illustrated history of Naas*, Naas: Naas Local History Group, 2007. Co-editor, Liam Kenny. NLI, 176 p.

Horner, Arnold, *Irish Historic Towns Atlas, 7: Maynooth*, Dublin: RIA, 1995. NLI, ILB 941 p 13 (4).

IGRS, *Tombstone inscriptions, Vol. 1*, Dublin: IGRS Tombstone Committee, 2001. NLI, 850 p.

—— *Index to Ballyna Roman Catholic registers, 1785–1899*. KAS, 1988. NLI Ir 9293 i 4.

Kavanagh, Michael V., *A contribution towards a bibliography of the history of County Kildare in printed books*, Kildare: Kildare County Library Council. NLI Ir 94135 k 1, 328 p.

Leadbeater, Mary, *The Annals of Ballitore*, London: 1862. Shackleton. NLI Ir 92 l 8.

—— *Lest we forget: Kildare and the Great Famine*, Naas: Kildare County Council, 1996. NLI Ir 94108 L 21, 106 p.

McAuliffe, E.J., *An Irish genealogical source: the roll of the Quaker School at Ballitore, County Kildare: with an index and notes on certain families*, Blackrock, Co. Dublin: Irish Academic Press, 1984. NLI Ir 92001 m 26, 49 p.

MacKenna, John, *Castledermot and Kilkea: a social history, with notes on Ballytore, Graney, Moone and Mullaghmast*, Athy: Winter Wood Books, 1982. NLI Ir 94135 m 5, 60 p.

Mac Suibhne, Peadar, *Rathangan*, Maynooth: Tomás Ó Fiaich, 1975. NLI Ir 94135 m 3, 323 p.

Magee, Sean, *Weavers of Prosporous, County Kildare, Balbriggan, County Dublin and Tullamore, County Offaly in memorials of 1826*, Dún Laoghaire: Dún Laoghaire Genealogical Society, 1998. NLI Ir 9291 g 7.

Mahon Behan, Vera, *Athy and district*. NLI, 56 p.

Naas Local History Group, *Nás na Ríogh: . . . an illustrated history of Naas*, Naas: Naas Local History Group, 1990. NLI Ir 94135 n 2, 144 p.

Nelson, Gerald, *A History of Leixlip*, Naas: Kildare County Library, 1990. NLI Ir 94135.n.1, 68 p.

Nolan, W., *Kildare history and society: interdisciplinary essays on the history of an Irish county*, Dublin: Geography Publications, 2006. Co-editor, Thomas McGrath. NLI, 807 p.

Ó Conchubhair, Séamus, *A History of Kilcock and Newtown*, 1987.

Ó Dálaigh, Brian, *Irish villages: studies in local history*, Dublin: Four Courts Press, 2003. Carbury. NLI, 326 p.

O'Donovan, John, *Ordnance Survey letters, Kildare, 1836, 1838, 1839*, Dublin: Fourmasters Press, 2002. NLI LO 8198, 230 p.

O'Dowd, Desmond J., *Changing times: religion and society in nineteenth-century Celbridge*, Dublin: Irish Academic Press, 1997. NLI Ir 94135 o 6, 73 p.

Ó Dubhshláine, Mícheál, *Are you going home now?: memories of old Kilkea*, Trá Lí: Tig Áine, 2006. NLI, 239 p.

Ó Muineog, Mícheál, *Kilcock GAA: A History*, 1989.

Paterson, J. (ed.), *Diocese of Meath and Kildare: an historical guide*, 1981. NLI Ir 941 p 75.

Quane, Michael, *Ballitore School*, Kildare: Kildare Archaeological Society, 1966/7. NLI P, pp. 174–209.

Reid, J.N.S., *Church of St Michael and All Angels, Clane*, 1983.

Ryan, Eileen, *Monasterevan parish, Co. Kildare: some historical notes* . . . Naas: 1958. NLI Ir 91413.r.1, 75 p.

Shackleton, Betsy, *Ballitore and its inhabitants seventy years ago*, Dublin: printed by Richard D. Webb & Son, 1862. NLI Oke 398, 110 p.

Shackleton, Jonathan, *The Shackletons of Ballitore (1580–1987)*, Dublin: the author, 1988. NLI GO 268.

Wolfe, Major R., *Wolfes of Forenaghts, Blackhall, Baronrath, Co. Kildare, Tipperary, Cape of Good Hope, &c.: also the old Wolfes of Co. Kildare, and the Wolfes of Dublin*, Guilford: W. Matthews, 1885. NLI Ir 9292 w 4, 17, 23, 107 p.

Local journals

The Bridge: Kilcullen community magazine. NLI Ir 94135 b 2.

Journal of the Kildare Archaeological Society. NLI Ir 794106 k 2.

Reportorium Novum. NLI Ir 27413 r 3.

Directories

1788	Richard Lucas, *General Directory of the Kingdom of Ireland*. NLI Pos. 3729. Reprinted in Veale, *Lucas, IG*, 1965, 1966, 1967, 1968.
1824	J. Pigot & Co., *City of Dublin and Hibernian Provincial Directory*. NLI; LDS film 451787. Online: Hayes.
1846	Slater's *National Commercial Directory of Ireland*. PRONI; NLI LO; LDS film 1696703 item 3. Online: Hayes.
1856	Slater, *Royal National Commercial Directory of Ireland*. NLI; LDS film 1472360 item 1.
1870	Slater, *Directory of Ireland*. NLI.
1881	Slater, *Royal National Commercial Directory of Ireland*. NLI. Online: FindMyPast.
1894	Slater, *Royal Commercial Directory of Ireland*. NLI.

Gravestone inscriptions

Parts (at least) of seven Co. Kildare graveyards are transcribed at <*www. interment.net*>.

Ardkill: Ballyshannon, GO. Ms. 622, p. 108.

Ballaghmoon: Ballaghmoon, Kildare County Library, IGRS, Vol. 1.

Ballynafagh: Ballynafagh, C of I, Kildare County Library.

Belan: Belan, Kildare County Library, IGRS, Vol. 1.

Castledermot: Castledermot town, C of I, Kildare County Library. Also IGRS, Vol. 1.

—— Ballyhade, Kildare County Library, IGRS, Vol. 1.

—— St James, Kildare County Library.

—— Franciscan Friary, Kildare County Library.

—— Prumplestown, Kildare County Library.

Clane: Clane town, C of I, Kildare County Library.

Curragh Military Cemetery: Online: <*www.curragh.info*>.

Donadea: Donadea South, C of I, Kildare County Library.

Dunmanoge: Kildare County Library, IGRS, Vol. 1.

Dunmanoge: Maganey Upper, RC, GO Ms. 622, p. 108.

—— Castleroe Rath, Kildare County Library.

—— Levistown, Kildare County Library.

Dunmurraghill: Dunmurraghill, Kildare County Library.

Fontstown: Fontstown Lower, GO Ms. 622, p. 148/9.

Graney: Knockpatrick, Kildare County Library, IGRS, Vol. 1.

Harristown: Harristown Lower, GO. Ms.622, 126/7.

Kilcock: Kilcock, Church Lane, C of I, Kildare County Library.

Kilcullen: Oldkilcullen, *Co. Carlow Tombstone Inscriptions*, Vol. 3. NLI Ir 9295 c 3.

—— Kineagh, Kildare County Library, IGRS, Vol. 1.

Kildare: Church and Friary Lane, C of I, IGRS, Vol. 1.

Kilkea: Kilkea Lower, Kildare County Library.

Killelan: Killelan, Kildare County Library, IGRS, Vol. 1.

—— Killeen Cormac, Kildare County Library, Also IGRS, Vol. 1.

Kilteel: *JKAS*, 1981/2. NLI Ir 794106 k 2.

Moone: Kildare County Library, IGRS, Vol. 1.

—— Moone Abbey, Kildare County Library, IGRS, Vol. 1.

Narraghmore: Moyleabbey, Kildare County Library, IGRS, Vol. 1.

—— Mullamast, Kildare County Library.

St Michael's: Athy, GO Ms. 622, 89.

Straffan: Barberstown, *JKAS*, 1977/8.

Taghadoe: C of I, Kildare County Library.

Tankardstown: Levistown, Kildare County Library.

Timahoe: Timahoe East, Kildare County Library.

Timolin: C of I, IGRS, Vol. 1, Kildare County Library.

—— Ballitore, Quaker, Kildare County Library.

Estate records

[No landlord given]. Map and survey, 1840. NLI Ms. 21.F.103(6). All tenants. Covering townlands in the civil parishes of Ballybought, Ballymore Eustace, Ballysax, Bodenstown, Carn, Carnalway, Churchtown, Fontstown, Gilltown, Jago, Kilberry, Kill, Killashee, Naas, Narraghmore, Rathmore and Sherlockstown.

[No landlord given]. Maps, 1707–1838. NLI Ms. 21.F.34(1–38). Most tenants. Covering townlands in the civil parishes of Aghavallen, Balraheen, Brideschurch, Carragh, Carrick, Downings, Dunfierth, Greatconnell, Kilcock, Kilcullen, Killelan, Kilrainy, Kineagh, Moone, Naas, Nurney and Rathernan.

Aylmer, Michael. Rent roll, 1796. NLI Ms. 9056. Major tenants only. Covering townlands in the civil parishes of Kill, Lyons and Mylerstown.

Christ Church, Dublin, Dean and Chapter of. Maps and rentals, 1692–1838. NLI Mss. 2789–90. Major tenants only. Covering townlands in the civil parishes of Ardkill and Kilcullen.

Cloncurry, Lord. Accounts and rentals, 1814–53. NLI Ms. 8183. Major tenants only. Covering townlands in the civil parishes of Castledermot, Cloncurry, Clonshanbo, Donadea, Lyons and Rathangan.

Colleys, Hon. Misses. Maps and rentals, with detailed comments, 1744. NLI Ms. 9212. Major tenants only. Covering townlands in the civil parishes of Ardkill, Carbury, Carrick, Kilmore and Mylerstown.

Deane, J.W. Rentals, 1845–81. NLI Mss. 14281–2. All tenants. Covering townlands in the civil parishes of Kilkea and Timolin.

de Burgh. Maps and rentals, 1787–1850. NLI Pos. 4576 (De Burgh Papers). Coverage unclear. Covering townlands in the civil parish of Naas.

Drogheda, Earl of. Rentals, 1746–1801. NLI Mss. 12720–23. Principally major tenants. Covering townlands in the civil parishes of Ballybrackan, Cadamstown, Fontstown, Harristown, Lackagh, Monasterevin and Narraghmore.

Drogheda, Earl of. Rentals, 1810–15. NLI Mss. 12724–33. All tenants. Covering townlands in the civil parishes of Ballybrackan, Fontstown, Harristown, Kilrush, Monasterevin and Narraghmore.

Drogheda, Earl of. Rentals, 1838–83. NLI Mss. 9737–8. Most tenants (?). Covering townlands in the civil parishes of Ballybrackan, Fontstown, Harristown, Monasterevin and Narraghmore.

Edgeworth, Richard. Rental book with details of leases, 1796. NAI M.1503. All tenants. Covering townlands in the civil parish of Kilkea.

Fitzgerald, Maurice. Accounts, 1768–82. NLI Ms. 23458. Major tenants only. Covering townlands in the civil parishes of Feighcullen and Rathangan.

Fitzwilliam, Earl. NLI Mss. 6069–72, rentals, 1796. NLI Mss. 6069–72, rentals, 1796–1808. NLI Mss. 6077–81, rentals, 1813–25. Most tenants. Covering townlands in the civil parish of Naas.

Kildare, Earl of. NLI Pos. 1431 (BM Harleian Ms. 7200), rent roll, 1684. Principally major tenants. Covering townlands in the civil parishes of Ballaghmoon,

Ballybrackan, Balraheen, Castledermot, Churchtown, Clane, Cloncurry, Donaghmore, Duneany, Dunmanoge, Dunmurry, Feighcullen, Fontstown, Graney, Grangerosnolvan, Harristown, Kilberry, Kilcock, Kildare, Kilkea, Killelan, Kineagh, Lackagh, Laraghbryan, Leixlip, Moone, Morristownbiller, Naas, Narraghmore, Oughterard, Pollardstown, Rathangan, Rathernan, St John's, St Michael's, Taghadoe, Tankardstown, Thomastown, Tipper and Walterstown.

Lattin, George. Mansfield papers. Rent ledgers, 1742–73. NLI Mss. 9635–6. All tenants. Covering townlands in the civil parishes of Forenaghts, Greatconnell, Killashee, Ladytown and Naas.

Leinster, Duke of. Lease books, 1780–1850. NLI Mss. 19908–910. All tenants. Covering townlands in the civil parishes of Ballybrackan, Ballysax, Cloncurry, Duneany, Dunmurry, Feighcullen, Grangeclare, Harristown, Haynestown, Kildare, Naas, Oughterard, Pollardstown, Rathangan, Rathernan, Rathmore, Thomastown, Tipper, Tipperkevin and Walterstown. NLI Mss. 19911–12, lease books, 1780–1850. Covering townlands in the civil parishes of Ballaghmoon, Castledermot, Dunmanoge, Graney, Grangerosnolvan, Kilkea, Killelan, Kineagh, Moone, Narraghmore and Tankardstown. NLI Mss. 19921–2, tenants registers. All tenants. Covering townlands in the civil parishes of Ballybrackan, Ballysax, Castledermot, Duneany, Dunmurry, Feighcullen, Grangeclare, Kildare, Pollardstown, Thomastown and Walterstown.

Magan, William Henry. Maps, 1848. NLI Ms. 14.A.27. All tenants. Covering townlands in the civil parishes of Ballyshannon, Cloncurry and Kilrush.

Mansfield, John. Map, 1813. NLI Ms. 16.H.34(5). All tenants. Covering townlands in the civil parish of Carragh.

Oxmantown, Lord. Accounts, 1798–9. NAI M.1279. Major tenants only. Covering townlands in the civil parish of Clane.

Rockingham, Marquis of. Rent roll, 1735–48. NLI Ms. 6054. Most tenants. Covering townlands in the civil parish of Naas. NLI Ms. 6053, accounts and rentals. Major tenants only. Covering townlands in the civil parishes of Kilcullen, Naas and Tipperkevin. NLI Mss. 6062–3, rentals, 1778–81. Most tenants. Covering townlands in the civil parishes of Carragh, Naas and Tipperkevin.

Sabine, Joseph. Maps and rentals, 1777–83. NLI Ms. 679. Principally major tenants. Covering townlands in the civil parishes of Ballymore Eustace and Ladytown.

Sarsfield-Vesy. Rentals and accounts, NAI; see RDKPRI 56. Covering townlands in the civil parishes of Carn, Clane, Feighcullen, Morristownbiller, Naas and Tully.

Valentia, Viscount. Maps and rentals, 1773. NLI Ms. 19024. Major tenants only. Covering townlands in the civil parishes of Ballysax, Cloncurry and Lullymore.

KILKENNY

Census returns and substitutes

1641   Book of Survey and Distribution. NLI Ms. 975.

1641   Testimonies of 212 Carlow and Kilkenny witnesses to the 1641 Rebellion. Online: 1641.

1650–1800   Dunnamaggan. *Old Kilkenny Review*, 1992, 958.

1654   Kilkenny town. *Civil Survey*, Vol. 8. NLI I 6551 Dublin.

1659   Pender's 'Census'. Reprinted GPC, 1997; IMC, 2002. LDS film 924648.

1664   Hearth Money Rolls, parishes of Agherney, Aghavillar, Bellaghtobin, Belline, Burnchurch, Callan, Castleinch, Clone, Coolaghmore, Coolcashin, Danganmore, Derrinahinch, Dunkitt, Earlstown, Eyverk, Fartagh, Inishnagg and Stonecarthy, Jerpoint, Kells, Kilbeacon and Killahy, Kilcolm, Kilferagh, Kilkredy, Killamery, Killaloe, Killree, Kilmoganny, Kiltackaholm. Knocktopher and Kilkerchill, Muckalee and Lismatigue, Outrath, Ratbach, Rathpatrick, Tullaghanbrogue, Tullaghmaine and Urlingford. *IG*, 1974–5.

1684–1769   Registers of Kilkenny College. NLI Pos. 4545.

1702   Partial parishioners lists, St Mary's and St Canice's parishes, Kilkenny town. NAI List 63 (Priim 8, 11, 15, 16).

1715   Protestant males between 16 and 60 in St John's parish, Kilkenny town. NAI.

1750–1844   Inistiogue emigrants in Newfoundland. Whelan, *Kilkenny History and Society*.

1752   Burgesses and Freemen of Inistioge, *IG*, Vol. 10, 1, 1998, pp. 113–17.

1766   Portnascully, Catholic householders. GO 683–4; also LDS film 100158.

1775   Landowners. GO 443.

1785   Freeholders (incomplete). GO 443; LDS film 100158.

1785–1819   Freeholders: 1785 (incomplete), GO 443; LDS film 100158; 1786–1809 (Iverk only) GO 684; LDS film 100158; 1809–1819, NLI Ms. 14181.

1785–1879   'Kilkenny city deeds', *Old Kilkenny Review*, Vol. 2, No. 4.

1797   Chief Catholic inhabitants, parishes of Graiguenamanagh and Knocktopher. *IA*, 1978.

1811–58   Registers and Accounts of St Kieran's College. NLI Pos. 973.

1819   Memorial of the inhabitants of Ballyraggett for the appointment of a Butter Master. c.50 names. NAI OP 1832/49.

1821   Extracts only for Pollrone, *IA* 1976, 1977. Extracts from the 1821 census, parishes of Aglish, Clonmore, Fiddown, Kilmacow, Polerone, Rathkyran and Whitechurch. GO 684 (Walsh-Kelly Notebooks). Also *IG*, Vol. 5, 1978; Veale, *Census*.

1822–30   *Co. Kilkenny, Division of Kilkenny and Thomastown, applicants for the vote.* (Kilkenny, 1,285 names; Thomastown, 2,525 names). NLI ILB 324.

1823–38   Tithe Books. Part online: Connors.

1831	Extracts from the 1831 census, parishes of Aglish, Clonmore, Kilmacow, Polerone, Rathkyran and Tybroghney. GO 684 (Walsh-Kelly Notebooks).
1841	Extracts from the 1841 census, parishes of Aglish and Rathkyran. GO 684 (Walsh-Kelly Notebooks). Townlands of Aglish and Portnahully only. *IA*, 1977.
1842	Voters. NAI OP 1842/79.
1847–53	Assisted emigration from Castlecomer Union, Lyng, *Castlecomer.* Online: Connors. c.650 names.
1849–50	Griffith's Valuation. Online: Askaboutireland.
1851	Parish of Aglish. *IA*, 1977. Also GO 684 (Walsh-Kelly Notebooks).
1901	Census. Online: NAI.
1911	Census. Online: NAI.

Online

1641	<www.1641.tcd.ie>	
Askaboutireland	<www.askaboutireland.ie>	
Celtic Cousins	<www.celticcousins.net>	Walsh-Kelly parish extracts
Connors	<www.connorsgenealogy.com>	
Genweb, Kilkenny	<www.rootsweb.ancestry.com/~irlkik>	
Hayes, John	<www.failteromhat.com>	

Publications

Local histories etc.

Alsworth, W.J., *History of Thomastown and District*, 1953. NLI JP 1996.

Bennett McCuaig, Carol, *Leinster to Lanark*, Renfrew, Ont.: Juniper Books, 2010. Post-1798 emigrants from Cos. Carlow, Kilkenny, Wexford and Wicklow to Lanark County, Ottawa. NLC, 284 p.

Bradley, John, *Irish Historic Towns Atlas, 10: Kilkenny*, Dublin: RIA, 2000. NLI.

—— *Kilkenny through the centuries: chapters in the history of an Irish city*, Kilkenny: Kilkenny Borough Council, 2009. NLI, 527 p.

Brennan, M., *Schools of Kildare and Leighlin, 1775–1835*, Dublin: M.H. Gill & Son, 1935. NLI Ir 37094135 b 4, 616 p.

Brennan, T.A., *A History of the Brennans of Idaugh in Co. Kilkenny*, New York: 1979. NLI Ir 9292 b 45.

Burtchaell, G., *Genealogical memoirs of the members of Parliament for the county and city of Kilkenny . . . 1295–1888*, Dublin: Sealy, Bryers & Walker, 1888. NLI Ir 920041 b 3, 276 p.

Carrigan, Rev. William, *The History and Antiquities of the Diocese of Ossory*, Kilkenny: Roberts Books, 1980. Reprint of 1905 edition. NLI Ir 27413 c 9, 4 vols.

Carville, Geraldine, *Norman splendour: Duiske Abbey, Graignamanagh*, Belfast: Blackstaff Press, 1979. NLI Ir 270 c 30, 119 p.

—— A town remembers: Duiske Abbey, Graignamanagh: an illustrated history and guide, 1980. NLI 4A 1771, 48 p.

—— County Kilkenny Tombstone Inscriptions, Vol. 5, St Mullins: Muintir na Tíre, 1988–9. 200 p. Kilkenny County Library.

Coyle, James, The Antiquities of Leighlin, Dublin: Browne & Nolan, n.d. NLI Ir 94138 c 1.

Doyle, Pat, County Kilkenny Tombstone Inscriptions, Vol. 4: Paulstown and Goresbridge, St Mullins: Muintir na Tíre, 1987, 297 p. Kilkenny County Library.

Dunleavy, John J., A short history of Paulstown, Kilkenny: the author, 2007. NLI, 43 p.

Gulliver, P.H., Merchants and shopkeepers: a historical anthropology of an Irish market town, 1200–1991, Toronto: University of Toronto Press, 1995. Co-author, Marilyn Silverman. NLI Ir 94139 g 1, 440 p.

Healy, William, History and antiquities of Kilkenny county and city, Kilkenny: 1893. NLI Ir 94139 h 1.

Hogan, John, Kilkenny: the ancient city of Ossory, the seat of its kings, the see of its bishops and the site of its cathedral, Kilkenny: P.M. Egan, 1884. NLI Ir 94139 h 2, 462 p.

Holahan, J., Notes on the antiquities of the united parishes of Ballycallan, Kilmanagh and Killaloe: with notices of the late parish priests . . . Kilkenny: Journal office, 1875. NLI Ir 274144 h 1, 50 p.

Hore, H.F., The Social State of the Southern and Eastern Counties of Ireland in the Sixteenth Century, being the presentments of the gentlemen, commonalty, and citizens of Carlow, Cork, Kilkenny, Tipperary, Waterford, and Wexford, made in the reigns of Henry VIII. and Elizabeth: Printed from the originals in the Public Record Office, London: Edited by the late Herbert J. [i.e. F.] Hore . . . and the Rev. James Graves. Dublin: 1870. NLI Ir 794105 r 2.

IGRS, Tombstone inscriptions, Vol. 1, Dublin: IGRS Tombstone Committee, 2001. NLI, 850 p.

Joyce, John, Graiguenamanagh and the South Carlow-Kilkenny area in 1798, Graignamanagh Historical Society, 1998. NLI 1A 337, [20] p.

—— Graiguenamanagh: a town and its people: an historical and social account of Graiguenamanagh and Tinnahinch, Graiguenamanagh: Graigue Publications, 1993. NLI Ir 94139 j 2, 198 p.

Kehoe, Imelda, A history of St. Mary's Church, Gowran, Gowran: Gowran Development Association, 1992. NLI Ir 200 p 104(2), 32 p.

Kenealy, M., 'The parish of Aharney and the Marum family', Old Kilkenny Review, 1976. NLI, Ir 94139 o 3.

Kennedy, Edward, The land movement in Tullaroan, County Kilkenny, 1879–91, Dublin: Four Courts Press, 2004. NLI, 68 p.

Kennedy, Joseph, Callan 800, 1207–2007: history and heritage, Callan: Callan Heritage Society, 2007. NLI, 582 p.

Kilkenny Archaeological Society, St. Patrick's, Kilkenny: gravestone inscriptions: with historical notes on the parish, Kilkenny: Kilkenny Archaeological Society, 1990? NLI Ir 9295 k 1, 100 p.

Kirwan, John, *The Kirwan's of Lowergrange, Goresbridge, Co. Kilkenny and their associated familie*, 1995. NLI, 1 sheet.

Laffan, Kathleen, *Kilmacow . . . A south Kilkenny parish*, Kilkenny: Kilkenny People, 1998. NLI. 552 p.

Litton, Helen, *An index to the Rev. William Carrigan's 'The history and antiquities of the Diocese of Ossory'*, Kilkenny: Diocese of Ossory, 2005. NLI, 268 p.

Lyng, Tom, *Castlecomer connections: exploring history, geography, and social evolution in North Kilkenny environs*, Castlecomer: Castlecomer History Society, 1984. NLI Ir 94139 L 4, 429 p.

Murphy, Phillip E., *The O'Leary footprint: an anthology of the publications of the O'Leary family on Graignamanagh, Tinnahinch, Ullard and St. Mullins, 1895–1926*, Graignamanagh: O'Leary Archive, 2004. NLI, 420 p.

Neely, W.G., *Kilkenny: an urban history, 1391–1843*, Belfast: Institute of Irish Studies, 1989. NLI Ir 94139 n 2, 306 p.

Nolan, Pat, *An index to articles in the Old Kilkenny Review, 1946–2005*, Kilkenny: Irish Origins Research Agency, 2006. NLI.

Nolan, W., *Fassidinin: Land, Settlement and Society in South East Ireland, 1600–1850*, Dublin: Geography Publications, 1979. NLI Ir 94139 n 1, 259 p.

O'Donovan, John, *Ordnance Survey letters, Kilkenny (1839)*, Dublin: Fourmasters Press, 2003. NLI LO 8196, 250 p.

O'Dwyer, Michael, *Coolagh: its history and heritage*, Coolagh: Coolagh Centenary Committee, 1996. NLI Ir 94139 c 3, 213 p.

—— *The famine in the Kilkenny/Tipperary region: a history of the Callan Workhouse and Poor Law Union, 1845–52*, Callan: Callan Heritage Society, 2008. NLI, 119 p.

O'Shea, Mary, *Parish of Templeorum: a historical miscellany, 1999–2000*, Raheen: the author, 2000. NLI, 72 p.

O'Sullivan, Michael, *Rathpatrick Graveyard, Co. Kilkenny, memorial inscriptions*, Waterford: Michael O'Sullivan, 1998. NLI Ir 9295 p, 21 p.

Phelan, M., 'Callan doctors', *Old Kilkenny Review*, 1980. NLI, Ir 94139 o 3.

Phelan, M.M., *Kilkenny Gravestone Inscriptions, 1: Knocktopher*, Kilkenny: Kilkenny Archaeological Society, 1988. NLI 2A 3457, 44 p.

Prim, J.G.A., 'Documents connected with the city of Kilkenny militia in the 17th and 18th centuries', *Kilkenny and South-East of Ireland Archaeological Society Journal*, 1854, 5, 231 74. NLI.

—— *The History . . . of St. Canice, Kilkenny*, Dublin: Hodges, Smith & Co., 1857. Co-author, James Graves. NLI Ir 7266 g 5/1, 360 p.

Shaw, William, *Survey of Tullaroan, or Grace's Parish, in the cantred of Grace's Country, and county of Kilkenny; taken from the statistical account, or parochial survey of Ireland*, Dublin: Faulkner Press, 1819. NLI Ir 94137 m 1, 160 p.

Silverman, M., *In the Vally of the Nore: Social History of Thomastown, Co. Kilkenny, 1843–1983*, Dublin: Geography Publication, 1986. Co-editor, P. Gulliver.

Sullivan, Joe, *To school by the banks: a history of the origins and development of the primary schools in Carrigeen, Co. Kilkenny*, Carrigeen: Carrigeen School Centenary Committee, 2000. NLI, 163 p.

Thomastown Vocational School, *Thomastown: through the mists of time*, Kilkenny: Transition Year, Thomastown Vocational School. NLI Ir 94139 t 1, 138 p.

Veale, Tom, *Census extract, 1821: Mooncoin area of Co. Kilkenny, Ireland: surname index*, Dublin: Veale, 1997. NLI Ir 94139 v 1, 97 p.

—— *Index of Surnames in 'The New Commercial Directory for the cities of Waterford and Kilkenny and the towns of Clonmel, Carrick-on-Suir, New Ross and Carlow'*, Dublin: Veale, 1996. NLI Ir 9414 p.

—— *Richard Lucas, 1788: directory extract for south east of Ireland*, Dublin: Veale, 1995 NLI Ir 9414.

Walsh, Christopher, *A place of memories*, Tullaroan: Christopher Walshe, 1991. NLI Ir 94139 w 1.

Walsh, Jim, *Sliabh Rua: a history of its people and places*, Slieverue: Slieverue Parish Pastoral Council, 2001. NLI, 612 p.

Whelan, Kevin, *Kilkenny History and Society*, Dublin: Geography Publications, 1990. Co-editor, W. Nolan. NLI Ir 94139 k 8, 715 p.

Local journals
Deenside. NLI Ir 914139 d 3.
Journal of the Butler Society. NLI Ir 9292 b 28.
Kilkenny and South-East of Ireland Archaeological Society Journal. NLI J 7914 (to 1890); Ir 794105 r 1 (after 1890).
Old Kilkenny Review. NLI Ir 94139 o 3.
Transactions of the Ossory Archaeological Society. NLI Ir 794105 o 1.

Directories

1788	Richard Lucas, *General Directory of the Kingdom of Ireland*. NLI Pos. 3729. Reprinted in Veale, *Lucas, IG*, 1965, 1966, 1967, 1968.
1820	J. Pigot, *Commercial Directory of Ireland*. PRONI; NLI Ir 9141 p 107; LDS film 962702 item 1.
1824	J. Pigot & Co., *City of Dublin and Hibernian Provincial Directory*. NLI; LDS film 451787. Online: Hayes.
1839	T. Shearman, *New Commercial Directory for the cities of Waterford and Kilkenny, Towns of Clonmel, Carrick-on-Suir, New Ross and Carlow*. Indexed in Veale, *Index*.
1846	Slater's *National Commercial Directory of Ireland*. PRONI; NLI LO; LDS film 1696703 item 3. Online: Hayes.
1856	Slater, *Royal National Commercial Directory of Ireland*. NLI; LDS film 1472360 item 1.
1870	Slater, *Directory of Ireland*. NLI.
1881	Slater, *Royal National Commercial Directory of Ireland*. NLI. Online: FindMyPast.

1884　　　George Henry Bassett, *Kilkenny City and County Guide and Directory.*
1885　　　George Henry Bassett, *Wexford County Guide and Directory.* Reprinted
　　　　　Kilkenny: Grangesilvia Publications, 2001. NLI.
1894　　　Slater, *Royal Commercial Directory of Ireland.* NLI.

Gravestone inscriptions
Kilkenny Archaeological Society has transcripts of seventy-three graveyards at
Rothe House in Kikenny. Parts (at least) of nine Co. Kilkenny graveyards are
transcribed at <*www.interment.net*>.

Ballygurrim: Jamestown, IGRS, Vol. 1 (16).
Ballytarsney: IGRS, Vol. 1 (24).
Clonmore: IGRS, Vol. 1 (30).
Danesfort: GO Ms. 622, p. 147.
Dunkitt: IGRS, Vol. 1 (113).
Fiddown: Fiddown, C of I, GO Ms. 622 p. 150.
Gaulskill: Ballynamorahan, C of I, IGRS, Vol. 1 (39).
Graiguenamanagh: *Kilkenny Tombstones,* Vol. 5.
Grangesilvia: Goresbridge, *Kilkenny Tombstones,* Vol. 4.
Jerpointchurch: Kilvinoge, IGRS, Vol. 1 (10).
Kilbeacon: Garrandarragh, RC, IGRS, Vol. 1 (42).
Kilbride: Kilbride, IGRS, Vol. 1 (13).
Kilcolumb: Rathinure, IGRS, Vol. 1 (53).
Kilmacahill: Paulstown, *Kilkenny Tombstones,* Vol. 4.
Killahy: Killahy, IGRS, Vol. 1 (13).
Kilmacow: Kilmacow, C of I, IGRS, Vol. 1 (119).
Knocktopher: Knocktopher town, *Kilkenny Gravestone Inscriptions, 1.*
—— Sheepstown, IGRS, Vol. 1 (4).
Muckalee: Muckalee, IGRS, Vol. 1 (23).
Portnascully: Portnascully, IGRS, Vol. 1 (52).
Rathpatrick: O'Sullivan, *Rathpatrick Graveyard.*
Rosbercon: Rosbercon town, C of I, Cantwell, *West Wexford* (9).
—— Rosbercon, RC, Cantwell, *West Wexford* (9).
St Canice: St Canice's interior, J.G.A. Prim, *St. Canice.*
St Mary's: Kilkenny, St Mary's Lane, C of I, *Old Kilkenny Review,* 1979, 1980, 1981.
Tubbrid: Tubbrid, IGRS, Vol. 1 (3).
Ullard: *Kilkenny Tombstones,* Vol. 5.
Ullid: Ullid, IGRS, Vol. 1 (15).

Estate records
Tuthill. Rental, 1812. NAI M. 5825 (48). Principally major tenants. Covering
　　townlands in the civil parish of Dunnamaggan.

LAOIS (QUEEN'S COUNTY)

Census returns and substitutes

1641	Testimonies of 273 Queen's Co. witnesses to the 1641 Rebellion. Online: 1641.
1641	Book of Survey and Distribution. NLI Ms. 972.
1659	Pender's 'Census'. Reprinted GPC, 1997; IMC, 2002. LDS film 924648. Online: IGPweb.
1664	Hearth Money Roll. NAI Thrift Abstracts 3737.
1668–9	Hearth Money Roll. Baronies of Maryborough and Clandonagh (Upper Ossory). NAI Thrift Abstracts 3737.
1758–75	Freeholders. JKAS, Vol. 8, pp. 309–327. Online: IGPweb, Laois.
1766	Lea parish. RCBL; also LDS film 258517. Lea, Mountmellick: Online: PRONI name search.
1821	Mountrath. NAI m6225(1)–(5).
1823–38	Tithe Books.
1832–40	Owners and occupiers, Lea parish. NLI Ms. 4723/4.
1844	Register of Arms, baronies of Clandonagh (Upper Ossory), Maryborough and Cullenagh. 433 names. NAI.
1847	Voters. NLI ILB O4 P12.
1851–2	Griffith's Valuation. Online: Askaboutireland.
1901	Census. Online: NAI.
1911	Census. Online: NAI.

Online

1641	*<www.1641.tcd.ie>*
Askaboutireland	*<www.askaboutireland.ie>*
Connors	*<www.connorsgenealogy.com>*
Hayes, John	*<www.failteromhat.com>*
IGPweb, Laois	*<www.igp-web.com/laois/records.htm>*
NAI	*<www.census.nationalarchives.ie>*
PRONI name search	*<www.proni.gov.uk>*

Publications

Local histories etc.

Athy Union, *Athy Union list of destitute persons relieved out of the workhouse in the Stradbally District, Athy Union*, Naas: Athy Union, 1845. NLI, Poster.

Brennan, M., *Schools of Kildare and Leighlin, 1775–1835*, Dublin: M.H. Gill & Son, 1935. NLI Ir 37094135 b 4, 616 p.

Campbell, Rosaleen, *Tombstone Inscriptions of Castlebrack*, Castlebrack: 1990. NLI Ir 9295 p 2(3), 32 p.

Coyle, James, *The Antiquities of Leighlin*, Dublin: Browne & Nolan, n.d. NLI Ir 94138 c 1.

Dunne, Bridie, *Clonaghadoo: people and places, 1845–2007*, Mountmellick: the author, 2007. NLI, 204 p.

Dwyer, Philip, *The Diocese of Killaloe, from the Reformation to the Close of the Eighteenth Century*, Dublin: Hodges, Foster & Figgis, 1878. NLI Ir 94143 d 11, 602 p. Reprinted Newmarket-on-Fergus: O'Brien Book Publications, 1997.

Feehan, John, *The Landscape of Slieve Bloom: a study of the natural and human heritage*, Dublin: Blackwater Press, 1979. NLI Ir 91413 f 4, 284 p.

Flynn, Michael, *An outline history of the Flynn family of Coolroe, Ballybrittas, Co. Leix . . . details of the Devoy family of Ballybrittas . . . the Lapham and Beasley families*, Mullingar: the author, 1995. NLI Ir 9292 d 37.

Flynn, Thomas S., *The Dominicans of Aghaboe (c.1382–c.1782)*, Dublin: Dominican Publications, 1975. NLI Ir 270 p 10, 57 p.

Hovenden, Robert, *Lineage of the family of Hovenden (Irish branch) by a member of the family*, London: 1892. NLI Ir 9292 h 6, 8 p.

Jolly, M.A., *A Portarlington settler and his descendants*, London: Spottiswoode, Ballantyne & Co., 1935. NLI GO 415, 6 p.

Lane, Pádraig G. (ed.), *Laois: history and society*, Dublin: Geography Publications, 1999. NLI, 748 p.

Langdon, Thomas P., *The descendants of Edward and Esther (Lalor) Greene of Stradbally Parish, Queen's County, Ireland, and Middletown, CT*, Southington, Conn.: T.P. Langdon, 1997. LC CS71.G8 1997b.

Mac Suibhne, Peadar, *Parish of Killeshin, Graigcullen*, Carlow: St Patrick's College, 1975. NLI Ir 94136 m 3, 192 p.

Meehan, Patrick, *Members of Parliament for Laois and Offaly, 1801–1918*, Port Laoise: Leinster Express, 1983. NLI Ir 328 m 6, 246 p.

Merrigan, Michael, *Croasdaile's History of Rosenallis, Co. Laois, Ireland*, Dún Laoghaire: Dún Laoghaire Genealogical Society, 1998. NLI Ir 9291 g 7, 70 p.

O'Brien, Edward, *An historical and social diary of Durrow, County Laois, 1708–1992*, Durrow: Millfield Press, 1992. NLI Ir 94137 o 8.

O'Byrne, Daniel, *The history of the Queen's county: containing an historical and traditional account of is foundries, duns . . . and an account of some noble families of English extraction*, Dublin: J. O'Daly, 1856. NLI Ir 94137 o 2, 159 p.

O'Dea, Kieran, *Errill Cemetary*, Kilkenny: Errill Tidy Towns Committee, 1994. NLI, 46 p.

O'Donovan, John, *Ordnance Survey letters, Queen's Co. (1838)*, Dublin: 1926. NLI Ir 9141 O 16, 2 vols.

O'Hanlon, John, *History of the Queen's County*, Dublin: Sealy, Bryers & Walker, 1907–1914. Co-author, Edward O'Leary. NLI Ir 94137 o 3, 2 vols.

O'Shea, Christopher, *Aspects of Local History*, Pallaskenny: Salesian Press, 1977. NLI Ir 941 p 56, 39 p.

—— *Owen and Perrin family history: an account of the family of Owen of Rathdowney, Ireland . . .* Chichester, Sussex: H. Owen, 1981. NLI Ir 9292 o 43, 186 p.

Paterson, J. (ed.), *Diocese of Meath and Kildare: an historical guide*, 1981. NLI Ir 941 p 75.

Powell, John S., *Huguenot records from Portarlington: 'your humble servant': notes and letters from Portarlington, 1692–1768: a selection of documents* (Documents of Portarlington series, No. 4), York: Frenchchurch, 1999. NLI.

—— *'Shot a buck . . .': the Emo estate, 1798–1852* (Documents of Portarlington series, No. 3), York: Frenchchurch, 1998. NLI.

Redmond, Paul, *Gravestone Inscriptions from Killeshin, Sleaty, Graiguecullen, Mayo, Arles, Doonane, Castletown, Rathsapick, Shrule, Rathnure etc. with historical notes*, 1997. NLI Ir 3991 r 16, 119 p.

Rudd, Norman N., *An Irish Rudd family, 1760–1988: progeny of Gordon Arthur Rudd and Alicia Wellwood, Rathsarn Parish, Queen's County, Ireland: Rudd origins and other Irish Rudds*, Rudd Family Research Association, 1992. NLI Ir 9292 r 22, 488 p.

An Tóstal, *The story of Abbeyleix: An Tóstal souvenir, 1953*, Abbeyleix: An Tóstal, 1953. NLI Ir 94137 s 1, 76 p.

Walker, Linus H., *Beneath Slievemargy's brow*, Port Laoise: Leinster Express, 2001. NLI, 302 p.

Walsh, Hilary D., *Borris-in-Ossory, Co. Laois: an Irish rural parish and its people*, Kilkenny: Kilkenny Journal, 1969. NLI Ir 94137 w 1, 256 p.

Local journals
Laois Heritage: Bulletin of the Laois Heritage Society. NLI Ir 9413705 l 1.

Directories

1788   Richard Lucas, *General Directory of the Kingdom of Ireland.* NLI Pos. 3729. Reprinted in Veale, *Lucas, IG*, 1965, 1966, 1967, 1968.

1824   J. Pigot & Co., *City of Dublin and Hibernian Provincial Directory.* NLI; LDS film 451787. Online: Hayes.

1846   Slater's *National Commercial Directory of Ireland.* PRONI. NLI LO; LDS film 1696703 item 3. Online: Hayes.

1856   Slater, *Royal National Commercial Directory of Ireland.* NLI; LDS film 1472360 item 1.

1870   Slater, *Directory of Ireland.* NLI.

1881   Slater, *Royal National Commercial Directory of Ireland.* NLI. Online: FindMyPast.

1894   Slater, *Royal Commercial Directory of Ireland.* NLI.

Gravestone inscriptions

Irish Midlands Ancestry has transcripts for a large number of graveyards in the county. Contact details will be found in Chapter 15. Published or publicly available transcripts are given below.

Castlebrack: Rosaleen Campbell, *Tombstone Inscriptions of Castlebrack*, Castlebrack: 1990. NLI Ir 9295 p 2(3).

Dysartenos: Dunamaise, Holy Trinity. <*www.interment.net*>.

318   TRACING YOUR IRISH ANCESTORS

Killabban, Mayo: Redmond, *Gravestone Inscriptions*.
Killabban, Castletown: Redmond, *Gravestone Inscriptions*.
Killeshin, Graigue: Redmond, *Gravestone Inscriptions*.
Killeshin: Redmond, *Gravestone Inscriptions*.
Kyle: Kildare County Library.
Rathaspick, Doonane: Redmond, *Gravestone Inscriptions*.
Shrule: Redmond, *Gravestone Inscriptions*.
Sleaty: Redmond, *Gravestone Inscriptions*.
Stradbally: Carricksallagh ('Oak Vale'). <*www.interment.net*>.
Main St, C of I. <*www.interment.net*>.
Rathsaran: Online: Genweb, Laois.
Rathdowney: Errill, Published: Kieran O'Dea, *Errill Cemetery*, Erril: Errill Tidy Towns Committee, 1994.

Estate records
Fitzmaurice, James. Rent book, 1851–71. NLI Ms. 19451. Most tenants. Covering townlands in the civil parish of Killeshin.

LEITRIM

Census returns and substitutes
1600–1868	Roll of all the gentlemen. NLI P 2179.
1659	Pender's 'Census'. Reprinted GPC, 1997; IMC, 2002. LDS film 924648.
1726–7	Protestant householders. Edgeworth Papers, NAI M1501. Annaduff, Kiltogher, Kiltubbrid, Fenagh, Mohill.
1791	Freeholders. GO 665; also LDS film 100213.
1792	Protestants in the barony of Mohill. IA, Vol. 16, No. 1.
1796	Spinning-Wheel Premium List. 1,875 names for Co. Leitrim. Online: Hayes.
1807	Freeholders, Mohill barony. NLI Ms. 9628.
1820	Voting freeholders. NLI Ms. 3830.
1821	Parish of Carrigallen. NLI Pos. 4646.
1823–38	Tithe Books.
1839–83	Workhouse records: Mohill (1839–83), Manorhamilton (1839–81) and Carrick-on-Shannon (1843–82) unions. Leitrim County Library.
1842	Voters. NAI OP 1842/4.
1852	Voters, Oughteragh, Cloonclare, Cloonlogher. *Bréifne*, Vol. 5, No. 20.
1856	Griffith's Valuation. Online: Askaboutireland.
1861	Catholic Householders, Mohill parish. Leitrim GC.
1901	Census. Online: NAI.
1911	Census. Online: NAI.

Online

Askaboutireland	<www.askaboutireland.ie>	
Grieves	<members.iinet.net.au/~sgrieves>	Gravestones
Hayes, John	<www.failteromhat.com>	Large compendium of transcribed records
Leitrim-Roscommon	<www.leitrim-roscommon.com>	1901, Griffith's, Townlands.
NAI	<www.census.nationalarchives.ie>	

Publications

Local histories etc.

Breen, Father Mark, *The Gray Family: Anskirt, Gortletteragh*. Leitrim County Library 929.2.Gra.

Clancy, Eileen, *Ballinaglera Parish, Co. Leitrim: aspects of its history and traditions*, Dublin: the authors, 1980. Co-author, P. Forde. NLI Ir 94121 c 2, 212 p.

Clancy, P.S., *Historical Notices of the Parish of Inishmagrath: Diocese of Kilmore, Co. Leitrim*, Carrick-on-Shannon: Maura Clancy, 1972. Leitrim County Library 941.71 LIN.

Day, Angelique, and McWilliams, Patrick (eds.), *Ordnance Survey Memoirs of Ireland, Vol. 40: Counties of South Ulster, 1834–8: Cavan, Leitrim, Louth, Monaghan and Sligo*, Belfast: Institute of Irish Studies, 1997. Co. Leitrim: Manorhamilton Union. NLI Ir 9141 o 80, 216 p.

Farrell, Noel, *Exploring Family origins in Carrick-on-Shannon*, Longford: Longford Leader, 1994. NLI 1B 1012, 47 p.

Freeman, T.W., *The Town and District of Carrick on Shannon*, 1949. NLI P. 1916.

Gallogly, Dan, *The diocese of Kilmore, 1800–1950*, Cavan: Bréifne Historical Society, 1999. NLI, 466 p.

—— *Sliabh an Iarainn Slopes: history of the town and parish of Ballinamore, Co. Leitrim*, Mullagh: Gallogly, 1991. NLI Ir 94121 g 1, 298 p.

Hackett, Raymond, *Carrigallen Parish: A History*, Carrigallen: 1996. Co-editor, Michael Reilly. Leitrim County Library 941.71.

Hayes-McCoy, G.A., *Index to 'The Compossicion Booke of Connoght, 1585'*, Dublin: IMC, 1945. NLI Ir 9412 c 1, 179 p.

Kelly, Liam, *Kiltubbrid*, Carrick-on-Shannon: Kiltubrid GAA, 1984. NLI Ir 397 k 4, 144 p.

—— *Kiltubrid, County Leitrim: snapshots of a parish in the 1890s*, Dublin: Four Courts Press, 2005. NLI, 64 p.

Logan, Patrick, *Outeragh: My Native Parish*, Dublin: 1963. NLI Ir 941 p 74, 24 p.

MacAtasney, Gerard, *Leitrim and the great hunger, 1845–50 '. . . a temporary inconvenience . . .'?* Leitrim: Carrick-on-Shannon and District Historical Society, 1997. NLI Ir 94121 m 2, 177 p.

MacNamee, James J., *History of the Diocese of Ardagh*, Dublin: Browne & Nolan, 1954. NLI Ir 274131 m 5, 858 p.

McNiffe, Liam, 'Short history of the barony of Rosclogher, 1840–60', *Breifny,* 1983–4.

—— *Manorhamilton parish church, 1783–1983: 'Glimpses of our history',* Cavan: Blacks, 1983. NLI Ir 200 p 48, 20 p.

Monahan, Rev. J., *Records Relating to the Diocese of Ardagh and Clonmacnoise,* Dublin: M.H. Gill & Son, 1886. NLI Ir 27413 m 3, 400 p.

O'Connell, Philip, *The Diocese of Kilmore: its History and Antiquities,* Dublin: Browne & Nolan, 1937. NLI Ir 274119 o 3, 579 p.

Ó Dálaigh, Brian, *Irish villages: studies in local history,* Dublin: Four Courts Press, 2003. Cloone. NLI. 326 p.

Ó Duigneáin, Proinnsíos, *North Leitrim in famine times, 1840–50,* Manorhamilton: P. Ó Duigneáin, 1987? NLI 3A 3555, 48 p.

O'Flynn, T., *History of Leitrim,* Dublin: C.J. Fallon, 1937. NLI Ir 94121 o 3, 109 p.

Reynolds, Sister Mary, *Gortletteragh National School,* Farnaught: the authors, 2009. NLI, 352 p.

Scott, Brendan, *Culture and society in early modern Bréifne/Cavan,* Dublin: Four Courts Press, 2004. NLI, 241 p.

Simington, Robert C., *The transplantation to Connacht, 1654–58,* Shannon: Irish University Press, for IMC, 1970. NLI Ir 94106 s 9, 306 p.

Slevin, Fiona, *By hereditary virtues: a history of Lough Rynn,* Coolabawn Publishing: 2006. NLI, 184 p.

Whelan, Michael, *The parish of Aughavas, Co. Leitrim: its history and its people,* Aughavas: Whelan, 1998. NLI Ir 94121 w 1, 371 p.

Local journals
Ardagh and Clonmacnoise Historical Society Journal. NLI Ir 794105.
Bréifne. NLI Ir 94119 b 2.
Breifny. NLI Ir 794106 b 1.
The Drumlin: A Journal of Cavan, Leitrim and Monaghan. NLI Ir 05 d 345.

Directories

1824	J. Pigot & Co., *City of Dublin and Hibernian Provincial Directory.* NLI; LDS film 451787. Online: Hayes.
1846	Slater's *National Commercial Directory of Ireland.* PRONI. NLI LO; LDS film 1696703 item 3. Online: Hayes.
1856	Slater, *Royal National Commercial Directory of Ireland.* NLI; LDS film 1472360 item 1.
1870	Slater, *Directory of Ireland.* NLI.
1881	Slater, *Royal National Commercial Directory of Ireland.* NLI. Online: FindMyPast.
1894	Slater, *Royal Commercial Directory of Ireland.* NLI.

Gravestone inscriptions

Leitrim Genealogy Centre and Leitrim County Library have transcripts for 105 graveyards in the county. Contact details will be found in Chapter 15. Eileen Hewson (<*www.kabristan.org.uk*>) has transcribed and published four volumes of transcripts for Co. Leitrim. They are available at NLI. It is not clear if the transcripts are complete for each graveyard. Other published or freely available transcripts are given below.

Cloonclare: Manorhamilton, C of I. Online: Grieves.

Killasnet: Lurganboy, Pres. Online: Grieves.

Kiltubbrid: Church and graveyard, C of I, RCBL.

Kinlough (part) <*www.interment.net*>.

Estate records

Bessborough, Earl of. Rental, 1805. NA M3374; major tenants only. NA M3370: valuation of estate, 1813. All tenants. NA M3383: tenants with leases, 1813. NA M3384: rental, 1813. All tenants. Covering townlands in the civil parishes of Fenagh and Kiltubbrid.

Clements. Rentals of the Woodford estate, 1812–28. NLI Mss. 3816–27. All tenants. Covering townlands in the civil parish of Carrigallen. NLI Mss. 12805–807, 3828: rental, 1812–24 (with gaps) of the townland of Bohey in the civil parish of Cloone.

Crofton, Sir Humphrey. Rental, March 1833, with tenants' names in alphabetical order. NLI Ms. 4531. Covering townlands in the civil parishes of Cloone, Kltoghert, Mohill and Oughteragh.

Johnson, William. Rental of the Drumkeeran estate, 1845–56. NLI Ms. 9465. All tenants. Covering townlands in the civil parish of Inishmagrath.

King. Rent roll and estate accounts, 1801–1818. NLI Ms. 4170. Major tenants only. Covering townlands in the civil parishes of Fenagh and Kiltubbrid.

King, John. Rent and miscellaneous accounts, 1757–86. NLI Mss. 3520, 3125. All tenants. Covering townlands in the civil parishes of Fenagh and Mohill.

Leitrim, Earl of. Rental and accounts, 1837–42. NLI Ms. 12787. All tenants. NLI Mss. 5728–33: rentals 1838–65. All tenants. NLI Mss. 5803–805: rentals 1842–55. All tenants. NLI Mss. 12810–12: rentals 1844–8. All tenants. NLI Mss. 179, 180: rentals 1844 and 1854. All tenants. Covering townlands in the civil parishes of Carrigallen, Cloone, Clooneclare, Inishmagrath, Killasnet, Kiltoghert and Mohill.

Newcomen, Viscount. Rental, 1822, NA M2797. Mainly larger tenants. Covering townlands in the civil parish of Drumlease.

O'Beirne, Francis. Rental, 1850. NLI Ms. 8647 (14). Mainly large tenants. Covering townlands in the civil parishes of Cloone, Drumlease and Kiltoghert.

St George, Charles Manners. Annual accounts and rentals. NLI Mss. 4001–4022. Covering townlands in the civil parish of Kiltoghert.

Tottenham, Nicholas Loftus. 26 maps. NLI Ms. 9837. Major tenants only. Covering townlands in the civil parishes of Clooneclare, Inishmagrath and Rossinver.

Tottenham, Ponsonby. Printed rental, 1802. NLI Ms. 10162. Mainly larger tenants. Covering townlands in the civil parishes of Clooneclare and Rossinver.

Wynne, Owen. Rentals and expense books, 1737–68. NLI Mss. 5780–82. Major tenants only. NLI Mss. 5830–31: rent ledgers 1738–53, 1768–73. Major tenants only, indexed. NLI Mss. 3311–13: a rental and two rent ledgers, yearly from 1798 to 1825, with all tenants. Covering townlands in the civil parishes of Clooneclare, Cloonlogher, Killanummery, Killasnet and Rossinver.

LIMERICK

Census returns and substitutes

1569	Freeholders. NLI Pos. 1700.
1570	Freeholders and gentlemen. JNMAS, 1964.
1586	Survey of leaseholders on the Desmond estates. NAI M.5037.
1641	Book of Survey and Distribution. NLI Ms. 973.
1654–6	*Civil Survey*, Vol. 4. NLI I 6551 Dublin.
1659	Pender's 'Census'. Reprinted GPC, 1997; IMC, 2002. LDS film 924648.
1660	Rental of lands in Limerick city and county. NLI Ms. 9091.
1664	Hearth Money Rolls, Askeaton. JNMAS, 1965.
1673	Valuation of part of Limerick city (estates of the Earls of Roscommon and Orrery), with occupiers' names and valuation. NLI Pos. 792.
1715–94	Limerick city freemen. LDS film 477000 from NA (Kew).
1746–1836	Freemen, Limerick. Also NLI Pos. 5526. JNMAS, 1944–5. Online: Celtic Cousins.
1761	Freeholders, Limerick city (16092) and county (16093). NLI Ms. 16092, Ms. 16093.
1766	Abington, Cahircomey, Cahirelly, Carrigparson, Clonkeen, Kilkellane, Tuogh. NAI Parl. Ret. 681/684. Protestants only Croagh, Kilscannel, Nantinan and Rathkeale. IA, 1977. Tuogh in Duggan, Cappamore. Online: Connors. Clonagh, Croagh (Crough), Doondonnell, Killscannell, Nantinan and Rathkeale: online PRONI name search.
1776	Freeholders entitled to vote. NAI M 1321–2. Voters. NAI M.4878.
1783	Burgesses of Kilmallock. NLI Ms. 10941.
1793–1821	Two lists of people resident in the area of Newcastle in 1793 and 1821. IA, Vol. 16, No. 1 (1984).
1798	Rebel prisoners in Limerick Jail. JNMAS, Vol. 10 (1), 1966.
1813	Chief inhabitants of the parishes of St Mary's and St John's, Limerick. IA, Vol. 17, No. 2, 1985.
1816–28	Freeholders. GO 623; also LDS film 100224.

1821	Some extracts. NAI Thrift Absracts.
1821	Fragments only, Kilfinane district. *JNMAS*, 1975.
1823–38	Tithe Books. Part online: Connors.
1829	Freeholders. GO 623.
1835	Householders, Parish of Templebredin. *JNMAS*, 1975.
1835–9	List of inhabitants of Limerick taking water (Waterworks accounts). NLI Pos. 3451.
1838–52	Reproductive Loan Fund records. Administered from Limerick city, for all areas of the city and county. More than 5,000 names. NA (Kew), T 91. Partly online: Moving Here.
1840	Freeholders, Barony of Coshlea. NLI Ms. 9452.
1840	Rate books: Kilfinnane, NLI Ms. 2026; Kilmallock, NLI Ms. 9449. With comments.
1843	Voters. NAI OP 1843/66.
1846	Survey of households in connection with famine relief. Loughill, Foynes and Shanagolden areas. NLI Ms. 582.
1848–51?	Undated lists of paupers in the Loughill E. Division, showing families, with name, age and address. Lists of inmates of Glin Union workhouse. NLI Ms. 13413.
1851	Some extracts. NAI Thrift Absracts.
1851–2	Griffith's Valuation. Online: Askaboutireland.
1852	'Analysis of the late election showing the entire list of the poll'. Limerick County Library.
1870	Rate Book for barony of Clanwilliam. NAI M 2434.
1901	Census. Online: NAI.
1911	Census. Online: NAI.

Online

Askaboutireland	*<www.askaboutireland.ie>*
Celtic Cousins	*<www.celticcousins.net>*
Connors	*<www.connorsgenealogy.com>*
Devries	*<www.macatawa.org/~devries/Irish.html>*
Hayes, John	*<www.failteromhat.com>*
Limerick Archives	*<www.limerickcity.ie>*
Limerick Library	*<www.limerickcity.ie/Library>*
Moving Here	*<www.movinghere.org.uk/search>*
PRONI name search	*<www.proni.gov.uk>*

Publications

Local histories etc.

Archdiocese of Cashel and Emly, *Pobal Áilbe: Cashel and Emly atlas*, Dublin: Ordnance Survey Office, 1970. NLI ILB 94143 a 3.

Barry, J.G., 'Cromwellian settlement of Co. Limerick', *Limerick Field Journal,* Vols. 1–8, 1897–1908. In effect an edition of the Books of Survey and Distribution. NLI Ir 794205 l 1.

Begley, Canon John, *The Diocese of Limerick,* Dublin: Browne & Nolan, 1906–1938. *Vol. 1: Ancient and Medieval,* 1906. *—Vol. 2: Sixteenth and Seventeenth Centuries,* 1927. *—Vol. 3: 1691 to the Present,* 1938. Reprinted Limerick: 1993. NLI.

Bennis, E.H., *Reminiscences of Old Limerick,* Limerick: George McKern & Sons, 1939. NLI GO 674, 30 p.

Bennis, Patricia M., *St. John's Fever and Lock Hospital, Limerick, 1780–1890,* Newcastle-upon-Tyne: Cambridge Scholars, 2009. NLI, 106 p.

Carroll, J., *Village by the Shannon,* Limerick: 1991, 144 p. Co-author, R. Tuohy. A history of Castleconnell.

Cochrane, Mary, *Clounleharde, Ireland to Mt Ararat, Gippsland: a history of the Dore family, 1841–1982,* Parkenham Gazette, 1982. NLI GO 414, 50 p.

Connellan, Canon Brendan, *Light on the Past: Story of St. Mary's Parish,* Limerick: Connellan, 2001. Limerick City Library, 254.0094194, 147 p.

Cronin, Patrick, *The auld town: a chronicle of Askeaton,* Limerick: Askeaton Civic Trust, 1995. NLI Ir 94144 c, 111 p.

—— *Eas Céad Tine, 'The Waterfall of the Hundred Fires',* Askeaton: 1999. 90 p. A history of Askeaton.

Curtin, Gerard, *A pauper warren: West Limerick, 1845–49,* Ballyhahill: Sliabh Luachra Books, 2000. NLI Ir 94144 c 19.

—— *Recollections of our native valley: A history of Loughill-Ballyhahill and the Owavaun Valley,* Ballyhahill: 1996. NLI Ir 94144 c 13, 405 p.

Donovan, Tom (ed.), *The Knights of Glin: Seven Centuries Of Change,* Glin: Glin Historical Society, 2009. 445 p.

Doody-Scully, Margaret, *From the bog to the bishop, 12,000 BC–2005 AD: Mahoonagh's religious bound together by their shared history,* Newcastle West, Co. Limerick: Gael Scoil ó Doghair, 2005. NLI, 400 p.

Dowd, Rev. James, *Limerick and its Sieges,* Limerick: M'Kern & Sons, 1896. NLI Ir 94144 d 2, 195 p.

—— *St Mary's Cathedral, Limerick,* Limerick: 1936. Revised by T.F. Abbott, who included notes on the cathedral organ, with a succession of bishops and list of deans. NLI Ir 7266 d 6.

Duggan, Eileen, *Cappamore: a parish history,* Cappamore: Cappamore Historical Society, 1992. NLI Ir 94145 c 22, 438 p.

Dunraven, Countess of, *Memorials of Adare Manor,* Oxford: 1865. NLI Ir 94144 d 3, c. 350 p.

Dwyer, Philip, *The Diocese of Killaloe, from the Reformation to the Close of the Eighteenth Century,* Dublin: Hodges, Foster & Figgis, 1878. NLI Ir 94143 d 11, 602 p. Reprinted Newmarket-on-Fergus: O'Brien Book Publications, 1997.

—— *Famine Ireland: Limerick: Extracts from British Parliamentary Papers, 1846–49, relating to Limerick City and County,* Limerick Corporation Public Library. Photocopied and bound into 2 vols., 274 p.

Farrell, Noel, *Rathkeale/Newcastle family roots: exploring family origins in Rathkeale and Newcastle West*, Longford: Noel Farrell, 2001. NLI 3B 500, 48 p.

Feheny, J.P.M., *Ballysteen: the people and the place*, Blarney: Iverus, 1998. NLI, 201 p.

Fennell, Paul D., *The Fennells of Manister, Co. Limerick, Eire*, Baltimore, Md.: Gateway Press, 2000. NLI Ir 9292 f 34, 309 p.

Ferrar, John, *The History of Limerick, Ecclesiastical, Civil and Military, from the earliest records to the year 1787*, Limerick: 1767. 2nd ed., much revised and enlarged, 1787. NLI J.94144.FER/1787, 492 p. Online: Google Books.

Fitzgerald, P., *The history, topography and antiquities of the city and county of Limerick*, Dublin: 1826–7. Co-author, J.J. McGregor. NLI. Online: Google Books.

Fitzgerald, Séamus, *Cappawhite and Doon*, Pallasgrean: S. Fitzgerald, 1983. NLI Ir 9141 p 43, 124 p.

Fleming, D.A., *Politics and provincial people: Sligo and Limerick, 1691–1761*, Manchester: Manchester University Press, 2010. NLI, 272 p.

Fleming, John, *Reflections, historical and topographical on Ardpatrick, Co. Limerick*, Limerick: the author, 1979. NLI Ir 94144 f 5, 165 p.

Gaughan, Rev. J.A., *The Knights of Glin: a Geraldine family*, Dublin: Humanities Press, 1978. NLI Ir 9292 g 17, 222 p.

Hamilton, G.F., *Records of Ballingarry*, Limerick: 1930. NLI Ir 94144 h 2.

Hannan, Kevin, *Limerick historical reflections*, Limerick: 1996. 352 p.

Hayes, Richard, 'The German colony in County Limerick,' *JNMAS*, 1937. Palatines. NLI.

—— 'Some notable Limerick doctors,' *JNMAS*, I, 3, 1938, pp. 113–23.

Herbert, Robert, *Worthies of Thomond: a compendium of short lives of the most famous men and women of Limerick and Clare*, Limerick: the author, 1946. NLI, 3 parts.

Hynes, G. Carew, *Dún Bleisce: a history*, Doon: Cumann Forbartha Dhún Bleisce, 1990. NLI Ir 94144 d 10, 200 p.

IGRS, *Tombstone inscriptions, Vol. 1*, Dublin: IGRS Tombstone Committee, 2001. NLI, 850 p.

Jackson, R.W., *The History of St Michael's Church, Limerick, 1844–1944*, Limerick: 1944.

Jones, Hank, *The Palatine Families of Ireland*, San Leandro, Calif.: 1965. NLI Ir 9292 p 6, 152 p.

Kerins, C., *Ballingarry, Granagh, and Clouncagh: archival records, 1800–1900*, Dublin: Christy Kerins, 2000. NLI Ir 94144 b 11, 184 p.

Knockea Book Committee, *Knockea National School, 1851–1965–2003*, 2004. NLI, 128 p.

Lee, Rev. Dr C., 'Statistics from Knockainy and Patrickswell parishes, 1819–1940,' *JCHAS*, Vol. 47, No. 165. NLI.

Lee, David, *Made in Limerick, Vol. 1: History of industries, trade and commerce*, Limerick: Limerick Civic Trust, 2003. Co-editor, Debbie Jacobs. NLI, 362 p.

—— *Made in Limerick, Vol. 2: History of trades, industries and commerce,* Limerick: Limerick Civic Trust, 2006. Co-editor, Debbie Jacobs. NLI, 344 p.

—— *Remembering Limerick,* Limerick: Limerick Civic Trust and FÁS, 1997. Essays on the 800th anniversary of the charter. NLI Ir 94144 r 1, 407 p.

Lenihan, Maurice, *Limerick: its history and antiquities,* Dublin: 1866. Facsimile reprint Cork: Mercier Press, 1967. 780 p. Reprinted, with new index, 1991. NLI Ir 94144 l 1.

Lyddy, Margaret, *St Joseph's Parish: A history,* Limerick: 1990. 31 p. Lists Quaker gravestones in Ballinacurra.

MacCaffrey, James, *The Black Book of Limerick,* Dublin: M.H. Gill & Son, 1907. NLI Ir 27414 m 1.

McNamara, Sarah, *Development of Limerick by Honan merchants: the unfolding of a hidden history,* Limerick: McNamara, 2003. Limerick City Library, 941.94, 96 p.

McNerney Winkler, Rosemary, *McNerney, McInerney genealogy: a family from Glin, Kilfergus Parish, County Limerick, Ireland,* Albuquerque, N. Mex.: R.M. Winkler, 2001. LC CS71.M475683 2001.

Meistrell, Rita J., *The James Sullivan family: Emigrants from Lisready Cripps, Loughill, County Limerick and their descendants,* Los Angeles: Rita J. Meistrell, 1999. NLI Ir 9292 m 87, 258 p.

Meredyth, Francis, *Descriptive and Historic Guide, St Mary's Cathedral,* Limerick: 1887.

Moloney, Rev. M., 'The Parish of St Patrick, Limerick', *JNMAS*, I, 1937, 102.

Nash, Róisín, *A bibliography of Limerick,* Limerick: 1962.

O'Connor, Patrick J., *Hometown: A Portrait of Newcastle West, Co. Limerick,* Oireacht na Mumhan Books. NLI.

—— *People make places: the story of the Irish Palatines,* Newcastle West: Oireacht na Mumhan Books, 1989. NLI Ir 941 o 71, 229 p.

O'Donovan, John, *Letters and extracts relative to ancient territories in Thomond,* Dublin: Ordnance Survey, 1841. NLI Ir 9141 O 19.

O'Flaherty, Eamon, *Irish Historic Towns Atlas, 21: Limerick,* Dublin: RIA, 2010. NLI.

Oram, Hugh, *Bygone Limerick: the city and county in days gone by,* Cork: Mercier Press, 2010. NLI, 125 p.

Ó Riain, Dónal, *The history and folklore of Parteen and Meelick,* Parteen: Ó Riain, 1991. NLI, 360 p.

O'Sullivan, Michael F., *A History of Hospital and its environs,* Cullen: Michael F. O'Sullivan, 1995. NLI Ir 94144 o 7, 135 p.

Ó Tuathaigh, Gearóid, *Limerick History and Society: Interdisciplinary essays on the History of an Irish County,* Dublin: Geography Publications, 2009. NLI, 697 p.

Potter, Mathew, *First citizens of the Treaty City: the mayors and mayoralty of Limerick, 1197–2007,* Limerick: Limerick City Council, 2007. NLI, 299 p.

—— *The government and the people of Limerick: the history of Limerick Corporation/City Council, 1197–2006,* Limerick: Limerick City Council, 2006. NLI, 583 p.

Prendergast, Frank, *St. Michael's Parish: Its Life and Times,* Limerick: St Michael's Parish, 2000. Limerick City Library, 254.0094194.

Press, Kate, *West Limerick families abroad,* Melbourne: Kate Press, 2001. Co-author, Valerie Thompson. NLA NLq 305.89162094 P935, 217 p.

Seoighe, Mainchín, *Bruree: the history of the Bruree district, i.e. the history of the parish of Bruree and of the old parish of Tankardstown,* Bruree: Rockhill Development Association, 1973. NLI Ir 94144 s 4, 184 p.

—— *Dromin Athlacca: the story of a rural parish in Co. Limerick,* Athlacca: Glór na nGael, 1978. NLI Ir 94144 s 3, 214 p.

—— *From Bruree to Corcomhide: the district where world statesman Éamon de Valera grew up and where the illustrious Mac Eniry family ruled,* Bruree: Bruree/Rockhill Development Association, 2000. NLI Ir 91414 s 15, 562 p.

—— *Portrait of Limerick,* London: R. Hale, 1982. Wide-ranging historical and geographical tour of city and county. NLI Ir 914144 s 6.

—— *Sean-Chill Mocheallóg / Old Kilmallock,* Cumann na Máighe, 1975. NLI Ir 941 p 87, 26 p.

Seymour, St John D., *The Diocese of Emly,* Dublin: Church of Ireland Print, 1913. NLI Ir 27414 s 1, 297 p.

Sheehan, John, *A corner of Limerick history: recollections and photographs,* Ballybrown: John Sheehan, 1989. History of Ballybrown. NLI Ir 94144 s 8, 311 p.

Spellisy, Seán, *Limerick, the Rich Land,* O'Brien's Bookshop: 1989. NLI Ir 94144 s 7, 286 p.

Stewart, Dorothy, *A Short history of St John's Church, Limerick,* Ballysimon: 1952. NLI Ir 2741 p 23, 12 p.

Tierney, Mark, *Murroe and Boher: history of an Irish country parish,* Dublin: Browne & Nolan, 1966. NLI Ir 94144 t 1, 251 p.

Tipperary Heritage Unit, *St. Ailbe's Heritage: A Guide to the History, Genealogy and Towns of the Archdiocese of Cashel and Emly,* Tipperary: Tipperary Heritage Unit, 1994. Tipperary County Library 929.3, 124 p.

Toomey, Thomas, *An antique and storied land: a history of the parish of Donoughmore, Knockea, Roxborough and its environs in County Limerick,* Limerick: 1991. Co-author, Harry Greensmyth. NLI Ir 94144.t.4, 374 p.

Tuthill, P.B., *Pedigree of the family of Villiers of Kilpeacon, Co. Limerick,* London: 1907.

Walter, J. and S., *A little of Limerick: an account of the Hickey, Scanlan, and Baggott families of Camperdown and Cobden,* 1999, 319 p.

Westropp, Westropp Manuscripts, RIA. Will abstracts mainly for Cos. Clare and Limerick.

Whelan, Frank, *Cappagh: a sense of history,* Ballingrane: Whelan, 2003. 2nd edition. NLI, 147 p.

White, John D., *The History of the Family of White of Limerick, Knockcentry, etc.,* 1887. NLI Ir 9292 w 10.

White, Rev. P., *History of Clare and the Dalcassian Clans of Tipperary, Limerick and Galway,* Dublin: 1893. Reprinted Newmarket-on-Fergus: O'Brien Book Publications, 1997. NLI Ir 94143 w 4, 398 p.

Local journals
The Dawn (Journal of the Bruff Historical Society). NLI Ir 94144 d.
The Glencorbry Chronicle.
Journal of the Newcastle West Historical Society. NLI Ir 94143 n 2.
Journal of the North Munster Archaeological Society. NLI Ir 794105 n 1.
Limerick Field Journal. NLI Ir 794205 l 1.
Lough Gur Historical Society Journal. Leitrim County Library.
Old Limerick Journal. NLI Ir 94144 o 2.
Shannonside Annual. NLI Ir 94146 s 2.

Directories

1769	John Ferrar, *Directory of Limerick*. Online: Celtic Cousins.
1788	Richard Lucas, *General Directory of the Kingdom of Ireland*. NLI Pos. 3729. Reprinted in Veale, *Lucas, IG*, 1965, 1966, 1967, 1968. Online: Celtic Cousins.
1809	Holden's *Annual London and country directory of the United Kingdoms and Wales, in three volumes, for . . . 1811*. Facsimile reprint, Norwich: M. Winton, 1996. NLI G 942 h 23; LDS film 258722 item 2.
1816	Holden's *Directory*.
1820	J. Pigot, *Commercial Directory of Ireland*. PRONI; NLI Ir 9141 p 107; LDS film 962702 item 1.
1824	J. Pigot & Co., *City of Dublin and Hibernian Provincial Directory*. NLI; LDS film 451787. Online: Hayes.
1838	Deane's *Limerick Almanack, Directory and Advertiser*.
1840–42	F. Kinder & Son, *The New Triennial and Commercial Directory . . . Limerick, Waterford and Kilkenny*.
1846	Slater's *National Commercial Directory of Ireland*. PRONI; NLI LO; LDS film 1696703 item 3. Online: Hayes.
1856	Slater, *Royal National Commercial Directory of Ireland*. NLI; LDS film 1472360 item 1.
1866	George Henry Bassett, *Directory of the City and County of Limerick, and of the Principal Towns in the Cos. of Tipperary and Clare*. NLI Ir 914144 b 5.
1867	Henry and Coughlan's *General Directory of Cork and Munster*. Online: FindMyPast.
1870	Slater, *Directory of Ireland*. NLI.
1875–80	George Henry Bassett, *Limerick Directory*.
1881	Slater, *Royal National Commercial Directory of Ireland*. NLI. Online: FindMyPast.
1886	Francis Guy, *Postal Directory of Munster*. NLI Ir 91414 g 8; LDS film 1559399 item 8.
1889	George Henry Bassett, *The Book of Tipperary* (Ballylooby).
1891	H. and E. Ashe, *The Limerick City and Counties of Limerick and Clare Directory, 1891–2*. Online: FindMyPast.

1893   Francis Guy, *Directory of Munster.* NLI Ir 91414 g 8.

1894   Slater, *Royal Commercial Directory of Ireland.* NLI.

Gravestone inscriptions

Limerick Genealogy has a large collection of transcripts for Limerick city and county. Contact details are in Chapter 15. Limerick city (Mount St Lawrence) burial registers, 1855–2008, are online at Limerick Archives.

Abbeyfeale: Main St, RC, O'K., Vol. 11.

Ardagh: Minsters Land, RC, *JNMAS*, 36, 1995, pp. 3–59.

Ardcanny: Melllon, *IA*, Vol. 9, No. 1, 1977.

Ardpatrick: Fleming, John, *Reflections . . . on Ardpatrick*, 1979.

Askeaton: C of I, IGRS, Vol. 1.

Athlacca: Athlacca South, C of I, Seoighe, *Dromin, Athlacca*, 1978.

Ballingarry: Hamilton, G.F., *Records of Ballingarry*, Limerick, 1930. NLI Ir 94144 h 2.

Bruff: Main St, C of I, *The Dawn*, 1986, pp. 142–51.

Newtown, *The Dawn*, 1986, pp. 142–51.

Bruree: Howardstown North, Seoighe, *Brú Rí: Records of the Bruree District*, 1973.

—— Ballynoe, C of I, Seoighe, *Brú Rí: Records of the Bruree District*, 1973.

Dromin: Dromin South, Seoighe, *Dromin, Athlacca*, 1978.

Galbally: Ballylooby. Online: Devries.

Grange: Grange Lower, *IA*. NLI Ir 9205 i 3.

Hospital: Barrysfarm, RC, *Lough Gur Historical Society Journal*, 1994, pp. 115–24; 1996, pp. 85–92; 1998, pp. 63–70.

Limerick, St Michael's: Ballinacurra (Bowman), Quaker, Lyddy, *St Joseph's Parish, A history.*

Kilbeheny: Churchquarter, C of I, *IG*.

Killeedy: Mountcollins, Casey, O'K., Vol. 11.

Knockainy: Loughgur, *Lough Gur Historical Society Journal*, 1 (1985), pp. 51–61.

—— Patrickswell, RC, *Lough Gur Historical Society Journal*, 2 (1986), pp. 71–9.

Knocklong: Grange, *Lough Gur Historical Society Journal*, 1989, pp. 75–81.

Nantinan: C of I, *IA*. NLI Ir 9205 i 3.

Rathkeale: Church St, C of I, *IA*. NLI Ir 9205 i 3, Vol. 14, No. 2, 1982.

Stradbally: Stradbally North, Shannon Lodge, C of I, IGRS, Vol. 1.

Tankardstown: Tankardstown Sough, Seoighe, *Brú Rí: Records of the Bruree District*, 1973.

Tullabracky: *The Dawn*, 1988, pp. 125–45.

Estate records

[**No landlord given**]. NAI M. 3668 (12), Map, 1840. All tenants. Covering townlands in the civil parishes of Newcastle.

[**No landlord given**]. Rental, townlands of Leheys and Ballinree, 1815–18. NLI Ms. 13413 (7). Major tenants only. Civil parishes of Robertstown and Shanagolden.

Ashtown, Lord. Rent ledger, 1839–82. NLI Mss. 5823–5. All tenants. Covering townlands in the civil parishes of Athneasy, Ballingarry (Coshlea), Crecora, Darragh, Emlygrennan, Galbally, Kilbreedy Major, Kilfinnane, Kilflyn, Knocklong and Particles.

Bourke. Major-General Richard. Rent rolls, 1831. NLI Mss. 19787, 19790–98. Principally major tenants. Covering townlands in the civil parishes of Abington, Ballingarry (Connello), Ballybrood, Ballynaclogh, Doon and Uregare.

Castle Oliver estate. NLI Ms. 10933 (Part 1), some tenants only, 1827–32. Coverage unclear. Covering townlands in the civil parishes of Ballingarry (Connello), Ballingarry (Coshlea), Darragh, Emlygrennan, Kilfinnane, Kilflyn, Knocklong, Particles, St Peter's and St Paul's.

Chetwood, Jonathan. Rent ledger, 1816–22. NLI Ms. 14250, Most tenants. Covering townlands in the civil parishes of Limerick, St Patrick's and Ludden.

Cloncurry, Lord. Rentals, 1825–50. NLI Mss. 3417, 5661–6, 5693–5, 9053. Principally major tenants. Covering townlands in the civil parishes of Abington and Loghill.

Collins. Tenants, 1859–89. NLI Ms. 17718. All tenants. Covering townlands in the civil parish of Abbeyfeale.

Courtenay, Viscount (Earls of Devon). Estate Rental, 1762, 1861–2, LCA, IE LA P6. Covering townlands in the civil parishes of Ardagh, Caherelly, Cloncrew, Clonelty, Dromcolliher, Glenkeen, Kilmoylan, Knocknagaul, Mahoonagh, Monagay, Newcastle and Rathkeale. Online.

Creaghe, John Fitzstephen. Printed LEC Rental, 1820–68. NAI M. 3703 (183). Principally major tenants. Covering townlands in the civil parishes of Kilfergus, St Peter's and St Paul's.

de Lacy Smith. Rental, 1740–44. NLI Ms. 869. Major tenants only. Covering townlands in the civil parishes of Ardcanny, Ballycahane, Kilcornan and Knockainy.

Fitzmaurice, James. Rent book, 1851–71. NLI Ms. 19451. Most tenants. Covering townlands in the civil parish of Templebredon.

Gascoigne, Richard Oliver. Leases, 1764–72. NLI Ms. 10930 (2) (Part 2). Principally major tenants. Covering townlands in the civil parishes of Abbeyfeale, Ballingarry (Connello), Croom, Grean and Kilcornan.

Gascoigne, Richard Oliver. Rent books, tenants lists etc., 1816–40. NLI Ms. 10930, 10936. Most tenants. Covering townlands in the civil parishes of Ballingarry (Connello), Darragh, Emlygrennan, Kilbreedy Major, Kilfinnane, Kilflyn, Knocklong, Particles and Uregare.

Greene, Henry. Tenants list, 1775–90. NAI M.5555(1). Major tenants only. Covering townlands in the civil parishes of Ballynaclogh, Cahernarry and Ludden.

Kingston, Earl of. Rental, 1840. NLI Ms. 3276. All tenants. Covering townlands in the civil parishes of Ballingarry (Coshlea), Ballylanders, Brigown, Effin, Glenkeen, Kilbeheny, Knockainy, Macroney and Templetenny.

Kingston, Earl of. Rental, 1840. NLI Ms. 3276. All tenants. Covering townlands in the civil parishes of Ballingarry (Coshlea), Ballylanders, Brigown, Effin, Glenkeen, Kilbeheny, Knockainy, Macroney and Templetenny.

Lefroy, Seyant. Rental, 1812. NLI Ms. 10932 (Part 1). Major tenants only. Covering townlands in the civil parishes of Kilbreedy Major, Kilmeedy, St Peter's and St Paul's.

Lefroy, Seycant. Rental, 1812. NLI Ms. 10930 (3) (Part 2). Major tenants only. Covering townlands in the civil parishes of Kilbreedy Major, Kilmeedy, St Peter's and St Paul's.

Lefroy, Thomas. Rental, Leases, 1807–1812. NLI Ms. 10933 (Part 6). Major tenants only. Covering townlands in the civil parishes of Kilbreedy Major and Kilmeedy.

Lloyd, Dr Thomas. Rent roll, 1843. NLI Ms. 11429 (2). Most tenants. Covering townlands in the civil parishes of Caherconlish, Doon, Fedamore, Knocknagaul, Oola and Particles.

Monsell. Rentals, 1840–48. NLI Ms. 7868, 7869. All tenants. Covering townlands in the civil parishes of Ballycahane, Kilkeedy, Killeely, Kiltallagh, Mungret, Rathronan.

Monsell, William. Rental, 1852–5. NLI Ms. 7870. Major tenants only. Covering townlands in the civil parishes of Athlacca, Donaghmore, Kilkeedy, Killeely, Killeenagarriff, Mungret, Rathronan and Stradbally.

Monteagle Papers. Rent book, 1800–1807. NLI Ms. 605A. Major tenants only. Covering townlands in the civil parishes of Cappagh, Kilmoylan, Loghill, Robertstown, Shanagolden, St Peter's and St Paul's.

Oliver estate. Rentals, 1775–1831 (intermittent). NLI Mss. 10930–34, 9091. Principally major tenants. Covering townlands in the civil parishes of Athneasy, Ballingaddy Ballingarry (Connello), Ballingarry (Coshlea), Darragh, Emlygrennan, Kilfinnane, Kilflyn, Knocklong, Particles, St Peter's and St Paul's and Uregare.

Sexton, Edmond. Tenants, 1725. NLI Ms. 16085. Major tenants only. Covering townlands in the civil parishes of Adare, Croom and Killeedy.

Tuthill. Rentals, 1745–1841. NAI M. 5825. Principally major tenants. Covering townlands in the civil parishes of Adare, Ballycahane, Bruree, Caherconlish, Caherelly, Crecora, Croagh, Croom, Doon, Fedamore, Grean, Kilfrush, Kilpeacon and Knocknagaul.

Wandesforde. Prior: Rent book, 1804–1819. NLI Ms. 14171. Principally major tenants. Covering townlands in the civil parishes of Clonagh, Cloncagh, Corcomohide, Darragh, Dromcolliher, Kilmeedy, Kilmoylan, Kilscannell and Rathkeale.

Webb, James. Rental, 1765–72. NLI Ms. 7867. Major tenants only. Covering townlands in the civil parishes of Adare, Ballycahane and Monasteranenagh.

LONGFORD

Census returns and substitutes

1641	Book of Survey and Distribution. NLI Ms. 965.
1659	Pender's 'Census'. Reprinted GPC, 1997; IMC, 2002. LDS film 924648. Online: IGPweb Longford.
1726–7	Protestant householders, Abbeylara, Abbeyshrule, Ardagh, Clonbroney, Clongesh, Kilcommock, Killashee, Rathreagh, Shrule, Taghshiny (Longford); Rathsapick, Russagh (Westmeath). List compiled for the distribution of religious books. NAI M1502.
1729	'Presbyterian exodus from Co. Longford', *Breifny*, 1977–8.
1740	Protestants, Shrule and Rathreagh (Longford); Rathaspick (Westmeath). RCBL GS 2/7/3/25.
1747–1806	Freeholders. Registration book. NAI M 2745.
1766	Abbeylara: Online: PRONI name search.
1790	Freeholders c.1790. NAI M 2486 8. NLI Pos. 1897; LDS film 100888.
1795–1862	Charlton Marriage Certificates. NAI M2800. Indexed in Accessions, Vol. 37.
1796	Spinning-Wheel Premium List. 2,550 names for Co. Longford. Online: Hayes.
1800–1835	Freeholders. GO 444; also LDS 100181.
1823–38	Tithe Books. Fully transcribed and indexed in Rymsza, *Co. Longford Residents*.
1828–36	Freeholders certificates. NAI M.2781.
1834	Granard RC parish; heads of household, with Catholic registers. NLI.
1838	Mullinanalaghta RC parish, Contributors to new church. *Teathbha*, 1 (3), 1978, pp. 244–51.
1843	Voters. NAI OP 1843/62.
1854	Griffith's Valuation. Online: Askaboutireland.
1901	Census. Online: NAI.
1911	Census. Online: NAI.

Online

Askaboutireland	*<www.askaboutireland.ie>*
IGPweb Longford	*<www.igp-web.com/longford>*
Hayes, John	*<www.failteromhat.com>*
Longford Ancestry	*<www.longfordancestry.com>*
Moffatt	*<www.longford.ca>*
NAI	*<www.census.nationarchives.ie>*
PRONI name search	*<www.proni.gov.uk>*

Publications

Local histories etc.

Brady, G., *In Search of Longford Roots*, Offaly Historical Society, 1987. NLI Ir 94136
t 1.

Brady, J., *A short history of the parishes of the diocese of Meath, 1867–1944*. NLI Ir
94132 b 2.

Butler, H.T and H.E., *The Black Book of Edgeworthstown, 1585, 1817,* 1927.

Cobbe, D., *75 Years of the Longford Leader,* 1972. NLI ILB 07.

Devaney, O., *Killoe: History of a Co. Longford Parish,* 1981. NLI Ir 9413 d 1.

Farrell, James, P., *History of the County of Longford,* Dublin: 1891. NLI Ir 94131 f 2.

Farrell, Noel, *Exploring Family origins in Longford,* Longford: Longford Leader,
1991.

Gearty, Sarah, *Irish Historic Towns Atlas, 22: Longford,* Dublin: RIA, 2010. NLI.

Gillespie, Raymond, *Longford: Essays in County History,* Dublin: Lilliput Press,
1991. Co-editor, Gerard Moran. Dublin City Library (1), 941.812.

Healy, John, *History of the Diocese of Meath,* Dublin: 1908. 2 vols.

Kelly, Francis, *Window on a Catholic parish: St Mary's, Granard, Co. Longford,*
Blackrock, Co. Dublin: Irish Academic Press, 1996. NLI Ir 27413 k 5, 63 p.

Lefroy, Sir J.H., *Notes and Documents relating to the Lefroy family . . . of
Carrickglas, Co. Longford,* London: Royal Artillery Institution, 1868. NLI Ir 9292
l 18, 233 p.

McGivney, J., *Placenames of the Co. Longford,* Longford: 1908.

MacNamee, James J., *History of the Diocese of Ardagh,* Dublin: Browne & Nolan,
1954. NLI Ir 274131 m 5, 858 p.

Mimnagh, John, *'To the four winds': famine times in north Longford,* Mullingar:
the author, 1997. NLI Ir 9413 m 3, 112 p.

Monahan, Rev. J., *Records Relating to the Diocese of Ardagh and Clonmacnoise,*
Dublin: M.H. Gill & Son, 1886. NLI Ir 27413 m 3, 400 p.

Morris, Martin, *Longford: History and Society,* Dublin: Geography Publications,
2010. Co-editor, Fergus O'Ferrall. NLI, 803 p.

Murray, Mary Celine, *Bibliography of the Co. Longford,* Longford, 1961; LDS film
1279275.

Murtagh, H., *Irish Midland Studies,* Athlone: Old Athlone Society, 1980. NLI Ir 941
m 58, 255 p.

O'Donovan, John, *Ordnance Survey letters, Longford (1838),* Dublin: 1926. NLI Ir
9141 O 11.

Rymsza, Guy, *County Longford Residents prior to the Famine,* South Bend, Ind.:
Dome Shadow Press, 2004. A transcription and complete index of the Tithe
Applotment Books of Co. Longford, I (1823–35). Longford County Library,
439 p.

Stafford, R.W., *St Patrick's Church of Ireland, Granard: Notes of Genealogical and
Historical Interest,* 1983. NLI Ir 914131 s 3.

Local journals
Ardagh and Clonmacnoise Historical Society Journal. NLI Ir 794105.
Teathbha. NLI Nl Ir 94131 t 1.

Directories

1824	J. Pigot & Co., *City of Dublin and Hibernian Provincial Directory.* NLI; LDS film 451787. Online: Hayes.
1846	Slater's *National Commercial Directory of Ireland.* PRONI; NLI LO; LDS film 1696703 item 3. Online: Hayes.
1856	Slater, *Royal National Commercial Directory of Ireland.* NLI; LDS film 1472360 item 1.
1870	Slater, *Directory of Ireland.* NLI.
1881	Slater, *Royal National Commercial Directory of Ireland.* NLI. Online: FindMyPast.
1894	Slater, *Royal Commercial Directory of I.* NLI.

Gravestone inscriptions
Ardagh: St Patrick's <*www.interment.net*>.
Ballymacormick: RC, Farrell, *Exploring Family origins in Longford.*
—— Ballinamore, Farrell, *Exploring Family origins in Longford.*
Granard: Granard, The Hill, C of I, Stafford, *St Patrick's.*
Killoe: Drumlish <*www.interment.net*>.
Templemichael: Longford town, Pres., Farrell, *Exploring Family origins in Longford.*
Church St: C of I, Farrell, *Exploring Family origins in Longford.*

Estate records
[**No landlord given**]. Survey and valuation, 1810–71. NAI M.1309. All tenants. Covering townlands in the civil parishes of Columbkille and Killoe.
Adair, John. Rentals, 1738–67. NLI Ms. 3859. Coverage unclear. Covering townlands in the civil parish of Clonbroney.
Aldborough estate. Rentals, 1846. NA M. 2971.
Barbon, James. Map, 1815. NAI M.771. All tenants. Covering townlands in the civil parish of Cashel.
Belmore, Earls of. Rentals for the Longford estate, 1740–1837. PRONI D.3007. Covering areas in the civil parish of Templemichael.
Buckingham, Duke of. Estate sale, 1848. NLI 14.A.20. All tenants. Covering townlands in the civil parish of Granard.
Coates, Thomas. Rental, 1822. NAI M1883(iv). Major tenants only. Covering townlands in the civil parish of Abbeyshrule.
Crofton, Sir Humphrey. Rental and account, 1832–3. NLI Ms. 4531. All tenants. Covering townlands in the civil parish of Killashee.
Dopping. Rentals, 1833–82. NLI Ms.9,993. All tenants. Covering townlands in the civil parish of Columbkille.

Edgeworth. Map, 1727. NLI 16. H.28(10). All tenants. Covering townlands in the civil parish of Clonbroney.

Edgeworth, Rev. Essez. Account Book of Tithes, 1719–27. NAI M1502. Most tenants. Covering townlands in the civil parishes of Ballymacormick, Clongesh, Granard, Kilcommock, Killoe, Mostrim and Templemichael.

Edgeworth, Richard. Rental, accounts, valuations, 1760–1849. NAI M1497, M.1503, M.1505. All tenants. Covering townlands in the civil parishes of Ardagh, Clonbroney, Granard. Mostrim and Templemichael.

Enery, John. Rental, 1750. NAI M1883(ii). All tenants. Covering townlands in the civil parishes of Agharra, Kilglass and Killoe.

Fetherstonh, Sir Thomas. Rental, 1820. NAI M.1314. All tenants. Covering townlands in the civil parish of Killoe.

Fox, James. Rental, 1819. NLI Pos. 4065. All tenants. Covering townlands in the civil parishes of Cashel, Mostrim and Rathcline.

Harman / King Harman. Rentals, accounts and maps, 1757–1846. NAI M. 1259, 1273, 1311, 1865, 1866, 1869, 1883, 1918, 1921, 1922, 1924. All tenants. Covering townlands in the civil parishes of Abbeyshrule, Agharra, Cashel, Columbkille, Forgney, Kilcommock, Kilglass, Killashee, Killoe, Mostrim, Noughaval, Rathcline, Shrule, Taghshinny and Templemichael.

Jessop, John H. Survey, 1801. NLI Ms. 10,209. All tenants. Covering townlands in the civil parishes of Ardagh, Ballymacormick, Clongesh, Forgney, Moydow, Taghsheenod and Taghshinny.

King, John. Rent and Miscellaneous accounts, 1757–86. NLI Mss. 3520, 3125. All tenants. Covering townlands in the civil parish of Rathcline.

Lorton, Lord. Tenants list, 1847. NLI Ms. 18,244. All tenants. Covering townlands in the civil parishes of Cashel, Clongesh, Granard. Mostrim, Shrule and Taghshinny.

'Magan' maps. 1789–92, Longford County Archives. Forty-five maps of the Granard and Ballymacormack areas, with names of occupiers and topographical detail.

Montfort, H. Rental, 1845–8. NLI Ms.16,843. Most tenants. Covering townlands in the civil parish of Killashee.

Newcommen, Viscount. Maps, 1826–7. NLI Ms. 2766. All tenants. Covering townlands in the civil parishes of Abbeylara, Ardagh Cashel, Clonbroney, Clongesh, Granard, Kilcommock. Killashee, Killoe and Templemichael.

Oxmantown, Lord. Accounts, 1798–9. NAI M.1279. Major tenants only. Covering townlands in the civil parish of Abbeyshrule, Agharra, Ballymacormick, Cashel, Columbkille, Forgney, Kilcommock, Kilglass, Killashee. Mostrim, Noughaval, Rathcline, Shrule, Taghsheenod and Taghshinny.

Rochfort. Poor Rent, 1851–4. NAI M.1262. Most tenants. Covering townlands in the civil parishes of Columbkille and Killoe.

Rosse, Countess Dowager of. Surveys, rentals, tithes, maps and valuations, 1810–37. NAI M. 1883(v), 1914–16, 1284, 1286, 1290, 1294–5, 1301. All tenants. Covering townlands in the civil parishes of Abbeyshrule, Agharra,

Columbkille, Ballymacormick, Cashel, Clonbroney, Forgney, Kilcommock, Kilglass, Killashee, Killoe, Mostrim, Noughaval, Rathcline, Taghsheenod, Taghshinny, Templemichael and Shrule.

LOUTH

Census returns and substitutes

1538–1940	A Genealogical Survey of the Townland of Dowdallshill, Dundalk, Co. Louth. Online: Hall.
1600	'Gentlemen of Co. Louth', *JCLAHS*, Vol. 4, No. 4, 1919/20.
1625–7	Leet Court Rolls. Jurors and litigants in Armagh Manor; Arboe, Ardtrea, Donaghmore (Tyrone); Termonfeckin (Louth). *SA*, Vol. 11, No. 9, 1957, pp. 295–322.
1641	Book of Survey and Distribution. NLI Ms. 974.
1659	Pender's 'Census'. Reprinted GPC, 1997; IMC, 2002. LDS film 924648.
1663	Hearth Money Roll, *JCLAHS*. Vol. 6, Nos. 2 and 4; Vol. 7, No. 3.
1666	Hearth Money Roll, Dunleer parish, *IG*, 1969.
1670/71	Armagh diocese gentry, clergy and parishioners supporting the Franciscans. *SA*, Vol. 15, No. 1, 1992, pp. 186–216.
1683	Co. Louth brewers and retailers. *JCLAHS*, Vol. 3, No. 3.
1683	Drogheda merchants. *JCLAHS*, Vol. 3, No. 3.
1715	Dunleer freemen, *IG*, 4(2), 1969, pp. 142–4.
1739–41	Corn census of Co. Louth. *JCLAHS*, Vol. 11, No. 4, pp. 254–86.
1756	Commissions of Array, giving lists of Protestants who took the oath. NLI Pos. 4011. Online: Hall.
1760	Ardee parish. *IG*, 1961. PRONI.
1766	Ardee, Ballymakenny, Beaulieu, Carlingford, Charlestown, Clonkeehan, Darver, Drumiskan, Kildermock, Kileshiel, Louth, Mapastown, Philipstown, Shanlis, Smarmore, Stickallen, Tallonstown, Termonfeckin. NAI M2476 (b); Creggan NAI Parl. Ret. 657, Nelson, *History of the Parish of Creggan . . . Carlingford*, Creggan. Online: PRONI name search.
1775	Collon cess payers. RCBL MIC 1/163. Online: Hall.
1782–92	Cess payers. Parishes of Cappoge, Drumcar, Dysart, Monasterboice and Mullary. *JCLAHS*, Vol. 9, No. 1.
1791	Landholders, Dromiskin parish. Leslie, *History of Kilsaran*.
1793–8	County Louth Assizes, 1793–9, from the *Freeman's Journal*. Online: Hall.
1796	Spinning-Wheel Premium List. 3,150 names for Co. Louth. Online: Hayes.
1798	Drogheda voters' list. *JCLAHS*, Vol. 20, 1984.
1801	Tithe Applotment, Stabannon and Roodstown. Leslie, *History of Kilsaran*.
1802	Drogheda voters. *JCLAHS*, Vol. 20, 1984.

1802	Carlingford. Protestants only. *JCLAHS*, Vol. 16, No. 3.
1804	Drogheda Militia. Online: Hall.
1806	Louth Militia, Enlisted Recruits. Online: Hall.
1816	Grand Jurors. NLI Ir 6551 Dundalk.
1821–32	Freeholders, 1821, NLI Ir 94132 L 3. 1822, Online: Hall, 1824–7: Online: Hall, 1832, Dundalk Voters' List: Online: Hall.
1823–38	Tithe Books.
1833	Memorial of the inhabitants of Drogheda about cholera. c.250 signatures. NAI OP 1833/51.
1834	Tallanstown parish census. *JCLAHS*, Vol. 14.
1836	Memorial from inhabitants of Dundalk. c.100 names. NAI OP 1838/26.
1837	Valuation of towns returning members of Parliament (occupants and property values): Drogheda, Dundalk. *Parliamentary Papers, 1837: Reports from Committees*, Vol. 2 (i), Appendix G.
1837	Marksmen (illiterate voters) in parliamentary boroughs: Drogheda, Dundalk. *Parliamentary Papers, 1837: Reports from Committees*, Vol. 2 (i), Appendix A.
1837–8	Memorials from inhabitants of Ardee. 1837 (c.90 names), 1838 (c.100 names). NAI OP 1838/26.
1839	Tenants of Lord Roden, Dundalk area. Online: Hall.
1842	Voters. NAI 1842/70. Online: Hall.
1852	Local census: Mosstown and Phillipstown. *JCLAHS*, 1975.
1852	Voting electors. NLI Ms. 1660.
1854	Griffith's Valuation. Online: Askaboutireland.
1854	Louth Patriotic Fund for the dependents of Crimean War soldiers. Online: Hall.
1855–6	Ardee Convent Building Fund. Online: Hall.
1865	Parliamentary voters. NLI P. 2491. Online: Hall.
1901	Census. Online: NAI.
1911	Census. Online: NAI.

Online

Askaboutireland	*<www.askaboutireland.ie>*	
Carlingford	*<carlingfordheritagecentre.com>*	
Hall, Brendan	*<www.jbhall.freeservers.com>*	Huge compendium of Co. Louth records
Hayes, John	*<www.failteromhat.com>*	
NAI	*<www.census.nationalarchives.ie>*	
PRONI name search	*<www.proni.gov.uk>*	

Publications

Local histories etc.

Bernard, Nicholas, *The Whole Proceedings of the Siege of Drogheda* [*and*] *Londonderry*, Dublin: 1736. NLI Ir94106.b2.

Boyle, Sean, *Looking Forward, Looking Back: Stories, Memories and Musings of Castlebellingham, Kilsaran, Stabannon*, Dundalk, 2004.

Conlon, Larry, *The Heritage of Collon, 1764–1984*, Ardee: Conlon, 1984. NLI Ir 94132 c 5, 87 p.

—— A copy of the book of the Corporation of Atherdee [Ardee] (manuscript). NLI Ms. 31778.

—— 'Cromwellian and Restoration settlements in the parish of Dundalk', *JCLAHS*, Vol. 19, 1, 1977.

D'Alton, John, *The history of Drogheda*, Dublin: McGlashan & Gill, 1844. NLI Ir 94132 d 1, 2 vols.

Day, Angelique, and McWilliams, Patrick (eds.), *Ordnance Survey Memoirs of Ireland, Vol. 40: Counties of South Ulster, 1834–8: Cavan, Leitrim, Louth, Monaghan and Sligo*, Belfast: Institute of Irish Studies, 1997. Co. Louth: Ballymascanlan, Carlingford, Castletown. NLI Ir 9141 o 80, 216 p.

Dooley, Terence A.M., *The murders at Wildgoose Lodge: agrarian crime and punishment in pre-famine Ireland*, Dublin: Four Courts Press, 2007. NLI, 285 p.

Duffner, P., *Drogheda: the Low Lane Church, 1300–1979*. NLI Ir 94132 d 7.

—— 'Families at Mosstown and Phillipstown in 1852', *JCLAHS*, Vol. 18, 3, 1975. NLI.

Garry, James, *Calvary Cemetery, St. Mary's, Drogheda: history and tombstone inscriptions*, Drogheda: Old Drogheda society, 2002. NLI Ir 187 p.

—— *The Cord Cemetery: history and tombstone inscriptions*, Drogheda: Old Drogheda society, 1999. NLI [Ir] 9295 g 2, 164 p.

—— *Clogherhead through the years*, Drogheda: Old Drogheda Society, 1999. NLI Ir 94132 g 24, 226 p.

—— *St. Peter's Parish Cemetery, Drogheda*, Drogheda: 1993. Louth County Library.

—— *The Streets and Lanes of Drogheda*, Drogheda: 1996. NLI Ir 91413 g 4/1, 120 p.

Gavin, Joseph, *Military barracks, Dundalk: a brief history*, Dublin: Defence Forces Printing Press, 1999. Co-author, Stephen O'Donnell. NLI Ir 355 g 9, 102 p.

Gerrard, Richard, *The story of Newtownstalaban*, Drogheda: Old Drogheda Society, 2003. NLI, 240 p.

Greene, Ted, *Drogheda: its place in Ireland's history*, Julianstown: the author, 2006. NLI, 410 p.

Hall, Brendan, *The Louth Rifles, 1877–1908*, Dún Laoghaire: Genealogical Society of Ireland, 2000. Co-editor, Donal Hall. NLI, 160 p.

—— *Officers and recruits of the Louth Rifles, 1854–76* (2nd ed.), Dún Laoghaire: Genealogical Society of Ireland, 2001. NLI Ir 94132 h 3, 188 p.

Hall, Donal, *The unreturned army: County Louth dead in the Great War, 1914–1918*, Dundalk: Louth Archaeological and Historical Society, 2005. NLI, 243 p.

Irish Countrywomen's Association, *A Local History Guide to Summerhill and Surrounding Areas.* NLI Ir 94132 i 1.

King, Philip, *Monasterboice heritage: a centenary celebration* . . . Monasterboice: Philip King, 1994. NLI Ir 94132 k 1, 352 p.

Leslie, Canon J.B., *History of Kilsaran Union of Parishes,* Dundalk: Tempest, 1908. NLI Ir 94132 l 1, 350 p.

L'Estrange, G., *Notes and Jottings concerning the parish of Charlestown Union,* Charlestown: Rectory Press, 1912. NLI Ir 94132 l 2, 94 p.

MacAllister, Robert Alexander Stewart, *Monasterboice, Co. Louth,* Dundalk: Tempest, 1946. NLI Ir 7941 m 11, 79 p.

McHugh, Ned, *Drogheda before the Famine: urban poverty in the shadow of privilege, 1826–45,* Maynooth: Irish Academic Press, 1998.

Mac Íomhair, D., *Tombstone Inscriptions from Fochart,* Dundalk: Dundalgan press, 1968. NLI Ir 94132 p 1, 20 p.

McNeill, Charles, *Dowdall deeds,* Dublin: Stationery Office, for IMC, 1960. Co-editor, A.J. Otway-Ruthven. NLI Ir 091 m 9, 416 p.

—— 'Some early documents relating to English Uriel, and Drogheda and Dundalk, 1: The Draycott family', *JCLAHS,* 5, 1924, pp. 270–75.

McQuillan, Jack, *The railway town: the story of the Great Northern Railway Works and Dundalk,* Dundalk: Dundalgan Press, 1993. NLI Ir 625 m 17, 212 p.

Martin, John (Jackie), *Memories of Kilkerley,* Kilkerley: the author, 2006. NLI, 77 p.

Murphy, Donald, *The Flanagans of Tobertoby, Co. Louth,* 1989. NLI, 94 p.

Murphy, Peter, *Together in Exile,* Nova Scotia: 1991. Carlingford emigrants to St John's, New Brunswick. Carlingford Library.

Murray, Rev. Lawrence P., *History of the Parish of Creggan in the Seventeenth and Eighteenth Centuries,* Dundalk: 1940.

Nelson, Simon, *History of the Parish of Creggan in Cos. Armagh and Louth from 1611 to 1840,* Belfast: PRONI, 1974. NLI Ir 941 p 43, 37 p.

—— 'Notes on the Volunteers, Militia and Yeomanry, and Orangemen of Co. Louth', *JCLAHS,* Vol. 18, 4, 1976.

—— 'Old title deeds of Co. Louth: Dundalk, 1718–1856', *JCLAHS,* Vol. 20, 1, 1981.

O'Neill, C.P., *History of Dromiskin, Darver Parish,* Dundalk: Annaverna Press, 1984. NLI Ir 94132 o 4, 101 p.

O'Sullivan, Harold, *Irish Historic Towns Atlas, 16: Dundalk,* Dublin: RIA, 2006. NLI.

Redmond, Brigid, *The Story of Louth,* Dublin: 1931. NLI Ir 9141 p 1.

Reynolds, F., *The Medieval Parishes of Clogherhead and Walshestown (1300–1857),* Drogheda: Reynolds, 2003. NLI, 25 p.

Ross, Noel, *Tombstone Inscriptions in Castletown Graveyard, Dundalk,* Dundalk: Old Dundalk Society, 1992. Co-author, Maureen Wilson. NLI Ir 9295 p1(1).

Sharkey, Noel, *The Parish of Haggardstown and Blackrock: A History,* Dundalk: Sharkey, 2003. Louth County Library R 941.825.

Tempest, H.S., *Descriptive and Historical Guide to Dundalk and District,* 1916. NLI Ir 94132 t 1.

Ua Dubhthaigh, Pádraic, *The book of Dundalk*, Sligo: Champion Publications, 1946. NLI Ir 914132 u 2, 148 p.

Local journals
Journal of the County Louth Archaeological and Historical Society. NLI Ir 794105 L 2.
Journal of the Old Drogheda Society. NLI Ir 94132 o 3.
Journal of the Termonfeckin Historical Society.
Seanchas Ardmhacha. NLI Ir 27411 s 4.

Directories

1820	J. Pigot, *Commercial Directory of Ireland*. PRONI; NLI Ir 9141 p 107; LDS film 962702 item 1.
1824	J. Pigot & Co., *City of Dublin and Hibernian Provincial Directory*. NLI; LDS film 451787. Online: Hayes.
1830	McCabe, *Drogheda Directory*. NLI Pos. 3986.
1846	Slater's *National Commercial Directory of Ireland*. PRONI; NLI LO; LDS film 1696703 item 3. Online: Hayes.
1856	Slater, *Royal National Commercial Directory of Ireland*. NLI; LDS film 1472360 item 1.
1861	Henderson, *Post Office Directory of Meath and Louth*.
1870	Slater, *Directory of Ireland*. NLI.
1881	Slater, *Royal National Commercial Directory of Ireland*. NLI. Online: FindMyPast.
1886	George Henry Basset, *Louth County Guide and Directory*. NLI Ir 914132 b 2/1.
1890	Tempest's *Almanack and Directory of Dundalk*. Annually from 1890.
1894	Slater, *Royal Commercial Directory of Ireland*. NLI.

Gravestone inscriptions

Many of the published transcripts are indexed online at <*www.jbhall.freeservers.com*>.

Ardee: Ardee, Market St, C of I, *IG*, 3 (1) 1956.
Ballymakenny: C of I, *SA*, 1983/4.
Ballymascanlan: C of I, *JCLAHS*, Vol. 17, No. 4, 1972.
—— Faughart Upper, HW.
Beaulieu: C of I, *JCLAHS*, Vol. 20, No. 1.
Carlingford: Church Lane, C of I, *JCLAHS*, Vol. 19, No. 2, 1978.
Church Lane: C of I, Online: Carlingford.
Mountbagnall (Newtown): Online: Carlingford.
Omeath: Online: Hall, Brendan.
Castletown: Ross, *Tombstone Inscriptions*.
Charlestown: C of I, L'Estrange, *Notes and Jottings*.
Clogher: Main St, C of I. Garry, *Clogherhead*.

Clonkeen: Churchtown, C of I, L'Estrange, *Notes and Jottings.*

Clonmore: C of I, *JCLAHS*, Vol. 20, No. 2.

Collon: Church St, LDS Family History Library, 941.825/k29c; also <*www. interment.net*>.

Darver: C of I, Cavan Heritage and Genealogy Centre. Also *Bréifne*, 1922.

Drogheda, St Mary's: Calvary, Garry, *Calvary*; also (part) <*www.interment.net*>.

Dromin: LDS Family History Library, 941.825/k29c.

Drumshallon: *JCLAHS*, Vol. 19, No. 3, 1979.

Dunany: *JCLAHS*, Vol. 20, No. 3, 1983.

Dundalk: Seatown, *Tempest's Annual*, 1967, 1971/2.

Dunleer: Main St, C of I, *JCLAHS*, Vol. 22, No. 4, 1992.

Dysart: *JCLAHS*, Vol. 19, No. 3, 1979.

Faughart: Dungooly, Mac Íomhair, *Tombstone Inscriptions from Fochart.*

Gernonstown: Castlebellingham, Leslie, *History of Kilsaran.*

Haynestown: *JCLAHS*, 1993.

Kildemock: Drakestown, *JCLAHS*, Vol. 13, No. 1.

—— Millockstown, Leslie, *History of Kilsaran.*

—— Kilsaran, Leslie, *History of Kilsaran.*

Killanny: RC, *Clogher Record*, 1966.

Killincoole: Online: Hall, Brendan.

Kilsaran: Leslie, *Kilsaran.*

Louth: Priorstate, *JCLAHS*, Vol. 19, No. 4, 1980.

—— Grange, *JCLAHS*, Vol. 19, No. 3, 1979.

Knockbridge: Online: Hall, Brendan.

Mansfieldstown: Mansfieldstown, Leslie, *History of Kilsaran.*

Mayne: Glebe East, *JCLAHS*, Vol. 20, No. 4, 1984.

Monasterboice: King, *Monasterboice.*

Mosstown: Mosstown North, LDS Family History Library, 941.825/k29c.

Port: *JCLAHS*, 21 (2), 1986, pp. 208–218.

Rathdrumin: Glebe, C of I, *JCLAHS*, Vol. 19, No. 1, 1970.

Richardstown: *JCLAHS*, Vol. 12, No. 1, 1926.

St Peter's, Drogheda: Calvary, Garry, *Calvary.*

Churchyard, *Journal of the Old Drogheda Society*, 1992.

The Cord: Garry, *The Cord.*

Parish cemetery: Garry, *St. Peter's.*

Salterstown: *JCLAHS*, Vol. 20, No. 3, 1983.

Shanlis: *JCLAHS*, Vol. 22, No. 1, 1989.

Smarmore: *JCLAHS*, Vol. 22, No. 1, 1989.

Stabannan: C of I, Leslie, *Kilsaran.*

Stickillin: *JCLAHS*, Vol. 22, No. 1, 1989.

Termonfeckin: *IG*, 8, No. 2 (1991), pp. 293–317; Vol. 8, No. 3 (1992), pp. 436–52.

Tullyallen: RC, *SA*, Vol. 7, No. 2, 1977.

Tullyallen: Newtownstalaban, *JCLAHS*, Vol. 17, No. 2, 1970.

Estate records

[Unknown]. Rental, 1809–1815, Louth County Archives, pp00001/001/03/001. Covering areas in the civil parish of Killanny.

[No landlord given]. 'Tenants in Culver House Park, Drogheda.' 30 tenants, with maps, 1809, *JCLAHS*, 11 (3), 1947, 206–208. Covering areas in the civil parish of St Peter's.

[No landlord given]. Families (all) in the townlands of Mosstown and Philipstown, 1852, *JCLAHS*, 18 (3), 1975, 232–7. Covering areas in the civil parish of Mosstown.

Anglesea. Tenants list for Anglesea estate, Carlingford parish, 1810, 1856, *JCLAHS*, 12 (2), 1950, pp. 136–51. Covering areas in the civil parish of Carlingford. Details of the Anglesea estate papers in PRONI; *JCLAHS*, Vol. 17, 1, 1973. (See also *JCLAHS*, 12, 2.)

Balfour. Tenants, Ardee parish, 1838, *JCLAHS*, 12 (3), 1951, pp. 188–90. Covering areas in the civil parish of Ardee.

Caraher. Cardistown, tenants on potato land, 1810–17, *JCLAHS*, 165 (3), 1967, pp. 177–83. Covering areas in the civil parish of Clonkeen.

Clanbrassil. Tenants on two Clanbrassil estate maps of Dundalk, 1782–8, *JCLAHS*, 15 (1), 1961, pp. 39–87. Covering areas in the civil parish of Dundalk.

Doyne, Philip. Rent roll, 1824–32, Louth County Archives, pp. 00001/001/08/001. Covering areas in the civil parishes of Cappoge and Gernonstown.

Drumgooter. A tenant farm in the eighteenth and nineteenth centuries (from a rent roll of the estate of Sir John Bellew), *JCLAHS*, Vol. 20, 4, 1984. Civil parish of Rathdrumin.

Filgate. Rent roll, 1792, Louth County Archives, pp00001/001. Covering areas in the civil parishes of Charlestown, Haggardstown, Louth, Monasterboice, Mullary, Shanlis and Tallanstown. Half-yearly rent roll showing rents due.

Foster, John. Rental and accounts of Collon Estate, 1779–81, *JCLAHS*, 10 (3), 1943, pp. 222–9. Covering areas in the civil parish of Collon.

McClintock. Tenants on the McClintock estate, Drumcar and Kilsaran, 1852, *JCLAHS*, 16 (4), 1968, pp. 230–32. Covering areas in the civil parishes of Drumcar and Kilsaran.

Roden. 'Papers from the Roden estate, Clanbrassel estate map, 1785', *JCLAHS*, Vol. 20, 1, 1981.

Tenants of Omeath. 1865, *JCLAHS*, Vol. 17, 1, 1973.

Trench. Rentals, Drogheda. NLI Ms. 2576.

MAYO

Census returns and substitutes

1600–1700	Mayo landowners in the seventeenth century, *JRSAI*, 1965, pp. 153–62.
1692–8	Foxford Quit Rent books. NAI M6968.
1693	List of those outlawed after the Williamite wars; in some instances addresses and family relationships are specified. *AH*, 22, 1–240.

1716	Ballinrobe Protestant freeholders requesting the building of walls. 70 names. *JGAHS*, 7, 1911/12, pp. 168–70.
1783	Ballinrobe householders. *AH*, Vol. 14.
1785	Lord Altamont's rent roll of Westport. 63 names. *Cathair na Mart*, Vol. 2, No. 1.
1786	Petition for a postal service between Westport and Castlebar. 70 inhabitants of Westport listed. *Cathair na Mart*, 16, 1996.
1796	Catholics migrating from Ulster to Co. Mayo, *SA*, 1958, pp. 17–50. See also 'Petition of Armagh migrants in the Westport area', *Cathair na Mart*, Vol. 2, No. 1 (Appendix). Online: Dees.
1796	Spinning-Wheel Premium List. 1,900 names for Co. Mayo. Online: Hayes.
1798	Persons who suffered losses in the 1798 Rebellion. Propertied classes only. c.650 names. NLI I 94107.
1818	Tithe collectors' account book, parishes of Kilfian and Moygawnagh. NAI M. 6085.
1820	Protestants in Killala. NAI MFCI 32.
1823–38	Tithe Books. Part online: Connors.
1823	Defendants at Westport petty sessions. NLI Ms. 14902.
1825	Petition to have the River Moy dredged (100 names, Ballina). NAI OP 974/131.
1831	750 names to a petition for poor relief in Coolcarney (Kilgarvan and Attymass). NAI OP 9974/116.
1832	Protestants in Foxford. NLI Ms. 8295.
1832–9	Freeholders. Alphabetical listing, showing residence and valuation. NAI OP 1839/138.
1833	Defendants at Mayo Lent Assizes. Alphabetical list, giving crime. *Claremorris in History*, Mayo Family History Society, 1987.
1835	Correspondence concerning distressed poor in parts of west Mayo, including parishes of Achill, Burrishoole and Doonfeeny. c.300 names. NAI OP 1835/350. See also *Cathair na Mart*, No. 17, 1997.
1835–9	Lord Lucan's rent rolls for Castlebar. Also 1848–73. Mayo County Library.
1836	Defendants at Mayo Summer Assizes. *Claremorris in History*, Mayo Family History Society, 1987.
1838	Memorial from Achill opposing Edward Nangle's request for the establishment of petty sessions. c.250 names (signatures and marks). NAI OP 1838/214.
1838–48	Reproductive Loan Fund records. Records of loan associations at Ballina (Carramore), Ballindangan, Ballinrobe, Castlebar, Claremorris, Newport, Swineford and Westport, covering more than 4,000 individuals. NA (Kew). T 91. Partly online: Moving Here.
1839	Crossmolina parishioners. 170 names of nominators of tithe apploters. NAI OP/1839/77.

1841	Some extracts only, for Newport. NAI Thrift Abstracts.
1842	Freeholders (excludes the baronies of Erris and Tirawley). NAI OP/1842/71.
1845	Defendants at Mayo Summer Assizes (notebook of Justice Jackson). NAI M55249.
1845	Clare Island tenants, *South Mayo Family History Research Journal*, 7, 1994, 46–7.
1850	Voters' lists, *South Mayo Family History Research Journal*, 1996, 27–41.
1856–7	Voters' registers, baronies of Costello (NAI M.3447), Clanmorris (NAI M.3448), Tirawley (NAI M.2782), Kilmaine (NAI M.2783) and Gallen (NAI M.2784).
1856–7	Griffith's Valuation. Indexed online: Hayes.
1901	Census. Online: NAI.
1911	Census. Online: NAI.

Online

Celtic Cousins	<www.celticcousins.net>
Connors	<www.connorsgenealogy.com>
Dees	<freepages.genealogy.rootsweb.com/~deesegenes>
Hayes, John	<www.failteromhat.com>
Moving Here	<www.movinghere.org.uk/search>

Publications

Local histories etc.

Achill Orphan Refuges, 'The ethnography of the Inishbofin and Inishark', PRIA, 3rd Ser., Vol. 3, 1893–6, pp. 360–80.

Achill: 15th report of the mission: Report of Achill Orphan Refuges, 1849. NLI Ir 266 a 8.

Butler, Patrick, *Turlough Park and the FitzGeralds*, Butler: 2002. NLI, 48 p.

Cantwell, Ian, *Memorials of the Dead, Counties Galway and Mayo (Western Seaboard)*, Eneclann CD ENEC004, Dublin: Eneclann, 2002. Galway County Library. Online: FindMyPast.

Clarke, P.J., *Mayo comrades of the Great War, 1914–1919*, Ballina: Padraig Corcoran, 2006. NLI, 360 p.

Comer, Michael, *Béacán/Bekan: portrait of an East Mayo parish*, Ballinrobe: Comer, 1986. Co-editor, Nollaig Ó Muraíle. NLI Ir 94123 b 1, 208 p.

Crossmolina Historical and Archaeological Society, *The Deel Basin: a historical survey*, 1985–90. NLI Ir 94123 c 5.

Donohoe, Tony, *History of Crossmolina*, Dublin: De Búrca, 2003. NLI, 627 p.

Farrell, Noel, *Exploring Family Origins in Ballina Town*, Longford: Noel Farrell, 2001?, 48 p.

—— *Exploring Family Origins in Castlebar and Westport*, Longford: Noel Farrell, 2006. NLI, 48 p.

Fitzgerald, Patricia, *An Gorta Mór i gCill Alaidhe* [*The Great Famine in Killala*], Killala: the authors, 1996. Co-author, Olive Kennedy. NLI 1A 1893, 66 p.

Garvey, Rosemary, *Kilkenny to Murrisk: a Garvey family history*, Killadoon: the author, 1992. NLI Ir 9292 g 30.

Hayes-McCoy, G.A., *Index to 'The Compossicion Booke of Connoght, 1585'*, Dublin: IMC, 1945. NLI Ir 9412 c 1, 179 p.

Higgins, Tom, *Through Fagan's Gates: the parish and people of Castlebar down the ages*, Castlebar: Higgins, 2001. NLI, 224 p.

Jennings, Martin, *Swinford re-echo: parish inscapes*, Swinford: Swinford Community Council, 1981. NLI Ir 94123 s 2, 92 p.

Jordan, Donald E., Jr, *Land and popular politics in Ireland: County Mayo from the plantation to the Land War*, Cambridge: Cambridge University Press, 1994. NLI Ir 94123 J 1, 369 p.

Kennedy, Gerald Conan, *North Mayo (Tirawley) history and folklore, landscape, environment, places of historic interest*, Killala: Morrigan Books, 1992. NLI Ir 941 p 122(3), 3 folded sheets.

Kingston, Rev. John, *Achill Island: the deserted village at Slievemore: a study . . .* Achill Island: Bob Kingston, 1990. NLI Ir 720 k 6.

Knight, P., *Erris in the Irish highlands and the Atlantic railway*, Dublin: M. Keene, 1836. NLI Ir 914123 k 2, 178 p.

Knox, H.T., *The history of Mayo to the close of the 16th century*, Dublin: Hodges, Figgis, 1908. NLI Ir 94123 k 2 (and LO), 451 p. Reprinted Dublin: De Búrca Rare Books, 1982.

—— *Notes on the Early History of the Dioceses of Tuam, Killala and Achonry*, Dublin: Hodges Figgis, 1904. NLI Ir 27412 k 1, 410 p.

McCarthy, Rosemary P., *The 'family tree': the Connors-Walsh family of Kiltimagh, County Mayo, and the USA, with branches in Great Britain . . .* New York: the author, 1979. LC CS71.O18 1979, 193 p.

McDonald, Theresa, *Achill, 5000 BC to 1900 AD: archaelogy, history, folklore*, IAS Publications, 1992. NLI Ir 94123 m 12.

McDonnell, Thomas, *The diocese of Killala: from its institution to the end of the penal times*, Ballina: R. & S. Monaghan, 1975. NLI Ir 27412 m 1, 143 p.

Mac Graith, Uinsionn, *The placenames and heritage of Dún Chaocháin in the Barony of Erris, County Mayo*, Béal an Átha: Comhar Dhún Chaocháin, 2004. Co-editor, Treasa Ní Ghearraigh. NLI, 172 p.

McGrath, Fiona, *Emigration and landscape: the case of Achill Island*, Dublin: Department of Geography, Trinity College, 1991. NLI Ir 900 p 10 (3).

MacHale, Edward, *The Parishes in the Diocese of Killala: (1) South Tirawley, (2) North Tirawley, (3) Erris, (4) Tireragh*, Killala: 1985. NLI Ir 27414 m 6, 166/104/88, 79 p.

Mac Néill, Eoin, *Clare Island survey: Place-names and family names*, Dublin: RIA Proceedings. Vol. 31, Sect. 1, Part 3, 1911–15. NLI Ir 92942 m 6, 42 p.

Mahon, Marie, *Claremorris in History*, Mayo Family History Society, 1987. NLI, 92 p.

Masterson, William G., *County Mayo: families of Ballycroy parish, 1856–1880*, Indianapolis, Ind.: the author, 1995. NLI Ir 9292 m 74.

—— *County Mayo, Ireland, Newport area families, 1864–1880*, Indianapolis, Ind.: W.G. Masterson, 2000. NLI Ir 9291 m 31, 157 p.

Meehan, Rosa, *The story of Mayo*, Castlebar: Mayo County Library, 2003. NLI 393 p.

Moffitt, Miriam, *The Church of Ireland community of Killala and Achonry, 1870–1940*, Dublin: Irish Academic Press, 1999. NLI Ir 283 m 4, 64 p.

Moran, Gerard, *The Mayo evictions of 1860: Patrick Lavelle and the 'War' in Partry*, Foilseacháin Náisiúnta Teoranta, 1986. NLI Ir 94123 m 9, 143 p.

Mulloy, Bridie, *Itchy feet and thirsty work: a guide to the history and folklore of Ballinrobe*, Ballinrobe: Lough Mask and Lough Carra Tourist Development Association, 1991. NLI Ir 94123.m.11, 268 p.

Mulloy, Sheila, *Victory or glorious defeat: biographies of participants in the Mayo rebellion of 1798*, Westport: Dublin: Carrowbaun Press, 2010. NLI, 311 p.

Ní Ghearaigh, Treasa, *Cill Ghallagáin graveyard in the parish of Kilcommon, County Mayo*, Béal an Átha: Comhar Dhún Chaocháin, 2009. NLI 96 p.

Ní Ghiobúin, Mealla C., *Dugort, Achill Island, 1831–1861: a study of the rise and fall of a missionary community*, Dublin: Irish Academic Press, 2001. NLI 2A 499, 78 p.

Noone, Sean, *Where the sun sets: Ballycroy, Belmullet, Kilcommon and Kiltane, County Mayo*, Ballina: Erris Publications, 1991. NLI Ir 94123 n 5, 351 p.

Ó Dálaigh, Brian, *Irish villages: studies in local history*, Dublin: Four Courts Press, 2003. Co-editors, Liam Clare and Karina Holton. Ballycastle. NLI, 326 p.

O'Donovan, John, *Ordnance Survey letters: Mayo . . . 1838*, Dublin: Fourmasters Press, 2009. NLI, 355 p.

—— *Tribes and customs of Hy Fiachra*, Kansas City, Mo.: Kansas City Irish Genealogical Foundation, 1993. NLI Ir 941 t 21.

O'Flaherty, Roderic, *A chorographical description of West or H-Iar Connaught: written AD 1684*, Dublin: for the Irish Archaeological Society, 1846. NLI Ir 94124 o 2. Reprinted Galway: Kenny's Bookshops and Art Galleries, 1978.

O'Hara, B., *Killasser: a history*, Galway: O'Hara, 1981. NLI Ir 94123 o 6, 104 p.

—— *Mayo: aspects of its heritage*, Galway: Regional Technical College, 1982. NLI Ir 94123 o 7, 313 p.

Ó Móráin, Pádraig, *A short account of the history of Burrishoole Parish*, Westport: CPR, 2004. NLI, 102 p.

O'Sullivan, William, The Strafford Inquisition of County Mayo (RIA Ms. 24 E 15), Dublin: IMC, 1958. NLI Ir 94123 o 4, 245 p.

People of Bohola, *Bohola: its history and its people*, Bohola: Sheridan Memorial Community Centre Committee, 1992. NLI, 312 p.

Quinn, David B., *History of Mayo*, Ballina: Brendan Quinn, 1993–2002. NLI, 5 vols. Articles first published in *Western People* in 1930s.

—— *St Muiredach's College, Ballina: Roll, 1906–79.* NLI Ir 259 m 2; Ir 37941 s 18.

Simington, Robert C., *The transplantation to Connacht, 1654–58*, Shannon: Irish University Press for IMC, 1970. NLI Ir 94106 s 9, 306 p.

Smith, Brian, *Tracing your Mayo Ancestors*, Dublin: Flyleaf Press, 1997. NLI GS, 96 p.

Sobolewski, Peter, *Kiltimagh: our life and times*, Kiltimagh: Kiltimagh Historical Society, 1996. Co-editor, Betty Solan. NLI, 94123 k, 318 p.

Suttle, Sam, *Roots and branches: a history of the Hughes family of Islandeady*, Dublin: 1999. NLI, 88 p.

Swinford Historical Society, *An Gorta Mór: famine in the Swinford Union*, Swinford: Swinford Historical Society, 1996. NLI Ir 94123 f 3, 80 p.

Walsh, Marie, *An Irish country childhood: memories of a bygone age*, London: Smith Gryphon, 1995. NLI Ir 92 w 242, Attymass.

Local journals
Cathair na Mart (Journal of the Westport Historical Society). NLI Ir 94123 c 4.
North Mayo Historical and Archaeological Journal. NLI Ir 94123 n 4.
South Mayo Family History Research Journal. Mayo County Library.

Directories

1824 J. Pigot & Co., *City of Dublin and Hibernian Provincial Directory*. NLI; LDS film 451787. Online: Hayes.

1846 Slater's *National Commercial Directory of Ireland*. PRONI; NLI LO; LDS film 1696703 item 3. Online: Hayes.

1856 Slater, *Royal National Commercial Directory of Ireland*. NLI; LDS film 1472360 item 1.

1870 Slater, *Directory of Ireland*. NLI.

1881 Slater, *Royal National Commercial Directory of Ireland*. NLI. Online: FindMyPast.

1894 Slater, *Royal Commercial Directory of Ireland*. NLI.

Gravestone inscriptions

Parts (at least) of fifteen Co. Mayo graveyards are transcribed at <*www.interment. net*>. Mayo South Family Heritage Centre has transcripts for 142 graveyards, mainly in the south of the county. Mayo North Family History Research Centre also has a large number of transcripts. Galway Family History Society has transcripts for Inishbofin, and Sligo Heritage and Genealogy Centre has transcripts for the parish of Kilmoremoy. Contact details will be found in Chapter 15.

Achill, Doogort East, Cantwell, *Memorials*.
Achill Sound, C of I. IGRS, Vol. 2.
Aghagower, Aghagower, RC, Cantwell, *Memorials*.
Aglish, Knockacroghery (Castlebar?), Cantwell, *Memorials*.
Ballintober, Ballintober (Abbey), Cantwell, *Memorials*.
Ballyovey, Gorteenmore (Tourmakeedy?), RC, Cantwell, *Memorials*.
Burrishoole, Tierna (Carrowkeel ?), Cantwell, *Memorials*.
Newport, Church Lane, C of I, Cantwell, *Memorials*.
Islandeady, Islandeady, Cantwell, *Memorials*.
Kilcommon (Erris), Fahy, Cantwell, *Memorials*.

Kilcommon or Pollatomish, Cantwell, *Memorials.*
Kilgalligan, Ní Ghearaigh, *Cill Ghallagáin.*
Kilteany, Cantwell, *Memorials.*
Bunnahowen, RC, Cantwell, *Memorials.*
Kilgeever, Louisburgh, Bridge St, C of I, Cantwell, *Memorials.*
Lecarrow (Killeen?), RC, Cantwell, *Memorials.*
Kilgeever, Cantwell, *Memorials.*
Kilmaclasser, Rushbrook (Fahy? Clogher Lough?), Cantwell, *Memorials.*
Kilmeena, Kilmeena, Cantwell, *Memorials.*
Kilmore, Binghamstown, C of I, Cantwell, *Memorials.*
Cross (Boyd), Cantwell, *Memorials.*
Termoncarragh, Cantwell, *Memorials.*
Oughaval, Drumin East, Cantwell, *Memorials.*

Estate records

Altamont, Lord. NAI M5788(2), rental of the Westport estate, 1787. Principally major tenants. The section on the town of Westport is published in *Cathair na Mart*, Vol. 2, No. 1, along with a rent roll for the town from 1815. Covering townlands in the civil parishes of Aghagower, Burriscarra, Burrishoole, Kilbelfad, Kilbride, Kilconduff, Kildacomoge, Kilfian, Killdeer, Kilmaclasser, Kilmeena, Moygownagh and Oughaval.

Arran, Earl of. NLI Ms. 14087: leases on the Mayo estate, 1720–1869, mentioning lives in the leases. NLI Ms. 14086: valuation survey of the Mayo estates, 1850–52. All tenants. Covering townlands in the civil parishes of Addergoole, Ardagh, Ballysakeery, Crossmolina, Kilbelfad, Kilcummin, Kilfian, Killala and Kilmoremoy.

Browne, Col. John. NLI Pos. 940. Account of the sales of the estates of Col. John Browne in Cos. Galway and Mayo, compiled in 1778, giving names of major tenants and purchasers, 1698–1704, and those occupying the estates in 1778. Covering townlands in the civil parishes of Addergoole, Aghagower, Aglish, Ballintober, Ballyhean, Ballyovey, Ballysakeery, Breaghwy, Burrishoole, Cong, Crossmolina, Drum, Islandeady, Kilcommon, Kilgeever, Killeadan, Kilmaclasser, Kilmainemore, Kilmeena, Manulla, Moygownagh, Oughaval, Robeen, Tonaghty and Turlough.

Clanmorris, Lord. NLI Ms. 3279. Rental, 1833. All tenants. Covering townlands in the civil parishes of Kilcommon, Kilmainemore, Mayo, Robeen, Rosslee, Tonaghty and Toomour.

Domville. NLI Ms. 11816. Rentals, 1833–6, 1843, 1847, 1851. All tenants. Covering townlands in the civil parishes of Killasser, Manulla and Robeen.

Knox, Henry. NAI 5630 (1). Rental, early nineteenth century. All tenants. Covering townlands in the civil parishes of Crossmolina, Doonfeeny, Kilfian and Kilmoremoy.

Medlicott, Thomas. NLI Ms. 5736 (3), Tithe Applotment Book, Achill. NLI Mss. 5736 (2), 5821. Rent rolls, showing lives in leases, 1774, 1776. Major tenants only.

Covering townlands in the civil parishes of Achill, Aghagower, Burrishoole, Kilcommon, Kilmeena and Kilmore.

O'Donel, Sir Neal. NLI Ms. 5738 and 5744: leaseholders on the estates, 1775–1859, 1828, giving lives mentioned in leases. Mainly major tenants. NLI Ms. 5736: Rental, 1788. Major tenants only. NLI Ms. 5281: Rental, 1805. Major tenants only. NLI Ms. 5743: Rental, 1810. Major tenants only. NLI Ms. 5281: Rental, 1828. Major tenants only. Covering townlands in the civil parishes of Achill, Aghagower, Burrishoole, Cong, Kilcommon, Kilgeever, Kilmore and Kilmaclasser.

O'Malley, Sir Samuel. NAI M1457 (published in *Cathair na Mart*, Vol. 6, No. 1). Valuation of the Mayo estates, 1845. All tenants. Covering townlands in the civil parishes of Aglish, Kilgeever and Kilmeena.

MEATH

Census returns and substitutes

1641	Testimonies of 212 witnesses to the 1641 Rebellion. Online: 1641.
1641	Book of Survey and Distribution. NLI Ms. 974.
1654–6	*Civil Survey*, Vol. 3. NLI I 6551 Dublin.
1659	Pender's 'Census'. Reprinted GPC, 1997; IMC, 2002. LDS film 924648.
1663	Hearth Money Roll, *JCLAHS*, Vol. 6, Nos. 2 and 4; Vol. 7, No. 3.
1670/71	Armagh diocese, gentry, clergy and parishioners supporting the Franciscans. *SA*, Vol. 15, No. 1, 1992, pp. 186–216.
1710	Voters in Kells, PRONI T 3163. NLI Headford papers.
1766	Ardbraccan. Protestants only. GO 537; also RCBL. Ardbraccan, Churchtown, Liscartan, Martry, Rataine. Online: PRONI name search.
1770	Freeholders. NLI Ms. 787–8; also LDS film 100181.
1781	Voters. NAI M4910–12.
1792	Hearth tax collectors' account and collection books, parishes of Colp, Donore, Duleek and Kilshalvan, NLI Ms. 26735; Ardcath, Ardmulchan, Ballymagarvy, Brownstown, Clonalvy, Danestown, Fennor, Kentstown, Knockcommon and Rathfeigh, NLI Ms. 26736; Athlumney, Danestown, Dowdstown, Dunsany, Kilcarn, Killeen, Macetown, Mounttown, Tara and Trevet, NLI Ms. 26737; St Mary's, Drogheda, NLI Ms. 26739, 26735.
1793	Hearth tax collectors' account and collection books, parishes of Ardagh, Dowth, Gernonstown, Killary, Mitchelstown, Siddan, Slane and Stackallan, NLI Ms. 26738.
1795–1862	Charlton Marriage Certificates. NAI. List 37, M2800. Indexed in NAI Accessions, Vol. 37.
1796	Spinning-Wheel Premium List. 1,450 names for Co. Meath. Online: Hayes.
1797–1801	Tithe Valuations, Athboy. NAI MFCI 53, 54.
1802	Drogheda Voters, *JCLAHS*, Vol. 20, 1984.
1802–1806	Protestants in the parishes of Agher, Ardagh, Clonard, Clongill, Drumconrath, Duleek, Emlagh, Julianstown, Kentstown, Kilbeg,

Kilmainhamwood, Kilskyre, Laracor, Moynalty, Navan, Robertstown, Raddenstown, Rathcore, Rathkenny, Rathmolyon, Ratoath, Skryne, Straffordstown, Stamullin, Tara, Trevet and Templekeeran. *IA*, 1973.

1804	Drogheda Militia. Online: Hall.
1813	Protestant children at Ardbraccan School. *IA*, 1973.
1815	Voters. PRONI T3163; also NLI Headford papers.
1816	Grand Jurors. NLI Ir 6551 Dundalk.
1821	Parishes of Ardbraccan, Ardsallagh, Balrathboyne, Bective, Churchtown, Clonmacduff, Donaghmore, Donaghpatrick, Kilcooly, Liscartan, Martry, Moymet, Navan, Newtownclonbun, Rathkenny, Rataine, Trim, Trimblestown and Tullaghanoge. NAI.
1823–38	Tithe Books.
1830	Census of landowners in Julianstown, Moorchurch, Stamullen and Clonalvey, *Ríocht na Midhe* 3 (4), 1966, pp. 354–8.
1833	Protestant cess-payers, parishes of Colp and Kilshalvan. *Ríocht na Midhe*, 4 (3), 1969, pp. 61–2.
1833	Memorial of the inhabitants of Drogheda about cholera. c.250 signatures. NAI OP 1833/51.
1837	Valuation of towns returning members of Parliament (occupants and property values), Drogheda and Dundalk. *Parliamentary Papers, 1837: Reports from Committees*, Vol. 2 (i), Appendix G.
1837	Marksmen (illiterate voters) in parliamentary boroughs, Drogheda and Dundalk. *Parliamentary Papers, 1837: Reports from Committees*, Vol. 2 (i), Appendix A.
1843	Voters, NLI Ms. 1660.
1848–9	Smith O'Brien Petition, Eneclann CD ENEC002. Almost 1,000 names for Kells.
1850	Register of land occupiers, with particulars of land and families, in the Unions of Kells and Oldcastle. NLI Ms. 5774.
1852	Voting electors. NLI Ms. 1660.
1855	Griffith's Valuation. Online: Askaboutireland.
1865	Parliamentary voters. NLI P. 2491.
1866–73	Emigrants from Stamullen Catholic parish, *IG*, 8, No. 2, 1991, pp. 290–92. Original with RC registers.
1871	Drumcondra and Loughbrackan. NLI Pos. 4184.
1901	Census. Online: NAI.
1911	Census. Online: NAI.

Online

1641	<www.1641.tcd.ie>
Ashbourne	<www.angelfire.com/ak2/ashbourne>
Askaboutireland	<www.askaboutireland.ie>
Hall, Brendan	<www.jbhall.freeservers.com>
Hayes, John	<www.failteromhat.com>

IGP Meath	<*www.igp-web.com/Meath*>
NAI	<*www.census.nationarchives.ie*>
PRONI name search	<*www.proni.gov.uk*>

Publications

Local histories etc.

Bernard, Nicholas, *The Whole Proceedings of the Siege of Drogheda [and] Londonderry*, Dublin: 1736. NLI Ir94106.b2.

Bolton, Michael D.C., *Headfort House*, Kells: Fieldgate Press, 1999. NLI, 57 p.

Brady, J., *A short history of the parishes of the diocese of Meath, 1867–1944*. NLI Ir 94132 b 2.

Carty, Mary Rose, *History of Killeen Castle*, Dunsany: Carty/Lynch, 1991. NLI Ir 94132 c 8, 87 p.

Clare, Linda, *On the edge of the Pale: the rise and decline of an Anglo-Irish community in County Meath, 1170–1530*, Dublin: Four Courts Press, 2006. Medieval Syddan. NLI, 64 p.

Cogan, A., *The diocese of Meath, ancient and modern*, Dublin: J.F. Fowler, 1874. NLI Ir 27413 c 3s, 3 vols.

Cogan, J., *Ratoath*, Drogheda: Drogheda Independent. NLI Ir 9141 p 84, 56 p.

Coldrick, Bryn, *Rossin, Co. Meath: an unofficial place*, Dublin: Four Courts Press, 2002. NLI 3B 726, 63 p.

Conlon, Larry, *The Heritage of Collon, 1764–1984*, Ardee: Conlon, 1984. NLI Ir 94132 c 5, 87 p.

Connell, Paul, *The Diocese of Meath under Bishop John Cantwell, 1830–66*, Dublin: Four Courts Press, 2004. NLI, 285 p.

Connell, Peter, *Changing Forces: Shaping a Nineteenth Century town: A Case Study of Navan*, Maynooth: Geography Depatyment, St Patrick's College, 1978. NLI Ir 94132 c 1.

—— *The land and people of County Meath, 1750–1850*, Dublin: Four Courts Press, 2004. NLI, 266 p.

Coogan, Oliver, *A History of Dunshaughlin, Culmullen and Knockmark*, Dunshaughlin: Coogan, 1988. NLI, 132 p.

—— *A short history of south-east Meath*, 1979.

Coogan, Tony, *Charlesfort: the story of a Meath estate and its people, 1668–1968*, Kells: the author, 1991. NLI Ir 94132 9 2(2), 72 p.

Curran, Olive C., *History of the Diocese of Meath, 1860–1993*, Mullingar: Diocese of Meath, 1995. NLI Ir 27413 h 6, 3 vols.

Cusack, Danny, *The Great Famine in County Meath: an Gorta Mór i gContae na Midhe: a 150th anniversary commemoration (1845–1995)*, Meath County Council, 1996. NLI Ir 94132 c 9/1, 98 p.

—— *Kilmainham of the woody hollow: a history of Kilmainhamwood for the centenary of the Church of the Sacred Heart, Kilmainhamwood (1898–1998)*, Kells: Kilmainhamwood Parish Council, 1998. NLI Ir 94132 c 11, 166 p.

D'Alton, John, *The history of Drogheda*, Dublin: McGlashan & Gill, 1844. NLI Ir 94132 d 1, 2 vols.

Duffner, P., *Drogheda: the Low Lane Church, 1300–1979*. NLI Ir 94132 d 7.

Duleek Heritage, *The parish of Duleek and 'over the ditches': a ramble calling at Bellewstown, Kilsharvan, Mount Hanover, Donore, Duleek, Athcarne, Riverstown, Cushenstown and Boolies*, Duleek: Duleek Heritage, 2001. NLI, 266 p.

Falsey, Olive, *Kildalkey: a parish history*, Falsey, 2001. NLI, 155 p.

Farrell, Noel, *Exploring family origins in Navan town*, Longford: Noel Farrell, 1998. Includes transcripts of 1901 and 1911 censuses, 1838 Thom's, 1941 electors, Griffith's etc. NLI 1B 2149, 48 p.

Farrell, Valentine, *Not so much to one side*, Upholland: Farrell, 1984. NLI Ir 94132 f 6, 214 p.

Fitzsimons, J., *The Parish of Kilbeg*, Kells: Kells Art Studios, 1974. NLI Ir 914132 f 3, 287 p.

French, Noel, *Bellinter House*, Trim: Trymme Press, 1993. NLI Ir 941 p 124(3).

—— Monumental Inscriptions from Some Graveyards in Co. Meath (typescript), 1990. NAI open shelves; also NLI Ir 9295 f 2.

—— *Navan by the Boyne*, Athboy: French, 1986. NLI, 116 p.

—— *Nobber: a step back in time*, Trim: Meath Heritage Centre, 1991. NLI Ir 941 p 103 (3), 56 p.

—— *A short history of Rathmore and Athboy*, 1995. NLI Ir 94132 f.

—— *Trim Traces and Places*, Trim, 1987. NLI, 54 p.

Garry, James, *The Streets and Lanes of Drogheda*, Drogheda: 1996. NLI Ir 91413 g 4/1, 120 p.

Gerrard, Richard, *The annals of St. Mary's Boys' School, Drogheda, 1865–2000*, Drogheda: St Mary's School, 2000. NLI Ir 370 g 26, 3 vols.

Gilligan, Jim, *Graziers and Grasslands: portrait of a rural Meath Community, 1854–1914*, Maynooth: Irish Academic Press, 1998. NLI.

Greene, Ted, *Drogheda: its place in Ireland's history*, Julianstown: the author, 2006. NLI, 410 p.

Healy, John, *History of the Diocese of Meath*, Dublin: 1908, 2 vols.

Hennessy, Mark, *Irish Historic Towns Atlas, 14: Trim*, Dublin: RIA, 2004. NLI.

IGRS, *Tombstone inscriptions, Vol. 2*, Dublin: IGRS Tombstone Committee, 2001. NLI 3B 29, c.900 p.

Irish Countrywomen's Association, *Kentstown in bygone days*, 1997. NLI Ir 94132 k 3, 132 p.

Kieran, Joan S., *An Outline History of the Parish of St Mary's Abbey, Ardee*, 1980. NLI Ir 91413 p 12, 5 p.

McCullen, John, *The Call of St Mary's: a hundred years of a parish*, Drogheda: McCullen, 1984. NLI Ir 27413 m 8, 92 p.

McHugh, Ned, *Drogheda before the Famine: urban poverty in the shadow of privilege, 1826–45*, Maynooth: Irish Academic Press, 1998.

Mac Lochlainn, Tadhg, *The Parish of Laurencetown and Kiltormer*, Ballinasloe: Mac Lochlainn, 1981. NLI Ir 94124 m 5, 73 p.

McNeill, Charles, *Dowdall deeds*, Dublin: Stationery Office, for IMC, 1960. Co-editor, A.J. Otway-Ruthven. NLI Ir 091 m 9, 416 p.

McNiffe, Liam, *A history of Williamstown, Kells*, Williamstown: McNiffe, 2003. NLI, 68 p.

—— *Studies in local history: Meath*, Navan: Costello Print, 1998. NLI Ir 94132 s 5, 216 p.

Matthews, Bredan, *A history of Stamullen*, Stamullen: Matthews, 2003. NLI, 138 p.

Murchan, Maureen, *Moynalty Parish: the millennium record: 'a moment in time'*, Moynalty: Millennium Record Book Committee, 2000. Co-editor, Joe McKenna. NLI Ir 94132 m 10, 468 p.

O'Boyle, Edna, *A history of Duleek*, Duleek: Duleek Historical Society, 1989. NLI Ir 94132 o 8, 129 p.

O'Donovan, John, *Ordnance Survey letters, Meath (1836)*, Dublin: Fourmasters Press, 2001. NLI LO 8193, 246 p.

—— *Parish Guide to Meath*, Dublin: Irish Church Publications, 1968. NLI Ir 270 p 2, 48 p.

Paterson, J. (ed.), *Diocese of Meath and Kildare: an historical guide*, 1981. NLI Ir 941 p 75.

Quane, Michael, *Gilson Endowed School, Oldcastle*, Meath Archaeological and Historical Society, 1968. NLI, 23 p.

Rathkenny Local History Group, *Rathkenny Parish: a local history*, Rathkenny: 1983. NLI, 176 p.

Ratoath Heritage Group, *Ratoath: past and present*, Ratoath: Ratoath Heritage Group, 2008. NLI, 508 p.

Rayfus, Colin E., *The 1865 Rathcore evictions*, Trim: C.E. Rayfus, 2008. NLI, 141 p.

Scott, Brendan, *Religion and reformation in the Tudor Diocese of Meath*, Dublin: Four Courts Press, 2006. NLI, 174 p.

Simms, Angret, *Irish Historic Towns Atlas, 4: Kells*, Dublin: RIA, 1990. NLI ILB 941 p 13 (2).

Local journals
Annala Dhamhliag: The Annals of Duleek. NLI I 94132 a 1.
Ríocht na Midhe. NLI Ir 94132 r 1.

Directories

1824	J. Pigot & Co., *City of Dublin and Hibernian Provincial Directory.* NLI; LDS film 451787. Online: Hayes.
1846	Slater's *National Commercial Directory of Ireland.* PRONI; NLI LO; LDS film 1696703 item 3. Online: Hayes.
1856	Slater, *Royal National Commercial Directory of Ireland.* NLI; LDS film 1472360 item 1.
1861	Henderson, *Post Office Directory of Meath and Louth.*
1870	Slater, *Directory of Ireland.* NLI.

1881   Slater, *Royal National Commercial Directory of Ireland*. NLI. Online: FindMyPast.

1894   Slater, *Royal Commercial Directory of Ireland*. NLI.

Gravestone inscriptions

Parts (at least) of thirty-three Co. Meath graveyards are transcribed at <*www. interment.net*>.

Agher: C of I, *IA*, Vol. 10, No. 2, 1978.
Agher: C of I, IGRS, Vol. 1.
Ardmulchan: French, *Monumental Inscriptions*.
Ardsallagh: French, *Monumental Inscriptions*.
Assey: IGRS, Vol. 2.
Athboy: Church Lane, C of I, *IA*, Vol. 12, Nos. 1 and 2, 1981, IGRS, Vol. 2.
Athlumney: IGRS, Vol. 2.
Balfeaghan: IGRS, Vol. 1.
Ballygarth: IGRS, Vol. 2.
Balrathboyne: Cortown, IGRS, Vol. 2.
Balsoon: *IA*, Vol. 7, No. 2, 1976, IGRS, Vol. 2.
Bective: Clady, IGRS, Vol. 2.
Castlejordan: C of I, IGRS, Vol. 2.
Churchtown: IGRS, Vol. 2.
Clonard: Tircroghan, IGRS, Vol. 2.
Colp: Mornington town, RC, *Journal of the Old Drogheda Society*, 1989.
—— Stagreenan: *Journal of the Old Drogheda Society*, 1977.
—— Colp West: C of I, LDS Family History Library.
Danestown: Danestown, *Ríocht na Midhe*, Vol. 5, No. 4, 1974, IGRS, Vol. 2.
Diamor: Clonabreaney, *Ríocht na Midhe*, Vol. 6, No. 2, 1976.
Donaghmore: Donaghmore, RC, French, *Monumental Inscriptions*.
Dowdstown: French, *Monumental Inscriptions*.
Drumlargan: *IA*, Vol. 12, Nos. 1 and 2, 1980.
Duleek: Church Lane, C of I, *IG*, Vol. 3, No. 12, 1967, IGRS, Vol. 2.
Dunboyne: Dunboyne, IGRS, Vol. 2. Also *IA*, Vol. 11, Nos. 1 and 2, 1979.
Dunmoe: French, *Monumental Inscriptions*.
Gallow: Gallow, IGRS, Vol. 2.
Gernonstown: French, *Monumental Inscriptions*.
Girley: Girley, French, *Monumental Inscriptions*.
Kells: Headford Place, *IG*, Vol. 3, No. 11, 1966.
Kilbride: Baytown, *Ríocht na Midhe*, Vol. 6, No. 3, 1977, IGRS, Vol. 2.
Kilcarn: French, *Monumental Inscriptions*.
Kilcooly: Kiltoome (Kilcooly?), IGRS, Vol. 2.
Kildalkey: IGRS, Vol. 2.
Killaconnigan: Killaconnigan, IGRS, Vol. 2.
Killeen: Killeen, *Ríocht na Midhe*, Vol. 4, No. 3, 1970.

Kilmore: Arodstown, *Ríocht na Midhe*, Vol. 6, No. 1, 1975, IGRS, Vol. 2.

—— Kilmore, C of I, *Ríocht na Midhe*, Vol. 6, No. 1, 1975.

Laracor: Moy, *IA*, Vol. 6, No. 2, 1974.

—— Summerhill Demesne: LDS Family History Library.

Loughan or Castlekeeran: IGRS, Vol. 2.

Loughcrew: C of I, *IA*, Vol. 9, No. 2, 1977.

Martry: Allenstown Demesne, French, *Monumental Inscriptions*.

Moymet: IGRS, Vol. 2.

Moynalty: Hermitage, French, *Monumental Inscriptions*.

Navan: Church Hill, C of I, MF CI 45, NAI.

Oldcastle: *Ríocht na Midhe*, Vol. 4, No. 2, 1968.

Rataine: IGRS, Vol. 2.

Rathfeigh: IGRS, Vol. 2.

Rathkenny: C of I, French, *Monumental Inscriptions*.

Rathmore: RC, *IA*, Vol. 7, No. 2, 1975, IGRS, Vol. 2.

Rathmore: Moyagher Lower, *IA*, Vol. 8, No. 1, 1976, IGRS, Vol. 2.

Ratoath: Main St, C of I, French, *Monumental Inscriptions*.

Scurlockstown: IGRS, Vol. 2.

Skreen: French, *Monumental Inscriptions*.

St Mary's, Drogheda, New Road, C of I, *Journal of the Old Drogheda Society*, 1986.

Stackallan: French, *Monumental Inscriptions*.

Tara: Castleboy, C of I, Meath Heritage Centre.

Trim: Tremblestown, RC, French, *Monumental Inscriptions*.

Tullaghanoge: French, *Monumental Inscriptions*.

Estate records

Balfour. Balfour tenants in the townlands of Belustran, Cloughmacow, Doe and Hurtle, 1838, *JCLAHS*, 12 (3), 1951, 190, civil parish of Nobber.

Edgeworth, Richard. Rental, NAI M 1503. 1760–68. All tenants. Covering townlands in the civil parish of Scurlockstown.

Gormanston. Estate rental books, 1747–1872. NLI Mss. 44385–9: parishes of Enniskeen, Kilberry, Nobber and Stamullin. Early rentals are indexed.

Newcomen estates. Maps of estates to be sold, 20 July 1827. NLI Ms.2766. All tenants. Covering townlands in the civil parishes of Clonmacduff and Moymet.

Reynell family. Rent books, 1834–48. NLI Ms. 5990.

Smythe, William Barlow. Collinstown. Farm account book. NLI Ms. 7909.

Trench estate. Rentals, Drogheda. NLI Ms. 2576.

Wellesley. Tenants of the Wellesley estate at Dangan, Ballymaglossan, Moyare, Mornington and Trim, 1816, *Ríocht na Midhe*, 4 (4), 1967, pp. 10–25, civil parishes of Ballymaglassan, Colp, Laracor, Rathmore and Trim.

MONAGHAN

Census returns and substitutes

	Medieval Clones families, *Clogher Record*, 1959.
1630	Muster Roll of Ulster. Armagh County Library; PRONI D.1759/3C/1, T. 808/15164; NLI Pos. 206.
1630–1800	Church of Ireland Marriage Licence Bonds, Diocese of Clogher. Online: Ulsterancestry.
1641	Index to the rebels of 1641 in the Co. Monaghan depositions. Online: 1641.
1659	Pender's 'Census'. Reprinted GPC, 1997; IMC, 2002. LDS film 924648.
1663–5	Hearth Money Roll, *History of Monaghan for two hundred years, 1660–1860*, Dundalk: 1921.
1738	Some Clones Inhabitants, *Clogher Record*, Vol. 2, No. 3, 1959.
1777	Some Protestant Inhabitants of Carrickmacross, *Clogher Record*, Vol. 6, No. 1, 1966.
1785	Male Protestants aged over seventeen, Magheracloone and Errigal Trough. LDS film 258517.
1796	Spinning-Wheel Premium List. 4,400 names for Co. Monaghan. Online: Hayes.
1821	Some abstracts only; see *Clogher Record*, 1991. NAI Thrift Abstracts.
1823	Some Church of Ireland members in the Aghadrumsee area, *Clogher Record*, 15 (1), 1994.
1823–38	Tithe Books.
1824	Protestant householders, Aghabog parish. RCBL D1/1/1.
1832	Donagh parish (with C of I records). PRONI MIC.1/127.
1834–42	Voters. NAI OP 1842/30.
1835–49	Shirley Estate Loan Book. Carrickmacross Library.
1841	Some abstracts only. NAI Thrift Abstracts.
1842–9	Workhouse records, Castleblayney Union. Monaghan Ancestral Research.
1843	Magistrates, landed proprietors etc. NLI Ms. 12,767.
1847	Poor Law Rate Book, Castleblayney, *Clogher Record*, Vol. 5, No. 1, 1963.
1851	Some abstracts only. NAI Thrift Abstracts.
1858–60	Griffith's Valuation. Online: Askaboutireland.
1901	Census. Online: NAI.
1911	Census. Online: NAI.
1912	The Ulster Covenant. Almost half a million original signatures and addresses of those who signed. Almost 11,000 names for Monaghan. Online: Covenant.

Online

Askaboutireland	<www.askaboutireland.ie>	
1641	<www.1641.tcd.ie>	
Clogher	<www.clogherhistoricalsoc.com>	Clogher Historical Society
Covenant	<www.proni.gov.uk/ulstercovenant>	
Hayes, John	<www.failteromhat.com>	
McGeough	<ahd.exis.net/monaghan>	Good maps
NAI	<www.nationalarchives.ie>	
PRONI	<www.proni.gov.uk>	
Ulsterancestry	<www.ulsterancestry.co.uk>	

Publications

Local histories etc.

[Unknown], *St. Macartan's College, 1840–1990*, Monaghan: St Macartan's College, 1990. Monaghan County Library 371.20094167.

Bailey, Mark E., *Border heritage: tracing the heritage of the City of Armagh and Monaghan County*, Norwich: TSO, 2008. NLI, 285 p.

Bráithre Críostaí Mhuineacháin, *Monaghan Memories: Na Bráithre Críostaí, Muineachán, 1867–1984*, Monaghan: Christian Brothers, 1984. Monaghan County Library 255.78094167/REFERENCE.

Brown, Dr L.T., *Shepherding the Monaghan Flock: The Story of First Monaghan Presbyterian Church, 1697–1997*, Monaghan: 1997. Monaghan County Library 262.3.

Carville, Gary, *Parish of Clontibret*, Castleblayney: 1984. NLI Ir 941 p 74, 59 p.

—— *A Clones miscellany: Compiled by Clones Community Forum*, Clones: Clones Community Forum, 2004. NLI, 170 p.

Copeland, Henry de Saussure, *Lynch family, 2nd–8th generations: line of Conlaw Peter Lynch, descendants of Conlaw Peter Lynch and Eleanor (MacMahon) Neison of Clones, Monaghan . . . and Cheraw, South Carolina*, the compiler, 1993. NLI GO 617, 5 p.

Cotter, Canon J.B.D., *A Short History of Donagh Parish*, Enniskillen: 1966.

Day, Angelique, and McWilliams, Patrick (eds.), *Ordnance Survey Memoirs of Ireland, Vol. 40: Counties of South Ulster, 1834–8: Cavan, Leitrim, Louth, Monaghan and Sligo*, Belfast: Institute of Irish Studies, 1997. Co. Monaghan: Aghabog, Aughnamullen, Ballybay, Clontibret, Currin, Donagh, Donaghmoyne, Ematris, Errigal Truagh, Inniskeen, Killanny, Kilmore, Magheracloone, Magheross, Monaghan, Muckno, Tydavnet and Tyholland. NLI Ir 9141 o 80, 216 p.

Doyle, Anthony, *Charles Powell Leslie (II)'s estates at Glaslough, County Monaghan, 1800–41: portrait of a landed estate business and its community in changing times*, Dublin: Irish Academic Press, 2001. NLI, 68 p.

Duffy, Joseph, *A Clogher Record Album: a diocesan history*, Enniskillen: Cumann Seanchais Chlochair, 1975. NLI Ir 94114 c 3, 340 p.

Duffy, Patrick, *Landscapes of South Ulster: a parish atlas of the Diocese of Clogher*, Belfast: Institute of Irish Studies, 1993. NLI ILB 270 d 1, 131 p.

Farrell, Noel, *Exploring family origins in Monaghan town*, Longford: Noel Farrell, 1998. NLI, 48p.

Gilsenan, M., *Hills of Magheracloone, 1884–1984:* Magheracloone: Magheracloone Mitchells GAA, 1985. NLI Ir 94117 g 1, 480 p.

Guest, Bill L., *American descendants of John Moorhead of Drumsnat, Monaghan County, Ireland*, Spring, Tex.?: B.L. Guest, 1992? LC CS71.M8398 1991, 50 p.

Haslett, A., *Historical sketch of Ballyalbany Presbyterian Church, Formerly Second Monaghan, Formerly Belanalbany, Formerly New Monaghan Secession Presbyterian Church [1750–1940]*, Belfast: 1940. Co-author, Rev. S.L. Orr. NLI Ir 285 o 4, 231 p.

Kelly, Dominic Michael, *Kellys of Killark: a family history*, Seaview Press, 2001. Magheracloone, Co. Monaghan. NLA; NLI 929.20994 K29, 353 p.

Killeevan Heritage Group, *From Carn to Clonfad: Killeevan Heritage Group takes a Journey through some pages out of the history of Currin, Killeevan and Aghabog*, Killeevan: Killeevan Heritage Group. Monaghan County Library 941.67.

Leslie, Seymour, *Of Glaslough in Oriel*, Glaslough: Glaslough Press, 1912. NLI Ir 9292 l 6, 114 p.

Livingstone, Peadar, *The Monaghan story: a documented history of the County Monaghan from the earliest times to 1976*, Enniskillen: Clogher Historical Society, 1980. NLI Ir 94117 L 2, 693 p.

Lockington, John W., *Full circle: a story of Ballybay Presbyterians*, Monaghan: Cahans. NLI

M., G.S., *A Family History of Montgomery of Ballyleck, County Monaghan, now of Beaulie*, Belfast: 1850. LHL 929.2/MONT.

Mac Annaidh, S., 'Cholera in Tonytallagh townland in Currin, 1834', *Clogher Record*, Vol. 16, No. 1, 1997, pp. 180–81.

McArdle Lafferty, Róisín, *Laggan School, 1823–1977: a commemorative history of a Co. Monaghan primary school*, Laggan: 2007. NLI 164 p 1.

McCluskey, Seamus, *Emyvale: McKenna country*, 1999. NLI, 247 p.

MacDonald, Brian, 'Church of Ireland members in the Aghadrumsee area in 1823', *Clogher Record*, Vol. 15, No. 1, 1994, pp. 107–121.

—— *Time of Desolation: Clones Poor Law Union, 1845–50*, Monaghan: Clogher Historical Society, 2002. Monaghan County Library 941.67.

McGeough, Paula, *Beyond the Big Bridge: A History of Oram and Surrounding Townlands*, Monaghan: 2002. Monaghan County Library 941.67.

McIvor, John, *Extracts from a Ballybay Scrapbook*, Monaghan: 1974. NLI Ir 9141 p 61, 51 p.

McKenna, J.E., *Parochial Records*, Enniskillen: 1920. 2 vols.

McMahon, Theo, *Old Monaghan, 1775–1995*, Monaghan: Clogher Historical Society, 1995. NLI Ir 94117 m 12, 224 p.

Madden, Lucy, The town of Clones, *IR*, No. 2, 1993, pp. 18–19.

Maisel, Rosemary Virginia, *The Patrick Kirwan family of Carrickmacross, County Monahan, Ireland*, Catonsville, Md.: R.V. Maisel, c.1991. LC CS71.K599 1991, 76 leaves.

Marshall, J.J., *History of the Town and District of Clogher, Co. Tyrone, parish of Errigal Keerogue, Tyrone, and Errigal Truagh in the Co. of Monaghan*, Dungannon: Tyrone Printing Co., 1930. NLI Ir 94114 m 2, 97 p.

—— *Monaghan Election Petition, 1826: minutes of evidence*. NLI Ir 32341 m 52.

Mulligan, Eamonn, *The Replay: A Parish History: Kilmore and Drumsnat*, Monaghan: Sean McDermotts GFC, 1984. Co-author, Fr Brian McCluskey. Kilmore and Drumsnatt. NLI Ir 94117 m 10, 376 p.

Murnane, Peadar, *At the ford of the birches: the history of Ballybay, it's people and vicinity*, Ballybay: Murnane Brothers, 1999. Co-author, James H. Murnane. NLI Ir 94117 m 19, 670 p.

Murphy, Sean, *Ardaghey past and present*, Ardaghey: Ardaghey Foróige Club, 1991. NLI Ir 94117.a.3, 132 p.

Nesbitt, David, *Full circle: a story of Ballybay Presbyterians*, Ballybay: Cahans Publications, 1999. NLI, 387 p.

O'Donnell, Vincent, *Ardaghey Church and people*, Ardaghey: St Naul's Church, 1995. NLI Ir 94113 a 5, 146 p.

Ó Dufaigh, Brendan, *The book of Clontibret*, Monaghan: Ó Dufaigh, 1997. NLI, 390 p.

Ó Mórdha, P., 'Early schools and schoolteachers in Clones', *Clogher Record*, Vol. 15, No. 1, 1994, pp. 48–50.

—— 'Some notes on Clones Workhouse', *Clogher Record*, Vol. 15, No. 1, 1994, pp. 74–5.

—— *The Story of the GAA in Currin and an outline of Parish History*, Currin: Currin GAA Club, 1986. NLI Ir 396.0.48, 208 p.

—— Summary of inquests held on Currin, Co. Monaghan, victims, 1846–55, *Clogher Record*, 15, No. 2, 1995, pp. 90–100.

Quinn, Daig, *St. Anne's Church, Drumcatton and Blackstaff, 1796 to 1996*, Carrickmacross: Drumcatton 200 Committee, 1996. Donaghmoyne. Monaghan County Library 941.697.

Rushe, Denis Carolan, *Historical Sketches of Monaghan*, Dublin: J. Duffy, 1895. NLI Ir 94117 r 1, 120 p.

—— *History of Monaghan for two hundred years, 1660–1860*, Dundalk: Tempest, 1921. NLI Ir 94117 r 3, 359 p.

—— *Monaghan in the 18th century*, Dublin and Dundalk: M.H. Gill, 1916. NLI Ir 94117 r 2, 139 p.

Shirley, E.P., *The history of the county of Monaghan*, London: Pickering, 1879. NLI Ir 94117 s 2, 618 p. Reprinted Bangor: Fox, 1988.

Swanzy, D., 'The Swanzys of Clontibret', *Clogher Record*, Vol. 16, No. 1, 1997, pp. 166–76.

Local journals
Clann MacKenna Journal. NLI Ir 9292 c 54.
Clogher Record. NLI Ir 94114 c 2.
The Drumlin: A Journal of Cavan, Leitrim and Monaghan. NLI Ir 05 d 345.
Macalla. NLI Ir 94116 m 8.

Directories

1824	J. Pigot & Co., *City of Dublin and Hibernian Provincial Directory*. NLI; LDS film 451787. Online: Hayes.
1846	Slater's *National Commercial Directory of Ireland*. PRONI; NLI LO; LDS film 1696703 item 3. Online: Hayes.
1854–	*Belfast and Province of Ulster Directory*. Also 1856, 1858, 1861, 1863, 1865, 1868, 1870, 1877, 1880, 1884, 1887, 1890, 1894, 1900. Online: PRONI; LDS (various years).
1856	Slater, *Royal National Commercial Directory of Ireland*. NLI; LDS film 1472360 item 1.
1865	R. Wynne, *Business Directory of Belfast*. NLI Ir 91411 b 2.
1870	Slater, *Directory of Ireland*. NLI.
1881	Slater, *Royal National Commercial Directory of Ireland*. NLI. Online: FindMyPast.
1894	Slater, *Royal Commercial Directory of Ireland*. NLI.
1897	Gillespie's *Co. Monaghan Alamanack and Directory*.

Gravestone inscriptions

Aghabog: Crover (Aghabog?), C of I, *Clogher Record*, 1982.
Ballybay: Six Pres. and C of I graveyards, Murnane, *At the Ford*.
Clones: Abbey Lane, *Clogher Record*, 1982–4.
—— The Diamond, C of I, *Clogher Record*, Vol. 13, No. 1, 1988.
Clontibret: Annayalla, RC, *Clogher Record*, Vol. 7, No. 2, 1974.
Gallagh, C of I, Monaghan Ancestral Research.
Clontibret, Pres., Monaghan Ancestral Research.
Donagh: Glaslough town, C of I, *Clogher Record*, Vol. 9, No. 3, 1978.
Donagh: *Clogher Record*, Vol. 2, No. 1, 1957.
Donagh: *Clogher Record*, Vol. 6, No. 1, 1966.
Drumsnat: Mullanacross, C of I, *Clogher Record*, Vol. 6, No. 1, 1966.
Ematris: Rockcorry town, C of I, *Clogher Record*, Vol. 6, No. 1, 1966.
Edergoole, Monaghan Ancestral Research.
Errigal Trough: Attiduff, St Joseph's, RC, HW.
Killanny: Aghafad, C of I, *Clogher Record*, Vol. 6, No. 1, 1966.
Killeevan: Drumswords, *Clogher Record*, 1985.
—— Killeevan Glebe, *Clogher Record*, 1982.
Killyfuddy: RC, HW.
Kilmore: Kilnahaltar (Kilmore?), C of I, *Clogher Record*, 1983, 1985.
Monaghan: Aghananimy, RC, Monaghan Ancestral Research.

Rackwallace: *Clogher Record*, Vol. 4, No. 3, 1962.

Tedavnet: Drumdesco (Urbeshanny?), RC, Monaghan Ancestral Research.

Tehallan: Templetate, C of I, GO.

Tullycorbet: Creevagh, Murnane, *At the ford of the birches.*

Corvoy (RC): Murnane, *At the ford of the birches.*

Estate records

[**No landlord given**]. Clones rent roll, 1821, *Clogher Record*, 13 (1), 1988.

[**No landlord given**]. Ballybay estate rentals, 1786, *Clogher Record*, Vol. 11, No. 1.

[**No landlord given**]. Castleblayney rent book, 1772, *Clogher Record*, Vol. 10, No. 3.

[**No landlord given**]. Emy and Glaslough estates, rent roll, 1752–60. Principally major tenants. Civil parishes of Donagh and Errigal Truagh. MG.

[**No landlord given**]. Rent book, 1772. Most tenants, Castleblayney rent book 1772, *Clogher Record*, 11 (1), 1982, civil parish of Muckno.

Anketell estate. Rentals, 1784–9, *Clogher Record*, Vol. 11, No. 3.

Balfour. Rentals of 1632 and 1636, *Clogher Record*, 1985.

Bath, Earl of. NLI Pos. 5894, Rentals, 1784–1809. Major tenants only. Covering townlands in the civil parishes of Donaghmoyne, Iniskeen, Magheracloone and Magheross.

Crofton. NLI Ms. 4530: rental, 1792. All tenants. NLI Ms. 8150: rentals 1769–1851, some full, some major tenants only. NLI Ms. 20783: rentals 1853, 1854, 1859. All tenants. Covering townlands in the civil parish of Aghnamullen, Errigal Trough and Tednavnet.

Dartry, Earl of (Viscount Cremorne). NLI Ms. 3181: maps with tenants' names, 1779. NLI Ms. 3282: rental, 1780. Major tenants only. NLI Ms. 3184: rental, 1790. Major tenants only. NLI Ms. 1696: leaseholders. NLI Ms. 3674: rental, 1796–7. Major tentants only. NLI Mss. 3186–7: rental, 1800–1801. Major tenants only. NLI 3189: rental, 1838. All tenants. NLI Ms. 1648: rental 1846. All tenants. NLI Ms. 1698: valuation, 1841–2. All tenants. Covering townlands in the civil parishes of Aghabog, Aghnamullen, Donagh, Ematris, Errigal Trough, Killeevan, Kilmore, Monaghan and Tyholland.

Forster, James. Five rent rolls, 1803–1808, 1812–24. Covering areas in the parishes of Aghabog, Killeevan, Tydavnet and Tyholland. MG.

Kane. Rentals, 1840–41; account books, 1842–4; arrears, 1848, 1849, 1852; rent receipts, 1851–2. Covering townlands in the parish of Tydavnet. MG.

Kane. Rentals and reports for the Kane estates, Errigal Truagh, 1764; also 1801, 1819–21, *Clogher Record*, 13 (3), 1990, civil parish of Errigal Trough.

Ker. Landholders, Newbliss, 1790–c.1830. Civil parish of Killeevan. *Clogher Record*, 1985.

Leslie. NLI 5783: rentals 1751–66. Major tenants only and leases. Donagh civil parish, NLI 5809 Rent rolls, 1751–80. NLI Ms. 13710 (part 3), 5809. Coverage unclear, Glaslough and Emy estates, civil parish of Donagh. NLI Ms. 5813, rental, 1839–40. All tenants. Covering townlands in the civil parishes of Aghabog, Drummully, Drumsnat, Errigal Trough and Kilmore.

Madden. Rentals and accounts, 1775–1929. PRONI D.3465. Covering townlands in the civil parishes of Currin and Killeevan.

Mayne, Edward. NAI M.7036 (18 and 19), rental, 1848 and 1853. All tenants.

Moutray. Rentals, 1757–1946. PRONI D2023/3/1. Covering townlands in the civil parish of Errigal Trough.

Murray-Ker. Full rentals, 1840–43 (NA BR Mon 8/1) and 1853–4 (NA BR Mon 9/1). Covering townlands in the civil parishes of Aghabog, Aghnamullen and Killeevan.

Rossmore estate. Maps with tenants' names, c.1820–52. Monaghan town and surrounding areas. MG.

Smyth, Edward. NAI 7069, rental, n.d. All tenants. Covering townlands in the civil parishes of Ballybay and Clontibret.

Weymouth estate. Magheross. Survey. Major tenants only. MG.

Wingfield estate. Rentals and arrears, 1852. County and town of Monaghan. MG.

OFFALY (KING'S COUNTY)

Census returns and substitutes

1641	Testimonies of 98 witnesses to the 1641 Rebellion. Online: 1641.
1641	Book of Survey and Distribution. NLI Ms. 972.
1659	Pender's 'Census'. Reprinted GPC, 1997; IMC, 2002. LDS film 924648.
1766	Ballycommon. JKAS, Vol. 7. GO 537. Online: PRONI name search.
1770	Voters. NLI Ms. 2050.
1793–1907	Register of tenants who planted trees, Geashill, 1793–1907, Eglish, 1809–1837, JKAS, 15 (3), 1973/4, pp. 310–18.
1802	Protestants in the parishes of Ballyboggan, Ballyboy, Castlejordan, Clonmacnoise, Drumcullin, Eglish, Gallen, Killoughey, Lynally, Rynagh and Tullamore. IA, 1973.
1821	Parishes of Aghacon, Birr, Ettagh, Kilcolman, Kinnitty, Letterluna, Roscomroe, Roscrea and Seirkieran. NAI CEN 1821/26–34.
1823–38	Tithe Books. NAI.
1824	Catholic householders, Lusmagh parish. In Roman Catholic parish registers. NLI.
1830	Contributors to new Catholic church in Lusmagh. In Roman Catholic parish registers. NLI.
1835	Tubber parish. NLI Pos. 1994.
1840	Eglish and Drumcullin parishes. In Roman Catholic parish registers. NLI Pos. 4175.
1842	Voters. OP 1842/27.
1852	Assisted passages from Kilconouse, Kinnitty parish. AH, Vol. 22, 1960.
1854	Griffith's Valuation Online: Askaboutireland.
1901	Census. Online: NAI.
1911	Census. Online: NAI.

Online

1641	<www.1641.tcd.ie>
From Ireland	<www.from-ireland.net>
Hayes, John	<www.failteromhat.com>
NAI	<www.census.nationalarchives.ie>
Offaly Historical and Archaeological Society	<www.offalyhistory.com>
PRONI name search	<www.proni.gov.uk>

Publications

Local histories etc.

Boruwlaski, Joseph, *Joseph Boruwlaski: his visit to Portarlington, 1795*, York: Frenchchurch Press, 1997. NLI, 5 p.

Brady, J., *A short history of the parishes of the diocese of Meath, 1867–1944*. NLI Ir 94132 b 2.

Byrne, Michael, *Durrow and its History: a celebration of what has gone before*, Tullamore: Esker Press, 1994. NLI Ir 9141 p 71, 303 p.

—— *Sources for Offaly History*, Tullamore: Offaly Research Library, 1977. NLI Ir 94136 b 1, 102 p.

—— *Tullamore Catholic Parish: a historical survey*, Tullamore: Tullamore Parish Committee, 1987. NLI Ir 27414 b 7, 188 p.

Carville, Geraldine, *Birr, the monastic city: St. Brendan of the water cress*, Bray: Kestrel Books, 1997. NLI Ir 94101 c 4, 103 p.

Clonbullogue Book Committee, *The Life, the times, the people*, Clonbullogue: Clonbullogue Book Committee, 1993. NLI Ir 94136 L 3, 416 p.

Cooke, William Antisell, *History of Birr*, Dublin: 1875. Genealogical Office.

Darby, Stephen, *Ballybryan: a step back in time*, Ballybryan: Ballybryan National School, 1994. NLI Ir 94136 d 3, 216 p.

Dwyer, Philip, *The Diocese of Killaloe, from the Reformation to the Close of the Eighteenth Century*, Dublin: Hodges, Foster & Figgis, 1878. NLI Ir 94143 d 11, 602 p. Reprinted Newmarket-on-Fergus: O'Brien Book Publications, 1997.

—— *Ferbane Parish and its Churches.* NLI Ir 91413 f 4.

Farrell, Noel, *Exploring family origins in Birr*, Longford: Noel Farrell, 1998. NLI 1B 1659.

—— *Exploring family origins in old Tullamore town*, Longford: Noel Farrell, 1998. NLI 1B 966.

Feehan, John, *The Landscape of Slieve Bloom: a study of the natural and human heritage*, Dublin: Blackwater Press, 1979. NLI Ir 91413 f 4, 284 p.

Finney, Charles W., *Monasteroris Parish, 8th May 1778–8th May 1978*, Monasteroris: 1978. NLI Ir 200 p 23, 14 p.

Gleeson, John, *History of the Ely O'Carroll Territory or Ancient Ormond*, Dublin: Gill, 1915. NLI Ir 94142 g 1. Reprinted Roberts Books, c.1982, with an introduction and bibliography by George Cunningham.

Healy, John, *History of the Diocese of Meath*, Dublin: 1908. 2 vols.

Irish Countrywomen's Association, *Approach the fountain: a history of Seir Kieran*, Seir Kieran: Seir Kieran ICA, 1992. NLI Ir 94136 p 2(4), 163 p.

Joyce, J. St George, *The King's County: epitome of its history, topography &c.*, Tullamore: Esker Press, 1998. Facsimile reprint of 1883 ed. NLI Ir 94136 j 2, 79 p.

Kearney, John, *Daingean: pages from the past*, Daingean: 1988. NLI, 48 p.

Kelly, Denis, *Famine: Gorta i Lusmá*, 1996. NLI, 50 p.

Magee, Sean, *Weavers of Prosperous, County Kildare, Balbriggan, County Dublin and Tullamore, County Offaly in memorials of 1826*, Dún Laoghaire: Dún Laoghaire Genealogical Society, 1998. NLI Ir 9291 g 7.

Meehan, Patrick, *Members of Parliament for Laois and Offaly, 1801–1918*, Portlaoise: Leinster Express, 1983. NLI Ir 328 m 6, 246 p.

—— *Memoir of the Warburton family of Garryhinch, King's Co.*, Dublin: 1842. 2nd ed. 1881.

Monahan, Rev. J., *Records Relating to the Diocese of Ardagh and Clonmacnoise*, Dublin: M.H. Gill & Son, 1886. NLI Ir 27413 m 3, 400 p.

Nolan, W., *Offaly: history and society*, Dublin: Geography Publications, 1998. NLI Ir 94136 o 10, 1,055 p.

O'Donovan, John, *Ordnance Survey Letters, King's Co. (1837–8)*, Dublin: 1926. NLI Ir 9141 O 11, 2 vols.

Offaly Historical Society, *Offaly Tombstone Inscriptions, Vols. 1–4*, Tullamore: Offaly Historical Society, 1981? NLI.

O'Reilly, Joe, *From Clonsast to Ballyburley*, Edenderry: O'Reilly, 1994. NLI Ir 94136 f 2, 176 p.

Ó Riain, Séamus, *Dunkerrin: a parish in Ely O Carroll: a history of Dunkerrin Parish from 1200 AD to the present time*, Dunkerrin: Dunkerrin History Committee, 1988. NLI Ir 94136 O 5, 256 p.

Palmer, A. Kingsmill, Canon, *Notes on the parish of Geashill and Killeigh: With an introduction by . . . R. Wyse Jackson . . . Bishop of Limerick*, Naas: Leinster Leader. NLI Ir 283 p 6, 22 p.

Paterson, J. (ed.), *Diocese of Meath and Kildare: an historical guide*, 1981. NLI Ir 941 p 75.

Pey, Brian, *Eglish and Drumcullen: a parish in Firceall*, Firceall Heritage Group, 2003. NLI, 435 p.

Ryan, Brendan, *A land by the river of God: a history of Ferbane Parish from earliest times to c.1900*, Ferbane: St Mel's Diocesan Trust, 1994. NLI Ir 94136 r 1, 348 p.

Sheil, Helen, *Falling into wretchedness: Ferbane in the late 1830s*, Dublin: Irish Academic Press, 1998. NLI Ir 94136 s 3, 64 p.

Simons, P. Frazer, *Tenants no more: Voices from an Irish townland, 1811–1901, and the great migration to Australia and America*, Richmond, Vic.: Prowling Tiger Press, 1996. Clay family from Gurteen, Co. Offaly, Methodist emigrants to the United States and Australia. NLI Ir 994 s 32, 288 p.

Trodd, Valentine, *Clonmacnois and West Offaly*, Banagher: 1998. NLI Ir 94136 t 5, 224 p.

—— *Midlanders: chronicle of a Midland parish*, Banagher: Scéal Publications, 1994. NLI Ir 94136 t 3, 226 p.

Local journals

Ardagh and Clonmacnoise Historical Society Journal. NLI Ir 794105.

Offaly Heritage: Journal of the Offaly Historical and Archaeological Society (2003–). NLI.

Directories

1824   J. Pigot & Co., *City of Dublin and Hibernian Provincial Directory.* NLI; LDS film 451787. Online: Hayes.

1846   Slater's *National Commercial Directory of Ireland.* PRONI; NLI LO; LDS film 1696703 item 3. Online: Hayes.

1856   Slater, *Royal National Commercial Directory of Ireland.* NLI; LDS film 1472360 item 1.

1870   Slater, *Directory of Ireland.* NLI.

1881   Slater, *Royal National Commercial Directory of Ireland.* NLI. Online: FindMyPast.

1894   Slater, *Royal Commercial Directory of Ireland.* NLI.

Gravestone inscriptions

Irish Midlands Ancestry has transcripts for a large number of graveyards in Co. Offaly. Contact details will be found in Chapter 15.

Ballykean: Stranure (Cloneygowan?), C of I, GO Ms. 622, p. 182.

Durrow: Durrow Demesne ('St Colmcille'), <*www.interment.net*>.

Kilclonfert: Kilclonfert, Byrne, *Kilclonfert.*

Killaderry: Phillipstown, Main St, *Offaly Tombstone Inscriptions*, Vol. 4.

Killaderry: *Offaly Tombstone Inscriptions*, Vol. 4.

Lusmagh: *Offaly Tombstone Inscriptions*, Vol. 3.

Monasteroris: *Offaly Tombstone Inscriptions*, Vol. 2.

Rahan: Rahan Demesne, C of I, *Offaly Tombstone Inscriptions*, Vol. 1.

Estate records

[**No landlord given**]. Rental and maps, 1855, NAI, M601, townlands of Ballyfarrell and Derrymore, civil parish of Killoughy.

[**No landlord given**]. Rentals, 1840–50. NLI Ms. 4337, 7 townlands, 154 tenants, civil parish of Clonsast.

Charleville, Earl of. Tullamore tenants, 1763, LDS Family History Library, 941.5 A1, civil parish of Kilbride.

Magan, William Henry. NLI Ms. 14.A.27, maps, 1848. All tenants. Covering townlands in the civil parish of Killaderry.

ROSCOMMON

Census returns and substitutes

1659	Pender's 'Census'. Reprinted GPC, 1997; IMC, 2002. LDS film 924648.
1749	Aughrim, Ardcarn, Ballintober, Ballynakill, Baslick, Boyle, Bumlin, Cam, Clontuskert, Cloocraff, Cloonfinlough, Cloonygormican, Creeve, Drimatemple, Dunamon, Dysart, Estersnow, Elphin, Fuerty, Kilbride, Kilbryan, Kilcolagh, Kilcooley, Kilcorkey, Kilgefin, Kilglass, Kilkeevin, Killinvoy, Killuken, Kilumnod, Kilmacallen, Kilmacumsy, Kilmore, Kilnamagh, Kilronan, Kiltoom, Kiltrustan, Lisonuffy, Ogulla, Oran, Rahara, Roscommon, St John's, St Peter's Athlone, Shankill, Taghboy, Termonbarry, Tibohine, Tisrara, Tumna. NAI MFS 6. See also Manning, *Elphin Index*. Online: FindMyPast.
1780	Freeholders. GO 442; also LDS film 100181.
1790–99	Freeholders, c.30 lists. NLI Ms. 10130.
1796	Spinning-Wheel Premium List. 1,650 names for Co. Roscommon. Online: Hayes.
1813	Freeholders. NLI ILB 324.
1821	Some extracts. NAI Thrift Abstracts.
1823–38	Tithe Books.
1830	Memorial of inhabitants, barony of Killyan, Co. Galway, upon relief for public works [1830?]. More than 130 names. Parishes of Athleague, Kilroran, Killyan and Tisrara (Co. Roscommon).
1830–47	Ballykilcline, Kilglass parish. Scally, *Hidden Ireland*. Online: Ballykilcline.
1837	Marksmen (i.e. illiterate voters), Athlone borough. *Parliamentary Papers, 1837: Reports from Committees*, Vol. 2 (1), Appendix A.
1837	Memorial for quarter sessions at Castlerea. Parishes of Kiltullagh and Loughglyn especially. Also mentioned: Baslick, Kilkeevin Ballintubber, Aughamore. c.260 names. NAI OP 1837/3.
1838	Memorial from inhabitants of Frenchpark for quarter sessions, c.250 names. NAI OP 1850/114.
1838–53	Reproductive Loan Fund records. Covering parishes of Ardcarn, Aughrim, Ballintober, Baslick, Boyle, Bumlin, Clooncraff, Cloonfinlough, Creeve, Elphin, Estersnow, Kilglass, Kilkeevin, Killukin (Boyle), Kilmore, Kilteevan, Kiltoom, Kiltullagh, Ogulla, Oran, Termonbarry and Tibohine. More than 9,000 names. NA (Kew). T 91. Partly online: Moving Here.
1841	Some extracts. NAI Thrift Abstracts.
1843	Petition for quarter sessions at Frenchpark, 'inhabitants of the western districts of Castlerea and Frenchpark.' More than 350 names and signatures. NAI OP 1850/114.
1843	Voters. NAI OP 1843/59.
1843	Workhouse records, Carrick-on-Shannon Union, 1843–82. Leitrim County Library.

1848	Male Catholic inhabitants of the parish of Boyle. NLI Pos. 4692.
1851	Some extracts. NAI Thrift Abstracts.
1857–8	Griffith's Valuation. Online: Askaboutireland.
1861	Athlone voters. Westmeath County Library. Also LDS film 1279285.
1901	Census. Online: NAI.
1911	Census. Online: NAI.

Online

Askaboutireland	*<www.askaboutireland.ie>*
Ballykilcline	*<www.ballykilcline.com>*
FindMyPast	*<www.findmypast.ie>*
Hayes, John	*<www.failteromhat.com>*
History	*<www.roscommonhistory.ie>*
IGP Roscommon	*<www.igp-web.com/roscommon>*
Leitrim-Roscommon	*<www.leitrim-roscommon.com>*
Moving Here	*<www.movinghere.org.uk/search>*
NAI	*<www.census.nationalarchives.ie>*

Publications

Local histories etc.

Notes on the O'Kellys and other families of Kilkeerin [Kilkeevin?] parish, Co. Roscommon (typescript). NLI Ir 9292 k 5.

Taughmaconnell: a history: compiled by the Taughmaconnell Historical and Heritage Group, Taughmaconnell: Taughmaconnell Historical and Heritage Group, 2000. NLI A 3A 328, 256 p.

Kingsland, Co. Roscommon: its people, past and present, Kingsland Reunion Committee, 1994. Roscommon County Library.

Athlone: Materials from printed sources relating to the history of Athlone and surrounding areas, 1699–1899, including an index volume. NLI Mss. 1543–7.

Beckett, Rev. M., *Facts and Fictions of Local History*, 1929. Kiltullagh district.

Beirne, Francis, *A history of the parish of Tisrara*, Tisrara: Tisrara Heritage Society, 1997. NLI Ir 94125 h 5, 219 p.

Burke, Francis, *Lough Ce and its annals: North Roscommon and the diocese of Elphin in times of old*, Dublin: 1895. NLI Ir 27412 b 1.

Clarke, Desmond, 'Athlone: a bibliographical study', *An Leabharlann*, No. 10, 1952, pp. 138–9.

Clonown Community Centre, *Clonown: the history, traditions and culture of a South Roscommon community*, Clonown: Clonown Community Centre, 1989. NLI Ir 94125.c.6, 180 p.

Coleman, Anne, *Riotous Roscommon: social unrest in the 1840s*, Dublin and Portland, Oreg.: Irish Academic Press, 1999. NLI Ir 94125 c 12, 64 p.

Coyle, Liam, *A parish history of Kilglass, Slatta, Ruskey*, Kilglass: Kilglass Gaels GAA Club, 1994. NLI Ir 94125 C 9, 559 p.

Drum Heritage Group, *Drum and its hinterland*, Drum: Drum Heritage Group, 1994. NLI Ir 94125 d 3, 368 p.

Dunn, Mary Lee, *Ballykilcline rising: from famine Ireland to immigrant America*, Amherst, Mass.: University of Massachusetts Press, 2008. NLI, 218 p.

Egan, Edward, *Bygone times: a near-forgotten history*, Drum: Drum Heritage, 2007. NLI, 540 p.

—— *Celebrating 21 years of living history in Drum: Drum Heritage, from its humble beginnings*, Drum: Drum Heritage Committee, 2008. NLI, 100 p.

—— *The Egans of Curraghboy: their direct descendants and family connections*, Kielty: Edward Egan, 2009. NLI, 231 p.

Egan, Patrick K., *The parish of Ballinasloe: its history from the earliest times to the present day*, Galway: Kenny's Bookshops, 1994. NLI Ir 94124 e 2, 355 p.

Farrell, Noel, *Exploring Family Origins in Athlone town*, Longford: Noel Farrell, 2006. NLI, 48 p.

—— *Exploring family origins in old Roscommon town*, Longford: Noel Farrell, 1998. NLI, 48 p.

Fisher Schmidt, Joanne C., *Tombstones of Ireland: counties Down and Roscommon*, Bowie, Md.: Heritage Books, c.2000. LC CS448.D68 S36 2000, 110 p.

Gacquin, William, *Roscommon before the Famine: the parishes of Kiltoom and Cam*, Dublin: Irish Academic Press, 1996. NLI Ir 94125 g 9, 64 p.

—— *Tombstone inscriptions, Cam Old Cemetery*, Cam: Cam Cemetery Committee, 1992. NLI Ir 941 p 120(1), 49 p.

Gibbon, Skeffington, *The recollections of Skeffington Gibbon, from 1796 to the present year, 1829*, Dublin: printed by Joseph Blundell, 1829. NLI Ir 92 g 94, 170 p.

Gormley, Mary, *Tulsk Parish in historic Magh Ai: aspects of its history and folklore compiled*, Roscommon: County Roscommon Historical and Archaeological Society, 1989. Baslick, Killukin (Roscommon), Ogulla. NLI Ir 94125 g 8, 160 p.

Grenham, John Joe, *Moore: the customs and traditions of a rural community*, Moore Community Council, 1983. Roscommon County Library 941.75.

Hayes-McCoy, G.A., *Index to 'The Compossicion Booke of Connoght, 1585'*, Dublin: IMC, 1945. NLI Ir 9412 c 1, 179 p.

Higgins, Jim, *The Tisrara medieval church*, Carrowntemple Four Roads: Tisrara Heritage . . . Committee, 1995. NLI Ir 7941 h 25.

Huggins, Michael, *Social conflict in pre-famine Ireland: the case of County Roscommon*, Dublin: Four Courts Press, 2007. NLI, 221 p.

Hunter, John, *Resource Co. Roscommon* (CD-ROM, Hunter, 3rd ed., 2010).

Hurley, Rev. Timothy, *St Patrick and the Parish of Kilkeevan, Vol. 1*, Dublin: Dollard, 1944. NLI Ir 27412 h 2, 618 p.

IGRS, *Tombstone inscriptions, Vol. 2*, Dublin: IGRS Tombstone Committee, 2001. NLI 3B 29, c.900 p.

Keaney, Marion, *Athlone: bridging the centuries*, Mullingar: Westmeath County Council, 1991. Co-editor, Gearóid Ó Briain. NLI Ir 94131 a 2.

Knox, H.T., *Notes on the Early History of the Dioceses of Tuam, Killala and Achonry*, Dublin: Hodges Figgis, 1904. NLI Ir 27412 k 1, 410 p.

Lenehan, Jim, *Politics and Society in Athlone, 1830–85: A Rotten Borough*, Irish Academic Press, 1999. NLI.

Manning, Peter, *Elphin Diocesan census, 1749: surname index*, Rainham, Kent: Manning, 1987. NLI Ir 27412 m 20.

Mattimoe, Cyril, *North Roscommon: its people and past*, Kildare: Cyril Mattimoe, 1992. NLI Ir 94125 m 8, 214 p.

Moran, James M., *Stepping on stones: Roscommon Mid-West, the Suck lowlands, the Ballinturly-Correal valley*, Cartur: James Moran, 1993. NLI Ir 94125 m 10.

—— *Vignettes*, Athleague: Moran/Cartur Publications, 1996. NLI Ir 94125 m 12, 296 p.

Murtagh, H., *Athlone besieged*, Athlone: Temple Printing Co., 1991. Eyewitness and other contemporary accounts of the Siege of Athlone (1690). NLI Ir 94107 p 21(1).

—— *Athlone: history and settlement to 1800*, Athlone: Old Athlone Society, 2000. NLI Ir 94131 m 6, 256 p.

—— *Irish Historic Towns Atlas, 6: Athlone*, Dublin: RIA, 1994. NLI ILB 941 p (13) 3.

O'Brien, Brendan, *Athlone Workhouse and the Famine*, Athlone: Old Athlone Society, 1995. Edited by Gearóid O'Brien. NLI Ir 300 p 207(8).

Scally, Robert, *The End of Hidden Ireland*, Oxford: Oxford University Press, 1997. Townland of Ballykilcline. NLI Ir 94125 s 7, 266 p.

Schmidt, Joanne, C.F., *Tombstones of Ireland. Counties Down and Roscommon*, Maryland, Heritage Books, 2000. 118 p.

Simington, Robert C., *The transplantation to Connacht, 1654–58*, Shannon: Irish University Press, for IMC, 1970. NLI Ir 94106 s 9, 306 p.

Stokes, George T., *Athlone, the Shannon and Lough Ree*, Dublin and Athlone: 1897. NLI Ir 91413 s 1.

Tonra, Henry, *The Parish of Ardcarne*, 2001. NLI, 244 p.

Vesey, Padraig, *The murder of Major Mahon, Strokestown, County Roscommon, 1847*, Dublin: Four Courts Press, 2008. NLI, 64 p.

Local journals

Journal of the Old Athlone Society. NLI Ir 94131 o 1.

Journal of the Roscommon Historical and Archaeological Society. NLI Ir 94125 r 5.

The Moylfinne: Journal of the Old Taughmaconnell Society. Roscommon County Library.

Directories

1824   J. Pigot & Co., *City of Dublin and Hibernian Provincial Directory.* NLI; LDS film 451787. Online: Hayes.

1846   Slater's *National Commercial Directory of Ireland.* PRONI; NLI LO; LDS film 1696703 item 3. Online: Hayes.

1856   Slater, *Royal National Commercial Directory of Ireland.* NLI; LDS film 1472360 item 1.

1870   Slater, *Directory of Ireland.* NLI.

1881   Slater, *Royal National Commercial Directory of Ireland*. NLI. Online: FindMyPast.

1894   Slater, *Royal Commercial Directory of Ireland*. NLI.

Gravestone inscriptions

Parts (at least) of ten Co. Roscommon graveyards are transcribed at *<www. interment.net>*.

Ardcarn (C of I): Schmidt, *Tombstones*.
Athleague: Glebe (C of I). Online: History.
Aughrim: RHGC.
Bumlin: Killinordin, RHGC.
Cam: IGRS, Vol. 2. Also Gacquin, *Tombstone inscriptions*.
Cloonfinlough: Ballintemple, RHGC.
Dysart: RHGC.
Elphin: Elphin Cathedral, C of I, GO Ms. 622, p. 151.
Estersnow (C of I): Schmidt, *Tombstones*.
Fuerty: RHGC.
Kilmore: (C of I): Schmidt, *Tombstones*.
Kiltrustan: RHGC.
Lissonuffy: RHGC.
Roscommon: Hill St, C of I, GO Ms. 622, p. 170; also RHGC.
St John's, Kilcommon (Lecarrow): Online: History.
New: Online: History.
St Peter's: Athlone, King St, C of I, NLI Pos. 5309 (with parish registers).
Taghboy: Jamestown?, GO Ms. 622, p. 170.
Taghmaconnell: IGRS, Vol. 2.
Tisrara: Mount Talbot (Tisrara?), C of I, IGRS, Vol. 2.
Carrowntemple: Higgins, *The Tisrara medieval church*.

Estate records

[No landlord given]. NLI Ms. 24880. Tenants list, Moore parish, 1834.

Blake Knox, Francis. NLI Ms. 3077. Rentals, 1845–66. Covering townlands in the civil parishes of Cloonfinlough and Rahara.

Boswell, Frances. NLI Pos. 4937. Rent ledger, c.1760–86. Major tenants only. Covering townlands in the civil parish of Kilronan.

Browne, John. NLI 16 1 14(8). Map of Carronaskeagh, Cloonfinlough parish, May 1811, with tenants' names.

Cleaver, Rev. William. Estate account book, 1834–40, James Hardiman Library, Galway, LE1: ring townlands in the civil parishes of Fuerty and Kilcorkey.

Clonbrock, Baron. NLI Ms. 19501. Tenants' ledger, 1801–1806, indexed. Covering townlands in the civil parish of Taughmaconnell.

Crofton. Estate account book, 1833–40, James Hardiman Library, Galway, LE1. Covering townlands in the civil parish of Kilmeane.

Crofton, Edward. NLI Ms. 19672. Rent roll, May 1778. Major tenants only. Covering townlands in the civil parishes of Baslick, Estersnow, Kilbryan, Kilgefin, Killinvoy, Killumod, Klmeane, Kiltrustan and Ogulla.

Crofton, Sir Humphrey. NLI Ms. 4531. Rental, March 1833, tenants' names alphabetically. Covering townlands in the civil parish of Tumna.

Dundas, Sir Thomas. NLI Mss. 2787, 2788. Rentals, 1792, 1804. Major tenants only. Covering townlands in the civil parishes of Boyle, Estersnow, Kilnamanagh and Tumna.

Evans, Walker. NLI Ms. 10152. Leases, c.1790. Covering townlands in the civil parish of Creeve.

Fox, James. NLI Pos. 4065, rental, 1819. All tenants. Covering townlands in the civil parish of Ogulla.

Gunning, Gen. John. NLI Ms. 10152. Rental, 1792. Major tenants only. Covering townlands in the civil parishes of Athleague, Fuerty and Kilcooley.

King. NLI Ms. 4170. Rent rolls and accounts, 1801–1818. Major tenants only. Covering townlands in the civil parishes of Creeve, Elphin and Kilmore.

King, John. NLI Mss. 3520, 3125, rent and miscellaneous accounts, 1757–86. All tenants. Covering townlands in the civil parishes of Creeve, Elphin, Kilmacumsy, Kilmore, Roscommon, Taghboy and Tisrara.

Lorton, Lord. NLI Mss. 3104/5. Lease books, 1740–1900, including many leases to small tenants, with lives mentioned in the leases. Covering townlands in the civil parishes of Ardcarn, Aughrim, Boyle, Creeve, Elphin, Estersnow, Kilbryan and Kilnamanagh.

Ormsby, Rev. Rodney. NLI Ms. 10152. Leases, c.1803, townland of Grange.

Pakenham-Mahon. NLI Ms. 10152: rent roll, 1725. Major tenants only. NLI Ms. 10152: rent roll, 1765–8. Major tenants only. NLI Ms. 2597: rent ledger, 1795–1804, indexed. NLI Mss. 5501–5503: rent ledgers, 1803–1818, 1824–36, part indexed. NLI Ms. 9473: tenants of Maurice Mahon, c.1817. NLI Ms. 9471: rentals and accounts, 1846–54. Covering townlands in the civil parishes of Bumlin, Cloonfinlough, Elphin, Kilgefin, Kilglass, Kilnamanagh, Kiltrustan, Lisonuffy and Shankill. Also NLI Ms. 9472; rent ledger 1840–48, Kilmacumsy parish.

St George, Charles Manners. NLI Mss. 4001–4022. Accounts and rentals (annual), 1842–6, 1850–55, 1861–71. Covering townlands in the civil parishes of Ardcarn, Killukin and Killumod.

Sandford. NLI 10,152: Rental (major tenants only), 1718. NLI Ms. 10,152: Leases, c.1750. NLI Ms. 10,152: Lands to be settled on the marriage of Henry Sandford, with tenants' names, 1750. NLI Mss. 4281–9: Annual Rentals, 1835–45. Covering townlands in the civil parishes of Ballintober, Baslick, Kilkeevin, Boyle, Kiltullagh and Tibohine.

Tenison, Thomas. NLI Ms. 5101. Rental and accounts, 1836–40. Covering townlands in the civil parishes of Ardcarn and Kilronan.

SLIGO

Census returns and substitutes

1659	Pender's 'Census'. Reprinted GPC, 1997; IMC, 2002. LDS film 924648.
1664	MacLysaght, *Hearth Money Rolls*.
1749	Parishes of Aghanagh, Ahamlish, Ballynakill, Ballysumaghan, Drumcliff, Drumcolumb, Killadoon, Kilmacallan, Kilmactranny, Kilross, Shancough, Sligo and Tawnagh. NAI MFS 6. See also Manning, *Elphin Index*. Online: FindMyPast.
1790	Voters. NLI Ms. 2169.
1795–6	Freeholders. NLI Ms. 3136.
1798	Persons who suffered losses in the 1798 Rebellion. Propertied classes only. c.250 names. NLI I 94107.
1822–48	Reproductive Loan Fund records, Templehouse Loan Association. Mainly parishes of Emlaghfad and Kilvarnet. NA (Kew) T/91.
1823–38	Tithe Books. Part online: Genweb, Sligo.
1832–7	Voters registered in Sligo borough, *Parliamentary Papers, 1837: Reports from Committees*, Vol. 2 (2), pp. 193–6.
1842–3	Voters. OP 1843/61.
1852	Sligo electors. NLI Ms. 3064.
1858	Griffith's Valuation. Online: Askaboutireland.
1901	Census. Online: NAI.
1911	Census. Online: NAI.

Online

Askaboutireland	*<www.askaboutireland.ie>*
FindMyPast	*<www.findmypast.ie>*
Genweb, Sligo	*<www.rootsweb.ancestry.com/~irlsli>*
Hayes, John	*<www.failteromhat.com>*
Leitrim-Roscommon	*<www.leitrim-roscommon.com>*
Murray	*<homepage.eircom.net/~kevm>*
NAI	*<www.census.nationalarchives.ie>*

Publications

Local histories etc.

Carroll, P.J., *Cillglas—Kilglas: the church by the stream: a history of the confiscation settlement and vesting of its lands*, Carroll, 1995. NLI, 32.

Clements, Roy, *Mainly Skreen and Dromard in Co. Sligo*, Dari Press, 2005. NLI, 121 p.

Day, Angelique, and McWilliams, Patrick (eds.), *Ordnance Survey Memoirs of Ireland, Vol. 40: Counties of South Ulster, 1834–8, Cavan, Leitrim, Louth, Monaghan and Sligo*, Belfast: Institute of Irish Studies, 1997. Co. Sligo: Emlaghfad, Killoran and Kilvarnet, Kilmactigue. NLI Ir 9141 o 80, 216 p.

Farry, M., *Killoran and Coolaney: a local history*, 1985. NLI Ir 94122 f 1.

Finn, J., *Gurteen, Co. Sligo: its history, antiquities and traditions*, Boyle: Roscommon Herald, 1981. NLI Ir 94122 p 1, 64 p.

Fleming, D.A., *Politics and provincial people: Sligo and Limerick, 1691–1761*, Manchester: Manchester University Press, 2010. NLI, 272 p.

Greer, James, *The windings of the Moy with Skreen and Tirerogh*, Dublin: Thom, 1923. NLI Ir 91412 g 3, 232 p. Reprinted Ballina: Western People, 1986.

Halloran, Canon Martin, *Templeboy 2000*, Templeboy: Halloran, 2000.

Hayes-McCoy, G.A., *Index to 'The Compossicion Booke of Connoght, 1585'*, Dublin: 1945. NLI Ir 9412 c 1, 179 p.

Heneghan, Susan, *Laethanta scoile: Castlerock townland, Castlerock school, and its surrounds, 2003*, Sligo: 2003. NLI, 131 p.

Henry, Patrick J., *Sligo: medical care in the past, 1800–1965*, 1995. NLI Ir 362 h 11, 144 p.

Higgins, John, *Keash and Culfadda: a local history*, Keash: Keash-Culfadda Local History Committee, 2001. Co-editors, Mary B. Timoney, Brother Thomas Connolly and John Kielty. NLI, 245 p.

IGRS, *Tombstone inscriptions, Vol. 2*, Dublin: IGRS Tombstone Committee, 2001. NLI 3B 29, c.900 p.

Jackson, R.W, *Freemasonry in Sligo, 1767 to 1867*, Beverley, Yorks: Wright & Hoggard, 1909. NLI, 16 p.

Johnston, Jack, *The Riverstown story: County Sligo*, Sligo: Riverstown Enterprise Development, 2005. NLI, 304 p.

Knox, H.T., *Notes on the Early History of the Dioceses of Tuam, Killala and Achonry*, Dublin: Hodges Figgis, 1904. NLI Ir 27412 k 1, 410 p.

McDonagh, J.C., *History of Ballymote and the Parish of Emlaghfad*, 1936. NLI Ir 94122 m 8Ir 94122 m 1.

McDonnell, Thomas, *The diocese of Killala: from its institution to the end of the penal times*, Ballina: R. & S. Monaghan, 1975. NLI Ir 27412 m 1, 143 p.

McGloin, Atlanta, *In the shadow of Carran Hill: historical perspectives of Gleann and its surroundings*, 1997. NLI Ir 94122 i 1, 195 p.

McGowan, Joe, *Inishmurray gale, stone and fire: portrait of a fabled island*, Mullaghmore: Aeolus, 1998. NLI Ir 94122 m 23, 64 p.

—— *In the shadow of Benbulben*, Mullaghmore: Aeolus, 1993. NLI Ir 94122 m 14, 336 p.

McGuinn, J., *Curry*, the author, 1984. NLI Ir 94122 m 8, 102 p.

MacHale, Edward, *The Parishes in the Diocese of Killala: (1) South Tirawley, (2) North Tirawley, (3) Erris, (4) Tireragh*, Killala: 1985. NLI Ir 27414 m 6, 166, 104, 88, 79 p.

MacLysaght, Edward, *Seventeenth century hearth money rolls, with full transcript for County Sligo*, Dublin: IMC, 1967. From NLI Ms. 2165. NLI Ir 94122 m 5.

MacNamee, James J., *History of the Diocese of Ardagh*, Dublin: Browne & Nolan, 1954. NLI Ir 274131 m 5, 858 p.

McTernan, John C., *At the foot of Knocknarea: a chronicle of Coolera in bygone days*, Coolera: Coolera-Strandhill GAA, 1990. Killaspugbrone. NLI Ir 94122.m.10, 188 p.

—— *Historic Sligo,* Sligo: Yeats Country Publications, 1965. A bibliographical introduction to the antiquities, history, maps and surveys, manuscripts, newspapers, historic families and notable individuals of Co. Sligo. NLI Ir 94122 m 4, 156 p.

—— *Memory harbour: the Port of Sligo: an outline of its growth and decline and its role as an emigration port,* Sligo: Avena Publications, 1992. NLI Ir 387 m 16, 96 p.

—— *Sligo: the light of bygone days: Vol. 1, Houses of Sligo & associated families,* Sligo: Avena, 2009. NLI, 514 p.

—— *Sligo: the light of bygone days: Vol. 2, Sligo familes: chronicles of sixty familes past & present,* Sligo: Avena, 2009. NLI, 409 p.

Manning, Peter, *Elphin Diocesan census, 1749: surname index,* Rainham, Kent: Manning, 1987. NLI Ir 27412 m 20.

Moffitt, Miriam, *The Church of Ireland community of Killala and Achonry, 1870–1940,* Dublin: Irish Academic Press, 1999. NLI Ir 283 m 4, 64 p.

O'Connell, Philip, *The Diocese of Kilmore: its History and Antiquities,* Dublin: Browne & Nolan, 1937. NLI Ir 274119 o 3, 579 p.

O'Connor, Watson B., *The O'Connor family: families of Daniel and Mathias O'Connor of Carsallagh House, Achonry, Co. Sligo . . . 1750,* New York: 1914.

O'Donovan, John, 'Ordnance Survey letters: Sligo, 1836,' 1928. Typewritten. NLI, Ir 9141 O 18, 181 f.

O'Rourke, T., *History and Antiquities of the Parishes of Ballysadare and Kilvarn,* 1878. Including histories of the O'Haras, Coopers, Percevals and other families. NLI I 94122.

—— Petition by Sligo Protestants, 1813. NLI P. 504.

Ridge, John T., *Sligo in New York: the Irish from County Sligo, 1849–1991,* New York: County Sligo Social and Benevolent Association, c.1991. NLI Ir 947 r 21, 157 p.

Simington, Robert C., *The transplantation to Connacht, 1654–58,* Shannon: Irish University Press, for IMC, 1970. NLI Ir 94106 s 9, 306 p.

Sligo Family Research, *Doo Chapel, Kilmorgan,* Sligo: Sligo Family Research, 1980? NLI, 7 p.

Timoney, Martin A., *A celebration of Sligo: first essays for Sligo Field Club,* Sligo: Sligo Field Club, 2002. NLI. 336 p.

Wood Martin, W.G., *History of Sligo, county and town, from the close of the Revolution of 1688 to the present time,* Dublin: Hodges, Figgis & Co., 1892. NLI Ir 94122 w 1, 3 vols., 510 p.

—— *Sligo and the Enniskilleners, from 1688–91,* Dublin: 1882.

Directories

1820   J. Pigot, *Commercial Directory of Ireland.* PRONI; NLI Ir 9141 p 107; LDS film 962702 item 1.

1824   J. Pigot & Co., *City of Dublin and Hibernian Provincial Directory.* NLI; LDS film 451787. Online: Hayes.

1839   *Directory of the Towns of Sligo, Enniskillen, Ballyshannon, Donegal . . .*

1846	Slater's *National Commercial Directory of Ireland*. PRONI; NLI LO; LDS film 1696703 item 3. Online: Hayes.
1856	Slater, *Royal National Commercial Directory of Ireland*. NLI; LDS film 1472360 item 1.
1870	Slater, *Directory of Ireland*. NLI.
1881	Slater, *Royal National Commercial Directory of Ireland*. NLI. Online: FindMyPast.
1889	*Sligo Independent County Directory*.
1894	Slater, *Royal Commercial Directory of Ireland*. NLI.

Gravestone inscriptions

Parts (at least) of 8 Co. Sligo graveyards are transcribed at <*www.interment.net*>. Sligo Heritage and Genealogy Centre has transcripts for 146 graveyards in the county. Contact details will be found in Chapter 15. Published transcripts are given below. Eileen Hewson (<*www.kabristan.org.uk*>) has transcribed and published almost 4,500 inscriptions in five volumes for Co. Sligo. Most are available at NLI. It is not clear if the transcripts are complete for each graveyard.

Calry C of I, IGRS, Vol. 2.
St John's, Sligo Abbey, IGRS, Vol. 2.

Estate records

Boswell, Francis. NLI Pos. 4937. Rental, c.1760–86. Major tenants only. Covering townlands in the civil parishes of Ahamlish and Drumrat.

Cooper family. NLI Mss. 3050–60: eleven volumes of rentals and rent ledgers, 1775–1872. Major tenants only. NLI Ms. 3076: rental 1809/1810. Major tenants only. NLI Mss. 9753–7: rentals and accounts. Major tenants only. Covering townlands in the civil parishes of Achonry, Ahamlish, Ballysadare, Ballysumaghan, Drumcolumb, Drumcliff, Killery, Killaspugbrone, Kilmacallan, Kilmorgan, Kilross, Tawnagh and Templeboy.

Crofton, Sir Malby. NAI M938X: rental, 1853, with all tenants. NAI M940X: leases on the estate, including many small tenants, and mentioning lives in the leases. Covering townlands in the civil parishes of Dromard and Templeboy.

Dundas, Sir Thomas. NLI Mss. 2787, 2788: rentals, 1792, 1804. Major tenants only. Covering townlands in the civil parishes of Aghanagh, Drumrat, Emlaghfad, Kilcolman, Kilfree, Kilglass, Kilmacallan, Kilmacteigue, Kilmactranny, Kilmoremoy, Kilshalvey and Skreen.

Lorton, Lord. NLI Mss. 3104, 3105: lease books, 1740–1900, including many leases to small tenants, with lives mentioned in leases. Covering townlands in the civil parishes of Aghanagh, Drumcolumb, Kilfree, Killaraght, Kilmacallan, Kilshalvey and Toomour.

O'Hara the younger, Charles. NLI Pos. 1923. Rent roll. c.1775. All tenants, giving lives named in leases. Covering townlands in the civil parishes of Achonry, Ballysadare, Killoran and Kilvarnet.

Strafford, Earl of (and others). NLI Ms. 10223. Estate rentals, 1682 and 1684. Major tenants only. Includes a large part of Sligo town. Covering townlands in the civil parishes of Ahamlish, Ballysadare, Ballysumaghan, Calry, Cloonoghill, Dromard, Drumcliff, Kilfree, Killoran, Killaspugbrone, Kilmacallan, Kilmacowen, Kilmacteigue, Kilross, St John's, Skreen, Templeboy and Toomour.

Wynne, Owen. NLI Mss. 5780–82: rentals and expense books, 1737–68. Major tenants only. NLI Mss. 5830–31: rent ledgers, 1738–53, 1768–73. Major tenants only, indexed. NLI Mss. 3311–13: a rental and two rent ledgers, yearly from 1798 to 1825, with all tenants. Covering townlands in the civil parishes of Ahamlish, Ballysadare, Calry, Drumcliff, Killoran, St John's, Tawnagh and Templeboy.

TIPPERARY

Census returns and substitutes

1595	Freeholders. NLI Pos. 1700.
1641	Testimonies of 203 witnesses to the 1641 Rebellion. Online: 1641.
1641	Book of Survey and Distribution. NLI Ms. 977.
1641–63	Proprietors of Fethard. *IG*, Vol. 6, No. 1, 1980.
1653	Names of soldiers and adventurers who received land in the county under the Cromwellian settlement. Prendergast, *The Cromwellian Settlement*.
1654	*Civil Survey*, Vols. 1 and 2. Dublin. NLI 6551. Part online: Pitskar.
1659	Pender's 'Census'. Reprinted GPC, 1997; IMC, 2002. LDS film 924648. Onine: Genweb Tipperary.
1666–8	Three Hearth Money Rolls. Laffan, *Tipperary's Families*. Part online: Rootsweb Tipperary.
1703	Minister's money account, Clonmel. *AH*, 34.
1750	Catholics in the parishes of Barnane, Bourney, Corbally, Killavanoge, Killea, Rathnaveoge, Roscrea, Templeree and Templetouhy. *IG*, 1973.
1766	Ballingarry, Uskeane GO 536; Athassel, Ballintemple, Ballycahill, Ballygriffin, Boytonreth, Brickendown, Bruis, Clerihan, Clonbeg, Clonbolloge, Cloneen, Clonoulty, Clonpet, Colman, Cordangan, Corrogue, Cullen, Dangandargan, Drum, Dustrileague, Erry, Fethard, Gaile, Grean, Horeabbey, NAI. Parl. Ret. 682–701. Index online: Genweb Tipperary. Burgesbeg, Ballingarry, Uskane: PRONI name search.
1776	Voters. NAI M.4910 12.
1776	Freeholders. NAI M.1321–2; also GO 442. Online: Rootsweb Tipperary.
1790–1801	Tithe Book, Ardmayle and Ballysheehan parishes. NLI Pos. 5553.
1799	Census of Carrick-on-Suir. BL Add. Ms. 11722; NLI Pos. 28; Carrick-on-Suir heritage centre.
1813	Valuation of Roscrea. NAI MFCI 3.
1821	Clonmel. NAI m 242(2); Modreeny (extracts only), GO 572.

1823–38	Tithe Books. Part online: Connors, Genweb Tipperary.
1828	Clonmel, houses and occupiers. *Parliamentary Papers, 1837: Reports from Committees*, Vol. 11 (2).
1832–7	Registered voters, Clonmel and Cashel boroughs. *Parliamentary Papers, 1837: Reports from Committees*, Vol. 2 (2).
1835	Census of Newport and Birdhill. NLI Pos. 1561 Templebredin, *JNMAS*, 1975.
1837	Protestant parishioners, Clogheen union, 1837, 1877, 1880. *IA*, Vol. 17, No. 1, 1985.
1838–53	Reproductive Loan Fund records. Tipperary Town Loan Association. Covering parishes of Bruis, Clonpet, Cordangan, Corroge, Solloghodbeg, Solloghodmore, Templenoe and Tipperary. c.450 individuals. NA (Kew) T 91. Partly online: Moving Here.
1851	Griffith's Valuation. Online: Askaboutireland.
1864–70	Protestants in the parishes of Shanrahan and Tullagherton, *IA*, 16 (2), 1984, pp. 61–7.
1901	Census. Online: NAI.
1911	Census. Online: NAI.

Online

1641	*<www.1641.tcd.ie>*
Askaboutireland	*<www.askaboutireland.ie>*
Connors	*<www.connorsgenealogy.com>*
Devries	*<www.macatawa.org/~devries/CahirCoTipperary.html>*
Genweb Tipperary	*<www.irelandgenweb.com/~irltip>*
Grieves	*<members.iinet.net.au/~sgrieves>*
Hayes, John	*<www.failteromhat.com>*
IGP Tipperary	*<www.igp-web.com/tipperary>*
Limerick Archives	*<www.limerickcity.ie>*
Moving Here	*<www.movinghere.org.uk/search>*
NAI	*<www.census.nationalarchives.ie>*
Pitskar	*<freepages.genealogy.rootsweb.com/~irish>*
PRONI name search	*<www.proni.gov.uk>*
Tipperary Historical Society	*<tipperarylibraries.ie/ths>*

Publications

Local histories etc.

Archdiocese of Cashel and Emly, *Pobal Áilbe: Cashel and Emly atlas*, Dublin: Ordnance Survey Office, 1970. NLI ILB 94143 a 3.

Bateman, Paul, *Heffernans from Clonbonane, Co. Tipperary*, Canberra?: the author, 1991. NLI Ir 9292 H 18, 133 p.

Bell, Eileen, *Around New Inn and Knockgraffon*, Cashel: Lion Print, 2003. NLI, 120 p.

Burke, William P., *History of Clonmel*, Waterford: 1907. Incluning Grubb, *Commercial Directory of Clonmel*. NLI Ir 94142 b 1. Online: Rootsweb Tipperary.

Butler, David J., *South Tipperary, 1570–1841: Religion, land and rivalry*, Dublin: Four Courts Press, 2007. NLI, 336 p.

Carville, Geraldine, *The heritage of Holy Cross*, Belfast: Blackstaff Press, 1973. NLI Ir 271 c 27, 175 p.

Collins, Michael, *The Famine in Newport*, Newport: Newport Historical and Archaeological Society, 1996? NLI, 56 p.

Dunne, Katie, *Grangemockler: Church and People, 1897–1997*, Grangemockler: Grangemockler Centenary Committee, 1997. NLI.

—— 'Emigration from the workhouse of Nenagh Union, Co. Tipperary, 1849–60', *IA*, 17 (1), 1985.

Farrell, Noel, *Carrick-on-Suir family roots: exploring family origins in Carrick-on-Suir, County Tipperary*, Longford: Noel Farrell, 2001. NLI, 48 p.

—— *Exploring Family Origins in Nenagh*, Longford: Noel Farrell, 2006. NLI, 48 p.

—— *Exploring Family Origins in Tipperary town*, Longford: Noel Farrell, 2006. NLI, 48 p.

Fitzgerald, Séamus, *Cappawhite and Doon*, Pallasgrean: S. Fitzgerald, 1983. NLI Ir 9141 p 43, 124 p.

Flood, John, *Kilcash: a history, 1190–1801*, Dublin: Geography Publications, 1999. Co-author, Phil Flood. NLI Ir 94142 F 6, 135 p.

Flynn, Paul, *The book of the Galtees and the Golden Vale: a border history of Tipperary, Limerick and Cork*, Dublin: Hodges, Figgis & Co., 1926. NLI Ir 94142 f 2, 417 p.

Gleeson, John, *Cashel of the kings: a history of the ancient capital of Munster from the date of its foundation until the present day*, Dublin: J. Duffy & Co., 1927. NLI Ir 94142 g 2, 312 p. Reprinted Dublin: Edmund Burke, 2001.

—— *History of the Ely O'Carroll Territory or Ancient Ormond*, Dublin: Gill, 1915. Reprinted Roberts Books, c.1982, with an introduction and bibliography by George Cunningham. NLI Ir 94142 g 1.

Gorman, Edward, *Records of Moycarkey and Two Mile Borris, with some fireside stories*, Galway: Printinghouse, 1955. NLI Ir 94142 g 4, 58 p.

Grace, Daniel, *Cloughjordan heritage*, Cloughjordan. Co-editor, Edward J. Whyte PP. NLI Ir 914142 c 37.

—— *The Great Famine in Nenagh Poor Law Union, Co. Tipperary*, Nenagh: Relay Books, 2000. NLI Ir 94142 g 8, 230 p.

—— *Portrait of a parish: Monsea and Killodiernan, Co. Tipperary*, Nenagh: Relay Publications, 1996. NLI Ir 94142 g 5, 346 p.

Griffin, Kevin M., *Ballina/Boher parish: our history and traditions*, Killaloe: Ballina Killaloe Print, 2000. Co-author, Kevin A. Griffin. NLI Ir 94142 g 9, 389 p.

Gwynn, A., *A history of the diocese of Killaloe*, Dublin: M.H. Gill & Son, 1962. NLI Ir 27414.g.3, 566 p.

Harvey, N., *Parochial history of Waterford and Lismore during the 18th and 19th centuries*, 1912. NLI Ir 94141 p 1, 290 p.

Hayes, W.J., *The Keeffes of the Jockey*, Roscrea: Lisheen Publications, 2001. NLI A 2A 272, 80 p.

—— *Moyne-Templetuohy: a life of its own: the story of a Tipperary parish*, Tipperary: Moyne-Templetuohy History Group, 2001. NLI, 3 vols.

—— *Newport, Co. Tipperary: the town, its courts and gaols*, Roscrea: Lisheen Publications, 1999. NLI, 72 p.

—— *Old church and graveyard, Townparks, Templemore*, Templemore: Sister Áine Historical Society, 1995. NLI Ir 9293 h 2, 141 p.

—— *Thurles: a guide to the cathedral town*, Roscrea: Lisheen Publications, 1999. NLI, 54 p.

—— *The Tipperary Gentry, Vol. 1*, Dublin and Bunclody: Irish Family Names, 2003. Co-author, Art Kavanagh. NLI. 248 p.

—— *Tipperary Remembers*, 1976. NLI Ir 914142 H 9.

Higgins, Noreen, *Tipperary's tithe war, 1830–38: parish accounts of resistance against a church tax*, Tipperary: St Helen's Press, 2002. NLI, 289 p.

Hore, H.F., *The Social State of the Southern and Eastern Counties of Ireland in the Sixteenth Century, being the presentments of the gentlemen, commonalty, and citizens of Carlow, Cork, Kilkenny, Tipperary, Waterford, and Wexford, made in the reigns of Henry VIII. and Elizabeth: Printed from the originals in the Public Record Office, London. Edited by the late Herbert J. [i.e. F.] Hore . . . and the Rev. James Graves*, Dublin: 1870. NLI Ir 794105 r 2.

IGRS, *Tombstone inscriptions, Vol. 2*, Dublin: IGRS Tombstone Committee, 2001. NLI 3B 29, c.900 p.

Kenny, Michael, *Glankeen of Borrisoleigh: a Tipperary Parish*, Dublin: J. Duffy & Co., 1944. NLI Ir 94142 k 2, 6 p.

Laffan, Thomas, *Tipperary's families: being the hearth money records for 1665–6–7 . . .* Dublin: James Duffy & Co., 1911. NLI Ir 9292 l 11, 205 p.

Lonergan, Eamonn, *A workhouse story: a history of St. Patrick's Hospital, Cashel, 1842–1992*, Clonmel: Lonergan, 1992. NLI Ir 360 L 6, 223 p.

Mac Carthaigh, Mícheál, *A Tipperary parish: a history of Knockavilla-Donaskeigh*, Carrigrohane, Co. Cork: S. Moran, 1986. NLI Ir 94142 m 5, 302 p.

Marnane, Denis G., *Cashel: History and Guide*, Dublin: Nonsuch Press, 2007. NLI, 159 p.

—— *Finding Tipperary: a guide to the resources of the Tipperary Studies Department, Tipperary County Library*, Thurles: County Tipperary Joint Libraries Committee, 2007. NLI, 184 p.

—— *Land and violence: a history of West Tipperary from 1660*, Tipperary: Marnane, 1985. NLI Ir 94142 m 4, 196 p.

Meskell, Peter, *History of Boherlahan-Dualla*, Middleton: Litho Press Co., 1987.

Moloney, Bernie, *Times to cherish: Cashel and Rosegreen parish history, 1795–1995*, Cashel: Cashel and Rosegreen Parish, 1994. NLI Ir 27414 T 2, 224 p.

Murphy, Ignatius, *The Diocese of Killaloe, 1800–1850*, Dublin: Four Courts Press, 1992. NLI Ir 27414 m 7, 488 p.

—— *The Diocese of Killaloe, 1850–1904*, Dublin: Four Courts Press, 1995. NLI Ir 27414 m 9, 527 p.

—— *The Diocese of Killaloe in the eighteenth century*, Dublin: Four Courts Press, 1991. NLI Ir 27414 m 8, 373 p.

Murphy, Nancy, *More of Nenagh's yesterdays*, Nenagh: Relay Publications, 1997. NLI Ir 9141 m 102, 128 p.

—— *Tracing Northwest Tipperary Roots*, Nenagh: 1982.

Neely, W.G., *Kilcooley: land and parish in Tipperary*, W.G. Neely, 1983. NLI Ir 94142 n 1, 168 p.

Nolan, W., *Tipperary: History and Society*, Dublin: Geography Publications, 1985. Co-editor, Thomas G. McGrath. NLI Ir 94142 t 6, 493 p.

O'Brien, Bridie, *How we were: in the parish of Kilbarron-Terryglass, Co. Tipperary*, Nenagh: Relay Books, 1999. NLI Ir 94142 o 7, 396 p.

O'Donnell, Seán, *Clonmel, 1840–1900: anatomy of an Irish town*, Dublin: Geography Publications, 2000. NLI, 337 p.

O'Dwyer, Michael, *The famine in the Kilkenny/Tipperary region: a history of the Callan Workhouse and Poor Law Union, 1845–52*, Callan: Callan Heritage Society, 2008. NLI, 119 p.

O'Keeffe, Tadhg, *Irish Historic Towns Atlas, 13: Fethard*, Dublin: RIA, 2003. NLI.

Ó Néill, Col. Eoghan, *The Golden Vale of Ivowen: Land and people of the valley of the Suir, County Tipperary*, Dublin: Geography Publications, 2001. NLI, 604 p.

Ó Riain, Séamus, *Dunkerrin: a parish in Ely O Carroll: a history of Dunkerrin Parish from 1200 AD to the present time*, Dunkerrin: Dunkerrin History Committee, 1988. NLI Ir 94136 O 5, 256 p.

O'Riordan, Ed, *Hard days and happy days: the history of Skeheenarinky National School, 1858 to 2008*, Skeheenarinky: Skeheenarinky National School Parents' Association, 2008. Co-editor, Karol DeFalco. NLI, 286 p.

O'Riordan, Edmund, *Famine in the Valley*, Cahir: Galty Vee Valley Tourism, 1995. NLI Ir 94142 o 4, 85 p.

—— *Historical guide to Clogheen*, O'Riordan, 1996. Tipperary County Library 941.92, 76 p.

Poulacapple National School, *Centenary of a rural school: Poulacapple, 1891–1991*, Poulacapple: 1991. NLI Ir 94142 p 5(2), 144 p.

Power, Martin, *Dear land—native place: Monsea and Dromineer: a history*, Nenagh: Nenagh Guardian, 1998. NLI Ir 94142 p 7, 390 p.

Power, V. Rev. P., *Waterford and Lismore: A Compendious History of the Dioceses*, Dublin: Cork University Press, 1937. NLI Ir 274141 p 1, 402 p.

Power, Thomas P., *Land, politics and society in eighteenth-century Tipperary*, Oxford: Oxford University Press, 1993. NLI Ir 94142 p 3, 376 p.

Prendergast, John, *The Cromwellian Settlement of Ireland*, Dublin: 1865. Reprinted London: Constable, 1996. NLI Ir 94106 p 14, 304 p.

Pyke, D., *Parish Priests and Churches of St Mary's, Clonmel*, 1984. NLI Ir 274 p 40, 54 p.

Resch, M.L., *The descendants of Patrick Halloran of Boytonrath, Co. Tipperary*, Baltimore, Md.: Gateway Press, 1987. NLI Ir 9292 r 12, 627 p.

Ryan, C.A., *Tipperary Artillery, 1793–1889*, 1890. NLI Ir 355942 t 1.

Ryan, Senator Willie, *Golden-Kilfeacle: the parish and its people*, Tipperary: Kilfeacle, 1997. NLI Ir 94142 r 2, 371 p.

Seymour, St John D., *The Diocese of Emly*, Dublin: Church of Ireland Print., 1913. NLI Ir 27414 s 1, 297 p.

Sheehan, E.H., *Nenagh and its Neighbourhood*, Nenagh: Nancy Murphy, 1976. Including many family records. NLI Ir 914142 s 4, 98 p.

Shelley, John R., *A short history of the 3rd Tipperary Brigade*, Cashel: Shelley, 1996. NLI Ir 94142 s 5, 103 p.

Tierney, Mark, *Murroe and Boher: history of an Irish country parish*, Dublin: Browne & Nolan, 1966. NLI Ir 94144 t 1, 251 p.

Treacy, Brendan, *Nenagh through the mists of time*, Nenagh: Brendan Treacy, 2009. NLI, 224 p.

—— *Nenagh yesterday*, Nenagh: Nenagh Relay Publications, 1993. NLI Ir 94142 t 4, 144 p.

Veale, T., *Index of Surnames in 'The New Commercial Directory for the cities of Waterford and Kilkenny and the towns of Clonmel, Carrick-on-Suir, New Ross and Carlow'*, Dublin: Veale, 1996. NLI Ir 9414 p.

—— *Richard Lucas, 1788: directory extract for south east of Ireland*, Dublin: Veale, 1995. NLI Ir 9414 v.

Walsh, Paul P., *A history of Templemore and its environs*, Templemore: Paul P. Walsh, 1991. NLI Ir 94142 w 2, 141 p.

Watson, Col. S.J., *A Dinner of Herbs: a history of Old St Mary's Church, Clonmel*, Clonmel: Watson Books, 1988. Tipperary County Library 284.094193, 259 p.

White, James (ed.), *My Clonmel Scrap Book*, Clonmel: Tentmaker Publications, 1995. Reprint of 1907 edition. NLI Ir 94142 w 3, 376 p.

White, John D., *The History of the Family of White of Limerick, Knockcentry, etc.*, 1887. NLI Ir 9292 w 10.

White, Rev. P., *History of Clare and the Dalcassian Clans of Tipperary, Limerick and Galway*, Dublin: 1893. Reprinted Newmarket-on-Fergus: O'Brien Book Publications, 1997. NLI Ir 94143 w 4, 398 p.

Williams, Richard, *In and out of school: in the home of the MacDonaghs*, Nenagh: Nenagh Guardian, 1999. Cloghjordan. NLI Ir 94142 w 5. 312 p.

Local journals
Boherlahan/Dualla Historical Journal (1998–). NLI.
Clonmel Historical and Archaeological Society Journal. NLI Ir 94142 c 2.
Cois Deirge. NLI Ir 94142 c 4.
Éile (Journal of the Roscrea Heritage Society). NLI Ir 94142 e 1.
Journal of the North Munster Archaeological Society. NLI Ir 794105 n 1.
Tipperary Historical Journal / Irisleabhar Staire Thiobraid Árann. NLI Ir 94142 t 2.

Directories
1788   Richard Lucas, *General Directory of the Kingdom of Ireland.* NLI Pos. 3729. Reprinted in Veale, *Lucas, IG*, 1965, 1966, 1967, 1968.

1820	J. Pigot, *Commercial Directory of Ireland*. PRONI; NLI Ir 9141 p 107; LDS film 962702 item 1.
1824	J. Pigot & Co., *City of Dublin and Hibernian Provincial Directory*. NLI; LDS film 451787. Online: Hayes; part online: Rootsweb Tipperary.
1839	T. Shearman, *New Commercial Directory for the cities of Waterford and Kilkenny, Towns of Clonmel, Carrick-on-Suir, New Ross and Carlow*.
1846	Slater's *National Commercial Directory of Ireland*. PRONI; NLI LO; LDS film 1696703 item 3. Online: Hayes.
1856	Slater, *Royal National Commercial Directory of Ireland*. NLI; LDS film 1472360 item 1. Part online: Rootsweb Tipperary.
1866	George Henry Bassett, *Directory of the City and County of Limerick, and of the Principal Towns in the Cos. of Tipperary and Clare*. NLI Ir 914144 b 5.
1867	Henry and Coughlan's *General Directory of Cork and Munster*. Online: FindMyPast.
1870	Slater, *Directory of Ireland*. NLI.
1881	Slater, *Royal National Commercial Directory of Ireland*. NLI. Online: FindMyPast.
1886	Francis Guy, *Postal Directory of Munster*. NLI Ir 91414 g 8; LDS film 1559399 item 8.
1889	George Henry Bassett, *The Book of Tipperary*. NLI Ir 914142 b 25. Online: Pitskar.
1889	Francis Guy, *City and County Cork Almanack and Directory*.
1894	Slater, *Royal Commercial Directory of Ireland*. NLI.

Gravestone inscriptions

Tipperary North Family History Research Centre has some transcriptions from more than 150 graveyards in the north of the county, online at <*www.rootsireland. ie*>. South Tipperary County Archives (<*www southtipparchives.ie*>) holds fifteen burial registers from cemeteries in the south of the county.

Ardfinnan: Rochestown. Online: Devries.
Ballyclerahan: IGRS, Vol. 2.
Bansha: Online: Devries.
Barnane-Ely: Barnane. Online: Grieves.
Cahir-Kilcommon (Quaker): Online: Devries.
Kilcommon (C of I): Online: Devries.
Loughloher: Online: Devries.
Old Church: Online: Devries.
Derrygrath: Online: Devries.
Drom: Online: Grieves.
Glenkeen: Kylanna. Online: Grieves.
Holycross: C of I, GO Ms. 622 P. 176/7.
Inch: Dovea C of I. Online: Grieves.

Inch Old: Online: Grieves.

Inishlounaght: Marlfield. Online: Devries.

Kilfithmone: C of I. Online: Grieves.

Kilgrant: Powerstown RC. Online: Grieves.

Old Powerstown: Online: Grieves.

Kilmore: *IG*, Vol. 2, No. 10, 1953.

Kiltinan: GO Ms. 622, p. 144.

Knigh: IGRS, Vol. 2, NAI open shelves.

Loughmoe West: Online: Grieves.

Mortlestown: Online: Devries.

Newchapel: IGRS, Vol. 2.

Outeragh: Online: Devries.

Shanrahan: Online: Devries.

St Patricksrock, Cashel, The Rock: IGRS, Vol. 2.

Tullaghorton: Castlegrace. Online: Devries.

Doughill. Online: Devries.

Twomileborris: Littleton, GO Ms. 622, p. 171.

Uskane: *IG*, Vol. 3, No. 2, 1957.

Whitechurch: Online: Devries.

Estate records

Burton, Edward William. Rental, 1828. All tenants. NLI Ms. 8683. Covering areas in the civil parish of Kilmurry.

Courtenay, Viscount. Estate rental, 1762. Townlands in the parishes of Castletownarra and Glenkeen. LCA IE LA P6. Online: Limerick Archives.

Kingston, Earl of. NLI Ms. 3276, rental, 1840. All tenants. Covering townlands in the civil parishes of Glenkeen and Templetenny.

Newcommen, Viscount. NLI Ms. 2766, maps, 1826–7. All tenants. Covering townlands in the civil parishes of Bourney, Dolla, Dolla, Kilnaneave, Peppardstown and Templederry.

TYRONE

Census returns and substitutes

1612–13	Survey of Undertakers Planted in Co. Tyrone. *Historical Manuscripts Commission Report*, No. 4 (Hastings Mss.), 1947, pp. 159–82.
1625–7	Leet Court Rolls. Jurors and litigants in Armagh Manor; Arboe, Ardtrea, Donaghmore (Co. Tyrone); Termonfeckin (Co. Louth). SA, Vo. 11, No. 9, 1957, pp. 295–322.
1630	Muster Roll of Ulster. Armagh County Library; PRONI D.1759/3C/1, T. 808/15164; NLI Pos. 206. Online: Genweb Tyrone.
1631	Muster Roll, Co. Tyrone. PRONI T.934.
1654–6	*Civil Survey*, Vol. 3. NLI I 6551 Dublin.
1661	Books of Survey and Distribution. PRONI T.370/C and D.1854/1/23.

1664	Hearth Money Roll. NLI Mss. 9583/4; PRONI T283/D/2. Clogher diocese in *Clogher Record* (1965); Dungannon barony in SA (1971).
1665	Subsidy roll. PRONI T.283/D/1; NLI Pos. 206.
1666	Hearth Money Roll. PRONI T.307. Online: Rootsweb Tyrone.
1699	Protestants in the parishes of Drumragh, Bodoney and Cappagh. GO Sources Box 6.
1740	Protestants, Derryloran and Kildress. PRONI T.808/15258: RCBL; LDS film 1279327. Online: PRONI name search.
1766	Aghaloo, Artrea, Carnteel, Clonfeacle, Derryloran, Donaghendry, Drumglass, Dungannon, Kildress, Tullyniskan, Errigal Keerogue. PRONI T.808/15264–7. Online: PRONI name search. Also NAI Parliamentary returns, 648–66, LDS film 258517.
1775	Arboe. With Arboe Church of Ireland registers. PRONI T.679/111, 115–19; D.1278.
1775	Dissenters' petitions, Ardstraw and Newtownstewart, Dungannon town and neighbourhood, Strabane town and neighbourhood, Coagh, Cookstown. Online: PRONI name search.
1780	Householders, Ternonmaguirk. RCBL GS 2/7/3/25.
1795–8	Voters' list, Dungannon barony. PRONI TYR5/3/1. Online: Freeholders.
1796	Spinning-Wheel Premium List. 7,150 names for Co. Tyrone. Online: Hayes.
1821	Some extracts, Aghaloo. NAI Thrift Abstracts.
1823–38	Tithe Books.
1828–57	Caledon estate. Seven volumes of cash books, containing entries of payments made to emigrating tenants. PRONI D.266/337.
1830	Census of the C of I parish of Donaghenry, Co. Tyrone, c.1830. PRONI C.R.1/38.
1832	Memorial of the . . . inhabitants of Strabane protesting at vexatious prosecutions. c.70 names. NAI OP 964/16.
1832	Census of rural deanery of Derryloran, 1832. PRONI T.2574.
1834	Valuation of Dungannon. *Parliamentary Papers, 1837: Reports from Committees*, Vol. 2 (i), Appendix G.
1834	Clonoe (Coalisland). NLI Pos. 5579.
1838	Memorial from inhabitants of Dungannon to reinstate Richard Murray JP. c.150 signatures. NAI OP 1838/171.
1840	Ratepayers for the Union of Armagh. PRONI D/1670/13/6.
1842	Voters. NAI OP 1842/77.
1842	Workhouse records, Clogher (1842–9), Irvinestown (1845–1918), Enniskillen (1845–1913) and Strabane (1861–83) unions. PRONI; also LDS films 259162–3, 259187–90, 25914–53 and 259164–5, respectively.
1851	Griffith's Valuation. Online: Askaboutireland.
1851–2	Clogherny C of I parishioners. PRONI DIO 4.32C/9/4/2.
1866	Parishioners' list. C of I parish of Termonmaguirk. Local custody.

1901	Census. Online: NAI.
1911	Census. Online: NAI.
1912	The Ulster Covenant. Almost half a million original signatures and addresses of those who signed. c.29,000 names for Co. Tyrone. Online: Covenant.

Online

Askaboutireland	*<www.askaboutireland.ie>*
Bready	*<www.breadyancestry.com>*
Clogher Historical Society	*<www.clogherhistoricalsoc.com>*
Freeholders	*<www.proni.gov.uk/freeholders>*
Hayes, John	*<www.failteromhat.com>*
Headstones	*<www.historyfromheadstones.com>*
PRONI name search	*<www.proni.gov.uk>*
Rootsweb Tyrone	*<freepages.genealogy.rootsweb.ancestry.com/~tyrone>*

Publications

Local histories etc.

Provisional list of pre-1900 School Registers in the Public Record Office of Northern Ireland, UHGGN, 9, 1986, pp. 60–71.

[Unknown], *Ballymagrane Presbyterian Church: a short history of the congregation*, Ballymagrane: Ballymagrane Presbyterian Church, 1959. NLI, 24 p.

—— *Donoughmore Presbyterian Church, 1658–1958*, Omagh: Stule Press, 1958. NLI, 24 p.

—— *Drumquin . . . A Collection of Writings and Photographs of the Past.* NLI Ir 91411 p 10.

Bailie, W.D., *Benburb Presbyterian Church, 1670–1970*, Benburb: Benburb Presbyterian Church, 1970. NLI, 11 p.

Belmore, Earl of, *Parliamentary Memoirs of Fermanagh and Tyrone, 1613–1885*, Dublin: Alex Thom & Co., 1887. NLI Ir 94118 b 1, 368 p.

Bradley, Rev. John, *The life and times of Father Bernard Murphy, Termon, Carrickmore, 1832–97*, Belfast: Eddie Murphy, 1994. Updated 1994. NLI Ir 92 m 511, 96 p.

Bradley, William John, *Gallon: the history of three townlands in County Tyrone from the earliest times to the present day*, Derry: Guildhall Press, c.2000. NLI, 216 p.

Conlon, Bernard, *The travels of Bernard Conlon: Sessiamagaroll to San Francisco, New York, New Zealand and New South Wales: Recorded as a memoir by his son, Proinsias Ó Conluain*, Dungannon: O'Neill Country Historical Society, 2004. NLNZ, 36 p.

Cox, Michael, *Overlooking the River Mourne: four centuries of family farms in Edymore and Cavanalee in County Tyrone*, Belfast: UHF, 2006. NLI, 157 p.

Daly, Edward, *The clergy of the Diocese of Derry: an index*, Dublin: Four Courts Press, 2009. NLI, 244 p.

Day, Angelique, and McWilliams, Patrick (eds.), *Ordnance Survey Memoirs of Ireland Series*, Belfast: Institute of Irish Studies and RIA, 1990–97.

—*Vol. 5: Co. Tyrone I* (1990): Aghaloo, Artrea, Ballinderry, Ballyclog, Bodoney, Carnteel, Clogherny, Clonoe, Desertcreat, Donaghenry, Drumglass, Errigal Keerogue, Kildress, Killyman, Lissan, Pomeroy, Tamlaght, Tullyniskan. NLI Ir 914111 o 14.

—*Vol. 20: Co. Tyrone II* (1993): Aghaloo, Artrea, Ballinderry, Ballyclog, Bodoney, Carnteel, Clogherny, Clonoe, Desertcreat, Donaghenry, Drumglass, Errigal Keerogue, Kildress, Killyman, Lissan, Pomeroy, Tamlaght, Tullyniskan. NLI Ir 9141 o 28.

Donnelly, T.P., *A History of the Parish of Ardstraw West and Castlederg*, 1978. NLI Ir 94114 d 6.

Duffy, Joseph, *A Clogher Record Album: a diocesan history*, Enniskillen: Cumann Seanchais Chlochair, 1975. NLI Ir 94114 c 3, 340 p.

Elliott, David R., *Enniskillen Poor Law Union outdoor relief register (1847–99), covering parts of counties Fermanagh, Cavan, and Tyrone*, Parkhill, Ont.: Kinfolk Finders, 2009. NLI, 88 p.

Gartland, Joseph, *The Gartlands of Augher, Tyrone*, Dedham, Mass.: Joseph A. Gartland Jr, 1983. Gartland, Healy, Kerr, Grady and Magee families. NLI GO 218, 213 leaves.

Gebbie, John H., *Ardstraw (Newtownstewart): historical survey of a parish, 1600–1900*, Omagh: Strule Press, 1968. NLI Ir 94114 g 2, 143 p.

Glasgow, John, *History of the Third Presbyterian Church, Cookstown, 1835–1935: a century in progress*, Cookstown: Mid-Ulster Printing Co., 1935. NLI, 44 p.

Gortin and District Historical Society, *Meetings and memories in Lower Badoney*, Gortin and District Historical Society, 1995–2000. NLI, 2 vols.

Historical Committee of the Grouped Parishes, *The changing years: in the grouped parishes of Ardstraw, Baronscourt and Badoney Union*, Omagh: Grahams Printers, 2000. NLI, 157 p.

Hutchison, W.R., *Tyrone precinct: a history of the plantation settlement of Dungannon and Mountjoy to modern times*, Belfast: W.E. Mayne, 1951. NLI Ir 94114 h 2, 236 p.

Johnson, Norman, *Methodism in Omagh: an historical account of Methodism, over two centuries, in the Omagh and Fintona Circuit*, Omagh: Omagh Methodist Church, 1982. Co-author, Desmond Preston. NLI Ir 27411 p 5, 36 p.

Johnstone, John, *Clogher Cathedral Graveyard*, Omagh: Graham, 1972. NLI Ir 9292 p 9, 54 p.

Kerr, Peter, 'Families and holdings in the townland of Innishatieve, Carrickmore', *SA*, 15, No. 2, 1993, pp. 151–235.

Keys, John, *Fivemiletown Methodist Church jubilee, 1897–1947: a short account of the Fivemiletown circuit*, Cookstown: Mid-Ulster Printing Co., 1947. NLI, 1A 2063, 16 p.

Law, Herbert Innes, *Edenderry Parish, Diocese of Derry*, 2001. NLI, 128 p.

Mac an Ultaigh, Críostóir, *Urney: a portrait of an Irish parish*, Urney: Urney GAA Club, 1994. NLI Ir 396 m 73, 145 p.

McEvoy, J., *County of Tyrone, 1802: a statistical survey by John McEvoy: with introduction by W.H. Crawford*, Belfast: Friar's Bush Press, 1991. NLI Ir 3141 m 13.

McGrew, William J., *Tombstones of the Omey:* [15 graveyards transcribed within Omagh District, Co. Tyrone (1688–1900)], Omagh: Omagh Branch, NIFHS, 1998. NLI Ir 9295 m 6, 184 p.

McKee, Rev. W.J.H., *Aspects of Presbyterianism in Cookstown*, Belfast: Presbyterian Historical Society of Ireland, 1995. Examination of the beginnings of Presbyterianism in Cookstown.

Marsh, Robert G., *Brackaville: a parish of the Church of Ireland*, Dungannon: Tyrone Printing Co., 1981. NLI, 79 p.

Marshall, J.J., *Annals of Aughnacloy and of the parish of Carnteel, County Tyrone*, Dungannon: Tyrone Printing Co., 1925. NLI P 1167(3), 76 p.

—— *History of Dungannon*, Dungannon: Tyrone Printing Co., 1929. NLI Ir 94114 m 3, 137 p.

—— *History of the territory of Minterburn and Town of Caledon (formerly Munter Birn, and Kenard), Co. Tyrone*, Dungannon: Tyrone Printing Co., 1923. NLI Ir 94114 m 1, 39 p.

—— *History of the Town and District of Clogher, Co. Tyrone, parish of Errigal Keerogue, Tyrone, and Errigal Truagh in the Co. of Monaghan*, Dungannon: Tyrone Printing Co., 1930. NLI Ir 94114 m 2, 97 p.

—— *Vestry book of the Parish of Aghalow, Caledon, Co. Tyrone: with an account of the family of Hamilton of Caledon, 1691–1807*, Dungannon: Tyrone Printing Co., 1935. NLI Ir 27411 a 2, 66 p.

Meehan, C.P., *Tyrone: 1901 census index*, Alberta: Largy Books, 1995, NLI.

Mongan, Norman, *Notes on an Erenagh family: the sacred clan of O Mongan of Ballymongan and Termonomongan*, Norman Charles Mongan, 1987. NLI, GO 686, 37 p.

Montgomery, S.D., *Ministries in miniature: Aughnacloy Presbyterian Church, 1697–1938*, Omagh: Aughnacloy Presbyterian Church, 1938. NLI, 36 p.

Murphy, H.B., *Three hundred years of Presbyterianism in Clogher*, Belfast: News Letter, 1958. NLI Ir 285 m 42, 159 p.

Ó Dálaigh, Brian, *Irish villages: studies in local history*, Dublin: Four Courts Press, 2003. Pomeroy. NLI 326 p.

O'Daly, B., 'Material for a history of the parish of Kilskeery', *Clogher Record*, 1953/4/5. NLI.

O'Kane, William, *Heather, peat and stone: the parishes and townlands of County Tyrone*, Dungannon: Irish World, 1992. NLI Ir 94114 h 6, 165 p.

Roulston, William, *The Parishes of Leckpatrick and Dunnalong*, Ulster Local History Trust, 2000. UHF. Online: Bready.

—— *Restoration Strabane, 1660–1714: economy and society in provincial Ireland*, Dublin: Four Courts Press, 2007. NLI, 64 p.

—— *Three centuries of life in a Tyrone parish: A history of Donagheady from 1600 to 1900*, Strabane: Strabane History Society, 2010. NLI, 400 p.

Rutherford, J., *Donagheady Presbyterian Churches and Parish*, Belfast: McGraw, Stevenson & Orr, 1953. NLI Ir 285 r 7, 117 p.

Stewart, Austin, *Coalisland, County Tyrone, in the Industrial Revolution, 1800–1901*, Dublin: Four Courts Press, 2002, 64 p.

Todd, Sheelagh, *Register of gravestones in Leckpatrick Old Burial Ground*, the author, 1991. NLI Ir 9295 p 1(4), 105 p.

Local journals
Clogher Record. NLI Ir 94114 c 2.
Derriana. NLI I r 27411 d 4.
Dúchas Néill: Journal of the O'Neill Country Society.
North Irish Roots: Journal of the North of Ireland Family History Society. NLI Ir 92905 n 4.
Irish Family Links. NLI Ir 9292 f 19.
Seanchas Ardmhacha. NLI Ir 27411 s 4.
Ulster Journal of Archaeology. NLI Ir 794105 u 1.

Directories
Thirty Belfast and Ulster directories are online at PRONI.

1819	Thomas Bradshaw's *General directory of Newry, Armagh, and the towns of Dungannon, Portadown, Tandragee, Lurgan, Waringstown, Banbridge, Warrenpoint, Rosstrevor, Kilkeel, Rathfriland, 1820*. PRONI; NLI Ir 91411 b 18; LDS film 258723.
1820	J. Pigot, *Commercial Directory of Ireland*. PRONI; NLI Ir 9141 p 107; LDS film 962702 item 1.
1824	J. Pigot & Co., *City of Dublin and Hibernian Provincial Directory*. NLI; LDS film 451787. Online: Hayes.
1839	Martin, *Belfast Directory*. Also 1841, 1842. PRONI; NLI Ir 9141111 m 4.
1846	Slater's *National Commercial Directory of Ireland*. PRONI; NLI LO; LDS film 1696703 item 3. Online: Hayes.
1854–	*Belfast and Province of Ulster Directory*. Also 1856, 1858, 1861, 1863, 1865, 1868, 1870, 1877, 1880, 1884, 1887, 1890, 1894, 1900. PRONI; LDS (various years).
1856	Slater, *Royal National Commercial Directory of Ireland*. NLI; LDS film 1472360 item 1.
1865	R. Wynne, *Business Directory of Belfast*. NLI Ir 91411 b 2.
1870	Slater, *Directory of Ireland*. NLI.
1872	*Tyrone Almanac and Directory*. NLI Ir 914114 t 2.
1881	Slater, *Royal National Commercial Directory of Ireland*. NLI. Online: FindMyPast.
1882	*Omagh Almanac*. NLI Ir 914114 o 1.

1887   *Derry Almanac and Directory*, annually from 1887. NLI Ir 914112 d 1.

1888   George Henry Bassett, *The Book of Armagh* (Moy). NLI Ir 94116 b 3.

1891   *Omagh Almanac*. NLI Ir 914114 o 1.

1894   Slater, *Royal Commercial Directory of Ireland*. NLI.

Gravestone inscriptions

Heritage World has transcripts of 112 graveyards in Co. Tyrone. The Ulster Historical Foundation has transcripts for 53 graveyards. These are searchable online for a fee at <*www.historyfromheadstones.com*>. Published or freely available transcripts are given below. Eileen Hewson (<*www.kabristan.org.uk*>) has transcribed and published almost 5,000 inscriptions in six volumes for Strabane and Co. Tyrone. Most are available at NLI. It is not clear if the transcripts are complete for each graveyard.

Cappagh: Dunmullin. McGrew, *Tombstones of the Omey.*

Killclogher: RC. McGrew, *Tombstones of the Omey.*

Knockmoyle: RC. McGrew, *Tombstones of the Omey.*

Mountjoy Forest East Division: C of I. McGrew, *Tombstones of the Omey.*

Edenderry (Omagh): Pres. McGrew, *Tombstones of the Omey.*

Lislimnaghan, Omagh: C of I. McGrew, *Tombstones of the Omey.*

Carnteel: Pres. Johnstone, *Clogher Cathedral Graveyard.*

Clogherny: Donaghane (Donaghanie?). McGrew, *Tombstones of the Omey.*

Donacavey: *Clogher Record*, Vol. 7, No. 2, 1970.

Drumglass: Dungannon, Old Drumglass. RC. *SA*, Vol. 7, No. 2, 1974.

Drumragh: Clanabogan (C of I): McGrew, *Tombstones of the Omey.*

Drumragh (Old): RC. McGrew, *Tombstones of the Omey.*

Kilskeery: C of I. *Clogher Record*, Vol. 8, No. 1, 1973.

Leckpatrick: Todd, *Register of gravestones.*

Termonmaguirk: Drumnakilly. C of I. McGrew, *Tombstones of the Omey.*

Estate records

Abercorn, Dukes of. Rentals, 1794–1911. PRONI D623/C/4. Covering areas in the civil parishes of Ardstraw, Donaghedy, Leckpatrick and Urney.

Alexander, Earls of Caledon. Rentals, 1766–1916. PRONI D.2433. Covering areas in the civil parishes of Aghaloo, Clonfeacle, Eglish and Tynan. May cover areas in other parishes.

Auchinleck. Rentals, 1830–1900. PRONI D674. Covering areas in the civil parish of Drumragh (the Omagh area).

Belmore, Earls of. Rentals, 1789–1893. PRONI D1716/21–6. Covering areas in the civil parish of Clogherny (Beragh area).

Belmore, Earls of. Rentals, 1777–1913. PRONI D.3007. Covering areas in the civil parish of Termonmaguirk.

Bruce. 45 maps of the estate with tenants' names, revised 1906 and 1911, 1838. PRONI D1154/2/B/1. Covering areas in the civil parish of Clonfeacle.

Burges. Maps, with observations on the tenancies, 1798. PRONI. Covering areas in the civil parish of Donaghmore.

Cairns, George. Rental, 1793–5. PRONI D2559/3/3, 4. Covering areas in the civil parish of Clogher.

Caledon. Rentals, 1828–1916. PRONI D.2433. Covering areas in the civil parishes of Aghaloo and Eglish.

Charlemont. Rentals, 1798–1802. NLI Ms. 2702. Major tenants only. Covering areas in the civil parishes of Clonfeacle and Donaghmore.

Eccles. Rental of Fintona estate, 1746–1850. PRONI T1612. Covering areas in the civil parish of Donacavey.

Goff. 22 maps of the estate giving tenant names, 1868. PRONI D751/1–22. Covering areas in the civil parishes of Carnteel, Donaghmore, Killeeshil and Pomeroy.

Greer. Valuation and accounts, 1823. PRONI T2642/1–4. Covering areas in the civil parishes of Desertcreat, Drumglass and Killyman.

Lenox-Conyngham. Rentals, 1786–1914. PRONI D.1449/1–7. Covering areas in the civil parishes of Arboe, Artrea and Tamlaght.

Leslie. Rental, 1846. NLI Ms. 5813. All tenants. Valuation, with names and observations, 1833. NLI Ms. 5813. All tenants. Covering areas in the civil parishes of Carnteel and Errigal Keerogue.

Lindsay. Rentals, 1745–61. NLI Ms. 5204. All tenants. Rentals, 1778–1817. NLI Ms. 5205. All tenants. Survey, 1800. NLI Ms. 2584. Major tenants only. Rentals, 1808–1817. NLI Ms. 5206. All tenants. Rentals, 1836–48. NLI Ms. 5208. All tenants. Covering areas in the civil parishes of Artrea, Derryloran, Desertcreat and Donaghenry.

Lowry. Rental, 1818–1943. PRONI D1132. Covering areas in the civil parish of Pomeroy.

MacKenzie, Alexander. Rentals, 1825. NLI Ms. 18980. All tenants. Covering areas in the civil parish of Drumglass.

Maxwell. Valuation, with names, 1807. NLI Ms. 5379. All tenants. Survey and valuation, 1830. NLI Ms. 5380. All tenants. Covering areas in the civil parish of Urney.

Montgomery, Hugh. Rental, 1792–4. PRONI D464/74. Covering areas in the civil parish of Clogher.

Montgomery. Rent rolls and more, 1650–1900. PRONI D627. Covering areas in the civil parish of Clogher.

Montgomery. Rental, 1792–4. PRONI D.464/74. Covering areas in the civil parish of Clogher.

Moutray. Rent accounts, 1807–1838. PRONI D1716/17. Covering areas in the civil parish of Carnteel. May cover other parishes.

Moutray. Rentals, 1757–1946. PRONI D2023/3/1. Covering areas in the civil parishes of Carnteel, Clogher, Errigal Keerogue and Errigal Trough.

Ogilby. Rentals, 1834–79. PRONI D15550/16. Covering areas in the civil parish of Donaghedy (Dunamanagh).

Powerscourt. Rentals, 1809. NLI Ms. 19191. All tenants. Rentals, 1835, 1838. NLI Ms. 19192. All tenants. Covering areas in the civil parish of Clonfeacle.

Ranfurly, Earls of. Rentals (58 volumes), 1750–1898. PRONI D285/158–215. Covering areas in the civil parishes of Clonfeacle, Donaghmore, Drumglass and Killyman

Ranfurly, Earls of. Rentals, 1830–97. PRONI D804/1. Covering areas in the civil parishes of Clonfeacle, Donaghmore, Drumglass and Killyman.

Stewart. Rentals, 1786–8. NLI Ms. 766. All tenants. Covering areas in the civil parishes of Artrea, Carnteel, Clonfeacle, Derryloran, Desertcreat, Donaghenry, Donaghmore, Kildress, Killeeshil and Pomeroy.

Stewart. Survey, with tenants' names, 1767. NLI Ms. 9627. Major tenants only. Covering areas in the civil parish of Derryloran.

Stewart. Survey, with tenants' names, 1730. NLI Ms. 8734 (1). Major tenants only. Covering areas in the civil parishes of Carnteel, Clonfeacle and Killeeshil.

Stewart, John. Leases and rentals, 1789–1842. PRONI D1021. Covering areas in the civil parish of Termonmaguirk.

Story. Rentals, 1791–1830. PRONI MIC42/1. Covering areas in the civil parish of Clogher.

Verner. Rentals, 1788–92, 1820–32, 1854–64, 1860–68. PRONI D236/487A-C, E. Covering areas in the civil parishes of Carnteel, Donaghmore, Errigal Keerogue, Killeeshil and Killyman.

Verner/Wingfield. Rental. PRONI D/2538, 1830. Covering areas in the civil parishes of Cappagh, Clogherny, Donaghmore, Errigal Keerogue, Killeeshil and Termonmaguirk. May cover further parishes.

Waring Maxwell, John. Rent rolls, 1800. PRONI D2559/3/8–11. Covering areas in the civil parish of Clogher.

Waring Maxwell, Robert. Rent rolls, 1838–43. PRONI D2559/3/17, 20, 21, 23, 24. Covering areas in the civil parish of Clogher.

WATERFORD

Census returns and substitutes

1542–1650	Freemen of Waterford. *IG*, Vol. 5, No. 5, 1978.
1641	Testimonies of 285 witnesses to the 1641 Rebellion. Online: 1641.
1641	Houses and tenants, Waterford city. *JCHAS*, Vol. 51, 1946. Also NAI, Quit Rent Office Papers.
1641	Book of Survey and Distribution. NLI Ms. 970.
1659	Pender's 'Census'. Reprinted GPC, 1997; IMC, 2002. LDS film 924648.
1662	Subsidy Roll of Co. Waterford. *AH*, 30, 1982, pp. 47–96.
1663	Inhabitants of Waterford city, including occupations. *JCHAS*, Vol. 51.
1664–6	*Civil Survey*, Vol. 6.
1700	Members of some Waterford guilds. *JWSEIAS*, Vol. 7, 1901, pp. 61–5.
1703	Minister's money account, Clonmel. *AH*, 34.
1766	Killoteran householders. NAI Parl. Ret. 1413; GO 684; LDS film 100158.
1772	Hearth Money Rolls. For parts of Co. Waterford only. *JWSEIAS*, Vol. 15, 1912.

1775	Gentry of Co. Waterford. *JWSEIAS*, Vol. 16, No. 1, 1913.
1778	Inhabitants of Waterford city. *Freeman's Journal*, 29 October 1778, 5 November 1778.
1792	Leading Catholics of Waterford. *IA*, Vol. 8, No. 11.
1792	Rent and arrears due to Waterford Corporation, 1. NLI P 3000.
1807	Waterford city voters. *IA*, Vol. 8, No. 11.
1821	Townland of Callaghane, parish of Ballygunner, *Decies*, 16. Extracts from Waterford city, *IG*, 1968/9. Clonmel, NAI m 242(2). Index to Waterford city, Veale, *Extract*. Online: IGPweb Waterford.
1823–38	Tithe Books.
1839	Waterford city Polling List. *IG*, 8 (2), 1991, pp. 275–89.
1841	Memorial of inhabitants of Waterford city. More than 1,500 names and signatures, unindexed. NAI OP 1841/43.
1843	Voters. NAI OP 1843/65.
1847	Principal fishermen, Ring. Alcock, *Facts . . .*
1848–51	Griffith's Valuation. Online: Askaboutireland; also Waterford Library.
1848–9	Smith O'Brien Petition. More than 3,000 names for Waterford city. Online: FindMyPast
1864–1901	Civil death registers. Online: Waterford Library.
1901	Census. Online: NAI.
1911	Census. Online: NAI.

Online

1641	<www.1641.tcd.ie>	
Askaboutireland	<www.askaboutireland.ie>	
Celtic Cousins	<www.celticcousins.net>	Walsh-Kelly parish extracts
Hayes, John	<www.failteromhat.com>	
IGPweb Waterford	<www.igp-web.com/Waterford>	
NAI	<www.census.nationalarchives.ie>	
Waterford Archives	<www.waterfordcoco.ie>	
Waterford Historical and Archaeological Society	<www.iol.ie/~mnoc/forHSoc.html>	
Waterford Library	<www.waterfordcountylibrary.ie>	

Publications

Local histories etc.

Abbesyside Reference Committee, *Abbeyside reference archive*, Abbeyside: Abbeyside Reference Committee, 1995. NLI, 12 p.

Brennan, T.A., *The Gearons of Janeville, Tallow, county Waterford*, New York: 1966. NLI GO 466, 12 leaves.

Broderick, Eugene, *Waterford's Anglicans: religion and politics, 1819–72*, Newcastle: Cambridge Scholars, 2009. NLI, 394 p.

Butler, M., *A history of the barony of Gaultier . . . With a map of Gaultier*, Waterford: Downey & Co., 1913. NLI Ir 94141 b 1, 217 p.

Cowman, Des, *The Famine in Waterford, 1845–50: Teacht na bPrátaí Dubha*, Dublin: Geography Publications, 1995. Associate editor, Donald Brady. NLI, Ir 94141 f 2, 344 p.

—— *The making and breaking of a mining community: the Copper Coast, Co. Waterford, 1825–75*, Dublin: Mining Heritage Trust of Ireland, 2006. NLI, 188 p.

—— *Perceptions and promotions: the role of Waterford Chamber of Commerce, 1787–1987*, Waterford: Waterford Chamber of Commerce, 1988. NLI, 76 p.

Cuffe, Major O.T., *Records of the Waterford Militia, 1584–1885*, London: 1885. NLI Ir 355942 c 3, 112 p.

Desmond, Michael, *Ballymacarbry and Fourmilewater: a history from 1650 to 1850*, Clonmel: the author, 2004. NLI, 58 p.

Dickson, David, *Old world colony: Cork and South Munster, 1630–1830*, Cork: Cork University Press, 2005. NLI, 726 p.

Downey, Edmund, *The story of Waterford to the middle of the 18th century*, Kilkenny: 1891. NLI Ir 94191.

Farrell, Noel, *County Waterford, Dungarvan family roots: exploring family origins in Dungarvan*, Longford: Noel Farrell, 2001. NLI 3B 184, 48 p.

Fitzpatrick, Thomas, *Waterford during the Civil War, 1641–53*, Waterford: Downey, 1912. NLI Ir 94106 f 5, 144 p.

Fraher, William, *Desperate haven: the Poor Law, famine and aftermath in Dungarvan Union*, Dungarvan: Dungarvan Museum Society, 1996. NLI Ir 94141 d 6, 415 p.

—— *A guide to historic Dungarvan: incorporating a town trail*, Dungarvan: Dungarvan Museum Society, 1991. NLI Ir 941 p 103 (2), 48 p.

Hansard, Joseph, *The history, topography and antiquities of Waterford . . .* [1870], Waterford: Waterford County Council, 1997. Edited by Donal Brady. NLI, Ir 94141 h 3, 300 p.

Harvey, N., *Parochial history of Waterford and Lismore during the 18th and 19th centuries*, 1912. NLI Ir 94141 p 1, 290 p.

Hore, H.F., *The Social State of the Southern and Eastern Counties of Ireland in the Sixteenth Century*, Dublin: 1870. NLI Ir 794105 r 2 [See 'Carlow'].

Hunt, Tom, *Portlaw, County Waterford, 1825–76: portrait of an industrial village and its cotton industry*, Dublin: Irish Academic Press, 2000. NLI, 80 p.

IGRS, *Tombstone inscriptions, Vol. 2*, Dublin: IGRS Tombstone Committee, 2001. NLI 3B 29, c.900 p.

Keohan, Edmond, *Illustrated history of Dungarvan*, Waterford: Waterford News, 1924. NLI Ir 94141 k 1, 156 p.

Kerr, Elizabeth M.F., 'Methodist New Chappell, Waterford', *IG*, 10, 4, 2001, pp. 396–400.

McEneaney, Eamonn, *A History of Waterford and its mayors from the 12th century to the 20th century*, Waterford: Waterford Corporation, 1995. NLI Ir 94141 h 2, 240 p.

McRonald, Malcolm, *The Irish boats, Vol. 2: Liverpool to Cork and Waterford*, Stroud, Glos.: Tempus, 2006. NLI, 256 p.

Nolan, W., *Waterford: History and Society*, Dublin: Geography Publications, 1986. NLI Ir 94141 w 6, 754 p.

O'Brien, Niall, *Blackwater and Bride: navigation and trade, 7,000 BC to 2007*, Ballyduff Upper: Niall O'Brien Publishing, 2008. NLI, 562 p.

Ó Cadhla, Stiofán, *The holy well tradition: the pattern of St Declan, Ardmore, County Waterford, 1800–2000*, Dublin: Four Courts Press, 2002. NLI, 63 p.

Ochille, F., *The Holy City of Ardmore, Co. Waterford*, Youghal: J.W. Lindsay, 1852. NLI, Dix Youghal [1852], 73 p.

Ó Dálaigh, Brian, *Irish villages: studies in local history*, Dublin: Four Courts Press, 2003. Co-editors, Liam Clare and Karina Holton. Portlaw. NLI.

O'Donnell, Seán, *Clonmel, 1840–1900: anatomy of an Irish town*, Dublin: Geography Publications, 2000. NLI, 337 p.

Ó Fiannusa, Pádraig, *Tuath Chois Móire—Cois Bríde: a miscellany of local history and tradition, local toponymy . . .* Ceapach Chuinn: Ó Fiannusa, 1980. NLI Ir 94141 o 2, 151 p.

O'Sullivan, Michael, *Holy Trinity Church, Ballybricken, Waterford city: memorial inscriptions*, Waterford: Michael O'Sullivan, 1998. NLI Ir 9295 h 1, 119 p.

—— *Kilbarry Graveyard, Waterford, Ireland: memorial inscriptions*, Waterford: Michael O'Sullivan, 1995. NLI Ir 9295 p, 12 p.

—— *Killotteran, Co. Waterford: memorial inscriptions*, Waterford: Michael O'Sullivan, 1995. NLI Ir 9295 p, 12 p.

—— *Lisnakill Graveyard, Co. Waterford: memorial inscriptions*, Waterford: Michael O'Sullivan, 1999. NLI Ir 9295 p, 10 p.

—— *Memorial inscriptions and obituaries, Abbey Church, Kilculliheen, Waterford*, Waterford: Michael O'Sullivan, 1995. NLI, 235 p.

—— *Memorial Inscriptions, Quaker Cemetery, Newtown, Waterford City, Ireland*, Waterford: Michael O'Sullivan, 1996. NLI, 69 p.

Power, V. Rev. P., *A short history of County Waterford*, Waterford: Waterford News, 1933. NLI Ir 94141 p 2, 98 p.

—— *Waterford and Lismore: A Compendious History of the Dioceses*, Dublin: Cork University Press, 1937. NLI Ir 274141 p 1, 402 p.

—— Power-O'Shee papers (Gardenmorris, Co. Waterford), *AH*, 20, pp. 216–58.

Pyke, D., *Parish Priests and Churches of St Mary's, Clonmel*, 1984. NLI Ir 274 p 40, 54 p.

Reilly, Joseph F., *Reilly of Ballintlea, Kilrossanty, Co. Waterford . . . with American descendants*, Hartland, Vt.: the author, 1981. NLI Ir 9292 r 21, 42 p.

Ryland, R.H., *The history, topography and antiquities of the county and city of Waterford*, London: J. Murray, 1824. Reprinted Kilkenny: Wellbrook, 1982. NLI Ir 9141 r 1, 419 p.

Smith, Charles, *The ancient and present state of the county and city of Waterford: being a natural, civil, ecclesiastical, historical and topographical description thereof*, Dublin: A. Reilly, 1774. Reprinted Cork: Mercier Press, 1969. NLI Ir 94141 s 1.

Society of Friends, Waterford, *Facts from the fisheries: contained in four quarterly reports from the Ring District, County Waterford*, Waterford: 1848. NLI Dix Waterford 1848, 48 p.

Taylor, Andy, *Echoes from a seashell*, the author, 1990. Tramore. NLI, Ir 94141.t.2, 222 p.

—— *Ussher Papers (Cappagh, Co. Waterford)*, AH, 15, 63–78.

Veale, T., *Extract from 1821 census, Waterford city: surname index*, Dublin: Tom Veale, 1993. 40 p. NLI Ir 94141 p.

—— *Index of Surnames in 'The New Commercial Directory for the cities of Waterford and Kilkenny and the towns of Clonmel, Carrick-on-Suir, New Ross and Carlow'*, Dublin: Veale, 1996. NLI Ir 9414 p.

—— *Richard Lucas, 1788: directory extract for south east of Ireland*, Dublin: Veale, 1995. NLI Ir 9414 v.

Walsh, Joseph J., *Waterford's yesterdays and tomorrows and an outline of Waterford history*, Waterford: 1968. NLI, Ir 94141 w 3, 196 p.

—— *Waterford Historical Society Proceedings*. Newspaper cuttings relating to Waterford in 9 vols. NLI ILB 94141.

Watson, Col. S.J., *A Dinner of Herbs: a history of Old St Mary's Church, Clonmel*, Clonmel: Watson Books, 1988. Tipperary County Library 284.094193, 259 p. Cashel Library.

White, James (ed.), *My Clonmel Scrap Book*, Clonmel: Tentmaker Publications, 1995. Reprint of 1907 edition. NLI Ir 94142 w 3, 376 p.

Young, John M., *A maritime and general history of Dungarvan, 1690–1978*, Dungarvan: the author, 1978. NLI Ir 94141 y 1, 87 p.

Local journals
Decies. NLI Ir 9414 d 5. Online: Waterford Library.
Journal of the Waterford and South-East of Ireland Archaeological Society. NLI Ir 794105 w 1.
Online: Waterford Library.

Directories
1788	Richard Lucas, *General Directory of the Kingdom of Ireland*. NLI Pos. 3729. Reprinted in Veale, *Lucas, IG*, 1965, 1966, 1967, 1968.
1809	Holden, *Triennal Directory*.
1820	J. Pigot, *Commercial Directory of Ireland*. PRONI; NLI Ir 9141 p 107; LDS film 962702 item 1.
1824	J. Pigot & Co., *City of Dublin and Hibernian Provincial Directory*. NLI; LDS film 451787. Online: Waterford Library; Hayes.
1839	T. Shearman, *New Commercial Directory for the cities of Waterford and Kilkenny, Towns of Clonmel, Carrick-on-Suir, New Ross and Carlow*. Indexed in Veale, *Index*. Online: Waterford Library.
1839	T.S. Harvey, *Waterford Directory*.

1846 Slater's *National Commercial Directory of Ireland*. PRONI; NLI LO; LDS film 1696703 item 3. Online: Hayes; Waterford Library.

1856 Slater, *Royal National Commercial Directory of Ireland*. NLI; LDS film 1472360 item 1. Online: Waterford Library.

1866 T.S. Harvey, *Waterford Almanac and Directory*. Archive CD Books Ireland.

1867 Henry and Coughlan's *General Directory of Cork and Munster*. Online: FindMyPast.

1869 Newenham Harvey, *Waterford Directory*. Waterford City Library.

1870 Slater, *Directory of Ireland*. NLI.

1877 Harvey's *Waterford Almanack and Street Directory for 1877*. Online: Waterford Library.

1881 Slater, *Royal National Commercial Directory of Ireland*. NLI. Online: Waterford Library.

1884 George Henry Bassett, *Kilkenny City and County Guide and Directory*.

1886 Francis Guy, *Postal Directory of Munster*. NLI Ir 91414 g 8; LDS film 1559399 item 8.

1894 Slater, *Royal Commercial Directory of Ireland*. NLI.

Gravestone inscriptions

Affane: Affane Hunter, C of I, *IG*, Vol. 2, No. 9, 1952.
Ballygunner: Ballygunnertemple, IGRS, Vol. 2.
Ballynakill: C of I, IGRS, Vol. 2.
Ballynakill: Ballynakill House, IGRS, Vol. 2.
Clashmore: Clashmore town, C of I, *IG*, Vol. 2, No. 8, 1950.
Corbally: Corbally Beg, RC, IGRS, Vol. 2.
Crooke: RC, IGRS, Vol. 2.
Drumcannon: IGRS, Vol. 2.
Dunhill: IGRS, Vol. 2.
Dysert: Churchtown, C of I, *Decies*, No. 25, 1984.
Faithlegg: Coolbunnia (Faithlegg?), RC, IGRS, Vol. 2.
Fenoagh, Curraghnagarragha: IGRS, Vol. 2.
Islandikane: Islandikane South, IGRS, Vol. 2.
Kilbarry: IGRS, Vol. 2, also O'Sullivan, *Kilbarry Graveyard*.
Kilburne: Knockeen, IGRS, Vol. 2.
Kilculliheen: Abbeylands (C of I), O'Sullivan, *Memorial inscriptions*.
Kill St Lawrence: IGRS, Vol. 2.
Killea: Commons (Killea Old?), RC, IGRS, Vol. 2.
Killoteran: C of I, IGRS, Vol. 2, also O'Sullivan, *Killoteran, Co. Waterford*.
Kilmeadan: Coolfin (Kilmeadan?), IGRS, Vol. 2.
Lisnakill: IGRS, Vol. 2, also O'Sullivan, *Lisnakill Graveyard*.
Mothel: C of I, *Decies*, Nos. 38, 39, 40, 41, 42.
Newcastle: Ardeenloun East (Newcastle?), IGRS, Vol. 2.
Rathgormuck: *Decies*, No. 37.

Reisk: IGRS, Vol. 2.

St John's Without, Lower Newton Road (Quaker), O'Sullivan, *Quaker Cemetery.*

John's Lane (Quaker), O'Sullivan, *Quaker Cemetery.*

Stradbally: Faha Chapel of Ease, *Decies,* No. 17, 1981.

Stradbally: *Decies,* No. 16, 1981.

Trinity Without: Waterford, Chapel Lane, RC (Ballybricken), Power, *Catholic Records,* also O'Sullivan, *Holy Trinity Church, Ballybricken.*

Whitechurch: Ballykennedy (Whitechurch?), C of I, IA, NLI Ir 9205 i 3, Vol. 5, No. 1, 1973.

Estate records

[**No landlord given**]. Rentals, 1849, *Decies,* No. 27, 1984. All tenants. Covering areas in the civil parishes of Lismore and Mocollop.

Bellew. Tenants list, 1760, JWSEIAS, Vol. 19, No. 4, 1911. All tenants. Covering areas in the civil parish of Dungarvan.

Boyle/Cavendish. The Lismore Papers. Rentals, valuations, lease books and account books for the estates of the Earls of Cork and the Dukes of Devonshire, 1570–1870. NLI Mss. 6136–898. Generally covering only major tenants. A detailed listing is given in NLI Special List 15 (Online). Covering townlands in the civil parishes of Dungarvan, Lismore and Mocollop. May cover areas in other parishes. See also 'Lismore Castle Estate Emigration Database'. Online: Waterford Archives.

Chearnley family. Rental, 1752. NLI, Ms. 8811. Major tenants only. Covering areas in the civil parishes of Lismore and Mocollop.

Crown lands. Rental, 1784, NAI, M.3199. All tenants. Covering areas in the civil parishes of Crooke, Faithlegg and Kill St Nicholas.

Cunningham, Patrick. LEC Rental, 1869, NAI, M 1834. Coverage unclear. Covering areas in the civil parish of Fenoagh.

Dawson, Richard. Rental, 1781–1901. NLI, Ms. 3148. Major tenants only. Covering areas in the civil parishes of Colligan, Dungarvan, Fews, Kilgobnet, Kilrossanty, Lismore and Mocollop, Modelligo and Templemichael.

Fox, James. Rental, 1745–73. NLI, Pos. 4065. Major tenants only. Covering areas in the civil parishes of Drumcannon and Kilbarry.

Lane Fox, George. Tenants list, 1857, *Decies,* No. 26, 1984. All tenants. Covering areas in the civil parish of Kilbarry.

Mansfield, John. Rent ledger, 1783–94. NLI, Ms. 9633. Major tenants only. Covering areas in the civil parishes of Clashmore, Clonea, Dungarvan, Kilmolash, Lisgenan or Grange, Modelligo and Rathgormuck.

Middleton, Lord. Estate survey, 1784. NLI, Ms. 9977. Coverage unclear. Covering areas in the civil parish of Kilronan.

Newport-Bolton family. Rental, 1840–76. NLI, Ms. 8488. All tenants. Covering areas in the civil parishes of Drumcannon and Kilmacomb.

Osborne family. Rentals, 1850, NAI, D. 6057. All tenants. Rentals, 1863–77, NAI, M. 3052. All tenants. Covering areas in the civil parishes of Clashmore, Colligan,

Dungarvan, Kilbarrymeaden, Kilgobnet, Killaloan, Kilronan, Kilrossanty, Monksland, Rathgormuck, Ringagonagh, St Mary's, Clonmel, Stradbally and Whitechurch.

Power, Anne. Rental, 1853, NAI, M.1830. All tenants. Covering areas in the civil parish of Dysert.

St George, Charles Manners. Rentals and accounts, 1842–71. NLI, Mss. 4001–4022. All tenants. Covering areas in the civil parishes of Affane, Fews and Whitechurch.

Sargeant, Francis. Rentals, 1798. NLI, Ms. 10,072. All tenants. Covering areas in the civil parish of Clashmore.

WESTMEATH

Census returns and substitutes

1640	Irish Proprietors in Moate and District, in Cox, *Moate*.
1641	Book of Survey and Distribution. NLI Ms. 965.
1659	Pender's 'Census'. Reprinted GPC, 1997; IMC, 2002. LDS film 924648.
1666	Hearth Money Roll of Mullingar. *Franciscan College Journal*, 1950.
1726–7	Protestant householders, Abbeylara, Abbeyshrule, Ardagh, Clonbroney, Clongesh, Kilcommock, Killashee, Rathreagh, Shrule and Taghshiny (Co. Longford), Rathsapick and Russagh (Co. Westmeath). List compiled for the distribution of religious books. NAI M1502.
1731	Protestants, Shrule and Rathreagh (Co. Longford), Rathaspick (Co. Westmeath). RCBL GS 2/7/3/25.
1749	St Peter's, Athlone. NAI MFS 6.
1761–88	Freeholders. NLI Mss. 787/8.
1763	Poll Book. GO 443.
1766	Russagh. LDS film 258517. Online: PRONI name search.
1796	Spinning-Wheel Premium List. 1,250 names for Co. Westmeath. Online: Hayes.
1802–1803	Protestants in the parishes of Ballyloughloe, Castletown Delvin, Clonarney, Drumraney, Enniscoffey, Kilbridepass, Killalon, Kilcleagh, Killough, Killua, Killucan, Leney, Moyliscar and Rathconnell. *IA*, 1973.
1823–38	Tithe Books.
1832	Voters. *IG*, Vol. 5, No. 2 and 6; Vol. 6, No. 1 (1975, 1979, 1980).
1834	Census transcript, Rosemount area. Sheehan, *Kilcrumreragh*.
1835	Tubber parish. NLI Pos. 1994.
1837	Marksmen (i.e. illiterate voters), Athlone borough. *Parliamentary Papers, 1837: Reports from Committees*, Vol. 2 (1), Appendix A.
1843	Westmeath voters. NAI OP 1843/60.
1854	Griffith's Valuation. Online: Askaboutireland.
1855	Partial census of Streete parish, c.1855. NLI Pos. 4236.

1861	Athlone Voters. Westmeath County Library; also LDS film 1279285.
1863–71	Census for the parish of Rathaspick and Russagh. PRONI T.2786.
1901	Census. Online: NAI.
1911	Census. Online: NAI.

Online

Askaboutireland	*<www.askaboutireland.ie>*
Hayes, John	*<www.failteromhat.com>*
Leitrim-Roscommon	*<www.leitrim-roscommon.com>*
NAI	*<www.census.nationalarchives.ie>*
PRONI name search	*<www.proni.gov.uk>*
Rootsweb Westmeath	*<www.rootsweb.com/~irlwem2>*

Publications

Local histories etc.

Athlone: Materials from printed sources relating to the history of Athlone and surrounding areas, 1699–1899. NLI, Mss. 1543–7. Including an index volume.

Genealogies of the grand jurors of Co. Westmeath, 1727–1853. NLI Ir 94131 g 1.

Andrews, J.H., *Irish Historic Towns Atlas 5: Mullingar*, Dublin: RIA, 1992. NLI.

Brady, J., *A short history of the parishes of the diocese of Meath, 1867–1944.* NLI Ir 94132 b 2.

Brady, Rev. John, *The parish of Mullingar*, Mullingar: the parish, 1962. NLI Ir 274108 p 12, 31 p.

Clarke, Desmond, 'Athlone, a bibliographical study', *An Leabharlann*, No. 10, 1952, pp. 138–9.

Clarke, Joe, *Coosan school, 1836–1988: school memories and local history*, 1988. NLI, 48 p.

Clarke, M.V., Register of the Priory of the Blessed Virgin Mary at Tristernagh, IMC. NLI Ir 271 c 22.

Cox, Liam, *Moate, Co. Westmeath: a history of the town and district*, Athlone: 1981. NLI Ir 994131 c 2; also LDS film 1279227.

Egan, Oliver, *Tyrellspass, Past and Present*, Tyrellspass: Tyrellspass Town Development Committee, 1986. NLI Ir 271 c 22, 212 p.

Farrell, Mary, *Mullingar: essays on the history of a midlands town in the 19th century*, Mullingar: Westmeath County Library, 2002. NLI, 207 p.

Farrell, Noel, *Exploring Family Origins in Mullingar Town*, Longford: Noel Farrell, 2005, 48 p.

—— *Exploring Family Origins in Athlone Town*, Longford: Noel Farrell, 2006. NLI, 48 p.

Grouden, Breda, *The contribution of the Clibborn family to Moate town and district*, Moate: Moate Historical Society, 1990. NLI Ir 941 P 108(4), 40 p.

Healy, John, *History of the Diocese of Meath*, Dublin: 1908, 2 vols.

Hunt, Tom, *Sport and society in Victorian Ireland: the case of Westmeath*, Cork: Cork University Press, 2007. NLI, 357 p.

IGRS, *Tombstone inscriptions, Vol. 2*, Dublin: IGRS Tombstone Committee, 2001. NLI 3B 29, c.900 p.

Keaney, Marian, *Westmeath Local Studies: a guide to sources*, Mullingar: Longford-Westmeath Joint Library Committee, 1982. NLI Ir 94131 k 1, 50 p.

—— *Athlone: bridging the centuries*, Mullingar: Westmeath County Council, 1991. Co-editor, Gearóid Ó Briain. NLI Ir 94131 a 2.

Lenehan, Jim, *Politics and Society in Athlone, 1830–85: A Rotten Borough*, Dublin: Irish Academic Press, 1999. NLI.

MacNamee, James J., *History of the Diocese of Ardagh*, Dublin: Browne & Nolan, 1954. NLI Ir 274131 m 5, 858 p.

McCormack, Stan, *Kilbeggan, 2000: Millennium book of photographs*, Kilbeggan: Kilbeggan Community Group, 1999. Westmeath County Library 941.815, 186 p.

—— *Kilbeggan, Past and Present*, Kilbeggan: the author, 2006. Westmeath County Library 941.815, 328 p.

—— *Against the Odds: Kilbeggan Races, 1840–1994*, Kilbeggan: the author, 1995. Westmeath County Library 798.450941, 254 p.

—— *Westmeath, 1798: a Kilbeggan rebellion*, Westmeath: the authors, 1998. Co-author, Kathleen Flynn. NLI Ir 94131 f 2, 172 p.

Monahan, Rev. J., *Records Relating to the Diocese of Ardagh and Clonmacnoise*, Dublin: M.H. Gill & Son, 1886. NLI Ir 27413 m 3, 400 p.

Moyvoughley Historical Committee, *Moyvoughley and its hinterland*, Moyvoughley: 2000. NLI Ir 94131 m 5, 400 p.

Murtagh, H., *Irish midland studies: essays in commemoration of N.W. English*, Athlone: Old Athlone Society, 1980. NLI Ir 941 m 58, 255 p.

—— *Irish Historic Towns Atlas, 6: Athlone*, Dublin: RIA, 1994. NLI ILB 941 p (13) 3.

—— *Athlone besieged*, Athlone: Temple Printing Co., 1991. Eyewitness and other contemporary accounts of the Siege of Athlone (1690 and 1691). NLI Ir 94107 p 21(1).

—— *Athlone: history and settlement to 1800*, Athlone: Old Athlone Society, 2000. NLI Ir 94131 m 6, 256 p.

O'Brien, Brendan, *Athlone Workhouse and the Famine*, Athlone: Old Athlone Society, 1995. Edited by Gearóid O'Brien. NLI Ir 300 p 207(8).

O'Brien, Gearóid, *St Mary's Parish, Athlone: a history*, Longford: St Mel's Trust, 1989. NLI Ir 27412 o 3, 213 p.

—— *Clonbonny: a centre of learning*, Athlone: 1995. NLI Ir 300 p 207(9), 64 p.

O'Brien, Seamus, *Famine and community in Mullingar Poor Law Union, 1845–9: mud cabins and fat bullocks*, Dublin and Portland, Oreg.: Irish Academic Press, 1999. NLI Ir 94132 o 13, 64 p.

O'Donovan, John, *Ordnance Survey Letters, Westmeath (1838)*, Dublin: 1926. NLI, Ir 9141 O 22, 2 vols.

Paterson, J. (ed.), *Diocese of Meath and Kildare: an historical guide*, 1981. NLI Ir 941 p 75.

Ryan, Hazel A., *Athlone Abbey Graveyard Inscriptions*, Mullingar: Longford-Westmeath Joint Library Committee, 1987. NLI Ir 9295 p 2(1).

Sheehan, Jeremiah, *Westmeath, as others saw it: excerpts from the writings of 35 authors, who recorded . . . observations on various aspects of Westmeath and its people, from 900 AD to the present*, Moate: J. Sheehan, 1982. NLI Ir 94131 S 5, 224 p.

—— *A pre-famine survey of Kilcrumreragh: A unique social document of Rosemount, 1834*, Moate: Moate Historical Society, 1997.

—— *Worthies of Westmeath: a biographical dictionary of brief lives of famous Westmeath people*, Westmeath: Wellbrook Press, 1987. Westmeath County Library 920.041815, 130 p.

SS. Peter and Paul Foróige, *Our local history: Streamstown, Horseleap and Boher*, Kilbeggan: Foróige, 1990. NLI Ir 94131.0.4, 246 p.

Stokes, George T., *Athlone, the Shannon and Lough Ree*, Dublin and Athlone: 1897. NLI Ir 91413 S 1.

Tormey, John, *Rathaspic and Russagh: a history of the parish*, Mullingar: Tormey & Wallace, 1983. Co-author, Peter Wallace. NLI Ir 94131 t 2, 176 p.

Upton, Upton Papers, RIA. NLI Pos. 1997. Wills and deeds mainly relating to Co. Westmeath. Originals in RIA; microfilm in NLI.

Woods, James, *Annals of Westmeath*, Dublin: Sealy, Bryers & Walker, 1907. NLI Ir 94131 W 1, 345 p.

Local journals
Ardagh and Clonmacnoise Historical Society Journal. NLI Ir 794105.
Irish Midland Studies. NLI Ir 941 m 58.
Journal of the Old Athlone Society. NLI Ir 94131 o 1.
Ríocht na Midhe. NLI Ir 94132 r 1.

Directories
1820	J. Pigot, *Commercial Directory of Ireland*. PRONI; NLI Ir 9141 p 107; LDS film 962702 item 1.
1824	J. Pigot & Co., *City of Dublin and Hibernian Provincial Directory*. NLI; LDS film 451787. Online: Hayes.
1846	Slater's *National Commercial Directory of Ireland*. PRONI; NLI LO; LDS film 1696703 item 3. Online: Hayes.
1856	Slater, *Royal National Commercial Directory of Ireland*. NLI; LDS film 1472360 item 1.
1870	Slater, *Directory of Ireland*. NLI.
1881	Slater, *Royal National Commercial Directory of Ireland*. NLI. Online: FindMyPast.
1894	Slater, *Royal Commercial Directory of Ireland*. NLI.

Gravestone inscriptions

Parts (at least) of eight Co. Westmeath graveyards are transcribed at <*www. interment.net*>.

Ardnurcher or Horseleap, Ardnurcher. Online: Rootsweb Westmeath.
Ballyloughloe, Labaun (Mount Temple?), C of I, *ia*, Vol. 4, No. 2, 1972.
Carrick, GO Ms. 622, p. 171.
Foyran, Castletown (Finnea), GO Ms. 622, p. 107.
Kilcleagh, Killomenaghan, Cox, *Moate.*
Kilcleagh, Moate, Main St, C of I, Cox, *Moate.*
—— Moate, Main St, Quaker, Cox, *Moate.*
Killua, French, *Monumental Inscriptions.*
Mullingar, Church St, C of I, DSHC.
St Feighin's, Fore, RC, IGRS, Vol. 2.
St Mary's, Athlone, Church St, C of I, NLI Pos. 5309 (with parish registers).
—— Athlone, Abbey ruins, Ryan, *Athlone Abbey*, IGRS, Vol. 2.
Stonehall, C of I, GO Ms. 622, p. 183.
Street, Barradrum (Street?), C of I, *Ríocht na Midhe*, Vol. 4, No. 3, 1969.

Estate records

[**No landlord given**]. Rent accounts, 1766–82. NLI Ms. 3157. Major tenants only. Covering areas in the civil parish of Kilcleagh.

[**No landlord given**]. Rental, 1831–3. NAI M.5872. Most tenants. Covering areas in the civil parish of Foyran.

Adams, Randal. Maps, 1697. *AH*, No. 10, 1941. Principally major tenants. Covering areas in the civil parishes of Ardnurcher or Horseleap, Castletownkindalen, Churchtown, Mullingar and Rathconrath.

Boyd, G.A. Rentals, 1842–54. NLI Ms. 3108. All tenants. Covering areas in the civil parishes of Ardnurcher or Horseleap, Ballymore, Castlelost, Castletownkindalen, Clonfad, Drumraney, Dysart, Kilbride, Kilcumreragh, Lynn, Moylisker, Mullingar, Newtown, Pass of Kilbride, Rahugh, Rathconnell and Rathconrath.

Buckingham, Duke of. Estate sale and map, 1848. All tenants. NLI Ms. 14.A.20. Covering areas in the civil parishes of Foyran, Kilcleagh, Lickbla and Rathgarve.

Caulfield, Col. W. Maps, 1811–37. NLI 21.F.125. Principally major tenants. Covering areas in the civil parishes of Piercetown and Rathconrath.

Clonbrock. Rental, 1624–95. NLI Ms. 35,722. Major tenants only. Covering areas in the civil parishes of Ballymore, Drumraney and Killare.

Dobbyn, George. Rental, 1849. NLI D 26410. Most tenants. Covering areas in the civil parishes of Mullingar and Rathconnell.

Eustace, Charles Stannard. Map, 1847. NLI 21.F.80 (27). Most tenants. Covering areas in the civil parishes of Ballymore, Kilcleagh and Templepatrick.

Gibbons, James. Valuation, 1818–21. NAI M6994. Coverage unclear. Covering areas in the civil parishes of Castlelost and Kilbride.

Harman. Tenants' names, 1846. NAI M.1865. All tenants. Covering areas in the civil parish of St Mary's, Athlone.

Harman, Mrs Frances. Rent roll, 1757–8. NAI M.1311. All tenants. Covering areas in the civil parish of Noughaval.

Hinds, George. Map, 1843. NLI 16.J.10 (8). Principally major tenants. Covering areas in the civil parish of Castletowndelvin.

Hodson, Sir George. Rent ledger, 1840–49. NLI Ms. 16409. Principally major tenants. Covering areas in the civil parish of Mullingar.

Hopkins, Sir Francis. Rent Rolls, 1795–1839. NLI Ms. 3195. Major tenants only. Covering areas in the civil parish of Killua.

Ireland, Sophia Mary. Rental, 1851. NAI M5595. Most tenants. Covering areas in the civil parish of Noughaval.

Jones, Walter. Map of the lands of Anaugh, 1752. NLI 21.F.80 (1). Coverage unclear. Covering areas in the civil parish of St Mary's, Athlone.

Lyons. Rent roll and timber accounts, 1786–92. NLI Ms. 4249. All tenants. Covering areas in the civil parishes of Killulagh and Mullingar.

Lyons, John Charles. Map, 1834. NLI 21.F.80 (15). All tenants. Covering areas in the civil parishes of Lynn and Mullingar.

Magan, William Henry. Maps, 1848. NLI Ms. 14.A.27. All tenants. Covering townlands in the civil parishes of Ardnurcher or Horseleap, Castletowndelvin, Castletownkindalen, Churchtown, Conry, Kilcleagh, Kilcumreragh, Killare, Kilmacnevan, Lynn and Rathconrath.

Maunsell, George Meares. Map of part of the lands of Ballymore, 1827. NLI 16.J.10(6). Most tenants.

Meares. Papers, 1650–1750. NLI Ms. 33,003. Coverage unclear. Covering areas in the civil parishes of Ballymorin, Killare, Piercetown, Rathconrath and Templepatrick.

Moland, Thomas. Maps, 1782. NLI Ms. 32,505. Major tenants only. Covering areas in the civil parishes of Lynn and Mullingar.

Nugent. Rent accounts, 1736–62. NLI Ms. 5991. Major tenants only. Covering areas in the civil parish of Rathconnell.

Oxmantown, Lord. Accounts, 1798–9. NAI M.1279. Major tenants only. Covering townlands in the civil parishes of Drumraney, Noughaval and St Mary's, Athlone.

Pratt, John. Accounts of rents, 1710–39. NLI Mss. 2587, 5247. Coverage unclear. Covering areas in the civil parishes of Killucan, Mullingar and Rathconnell.

Reynell. Rentals, 1834–48. NLI Ms. 5990. All tenants. Covering areas in the civil parishes of Killua, Killulagh, Mullingar and Rathconnell.

Rochfort. Poor Rent, 1851–4. NAI M.1262. Most tenants. Covering areas in the civil parishes of Columbkille, Kilcumreragh, Killoe and Kilmanaghan.

Rosse, Countess Dowager of. Rents and arrears, 1836–7. NAI M.1291, 1301. All tenants. Covering areas in the civil parishes of Drumraney, Noughaval and St Mary's, Athlone.

Smyth, Ralph. Maps and surveys, 1783–1813. NLI Ms. 2799. Principally major tenants. Covering areas in the civil parishes of Durrow, Dysart, Mullingar, Portloman, Rahugh and Templeoran.

Smythe, Ralph. Rent ledger, 1775–9. NLI Ms. 9986. All tenants. Covering areas in the civil parishes of Faughalstown and St Feighin's.

Smythe, William Barlow. Rent book, 1835–47. NLI Ms. 9982. All tenants. Covering areas in the civil parishes of Faughalstown and St Feighin's.

Smythe, William Barlowe. Map, 1831–6. NLI Ms. 83. Most tenants. Covering areas in the civil parishes of Faughalstown, Kilcumny and St Feighin's.

Smythe, William. Map and survey, 1831–40. NLI 21.F.80 (3). Coverage unclear. Covering areas in the civil parishes of Faughalstown and St Feighin's.

Smythe, William. Rent ledger, 1802–1809. NLI Ms. 9985. All tenants. Covering areas in the civil parish of St Feighin's.

Smythe, William. Rent ledger, receipts, 1723–37. NLI Ms. 9990. Most tenants. Covering areas in the civil parish of St Feighin's.

Talbot, Sir John. Rental, 1841. NAI M2246. Major tenants only. Covering areas in the civil parishes of Dysart, Lackan, Leny, Lickbla, Mullingar, Multyfarnham, Portloman, Templeoran and Tyfarnham.

Temple, Gustavus Handcock. Maps, 1786. NLI 14.A.29. Principally major tenants. Covering areas in the civil parishes of Ballyloughloe, Bunown, Churchtown, Drumraney, Dysart, Kilkenny West, Mullingar, Noughaval and St Mary's, Athlone.

Towers, Thomas. Rental, 1801–1804, NLI Ms. 4847. Major tenants only. Covering areas in the civil parish of Mayne.

Wilson's Hospital. Rentals, 1822–60. NLI Mss. 1000, 3098. All tenants. Covering areas in the civil parishes of Bodenstown, Castlelost, Churchtown, Foyran, Piercetown, Portloman, Portnashangan, St Mary's, Stonehall and Taghmon.

WEXFORD

Census returns and substitutes

1618	Herald's Visitation of Co. Wexford. GO 48; NLI Pos. 957.
1641	Testimonies of 611 witnesses to the 1641 Rebellion. Online: 1641.
1641	Book of Survey and Distribution. NLI Ms. 975.
1654–6	*Civil Survey*, Vol. 9. NLI I 6551 Dublin.
1659	Pender's 'Census'. Reprinted GPC, 1997; IMC, 2002. LDS film 924648.
1665–1839	'Free burgesses of New Ross', *Proceedings of the Royal Society of Antiquaries of Ireland*, Ser. 5, Vol. 1, Part 1 (1890), pp. 298–309.
1766	Edermine, Protestants only. GO 537; LDS film 258517; Ballynaslaney NAI. M2476. Ballynaslaney, Clonmore, Edermine. Online: PRONI name search.
1776	Freemen of Wexford, *IG*, 5, Nos. 1, 3, 4, 1973.
1789	Protestant householders in the parish of Ferns. *IA*, Vol. 13, No. 2, 1981.

1792	Some Protestant householders in the parishes of Ballycanew and Killisk. *IA*, Vol. 13, No. 2, 1981.
1798	Protestants murdered in the 1798 Rebellion. Cantwell, *Memorials of the Dead . . . supplementary volume*, Dublin: 1986, Vol. 10, p. 432.
1798	Persons who suffered losses in the 1798 Rebellion. Propertied classes only. c.2,000 names. NLI I 94107.
1817	Emigrants from Cos. Carlow and Wexford to Canada. Whelan, *Wexford: History and Society.* Online: ShipsList.
1823–38	Tithe Books.
1840	Wexford electors. NAI OP 1840/103.
1842	Voters. NAI OP 1842/82.
1842–1921	Shillelagh Workhouse admission and discharge registers. Bray Public Library.
1846	Memorial of the poor fishermen and labourers of Fethard. c.82 names, with occupations and numbers in family. NAI OP 1846/152.
1853	Griffith's Valuation. Online: Askaboutireland.
1861	Catholics in Enniscorthy parish. With Catholic records. NLI.
1867	Marshallstown. *IG*, Vol. 6, No. 5, 1984, pp. 652–69.
1901	Census. Online: NAI.
1911	Census. Online: NAI.

Online

1641	<www.1641.tcd.ie>
Askaboutireland	<www.askaboutireland.ie>
FindMyPast	<www.findmypast.ie>
Hayes, John	<www.failteromhat.com>
Kilmore	<www.kilmoregenealogy.com>
Leitrim-Roscommon	<www.leitrim-roscommon.com>
NAI	<www.census.nationalarchives.ie>
PRONI name search	<www.proni.gov.uk>
Shipslist	<www.theshipslist.com>

Publications

Local histories etc.

Bennett McCuaig, Carol, *Leinster to Lanark*, Renfrew, Ont.: Juniper Books, 2010. Post-1798 emigrants from Cos. Carlow, Kilkenny, Wexford and Wicklow to Lanark County, Ottawa. NLC, 284 p.

Breen, Gerry, *Rosslare in history*, Rosslare: Rosslare Historical Society, 2007. NLI, 115 p.

Brennan, M., *Schools of Kildare and Leighlin, 1775–1835*, Dublin: M.H. Gill & Son, 1935. NLI Ir 37094135 b 4, 616 p.

Browne, Bernard, *Old Ross: the town that never was: a community biography*, Sean-Ros Press, 1993. NLI Ir 94138 b 7, 133 p.

Butler, Thomas C., *A parish and its people: history of Carrig-on-Bannow Parish*, Wellingtonbridge: 1985. NLI Ir 94138 b 4, 254 p.

Cantwell, Brian, Memorials of the Dead, Wexford, Vols. 5–9 (typescript), 1984. NLI Ir 9295 c 2, Master Index, Vol. 10.

Coyle, James, *The Antiquities of Leighlin*, Dublin: Browne & Nolan. NLI Ir 94138 c 1.

Culleton, Edward, *By bishop's rath and Norman fort: the story of Piercestown-Murrintown*, Wexford: Drinagh Enterprises, 1994. Wexford County Library, 285 p.

de Vál, Séamas S., *Bun Clóidí: a history of the district down to the beginning of the twentieth century*, Bun Clóidí: the author, 1989. NLI Ir 94138 b 5, 319 p.

—— *Templeudigan, yesterday and today*, Templeudigan: Templeudigan Historical Society, 2001. Wexford County Library, 184 p.

Doyle, Martin, *Notes and Gleanings Relating to the County of Wexford*, Dublin: 1868.

Farrell, Noel, *Exploring family origins in Enniscorthy*, Longford: Noel Farrell, 1998. NLI 1B 2233.

—— *Exploring family origins in New Ross*, Longford: Noel Farrell, 1998. NLI 1B 1174.

Flood, W.H. Grattan, *History of the Diocese of Ferns*, Waterford: Downey, 1916. NLI Ir 27413 f 1, 246 p.

—— *History of Enniscorthy, County Wexford*, Enniscorthy: Flood, 1898. NLI Ir 941382 f 1, 233 p.

—— *History of Hooke (Templetown) parish, County Wexford*, Wexford: the author, 1968. Wexford County Library, 28 p.

Forde, Walter, *In Ibar's footsteps: St Ibar's Church, Castlebridge, 1855–2005*, Castlebridge: Kara Publications, 2005. NLI, 164 p.

Griffiths, George, *The chronicles of the county of Wexford . . . brought down to the year 1877*, Enniscorthy: 1890. NLI J 94138, 478 p.

Hay, Edward, *History of the Insurrection of County Wexford in 1798*, Dublin: J. Duffy, 1847. NLI J 94107.

Hennessy, Patrick, *Davidstown, Courtnacuddy (a Wexford Parish): Some of Its History*, Enniscorthy: Hennessy, 1986. NLI Ir 94138 h 3, 138 p.

Hore, H.F., *The Social State of the Southern and Eastern Counties of Ireland in the Sixteenth Century*, Dublin: 1870. NLI Ir 794105 r 2. (See 'Carlow'.)

Hore, P.H., *History of the town and county of Wexford*, London: 1900–1911. NLI Ir 94138 h 2, 6 vols.

Hurley Binions, Gloria, *Rathnure and Killane: a local history*, Killane: Binions, 1997. NLI Ir 94138 r 8, 151 p.

Jeffrey, William H., *The Castles of Co. Wexford*, Wexford: Old Wexford Society, 1979. Wexford County Library.

Kavanagh, Art, *The Wexford gentry*, Vols. 1 and 2, Bunclody: Irish Family Names, 1994/6. NLI Ir 9291 k 4.

Kinsella, A., *The Waveswept Shore: A history of the Courtown district*, Wexford: Kinsella, 1982. Wexford County Library, 162 p.

Kirk, Francis J., *Some Notable Conversions in the Co. of Wexford*, London: Burns & Oates, 1901. NLI Ir 2828 k 1, 114 p.

Lalor, Stephen, *The story of New Ross, 1207–2007*, Dublin: the author, 2007. NLI, 82 p.

Lambert, Richard, *Rathangan: a County Wexford parish: its emerging story*, Rathangan: Lambert, 1995. NLI Ir 94138 L 3, 282 p.

McDonald, Danny, *Tomhaggard: a sacred place*, Tomhaggard: Tomhaggard Heritage Group, 2002. NLI, 120 p.

Mac Suibhne, Peadar, *Clonegal Parish*, Carlow: Newark Printers, 1975. NLI Ir 2741 m 14, 190 p.

Monageer Comóradh '98, *Monageer Parish: a rural district in 1798: a short history*, Monageer: Monageer Comóradh '98, 1998. NLI, 59 p.

Murphy, Hilary, *The parish of Mulrankin, ancient and modern*, Wexford: Mulrankin-Tomhaggard Parish Council, 2004. NLI, 196 p.

Murphy, Rory, *Memorials to the dead: Templeshanbo*, Bunclody: Glór na nGael, 1990. NLI Ir 94138.m.4, 59 p.

Murray, Patsy, *A history of Coolgreany*, Coolgreany: Coolgreany Historical Society, 1992. NLI Ir 94138 m 5, 88 p.

Ó Dálaigh, Brian, *Irish villages: studies in local history*, Dublin: Four Courts Press, 2003. Co-editors, Liam Clare and Karina Holton. Kilmore Quay. NLI.

O'Donovan, John, *Ordnance Survey letters, Wexford (1840)*, Dublin: 1927. NLI, Ir 9141 O 23, 2 vols.

Rees, J., *A farewell to famine*, Arklow: Arklow Enterprise Centre, 1994. NLI Ir 94138 r 6, 174 p.

Roche, Richard, *The Texas connection*, Wexford: Wexford Heritage Committee, 1989. The story of the Wexford colony in Refugio, Texas. NLI Ir 942 r 10, 59 p.

Rossiter, Nicholas, *Wexford Port: a history*, Wexford: Wexford Council of Trade Unions, 1989. NLI Ir 94138 r 4, 95 p.

Rowe, David, *Historical, genealogical and architectural notes on some houses of Wexford*, Whitegate, Co. Clare: Ballinakella Press, 2004. Co-author, Eithne Scallan. NLI.

Urwin, Margaret, *County Wexford family in the land war: by the O'Hanlon Walshs of Knocktartan*, Dublin: Four Courts Press, 2002. NLI 3B 445, 64 p.

Vandeleur, Rev. W.E., *Notes on Ardamine and Killena Parishes*, Dundalk: Dundalgan Press, 1928. Wexford County Library, 24 p.

—— *Notes on the history of Kiltennel*, Dundalk: W. Tempest, 1927. Wexford County Library, 16 p.

Veale, T., *Index of Surnames in 'The New Commercial Directory for the cities of Waterford and Kilkenny and the towns of Clonmel, Carrick-on-Suir, New Ross and Carlow'*, Dublin: Veale, 1996. NLI Ir 9414 p.

—— *Richard Lucas, 1788: directory extract for south east of Ireland*, Dublin: Veale, 1995 NLI Ir 9414 v.

Whelan, Kevin, *A History of Newbawn*, Newbawn: Macra na Feirme, 1989. Wexford County Library, 118 p.

—— *Tintern Abbey, Co. Wexford: Cistercians and Colcloughs: 8 centuries of occupation*, Saltmills: Friends of Tintern, 1990. NLI Ir 700 p 77 (5).

—— *Wexford History and Society*, Dublin: Geography Publications, 1987. Associate editor, William Nolan. NLI LO, 564 p.

White, W.D., *Heirs to a heritage: a story of the people and places of the Clonegal area of Clonegal Parish*, Clonegal, Co. Carlow: 1992. NLI Ir 941 p 132(2), 72 p.

Local journals

Journal of the Old Wexford Society, NLI Ir 94138 o 5.

Journal of the Taghmon Historical Society. NLI.

Journal of the Wexford Historical Society. NLI Ir 94138 o 5.

The Past (Journal of the Uí Cinnsealaigh Historical Society). NLI Ir 941382 p 1.

Directories

1788	Richard Lucas, *General Directory of the Kingdom of Ireland*. NLI Pos. 3729. Reprinted in Veale, *Lucas*, IG, 1965, 1966, 1967, 1968.
1820	J. Pigot, *Commercial Directory of Ireland*. PRONI; NLI Ir 9141 p 107; LDS film 962702 item 1.
1824	J. Pigot & Co., *City of Dublin and Hibernian Provincial Directory*. NLI; LDS film 451787. Online: Hayes.
1839	T. Shearman, *New Commercial Directory for the cities of Waterford and Kilkenny, Towns of Clonmel, Carrick-on-Suir, New Ross and Carlow.* Indexed in Veale, *Index*.
1846	Slater's *National Commercial Directory of Ireland*. PRONI; NLI LO; LDS film 1696703 item 3. Online: Hayes.
1856	Slater, *Royal National Commercial Directory of Ireland*. NLI; LDS film 1472360 item 1.
1867	Coghlan, P.J., *A directory for the Co. of Wexford . . . townlands, gentlemen's seats and noted places*, Galway. NLI Ir 914138 c 4, 59 p.
1870	Slater, *Directory of Ireland*. NLI.
1872	George Griffith, *County Wexford Almanac*. NLI Ir 914138 g 2.
1881	Slater, *Royal National Commercial Directory of Ireland*. NLI. Online: FindMyPast.
1885	George Henry Bassett, *Wexford County Guide and Directory*. NLI Ir 914138 b 8.
1894	Slater, *Royal Commercial Directory of Ireland*. NLI.

Gravestone inscriptions

Parts (at least) of seven Co. Wexford graveyards are transcribed at <*www.interment.net*>.

Brian J. Cantwell, *Memorials of the Dead, Co. Wexford* (complete), Vols. 5–9. Master index: Vol. 10. NLI Ir 9295 c 2; NAI search room. Online: FindMyPast.

Estate records

Co. Wexford rent lists, eighteenth century. NLI Ms. 1782.

Alcock estate. Tenants, Clonmore, 1820. NLI Ms. 10169.

Baron Farnham estate. Rent books for Bunclody, 1775–1820. NLI Mss. 787–8.

Farnham. Tenants and tradesmen from Baron Farnham's Estate of Newtownbarry, 1774, *Irish Family History Society Newsletter*, 10, 1993, pp. 5–7.

WICKLOW

Census returns and substitutes

1641	Testimonies of 164 witnesses to the 1641 Rebellion. Online: 1641.
1641	Book of Survey and Distribution. NLI Ms. 969.
1669	Hearth Money Roll. NAI m 4909; also GO 667.
1745	Poll Book. PRONI 2659.
1766	Parishes of Drumkay, Dunganstown, Kilpoole, Rathdrum and Rathnew. GO 537; also Wicklow Heritage Centre and LDS film 258517. Dunganstown, Rathdrum and Wicklow: Online: PRONI name search.
1792–6	Valuation of the corn tithes of Newcastle, with names of tenants. NLI Ms. 3980.
1798	Persons who suffered losses in the 1798 Rebellion. Propertied classes only. c.950 names. NLI I 94107.
1823–38	Tithe Books. NAI.
1837	Memorial from inhabitants of Ballinacor South and Shillelagh for quarter law sessions at Tinahely. More than 1,500 names, most (?) from Tinahely district. NAI OP 1837/133. See Magee, *Shillelagh and Ballinacor South.*
1842–8	Emigrants list, Shilelagh, NLI Mss. 18,429, 18,524. See also *West Wicklow Historical Journal*, No. 1 et seq.
1842–1921	Shillelagh Workhouse admission and discharge registers. Bray Public Library.
1843–54	Wicklow voters, 1843–51. NAI OP 1843/64, 1849/5, 1854/21, 1851/60.
1849–1914	Rathdrum Workhouse admission and discharge registers. Bray Public Library.
1852–3	Griffith's Valuation. Online: Askaboutireland.
1901	Census. Online: NAI.
1911	Census. Online: NAI.

Online

1641	<www.1641.tcd.ie>
Askaboutireland	<www.askaboutireland.ie>
Carnew Historical Society	<www.carnewhistoricalsociety.com>
CMC, Wicklow	<www.cmcrp.net/Wicklow>
FindMyPast	<www.findmypast.ie>
Hayes, John	<www.failteromhat.com>

IGP Wicklow	<*www.igp-web.com/Wickow/index.html*>
NAI	<*www.census.nationalarchives.ie*>
PRONI name search	<*www.proni.gov.uk*>

Publications

Local histories etc.

Bennett McCuaig, Carol, *Leinster to Lanark*, Renfrew, Ont.: Juniper Books, 2010. Post-1798 emigrants from Cos. Carlow, Kilkenny, Wexford and Wicklow to Lanark County, Ottawa. NLC, 284 p.

Bland, F.E., *The Story of Crinken, 1840–1940*, Bray: 1940. NLI Ir 941 p 26, 26 p.

Brien, C., *In the Land of Brien: a short history of the Catholic Church and other institutions in Bray and district from earliest times*, Bray: 1984.

Cantwell, Brian, Memorials of the Dead, Wicklow, Vols. 1–4 (typescript), 1978, Master index, Vol. 10. NLI Ir 9295 c 2.

Carville, Geraldine, *Baltinglass: abbey of the three rivers*, Moone, Co. Kildare: West Wicklow Historical Society, 1984. NLI Ir 94134 c 5, 87 p.

Chavasse, C., *The story of Baltinglass: a history of the parishes of Baltinglass, Ballynure and Rathbran in County Wicklow, Kilkenny Journal*, 1970. NLI Ir 9141 p 40, 75 p.

Clare, Liam, *Enclosing the commons: Dalkey, the Sugar Loaves and Bray, 1820–70*, Dublin: Four Courts Press, 2004. NLI 4A 3362, 64 p.

—— *Victorian Bray: a town adapts to changing times*, Dublin: Irish Academic Press, 1998. NLI Ir 94134 c 14, 82 p.

Clarke, Sheila, *Ashford: a journey through time*, Blackrock, Co. Dublin: Ashford Books, 2003. NLI, 215 p.

Cleary, Jimmy, *Wicklow Harbour: a history*, Wicklow: Wicklow Harbour Commissioners, 2001. Co-author, Andrew O'Brien. NLI, 78 p.

Corbett, R. John H., *A short history of Glenealy and its Church of Ireland parish bicentenary, 1792–1992*, Glenealy: the parish, 1992. NLI Ir 200 p 91(6), 21 p.

County Wicklow Heritage Project, *The last county: the emergence of Wicklow as a county, 1606–1845*, Wicklow: County Wicklow Heritage Project, 1993. NLI Ir 94134 p 3(4), 80 p.

Coyle, James, *The Antiquities of Leighlin*, Dublin: Browne & Nolan. NLI Ir 94138 c 1.

Davies, K.M., *Irish Historic Towns Atlas, 9: Bray*, Dublin: RIA, 1998. NLI.

de Lion, C., *The vale of Avoca*, Dublin: Kamac Publications, 1967/91. NLI Ir 914134 p 4, 48 p.

Doran, A.L., *Bray and environs*, Bray: 1903. Reprinted 1985.

Earl, L., *The battle of Baltinglass*, London: Alfred Knopf, 1952. NLI Ir 94134 e 1, 241 p.

Eustace, E.A.R., *Short history of Ardoyne Parish*, Carlow: 1967.

Evans, Major E.B., *A history of the County Wicklow regiment of militia . . . officers from 1793*, 1885. NLI Ir 355942 e 2, 58 p.

Farrell, Noel, *Exploring family origins in Arklow town*, Longford: Noel Farrell, 1998. NLI, 48 p.

Flannery, Judith, *Christ Church, Delgany, 1789–1990: between the mountains and the sea: a parish history*, Delgany: Select Vestry of Delgany Parish, 1990. NLI Ir 27413 f 3, 162 p.

Flynn, A., *Famous Links with Bray*, Bray: 1985. NLI Ir 941 p 85, 51 p.

—— *History of Bray*, Cork: Mercier Press, 1986. NLI Ir 94134 f 1.

Flynn, Michael, *Outline histories . . . Kelly of Youngstown, Kilmead, Athy, Co. Kildare, Murphy of Togher, Roundwood, Co. Wicklow, Masterson family of Ardellis, Athy, Co. Kildare (with descendants)*, Mullingar: Michael P. Flynn, 1997. NLI Ir 9292 f.

Forde, F., *Maritime Arklow*, Arklow: 1988.

Garner, W., *Bray: architectural heritage*, Dublin: 1980.

Gurrin, Brian, *A century of struggle in Delgany and Kilcoole: an exploration of the social implications of population change in north-east Wicklow, 1666–1779*, Dublin: Irish Academic Press, 2000. NLI, 80 p.

Hannigan, Ken, *Wicklow: History and Society*, Dublin: Geography Publications, 1994. Co-editor, William Nolan. NLI Ir 94134 w 8, 1,005 p.

Heavener, Robert, *Credo Dunganstown: an age-old Irish parish with a living message for Everyman today*, Jordanstown, Co. Antrim: Cromlech Books, 1993. NLI Ir 27413 h 7, 145 p.

Irish Countrywomen's Association, *Avoca Local History Guide: presented by Avoca Guild*, ICA, Avoca: ICA, 1987. NLI Ir 94134 p 3(3), 52 p.

Jennings, Robert, *Glimpses of an ancient parish: Newcastle, Co. Wicklow, 1189–1989*, 1989. NLI Ir 94134 p 3(2), 42 p.

—— *Kilcoole, County Wicklow: History and folklore, historical walks and drives*, Kilcoole: Kilcoole Millennium and Residents' Association, 1998. NLI Ir 94134 j 1, 130 p.

—— *Newcastle down the years*, Newcastle: Newcastle Residents' Association, 2008. NLI, 119 p.

Mac Eiteagáin, Darren, *Ballynagran: an historical perspective*, Wicklow: Ashford Historical Society, 1994. NLI 1A 456, 21 p.

Mac Suibhne, Peadar, *Clonegal Parish*, Carlow: 1975. NLI Ir 2741 m 14, 190 p.

Magee, Seán, *Shillelagh and Ballinacor South, Co. Wicklow, 1837: A Memorial*, Dún Laoghaire: Dún Laoghaire Genealogical Society, 1997. NLI Ir 9291 g 7, 64 p.

Mansfield, C., *The Aravon Story*, Dublin: 1975. History of Aravon School. NLI Ir 372 p 237, 26 p.

Martin, C., *A drink from Broderick's Well, Dublin*, Dublin: 1980. NLI Ir 94134 m 4, 167 p.

—— *The Woodcarvers of Bray, 1887–1914*, Bray: 1985.

Morris, J., *The story of the Arklow lifeboats*, Coventry: 1987.

Murphy, Hilary, *The Kynoch era in Arklow, 1895–1918*, Wexford: Murphy, 1976. NLI Ir 600 p 29, 76 p.

O'Donovan, John, Ordnance Survey letters, Wicklow (1838), Bray: 1928. Typewritten. NLI Ir 9141 O 24, 172 f.

O'Reilly, George H., *Newcastle, County Wicklow, school registers, 1864–1947*, Dún Laoghaire: Dún Laoghaire Genealogical Society, 1997. NLI Ir 9291 g 7, 159 p.

—— *Corn growers, carriers and traders, County Wicklow, 1788, 1789 and 1790*, Dún Laoghaire: Dún Laoghaire Genealogical Society, 1997. Co-author, James O. Coyle. NLI Ir 9291 g 7, 27 p.

Power, Pat, *People of the rebellion: Wicklow, 1798*, Dún Laoghaire: Dún Laoghaire Genealogical Society, 1999. NLI Ir 9291 g 7, 116 p.

Power, P.J., *The Arklow calendar: a chronicle of events from earliest times to 1900 AD*, Arklow: Elizabeth Press, 1981. NLI Ir 94134 p 1, 129 p.

Rees, J., *Arklow: last stronghold of sail: Arklow ships, 1850–1985*, Arklow: Arklow Historical Society, 1985. Co-author, L. Charlton. NLI Ir 386 r 7, 178 p.

—— *Fitzwilliam tenants listed in the Coolattin Estate emigration, 1847–56*, Wicklow: Dee-Jay Publications, 1998. NLI Ir 94108 r 23, 84 leaves.

—— *Surplus people: the Fitzwilliam clearances, 1847–56*, Cork: Collins Press, 2000. NLI, 156 p.

Scott, G.D., *The stones of Bray*, Dublin: Hodges, Figgis, 1913. Barony of Rathdown. NLI Ir 914133 b 2.

Stokes, A.E., *The parish of Powerscourt*, Bray: Old Bray Society, 1986. NLI, 16 p.

Taylor, R.M., *St. Mary's Church, Blessington, 1683–1970*, Greystones: 1970.

Veale, T., *Richard Lucas, 1788: directory extract for south east of Ireland*, Dublin: Veale, 1995. NLI Ir 9414 v.

White, W.D., *Heirs to a heritage: a story of the people and places of the Clonegal area of Clonegal Parish*, Clonegal, Co. Carlow: 1992. NLI Ir 941 p 132(2), 72 p.

Local journals
Ashford and District Historical Journal. NLI Ir 94134.a.
Bray Historical Record. NLI Ir 94134 o 3.
Carnew Historical Society Journal. NLI.
Journal of the Arklow Historical Society. NLI Ir 94134 a.
Journal of the Cualann Historical Society. NLI Ir 94134 b.
Journal of the Greystones Historical and Archeological Society. NLI Ir 94134 g V.1.
Journal of the West Wicklow Historical Society. NLI Ir 94134 w 5.
Report of the Old Bray Society. NLI Ir 94134 o 3.
Reportorium Novum. NLI Ir 27413 r 3.
Roundwood and District History and Folklore Journal. NLI Ir 94134 r 1.

Directories
1788	Richard Lucas, *General Directory of the Kingdom of Ireland.* NLI Pos. 3729. Reprinted in Veale, *Lucas, IG*, 1965, 1966, 1967, 1968.
1824	J. Pigot & Co., *City of Dublin and Hibernian Provincial Directory.* NLI; LDS film 451787. Online: Hayes.
1846	Slater's *National Commercial Directory of Ireland.* PRONI; NLI LO; LDS film 1696703 item 3. Online: Hayes.

1856	Slater, *Royal National Commercial Directory of Ireland*. NLI; LDS film 1472360 item 1.
1870	Slater, *Directory of Ireland*. NLI.
1881	Slater, *Royal National Commercial Directory of Ireland*. NLI. Online: FindMyPast.
1894	Slater, *Royal Commercial Directory of Ireland*. NLI.

Gravestone inscriptions

Parts (at least) of fifteen Co. Wicklow graveyards are transcribed at <*www. interment.net*>.

Brian J. Cantwell, *Memorials of the Dead, Co. Wicklow* (complete), Vols. 1–4; master index: Vol. 10. NLI Ir 9295 c 2; NAI search room. Online: FindMyPast.

Estate records

Adair. Rent ledger, n.d. NLI Ms. 16410. Principally major tenants. Covering areas in the civil parish of Kilmacanoge.

Cobbe. Rental and maps, 1771, 1830–82. NLI Pos. 4033. All tenants. Covering areas in the civil parish of Boystown.

Commissioners of Education. Valuation, 1816. NLI Ms. 16925. Most tenants. Covering areas in the civil parish of Ballykine.

Fitzwilliam, Earl. NLI Ms. 6068: lease book, 1795–1808; Ms. 6074: rental, 1811–12; Ms. 6076: rental, 1809–1811; Ms. 6082: occupiers, 1827–68; Mss. 6001–6051: rentals, 1782–1855; Mss. 6083–7: rentals, 1828–33; Mss. 6088–6118: rentals, 1834–66. Most tenants. Covering areas in the civil parishes of Aghowle, Ardoyne, Carnew, Crecrin, Crosspatrick, Derrylossary, Dunganstown, Glenealy, Hacketstown, Kilcommon (Arklow), Kilcommon (Ballinacor), Killiskey, Kilpipe, Kilpoole, Kiltegan, Liscolman, Moyacomb, Moyne, Mullinacuff, Newcastle Lower, Preban, Rathdrum and Rathnew.

Hatch. NLI Mss. 11996–7: rent survey, 1817 (most tenants); Ms. 11341: rental, 1750; Ms. 11995: rental, 1785 (major tenants). Covering areas in the civil parishes of Aghowle, Calary, Derrylossary, Newcastle Lower and Rathnew.

Hepenstal, Rev. L.W. Map, 1818. NLI Ms.16.J.22 (1). Most tenants. Covering areas in the civil parishes of Ballinacor, Ballykine, Ballynure, Donaghmore and Knockrath.

Hodson. NLI Mss. 16390–96, rent ledger, 1799–1887. Principally major tenants. Covering areas in the civil parishes of Bray, Calary, Kilmacanoge and Powerscourt.

Hodson, Sir George. NLI Ms. 16418, rent ledger, 1841–50. Principally major tenants. Covering areas in the civil parishes of Bray, Calary and Kilmacanoge.

Kemmis. NLI Ms. 15161, 1803–1923. Principally major tenants. Covering areas in the civil parishes of Ballinacor, Ballykine, Kilpipe and Knockrath.

Miley, Rev. Edward. NAI M 5679, rental, n.d. Most tenants. Covering areas in the civil parish of Kilbride (Talbotstown).

Ormonde, Duke of. NLI Ms. 23789, 1706, rental. Principally major tenants. Covering areas in the civil parishes of Arklow and Kilcommon (Arklow).

Paul, Sir. R.J. Map, 1843. NLI Ms. 21.F.136. Most tenants. Covering areas in the civil parish of Ballynure.

Pembroke estate. NLI M 2011, rent rolls, 1754–1806. Most tenants. Covering areas in the civil parish of Bray.

Percy, Anthony. NLI Ms. 10265, n.d. Major tenants only. Covering areas in the civil parishes of Donaghmore and Rathnew.

Powerscourt. NLI Ms. 16386: register of leases, 1775–1862 (many with comments); Ms. 4882: rental, 1836–41; Ms. 19298: rentals, 1840–50; Mss. 19189–90: rentals 1803–1813; Mss. 19197–9: rentals 1841–4; Mss. 19202–209: rentals, 1846–57. Most tenants. Covering areas in the civil parishes of Bray, Calary, Castlemacadam, Derrylossary, Kilmacanoge, Newcastle Lower, Powerscourt and Rathnew.

Proby. NLI Ms. 3149, rental, 1826. All tenants. Covering areas in the civil parishes of Arklow, Ballintemple, Inch, Kilbride (Arklow) and Killahurler.

Putland, George. NLI Mss. 12768–78, rentals, 1814–27. Principally major tenants. Covering areas in the civil parishes of Castlemacadam, Garrycloyne, Matehy and Templeusque.

Ram. NLI Ms. 8238, rental, 1810–20. Principally major tenants. Covering areas in the civil parishes of Ballinacor, Donaghmore and Kilcommon (Ballinacor).

Rockingham, Marquis of. NLI Mss. 6055, 6056: rentals, 1748, 1754, most tenants; Mss. 6058, 6059: rentals, 1763, 1770; most tenants. Covering areas in the civil parishes of Aghowle, Ardoyne, Carnew, Crecrin, Crosspatrick, Hacketstown, Kilcommon (Ballinacor), Kilpipe, Kiltegan, Liscolman, Moyacomb, Moyne, Mullinacuff and Preban.

Stone, Richard. NLI Ms. 16584, rent ledger, 1712–18. Major tenants only. Covering areas in the civil parishes of Delgany, Drumkay, Dunganstown, Glenealy, Kilbride (Arklow), Kilcoole, Killiskey, Knockrath, Preban and Rathnew.

Westby, William Jones. NLI Mss. 14291–2, rentals, 1836–41. Most tenants. Covering areas in the civil parishes of Hacketstown and Kiltegan.

Wicklow papers. NLI Ms. 9580, rental, 1704–1705. Principally major tenants. Covering areas in the civil parishes of Arklow, Calary, Kilcoole, Killiskey, Kiltegan, Newcastle Lower and Newcastle Upper.

Chapter 14

ROMAN CATHOLIC PARISH REGISTERS

What follows is a listing of all copies of Roman Catholic parish registers, microfilm and database transcript, to be found at present (2011) in the National Library of Ireland, the Public Record Office of Northern Ireland, the LDS Family History Library and local heritage centres, as well as any that have been published or transcribed online. The aim is to assist research by providing an overview of the dates and locations of records available, in any sense, to the public. For this reason, and because such an undertaking is beyond the scope of the present work, no attempt has been made to list the dates of the originals held in local custody, except where no other copy is known. Online references are detailed in that section of the county source lists, except for LDS records; 'Familysearch' refers to the main LDS site, <*www.familysearch.org*>, where any Irish parish records are included as part of the International Genealogical Index (IGI). The transcripts in the IGI are not complete, including only dates and personal names. The same is true of the transcripts in the LDS CD-ROM set *British Isles Vital Records Index* (2nd ed., 2001), which includes some thirteen parishes, mainly for Co. Roscommon, and overlaps to some extent with the IGI. It should be added that it can be very hard to pin down exactly what the IGI includes. It is perfectly possible that I have missed something.

The parish names used in the tables are those found on the accompanying maps. For the most part these are the names used in the nineteenth-century records. Once again, some caution is needed in using the maps. Based largely on Lewis's *Topographical Dictionary of Ireland* (1837), they attempt to show all parishes with baptism, marriage or burial records before 1880. The problems are therefore obvious. To put it at its kindest, the maps can only be taken as indicative, to be used primarily in identifying which parishes adjoin each other. In the case of Dublin city and county, the rapid creation and subdivision of parishes from the 1850s made it impossible to include them all on the maps, though any available records are listed.

Antrim

Most but not all UHF
records appear to be online
at <*www.rootsireland.ie*>.

Parish (Diocese)	Baptisms	Marriages	Burials	Location	Reference
Aghagallon	Apr 1 1828–Dec 20 1880	May 25 1828–Nov 8 1880	Mar 29 1828–July 5 1848	NLI	Pos. 5467
(Down and Connor)			May 25 1872–Dec 22 1880		
	1828–89	1828–89	1828–48; 1873–81	PRONI	MIC.1D/6.63
	1828–1900	1828–1900	1828–1900	UHF	
Ahoghill	1833–63	1833–63	1833–63	NLI	Pos. 5472
(Down and Connor)	Jan 10 1964–Dec 25 1880	Apr 3 1864–Dec 25 1880			
	1833–81	1833–81	1833–47 (patchy)	PRONI	MIC.1D/68
	1864–1900	1866–1900		UHF	
Antrim	Jan 19 1874–Dec 3 1880			NLI	Pos. 5472
(Down and Connor)	1873–81			PRONI	MIC.1D/68
	1873–1900	1873–1900		UHF	
Armoy	Apr 23 1848–Mar 10 1872	May 18 1848–Jan 7 1872		NLI	Pos. 5473
(Down and Connor)	Oct 12 1873–Dec 23 1880	Nov 29 1973–Oct 24 1880			
	1848–80	1848–82		PRONI	MIC.1D/69
	1872–1900	1872–1900		UHF	
Ballintoy	Apr 14 1872–Nov 6 1880	May 20 1872–Mar 27 1879		NLI	Pos. 5473
(Down and Connor)	1872–82	1872–82		PRONI	MIC.1D/69
	1872–1900	1872–1900		UHF	
Ballyclare	July 4 1869–Dec 25 1880	Feb 26 1870–Dec 29 1880		NLI	Pos. 5467
(Down and Connor)	(original and transcript)	(original and transcript)			
	1869–81	1870–72		PRONI	MIC.1D/63
	1869–1900	1870–1900		UHF	

Parish (Diocese)	Baptisms	Marriages	Burials	Location	Reference
Ballymoney	Mar 9 1853–Oct 15 1880	Apr 1853–June 30 1879		NLI	Pos. 5473
(Down and Connor)	1853–82	1853–79		PRONI	MIC.1D/69A
	1853–1900	1853–1900	1879–87	UHF	
Blaris	See Down				
(Down and Connor)					
Braid	Sept 1878–Dec 22 1880	Nov 2 1878–Dec 25 1880		NLI	Pos. 5473
(Down and Connor)	1878–81	1878–81		PRONI	MIC.1D/69A
	1878–81	1878–81		UHF	
Carnlough	Aug 4 1869–Dec 18 1880	Aug 15 1869–Oct 21 1880		NLI	Pos. 5474
(Down and Connor)	1825–80	1869–82		PRONI	MIC.1D/70–71
	1857–69	1869–1900		UHF	
Carrickfergus	Aug 15 1821–Nov 23 1828	Sept 21 1821–Nov 9 1828		NLI	Pos. 5472
(Down and Connor)	Dec 14 1828–Feb 9 1841	Dec 28 1828–Oct 1 1840			
	Mar 8 1852–May 12 1872	Apr 11 1852–June 3 1872			
	1852–72	1852–72		PRONI	MIC.1D/68, 90
	1820–1900	1821–1900		UHF	
Culfeightrin	July 3 1825–Apr 7 1834	Nov 1834–Dec 1838		NLI	Pos. 5472; with
(Down and Connor)	(also a transcript)				Cushendun
	Dec 20 1834–Dec 26 1838	Jan 1 1839–June 9 1844			and
	May 1839–Feb 5 1847	Aug 3 1845–Mar 6 1848			Ennispollan,
	1845–Apr 17 1848	June 2 1848–Feb 27 1867			Pos. 5473
	May 7 1848–May 15 1867	June 18 1867–Nov 14 1880			
	1825–81	1834–1880		PRONI	MIC.1D/68, 69A
	1848–1900	1894–1900		UHF	
Cushendun	Apr 1848–Feb 24 1852	May 1 1848–Feb 24 1852		NLI	Pos. 5473
(Down and Connor)	June 8 1862–Nov 11 1880	June 15 1862–Sept 28 1880			
	1848–52	1848–52	1845–52	PRONI	MIC.1D/59 A-B
	1862–81	1862–81			
	1834–1900	1845–1900		UHF	
Drumaul	Oct 5 1825–May 25 1832	Apr 21 1835–Oct 23 1842	Apr 21 1835–Oct 23 1842	NLI	Pos. 5474 to
(Down and Connor)	May 27 1832–Aug 1835	Oct 30 1842–May 13 1854			1842;
	Aug 30 1835–Aug 14 1842	May 16 1858–Nov 14 1867			remainder on
	Aug 23 1842–Sept 5 1854	(fragmented)			Pos. 5475
	Aug 1855–Jan 1 1868	1871–July 4 1873			
	Sept 5 1871–May 18 1873	Oct 13 1872–Nov 11 1880			
	Jan 2 1866–Jan 1 1868				
	Feb 2 1872–Dec 26 1880				
	1825–81	1825–84	1837–48	PRONI	MIC.1D/70–71
	1825–1900	1825–1900	1837–48	UHF	
Dunean	May 16 1834–June 1844	May 16 1835–May 2 1844		NLI	Pos. 5474
(Down and Connor)	June 4 1844–Apr 13 1847	June 14 1844–Feb 20 1847			
	Sept 26 1847–Feb 3 1861	Oct 10 1847–Dec 29 1880			
	1834–61	1835–61		PRONI	MIC.1D/70
	1834–1900	1835–1900		UHF	
Dunloy	June 17 1860–Dec 26 1876	June 4 1877–Nov 23 1880	Apr 26 1877–Dec 24 1880	NLI	Pos. 5475
(Down and Connor)	Apr 25 1877–Nov 21 1880				
	1840–81	1877–81	1877–81	PRONI	MIC. 1D/71
	1860–1900	1877–1900	1877–1900	UHF	
Glenariffe	1872–1900			UHF	
(Down and Connor)					

Parish (Diocese)	Baptisms	Marriages	Burials	Location	Reference
Glenarm	Dec 18 1825–Mar 6 1859	Oct 6 1825–Mar 6 1859			
(Down and Connor)	June 7 1857–Dec 8 1862 (transcript)	May 3 1859–Dec 30 1880	Jan 24 1931–May 15 1838	NLI	Pos. 5475
	June 6 1865–Dec 26 1880 (transcript)				
	1865–80	1825–80	1831–8	PRONI	MIC.1D/71
	1836–1900	1859–1900		UHF	
Glenavy and Killead	May 30 1849–Dec 31 1880	Mar 25 1848–Dec 31 1880		NLI	Pos. 5467
(Down and Connor)	1849–81	1848–83		PRONI	MIC.1D/63
	1849–1900	1848–1900		UHF	
Glenravel	June 25 1825–1832	June 25 1825–1832 (also	June 25 1825–1832	NLI	Pos. 5474
(Down and Connor)	July 3 1825–Sept 30 1856	a transcript)	July 8 1832–Sept 13 1841		
	July 8 1832–Sept 13 1841	Nov 19 1864–Jan 11 1869			
	Feb 15 1864–July 21 1878	Oct 20 1878–Nov 25 1880			
	Oct 10 1878–Dec 24 1880				
	July 8 1832–Sept 13 1841				
	1825–56	1825–41	1825–41	PRONI	MIC.1D/70
	1864–81	1864–9	1864–9		
		1878–82			
	1825–1900	1873–1900	1825–69	UHF	
Greencastle	Mar 21 1854–Dec 25 1880	Apr 3 1854–Oct 21 1880		NLI	Pos. 5475
(Down and Connor)	1854–81	1854–81		PRONI	MIC.1D/71
	1854–1900	1854–1900		UHF	
Hannastown, Rock	Oct 7 1877–Dec 30 1880	Oct 13 1877–Nov 7 1880		NLI	Pos. 5467
and Derriaghy	1877–80	1877–80		PRONI	MIC.1D/63
(Down and Connor)	1848–1900	1848–1900	UHF		
Kirkinriola	1848–Dec 25 1880	Jan 22 1847–Nov 27 1880		NLI	Pos. 5473
(Down and Connor)	Jan 30 1866–Dec 25 1880 (transcript)	Jan 10 1840–July 28 1842			
		Dec 28 1847–Nov 27 1880 (transcripts)			
	1848–81	1840–42		PRONI	MIC.1D/69A
		1847–82			
	1836–1900	1836–42	1852–87	UHF	
		1847–1900			
Larne	Aug 15 1821–Nov 23 1828	Sept 21 1821–Nov 9 1828		NLI	Pos. 5472
(Down and Connor)	Dec 14 1828–Feb 9 1841	Dec 28 1828–Oct 1 1840			
	Mar 8 1852–May 12 1872	Apr 11 1852–June 3 1872			
	1821–83	1821–83		PRONI	MIC.1D/68, 90
	1820–1900	1821–1900		UHF	
Larne: St Mac Nissi	1828–1900	1828–1900		UHF	
(Down and Connor)					
Layde	Apr 8 1838–Mar 31 1844	July 1 1837–May 26 1844		NLI	Pos. 5472
(Down and Connor)	Jan 12 1858–July 4 1871	Mar 25 1860–Mar 15 1872			
	Apr 23 1871–Nov 28 1880	Apr 27 1872–Nov 14 1880			
	1838–44	1837–44		PRONI	MIC.1D/68
	1858–81	1860–81			
	1858–1900	1860–1900		UHF	
Loughguile	May 13 1845–June 1 1868	May 4 1845–May 14 1868		NLI	Pos. 5473
(Down and Connor)	June 21 1868–Nov 1 1869	June 5 1868–Nov 2 1869			
	Nov 10 1869–Dec 20 1880				
	1845–81	1845–69		PRONI	MIC.1D/69A
	1825–1900	1825–1900		UHF	

Parish (Diocese)	Baptisms	Marriages	Burials	Location	Reference
Portglenone	Jan 14 1864–Nov 28 1880	Feb 13 1864–Sept 30 1880		NLI	Pos. 5475
(Down and Connor)	1864–81	1864–82		PRONI	MIC.1D/71
	1864–1900	1864–1900		UHF	
Portrush	July 7 1844–Dec 23 1880	May 14 1848–Nov 4 1880		NLI	Pos. 5476
(Down and Connor)		(also a transcript)			
	1844–81	1848–89		PRONI	MIC.1D/72
Ramoan	Oct 21 1838–Dec 14 1880	Oct 13 1838–Sept 16 1880		NLI	Pos. 5476
(Down and Connor)	1838–81	1838–83		PRONI	MIC.1D/72
	1838–1900	1838–1900		UHF	
Rasharkin	Aug 16 1848–Nov 13 1880	July 20 1848–Dec 4 1880		NLI	Pos. 5476
(Down and Connor)	1848–81	1848–81		PRONI	MIC.1D/72
	1847–1900	1847–1900		UHF	
Rathlin Island	1856–80	1857–80		PRONI	MIC.1D/92
(Down and Connor)	1856–1900	1857–1900		UHF	

Armagh

All Armagh Ancestry (AA)
and Irish World (IW)
records are searchable
online at
<www.rootisireland.ie>.

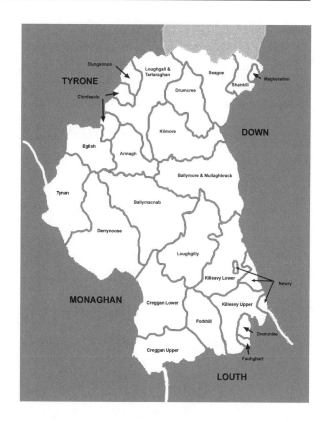

Parish (Diocese)	Baptisms	Marriages	Burials	Location	Reference
Armagh (Armagh)	1796–1880	1802–1803		PRONI	MIC.1D/41–2
		1806–1810			
		1816–81			
	1796–1900	1802–1810		AA	
		1816–23			
		1835–1900			

Parish (Diocese)	Baptisms	Marriages	Burials	Location	Reference
Armagh (Armagh) (contd.)	July 15 1796–Oct 29 1810	Jan 4 1802–May 13 1803		NLI	Pos. 5590;
	Nov 1810–Nov 3 1835	Jan 2 1817–Nov 11 1835			Baptisms from
	Nov 3 1835–Dec 7 1843	Nov 17 1835–Dec 25 1880			1843 Pos. 5591
	Dec 6 1843–May 8 1861				
	May 12 1861–May 17 1870				
	May 15 1870–Dec 30 1880				
Ballymacnab (Armagh)	1820–1900	1844–1900		AA	
	1844–81	1944–1880		PRONI	MIC.1D/37–8
	Jan 6 1844–Aug 21 1870	Jan 16 1844–Dec 16 1880		NLI	Pos. 5586
	Aug 20 1870–Dec 24 1880				
Ballymore and Mullabrack (Armagh)	1798–1802 1831–1900	1831–1900		AA	
	1843–65	1843–65		PRONI	MIC.1D/37
	1859–80	1859–80			
	1843–56	1843–56			
	1859–80	1859–80		LDS	0926031
	Oct 9 1843–May 27 1853	Oct 21 1843–Oct 1853		NLI	Pos. 5586
	Oct 7 1853–Nov 20 1856	Oct 16 1853–Nov 23 1856			
	June 5 1859–Dec 12 1880	July 24 1859–Nov 12 1880			
Clonfeacle (Armagh)	See Tyrone				
Creggan Lower (Armagh)	1845–80	1845–81		PRONI	MIC.1D/40
	1845–1900	1845–1900		AA	
	See NLI	See NLI		LDS	0926034
	Feb 14 1845–Dec 30 1880	Feb 13 1845–Nov 27 1880		NLI	Pos. 5589
Creggan Upper (Armagh)	1796–1803	1796–1803		PRONI	MIC.1D/43
	1812–29	1812–29			
	1845–81	1845–81			
	1796–1803	1796–1803		AA	
	1812–1900	1812–1900			
	Aug 5 1796–Jan 19 1803	Aug 8 1796–Feb 16 1803		NLI	Pos. 5592
	Sept 23 1812–Mar 28 1822	Dec 18 1812–Mar 22 1822			
	Apr 2 1822–May 29 1829	Apr 8 1822–July 24 1829			
	May 26 1845–May 31 1871	May 8 1845–Mar 1 1870			
	Jan 2 1870–Dec 28 1880	May 13 1871–Nov 26 1880			
Derrynoose (Armagh)	1814–19	1808–1814	1823–51	AA	
	1823–30	1823–33			
	1832–7	1846–1900			
	1846–1900				
	1835–7	1846–81	1846–51	PRONI	MIC.1D/40
	1846–81			LDS	1279356 item 1
	See NLI				
	Feb 1 1835–Jan 29 1837	July 17 1846–Jan 31 1875	July 22 1846–Apr 1851	NLI	Pos. 5589
	Dec 1846–Jan 28 1866	Feb 8 1875–Dec 9 1880			
	Feb 1 1866–Dec 30 1880				
Dromintee (Armagh)	1853–79	1853–77		PRONI	MIC.1D/41
	1853–1900	1853–77		AA	
		1883–4			
		1887–1900			
	June 7 1853–Aug 31 1879	Nov 8 1853–Dec 13 1877		NLI	Pos. 5590

Parish (Diocese)	Baptisms	Marriages	Burials	Location	Reference
Drumcree (Armagh)	1844–81 (some gaps)	1844–81 (some gaps)	1863–80	PRONI	MIC.1D/37; C.R.2/8
	1844–99	1844–1900	1863–1900	AA	
	Jan 1 1844–June 30 1864	Feb 9 1844–Nov 23 1863	May 26–Dec 22 1863	NLI	Pos. 5586
	June 17 1864–Dec 31 1880	July 23 1864–Nov 27 1880	June 24 1864–Dec 30 1880		
Dungannon (Armagh)	See Tyrone				
Eglish (Armagh)	1862–1900	1862–1900	1877–1900		IW
	1862–81	1862–82		PRONI	MIC.1D/36
	1862–1900	1862–1900	1877–1900	AA	
	Jan 21 1862–Nov 4 1880	Jan 27 1862–Nov 5 1880		NLI	Pos. 5585
Faughart (Armagh)	1851–1900	1851–1900		AA	
	1851–1900	1851–1900		Louth CL	
	1861–81 (indexed)	1851–82		PRONI	MIC.1D/47
	1851–96	indexed 1851–1900			
	Apr 16 1851–Dec 23 1880 (indexed)	Apr 21 1851–Nov 24 1880		LDS	0926040 item 1–5
	Apr 16 1851–Dec 23 1880 (indexed)	Apr 21 1851–Nov 24 1880		NLI	Pos. 5596
Forkhill (Armagh)	1845–79	1844–78		PRONI	MIC.1D/38
	1845–1900	1844–1900		AA	
	See NLI			LDS	0926041 item 1–2
	Jan 1 1845–Apr 29 1879	Jan 12 1844–Dec 29 1880		NLI	Pos. 5587
Killeavy Lower (Armagh)	1835–81	1835–62	1858–62	PRONI	MIC.1D/39
		1868–9			
		1874–8			
	1835–1900	1835–62		AA	
		1868–1900			
	See NLI			LDS	0926042
	Jan 4 1835–Jan 27 1860	Jan 6 1835–Jan 26 1860	Aug 1858–Jan 30 1860	NLI	Pos. 5588
	Jan 1 1860–Dec 29 1880	Jan 15 1860–Dec 29 1862	Jan 9 1860–Dec 24 1862		
		May 21 1874–Nov 29 1878			
Killeavy Upper (Armagh)	1832–80	1832–82		PRONI	MIC.1D/39
	1832–1900	1832–1900		AA	
	See NLI			LDS	0926042
	Oct 22 1832–Oct 31 1868	Nov 4 1832–Oct 13 1868		NLI	Pos. 5588
	Nov 7 1868–Dec 31 1880	Dec 30 1868–Dec 29 1880			
Kilmore (Armagh)	1845–81	1845–81		PRONI	MIC.1D/38
	1845–1900	1845–1900		AA	
	Jan 7 1845–Dec 19 1880	Jan 3 1845–Dec 31 1880		NLI	Pos. 5587
Loughgall and Tartaraghan (Armagh)	1834–1900	1833–1900		AA	
	1835–81	1833–80		PRONI	MIC.1D/38
	Jan 1835–Aug 29 1852	Aug 20 1833–Jan 5 1854		NLI	Pos. 5587
	Oct 8 1854–May 2 1858	Feb 8 1860–Nov 22 1880			
	July 12–Dec 27 1857				
	Sept 18 1859–Dec 28 1880				
Loughgilly (Armagh)	1825–44	1825–44		PRONI	MIC.1D/38
	1849–81	1849–81			
	1825–1900	1825–1900		AA	
	May 17 1825–Dec 31 1844	Feb 12 1825–Nov 29 1844		NLI	Pos. 5587
	Feb 4 1849–Dec 19 1880	Feb 18 1849–Dec 20 1880			

Parish (Diocese)	Baptisms	Marriages	Burials	Location	Reference
Magheralinn (Dromore)	See Down				
Newry (Dromore)	1818–84 (indexed from 1858)	1820–1917	1818–62	PRONI	MIC.1D/26–8
	1818–1900	1825–1900		UHF	
	See NLI			LDS	0926087 item 1–3
	Sept 18 1818–Nov 4 1819	May 16 1820–May 1825	Nov 6 1818–Apr 28 1819	NLI	Pos. 5501
	May 4 1820–July 1825	Aug 21 1825–Oct 23 1826	1820–July 17 1820		1818–26; Pos.
	Aug 21 1825–Sept 24 1826	Nov 6 1826–Jan 15 1851	Sept 11 1825–Oct 7 1826		5502 1826–80;
	Oct 1826–May 1843	Jan 21 1851–Dec 29 1880	Nov 8 1826–May 31 1862		Pos. 5503
	May 1843–Dec 1880				Index
	Index from 1858				
Seagoe (Dromore)	1836–81	1837–81	1837–80	PRONI	MIC.1D/23–4
	1836–1900	1836–1900		AA	
	See NLI			LDS	0926088 item 1–4
	Sept 1836–Feb 25 1870	Oct 16 1836–Feb 5 1860	Apr 13 1837–Jan 27 1860	NLI	Pos. 5498
	Mar 3 1870–Dec 26 1880	Feb 10 1860–Nov 18 1880	Feb 16 1860–Dec 5 1880		
Shankill (Dromore)	1822–81	1866–81	1866–81	PRONI	MIC.1D/23
	1822–1900	1822–1900	1825–1900	AA	
	See NLI			LDS	0926089
	Sept 13 1822–Dec 30 1865 (modern transcript with gaps)	Jan 19 1866–Dec 28 1880	Jan 5 1866–Dec 27 1880	NLI	Pos. 5498
	Jan 1 1866–Dec 31 1880				
Tynan (Armagh)	1822–34	1822–34		PRONI	MIC.1D/40
	1838–42	1845–77			
	1845–84				
	1822–1900	1822–34		AA	
		1836			
		1888–1900			
	See NLI			LDS	09799710 item 6–8
	June 2 1822–Aug 11 1834	June 6 1822–Oct 26 1834		NLI	Pos. 5589
	Aug 12 1838–July 25 1842	June 22 1845–Oct 18 1877			
	May 17 1845–Sept 2 1880				

Belfast

All parishes are in the
diocese of Down and
Connor. All UHF records are
searchable online at
<*www.rootisireland.ie*>.

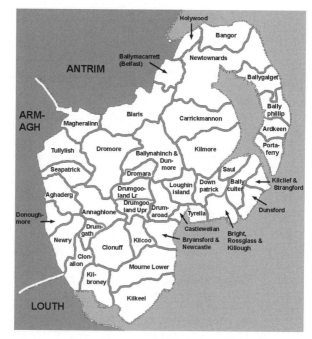

Parish	Baptisms	Marriages	Burials	Location	Reference
Ballymacarrett	1841–88	1841–88		PRONI	MIC.1D/65
	Oct 11 1841–Oct 7 1865	Oct 8 1841–May 7 1865		NLI	Pos. 5469
	Nov 5 1865–Dec 29 1880	Oct 12 1865–Dec 30 1880			
Holy Cross	1834–1900	1868–1900		UHF	
	1868–81	1868–81		PRONI	MIC.1D/65
	Sept 20 1868–Dec 31 1880	Sept 12 1868–Dec 25 1880		NLI	Pos. 5469
Holy Family	1869–1900	1895–1900		UHF	
	No records microfilmed			NLI	
	No records microfilmed			PRONI	
Holy Rosary	1888–1900	1895–1900		UHF	
	No records microfilmed			NLI	
	No records microfilmed			PRONI	
Sacred Heart	1891–1900	1890–1900		UHF	
	No records microfilmed			NLI	
	No records microfilmed			PRONI	
St Brigid's	1886–1900	1891–1900		UHF	
	No records microfilmed			NLI	
	No records microfilmed			PRONI	
St Joseph's		1872–1900		UHF	
	1872–81	1872–81		PRONI	MIC.1D/67
	Dec 22 1872–Dec 27 1880	Sept 24 1872–Dec 1 1880		NLI	Pos. 5471
St Malachy's	1858–81	1858–81		PRONI	MIC.1D/64
	1858–1900	1858–1900		UHF	
	May 10 1858–Dec 28 1880	June 9 1858–Dec 26 1880		NLI	Pos. 5468
	Jan 1 1870–Dec 28 1880	(many pages			
	(transcript)	mutilated)			

Parish	Baptisms	Marriages	Burials	Location	Reference
St Mary's	1867–81	1867–81		PRONI	MIC.1D/67
	1867–1900	1867–1900		UHF	
	Feb 18 1867–Sept 21 1876	Feb 18 1867–Dec 27 1880		NLI	Pos. 5471
	Sept 22 1876–Dec 31 1880				
St Mathew's	1841–1900	1841–1900		UHF	
	No records microfilmed			NLI	
	No records microfilmed			PRONI	
St Patrick's	1794–1900	1798–1900		UHF	
	1798–1811	1798–1812		PRONI	MIC.1D/66–7
	1814–67	1814–67			
	1875–80				
	Apr 5 1798–Oct 20 1811	Apr 19 1798–June 18 1812		NLI	Pos. 5470, 5471
	Jan 23 1814–Aug 18 1841	Jan 29 1814–Aug 17 1841			
	Aug 18 1841–July 15 1853	Aug 17 1841–July 28 1853			
	July 14 1853–July 17 1867	July 25 1853–July 2 1867			
	Aug 10 1875–June 7 1880				
St Paul's	1887–	1887–		Local custody	
	1887–1900	1887–1900		UHF	
	No records microfilmed			NLI	
	No records microfilmed			PRONI	
St Peter's	1866–81	1866–81		PRONI	MIC.1D/64–5
	1866–1900	1866–1900		UHF	
	Oct 31 1866–May 8 1871	Oct 22 1866–Dec 29 1880		NLI	Pos. 5468;
	May 14 1871–Feb 17 1875				Pos. 5469
	Feb 22 1875–Aug 2 1879				
	Aug 2 1879–Dec 29 1880				
St Vincent de Paul	1894–1900	1896–1900		UHF	
	No records microfilmed			NLI	
	No records microfilmed			PRONI	
Union Workhouse	1884–1900			UHF	
	No records microfilmed			NLI	
	No records microfilmed			PRONI	

Carlow

All parishes are in the diocese of Kildare and Leighlin. The location of the Carlow Genealogy Project (CGP) records is unclear. They may be available via Carlow County Library.

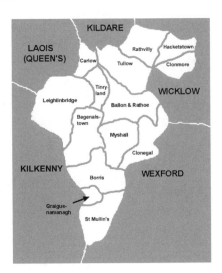

Parish	Baptisms	Marriages	Burials	Location	Reference
Ballon and Rathoe	1781–1899	1782–1899		CGP	
	Jan 2 1785–Sept 10 1795	Aug 10 1782–Dec 10 1795	Aug 9 1825–Dec 6 1834	NLI	Pos. 4189
	July 2 1816–Dec 26 1830	Jan 8 1820–Dec 14 1825	Jan 15 1861–Dec 28 1871		
	Jan 9 1820–Feb 14 1825	Aug 10 1816–Nov 26 1880			
	(not a duplicate)				
	Jan 6 1831–Dec 27 1867				
Ballynakill	1794–1899	1800–1899	1794–1815	IMA	
	Oct 14 1794–Mar 19 1815	Oct 27 1794–Feb 7 1815		NLI	Pos. 4200
	Jan 16 1820–May 26 1820	Jan 15 1820–July 7 1820			
	Nov 4 1820–Sept 19 1872	Nov 3 1820–Nov 25 1875			
	Sept 29 1872–June 11 1876	May 22 1877–Nov 3 1880			
	Apr 1 1877–Nov 3 1880				
Borris	1782–1899	1782–1899		CGP	
	See NLI			LDS	0926107
	May 2 1782–Dec 23 1813	Jan 26 1782–Dec 4 1813		NLI	Pos. 4196
	Feb 2 1825–Mar 15 1840	Feb 8 1825–Mar 3 1840			
	Mar 22 1840–Dec 30 1855	Apr 28 1840–Nov 23 1868			
	Jan 1 1856–Dec 30 1876	Feb 2 1869–Nov 27 1880			
	Jan 7 1877–Dec 25 1880				
Carlow	1774–1899	1769–1899		CGP	
	See NLI			LDS	0926119
					item 1–2
	June 1774–Jan 1789 (gaps)	Nov 8 1769–Aug 20 1786		NLI	Pos. 4193
	Dec 7–Dec 17 1793	1791 (some)			
	Jan 19 1794–Dec 17 1795	1794 (some)			
	Jan 1799–May 1804	Jan 1 1820–June 17 1845			
	Jan 10–Apr 15 1806	Jan 22 1845–Apr 14 1856			
	Jan 2–Feb 5 1807	May 10 1856–Nov 22 1880			
	Jan 1–May 8 1809				
	Jan 5–12 1811				
	1820–June 1845				
	Jan 1 1845–1880				
	Index 1834–49				
Clonegal	1833–99	1833–99		CGP	
	See NLI			LDS	0926110
	Jan 7 1833–Nov 27 1842	Feb 14 1833–May 20 1871		NLI	Pos. 4197
	Nov 27 1842–Dec 5 1852	May 25 1871–Nov 16 1880			
	Dec 5 1852–Mar 29 1868				
	Apr 2 1868–Apr 30 1871				
	(all transcripts)				
	June 5 1871–Nov 16 1880				
	(original)				
	1833–1900	1833–1900		WFHC	
Clonmore	1813–99	1819–99	1861–99	CGP	
	Nov 23 1819–Apr 9 1833	Feb 10 1813–Feb 19 1833		NLI	Pos. 4198
	Apr 7 1833–Feb 26 1860	May 4 1833–Feb 19 1860			
	Mar 4 1860–Dec 11 1880	May 16 1860–Dec 11 1880			
	1819–1900	1813–1900		WFHC	

Parish	Baptisms	Marriages	Burials	Location	Reference
Dunleckney	1820–99	1820–99		CGP	
	See NLI			LDS	0926113
	Jan 1 1820–June 27 1841	Jan 8 1820–June 26 1841		NLI	Pos. 4195
	July 1 1841–Dec 25 1857	July 8 1841–Nov 28 1857			
	Jan 3 1858–Nov 27 1880	Jan 19 1858–Nov 27 1880			
Graignamanagh	Apr 22 1838–Dec 27 1868	July 5 1818–Nov 26 1868		NLI	Pos. 4198
	Jan 1 1869–Dec 24 1880	Jan 17 1869–Nov 3 1880			
	1818–1900	1818–1900		RHK	
Hacketstown	1827–99	1828–99		CGP	
	See NLI			LDS	0926115 item 1
	1815–20 (a few entries)	Aug 31 1820–Dec 1 1827		NLI	Pos. 4191
	Aug 29 1820–Apr 20 1823	Mar 3 1829–Nov 28 1863			
	July 10 1826–Sept 7 1826	Nov 20 1861–Sept 25 1870			
	Oct 14 1827–Mar 23 1877	Feb 2 1877–Aug 1 1878			
	Jan 4 1862–Mar 23 1878	May 9 1878–Nov 25 1880			
	Mar 10 1878–Dec 26 1879				
	1828–1900	1820–1900		WFHC	
Leighlinbridge	1783–1900	1783–1899	1898–9	CGP	
	See NLI			LDS	1363869
	Jan 1 1783–Oct 22 1786	Feb 9 1783–Jan 14 1788		NLI	Pos. 4195
	Dec 1 1819–June 26 1827	July 12 1827–Nov 22 1880			
	July 6 1827–Nov 16 1844				
	Nov 17 1844–Sept 29 1867				
	Jan 2 1859–Dec 26 1880				
	Jan 12 1820–Feb 27 1827				
Myshall	1846–99	1846–99		CGP	
	See NLI			LDS	0926123
	Feb 11 1822–May 3 1846	Sept 17 1822–Jan 30 1845		NLI	Pos. 4198
	Oct 25 1846–Dec 25 1880	(pages missing and mutilated)			
		Feb 17 1846–Nov 27 1880			
Rathvilly	1797–1899	1800–1899	1844–99	CGP	
	Oct 19 1797–Jan 15 1813	Oct 5 1800–Feb 13 1812		NLI	Pos. 4189
	June 29 1813–Apr 25 1842	June 29 1813–Nov 27 1880			
	Apr 25 1842–Dec 12 1880				
	1797–1900	1799–1900	1860–84	WFHC	
St Mullins	1796–1899	1796–1899	1875–99	CGP	
	May 8 1796–Sept 28 1800	June 20 1796–Feb 5 1807		NLI	Pos. 4196
	Feb 1 1801–Apr 16 1807	Jan 8 1808–May 20 1809			
	Sept 4 1807–Mar 3 1810	Jan 24 1820–June 10 1832			
	Jan 19 1812–Apr 16 1814	Oct 25 1807–Mar (?) 8 1813			
	Feb 8 1816–Mar (?) 25 1816	Aug 10 1832–Nov 30 1871			
	Jan 6 1820–July 30 1832	Feb 6 1872–Nov 25 1880			
	Aug 10 1832–Nov 30 1871				
	Jan 4 1872–Dec 30 1880				
Tinryland	1813–99	1813–99	1898–9	CGP	
	Mar 28 1813–May 24 1833	June 20 1813–Feb 28 1843		NLI	Pos. 4192
	June 2 1833–Dec 20 1857	Apr 25 1843–Nov 26 1857			
	Jan 6 1858–Nov 27 1880	Jan 21 1858–Nov 27 1880			

Parish	Baptisms	Marriages	Burials	Location	Reference
Tullow	1748–1899	1748–1899	1767–75	CGP	
			1861–99		
	Aug 13 1763–Jan 10 1781	May 5 1775–Feb 20 1776		NLI	Pos. 4194
	Jan 19 1798–Jan 1 1802	(2 entries for 1777)			
	June 5 1807–July 4 1831 (?)	Jan 18 1799–Feb 27 1800			
	Aug 23 1830–Apr 18 1858	June 19 1807–May 20 1830			
	Apr 22 1858–Oct 9 1876	(transcript many gaps)			
	Oct 10 1876–Dec 21 1880	Nov (?) 20 1830–Feb 20			
		1860			
		Apr 30 1860–Nov 18 1880			

Cavan

All Cavan Heritage
and Genealogy
Centre (CHGC)
records are
searchable online at
<*www.rootis
ireland.ie*>.

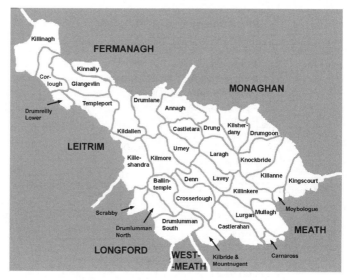

Parish (Diocese)	Baptisms	Marriages	Burials	Location	Reference
Annagh	1845–1920	1847–1900		CHGC	
(Kilmore)	Nov 12 1845–Oct 25 1864	July 1847–Dec 1880		NLI	Pos. 7505, 5342
	(Anna East)	(Anna East)			
	Jan 1849–Sept 1875	Nov 1864–Aug 1899			
	(Anna West)	(Anna West)			
	Oct 3 1875–Dec 29 1880				
	1875–81			PRONI	MIC.1D/75
Ballintemple	1862–99	1862–99		CHGC	
(Kilmore)	Oct 16 1862–Dec 26 1880	Oct 20 1862–Nov 20 1880		NLI	Pos. 5343
	1862–81	1862–81		PRONI	MIC.1D/76
Carnaross (Meath)	See Meath				
Castlerahan and	1752–1920	1752–1920	1752–1899	CHGC	
Munterconnaught	Feb 6 1752–July 1771	Sept 5 1751–June 8 1771	Sept 1751–June 1758	NLI	Pos. 5348
(Kilmore)	Feb 3 1773–Nov 4 1776	Feb 4 1773–Feb 26 1775	Dec 1761–July 1769		
	Nov 6 1814–Aug 16 1820	Nov 20 1814–June 7 1820	Feb 1773–Oct 1775		
	Oct 26 1828–May 2 1841	May 17 1832–Nov 27 1841	Dec 1814–Oct 1820		
	Aug 1854–Feb 17 1879	Aug 7 1855–Nov 26 1878	May 26 1832–Oct 24 1841		

Parish (Diocese)	Baptisms	Marriages	Burials	Location	Reference
Castlerahan and	1752–71	1751–71	1751–8	PRONI	MIC.1D/81
Munterconnaught	1773–6	1773–5	1761–9		
(Kilmore)	1814–20	1814–20	1773–5		
(contd.)	1828–41	1832–41	1814–20		
	1854–79	1855–78	1832–41		
Castletara	1763–1920	1763–1920		CHGC	
(Kilmore)	June 26 1763–June 12 1809	June 12 1763–Apr 29 1793		NLI	Pos. 5350, 6430
	Apr 19 1862–Dec 26 1880	Oct 28 1808–June 11 1809			
	1763–1809	1763–93		PRONI	MIC.1D/83–4
	1862–81	1808–1809			
Corlough	1877–1911	1877–1911		CHGC	
(Kilmore)	See NLI			LDS	0926129 item 3
	Feb 12 1877–Dec 16 1880	Feb 12 1877–Oct 21 1880	Feb 16 1877–Dec 19 1880	NLI	Pos. 5346
	1877–81	1877–82	1877–81	PRONI	MIC.1D/79
Crosserlough	1843–1920	1843–1920	1843–99	CHGC	
(Kilmore)	See NLI			LDS	0926130
	Oct 1843–Feb 17 1876	Dec 1866–Dec 13 1880	Dec 1866–Dec 13 1880	NLI	Pos. 5344
	Dec 1866–Dec 13 1880	Oct 10 1868–Nov 27 1880			
	Apr 2 1876–Aug 6 1880				
	1843–81	1843–81	1843–76	PRONI	MIC.1D/77
Denn (Kilmore)	1856–99	1856–99		CHGC	
	Oct 19 1856–Jan 16 1874	Oct 20 1856–Oct 28 1858		NLI	Pos. 5350
	(transcript–many gaps)				
	1856–74 (gaps)	1856–8		PRONI	MIC.1D/83
Drumgoon (Kilmore)	1829–1920	1829–1920		CHGC	
	Feb 22 1829–July 25 1872			NLI	Pos. 5348
	Oct 1 1872–Sept 12 1879				
	1829–79	1829–72		PRONI	MIC.1D/81
Drumlane (Kilmore)	1835–1920	1835–1920		CHGC	
	Jan 1836–Nov 20 1867	Sept 1 1870–Dec 8 1880		NLI	Pos. 5342
	(out of order)				
	Jan 6 1868–Dec 12 1880				
	1836–81	1870–80		PRONI	MIC.1D/75
Drumlumman South	1837–99	1837–99	1837–99	CHGC	
(Ardagh and	See NLI			LDS	1279229 item 7
Clonmacnoise)	Nov 13 1837–Aug 3 1873	Dec 2 1837–June 18 1873	Dec 21 1837–Sept 17 1869	NLI	Pos. 4236
	May 5 1875–Dec 5 1880	Feb 27 1876–Nov 30 1880	Feb 16 1876–Dec 18 1880		
Drumreilly Lower	See Leitrim				
(Kilmore)					
Drung (Kilmore)	1847–1920			CHGC	
See also Kilsherdany	1847–82	1847–82		NLI	Ms. 25,553
	1847–83			PRONI	C.R.2/10
Glangevlin (Kilmore)	1867–99	1867–1920		CHGC	
	See NLI			LDS	0979703 item 5
	Mar 2 1867–Dec 29 1880	Jan 28 1867–Nov 15 1880		NLI	Pos. 5345
	1867–81	1867–81		PRONI	MIC.1D/78
Kilbride and	See Meath				
Mountnugent					
(Meath)					

Parish (Diocese)	Baptisms	Marriages	Burials	Location	Reference
Kildallen (Kilmore)	1867–1900	1867–1900		CHGC	
	Apr 15 1867–Dec 31 1880	Jan 1 1867–Dec 9 1880		LDS	0979703 item 2
	Apr 15 1867–Dec 31 1880	Jan 1 1867–Dec 9 1880		NLI	Pos. 5345
	1867–81	1867–81		PRONI	MIC.1D/78
Killanne (Kilmore)	1835–1920	1835–1920		CHGC	
	See NLI			LDS	0926132 item 2
	Jan 28 1835–Nov 20 1849	Jan 12 1835–Feb 12 1850		NLI	Pos. 5349
	Jan 13 1868–Nov 19 1880	Jan 28 1868–Sept 22 1880			
	1835–49	1835–50		PRONI	MIC.1D./82
	1868–80	1868–80			
Killeshandra	1835–1920	1835–1920	1835–99	CHGC	
(Kilmore)	See NLI			LDS	099703 item 7
	Jan 4 1835–Oct 14 1840	Jan 7 1835–Sept 1 1840		NLI	Pos. 5345/6
	Dec 24 1840–Aug 24 1844	Aug 19 1849–May 20 1852			
	Mar 15 1845–July 17 1852	Aug 1 1853–Oct 15 1868			
	Aug 1 1853–Oct 15 1868	Sept 28 1868–Nov 15 1880			
	Oct 3 1868–Dec 31 1880				
	1835–80	1835–40		PRONI	MIC.1D/78–9
		1849–81			
Killinagh (Kilmore)	1860–1900	1860–1900	1875–99	CHGC	
	Apr 1 1869–Dec 31 1880	June 28 1869–Nov 28 1880	Feb 21 1875–Dec 27 1880	NLI	Pos. 5350
	1869–81	1869–81	1875–81	PRONI	MIC.1D/83
Killinkere and	1766–1920	1766–1920	1842–99	CHGC	
Mullagh (Kilmore)	May 27 1766–Oct 19 1790	Dec 23 1766–Aug 29 1789		NLI	Pos. 5349
	Jan 1 1842–Apr 11 1862	Jan 22 1842–Nov 32 1861			
	Mar 5 1864–Dec 12 1880	June 4 1864–Nov 19 1880			
	1766–90	1766–89		PRONI	MIC.1D/82
	1842–61	1842–61			
	1864–80	1864–80			
Kilmore (Kilmore)	1859–1909	1859–1909	1859–1909	CHGC	
	May 1 1859–Dec 31 1880	May 1 1859–Dec 31 1880	May 1 1859–Dec 31 1880	NLI	Pos. 5343
	1859–81	1859–81	1859–81	PRONI	MIC.1D/76
Kilsherdany	1803–1899	1803–1899		CHGC	
(Kilmore)	June 26 1803–Nov 26 1814	July 10 1803–Jan 18 1814		NLI	Pos. 5342
	Nov 19 1826–Apr 29 1849	Jan 12–May 20 1835			
	Oct 4 1855–Jan 10 1860	1843–Apr 29 1849			
		Oct 1 1855–Aug 16 1857			
	1803–1814	1803–1814		PRONI	MIC.1D/48
	1826–49	1835			
	1855–60	1843–9			
		1855–7			
Kingscourt (Meath)	1838–1920	1838–1920		CHGC	
	See NLI			LDS	0926175
	Oct 16 1838–Aug 13 1854	Aug 15 1838–May 27 1861	Sept 1846–May 30 1858	NLI	Pos. 4183
	Jan 1 1864–Dec 31 1880				
Kinnally (Kilmore)	1835–99	1835–1900	1852–7	CHGC	
	Dec 11 1835–Mar 28 1853	Dec 3 1835–Apr 29 1853	Apr 5 1853–Mar 7 1857	NLI	Pos. 5346
	Apr 5 1853–Mar 7 1857	Apr 5 1853–Mar 7 1857			
	Mar 16 1857–Dec 17 1880				
	1835–81	1835–57	1853–7	PRONI	MIC.1D/79

Parish (Diocese)	Baptisms	Marriages	Burials	Location	Reference
Knockbride (Kilmore)	1835–1920	1835–1920		CHGC	
	See NLI			LDS	0926133 item 3
	May 15 1835–Aug 19 1860	Jan 15 1835–Aug 20 1860	Jan 11 1835–1860	NLI	Pos. 5349
	Sept 7 1860–May 20 1879	Sept 12 1860–Jan 25 1877	Sept 10 1860–Mar 6 1875		
	1835–79	1835–79	1835–75	PRONI	MIC.1D/82
Laragh (Kilmore)	1876–1920	1835–1920		CHGC	
	May 2 1876–Dec 1 1880			NLI	Pos. 5342
	1876–81			PRONI	MIC.1D/75
Lavey (Kilmore)	1867–99	1867–99		CHGC	
	Jan 12 1867–Sept 19 1880			NLI	Pos. 5342
	1867–81			PRONI	MIC.1D/75
Lurgan (Kilmore)	1755–1899	1755–1920		CHGC	
	See NLI			LDS	0926134
	Jan 6 1755–Aug 1 1795	Feb 1755–Aug 29 1770	Nov 12 1821–Oct 5 1840	NLI	Pos. 5347
	(very patchy)	Jan 14 1773–Sept 6 1780	Oct 1 1840–Mar 30 1855		
	Nov 1 1821–Sept 30 1840	Nov 21 1821–Sept 23 1840			
	Oct 10 1840–Dec 31 1875	Oct 10 1840–Nov 27 1875			
	Jan 4 1876–Dec 24 1880				
	1755–95 (gaps)	1855–1770	1821–55	PRONI	MIC.1D/80–81
	1821–81	1773–80			
		1821–75			
Moybologue (Kilmore)	See Meath				
Mullagh (Kilmore)	June 29 1842–Feb 28 1872	June 29 1842–July 6 1872	Sept 29 1842–Feb 3 1857	NLI	Pos. 5347
	1760–90	1766–89	1842–57	PRONI	MIC.1D/80, 82
	1842–72	1842–72			
Mullahoran (Ardagh and Clonmacnoise)	1859–1902	1859–1902	1859–1937	CHGC	
	1859–1902	1859–1902	1859–75	LDS	1279229 item 10
			1925–37		
	Jan 21 1859–Dec 26 1880	Jan 31 1859–Dec 6 1880	Feb 7 1859–Feb 26 1875	NLI	Pos. 4237
Scrabby (Ardagh and Clonmacnoise)	See Longford				
Templeport (Kilmore)	1836–1904	1836–1904	1827–99	CHGC	
	See NLI			LDS	0979703 item 6
	Sept 4 1836–July 14 1870	Nov 18 1836–July 4 1870	Feb 26 1827–Dec 1845	NLI	Pos. 5345
	July 26 1870–Dec 24 1880	Sept 15 1870–Oct 16 1880	July 26 1870–Dec 16 1880		
	1836–80	1836–82	1827–45	PRONI	MIC.1D/78
			1870–80		
Urney (Kilmore)	1812–1920	1812–1920		CHGC	
	July 6 1812–Dec 12 1829	July 19 1812–Feb 23 1830		NLI	Pos. 5342/3
	Dec 1829–July 24 1859	Feb 23 1830–Aug 3 1859			
	Jan 1 1860–Dec 30 1880	Sept 14 1859–Nov 27 1880			
	1812–81	1812–80		PRONI	MIC.1D/75–6

Clare

All Limerick Genealogy (LG) transcripts are online at <*www.rootsireland.ie*>.

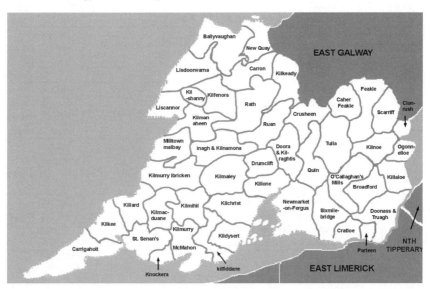

Parish (Diocese)	Baptisms	Marriages	Burials	Location	Reference
Ballyvaughan	1854–1900			CCL	
Galway	1854–1900	Not specified		Clare HGC	
	Sept 1 1854–July 29 1876	Aug 18 1876–Dec 31 1880		NLI	Pos. 2440
Broadford (Killaloe)	1845–1900	Not specified		Clare HGC	
	See NLI			LDS	0979694 item 3
	Jan 19 1844–Dec 19 1880	Feb 10 1844–Nov 27 1880		NLI	Pos. 2476
Caher Feakle	1842–1900	Not specified		Clare HGC	
(Killaloe)	Feb 16 1842–Mar 27 1861	Jan 16 1842–Feb 12 1861		NLI	Pos. 2487
	Mar 25 1861–Jan 28 1873	Nov 15 1862–July 28 1880			
	Feb 4 1873–Dec 26 1880				
Carrigaholt (Killaloe)	1853–1900	Not specified		Clare HGC	
	See NLI			LDS	0926099
	Feb 8 1853–Mar 17 1878	Jan 12 1852–Mar 17 1878		NLI	Pos. 2485
	Feb 19 1878–Dec 15 1880	Mar 5 1878–Nov 15 1880			
Carron (Galway)	1854–1900	Not specified		Clare HGC	
	See NLI			LDS	0926063
	Oct 26 1853–Dec 25 1880	Nov 24 1856–June 22 1880		NLI	Pos. 2440
Clonrush (Killaloe)	1846–1900	Not specified		Clare HGC	
	See NLI			LDS	0926093 item 1
	July 1846–Mar 3 1880	Jan 22 1846–Feb 10 1880		NLI	Pos. 2476
Cratloe (Limerick)	1802–1900	Not specified		Clare HGC	
	Nov 26 1802–Dec 30 1856	Jan 15 1822–Dec 10 1856		NLI	Pos. 2410/11
	Jan 16 1857–Nov 19 1877	Feb 3 1857–Sept 8 1877			
	1802–1833	1822–1901		LG	
Crusheen (Killaloe)	1860–1900	Not specified		Clare HGC	
	See NLI			LDS	0926093 item 2
	Feb 1860–Dec 29 1880			NLI	Pos. 2472

Parish (Diocese)	Baptisms	Marriages	Burials	Location	Reference
Doonass and Truagh	1851–1900	Not specified		Clare HGC	
(Killaloe)	See NLI			LDS	0979694 item 2
	July 27 1851–Dec 12 1880	Sept 6 1851–Nov 29 1880		NLI	Pos. 2476
Doora and Kilraghtis	1821–1900	Not specified		Clare HGC	
(Killaloe)	Mar 1 1821–Jan 23 1863	Jan 10 1823–Dec 5 1880		NLI	Pos. 2472
	Mar 1862–Dec 23 1880				(B.to 1862); remainder 2474
Drumclift (Killaloe)	1841–1900	Not specified		Clare HGC	
	Mar 19 1841–Oct 1 1879	Apr 3 1837–Dec 1 1880		NLI	Pos. 2472
	1841–1900	1837–1900		Online	<www.ennis parish.com>
Feakle (Killaloe)	1860–1900	Not specified		Clare HGC	
	1842–61	1842–61		LDS	0979696 items
	1860–80	1860–80			5,7; 0979694 it 5
	Apr 22 1860–Dec 25 1880	Sept 21 1860–Aug 17 1880		NLI	Pos. 2476
Inagh and Kilnamona	1850–1900	Not specified		Clare HGC	
(Killaloe)	Feb 23 1850–Oct 1 1865 (indexed)	Apr 14 1850–July 26 1865 (indexed)		NLI	Pos. 2472
	Oct 6 1865–Dec 25 1880	Oct 9 1865–July 29 1880			
Kilchrist (Killaloe)	1846–1900	Not specified		Clare HGC	
	See NLI			LDS	0926092
	Oct 2 1846–Dec 29 1880	Nov 1 1846–June 20 1880		NLI	Pos. 2471
Kildysart (Killaloe)	1829–1900	Not specified		Clare HGC	
	July 1829–Nov 1866 (indexed transcript with parish history)	Jan 1867–Dec 22 1880		NLI	Pos. 2475
	Nov 14 1866–Dec 28 1880				
Kilfenora (Galway)	1836–1900	Not specified		Clare HGC	
	See NLI			LDS	0926065
	June 1 1836–May 15 1847	Dec 2 1865–Nov 26 1880		NLI	Pos. 2440
	Sept 3 1854–Sept 12 1876				
	Oct 8 1876–Dec 27 1880				
Kilfiddane (Killaloe)	1868–1900	Not specified		Clare HGC	
	Aug 15 1868–Dec 20 1880	Jan 8 1869–Feb 10 1880		NLI	Pos. 2485
Kilkee (Killaloe)	1836–1900	Not specified		Clare HGC	
	See NLI			LDS	0926100
	Mar 3 1869–Dec 12 1880			NLI	Pos. 2485
Killaloe (Killaloe)	1828–1900	Not specified		Clare HGC	
	May 24 1828–June 19 1844	Feb 26 1829–Sept 7 1880		NLI	Pos. 2477
	June 23 1844–Jan 21 1855				
	Feb 1 1855–Dec 8 1880				
Killard (Killaloe)	1855–1900	Not specified		Clare HGC	
	See NLI			LDS	0979696 item 2–3
	May 13 1855–Dec 29 1880 (transcript)		Feb 12 1867–Oct 31 1880	NLI	Pos. 2487
Killkeady (Killaloe)	1833–1900	Not specified		Clare HGC	
	Feb 1833–40 (transcript)	Feb 20 1871–July 24 1880		NLI	Pos. 2473
	1840–55 (transcript)				
	1855–66 (transcript)				
	Dec 24 1870–Dec 31 1880				

Parish (Diocese)	Baptisms	Marriages	Burials	Location	Reference
Killone (Killaloe)	1834–1900	Not specified		Clare HGC	
	See NLI			LDS	0979693
					item 1–2
	Jan 25 1863–July 21 1880 (Killone)	Feb 17 1853–Dec 15 1880 (Killone)		NLI	Pos. 2471
	Dec 10 1853–Dec 15 1880 (Clarecastle)	Jan 21 1854–Nov 19 1880 (Clarecastle)			
Kilmacduane (Killaloe)	1854–1900	Not specified		Clare HGC	
	Jan 17 1854–Dec 30 1880	May 1 1853–Nov 29 1867		NLI	Pos. 2485
Kilmaley (Killaloe)	1829–1900	Not specified		Clare HGC	
	See NLI			LDS	0926094
	Sept 23 1828–Dec 31 1880			NLI	Pos. 2474
Kilmanaheen (Galway)	1823–1900	Not specified		Clare HGC	
	See NLI			LDS	0926067
	Jan 15 1870–Sept 8 1880			NLI	Pos. 2440
Kilmihil (Killaloe)	1849–1900	Not specified		Clare HGC	
	Mar 20 1849–Jan 12 1870 (indexed)	Jan 20 1849–Sept 19 1869 (indexed)		NLI	Pos. 2485
	Jan 1 1870–Dec 29 1880	Apr 8 1869–Nov 13 1880			
Kilmurry Ibricken (Killaloe)	1839–1900	Not specified		Clare HGC	
	See NLI			LDS	0926101
	Apr 25 1839–Apr 12 1876	Apr 13 1839–Aug 14 1852		NLI	Pos. 2486
	Jan 1 1876–Dec 26 1880	Sept 1855–Aug 2 1863			
	(transcript)	Feb 11 1863–Oct 15 1876			
		Feb 5 1876–Nov 27 1880			
Kilmurry McMahon (Killaloe)	1842–1900	Not specified		Clare HGC	
	Nov 1 1845–Dec 19 1880	Sept 20 1837–Oct 16 1880	Nov 5 1844–Apr 1848	NLI	Pos. 2485
Kilnoe (Killaloe)	1832–1900	Not specified		Clare HGC	
	Nov 1 1832–Dec 31 1880	Nov 2 1832–July 4 1880		NLI	Pos. 2477
Kilshanny (Galway)	1869–1900	Not specified		Clare HGC	
	No records microfilmed			NLI	
Knockera (Killaloe)	1859–1900	Not specified		Clare HGC	
	Jan 23 1859–Dec 30 1880	Feb 10 1859–Nov 23 1880		NLI	Pos. 2485
Limerick city: Parteen (Limerick)	Sept 26 1831–Feb 14 1877	July 1 1814–Nov 9 1819		NLI	Pos. 2410
		Feb 4 1821–Jan 10 1836			
		Feb 9 1847–Jan 22 1877			
	1831–1900	Not specified		Clare HGC	
	1831–1902	1814–1900		LG	
Liscannor (Galway)	1843–1900	Not specified		Clare HGC	
	June 15 1843–July 4 1854	Feb 17 1866–Oct 4 1880		NLI	Pos. 2440
	July 3 1854–Feb 27 1873	(transcript)			
		May 25 1873–Oct 4 1880			
Lisdoonvarna (Galway)	1854–1900	Not specified		Clare HGC	
	June 1 1854–Nov 19 1876	Jan 12 1860–Nov 23 1880		NLI	Pos. 2440
Milltownmalbay (Killaloe)	1831–1900	Not specified		Clare HGC	
	Nov 16 1831–July 8 1855	Nov 24 1856–Dec 1 1858		NLI	Pos. 2486
	May 1 1855–Dec 1 1858	Feb 9 1859–Nov 27 1880			
	Dec 4 1858–Dec 31 1880				

Parish (Diocese)	Baptisms	Marriages	Burials	Location	Reference
New Quay (Galway)	1836–1900	Not specified		Clare HGC	
	See NLI			LDS	0979691 item 1
	Oct 4 1847–Aug 31 1854 (transcript)	Feb 5 1848–Apr 20 1863 (transcript)		NLI	Pos. 2441
	Oct 3 1854–Dec 30 1880				
Newmarket-on-Fergus (Killaloe)	1828–1900	Not specified		Clare HGC	
	See NLI			LDS	0926095 item 2
	Apr 29 1828–Feb 25 1866	1828–Aug 13 1865		NLI	Pos. 2471–2
O'Callaghan's Mills (Killaloe)	1835–1900	Not specified		Clare HGC	
	See NLI			LDS	0979694 item 6
	Jan 4 1835–Dec 31 1880	Jan 14 1835–Nov 14 1880		NLI	Pos. 2476
Ogonnelloe (Killaloe)	1832–1900	Not specified		Clare HGC	
	See NLI			LDS	0979694 item 1
	Mar 29 1832–Feb 25 1869 (transcript)	Feb 9 1857–Feb 9 1869 (transcript)		NLI	Pos. 2476
Quin (Killaloe)	1815–1900	Not specified		Clare HGC	
	See NLI			LDS	0926096
	Jan 4 1816–Mar 1 1855	Jan 29 1833–Feb 14 1855		NLI	Pos. 2473
	Jan 1855–Dec 31 1880	Jan 10 1855–June 26 1880			
Rath (Killaloe)	1819–1900	Not specified		Clare HGC	
	Apr 4 1819–Dec 25 1836	Jan 27 1818–Feb 25 1844		NLI	Pos. 2474 (B.
	Feb 216 1837–Nov 15 1862	Feb 27 1859–Nov 26 1862			to 1862);
	Oct 31 1862–Dec 23 1880	Nov 10 1862–June 27 1880			remainder 2475
Ruan (Killaloe)	1845–1900	Not specified		Clare HGC	
	Aug 18 1845–Dec 23 1880	July 2 1846–June 23 1880		NLI	Pos. 2473
Scarriff (Killaloe)	1852–1900	Not specified		Clare HGC	
	See NLI			LDS	0926097
	May 5 1852–Mar 24 1872	Nov 22 1852–Apr 20 1872		NLI	Pos. 2476
	Mar 24 1872–Dec 31 1880	Apr 20 1872–June 15 1880			
Sixmilebridge (Killaloe)	1828–1900	Not specified		Clare HGC	
	Dec 15 1828–Aug 28 1839	Jan 25 1829–July 29 1839		NLI	Pos. 2474
	Jan 28 1840–Dec 23 1864	May 1840–Nov 26 1864			
	Jan 6 1865–Dec 26 1880	Feb 12 1865–Oct 12 1880			
St Senan's (Killaloe)	1827–1900	Not specified		Clare HGC	
	See NLI			LDS	0979696 item 4
	Aug 1 1827–Dec 8 1831	Jan 7 1829–Dec 6 1880		NLI	Pos. 2487
	Jan 14 1833–Sept 29 1863				
	Oct 1 1863–Dec 31 1880				
Tulla (Killaloe)	1819–1900	Not specified		Clare HGC	
	See NLI			LDS	0979693 item 4
	Jan 1819–Mar 28 1846	Jan 1 1819–Feb 24 1846		NLI	Pos. 2471
	Apr 21 1846–Dec 28 1861 (indexed)	Apr 20 1846–Nov 30 1861 (indexed)			
	Jan 1 1862–Dec 29 1880 (indexed)	Jan 21 1862–Oct 21 1880			

Cork East

Cork city parishes are all in the diocese of Cork and Ross. With the exception of St Mary's and St Patrick's, all Cork and Ross diocese NLI records are online at <*www.irishgenealogy.ie*>. All Mallow Heritage Centre (MHC) transcripts are online at <*www.rootsireland.ie*>.

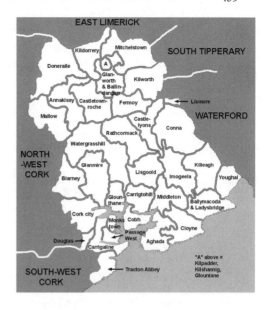

Parish (Diocese)	Baptisms	Marriages	Burials	Location	Reference
Aghada (Cloyne)	1792–1895	1785–1897		MHC	
	Jan 1 1815–Mar 26 1837	May 11 1838–Nov 26 1880		NLI	Pos. 4990
	Mar 12 1838–Nov 26 1880				
Annakissy (Cloyne)	1805–1895	1806–1875		MHC	
	June 16 1806–Dec 28 1829	July 28 1805–Nov 19 1835		NLI	Pos. 5001
	Jan 3 1830–Dec 26 1880	Jan 21–June 4 1837			
		July 9 1837–Nov 27 1880			
Ballymacoda and	1835–99	1836–99		MHC	
Ladysbridge (Cloyne)	Nov 10 1835–Aug 28 1880	Sept 22 1835–Nov 11 1879		NLI	Pos. 4991
Blarney (Cloyne)	1820–96	1779–1813		MHC	
		1821–95			
	Aug 12 1791–June 6 1792	Sept 24 1778–Mar 2 1813		NLI	Pos. 5006;
	Feb 2 1821–Dec 19 1825	Feb 15 1821–Nov 26 1825			marriages
	Oct 29 1826–May 25 1845	Dec 17 1826–Aug 26 1849			from 1848 on
	June 1 1845–Dec 22 1880	Jan 11 1848–Nov 8 1880			Pos. 5007
Carrigaline	Jan 1 1826–Dec 19 1880	Jan 23 1826–Nov 18 1880		NLI	Pos. 4790.
(Cork and Ross)					Online: <*www.*
					irishgene
					alogy.ie>
	1826–80	1826–80		Published	Thompson,
					Families
Carrigtohill (Cloyne)	1817–1922	1818–1922		MHC	
	Dec 2 1817–July 1873	Nov 22 1817–Oct 13 1878		NLI	Pos. 4989
	July 19 1873–Nov 5 1880				
Castlelyons (Cloyne)	1791–1910	1830–1922		MHC	
	Aug 12 1791–Dec 28 1828	Jan 17 1830–Nov 19 1880		NLI	Pos. 4994
	Jan 3 1830–Dec 22 1880				

Parish (Diocese)	Baptisms	Marriages	Burials	Location	Reference
Castletownroche (Cloyne)	1810–1922	1811–1922		MHC	
	Aug 25 1811–Dec 29 1834	Sept 19 1811–Oct 1845		NLI	Pos. 4995;
	Jan 2 1835–Dec 27 1866	Nov 29 1845–Oct 13 1880			baptisms from 1835, marriages from 1845, Pos. 4996
Cloyne (Cloyne)	1791–1922	1791–1895		MHC	
	Sept 2 1791–Nov 4 1793	Feb 3 1786–Feb 17 1801		NLI	Pos. 4989
	Oct 5 1803–July 30 1812	Apr 14 1801–Dec 2 1820			baptisms; Pos.
	Jan 2 1821–Dec 29 1831	Jan 11 1821–Nov 26 1831			4990
	July 1 1833–Dec 29 1878	Jan 10 1832–May 18 1880			marriages
Cobh (Cloyne)	1812–1908	1812–99		MHC	
	1812–Dec 31 1820			NLI	Pos. 4986;
	Jan 22 1821–May 24 1827				baptisms from
	June 5 1827–May 1842				1821,
	Aug 1842–May 31 1863				marriages
	June 4 1863–Dec 30 1877				from 1812 on
	Jan 3 1878–Dec 19 1880				Pos. 4987
Conna (Cloyne)	1832–1911	1844–1922		MHC	
	Sept 1834–Sept 1844 (some gaps)	Oct 30 1845–Nov 13 1880		NLI	Pos. 4996
	Dec 16 1845–Dec 26 1880				
Cork city: Blackrock (Cork and Ross)	July 10 1810–May 31 1811	Sept 16 1810–May 18 1811		NLI	Pos. 4791
	Feb 5 1832–Aug 15 1837	Feb 7 1832–Aug 15 1837			
	Feb 3 1839–June 17 1839	Feb 13 1841–Oct 9 1847			
	Jan 6 1841–Aug 16 1847	Jan 18 1848–Nov 2 1880			
	Jan 13 1848–Dec 5 1880				
Cork city: SS. Peter and Paul (Cork and Ross)	Apr 24 1766–Oct 22 1766	Apr 30 1766–Sept 18 1776 NLI		Pos. 4785,	
	Nov 14 1780–Jan 21 1798	Oct 22 1780–Oct 6 1803			4786, 4887;
	Jan 21 1798–Sept 23 1803	Jan 22 1809–Aug 23 1810			Online: <www.
	Jan 1 1809–June 17 1811	July 22 1814–Aug 30 1817			irishgene
	Apr 1834–May 31 1840	May 5 1834–May 30 1840			alogy.ie>
	Jan 15 1837–Dec 30 1855	(scraps 1825 and 1827)			
	Feb 1 1856–Sept 13 1870	Jan 17 1838–Dec 3 1853			
	Mar 3 1870–Dec 25 1880	Jan 3 1856–Nov 27 1880			
Cork city: St Finbarr's (South) (Cork and Ross)	Aug 10 1756–Sept 7 1757	Bans 1753–74 (many gaps)		NLI	Pos. 4778–80;
	July 5 1760–Sept 17 1763	Apr 22 1775–Sept 3 1789			Online: <www.
	Mar 22 1772–July 30 1777	Jan 7 1789–June 20 1810			irishgene
	Jan 15 1789–Dec 30 1802	June 21 1810–Jan 14 1860			alogy.ie>
	Jan 1 1803–Dec 1834	Jan 1 1860–Dec 2 1877			
	Jan 3 1835–Dec 19 1856	Jan 8 1878–Nov 27 1880			
	Jan 12 1857–Jan 6 1878				
	Jan 7 1878–Dec 31 1880				
Cork city: St Mary's (Cork and Ross)	July 1748–May 1764	July 10 1748–May 30 1764		NLI	B.1748–64, Pos.
	Mar 1765–Nov 1788 (gaps)	Apr 16 1765–Nov 19 1788			4780; B.
	Aug 1780–Dec 1788 (gaps)	Jan 7 1789–Dec 26 1812			1773–1807, Pos.
	Jan–May 1786	Jan 7 1813–Nov 25 1845			4781; B.
	Jan 1789–Jan 1807(gaps)	Mar 1831–4 (odd pages)			1789–1834,
	Jan 1808–Mar 1834	Jan 14 1845–Dec 30 1880			Pos. 4782; B.
	Mar 1831–4 (gaps)	1846–53 (odd pages)			1833–59, Pos.
	Nov 1833–Oct 1853				4783; B.

Parish (Diocese)	Baptisms	Marriages	Burials	Location	Reference
Cork city: St Mary's (Cork and Ross) *(contd.)*	1846–53 (gaps) 1852–80				1869–80, Pos. 4874; M. 1748–88, Pos. 4784; M. 1789–1880, Pos. 4785
Cork city: St Patrick's (Cork and Ross)	Oct 7 1831–Jan 3 1851 Nov 30 1836–Mar 27 1872 Apr 1 1872–Dec 29 1880	July 16 1832–June 29 1851 (very few for 1831–4) Nov 19 1836–Dec 20 1880		NLI	Pos. 4788
Doneraile (Cloyne)	1815–1922 Apr 16 1815–Sept 17 1836 Dec 21 1836–May 12 1867 Mar 1 1866–Dec 28 1880	1815–95 Jan 26 1815–May 14 1867 Mar 4 1866–Dec 2 1880		MHC NLI	Pos. 5000
Douglas (Cork and Ross)	Nov 15 1812–Aug 30 1851 Sept 27 1851–Dec 23 1867 Feb 26 1867–Dec 17 1880	Nov 25 1812–July 25 1851 Aug 23 1851–Mar 3 1867 Mar 2 1867–Nov 13 1880		NLI	Pos. 4790. Online: <*www.irishgenealogy.ie*>
Fermoy (Cloyne)	1827–99 Jan 1 1828–Aug 27 1848 Jan 4 1849–Dec 27 1880 Workhouse: Apr 28 1854–Sept 17 1880	1828–99 May 18 1828–Dec 21 1880		MHC NLI	Pos. 4993 baptisms; Pos. 4994 marriages
Glanmire (Cork and Ross)	1818–28 1828–41 1842–71 to date May 10 1818–Oct 12 1828 Oct 13 1828–Dec 31 1841	1818–28 1828–41 1842–71 to date May 29 1818–Oct 6 1828 Nov 11 1828–Dec 1841 Feb 11 1871–Oct 2 1880		Local custody NLI	Pos. 4789; marriages from 1871 on Pos. 4790
Glanworth and Ballindangan (Cloyne)	1836–99 Jan 1 1836–Dec 12 1880 Ballindangan, Sept 1870– Dec 29 1880	1836–99 Glanworth only, Jan 12 1836–Oct 19 1880		MHC NLI	Pos. 4996
Glountane (Cloyne)	1829–95 May 20 1829–Aug 1844 May 16 1847–Dec 21 1880	1858–95		MHC NLI	Pos. 5008
Glounthane (Cork and Ross)	Aug 20 1864–Dec 25 1880 1813–	Oct 8 1864–Nov 25 1880 1813–		NLI Local custody	Pos. 4789
Imogeela (Cloyne)	1835–99 Feb 1 1833–Dec 19 1880	1834–99 Sept 22 1833–Sept 6 1879		MHC NLI	Pos. 4991
Kildorrery (Cloyne)	1824–99 May 15 1824–Sept 30 1853	1803–1895 Jan 25 1803–Aug 15 1880		MHC NLI	Pos. 4994
Killeagh (Cloyne)	1829–96 Mar 29 1829–Sept 30 1880	1823–97 Nov 1 1822–July 10 1880		MHC NLI	Pos. 4992
Kilpadder (Cloyne)	Feb 12 1858–Nov 20 1869			NLI	Pos. 5008
Kilshannig (Cloyne)	Apr 10 1842–June 23 1850			NLI	Pos. 5008
Kilworth (Cloyne)	1829–99 Sept 19 1829–Oct 9 1876	1830–99 Oct 3 1829–Dec 16 1880		MHC NLI	Pos. 4996

Parish (Diocese)	Baptisms	Marriages	Burials	Location	Reference
Lisgoold (Cloyne)	1807–1895	1822–99		MHC	
	July 13 1807–July 26 1821	Oct 16 1821–Nov 13 1880		NLI	Pos. 4991
	July 31 1821–Apr 29 1853				
	May 8 1853–Dec 31 1880				
Lismore	See Waterford				
Mallow (Cloyne)	1809	1758–1922		MHC	
	1817–28				
	1832–1922				
	Jan 1–July 17 1809	Apr 17 1757–Nov 22 1823		NLI	Pos. 4997;
	June 28 1817–Feb 19 1818	Oct 6 1805–Sept 6 1820			baptisms from
	Aug 27 1820–June 23 1828	Apr 30 1832–Jan 31 1841			1847,
	Jan 2 1825–July 31 1828	Feb 2 1844–Oct 17 1880			marriages
	Jan 2 1825–Dec 28 1828				from 1844 on
	Apr 13 1832–Dec 14 1840				Pos. 4998
	Jan 4 1841–80				
Middleton (Cloyne)	1819–99	1810–54		MHC	
		1866–99			
	Sept 24 1819–Dec 29 1863	Oct 31 1819–Apr 21 1864		NLI	Pos. 4986
	Jan 3 1864–Dec 30 1880	Jan 16 1864–Dec 31 1880			
Mitchelstown (Cloyne)	1792–1801	1815–99		MHC	
	1815–99				
	Jan 1 1792–July 13 1801	Jan 7 1822–Nov 27 1845		NLI	Pos. 4992;
	Sept 11 1814–Aug 1833	July 13 1845–Nov 1 1880			from 1845, Pos.
	Sept 12 1833–Nov 1845				4993
	July 6 1845–Dec 26 1880				
Monkstown (Cork and Ross)	May 2 1875–Dec 26 1880	June 5 1875–Nov 29 1880		NLI	Pos. 4791. Online: <www.irishgene alogy.ie>
Newmarket (Cloyne)	1833–99	1822–99		MHC	
	Nov 17 1821–Dec 24 1833	Jan 10 1822–Sept 16 1865		NLI	Pos. 5010
	July 8 1833–Oct 8 1865	Mar 9 1866–Aug 21 1880			baptisms; Pos.
	Mar 13 1866–Dec 30 1880				5011 marriages
Passage West (Cork and Ross)	Apr 5 1795–May 15 1832	Aug 23 1813–Sept 21 1816		NLI	Pos. 4791, 4792
	July 3 1813–Sept 29 1816	May 1 1832–Aug 26 1844			
	May 1 1832–Sept 14 1844	Sept 12 1844–Feb 12 1865			
	Sept 4 1844–Feb 12 1865	Mar 1 1859–Oct 19 1880			
	Mar 6 1859–Dec 30 1880				
Rathcormack (Cloyne)	1792–1899	1829–99		MHC	
	Jan 10 1792–Mar 1850	Jan 7 1829–June 2 1866		NLI	Pos. 4995
	Mar 4 1850–June 7 1866				
	June 12 1866–Dec 28 1880				
Tracton Abbey (Cork and Ross)	Dec 12 1802–Dec 25 1853	June 6 1840–Feb 10 1880		NLI	Pos. 4789. Online: <www.irishgene alogy.ie>
	Jan 24 1853–Dec 10 1880				
Youghal (Cloyne)	1803–1899	1802–1906		MHC	
	Sept 15 1803–Mar 2 1830	Feb 16 1830–June 29 1862		NLI	Pos. 4988;
	Feb 1 1830–Aug 1846	June 7 1866–Nov 27 1880			marriages
	Sept 4 1846–Aug 21 1875				from 1866 on
	Sept 1 1875–Nov 30 1880				Pos. 4989

Cork North-West

All Cork and Ross diocese NLI records are online at *<www.irishgenealogy.ie>*. All Mallow Heritage Centre (MHC) transcripts are online at *<www.rootsireland.ie>*.

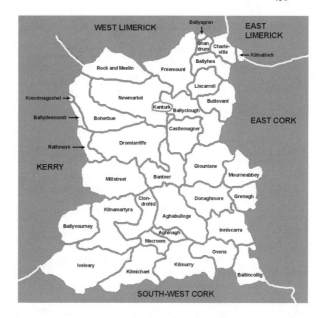

Parish (Diocese)	Baptisms	Marriages	Burials	Location	Reference
Aghabulloge (Cloyne)	1820–95	1820–95		MHC	
	Jan 4 1820–Apr 13 1856	Jan 5 1820–Nov 20 1880		NLI	Pos. 5007
	Jan 5 1856–Dec 19 1880				
Aghinagh (Cloyne)	1848–95	1858–95		MHC	
	Apr 3 1848–Dec 12 1880			NLI	Pos. 5007
Ballyagran	See West Limerick				
Ballyclough (Cloyne)	1807–1895	1805–1899		MHC	
	Aug 15 1807–Dec 30 1818	Jan 19 1805–Dec 2 1827		NLI	Pos. 5009
	Jan 3 1819–Dec 14 1845	Feb 3 1828–Aug 18 1867			(baptisms to
	Jan 4 1846–July 15 1880				1845; Pos. 5010
Ballincollig	Jan 16 1820–Mar 19 1828	Jan 12 1825–Feb 19 1828		NLI	Pos. 4791
(Cork and Ross)	Aug 26 1828–Dec 30 1857	Aug 28 1828–Nov 28 1857			
	Jan 3 1858–Dec 24 1880	Oct 25 1873–Aug 29 1880			
Ballydesmond	1888–1911	1888–1911		Online	*<www. irish genealogy.ie>*
(Kerry)					
	1888–1900 (Vol. 14)	1888–1900 (Vol. 11)		Published	O'K
Ballyhea (Cloyne)	1809–1899	1811–99		MHCC	
	Jan 12 1809–July 24 1873	June 23 1811–July 20 1873		NLI	Pos. 4992
	Nov 12 1871–Dec 2 1880	Nov 8 1871–July 18 1880			
Ballyvourney	1810–68 (gaps)			LDS	BFA 823808
(Cloyne)	1822–95	1871–99		MHC	
	Apr 11 1825–Dec 29 1829			NLI	Pos. 5007
	1810–24			Online	Grogan
	1810–68 (Vol. 11)			Published	O'K
Banteer (Cloyne)	1828–99	1828–99		MHC	
	Jan 1 1847–Dec 24 1880	Feb 2 1847–Dec 9 1880		NLI	Pos. 5011
Boherbue	See Kerry				

Parish (Diocese)	Baptisms	Marriages	Burials	Location	Reference
Buttevant (Cloyne)	1814–1907	1820–1920		MHC	
	July 1 1814–Dec 27 1879	July 23 1814–Sept 14 1880		NLI	Pos. 4998
Castlemagner	1832–99	1832–98		MHC	
(Cloyne)	May 7 1832–Dec 26 1880	May 8 1832–Oct 12 1880		NLI	Pos. 5009
Charleville (Cloyne)	1827–1922	1774–1814		MHC	
		1828–1922			
	May 2 1827–Dec 31 1880	Aug 10 1774–Nov 15 1792		NLI	Pos. 5001;
		Nov 23 1794–July 3 1822			from 1827, Pos.
		June 3 1827–Dec 9 1880			5002
Clondrohid (Cloyne)	1807–1895	1822–94		MHCC	
	1807–1822	Apr 21 1822–June 1 1847		NLI	Pos. 5002;
	Apr 11 1822–Oct 22 1843	Jan 18 1848–Nov 21 1880			from 1844,
	June 2 1844–Dec 30 1880				Pos. 5003
Donaghmore	1803–1895	1790–1899		MHC	
(Cloyne)	Apr 1 1803–Dec 13 1815	Jan 18 1790–Feb 3 1828		NLI	Pos. 5003
	Oct 1 1815–Apr 3 1828	Feb 7 1828–Jan 7 1835			baptisms to
	Apr 6 1828–Oct 21 1834	Oct 23 1834–Sept 17 1875			1828; Pos. 5004
	Oct 23 1834–Sept 17 1875	Feb 13 1870–July 8 1880			remainder
	Jan 1 1870–July 8 1880				
Dromtarriffe	Feb 6 1832–July 26 1851	Jan 25 1832–July 17 1852		NLI	Pos. 4264
(Kerry)	Aug 1 1851–Dec 26 1880	Jan 25 1852–July 27 1880			
	1832–75	1832–80		LDS	0883884 item
					5; 0883696 13
	1832–40 (Vol. 4)	1832–65 (Vol. 2)		Published	o'к
	1841–8 (Vol. 3)	1865–1900 (Vol. 14)			
	1851–65 (Vol. 4)				
	1865–1900 (Vol. 6)				
	1832–90	1832–88		Online	<www.irish genealogy.ie>
Freemount	Sept 10 1827–Mar 22 1840	Oct 15 1827–Oct 2 1880		NLI	Pos. 5008
(Cloyne)	July 15–Dec 28 1843				
	Jan 10 1858–Dec 18 1880				
	1827–43	1823–95		MHC	
	1859–96				
Glountane	May 20 1829–Aug 1844			NLI	Pos. 5008
(Cloyne)	May 16 1847–Dec 21 1880				
	1829–95	1858–95		MHC	
Inniscarra (Cloyne)	1814–95	1814–99		MHC	
	July 3 1814–Sept 29 1844	Aug 7 1814–June 1 1871		NLI	Pos. 5005
	Jan 1 1845–Dec 31 1879	July 15 1871–Nov 25 1880			baptism to
					1844; Pos. 5006
					remainder
Iveleary	Nov 1 1816–Aug 29 1843	Nov 20 1816–May 9 1880		NLI	Pos. 4794 b.
	Sept 3 1843–Dec 30 1880				–1843; rest Pos.
					4795. Online:
					<www.irish
					genealogy.ie>
	1816–75	1816–80		LDS	0883696;
					0883784
	1816–63 (Vol. 7)	1816–99 (Vol. 7)		Published	o'к
	1853–1900 (Vol. 9)				
	1816–1900	1816–1900		Online	Grogan

Parish (Diocese)	Baptisms	Marriages	Burials	Location	Reference
Kanturk (Cloyne)	July 28 1822–Oct 16 1849	Feb 20 1824–Jan 19 1850		NLI	Pos. 5008
	Sept 21 1849–Dec 26 1880	Sept 29 1849–Dec 26 1880			
	Workhouse: Sept 1 1844–				
	Aug 18 1867				
	1822–1922	1824–1922		MHC	
Kilmallock	See Limerick East				
Kilmichael (Cork and Ross)	Oct 6 1819–Feb 23 1847	Jan 9 1819–Feb 12 1850		NLI	Pos. 4797; marriage from 1851 on Pos. 4798. Online: <www.irish genealogy.ie>
	Mar 10 1847–Dec 23 1880	Jan 23 1851–Aug 7 1880			
Kilmurry	June 2 1786–Feb 1812	1803–1805 (fragmented)		NLI	Pos. 4803. Online: <www.irish genealogy.ie>
	Feb 22 1812–Dec 20 1825	Feb 22 1812–Nov 24 1825			
	Jan 8 1826–Dec 30 1838	Jan 8 1826–Dec 1 1838			
	Dec 14 1838–June 29 1872	Jan 30 1839–Nov 13 1880			
	July 2 1872–Dec 31 1880				
	June 1 1829–Dec 29 1880	Oct 22 1829–Sept 24 1880		NLI	Pos. 4999. Online: <www.irish genealogy.ie>
Kilnamartyra (Cloyne)	Jan 30 1803–Dec 16 1820	Jan 8 1803–June 4 1833		NLI	Pos. 5003
	Jan 16 1821–Dec 11 1880	Sept 1839–Feb 10 1880			
	1803–1894	1803–1895		MHC	
Knocknagoshel	See Kerry				
Liscarroll (Cloyne)	Mar 1 1812–Oct 14 1837	Feb 14 1813–Oct 15 1837		NLI	Pos. 4999
	Nov 24 1833–Dec 19 1880	July 6 1831–Oct 28 1880			
	1812–1909	1813–1922		MHC	
Macroom (Cloyne)	Apr 11–18 1803	Jan 20 1808–Aug 14 1813		NLI	Pos. 5004 b. to 1823; Pos. 5005 remainder
	Sept 28 1805–Apr 7 1814	Sept 19 1813–Nov 7 1880			
	Jan 5 1814–June 30 1823				
	July 1 1823–Oct 26 1843				
	Dec 21 1843–Dec 31 1880				
		1864–6 (Vol. 14)		Published	O'K
		1831–1947 (Vol. 14)			
	1805–1817	1780–1899		MHC	
	1824–98				
Millstreet (Kerry)	Dec 4 1853–July 14 1865	Jan 14 1855–Nov 6 1880		NLI	Pos. 4267
	July 23 1865–Dec 31 1878				
	Jan 12 1873–Dec 21 1880				
	1822–3	1855–80		LDS	0883884 item 6; 0883697 2
	1853–75				
	1822–3 (Vol. 11)	1855–70 (Vol. 2)		Published	O'K
	1859–1900 (Vol. 11)	1870–1900 (Vol. 11)			
	1860–62 (Vol. 11)				
Mourneabbey (Cloyne)	June 1 1829–Dec 29 1880	Oct 22 1829–Sept 24 1880		NLI	Pos. 4999
	1829–1907	1829–1907		MHC	

Parish (Diocese)	Baptisms	Marriages	Burials	Location	Reference
Newmarket (Cloyne)	Nov 17 1821–Dec 24 1833	Jan 10 1822–Sept 16 1865		NLI	Pos. 5010
	July 8 1833–Oct 8 1865	Mar 9 1866–Aug 21 1880			baptisms; Pos.
	Mar 13 1866–Dec 30 1880				5011 marriages
	1833–1906	1822–1922		MHC	
Ovens	Sept 24 1816–May 24 1825	Sept 24 1816–May 24 1825		NLI	Pos. 4795.
(Cork and Ross)	Sept 11 1825–Sept 8 1833	Sept 22 1825–Aug 27 1833			Online:
	Oct 27 1834–Dec 30 1877	Oct 25 1834–Feb 14 1837			<www.irish
		Jan 22 1839–Nov 13 1877			genealogy.ie>
Rathmore	See Kerry				
Rock and Meelin	1866–99	1867–99		MHC	
(Cloyne)	Mar 17 1866–Dec 26	Apr 14 1866–Mar 1		NLI	Pos. 5009
	1880	1880			
Shandrum (Cloyne)	1793–1917	1793–1922		MHC	
	Mar 1 1829–Dec 26 1880			NLI	Pos. 5001

Cork South-West

All Cork and Ross diocese NLI records are online at <www.irishgenealogy.ie>.

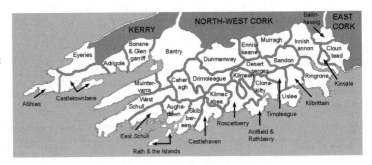

Parish (Diocese)	Baptisms	Marriages	Burials	Location	Reference
Adrigole (Kerry)	Jan 1 1830–Dec 9 1849	Jan 1831–Oct 26 1849		NLI	Pos. 4287
	Aug 12 1855–Jan 20 1879	Sept 1 1855–Aug 10 1878			
	1830–1910	1831–1910		Online	<www.irish
					genealogy.ie>
Allihies (Kerry)	Oct 6 1822–June 10 1860	Jan 1823–Feb 27 1826		NLI	Pos. 4286
	Sept 10 1859–Dec 29 1874	Jan 10 1832–Feb 12 1861			
	Jan 1 1875–Dec 26 1880	Jan 8 1860–Feb 13 1872			
		Oct 7 1871–Aug 20 1880			
	1822–	1823–		Published	O'Dwyer,
					Allihies
	1810(?)–1911	1823–72		Online	<www.irish
					genealogy.ie>
Ardfield and	Jan 1 1801–Apr 5 1837	May 1800–July 2 1837		NLI	Pos. 4771.
Rathberry (Cork and	(1802 missing)	(1812–16 missing)			Online:
Ross)	Apr 7 1832–Dec 27 1876	May 17 1832–May 30 1880			<www.irish
					genealogy.ie>
Aughadown	June 1822–Oct 12 1838	Oct 15 1822–Feb 28 1865		NLI	Pos. 4775.
(Cork and Ross)	Oct 20 1838–Jan 28 1864				Online:
	Jan 1 1865–Dec 31 1880				<www.irish
					genealogy.ie>

Parish (Diocese)	Baptisms	Marriages	Burials	Location	Reference
Ballingarry	Apr 27 1836–Dec 27 1878	Apr 21 1836–Nov 30 1878		NLI	Pos. 4801. Online: <*www.irish genealogy.ie*>
	1809–1835			Local	
	1836–80			custody	
Ballinhassig (Cork and Ross)	Mar 8 1821–Dec 24 1874 Mountain parish: Oct 10 1858–Dec 20 1877 Jan 9 1875–Dec 20 1880	July 15 1821–Sept 29 1877 Feb 6 1875–Nov 23 1880		NLI	Pos. 4795; from 1875 on Pos. 4796. Online: <*www.irish genealogy.ie*>
Ballymartle	Nov 20 1841–Dec 12 1859 1809–1835 1836–80	Aug 28 1841–Jan 12 1860		NLI Local custody	Pos. 4801 Online: <*www.irish genealogy.ie*>
Bandon (Cork and Ross)	Jan 5 1794–Dec 30 1803 Jan 2 1804–Oct 25 1811 Jan 1 1814–Dec 31 1822 Jan 1 1823–Dec 30 1835 Jan 1 1836–Jan 27 1855 Jan 7 1855–Dec 30 1880	July 29 1794–Dec 1 1803 (some entries for 1790 also) Jan 10 1804–Sept 25 1811 Jan 9 1814–Mar 7 1848 Jan 9 1848–Nov 27 1880		NLI	Pos. 4793; baptisms from 1823, marriages from 1848 on Pos. 4794. Online: <*www.irish genealogy.ie*>
Bantry (Cork and Ross)	1788 1791–2 (parts) Nov 1794–July 1799 (parts) Jan 1808–May 1809 1812–14 (parts) July 1822–June 11 1824 Mar 31 1823–Dec 31 1866 Jan 1 1867–Sept 28 1875 Oct 1 1875–Dec 28 1880	May 7 1788–May 28 1823 May 1823–Dec 5 1857 Jan 7 1872–Nov 5 1880		NLI Online:	Pos. 4802; baptisms from 1875, marriages from 1872 on Pos. 4803. <*www.irish genealogy.ie*>
Bonane and Glengarriff (Kerry)	July 22 1846–Dec 25 1856 Jan 3 1857–Dec 21 1877 Jan 9 1878–Dec 26 1880 1846–1911	July 18 1847–Nov 29 1856 Feb 1 1857–Feb 9 1875 Feb 2 1876–Feb 10 1880 1847–1910		NLI Online	Pos. 4288 <*www.irish genealogy.ie*>
Caheragh (Cork and Ross)	June 10 1818–Sept 1858 Oct 1858–Dec 27 1880	June 23 1818–Aug 25 1858 Nov 27 1858–Dec 4 1880		NLI	Pos. 4799. Online: <*www.irish genealogy.ie*>
Castlehaven (Cork and Ross)	Oct 14 1842–Dec 30 1880			NLI	Pos. 4774. Online: <*www.irish genealogy.ie*>
Castletownbere (Kerry)	Sept 1819–Apr 25 1854 May 4 1854–Dec 28 1859 1 1859–Sept 22 1878 1819– 1819–1908(?)	July 1819–Feb 5 1859 Jan 8 1858–Nov 20 1880 1819– 1819–1911		NLI Published Online	Pos. 4284 O'Dwyer, *Castletownbere* <*www.irish genealogy.ie*>

Parish (Diocese)	Baptisms	Marriages	Burials	Location	Reference
Clonakilty (Cork and Ross)	Aug 3 1809–Mar 1827 Jan 1 1827–Dec 31 1873	Jan 8 1811–Nov 17 1880		NLI	Pos. 4772. Online: <*www.irish genealogy.ie*>
Clountead, Ballingarry and Ballymartle	Apr 27 1836–Dec 27 1878 Jan 1 1879–Dec 26 1880	Apr 21 1836–Nov 30 1878 NLI Jan 30 1879–Oct 30 1880		Pos. 4801,	 Online: <*www.irish genealogy.ie*>
	1809–1835 1836–80			Local custody	
Desertserges	June 14 1817–May 28 1855 June 11 1855–Dec 17 1880	(with Enniskeane) Sept 29 1813–Sept 26 1880		NLI	Pos. 4798 Online: <*www.irish genealogy.ie*>
	Confirmations from 1860			Online	Swanton
Drimoleague (Cork and Ross)	July 20 1817–Oct 20 1846 Oct 25 1846–June 12 1876 June 4 1876–Dec 26 1880	July 20 1817–Nov 14 1863 Dec 8 1876–Dec 10 1880 (1878 missing)		NLI	Pos. 4801. Online: <*www.irish genealogy.ie*>
Dunmanway (Cork and Ross)	June 21 1818–Apr 24 1838 July 1 1837–Dec 29 1880	June 21 1818–Nov 27 1880		NLI	Pos. 4805. Online: <*www.irish genealogy.ie*>
Enniskeane	Nov 24 1813–July 1837 Aug 1 1837–Dec 30 1880	(with Desertserges) Sept 29 1813–Sept 26 1880		NLI	Pos. 4798. Online: <*www.irish genealogy.ie*>
	Partial	Confirmations from 1860		Online	Swanton
Eyeries (Kerry)	Apr 1843–Mar 25 1873 Jan 5 1873–Dec 31 1880	Feb 1824–Feb 23 1873 Feb 6 1873–Aug 28 1880		NLI	Pos. 4286
	1843–	1824–		Published	O'Dwyer, Eyeries
	1843–1911	1823–1910		Online	<*www.irish genealogy.ie*>
Innishannon (Cork and Ross)	Aug 20 1825–Dec 29 1846 Jan 4 1847–Nov 30 1880	Aug 16 1825–Oct 9 1880		NLI	Pos. 4797. Online: <*www.irish genealogy.ie*>
Kilbrittain (Cork and Ross)	Aug 1810–Sept 8 1814 July 9 1811–Feb 1848 Mar 29 1850–Mar 30 1851 Apr 6 1852–Apr 23 1863 Apr 16 1863–Dec 28 1880	Aug 1810–Sept 8 1814 Aug 2 1810–June 7 1863 (with Rathclareen) Nov 7 1863–Sept 12 1880		NLI	Pos. 4796. Online: <*www.irish genealogy.ie*>
Kilmacabea (Cork and Ross)	June 9 1832–Dec 24 1880	July 10 1832–Feb 28 1865 May 28 1865–Sept 14 1880		NLI	Pos. 4771. Online: <*www.irish genealogy.ie*>
Kilmeen and Castleventry (Cork and Ross)	Aug 1821–Feb 13 1858 Feb 19 1858–Dec 31 1880			NLI	Pos. 4772. Online: <*www.irish genealogy.ie*>

Parish (Diocese)	Baptisms	Marriages	Burials	Location	Reference
Kinsale (Cork and Ross)	Jan 20 1805–July 20 1806 Jan 1 1815–Sept 4 1821 Sept 3 1817–Dec 28 1829 Aug 29 1828–May 2 1859 May 16 1859–Dec 23 1880	Aug 31 1828–Apr 26 1859 May 16 1859–Dec 23 1880		NLI	Pos. 4800; b. and m. from 1859 on Pos. 4801. Online: <*www.irish genealogy.ie*>
Lislee Cork and Ross)	Aug 1 1804–Oct 1 1836 (Transcript made in 1873) June 23 1835–Aug 27 1873	Nov 12 1771–Aug 31 1873 (Transcript made in 1873) Feb 13 1836–Mar 16 1873 (Original)		NLI 1835 on Pos.	Pos. 4776; b. and m. from 4777. Online: <*www.irish genealogy.ie*>
Muintervarra (Cork and Ross)	May 5 1820–Feb 16 1856 Mar 2 1856–Dec 24 1880	Feb 4 1819–Sept 30 1880		NLI	Pos. 4799. Online: <*www.irish genealogy.ie*>
Murragh (Cork and Ross)	Jan 1834–Dec 29 1864	Jan 26 1834–Oct 8 1864 Jan 7 1865–Nov 27 1880		NLI	Pos. 4796. Online: <*www.irish genealogy.ie*>
Rath and The Islands (Cork and Ross)	July 21 1818–Sept 15 1851 Oct 4 1851–Dec 28 1880	Jan 31 1819–Aug 18 1851 Feb 5 1852–Nov 25 1880		NLI	Pos. 4773; baptisms and marriages from 1853 on Pos. 4774. Online: <*www.irish genealogy.ie*>
Ringrone (Cork and Ross)	Sept 16 1819–Nov 19 1854 Jan 6 1855–Dec 24 1880	Sept 30 1819–June 12 1857 Jan 20 1856–Nov 16 1880		NLI	Pos. 4802. Online: <*www.irish genealogy.ie*>
Roscarberry (Cork and Ross)	Nov 13 1814–Dec 28 1880	Jan 12 1820–Oct 20 1880		NLI	Pos. 4773. Online: <*www.irish genealogy.ie*>
Schull East (Cork and Ross)	Oct 24 1807–Sept 30 1815 Jan 1816–Dec 27 1839 Jan 1 1840–Dec 31 1870 Jan 1 1871–Dec 27 1880	Feb 1809–Nov 5 1815 Jan 21 1816–Nov 25 1832 Jan 31 1833–Sept 17 1870 Feb 4 1871–Dec 21 1880		NLI	Pos. 4804; baptisms and marriages from 1871 on Pos. 4805. Online: <*www.irish genealogy.ie*>
Schull West (Cork and Ross)	Jan 1 1827–Feb 24 1864 Nov 15 1863–Dec 20 1880	Jan 25 1827–Feb 9 1864 (with gaps) Apr 9 1864–Apr 27 1880		NLI	Pos. 4800. Online: <*www.irish genealogy.ie*>

Parish (Diocese)	Baptisms	Marriages	Burials	Location	Reference
Skibbereen (Cork and Ross)	Mar 27 1814–Dec 31 1826 Jan 6 1827–Dec 31 1864 Jan 1 1865–Oct 16 1880	Nov 3 1837–Oct 16 1880		NLI	Pos. 4774; baptisms from 1865, marriages from 1837 on Pos. 4775. Online: <www.irish genealogy.ie>
Timoleague (Cork and Ross)	Nov 1842–Dec 24 1880	Apr 6 1843–Feb 10 1880		NLI	Pos. 4773. Online: <www.irish genealogy.ie>
Watergrasshill (Cork and Ross)	Jan 5 1836–Dec 24 1855 Jan 21 1856–Dec 21 1880			NLI	Pos. 4790. Online: <www.irish genealogy.ie>

Derry/Londonderry

All Irish World (IW) and Derry Genealogy Centre (DGC) records are online at <www.rootsireland.ie>.

Parish (Diocese)	Baptisms	Marriages	Burials	Location	Reference
Arboe (Armagh)	1827–1900	1827–1900		IW	
	Nov 9 1827–Dec 30 1860	Nov 12 1827–Dec 12 1861		LDS	0926029
	Jan 1 1861–Dec 10 1880	Jan 5 1862–Dec 27 1880			
	See NLI			NLI	Pos. 5583
	1827–80	1827–81		PRONI	MIC.1D/34
Ardtrea and Desertlin (Armagh)	1832–1900	1830–1900		IW	
	See NLI			LDS	0926030
	July 1 1832–Mar 28 1834	Apr 14 1830–July 12 1843		NLI	Pos. 5584
	Jan 20 1838–Feb 16 1843	Nov 12 1854–Feb 6 1869			
	Nov 1 1854–Feb 21 1869				
	Jan 18 1864–June 14 1880				

Parish (Diocese)	Baptisms	Marriages	Burials	Location	Reference
Ardtrea and Desertlin	1832–4	1830–43		PRONI	MIC.1D/35
		1830–43		DGC	
		1854–71			
		1878			
		1882			
		1884–6			
		1898–1900			
Ballinascreen (Derry)	Nov 20 1825–Feb 21 1834	Nov 29 1825–Feb 11 1834		NLI	Pos. 5764
	June 5 1836–May 31 1863	Apr 3 1834–May 17 1863			
	June 1 1863–Dec 28 1880	June 3 1863–Oct 17 1880			
	1836	1834–85	1831–2	PRONI	MIC.1D/59
	1846–81		1848–51		
	1836	1834–1900	1848–51	DGC	
	1846–1900		1882–4		
Ballinderry (Armagh)	1826–1900	1826–1900		IW	
	Dec 19 1826–Oct 30 1838	Jan 10 1827–Nov 7 1880		NLI	Pos. 5581
	Sept 25 1841–Dec 18 1880				
	1826–39	1827–80		PRONI	MIC.1D/32
	1841–81				
Ballymoney (Down and Connor)	See Antrim				
Ballyscullion (Derry)	Sept 8 1844–Dec 22 1880	Sept 14 1844–Nov 2 1880		NLI	Pos. 5763
	1844–81	1844–83		PRONI	MIC.1D/58
	1844–1900	1844–1900		DGC	
Banagher (Derry)	Jan 16 1848–July 21 1878 (incomplete)	Dec 24 1851–Jan 6 1878		NLI	Pos. 5764
	1848–78 (incomplete)	1857–78 (incomplete)		PRONI	MIC.1D/59
	1848–1900	1850–78		DGC	
		1884–1900			
Coleraine (Derry)	Aug 4 1843–Aug 2 1863			NLI	Pos. 5767
	Aug 29 1863–Dec 13 1880				
	1843–80			PRONI	MIC.1D/62
	1843–1900	1864–1900		DGC	
Coleraine (Down and Connor)	May 5 1848–Dec 27 1880	May 15 1848–Oct 16 1880		NLI	Pos. 5474
	1848–81	1848–81		PRONI	MIC.1D/70
Cumber Upper (Derry)	1853–4	1863–1900		DGC	
	1863–1900				
	May 18 1863–Dec 27 1880	Sept 20 1863–Dec 28 1880		NLI	Pos. 5762
	1863–81	1863–82		PRONI	MIC.1D/57
Derry city: St Columb's (Derry)	Oct 12 1823–Sept 10 1826	Nov 28 1823–Sept 6 1826	Apr 19 1863–Dec 30 1863	NLI	Pos. 5762
	Sept 3 1836–Dec 1851 (3 sections)	Mar 28 1835–July 20 1836			
		Jan 4 1841–Nov 6 1851			
	Jan 1 1852–Apr 17 1863	(transcript) Apr 6			
	Jan 1 1864–July 23 1880	(1854?)–Dec 30 1863 (fragmented)			
	1823–6	1823–6	1863	PRONI	MIC.1D/57
	1836–81	1835–6			
		1841–63			
	1823–6	1823–6		DGC	
	1833–1900	1835–7			
		1841–1900			

Parish (Diocese)	Baptisms	Marriages	Burials	Location	Reference
Derry city: St Eugene's Cathedral (Derry)	June 11 1873–Dec 30 1880			NLI	Pos. 5762
	1873–81			PRONI	MIC.1D/57
	1873–1900	1873–1900		DGC	
Derry city: Waterside (Derry)	Jan 6 1864–Nov 29 1874 Dec 1 1874–Dec 26 1880	Jan 7 1864–Nov 30 1880		NLI	Pos. 5761
	1864–81	1864–80		PRONI	MIC.1D/56
	1864–1900	1864–1900		DGC	
Desertcreight (Armagh)	See Tyrone				
Desertmartin and Kilcronaghan (Derry)	Nov 1 1848–Dec 19 1880	Nov 13 1848–Nov 27 1880	Nov 11 1848–Dec 6 1880	NLI	Pos. 5765
	1848–81	1848–80	1848–82	PRONI	MIC.1D/60
	1848–1900	1848–1900	1848–83	DGC	
Dungiven (Derry)	July 4 1847–May 4 1853 Sept 7 1863–Dec 26 1880	Sept 29 1864–Dec 26 1880	Mar 4 1870–Dec 31 1871	NLI	Pos. 5764
	1825–34	1825–34	1825–32	PRONI	MIC.1D/59
	1847–81	1864–82	1870–71		
	1825–34	1825–34	1825–32	DGC	
	1847–1900	1864–1900	1870–71		
Errigal (Derry)	Apr 26 1846–Dec 15 1880	Feb 25 1873–Dec 23 1880		NLI	Pos. 5764
	1846–81	1873–80		PRONI	MIC.1D/59
	1846–1900	1872–1900		DGC	
Faughanvale (Derry)	Nov 4 1860–Nov 2 1880	Sept 1863–Dec 25 1880		NLI	Pos. 5762
	1863–81	1860–80		PRONI	MIC.1D/57
	1863–1900	1860–1900		DGC	
Greenlough (Derry)	Oct 5 1846–Dec 29 1880	June 14 1846–Dec 25 1880	June 21 1846–Aug 18 1870	NLI	Pos. 5763
	1846–81	1846–82	1846–70	PRONI	MIC.1D/58
	1845–1900	1846–1900		DGC	
Kilrea (Derry)	Aug 23 1846–Dec 26 1860 Jan 1861–Aug 1865	Aug 23 1846–Dec 26 1860 Jan 1861–Mar 12 1877	Aug 23 1846–Dec 26 1860 Jan 1861–Mar 12 1877	NLI	Pos. 5763 and Pos. 5764
	1846–65	1846–77	1846–77	PRONI	MIC.1D/58–59
	1846–65	1846–1900	1846–77	DGC	
	1874–1900				
Limavady (Derry)	Dec 1855–Dec 25 1962 Jan 12 1862–Dec 26 1880 Jan 3 1862–June 9 1879 (Ballykelly)	Apr 9 1856–Dec 18 1861 Apr 20 1862–Dec 23 1880	May 2 1859–Dec 10 1869	NLI	Pos. 5761
	1855–80	1856–81	1859–69	PRONI	MIC.1D/56
	1855–1900	1856–1900	1859–69	DGC	
Lissan (Armagh)	1822–1900	1822–1900		IW	
	July 22 1823–Dec 30 1880	Sept 1 1839–Nov 20 1880		NLI	Pos. 5585
	1839–81	1839–80		PRONI	MIC.1D/36
		1822–30		DGC	
		1839–1900			
Maghera and Killylough (Derry)	Mar 17 1841–Oct 18 1857 Oct 25 1857–Dec 28 1880	May 13 1841–May 11 1853 Oct 25 1857–Nov 16 1880	May 18 1848–Sept 7 1857 Oct 29 1857–Sept 15 1880	NLI	Pos. 5763
	1841–81	1841–53	1848–80	PRONI	MIC.1D/58
		1857–82	1887–8		
	1841–1900	1841–1900	1848–88	DGC	
Magherafelt (Armagh)	Jan 4 1834–July 26 1857 Jan 10 1858–Dec 26 1880	Jan 2 1834–Apr 21 1857 Feb 10 1858–Dec 16 1880		NLI	Pos. 5579
	1834–80	1834–81		PRONI	MIC.1D/30–31
	1830–1900	1858		DGC	

Parish (Diocese)	Baptisms	Marriages	Burials	Location	Reference
Tamlaghtard (Derry)	Sept 13 1863–Dec 24 1880	Oct 29 1863–Nov 16 1880	Sept 28 1863–Jan 2 1880	NLI	Pos. 5761
	1863–81	1863–81	1863–80	PRONI	MIC.1D/56
	1833–1900	1833–1900	1863–80	DGC	
Termoneeny (Derry)	Sept 27 1837–Aug 1839	Sept 27 1837–Aug 1839	Sept 27 1837–Aug 1839	NLI	Pos. 5763
	June 22 1852–Aug 15 1865	Apr 19 1852–Aug 15 1865			
	Oct 27 1867–Aug 18 1871	Jan 12 1868–Feb 12 1871			
	Nov 27 1871–Dec 30 1880	Dec 7 1873–Dec 28 1880			
	1837–1900	1837–1900		Online index	Lavey
	1837–9	1837–9	1837–9	PRONI	MIC.1D/58
	1852–65	1852–65			
	1867–81	1868–71			
		1873–80			
	1837–9	1837–9	1837–9	DGC	
	1852–65	1852–1900	1868–1900		
	1867–1900				

Donegal

All Donegal Ancestry (DA) records are online at <www.rootsireland.ie>.

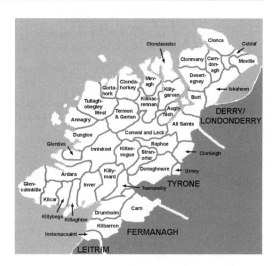

Parish (Diocese)	Baptisms	Marriages	Burials	Location	Reference
All Saints (Raphoe)	1843–86	1843–86		DA	
	1884–1911	1886–1921		LDS	1279235 items 7–10
	Dec 10 1843–Mar 25 1870	Nov 30 1843–Mar 20 1870		NLI	Pos. 4598
	Dec 1 1856–Dec 13 1880				
	Mar 22 1857–Dec 25 1880				
	Apr 30 1870–Nov 7 1880				
	1843–81	1843–70		PRONI	MIC.1D/85
Annagry (Raphoe)	1895–			Local custody	

Parish (Diocese)	Baptisms	Marriages	Burials	Location	Reference
Ardara (Raphoe)	1867–1912	1856–1921		LDS	1279234 items 7–10 and others
	Jan 6 1869–Nov 18 1877 Jan 3 1878–Dec 31 1880	May 13 1867–Apr 2 1875		NLI	Pos. 4599
	1869–80	1867–75		PRONI	MIC.1D/86
	1868–1904	1856–85		DA	
Aughnish (Raphoe)	1873–99	1873–81		DA	
	See NLI			LDS	1279234 items 27–29
	Nov 24 1873–Dec 18 1880	Dec 18 1873–Dec 12 1880		NLI	Pos. 4598
	1873–81	1873–81		PRONI	MIC.1D/85
Burt and Inch (Derry)	1859–1900	1850	1860–1866	DA	
		1856–1900	1898–9		
	Nov 20 1859–Sept 26 1880	Jan 7 1856–Sept 30 1880	Apr 21 1860–July 9 1866	NLI	Pos. 5766
	1859–80	1856–80	1860–1866	PRONI	MIC.1D/55
Carn (Clogher)	See Fermanagh				
Carndonagh (Derry)	1846–1900	1846–1900	1846–51	DA	
	Jan 23 1847–Oct 16 1873	Jan 12 1849–Sept 11 1873		NLI	Pos. 5765
	Nov 23 1873–Dec 26 1880	Nov 23 1873–Nov 7 1880			
	1847–81	1849–81		PRONI	MIC.1D/54
Clonca (Derry)	1851–2	1870–1900		DA	
	1856–1900				
	Nov 2 1856–Dec 8 1880	Apr 22 1870–Dec 26 1880		NLI	Pos. 5765
	May 5 1868–Dec 26 1880	Jan 14 1877–Dec 6 1880			
	1856–81	1870–85		PRONI	MIC.1D/54
Clondahorkey (Raphoe)	1877–99	1877–99		DA	
	1877–1913	1877–1920		LDS	1279235 item 1–3
	Oct 7 1877–Dec 28 1880	Jan 28 1879–Nov 2 1880		NLI	Pos. 4599
	1877–81	1877–82		PRONI	MIC.1D/86
Clondavadoc (Raphoe)	1847–99	1847–99	1847–99	DA	
	Feb 21 1847–Jan 29 1871	Feb 24 1847–July 12 1869	Feb 21 1847–Feb 5 1869	LDS	1279236 items 2
	Feb 21 1847–Jan 29 1871	Feb 24 1847–July 12 1869	Feb 21 1847–Feb 5 1869	NLI	Pos. 4600
	1847–71	1847–69	1847–69	PRONI	MIC.1D/87
Clonleigh (Derry)	1773–95	1778–9		DA	
	1836–7	1781, 1785, 1791			
	1853–1900	1842–1900			
	Apr 1 1773–Feb 22 1795	Aug 1788–Sept 14 1781 [sic]		NLI	Pos. 5766
	Jan 10 1836–May 18 1837	1843–79			
	Mar 3 1853–Sept 7 1879	Nov 14 1853–Apr 20 1870			
	Mar 12 1853–Mar 25 1870	Sept 16 1879–Nov 13 1880			
	May 1 1864–Dec 31 1880				
	1773–95	1778–81		PRONI	MIC.1D/61
	1836–7	1843–81			
	1853–80				
Clonmany (Derry)	1852–1900	1852–1900		DA	
	Jan 12 1852–Dec 30 1880			NLI	Pos. 5765
	1852–81			PRONI	MIC.1D/54

Parish (Diocese)	Baptisms	Marriages	Burials	Location	Reference
Conwal and Leck	1853–99	1853–99		DA	
(Raphoe)	1851–1950	1854–1962		LDS	1279236 item 22–26 and others
	May 15 1853–Mar 13 1862	May 15 1853–Mar 13 1862		NLI	Pos. 4598
	Sept 1854–Jan 4 1855	Jan 8 1857–Nov 22 1863			
	May 26 1856–Dec 30 1862	Feb 1 1877–Nov 27 1880			
	Mar 29 1868–Dec 31 1880				
	Oct 11 1874–Dec 26 1880				
	1874–81	1877–81		PRONI	MIC.1D/85
Culdaff (Derry)	1838–1900	1838–43	1867–87	DA	
		1848–1900			
	Jan 3 1838–Nov 6 1841	Jan 14 1849–Dec 19 1880		NLI	Pos. 5766
	June 7 1847–Dec 13 1880				
	1838–41	1849–80		PRONI	MIC.1D/55
	1847–80				
	1838–1900	1838–43	1867–87	DGC	
		1848–1900			
Desertegney (Derry)	1864–1900	1871–1900		DA	
	Dec 3 1864–Dec 21 1880	Nov 9 1871–Dec 30 1880		NLI	Pos. 5765
	1864–81	1871–2		PRONI	MIC.1D/54
Donaghmore (Derry)	1840–1900	1846–1900		DA	
	Nov 16 1840–Dec 20 1863	Apr 16 1846–Nov 28 1863		NLI	Pos. 5767
	Jan 1 1864–Dec 18 1880	Jan 1 1864–Nov 14 1880			
	1840–80	1846–83		PRONI	MIC.1D/62
Drumholm (Raphoe)	1866–1912	1866–1947		LDS	1279237 item 10–11
	June 17 1866–Dec 28 1880	Aug 12 1866–Sept 28 1880		NLI	Pos. 4599
	1866–81	1866–81		PRONI	MIC.1D/86
Dungloe (Raphoe)	1876–1921	1878–1921		LDS	1279236 items 14–19 and others
	Nov 1 1876–Dec 31 1880			NLI	Pos. 4600
	1876–81			PRONI	MIC.1D/87
Glencolmkille	1879–1949	1879–1949		LDS	1279235 items 6, 11
(Raphoe)	1880 earliest			Local custody	
	No records microfilmed			NLI	
	No records microfilmed			PRONI	
Glenties (Raphoe)	Nov 30 1866–Nov 6 1880			NLI	Pos. 4599
	No records microfilmed			PRONI	
Gortahork (Raphoe)	1856–96	1856–80		LDS	1279234 items 4, 5
	1887–1959	1900–1939			
	Nov 11 1849–Apr 14 1861	Aug 20 1861–Dec 3 1880	Nov 2 1849–Aug 6 1869	NLI	Pos. 4600
	Nov 23 1871–Dec 26 1880				
	1849–61	1861–80	1849–69	PRONI	MIC.1D/87
	1871–80				
	1856–99	1856–80		DA	

Parish (Diocese)	Baptisms	Marriages	Burials	Location	Reference
Inniskeel (Raphoe)	1866–1917	1866–1923		LDS	1279237 items 4–7 and others
	Oct 11 1866–Dec 29 1880			NLI	Pos. 4599
	1866–81			PRONI	MIC.1D/86
Innismacsaint	July 25 1848–Nov 22 1880	Sept 5 1847–Oct 21 1880		LDS	979704 item 6
(Clogher)	July 25 1848–Nov 22 1880	Sept 5 1847–Oct 21 1880		NLI	Pos. 5569
	1847–80	1847–80		PRONI	MIC.1D/12
Inver (Raphoe)	1861–99	1861–99		DA	
	Jan 30 1861–Dec 25 1880	Feb 3 1861–June 27 1867 Nov 26 1875–Dec 27 1880		LDS	0926210
	Jan 30 1861–Dec 25 1880	Feb 3 1861–June 27 1867 Nov 26 1875–Dec 27 1880		NLI	Pos. 4599
	1861–81	1861–7 1875–81		PRONI	MIC.1D/86
Iskaheen (Derry)	1858–1900			DA	
	1858–1923	1858–1921		LDS	1279235 item 17–20
	Sept 19 1858–Dec 26 1880			NLI	Pos. 5766
	1858–80			PRONI	MIC.1D/55
Kilbarron (Raphoe)	Nov 19 1854–Jan 4 1858 Jan 1 1858–Oct 11 1866 Oct 14 1866–Dec 8 1880	Jan 7 1858–Nov 20 1880		NLI	Pos. 4601
	1854–81	1858–81		PRONI	MIC.1D/88
	1858–79	1860–73		DA	
Kilcar (Raphoe)	1848–1911	1901–1921	1906–1958	LDS	1279236 items 4–7
	Jan 4 1848–Dec 29 1880			NLI	Pos. 4599
	1848–81			PRONI	MIC.1D/86
	1849–61			DA	
Killaghtee (Raphoe)	1857–86	1857–86		LDS	1279234 item 6
	Jan 12 1845–Apr 18 1847 Oct 10 1850–Oct 9 1853 July 26 1857–Nov 24 1880	Sept 20 1857–Nov 7 1880		NLI	Pos. 4601
	1845–7 1850–1853 1857–81	1857–81		PRONI	MIC.1D/88
Killybegs (Raphoe)	1850–1911	1850–1914		LDS	1279234 items 24–26
	Oct 12 1850–Dec 29 1880			NLI	Pos. 4601
	1850–81			PRONI	MIC.1D/88
Killygarvan (Raphoe)	1868–99	1879–99		DA	
	Oct 11 1868–Dec 26 1880	Feb 2 1873–Jan 15 1879		NLI	Pos. 4598
	1868–80	1873–9		PRONI	MIC.1D/85
Killymard (Raphoe)	Sept 20 1874–Dec 25 1880			LDS	
	Sept 20 1874–Dec 25 1880			NLI	4599
	1874–81			PRONI	MIC.1D/86
Kilmacrennan	1862–99	1863–99		DA	
(Raphoe)	1862–1912	1863–1973		LDS	1279235 items 24–28
	Nov 2 1862–Sept 26 1880			NLI	Pos. 4598
	1862–80			PRONI	MIC.1D/85

Parish (Diocese)	Baptisms	Marriages	Burials	Location	Reference
Kilteevogue (Raphoe)	1855–1910	1855–1913		LDS	1279234 items 22–23 and others
	Dec 2 1855–Apr 8 1862	Nov 8 1855–Mar 23 1862		NLI	Pos. 4598
	Apr 1 1870–Dec 8 1880	May 5 1870–Dec 1880			
	1855–62	1855–62		PRONI	MIC.1D/85
	1870–80	1870–82			
	1854–99	1855–99		DA	
Mevagh (Raphoe)	1853–9	1878–1921		LDS	1279234 items 11–16
	1871–1927				
	Jan 1 1871–July 28 1878 (transcript)			NLI	Pos. 4600
	1871–8			PRONI	MIC.1D/87
Moville (Derry)	1847–1900	1847–1900	1847–54	DA	
	Nov 7 1847–Dec 28 1880	Nov 4 1847–Dec 12 1880	Nov 2 1847–July 23 1854	NLI	Pos. 5762
	1852–4 (part?)	1850–67	1850–54 (part)	Online	Palmer
	1847–80	1847–80	1847–54	PRONI	MIC.1D/55
Raphoe (Raphoe)	1863–99	1876–99		DA	
	1876–1949	1876–1936 (gaps)		LDS	1279235 item 14–16
	Feb 13 1876–Dec 11 1880	Feb 10 1876–Nov 7 1880		NLI	Pos. 4598
	1876–81	1876–81		PRONI	MIC.1D/85
Stranorlar (Raphoe)	1877–99	1877–99		DA	
	1877–1926	1877–1921	1905–1935	LDS	1279235 items 21–3
	1860 earliest			Local custody	
	No records microfilmed			NLI	
Tawnawilly (Raphoe)	1872–1932	1873–1911		LDS	1279234 items 17–19 and others
	Dec 12 1872–Dec 30 1880	Jan 9 1873–Oct 2 1880		NLI	Pos. 4599
	1872–81	1873–82		PRONI	MIC.1D/86
Termon and Gartan (Raphoe)	1882–1949	1880–1928		LDS	1279237 item 8–9
	1862 earliest			Local custody	
	No records microfilmed			NLI	
Tullaghobegley West (Raphoe)	1868–1935	1866–1943		LDS	1279234 items 8–13 and others
	Jan 6 1868–Mar 17 1871			NLI	Pos. 4600
	May 11 1873–Dec 29 1880				
	1868–71			PRONI	MIC.1D/87
	1873–81				
	1856–1900	1856–1900		DA	
Urney (Derry)	From 1866	From 1866		Local custody	

Down

Most but not all UHF records appear to be online at <*www.rootsireland.ie*>.

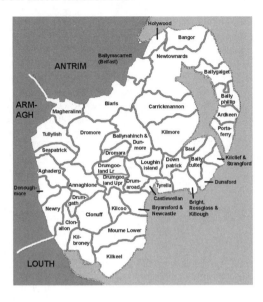

Parish (Diocese)	Baptisms	Marriages	Burials	Location	Reference
Aghaderg (Dromore)	Jan 5 1816–Aug 20 1840	Feb 1 1816–Sept 5 1839	Sept 22 1838–Nov 1840	NLI	Pos. 5504
	Sept 11 1840–Aug 25 1876	Oct 4 1839–Aug 17 1876	Jan 30. 1843–Aug 9 1876		
	1816–76	1816–76	1816–76	PRONI	MIC.1D/29
	1840–76	1839–76	1843–75	UHF	
Annaghlone (Dromore)	See NLI			LDS	0926074 item 1–2
	Sept 21 1834–Mar 4 1851	May 22 1851–Nov 18 1880	Apr 13 1851–Nov 28 1880	NLI	Pos. 5499
	Mar 29 1851–Nov 15 1880				
	1834–81	1851–81	1851–82	PRONI	MIC.1D/24
	1834–1900	1836–1900		UHF	
Ardkeen (Down and Connor)	Jan 11 1828–Nov 26 1838	Jan 13 1828–June 3 1839		NLI	Pos. 5478
	June 2 1852–Dec 22 1880	June 9 1852–Dec 24 1880			
	1828–38	1828–39		PRONI	MIC.1D/74
	1852–82	1852–89			
	1828–1900	1828–37		UHF	
		1853–1900			
Ballyculter (Down and Connor)	Jan 17 1844–May 21 1864	Aug 27 1843–Apr 15 1880		NLI	Pos. 5477
	Nov 19 1870–Dec 1 1880 (transcript)				
	1844–64	1843–82		PRONI	MIC.1D/73
	1870–81				
Ballygalget (Down and Connor)	Jan 11 1828–Apr 18 1835	June 9 1852–Sept 5 1866		NLI	Pos. 5478
	June 18 1852–Feb 20 1853 (transcript)	Mar 4 1867–Oct 20 1880			
	June 2 1852–Feb 28 1864				
	Nov 10 1866–Dec 19 1880				
	1828–35	1852–82		PRONI	MIC.1D/74
	1872–64				
	1866–81				
	1828–99	1852–99	1894–9	UHF	

Parish (Diocese)	Baptisms	Marriages	Burials	Location	Reference
Ballynahinch and Dunmore (Dromore)	See NLI			LDS	0926075 item 1–2
	May 1 1827–July 1 1836 Apr 14 1836–July 28 1864 July 1 1863–Dec 31 1880	Mar 3 1829–July 25 1864		NLI	Pos. 5500
	1827–81	1829–64		PRONI	MIC.1D/25
	1827–1900	1826–1900		UHF	
Ballyphillip and Portaferry (Down and Connor)	Mar 20 1843–Dec 31 1880 (transcript)	Mar 20 1843–Dec 31 1880 (transcript)		NLI	Pos. 5478
	1843–81	1843–81	1843–81 (partial)	PRONI	MIC.1D/74
	1843–1900	1843–1900	1843–1900	UHF	
Bangor (Down and Connor)	1855–			Local custody	
	No records microfilmed			NLI	-
	No records microfilmed			PRONI	
Blaris (Down and Connor)	1840–	1840–		Local custody	
	No records microfilmed			NLI	-
	No records microfilmed	Subscriptions in Holy Trinity cemetery		PRONI	T.1602
Bright, Rossglass and Killough (Down and Connor)	Nov 10 1856–Nov 26 1880 (also a transcript)	Nov 22 1856–Sept 17 1880		NLI	Pos. 5478
	1856–81	1856–81		PRONI	MIC.1D/74
	1856–1900	1856–1900	1877–1900	UHF	
Bryansford and Newcastle (Down and Connor)	Feb 24 1845–Dec 30 1880	Mar 25 1845–Dec 28 1880	Apr 18 1860–Nov 8 1880	NLI	Pos. 5477
	1845–81	1845–85	1860–82	PRONI	MIC.1D/73
	1845–1900	1845–1900	1860–1900	UHF	
Carrickmannon and Saintfield (Down and Connor)	Oct 1 1837–Dec 4 1880	Oct 18 1845–Nov 17 1880		NLI	Pos. 5467
	1837–81	1845–83		PRONI	MIC.1D/63
	1837–1900	1845–1900		UHF	
Castlewellan (Down and Connor)	Nov 18 1859–Dec 25 1880	Nov 18 1859–Dec 25 1880		NLI	Pos. 5477
		1859–81		PRONI	MIC.1D/73
	1859–99	1859–99	1866–8	UHF	
Clonallon (Dromore)	See NLI		LDS		0926077
	Nov 28 1826–Nov 17 1838 Nov 19 1838–Jan 9 1869	Nov 23 1826–Dec 30 1880		NLI	Pos. 5497
	1826–69	1826–82		PRONI	MIC.1D/22
	1826–1900	1826–1900		UHF	
Clonuff (Dromore)	See NLI			LDS	0926078
	Sept 15 1850–Dec 26 1880	Aug 4 1850–Dec 30 1880	July 3 1850–Dec 6 1880	NLI	Pos. 5504
	1850–80	1850–80	1850–81	PRONI	MIC.1D/29
	1850–1900	1850–1900		UHF	
Donoughmore (Dromore)	See NLI			LDS	0926079
	May 30 1835–July 22 1874 Sept 30 1871–Dec 20 1880	Sept 2 1825–Sept 25 1880	Oct 17 1840–71	NLI	Pos. 5497
	1835–80	1825–82	1840–71	PRONI	MIC.1D/22
Downpatrick (Down and Connor)	Oct 6 1851–Dec 29 1880	Feb 16 1853–Nov 8 1880	Aug 22 1851–Dec 31 1880	NLI	Pos. 5478
	1851–82	1853–82	1851–82	PRONI	MIC.1D/74
	1851–1900	1852–1900		UHF	

Parish (Diocese)	Baptisms	Marriages	Burials	Location	Reference
Dromara (Dromore)	See NLI			LDS	0926080
	Jan 14 1844–Dec 19 1880	Jan 14 1844–Dec 18 1880	Jan 10 1844–Sept 12 1880	NLI	Pos. 5499
	1844–80	1844–80	1844–80	PRONI	MIC.1D/24; C.R.2/3
	1844–1900	1844–1900		UHF	
Dromore (Dromore)	1823–81			LDS	
	Mar 3 1823–Jan 17 1845	Sept 8 1821–Dec 31 1844	Nov 9 1821–Jan 5 1845	NLI	Pos. 5504
	Jan 1 1845–Dec 30 1880	Feb 4 1845–Nov 17 1880	Nov 15 1847–Dec 27 1880		
	1823–81	1821–82	1821–82	PRONI	MIC.1D/29
	1823–1900	1821–1900	1845–1900	UHF	
Drumaroad (Down and Connor)	Jan 20 1853–Oct 24 1880	May 22 1853–Nov 3 1880		NLI	Pos. 5476
	1853–81	1853–80		PRONI	MIC.1D/72
	1853–1900	1853–1900		UHF	
Drumgath (Dromore)	See NLI			LDS	0926084 item 1–2
	Apr 13 1829–Dec 10 1880	July 6 1837–Nov 14 1880	June 5 1837–Nov 24 1880	NLI	Pos. 5499
	1829–81	1837–80	1837–80	PRONI	MIC.1D/24
Drumgooland Lower (Dromore)	Mar 24 1832–Dec 3 1880	Apr 27 1832–Nov 18 1880	Mar 11 1832–Nov 14 1880	LDS	0926083
	Mar 24 1832–Dec 3 1880	Apr 27 1832–Nov 18 1880	Mar 11 1832–Nov 14 1880	NLI	Pos. 5497
	1832–81	1832–81	1832–81	PRONI	MIC.1D/22
	1832–1900	1886–1900		UHF	
Drumgooland Upper (Dromore)	1817–1946	1827–		LDS	0990108 item 4; 0994208 item 1
	May 26 1827–Dec 28 1880	Aug 9 1827–Dec 28 1880	May 6 1828–Nov 2 1880	NLI	Pos. 5497
	1827–80	1827–80	1828–81	PRONI	MIC.1D/22
	1827–1900	1827–1900		UHF	
Dunsford (Down and Connor)	Apr 1845	Apr 1845	Feb 27 1848–Dec 19 1880	NLI	Pos. 5476
	Feb 28 1848–Nov 24 1880	Feb 22 1848–Feb 28 1868			
	1845–81	1845–80	1848–68	PRONI	MIC.1D/72
	1880–1900			UHF	
Holywood (Down and Connor)	Nov 18 1866–Dec 25 1880	May 3 1867–Nov 4 1880		NLI	Pos. 5471
	1866–80	1867–83		PRONI	MIC.1D/67
	1866–1900	1867–1900		UHF	
Kilbroney (Dromore)	See NLI			LDS	0990108 item 4; 0926085 item 1–3
	Jan 1 1808–Jan 22 1843	Jan 29 1808–Dec 6 1853	Jan 1 1808–Jan 7 1843	NLI	Pos. 5499
	Jan 2 1843–Dec 19 1880	Mar 22 1848–Dec 30 1880	Jan 4 1843–Dec 30 1880		
	1808–1881	1808–1881	1808–1881	PRONI	MIC.1D/24–25
	1808–1900	1848–1900	1808–1900	UHF	
Kilclief and Strangford (Down and Connor)	Jan 14 1866–July 26 1867	Nov 25 1865–Oct 26 1868		NLI	Pos. 5476
	Oct 9 1870–Nov 19 1880	Jan 8 1871–Jan 13 1881			
	1866–81	1865–81		PRONI	MIC.1D/72
	1898–1900	1898–1900		UHF	
Kilcoo (Down and Connor)	Oct 22 1832–Dec 1 1880			NLI	Pos. 5476
	1832–80			PRONI	MIC.1D/72
	1832–99	1899		UHF	

Parish (Diocese)	Baptisms	Marriages	Burials	Location	Reference
Kilkeel (Down and Connor)	July 1839–Sept 12 1877	May 9 1838–Apr 18 1876		NLI	Pos. 5477
	May 26 1845–Dec 27 1880 (transcript)	Oct 30 1867–Apr 19 1869			
	May 3 1857–Aug 9 1878				
	1839–81	1839–76		PRONI	MIC.1D/73
	1837–1900	1839–1900	1869–1900	UHF	
Kilmore (Down and Connor)	1837–1900	1896–1900	1896–1900	UHF	
Loughinisland (Down and Connor)	1806–Oct 24 1852	Nov 1 1805–Oct 23 1852	Nov 10 1805–Oct 5 1852 (some pages missing)	NLI	Pos. 5477
	1806–1852	1805–1852	1805–1852	PRONI	MIC.1D/73
	1806–1900	1805–1900	1730–1899	UHF	
Magheralinn (Dromore)	See NLI			LDS	0926086
	1815–16	1815–16			
	Jan 1 1817–Dec 20 1845	Jan 5 1817–Dec 27 1845	Jan 1 1817–Oct 4 1845	NLI	Pos. 5501
	Dec 6 1845–June 4 1871	Dec 26 1845–May 12 1871	Jan 1 1846–May 11 1871		
	July 17 1871–Dec 9 1880	July 10 1871–Dec 18 1880	Oct 3 1871–Dec 6 1880		
	1815–81	1815–82	1815–80	PRONI	MIC.1D/26
	1815–1900	1814–1900	1848–1900	UHF	
Mourne Lower (Down and Connor)	Aug 28 1842–Dec 18 1867	Sept 11 1839–Nov 21 1866		NLI	Pos. 5478
	Jan 11 1868–Dec 14 1880	Aug 25 1867–Oct 10 1880			
	1842–81	1839–80		PRONI	MIC.1D/74
	1842–1900	1839–1900		UHF	
Newry (Dromore)	See Armagh				
Newtownards (Down and Connor)	June 17 1864–Dec 23 1880			NLI	Pos. 5467
	1864–81			PRONI	MIC.1D/63
	1856–1900	1855–1900		UHF	
Saul (Down and Connor)	May 17 1868–Dec 10 1880	May 1 1868–Dec 21 1880		NLI	Pos. 5478
		1868–80	1868–81	PRONI	MIC.1D/74
	1785–1900	1785–1900		UHF	
Seapatrick (Dromore)	See NLI			LDS	0926076
	Jan 24 1843–Dec 14 1880	July 10 1850–Oct 4 1880	July 31 1850–Dec 16 1880	NLI	Pos. 5501
	1843–81	1850–82	1833–80	PRONI	MIC.1D/26
	1843–1900	1850–1900	1850–1900	UHF	
Tullylish (Dromore)	See NLI			LDS	0926090 item 1–3
	Jan 1 1833–Apr 14 1844	Jan 10 1833–Apr 8 1844	Jan 18 1833–Apr 17 1844	NLI	Pos. 5500
	May 7 1844–Aug 13 1844	Feb 4 1845–Dec 31 1880	May 1 1844–Dec 30 1880		
	Apr 26 1846–Feb 5 1856 (Clare and Gilford)	Apr 26 1846–Nov 25 1853 (Clare and Gilford)	Apr 26 1846–Nov 25 1853 (Clare and Gilford)		
	Jan 21 1843–Dec 31 1880				
	1833–81	1833–81	1833–81	PRONI	MIC.1D/25
	1853–1900	1853–1900	1853–1900	UHF	
Tyrella (Down and Connor)	Apr 21 1854–Dec 26 1880	July 10 1854–Dec 5 1880		NLI	Pos. 5476
	1854–81	1854–81		PRONI	MIC.1D/72
	1854–1900	1855–1900		UHF	

Dublin

All parishes are in the archdiocese of
Dublin. Swords Heritage Centre (SHC)
and Dún Laoghaire Heritage Society
(DLHS) transcripts are online at
<*www.rootsireland.ie*>.

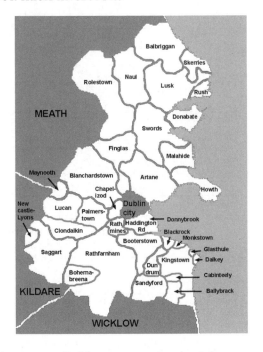

Parish (Diocese)	Baptisms	Marriages	Burials	Location	Reference
Artane, Coolock, Clontarf, Santry	1774–	1774–		Local custody	
	1771–1873	1771–1873		NAI	97/37/2
	1771–1899	1771–1880		SHC	
Balbriggan	July 17 1770–Feb 15 1778	July 17 1770–Feb 15 1778		NLI	Pos. 9209
	Aug 22 1796–Oct 5 1813	Aug 29 1796–June 17 1810			
	Oct 27 1816–May 22 1860	Feb 12 1817–Nov 25 1856			
	Jan 1 1856–July 19 1893	Jan 12 1856–Nov 28 1900			
	May 21 1861–Feb 26 1871	Nov 25 1861–Feb 14 1871			
	July 23 1893–Oct 14 1901				
	1770–1899	1796–1899		SHC	
Ballybrack	1861–1900 (?)	1861–1900 (?)		DLHS	
	1841–	1860–		Local custody	
	No registers microfilmed	Jan 9 1860–Nov 15 1908 (Index)		NLI	Pos. 9211
Blackrock	1854–1900			DLHS	
	1850–	1922–		Local custody	
	July 23 1854–Oct 28 1900			NLI	Pos. 9212
Blanchardstown	Dec 3 1774–Dec 8 1824	Jan 1775–Nov 7 1824		NLI	Pos. 6613, 6617
	Jan 5 1824–Dec 28 1856	Aug 8 1824–Nov 11 1856			
	Apr 25 1852–Dec 26 1880	Jan 18 1857–Nov 25 1880			
	1771–1860	1771–1899		SHC	
Bohernabreena	1868–1901			Online	<*www.irish genealogy.ie*>
	1868–			LDS	
	No registers microfilmed			NLI	

Parish (Diocese)	Baptisms	Marriages	Burials	Location	Reference
Booterstown	1755–1900	1755–1900		DLHS	
	Oct 13 1755–Dec 20 1790	June 4 1756–Dec 20 1794		NLI	Pos. 9084 (b.);
	Jan 1 1791–Oct 20 1816	Jan 1 1791–Sept 31 [sic] 1816			9085 (m)
	Jan 3 1817–Dec 29 1845	Oct 5 1816–Dec 26 1845			
	Jan 4 1846–July 2 1854	Jan 11 1846–Feb 11 1856			
	July 2 1854–Mar 7 1902	Jan 13 1856–Oct 34 1899			
Cabinteely	1862–1900			DLHS	
	1859–	1859–		Local custody	
	Sept 25 1863–Sept 13 1903	Apr 30 1866–Nov 22 1910		NLI	Pos. 9211
Chapelizod	1850–1900			Online	<www.irish genealogy.ie>
	1846–	1846–		Local custody	
	Oct 7 1849–Dec 15 1901	Nov 1849–July 29 1901		NLI	Pos. 9199
Clondalkin	1778–1896	1778–1900		Online	<www.irish genealogy.ie>
	1778–1800	June 11 1778–Feb 24 1800		NLI	Pos. 6612
	June 1812–May 1822	Aug 23 1812–Feb 19 1822			
	1823–26	Aug 3 1835–Aug 28 1842			
	Jan 1837	Apr 20 1856–Nov 28 1880			
	Aug 1809–Feb 1813				
	June 1813–June 1818				
	June 1822–Aug 1830				
	Dec 1830–Aug 1833				
	1834–7				
	July 1848				
	Apr 1849–Aug 1852				
	Transcript 1809–1852				
	1853–188				
Coolock	1879–	1879–		Local custody	
	No registers microfilmed			NLI	
Dalkey	1861–1900			DLHS	
	1861–	1894–		Local custody	
	Jan 13 1861–Dec 7 1899	Apr 13 1894–Oct 25 1910		NLI	Pos. 9212
Donabate	Nov 3 1760–Dec 27 1807	Feb 1 1761–June 6 1805		NLI	Pos. 6618
	July 4 1824–Oct 5 1869	Feb 9 1865–Nov 29 1880			
	Feb 28 1869–Oct 17 1880				
	1760–1899	1761–1899		SHC	
Donnybrook See also Haddington Road	1865–	1865–		Local custody	
	Apr 15 1871–Feb 24 1902	Jan 21 1877–Nov 19 1905		NLI	Pos. 9309. Online: <www.irish genealogy.ie>
Dundrum	1854–1900	1865–1900		DLHS	
	July 2 1854–Dec 1 1901 Separate index	Sept 26 1865–Nov 17 1901		NLI	Pos. 9309

Parish (Diocese)	Baptisms	Marriages	Burials	Location	Reference
Fairview	June 18 1879–Dec 23 1880	June 10 1879–Nov 27 1880		NLI	Pos. 6609
Finglas	Mar 4 1788–July 31 1788	Nov 20 1757–July 11 1760		NLI	Pos. 6613
	Dec 6 1784–Oct 16 1823	Dec 12 1784–July 17 1794			
	Nov 5 1823–Nov 18 1827	Oct 11 1821–Aug 10 1823			
	Jan 6 1828–Nov 27 1828	Nov 5 1823–Nov 18 1827			
	Dec 7 1828–May 30 1841	Jan 6 1828–Nov 27 1828			
	June 1 1841–Feb 20 1854	Jan 8 1829–June 1 1841			
	Jan 3 1854–Dec 12 1880	June 1 1841–Feb 20 1854			
		Jan 24 1854–Nov 24 1880			
	1812–99	1812–99		SHC	
Garristown	Jan 4 1857–Dec 27 1874	July 27 1857–Oct 29 1880		NLI	Pos. 6617
	Jan 1 1875–Nov 25 1880				
	1857–99	1857–99		SHC	
Glasthule	1865–1900	1860–1900 (Ballybrack)		DLHS	
	1865–			Local custody	
	May 27 1865–Dec 24 1902			NLI	Pos. 9211
	Separate index				
Haddington Road	1798–1876	1798–1876		Online	<www.irish genealogy.ie>
	Apr 16 1798–Aug 16 1829	Apr 16 1798–Aug 16 1829		NLI	Pos. 9214
	Jan 1 1830–Feb 13 1845	Jan 1 1830–Feb 13 1845			
	Jan 21 1845–July 16 1849	Jan 21 1845–July 16 1849			
	Jul 17 1849–Mar 5 1866	Jul 17 1849–Dec 26 1876			
	Mar 12 1866–Dec 26 1876	Jan 7 1877–Dec 1 1905			
	Jan 1 1877–Mar 19 1907	See also Pos. 9215 for miscellaneous indexes 1798–1916			
Howth	Dec 24 1784–Dec 26 1800	Jan 9 1785–Dec 1 1800		NLI	Pos. 6618
	Aug 6 1806–Aug 31 1831	Aug 5 1806–Nov 16 1815			
	Aug 26 1831–Dec 28 1853	May 13 1818–Nov 25 1824			
	Jan 6 1854–Dec 25 1880	Jan 1 1826–July 13 1831			
		Sept 2 1831–Dec 30 1856			
		Jan 6 1857–Nov 14 1880			
	1784–1899	1784–1899		SHC	
Kingstown	1755–1900	1755–1900		DLHS	
	1769–	1769–		Local custody	
	Dec 4 1768–July 31 1861 (Indexed)	Jan 27 1769–Mar 27 1932 (Indexed to 1861)		NLI	Pos. 9071 (B. to 1861); Pos. 9072 (B. to 1914); Pos. 9073 (M)
	Aug 9 1861–Mar 22 1914 (Indexed)				
Lucan	1818–1901	1818–1900		Online	<www.irish genealogy.ie>
	Sept 1818–July 1834	Sept 5 1818–July 13 1835		NLI	Pos. 6612.
	Aug 23 1835–Aug 28 1842	Jan 11 1831–Nov 22 1834			Pos. 9310 from
	Feb 4 1849–Jan 26 1862	Aug 3 1835–Sept 18 1842			1885
	Mar 3 1885–Oct 27 1907	Feb 18 1849–Nov 1861			
		Sept 15 1887–Oct 28 1908			

Parish (Diocese)	Baptisms	Marriages	Burials	Location	Reference
Lusk	Sept 1757–Aug 6 1801	Nov 20 1757–Jan 12 1801		NLI	Pos. 6616
	Mar 11 1802–Dec 27 1835	(poor condition)			
	(early years very faint)	Mar 11 1802–Dec 27 1835			
	Aug 3 1856–Dec 21 1880	(early years very faint)			
		Mar 6 1856–Nov 22 1880			
	1701–1899	1701–1899		SHC	
Malahide	1856–			Local custody	
	Apr 20 1856–Apr 13 1901 Index	May 7 1856–June 24 1901		NLI	Pos. 9310
	1856–1900	1856–99		SHC	
		[See also Swords]			
Maynooth	See Kildare				
Monkstown	1855–1900	1865–1900		DLHS	
	1865–	1881–		Local custody	
Naul	1832–	1836–		Local custody	
	1832–99	1833–99		SHC	
Newcastle-Lyons	1773–	1773–		Local custody	
	No records microfilmed			NLI	
Palmerstown	1798–1862	1838–58		Online	<www.irish genealogy.ie>
	Aug 26 1798–Dec 31 1799	Sept 24 1837–Sept 27 1857		NLI	Pos. 6612
	Sept 3 1837–Apr 24 1864				
Rathfarnham	1777–1857	1777–1864		Online	<www.irish genealogy.ie>
	Jan 1 1777–May 1781	Feb 5 1777–May 19 1781	News cuttings, Parochial notes	NLI	Pos. 8972
	May 1781–Nov 14 1781	May 26 1781–Nov 18 1781			
	Nov 18 1781–Dec 1 1788	Sept 22 1807–Jan 9 1832			
	Sept 18 1807–Jan 15 1832	Jan 23 1832–Jan 8 1852			
	Jan 22 1832–Feb 1 1852	Jan 5 1852–Nov 21 1858			
	Jan 1 1852–Feb 7 1857	Nov 19 1862–Nov 3 1864			
	Jan 7 1861–1917	Nov 12 1864–Mar 4 1787			
		Feb 12 1878–July 24 1933			
Rathgar	1874–	1874–		Local custody	
	No records microfilmed			NLI	
Rathmines	1823–	1823–		Local custody	
	Nov 23 1823–Feb 12 1840	Nov 23 1823–Feb 12 1840		NLI	Pos. 9200 (bapt to 1886, marr. to 1881)
	Mar 22 1840–Dec 10 1850	Mar 22 1840–Dec 10 1850			
	Dec 9 1848–Aug 26 1860	Dec 9 1848–Aug 26 1860			Pos. 9201.
	Dec 9 1848–Nov 28 1881	Dec 17 1848–Dec 10 1881			Online:
	Dec 15 1881–Jun 26 1886	Jan 7 1882–Aug 1 1886			<www.irish
	Aug 8 1886–Feb 13 1899	Aug 10 1886–Jan 21 1901			genealogy.ie>
	Feb 15 1899–Oct 9 1906	All with indexes			
	All with indexes				

Parish (Diocese)	Baptisms	Marriages	Burials	Location	Reference
Rolestown	Jan 2 1857–Dec 27 1880	Jan 19 1857–Nov 20 1880		NLI	Pos. 6617
	1857–99	1857–99		SHC	
Rush	July 12 1785–Dec 27 1828	Sept 22 1785–Dec 27 1796		NLI	Pos. 6617
	Mar 13 1829–Dec 27 1856	July 14 1799–Apr 28 1810			
	Dec 31 1856–Dec 28 1880	Aug 16 1813–Dec 3 1828			
		1829–Sept 29 1856			
		Jan 1 1857–Nov 27 1880			
	1785–1899	1785–1899		SHC	
Saggart	1832–99	1832–78		Online	<www.irish genealogy.ie>
	Oct 4 1832–Feb 1862	May 21 1832–Aug 14 1878		NLI	Pos. 6483
	May 13 1878				
	Jan 12 1862–Dec 26 1880				
Sandyford	1823–1900	1823–56		Online	<www.irish genealogy.ie>
	1823–	1823–		Local custody	
	Mar 8 1841–Dec 28 1856	Nov 16 1823–Nov 24 1856		NLI	Pos. 9308
	Jan 22 1857–Dec 18 1904	Mar 8 1841–Dec 28 1856			
	Jan 4 1857–Oct 22 1905	Jan 13 1857–Nov 21 1909			
		Jun 1 1876–Nov 17 1901			
Sandymount	1865–	1865–		Local custody	
	No registers microfilmed			NLI	
Skerries	Oct 12 1751–Dec 31 1781	June 22 1751–Nov 17 1781		NLI	Pos. 6614
	Jan 6 1872–June 23 1814	Jan 10 1782–July 5 1814			
	July 12 1814–Dec 23 1853	(poorly filmed)			
	Jan 1 1854–Dec 23 1880	Aug 15 1814–Mar 25 1856			
		Apr 24 1856–Nov 6 1880			
	1751–1899	1751–1899		SHC	
Swords	Dec 26 1763–July 7 1777	Oct 3 1763–June 7 1777		NLI	Pos. 6616
	June 2 1802–Nov 29 1819	June 24 1802–Nov 25 1819			
	Dec 3 1819–Sept 15 1828	Dec 26 1819–Dec 15 1828			
	Sept 15 1828–Dec 4 1845	Jan 19 1829–Dec 3 1845			
	Dec 2 1845–Mar 23 1856	Jan 12 1846–Nov 26 1856			
	(Indexed)	Feb 2 1857–Nov 7 1880			
	Mar 28 1858–Dec 21 1880				
	1763–1802	1763–77		SHC	
	1835–99	1802–1899			
Terenure	1870–	1894–		Local custody	
	No registers microfilmed			NLI	

Dublin City

All parishes are in the
archdiocese of Dublin. All
Dublin City records before 1880
are online in one form or
another, almost all at
<*www.irishgenealogy.ie*>.

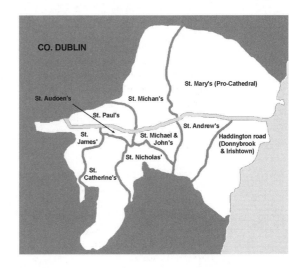

Parish (Diocese)	Baptisms	Marriages	Burials	Location	Reference
Aughrim St	1888–	1888–		Local custody	
Berkeley Road	1890–	1890–		Local custody	
Cabra	1909–	1856–		Local custody	
Harrington St	May 8 1865–Apr 21 1873	Feb 1865–Jan 10 1893		NLI	Pos. 9312
	Apr 22 1873–Feb 17 1880	Jan 16 1893–Nov 17 1912			(bapt. to 1890)
	Feb 17 1880–Jun 16 1885	Index on Pos. 9314			Pos. 9313
	Jun 19 1885–Jun 27 1890				(bapt. to 1901)
	Jun 27 1890–Nov 23 1897				Pos. 9314
	Nov 23 1897–Dec 24 1901				(marr.)
	Index on Pos. 9311				Online: <*www.irish genealogy.ie*>
St Agatha's	1852–1900	1853–1900		Online	<*www.irish genealogy.ie*>
	Dec 15 1852–Dec 31 1800	Jan 7 1853–Dec 16 1880		NLI	Pos. 6611
	Dec 29 1879–Dec 31 1880				
St Andrew's	1742–1900	1741–1900		Online	<*www.irish genealogy.ie*>
	Jan 1741/2–July 1752	Jan 1741/2–July 1751		NLI	Pos.
	July 1750–June 1773	Oct 1751–June 1773			6605–6610
	Sept 1751–June 1776	June–Oct 1756			
	Feb 1777–Sept 1787	Mar 1759–May 1776			
	Oct 1772–Sept 1790	June 1792–May 1793			
	Aug 1779–May 1793	July 1773–Dec 1778			
	Aug 1790–Jan 1801	July 1776–Oct 1777			
	Jan 1792–1801	Apr 1789–May 1793			
	Mar–Apr 1802	Sept 1790–Oct 1801			
	Jan 1801–1812	Apr–Aug 1804			
	Jan 1811–July 1822	Jan 1801–Dec 1880			
	June 1810–Dec 1880				

Parish (Diocese)	Baptisms	Marriages	Burials	Location	Reference
St Audoën's	1778–1900	1747–1900		Online	<www.irish genealogy.ie>
	Dec 1778–Dec 1799	Feb 8 1747–Aug 13 1785		NLI	Pos. 6778
	June 22 1800–Aug 19 1825	Jan 1800–Aug 30 1825			
	Sept 22 1825–July 14 1833	Oct 3 1825–June 14 1833			
	July 1833–Sept 19 1856	Aug 4 1833–June 21 1859			
	(poor condition)	Oct 14 1856–Dec 12 1880			
	June 11 1878–Dec 31 1880				
St Catherine's	1740–1880	1740–1880		Online	<www.irish genealogy.ie>
	May 1740–Dec 1749	May 1740–Dec 1749		NLI	Pos. 7138–41
	Jan 1750–Aug 1765	Jan 1750–Aug 1765			
	Feb 1761–Oct 1766	June 1765–Dec 1792			
	June 1765–Feb 1794	Feb–July 1794			
	Dec 10 1797	1799 (scraps)			
	Nov 1799–Dec 1805	1800–1818			
	Nov 1799–Dec 1810	1811–21			
	Feb 1806–Nov 1819	1823–8			
	Jan 1811–Sept 1821	1822–51 (gaps)			
	Mar–Dec 1820	1849–63 (John's Lane)			
	June 1821–Dec 1880 (gaps)	1852–Nov 1856			
		1857–80			
St James's	1752–1882	1806–1896		Online	<www.irish genealogy.ie>
	Sept 1752–1784	1754–5		NLI	Pos. 7228–7232
	Apr 1785–Aug 1798/9	Oct 8 1804–Dec 13 1833			
	Apr 1800–1880	1856–8			
	Multiple registers for	Mar 4 1832–Nov 26 1856			
	all periods	June 3 1859–May 1868			
	Many registers poorly	Aug 23 1868–Dec 29 1880			
	legible, many entries out	Many entries are not in			
	of chronological order	chronological order			
St Laurence O'Toole's	July 20 1853–June 4 1875	June 19 1856–Dec 26 1880		NLI	Pos. 6611
	June 7 1875–Dec 31 1880				
St Mary's (Pro-Cathedral)	1741–1900	1741–1900		Online	<www.irish genealogy.ie>
	1741–1900	1741–1900		NLI	Pos. 9148–9167
	Partial index to				
	baptisms 1810–1839 on				
	Pos. 9162				
St Michael and John's	1743–1899	1742–1899		Online	<www.irish genealogy.ie>
	Jan 1 1768–Jan 1857	Jan 8 1784–Dec 1851		NLI	Pos. 7358–60
	Mar 2 1856–Dec 30 1880	Jan 11 1852–Nov 28 1880			
	Indexed 1876–80	Indexed c. 1743–42			
St Michan's	1726–1888	1726–1884		Online	<www.irish genealogy.ie>

Parish (Diocese)	Baptisms	Marriages	Burials	Location	Reference
St Michan's *contd.*	Feb 1726–Jan 1734	Feb 25 1726–July 19 1730		NLI	Pos. 8829–31
	Jan 1735–Dec 1739	June 1730–Jan 1734			
	Sept 1739–Oct 1744	Jan 1735–Dec 1739			
	June 1755–Sept 1763	Dec 1739–Sept 1744			
	Oct 1744–Mar 1768	Oct 1744–May 29 1763			
	Sept 1770	Mar 18 1756–Oct 26 1763			
	Aug 1795–June 1854	Aug 16 1795–Aug 23 1823			
	May 1830–June 1850	Sept 1823–Mar 1856			
	May 1850–July 1854	Mar 31 1856–1884			
	July 9 1854–Dec 7 1869	Indexed			
	Nov 2 1868–Nov 20 1869				
	Nov 10 1869–Jan 30 1888				
St Nicholas' (Without)	Jan 3 1742–Aug 21 1752	Sept 29 1767–Dec 13 1801	Apr 7 1829–May 2 1856	NLI	Pos.
	Jan 11 1767–Dec 26 1801	Dec 21 1783–Dec 22 1796	Dec 3 1857–May 22 1905		7267–7270;
	Aug 15 1772–Nov 26 1780	Mar–Oct 1791			7275; 7277;
	Dec 1 1782–Jan 2 1785	Jan–Feb 1793			7368
	Mar 22 1788–Sept 20 1790	Jan 2 1802–Aug 16 1828			
	1781–94 (scraps)	Jan 1 1807–June 1 1807			
	1823 (fragment)	Nov 20 1814			
	Nov 21 1824–1857	1824–7			
	1858–80 (index)	1822–July 29 1866			
		Sept 14 1856–Sept 13 1865			
St Paul's	1731–1886	1731–1886	NAI 97/37/2–6	NAI	
	1731–1882 (indexed)	1731–1889 (indexed)		NLI	Pos. 8828–8838
	1731–1878	1732–1900		SHC	

Fermanagh

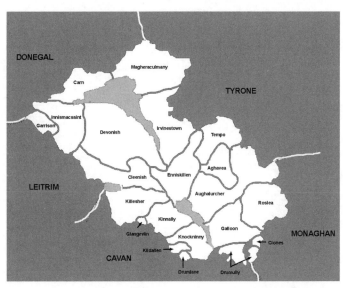

Parish (Diocese)	Baptisms	Marriages	Burials	Location	Reference
Aghavea (Clogher)	Mar 31 1862–Dec 26 1880	May 11 1866–June 15 1880		NLI	Pos. 5572
	1862–82	1866–81			
		1896–7		PRONI	MIC.1D/15

Parish (Diocese)	Baptisms	Marriages	Burials	Location	Reference
Aughalurcher (Clogher)	See NLI			LDS	979704 item 6
	Oct 19 1835–Dec 28 1880			NLI	Pos. 5569
	1835–83			PRONI	MIC.1D/12; CR.2/12
Carn (Clogher)	See NLI			LDS	0926049 item 1
	Mar 19 1851–Oct 28 1877	Jan 9 1836–Nov 23 1880		NLI	Pos. 5569
	Nov 18 1877–Dec 30 1880				
	1851–81	1836–81		PRONI	MIC.1D/12–13
Cleenish (Clogher)	See NLI			LDS	979705 item 1–4
	Dec 28 1835–Sept 8 1839	Apr 8 1866–Nov 14 1880		NLI	Pos. 5571
	Feb 8 1859–Jan 25 1868				
	Apr 8 1866–Dec 3 1880				
	1835–9	1866–81		PRONI	MIC.1D/14
	1859–81				
Clones (Clogher)	See Monaghan				
Devonish (Clogher)	See NLI			LDS	926050
	Feb 12 1853–Aug 1879			NLI	Pos. 5567
	Arranged chronologically by letter				
	1853–79			PRONI	MIC.1D/10
Drumlane (Kilmore)	See Cavan				
Drumully (Clogher)	Jan 6 1845–Apr 2 1866	July 14 1864–Oct 31 1880		NLI	Pos. 5572
	July 7 1864–Dec 26 1880				
	1845–81	1864–81		PRONI	MIC.1D/15
Enniskillen (Clogher)	1838–Sept 27 1868	Feb 10 1818–Dec 26 1880		NLI	Pos. 5567 to 1868; remainder on Pos. 5568
	Sept 30 1868–Dec 26 1880				
	1838–81	1817–80		PRONI	MIC.1D/10–11
Galloon (Clogher)	Jan 1 1853–Feb 27 1859	May 10 1847–July 24 1879		NLI	Pos. 5572
	June 14 1863–Dec 30 1880				
	1853–9	1847–79		PRONI	MIC.1D/15
	1863–81				
Garrison (Clogher)	See NLI			LDS	979704 item 3–5
	July 12 1860–Apr 14 1874	Jan 12 1860–May 19 1873		NLI	Pos. 5569
	Oct 31 1871–Dec 23 1880	Oct 2 1871–Oct 4 1880			
	1860–81	1860–80		PRONI	MIC.1D/12
Glangevlin (Kilmore)	See Cavan				
Innismacsaint (Clogher)	See Donegal				
Irvinestown (Clogher)	See NLI			LDS	979705 item 7–10
	Nov 29 1846–July 3 1874	Dec 22 1851–Aug 28 1874		NLI	Pos. 5571
	Aug 18 1874–Dec 21 1880	Aug 7 1874–Aug 7 1880			
	1846–81	1851–82		PRONI	MIC.1D/14
Kildallen (Kilmore)	See Cavan				
Killesher (Kilmore)	See NLI			LDS	0926133 item 1
	Sept 2 1855–Dec 16 1880	Sept 2 1855–Dec 16 1880	Sept 2 1855–Dec 16 1880	NLI	Pos. 5345
	1855–81	1855–81	1855–81	PRONI	MIC.1D/78
Kinnally (Kilmore)	See Cavan				

Parish (Diocese)	Baptisms	Marriages	Burials	Location	Reference
Knockninny	See NLI			LDS	979703 item 1
(Kilmore)	May 21 1855–Nov 27 1870	Jan 1855–Nov 24 1870		NLI	Pos. 5349
	1855–70	1855–70		PRONI	MIC.1D/78
Magheraculmany	See NLI			LDS	979705 item
(Clogher)					11–14
	Aug 24 1836–Jan 11 1857	Nov 13 1837–Nov 1 1844		NLI	Pos. 5571
	Mar 22 1857–Dec 26 1869	Apr 24 1857–Dec 6 1869			
	Jan 2 1870–Dec 29 1880	Nov 12 1844–Apr 13 1857			
		Jan 15 1870–Dec 27 1880			
	1836–81	1837–81		PRONI	MIC.1D/14;
					C.R.2/1
Roslea (Clogher)	See NLI			LDS	0926057
	Jan 6 1862–Dec 26 1880	Jan 19 1862–Nov 26 1880		NLI	Pos. 5577
	1862–81	1862–81		PRONI	MIC.1D/20
Tempo (Clogher)	Nov 1 1845–Oct 13 1870	Oct 11 1845–Nov 23 1870		NLI	Pos. 5570
	Aug 2 1871–Dec 18 1880	Jan 3 1871–Nov 8 1880			
	1845–81	1845–		PRONI	MIC.1D/13

Galway East

Most but not all East Galway Family History Society (EGFHS) transcripts appear to be online at *<www.rootsireland.ie>*, as are Galway Family History Society West (GFHSW) transcripts.

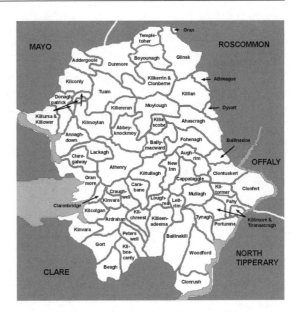

Parish (Diocese)	Baptisms	Marriages	Burials	Location	Reference
Abbeyknockmoy	1821–1900	1844–1900	1847–8	GFHSW	
(Tuam)	1821–32	1837–44	1847–8	LDS	1279210 item
	1837–58	1894–1901			9–14
	1841–54				
	1894–1915				
	No records microfilmed			NLI	
Addergoole (Tuam)	1858–1900	1859–1900		GFHSW	
	1858–91	1859–84		LDS	1279208 item
	1878–1918				1–2
	Aug 7 1858–Nov 18 1877	Jan 10 1859–Dec 11 1880		NLI	Pos. 4210
	Jan 8 1878–Dec 31 1880				

Parish (Diocese)	Baptisms	Marriages	Burials	Location	Reference
Ahascragh (Elphin)	1840–1900	1866–1900		EGFHS	
	See NLI			LDS	09899751 item 1–2
	Jan 10 1840–May 6 1880	Jan 29 1866–Nov 26 1880		NLI	Pos. 4616, 4617
	Aug 15 1870–Dec 31 1880 (Ahascragh only)	(Ahascragh only)			
	1840–1900	1866–1900		RHGC	
Annaghdown (Tuam)	1834–1900	1834–1900		GFHSW	
	1834–1909 (gaps)	1834–1909 (gaps)		LDS	1279206 item 1–2
	Sept 1834–Sept 12 1869	Mar 15 1834–Nov 29 1868		NLI	Pos. 4219
	Feb 2 1875–Jan 4 1880	Feb 6 1875–June 12 1880			
Ardrahan (Galway)	1839–1900	1845–1900	1878	GFHSW	
	See NLI			LDS	0926062
	May 30 1839–Mar 22 1846	Mar 26 1845–Feb 20 1850		NLI	Pos. 2442
	Nov 18 1866–Nov 15 1880	Feb 3 1867–Sept 13 1887			
Athenry (Tuam)	1858–1900	1858–1900		GFHSW	
	1858–1919	1858–1901		LDS	1279207 item 6–7; 1279209 4–5
	Aug 3 1858–Sept 21 1878	Aug 15 1858–Oct 1 1878		NLI	Pos. 4219
Athleague	See Roscommon				
Aughrim (Clonfert)	1828–1900	1829–1900	1825–30	EGFHS	
	1828–1901	1828–1921	1892–1901	LDS	1279215 item 9–12
	Mar 27 1828–Dec 28 1880			NLI	Pos. 2431
Ballinakill (East Galway) (Clonfert)	1839–50	1870–1900		EGFHS	
	1860–1900				
	1839–51	1891–1903		LDS	0979689 item 12, 14; 1279216 22
	1858–9				
	1859–80				
	1890–1902				
	Apr 15 1839–Oct 22 1851			NLI	Pos. 2434
	Feb 5 1859–Dec 24 1880				
	Nov 20 1858–Dec 26 1859				
Ballinasloe (Clonfert)	1820–1900	1820–1900	1825–30	EGFHS	
	1820–1900	1853–1902		LDS	1279217 item 9–17
	Sept 23 1820–July 27 1832	Sept 23 1820–July 27 1832	Sept 23 1820–July 27 1832;	NLI	Pos. 2432
	July 19 1832–Feb 21 1841	July 19 1832–Feb 21 1841	July 19 1832–Feb 21 1841		
	June 7 1841–June 14 1847				
	July 6 1847–May 30 1862				
	June 6 1862–Dec 31 1880				
Ballymacward (Clonfert)	1841–3	1885–1900		EGFHS	
	1856–90				
	1855–1901	1885–1902		LDS	1279226 item 26–28
	Oct 1 1841–Nov 15 1843			NLI	Pos. 2431
	May 2 1855–Feb 15 1874				
	May 12 1855–Dec 30 1880				

Parish (Diocese)	Baptisms	Marriages	Burials	Location	Reference
Beagh (Galway)	1855–1900			EGFHS	
	See NLI			LDS	0979692 item 1–2
	Feb 5 1851–June 25 1851	Mar 1849–Feb 23 1850		NLI	Pos. 2442
	Jan 14 1855–Apr 3 1881	May 19 1860–Oct 18 1881			
	1855–62			Online	*<www.celtic cousins.net>*
Boyounagh (Tuam)	1838–1900	1838–65		EGFHS	
	1859–1908			LDS	1279211 item 9
	Oct 5 1838–June 11 1858	Oct 9 1838–July 17 1865		NLI	Pos. 4211
	Dec 11 1859–Oct 25 1863				
	Oct 8 1865–Dec 26 1880				
Cappataggle (Clonfert)	1799–1900	1806–1863	1806–1849	EGFHS	
		1893–1900			
	1809–1844	1831–44	1827–44	LDS	1279215 item 31–3; 1279216 1–2
	1844–1917	1844–65	1844–69		
	Jan 6 1809–Mar 10 1814	Jan 6 1809–Mar 10 1814	Jan 6 1809–Mar 10 1814	NLI	Pos. 2431
	Jan 1 1814–May 29 1827	Jan 1 1814–May 29 1827	Jan 1 1814–May 29 1827		
	Sept 23 1827–June 24 1844	Sept 23 1827–June 24 1844	Sept 23 1827–June 24 1844		
	June 26 1844–Sept 15 1869	Nov 1 1831–June 25 1844	June 26 1844–Sept 15 1869		
		July 18 1844–July 30 1863			
Carabane (Clonfert)	1831–1900	1834–1900		EGFHS	
	1831–1902	1832–1912		LDS	0979689 item 15; 1279216 15–17
	July 14 1831–Mar 6 1878	July 24 1831–Jan 29 1878		NLI	Pos. 2434
Claregalway (Galway)	1849–1902	1849–1908	1849–76	GFHSW	
	Nov 11 1849–Dec 29 1880	Nov 12 1849–Nov 23 1880	Nov 11 1849–Nov 1876	NLI	Pos. 2429
Clarenbridge (Galway)	1854–1900	1837–1900		GFHSW	
	See NLI			LDS	0979690 item 1
	Aug 7 1854–Mar 29 1881	June 13 1837–Feb 18 1882		NLI	Pos. 2442
Clonfert (Clonfert)	1884–1900			EGFHS	
	1893–1901	1894–1904		LDS	1279215 item 13–14
	No records microfilmed			NLI	
Clonrush Killaloe	See Clare				
Clontuskert (Clonfert)	1827–1900	1827–82	1827–88	EGFHS	
	1827–1901	1827–1901		LDS	1279215 item 1–2
	Oct 2 1827–Dec 20 1880	Oct 2 1827–Oct 4 1868	Oct 2 1827–Oct 4 1868	NLI	Pos. 2431
	(modern transcript)	Mar 2 1870–Dec 5 1880			
	Oct 2 1827–Oct 4 1868				
	Mar 2 1870–Dec 5 1880				
Craughwell (Galway)	1847–94	1847–58	1847–50	EGFHS	
	Nov 20 1847–Mar 28 1881	July 6 1856–Nov 25 1876		LDS	0979692 item 8
	Nov 20 1847–Mar 28 1881	July 6 1856–Nov 25 1876		NLI	Pos. 2442
Donaghpatrick (Tuam)	1844–1900	1844–1900		GFHSW	
	1857–1901	1857–1905		LDS	1279206 item 12
	Apr 8 1844–June 30 1844	Apr 8 1844–Dec 6 1846		NLI	Pos. 4219
	Nov 12 1849–June 9 1861	Dec 8 1849–June 15 1861			
	Aug 1 1863–Dec 27 1880	Sept 12 1863–Nov 18 1880			

Parish (Diocese)	Baptisms	Marriages	Burials	Location	Reference
Dunmore (Tuam)	1833–1900	1833–1900		GFHSW	
	1833–60	1833–60		LDS	1279210 item
	1877–1910				4–8
	Mar 2 1833–Mar 1 1846	Mar 17 1833–Sept 6 1860		NLI	Pos. 4211
	Dec 12 1853–Oct 21 1859	Jan 13 1861–Sept 9 1877			
	(two sections, 1856–9)				
	Dec 14 1847–Jan 20 1854				
	Sept 16 1877–Dec 30 1880				
Dysart (Elphin)	See Roscommon				
Fahy (Clonfert)	1873–1900	1876–1900		EGFHS	
	1893–1903	1894–1908		LDS	1279216 item
					24–25
	No records microfilmed			NLI	
Fohenagh (Clonfert)	1828–1900	1828–85		EGFHS	
	1827–77	1827–77		LDS	1279215 4–8;
	1889–1902	1890–1905			0926058
	Aug 1 1827–Apr 4 1877	Aug 1 1827–Apr 4 1877	Aug 1 1827–Apr 4 1877	NLI	Pos. 2431
Glinsk (Elphin)	1836–1900	1836–1900		EGFHS	
	Sept 5 1836–Jan 28 1846	Nov 1 1836–Apr 24 1865	Sept 14 1836–Sept 20 1839	NLI	Pos. 4620
	Nov 2 1846 (?)–June 22	July 6 1865–Nov 1 1880			
	1848				
	Mar 15 1849–Sept 23 1866				
	Oct 6 1866–Dec 26 1880				
	1836–1900	1836–1900	1836–9	RHGC	
Gort (Galway)	1848–1900	1853–1900		EGFHS	
	See NLI			LDS	0979691 item 3
	Feb 14 1848–Feb 13 1862	Dec 6 1853–Feb 20 1862		NLI	B. to 1872, M.
	July 17 1854–Dec 28 1872	Feb 23 1862–Feb 17 1863			to 1862: Pos.
	Feb 18 1862–Feb 17 1863				2441;
	Jan 5 1873–Mar 2 1881				remainder
					2442
Kilbeacanty (Galway)	1855–1900	1881–1900		EGFHS	
	See NLI			LDS	0979692 item 3
	Aug 6 1854–Jan 7 1881			NLI	Pos. 2442
Kilchreest (Galway)	1855–1900	1865–97		EGFHS	
	See NLI			LDS	0926064
	Feb 1 1855–June 25 1881	Feb 2 1865–Feb 23 1886		NLI	Pos. 2442
Kilcolgan (Galway)	1854–1900	1871–1900		GFHSW	
	See NLI			LDS	0979691 item 10
	Nov 12 1854–July 21 1881	Jan 29 1871–Sept 6 1884		NLI	Pos. 2442
Kilconly (Tuam)	1872–1900	1872–1900		GFHSW	
	1872–1913			LDS	1279214 item 4
	Mar 3 1872–Dec 29 1880			NLI	Pos. 4212
Kilkerrin and	1892–1900	1884–93		EGFHS	
Clonberne (Tuam)	1892–1903	1893–35	1920–1926	LDS	1279213 item
					8–9
	No records microfilmed			NLI	

Parish (Diocese)	Baptisms	Marriages	Burials	Location	Reference
Killascobe (Tuam)	1806–1810	1807–1900		EGFHS	
	1867–1900				
	1806–1902	1806–1902		LDS	1279259 item 13
	July 13 1867–Dec 24 1880	May 7 1807–July 20 1819		NLI	Pos. 4220
		Nov 25 1825–June 8 1847			
		July 25 1849–Dec 15 1880			
Killeenadeema	1836–1900	1836–1900		EGFHS	
(Clonfert)	1836–1932	1837–1915		LDS	1279216 item 18–19
	May 1 1836–Dec 12 1880	Apr 24 1836–Oct 2 1880		NLI	Pos. 2434
Killereran (Tuam)	1870–1900	1851–1900		GFHSW	
	1870–1900	1851–79		LDS	1279214 item 1–2
		1888–1900			
	June 12 1870–Dec 26 1880	Feb 26 1851–Aug 8 1858		NLI	Pos. 4220
		Oct 24 1870–July 1 1879			
Killian (Elphin)	1804–1900	1804–1900	1804–1900	EGFHS	
	See NLI			LDS/online	0989748/ Familysearch
	Apr 22 1804–July 26 1833	Apr 21 1804–Feb 28 1843	Oct 21 1844–Dec 5 1859	NLI	Pos. 4613, 4614
	Oct 19 1844–Dec 29 1863	Oct 13 1844–Mar 31 1863			
	Dec 13 1859–Mar 23 1861	Jan 16 1860–Oct 5 1865			
	May 12 1860–Nov 21 1880	(Newbridge)			
	(Newbridge)	Jan 24 1864–Nov 18 1880			
	Jan 14 1864–Nov 21 1879				
	1804–1900	1804–1900	1844–59	RHGC	
Killimore and	1831–91	1831–41		EGFHS	
Tiranascragh		1851–97			
(Clonfert)	1831–1901	1831–1902		LDS	1279215 items 3–8
	Oct 8 1831–Dec 29 1846	Nov 7 1831–July 27 1880		NLI	Pos. 2433
	Jan 1 1847–Sept 10 1879				
Killursa and Killower	1880–1916	1880–1920		GFHSW	
(Tuam)	1880–1912	1880–1916		LDS	1279207 items 13–14
	No records microfilmed			NLI	
Kilmoylan (Tuam)	1835–1900	1813–1900		GFHSW	
	1835–1906	1813–94	1835–68	LDS	1279207 item 1–5
	Dec 18 1835–Aug 5 1860	Oct 14 1813–July 20 1872		NLI	Pos. 4220
	Aug 4 1872–July 9 1879	Aug 1 1871–Nov 26 1880			
Kiltormer (Clonfert)	1834–1900	1834–1900		EGFHS	
	1834–1903	1834–1926	1834–6	LDS	1279217 item 24–27
	Mar 12 1834–July 15 1860	Feb 9 1834–May 20 1860		NLI	Pos. 2433
	May 22 1862–Dec 20 1880	Sept 30 1860–Sept 28 1873			
Kiltullagh (Clonfert)	1844–1900	1826–1900	1830–41	EGFHS	
	1844–1901	1826–1902	1830–41	LDS	1279216 item 10–14
	June 25 1844–Jan 15 1854	Jan 30 1830–Aug 4 1880	Sept 5 1830–May 23 1837	NLI	Pos. 243434
	Dec 21 1862–Oct 12 1872				

Parish (Diocese)	Baptisms	Marriages	Burials	Location	Reference
Kinvara (Galway)	1831–1900	1831–1900		GFHSW	
	1831–53			LDS	0926068
	June 28 1831–May 15 1837	July 9 1831–May 13 1837	List of the inhabitants	NLI	B. and M. to
	June 23 1843–Aug 29 1853	June 26 1843–Aug 12 1853	showing Christmas dues		1853: Pos. 2442;
	July 31 1854–Sept 29 1867	Nov 17 1867–Jan 18 1881	1834		remainder
	Oct 11 1867–Mar 27 1881		Easter dues 1835 and		2443
			remembrance masses		
			July 27 1835–May 13 1837.		
			Also list of certificates		
			issued 1844–55		
Lackagh (Tuam)	1842–1900	1841–1900	1858–76	GFHSW	
	See NLI			LDS	0976227 item
					2–3
	July 1842–Sept 24 1847	Sept 10 1841–Dec 20 1847		NLI	Pos. 4220
	Apr 1 1848–Sept 25 1853	Sept 25 1853–Mar 1 1880			
	Sept 5 1853–Dec 26 1880				
Leitrim (Clonfert)	1815–40	1816–30	1816–30	EGFHS	
	1846–1900	1842–50	1847–87		
		1887–1900			
	See NLI			LDS	1279215 item
					15–16
	May 22 1815–Aug 3 1819	May 22 1815–Aug 3 1819	May 22 1815–Aug 3 1819	NLI	Pos. 2434
	Oct 13 1819–Dec 28 1822	Oct 13 1819–Dec 28 1822	Oct 13 1819–Dec 28 1822		
	Jan 4 1823–June 1 1829	Jan 4 1823–June 1 1829	Jan 4 1823–June 1 1829		
	Sept 30 1850–Dec 17 1880	Dec 9 1846–Nov 28 1880	Dec 16 1846–Sept 18 1880		
Loughrea (Clonfert)	1810–1900	1786–1900	1817–26	EGFHS	
	1810–1901	1810–1901	1817–26	LDS	1279216/7 item
					29–32; 1–8
	Apr 29 1827–Dec 27 1848	May 12 1827–Nov 24 1880		NLI	Pos. 2435
	Jan 1 1849–July 27 1863	July 21 1868–Dec 21 1880			
	July 21 1863–Aug 8 1871				
	July 21 1868–Dec 21 1880				
Moylough (Tuam)	1848–1900	1837–1900		EGFHS	
	1848–1903	1848–1903		LDS	1279210 item
					4–8
	Jan 16 1848–Oct 28 1863	Nov 20 1848–Sept 29 1863		NLI	Pos. 4220
	Sept 20 1860–July 1870	Dec 17 1860–Dec 7 1870			
	Jan 11 1871–Dec 8 1880	Jan 12 1871–Oct 23 1880			
	Jan 2 1873–Dec 31 1880	Feb 17 1873–Oct 18 1880			
Mullagh (Clonfert)	1863–1900	1863–1900		EGFHS	
	1863–1903	1846–1920		LDS	1279218 item
					7–9
	Feb 11 1859–Dec 24 1880	Apr 26 1863–Oct 22 1880		NLI	Pos. 2434
	1846–85 (incomplete)	1846–85 (incomplete)			
	Jan 3 1863–Sept 13 1880	Jan 3 1863–Sept 13 1880			
New Inn (Clonfert)	1827–1900	1827–1900		EGFHS	
	1827–1903	1827–1908	1893–1930	LDS	1279216 item
					3–9
	Oct 17 1827–Apr 23 1840	Oct 28 1827–May 15 1842		NLI	Pos. 2431
	Aug 11 1841–Dec 5 1880	July 29 1839–Nov 15 1880			

Parish (Diocese)	Baptisms	Marriages	Burials	Location	Reference
Oran (Elphin)	See Roscommon				
Oranmore (Galway)	1833–1900	1833–1900	1848–1900	GFHSW	
	See NLI			LDS	0979690 item 1
	Mar 11 1833–Apr 29 1839	May 2 1833–July 18 1838	Jan 7 1833–Dec 24 1837	NLI	Pos. 2438
	May 25 1833–Dec 28 1843	Aug 24 1843–Nov 8 1880			
	Dec 28 1843–Dec 25 1880				
Peterswell (Galway)	1854–1900	1856–1900		EGFHS	
	See NLI			LDS	0979692 item 4
	Jan 27 1854–Jan 15 1881	Jan 28 1856–July 24 1886		NLI	Pos. 2442
Portumna (Clonfert)	1830–1900	1832–90		EGFHS	
	1830–91	1830–90		LDS	1279216 items 20–21
	Oct 6 1830–Feb 1 1878	Oct 27 1830–Nov 1 1876		NLI	Pos. 2433
	Feb 22 1878–Dec 24 1880	Feb 6 1878–Oct 14 1880			
Templetoher (Tuam)	1856–1900	1859–72	1858–70	EGFHS	
	1856–1900	1858–89		LDS	1279259 item 11, 12
	Aug 25 1858–Jan 25 1872	Sept 11 1858–Feb 11 1872		NLI	Pos. 4213
Tuam (Tuam)	1790–1900	1790–1900		GFHSW	
	1790–1929	1795–1901		LDS	1279208/9 items 7–15; 1
	Mar 3 1790–July 2 1804	Jan 26 1799 (?)–Mar 6 1832		NLI	Pos. 4221, 4222
	Oct 14 1811–Oct 5 1829	Oct 17 1832–Dec 26 1880			
	Nov 1 1829–Apr 12 1845				
	May 1 1845–Oct 1 1857				
	Oct 3 1858–July 13 1873				
Tynagh (Clonfert)	1816–42	1809–1842		EGFHS	
	1846–64	1846–64			
	1874–1900				
	May 1 1816–Dec 31 1842	May 22 1809–Dec 10 1842		NLI	Pos. 2433
	Sept 25 1846–Dec 31 1880	Sept 26 1846–Feb 10 1863			
Woodford (Clonfert)	1821–43	1821–36		EGFHS	
	1851–61	1865–89			
	1821–60	1821–66		LDS	1279217/8, 18, 19–21, 1–6
	1865–1908	1881–9			
	Apr 20 1821–Nov 25 1843	Apr 22 1821–Nov 25 1843		NLI	Pos. 2433
	Mar 6 1851–Aug 4 1861	Mar 1 1851–July 23 1861			Online
	Apr 22 1865–Sept 13 1868	July 27 1865–Feb 9 1869			<homepages.
	Feb 20 1869–Oct 16 1880	Feb 18 1871–Feb 19 1880			rootsweb.
	1865–89				ancestry.
					com/~egan>

Galway West

All Galway
Family History
Society West
(GFHSW)
transcripts are
online at
<*www.roots
ireland.ie*>.

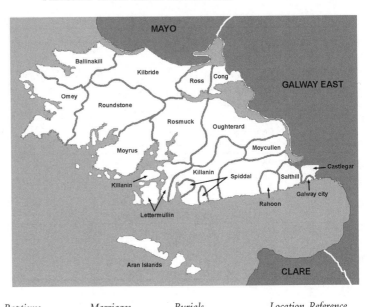

Parish (Diocese)	Baptisms	Marriages	Burials	Location	Reference
Aran Islands (Tuam)	1872–1900	1872–1900		GFHSW	
	1872–1905	1872–1905		LDS	1279214 item 8
	Nov 7 1874–Dec 23 1880	Feb 20 1872–Dec 21 1880		NLI	Pos. 4219
Ballinakill (Tuam)	1869–1900	1869–1900		GFHSW	
	1869–1903	1870–1903		LDS	1279212 item 17–19
	July 23 1869–Dec 26 1880	July 25 1869–Dec 5 1880		NLI	Pos. 4218
	May 14 1876–Dec 26 1880 (separate register)	Jan 12 1875–Nov 17 1880			
Castlegar (Galway)	1827–1908	1827–1912	1829–1908	GFHSW	
	See NLI			LDS	0979690
	Mar 8 1827–Dec 31 1841	Mar 8 1827–Dec 15 1841	Mar 25 1827–Oct 28 1841	NLI	Pos. 2438
	Jan 2 1842–July 31 1863	Jan 8 1842–Oct 24 1864	Jan 9 1842–July 3 1864		
	Nov 3 1864–Nov 21 1880	Nov 3 1864–Nov 21 1880	Nov 13 1864–Nov 14 1880		
Cong and The Neale	See Mayo (South)				
Galway city: St Nicholas	See NLI			LDS	0926070
	Apr 21 1690–Dec 28 1690			NLI	Pos. 2436
	Mar 31 1723– Mar 10 1726				
Galway city: St Nicholas East	1810–58	1789–1858	1789–1858	GFHSW	
	See NLI			LDS	0926070
	Nov 15 1810–Dec 30 1821	Jan 7 1789–Nov 29 1824	Sept 1 1788–Dec 17 1809	NLI	Pos. 2436 and
	Oct 1 1831–Dec 1858	Oct 17 1831–Dec 23 1858	Oct 1 1831–Dec 26 1858		2437
Galway city: St Nicholas North	1818–67	1818–68	1818–68	GFHSW	
	See NLI			LDS	0926070
	Apr 5 1818–Mar 30 1835	Apr 12 1818–Aug 22 1868	Apr 5 1818–Mar 31 1861	NLI	Pos. 2436 and
	Apr 7 1835–Oct 28 1867	1866–8 (2 pages only)			437
Galway city: St Nicholas North and East	1859–1900	1859–1900	1859–1900	GFHSW	
	See NLI			LDS	0926070
	Feb 2 1859–Dec 26 1880	Feb 3 1859–Nov 30 1880	Feb 20 1859–Dec 31 1880	NLI	Pos. 2437

Parish (Diocese)	Baptisms	Marriages	Burials	Location	Reference
Galway city: St Nicholas South and West	1814–1900	1809–1900	1810–1900	GFHSW	
	As NLI	As NLI	As NLI	LDS	0926070
	Apr 21 1690–Dec 28 1690	1809–1821 (3 pages only)	1811–69 (5 pages only)	NLI	Pos. 2436
	Mar 31 1723–	Mar 12 1814–Dec 26 1826	Mar 5 1814–Nov 16 1826		
	Mar 10 1726	Feb 13 1822–Sept 29 1859	Aug 15 1847–July 3 1859		
	1805–1821 (2 pages only)	Aug 13 1828–Oct 13 1845	Aug 13 1828–Oct 13 1845		
	Feb 27 1814–Dec 13 1826	Jan 9 1846–Jan 31 1852	Feb 7 1846–Dec 21 1851		
	Oct 16 1822–Aug 20 1866	Nov 4 1959–Oct 8 1868	Nov 8 1859–Sept 8 1868		
	Aug 13 1828–Oct 13 1845	Nov 9 1872–Dec 31 1880	Nov 25 1872–Dec 5 1880		
	Jan 6 1846–Apr 12 1853				
	1859–68				
	1872–80				
Kilbride (Tuam) See also Ross	As NLI			LDS	0926221
	Dec 11 1853–Nov 12 1880 (transcript)			NLI	Pos. 4214
	1853–1900	1853–1900		GFHSW	
Killanin (Galway)	1834–1900	1875–1900	1881–8	GFHSW	
	Jan 1 1875–Dec 26 1880	Jan 26 1875–Dec 6 1880		LDS	0926228 item 2
	Jan 1 1875–Dec 26 1880	Jan 26 1875–Dec 6 1880		NLI	Pos. 2439
Lettermullin (Tuam)	1853–1900	1853–1900		GFHSW	
	1861–1900	1853–95		LDS	127921 item 11–13
	Aug 17 1853–May 16 1880	July 18 1853–Nov 1 1880		NLI	Pos. 4218
	Aug 18 1872–Nov 21 1880 (Killeen)				
Moycullen (Galway)	1848–1900	1849–1900	1848–1900	GFHSW	
	See NLI			LDS	0926071
	Jan 2 1786–Mar 9 1823	Jan 8 1786–Jan 13 1823	Jan 4 1786–Mar 13 1823	NLI	Pos. 2441
	Jan 4 1837–May 3 1841	Oct 1 1843–Oct 3 1848	Nov 1848–Dec 21 1880		
	Oct 6 1843–Oct 3 1848	Feb 18 1849–Nov 16 1880			
	Nov 4 1848–Dec 26 1880				
	1793–1812	1793–1812		Published	AH, No. 14, pp. 126–34
Moyrus (Tuam)	1853–1900	1854–1900		GFHSW	
	1852–1903	1852–1903		LDS	1279212 items 8–10
	Dec 8 1853–Sept 20 1873	Sept 9 1852–Sept 6 1874		NLI	Pos. 4218
	Oct 18 1874–Nov 7 1880	Nov 1 1874–Nov 20 1880			
Omey (Tuam)	1838–1900 (Clifden)	1838–1900 (Clifden)	1869–77 (Ballyconeely)	GFHSW	
	1864–1900 (Ballyconeely)	1864–1900 (Ballyconeely)			
	1881–1900 (Omey/Ballindoon)	1885–1900 (Omey/Ballindoon)			
	1838–1924	1839–1938	1869–72	LDS	1279213 item 1–7; 1279213 1
	Jan 7 1838–Oct 7 1855	Sept 15 1839–May 6 1855		NLI	Pos. 4218
	July 1856–Oct 26 1874	(various groups of entries for different dates)			
	Oct 2 1864–Aug 7 1880 (Ballyconneely)	Aug 19 1858–Feb 27 1874 (various groups of entries for different dates)			
		Oct 29 1864–Dec 18 1873			
		June 26 1874–Dec 14 1880			

Parish (Diocese)	Baptisms	Marriages	Burials	Location	Reference
Oughterard (Galway)	1809–1900	1809–1900	1827–74	GFHSW	
	1809–1821	1809–1816	1827–74	LDS	0979690 item 3
	1827–80	1827–80			
	June 27 1809–Aug 18 1821	July 27 1809–Feb 23 1816	Mar 8 1827–Feb 4 1874	NLI	Pos. 2438
	Mar 9 1827–Dec 30 1880	Mar 20 1827–Dec 28 1880			
Rahoon (Galway)	1806–1913	1806–1913	1806–1913	GFHSW	
	See NLI			LDS	0926069
	Jan 3 1819–Dec 31 1832	Jan 3 1819–Dec 27 1832	Jan 3 1819–July 23 1826	NLI	Pos. 2437
	Jan 1 1833–Jan 28 1845		2 pages for 1830		
	Apr 17 1845–Mar 25 1877				
Rosmuck (Galway)	1840–1900	1863		GFHSW	
	Aug 11 1840–Dec 27 1880			NLI	Pos. 2439
Ross (Tuam)	1853–1900	1853–1900		GFHSW	
See also Kilbride	1853–1919	1883–1903		LDS	1279259 item 6–10
	Dec 25 1853–Apr 29 1871			NLI	Pos. 4216
	Jan 10 1873–Dec 19 1880				
Roundstone (Tuam)	1872–1900	1872–1900		GFHSW	
	1872–1910	1872–1900		LDS	1279212 items 8–10
	Aug 3 1872–Dec 26 1880	Aug 4 1872–Dec 19 1880		NLI	Pos. 4218
Salthill (Galway)	No records microfilmed			NLI	
Spiddal (Galway)	1861–1900	1873–1900	1873–1900	GFHSW	
	See NLI			LDS	0979690 item 4
	Feb 7 1861–Mar 25 1873	Apr 29 1873–Nov 3 1880	Apr 22 1873–Dec 8 1880	NLI	Pos. 2438
	Apr 13 1873–Dec 25 1880				

Kerry

All parishes are in the diocese of Kerry. All online records are at <*www.irishgenealogy.ie*>.

Parish (Diocese)	Baptisms	Marriages	Burials		Location	Reference
Abbeydorney	Oct 2 1835–Sept 10 1844	Jan 24 1837–July 20 1859			NLI	Pos. 4274
	Feb 27 1851–Sept 6 1859	Nov 2 1859–Nov 10 1880				
	Nov 7 1880–Dec 6 1880					
	1835–1900	1837–1900			Online	
Ardfert	1818–46	1825–46			LDS	0883784 item 6; 0883740 item 3
	Mar 1819–Nov 1819	Feb 15 1825–Jan 25 1826			NLI	Pos. 4272
	July–Sept 1824	Jan 10 1835–Feb 24 1846				
	Feb 8 1835–Oct 2 1846	Nov 4 1859–Nov 30 1880				
	Oct 1 1859–Dec 20 1874					
	Dec 24 1984–Dec 26 1880					
	1856–1900	1859–1900			Online	
	1818–39	1825–43 (Vol. 8)			Published	o'ĸ
	1839–46 (Vol. 8)					
Ballanvohir	Apr 2 1829–Mar 12 1834	May 1 1829–June 3 1835			NLI	Pos. 4274
	Mar 23 1837–Mar 19 1839	May–Oct 1837				
	Oct 2 1851–Dec 26 1880	Sept 1855–Nov 14 1880				
	(transcript)	(transcript)				
	1819–1900	1809–1908			Online	
Ballybunion	Nov 1 1831–Jan 4 1870	Feb 7 1837–Nov 13 1869			NLI	Pos. 4280
	Jan 2 1870–Dec 27 1880	Jan 15 1870–Nov 21 1880				
	1831–1901	1831–1905			Online	
Ballyheigue	Dec 1 1857–Dec 17 1880	Jan 13 1858–Feb 10 1880			NLI	Pos. 4273
	1857–1900	1858–1900			Online	
Ballylongford	Mar 20 1823–May 12 1838	June 1826–Jan 1827			NLI	Pos. 4284
	(very fragmented)	Feb 1828–Aug 1828				
	Oct 1869–Dec 31 1880	Jan 1832–Nov 1837				
		(very fragmented)				
	1823–1900	1826–1900			Online	
Ballymacelligot	Oct 4 1868–Dec 19 1880	Nov 14 1868–July 30 1880			NLI	Pos. 4273
	1868–1900	1868–1900			Online	
Beaufort	Mar 10 1844–Jan (?) 1880	Jan 7 1843–Feb 25 1879			NLI	Pos. 4265
	1844–1902	1843–1911			Online	
Boherbue	1833–75	1863–80			LDS	0883696 item 12; 0883884 item 4
	July 22 1833–Dec 7 1860	Mar 22 1863–Nov 25			NLI	B. to 1865, Pos. 4265; remainder 4266
	Feb 8 1863–Dec 29 1873	1880				
	Jan 6 1873–Dec 24 1880					
	1833–1904	1863–1907			Online	
	1833–64 (Vol. 2)	1863–70 (Vol. 3)			Published	o'ĸ
	1863–1900 (Vol. 11)	1863–1900 (Vol. 11)				
		1903–1947 (Vol. 14)				
Bonane and Glengarriff	July 22 1846–Dec 25 1856	July 18 1847–Nov 29 1856			NLI	Pos. 4288
	Jan 3 1857–Dec 21 1877	Feb 1 1857–Feb 9 1875				
	Jan 9 1878–Dec 26 1880	Feb 2 1876–Feb 10 1880				
	1846–1911	1847–1910			Online	

Parish (Diocese)	Baptisms	Marriages	Burials	Location	Reference
Brosna	1866–75			LDS	1238660 item 3
	Mar 15 1868–May 14 1878			NLI	Pos. 4283
	1867–1900	1890–1900		Online	
	1866–1900 (Vol. 8)	1872–1900 (Vol. 8)		Published	O'K
Cahirciveen	Nov 11 1846–June 24 1863			NLI	Pos. 4285
	(some pages mutilated)				
	Apr 16 1863–Jan 18 1879				
	(transcript)				
	1845–1906	1863–1900		Online	
Cahirdaniel	Feb 1831–July 29 1867	May 1831–Feb 18 1868		NLI	B., Pos. 4287;
	(mutilated)	(many pages mutilated)			M. 4288
	1831–1910	1831–1910		Online	
Castleisland	1829–1913	1825–1918		LDS	1279379
	Apr 1823–Dec 29 1859	Oct 10 1822–Aug 10 1858		NLI	M. and B. to
	Jan 1 1859–Aug 29 1869	Feb 8 1859–May 6 1880			1869, Pos.
	Feb 15 1870–Dec 18 1880				4276;
					remainder
					4277
	1823–1900	1822–1900		Online	
	1823–58 (Vol. 6)	1822–91 (Vol. 7)		Published	O'K
	1859–69 (Vol. 4)	1878–1900 (Vol. 7)			
	1870–1872 (Vol. 6)				
Dingle	Feb 25 1825–Apr 20 1837	May 1 1821–Dec 30 1859		NLI	Pos. 4277 to
	Sept 30 1837–Dec 6 1859	Jan 28 1860–Oct 13 1880			1859;
	Jan 1 1860–Sept 15 1869				remainder
	Sept 11 1869–Jan 12 1880				4278
	1823–99	1821–1900		Online	
Dromod	Feb 1850–Aug 5 1867	Jan 29 1850–Mar 5 1867		NLI	Pos. 4288
	Apr 13 1867–Dec 31 1880	Apr 13 1867–Dec 31 1880			
	1850–1901	1850–1900		Online	
Duagh	Jan 1 1819–Dec 2 1833	Jan 24 1832–Nov 10 1833	May 9 1844–Dec 6 1846	NLI	Pos. 4282
	Dec 2 1833–Nov 27 1852	Jan 26 1834–Aug 14 1852			
	1853–Sept 28 1871 (some	1853–June 18 1871 (some			
	early pages missing)	early pages missing)			
	Oct 1 1871–Dec 27 1880	Jan 18 1872–Oct 19 1880			
	1800–1906	1827–1911		Online	
Fossa	Jan 11 1857–Dec 17 1880	Jan 21 1858–Sept 26 1880		NLI	Pos. 4265
	1857–1902	1858–1911		Online	
Glenbeigh	Mar 17 1830–Aug 1837	Mar 1830–Feb 1835		NLI	Pos. 4285
	(fragmented)	(fragmented)			
	June 21 1841–Mar 25 1870				
	(fragmented pages missing)				
	Apr 9 1870–Dec 30 1880				
	1825–1900	1830–98		Online	
Glenflesk	1820–75	1831–80 (gaps)		LDS	0883747 item
					2, 19
	Sept 1821–Mar 12 1873	Feb 13 1831–Feb 25 1873		NLI	Pos.4266
	1820–94	1831–94		Online	
	1820–32 (Vol. 7)	1831–1900 (Vol. 6)		Published	O'K
	1832–62 (Vol. 7)				
	1862–94 (Vol. 8)				

Parish (Diocese)	Baptisms	Marriages	Burials	Location	Reference
Keel	Feb 5 1804–July 8 1813	Feb 4 1804–Mar 15 1818		NLI	Pos. 4273
	Jan 9 1815–Oct 1817	May 1818–June 18 1834			
	Apr 7 1818–June 30 1834	Aug 28 1834–Feb 4 1845			
	July 6 1834–Mar 1845	Apr 9 1845–July 31 1880			
	Feb 29 1845–Nov 1 1880				
	1804–1900	1804–1908		Online	
Kilcummin	1821–75	1823–59		LDS	0883784 item
		1873–80			5, 0883740
					item 5
	Jan 10 1821–Aug 31 1859	Jan 31 1823–Sept 23 1859		NLI	Pos. 4265
	Feb 8 1873–May 11 1880	Feb 8 1873–May 11 1880			
	1821–1901	1823–1900		Online	
	1821–1900 (Vol. 5)	1823–59 (Vol. 5)		Published	O'K
		1873–1900 (Vol. 5)			
Kilgarvan	Apr 15 1818–Aug 23 1846	Nov 4 1818–Aug 1 1846		NLI	Pos. 4290
	Aug 10 1846–Nov 30 1853	Sept 23 1846–Apr 16 1864			
	Dec 2 1863–Dec 31 1880	Sept 6 1864–May 1880			
	1818–96	1818–95		Online	
Killarney	1785–1839	1792–1880		LDS	0883697 item
					4, 5; 0883851 1
	Aug 5 1792–June 24 1803	Aug 15 1792–June 27 1803		NLI	Pos. 4262 to
	June 27 1803–July 12 1809	June 29 1803–July 18 1809			1830; B. to
	July 16 1809–Sept 5 1816	July 16 1809–Sept 1 1816			1865. M. to
	Sept 3 1816–Apr 15 1824	Sept 2 1816–May 23 1824			1857, 4263;
	Apr 16 1824–Jan 17 1830	June 11 1824–Jan 28 1830			remainder
	Jan 3 1830–Dec 25 1880	Feb 1 1830–May 24 1857			4264
		Jan 7 1858–Nov 9 1880			
	1785–1900	1792–1906		Online	
	1785–1803 (Vol. 5)	1792–1839 (Vol. 5)		Published	O'K
	1803–1833 (Vol. 6)	1839–90 (Vol. 7)			
	1833–40 (Vol. 7)	1891–1900 (Vol. 7)			
	1840–65 (Vol. 8)				
	1865–1900 (Vol. 14)				
Killeentierna	1801–1875	1803–1880		LDS	0883740 item
					4, 0883818
					item 18
	June 14 1801–Dec 24 1809	June 12 1803–Feb 28 1828		NLI	Pos. 4272
	July 24 1823–Nov 14 1880	Jan 8 1830–July 10 1880			
		(transcript)			
	1801–1911	1803–1884		Online	
	1801–1809 (Vol. 4 and 6)	1803–1900 (Vol. 6)		Published	O'K
	1823–70 (Vol. 4 and 6)				
	1871–1900 (Vol. 6)				
Killiny	Dec 7 1828–Dec 31 1864	Feb 28 1829–Nov 13 1864		NLI	Pos. 4275 to
	Jan 31 1865–June 16 1879	Jan 18 1865–Sept 11 1880			1864;
					remainder 4276
	1828–1910	1829–1911		Online	
Killorglin	No records microfilmed			NLI	
	1798–1911	1798–1911		Online	

Parish (Diocese)	Baptisms	Marriages	Burials	Location	Reference
Killury	Dec 10 1782–July 1786	Feb 13 1809–Feb 16 1836		NLI	Pos. 4278, 4279
	Nov 4 1806–Nov 29 1819	(many pages illegible)			
	July 18 1820–Apr 29 1835				
	Sept 4 1831–June 29 1845				
	Aug 31 1845–Apr 20 1858				
	May 8 1858–Dec 25 1880				
	1782–1900	1809–1900		Online	
Kilmelchidar	Jan 14 1807–Jan 19 1808	Jan 1808–Aug 5 1808		NLI	Pos. 4274 to
	Jan 1 1808–June 29 1828	Feb 5 1808–May 31 1828			1828;
	July 1 1828–July 30 1871	July 24 1828–Nov 1880			remainder
	Aug 24 1871–Dec 19 1880				4275
	1808–1895	1808–1897		Online	
Kilnaughten	Oct 1 1859–Dec 26 1880	July 26 1859–May 29 1880		NLI	Pos. 4280
	1859–1903	1859–1900		Online	
Knocknagoshel	No records microfilmed			NLI	
	1866–1907			Online	
Listowel	Aug 1802–June 1826	Jan 8 1837–May 26 1828		NLI	Pos. 4281
	Oct 1826–Dec 1833	Nov 10 1842–Feb 28 1842			
	Jan 1837–May 1838	Sept 2 1843–Feb 12 1844			
	Nov 1842–May 1843	Mar 9 1846–July 10 1846			
	Sept 1843–Feb 1844	June 25 1850–Jan 1851			
	Mar 1846–July 1846	Feb 6 1851–May 5 1853			
	May 1850–Jan 1851	June 7 1855–May 30 1855			
	Mar 1852–May 1853	June 18 1855–Nov 21 1880			
	May 1855–July 1855				
	Jan–July 1841				
	May 1856–80				
	1802–1906	1837–1906		Online	
Lixnaw	Aug 4 1810–Mar 27 1843	Jan 15 1810–June 6 1852		NLI	B. to 1849 Pos.
	Apr 2 1843–Feb 20 1845	Aug 17 1856–Nov 27 1875			4281;
	June 4 1848–Dec 25 1875	Jan 17 1876–Dec 1 1880			remainder
	Feb 14 1876–Dec 1 1880				4282
	1810–1901	1810–1901		Online	
Milltown	Oct 9 1825–Sept 20 1840	Oct 7 1821–Nov 1832		NLI	Pos. 4266
	Oct 1 1841–Aug 21 1859	Oct 17 1841–June 6 1861			
	1820–95	1821–94		Online	
Molahiff	Jan 1 1830–Sept 22 1872	Jan 13 1830–Mar 13 1872		NLI	Pos. 4267
	(very poor condition)	(very poor condition)			
	Sept 29 1859–June 8 1871				
	(Aglis)				
	Jan 20 1871–Aug 10 1872				
	Oct 1872–Oct 23 1880				
	(damaged)				
	1827–94	1832–94		Online	
	1872–1900 (Vol. 8)	1881–1900 (Vol. 8)		Published	O'K
Moyvane	July 21 1855–Oct 7 1877	Oct 4 1855–Nov 27 1880		NLI	Pos. 4283
	1830–1911	1831–1905		Online	
Prior	No records microfilmed			NLI	
	1853–1904	1851–1900		Online	

Parish (Diocese)	Baptisms	Marriages	Burials	Location	Reference
Rathmore	1837–75	1839–1880		LDS	0883875 item 11, 0883698 item 2
	Sept 19 1837–Mar 14 1841 Jan 14 1844–Dec 20 1874	Jan 26 1839–May 3 1874		NLI	Pos. 4268
	1837–1900	1830–88		Online	
	1837–46 (Vol. 1) 1846–74 (Vol. 1) 1875–1900 (Vol. 5)	1839–74 (Vol. 1) 1875–1900 (Vol. 5)		Published	o'к
Sneem	Aug 17 1845–Nov 26 1848 Nov 1 1857–Dec 25 1880	Feb 2 1858–Nov 27 1880		NLI	Pos. 4288
	Aug 1845–Sept 1848			NLI	Ms. 2729
	1833–1900	1858–1900		Online	
Spa	Nov 11 1866–Dec 31 1880	Jan 27 1867–Nov 11 1880		NLI	Pos. 4274
	1866–1911	1867–1911		Online	
Templenoe	Jan 1 1819–Dec 24 1838 Jan 2 1839–Dec 30 1858 Jan 2 1859–Dec 19 1870 Jan 1 1871–Aug 1 1876 Aug 6 1876–Feb 16 1879	Jan 26 1819–Mar 2 1824 Jan 17 1826–June 30 1838 Jan 23 1839–Nov 27 1858 Jan 9 1859–Oct 24 1880		NLI	Pos. 4289
	1819–1907	1819–1907		Online	
Tralee	Jan 1 1772–Feb 24 1795 Mar 1 1795–Dec 28 1813 Jan 14 1818–July 30 1832 Aug 1 1832–July 30 1843 Aug 1 1843–June 22 1856 June 24 1856–Dec 22 1867 Jan 1 1868–June 4 1874	May 1 1832–Nov 26 1853 Nov 18 1853–June 21 1856 June 24 1856–Feb 1 1876		NLI	B. to 1845, Pos. 4269; B. to 1874, M. to 1832, 4270; remainder 4271
	1772–1900	1774–1900		Online	
Tuosist	Apr 22 1844–May 26 1880 (some pages missing)			NLI	Pos. 4287
	1844–91	1879–82		Online	
Valentia	Mar 7 1825–July 5 1864 May 15 1867–Dec 14 1880	Feb 5 1827–Apr 1856		NLI	Pos. 4287
	1825–1902	1827–55		Online	

Kildare

All Kildare Genealogy (KG) database
transcripts are online at
<*www.rootsireland.ie*>.

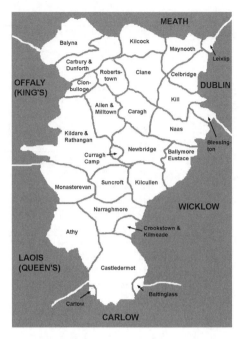

Parish (Diocese)	Baptisms	Marriages	Burials	Location	Reference
Allen and Milltown	1820–99	1820–99		KG	
(Kildare and Leighlin)	Oct 15 1820–Oct 31 1852	Oct 17 1820–Oct 26 1876		NLI	Pos. 4206
Athy (Dublin)	1753–1899	1753–1899		KG	
	Dec 7 1779–Mar 21 1797	Jan 14 1780–Feb 12 1797		NLI	Pos. 6479/80
	Sept 11 1803–Aug 21 1807	Sept 21 1803–Feb 2 1810			
	Aug 23 1807–Nov 26 1816	Feb 9 1812–June 25 1812			
	Dec 10 1821–Mar 5 1837	July 17 1815–Mar 7 1816			
	Mar 17 1837–Aug 14 1853	June 24 1822–Jan 25 1837			
	Aug 21 1853–Apr 7 1873	Apr 6 1837–Nov 22 1853			
	Apr 9 1873–Dec 31 1880	Jan 10 1854–Nov 26 1880			
Ballymore Eustace	1839–99	1839–99		KG	
(Dublin)	Mar 8 1779–Apr 27 1792	Oct 18 1779–Nov 27 1794		NLI	Pos. 6481
	Jan 10 1787–Mar 1 1790	Feb 21 1787–June 11 1796			
	May 3 1792–Apr 6 1796	May 15 1797–July 19 1830			
	Jan 5 1797–Oct 28 1830	Apr 22 1826–Dec 1 1838			
	Apr 23 1826–Dec 26 1838	Jan 27 1839–Nov 26 1863			
	Jan 1 1839–Apr 27 1854	Jan 25 1864–Oct 25 1880			
	May 7 1854–Dec 31 1880				
	1779–1838	1779–1900		WFHC	
Baltinglass	See Wicklow				
Balyna (Kildare and	1785–1899	1797–1899	1887–99	KG	
Leighlin)	Oct 17 1785–Oct 27 1801	Nov 5 1797–May 23 1799		NLI	Pos. 4206
	Nov 6 1801–July 17 1803	Nov 13 1801–Jan 31 1802			
	Aug 24 1807–Oct 21 1811	Oct 1 1807–Oct 26 1811			
	Jan 15 1815–Feb 22 1815	Jan 25 1815–Feb 7 1815			
	Feb 1 1818–Apr 12 1829	Apr 7 1817–Aug 21 1830			
	Feb 1 1818–Dec 21 1865	Mar 23 1818–Nov 15 1880			
	(1818–29 duplicate entries)	(1818–30 duplicate entries)			
	Jan 27 1866–Dec 23 1880				

Parish (Diocese)	Baptisms	Marriages	Burials	Location	Reference
Balyna (Kildare and Leighlin) *(contd.)*	1785–1899	1785–1899		Published	*JKAS*, 1988, NLI Ir 9293 i 4
Blessington (Dublin)	Apr 4 1852–Nov 14 1880 1852–80 (Church of Kilbride) 1821–1900	Feb 22 1852–Dec 4 1880 1877–80 (Church of Kilbride) 1823–1900		NLI WFHC	Pos. 6483, 6615
Caragh (Kildare and Leighlin)	1849–99 June 19 1849–Aug 12 1866 Aug 6 1849–July 4 1875 June 17 1866–Apr 19 1874 (transcript)	1857–99 Feb 7 1850–Nov 23 1859 Feb 7 1850–June 30 1875 (transcript)		KG NLI	Pos. 4206
Carbury and Dunforth (Kildare and Leighlin)	1821–99 Oct 1 1821–May 22 1850 June 9 1850–Dec 5 1880	1821–87 Nov 2 1821–Oct 27 1850 Oct 6 1850–Nov 14 1880	1847–1978 Feb 18 1869–June 9 1879	KG NLI	Pos. 4206
Carlow	See Carlow				
Castledermot (Dublin)	1789–1899 Nov 5 1789–Feb 3 1821 1822–Oct 18 1829 1829–Nov 9 1842 Dec 4 1842–Dec 10 1856 (index 1854–80) Jan 18 1857–Dec 26 1880	1789–1899 Nov 5 1789–Feb 3 1821 May 1822–Dec 14 1829 Jan 18 1830–Nov 2 1842 Jan 10 1843–Dec 27 1856 Feb 15 1857–Dec 19 1880		KG NLI	Pos. 6480/81
Celbridge (Dublin)	1857–82 From 1767 Jan 4 1857–Dec 19 1880	From 1767		KG Local custody NLI	Pos. 6613
Clane (Kildare and Leighlin)	1821–99 Mar 17 1785–Sept 4 1785 Feb 1 1786–July 3 1786 Dec 8 1788–Apr 8 1789 Feb 28 1825–Feb 28 1827 Sept 6 1829–May 31 1840 June 2 1840–Dec 26 1880	1821–99 Apr 10 1825–June 2 1828 Nov 15 1829–June 5 1840 July 19 1840–Nov 23 1880		KG NLI	Pos. 4206
Clonbulloge	See Offaly (King's County)				
Crookstown and Kilmeade (Dublin)	1853–6 Apr 28 1837–Aug 17 1840 Aug 1840–Aug 7 1843 Apr 28 1843–July 7 1846 Aug 9 1849–May 5 1853 May 5 1853–Mar 17 1856	1853–6 July 1 1837–Aug 8 1840 July 1 1842–July 25 1846 Jan 16 1853–Feb 5 1856		KG NLI	Pos. 6485
Curragh Camp (Kildare and Leighlin)	1855–93 Aug 5 1855–July 9 1871 Nov 12 1871–Dec 19 1880	1855–89 Sept 15 1855–Jan 15 1871 Dec 3 1871–Sept 13 1880	1877–90	KG NLI	Pos. 4207
Kilcock (Kildare and Leighlin)	1771–1899 1770–91 July 6 1771–Dec 4 1786 Aug 14 1816–Dec 23 1826 Oct 9 1831–June 28 1834 July 8 1834–Dec 19 1880	1770–1899 1770–91 Jan 28 1770–May 28 1787 Feb 27 1791–May 1 1791 Aug 7 1816–Sept 29 1822 July 8 1834–Nov 16 1880	1889–97	KG LDS NLI	0926117 item 1 Pos. 4207

Parish (Diocese)	Baptisms	Marriages	Burials	Location	Reference
Kilcullen (Dublin)	1777–1899	1786–1899		KG	
	Oct 22 1777–Sept 1 1818	May 11 1786–Nov 20 1806		NLI	Pos. 6484
	Apr 25 1829–Sept 13 1840	Apr 24 1810–Oct 27 1816			
	Jan 11 1857–Dec 14 1880	May 11 1829–Nov 14 1831			
		Apr 11 1836–June 23 1840			
		Jan 25 1857–Nov 26 1880			
Kildare and	1815–99	1815–99		KG	
Rathangan (Kildare	Nov 1 1815–Dec 31 1837	Nov 1 1815–Nov 30 1837		NLI	Pos. 4208
and Leighlin)	Jan 6 1838–Mar 28 1864	Jan 17 1838–Feb 7 1864			
	Apr 3 1864–Nov 28 1880	Apr 18 1864–Nov 28 1880			
Kill (Kildare and	1813–99	1813–99		KG	
Leighlin)	See NLI			LDS	0926115 item 2
	Nov 9 1840–June 30 1872	Feb 27 1843–Apr 8 1872		NLI	Pos. 4208
	June 23 1872–Dec 19 1880				
Maynooth (Dublin)	1814–99	1806–1899		KG	
	Aug 24 1814–Sept 10 1827	Jan 12 1806–Aug 27 1827		NLI	Pos. 6615
	Sept 15 1827–Feb 1 1857	Sept 16 1827–Nov 24 1856			
	Jan 4 1857–Dec 24 1880				
Monasterevan	1819–99	1818–1900		KG	
(Kildare and Leighlin)	Jan 1 1819–Feb 22 1835	Sept 11 1819–Feb 26 1835		NLI	Pos. 4203
	Mar 28 1829–Aug 15 1835	Jan 15 1835–July 17 1855			
	Jan 4 1835–June 24 1855	July 10 1855–Nov 25 1880			
	June 29 1855–Dec 26 1880				
Naas (Kildare and	1813–99	1813–99	1859–95	KG	
Leighlin)	Mar 1 1813–Jan 24 1865	Feb 28 1813–Aug 15 1877	Mar 14 1861–Dec 30 1868	NLI	Pos. 4208
	Feb 5 1865–Dec 28 1880	June 5 1876–Oct 26 1880			
Narraghmore	1827–99	1827–99		KG	
(Dublin)	Apr 27 1827–Apr 26 1837	Oct 26 1827–June 11 1837		NLI	Pos. 6485
	Mar 23 1856–Dec 30 1880	Apr 3 1856–Nov 23 1880			
	Feb 8 1868–Dec 27 1880				
Newbridge (Kildare	1786–1899	1786–1899	1889–94	KG	
and Leighlin)	Aug 2 1786–Jan 18 1795	Aug 6 1786–Jan 20 1795		NLI	Pos. 4209
	Jan 14 1820–Aug 18 1832	Jan 17 1820–Aug 15 1846			
	Jan 1 1834–Oct 1 1846	Oct 25 1849–Sept 25 1861			
	Oct 23 1836–Dec 31 1843	Sept 21 1846–Sept 25 1862			
	Sept 20 1846–Aug 5 1860	Oct 1 1861–Nov 24 1880			
	(index to 1861)				
	Mar 4 1849–Sept 22 1861				
	Oct 5 1861–Nov 24 1867				
	May 12 1867–Dec 27 1880				
Rathangan (Kildare	1880–99	1880–99	1888–92	KG	
and Leighlin)	No records microfilmed			NLI	
Suncroft (Kildare	1805–1899	1805–1899	1892–9	KG	
and Leighlin)	Mar 29 1805–Dec 26 1880	May 15 1805–July 29 1880		NLI	Pos. 4209

Kilkenny

All Rothe House, Kilkenny
(RHK), database transcripts are
online at *<www.rootsireland.ie>*.

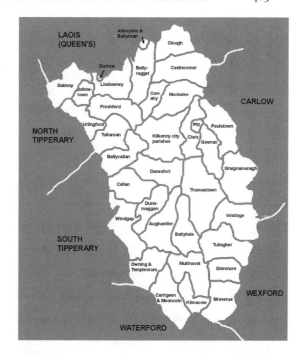

Parish (Diocese)	Baptisms	Marriages	Burials	Location	Reference
Abbeyleix and Ballyroan (Kildare and Leighlin)	See Laois (Queen's County)				
Aughaviller (Ossory)	Oct 22 1847–Dec 14 1880	Feb 24 1848–Nov 2 1880		NLI	Pos. 5022
	1848–1900	1848–79		RHK	
Ballycallan (Ossory)	See NLI			LDS	0926187
	May 26 1845–Dec 30 1880	July 22 1845–Nov 25 1880		NLI	Pos. 5027
	1820–1900	1820–1900		RHK	
Ballyhale (Ossory)	Aug 26 1823–Apr 4 1876			NLI	Pos. 5021
	1823–1900	1876–1910		RHK	
Ballyragget (Ossory)	See NLI			LDS	0979702 item 4
	Aug 31 1856–Dec 31 1880	Apr 10 1856–Nov 18 1880		NLI	Pos. 5017
	1856–1900	1856–1900		RHK	
Callan (Ossory)	See NLI			LDS	0926189
	Jan 27 1821–Oct 29 1844	Jan 28 1821–Oct 16 1844		NLI	Pos. 5025
	Nov 14 1844–June 11 1875	Nov 4 1844–Feb 15 1874			
	Nov 28 1871–Dec 28 1880	Jan 28 1871–Nov 25 1880			
	1821–1900	1821–1900		RHK	
Carrigeen and Mooncoin (Ossory)	Sept 12 1779–Nov 19 1780	Jan 26 1772–Mar 4 1783		NLI	Pos. 5018
	Oct 21 1781–Feb 7 1782	Jan 16 1789–Feb 21 1814			
	Feb 8 1782–Oct 14 1797	Feb 21 1816–Sept 27 1836			
	Dec 3 1797–Feb 13 1816	Jan 16 1837–May 12 1879			
	Feb 20 1816–Dec 29 1836				
	Jan 5 1837–Dec 29 1878				
	1779–1900	1772–1900		RHK	

Parish (Diocese)	Baptisms	Marriages	Burials	Location	Reference
Castlecomer (Ossory)	See NLI			LDS	0926190; 0979702 item 1–3
	Jan 1 1812–Oct 2 1818	Aug 13 1831–June 6 1847		NLI	Pos. 5019
	Dec 24 1828–June 3 1847	July 15 1847–Nov 24 1880			
	Apr 12 1847–Dec 7 1880				
	1812–18	1835–1900		RHK	
	1828–1900				
Clara (Ossory)	No records microfilmed			NLI	
	1778–1808	1835–1900		RHK	
	1835–1900				
Clough (Ossory)	See NLI			LDS	0926190; 0979702 item 1–3
	Jan 1 1812–Oct 2 1818	Aug 13 1831–June 6 1847		NLI	Pos. 5017
	Dec 24 1828–June 3 1847	Aug 3 1859–Nov 11 1880			
	Jan 3 1858–Nov 21 1880				
	1833–1900	1833–1911		RHK	
Conahy (Ossory)	See NLI			LDS	0926191 item 2–3
	June 2 1832–Dec 22 1876	June 17 1832–Nov 22 1880		NLI	Pos. 5016
	Jan 8 1877–Dec 28 1880				
	1832–1900	1832–1900		RHK	
Danesfort (Ossory)	See NLI			LDS	0926193
	Jan 1819–Feb 13 1869	Jan 8 1824–June 3 1868		NLI	Pos. 5025
	(many pages missing)	(many pages missing)			
	1819–1900	1823–63		RHK	
	(gaps in 1870s)	1874–1900			
Dunamaggan (Ossory)	Sept 25 1826–June 7 1840	Oct 20 1826–June 16 1842		NLI	Pos. 5022
	Apr 25 1843–May 12 1845	Feb 25 1843–Apr 29 1844			
	May 17 1844–Dec 20 1880	Feb 24 1870–Nov 25 1880			
	1826–1900	1826–44		RHK	
		1876–1900			
Durrow (Ossory)	1789–1900	1811–99		IMA	
	Jan 1 1789–Mar 30 1792	July 29 1811–Mar 27 1820		NLI	Pos. 5013
	Jan 2 1801–Feb 28 1805	May 23 1822–Sept 18 1827			
	(also a transcript)	July 17 1832–May 28 1860			
	June 9 1811–Jan 27 1820	June 9 1861–Nov 18 1880			
	May 19 1822–Feb 18 1827				
	May 26 1832–Feb 15 1857				
	Mar 8 1857–Dec 28 1880				
Freshford (Ossory)	See NLI			LDS	0926192 item 1–7
	Jan 12 1773–Aug 31 1797	Aug 13 1775–Nov 11 1779		NLI	Pos. 5015
	Mar 27 1800–Feb 9 1825	Feb 1 1801–Nov 28 1877			
	Jan 2 1825–Dec 28 1847	Jan 7 1878–Nov 24 1880			
	Jan 2 1848–Jan 3 1878				
	Jan 5 1878–Dec 25 1880				
	1772–97	1775–1900		RHK	
	1800–1900	(patchy)			

Parish (Diocese)	Baptisms	Marriages	Burials	Location	Reference
Galmoy (Ossory)	See NLI			LDS	0979701 item 4–5
	Sept 10 1805–May 2 1807	Sept 16 1861–Jan 29 1880		NLI	Pos. 5017, 6955
	June 6 1861–Dec 15 1880				
	1861–1900	1861–1900		RHK	
Glenmore (Ossory)	Mar 28 1831–Dec 11 1880	Jan 17 1831–Aug 31 1880		NLI	Pos. 5022
	1801–1900	1802–1900		RHK	
Gowran (Ossory)	See NLI			LDS	0926194 item 1–5
	Jan 1 1809–July 20 1828	Jan 11 1810–Nov 28 1828		NLI	Pos. 5026, 5027
	July 1 1828–May 4 1852	July 17 1828–Apr 28 1852			
	May 8 1852–Dec 20 1880	July 1 1852–Feb 24 1879			
	1809–1911	1810–1900		RHK	
Graignamanagh (Kildare and Leighlin)	Apr 22 1838–Dec 27 1868	July 5 1818–Nov 26 1868		NLI	Pos. 4198
	Jan 1 1869–Dec 24 1880	Jan 17 1869–Nov 3 1880			
	1818–1900	1818–1900		RHK	
Inistiogue (Ossory)	Dec 2 1810–Feb 2 1829	Jan 22 1827–Oct 9 1876		NLI	Pos. 5021, 5022
	Feb 3 1829–Dec 22 1876	Oct 27 1840–Feb 1 1877			
	Oct 20 1840–Feb 4 1877				
	1810–1900	1758–77		RHK	
		1827–1900			
Johnstown (Ossory)	1815–80	1851–80		LDS	0979700 item 2
	Aug 16 1814–Jan 26 1845	Feb 2 1851–Nov 13 1880		NLI	Pos. 5012
	Mar 1 1845–Dec 18 1880				
	1815–1900	1850–1900		RHK	
Kilkenny city: St Canice's (Ossory)	1768–1810	1768–1810	1777–9	LDS	0926195
	Apr 6 1768–Jan 15 1785	June 12 1768–Nov 27 1810		NLI	Pos. 5029, 5030
	Jan 18 1785–Dec 30 1810	Jan 10 1811–Nov 26 1844			
	Jan 7 1811–Dec 22 1844	Jan 7 1845–Nov 24 1880			
	Jan 3 1845–Dec 30 1880				
	1768–1900	1768–1900		RHK	
Kilkenny city: St John's (Ossory)	Jan 1809–July 8 1830	June 24 1809–July 5 1830		NLI	Pos. 5030
	Feb 1 1842–Feb 17 1877	Apr 11 1842–May 30 1872			
	1789–1900	1789–1900		RHK	
Kilkenny city: St Mary's (Ossory)	1754–1833	1754–1858	1754–87	LDS	0926196 item 1–3; 0926197 1–5
	Jan 1 1754–Aug 23 1782	Jan 1754–Sept 3 1809		NLI	Pos. 5028, 5029
	Aug 6 1784–Dec 1810	Oct 23 1762–Apr 26 1766			
	Oct 5 1762–Aug 21 1766	Jan 9 1798–Aug 27 1799			
	Feb 4 1811–Oct 7 1816	Jan 24 1801–Feb 7 1842			
	Oct 12 1816–May 7 1833	Feb 4 1811–Oct 7 1816			
	May 2 1833–Oct 13 1858	Nov 3 1816–Oct 13 1858			
	Oct 28 1858–Dec 27 1880	Nov 8 1858–Nov 18 1880			
	1754–1900	1754–1900	1754–86	RHK	
Kilkenny city: St Patrick's (Ossory)	Aug 11 1800–Mar 31 1867	July 19 1801–Jan 26 1868		NLI	Pos. 5027, 5028
	Apr 2 1867–Dec 31 1880				
	1800–1900	1800–1900		RHK	
Kilkenny city: Workhouse (Ossory)	Apr 30 1876–Dec 6 1880			NLI	Pos. 5030
	1876–99			RHK	

Parish (Diocese)	Baptisms	Marriages	Burials	Location	Reference
Kilmacow (Ossory)	See NLI			LDS	0926198
	July 2 1858–Dec 31 1880	Aug 9 1858–Nov 18 1880	June 30 1858–Dec 24 1880	NLI	Pos. 5023, 5024
	1858–80			Online	<www.roots web.com/~ irlkik>
	1836–1900	1798–1853 (gap 1858–1900)			RHK
Lisdowney (Ossory)	See NLI			LDS	0979701 item 1–3; 0926199 1–3
	May 26 1817–Oct 2 1853	Sept 12 1771–Apr 28 1778		NLI	Pos. 5017
	Apr 15 1854–Aug 20 1877	Nov 26 1828–Aug 13 1853			
	Oct 30 1853–Dec 29 1880	Nov 17 1853–Oct 27 1880			
	1817–1900	1817–1900			RHK
Muckalee (Ossory)	See NLI			LDS	0926200 item 1–5
	Oct 30 1801–Sept 1806 (very damaged)	Apr 19 1809–June 25 1853		NLI	Pos. 5026
	June 15 1840–Jan 8 1854	Apr 28 1853–Nov 28 1857			
	May 1 1853–Dec 28 1857	Jan 28 1858–Feb 19 1873			
	Jan 5 1858–Jan 28 1873				
	May 12 1871–Jan 28 1873				
	Aug 3 1873–Dec 5 1880				
	1801–1806	1809–1911			RHK
	1840–1900				
Mullinavat (Ossory)	See NLI			LDS	0926201
	Feb 21 1843–Dec 15 1880	May 18 1843–Mar 1 1880		NLI	Pos. 5021
	1836–1900	1842–83			RHK
		1887–1900			
Owning and Templeorum (Ossory)	Oct 7 1803–June 21 1815	Aug 5 1815–Nov 29 1849	Sept 12 1803–Mar 1806	NLI	Pos. 5019, 5020
	Sept 15 1815–May 8 1846	Nov 25 1851–Oct 24 1864	Apr 29 1808–June 17 1815		
	May 10 1846–1851	Jan 19 1851–Nov 22 1864			
	1851–4 (many large gaps)	Jan 30 1865–Nov 6 1880			
	Jan 31 1851–Dec 27 1864				
	Jan 3 1865–Dec 29 1880				
	1803–1900	1815–1900			RHK
Paulstown (Kildare and Leighlin)	See NLI			LDS	0926124
	July 9 1824–Apr 19 1846	Jan 21 1824–Nov 28 1840		NLI	Pos. 4198
	May 20 1852–May 30 1869	Jan 21 1841–Feb 11 1861			
	June 3 1855–Mar 4 1860	Jan 22 1861–Nov 25 1869			
	Mar 11 1860–May 1 1870	Feb 28 1870–Nov 27 1880			
	Jan 2 1870–Dec 12 1880				
	1840s (sporadic)	1824–1900			RHK
	1824–1900				
Pitt (Ossory)	July 8 1855–Dec 31 1880	Aug 13 1855–Oct 14 1880		NLI	Pos. 5028
Slieverue (Ossory)	Nov 26 1766–Apr 14 1778	Feb 2 1766–May 23 1778	Dec 1766–Feb 21 1778	NLI	Pos. 5031
	Feb 27 1781–June 25 1799	May 26 1791–July 9 1801			
	Apr 1777–Sept 18 1801	Oct 1 1801–Nov 25 1836			
	Oct 4 1801–Dec 31 1836	Jan 1837–Nov 16 1880			
	Dec 26 1836–Dec 26 1880				
	1766–1900	1766–1900			RHK

Parish (Diocese)	Baptisms	Marriages	Burials	Location	Reference
Thomastown	See NLI			LDS	0926202
(Ossory)	June 23 1782–Sept 27 1809	Jan 1786–Aug 10 1806		NLI	Pos. 5024
	Jan 9 1810–Mar 28 1834	May 27 1810–Aug 8 1833			
	Mar 17 1834–Dec 23 1880	Aug 7 1833–Nov 22 1880			
	1782–1900	1785–1806		RHK	
	1847–1900 (Tullaherin)	1810–1900			
		1847–1900 (Tullaherin)			
Tullagher (Ossory)	Apr 6 1817–June 28 1819	Jan 27 1835–Nov 3 1877		NLI	Pos. 5020, 5021
	Jan 26–Mar 17 1825				
	Jan 6 1830–July 12 1840				
	July 12 1840–Dec 29 1877				
	Feb 1 1834–Dec 31 1877				
	1817–1900	1817–1900		RHK	
	1825–1910				
Tullaroan (Ossory)	See NLI			LDS	0926204
	Mar 5 1843–Apr 15 1876	Apr 27 1843–Feb 7 1880		NLI	Pos. 5026
	1843–1900	1843–1900		RHK	
Urlingford (Ossory)	May 5 1805–Feb 15 1844	May 9 1805–Nov 7 1843		NLI	Pos. 5016
	May 5 1805–July 11 1823	Aug 5 1843–Sept 1870			
	(transcript)	Feb 20 1871–July 20 1880			
	Feb 16 1844–Oct 18 1857				
	Feb 15 1846–Dec 3 1870				
	Aug 21 1869–Dec 26 1880				
	Dec 16 1870–Dec 18 1880				
	1805–1900	1805–1900		RHK	
Windgap (Ossory)	See NLI			LDS	0926205
	Aug 18 1822–Feb 27 1852	Sept 14 1822–Mar 1 1880		NLI	Pos. 5023
	(transcript)	(transcript)			
	Mar 10 1852–Dec 27 1869				
	(transcript)				
	Jan 5 1870–Dec 10 1880				
	1822–1900	1822–75		RHK	
		1889–1900			

Laois (Queen's County)

All Irish Midlands Ancestry (IMA) database transcripts are online at <www.rootsireland.ie>.

Parish (Diocese)	Baptisms	Marriages	Burials	Location	Reference
Abbeyleix and Ballyroan (Kildare and Leighlin)	1824–99 June 6 1824–Aug 23 1830 Jan 19 1838–Dec (?) 26 1849 Apr 6 1850–Jan 5 1879 Jan 6 1878–Dec 5 1880 Index 1850–78	1824–99 July 2 1824–July 28 1830 Jan 30 1838–Nov 22 1880		IMA NLI	Pos. 4199
Aghaboe (Ossory)	1795–1899 1796–1880 1795–1825 (some large gaps) June 18 1826–Dec 19 1850 Jan 28 1849–Dec 12 1880	1794–1910 1794–1880 July 4 1794–Feb 1807 Nov 1 1816–Aug 10 1824 Aug 2 1825–Aug 4 1846 June 25 1850–May 20 1880		IMA LDS NLI	0979700 item 1 Pos. 5012
Arles (Kildare and Leighlin)	1821–99 1821–56 (arranged by townland, possibly some missing) Mar 20 1831–Jan 22 1843 Jan 6 1843–Aug 15 1861 Jan 1 1849–Dec 27 1858 (not a duplicate) Jan 9 1859–Dec 26 1880	1821–99 1821–56 (arranged by townland, possibly some missing) Sept 28 1831–Feb 27 1843 Aug 30 1843–July 24 1861 June 19 1850–Nov 25 1858 (not a duplicate) Jan 17 1859–Nov 24 1880	1821–56 (arranged by townland, possibly some missing)	IMA NLI	Pos. 4190
Athy	See Kildare				
Ballyadams (Kildare and Leighlin)	1820–99 Jan 3 1820–Feb 28 1847 Feb 9 1845–June 14 1874 (transcript) June 14 1874–Dec 20 1880	1820–99 Jan 12 1820–Nov 24 1853 Mar 341 1845–Apr 25 1874 (transcript)		IMA NLI	Pos. 4200
Ballynakill (Kildare and Leighlin)	1794–1899 Oct 14 1794–Mar 19 1815 Jan 16 1820–May 26 1820 Nov 4 1820–Sept 19 1872 Sept 29 1872–June 11 1876 Apr 1 1877–Nov 3 1880	1800–1899 Oct 27 1794–Feb 7 1815 Jan 15 1820–July 7 1820 Nov 3 1820–Nov 25 1875 May 22 1877–Nov 3 1880	1794–1815	IMA NLI	Pos. 4200
Ballyragget	See Kilkenny				

Parish (Diocese)	Baptisms	Marriages	Burials	Location	Reference
Borris-in-Ossory	1840–1926	1840–1926		IMA	
(Ossory)	See NLI			LDS	0926188
	May 4 1840–Mar 12 1878	July 20 1840–Sept 23 1880		NLI	Pos. 5014
	Nov 17 1855–Nov 25 1879	Nov 17 1855–Nov 25 1879			
Camross (Ossory)	1816–99	1820–99		IMA	
	May 12 1816–Sept 1 1829	Jan 21 1820–Mar 1830		NLI	Pos. 5014
	Mar 12 1821–Dec 27 1829	Aug 18 1839–Feb 8 1842			
	May 1818–Oct 6 1820	Aug 30 1846–1851			
	July 12 1823–Mar 18 1830	Aug 9 1855–Sept 17 1865			
	Oct 14 1838–Sept 11 1865	Oct 26 1865–Nov 25 1880			
	(many pages missing				
	1838–50)				
	Oct 8 1865–Dec 26 1880				
Cappinrush (Kildare	1824–99	1819–99		IMA	
and Leighlin)	Oct 20 1824–Aug 3 1862	Aug 1 1819–July 27 1862		NLI	Pos. 4201
	July 6 1862–Dec 26 1880	July 24 1862–Oct 19 1880			
Clonaslee (Kildare	1849–1906	1849–99	1892–1970	IMA	
and Leighlin)	Jan 15 1849–Dec 20 1880	Feb 20 1849–Oct 14 1880		NLI	Pos. 4202
Durrow (Ossory)	1789–1900	1811–99		IMA	
	Jan 1 1789–Mar 30 1792	July 29 1811–Mar 27 1820		NLI	Pos. 5013
	Jan 2 1801–Feb 28 1805	May 23 1822–Sept 18 1827			
	(also a transcript)	July 17 1832–May 28 1860			
	June 9 1811–Jan 27 1820	June 9 1861–Nov 18 1880			
	May 19 1822–Feb 18 1827				
	May 26 1832–Feb 15 1857				
	Mar 8 1857–Dec 28 1880				
Emo (Kildare and	1875–99	1875–99		IMA	
Leighlin)	July 4 1875–Dec 19 1880	Apr 26 1875–Nov 25 1880		NLI	Pos. 4203
Galmoy	See Kilkenny				
Killeshin (Kildare	1820–99	1822–99		CGP	
and Leighlin)	Nov 23 1819–Oct 16 1843	Jan 20 1822–Nov 24 1846		NLI	Pos. 4190
	Feb 12 1840–June 2 1844	Jan 26 1840–May 19 1844			
	Aug 16 1846–Aug 5 1849	Nov 27 1846–Aug 5 1849			
	Oct 10 1846–Dec 28 1856	Nov 27 1846–Nov 27 1856			
	Jan 4 1857–Dec 19 1880	Jan 27 1857–Nov 21 1880			
Kyle and Knock	See NLI			LDS	0979695 item 6
(Killaloe)	Jan 26 1845–Dec 23 1880	Feb 13 1846–Sept 8 1880		NLI	Pos. 2479
	1845–1911	1846–1911		NTGC	
Leighlinbridge	See Carlow				
(Kildare and Leighlin)					
Lisdowney	See Kilkenny				
Maryborough	1826–1909	1828–99	1876–1916	IMA	
(Kildare and Leighlin)	May 14 1826–Feb 4 1838	Apr 27 1826–Jan 30 1838		NLI	Pos. 4201
	Feb 4 1838–Nov 16 1851	Feb 14 1838–Jan 8 1855			
	1845–73 (alphabetical	1850–1940 (alphabetical			
	transcript)	transcript)			
	Apr 28 1873–Dec 27 1880	Jan 10 1858–Nov 25 1880			
Mayo and Doonane	1814–99	1815–99		IMA	
(Kildare and Leighlin)	See NLI			LDS	0926112
	June 21 1843–Sept 17 1877	May 1843–Sept 2 1877		NLI	Pos. 4190
	Sept 24 1877–Dec 12 1880	Feb 14 1878–Nov 27 1880			

Parish (Diocese)	Baptisms	Marriages	Burials	Location	Reference
Mountmellick (Kildare and Leighlin)	1814–99	1814–99	1890–1948	IMA	
	See NLI			LDS	0926121
	Jan 1 1814–Dec 23 1837	Feb 2 1814–Apr 27 1843		NLI	Pos. 4204
	Aug 6 1837–May 27 1860	July 7 1843–Nov 21 1872			
	1837–59 (alphabetical transcript)	Jan 19 1873–Aug 29 1880			
	Apr 19 1860–Dec 26 1880				
	Feb 26 1864–Feb 4 1879				
	1860–86 (alphabetical transcript)				
Mountrath (Kildare and Leighlin)	1823–1902	1827–99	1882–99	IMA	
	See NLI			LDS	0926122
	Oct 12 1823–Apr 21 1867	Oct 12 1823–Apr 21 1867		NLI	Pos. 4201
	May 13 1867–Dec 26 1880	May 13 1867–Dec 26 1880			
Offerlane (Ossory)	1772–1880	1784–1880		IMA	
	May 8 1782–Sept 8 1816	Sept 21 1784–May 9 1816		NLI	Pos. 5018
	May 4 1831–May 27 1880	Feb 9 1831–Feb 11 1855			
		Sept 17 1857–May 4 1880			
Portarlington	See Offaly (King's County)				
Raheen (Kildare and Leighlin)	1819–99	1819–99	1884–1925	IMA	
	Apr 5 1819–Dec 19 1880	Jan 20 1820–Sept 30 1880		NLI	Pos. 4202, 4205
	Jan 1 1843–Aug 27 1875	Nov 30 1866–May 30 1868			
	Feb 4 1844–Sept 10 1875	Aug 15 1844–Feb 13 1855			
		July 4 1860–May 24 1866			
		Jan 20 1870–Jan 10 1875			
Rathdowney (Ossory)	1763–1900	1764–1895		IMA	
	July 13 1763–Nov 28 1781	May 18 1769–Nov 7 1781		NLI	Pos. 5013, 5014
	Sept 14 1782–July 20 1789	Sept 7 1782–July 15 1789			
	May 6 1790–Nov 20 1791	Sept 15 1789–Nov 22 1791			
	Apr 14–Sept 1 1810	Jan 14–May 3 1808			
	June 2 1839–Jan 29 1840	Oct 6 1839–Mar 3 1840			
	Apr 26 1840–Dec 31 1880	May 27 1840–Nov 9 1880			
Roscrea	See Tipperary North				
Rosenallis (Kildare and Leighlin)	1766–1901	1765–1899	1921–87	IMA	
	Oct 21 1765–Jan 19 1777	Oct 12 1765–June 10 1777	Oct 14 1824–Sept 21 1827	NLI	Pos. 4205
	Feb 1 1782–Aug 13 1782	Feb 7 1782–June 10 1782			
	Aug 3 1823–Dec 27 1879	July 1823–July 24 1859			
		Jan 18 1865–Oct 26 1880			
Stradbally (Kildare and Leighlin)	1820–99	1820–99	1893–1983	IMA	
	Jan 2 1820–May 18 1855	Jan 20 1820–June 24 1849		NLI	Pos. 4202
	Jan 26 1851–Dec 26 1880	Feb 24 1851–Nov 4 1880			

Leitrim

All Leitrim Genealogy Centre database transcripts are online at
<*www.rootsireland.ie*>.

Parish (Diocese)	Baptisms	Marriages	Burials	Location	Reference
Annaduff (Ardagh and Clonmacnois)	1849–1984	1849–1983	1849–86 1930–84	LDS	1279224 item 18–20; 1279225 1–3
	1849–1900	1849–1900	1849–1900	Leitrim GC	
	Feb 29 1849–Dec 31 1880	Feb 12 1849–Feb 10 1880	Feb 5 1849–Dec 21 1880	NLI	Pos. 4236
Aughavas (Ardagh and Clonmacnois)	1845–1968	1845–1920	1845–99	LDS	1279224 item 15–17
	1845–1900	1845–1900	1845–1900	Leitrim GC	
	May 19 1845–Feb 4 1876	Aug 28 1845–July 4 1879	May 11 1845–July 2 1880	NLI	Pos. 4240
	Jan 1 1876–Dec 23 1880	Jan 10 1876–Nov 14 1880	May 5 1876–Nov 18 1880		
Ballinaglera (Kilmore)	1883–1900	1887–1900		Leitrim GC	
Bornacoola (Ardagh and Clonmacnois)	1824–97	1824–38 1850–97	1833–92	LDS	1279224 item 13–14
	1824–37 1850–1900	1824–37 1850–1900	1854–1900	Leitrim GC	
	Jan 4 1871–Dec 31 1880	June 13 1836–Sept 28 1837 May 9 1850–Nov 1 1880		NLI	Pos. 4234
Carrigallen (Kilmore)	1829–1900 (Many gaps)	1841–1900 (Many gaps)	1841–60	Leitrim GC	
	Nov 2 1829–Feb 7 1830 Dec 30 1838–Dec 12 1880 (many pages missing)	Jan 27 1841–Apr 24 1848 1854–Dec 10 1875 (some pages missing)	Mar 12 1842–June 25 1860	NLI	Pos. 5350
	1829–91 (gaps)	1841–90 (gaps)	1841–60	PRONI	MIC.1D/7, 83
Clooneclare (Kilmore)	1841–1900	1850–1900		Leitrim GC	
	Apr 29 1841–Dec 1885	Nov 12 1850–Sept 9 1884		NLI	Pos. 7505

Parish (Diocese)	Baptisms	Marriages	Burials	Location	Reference
Cloone-Conmaicne (Ardagh and Clonmacnois)	1820–1927	1823–1921	1850–78 1919–21	LDS	1279223 item 12–14
	1823–1900	1823–1900	1823–78	Leitrim GC	
	Feb 1 1820–Mar 12 1820 Jan 1 1834–May 27 1834 Nov 13 1834–Jan 13 1841 Jan 2 1843–Oct 4 1849 Jan 6 1850–Nov 20 1880	Jan 6 1823–Jan 6 1839 Jan 12 1843–Feb 14 1879	Jan 6 1823–Feb 17 1845 Jan 13 1850–Feb 25 1878	NLI	Pos. 4241
Drumlease (Kilmore)	1859–1900	1859–1900		Leitrim GC	
	Aug 21 1859–Apr 12 1879	Sept 15 1859–Oct 31 1880		NLI	Pos. 5344
	1859–79	1859–81		PRONI	MIC.1D/77
Drumreilly Lower (Kilmore)	See NLI			LDS	0926129 item 4
	1867–1900	1893–1900		Leitrim GC	
	Mar 4 1867–Dec 26 1880			NLI	Pos. 5345
	1867–80			PRONI	MIC.1D/78
Drumreilly Upper (Kilmore)	1878–1900	1870–1900		Leitrim GC	
Ennismagrath (Kilmore)	1834–1900	1834–1900	1834–1900	Leitrim GC	
	1881–1900	1881–1900	1881–1900		
	Jan 1835–July 1839 1834	1830–39	1833–9	NLI	Pos. 7505
Fenagh (Ardagh and Clonmacnois)	1825–9 1843–9 1852–83	1825–99	1825–94	LDS	1279223 item 1–3
	1825–1900	1826–1900	1825–94	Leitrim GC	
	June 5 1825–Oct 13 1829 Nov 24 1834–Apr 12 1843 June 5 1843–Nov 4 1852 Nov 22 1852–Dec 9 1880 (indexed)	Oct 4 1826–Feb 18 1832 June 15 1835–Mar 22 1842 Jan 17 1844–Feb 9 1880	June 1825–Feb 21 1834 Nov 24 1834–Dec 21 1841	NLI	Pos. 4239
Glenade (Kilmore)	1867–1900	1866–1900		Leitrim GC	
	Nov 10 1867–Dec 16 1880	Nov 10 1867–June 15 1880		NLI	Pos. 5344
	1867–81	1873–80		PRONI	MIC.1D/77
	1867–99	1867–99		SHGS	
Gortletteragh (Ardagh and Clonmacnois)	1830–40 1848–95	1826–35 1852–95	1826–39 (gaps) 1851–69	LDS	1279224 item 4–6
	1830–1840 1849–1900 [sic]	1826 1831–4 1849–1900	1826–38 1852–68	Leitrim GC	
	Apr 4 1830–Aug 1 1840 July 16 1848–Mar 6 1874 Mar 30 1874–Dec 31 1880	Jan 6 1826–Sept 12 1827 Feb 16 1830–Apr 30 1835 May 22 1848–Feb 17 1874 (disordered)	Jan 10 1826–Sept 15 1826 Mar 29 1830–Feb 17 1831 Mar 9 1839–July 29 1839 Aug 1 1851–July 29 1869	NLI	Pos. 4238
Killargue (Kilmore)	1853–1900	1852–1900		Leitrim GC	
	Sept 26 1852–Dec 26 1880	Nov 2 1852–Feb 4 1880		NLI	Pos. 5344
	1852–81	1852–81		PRONI	MIC.1D/77
Killasnet (Kilmore)	1852–1869 1874–1875 1878–1897	1852–70 1879–99	1852–66	Leitrim GC	

Parish (Diocese)	Baptisms	Marriages	Burials	Location	Reference
Killasnet (Kilmore) (contd.)	Mar 28 1852–Apr 1868	Mar 28 1852–Apr 1868	Mar 28 1852–Apr 1868	NLI	Pos. 5350
	Feb 23 1868–Jan 31 1869	Jan 30 1868–May 21 1871			
	Nov 29 1878–Nov 23 1880	Nov 11 1878–Nov 15 1880			
	1852–69	1852–71		PRONI	MIC.1D/83
	1878–81	1878–81			
Killenummery (Ardagh and Clonmacnois)	1828–1920	1828–83	1838–46	LDS	1279223 item 6–7
		1908–1910			
		1922–3			
	1828–45	1827–45	1829–1900	Leitrim GC	
	1849–1900	1849–1900			
	May 8 1828–Aug 7 1846	June 22 1827–Aug 16 1846	May 18 1838–Apr 15 1846	NLI	Pos. 4241
	Nov 1 1848–Dec 30 1880	Nov 10 1848–Dec 28 1880			
	1828–99	1827–99		SHGS	
Kiltoghart (Ardagh and Clonmacnois)	1826–91	1841–91	1841–79	LDS	1279223 item 4–5
	1826–1900	1832–1900	1832–53	Leitrim GC	
			1867–1900		
	Aug 16 1826–Apr 23 1854	July 19 1832–May 3 1854	Aug 10 1832–Apr 10 1854	NLI	Pos. 4240
	May 7 1854–Dec 30 1880	July 30 1854–Nov 24 1880	May 31 1854–Aug 11 1874		
	(Gowel) Mar 4 1866–Dec 26 1880	(Gowel) May 13 1866–Feb 29 1876	(Gowel) Apr 11 1866–Sept 10 1877		
Kiltubrid (Ardagh and Clonmacnois)	1841–74	1841–73	1847–73	LDS	1279223 item 9–11
	1880–1924	1883–1922			
	1841	1841	1847–1900	Leitrim GC	
	1847–1900	1847–1900			
	Jan 6 1841–Apr 27 1874	Jan 7 1841–May 22 1873	Jan 15 1847–May 1 1873	NLI	Pos. 4234
Kinlough (Kilmore)	1835–1900	1840–1900	1867–1900	Leitrim GC	
		1855, 1853 missing			
	July 12 1835–Mar 1860	Nov 26 1840–Dec 16 1880		NLI	Pos. 5344
	Apr 8 1860–Dec 24 1880				
	1835–81	1840–81		PRONI	MIC.1D/77
Mohill (Ardagh and Clonmacnois)	1836–1905	1836–1905	1836–83	LDS	1279224 item 1–3
		1910–16			
	1836–1900	1836–1900	1836–1900	Leitrim GC	
	Aug 4 1836–May 7 1854	July 14 1836–May 18 1854	July 3 1836–May 9 1854	NLI	Pos. 4239
	June 11 1854–Dec 23 1880	Aug 28 1854–July 19 1879	May 22 1854–July 27 1879		
	Including workhouse baptisms, 1846–55				
Murhan (Ardagh and Clonmacnois)	1861–95			LDS	1279223 item 8
	1861–1900	1867–1900		Leitrim GC	
	May 18 1861–Dec 21 1880	June 10 1868–Nov 20 1880		NLI	Pos. 4240
Oughteragh (Kilmore)	1841–1900	1841–1900		Leitrim GC	
	Nov 9 1869–Dec 28 1880	Jan 17 1870–Nov 20 1880		NLI	Pos. 5346/7
	May 26 1871–Dec 16 1880				
	1869–81	1787–1881		PRONI	MIC.1D/79–80
Rossinver (Kilmore)	1851–1900	1844–69		Leitrim GC	
		1875–1900			
	Aug 17 1851–Jan 29 1875 (many gaps)	Aug 28 1844–Sept 8 1870		NLI	Pos. 5350
	1851–75 (very poor condition)	1844–70 (very poor condition)		PRONI	MIC.1D/83

Limerick East

All Limerick Genealogy (LG)
transcripts are online at
<*www.rootsireland.ie*>.

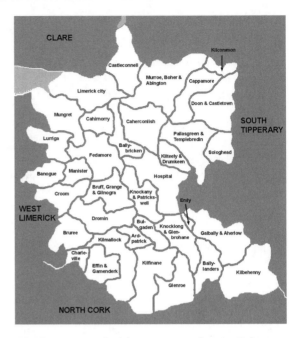

Parish (Diocese)	Baptisms	Marriages	Burials	Location	Reference
Ardpatrick (Limerick)	1861–1900	1861–1900		LG	
Ballybricken and	1801–1841	1801–1841	1801–1841 (scraps)	LDS	1279253 item 2
Bohermore	1800–1900	1805–1900		LG	
(Cashel and Emly)	Nov 9 1800–July 25 1841	Aug 10 1805–Oct 27 1841		NLI	Pos. 2509
	Aug 2 1841–Dec 26 1880	Nov 6 1841–Oct 23 1880			
	1800–1900	1801–1900		TFHR	
Ballylanders	1842–1900	1848–1900		LG	
(Cashel and Emly)	Mar 6 1849–Dec 25 1877	Jan 3 1857–Nov 25 1877 (modern transcript)		NLI	Pos. 2500
	1842–99	1841–1900		TFHR	
Banogue (Limerick)	1861–1900	1861–1900		LG	
	Sept 21 1861–Dec 21 1880	Oct 6 1861–Apr 27 1880		NLI	Pos. 2427
Bruff, Grange and	1781–1900	1781–1900		LG	
Gilnogra	Jan 6 1808–July 30 1827	Jan 27 1808–July 8 1827		NLI	B and M to
(Limerick)	Aug 10 1827–Nov 10 1845	Sept 20 1827–Oct 22 1845			1827 Pos. 2428;
	Nov 2 1845–Dec 23 1880	Nov 17 1845–Nov 23 1880			remainder 2429
Bruree (Limerick)	1825–1900	1824–1900		LG	
	Jan 6 1842–Mar 11 1868	July (?) 28 1861–Oct 13 1880		NLI	Pos. 2428
	Mar 22 1868–Dec 23 1880				
Bulgaden (Limerick)	1812–1900	1812–1900		LG	
	Mar 22 1812–Sept 27 1832	June 4 1812–Jan 27 1833		NLI	Pos. 2428
	Oct 6 1832–Jan 5 1854	Feb 5 1833–Nov 30 1853			
	Jan 23 1854–Dec 31 1880	Feb 2 1854–Nov 27 1880			
Caherconlish	1841–1900	1841–1900		LG	
(Cashel and Emly)	Jan 19 1841–Dec 30 1880	Feb 6 1841–Oct 8 1880		NLI	Pos. 2508
	1841–1900	1841–1900		TFHR	

Parish (Diocese)	Baptisms	Marriages	Burials	Location	Reference
Cahirnorry	1830–1900	1827–1900		LG	
(Limerick)	Jan 3 1830–Jan 2 1840	July 12 1827–Dec 2 1843		NLI	Pos. 2419
	Jan 4 1840–Dec 15 1880	Jan 11 1844–Nov 8 1880			
Cappamore	1842–1900	1843–1900		LG	
(Cashel and Emly)	Apr 4 1845–Dec 31 1880	Feb 25 1845–Nov 14 1880		NLI	Pos. 2508
	1842–1900	1843–1900		TFHR	
Castleconnell	1850–1900	1863–1900		LG	
(Killaloe)	Feb 5 1850–Jan 10 1864	Aug 10 1863–Nov 27 1880		NLI	Pos. 2477
	Aug 10 1863–Dec 31 1880				
Charleville	See Cork North-West				
Croom (Limerick)	1828–1900	1788, 1806–1899		LG	
	Oct 29 1828–Oct 30 1844	Dec 1770–July 23 1794	Dec 1770–July 23 1794	NLI	Pos. 2427
	Oct 4 1844–Dec 30 1880	Aug 23 1807–Feb 26 1810			
		May 6 1806–Mar 3 1829			
		May 2 1829–Sept 28 1844			
		Sept 29 1844–Nov 27 1880			
Doon and Castletown	1824–1900	1839–1900		LG	
(Cashel and Emly)	Mar 25 1824–Dec 27 1874	Jan 20 1839–Feb 17 1874		NLI	Pos. 2497
	1824–1900	1839–1900		TFHR	
Dromin (Limerick)	1817–1900	1817–1900		LG	
	May 19 1817–Sept 19 1837	June 23 1817–Dec 1 1837		NLI	Pos. 2426
	Mar 21 1849–Dec 16 1880	Mar 21 1849–Nov 14 1880			
Effin and Gamenderk	1843–1900	1843–1900		LG	
(Limerick)	Mar 1843–Dec 31 1880	Apr 24 1843–Nov 1880		NLI	Pos. 2427
Emly	See Tipperary South				
Fedamore (Limerick)	1807–1822	1807–1825		LG	
	1854–1902	1854–1900			
	Oct 29 1806–July 16 1813	Jan 9 1814–Nov 26 1825		NLI	Pos. 2409,
	Jan 1 1814–Jan 29 1822	Aug 1854–Dec 27 1880			2429, 2430
	July 30 1854–Dec 25 1880	Oct 29 1806–July 16 1813			
	Jan 4 1826–May 31 1833	Jan 7 1826–June 12 1833			
	(Manister)	(Manister)			
	June 2 1833–Dec 26 1880	June 20 1833–Aug 6 1880			
	(Manister)	(Manister)			
Galbally and Aherlow	1810–1900	1809–1900		LG	
(Cashel and Emly)	Mar 9 1810–June 23 1828	Oct 1809–Aug 34 1880		NLI	Pos. 2499
	(July 1820–21 missing)	(Mar 1820–July 1821			
	December 1828–June 1871	missing)			
	1810–1900	1809–1900		TFHR	
Glenroe (Limerick)	1853–1900	1853–1900		LG	
	June 27 1853–Dec 26 1880	Aug 2 1853–Mar 19 1880		NLI	Pos. 2428
Hospital	1810–1900	1812–1900		LG	
(Cashel and Emly)	Jan 11 1810–Jan 10 1842	Feb 10 1812–Jan 16 1842		NLI	Pos. 2507
	Jan 20 1842–Dec 29 1880	Jan 22 1842–Nov 6 1880			
	1810–99	1812–99		TFHR	
Kilbehenny	1824–1900	1825–1900		LG	
(Cashel and Emly)	Dec 17 1824–Apr 30 1843	Jan 30 1825–Feb 28 1843		NLI	Pos. 2500
	May 4 1843–Jan 23 1870	May 1 1843–Jan 20 1870			
	1824–99	1825–99		TFHR	

Parish (Diocese)	Baptisms	Marriages	Burials	Location	Reference
Kilfinane (Limerick)	1831–1900	1832–1900		LG	
	June 1832–July 30 1856	Aug 20 1832–July 39 1856		NLI	Pos. 2429; B
	Aug 14 1856–Apr 22 1859	Sept 5 1856–Mar 8 1859			and M
	Mar 23 1859–Mar 8 1880	May 4 1859–Aug 18 1880			1861–80, 2423
	July 1 1861–Dec 28 1880	Aug 18 1861–Sept 13 1880			
	(Ardpatrick)	(Ardpatrick)			
Kilmallock	1837–1900	1837–1900		LG	
(Limerick)	Oct 22 1837–Dec 19 1880	Nov 2 1837–Nov 24 1880		NLI	Pos. 2427
Kilteely and	1815–29	1816–29		LG	
Drumkeen	1832–99	1832–99			
(Cashel and Emly)	Dec 3 1815–Apr 5 1829	Nov 14 1832–Nov 17 1880		NLI	Pos. 2506
	Sept 3 1832–Dec 20 1880				
	1810–99	1815–99		TFHR	
Knockany and	1808–1900	1808–1900	1819–21	LG	
Patrickswell	Mar 14 1808–Nov 24 1821	Apr 25 1808–Oct 21 1821			
(Cashel and Emly)	Dec 3 1921–Nov 22 1841	Jan 20 1822–Feb 23 1841			
	May 3 1841–Dec 22 1880	May 3 1841–Oct 188 1880	June 1 1819–Mar 29 1821	NLI	Pos. 2505
	1808–1899	1808–1899		TFHR	
Knocklong and	1809–1900	1809–1900		LG	
Glenbrohane	Apr 26 1809–June 5 1819	Apr 12 1809–Oct 17 1819		NLI	Pos. 2509
(Cashel and Emly)	Sept 14 1823–June 11 1830	Jan 28 1824–Oct 1 1831			
	Jan 30 1832–July 30 1854	Jan 7 1832–Feb 4 1854			
	Nov 30 1854–Jan 15 1878	Aug 20 1854–Jan 15 1878			
	1809–1899	1809–1899		TFHR	
Limerick city:	1831–1900	Not specified		Clare HGC	
Parteen (Limerick)	Sept 26 1831–Feb 14 1877	July 1 1814–Nov 9 1819		NLI	Pos. 2410
		Feb 4 1821–Jan 10 1836			
		Feb 9 1847–Jan 22 1877			
Limerick city:	1788–1900	1821–1900		LG	
St John's (Limerick)	May 2 1788–Dec 30 1797	July 21 1821–Dec 15 1850		NLI	Pos. 2411 to
	Jan 1 1825–Jan 26 1829	Jan 11 1851–June 23 1877			1850;
	Jan 26 1829–Oct 31 1841				remainder
	Nov 1 1841–Dec 31 1849				2412
	Jan 5 1850–June 30 1877				
Limerick city: St	1745–1900	Not specified		Clare HGC	
Mary's (Limerick)	1745–1900	1745–1900		LG	
	Jan 2 1745–Apr 13 1795	Oct 29 1745–Apr 13 1795		NLI	Pos. 2412 to
	Mar 2 1795–Oct 13 1816	Apr 13 1795–Oct 3 1816			1816;
	Nov 1 1816–Dec 31 1836	Aug 30 1816–Nov 30 1836			remainder
	Jan 6 1837–June 24 1862	Jan 7 1837–June 19 1862			2413
Limerick city: St	1776–1900	1772–1900		LG	
Michael's (Limerick)	Aug 16 1776–Oct 18 1801	Feb 3 1772–Sept 12 1802		NLI	Pos. 2415 to
	Jan 12 1803–Feb 23 1807	Mar 28 1803–July 28 1804			1838; 2416 to
	Oct 14 1807–Apr 12 1813	Oct 18 1807–Aug 21 1808			1861;
	Jan 3 1814–Sept 13 1819	June 3 1810–May 6 1813			remainder
	Jan 19 1820–Mar 28 1824	May 6 1821–Mar 2 1824			2417
	May 13 1824–Dec 8 1838	June 6 1814–Nov 26 1819			
	Feb 14 1825–Oct 1 1830	May 13 1824–Dec 4 1838			
	Dec 9 1838–Dec 27 1852	Feb 6 1826–Nov 14 1828			
	Dec 27 1852–Feb 8 1876	Dec 26 1838–June 30 1877			

Parish (Diocese)	Baptisms	Marriages	Burials	Location	Reference
Limerick city: St	1764–1900	1764–1900		LG	
Munchin's (Limerick)	Nov 1 1764–Apr 4 1784	Nov 4 1764–Feb 24 1784		NLI	Pos. 2413 to
	Apr 8 1784–June 30 1792	May 11 1784–May 25 1792			1819;
	Oct 3 1798–Aug 30 1819	Oct 2 1798–May 12 1819			remainder
	Sept 4 1819–Oct 31 1835	Sept 2 1819–Nov 10 1835			2414
	Nov 16 1824–June 19 1828	Jan 24 1825–May 21 1828			
	Feb 15 1836–Sept 29 1877	Dec 3 1837–Aug 5 1877			
Limerick city: St	1805–1900	1806–1900		LG	
Patrick's (Limerick)	Jan 7 1812–Apr 30 1844	Jan 15 1812–Sept 17 1740		NLI	Pos. 2410
	May 8 1844–Apr 30 1830	Feb 11 1841–Oct 24 1880			
	May 8 1834–Dec 27 1875				
Lurriga (Limerick)	1801–1900	1802–1900		LG	
	Oct 2 1801–Mar 13 1826	Apr 26 1802–Nov 26 1825		NLI	Pos. 2409
	Mar 16 1826–Dec 30 1843	Jan 10 1826–Dec 2 1843			
	Jan 5 1844–Dec 20 1880	Jan 20 1844–Dec 14 1880			
Mungret (Limerick)	1844–1900	1844–1900		LG	
	Nov 3 1844–Dec 19 1880	Nov 27 1844–Nov 12 1880		NLI	Pos. 2409/10
Murroe, Boher and	1814–1900	1815–1911		LG	
Abington	June 15 1814–Nov 3 1845	Nov 29 1815–Nov 2 1845		NLI	Pos. 2508
(Cashel and Emly)	Nov 3 1845–Dec 25 1880	Nov 16 1845–Sept 1 1880			
	1814–99	1815–99		TFHR	
Pallasgreen and	1811–1900	1811–1900		LG	
Templebredin	Jan 2 1811–Dec 29 1833	Jan 9 1811–Jan 29 1838		NLI	Pos. 2498
(Cashel and Emly)	Jan 1 1934–Oct 13 1861	Feb 8 1838–Oct 13 1861			
	Oct 20 1861–Dec 26 1880	Oct 26 1861–Dec 11 1880			
	1811–99	1811–99		TFHR	
Sologhead	1809–1880	1810–80		LG	
(Cashel and Emly)	Oct 18 1809–Feb 27 1823	Jan 7 1810–Nov 24 1828		NLI	Pos. 2498 to
	Mar 2 1823–Apr 30 1828	Oct 14 1832–Jan 30 1854			1828;
	Feb 25 1837–Jan 23 1854	Feb 7 1854–Nov 27 1880			remainder on
	Feb 12 1854–Dec 31 1880				Pos. 2499
	1809–1900	1810–1900		TFHR	

Limerick West

All parishes are in the diocese of Limerick. All Limerick Genealogy (LG) transcripts are online at <www.rootsireland.ie>.

Parish (Diocese)	Baptisms	Marriages	Burials	Location	Reference
Abbeyfeale	1829–1900	1825–1900		LG	
	Feb 11 1829–Oct 1843	Nov 5 1856–Nov 1880		NLI	B. 1829–43,
	Aug 4 1856–Dec 30 1880				Pos. 6779; remainder 2426
Adare	1832–1900	1832–1900		LG	
	July 7 1832–Dec 25 1848	July 4 1832–Dec 2 1848		NLI	Pos. 2420
	Jan 4 1849–May 29 1865	Feb 17 1849–Feb 21 1865			
Ardagh	1845–1900	1841–1900		LG	
	Mar 24 1845–Dec 31 1869	Oct 25 1841–Nov 13 1869		NLI	Pos. 2424
Askeaton	1829–1900	1829–1900		LG	
	Jan 9 1829–Sept 1 1861	Jan 2 1829–July 21 1861		NLI	Pos. 2419
	Sept 1 1861–Dec 26 1880	Oct 3 1861–July 18 1880			
Athea	1830–1900	1827–1900		LG	
	Apr 16 1830–July 20 1856	Nov 1 1827–Feb 5 1856		NLI	Pos. 2424
	Dec 10 1850–July 26 1879	Feb 23 1851–July 19 1879			
Ballingarry	1825–1900	1825–1900		LG	
	Jan 21 1825–May 29 1828	Jan 23 1825–Feb 16 1836		NLI	Pos. 2421
	Dec 17 1849–Dec 18 1880	Jan 12 1850–Oct 16 1880			
Ballyagran	1841–1900	1841–1900		LG	
	Sept 10 1841–Nov 17 1844	Sept 16 1841–Sept 21 1844		NLI	Pos. 2430
	Jan 4 1847–Aug 30 1847	Jan 15 1847–Oct 1 1847			
	Sept 22 1850–May 21 1860	Jan 4 1851–Nov 4 1859			
	Sept 14 1860–Oct 30 1880	June 19 1860–Dec 25 1879			
	June 2 1861–Nov 8 1880	Jan 15 1861–Nov 8 1880			
Cappagh	1841–1900	1841–1900		LG	
	Jan 1 1841–Nov 3 1880	Jan 14 1841–Apr 20 1880		NLI	Pos. 2421

Parish (Diocese)	Baptisms	Marriages	Burials	Location	Reference
Croagh	1836–1900	1844–1900		LG	
	Aug 10 1836–June 11 1843	Jan 9 1844–Oct 16 1880		NLI	Pos. 2420
	Nov 3 1843–Oct 31 1859				
	Nov 13 1859–Dec 15 1880				
Drumcollogher	1830–1900	1830–1900		LG	
	Mar 4 1830–Sept 30 1850	Jan 24 1830–Sept 14 1850		NLI	Pos. 2423
	Nov 11 1851–Nov 10 1864	Oct 1 1851–Oct 17 1864			
	Nov 16 1864–Dec 27 1880	May 26 1866–Oct 12 1880			
Feenagh	1832–99	1850–51		LG	
		1853–99			
	Aug 29 1854–Dec 28 1880	July 27 1854–Dec 18 1880		NLI	Pos. 2424
Freemount	See Cork North-West				
Glin	1851–1900	1851–1900		LG	
	Oct 30 1851–Dec 31 1880	Oct 18 1851–Oct 4 1881		NLI	Pos. 2426
Kilcolman	1827–1900	1828–1900		LG	
	Oct 28 1827–Dec 30 1843	Jan 13 1828–Nov 10 1843		NLI	Pos. 2421
	Jan 8 1844–Sept 26 1859	Jan 13 1844–Nov 21 1880			
	Oct 22 1859–Aug 5 1877				
Kilcornan	1825–1900	1825–1900		LG	
	Apr 9 1825–1833	Apr 11 1825–1833		NLI	Pos. 2420
	Jan 26 1834–July 26 1848	Dec 22 1833–Mar 7 1848			
	July 30 1848–May 27 1883	Sept 10 1848–Feb 6 1883			
Kildimo	1831–1900	1831–1900		LG	
	Jan 1 1831–Nov 21 1845	Jan 14 1831–Nov 30 1845		NLI	Pos. 2419
	Jan 7 1846–Dec 31 1880	Jan 8 1846–Aug 1 1880			(B. 1846–80);
					Pos. 2420
Killeedy	1840–99	1841–1910		LG	
	Aug 11 1840–Mar 1 1874	Dec 13 1840–Feb 14 1874		NLI	Pos. 2423
Knockaderry	1816–20	1816–20		LG	
	1838–40	1838–99			
	1841–99				
	Feb 24 1838–Dec 27 1880	Feb 24 1838–Dec 15 1880		NLI	Pos. 2421
Loughill	1855–1900	1855–1900		LG	
	Oct 28 1855–Dec 26 1880	Nov 1 1855–July 4 1880		NLI	Pos. 2420
Mahoonagh	1812–1900	1810–1900		LG	
	Mar 24 1812–Aug 30 1830	Aug 31 1810–Feb (?) 1826			
	June 14 1832–July 5 1838	Jan 1826–May 1 1839			
	Nov 14 1839–June 19 1869	Feb 9 1840–Aug 10 1869		NLI	Pos. 2424/25
Monagea	1776–1900	1777–1900		LG	
	Jan 11 1809–July 21 1813	Jan 8 1777–Feb 29 1792		NLI	Pos. 2423
	Mar 25 1829–Dec 19 1831	Feb 1 1829–Dec 27 1880			
	Aug 19 1833–Nov 30 1841				
	Dec 31 1841–Nov 3 1880				
Newcastle West	1815–1905	1815–99		LG	
		1908–1911			
	May 28 1815–Oct 27 1831	Apr 20 1815–Nov 19 1831		NLI	Pos. 2425
	Nov 3 1831–Dec 28 1851	Nov 3 1831–Dec 28 1851			
	Jan 2 1852–Nov 29 1874	Jan 25 1852–Feb 2 1871			
Newcastle Union	Nov 14 1852–July 4 1869			NLI	Pos. 2425
Workhouse	June 17 1869–Dec 16 1880				

Parish (Diocese)	Baptisms	Marriages	Burials	Location	Reference
Rathkeale	1811–1900	1811–1900		LG	
	Jan 1 1811–July 12 1823	Jan 1 1811–Feb 7 1825		NLI	Pos. 2422
	Sept 23 1831–May 12 1839	Jan 7 1811–May 7 1839			
	June 1 1839–Dec 27 1846	(duplicates included)			
	Jan 4 1847–Feb 15 1861	May 7 1839–Feb 12 1861			
	Feb 20 1861–Dec 26 1875	Apr 13 1861–Jan 1 1876			
Shanagolden	1824–1900	1824–1900		LG	
	Apr 28 1824–July 23 1835	Apr 27 1824–Oct 6 1877		NLI	Pos. 2418/19
	Aug 3 1835–Aug 29 1842				
	Sept 3 1842–Sept 20 1862				
	Oct 2 1862–Nov 7 1877				
Templeglantine	1864–1900	1864–1900		LG	
	Dec 4 1864–July 15 1879	Jan 14 1865–June 8 1879		NLI	Pos. 2426
Tournafulla	1867–1900	1867–1900		LG	
	Jan 13 1867–Apr 3 1875	July 31 1867–Aug 31 1880		NLI	Pos. 2424

Longford

All Longford Genealogy Centre (LGC) transcripts are online at <*www.rootsireland.ie*>.

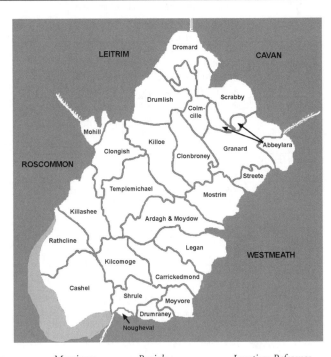

Parish (Diocese)	Baptisms	Marriages	Burials	Location	Reference
Abbeylara (Ardagh and Clonmacnois)	1854–1984	1854–1984	1854–1984	LDS	1279229 item 3–5
	1822–97	1855–99	1854–1901	LGC	
	July 9 1854–Dec 28 1880	July 12 1854–Dec 2 1879	Aug 9 1854–Dec 29 1880	NLI	Pos. 4236
Ardagh and Moydow (Ardagh and Clonmacnois)	1793–1815	1793–1984	1822–1984	LDS	1279220; 1279270
	1823–1977				
	1793–1901	1792–1901	1822–1901	LGC	
	Feb 12 1793–Jan 6 1816	Feb 12 1793–Oct 29 1842	Nov 26 1822–Oct 24 1842	NLI	Pos. 4235
	Oct 6 1822–Oct 28 1842	Nov 10 1842–Nov 10 1880	Nov 1 1842–Mar 13 1876		
	Nov 1 1842–Nov 11 1880				
	1793–1895	1792–1895	1822–95	Online	IGPweb

Parish (Diocese)	Baptisms	Marriages	Burials	Location	Reference
Carrickedmond (Ardagh and Clonmacnois)	1835–1901	1835–87 1890–1901	1835–69	LDS	1279222 item 1–3
	1820–1901	1820–1901	1820–1901	LGC	
	Apr 8 1835–Mar 30 1844 May 30 1848–Dec 3 1880	Jan 18 1835–Aug 19 1842 May 31 1848–June 14 1880	Jan 28 1835–Nov 17 1842 May 26 1848–Jan 2 1869	NLI	Pos. 4239
Cashel (Ardagh and Clonmacnois)	1830–1910	1830–1910	1830–31 1839–80	LDS	1279221 item 3–4
	1866–99	1830–99	1830–80	LGC	
	May 15 1830–Apr 21 1910	May 15 1830–Apr 21 1910	June 22 1830–Mar 27 1831 Apr 13 1867–May 10 1880	NLI	Pos. 9359
Clonbroney (Ardagh and Clonmacnois)	1848–1911	1853–1911	1853–92	LDS	1279229 item 11–13; 1279270 7–9
	1828–1901	1828–1901	1828–1901	LGC	
	Jan 25 1849–Mar 2 1862 Mar 13 1862 –Nov 9 1880	Jan 8 1854–Feb 27 1862 Feb 16 1863–July 1880	Jan 8 1854–Feb 27 1862 Mar 5 1862–Jan 10 1878	NLI	Pos. 4233
	1828–1901	1828–99	1828–92	Online	IGPweb
Clongish (Ardagh and Clonmacnois)	1829–87	1829–79	1829–81	LDS	1279219 item 11–12
	1829–1920	1829–1920	1829–1920	LGC	
	Oct 25 1829–Mar 12 1857 Aug 3 1829–Sept 23 1879 Mar 15 1857–Dec 26 1880	Aug 3 1829–Sept 23 1879	Aug 22 1829–Dec 15 1880	NLI	Pos. 4233
	1829–41			Online	IGPweb
Colmcille (Ardagh and Clonmacnois)	1833–1984	1833–71 1876–1983	1932–71	LDS	1279229 item 1–2, 14–15; 1279228
	1833–1901	1833–1901	1836–1901	LGC	
	July 1845–Feb 11 1873	Aug 3 1845–May 22 1871	July 22 1845–Dec 21 1858	NLI	Pos. 4238
Dromard (Ardagh and Clonmacnois)	1854–1910	1853–85	1853–81	LDS	1279229 item 8–9
	1840–1901	1853–1901	1853–1901	LGC	
	Jan 14 1838–July 15 1845 Jan 10 1852–June 18 1855 May 22 1853–Dec 26 1880 Jan 3 1872–Dec 26 1880	Feb 13 1835–Apr 15 1855 Oct 5 1853–Nov 2 1868 Nov 26 1874–Nov 22 1880	Dec 11 1853–Oct 15 1868 July 26 1874–Dec 20 1880	NLI	Pos. 4241
Drumlish (Ardagh and Clonmacnois)	1834–89	1834–89	1834–89	LDS	1279221 item 5
	1834–1901	1834–1901	1834–1901	LGC	
	Jan 1 1834–Mar 13 1868 Mar 4 1874–Dec 30 1880	Jan 12 1834–Feb 25 1868 Jan 1 1870–June 16 1872 Jan 15 1877–Nov 8 1880	Jan 2 1834–Mar 13 1868 Feb 16 1870–July 10 1872 Aug 13 1876–Dec 13 1880	NLI	Pos. 4234
Drumraney (Meath)	See Westmeath				
Granard (Ardagh and Clonmacnois)	1779–1928	1782–1900	1782–1862	LDS	12792298 item 1–6; 1279270 13–
	1779–1950	1782–1950	1811–1950	LGC	
	Jan 1 1779–Apr 2 1811 1812–18 (fragments) Oct 20 1816–Feb 26 1832 Jan 1832–June 2 1869 Jan 2 1820–Dec 26 1880	Dec 3 1782–May 25 1815 Sept 10 1816–July 14 1836 July 18 1836–May 6 1869 June 30 1869–Dec 8 1880	Dec 18 1782–Aug 8 1816 Apr 29 1818–Apr 28 1820 Sept 16 1816–Dec 27 1847 Jan 3 1848–May 24 1865	NLI	Pos. 4237
	1778–1894	1811–65	1811–65	Online	IGPweb

Parish (Diocese)	Baptisms	Marriages	Burials	Location	Reference
Kilcomoge (Ardagh and Clonmacnois)	1859–1984	1859–1981	1859–80	LDS	12792222 item 5–7; 12879270 4–6
	1859–1901	1859–1901	1859–1901	LGC	
	Sept 7 1859–Dec 19 1880	Sept 13 1859–Feb 4 1880	Nov 13 1859–Nov 18 1880	NLI	Pos. 4234
	1859–80	1859–80	1859–80	Online	IGPweb
Killashee (Ardagh and Clonmacnois)	1840–1901	1828–1901	1841–1901	LGC	
	Nov 1 1826–Nov 4 1843	Nov 19 1826–Oct 23 1843	Nov 15 1826–Aug 3 1843	NLI	Pos. 4235
	Apr 9 1848–July 4 1868	June 18 1848–Apr 5 1868			
	June 4 1865–Nov 24 1880	May 18 1864–Oct 9 1880	Nov 20 1858–May 11 1868		
Killoe (Ardagh and Clonmacnois)	1826–1917	1826–68	1826–68	LDS	1279221 item 6–14
	1826–1917	1826–1917	1826–1901	LGC	
	Jan 1 1826–July 21 1832	May 29 1826–July 18 1832	Jan 2 1826–June 10 1853	NLI	Pos. 4238
	Jan 1 1826–Aug 31 1852	Jan 2 1826–Oct 21 1852	Aug 23 1853–Dec 29 1868		
	Feb 4 1853–Oct 7 1868	Sept 5 1854–Dec 16 1868	Jan 20 1869–Dec 26 1880		
	Apr 11 1869–Dec 18 1880	Jan 31 1869–Nov 1 1880			
	1826–1917	1826–1917	1826–84	Online	IGPweb
Legan (Ardagh and Clonmacnois)	1855–1905	1855–1905	1855–90	LDS	1279221 item 15
	1855–1901	1855–1901	1855–1901	LGC	
	Jan 5 1855–Dec 29 1880	Jan 7 1855–Dec 11 1880	Jan 20 1855–Dec 25 1880	NLI	Pos. 4234
Mohill (Ardagh and Clonmacnois)	See Leitrim				
Mostrim (Ardagh and Clonmacnois)	1838–95	1838–94	1838–88	LDS	1279219 item 10
	1837–1920	1838–1920	1838–1920	LGC	
	June 8 1838–Dec 29 1880	June 11 1838–Oct 29 1880	May 23 1838–Dec 9 1880	NLI	Pos. 4233
Moyvore (Meath)	1832–1900	1832–1900	1831–65	DSHGC	
	See NLI			LDS	0926167 item 1–2
	Sept 5 1831–Feb 8 1862	Feb 12 1832–Sept 28 1862	Aug 6 1831–Apr 1863	NLI	Pos. 4171
	Feb 18 1862–Dec 25 1880	Mar 2 1862–Dec 25 1880	May 1863–Sept 5 1865		
Nougheval (Meath)	See Westmeath				
Rathcline (Ardagh and Clonmacnois)	1840–89	1840–1903	1835–69	LDS	1279222 item 4
			1839–99		
	1840–1901	1840–1901	1841–1901	LGC	
	Jan 12 1840–Mar 9 1904	Jan 12 1840–Mar 9 1904	Dec 10 1839–Mar 17 1899	NLI	Pos. 9539
Scrabby (Ardagh and Clonmacnois)	1836–99	1836–99		Clare HGC	
	1833–1920	1833–71	1833–60	LDS	1279228 item 10–13
		1877–1906			
	1833–1901	1833–1901	1835–1901	LGC	
	Feb 12 1833–Mar 15 1854	Feb 17 1833–Feb 22 1855	Sept 9 1835–Mar 1854	NLI	Pos. 4237
	Mar 4 1855–Dec 28 1867	Apr 15 1855–June 29 1871	Apr 7 1856–Aug 20 1860		
	Apr 4 1870–Sept 29 1880	June 11 1877–Nov 13 1880			
Shrule (Ardagh and Clonmacnois)	1820–74	1820–74	1830–76	LDS	1279219 item 13–14; 1279221 1–2
	1875–1902	1875–1903			
	1820–87	1820–88	1820–99	LGC	
	Mar 26 1820–Oct 26 1830	May 12 1829–Oct 25 1830	Mar 14 1820–Sept 12 1830	NLI	Pos. 4235
	Nov 1 1830–Dec 24 1874	Dec 26 1830–Nov 8 1874	Nov 8 1830–Aug 17 1876		

Parish (Diocese)	Baptisms	Marriages	Burials	Location	Reference
Streete (Ardagh	1821–63	1820–1900	1772–1995	DSHGC	
and Clonmacnois)	1820–1901	1820–26	1834–81	LDS	1279228 item
		1835–1881	1887–1913		7–9
		1887–1902			
	July 6 1820–July 14 1827	Aug 10 1820–Jan 22 1828	Sept 27 1823–Aug 13 1829	NLI	Pos. 4236
	Nov 21 1831–Dec 20 1831	Jan 4 1835–Nov 19 1880	Dec 14 1834–Jan 8 1841		
	Dec 15 1834–Dec 29 1880		July 19 1842–Dec 29 1880		
Templemichael	1802–1920	1820–1900	1802–1869	LDS	1279219 item
(Ardagh and					1–9
Clonmacnois)	1811–1930	1810–1930	1802–1930	LGC	
	Jan 5 1802–Jan 3 1808	Jan 20 1802–Feb 26 1829	Jan 30 1802–Feb 19 1829	NLI	Pos. 4232
	June 6 1808–Jan 28 1829	Mar 1 1829–June 9 1868	Mar 1 1829–Oct 4 1865		
	Mar 1 1829–June 11 1862	June 4 1868–Dec 13 1880			
	June 12 1862–July 7 1868				
	June 3 1868–Dec 31 1880				

Louth

All parishes are in the archdiocese of Armagh. All Louth County Library transcripts are online at <www.rootsireland.ie>.

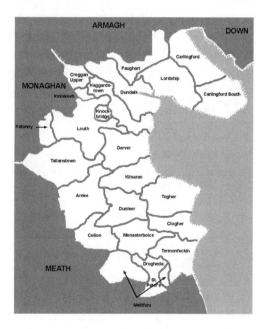

Parish (Diocese)	Baptisms	Marriages	Burials	Location	Reference
Ardee	1763–1815	1763–1900	1810–21	Louth CL	
	1819–1900				
	Apr 10 1763–June 24 1802	Aug 8 1769–June 10 1802	July 1 1802–Oct 31 1810	NLI	Pos. 5601
	July 20 1802–Oct 25 1810	Aug 10 1802–Oct 29 1810	Mar 7 1821–Feb 7 1825		
	Mar 4 1821–Dec 11 1880	Mar 5 1821–Feb 9 1826			
	1763–1810	1769–1800	1765–1810	PRONI	MIC.1D/52
	1821–81	1821–6	1821–25		
Carlingford	1835–1900	1835–1900	1835–40	Louth CL	
			1842–8		
			1853		
			1867–89		

Parish (Diocese)	Baptisms	Marriages	Burials	Location	Reference
Carlingford (contd.)	Apr 2 1835–Aug 13 1848	Apr 23 1838–Aug 12 1848	Apr 7 1835–Aug 12 184	NLI	Pos. 5594
	Aug 13 1848–Dec 22 1880	Sept 13 1848–Dec 30 1880	Oct 29 1867–Dec 30 1880		
	1835–81	1835–81	1835–48	PRONI	MIC.1D/45
			1869–82		
Carlingford South	June 4 1811–Aug 13 1838	Feb 19 1811–July 17 1838		LDS	0926033
	Aug 14 1838–Dec 29 1880	Sept 19 1838–Dec 11 1880			
	1811–1900	1811–30	1811–38	Louth CL	
		1832–1900	1842–3		
			1846–73		
			1877–88		
	June 4 1811–Aug 13 1838	Feb 19 1811–July 17 1838		NLI	Pos. 5593
	Aug 14 1838–Dec 29 1880	Sept 19 1838–Dec 11 1880			
	1811–81	1811–82		PRONI	MIC.1D/44
Clogher	1744–99	1742–99	1742–99	Louth CL	
	1833–1900	1833–1900			
	Nov 2 1744–Oct 17 1777	Feb 12 1742–Aug 25 1771	Nov 30 1744–July 21 1772	NLI	Pos. 5599
	Apr 4 1780–Dec 30 1799	Apr 4 1780–Sept 18 1799	Mar 20 1780–1799		
	Mar 9 1833–Oct 23 1836	Apr 11 1833–Oct 27 1836	(incomplete)		
	Aug 5 1837–Dec 21 1880	Aug 18 1837–Nov 21 1880			
	1744–77	1742–71	1744–72	PRONI	MIC.1D/53
	1780–99	1780–99	1780–99 (gaps)		
	1833–81	1833–81			
Collon	1787–93	1772–3		Louth CL	
	1796–9	1788–9			
	1804–1807	1791–2			
	1810	1803–1807			
	1819–45	1817–45			
	1847–1900	1848–1900			
	Apr 2 1789–Mar 1807	Jan 1789–Feb 1807		NLI	Pos. 5597
	Aug 15 1819–Dec 29 1836	Dec 2 1817–Dec 21 1835			
	Jan 6 1836–Dec 14 1880	(fragmented and			
		disordered)			
	Feb 7 1836–Sept 19 1845				
	Mar 11 1848–Nov 27 1880				
	1789–1807	1789–1807		PRONI	MIC.1D/48
	1819–81	1817–45			
		1848–81			
Creggan Upper	See Armagh				
Darver	See NLI			LDS	0926035
	1787–1900	1787–1900	1871–9	Louth CL	
	June 29 1787–Oct 26 1819	July 27 1787–June 23 1836		NLI	Pos. 5596
	Nov 1819–Mar 30 1836	May 3 1837–Feb 29 1848			
	Nov 23 1833–1846	Feb 4 1847–Nov 17 1880			
	June 18 1846–Dec 31 1880				
	1787–1880	1837–83	1871–9	PRONI	MIC.1D/47
Drogheda: St Peter's	See NLI			LDS	0926036/7
	1744–1804	1804	1879	Louth CL	
	1815–99	1819–25	1885		
		1828–1900			
	Jan 9 1744–May 2 1757	Nov 1 1815–July 24 1842		NLI	Pos. 5597;
	Aug 25 1764–Oct 27 1771	(very poor)			From 1815 Pos.

Parish (Diocese)	Baptisms	Marriages	Burials	Location	Reference
Drogheda: St Peter's (contd.)	Apr 7 1777–Feb 26 1778	July 26 1842–Jan 4 1866			5598
	June 14 1781–Oct 1 1783	Jan 3 1866–Dec 26 1880			
	Nov 28 1783–Apr 1795				
	Oct 1803–Dec 19 1804				
	Nov 1815–July 24 1842				
	(very poor)				
	July 29 1842–Dec 1880				
	1744–57	1815–80		PRONI	MIC.1D/48–49
	1764–71				
	1777–8				
	1781–95				
	1803–1804				
	1815–81				
Dundalk	See NLI			LDS	0979711 item 1–4
	1790–1802	1790–1802	1790–1831 (gaps)	Louth CL	
	1814–1900	1817–1900			
	Aug 4 1790–Sept 30 1802	Aug 15 1790–Nov 19 1802	Aug 17 1790–Nov 27 1802	NLI	Pos. 5595
	May 25 1814–Aug 30 1831	Oct 27 1817–Aug 20 1831			
	Aug 29 1831–Dec 31 1844				
	Jan 25 1845–Jan 18 1868				
	Jan 21 1868–Dec 31 1880				
	1790–1802	1790–1802	1790–1802	PRONI	MIC.1D/46
	1814–81	1817–31			
Dunleer	See NLI			LDS	0926039
	1798–1900	1772–1900	1832–58	Louth CL	
			1877–98		
	Oct 29 1847–Dec 26 1880	Nov 13 1772–Feb 21 1798	Dec 3 1847–Dec 7 1858	NLI	Pos. 5602
		Jan 28 1848–Nov 24 1880	Jan 1 1877–Dec 6 1880		
	1847–81	1772–98	1847–58	PRONI	MIC.1D/50
		1848–82	1877–82		
Faughart	See NLI			LDS	0926040 item 1–5
	1851–1900	1851–1900		Louth CL	
	Apr 16 1851–Dec 23 1880	Apr 21 1851–Nov 24 1880		NLI	Pos. 5596
	(indexed)				
	1861–81 (indexed)	1851–82		PRONI	MIC.1D/47
	1851–96	indexed 1851–1900			
Haggardstown	1752–1900	1752–1900	1752–1806	Louth CL	
			1832–8		
	Jan 12 1752–May 28 1789	Jan 21 1752–Oct 17 1789	Jan 8 1752–Sept 12 1789	NLI	Pos. 5594
	May 29 1789–Aug 21 1838	June 11 1789–Aug 27 1838	Sept 4 1789–Mar 11 1806		
	July 5 1838–Nov 27 1880	Nov 1 1838–Nov 25 1880	Sept 9 1831–Aug 27. 1838		
	1752–1880	1752–1880	1752–1806	PRONI	MIC.1D/45
			1831–8		
Inniskeen	See Monaghan				
Kilsaran	1809–1900	1809–1900		Louth CL	
	Jan 1 1809–May 8 1824	Jan 23 1809–Oct 228 1826		NLI	Pos. 5599
	Aug 3 1831–June 28 1836	Aug 30 1831–Nov 14 1836			
	Juny 19 1853–Dec 27 1880	Sept 11 1853–Nov 27 1880			
	1809–1824	1809–1826		PRONI	53
	1831–6	1831–6			
	1853–81	1853–82			

Parish (Diocese)	Baptisms	Marriages	Burials	Location	Reference
Knockbridge	See NLI			LDS	0926043
	1851	1858–69		Louth CL	
	1858–69	1889–1900			
	1881–1900				
	Nov 3 1858–1869	Sept 19 1858–1869		NLI	Pos. 5594
	1858–69	1858–69		PRONI	MIC.1D/45
Lordship	See NLI			LDS	0926044/5
	1833–1900	1833–1900		Louth CL	
	Jan 7 1838–Aug 27 1864	Jan 21 1838–Aug 28 1864		NLI	Pos. 5595
	Sept 4 1864–Dec 30 1880	Sept 1 1864–Nov 25 1880			
	1838–81	1838–80		PRONI	MIC.1D/46–47
Louth	1833–1900	1835–1900		Louth CL	
	Mar 12 1833–Sept 25 1871	Apr 8 1833–Dec 18 1873		NLI	Pos. 5593
	Oct 14 1873–Dec 4 1880	Jan 23 1874–Dec 7 1880			
	1833–71	1833–81		PRONI	MIC.1D/44
	1873–81				
Mellifont	1821–1900	1821–1900		Louth CL	
	Dec 2 1821–Dec 29 1848	Dec 14 1821–Dec 9 1848		NLI	Pos. 5599
	1821–81	1821–82		PRONI	MIC.1D/53
Monasterboice	1814–30	1814–72	1814–22	Louth CL	
	1834–1900				
	Nov 1 1814–Oct 30 1830	Nov 2 1814–Sept 28 1830	Nov 5 1814–Nov 30 1815	NLI	Pos. 5600
	Jan 9 1834–Dec 23 1859	Oct 21 1830–Nov 20 1872	Jan 4 1820–Dec 8 1822		
	Jan 6 1860–Dec 19 1880	Jan 20 1870–Nov 20 1872	Sept 12 1830–Jan 10 1850		
	1814–30	1814–72	1814–50 (gaps)	PRONI	MIC.1D/51–52
	1834–81		1857–8		
			1876–7		
Tallanstown	See NLI			LDS	0979712 item 4–9
	1817–25	1804–1900 (gaps)		Louth CL	
	1835–1900				
	Nov 9 1817–Apr 13 1825	Apr 4 1804–Mar 16 1816		NLI	Pos. 5602
	Sept 25 1830–Nov 6 1835	Apr 17 1816–June 1 1863			
	1 Nov 9 1835–Sept 28 1875	Aug 31 1867–Nov 25 1880			
	Oct 12 1875–Dec 27 1880				
	1817–25	1804–1863		PRONI	MIC.1D/50
	1830–81	1867–84			
Termonfeckin	See NLI			LDS	0926044/5
	1823–1900	1799–1810	1799–1810	Louth CL	
		1823–53	1827–33		
		1855–1900			
	Apr 3 1823–Feb 3 1853	Apr 14 1823–Nov 27 1852	Jan 1 1827–Oct 11 1833	NLI	Pos. 5600
	Jan 6 1853–Dec 17 1880	Apr 12 1853–Nov 9 1880			
	1823–81	1823–81	1827–33	PRONI	MIC.1D/51
Togher	1791–1900	1791–1900	1791–1817	Louth CL	
	Nov 1 1791–Apr 24 1828	July 31 1791–Mar 17 1828	June 3 1791–May 8 1817	NLI	Pos. 5597
	Aug 8 1869–Dec 31 1880	Feb 24 1873–Nov 13 1880			
	1791–1828	1873–81	1791–1817	PRONI	MIC.1D/48
	1869–81				

Mayo

All Mayo North Family History Research Centre (MNFHRC) and South Mayo Family Research Centre (SMFRC) transcripts up to 1900 are online at <www.roots ireland.ie>. NLI microfilms marked with an asterisk (*) are online at <www. ancestry.com>.

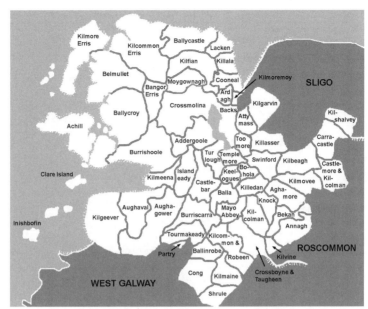

Parish (Diocese)	Baptisms	Marriages	Burials	Location	Reference
Achill (Tuam)	1868–1911	1867–1913		LDS	1279259 item 3–5
	1868–1900	1867–1913		MNFHRC	
	Dec 29 1867–Dec 26 1880	Oct 18 1867–June 25 1880		NLI	Pos. 4222
Addergoole (Killala)	1840–80	1840–78		LDS	1279205 item 9–11
	1840–1900	1840–1900		MNFHRC	
	Jan 15 1840–Mar 2 1866	Jan 13 1840–Mar 10 1878		NLI	Pos. 4229
	Mar 2 1866–June 11 1878				
	June 16 1878–Dec 26 1880				
	1842–62			Online	Dees
Aghamore (Tuam)	1864–1901	1864–1921		LDS	1279206 item 13–15
	Feb 2 1864–Dec 26 1880 (transcript)	Dec 22 1864–Sept 22 1880		NLI	Pos. 4217
	1864–1900	1864–1900		SMFRC	
Annagh (Tuam)	1854–1924	1852–1902		LDS	1279208 item 3–6
	Nov 17 1851–Dec 30 1870	June 14 1852–June 30 1870		NLI	Pos. 4217
	Jan 6 1871–Dec 26 1880	Nov 20 1870–Dec 1 1880			
	1851–1900	1852–1900	1954–95	SMFRC	
Ardagh (Killala)	1870–80			LDS	1279204 item 23
	1866–1900	1882–1908		MNFHRC	
	Feb 5 1870–July 14 1880			NLI	Pos. 4230

Parish (Diocese)	Baptisms	Marriages	Burials	Location	Reference
Attymass (Achonry)	See NLI			LDS	0926002 item 1–2
	1875–1900	1874–97		MNFHRC	
	June 16 1875–Aug 22 1880	Feb 1 1874–Oct 15 1880		NLI	Pos. 4224*
Aughagower (Tuam)	1828–36	1854–1903		LDS	1279209 item 19–20; 1279210, 1–3
	1842–54				
	1854–1903				
	1828–1900	1828–1900		MSFHC	
	Apr 9 1828–May 17 1836	Nov 16 1854–Dec 7 1880		NLI	Pos. 4210
	Mar 17 1842–Aug 20 1854				
	Sept 24 1854–Dec 18 1880				
	1828–36			Online	Dees
	1842–6				
Aughaval (Tuam)	1845–1905	1823–1905		LDS	12792210/1 item 17–22, 1–4; more
	July 9 1845–Nov 14 1858 (not precisely ordered)	Apr 9 1823–Oct 6 1837 (not precisely ordered)		NLI	Pos. 4210
	Jan 18 1859–Mar 24 1872	Aug 10 1834–May 25 1857			
	Jan 19 1862–Mar 11 1874	(not precisely ordered)			
	Apr 7 1872–Dec 26 1880	Feb 4 1857–Feb 1 1861			
	Mar 15 1874–Dec 29 1880	Jan 15 1862–Dec 20 1880			
	1848–73	1825–60		Online	Dees
	1845–1900	1831–1900	1921–98	SMFRC	
Backs (Killala)	Aug 28 1848–Dec 11 1859 (Rathduff)	Dec 1 1848–Apr 14 1860 (Rathduff)		NLI	Pos. 4230
	Jan 2 1861–Sept 14 1879 (Rathduff)	Jan 27 1865–Dec 2 1869 (Rathduff)			
	Oct 12 1854–Oct 2 1856 (Knockmore)	Feb 24 1874–Sept 1879 (Rathduff)			
	Mar 4 1858–Aug 16 1879 (Knockmore)	Sept 25 1860–Nov 21 1861 (Knockmore)			
		Jan 13 1869–July 13 1879 (Knockmore)			
	1829–1900	1815–97		MNFHRC	
	1830–51	1829–50		LDS	1279205 item 5–8
	1854–79	1848–64			
	1848–79	1865–80			
	1865–80				
	1854–63			Online	Dees
Balla (Tuam)	May 28 1837–Dec 27 1880	July 3 1837–Oct 3 1880		NLI	Pos. 4213
	1837–1900	1837–1900		SMFRC	
	1837–1905	1837–1905		LDS	1279209 item 2–3
	1837–41			Online	Dees
Ballinrobe (Tuam)	1843–1903	1850–1911		LDS	1279209 item 8–10; 0926219
	Aug 20 1843–Dec 20 1851 (inc. some marriages)	Oct 24 1850–Apr 30 1856		NLI	Pos. 4215
	Nov 7 1850–Apr 17 1856	Jan 14 1861–Nov 7 1880			
	Jan 18 1861–Nov 7 1880				
	June 19 1871–Dec 29 1880				
	1843–1900	1850–1900		SMFRC	

Parish (Diocese)	Baptisms	Marriages	Burials	Location	Reference
Ballycastle (Killala)	1853–80	1869–80		LDS	1279204 item 20–21
	1853–1900	1869–1900		MNFHRC	
	Aug 8 1864–Dec 15 1880	Jan 15 1869–Sept 3 1880		NLI	Pos. 4229
Ballycroy (Killala)	1885–1900	1869–1900		MNFHRC	
	No records microfilmed			NLI	
Bangor Erris (Killala)	1860–81	1860–81		LDS	1279205 item 12, 16
	1860–1901	1860–1901		MNFHRC	
	Aug 1 1860–Dec 26 1880	Sept 4 1860–Mar 28 1880		NLI	Pos. 4231
Bekan (Tuam)	Aug 3 1832–Feb 2 1844 (some missing)	May 7 1832–Aug 6 1844 (some missing)		NLI	Pos. 4219
	Dec 15 1844–May 20 1861 (some missing)	Aug 8 1844–May 22 1872 (some missing)			
	Sept 15 1851–May 7 1871				
	1832–1900	1832–1900		SMFRC	
Belmullet (Killala)	1842–80	1836–80		LDS	1279205 item 13–15
	1841–1900	1836–1900		MNFHRC	
	Feb 15 1841–Dec 19 1872	Jan 8 1836–May 11 1845		NLI	Pos. 4231
	Dec 21 1872–Dec 26 1880	Aug 23 1857–Nov 2 1880			
Bohola (Achonry)	1857–1925	1857–1925		MNFHRC	
	Oct 1857–Dec 26 1880	Oct 29 1857–May 30 1880		NLI	Pos. 4224*
Burriscarra (Tuam)	1839–95	1839–1903		LDS	1279210 item 15–16; 0979699 1–2
	Sept 1 1839–Dec 24 1880	Sept 29 1839–Mar 1 1880		NLI	Pos. 4213
	1839–81 (extracts?)	1839–49 (part?)		Online	Dees
	1839–1900	1839–1900	1922–99	SMFRC	
Burrishoole (Tuam)	1872–1920	1872–1911		LDS	1279207 item 9–11
	1872–1900	1872–1900		MNFHRC	
	Jan 30 1872–Nov 27 1880			NLI	Pos. 4222
Carracastle (Achonry)	1853–1908	1847–1903		LDS	1279233 item 1–2
	1853–1925	1847–1925		MNFHRC	
	Jan 17 1853–Dec 26 1880	July 1 1847–Nov 21 1880		NLI	Pos. 4223
Castlebar (Tuam)	1838–1984	1824–1982		LDS	1279260/1
	Jan 2 1838–Apr 17 1855 (in disorder)	June 16 1824–Apr 17 1843		NLI	Pos. 4214
	Feb 25 1855–June 16 1872	June 27 1843–Dec 9 1880			
	June 22 1872–Dec 28 1880				
	Extracts	1828–31		Online	Dees
		1883–96			
	1838–1900	1824–1900		SMFRC	
Castlemore and Kilcolman (Achonry)	1851–1911	1830–1963		LDS	1279232 item 1–9
	Nov 1851–Nov 17 1861	Aug 10 1830–Oct 2 1867		NLI	Pos. 4226
	Jan 25 1864–June 2 1872	Feb 4 1868–Nov 10 1880			
	Jan 5 1860–Feb 6 1876				
	1861				
	1864–72 (transcript)				
	Feb 13 1876–Dec 31 1880				

Parish (Diocese)	Baptisms	Marriages	Burials	Location	Reference
Castlemore and	1851–1900	1830–1900		RHGC	
Kilcolman (Achonry)	1851–1900			SHGS	
(contd.)					
Clare Island (Tuam)	See NLI			LDS	0926220 item 3
	Oct 14 1851–Nov 21 1880			NLI	Pos. 4211
Cong and The Neale	1870–1924	1870–1900		LDS	1279214 item
(Tuam)					6–7
	Feb 28 1870–Dec 20 1880			NLI	Pos. 4214
	(transcript)				
	1870–1900	1870–1900		SMFRC	
Cooneal (Killala)	c 1830–c 1870	c 1830–c 1870		LDS	1279204 item 24
	1844–81	1843–81		MNFHRC	
	Nov 26 1843–Dec 19 1880	Oct 10 1843–Dec 21 1880		NLI	Pos. 4230
Crossboyne and	1825–1913	1791–1876		LDS	1279211 item
Taugheen (Tuam)					5–8
	July 7 1862–Feb 3 1877	Jan 9 1877–July 29 1880		NLI	Pos. 4217
	May 10 1877–Dec 26 1880				
	1825–1913	1791–1990	1918–44	SMFRC	
Crossmolina (Killala)	1831–80	1831–80		LDS	1279204 item 22
	1831–1900	1832–1900		MNFHRC	
	Aug 27 1831–Aug 8 1841	Nov 18 1832–Feb 10 1841		NLI	Pos. 4230
	Apr 23 1845–Dec 28 1880	Mar 10 1846–Dec 27 1880			
	1831–8?			Online	Dees
	1865–75				
Inishbofin (Tuam)	1867–1900	1867–1900		GFHSW	
	1867–1903	1877–8		LDS	1279213 item 10
	Oct 14 1867–Dec 15 1880	Nov 18 1867–Oct 25 1880		NLI	Pos. 4219
Islandeady (Tuam)	1839–1913	1839–98		LDS	1279213 item
					11–14
	Sept 7 1839–Dec 30 1866	Sept 17 1839–Sept 2 1880		NLI	Pos. 4212
	Jan 6 1867–May 14 1876				
	1839–1903 (part)			Online	Dees
	1839–1900	1839–1900		SMFRC	
Keelogues (Tuam)	1847–1909	1872–1909		LDS	1279259 item
					1–2
	1847–1909	1847–1909		MNFHRC	
	Aug 15 1847–Dec 24 1880	Aug 10 1847–Sept 4 1880		NLI	Pos. 4215
Kilbeagh (Achonry)	1855–1924	1845–1902		LDS	1279230 item
					1–6
	1847–1900	1844–1900		MNFHRC	
	Jan 1 1855–Dec 26 1880	May 18 1845–Mar 13 1866		NLI	Pos. 4224
		Jan 22 1855–Sept 12 1880			
Kilcolman (Tuam)	1835–1913	1806–1898		LDS	1279207 item
					15–20
	Apr 7 1835–Jan 29 1838	June 8 1806–Feb 4 1830		NLI	Pos. 4217
	Mar 26 1839–May 16 1858	Jan 7 1835–Mar 7 1836			
	May 16 1858–May 28 1873	Dec 29 1838–June 25 1871			
	1835–1912	1806–1890		Online	Dees
	1835–1900	1805–1900		SMFRC	

Parish (Diocese)	Baptisms	Marriages	Burials	Location	Reference
Kilcommon and Robeen (Tuam)	1857–80	1857–80		LDS	1279209 item
	1896–1924	1865–99			11–12; 0926223
		1896–1924			
	Oct 5 1857–Dec 24 1880	Oct 10 1857–June 24 1880		NLI	Pos. 4216
	Dec 8 1865–Dec 24 1880	Nov 25 1865–Apr 24 1880			
	(Roundfort)	(Roundfort)			
	1857–2000	1857–2000	1924–98	SMFRC	
Kilcommon Erris (Killala)	1883–1900	1843–8		MNFHRC	
	No records microfilmed			NLI	
Kilfian (Killala)	1826–36	1826–36	1826–32	LDS	1279205 item 2
		1843–4			
	1826–36	1826–36	1826–36	MNFHRC	
	Oct 1 1826–Apr 7 1836	July 2 1826–Oct 2 1844	Oct 6 1826–Feb 6 1832	NLI	Pos. 4230
Kilgarvin (Achonry)	See NLI			LDS	
	1870–1900	1844–81		MNFHRC	
		1897–1925			
	Mar 15 1870–Dec 31 1880	Nov 16 1844–May 4 1880		NLI	Pos. 4224*
Kilgeever (Tuam)	1850–72	1844–5		LDS	1279224 item 2;
	1894–1922	1906–1922			0926224 1; and
	1872–80 (Louisburgh)	1872–80			more
		(Louisburgh)			
	Feb 20 1850–Mar 7 1869			NLI	Pos. 4212
	(transcript)				
	Aug 1 1872–Dec 12 1880				
	1844–78			Online	Dees
	1850–1900	1850–1900		SMFRC	
Killala (Killala)	1852–80	1873–80		LDS	1279204 item
					17–19
	1852–1900	1873–1900		MNFHRC	
	Apr 6 1852–Aug 25 1873	Dec 14 1873–Nov 3 1880		NLI	Pos. 4231
	Sept 21 1873–Dec 23 1880				
Killasser (Achonry)	1847–1902	1847–1921		LDS	1279232 item
					16–17
	1848–1900	1847–1900	1847–8	MNFHRC	
	Nov 1 1847–Dec 31 1880	Dec 13 1847–June 5 1880	Nov 1 1847–Apr 3 1862	NLI	Pos. 4223
Killedan (Achonry)	1860–1909	1834–1909		LDS	1279231 item
					3–6
	Feb 2 1861–Dec 29 1880	May 22 1834–Apr 3 1862		NLI	Pos. 4224
		Nov 6 1861–Aug 8 1880			
	1861–1900	1835–1900		SMFRC	
Kilmaine (Tuam)	1854–1909	1855–1909		LDS	1279214 item 3–
					4; 0926225 2–4
	June 30 1854–Dec 31 1877	May 19 1855–Oct 20 1877		NLI	Pos. 4216
	Jan 20 1878–Dec 24 1880				
	1854–1900	1854–1900		SMFRC	
Kilmeena (Tuam)	1858–	1858–		Local Catholic parish	
	No records microfilmed			NLI	
	1870–1900	1870–1900		SMFRC	

Parish (Diocese)	Baptisms	Marriages	Burials	Location	Reference
Kilmore Erris (Killala)	1860–81	1860–81		LDS	1279205 item 17–18
	1859–1900	1860–1900		MNFHRC	
	June 24 1860–Dec 27 1880	Sept 1 1860–Nov 4 1880		NLI	Pos. 4231
Kilmoremoy (Killala)	See Sligo				
Kilmovee (Achonry)	1854–1913	1824–48			
	1855–1925			LDS	1279230 item 7–9; 0926017
	Feb 21 1854–Dec 21 1880	Nov 3 1824–Aug 28 1848		NLI	Pos. 4224*
	June 18 1854–Dec 19 1880	Oct 12 1854–Dec 21 1880			
	1854–1913	1824–80		Online	<www.east
	1854–1913	1824–1913		SMFRC	mayo.org>
Kilshalvey (Achonry)	See Sligo				
Kilvine (Tuam)	1872–1911	1872–1908		LDS	1279206 item 10
	No records microfilmed			NLI	
	1870–1900	1870–1900		SMFRC	
Knock (Tuam)	1868–1913	1875–1943		LDS	1279206 item 3–5
	Dec 17 1868–Dec 29 1880	Sept 7 1875–Dec 5 1880		NLI	Pos. 4218
	1868–1924	1874–1924		SMFRC	
Lacken (Killala)	1852–74	1854–69		LDS	1279205 item 4
	1852–1900	1854–1900		MNFHRC	
	Aug 19 1852–Nov 24 1874 (transcript—many gaps)	Mar 29 1854–Feb 7 1869 (transcript—many gaps)		NLI	Pos. 4230
Mayo Abbey (Tuam)	1841–99	1841–1906		LDS	1279209 item 6–7
	Apr 4 1841–Dec 20 1880	Sept 10 1841–June 5 1880		NLI	Pos. 4215
	1841–1990	1841–1990	1930–98	SMFRC	
Moygownagh (Killala)	1877–1925	1881–1925		MNFHRC	
	No records microfilmed			NLI	
Partry (Tuam) See also Tourmakedy	Oct 23 1869–July 15 1868	Jan 7 1870–July 11 1878		NLI	Pos. 4216
Shrule (Galway)	July 7 1831–Aug 12 1864	July 1 1831–June 23 1848 Oct 26 1855–May 10 1864		NLI	Pos. 2438
	1831–1900	1831–1900		SMFRC	
Swineford (Achonry)	1822–1915	1808–1915		LDS	1279233 item 5–9; 0926020
	1822–5	1808–1825		MNFHRC	
	1842–1900	1842–78			
	Mar 19 1822–June 26 1826	June 7 1808–July 3 1846		NLI	Pos. 4225
	May 12 1841–Aug 23 1850	July 3 1846–Mar 31 1878			
	Sept 1 1850–May 7 1859	Apr 24 1878–Nov 23 1915			
	July 2 1859–Sept 29 1875				
	Oct 2 1875–Dec 31 1900				
Templemore (Achonry)	May 20 1872–Mar 11 1880			LDS	0926021
	1888–1925	1872–1925		MNFHRC	
	May 20 1872–Mar 11 1880			NLI	Pos. 4224
Toomore (Achonry)	1871–93	1833–1911		LDS	12792031 item 18–19; 0926022
	1871–1900	1833–40 1870–1900		MNFHRC	
	Dec 30 1871–Jan 6 1880	Apr 30 1833–Mar 17 1840 Jan 20 1870–Dec 22 1880		NLI	Pos. 4223

Parish (Diocese)	Baptisms	Marriages	Burials	Location	Reference
Tourmakeady (Tuam)	1862–85	1870–78 1883–1903		LDS	1279206 item 16
	Aug 26 1869–Dec 26 1880 (transcript)	1869–Sept 5 1880		NLI	Pos. 4216
	1860–1900	1847–1900		SMFRC	
Turlough (Tuam)	1847–1911	1847–1909		LDS	1279212 item 5–7
	1847–1925	1849–1925		MNFHRC	
	Aug 1 1847–Dec 7 1865 Dec 8 1865–Dec 25 1880	Aug 8 1847–June 8 1880		NLI	Pos. 4213

Meath

All parishes are in the diocese of Meath except where noted. All Meath Heritage and Genealogy Centre (MHGC) transcripts up to 1900 are online at <*www.roots ireland.ie*>. NLI microfilms marked with an asterisk (*) are online at <*www.ancestry.com*>.

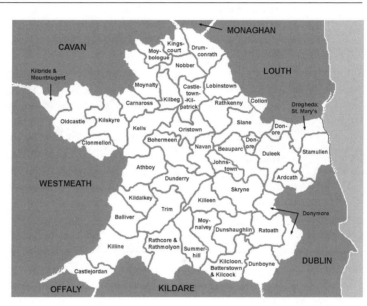

Parish (Diocese)	Baptisms	Marriages	Burials	Location	Reference
Ardcath	1795–1900	1797–1900		MHGC	
	Oct 25 1795–June 29 1879	June 18 1797–June 30 1879		NLI	Pos. 4180*
Athboy	1794–1900	1794–1900	1794–1847	MHGC	
	Apr 18 1794–Nov 15 1799	May 5 1794–Nov 7 1799	Apr 23 1794–Mar 27 1798	NLI	Pos. 4173*
	Mar 3 1807–May 16 1826	Apr 9 1807–Oct 24 1864	Mar 18 1807–Feb 23 1826		
	Jan 14 1827–Jan 12 1858	Feb 6 1865–Nov 25 1880	Jan 2 1865–Sept 23 1873		
	Jan 1 1858–Dec 29 1880				
Balliver	See NLI			LDS	0926163 item 1
	1837–1901			MHGC	
	Feb 12 1837–Dec 9 1880	Apr 7 1837–July 12 1880	Feb 12 1837–Nov 16 1880	NLI	Pos. 4179*
Beauparc	1815–1900	1816–1900		MHGC	
	Dec 17 1815–Sept 8 1880	Jan 10 1816–July 22 1881		NLI	Pos. 4180*
Bohermeen	See NLI			LDS	0926164
	1832–1900	1831–1900	1833–68	MHGC	
	June 2 1832–Dec 31 1880	Apr 22 1831–May 30 1881	Jan 5 1833–May 5 1842 Jan 15 1865–Mar 13 1868	NLI	Pos. 4182*

Parish (Diocese)	Baptisms	Marriages	Burials	Location	Reference
Carnaross	See NLI			LDS	0926165 item 1–2
	1806–1900	1805–1900	1805–1856	MHGC	
	Aug 25 1806–Oct 14 1807	June 1805–Feb 12 1820	June 9 1805–Sept 13 1856	NLI	Pos. 4184
	May 21 1808–Sept 28 1815	Feb 16 1823–Feb 24 1825			
	June 2 1827–Feb 6 1859	Jan 27 1828–Apr 12 1861			
	Feb 27 1859–Apr 2 1881	July 12 1861–May 11 1882			
Castlejordan	See Offaly (King's County)				
Castletown-Kilpatrick	1805–1900	1816–1900		MHGC	
	Dec 18 1805–Jan 22 1821	May 22 1816–May 19 1822		NLI	Pos. 4184
	Apr 12 1821–May 28 1822	Jan 24 1824–Apr 18 1841			
	Jan 7 1826–Sept 26 1832	Nov 10 1842–Nov 13 1873			
	Oct 3 1832–May 11 1841	Nov 13 1873–Nov 27 1880			
	Apr 1 1841–Nov 27 1873				
	Nov 27 1873–Nov 27 1880				
Clonmellon	1759–1901	1757–1901	1757–1993	DSHGC	
	1759–1900	1757–1900	1759–1849	MHGC	
	Jan 6 1759–Sept 18 1784 (some gaps)	Jan 17 1757–Aug 20 1784 (some gaps)	Jan 30 1757–Sept 17 1784 (some gaps)	NLI	Pos. 4187
	Feb 3 1785–Apr 29 1791	Aug 16 1784–Sept 4 1809	Dec 25 1878–Oct 29 1809		
	Jan 3 1815–Mar 24 1815	Jan 19 1815–Feb 21 1815	Nov 7 1819–July (15?) 1850		
	May 1 1791–Mar 10 1809	July 19 1819–July 29 1845			
	Apr 5 1809–Nov 2 1809	Jan 10 1846–June 19 1872			
	Jun 18 1819–July 10 1845				
	July 11 1845–Aug 25 1872				
Collon	See Louth				
Donore	1840–1900	1840–1900	1840–41	MHGC	
	Jan 1 1840–Feb 5 1881	Apr 27 1840–Sept 7 1881	(1841–50 missing)	NLI	Pos. 4181*
Donymore	1836–1900	1836–1900	1833–63	MHGC	
	Apr 30 1802–June 23 1823	June 17 1802–June 7 1823	June 7 1802–Apr 14 1823	NLI	Pos. 4179*
	Aug 14 1823–Nov 16 1880	July 23 1823–Nov 16 1880	Nov 2 1833–Apr 11 1863		
Drogheda: St Mary's	See NLI			LDS	0926169
	1835–1900	1870–1900	1870–71	MHGC	
	Apr 30 1835–June 9 1867	Apr 24 1870–Feb 2 1881	NLI	Pos. 4180*	
	June 9 1867–Nov 23 1875				
	Jan 2 1872–Jan 11 1881				
Drumconrath	1811–1900	1811–1900	1861–72	MHGC	
	Oct 1811–Aug 25 1861	Sept 31 [sic] 1811–Sept 22 1861		NLI	Pos. 4184
	Sept 15 1861–Feb 9 1881				
	Oct 4 1861–Feb 7 1881	Aug 11 1861–Mar 25 1872			
Duleek	See NLI			LDS	0926168
	1852–1901	1852–1911		MHGC	
	Feb 2 1852–Mar 7 1880	Feb 24 1852–June 21 1881		NLI	Pos. 4181*
Dunboyne	1798–1900	1787–1900	1787–1877	MHGC	
	Sept 2 1798–Apr 19 1823	June 31 [sic] 1787–Nov 22 1863	June 7 1787–Oct 31 1877	NLI	Pos. 4176*
	May 1 1823–Aug 11 1844				
	Sept 6 1844–Dec 16 1877	Feb 2 1834–Aug 26 1836			
		Jan 12 1864–Dec 29 1877			
Dunderry	1837–1900	1841–1901		MHGC	
	Oct 11 1837–Oct 24 1857	Oct 15 1841–May 31 1869		NLI	Pos. 4187
	Aug 10 1841–July 17 1869	May 10 1871–Oct 7 1883			
	May 3 1870–Mar 20 1881				

Parish (Diocese)	Baptisms	Marriages	Burials	Location	Reference
Dunshaughlin	See NLI			LDS	0926166
	1789–1880	1801–1880	1789–1872	MHGC	
	Jan 1 1789–Oct 9 1791	Oct 25 1800–July 26 1801	Oct 9 1791–Jan 24 1828	NLI	Pos. 4177*
	Jan 8 1849–Apr 14 1880	Aug 2 1801–Feb 11 1834	Jan 7 1863–Dec 23 1872		
	Feb 13 1849–Apr 1880				
Johnstown	See NLI			LDS	0926170
	1839–1900	1839–1900		MHGC	
	Jan 12 1839–Apr 24 1881	Jan 2 1839–Aug 29 1881		NLI	Pos. 4182*
Kells	1791–1900	1791–1900	1784–1828	MHGC	
	July 12 1791–Dec 2 1827	Aug 1 1791–Dec 26 1873	June 13 1794–Mar 30 1824	NLI	Pos. 4185
	July 17 1828–Nov 28 1831				
	Jan 27 1832–Dec 31 1873				
	(some for 1830)				
Kilbeg	See NLI			LDS	0926173 item 4
	1815–1900	1829–1900	1830–70	MHGC	
	Dec 1817–Jan 8 1852	Jan 15 1810–June 16 1813		NLI	Pos. 4184
	Mar 17 1858–Dec 24 1869	Jan 15 1830–May 21 1852			
		May 23 1858–Oct 10 1869			
Kilbride and	1832–1900	1832–99		CHGC	
Mountnugent	1830–1900	1830–63	1906–1983	DSHGC	
	See NLI			LDS	0926174
	Jan 1 1832–Jan 27 1864	Jan 1 1832–Nov 22 1863		NLI	Pos. 4172*
	Jan 13 1864–Nov 27 1880	Feb 4 1864–Nov 27 1880			
Kilcloon, Batterstown	1836–1900	1836–1900		MHGC	
and Kilcock. See also	Feb 21 1836–Dec 12 1880	Apr 14 1836–June 14 1880		NLI	Pos. 4177*
Kilcock (Kildare)	Feb 21 1836–Dec 12 1880	Apr 14 1836–June 14 1880			
	(transcript)	(transcript)			
Kildalkey	1782–1901	1782–1901		MHGC	
	No records microfilmed			NLI	
Killeen	1742–1900 (Kilmessan)	1742–1900 (Kilmessan)	1756–1900 (Kilmessan)	MHGC	
	1790–1896	1790–1896	1790–1896	MHGC	
	July 2 1742–Aug 26 1750	Feb 2 1865–Aug 26 1880	July 2 1742–Aug 26 1750	NLI	Pos. 4178*
	Jan 2 1791–Mar 25 1832	(Kilmessan)	Jan 2 1791–Mar 25 1832		
	Apr 10 1832–Dec 30 1864		Apr 10 1832–Oct 24 1871		
	(Killmessan)		(Killmessan)		
	Mar 25 1832–Dec 6 1880		Mar 25 1832–Dec 6 1880		
	(Dunsany, Killeen)		(Dunsany, Killeen)		
	Jan 21 1865–Nov 26 1880				
	(Kilmessan)				
Killine	1829–77	1829–77	1829–55	MHGC	
	Jan 29 1829–Jan 15 1833	Jan 29 1829–Jan 15 1833	Jan 29 1829–Jan 15 1833	NLI	Pos. 4179*
	Feb 4 1833–Mar 4 1878	Mar 1833–Nov 29 1877	Feb 3 1833–Feb 9 1855		
Kilskyre	See NLI			LDS	0926173 item 1–3
	1784–1901	1784–1900		MHGC	
	Apr 22 1784–Dec 30 1838	Jan 22 1784–Nov 2 1790	Jan 9 1784–Aug 29 1790	NLI	Pos. 4186
	Jan 1 1839–Oct 19 1841	June 12 1808–July 31 1841	Nov 29 1859–Oct 27 1873		
	(Ballinlough separately)	Jan 28 1842–Feb 16 1874			
	Nov 10 1841–Mar 4 1873	Apr 13 1874–Oct 30 1880			

Parish (Diocese)	Baptisms	Marriages	Burials	Location	Reference
Kingscourt	1838–1920	1838–1920		CHGC	
	See NLI			LDS	0926175
	Oct 16 1838–Aug 13 1854	Aug 15 1838–May 27 1861	Sept 1846–May 30 1858	NLI	Pos. 4183*
	Jan 1 1864–Dec 31 1880				
			Sept 1846–Nov 1850	Online	Genweb
Lobinstown	1823–1900	1823–1900		MHGC	
	Oct 8 1823–Apr 5 1881	Sept 28 1823–May 19 1881		NLI	Pos. 4183*
Moybologue	Feb 28 1867–Dec 18 1880	May 12 1868–Oct 14 1880		NLI	Pos. 5349
	1867–81	1868–82		PRONI	MIC.1D/82
Moynalty	See NLI			LDS	0926176 item 2
	1830–1900	1829–1900	1830–79	MHGC	
	July 25 1830–Apr 4 1880	Dec 1 1829–Jan 31 1883	Mar 2 1830–Jan 10 1880	NLI	Pos. 4187
Moynalvey	See NLI			LDS	0926177
	1811–1900	1783–1900		MHGC	
	Oct 4 1811–Oct 5 1828	Nov 4 1783–Nov 6 1786	Oct 15 1811–Sept 29 1828	NLI	Pos. 4178*
	Mar 25 1831–Dec 24 1877	Oct 7 1811–Sept 29 1828	Oct 28 1877–Dec 18 1880		
	Jan 13 1878–Dec 26 1880	Apr 24 1831–Nov 1 1880			
Navan	1782–1901	1853–1901		MHGC	
	Jan 14 1782–May 20 1813	Apr 4 1853–Oct 21 1868	June 18 1868–July 4 1880	NLI	Pos. 4181*
	Sept 7 1842–Jan 1881	Oct 25 1868–Nov 19 1881			
	Oct 22 1868–Dec 29 1880				
Nobber	See NLI			LDS	0926179
	1754–1900	1757–1900	1757–1866	MHGC	
	July 22 1754–Feb 10 1821	Jan 17 1757–Feb 7 1821	Feb 6 1757–Jan 23 1821	NLI	Pos. 4183*
	Jan 6 1821–July 12 1865	Mar 5 1821–May 11 1865	Jan 23 1821–Feb 10 1866		
Oldcastle	See NLI			LDS	0926180
	1789–1900	1789–1900		MHGC	
	Jan 5 1789–Feb 9 1807	Apr 28 1789–Feb 10 1807	Mar 27 1789–Feb 4 1807	NLI	Pos. 4188
	Nov 6 1808–Mar (?) 28	Nov 7 1808–Nov 28 1840	Nov 3 1808–Jan 2 1809		
	1834	Jan 9 1841–June 29 1846			
	Feb 18 1834–Nov 14 1877	July 12 1846–Nov 17 1877			
Oristown	See NLI			LDS	0926181
	1774–1900	1763–1900	1771–1831	MHGC	
	Dec 25 1757–July 25 1784	Nov 1 1763–May 27 1780		NLI	Pos. 4186
	(some gaps)	Jan 27 1783–June 7 1784			
	1774–8 (various dates)	Apr 24 1797–Apr 17 1801			
	Apr 30 1797–May 16 1814	Sept 15 1801–Aug 3 1842			
	(some gaps)	Mar 7 1848–Sept 19 1880			
	Feb 14 1831–Dec 22 1840				
	(some gaps)				
	Nov 14 1847–Dec 26 1880				
Rathcore and	1878–1911	1879–1912		MHGC	
Rathmolyon	No records microfilmed			NLI	
Rathkenny	1784–1900	1867–1900	1796–1816	MHGC	
	Nov 30 1784–Dec 6 1815	Nov 27 1784–Sept 10 1788		NLI	Pos. 4182*
	Nov 30 1784–Dec 6 1815	1785–1816 (some			
	July 12 1818–Feb 22 1861	entries only)			
	Aug 5 1866–Mar 1 1876	Aug 3 1818–Dec 5 1844			
		May 21 1846–Nov 22 1857			
		Oct 1 1866–Feb 10 1876			

Parish (Diocese)	Baptisms	Marriages	Burials	Location	Reference
Ratoath	See NLI			LDS	0926182
	1781–1900	1780–1900	1789–1814	MHGC	
	May 10 1781–Jan 23 1818	Jan 1780–May 7 1818	June 26 1789–Apr 15 1818	NLI	Pos. 4177*
	Aug 1 1818–Dec 29 1880	Aug 17 1818–Dec 13 1880			
Skryne	1841–1900	1842–1900		MHGC	
	Nov 28 1841–Dec 12 1880	Jan 16 1842–May 19 1880		NLI	Pos. 4179*
Slane	See NLI			LDS	0926183 item 1
	1851–1900	1851–1900		MHGC	
	Jan 1 1851–May 29 1881	Jan 7 1851–Nov 26 1881		NLI	Pos. 4187
Stamullen	See NLI			LDS	0926183 item 2
	1831–1901	1830–1901		MHGC	
	Jan 1 1831–Dec 22 1879	May 3 1830–Nov 29 1879	Jan 3 1834–Dec 27 1877	NLI	Pos. 4182
Summerhill	See NLI			LDS	0926184
	1812–1900	1812–1900	1812–36	MHGC	
	Apr 13 1812–Apr 26 1854	Apr 16 1812–Feb 26 1854	Apr 14 1812–Nov 11 1836	NLI	Pos. 4178*
	May 10 1854–Dec 12 1880				
		July 13 1854–Sept 30 1880			
Trim	See NLI			LDS	0926185 item 1–2
	1829–1901	1829–1901	1831–41	MHGC	
	July 25 1829–Dec 29 1880	July 30 1829–Nov 27 1880	Jan 7 1831–Apr 12 1841	NLI	Pos. 4179*

Monaghan

All parishes are in the diocese of Clogher. Some Monaghan Genealogy (MG*) transcripts are now (2011) online at <www.rootsireland.ie>.

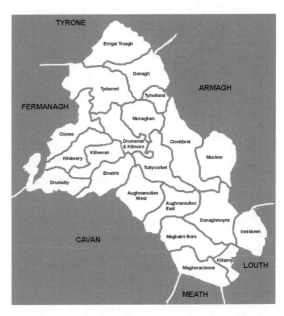

Parish (Diocese)	Baptisms	Marriages	Burials	Location	Reference
Aughnamullen East	See NLI			LDS	0979707 item 1–3
	1878–1900			MG	
	July 26 1857–Oct 26 1876	July 26 1857–Oct 26 1876	July 26 1857–Oct 26 1876	NLI	Pos. 5576
	Aug 3 1878–Dec 9 1880	Aug 20 1878–Nov 1 1880			
	1857–81	1857–81	1857–81	PRONI	MIC.1D/19

Parish (Diocese)	Baptisms	Marriages	Burials	Location	Reference
Aughnamullen West	1868–80			MG	
	Feb 14 1841–Dec 23 1867	Feb 2 1841–Nov 30 1867		NLI	Pos. 5575
	Jan 3 1868–Nov 14 1880	Jan 9 1868–Nov 27 1880			
	1841–81	1841–81		PRONI	MIC.1D/18
Clones	1848–80	1821–66		MG	
	July 23 1848–Apr 30 1854	May 30 1821–Mar 3 1840		NLI	Pos. 5577;
	Apr 22 1855–Feb 18 1866	Oct 1 1840–Feb 9 1866			marriages
	Feb 25 1866–Dec 29 1880	Apr 17 1866–Nov 21 1880			from 1878 on
					Pos. 5578
	1848–81	1821–81		PRONI	MIC.1D/20–21
Clontibret	1861–80			MG	
	Feb 12 1861–July 4 1874	Aug 27 1861–Dec 21 1880		NLI	Pos. 5573
	Sept 2 1872–Dec 24 1880				
	July 4 1874–Dec 31 1880				
	1860–81	1861–81		PRONI	MIC.1D/16
Donagh	1835–80	1836–60		MG	
	May 2 1836–Feb 28 1878	May 2 1836–Feb 28 1878		NLI	Pos. 5574
	(illegible in many parts)	(illegible in many parts)			
	Jan 14 1861–Dec 30 1880	Sept 30 1860–Nov 25 1880			
	1836–81	1836–82		PRONI	MIC.1D/17;
					C.R.2/11
Donaghmoyne	1841–78			MG*	
	Jan 19 1863–Jan 28 1878	Oct 11 1872–Oct 7 1880		NLI	Pos. 5572
	Jan 15 1869–Dec 10 1880				
	1863–80	1872–80		PRONI	MIC.1D/15
Drumsnat and	Feb 16 1836–June 13 1872	Feb 16 1836–June 13 1872	Feb 16 1836–June 13 1872	NLI	Pos. 5575
Kilmore	1875–80	1875–80	1875–80		
	1875–81	1836–72	1875–83	PRONI	MIC.1D/18;
					C.R.2/13
Drumully	1845–81			MG*	
	Jan 6 1845–Apr 2 1866	July 14 1864–Oct 31 1880		NLI	Pos. 5572
	July 7 1864–Dec 26 1880				
	1845–81	1864–81		PRONI	MIC.1D/15
Ematris	1848–76			MG*	
	May 14 1848–Mar 22 1860	Feb 2 1850–Nov 2 1861		NLI	Pos. 5578
	Mar 15 1861–Mar 9 1876				
	1848–76	1850–61		PRONI	MIC.1D/21
Errigal Truagh	Nov 1 1835–June 20 1852	Dec 1 1837–July 28 28 1849		LDS	0979706 item
	Mar 24 1861–Dec 29 1880	Jan 28 1862–May 27 1880			1–3
	1835–93			MG*	
	Nov 1 1835–June 20 1852	Dec 1 1837–July 28 28 1849		NLI	Pos. 5576
	Mar 24 1861–Dec 29 1880	Jan 28 1862–May 27 1880			
	1835–52	1837–49		PRONI	MIC.1D/19
	1861–81	1862–81			
Inniskeen	See NLI			LDS	0926053
	1845–87			MG*	
	July 3 1837–Oct 27 1862	Apr 7 1839–Nov 26 1850		NLI	Pos. 5575
	July 12 1863–Dec 29 1880				
	1837–81	1839–50		PRONI	MIC.1D/5;
					C.R.2/2
Killanny	Jan 9 1857–Dec 26 1880	Jan 20 1862–Dec 28 1880		NLI	Pos. 5574
	1857–81	1862–82		PRONI	MIC.1D/17

Parish (Diocese)	Baptisms	Marriages	Burials	Location	Reference
Killeevan	1841–2			MG	
	Jan 29 1871–Dec 1880	Jan 29 1871–Aug 25 1880		NLI	Pos. 5577
	1871–81	1871–81		PRONI	MIC.1D/20
Kilskeery	See NLI			LDS	0926054 item 1–4
	Oct 3 1840–June 15 1862	Aug 30 1840–May 27 1862		NLI	Pos. 5568
	June 19 1862–Feb 18 1870	July 17 1862–Feb 27 1870			
	Jan 27 1870–Dec 24 1880	Feb 3 1870–Mar 1 1880			
	1840–81	1840–82		PRONI	MIC.1D/11
Maghaire Rois	See NLI			LDS	0926055 item 1–2
	1858–80			MG*	
	Jan 6 1858–Apr 19 1870	Feb 21 1838–Jan 31 1844		NLI	Pos. 5578
	Jan 1 1878–Dec 31 1880	Jan 17 1858–Apr 19 1870			
	1858–70	1838–44		PRONI	MIC.1D/21
	1878–80	1858–81			
Magheracloone	May 2 1836–Nov 8 1863	Oct 9 1826–Mar 8 1859		NLI	Pos. 5574
	Jan 16 1865–Dec 10 1880	Apr 9 1866–Nov 21 1880			
	1836–63	1826–59		PRONI	MIC.1D/17;
	1865–81	1866–80			C.R.2/17
Monaghan	1847–1900			MG*	
	Nov 6 1835–Dec 21 1847	Feb 6 1827–June 7 1850		NLI	Pos. 5570
	June 12 1849–Apr 21 1850 (indexed)	Jan 12 1857–Nov 16 1880			
	Jan 4 1857–May 27 1875				
	May 29 1875–Dec 26 1880				
	1835–47			PRONI	MIC.1D/13;
	1849–81 (indexed)	1827–80			C.R.2/6
Muckno	See NLI			LDS	0979707 item 4–6
	Nov 1 1835–Apr 15 1862	Oct 31 1835–Apr 8 1862		NLI	Pos. 5576;
	Apr 21 1862–Jan 12 1869	Apr 28 1862–Oct 20 1868			marriages
	Dec 4 1868–Dec 31 1880	Nov 15 1868–Dec 9 1880			from 1868 on Pos. 5577
	1835–81	1835–81		PRONI	MIC.1D/19–20
Tullycorbet	1862–75	1862–76		MG	
	1876–1900 (Ballybay)	May 27 1862–June 15 1876		NLI	Pos. 5573
	Apr 1862–July 22 1876 (indexed)				
	July 3 1876–Dec 13 1880				
	1862–81	1862–76		PRONI	MIC.1D/16
Tydavnet	1835–80			MG*	
	Nov 1 1835–Dec 12 1862	Apr 18 1825–Oct 19 1865		NLI	Pos. 5573;
	Jan 1 1863–Nov 24 1871	Jan 9 1876–Nov 26 1880			baptism from 1871,
	Nov 22 1871–Dec 31 1880				marriages from 1876 on Pos. 5574
	1835–81	1825–65		PRONI	MIC.1D/2,
		1876–81			16–17

Parish (Diocese)	Baptisms	Marriages	Burials	Location	Reference
Tyholland	1835–80			MG	
	May 1 1835–Jan 12 1851	Jan 1 1827–July 26 1851	Jan 19 1851–Dec 19 1863	NLI	Pos. 5572
	Jan 19 1851–Dec 19 1863	Jan 19 1851–Dec 19 1863			
	Dec 18 1865–Dec 14 1876	Feb 1 1866–Nov 28 1872			
	Dec 12 1877–Dec 27 1880	Dec 3 1877–Nov 5 1880			
	1835–81	1827–82		PRONI	MIC.1D/3, 15

Offaly (King's County)

All Irish Midlands Ancestry (IMA) transcripts are online at <www.rootsireland.ie>. NLI microfilms marked with an asterisk (*) are online at <www.ancestry.com>.

52

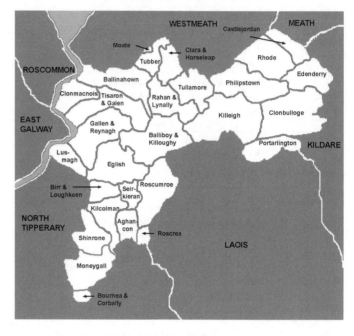

Parish (Diocese)	Baptisms	Marriages	Burials	Location	Reference
Aghancon (Killaloe)	1830–99	1830–99		IMA	
	Nov 5 1870–Dec 14 1880	Jan 27 1870–Oct 1 1880		NLI	Pos. 2479
Balliboy and Killoughy (Meath)	1821–99	1821–99	1828–81	IMA	
	See NLI			LDS	0926171
	Jan 5 1821–Dec 30 1833	June 29 1821–Dec 5 1833	Feb 1 1826–Dec 30 1880	NLI	Pos. 4175
	Jan 5 1834–Dec 27 1880	Jan 10 1834–Oct 28 1880			
Ballinahown (Ardagh and Clonmacnois)	1821–99	1822–1900	1821–46	IMA	
	1821–1905 (some gaps)	1823–1974	1821–8	LDS	1279227 item 1–6
			1829–45		
			1854–81		
			1882–94		
	Aug 12 1821–Dec 21 1824	Jan 7 1830–Aug 29 1845	Nov 21 1829–Sept 9 1845	NLI	Pos. 4235
	Feb 12 1826–Feb 25 1839	Oct 15 1854–Dec 26 1880	Sept 2 1854–Dec 26 1880		
	Feb 6 1841–Sept 21 1845				
	July 23 1854–Dec 24 1880				
Birr and Loughkeen (Killaloe)	1838–1913	1838–1905	1869–1970	IMA	
	See NLI			LDS	0926091
	May 5 1838–Jan 6 1847	May 5 1838–Nov 28 1846		NLI	Pos. 2478
	Jan 3 1847–Dec 30 1880	Jan 7 1847–Nov 27 1880			
Bournea and Corbally	See North Tipperary				

Parish (Diocese)	Baptisms	Marriages	Burials	Location	Reference
Castlejordan (Meath)	1826–1900	1826–70	1919–93	DSHGC	
	Nov 5 1826–Aug 28 1870	Nov 9 1826–Aug 21 1870	Nov 15 1848–July 31 1849	NLI	Pos. 4173*
	Sept 4 1870–Dec 29 1880	Sept 5 1870–Oct 8 1880			
Clara and Horseleap	See Westmeath				
Clonbulloge (Kildare	1819–99	1808–1899		IMA	
and Leighlin)	Nov 7 1819–June 14 1869	Jan 2 1808–June 14 1869		NLI	Pos. 4202
	June 20 1869–Dec 26 1880	July 1 1869–Oct 30 1880			
Clonmacnois	1826–1908	1826–88		IMA	
(Ardagh and	1826–1908	1826–1908	1892–1906	LDS	1279227 item
Clonmacnois)					7, 8
	Apr 19 1826–Feb 28 1846	Apr 24 1826–Dec 14 1840	Jan 2 1841–Feb 18 1842	NLI	Pos. 4243
	Jan 6 1841–July 31 1842	Feb 2 1841–Feb 8 1842	Feb 3 1848–Sept 29 1880		
	Feb 1 1848–Dec 21 1880	Feb 21 1848–Nov 25 1880			
	Jan 16 1876–Nov 14 1880	Feb 17 1876–Sept 12 1880			
Edenderry (Kildare	1820–99	1820–99	1935–81	IMA	
and Leighlin)	Jan 2 1820–Dec 29 1838	Jan 9 1820–Nov 20 1837		NLI	Pos. 4207
	Jan 6 1839–Jan 2 1880	Sept 17 1838–Jan 7 1880			
Eglish (Meath)	1809–1899	1820–99	1807–1899	IMA	
	Jan 1 1809–Dec 23 1810	Feb 21 1819–Mar 3 1829	Feb 26 1819–Apr 18 1829	NLI	Pos. 4175
	Feb 13 1819–May 16 1852	June 4 1829–Nov 27 1880	June 15 1837–May 12 1846		
	May 23 1852–Dec 18 1880		Jan 8 1848–Mar 16 1849		
			Jan 1851		
Gallen and Reynagh	1811–99	1797–1899	1803–1832	IMA	
(Ardagh and	1816–1973	1797–1983	1893–1980	LDS	1279226 item
Clonmacnois)					10–18
	Nov 16 1811–Sept 4 1812	Oct 16 1797–July 23 1837	Nov 15 1803–Nov 28 1804	NLI	Pos. 4242*
	Sept 28 1816–July 6 1817	Oct 13 1816–Apr 20 1822	Nov 13 1819–Apr 30 1820		
	Oct 2 1816–Mar 29 1822	Aug 25 1822–June 15 1825	Aug 25 1822–June 15 1825		
	July 13 1818–Sept 12 1827	Feb 18 1838–Dec 31 1880	Jan 2 1827–Sept 7 1827		
	Aug 25 1822–June 15 1825		Apr 24 1829–Sept 27 1831		
	Mar 6 1829–Oct 2 1837				
	Feb 18 1838–Dec 31 1880		1807, 1809, 1811 (a few		
			deaths recorded)		
Kilcolman (Killaloe)	1830–99	1830–99		IMA	
	See NLI			LDS	0979695 item 2
	Mar 7 1830–Nov 27 1869	Apr 29 1830–Feb 24 1868		NLI	Pos. 2479
Killeigh (Kildare	1844–99	1844–99		IMA	
and Leighlin)	Apr 23 1844–Dec 11 1875	1859–July 30 1875		NLI	Pos. 4203
	Jan 1 1876–Nov 19 1880	Feb 17 1876–Nov 19 1880			
Lusmagh (Clonfert)	1833–99	1832–99	1837–82	IMA	
	1833–1925	1832–1925	1833–1925	LDS	1279215 item
					28–30
	Dec 5 1827–May 3 1829	July 8 1832–Nov 25 1880	Jan 5 1837–Dec 15 1880	NLI	Pos. 2433
	Apr 22 1833–Dec 29 1880				
Moate	See Westmeath				
Moneygall (Killaloe)	1820–1911	1820–99		IMA	
	See NLI			LDS	0979695 item 1
	Jan 8 1820–Aug 21 1873	Jan 24 1820–June 14 1873		NLI	Pos. 2479
	1820–1900	1820–1900		NTGC	

Parish (Diocese)	Baptisms	Marriages	Burials	Location	Reference
Philipstown (Kildare	1795–1899	1820–1899	1880–1919	IMA	
and Leighlin)	Aug 12 1795–Sept 23 1798	Jan 7 1820–May 3 1855		NLI	Pos. 4202
	Jan 6 1820–Feb 18 1855	Jan 27 1851–Dec 2 1866			
	Nov 4 1850–Dec 30 1866	Feb 1 1867–Nov 24 1880			
	Jan 1 1867–Dec 26 1880				
Portarlington	1820–99	1820–99	1904–1960	IMA	
(Kildare and Leighlin)	Jan 1 1820–Nov 22 1846	Nov 24 1822–July 16 1845		NLI	Pos. 4205
	(indexed)	July 21 1845–June 21 1876			
	Nov 25 1846–Feb 27 1876	Jan 14 1876–Nov 27 1880			
	(indexed)				
	Mar 5 1876–Dec 26 1880				
	(indexed)				
Rahan and Lynally	1810–99	1810–99		IMA	
(Meath)	July 6 1810–Apr 28 1816	July 31 1810–Feb 28 1816		NLI	Pos. 4174
	Jan 2 1822–Dec 27 1835	Jan 9 1822–Jan 29 1880			
	Jan 1 1836–Mar 31 1845				
	Apr 5 1845–Feb 7 1880				
Rhode (Kildare and	1829–99	1829–99		IMA	
Leighlin)	Jan 29 1829–June 16 1879	Aug 4 1829–Feb 23 1878		NLI	Pos. 4205
	June 22 1879–Dec 14 1880	(gaps)			
	Jan 3 1866–Dec 14 1880				
Roscrea (Killaloe)	See North Tipperary				
Roscumroe (Killaloe)	1833–99	1833–99	1936–83	IMA	
	See NLI			LDS	0979695 item 4–5
	Feb 13 1833–Dec 21 1880	Jan 9 1833–Nov 1 1871		NLI	Pos. 2479
		Jan 28 1872–June 26 1880			
Seirkieran Ossory	1830–1901	1830–99	1877–1902	IMA	
	1870–80	1870–80		LDS	0979695 item 3
	Apr 11 1830–May 3 1857	July 4 1830–June 14 1857		NLI	Pos. 5013
	June 19 1857–Dec 17 1880	July 9 1857–Nov 27 1880			
Shinrone (Killaloe)	1842–99	1842–99		IMA	
	Feb 21 1842–Feb 7 1876	Apr 10 1842–Feb 7 1876		NLI	Pos. 2480
	Jan 4 1875–Dec 13 1880				
	(most of 1875 missing)				
Tisaron and Galen	1819–99	1819–99	1821–1960	IMA	
(Ardagh and	1819–1984	1819–33	1821–77	LDS	1279226 item
Clonmacnois)		1877–1984	1883–9		4–9
			1929–84		
	Oct 17 1819–July 24 1865	Nov 26 1819–Nov 26 1833	Dec 19 1821–Aug 9 1835	NLI	Pos. 4243
	June 21 1876–Apr 28 1877		Mar 6 1855–Jan 24 1876		
Tubber	See Westmeath				
Tullamore (Meath)	1819–1899	1801–1899	1893–1963	IMA	
	See NLI			LDS	0926186
	June 14 1809–Feb 20 1810	Apr 26 1801–Sept 29 1807		NLI	Pos. 4174
	Nov 1 1820–Feb 24 1822	Apr 9–10 1809			
	Feb 1 1827–Jan 31 1836	Nov 2 1820–Feb 19 1822			
	Mar 1 1836–Dec 26 1880	Feb 1 1827–Dec 29 1880			

Roscommon

All parishes are in the diocese of Elphin, except as noted. Most but not all Roscommon Heritage and Genealogy Centre (RHGC) transcripts listed below are online at <*www.rootsireland.ie*>.

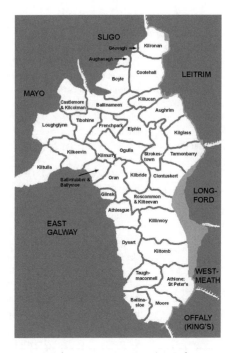

Parish (Diocese)	Baptisms	Marriages	Burials	Location	Reference
Athleague	Jan 4 1808–May 10 1828	June 23 1808–Feb 11 1834	Jan 3 1807–1837	NLI	Pos. 4613
	Aug 20 1834–Sept 1835	Mar 15 1836–Aug 25 1865			
	Oct 12 1835–July 25 1864	Jan 26 1865–Mar 5 1878			
	Jan 8 1865–Dec 23 1880				
	1808–1900	1808–1900	1808–1837	RHGC	
Athlone: St Peter's	See NLI			LDS	0989750/ Online: Familysearch
	Jan 4 1798–Feb 24 1810	Jan 7 1789–Jan 12 1817	Jan 3 1789–Dec 15 1816	NLI	Pos. 4615, 4616
	Feb 25 1810–Jan 31 1845	Jan 14 1817–Feb 4 1845	Jan 5 1817–May 25 1854		
	Feb 1 1845–Sept 30 1864	Mar 28 1845–Sept 18 1864	July 16 1845–Oct 26 1880		
	Oct 2 1864–Aug 12 1877	Oct 3 1864–Nov 22 1880			
	Aug 12 1877–Dec 31 1880				
	1789?–1900	1789–1900	1789–1880	RHGC	
Aughrim	Aug 13 1816–Dec 23 1837	Aug 21 1816–Dec 9 1837		NLI	Pos. 4610, 4611
	Feb 27 1825–Feb 2 1860	Mar 18 1825–Nov 19 1859			
	Jan 18 1865–Dec 27 1880	Jan 9 1865–Sept 13 1880			
	Jan 21 1865–Dec 31 1880	Feb 12 1865–Oct 4 1880			
	(Kilmore and Clonaff)	(Kilmore)			
	1816–1900	1816–1900		RHGC	
Ballinameen	See NLI			LDS	0989738 item 1–3
	Nov 20 1859–July 22 1871	Feb 5 1860–Oct 31 1880		NLI	Pos. 4605
	Sept 3 1871–Dec 14 1880				
	1859–1900	1860–1900		RHGC	

Parish (Diocese)	Baptisms	Marriages	Burials	Location	Reference
Ballinasloe (Clonfert)	1820–1900	1820–1900	1825–30	EGFHS	
	1820–1900	1853–1902		LDS	1279217 item 9–17
	Sept 23 1820–July 27 1832	Sept 23 1820–July 27 1832	Sept 23 1820–July 27 1832	NLI	Pos. 2432
	July 19 1832–Feb 21 1841	July 19 1832–Feb 21 1841	July 19 1832–Feb 21 1841		
	June 7 1841–June 14 1847				
	July 6 1847–May 30 1862				
	June 6 1862–Dec 31 1880				
Ballintubber and Balllymoe	Dec 21 1831–Dec 26 1863 (poor condition)	Aug 7 1831–Jan 17 1864		NLI	Pos. 4618
		Feb 15 1840–Oct 14 1850			
	Feb 18 1840–Nov 12 1865	Apr 23 1855–Sept 16 1862			
	Feb 26 1864–Nov 25 1880	Jan 12 1863–Aug 5 1880			
	1831–1900	1831–1900		RHGC	
Boyle	See NLI			LDS	0989743/ Familysearch
	Feb 13 1793–May 13 1796	Nov 13 1792–Jan 23 1797	July 2 1848–Sept 18 1964	NLI	Pos. 4607, 4608
	Mar 13 1803–Mar 1806	July 1803–June 1804			
	Jan 4–Mar 9 1811	July 4 1808–Dec 30 1827			
	Apr 18 1814–Sept 30 1827	Sept 24 1828–June 16 1848			
	Sept 2 1827–June 27 1848	July 3 1848–June 30 1864			
	July 1 1848–Sept 18 1864	Oct 6 1864–Set 25 1880			
	Sept 30 1864–Dec 29 1880				
	1793–1900	1792–1900	1848–64	RHGC	
Castlemore and Kilcolman	See Mayo				
Clontuskert	See NLI	See NLI		LDS	0989747
	Jan 3 1865–Nov 7 1880	Feb 9 1865–Feb 22 1879		NLI	Pos. 4612
	Aug 23 1874–Nov 16 1878 (Kilgefin)	Jan 18 1875–Feb 6 1879			
	1865–1900	1865–1900		RHGC	
Cootehall	See NLI			LDS	0989746/ Familysearch?
	Mar 26 1843–Mar 25 1861	Apr 6 1843–June 3 1860		NLI	Pos. 4612
	Apr 7 1861–Aug 4 1869	Apr 14 1861–Sept 23 1880			
	Apr 29 1869–Dec 24 1880				
	1843–1900	1843–1900		RHGC	
Dysart	1850–1900	1862–1900	1862–1900	EGFHS	
	See NLI			LDS	0989755/ Familysearch?
	July 6 1850–Oct 26 1862	Dec 23 1862–Aug 31 1880		NLI	Pos. 4616
	Dec 7 1862–Dec 30 1880	Feb 2 1865–July 9 1870			
	Jan 6 1865–Dec 18 1871	(Tisara)			
	1850–1900	1862–1900	1862–65	RHGC	
Elphin	June 11 1807–Dec 23 1808	May 6 1807–Sept 11 1808		NLI	Pos. 4609, 4610
	Dec 10 1808–Feb 16 1810	Dec 10 1808–Dec 21 1824			
	Jan 1 1809–July 21 1815	May 3 1824–Oct 4 1830			
	May 23 1810–Apr 29 1818	Mar 31 1864–Dec 20 1880			
	Aug 1 1818–Sept 26 1825				
	Mar 9 1825–Oct 13 1843				
	Nov 12 1841–July 28 1860				
	Jan 13 1866–Nov 19 1880				
	1808–1900	1807–1900	1807–1838	RHGC	

Parish (Diocese)	Baptisms	Marriages	Burials	Location	Reference
Frenchpark	Jan 7 1865–Dec 27 1880			NLI	Pos. 4618
	1865–1900	1865–1900		RHGC	
Kilglass (Elphin)	Jan 7 1865–Dec 27 1880			NLI	Pos. 4618
	1865–1900	1865–1900		RHGC	
Glinsk	1836–1900	1836–1900		EGFHS	
	Sept 5 1836–Jan 28 1846	Nov 1 1836–Apr 24 1865	Sept 14 1836–Sept 20 1839	NLI	Pos. 4620
	Nov 2 1846 (?)–June 22 1848	July 6 1865–Nov 1 1880			
	Mar 15 1849–Sept 23 1866				
	Oct 6 1866–Dec 26 1880				
	1836–1900	1836–1900	1836–90	RHGC	
Kilbride	July 12 1835–Sept 6 1849	Sept 10 1838–Oct 15 1846		LDS	0989749 item 1–2
	Apr 12 1868–Dec 12 1880				
	July 12 1835–Sept 6 1849	Sept 10 1838–Oct 15 1846		NLI	Pos. 4614
	Apr 12 1868–Dec 12 1880				
	1835–1900	1838–1900		RHGC	
Kilglass	Oct 20 1865–Dec 24 1880			NLI	Pos. 4611
	pre-1850 (reconstructed)			Online	<www.pure golduk.com/ bren>
	1865–1900	1865–1900		RHGC	
Kilkeevin	Nov 15 1804–May 15 1809	Nov 17 1804–July 31 1809	Feb 20 1805–May 6 1809	NLI	Pos. 4619
	Jan 17 1816–Aug 31 1819	Jan 15 1816–Apr 27 1820	Jan 26 1816–Oct 4 1819		
	Jan 6 1826–Jan 23 1840	Oct 28 1838–Dec 29 1839	Jan 1 1852–1855		
	Jan 4 1840–Jan 28 1860	May 20 1839–Jan 23 1860			
	Jan 1 1860–Dec 31 1864	Jan 11 1860–Nov 15 1864			
	Jan 1 1865–Jan 27 1878				
	Jan 1878–Dec 27 1880				
	1804–1900	1804–1900	1805–1855	RHGC	
Killinvoy	See NLI			LDS	0989752/ Familysearch
	July 26 1841–July 7 1859	July 17 1841–Feb 15 1858	1854–80	NLI	Pos. 4617
	Jan 8–Feb 19 1860	Nov 9 1854–Sept 24 1864			
	May 25 1854–Sept 25 1864	Nov 8 1864–Nov 7 1880			
	Oct 1 1864–Dec 20 1880				
	1841–1900	1841–1900	1854–81	RHGC	
Killucan	See NLI			LDS	0989741/ Familysearch
	June 24 1811–June 27 1833	Apr 7 1825–June 17 1833	Oct 11 1820–Mar 4 1826	NLI	Pos. 4606
	July 4 1833–June 24 1850	July 11 1833–Dec 5 1850			
	June 24 1850–Nov 27 1864	Jan 16 1851–Oct 9 1864			
	Dec 4 1864–Dec 26 1880	Nov 24 1864–Nov 13 1880			
	1811–1900	1825–1900	1820–26	RHGC	
Kilmurry	Jan 15 1865–Sept 7 1880	Feb 8 1869–Feb 9 1880 (?)		NLI	Pos. 4611
	1865–1900	1865–1900		RHGC	
Kilronan (Ardagh and Clonmacnois)	1824–9	1823–9	1835–72	LDS	1279224 item 7–12/Family search
	1835–1976	1835–72			
		1877–1984			
	Jan 1 1824–July 27 1829	Oct 24 1823–June 10 1829	Jan 16 1835–July 18 1872	NLI	Pos. 4242
	Jan 1 1835–Mar 25 1876	Jan 7 1835–Sept 16 1872			
	1824–1900	1823–1900	1835–72	RHGC	

Parish (Diocese)	Baptisms	Marriages	Burials	Location	Reference
Kiltomb	See NLI			LDS	0989751 item 3–5
	Oct 11 1835–May 26 1845	Oct 20 1835–July 2 184	June 24 1837–Mar 31 1845	NLI	Pos. 4617
	Apr 1 1848–Dec 26 1864	Jan 16 1848–Dec 27 1864	Jan 15 1857–May 17 1862		
		Jan 9 1865–Nov 19 1880	Jan 6–Nov 23 1865		
	1835–1900	1835–1900	1837–65	RHGC	
Kiltulla	See NLI			LDS	0926226
	Sept 11 1839–Oct 27 1860	Aug 25 1839–Oct 7 1860		NLI	Pos. 4212
	Nov 11 1860–Nov 21 1880	Nov 19 1860–Apr 16 1874			
		Jan 3 1877–Dec 26 1880			
	1839–1900	1839–1900		RHGC	
Loughglynn	See NLI			LDS	0989753/ Familysearch
	Mar 10 1817–Nov 20 1826	Apr 10 1817–Mar 24 1827	Jan 14 1850–June 18 1854	NLI	Pos. 4617, 4618
	Dec 15 1829–July 30 1835	Feb 10 1836–Apr 24 1840	1868–80		
	July 6 1835–Nov 24 1840	Dec 23 1849–Feb 16 1858			
	Dec 17 1849–Apr 17 1863	Jan 11 1865–Oct 18 1880			
	Jan 1 1865–Mar 10 1878	Jan 30 1865–May 5 1867			
	Jan 10 1865–May 19 1867 (Lisacul and Erritt)				
	Feb 10 1878–Dec 19 1880 (Lisacul and Erritt)				
	1817–1900	1817–1900	1850–80	RHGC	
Moore	1876–1938	1877–1907		LDS	1279214 item 9–10
	Sept 17 1876–Dec 26 1880	Jan 22 1877–Nov 19 1880		NLI	Pos. 4220
	1872–1900	1872–1900		RHGC	
Ogulla	Jan 7 1865–Dec 26 1880	Jan 28 1864–May 6 1880		NLI	Pos. 4611
	1865–1900	1864–1900		RHGC	
Oran	No registers microfilmed			NLI	
	1864–1900	1864–1900		RHGC	
Roscommon and Kilteevan	See NLI			LDS	0989748/ Familysearch
	Oct 1 1837–Sept 22 1864	Jan 10 1820–Aug 27 1864		NLI	Pos. 4614
	Mar 26 1864–Dec 30 1880				
	1837–1900	1820–1900	1821–4	RHGC	
Strokestown	As NLI			LDS	0989745/ Familysearch
	Oct 1830–May 1835	Oct 24 1830–June 15 1835		NLI	Pos. 4608, 4609
	July 1835–Jan 1846	June 17 1833–Oct 30 1864			
	Jan 1831–Feb 1833 (Lisonuffy and Cloonfinlough)	Oct 18 1830–May 30 1833 (Lisonuffy and Cloonfinlough)			
	June 1842–Dec 1842	July 6 1835–Sept 27 1849 (Lisonuffy and Cloonfinlough)			
	Dec 1851–Nov 1852	Jan 9 1965–Nov 11 1880			
	Nov 1853–Dec 1864				
	May 1857–Nov 1862				
	Apr 1865–Nov 1866				
	Jan 1865–Dec 1880				
	1830–1900	1830–1900		RHGC	

Parish (Diocese)	Baptisms	Marriages	Burials	Location	Reference
Tarmonbarry	Jan 22 1865–Dec 23 1880 Jan 6 1865–Dec 19 1880 (Lisonuffy and Bumlin)	Jan 26 1865–Dec 31 1880		NLI	Pos. 4611
	1865–1900	1865–1900		RHGC	
Taughmaconnell	1842–1900	1863–1900		EGFHS	
(Clonfert)	July 31 1842–Dec 15 1880	Jan 13 1863–Aug 19 1880		LDS	0926061
	July 31 1842–Dec 15 1880	Jan 13 1863–Aug 19 1880		NLI	Pos. 2432
	1842–1900	1842 [sic]–1900		RHGC	
Tibohine	Jan 1 1833–Sept 24 1864	Jan 7 1833–June 11 1864		NLI	Pos. 6955 to
	May 5 1875–Dec 18 1880	Feb 7 1865–Apr 25 1880			1864. Pos. 4619 thereafter
	1833–1900	1833–1900		RHGC	
	See NLI			Online	Familysearch

Sligo

All Sligo Heritage and Genealogy Society (SHGS) transcripts are online at <*www.roots ireland.ie*>.

Parish (Diocese)	Baptisms	Marriages	Burials	Location	Reference
Achonry (Achonry)	1878–1908	1864–1942		LDS	1279231 item 20–21
	1878–Oct 8 1880	Aug 3 1865–Aug 16 1880		NLI	Pos. 4227
	1878–99	1865–1905		SHGS	
Ahamlish (Elphin)	Nov 27 1796–May 28 1829	Dec 3 1796–Dec 27 1830	Nov 26 1796–Oct 1822	NLI	Pos. 4602
	Jan 4 1831–Nov 29 1835	Jan 22 1831–Sept 22 1857	Jan 13 1827–Sept 24 1830		
	Sept 9 1836–Nov 25 1845	Nov 2 1857–Dec 29 1863	Jan 3 1831–July 24 1845		
	Jan 2 1846–Dec 31 1863	Jan 18 1864–June 3 1880			
	Jan 8 1864–Mar 19 1879				
	1796–1900	1796–1899	1796–1845	SHGS	

Parish (Diocese)	Baptisms	Marriages	Burials	Location	Reference
Aughanagh (Elphin)	As NLI	As NLI	As NLI	LDS	0989739/ 0989740/ Familysearch
	May 9 1803–Jan 19 1808 (trans.)	Jan 11 1800–June 15 1802	Mar 3 1800–Mar 12 1802	NLI	Pos. 4606
	Oct 13 1816–Dec 22 1818 (trans.)	Apr 7 1829–Mar 8 1850	July 12–Sept 16 1816		
	Jan 3 1821–Sept 20 1825 (trans.)	Nov 1858–Feb 27 1863	Nov 30 1822–Sept 20 1846		
	Nov 1803–Nov 1807	Nov 20 1864–Oct 10 1880	Nov 10 1858–Oct 17 1874		
	1817–Nov 1818				
	Jan 1821–1841				
	Jan 1844–1846				
	1848–52				
	1856–64				
	1864–80				
	1803–1900			RHGC	
	1803–1899	1841–99		SHGS	
Ballysodare and Kilvarnet (Achonry)	1842–97	1858–1933		LDS	1279230 item 10–13
	Apr 25 1842–Aug 14 1853	Jan 14 1858–Dec 5 1880		NLI	Pos. 4227
	Feb 28 1858–Dec 26 1880				
	1842–99	1858–99		SHGS	
Castleconnor (Killala)	1835–80	1835–80	1855–80	LDS	1279204 item 1–2
	Jan 14 1855–Dec 26 1880	Oct 26 1854–Nov 2 1880		NLI	Pos. 4230
	1835–80	1836–76	1854–80	Online	Genweb, Sligo
	1835–1905	1835–99	1847–96	SHGS	
Castlemore and Kilcolman	See Mayo				
Cloonacool (Achonry)	1859–1908	1859–1921		LDS	1279230/1 item 18/1–2
	Oct 27 1859–Nov 9 1880	Oct 9 1859–Nov 9 1880		NLI	Pos. 4227
	1859–99	1859–1914		SHGS	
Curry (Achonry)	1867–1923	1867–1903		LDS	1279231 item 14–15
	Oct 6 1867–Dec 25 1880	Nov 3 1867–Dec 15 1880		NLI	Pos. 4227
	1867–1906	1867–99		SHGS	
Dromard and Skreen (Killala)	1817–92	1835–80	1853–80	LDS	1279204 item 6–11; 0926025
	Jan 1 1823–Aug 9 1859	Nov 13 1817–Feb 16 1860	Sept 25 1825–Feb 29 1828	NLI	Pos. 4229
	July 17 1848–Sept 29 1877	Feb 12 1878–Dec 11 1880			
	Sept 27 1877–Dec 31 1880	July 12 1848–Aug 18 1869			
	1823–68 (?)	1818–59 (?)		Online	<www.pure golduk.com/ bren>
	1823–92	1817–99	1825–43	SHGS	
Drumcliff (Elphin)	See NLI			LDS	0989735 item 1–3
	May 2 1841–Dec 31 1864 (transcript)	Jan 15 1865–Nov 28 1880		NLI	Pos. 4603
	Jan 1 1865–May 2 1880				
	1841–99	1865–99		SHGS	

Parish (Diocese)	Baptisms	Marriages	Burials	Location	Reference
Drumrat (Achonry)	Nov 12 1843–June 24 1847	Jan 12 1842–May 5 1851		NLI	Pos. 4228
	Sept 25 1842–Mar 6 1855	Dec 1872–May 15 1881			
	Jan 10 1874–July 3 1880				
	1843–1900	1833–1890		SHGS	
Easkey (Killala)	June 1864–Dec 28 1880			NLI	Pos. 4230
	1864–99			Online	<*www.pure goldduk.com/ bren*>
	1864–99	1898–1939		SHGS	
Emlefad and	July 4 1856–Oct 7 1877	Aug 12 1824–Jan 7 1866		NLI	Pos. 4228
Kilmorgan (Achonry)	Nov 27 1874–Dec 26 1880	Feb 11 1866–Feb 22 1875			
	1856–99	1824–99		SHGS	
Geevagh (Elphin)	Feb 25 1873–May 20 1880	Jan 13 1851–Nov 25 1880		NLI	Pos. 4607
	1873–80	1851–80		LDS	989742/ Familysearch
	1851–99	1851–99		SHGS	
Glenade	See Leitrim				
Kilfree and Killaraght	May 4 1873–Nov 27 1880	Feb 19 1844–Dec 11 1868		NLI	Pos. 4227
(Achonry)	May 22 1868–Nov 20 1880				
	1873–99	1844–99		SHGS	
Kilglass (Killala)	Oct 17 1825–July 7 1867	Nov 2 1825–May 30 1867	Nov 2 1825–June 15 1867	NLI	Pos. 4229
	Aug 15 1867–Dec 28 1880	Nov 21 1867–Dec 22 1880			
	1825–76?	1826–67	Mar 1825–June 1867	Online	<*www.pure goldduk.com/ bren*>
	1825–1900	1825–1900	1825–67	SHGS	
Killenummery	See Leitrim				
Killoran (Achonry)	Apr 19 1878–Dec 24 1880	Apr 22 1846–Nov 11 1880		NLI	Pos. 4228
	1878–81	1846–1912		SHGS	
Kilmactigue	Apr 8 1845–Dec 27 1856	Jan 23 1848–Sept 4 1880		NLI	Pos. 4226
(Achonry)	Jan 5 1857–June 18 1864				
	July 1 1864–July 24 1880				
	1845–99	1848–99		SHGS	
Kilmoremoy (Killala)	1823–52	1823–42	1823–42	LDS	1279205 item
	1850–67	1849–68			15–16; 1279205,
	1868–79				3
	1823–1923	1823–39	1823–1931	MNFHRC	
	May 15 1823–Oct 14 1836	May 15 1823–Oct 4 1842	Apr 29 1823–Aug 12 1836	NLI	Pos. 4231
	May 9 1849–July 16 1849	Oct 22 1850–Feb 4 1868	Sept 12 1840–May 3 1844		
	July 23 1851–Sept 8 1867	Feb 2 1868–Dec 31 1880			
	Feb 2 1868–Dec 31 1880				
Kilshalvey (Achonry)	1840–1908	1833–1930 (gaps)		LDS	1279233 item 10–11; 09260018
	Jan 3 1842–Dec 22 1877	Apr 30 1833–Apr 18 1876		NLI	Pos. 4228
	Mar 31 1860–Aug 12 1877				
	1842–99	1840–89		SHGS	
Kinlough (Kilmore)	1835–1900		1867–1900	Leitrim GC	
		1840–54			
		1856–99			
	July 12 1835–Mar 1860	Nov 26 1840–Dec 16 1880		NLI	Pos. 5344
	Apr 8 1860–Dec 24 1880				
	1835–81	1840–81		PRONI	MIC.1D/77

Parish (Diocese)	Baptisms	Marriages	Burials	Location	Reference
Rossinver (Kilmore)	1851–1900	1844–69		Leitrim GC	
		1875–1900			
	Aug 17 1851–Jan 29 1875 (many gaps)	Aug 28 1844–Sept 8 1870		NLI	Pos. 5350
	1851–75 (very poor condition)	1844–70 (very poor condition)		PRONI	MIC.1D/83
Sligo: St John's (Elphin)	See NLI			LDS	0989736 item 1–4
	Oct 3 1858–Feb 6 1854	Oct 7 1858–Dec 21 1880		NLI	Pos. 4615, 4616
	Feb 7 1864–May 24 1870				
	June 23 1870–Apr 1 1877				
	1831–99	1831–99	1831–48	SHGS	
Taunagh (Elphin)	See NLI			LDS/Online	0989737/ Familysearch
	Nov 1 1803–Dec 28 1834	Nov 28 1803–Jan 25 1809	June 15 1836–Jan 21 1843	NLI	Pos. 4604
	May 3 1836–Dec 27 1864	May 12 1836–Dec 12 1862			
	Jan 3 1865–Dec 29 1880	Jan 29 1865–Dec 29 1880			
	1803–1900	1803–1899	1836–43	SHGS	
Templeboy (Killala)	1815–38		1815–38	LDS	1279204 item 13, 14
	1875–80				
	Sept 5 1815–Nov 26 1816	Oct 22 1815–Dec 28 1837		NLI	Pos. 4230
	May 30 1826–Nov 13 1838	Jan 20 1868–Oct 23 1880			
	June 21 1868–Dec 26 1880 (Kilmacshalgan)	(Kilmacshalgan)			
	(Kilmacshalgan)	Dec 2 1875–Sept 5 1880			
	Nov 1 1875–Dec 15 1880 (Templeboy)	(Templeboy)			
	1815–99	1815–99	1815–33	SHGS	
	1868–1903	1868–91			
	(Kilmacshalgan)	(Kilmacshalgan)			

Tipperary North

All North Tipperary Genealogy Centre (NTGC) transcripts are online at <www.rootsireland.ie>.

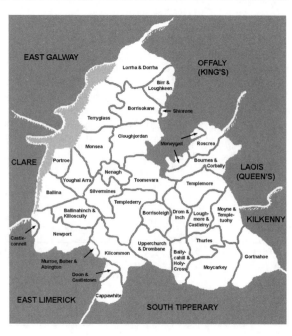

Parish (Diocese)	Baptisms	Marriages	Burials	Location	Reference
Ballina (Cashel and Emly)	Mar 1832–Nov 25 1871	May 1832–Feb 1872		NLI	Pos. 2507
	1832–1903	1832–1903		NTGC	
	1832–1911	1832–72		TFHR	
Ballinahinch and Killoscully (Cashel and Emly)	July 7 1839–Feb 7 1874	Jan 26 1853–Feb 4 1874		NLI	Pos. 2503
	1839–99	1853–99		NTGC	
	1839–99	1853–99		TFHR	
Ballycahill and Holy-Cross (Cashel and Emly)	Jan 2 1835–Oct 16 1878	Jan 1 1835–Dec 29 1878		NLI	Pos. 2493
	1835–1900	1835–1900		TFHR	
Birr and Loughkeen (Killaloe)	See Offaly (King's County)				
Borrisokane (Killaloe)	June 24 1821–Dec 29 1835	July 30 1821–Nov 28 1835		NLI	Pos. 2483
	Jan 1 1836–Sept 3 1844	(many pages illegible)			
	Sept 8 1844–Dec 30 1880	Jan 21 1836–Jan 21 1844			
	Oct 2 1844–Nov 16 1880				
	1821–1911	1821–1911		NTGC	
Borrisoleigh (Cashel and Emly)	Nov 9 1814–Dec 31 1826	Nov 24 1814–Dec 2 1826		NLI	Pos. 2488 to 1826; remainder on Pos. 2489
	Jan 2 1827–July 31 1843	Jan 17 1827–July 31 1843			
	Aug 1 1843–Dec 24 1880	Aug 1843–Nov 15 1880			
	1814–1900	1814–98		TFHR	
Bournea and Corbally (Killaloe)	July 10 1836–Dec 1 1866	June 28 1836–Dec 1 1866		NLI	Pos. 2478
	Jan 27 1867–Dec 30 1880	Jan 27 1867–May 30 1880			
	(1873 missing)	(1873 missing)			
	1836–66	1836–66		NTGC	
Cappawhite (Cashel and Emly)	Oct 5 1815–Jan 29 1846	Feb 13 1804–Jan 25 1846		NLI	Pos. 2497
	Feb 4 1846–Nov 13 1878	Feb 3 1846–Oct 6 1878			
	1815–1900	1803–1900		TFHR	
Castleconnell (Killaloe)	See Limerick				
Cloughjordan (Killaloe)	Aug 25 1833–Nov 3 1858	May 22 1833–Nov 17 1858		NLI	To 1858, Pos. 2481; remainder 2482
	Nov 8 1858–Dec 26 1880	Jan 7 1859–Nov 25 1880			
	1833–1911	1833–1911		NTGC	
Doon and Castletown (Cashel and Emly)	1824–1900	1839–1900		LG	
	Mar 25 1824–Dec 27 1874	Jan 20 1839–Feb 17 1874		NLI	Pos. 2497
	1824–1900	1839–1900		TFHR	
Drom and Inch (Cashel and Emly)	Mar 25 1827–Aug 24 1840	May 5 1827–Oct 16 1880		NLI	Pos. 2491
	Aug 18 1840–Dec 26 1880				
	1809–1900	1807–1880		TFHR	
Gortnahoe (Cashel and Emly)	Sept 10 1805–Dec 20 1830	Oct 3 1805–Nov 27 1830		NLI	Pos. 2493
	Apr 1 1831–Nov 28 1843	Oct 30 1831–Dec 31 1843			
	Jan 28 1844–Aug 27 1878	Jan 15 1844–Oct 7 1880			
	1805–1900	1805–1900		TFHR	
Kilcommon (Cashel and Emly)	Mar 7 1813–Jan 30 1840	June 12 1813–Jan 26 1840		NLI	Pos. 2506 to 1846; remainder on Pos. 2507
	Feb 1 1840–Apr 23 1847	May 30 1840–Apr 28 1847			
	May 1 1847–Dec 31 1880	May 2 1847–Nov 25 1880			
	1813–1900	1813–1900		NTGC	
	1813–95	1813–99		TFHR	

Parish (Diocese)	Baptisms	Marriages	Burials	Location	Reference
Lorrha and Dorrha (Killaloe)	Oct 4 1829–Dec 8 1844	Oct 18 1829–Nov 24 1844		NLI	Pos. 2480
	Jan 1 1845–Sept 4 1880	Jan 20 1845–Nov 27 1880			
	1829–1911	1829–1903		NTGC	
		1908–1911			
Loughmore and Castleiny (Cashel and Emly)	Mar 25 1798–July 28 1840	Apr 16 1798–June 26 1840		NLI	Pos. 2490
	Aug 1 1840–Dec 29 1880	Sept 6 1840–Oct 20 1880			
	1798–1900	1798–1900		NTGC	
	1798–1899	1798–1899		TFHR	
Moneygall (Killaloe)	See Offaly (King's County)				
Monsea (Killaloe)	Feb 1 1834–Dec 9 1865	Feb 2 1834–Nov 13 1870		NLI	Pos. 2481
	1834–1911	1834–1911		NTGC	
Moycarkey (Cashel and Emly)	Oct 13 1793–Nov 19 1796	Oct 6 1793–Oct 16 1796		NLI	Pos. 2488
	Jan 1 1800–Feb 3 1800	Jan 12 1810–Nov 8 1817			
	1801 (scraps)	Jan 17 1830–Feb 3 1822			
	Jan 2 1801–Oct 22 1809	Feb 5 1833–May 2 1854			
	June 7 1810–Nov 22 1810	Sept 13 1854–Oct 26 1880			
	Jan 12 1817–Apr 11 1818				
	Jan 2 1830–Jan 24 1833				
	Feb 4 1833–June 22 1854				
	July 1854–Dec 1880				
	1793–1900	1793–1900		TFHR	
Moyne and Templetuohy (Cashel and Emly)	Jan 4 1809–Mar 28 1848	Feb 1804–Nov 8 1880		NLI	Pos. 2491
	Apr 2 1848–Dec 31 1880				
	1809–1900	1804–1900		TFHR	
Nenagh (Killaloe)	Jan 1 1792–Nov 1809	Jan 8 1792–Feb 26 1797		NLI	Pos. 2483 (B. to 1809); remainder, 2484
	Nov 22 1830–Nov 1842	Sep 27 1818–Sept 28 1840			
	Jan 1845–Apr 19 1858	Sept 30 1840–Mar 4 1851			
	Jan 3 1859–Dec 27 1880	July 7 1850–Nov 27 1880			
	1792–1809	1792–7		NTGC	
	1830–42	1818–1911			
	1845–1911				
Newport (Cashel and Emly)	Oct 18 1795–Sept 30 1809	Apr 20 1795–Feb 8 1809	Mar 24 1795–May 18 1844	NLI	Pos. 2505 to 1847; remainder on Pos. 3506
	July 16 1812–Mar 18 1830	July 26 1812–Nov 28 1829	Feb 28 1813–May 20 1839		
	Feb 28 1813–May 20 1839	Feb 28 1813–May 20 1839			
	Mar 20 1830–May 25 1847	Jan 15 1830–May 23 1847			
	May 27 1847–July 17 1859	June 5 1847–Feb 24 1859			
	Nov 1 1859–Dec 31 1880	Nov 2 1859–Dec 9 1880			
	1795–1809	1795–1809		NTGC	
	1812–1900	1812–1900			
	1795–1900	1795–1900		TFHR	
Portroe (Killaloe)	Nov 11 1849–Dec 13 1880 (transcript)	Nov 18 1849–Nov 14 1880 (transcript)		NLI	Pos. 2483
	1849–1911	1849–1911		NTGC	
Roscrea (Killaloe)	1810–32	1810–32		LDS	0979696 item 1
	Jan 1 1810–June 13 1822	Feb 10 1810–Aug 4 1822		NLI	Pos. 2479 (B. and M. to 1832; remainder 2480
	June 17 1822–July 31 1832	Apr 30 1823–Aug 4 1832			
	Aug 5 1832–Dec 26 1863	Aug 14 1832–Nov 27 1842			
	Jan 1 1864–Dec 24 1880	Jan 20 1842–Nov 13 1880			
	1810–80	1810–80		NTGC	
Shinrone	See Offaly (King's County)				

Parish (Diocese)	Baptisms	Marriages	Burials	Location	Reference
Silvermines (Killaloe)	Nov 29 1840–Dec 16 1880	Jan 28 1841–Oct 2 1880		LDS	0926098
	Nov 29 1840–Dec 16 1880	Jan 28 1841–Oct 2 1880		NLI	Pos. 2481
	1840–1911	1841–1911		NTGC	
Templederry	Sept 13 1840–Feb 13 1850	Feb 11 1839–Feb 12 1850		NLI	Pos. 2482
(Killaloe)	1842–Apr 4 1869	Dec 13 1846 (?)–Feb 9 1869			
	Mar 25 1869–Dec 30 1880				
	1840–1911	1839–1911		NTGC	
Templemore (Cashel	Aug 16 1807–Nov 25 1821	Nov 15 1807–Apr 10 1825		NLI	Pos. 2491
and Emly)	(transcript)	Nov 30 1809–Jan 13 1820			baptism to
	Nov 16 1809–Jan 31 1829	Feb 11 1834–Oct 23 1849			1835, marriages
	Nov 28 1821–Nov 19 1835	Nov 10 1849–Sept 12 1880			to 1825;
	Jan 10 1836–Oct 28 1849				remainder on
	Nov 4 1849–Dec 27 1880				Pos. 2492
	1809–1900	1809–1900		TFHR	
Terryglass (Killaloe)	See NLI			LDS	0926102
	July 1 1827–May 4 1837	Sept 11 1827–Nov 20 1880		NLI	Pos. 2482
	May 6 1837–July 7 1846				
	July 12 1846–Dec 10 1880				
	(transcripts)				
	1827–1911	1827–1911		NTGC	
Thurles (Cashel and	Mar 9 1795–Jan 19 1810	Apr 13 1795–Nov 18 1804		NLI	Pos. 2489 to
Emly)	July 9 1805–Nov 17 1821	Jan 7 1805–Feb 15 1820			1833;
	Aug 10 1822–Dec 29 1833	Aug 13 1822–Dec 30 1833			remainder on
	Jan 1 1834–Apr 28 1870	Jan 13 1834–Feb 14 1870			Pos. 2490
	1795–1924	1795–1924		TFHR	
Toomevara (Killaloe)	See NLI			LDS	0926103
	Mar 10 1831–June 6 1856	Aug 31 1830–Sept 16 1836		NLI	Pos. 2481
	May 25 1861–Dec 27 1880	June 18 1861–Nov 12 1880			
	1831–56	1830–36		NTGC	
	1861–1911	1861–1911			
Upperchurch and	Oct 27 1829–Dec 15 1846	Feb 12 1829–Nov 15 1846		NLI	Pos. 2495
Drombane (Cashel	Dec 8 1846–Feb 29 1876	Jan 24 1847–Feb 29 1876			
and Emly)	1829–1900	1829–1900		TFHR	
Youghal Arra	Oct 26 1828–Dec 31 1846	Oct (?) 1 1820–May 16 1880		NLI	Pos. 2483–4
(Killaloe)	Jan 16 1847–Dec 21 1880				
	1828–1911	1820–1911		NTGC	

Tipperary South

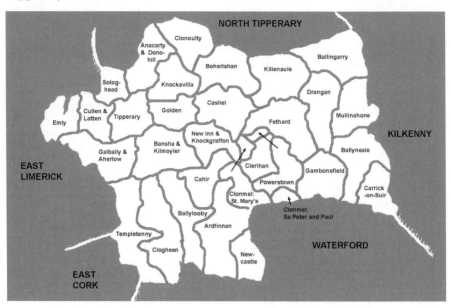

All Brú Boru Heritage Centre (BBHC) transcripts are online at <*www.rootsireland.ie*>.

Parish (Diocese)	Baptisms	Marriages	Burials	Location	Reference
Anacarty and	May 13 1821–Oct 1835	May 13 1821–Feb 11 1839		NLI	Pos. 2496
Donohill (Cashel	Oct 2 1835–Dec 20 1880	Feb 11 1839–Oct 28 1880			
and Emly)	1804–1899	1805–1899		TFHR	
Ardfinnan	1809–1880	1814–22		BBHC	
(Waterford and		1827–80			
Lismore)	Dec 8 1809–Nov 30 1826	Apr 20 1814–Feb 18 1822		NLI	Pos. 2457
	(some pages missing)	Jan 24 1827–June 26 1845			
	Jan 4 1827–June 30 1845	Aug 3 1845–Oct 26 1880			
	July 2 1845–Dec 31 1880				
	1810–1911	1817–1911		WHGC	
Ballylooby	1828–80	1828–80		BBHC	
(Waterford and	May 25 1828–Mar 16 1843	May 25 1828–July 14 1880		NLI	Pos. 2457, 2458
Lismore)	Mar 18 1843–Jan 14 1862				
	Jan 1 1862–Dec 27 1880				
	1828–1911	1828–1911		WHGC	
Ballyneale	1839–80			BBHC	
(Waterford and	Jan 2 1839–Dec 2 1880			NLI	Pos. 2453
Lismore)	1839–1911	1839–1911		WHGC	
Bansha and Kilmoyler	Nov 5 1820–Jan 13 1855	Jan 22 1822–Oct 24 1880		NLI	Pos. 2497
(Cashel and Emly)	(modern transcript)	(modern transcript)			
	Jan 15 1855–Dec 25 1880				
	1820–99	1821–99		TFHR	
Boherlahan (Cashel	Apr 27 1810–Dec 20 1823	May 16 1810–Jan 21 1824		NLI	Pos. 2504
and Emly)	Dec 21 1823–Dec 28 1839	Feb 2 1824–Jan 30 1840			
	Dec 29 1839–May 17 1868	Feb 1 1840–Feb 24 1868			
	1736–40	1736–40		TFHR	
	1810–1900	1810–1900			

Parish (Diocese)	Baptisms	Marriages	Burials	Location	Reference
Cahir (Waterford and Lismore)	1776–93	1776–1880		BBHC	
	1809–1880				
	June 9 1776–Mar 10 1793	July 14 1776–Nov 28 1835		NLI	Pos. 2459,
	Aug 29 1809–Mar 3 1823	Jan 8 1836–Oct 1866			2460
	Mar 9 1823–Dec 28 1831	Nov 3 1864–Nov 20 1880			
	Jan 25 1832–Jan 13 1845				
	Jan 1 1845–Dec 28 1880				
	1776–1911	1776–1911		WHGC	
Carrick-on-Suir (Waterford and Lismore)	1784–1880	1788–1880		BBHC	
	Sept 12 1784–Sept 30 1787	Jan 7 1788–Oct 15 1803		NLI	Pos. 2455,
	Jan 2 1788–Apr 24 1803	Jan 10 1806–Feb 7 1815			2456, 2457
	May 31 1805–Dec 29 1805	Jan 7 1823–Oct 14 1825			
	Jan 3 1806–July 2 1819	Jan 8 1826–Feb 3 1845			
	Jan 3 1823–Oct 10 1826	Jan 30 1845–Nov 13 1880			
	Apr 7 1834–Apr 6 1845				
	Apr 7 1845–Dec 23 1864				
	Dec 28 1869–Dec 26 1880				
	1776–1911	1776–1911		WHGC	
Cashel (Cashel and Emly)	Nov 11 1793–July 19 1831	Jan 5 1793–May 16 1831		NLI	Pos. 2501
	July 24 1831–Dec 23 1839	July 27 1831–Nov 22 1880			
	Aug 21 1839–Mar 31 1866				
	Apr 1 1866–Dec 16 1880				
	1793–1903	1793–1896		TFHR	
Clerihan (Cashel and Emly)	Apr 27 1852–Dec 25 1880	Aug 1 1852–Aug 7 1880		NLI	Pos. 2501
	1852–1900	1852–1900		TFHR	
Clogheen (Waterford and Lismore)	1778–1880	1814–80		BBHC	
	Jan 4 1778–May 18 1789 (some gaps)	July 11 1814–Apr 21 1867		NLI	Pos. 2453, 2454
	Mar 17 1809–June 5 1814				
	June 1 1815–July 20 1851				
	Aug 29 1851–June 4 1868				
	Apr 12 1868–Dec 27 1880				
	1778–1911	1814–1911		WHGC	
Clonmel: SS. Peter and Paul (Waterford and Lismore)	1836–80	1836–80		BBHC	
	Feb 11 1836–Sept 21 1859	Feb 11 1836–Nov 22 1880		NLI	Pos. 2463
	Sept 21 1859–Dec 29 1880				
	1836–1911	1836–1911		WHGC	
Clonmel: St Mary's (Waterford and Lismore)	1790–1880	1797–1880		BBHC	
	Feb 4 1790–Dec 26 1790	Apr 24 1797–Feb 10 1836		NLI	Pos. 2460,
	Mar 1 1793–Dec 31 1793				2461. 2462
	Jan 11 1795–Mar 28 1797				
	Apr 5 1797–Aug 5 1823				
	Aug 5 1823–Dec 28 1842				
	Jan 1 1843–Jan 7 1874				
	Jan 1 1864–Sept 20 1878				
	1790–1911	1798–1911		WHGC	
Clonoulty (Cashel and Emly)	Oct 1 1804–June 7 1809	Oct 7 1804–June 7 1809	June 2 1818–Apr 25 1821	NLI	Pos. 2502 to
	July 1809–June 10 1821	Oct 1 1809–May 27 1821			1855;
	June 20 1821–Jan 1 1837	June 12 1821–Nov 4 1836			remainder on
	Jan 2 1837–Nov 11 1855	Jan 10 1837–Nov 11 1855			Pos. 2503
	Jan 9 1856–Dec 28 1880	Jan 11 1856–Oct 13 1880			
	1804–1900	1804–1898		TFHR	

Parish (Diocese)	Baptisms	Marriages	Burials	Location	Reference
Cullen and Latten	Dec 4 1846–Dec 26 1880	Sept 10 1846–Nov 28 1880		NLI	Pos. 2498
(Cashel and Emly)	1846–99	1846–99		TFHR	
Drangan (Cashel	May 13 1847–Dec 28 1880	Jan 3 1847–June 13 1880		NLI	Pos. 2492 to
and Emly)					1846;
					remainder on
					Pos. 2493
	1811–98	1804–1898		TFHR	
Emly (Cashel and	July 31 1810–May 4 1839	Apr 27 1809–Oct 20 1838		NLI	Pos. 2500
Emly)	May 10 1839–Dec 24 1880	Jan 26 1839–Nov 25 1880			
	1810–99	1809–1898		TFHR	
Fethard (Cashel and	Jan 2 1806–June 30 1828	Jan 12 1806–Apr 27 1820		NLI	Pos. 2504
Emly)	June 1 1828–Feb 27 1835	Jan 18 1824–Jan 9 1838			
	Mar 1 1835–Jan 30 1847	Jan 14 1838–Nov 11 1880			
	Dec 1 1847–Dec 25 1880				
	1806–1900	1806–1900		TFHR	
Galbally and Aherlow	1810–1900	1809–1900		LG	
(Cashel and Emly)	Mar 9 1810–June 23 1828	Oct 1809–Aug 34 1880		NLI	Pos. 2499
	(July 1820–21 missing)	(Mar 1820–July 1821			
	December 1828–June 1871	missing)			
	1810–1900	1809–1900		TFHR	
Gambonsfield and	1840–80	1840–80		BBHC	
Kilcash (Waterford	Jan 1 1840–Feb 1 1856	Jan 11 1840–Jan 11 1856		NLI	Pos. 2452, 2453
and Lismore)	Feb 16 1856–Dec 27 1880	Jan 14 1856–Dec 29 1880			
	1840–1911	1840–1911		WHGC	
Golden (Cashel and	May 20 1833–Dec 14 1880	May 20 1833–Nov 7 1880		NLI	Pos. 2503
Emly)	1833–99	1833–99		TFHR	
Killenaule (Cashel	Dec 25 1742–Jan 6 1802	Aug 20 1812–Sept 19 1827		NLI	Pos. 2494
and Emly)	Jan 2 1814–Aug 10 1827	Oct 14 1827–Nov 29 1851			
	Aug 10 1827–Feb 29 1852	Feb 1 1852–Nov 25 1880			
	Mar 1 1852–Dec 28 1880				
	1742–1900	1741–1900		TFHR	
Knockavilla (Cashel	May 10 1834–Dec 26 1880	July 10 1834–Nov 15 1880		NLI	Pos. 2503
and Emly)	1834–1905	1834–1905		TFHR	
Mullinahone (Cashel	July 3 1809–Apr 27 1835	Feb 26 1810–Mar 3 1835		NLI	Pos. 2488
and Emly)	Apr 30 1835–Dec 25 1880	(transcript)			
		May 18 1835–Sept 23 1880			
	1810–99	1810–67		TFHR	
New Inn and	Mar 14 1820–Mar 31 1847	June 10 1798–Nov 26 1834		NLI	Pos. 2502
Knockgraffon	Apr 3 1847–Dec 22 1880	Jan 8 1835–Oct 2 1880			
(Cashel and Emly)	1820–96	1798–1900		TFHR	
Newcastle	See Waterford				
Powerstown	1808–1880	1808–1880		BBHC	
(Waterford and	Sept 8 1808–Oct 18 1845	Aug 11 1808–Nov 27 1880		NLI	Pos. 2455
Lismore)	Oct 20 1845–Nov 16 1880				
	1808–1811	1808–1811		WHGC	
Sologhead	See Limerick East				
Templetenny	1817–80	1818–80		BBHC	
(Waterford and	Nov 9 1817–June 2 1872	Jan 25 1818–Nov 13 1875		NLI	Pos. 2458/9
Lismore)	June 20 1872–Dec 24 1880	Feb 7 1876–Nov 28 1880			
	1817–1911	1818–1911		WHGC	

Parish (Diocese)	Baptisms	Marriages	Burials	Location	Reference
Tipperary (Cashel and Emly)	Jan 1 1810–Sept 30 1822	Feb 11 1793–May 20 1809		NLI	Pos. 2495 to
	Oct 1 1822–Oct 6 1833	Jan 10 1810–Nov 30 1844			1848;
	Jan 1 1833–Dec 31 1848 (transcript)	Jan 8 1845–Nov 25 1880			remainder on Pos. 2496
	Jan 1849–Dec 28 1868				
	Jan 11 1869–Dec 31 1880				
	1780–1899	1793–1900		TFHR	

Tyrone

All Irish World (IW) Heritage Centre transcripts are online at <*www.roots ireland.ie*>.

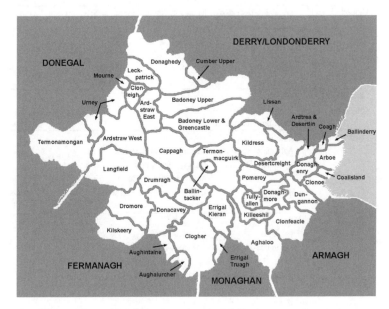

Parish (Diocese)	Baptisms	Marriages	Burials	Location	Reference
Aghaloo (Armagh)	Jan 1 1846–Dec 31 1880	Jan 2 1832–May 29 1834		NLI	Pos. 5585
		Oct 2 1837–Nov 21 1880			
	1846–81	1832–80		PRONI	MIC.1D/36
Arboe	See Derry/Londonderry				
Ardstraw East (Derry)	Dec 18 1861–Dec 24 1880	Dec (?) 8 1860–Oct 13 1880		NLI	Pos. 5765
	1860–80		1860–81	PRONI	MIC.1D/60
Ardstraw West (Derry)	June 3 1846–Mar 10 1850	May 15 1843–Apr 7 1878		NLI	Pos. 5767
	Jan 18 1852–Jan 30 1877	Feb 10–Oct 27 1880			
	Nov 23 1873–Dec 19 1880				
	Dec 25 1877–Dec 26 1880				
	1846–81	1843–78		PRONI	MIC.1D/62
		1880			
Ardtrea and Desertlin	See Derry/Londonderry				
Aughalurcher	See Fermanagh				
Aughintaine (Clogher)	Nov 14 1870–Dec 28 1880	Nov 18 1870–Jan 13 1880		LDS	0979704 item 1–2
	Nov 14 1870–Dec 28 1880	Nov 18 1870–Jan 13 1880		NLI	Pos. 5569
	1870–81	1870–83		PRONI	MIC.1D/12
Badoney Lower and Greencastle (Derry)	Oct 31 1866–Dec 24 1880			NLI	Pos. 5765
	1865–81	1865–80		PRONI	MIC.1D/60
	1865–1900	1865–93		DGC	

Parish (Diocese)	Baptisms	Marriages	Burials	Location	Reference
Badoney Upper (Derry)	1866–81 1865–81 (Plumbridge)	1865–81 (Plumbridge)		IW	
	Oct 31 1866–Dec 24 1880			NLI	Pos. 5765
	1866–81			PRONI	MIC.1D/60
Ballinderry	See Derry/Londonderry				
Ballintacker (Armagh)	1832–1900	1834–1900		IW	
	Sept 26 1832–Dec 26 1880	July 11 1834–Dec 3 1880		NLI	Pos. 5584
	1832–81	1834–82		PRONI	MIC.1D/35
Cappagh (Derry)	July 16 1843–Dec 6 1880 June 12 1846–Oct 1863 (1 page only)	July 24 1843–Nov 20 1880	July 21 1843–Jan 13 1865	NLI	Pos. 5766; baptisms from 1846 on Pos. 5765
	1843–83	1843–83	1843–65	PRONI	MIC.1D/60–61
	1843–1900	1843–1900	1843–65	DG	
Carrickmore (Armagh)	1881–1900	1881–1900		IW	
	No records microfilmed			NLI	
	No records microfilmed			PRONI	
Clogher (Clogher)	1856–81			IW	
	Apr 12 1856–Apr 13 1857 Apr 18 1857–Dec 23 1880	Sept 28 1825–Nov 10 1835 Mar 1940–Feb 19 1857 Apr 22 1857–Oct 21 1880		NLI	Pos. 5567. Also <www. ancestry.com>
	1856–81	1825–35	1840–81	PRONI	MIC.1D/10; C.R.2/14
Clonfeacle (Armagh)	1814–1900	1814–1900		AA	
	1814–1900	1814–1900		IW	
	Oct 16 1814–Mar 22 1840 Aug 25 1840–Dec 26 1880	Nov 9 1814–Mar 19 1840 Apr 23 1840–Oct 14 1880		LDS	0979708 item 2–3
	Oct 16 1814–Mar 22 1840 Aug 25 1840–Dec 26 1880	Nov 9 1814–Mar 19 1840 Apr 23 1840–Oct 14 1880		NLI	Pos. 5580
	1814–81	1814–81		PRONI	MIC.1D/31
Clonleigh	See Donegal				
Clonoe (Armagh)	1810–1900	1806–1816 1823–1900		IW	
	Feb 15 1810–May 23 1816 July 21 1810–Feb 13 1812 Oct 2 1822–Apr 16 1850 Apr 14 1850–Dec 21 1880	Dec 3 1806–June 25 1816 Jan 6 1823–Jan 11 1850 Apr 26 1850–Nov 27 1880	Dec 11 1806–May 31 1816	NLI	Pos. 5579
	1810–16 1822–81	1806–1816 1823–81	1806–1816	PRONI	MIC.1D/30
Coagh (Armagh)	1865–1900	1865–1900		IW	
	Dec 21 1865–Oct 17 1880	Dec 25 1865–Nov 26 1879		NLI	Pos. 5582
	1865–82	1865–81 1884–91		PRONI	MIC.1D/33
Coalisland (Armagh)	1822–1900	1822–1900		IW	
	1861–77	1862–77	1861–8	LDS	0979709 item 3
	Dec 24 1861–Aug 18 1880	May 9 1862–Feb 6 1879	Nov 15 1861–Mar 4 1868	NLI	Pos. 5583
	1861–80	1862–79	1861–8	PRONI	MIC.1D/34
Cumber Upper	See Derry/Londonderry				
Desertcreight (Armagh)	1814–1900	1811–1900		IW	
	Jan 2 1827–Dec 28 1851 Jan 1 1852–Sept 10 1858 Oct 17 1858–Dec 19 1880	Jan 23 1827–Sept 8 1858 Jan 23 1859–Dec 4 1880		NLI	Pos. 5585
	1827–81	1827–81		PRONI	MIC.1D/36

Parish (Diocese)	Baptisms	Marriages	Burials	Location	Reference
Donacavey (Clogher)	See NLI			LDS	0926051 item 1–2
	Nov 24 1857–Dec 14 1880	Oct 26 1857–Nov 25 1880		NLI	Pos. 5571
	1857–81	1857–80		PRONI	MIC.1D/14
Donaghedy (Derry)	Apr 1 1854–June 28 1863 (Dunamanagh)	Nov 11 1857–July 11 1859 (Dunamanagh)	Dec 4 1857–July 15 1859	NLI	Pos. 5761, 5466
	Sept 1 1853–Dec 11 1880	(Dec?) 13 1862–May 31 1863			
	1854–80	1857–9	1857–9	PRONI	MIC.1D/55–56
		1862–3			
	1854–1900	1858–9	1857–9	DG	
		1862–1900			
Donaghenry (Armagh)	See NLI			LDS	0979709 item 2
	Jan 1 1822–Dec 22 1840	Jan 1 1822–Dec 26 1840	Jan 1 1822–Jan 27 1839		
	Feb 16 1849–Dec 23 1880	May 28 1853–Nov 16 1880	Jan 15 1854–May 18 1868	NLI	Pos. 5583
	1822–40	1822–41	1854–69	PRONI	MIC.1D/8, 34
	1849–81	1853–80			
Donaghmore (Armagh)	1837–1900	1837–1900		IW	
	1871–80			LDS	0979709 item 1
	Feb 24 1837–Dec 24 1870	Mar 7 1837–July 30 1868		NLI	Pos. 5582
	Jan 11 1871–Dec 31 1880				
	1837–80	1837–60		PRONI	MIC.1D/33–34
Dromore (Clogher)	Nov 1 1835–Dec 30 1864	Oct 21 1833–Nov 23 1864		LDS	0926052 item 1–2
	Jan 1 1865–Dec 19 1880	Jan 10 1865–Nov 23 1880			
	Nov 1 1835–Dec 30 1864	Oct 21 1833–Nov 23 1864		NLI	Pos. 5568
	Jan 1 1865–Dec 19 1880	Jan 10 1865–Nov 23 1880			
	1835–80 ?			Online	Rootsweb Tyrone
	1835–81	1833–81		PRONI	MIC.1D/11
Drumragh (Derry)	May–Nov 1846	June–Aug 1846	May–Sept 1846	NLI	Pos. 5765
	Nov 13 1853–Dec 22 1880	Nov 7 1853–Dec 26 1880	Nov 23 1853–Dec 11 1880		
	Indexed				
	1846	1846	1846	PRONI	MIC.1D/60;
	1853–81	1853–81	1853–81		C.R.2/9
	Baptisms indexed 1846–79				
Dungannon (Armagh)	1783–90	1783–8	1821–1900	IW	
	1821–1900	1821–1900			
	See NLI			LDS	0926038 item 1–3
	Oct 14 1821–Oct 30 1826	Oct 6 1821–Oct 30 1826	Oct 11 1821–June 7 1826	NLI	Pos. 5580;
	Oct 25 1826–Dec 2 1829	Oct 30 1826–Dec 10 1829	Nov 7 1826–Nov 24 1829		Baptisms and
	Apr 24 1830–July 9 1833	May 2 1831–May 26 1833	Apr 26 1831–May 30 1833		marriages
	Aug 11 1833–June 10 1834	Aug 23 1833–Nov 12 1834	Aug 13 1833–June 1 1834		from 1834, 5581
	Aug 3 1834–Dec 30 1851	June 16 1834–Dec 29 1851	July 3 1834–Dec 29 1854		
	Jan 4 1852–Dec 31 1880	Jan 3 1854–Nov 20 1880	Jan 4 1852–Dec 31 1880		
	1821–81	1821–81	1821–81	PRONI	MIC.1D/31–32
Errigal Kieran (Armagh)	1834–97	1864–1900		IW	
	Jan 3 1847–Dec 28 1880	Jan 14 1864–Dec 16 1880		NLI	Pos. 5584
	1847–81 (Ballygawley)			PRONI	MIC.1D/35
	1864–81 (Ballymacelroy)				
	See Monaghan				

Parish (Diocese)	Baptisms	Marriages	Burials	Location	Reference
Kildress (Armagh)	1835–1900	1835–1900	1835–42	AA	
	1835–1900	1835–1900	1835–42	IW	
	Jan 4 1835–Dec 6 1852	Mar 15 1835–Jan 29 1876	Mar 6 1835–Dec 24 1842	NLI	Pos. 5586
	Jan 11 1857–Aug 10 1859	Jan 7 1840–Feb 19 1851			
	Jan 6 1861–Feb 17 1865	Jan 10 1878–Dec 4 1880			
	Jan 2 1878–Dec 6 1880				
	1835–1900 (part?)			Online	Rootsweb Tyrone
	1835–81 (gaps)	1835–42		PRONI	MIC.1D/37
Killeeshil (Armagh)	1816–1900	1816–1900		IW	
	Aug 10 1845–Dec 27 1856	Sept 3 1845–Dec 31 1856	Aug 13 1845–Dec 16 1856	NLI	Pos. 5582
	Jan 14 1857–Dec 21 1880	Jan 14 1857–Dec 14 1880	Jan 14 1857–Jan 27 1875		
			Nov 4–Dec 1880		
	1816–80	1816–83	1816–75	PRONI	MIC.1D/33
			1880–81		
Kilskeery (Clogher)	Oct 3 1840–June 15 1862	Aug 30 1840–May 27 1862		LDS	0926054 item 1–4
	June 19 1862–Feb 18 1870	July 17 1862–Feb 27 1870			
	Jan 27 1870–Dec 24 1880	Feb 3 1870–Mar 1 1880			
	Oct 3 1840–June 15 1862	Aug 30 1840–May 27 1862		NLI	Pos. 5568
	June 19 1862–Feb 18 1870	July 17 1862–Feb 27 1870			
	Jan 27 1870–Dec 24 1880	Feb 3 1870–Mar 1 1880			
	1840–81	1840–82		PRONI	MIC.1D/11
Langfield (Derry)	Sept 6 1846–Dec 18 1880	Sept 17 1846–Oct 18 1880	July 18 1853–Feb 2 1856	NLI	Pos. 5765
	1846–80	1853–6		PRONI	MIC.1D/60
Leckpatrick (Derry)	Sept 13 1863–Dec 12 1880	Oct 25 1863–Nov 16 1880		NLI	Pos. 5767
	1863–81	1863–84		PRONI	MIC.1D/62
	1863–1900	1863–1900		DGC	
Lissan	See Derry/Londonderry				
Mourne (Derry)	Jan 6 1866–Dec 29 1880	Apr 1 1866–Dec 3 1880 (transcript)		NLI	Pos. 5766
	1866–81	1866–83		PRONI	MIC.1D/62
Pomeroy (Armagh)	1837–1900	1819–1900		IW	
	Feb 26 1837–Nov 24 1840	Mar 5 1837–Dec 11 1840	Mar 7 1837–Dec 5 1840	NLI	Pos. 5585
	Dec 5 1841–May 2 1852	Dec 5 1841–June 10 1865	Apr 20 1857–Apr 12 1861		
	Apr 21 1857–Aug 3 1865	July 11 1869–Dec 25 1880	July 27 1871–Dec 30 1880		
	Feb 1 1869–Dec 9 1880				
	1837–52	1837–65	1837–40	PRONI	MIC.1D/36
	1857–65	1869–82	1857–61		
	1869–81		1871–81		
Termonamongan (Derry)	Mar 28 1863–Dec 29 1880	Sept 12 1863–Nov 13 1880		NLI	Pos. 5765
	1863–81	1863–80		PRONI	MIC.1D/60
Termonmacguirk (Armagh)	1834–57	1834–57		IW	
	Dec 7 1834–Feb 9 1857	Oct 23 1834–Dec 31 1857		NLI	Pos. 5582
	1834–57	1834–57		PRONI	MIC.1D/33
Tullyallen (Armagh)	Jan 1 1816–Jan 2 1834	Jan 3 1816–Jan 2 1834	Jan 2 1816–May 29 1834	NLI	Pos. 5582; from 1849, Pos. 5599
	Mar 2 1837–Aug 24 1844	Apr 3 1837–July 29 1844	Mar 5 1837–Aug 22 1844		
	Jan 14 1849–Dec 25 1880	Jan 9 1849–Nov 14 1880			
	No records microfilmed			PRONI	
Urney (Derry)	1856–1900	1856–1900		DA	
	From 1866	From 1866		Local custody	
	No records microfilmed			NLI	
	No records microfilmed			PRONI	

Waterford

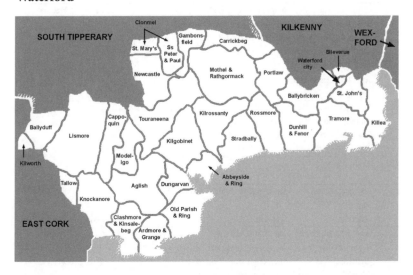

All parishes are in the diocese of Waterford and Lismore, except where indicated. All Waterford Heritage and Genealogy Centre (WHGC) transcripts are online. Copies of all NLI microfilms are also available at Waterford Central Library.

Parish (Diocese)	Baptisms	Marriages	Burials	Location	Reference
Abbeyside and Ring	July 6 1828–Dec 26 1842	July 24 1828–Feb 8 1842		NLI	Pos. 2469
	May 21 1842–Dec 29 1880	May 26 1842–Nov 18 1880			
	1828–1911	1828–1911		WHGC	
Aglish	May 17 1838–Dec 31 1880	Jan 25 1877–Nov 20 1880		NLI	Pos. 2464
	1831–1911	1833–1911		WHGC	
Ardmore and Grange	Oct 17 1823–Jan 19 1833	Nov 24 1857–Sept 23 1880	Jan 8 1826–Jan 11 1827	NLI	Pos. 2465
	Jan 1 1857–Dec 31 1880				
	1816–1911	1857–1911		WHGC	
Ballyduff	June 23 1849–Feb 6 1861	Nov 8 1853–Feb 12 1861		NLI	Pos. 2469,
	Apr 14 1876–June 4 1878	June 8 1861–Nov 18 1880			2470
	Jan 26 1879–Dec 21 1880				
	1849–1911	1853–1911		WHGC	
Cappoquin	Apr 14 1810–June 16 1870	Jan 7 1807–Aug 8 1871		NLI	Pos. 2467
	(indexed transcript)	July 23 1870–Oct 2 1880			
	June 19 1870–Dec 21 1880				
	1819–1911	1807–1911		WHGC	
Carrickbeg	Jan 1 1842–Oct 30 1846	Jan 11 1807–Jan 8 1867		NLI	Pos. 2450
	Feb 27 1847–Dec 28 1876	Nov 23 1866–Jan 9 1881			
	1842–1911	1807–1911		WHGC	
Clashmore and Kinsalebeg	Jan 6 1811–Oct 1 1845	Jan 23 1810–Aug 23 1879		NLI	Pos. 2462, 2464
	Oct 12 1845–Aug 23 1879				
	1811–1911	1810–1911		WHGC	
Clonmel: SS. Peter and Paul	See Tipperary South				
Clonmel: St Mary's	See Tipperary South				

Parish (Diocese)	Baptisms	Marriages	Burials	Location	Reference
Dungarvan	Feb 17 1787–Apr 27 1787	May 14 1809–Nov 29 1828		NLI	Pos. 2468,
	Sept 3 1811–May 17 1823	Jan 8 1829–Dec 2 1838			2469
	July 27 1823–Apr 30 1830	Feb 21 1838–Sept 1 1877			
	May 1 1830–July 13 1839	Sept 24 1877–Nov 12 1880			
	Jan 7 1838–July 26 1877				
	Sept 1 1877–Dec 28 1880				
	1787–1911	1809–1911		WHGC	
Dunhill and Fenor	Apr 4 1829–Nov 18 1843	Nov 26 1836–Feb 17 1874	Jan 1 1879–Nov 24 1881	NLI	Pos. 2448,
	Jan 5 1844–June 12 1881	Jan 14 1853–Nov 18 1880			2449
	Nov 16 1852–Feb 6 1876	(Fenor)			
	1829–1911	1837–1911		WHGC	
Gambonsfield and Kilcash	See Tipperary South				
Kilgobinet	Apr 7 1848–Oct 24 1872	Oct 10 1848–Apr 6 1880		NLI	Pos. 2464
	Mar 14 1873–Dec 25 1880				
	1848–1911	1848–1911		WHGC	
Killea	May 7 1815–July 20 1820	Jan 8 1780–Oct 9 1791		NLI	Pos. 2450
	Oct 10 1845–Dec 13 1863	Jan 13 1793–Feb 18 1798			
	(transcript)	(transcript)			
	Feb 17 1874–Dec 19 1880	Apr 3 1815–July 20 1820			
	(transcript)	Aug 29 1837–Aug 3 1838			
	Dec 24 1863–Mar 17 1881	Oct 5 1845–Apr 27 1882			
	(transcript)				
	1809–1911	1780–1911		WHGC	
Kilrossanty	July 4 1822–Aug 4 1858	Jan 16 1859–Sept 8 1880		NLI	Pos. 2465
	Jan 9 1859–Dec 27 1880				
	1822–1911	1859–1911		WHGC	
Kilworth	See Cork East				
Knockanore	May 4 1816–Apr 24 1823	Feb 7 1854–June 12 180		NLI	Pos. 2462
	Sept 1833–June 25 1872				
	June 17 1872–Dec 27 1880				
	1816–1911	1803–1911		WHGC	
Lismore	Mar 13 1820–Feb 14 1831	Nov 24 1822–Oct 8 1839		NLI	Pos. 2467, 2468
	July 11 1840–June 19 1848	Feb 27 1840–Nov 4 1866			
	Feb 21 1849–Apr 16 1858	May 1849–Feb 20 1857			
	Aug 27 1866–Dec 28 1880	Sept 1866–Nov 6 1880			
	1820–1911	1822–1911		WHGC	
Modeligo	July 28 1846–Dec 22 1880			NLI	Pos. 2470
	1815–1911	1820–1911		WHGC	
Mothel and Rathgormack	Mar 23 1831–June 17 1852	Mar 4 1845–Oct 16 1880		NLI	Pos. 2449
	June 20 1852–Jan 13 1881				
	1831–1911	1852–1911		WHGC	
Newcastle	July 1 1814–Dec 31 1845	Jan 7 1822–Oct 23 1880		NLI	Pos. 2454
	Jan 1 1846–Oct 31 1862				
	Nov 2 1862–Dec 29 1880				
	1814–1911	1822–1911		WHGC	
Old Parish and Ring	Jan 5 1813–Apr 24 1840	Jan 17 1813–Feb 13 1840		NLI	Pos. 2465
	Aug 12 1840–Aug 15 1859	Jan 24 1841–Mar 8 1859			
	1813–1911	1813–1911		WHGC	
Portlaw	Jan 26 1809–Oct 3 1825	Jan 15 1805–Feb 27 1881		NLI	Pos. 2449, 2450
	Dec 16 1825–Oct 24 1860	Feb 14 1814–Nov 19 1862			
	June 1 1858–Jan 23 1881	Nov 6 1860–Feb 21 1882			
	1809–1911	1805–1911		WHGC	

Parish (Diocese)	Baptisms	Marriages	Burials	Location	Reference
Rossmore	Mar 27 1797–Aug 1830	Apr 27 1797–Feb 11 1880		NLI	Pos. 2452
	Feb 1831–Feb 21 1869				
	1798–1911	1797–1911		WHGC	
Slieverue	See Kilkenny				
Stradbally	Nov 3 1806–May 30 1814	Aug 4 1805–Nov 28 1840		NLI	Pos. 2465,
	June 1 1814–Sept 22 1828	Sept 20 1840–Aug 2 1863			2466, 2467
	Sept 30 1828–July 29 1835	Sept 13 1863–Oct 13 1880			
	Aug 1 1835–Oct 13 1850				
	Oct 19 1850–Aug 28 1863				
	Aug 20 1863–Dec 9 1880				
	1797–1911	1805–1911		WHGC	
Tallow	Apr 19 1797–Mar 11 1831	Apr 20 1798–Apr 25 1803		NLI	Pos. 2470
	Apr 9 1831–Sept 19 1842	Oct 11 1808–Nov 13 1853			
	Jan 19 1856–Dec 31 1880				
	1797–1911	1799–1911		WHGC	
Touraneena	July 8 1852–Dec 11 1880	June 20 1852–Nov 14 1880		NLI	Pos. 2454
	1852–1911	1852–1911		WHGC	
Tramore	Jan 7 1798–Oct 24 1831	Jan 29 1786–July 29 1840		NLI	Pos. 2448
	1798–1911	1785–1911		WHGC	
Waterford city:	Jan 4 1795–Oct 13 1816	Jan 7 1797–Sept 6 1832		NLI	Pos. 2450, 2451
Ballybricken	Dec 1 1816–Apr 30 1832	Sept 10 1832–Sept 9 1843			(B.); 2452 (M.)
	May 1 1832–Apr 5 1841	Jan 8 1843–Nov 17 1874			
	Apr 6 1841–Jan 8 1844	Jan 7 1875–Nov 22 1880			
	Jan 8 1844–Jan 3 1875				
	Jan 3 1875–Dec 30 1880				
	1797–1911	1797–1911		WHGC	
Waterford city:	1729–52	Nov 26 1743–Jan 8 1787		NLI	Pos. 2444, 2445
Holy Trinity	1731–49 (St Stephen's)	(St Peter's)			
	1732–96 (St Michael's)	Sept 5 1747–Dec 20 1756			
	(gaps)	Feb 3 1761–Aug 30 1777			
	Nov 1737–Aug 1746	Jan 5 1791–June 28 1795			
	(St Peter's)	June 26 1796–Nov 24 1796			
	July 1752–Dec 1767	(St Michael's)			
	Jan 1768–July 1775	Jan 9 1797–Feb 20 1820			
	Feb 1793–Dec 1805	Aug 2 1819–Sept 9 1838			
	Jan 1806–July 1819	Sept 25 1838–Nov 1863			
	Dec 1809–Sept 1815				
	July 1819–Dec 1863				
	1729–1911	1747–1911		WHGC	
Waterford city:	Apr 7 1706–Mar 26 1730	Apr 7 1706–Mar 26 1730		NLI	Pos. 2446
St John's	Mar 5 1759–Mar 29 1787	Feb 10 1760–Feb 2 1808			
	Oct 1795–Aug 10 1807	Feb 2 1808–June 1 1817			
	Aug 2 1807–Mar 31 1816	Sept 12 1828–Nov 28 1856			
	June 1 1818–July 24 1828				
	Aug 17 1828–July 17 18370				
	1759–1911	1760–1911		WHGC	

Parish (Diocese)	Baptisms	Marriages	Burials	Location	Reference
Waterford city: SS. Patrick and Olaf	Apr 11 1731–Feb 10 1743	May 24 1743–Oct 29 1752		NLI	Pos. 2447
	Feb 13 1743–Oct 29 1752	Oct 30 1752–June 3 1772			
	Oct 30 1752–June 3 1772	Oct 10 1772–May 22 1783			
	June 6 1772–Sept 8 1791	Nov 23 1783–May 8 1791			
	May 9 1795–Mar 27 1798	Jan 25 1799–Dec 9 1800			
	Nov 18 1798–Mar 2 1801	Sept 12 1826–Sept 19 1839			
	Apr 9 1798–Jan 8 1799				
	Apr 3 1827–Oct 11 1839				
	1706–1911	1706–1911		WHGC	

Westmeath

All Dún na Sí Heritage and Genealogical Centre (DSHGC) transcripts listed below are online at <*www.roots ireland.ie*>. Some of the start and end dates supplied on the site itself appear to cover material other than parish registers. NLI microfilms marked with an asterisk (*) are online at <*www.ancestry.com*>.

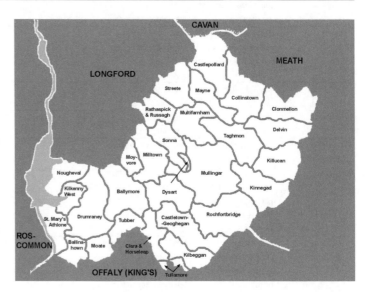

Parish (Diocese)	Baptisms	Marriages	Burials	Location	Reference
Ballinahown (Ardagh and Clonmacnois)	1821–99	1822–1900	1821–46	IMA	
	1821–1905 (some gaps)	1823–1974	1821–8	LDS	1279227 item 1–6
			1829–45		
			1854–81		
			1882–94		
	Aug 12 1821–Dec 21 1824	Jan 7 1830–Aug 29 1845	Nov 21 1829–Sept 9 1845	NLI	Pos. 4235
	Feb 12 1826–Feb 25 1839	Oct 15 1854–Dec 26 1880	Sept 2 1854–Dec 26 1880		
	Feb 6 1841–Sept 21 1845				
	July 23 1854–Dec 24 1880				
Ballymore (Meath)	1824–1900	1872–1900		DSHGC	
	See NLI			LDS	0926163 item 2–4
	Sept 22 1824–Sept 2 1841	Apr 1839–Sept 10 1870		NLI	Pos. 4171
	Mar 18 1839–Dec 30 1871	Feb 4 1872–Nov 27 1880			
	(some duplicates)				
	Sept 22 1824–Sept 2 1841				
	Mar 18 1839–Dec 30 1871				
	Jan 9 1872–Dec 31 1880				

Parish (Diocese)	Baptisms	Marriages	Burials	Location	Reference
Castlepollard (Meath)	Jan 4 1763–Mar 25 1765	1763–June 10 1790	Mar 10 1764–June 22 1790	NLI	Pos. 4164, 4165
	Oct 9 1771–June 30 1790	Mar 21 1793–Aug 15 1793	Jan 19 1793–June 13 1825		
	Jan 4 1795–Feb 16 1796	Jan 7 1795–June 16 1825			
	Feb 21 1796–Aug 19 1805	Nov 21 1825–Sept 14 1875			
	Aug 23 1805–June 24 1825				
	Nov 15 1825–Mar 20 1837				
	Mar 24 1837–Oct 17 1875				
	Oct 22 1875–Dec 22 1880				
Castletown-	1829–1900	1829–1900	1829–44	DSHGC	
Geoghegan (Meath)	Aug 2 1829–May 2 1835	Feb 8 1829–Mar 3 1835		NLI	Pos. 4169
	May 8 1835–Mar 29 1850	July 26 1835–Feb 10 1850			
	Mar 2 1846–Dec 12 1880	Oct 9 1846–May 27 1880			
	June 23 1861–Dec 26 1880	Jan 7 1862–Nov 26 1880			
Clara and Horseleap	1845–1910	1821–99	1825–68	IMA	
(Meath)	Feb 16 1845–Dec 26 1880	Nov 16 1821–Nov 25 1880	Jan 9 1825–Feb 23 1854	NLI	Pos. 4174
	Sept 2 1878–Dec 14 1880		Oct 2 1864–Oct 4 1868		
	(transcript)				
Clonmellon	See Meath				
Collinstown (Meath)	1807–1900	1784–1844	1809–1926	DSHGC	
	See NLI			LDS	0926165 item 3–4
	1807–1901	1784–1901	1784–1849	MHGC	
	Feb 24 1807–Apr 29 1815	June 21 1784–June 6 1837	Apr 24 1784–Oct 1949	NLI	Pos. 4168, 4169
	Mar 13 1821–Nov 18 1843	June 15 1837–Nov 26 1880			
	Mar 4 1844–June 6 1844				
	May 12 1844–Dec 24 1880				
Delvin (Meath)	1783–1900	1785–1900	1785–1985	DSHGC	
	Jan 1 1785–Mar 17 1789	Feb 7 1785–Mar 16 1789	Feb 7 1785–Mar 5 1789	NLI	Pos. 4172*
	July 23 1792–July 20 1812	July 30 1792–July 1812	July 7 1792–July 26 1812		
	July 5 1830–Dec 29 1880	Sept 30 1830–Oct 4 1880	Jan 3 1849–Apr 1 1855		
Drumraney (Meath)	1834–1900	1834–1900		DSHGC	
	See NLI			LDS	0926167 item 3–4
	Apr 26 1834–Dec 22 1880	May 2 1834–Sept 29 1880		NLI	Pos. 4171
Dysart (Meath)	1836–1900	1825–1900	1862–1900	DSHGC	
	Aug 10 1836–Aug 24 1862	Feb 5 1825–Feb 24 1862		NLI	Pos. 4168
	Apr 28 1861–Dec 30 1880				
Kilbeggan (Meath)	1818–1900	1821–1900	1818–84	DSHGC	
	Nov 4 1818–Aug 28 1824	Oct 23 1818–Nov 26 1859	Sept 28 1818–Dec 17 1843	NLI	Pos. 4176
	Apr 24 1825–Dec 9 1859	Jan 7 1860–Nov 16 1880			
	Jan 8 1860–Dec 5 1880				
Kilbride and	1832–1900	1832–99		CHGC	
Mountnugent	1830–1900	1830–63	1906–1983	DSHGC	
(Meath)	See NLI			LDS	0926174
	Jan 1 1832–Jan 27 1864	Jan 1 1832–Nov 22 1863		NLI	Pos. 4172
	Jan 13 1864–Nov 27 1880	Feb 4 1864–Nov 27 1880			
Kilkenny West	1829–1900	1829–1900	1829–1993	DSHGC	
(Meath)	Aug 5 1829–Dec 15 1880			NLI	Pos. 4171

Parish (Diocese)	Baptisms	Marriages	Burials	Location	Reference
Killucan (Meath)	1866–1900	1821–1900		DSHGC	
	See NLI			LDS	0926172
	May 7 1821–July 28 1838	May 11 1821–Sept 30 1847		NLI	Pos. 4166
	July 26 1838–Dec 27 1865	Oct 26 1847–Nov 27 1874			
	Jan 6 1866–Jan 19 1875	Jan 18 1875–Nov 26 1880			
	Jan 20 1875–Dec 28 1880				
Kinnegad (Meath)	1827–90	1844–99	1833–1975	DSHGC	
	June 22 1827–Jan 31 1869	July 18 1844–Jan 25 1869	Feb 7 1869–Dec 23 1880	NLI	Pos. 4170
	Jan 29 1869–Dec 29 1880	Feb 6 1869–Sept 8 1880			
Mayne (Meath)	1777–1820	1777–1820	1777–97	DSHGC	
	1824–35	1824–43	1824–69		
	1847–1900	1864–1900	1919–93		
	See NLI			LDS	0926176 item 1
	Aug 1777–May 29 1796	Nov 17 1777–Apr 24 1796	Aug 7 1777–Nov 27 1796	NLI	Pos. 4167
	Jan 22 1798–Nov 29 1820	Jan 7 1798–Dec 1 1820	Feb 2 1803–Sept 9 1820		
	Apr 2 1824–Apr 5 1835	May 9 1824–July 4 1843	Apr 2 1824–Aug 9 1844		
	Feb 21 1847–Aug 22 1863	Aug 20 1846–July 21 1850	Jan 1864–Oct 27 1869		
	(some pages missing)	Nov 2 1864–July 19 1880	Jan 4 1846–July 31 1850		
Milltown (Meath)	1791–1900	1781–1913	1781–1899	DSHGC	
	Jan 1 1781–Sept 12 1808	Apr 2 1809–Oct 3 1825	Jan 12 1781–Nov 17 1808	NLI	Pos. 4167
	Apr 2 1809–Oct 3 1825	Mar 1 1826–Nov 15 1849	Apr 2 1809–Oct 3 1825		
	Mar 1 1826–Nov 15 1849	Feb 18 1850–May 3 1860	Mar 1 1826–Nov 15 1849		
	Feb 18 1850–May 3 1860	May 3 1860–Oct 16 1869	Feb 18 1850–May 3 1860		
	May 3 1860–Oct 16 1869	Nov 15 1869–Nov 3 1872	May 3 1860–Oct 16 1869		
	Sept 21 1869–Nov 18 1872	Jan 14 1781–Feb 11 1805			
	Dec 10 1872–Dec 22 1880	Jan 13 1873–Oct 16 1880			
Moate (Ardagh and Clonmacnois)	1820–1900	1830–1900	1830–1900	DSHGC	
	1811–1900 (Ballyloughloe)	1824–1900 (Ballyloughloe)	1811–1900 (Ballyloughloe)		
	1830–1910	1830–1915	1830–36	LDS	1279227 item 9–11
			1835–1916		
	Jan 2 1830–Nov 30 1836	Jan 2 1830–Nov 30 1836	Feb 2 1837–May 13 1883	NLI	Pos. 9358
	Feb 2 1837–May 13 1883	Feb 2 1837–May 13 1883			
	May 17 1883–Aug 3 1911				
Moyvore (Meath)	1832–1900	1832–1900	1831–65	DSHGC	
	See NLI			LDS	0926167 item 1–2
	Sept 5 1831–Feb 8 1862	Feb 12 1832–Apr 28 1862	Aug 6 1831–Apr 1863	NLI	Pos. 4171
	Feb 18 1862–Dec 25 1880	Mar 21 1862–Dec 25 1880	May 1863–Sept 5 1865		
Mullingar (Meath)	1742–1900	1737–54	1830–1940	DSHGC	
		1779–82			
		1783–1824			
		1833–59			
		1860–1900			
	See NLI			LDS	0926178
	1741/2 (fragment)	Oct 26 1737–July 20 1754	May 6 1757–Oct 31 1797	NLI	Pos. 4161, 4162, 4163
	July 15 1742–Dec 19 1796	Jan 10 1779–Apr 21 1824	Jan 4 1833–May 26 1838		
	Jan 13 1797–May 2 1800	Jan 8 1833–Apr 9 1859	Feb 28 1843–1880		
	Jan 1 1800–Apr 13 1816	May 18 1860–July 12 1879			
	May 1 1825–Nov 23 1842	July 10 1879–Nov 27 1880			
	Nov 13 1843–Jan 24 1863				
	Jan 22 1863–Mar 12 1872				
	Mar 13 1872–Dec 31 1880				

Parish (Diocese)	Baptisms	Marriages	Burials	Location	Reference
Multifarnham (Meath)	1824–1900	1824–1900	1830–48	DSHGC	
	Feb 6 1824–Dec 28 1841	Feb 15 1824–Dec 9 1841	Jan 28 1831–July 16 1844	NLI	Pos. 4168
	Jan 1 1842–Dec 26 1880	Jan 7 1842–June 4 1880			
Nougheval (Meath)	1857–1908	1857–1908	1920–93	DSHGC	
	No records microfilmed			NLI	
Rathaspick and Russagh (Ardagh and Clonmacnois)	1826–1900	1821–42	1828–1993	DSHGC	
		1844–1900			
	1822–1984	1825–1983	1822–1909	LDS	1279229 item
			1928–84		16–22
	Mar 16 1822–Sept 9 1826	Dec 31 1819–Feb 7 1826	Mar 11 1822–Feb 20 1826	NLI	Pos. 4236
	July 24 1832–Apr 21 1833	Oct 27 1832–Oct 4 1833	Aug 2 1832–Nov 1833		
	May 1 1836–Dec 9 1843	Jan 11 1838–Nov 23 1843	Aug 15 1837–Oct 10 1843		
	Dec 17 1843–Oct 18 1846	Jan 7 1844–Nov 20 1880	Feb 8 1844–Dec 19 1880		
	Mar 28 1847–Dec 30 1880				
Rochfortbridge (Meath)	June 1 1823–Apr 9 1847	Dec 26 1816–Dec 1 1855		NLI	Pos. 4172*
	Apr 11 1847–Dec 28 1856	Jan 20 1856–Nov 26 1880			
	Jan 9 1857–Dec 27 1880				
	1821–1900	1816–1900		DSHGC	
Sonna (Meath)	1837–1900	1838–1900	1859–1993	DSHGC	
	Sept 23 1837–Dec 31 1880	Nov 26 1838–July 20 1880		NLI	Pos. 4168
St Mary's, Athlone (Ardagh and Clonmacnoise)	1813–1900	1813–1900	1813–1900	DSHGC	
	1813–27	1813–27	1813–27	LDS	1279224 item
	1834–1984	1834–1984			4–14; 1279226
					1–3
	Jan 1 1813–Sept 24 1826	Jan 1 1813–Sept 24 1826	Jan 1 1813–Sept 24 1826	NLI	Pos. 4242*
	Feb 4 1827–Mar 17 1827	Feb 4 1827–Mar 17 1827	Feb 4 1827–Mar 17 1827		
	May 3 1839–Apr 30 1852	June 5 1819–Apr 17 1827	June 4 1819–Dec 29 1826		
	Feb 1 1853–Dec 28 1855	(some deaths and	(some marriages and		
	Jan 1 1856–Feb 26 1868	baptisms included)	baptisms included)		
		Jan 24 1834–Dec 26 1851			
		Feb 9 1854–Feb 5 1863			
Streete (Ardagh and Clonmacnois)	1821–63	1820–1900	1772–1995	DSHGC	
	1820–1901	1820–26	1834–81	LDS	1279228 item
		1835–81	1887–1913		7–9
		1887–1902			
	July 6 1820–July 14 1827	Aug 10 1820–Jan 22 1828	Sept 27 1823–Aug 13 1829	NLI	Pos. 4236
	Nov 21 1831–Dec 20 1831	Jan 4 1835–Nov 19 1880	Dec 14 1834–Jan 8 1841		
	Dec 15 1834–Dec 29 1880		July 19 1842–Dec 29 1880		
Taghmon (Meath)	Sept 22 1781–Mar 7 1790	Jan 12 1782–July 16 1791	Sept 1 1809–Feb 25 1848	NLI	Pos. 4165
	June 8 1800–June 30 1800	Aug 7 1809–May 14 1848			
	Mar 24 1809–Dec 28 1840	Sept 2 1868–Nov 3 1880			
	Jan 1 1841–Dec 29 1850				
	Jan 2 1864–Dec 30 1880				
	1781–1900	1781–1900	1809–1900	DSHGC	
Tubber (Meath)	1820–1900	1824–1900	1824–73	DSHGC	
	1820–99	1820–99	1832–45	IMA	
	See NLI			LDS	0926185 item 2
	Nov 2 1821–Dec 25 1880	Nov 6 1824–Dec 13 1880		NLI	Pos. 4176
Tullamore	See Offaly (King's County)				

Wexford

All parishes are in the
diocese of Ferns. Copies of
all NLI Wexford
microfilms are also
available at Wexford
County Library. Wexford
Heritage and Genealogy
Service (WHGS) is no
longer in existence. None
of its records are at
present (2011) online,
though it is planned to
make them available on
<*www.rootsireland.ie*>. NLI
microfilms marked with
an asterisk (*) are online
at <*www.ancestry.com*>.

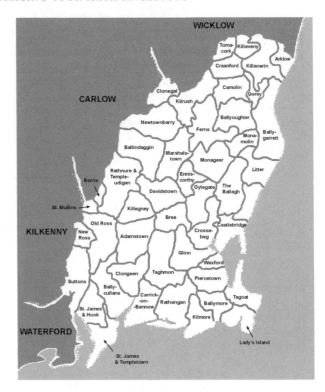

Parish	Baptisms	Marriages	Burials	Location	Reference
Adamstown	1849–1900	1892–1900		WHGS	
	(gaps 1864–92)				
	Jan 13 1807–Dec 30 1836	Dec 8 1849–Feb 13 1865	Sept 27 1823–Jan 30 1832	NLI	Pos. 4258
	Jan 7 1837–Oct 7 1848	Nov 26 1864–Oct 19 1880	(ages given)		
	Nov 10 1850–Sept 11 1864				
	Apr 13 1849–Mar 27 1861				
	Nov 20 1864–Oct 30 1880				
Arklow	See Wicklow				
Ballindaggin	July 18 1871–Dec 30 1880	July 2 1871–Nov 11 1880		NLI	Pos. 4251
Ballycullane	1827–1900	1827–96	1828–32	WHGS	
	Sept 13 1827–Sept 3 1880	Oct 7 1827–Sept 12 1880	Oct 10 1828–Jan 31 1832	NLI	Pos. 4259*
	(very poor condition)				
Ballygarrett	1828–1900	1830–1900	1830–69	WHGS	
	Nov 10 1828–Feb 19 1863	Aug 30 1828–Nov 13 1865	Aug 7 1830–Apr 18 1857		
			Oct 28 1865–Apr 19 1867	NLI	Pos. 4255
			(ages given)		
Ballymore	1813–1900	1802–1899		WHGS	
	May 22 1840–Dec 24 1880	Feb 13 1840–Oct 23 1880		NLI	Pos. 4246
Ballyoughter	Sept 30 1810–Dec 31 1811	Aug 20 1815–Feb 10 1868		NLI	Pos. 4255
	Aug 5 1815–Nov 28 1832	July 13 1871–Dec 27 1880			
	Aug 18 1844–Apr 19 1871				
	July 5 1871–Dec 27 1880				

Parish	Baptisms	Marriages	Burials	Location	Reference
Blackwater	1825–1900	1815–81	1840–83	WHGS	
	1815–Dec 28 1839	Jan 8 1815–Dec 10 1839	Jan 5 1843–Dec 20 1880	NLI	Pos. 4245*
	(early years barely legible)	Jan 13 1840–Nov 27 1880			
	Jan 4 1840–Dec 21 1880				
Borris	See Carlow				
Bree	Jan 3 1837–Dec 26 1880	Jan 23 1837–Nov 27 1880		NLI	Pos. 4251
Camolin	June 1 1853–Dec 10 1880	Mar 10 1853–Nov 7 1880	Jan 3 1858–Feb 7 1879	NLI	Pos. 4257
Carrick-on-Bannow	1873–1900			WHGS	
	Aug 29 1832–Nov 9 1873	Sept 11 1830–Sept 23 1873		NLI	Pos. 4244
	(some missing)	July 16 1873–Nov 27 1880			
	Aug 10 1873–Dec 31 1880				
Castlebridge	1832–1900	1832–92		WHGS	
	Oct 30 1832–Dec 31 1880	Dec 1 1832–Oct 27 1880		NLI	Pos. 4247
	July 17 1871–Dec 24 1880	Oct 6 1871–Oct 20 1880			
	(Screen)	(Screen)			
Clonegal	See Carlow				
Clongeen	1847–1900	1847–1900		WHGS	
	Jan 29 1847–Dec 30 1880	Apr 25 1847–Nov 25 1880	Jan 30 1856–Dec 3 1880	NLI	Pos. 4261
			(ages given)		
Craanford	1871–1900	1871–1900		WHGS	
	Jan 8 1856–Dec 3 1880	Nov 30 1871–Nov 28 1880		NLI	Pos. 4257
	Aug 26 1871–Oct 28 1880				
Crossabeg	1794–1900	1794–1900	1899–1900	WHGS	
	Jan 8 1856–Dec 3 1880			NLI	Pos. 4251
Davidstown	1801–1900	1840–59		WHGS	
	1805–Dec 24 1880	June 1808–Nov 27 1880		NLI	Pos. 4251
Enniscorthy	1794–1900	1794–1900		WHGS	
	May 16 1794–June 10 1804	May 3 1794–Sept 25 1805		NLI	Pos. 4249
	(also in transcript)	(also in transcript)			
	Mar 1 1806–May 23 1816	Sept 17 1805–May 12 1816			
	(also in transcript)	(also in transcript)			
	June 2 1816–Dec 31 1835	July 20 1816–Nov 28 1835			
	(also in transcript)	(also in transcript)			
	Jan 1 1836–Dec 30 1861	Jan 1 1836–Nov 30 1861			
	Jan 1 1836–Nov 6 1841	Mar 6 1821–Oct 28 1835			
	Jan 2 1862–Dec 23 1880				
Ferns	1819–1900	1840–1900	1840–59	WHGS	
	May 16 1819–Feb 14 1840	May 14 1819–Jan 10 1840		NLI	Pos. 4254
	Sept 6 1840–Dec 24 1880	Nov 2 1840–Nov 18 1880			
Glinn	1817–1900	1817–83	1867–83	WHGS	
	Jan 23 1817–Feb 3 1867	Jan 26 1817–Jan 17 1867	Jan 6 1823–Dec 21 1880	NLI	Pos. 4247
	Feb 7 1867–Dec 20 1880	Feb 5 1867–Nov 27 1880	(ages given)		
Gorey	May 26 1845–Nov 10 1880	June 5 1845–July 3 1847		NLI	Pos. 4256
		Aug 4 1847–May 2 1880			
Killanerin	Jan 1 1852–Oct 31 1880	Jan 25 1852–Oct 14 1880		NLI	Pos. 4255
Killaveny	Nov 20 1800–Dec 20 1836	Nov 14 1800–Sept 10 1836	Oct 19 1862–Mar 13 1867	NLI	Pos. 4257
	Jan 13 1837–Apr 29 1875	Jan 7 1837–May 4 1875	(Anacorra)		
	Oct 15 1857–Apr 10 1864	Aug 5 1860–Feb 6 1864			
	(Anacorra)	(Anacorra)			
	1800–1900	1801–1900		WFHC	

Parish	Baptisms	Marriages	Burials	Location	Reference
Killegney	1816–1900	1816–1900	1816–1900	WHGS	
	Mar 17 1816–Sept 20 1850	Mar 17 1816–Sept 20 1850	Mar 17 1816–Sept 20 1850	NLI	Pos. 4250
	(part of 1824 missing)	(part of 1824 missing)	(part of 1824 missing)		
	Jan 20 1853–Oct 24 1880	Feb 7 1853–Dec 2 1880	Feb 3 1861–Sept 12 1880		
			(ages given)		
Kilmore	1768–1900	1768–1850	1768–1850	WHGS	
	Apr 6 1752–Mar 30 1785	Apr 6 1752–Mar 30 1785	Apr 6 1752–Mar 30 1785	NLI	Pos. 4246
	June 24 1790–Nov 3 1794	June 24 1790–Nov 3 1794	June 24 1790–Nov 3 1794		
	Jan 2 1798–Mar 12 1826	Jan 2 1798–Mar 12 1826	Jan 2 1798–Mar 12 1826		
	(some pages missing)	(some pages missing)	(some pages missing)		
	July 7 1828–Sept 29 1854	Nov 4 1827–Sept 10 1856			
	Jan 1850–Dec 28 1880	Jan 26 1850–Oct 20 1880			
	1752–1854	1752–1812	1752–1866	Online	Kilmore
Kilrush	May 29 1841–Nov 16 1846			NLI	Pos. 4251
	Mar 6 1855–Dec 26 1880				
Lady's Island	1737–1900	1837–1900	1868–1900	WHGS	
	Aug 1737–May 24 1740	Feb 17 1753–Dec 2 1759		NLI	Pos. 4244
	May 16 1752–Mar 1763	Feb 16 1754–May 1800			
	Jan 1766–Dec 22 1802	(1798/9 missing)			
	Jan 18 1807–Feb 1 1818	Jan 18 1807–Feb 1 1818			
	Apr 26 1838–Dec 20 1880				
Litter	1818–1900	1875–98		WHGS	
	Oct 2 1798–Sept 8 1816	Jan 20 1788–Apr 14 1798		NLI	Pos. 4255
	Sept 13 1816–Dec 18 1853	Sept 25 1806–Oct 3 1880			
	Jan 3 1844–Dec 11 1880				
Marshalstown	May 16 1854–Dec 22 1880	Nov 28 1854–May 1 1880	Oct 10 1854–Nov 18 1856	NLI	Pos. 4248
			Feb 15 1860–Aug 2 1862		
			Oct 28 1876–Jan 16 1878		
Monageer	Nov 18 1838–Dec 13 1880	Nov 12 1838–Nov 3 1880	Aug 1 1838–Dec 22 1880	NLI	Pos. 4248
	(Monageer)	(Monageer)	(ages given—Monageer)		
	May 12 1842–Mar 18 1853	Jan 16 1847–Nov 23 1852	Oct 25 1847–Jan 25 1872		
	Oct 26 1869–Oct 10 1872	Oct 7 1869–Nov 2 1872	(Boolavogue)		
	May 5 1879–Dec 13 1880	July 1879–Nov 27 1880			
	(all Boolavogue)	(all Boolavogue)			
Monamolin	Feb 23 1839–Sept 24 1856	Nov 23 1834–Apr 1 1856		NLI	Pos. 4255
	Mar 15 1858–Oct 13 1880	Oct 20 1859–Aug 13 1880			
New Ross	1789–1900	1817–1900		WHGS	
	Nov 22 1789–Aug 23 1809	Feb 22 1859–Nov 30 1880	May 14 1794–July 22 1809	NLI	Pos. 4259, 4260
	Aug 27 1809–Aug 7 1841		Aug 2 1809–Nov 17 1814		
	Aug 1841–Apr 6 1870		Apr 9 1822–Feb 15 1859		
	Apr 10 1870–Dec 12 1880				
Newtownbarry	1834–Nov 1 1851	May 20 1834–June 29 1880	1834	NLI	Pos. 4251
	Apr 26 1857–Dec 29 1880		1857–8		
			1872–3		
Old Ross	Jan 9 1759–Aug 9 1759	Nov 3 1752–Feb 27 1759	May 16 1794–July 12 1808	NLI	Pos. 4259
	Jan 27 1778–Jan 29 1830	Jan 17 1778–Feb 29 1824	(ages given)		
	July 10 1851–Mar 8 1863	Aug 4 1851–Sept 21 1862	May 1863–Dec 27 1880		
	Feb 26 1863–Dec 19 1880	Apr 15 1863–Oct 28 1880			

Parish	Baptisms	Marriages	Burials	Location	Reference
Oylegate	1804–1900 (gap 1820–32)	1803–1900 (gap 1820–32)	1865–70	WHGS	
	Mar 4 1804–Dec 3 1820	Apr 18 1803–Oct 13 1820	Apr 7 1865–Dec 6 1870	NLI	Pos. 4254
	Aug 10 1832–Nov 30 1853	Oct 14 1832–Nov 19 1853	(ages given)		
	Sept 8 1848–Dec 23 1880	Sept 28 1848–Aug 12 1880	Oct 27 1860–Dec 16 1880		
	Nov 20 1860–Dec 24 1880	Nov 18 1860–Dec 16 1880	(Glenbryan—ages given)		
	(Glenbryan)	(Glenbryan)			
Piercetown	1811–1900	1812–1900		WHGS	
	Dec 18 1811–July 30 1854	Jan 10 1812–July 26 1854		NLI	Pos. 4250
	Jan 18 1839–July 28 1854	Jan 29 1839–Nov 27 1852			
	(Murrintown)	(Murrintown)			
	Aug 8 1854–Nov 13 1880	Aug 12 1854–Nov 13 1880			
Rathangan	1803–1850	1805–1850		WHGS	
	1846–54 (Cleariestown)	1844–54 (Cleariestown)		NLI	Pos. 4244
	Jan 27 1803–Aug 28 1805	June 25 1803–June 15 1806			
	Jan 19 1813–Feb 9 1853	Jan 7 1813–Nov 27 1852			
	June 19 1845–June 10 1850	Nov 26 1846–July 29 1854			
	Mar 30 1844–Oct 31 1854	Feb 15 1854–Aug 24 1880			
	Apr 2 1853–Dec 30 1880				
Rathnure and	1853–78	1847–53	1846–53	WHGS	
Templeudigan	Oct 3 1846–Jan 25 1853	Oct 17 1846–Jan 29 1853	Oct 18 1846–Jan 28 1853	NLI	Pos. 4248
	Feb 7 1853–Jan 23 1878	Feb 7 1853–Jan 31 1878	(ages given)		
	June 17 1877–Nov 30 1880	July 18 1877–July 13 1880	Feb 24 1853–Feb 9 1878		
	Mar 18 1878–Dec 31 1880	Mar 4 1878–Aug 28 1880	(ages given)		
			Feb 18 1878–Oct 16 1880		
			(ages given)		
St James and Hook	1835–73			WHGS	
	Nov 29 1835–Aug 10 1840	Nov 7 1875–Nov 29 1880	Oct 17 1835–May 28 1854	NLI	Pos. 4258
	Mar 28 1844–Sept 17 1873		(ages given)		
	Sept 23 1873–Dec 29 1880				
St James and	1793–1894	1792–1859		WHGS	
Templetown	(gaps 1798–1805, 1814–16)	(gap 1815–43)			
	Dec 23 1792–Oct 27 1793	Nov 18 1792–June 11 1815	Jan 2 1816–Apr 21 1879	NLI	Pos. 4245*
	Jan 7 1795–Nov 8 1798	Jan 8 1812–Nov 26 1842			
	Apr 6 1805–Mar 28 1815	Jan 18 1843–Nov 30 1860			
	Jan 5 1812–Dec 22 1815	Sept 17 1870–Nov 24 1880			
	Jan 1816–Oct 13 1880	Feb 9 1861–Nov 1880			
	Mar 6 1870–Dec 23 1880	June 18 1843–Nov 3 1880			
		(transcript)			
St Mullins	See Carlow				
Suttons	1826–1900	1825–94		WHGS	
	Nov 3 1824–Nov 7 1879	Feb 12 1825–Sept 26 1879	May 17 1827–Nov 26 1836	NLI	Pos. 4261
	Feb 19 1862–Dec 15 1880	Feb 22 1862–Nov 27 1880	Jan 13 1858–Dec 19 1880		
	(Ballykelly)	(Ballykelly)			
Taghmon	1801–1900			WHGS	
	May 26 1801–July 8 1832	May 29 1801–Mar 7 1835	Jan 3 1828–Dec 3 1846	NLI	Pos. 4247
	July 11 1832–Dec 21 1865	Apr 6 1866–Nov 27 1880	(ages given)		
	Mar 3 1866–Dec 19 1880		Feb 20 1866–Dec 23 1880		
			(ages given)		
Tagoat	1853–81	1853–81	1853–81	WHGS	
	Jan 16 1853–Dec 8 1875	Feb 8 1853–Nov 27 1875	Oct 16 1875–Aug 3 1880	NLI	Pos. 4245*
	Nov 16 1875–Dec 30 1880	Oct 31 1875–Nov 21 1880			

Parish	Baptisms	Marriages	Burials	Location	Reference
The Ballagh	Oct 29 1837–Jan 27 1853	Nov 4 1837–Nov 26 1852		NLI	Pos. 4248
	Feb 25 1875–Dec 26 1880	Nov 10 1874–July 20 1878			
	Oct 1863–Dec 17 1880				
Tomacork	Jan 1785–May 20 1786	June 18 1793–Feb 23 1797	May 12 1794–Dec 30 1797	NLI	Pos. 4256
	Feb 8 1791–Nov 24 1797	Jan 19 1807–Mar 1845	May 1 1847–Nov 13 1856		
	Jan 5 1807–May 6 1836	June 2 1847–Sept 12 1880	May 18 1864–Jan 11 1871		
	Nov 15 1832–May 27 1847		Apr 20 1873–Dec 24 1880		
	May 31 1847–Dec 28 1880				
	1785–1900	1807–1900		WFHC	
Wexford	1686–1900	1671–1900		WHGS	
	May 1671–85	May 1671–85		NLI	Pos. 4252
	(poorly legible)	(poorly legible)			(baptisms to
	Dec 13 1686–Jan 29 1689	Apr 4 1724–Dec 10 1822			1851); 4253
	Jan 13 1694–Mar 19 1710	Jan 9 1823–Nov 25 1867			(baptisms to
	Feb 19 1723–Aug 7 1787	Nov 26 1867–Nov 27 1880			1880); 4254
	June 2 1815–June 26 1838				(marriages)
	June 27 1838–Aug 25 1851				
	Aug 28 1851–Feb 15 1869				
	Mar 1 1869–Dec 31 1880				

Wicklow

All Wicklow Family History Centre (WFHC) transcripts are online at <www.rootsireland.ie>.

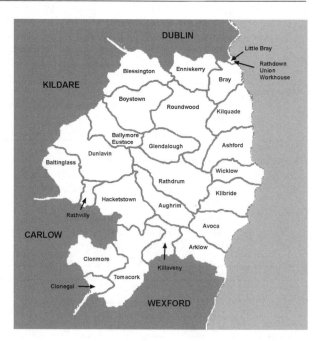

Parish (Diocese)	Baptisms	Marriages	Burials	Location	Reference
Arklow (Dublin)	May 25 1809–June 4 1809	Jan 7 1818–Nov 27 1843		NLI	Pos. 6474/5
	Dec 21 1817–Dec 31 1843	Jan 7 1844–Oct 27 1856			
	Jan 2 1844–Oct 27 1856	Jan 12 1857–Nov 26 1880			
	Jan 1 1857–Oct 2 1868				
	Oct 4 1868–Dec 29 1880				

Parish (Diocese)	Baptisms	Marriages	Burials	Location	Reference
Arklow (Dublin) (contd.)	1818–1961 (part?)			Online	<www.cmcrp.net>
	1817–80	1818–80		WFHC	
Ashford (Dublin)	Sept 18 1864–Dec 31 1880	Oct 6 1864–Nov 5 1880		NLI	Pos. 6477/8
	1864–1900	1864–1900		WFHC	
Aughrim (Dublin)	No records microfilmed			NLI	
	1868–1900			WFHC	
Avoca (Dublin)	June 15 1791–Feb 26 1805	June 15 1791–Feb 26 1805		NLI	Pos. 6476/7
	May 27 1809–Dec 21 1825	Oct 23 1778–Jan 26 1797			
	Oct 3 1825–June 5 1836	Nov 6 1812–Oct 25 1825			
	June 2 1836–Apr 23 1867	Oct 10 1825–Feb 6 1843			
	Mar 5 1843–Apr 18 1867	Apr 22 1844–Feb 28 1867			
	Apr 21 1867–Dec 25 1880	May 1 1867–Nov 2 1880			
	1792–1900	1778–1900		WFHC	
Ballymore Eustace (Dublin)	1838–99	1839–99		KHGS	
	Mar 8 1779–Apr 27 1792	Oct 18 1779–Nov 27 1794		NLI	Pos. 6481
	Jan 10 1787–Mar 1 1790	Feb 21 1787–June 11 1796			
	May 3 1792–Apr 6 1796	May 15 1797–July 19 1830			
	Jan 5 1797–Oct 28 1830	Apr 22 1826–Dec 1 1838			
	Apr 23 1826–Dec 26 1838	Jan 27 1839–Nov 26 1863			
	Jan 1 1839–Apr 27 1854	Jan 25 1864–Oct 25 1880			
	May 7 1854–Dec 31 1880				
	1792–1838	1779–1838	1779–1900	WFHC	
Baltinglass (Kildare and Leighlin)	See NLI			LDS	BFA 0926104 item 2
	May 31 1807–Feb 18 1810	Feb 2 1810–Apr 16 1811	Aug 12 1824–Sept 11 1830	NLI	Pos. 4192
	July 8 1810–Apr 4 1811	Nov 20 1813–Sept 12 1815			
	Oct 4 1813–Jan 19 1830	Apr (?) 25 1816–Apr 25 1831			
	Mar 7 1830–July 12 1857	Jan 28 1830–May 19 1857			
	May 12 1857–Nov 5 1865	July 23 1857–Feb 12 1866			
	Nov 12 1865–Dec 19 1880	May 3 1866–Dec 18 1880			
	1810–80	1810–80		WFHC	
Blackditches (Dublin)	June 9 1810–Aug 1825	June 18 1810–Aug 1825		NLI	Pos. 6483, 6615
	May 4 1830–June 10 1830	Aug 6 1826–June 7 1833			
	June 9 1826–Apr 25 1830	Feb 2 1833–Jan 25 1845			
	Feb 15 1833–Mar 4 1844	Apr 8 1844–May 8 1862			
	Mar 10 1844–May 8 1862	1862–80			
	1860–80				
	1810–1825	1810–1900		WFHC	
	1833–98				
Blessington (Dublin)	Apr 4 1852–Nov 14 1880	Feb 22 1852–Dec 4 1880		NLI	Pos. 6483, 6615
	1852–1880 (Church of Kilbride)	1877–80 (Church of Kilbride)			
	1821–1900	1823–1900		WFHC	

Parish (Diocese)	Baptisms	Marriages	Burials	Location	Reference
Bray (Dublin)	Bray, Little Bray, Shankill, Old Connaught and Shanganagh baptisms from St Michael's (Kingstown), 1768–1861 Aug 19 1792–Mar 4 1821 July 7 1822–Mar 9 1856 (indexed) Mar 16 1856–May 18 1886 May 16 1886–Mar 2 1905	Feb 19 1792–Mar 4 1821 Sept 8 1822–June 16 1856 (indexed) July 22 1856–Nov 11 1901		NLI	Pos. 9371
	1792–1900	1792–1900		WFHC	
Clonegal	See Carlow				
Clonmore	See Carlow				
Dunlavin (Dublin)	Oct 1 1815–Sept 29 1839 Oct 13 1839–Sept 8 1857 1857–Dec 15 1880 (ink badly faded)	Feb 14 1831–Oct 19 1839 (ink badly faded) Nov 12 1839–Nov 20 1857 (ink badly faded) Feb 12 1857–Nov 22 1880		NLI	Pos. 6484
	1816–1900	1831–1900		WFHC	
Enniskerry (Dublin)	Oct 7 1825–Sept 22 1861 Sept 11 1859–Dec 5 1880	Nov 1 1825–Sept 29 1861 Mar 6 1859–Nov 18 1880		NLI	Pos. 6478
	1826–1900	1826–1900		WFHC	
Glendalough (Dublin)	June 20 1807–Jan 18 1838 Aug 24 1839–May 1 1866 Apr 17 1857–Dec 24 1880	Jan 6 1808–June 27 1838 May 14 1840–July 24 1866 May 2 1857–Oct 6 1880		NLI	Pos. 6474
	1807–1837 1840–81	1808–1837 1840–81		WFHC	
Hacketstown	See Carlow				
Kilbride (Dublin)	Jan 1858–80	Feb 1858–80		NLI	Pos. 6615
	1820–36	1821–36		WFHC	
	1859–1900	1859–1900			
Killaveny (Ferns)	Nov 20 1800–Dec 20 1836 Jan 13 1837–Apr 29 1875 Oct 15 1857–Apr 10 1864 (Anacorra)	Nov 14 1800–Sept 10 1836 Jan 7 1837–May 4 1875 Aug 5 1860–Feb 6 1864 (Anacorra)	Oct 19 1862–Mar 13 1867 (Anacorra)	NLI	Pos. 4257
	1800–1900	1801–1900		WFHC	
Kilquade (Dublin)	Aug 23 1826–June 29 1855 Dec 17 1861–Feb 7 1863	Aug 12 1826–Sept 29 1862 Nov 4 1862–Nov 8 1880		NLI	Pos. 6478
	1826–1900	1826–1900		WFHC	
Little Bray (Dublin)	Dec 27 1891–May 25 1898	Feb 10 1866–Feb 13 1901		NLI	Pos. 9372
	1863–91	1863–91		WFHC	
Rathdown Union Workhouse (Dublin)	1841–1900 No registers microfilmed	1876–94		DLHS NLI	
Rathdrum (Dublin)	Jan 6 1795–Jan 29 1799 Oct 1 1816–July 29 1835 Aug 2 1835–Oct 3 1854 Sept 27 1854–June 12 1875 June 12 1875–Dec 21 1880	Nov 7 1816–Aug 5 1835 Aug 3 1835–Sept 22 1854 Nov 14 1854–Nov 3 1880		NLI	Pos. 6476
	1795–7 1816–1900	1817–1900		WFHC	

Parish (Diocese)	Baptisms	Marriages	Burials	Location	Reference
Rathvilly	See Carlow				
Roundwood (Dublin)	Jun 5 1881–Oct 11 1900	May 2 1857–Aug 4 1902		NLI	Pos. 9372
	1854–1900			WFHC	
Tomacork	See Wexford				
Wicklow (Dublin)	Jan 7 1747/8–Oct 9 1754	Jan 7 1747/8–Sept 1 1754		NLI	Pos. 6482
	Sept 9 1753–Dec 9 1775	Jan 19 1753–Nov 25 1761			
	Sept 27 1761–Dec 1762	Dec 19 1761–May 13 1777			
	Jan 1776–June 9 1781	Jan 11 1762–Feb 22 1778			
	1784/5 (4 entries)	Jan 22 1779–Oct 2 1780			
	May 15 1796–Dec 29 1830	Nov 20 1795–Feb 15 1874			
	Nov 29 1829–Dec 28 1862	June 23 1874–Nov 27 1880			
	Oct 17 1861–June 7 1874				
	July 1874–Dec 1880				
	1747–91	1747–1900		WFHC	
	1829–1900				

Chapter 15 ～

RESEARCH SERVICES, SOCIETIES, REPOSITORIES AND PUBLISHERS

1. RESEARCH SERVICES
A. Professional associations

The only association of professional researchers on the island of Ireland is the Association of Professional Genealogists in Ireland (APGI), <*www.apgi.ie*>, with members north and south. It is principally concerned with upholding research standards, rather than undertaking commercial research in its own right. APGI members are listed online.

B. The Irish Genealogical Project

In the early 1980s, as part of a series of Government-sponsored youth employment and training schemes, local history and heritage societies and other interested bodies began to organise the indexing of local parish records. With some exceptions, at the outset little thought was given to the potential value of these records. In the mid-1980s, as the number of areas covered by the indexing projects grew, their efforts were co-ordinated by an umbrella body, the Irish Family History Council, later to become the Irish Family History Foundation. An ambitious plan was drawn up under the aegis of this body to transcribe and computerise not only all the parish records of all denominations for the entire country but also all other sources of major genealogical interest: the Tithe Books, Griffith's Valuation, the civil records of births, marriages and deaths, the 1901 and 1911 census returns and local gravestone inscriptions. Expanded Government funding was secured for this plan, known as the Irish Genealogical Project, and in 1990, with the adherence of four centres in Northern Ireland, the International Fund for Ireland also became involved.

The general aim of the Project was to realise the tourist potential of Irish genealogy by creating a single organisation that could combine the experience and expertise of professional genealogists with the speed and accuracy of the local databases to provide a comprehensive, affordable, Ireland-wide research service. This aim will not now be met. The very strengths that made the local centres possible—their voluntary ethos, diversity of funding and structure, and solid local roots—have made it virtually impossible to co-ordinate their activities in a single service.

Originally a partner of the local centres, the state-funded <*www.irishgene alogy.ie*> now aims to complete the digitisation of church records in areas not covered by the centres themselves.

Although all the centres continue to supply offline addresses and contact details, the level of personal service most of them provide has diminished greatly as their records are transferred online to <*www.rootsireland.ie*>. Having the databases directly accessible is invaluable, though the payment system in use is more convenient for the centres than for the users. One persistent fear must be that some of the local sources accumulated by centres, such as gravestone transcriptions, will not make it online.

Area	Address	Comment
Co. Antrim	Ulster Historical Foundation 49 Malone Road Belfast BT9 6RY Tel. +44 (0) 28 90661988 Fax + 44 (0) 28 90661977 enquiry@uhf.org.uk <*www.ancestryireland.co.uk*>	Full commissioned research service. The UHF is a long-established, highly reputable research and publishing agency. The website offers paying access to most of its records, including parish and GRO databases, which are also available at <*www.rootsireland.ie*>.
Co. Armagh	Armagh Ancestry 40 English Street Armagh BT61 7BA Tel. +44 28 3752 1800 researcher@armagh.gov.uk No individual website.	Records online at <*www.rootsireland.ie*> are principally Roman Catholic registers and civil birth and marriage records of Co. Armagh.
Co. Cavan	Cavan Heritage and Genealogy Centre 1st Floor, Johnston Central Library Farnham Street Cavan Tel. + 353 (0) 49 4361094 cavangenealogy@eircom.net	No individual website. Full commissioned research service. Extensive collection of indexed and computerised records.
Co. Clare	Clare Heritage and Genealogical Centre Corrofin Co. Clare Tel. + 353 (0) 65 6837955 Fax + 353 (0) 65 6837540 <*www.clareroots.com*>	Full commissioned personal research service. No records online as yet (2011).

Area	Address	Comment
Cork North	Mallow Heritage Centre 27–28 Bank Place Mallow Co. Cork Tel. + 353 (0) 22 503020 <*www.mallowheritagecentre.com*> mallowhc@eircom.net	Full commissioned research service. Catholic records of North Cork and a substantial proportion of the Church of Ireland records for the same area. <*www.irishgenealogy.ie*> covers church records for Cork South and West.
Co. Derry/ Londonderry	Derry Genealogy Centre Harbour Museum Harbour Square Derry BT48 6AF Tel. +44 (0) 28 71377331 genealogy@derrycity.gov.uk	Full commissioned research service. No individual website.
Co. Donegal	Donegal Ancestry The Quay Ramelton Co. Donegal Tel. +353 (0) 74 9151266 info@donegalancestry.com <*www.donegalancestry.com*>	Partial commissioned research service. Of 41 Roman Catholic parishes in the county, 28 are transcribed. Holds a very substantial collection of non-Catholic records.
Co. Down	See Co. Antrim	
Dublin (city)	Dublin Heritage Group	No research service. Transcripts of church records database online at <*www.irishgenealogy.ie*>.
Dublin North	Fingal Genealogy Swords Historical Society Co. Ltd Carnegie Library North Street Swords Co. Dublin Tel. + 353 (0) 1 8400080 swordsheritage@eircom.net	No individual website. Full research service. Virtually all church records for north Co. Dublin, including some of the north city records.
Dublin South	Dún Laoghaire-Rathdown Heritage Craft Courtyard Marlay Park Grange Road Dublin 16 Tel. +353 (0) 1 2054700 cmalone@dlrcoco.ie	Partial commissioned research service. All the centre's records for south Co. Dublin are at <*www.rootsireland.ie*>.

Area	Address	Comment
Cos. Fermanagh and Tyrone	Irish World Family History Services Family History Suite 51 Dungannon Road Coalisland Co. Tyrone B71 4HP Tel. +44 (0) 28 87746065 *<www.irish-world.com>*	Full personalised research service. All the centre's database transcripts are online at *<www.rootsireland.ie>* and *<www.historyfromheadstones.com>*.
Galway East	East Galway Family History Society Ltd Woodford Heritage Centre Woodford Loughrea Co. Galway Tel. +353 (0) 90 9749309 galwayroots@eircom.net	No individual website. Full research service. All the centre's database transcripts are online at *<www.rootsireland.ie>*.
Galway West	West Galway Family History Society Ltd St Joseph's Community Centre Shantalla Galway Tel. + 353 (0) 91 860464 galwayfshwest@eircom.net	No individual website. Full commissioned research service. All the centre's database transcripts are online at *<www.rootsireland.ie>*.
Co. Kildare	Kildare Genealogy Riverbank Main Street Droichead Nua Co. Kildare Tel. +353 (0) 45 448350 kildaregenealogy@iol.ie	Full research service. All the centre's church database transcripts are online at *<www.rootsireland.ie>*.
Co. Kilkenny	Kilkenny Ancestry Rothe House Kilkenny Tel. +353 (0) 56 7722893 *<www.rothehouse.com>*	Full commissioned research service. All the centre's church record database transcripts are online at *<www.rootsireland.ie>*.
Cos. Laois and Offaly	Irish Midlands Ancestry Bury Quay Tullamore Co. Offaly Tel. +353 (0) 5793 21421 info@offalyhistory.com *<www.irishmidlandsancestry.com>*	Full commissioned research service. All the centre's database transcripts are online at *<www.rootsireland.ie>*.

Area	Address	Comment
Co. Leitrim	Leitrim Genealogy Centre c/o Leitrim County Library Ballinamore Co. Leitrim Tel. +353 (0) 71 9644012 Fax +353 (0) 71 9644425 leitrimgenealogy@eircom.net <*www.leitrimroots.com*>	Full commissioned research service. All the centre's church and civil record database transcripts are online at <*www.rootsireland.ie*>.
Co. Limerick	Limerick Genealogy Lissanalta House Dooradoyle Road Dooradoyle Co. Limerick Tel. +353 (0) 61 496542 <*www.limerickgenealogy.com*>	Full commissioned research service. All the centre's church and civil record database transcripts are online at <*www.rootsireland.ie*>.
Co. Longford	Longford Genealogy Centre 17 Dublin Street Longford Tel. +353 (0) 43 41235 email: longroot@iol.ie	No individual website. Partial commissioned research service. All the centre's church record database transcripts are online at <*www.rootsireland.ie*>.
Co. Louth	Louth County Library Roden Place Dundalk Co. Louth Tel. +353 (0) 42 9353190 referencelibrary@louthcoco.ie	No individual website. Partial commissioned research service. All the centre's Catholic church record database transcripts are online at <*www.rootsireland.ie*>.
Mayo North	Mayo North Family History Research Centre Enniscoe Castlehill Ballina Co. Mayo Tel. +353 (0) 96 31809 normayo@iol.ie <*mayo.irish-roots.net*>	Full commissioned research service. All the centre's church, civil and census record database transcripts are online at <*www.rootsireland.ie*>.
Mayo South	Mayo South Family Heritage Centre Main Street Ballinrobe Co. Mayo Tel. +353 (0) 94 9541214 soumayo@iol.ie <*mayo.irish-roots.net*>	Full commissioned research service. All the centre's church, civil and census record database transcripts are online at <*www.rootsireland.ie*>.

Area	Address	Comment
Co. Meath	Meath Heritage and Genealogy Centre Town Hall Castle Street Trim Co. Meath Tel. +353 (0) 46 9436633 meathhc@iol.ie	No individual website. Partial commissioned research service. All the centre's church record database transcripts are online at <www.rootsireland.ie>.
Co. Monaghan	Monaghan Genealogy 6 Tully Monaghan theomcmahon@eircom.net	No individual website. Partial commissioned research service. Some church record database transcripts are online at <www.rootsireland.ie>.
Co. Offaly	See Co. Laois	
Co. Roscommon	Roscommon Heritage and Genealogy Centre Church Street Strokestown Co. Roscommon Tel. +353 (0) 71 9633380 info@roscommonroots.com <www.roscommonroots.com>	Full commissioned research service. Almost all church and civil record database transcripts are online at <www.rootsireland.ie>.
Co. Sligo	Sligo Heritage and Genealogy Society Áras Reddan Temple Street Sligo Tel. +353 (0) 71 9143728 heritagesligo@eircom.net <www.sligoroots.com>	Full commissioned research service. All the centre's church record database transcripts are online at <www.rootsireland.ie>.
Co. Tipperary	Tipperary Family History Research Excel Heritage Centre Mitchell Street Tipperary Tel. +353 (0) 62 80555/80556 Fax +353 (0) 62 80552 research@tfhr.org <www.tfhr.org>	Partial commissioned research service. Roman Catholic registers for diocese of Cashel and Emly only.

Area	Address	Comment
Tipperary North	Tipperary North Family History Research Centre Governor's House Kickham Street Nenagh Co. Tipperary Tel. +353 (0) 67 33850 tipperarynorthgenealogy@eircom.net *<www.tipperarynorth.ie/genealogy>*	Full commissioned research service. All the centre's church, civil and census record database transcripts are online at *<www.rootsireland.ie>*.
Tipperary South	Brú Boru Heritage Centre Cashel Co. Tipperary Tel. +353 (0) 62 61122 bruboru@comhaltas.com	Full commissioned research service. All the centre's church transcripts (diocese of Waterford and Lismore only) and civil record transcripts are online at *<www.rootsireland.ie>*.
Co. Tyrone	See Co. Fermanagh	
Co. Waterford	Waterford Heritage Services Jenkins Lane Waterford Tel. +353 (0) 51 876123 mnoc@iol.ie *<www.waterford-heritage.ie>*	Full commissioned research service. Almost all Catholic records for diocese of Waterford and Lismore. Baptismal records are online at *<www.rootsireland.ie>* (November 2011).
Co. Westmeath	Dún na Sí Heritage and Genealogical Centre Moate Co. Westmeath Tel. +353 (0) 90 6481183 dunnasimoate@eircom.net	Partial commissioned research service. All the centre's church and census record database transcripts are online at *<www.rootsireland.ie>*.
Co. Wexford	No centre	It is promised (2011) that all the centre's church census record database transcripts will go online at *<www.rootsireland.ie>*.
Co. Wicklow	Wicklow Family History Centre Wicklow's Historic Gaol Kilmantin Hill Wicklow Tel. +353 (0) 404 20126 whf@eircom.net	*<www.wicklow.ie/FamilyHistoryCentre>* No individual website. Full research service. All the centre's church database transcripts are online at *<www.rootsireland.ie>*.

2. SOCIETIES
A. Ireland

Ballinteer Family History Society 29 The View Woodpark Ballinteer Dublin 16	Publishes *Gateway to the Past* annually. Members' facilities.	*<www.iol.ie/~ryanc/>*
Cork Genealogical Society c/o 22 Elm Drive Shamrock Lawn Douglas Cork	Annual *Journal* from 2001. Members' facilities only.	*<www.corkgenealogica lsociety.com>*
Cork Historical and Archaeological Society 13 Lislee Road Maryborough Douglas Cork	Publishes *Journal* annually.	*<www.ucc.ie/chas>*
Federation of Local History Societies (Cónascadh na gCumann Staire Áitiúla) c/o Dermot Ryan Winter's Hill Kinsale Co. Cork		*<homepage.eircom.net/~ localhist>*
Genealogical Society of Ireland 11 Desmond Avenue Dún Laoghaire Co. Dublin	Publishes *Genie Gazette*. Members' facilities only.	*<www.familyhistory.ie>*
Huguenot Society of Great Britain and Ireland Sunhaven Dublin Road Celbridge Co. Kildare		*<www.huguenotsociety. org.uk>*
Irish Family History Society PO Box 36 Naas Co. Kildare	Publishes *Irish Family History*.	*<www.ifhs.ie>*

Irish Genealogical Research Society Church of St Magnus the Martyr Lower Thames Street London EC3 6DN England	Publishes *The Irish Genealogist.*	<*www.igrsoc.org*>
North of Ireland Family History Society c/o School of Education Queen's University 69 University Street Belfast BT7 1HL	Publishes *North Irish Roots.*	<*www.nifhs.org*>
Raheny Heritage Society 68 Raheny Park Dublin 5.	Members' facilities only.	bjwray@eircom.net
Roscommon Family History Society Bealnamullia Athlone Co. Roscommon	Annual *Journal* since 2001. Also *The Moyfinne Journal.*	<*www.roscommonhistory.ie*>
Tipperary Historical Society Castle Avenue Thurles Co. Tipperary	Publishes *Tipperary Historical Journal* annually.	<*www.tipperarylibraries.ie/ths*>
Ulster Historical and Genealogical Guild UHF 49 Malone Road Belfast BT9 6RY	Publishes *Familia: Ulster Genealogical Review.*	<*www.ancestryireland.co.uk*>
Western Family History Association		<*www.wfha.info*>
Wicklow County Genealogical Society Summerhill Wicklow		

B. Abroad

Canadian Genealogy Centre
Library and Archives Canada
395 Wellington Street
Ottawa, Ont. K1A 0N4
Canada

<*www.genealogy.gc.ca*>

Federation of Family History Societies
PO Box 8857
Lutterworth, Leics. LE17 9BJ
England

<*www.ffhs.org.uk*>

Federation of Genealogical Societies
PO Box 200940
Austin, Tex. 78720-0940
USA

<*www.fgs.org*>

Irish Genealogical Society
   International
Suite 218
1185 Concord Street North
South St Paul, Minn. 55075
USA

Publishes *Septs.*

<*www.irishgenealogical.org*>

National Genealogical Society
Suite 300
3108 Columbia Pike
Arlington, Va. 22204-4304
USA

<*www.ngsgenealogy.org*>

New Zealand Society of Genealogists
PO Box 14036
Panmure
Auckland 1741
New Zealand

Publishes *New Zealand Genealogist.*

<*www.genealogy.org.nz*>

Society of Australian Genealogists
Richmond Villa
120 Kent Street
Sydney, NSW 2000
Australia

Publishes *Descent.*

<*www.sag.org.au*>

3. REPOSITORIES
A. Northern Ireland
Area libraries

See *<www.ni-libraries.net>*. Online catalogue.

General repositories

Church of Jesus Christ of Latter-Day Saints Family History Centre 403 Hollywood Road Belfast BT4 2GU	Tel. +44 (0) 28 90769839		Open Wednesday, Thursday and Saturday.
General Register Office Oxford House 49–55 Chichester Street Belfast BT1 4HL	Tel. +44 (0) 28 91513101	*<www.groni.gov.uk>*	Appointment advisable.
Linen Hall Library 17 Donegall Square, North Belfast BT1 5GB	Tel. +44 (0) 28 90321707	*<www.linenhall.com>*	Open Monday to Friday, 9:30 a.m. to 5:30 p.m., Saturday 9:30 a.m. to 4 p.m.
Presbyterian Historical Society 26 College Green Belfast BT7 1LN	Tel. +44 (0) 28 90727330	*<www.presbyterianhistoryireland.com>*	Open Tuesday and Wednesday, 9:30 a.m. to 4:30 p.m., Thursday 9:30 a.m. to 1 p.m.
Public Record Office of Northern Ireland 2 Titanic Boulevard Belfast BT3 9HQ	Tel. +44 (0) 28 90534800	*<www.proni.gov.uk>*	Open weekdays, 9:15 a.m. to 4:45 p.m., Thursday 10 a.m. to 8:45 p.m.
Society of Friends Library Meeting House Railway Street Lisburn Co. Antrim			Postal queries only.

B. Republic of Ireland

County libraries

See *<www.library.ie>*. Many county libraries have online catalogues.

General repositories

See also *<www.learnaboutarchives.ie>* and Seamus Helferty and Raymond Refaussé (eds.), *Directory of Irish Archives* (5th edition), Dublin: Four Courts Press, 2011.

Church of Jesus Christ of Latter-Day Saints Family History Centre The Willows Finglas Road Dublin 11			Open Tuesday to Saturday, various hours.
Cork Archives Institute Christ Church South Main Street Cork	Tel. +353 (0) 21 4277809	*<www.corkarchives.ie>*	Open Tuesday to Friday, 10 a.m. to 5 p.m.
Dublin City Library and Archive 138–142 Pearse Street Dublin 2	Tel. +353 (0) 1 6744999	*<www.dublinheritage.ie>*	Open Monday to Thursday, 10 a.m. to 8 p.m., Friday and Saturday 10 a.m. to 5 p.m.
Genealogical Office 2 Kildare Street Dublin 2	Tel. +353 (0) 1 6618811		Open Monday to Friday, 10 a.m. to 4:30 p.m.
General Register Office Research Room 3rd Floor Block 7 Irish Life Centre Lower Abbey Street Dublin 1	Tel. +353 (0) 1 6354000	*<www.groireland.ie>*	Research room open Monday to Friday, 9:30 a.m. to 4:30 p.m.
Land Valuation Office Irish Life Centre Lower Abbey Street Dublin 1	Tel. +353 (0) 1 8171000	*<www.valoff.ie>*	Open Monday to Friday, 9:30 a.m. to 12:30 p.m. and 2 to 4:30 p.m.
National Archives Bishop Street Dublin 8	Tel. +353 (0) 1 4072300	*<www.nationalarchives. ie>*	Open Monday to Friday, 10 a.m. to 5 p.m.

National Library of Ireland Kildare Street Dublin 2	Tel. +353 (0) 1 6030200	*<www.nli.ie>*	Open Monday to Wednesday, 10 a.m. to 9 p.m., Thursday and Friday 10 a.m. to 5 p.m., Saturday 10 a.m. to 1 p.m.
Registry of Deeds Henrietta Street Dublin 1	Tel. +353 (0) 1 6707500	*<www.landregistry.ie>*	Open Monday to Friday, 10 a.m. to 4:30 p.m.
Representative Church Body Library Braemor Park Dublin 14	Tel. +353 +353 (0) 1 4923979	*<www.library.ireland. anglican.org>*	Open Monday to Friday, 9:30 a.m. to 1 p.m. and 2 to 5 p.m.
Society of Friends Library Quaker House Stocking Lane Rathfarnham Dublin 16	Tel. +353 (0) 1 4956888	*<www.quakers-in-ireland.ie>*	Open Thursday, 11 a.m. to 1 p.m.

C. United Kingdom
England

British Postal Museum and Archive Freeling House Phoenix Place London WC1X 0DL	Tel. +44 (0) 20 72392570	*<www.postalheritage.org.uk>*
General Register Office for England and Wales Certificate Services Section PO Box 2 Southport PR8 2JD England		*<www.gro.gov.uk>*
National Archives Kew Richmond, Surrey TW9 4DU England	Tel. +44 (0) 20 88763444	*<www.nationalarchives.gov.uk>*

Scotland

General Register Office for Scotland New Register House Edinburgh EH1 3YT Scotland	Tel. +44 (0) 131 3144411	*<www.gro-scotland.gov.uk>*

For online records see also *<www.scotlandspeople.gov.uk>*.

Wales

Llyfrgell Genedlaethol Cymru / National Library of Wales Aberystwyth, Ceredigion SY23 3BU Cymru/Wales	Tel. +44 (0) 1970 632800	*<www.llgc.org.uk>*

4. PUBLISHERS

Eneclann Unit 1b Trinity College Enterprise Centre Pearse Street Dublin 2	Tel. + 353 (0) 1 6710338	*<www.eneclann.ie>*

Flyleaf Press 4 Spencer Villas Glenageary Co. Dublin	Tel. +353 (0) 1 2845906	*<www.flyleaf.ie>*

Genealogical Publishing Company, Inc. Suite 260 3600 Clipper Mill Road Baltimore, Md. 21211 USA	Tel. 1-800-296-6687	*<www.genealogical.com>*

Geography Publications 24 Kennington Road Templeogue Dublin 6W	Tel + 353 (0) 1 4566085	*<www.geographypublications.com>*

Irish Roots Media Ltd Blackrock Blessington Co. Wicklow	Tel. +353 (0) 87 9427815	*<www.irishrootsmagazine.com>*

INDEX